Frommer's®

France

Here's what the critics say about Frommer's:

"Done with style and verve. . . . These books (*Frommer's France* and *Frommer's Paris*) deliver the editorial goods."
—*France Insider's News*

♦

"Amazingly easy to use. Very portable, very complete."
—*Booklist*

♦

"The only mainstream guide to list specific prices. The Walter Cronkite of guidebooks—with all that implies."
—*Travel & Leisure*

♦

"Complete, concise, and filled with useful information."
—*New York Daily News*

♦

"The best series for travelers who want one easy-to-use guidebook."
—Meakin Armstrong, *US Air Magazine*

Other Great Guides for Your Trip:

Frommer's Europe

Frommer's Europe from $50 a Day

The Complete Idiot's Guide to Planning Your Trip to Europe

Frommer's Paris

Frommer's Paris from $70 a Day

Frommer's Provence & the Riviera

Frommer's Born to Shop France

Frommer's Born to Shop Paris

Frommer's® 99

France

By Darwin Porter & Danforth Prince

MACMILLAN • USA

ABOUT THE AUTHORS

France is a second home to **Darwin Porter,** a native of North Carolina, and **Danforth Prince,** who lived in France for many years. Darwin, who worked in television advertising and as a bureau chief for the *Miami Herald*, wrote the original edition of this guide back in 1971. Danforth, who began his association with Darwin in 1982, worked for the Paris bureau of the *New York Times* between renovations of a 14th-century château in the Loire Valley. Both these writers know their destination well, for they have made countless annual trips through the countryside and have lived and worked from Brittany to Provence.

MACMILLAN TRAVEL

A Simon & Schuster
Macmillan Company
1633 Broadway
New York, NY 10019

Find us online at **www.frommers.com**

ISBN 0-02-862276-6
ISSN 0899-3351

Editors: Vanessa Rosen and Leslie Shen
Production Editor: Stephanie Mohler
Photo Editor: Richard Fox
Design by Michele Laseau
Digital Cartography by John Decamillis and Rafaelle DeGennaro
Page Creation by Lissa Auciello-Brogan, David Faust, Natalie Hollifield, and Linda Quigley

SPECIAL SALES

Bulk purchases (10+ copies) of Frommer's and selected Macmillan travel guides are available to corporations, organizations, mail-order catalogs, institutions, and charities at special discounts, and can be customized to suit individual needs. For more information write to Special Sales, Macmillan General Reference, 1633 Broadway, New York, NY 10019.

Manufactured in the United States of America

Contents

List of Maps

An Invitation to the Reader

In researching this book, we discovered many wonderful places—hotels, restaurants, shops, and more. We're sure you'll find others. Please tell us about them, so we can share the information with your fellow travelers in upcoming editions. If you were disappointed with a recommendation, we'd love to know that, too. Please write to:

Frommer's France '99
Macmillan Travel
1633 Broadway
New York, NY 10019

An Additional Note

Please be advised that travel information is subject to change at any time—and this is especially true of prices. We therefore suggest that you write or call ahead for confirmation when making your travel plans. The authors, editors, and publisher cannot be held responsible for the experiences of readers while traveling. Your safety is important to us, however, so we encourage you to stay alert and be aware of your surroundings. Keep a close eye on cameras, purses, and wallets, all favorite targets of thieves and pickpockets.

What the Symbols Mean

✪ Frommer's Favorites

Our favorite places and experiences—outstanding for quality, value, or both.

The following abbreviations are used for credit cards:

AE	American Express	EURO	Eurocard
CB	Carte Blanche	JCB	Japan Credit Bank
DC	Diners Club	MC	MasterCard
DISC	Discover	V	Visa

Find Frommer's Online

Arthur Frommer's Outspoken Encyclopedia of Travel (www.frommers.com) offers more than 6,000 pages of up-to-the-minute travel information—including the latest bargains and candid, personal articles updated daily by Arthur Frommer himself. No other website offers such comprehensive and timely coverage of the world of travel.

The Best of France

France presents visitors with an embarrassment of riches—and you may find yourself bewildered at all the choices you'll have to make when planning your trip. We've tried to make the task easier for you by compiling a list of our favorite experiences and discoveries. In the following pages, you'll find the kind of candid advice we'd give our closest friends.

1 The Best Travel Experiences

- **Hunting Antiques:** The 18th- and 19th-century French aesthetic was gloriously different from those of England and North America, and many worthwhile objects bear designs with mythological references to the French experience. It's estimated that there are more than 13,000 antiques shops throughout the country. Stop wherever the sign ANTIQUAIRE or BROCANTE is displayed.

- **Dining Out:** The art of fine dining is still serious business in France. Even casual bistros with affordable menus are likely to offer fresh (seasonal) ingredients used in time-tested recipes that may comprise one of the most memorable meals of your life. Food here is as cerebral as it is sensual. For our favorite restaurants in France, see the two sections toward the end of this chapter.

- **Cycling in the Countryside:** The country that invented La Tour de France—the world's most impassioned bicycle race—offers thousands of options for leisurely bike trips. For a modest charge, trains throughout France will carry your bicycle to any point you specify, allowing you to avoid the urban congestion of Paris and other large cities. North America's oldest specialist is **Bike Tour France,** 5523 Wedgewood Dr., Charlotte, NC 28210-2432 (☎ **704/527-0955**). Best suited for tours through the Loire Valley and the Southwest, the company provides a technically sophisticated bicycle plus hotel accommodations as part of the price of tours that last 4 to 12 days. Routes are carefully selected to take in historic sites and beautiful scenery. See also "Special Interest Vacations" in chapter 3.

- **Cruising on a Luxury Barge:** Take a leisurely cruise on the canals and waterways of Burgundy, Brittany, Alsace, Languedoc, the Dordogne, or Provence. Many barges (originally used to transport lumber, coal, or grain) have been upgraded into luxury craft with superb dining facilities and comfortable accommodations. You can sit back and enjoy the lovely scenery, perhaps stopping here and there to sightsee or to visit local wineries. Contact **Première Selections,** a division of the Kemwel Company, 106 Calvert St., Harrison, NY 10528 (☎ **800/234-4000**). Inclusive fares for 3 nights begin at $1,160; for 6 nights, at $1,490. See also "Special Interest Vacations" in chapter 3.

- **Strolling Along the Seine in Paris:** Lovers still walk hand in hand alongside the river, while on its banks the *bouquinistes* still peddle their postcards, perhaps some 100-year-old pornography, or a tattered edition of a history of Indochina. Some visitors walk the full 7-mile stretch of the river through the city, but you may want to confine your stroll to central Paris, passing the Tuileries, the Louvre, and Notre-Dame and crossing one or more of the historic bridges, like pont Neuf, over the Seine and onto Ile de la Cité or Ile St-Louis and back again. See chapter 5.

- **Shopping in Parisian Boutiques:** The French ferociously guard their image as Europe's most stylish people. The citadels of Right Bank chic are found along rue du Faubourg St-Honoré and its extension, rue St-Honoré. The most glamorous shops sprawl for about a mile along these interconnected narrow streets, which stretch between the Palais Royal (to the east) and Palais de l'Elysée (to the west). Follow in the footsteps of Coco Chanel, Yves Saint Laurent, and Karl Lagerfeld for a shopper's tour of a lifetime. See chapter 5.

- **Touring the Loire Valley:** Exploring the châteaux scattered among the valley's rich fields and forests will familiarize you with the French Renaissance's architectural aesthetics and with the intrigues, dalliances, and scandals of the French kings and their courts. Nothing more evocatively conjures up the aristocratic ancien régime than a leisurely tour of these legendary châteaux. See chapter 7.

- **Climbing to the Heights of Mont-St-Michel:** Straddling the tidal flats between Normandy and Brittany, this is the most spectacular fortress in northern Europe. Believed to be protected by the archangel Michael himself, most of this Gothic marvel stands just as it did during the 1200s. See chapter 8.

- **Paying Tribute to Fallen Heroes on Normandy's D-Day Beaches:** On June 6, 1944, the largest armada ever assembled departed under cover of rough seas and dense fog from the English coast. Its success was anything but guaranteed, and for about a week the future of the civilized world hung in a bloody and brutal balance between the Nazi and Allied armies. Today you'll see only the sticky sands and wind-torn, gray-green seas of a rather chilly beach. But with just a bit of imagination, you can picture the struggles of the frightened yet determined young soldiers who established a bulkhead on the Nazi-occupied continent of Europe at a terrible price. See chapter 8.

- **Schussing Down the Alps:** France is noted for its world-class skiing and its luxurious resorts. Our favorites are Morzine and Avoriaz, Chamonix, Courchevel, and Megève. Here you'll find vertical cliffs only the experts should brave as well as challenging runs for intermediates and beginners; off the slopes, the après-ski scene roars into the wee hours. See chapter 12.

- **Touring Burgundy During the Grape Gathering:** Medieval lore and legend permeate the harvests in Burgundy, when thousands of workers (armed with vintner's shears and baskets) head over the rolling hills to gather the ripened grapes that have made the classified wines of Burgundy so famous. You can sample the local wines in any of the area restaurants, which always stock impressive collections. See chapter 13.

- **Partying on the Côte d'Azur:** Until Edwardian escapists "discovered" it about a century ago, the coastline of Provence was dotted with sleepy fishing villages; today this region is famous for its glamour and sense of hedonism, despite its desperate overcrowding (and impossible traffic jams). Our vote for best beach goes to the Plage de Tahiti, just outside St-Tropez, where there's lots of topless (and bottomless) action going on. If you bother to wear a bikini, it should be only the most daring. See chapter 21.
- **Touring the Riviera's Modern-Art Museums:** Since the 1890s, when Signac, Bonnard, and Matisse discovered St-Tropez, artists and their patrons have been drawn to the French Riviera. You can experience an unforgettable trip by driving across southern Provence, interspersing museum visits with wonderful meals, people watching, lounging on the beach, and stops at the area's architectural and artistic marvels. Highlights are Aix-en-Provence (Cézanne's studio and the Vasarély Museum), Biot (the Léger museum), Cagnes-sur-Mer (the Museum of Modern Mediterranean Art), Cap d'Antibes (the Grimaldi Château's Picasso collection), La Napoule (the Henry Clews Museum), and Menton (the Cocteau Museum). If that's not enough, Nice, St-Paul-de-Vence, and St-Tropez all have impressive modern-art collections. See chapter 21.

2 The Best Romantic Escapes

- **Deauville** (Normandy): Using the resort of Deauville to propel herself to stardom, Coco Chanel added greatly to its sense of glamour and romance. Play your hand at the casinos, if that's your thing; ride horses; stroll along the world's most discreetly elegant boardwalk; or simply revel in the resort's wonderful sense of style and nostalgia. See chapter 8.
- **La Baule** (Brittany): Consider an escape with your significant other to La Baule, a coastal resort in southern Brittany. The salt air; the moody, windswept Atlantic; and the lovely belle époque architecture help justify the name of its 5-mile beach, La Côte d'Amour. See chapter 9.
- **Talloires** (French Alps): The bracing climate, the history that goes back to the early Middle Ages, and the Gallic flair of the local innkeepers make for a memorable stay in Talloires. Accommodations range from a converted medieval monastery to an intimate B&B. The cuisine is world-class, as is the opportunity for quiet, relaxed romance. See chapter 12.
- **Les Baux** (Provence): During the Middle Ages, troubadours in southern Europe were encouraged to present their courtly love ballads to audiences at the craggy fortress of Les Baux. The romantic tradition continues today, with escapists from all over congregating in the weirdly eroded, rocky, arid Les Baux landscapes. The town contains an abundance of hideaways where you can concentrate on romance. See chapter 20.
- **St-Tropez** (Côte d'Azur): Somehow, any blonde manages to feel like Brigitte Bardot in sunny St-Tropez, and the sheer number of scantily clad satyrs and nymphs who slink through town in midsummer could perk up the most sluggish libido. The real miracle here is that the charm of the place actually manages to survive both its own hype and the hordes of visitors. See chapter 21.

3 The Best Driving Tours

- **La Route des Crêtes** (Alsace-Lorraine): The Vosges are one of the oldest mountain ranges in France and for many years formed one of the country's boundaries with Germany. Richly forested with tall hardwood trees and firs, they skirt the western edge of the Rhine and resemble Germany's Black Forest. Some parts of it are the closest thing in France to a wilderness. La Route des Crêtes, originally chiseled out of the mountains as a supply line, begins just west of Colmar, at the Col du Bonhomme. High points are Münster (home of the famous cheese), Col de la Schlucht (a resort with sweeping panoramas as far as the Jura and the Black Forest), and Markstein. At any point along the way, you can stop and strike out on some of the well-marked hiking trails. See chapter 11.

- **La Route des Grandes Alpes** (French Alps): One of the most panoramic drives in Western Europe stretches southward from the lakefront town of Evian to the coastal resort of Nice. En route, you'll see alpine uplands, larch forests, glaciers, and the foothills of Mont Blanc sheathed in mountain scenery. Plan on spending anywhere from 2 to 6 days for the drive, stopping for R and R along the way in such towns as Morzine, Avoriaz, Chamonix, and Megève. The route covers some 460 miles and crosses about 20 of France's dramatic mountain passes. Some sections are passable only in midsummer. See chapter 12.

- **La Côte d'Or** (Burgundy): Stretching only 37 miles from Santenay to Dijon, this route is for wine lovers. Rows of carefully terraced vines rise in tiers above the D122/N74/D1138 highways (La Route des Grands Crus), passing through the timeless towns of Puligny-Montrachet, Volnay, Beaune, Nuits-St-Georges, Vosne-Romanée, Gevrey-Chambertin, and Marsannay-la-Côte. Travel at your leisure, stopping wherever you like to sample and purchase the noble vintages whose growers are identified by signs sprouting from the sides of the highway. See chapter 13.

- **The Gorges of the Ardèche** (Rhône Valley): The river that carved these canyons (the Ardèche, a tributary of the Rhône) is the most temperamental of any French waterway: Its ebbs and flows have created the Grand Canyon of France. Riddled with alluvial deposits, canyons sometimes more than 950 feet deep, grottoes, and caves, the valley is one of the country's most unusual geological spectacles. A panoramic road (D290) runs along one rim of these canyons, providing views over a striking, arid landscape. Plan to park at many of the belvederes scattered along the route and walk for a few minutes on some of the well-marked footpaths. The drive, which you can do in a day even if you stop frequently for sightseeing, stretches in a southeast-to-northwest trajectory between the towns of Vallon-Pont-d'Arc and Pont St-Esprit. See chapter 14.

4 The Best Châteaux & Palaces

- **Château de Versailles** (Ile de France): This is the most spectacular palace in the world. Its construction was riddled with ironies and tragedies, and its hyperinflated costs can be partly blamed for the bloodbath of the French Revolution. Ringed with world-class gardens and a network of canals whose excavations required an army of laborers, the site also contains the Grand and Petit Trianons as well as miles of ornate corridors lined with the spoils of a vanished era. See chapter 6.

- **Palais de Fontainebleau** (Ile de France): Since the time of the earliest Frankish kings, the forest here has served as a royal hunting ground. Various dwellings had been erected for medieval kings in the heart of the forest, but in 1528, François I commissioned the core of the building that would be enlarged, expanded, and embellished by subsequent monarchs, including Henri II, Henri III, Catherine de Médici, Charles IX, and Louis XIII. Napoléon declared it his favorite château, delivering an emotional farewell to his troops from its horse-shoe-shaped staircase just after his 1814 abdication. See chapter 6.

- **Château de Chantilly** (Ile de France): This palace was begun in 1528 by Anne de Montmorency, a constable of France who advised six monarchs. To save costs, she ordered that her new building be placed atop the foundations of a derelict castle completed in 1386. Her descendants enlarged and embellished the premises, added the massive stables for which the place is admired today, and hired Le Nôtre to design gardens that later inspired Louis XVI to create similar (though larger) ones at Versailles. See chapter 6.

- **Château de Vaux-le-Vicomte** (Ile de France): Vaux-le-Vicomte symbolizes the dangers for status-seekers who refuse to curb themselves. It was built in 1661 for Nicolas Fouquet, Louis XIV's finance minister, and its lavishness made many wonder if some of the money for its construction had been pilfered from the treasury—which it had. This act did not amuse the Sun King, who had Fouquet jailed and his château confiscated. As a backhanded compliment to Fouquet, Louis swiftly hired the complex's designers (Mansard, Le Nôtre, Le Brun, Girardon, and de Legendre) to design his palace and gardens at Versailles. See chapter 6.

- **Château de Chambord** (Loire Valley): Despite the incorporation (probably by Michelangelo) of feudal trappings in its layout, this château was designed exclusively for pleasure—a manifestation of the political and military successes of a 21-year-old king, François I. Begun in 1519 as the Loire Valley's most opulent status symbol, Chambord heralded the end of the feudal age and the debut of the Renaissance. Ironically, after military defeats in Italy, a much-chastened François rarely visited here, opting instead to live in châteaux closer to Paris. See chapter 7.

- **Château d'Azay-le-Rideau** (Loire Valley): Many visitors consider this château among their three or four favorites, thrilling to its fairy-tale proportions and innate sense of beauty. Poised above the waters of the Indre (a tributary of the Loire), it boasts purely decorative remnants of medieval fortifications and an allure that prefigured the Renaissance embellishments of subsequent Loire Valley châteaux. See chapter 7.

- **Château de Chenonceau** (Loire Valley): Its builders daringly placed this palace on arched stone vaults above the rushing Cher, a tributary of the Loire. Built between 1513 and 1521, Chenonceau was later fought over by two of France's most influential women, each of whom imposed her will on Renaissance politics and the château's design. Henri II gave the palace to his mistress, Diane de Poitiers, whose allure, it was rumored, was kept alive by milk baths, morning horseback rides, and witchcraft. After the king's death, his scheming, unloved widow, Catherine de Médici, forced Diane to a less prestigious château nearby (Chaumont), thoroughly humiliating her in the process. See chapter 7.

- **Château de Villandry** (Loire Valley): Built in 1538, Villandry is a truly dignified palace. Most of its aesthetic appeal, however, derives from its 17 acres of formal gardens. Brought to their full magnificence after 1906 by the noted French scholar Dr. Carvallo, they're a mandatory stopover for anyone who wants to tour the great gardens of Europe. See chapter 7.

5 The Best Museums

- **Musée du Louvre** (Paris): Graced with an exterior that's a triumph of grandiloquent French architecture, its stately premises contain an embarrassment of artistic riches, with more paintings (around 300,000) than can be displayed at any one time. The collection somehow manages to retain its dignity despite the thousands of visitors who traipse through the corridors every day, particularly looking for the *Mona Lisa* and the *Venus de Milo*. In the 1980s the grandeur of its Cour Carrée was neatly offset by I. M. Pei's controversial Great Pyramid. See chapter 5.

- **Musée d'Orsay** (Paris): The spidery glass-and-iron canopies of an abandoned railway station were adapted into one of Europe's most thrilling museums. Devoted exclusively to 19th-century art, it contains paintings by most of the French impressionists, as well as thousands of sculptures and decorative objects whose design changed forever the way Europe interpreted line, movement, and color. See chapter 5.
- **Musée de la Tapisserie de Bayeux** (Bayeux, Normandy): This museum's star exhibit is a 900-year-old tapestry named in honor of medieval Queen Mathilda. Housed in a glass case, the Bayeaux tapestry is a long, narrow band of linen embroidered with depictions of the war machine that sailed from Normandy to conquer England in 1066. See chapter 8.
- **Musée Historique Lorrain** (Nancy, Alsace-Lorraine): Few other French museums reflect a specific province as pointedly as this one. Its eclectic collections include 16th-century engravings, 17th-century masterpieces by local painters, exhibits devoted to Jewish history in eastern France, antique furniture, wrought iron, and domestic accessories. See chapter 11.
- **Musée Ingres** (Montauban, the Dordogne): This museum, housed in a 17th-century archbishop's palace, was created in 1867 when Jean-Auguste-Dominique Ingres (one of the most admired classicists since the Revolution) bequeathed the city more than 4,000 drawings and paintings. See chapter 16.
- **Musée Toulouse-Lautrec** (Albi, Languedoc): The artist Toulouse-Lautrec was born in Albi in 1864. Much to his family's horror, he opted to move to a scandalous neighborhood in Paris, where his affectionate and amused depictions of the belle époque scene are priceless treasures today. Also on view here are works by Degas, Bonnard, and Matisse. See chapter 19.
- **Musée Fabre** (Montpellier, Languedoc): This museum occupies a historic villa where Molière once presented some of his plays. Today it boasts one of the worthiest collections of French, Italian, and Spanish paintings in the south of France. See chapter 19.
- **Musée Ile-de-France** (St-Jean-Cap-Ferrat, Côte d'Azur): This breathtaking villa is loaded with paintings and furniture that have remained more or less in their original positions since the donor's death in 1934. The source of the museum's grand ostentation was the baronne Ephrussi, scion of the Rothschilds, who scoured Europe in pursuit of her treasures. See chapter 21.
- **Fondation Maeght** (St-Paul-de-Vence, Côte d'Azur): Established as a showcase for modern art by the 20th-century collectors Aimé and Marguerite Maeght, this museum is an avant-garde compendium of works by Giacometti, Chagall, Braque, Miró, Matisse, and Barbara Hepworth. Built on many levels in a design by the fabled architect José Luís Sert, it boasts glass walls that allow views over the surrounding ancient arid landscapes of Provence. See chapter 21.

6 The Best Cathedrals

- **Notre-Dame de Paris** (Paris): A triumph of medieval French architecture, this structure's gray stone walls symbolize the power of Paris in the Middle Ages.

Begun in 1163, Notre-Dame is the cathedral of the nation. It's especially dazzling in the early morning and at sunset, when its image is reflected in the Seine. See chapter 5.

- **Notre-Dame de Chartres** (Chartres, Ile de France): No less a talent than Rodin declared this cathedral a French acropolis. The site it occupies was holy for both the prehistoric Druids and the ancient Romans. One of the first High Gothic cathedrals, the first to use flying buttresses, Chartres is one of the largest cathedrals in the world. It also contains what might be the finest stained-glass windows in history, more than 3,000 square yards of glass whose vivid hues and patterns of light are truly mystical. See chapter 6.

- **Notre-Dame de Rouen** (Rouen, Normandy): Consecrated in 1063 and rebuilt after a fire in 1200, this cathedral was immortalized in the late 19th century, when Monet spent hours painting a series of moody impressions of the facade at various times of day. Some sections of the cathedral are masterpieces of the Flamboyant Gothic style; others are plainer, though equally dignified. See chapter 8.

- **Notre-Dame de Reims** (Reims, Champagne): One of France's first Christian bishops, St. Rémi, baptized the pagan king of the Franks, Clovis, on this site in 496, thereby elevating Reims to one of the holiest sites in northern Europe. The cathedral commemorating that event was conceived as a religious sanctuary where the French kings would be anointed; it was suitably large, spectacular, and (in our eyes) rather cold. The coronation of every king between 1137 and 1825 was celebrated here. Damaged by World War I bombings, the cathedral was largely restored by American donations during the 1920s and 1930s. See chapter 10.

- **Notre-Dame d'Amiens** (Amiens, the Ardennes): A lavishly decorated example of High Gothic architecture, this cathedral boasts a soaring nave whose roof is supported by 126 breathtakingly slender pillars. It was begun in 1220 to house the head of St. John the Baptist, brought back from the Crusades in 1206, and at 469 feet long is the largest church in France. Amazingly, it escaped destruction during the bombings of the world wars, despite the fierce fighting that took place nearby. See chapter 10.

- **Notre-Dame de Strasbourg** (Strasbourg, Alsace-Lorraine): One of the largest buildings in the Christian world, this is also one of the most architecturally harmonious Gothic cathedrals of the Middle Ages. Built of russet-colored stone between 1176 and 1439, it's a perfect symbol of Alsatian pride and one of our favorite cathedrals. The monument's 16th-century astrological clock is a showstopper, gathering crowds daily for its 12:30pm exhibition of allegorical figures from myth and fable. See chapter 11.

7 The Best Vineyards & Wineries

One of the best sources for information about French wines is the **Centre d'Information, de Documentation, et de Dégustation (CIDD)**, 30 rue de la Sablière, 75014 Paris (☎ **01-45-45-44-20;** fax 01-45-42-78-20). Throughout the year, this self-funded school presents about a dozen courses addressing all aspects of wine tasting, producing, buying, and merchandising. Conducted in French and English, they're tailored to wine merchants, wine growers, and restaurant-industry professionals. The organization is a gold mine of information for anyone anticipating a tour of the vineyards.

- **Couly-Dutheil** (Chinon; ☎ **02-47-97-20-20**): The cellars here are suitably medieval, many carved into the rock undulating through the area's forests. Most of this company's production involves Chinon wines (mostly reds), though two that they're justifiably proud of are Borgeuil and St-Nicolas de Borgeuil, whose popularity in the North American market has grown in recent years. See chapter 7.

- **Champagne Taittinger** (Reims; ☎ 03-26-85-84-33): Taittinger is a grand marque of French champagne, one of the few whose ownership is still controlled by members of the family who founded it in 1930. It's one of the most visitor-friendly of the champagne houses. See chapter 10.
- **Domaines Schlumberger** (Guebwiller, near Colmar; ☎ 03-89-74-27-00): Established by Schlumberger beginning in 1810, these cellars are an unusual combination of early 19th-century brickwork and modern stainless steel; a visit will go far in enhancing your understanding of the subtle differences among wines produced by the seven varieties of grape cultivated in Alsace. See chapter 11.
- **Domaine Protheau** (Château d'Etroyes, Mercurey; ☎ 03-85-45-25-12): The 150 acres of grapevines straddle at least two appellations contrôlées, so you'll have a chance to immerse yourself in the subtle differences among reds (both pinot noirs and burgundies), whites, and rosés produced under the auspices of both Rully and Mercurey. The headquarters of the organization, founded in the 1740s, is a château built in the late 1700s and early 1800s. See chapter 13.

  Two miles away, you can visit the **Château Féodale de Rully** (☎ 03-85-87-20-42), a 12th-century stronghold of the comtes de Ternay. See chapter 13.
- **The Wine-Growing Region Around Bordeaux:** This region is among the most glamorous in France, with a strong English influence thanks to centuries of wine buying by London- and Bristol-based dealers. One of the area's prestigious growers is the **Société Duboscq**, Château Haut-Marbuzet, 33180 St-Estephe (☎ 05-56-59-30-54), which welcomes visitors daily. Free visits to the cellars are followed by a complimentary dégustation des vins of whichever of the company's products a client requests. See chapter 17.

8 The Best Luxury Hotels

- **Le Ritz** (Paris; ☎ 800/241-3333 in the U.S. and Canada, or 01-43-16-30-30): This hotel occupies a palace overlooking the octagonal borders of one of the most aesthetically perfect plazas in France: place Vendôme. The decor is pure opulence. Marcel Proust wrote parts of *Remembrance of Things Past* in an apartment here, and Georges-Auguste Escoffier perfected many of his lgendary recipes in its kitchens. See chapter 4.
- **Hôtel de Crillon** (Paris; ☎ 800/241-3333 in the U.S. and Canada, or 01-44-71-15-00): This hotel's majestic exterior was designed by the 18th-century architect Jacques-Ange Gabriel and forms part of the symmetrical backdrop for place de la Concorde. The decor encompasses the reigns of Cardinal Richelieu and Marie Antoinette, and nearly every surface is polished weekly by a battalion of well-trained attendants. See chapter 4.
- **Château d'Artigny** (Montbazon, Loire Valley; ☎ 02-47-34-30-30): The perfume king François Coty once lived and entertained lavishly at this mansion outside Tours—and you can do the same today, as it's been converted into one of the poshest hotels in the Loire Valley. You can live in the grandeur and total comfort once enjoyed by Elizabeth Taylor and other celebs, taking in the popular weekend soirées and musical evenings. See chapter 7.

- **Hôtel du Palais** (Biarritz, Basque Country; ☎ **800/223-6800** in the U.S. and Canada, or 05-59-41-64-00): Delectably beautiful, this place was built in 1845 as a pink-walled summer palace for Napoléon III and his empress, Eugénie. Adept at housing such guests as Edward VII of England, Alfonso XIII of Spain, and the duke of Windsor, the hotel is a belle époque fantasy. See chapter 18.
- **L'Oustau de Beaumanière** (Les Baux, outside Marseille, Provence; ☎ **04-90-54-33-07**): This Relais & Châteaux stands in the valley at the foot of Les Baux de Provence. The cuisine is superb, as are the luxurious accommodations, some of which are in buildings dating from the 16th and 17th centuries. See chapter 20.
- **Grand Hôtel du Cap-Ferrat** (St-Jean-Cap-Ferrat, Côte d'Azur; ☎ **04-93-76-50-50**): A destination in its own right, the Grand Hôtel occupies 14 prime acres on one of the world's most exclusive peninsulas. It's housed in a belle époque palace and since the turn of the century has been the temporary home for royals, aristocrats, and wealthy wanna-bes. See chapter 21.
- **Grand Hôtel du Cap-Eden Roc** (Cap d'Antibes, Côte d'Azur; ☎ **04-93-61-39-01**): Built during the grand Second Empire and set on 22 acres of splendidly landscaped gardens, this hotel is one of Europe's most legendary, evoking shades of the F. Scott Fitzgerald classic *Tender Is the Night*. Swimmers will revel in a pool blasted from the dark rock of the glamorous coastline of Cap d'Antibes. See chapter 21.
- **Hôtel Négresco** (Nice, Côte d'Azur; ☎ **04-93-16-64-00**): Built in 1913 as a layered wedding cake in the château style, the Négresco was a lavish holiday escape for the Edwardian era's most respected and most notorious figures. Among them was the actress Lillie Langtry, the long-term mistress of Britain's Edward VII. After her fall from grace, she sat in the Négresco's lobby, swathed in veils, refusing to utter a word. Following tasteful renovations, the hotel is better now than it was even during its Jazz Age heyday. See chapter 21.

9 The Best Affordable Hotels

- **Hôtel de Lutèce** (Paris; ☎ **01-43-26-23-52**): It slumbers sleepily from a position on Paris's "other island," the Ile St-Louis, which usually avoids the crush of visitors that swarm onto the more popular Ile de la Cité, just across the bridge. You'll still be right in the city, but you can imagine yourself in a country inn at this tasteful retreat on the Seine. See chapter 4.
- **Hostellerie Lechat** (Honfleur, Normandy; ☎ **02-31-14-49-49**): Views from its windows overlook a Norman 18th-century port favored by the French novelist Flaubert, and though its amenities aren't particularly grand, you'll get the feeling that Mme Bovary herself may be about to roll into view in her notorious carriage. The setting, which includes a rustically appealing restaurant, is charming and— even more surprising—the price tag is reasonable. See chapter 8.
- **Hôtel d'Avaugour** (Dinan, Brittany; ☎ **02-96-39-07-49**): Its exterior is as antique looking as the fortifications that ring the medieval harbor of Dinan, but a radical restoration transformed the interior into a site secure from the howling winds and driving rains of the Norman coast. Add to that its aesthetic appeal and the old-time flavor of Dinan's winding alleys and views out over the Channel, and you've got all the ingredients you'll need for an affordable escape. See chapter 9.
- **Hostellerie du Vieux-Pérouges** (Pérouges, Rhône Valley; ☎ **04-74-61-00-88**): This hotel, often described as a museum of the 13th century, is one of the most

significant in central France. Composed of a group of much-restored 13th-century buildings with low ceilings and thick walls, it vividly evokes the France of another day and doesn't overcharge for the privilege. See chapter 14.

- **Tulip Inn Le Bayonne Etche-Ona** (Bordeaux, Atlantic Coast; ☎ **05-56-48-00-88**): Like much of the rest of the neighborhood that surrounds it, this hotel was conceived during the 18th century as a showcase for French neoclassicism. Today, after a recent interior renovation, it offers modern comforts in an antique setting—and it's a great value. See chapter 17.

- **Hôtel du Donjon** (Carcassonne, Languedoc; ☎ **800/528-1234** in the U.S. and Canada, or 04-68-71-08-80): Built into the solid bulwarks of Carcassonne, one of France's most perfectly preserved medieval fortresses, is this small-scale hotel whose well-appointed furnishings provide a vivid contrast to the crude stone shell that contains them. A stay here truly allows you personal contact with a site that often provoked bloody battles between medieval armies. See chapter 19.

- **La Réserve** (Albi, Languedoc; ☎ **05-63-60-80-80**): This dignified farmhouse is surrounded by scrublands, vineyards, groves of olives, and cypresses. It's less expensive than many of the ultraluxurious hideaways along the nearby Côte d'Azur and has the added benefit of a location just outside the center of one of our favorite fortified sites in Europe, the medieval town of Albi. See chapter 19.

- **Hôtel Clair Logis** (St-Jean-Cap-Ferrat, Côte d'Azur; ☎ **04-93-76-04-57**): The real estate that surrounds this converted 19th-century villa is among the most expensive in Europe, but despite that, this hotel manages to keep its prices beneath levels that really hurt. If you check into a room here (each named after a flower that thrives in the 2-acre garden surrounding the place), you'll be in good company: even General de Gaulle, who knew the value of a centime, stayed here. See chapter 21.

10 The Best Historic Places to Stay

- **Hôtel Trianon Palace** (Versailles, Ile de France; ☎ **01-30-84-38-00**): Louis XIV nearly bankrupted the treasury of France during the construction of his nearby palace, but this hotel overlooking its gardens might have been even more influential. In 1919 the Versailles Peace Treaty was ratified by delegates who retired, after the momentous but ill-conceived event, to the same rooms housing guests today. In addition to all the history you'll get, you'll be pampered at this plush and elegant hotel, which boasts its own spa. See chapter 6.

- **Château de Locguénolé** (Hennebont, Brittany; ☎ **02-97-76-29-04**): No professional decorator could ever have accumulated the wide array of furnishings and artifacts that 500 years' occupancy by successive generations of the same family have managed to cram into this Breton manor house. Some visitors think it's the most charming hotel in southern Brittany, a fact that's very easy to believe once you experience its style and charm. See chapter 9.

- **Manoir du Stang** (La Forêt-Fouesnant, Brittany; ☎ **02-98-56-97-37**): Even the ivy that twines across the facade of this 16th-century Breton manor house looks as though it had been planted by someone very important, very long ago. Formal gardens segue into forested parkland, modern amenities are juxtaposed with enviable antiques—overall, the place is a gem that also happens to be a glamorous hotel. Some of the staff wear traditional Breton costumes, adding to the allure. See chapter 9.

- **Château de la Vallée Bleue** (La Châtre, Massif Central; ☎ **02-54-31-01-91**): If you happen to stay in a room named for Liszt, Chopin, Flaubert, or Delacroix, be assured that the nomenclature won't be accidental—those artists preceded you at this 19th-century monument and probably slept in the same rooms. The place was built by a doctor firmly committed to the well-being of his nearby patient, George Sand, famous author and feminist trendsetter whose masquerades as a man still provoke curiosity in this part of France. See chapter 15.

- **Château de Castel-Novel** (Varetz, the Dordogne; ☎ 05-55-85-00-01): This secluded château, with its 25-acre park, was a favorite with the novelist Colette, who once lived here. Her presence caused an illustrious entourage of political and literary luminaries to frequent the town. The more luxurious rooms, preferred by devoted literary fans, can be found in the main building along with Colette's library, which has since been turned into a charming salon. La Borderie is the château's more modern 10-room annex. You'll enjoy grilled lunches by the pool in summer and rich meals in the restaurant. See chapter 16.

- **Château de Brindos** (Anglet, Basque Country; ☎ 05-59-23-17-68): Built between 1923 and 1926 by the heiress to an American railway fortune (Virginia Gould) with her English husband (Reginald Wright), this château has an Art Deco facade, 14th-century Gothic ruins in its garden, and fireplaces and ceilings imported from other Renaissance palaces of Europe. Today it offers an alluring combination of the Gilded Age as interpreted by the Jazz Age, superb food, and some of the most spectacular architectural adornments in France's southwest. See chapter 18.

- **Château de Rochegude** (Rochegude, Provence; ☎ 04-75-97-21-10): During the thousand years of this château's existence, its owners have included popes, dauphins, and dozens of less prominent aristocrats who have showered it with taste and money. Today each guest room is outfitted in a different antique style inspired by a specific emperor or king. The setting is 20 acres of parkland adjacent to the Rhône, outside Orange. See chapter 20.

- **Château de Roussan** (St-Rémy-de-Provence, Provence; ☎ 04-90-92-11-63): One of its outbuildings was the home of the Renaissance psychic Nostradamus, and its main building, sheltered by a stone neoclassical facade erected in 1701, is among the most beautiful in Provence. Wandering around the place will evoke another time and another place, with absolutely none of the artificiality that dominates along the nearby Côte d'Azur. See chapter 20.

11 The Best Upscale Restaurants

- **Alain Ducasse** (Paris; ☎ 01-47-27-12-27): Achieving a coveted three-star rating from Michelin seemed hardly a daunting challenge to this brash chef who's taken Paris and Monaco by storm. Ducasse is the world's first six-star chef (three for Paris and three for his Louis XV in Monte Carlo). He's the darling of today's foodies and the spiritual heir of the legendary Escoffier. Who can outdo his homemade pasta bathed in cream, sweetbreads, truffles, and—get this—the combs and kidneys of a proud, strutting cock? See chapter 4.

- **Le Grand Véfour** (Paris; ☎ 01-42-96-56-27): Amid the arcades of the Palais Royal, this has been a dining spot since the reign of Louis XV, attracting over the years such notables as Colette, Victor Hugo, and the forever-loyal Jean Cocteau. Jean Taittinger of the champagne family runs it today, and his kitchen brings originality to the French classics—everything from pigeon in the style of Rainier of Monaco to French-roasted sole and sea scallops in a velvety pumpkin sauce. See chapter 4.

- **Taillevent** (Paris; ☎ 01-44-95-15-01): Dining here is still the social and gastronomic high point of a Paris visit. Its premises (an antique house near the Arc de Triomphe, laden with flowers) are suitably grand and its cuisine appropriately stylish to the Jackie O. lookalikes who sometimes dine here. See chapter 4.
- **Boyer-les-Crayères** (Reims, Champagne; ☎ 03-26-82-80-80): This restaurant's setting is a lavish but dignified château with soaring ceilings and a flawless French Empire decor. Built in 1904 as the home of the Pommery family (of champagne fortune) and surrounded by a 14-acre park, it's maintained by an impeccably trained staff who appreciate the nuances of elaborate service rituals. You can retire directly to your accommodations after consuming a bottle or two of the region's famous bubbly. See chapter 10.
- **L'Auberge de l'Ill** (near Colmar, Alsace-Lorraine; ☎ 03-89-71-89-00): After a meal here, you'll understand why France and Germany fought so bitterly for control of Alsace. Set amid well-tended farmland on the edge of the river Ill, this half-timbered manor house presents an almost idyllic setting. The food and wine served are rich, lush, and firmly rooted in the vineyards surrounding the place. See chapter 11.
- **Auberge du Père-Bise** (Talloires, French Alps; ☎ 04-50-60-72-01): A mysterious alchemy transformed what was a simple lakeside chalet into an illustrious restaurant. Set beside Lac d'Annecy in eastern France, it's outfitted like the prosperous provincial home of local gentry, yet it serves sublimely elegant food favored by many generations of people like the Rothschilds. See chapter 12.
- **A la Côte St-Jacques** (Joigny, Burgundy; ☎ 03-86-62-09-70): Set on the edge of Burgundy, beside the river Yonne, this is the quintessential *restaurant avec chambres*. Indulge your taste for supremely well-prepared food and wine, then totter off to one of about a dozen carefully furnished guest rooms scattered among several buildings in this historic compound. One of our favorite dishes is cassolette of morels and frogs' legs, especially sublime when accompanied by a half bottle of fine red burgundy. See chapter 13.
- **L'Espérance** (Vézelay, Burgundy; ☎ 03-86-33-39-10): Housed in an antique farmhouse at the base of a hill (La Colline de Vézelay) that has been a holy site for thousands of years, L'Espérance is run by one of Europe's most famous chefs, Marc Meneau, and his wife, Françoise. The place combines country comforts with world-class sophistication. See chapter 13.
- **Paul Bocuse** (Collonges-au-Mont-d'Or, near Lyon, Rhône Valley; ☎ 04-72-42-90-90): Bocuse was the enfant terrible of French gastronomy throughout most of his youth. Today he's the world's most famous living chef, catering to Europe's hardest-to-please customers. The cuisine is ostensibly Lyonnaise, but Bocuse has never allowed himself to be hemmed in by such provincialism, and his mind wanders the world for culinary inspiration. He creates his own signature dishes to delight the palates of his international fans—ranging from roast pigeon in puff pastry with foie gras to his celebrated black truffle soup. See chapter 14.

Impressions

Who can help loving the land that has taught us six hundred and eighty-five ways to dress eggs?

—Thomas Moore, *The Fudge Family in Paris* (1818)

- **Hôtel/Restaurant des Troisgros** (Roanne, Rhône Valley; ☎ **04-77-71-66-97**): The setting is the dining room of a once-nondescript hotel near a railway station. The cuisine, however, is a joyfully lush celebration of the agrarian bounty of France. Mingling specialties from all the regions, it attracts diners from as far away as Paris and Brussels. Years after they dine here, many people still speak reverently of their meal. See chapter 14.
- **Le Moulin de Mougins** (Mougins, Côte d'Azur; ☎ **04-93-75-78-24**): Occupying a 16th-century olive mill in a Provence pine forest, this restaurant is the creation of chef Roger Vergé, the most sophisticated media genius in the French culinary world. See chapter 21.

12 The Best Affordable Restaurants

- **Crémerie-Restaurant Polidor** (Paris; ☎ **01-43-26-95-34**): For many Parisians, the cuisine here evokes memories of what their grandmothers might have concocted for a family supper in the days after World War II. The unpretentious setting, where lace curtains filter the sunlight, was a favorite even of such iconoclasts as André Gide. See chapter 4.
- **Les Vapeurs** (Trouville, Normandy; ☎ **02-31-88-15-24**): An anomaly among the Norman coast's steeply priced brasseries, this choice overlooking the port is no-frills all the way, from its Art Deco decor to its fresh, well-priced seafood. People really seem to enjoy the festive ambience. See chapter 8.
- **Chez La Mère Pourcel** (Dinan, Brittany; ☎ **02-96-39-03-80**): The references this place makes to someone's grandmother (Mère Pourcel) are completely justified, since the cuisine hasn't changed very much in decades. That's just fine with its guests, many of whom drive from Paris for a day in the countryside and a well-priced dinner. See chapter 9.
- **La Table de Mengin** (Nancy, Alsace-Lorraine; ☎ **03-83-35-17-25**): The setting, in the antique heart of the capital of Lorraine, is as solidly bourgeois as you'd expect, and the cuisine appropriately sumptuous. You get all this for less, even much less, than equivalent cuisine as interpreted by the maestros of Paris or Nice. See chapter 11.
- **Au Chalet de Brou** (Bourg-en-Bresse, Rhône Valley; ☎ **04-74-22-26-28**): Located in a town famous for the quality of its poultry, this restaurant sits just across from the village church. It offers amazingly low prices on the wonderful local birds, and many food critics travel here from all over France for the hearty roast chicken. See chapter 14.
- **La Crémaillère** (Brive-la-Gaillarde, Périgord; ☎ **05-55-74-32-47**): This restaurant lacks the sensational aesthetic style of some of its more expensive competitors, but never mind: The food is affordable and, as many local artists and entrepreneurs will tell you, delectable. See chapter 16.
- **Le Bistro Latin** (Aix-en-Provence, Provence; ☎ **04-42-38-22-88**): The great deal here lies in the fixed-price menus, which are as carefully composed as a symphony. Prices are low, flavors are sensational, and hints of Italian zest pop up frequently in such dishes as risotto with scampi. See chapter 20.
- **Le Safari** (Nice, Côte d'Azur; ☎ **04-93-80-18-44**): This ever-popular, ever-crowded brasserie overlooking the cours Saleya market soaks up the Riviera sun. Dressed in jeans, waiters hurry back and forth, serving the regulars and the visitors alike on the sprawling terrace. This place makes one of the best salade niçoise concoctions in town, as well as a drop-dead spring lamb roasted in a wood-fired oven. See chapter 21.

2 Introducing France

France remains one of the world's most hyped, most talked about, and most written about destinations. It's packed with diversions and distractions of every sort—cultural, recreational, sensual, you name it. And perhaps that's why France has been called *le deuxième pays de tout le monde*—everyone's second country.

The French claim credit for developing the Gothic style of architecture and the cathedrals that stand as legacies of soaring stone for future generations. And ever since the Middle Ages, creators of everything from palaces to subway stations have drawn at least some inspiration from designs born in France. However, despite the thrilling monuments peppering the country, it would be wrong to assume that the culture's main contribution to the world is derived from stone, mortar, stained glass, and gilt. Its contributions to painting, literature, cuisine, fashion, and savoir faire are staggering.

When other parts of Europe were slumbering through the Dark Ages, Provence was alive with creativity as Provençal poetry evolved into a truly lyrical, evocative, and even erotic verse form. And Renaissance Paris, despite the frequent absences of its monarchs, who sequestered themselves with their entourages in remote Loire Valley châteaux, developed into one of Europe's most cosmopolitan cities, embellishing itself with majestic buildings and sculpture.

The passionate French tradition of scholarship helped build Europe's university system and synthesized the modern world's interpretation of human rights. In politics and ideology, France has always been a leader: Fueled by Enlightenment writings, whose most articulate voices were French, the 1789 Revolution toppled Europe's most deeply entrenched regime and cracked the foundations of dozens of other governments. Postrevolutionary Paris became a magnet for the greatest talents of the 19th and early 20th centuries.

Read on, as this chapter will introduce first-time visitors to France's subtle pleasures and open new doors to those who might already have spent time here.

1 The Regions in Brief

Though France covers only 212,741 square miles, no other country concentrates such a fabulous diversity of sights and scenery into so compact an area. It encompasses each of the characteristics that make up Europe: the north's flat, fertile lands; the central Loire Valley's

rolling green hills; the east's snowcapped alpine ranges; the southwest's towering Pyrénées; the Massif Central's plateaus and rock outcroppings; and the southeast's lushly semitropical Mediterranean coast. Even more noteworthy are the strong cultural and historic differences defining each region.

And all these contrasts beckon within easy traveling range. The train trip from Paris is just 4 hours to Alsace, 5 to the Alps, 7 to the Pyrénées, and 8 to the Côte d'Azur. **France's National Railroads (SNCF)** operate one of the finest lines in the world, with impressively fast service to and from Paris (though trains tend to crawl on routes unconnected with the capital).

You'll find some 44,000 miles of roadway at your disposal, most in good condition for fast long-distance driving. (But try not to stick to the Route Nationale network all the time. Nearly all France's scenic splendors lie along secondary roads, and what you'll lose in mileage you'll more than make up for in enjoyment.)

A "grand tour" of France is nearly impossible for the average visitor, who doesn't have a lifetime to explore the country. It would take you at least 2 weeks to tour each major province. You're going to be faced with hard choices about where to go given your time limit, interests, and budget. With this in mind, we've summarized the highlights of each region.

ILE DE FRANCE   Ile de France is an island only in the sense that its boundaries (following about a 50-mile radius from the center of Paris) are delineated by rivers with odd-sounding names like Essonne, Epte, Aisne, Eure, and Ourcq, plus a handful of canals. It was in this temperate basin that France was born. This region's spectacular attractions include **Paris, Versailles, Fontainebleau, Notre-Dame de Chartres,** and **Giverny,** yet it also incorporates endless dreary suburbs and even Disneyland Paris. Despite creeping industrialization, pockets of verdant charm remain, including the forests of Rambouillet and Fontainebleau and the artists' hamlet of Barbizon. See chapter 6.

LOIRE VALLEY   This area includes two ancient provinces, Touraine (centered around Tours) and Anjou (centered around Angers). It was beloved by royalty and nobility until Henry IV moved his court to Paris. Head here to see the most magnificent châteaux and castles in France. Irrigated by the Loire River and its many tributaries, this valley produces many superb and reasonably priced wines. See chapter 7.

NORMANDY   This region will forever be linked to the 1944 D-Day invasion. Some readers consider their visit to the D-Day beaches the most emotionally worthwhile part of their trip to France. Normandy boasts 372 miles of coastline and a longstanding maritime tradition. It's a popular weekend getaway from Paris, and many glamorous hotels and restaurants thrive here, especially around the casino town of **Deauville.** This area has hundreds of half-timbered houses reminiscent of medieval England, charming seaports like **Trouville,** and mighty ports like **Le Havre,** set where the Seine flows into the English Channel. Normandy's great attractions include **Rouen** cathedral, the abbey of **Jumièges,** and medieval **Bayeux.** See chapter 8.

BRITTANY   Jutting out into the Atlantic, the westernmost (and one of the poorest) regions of France is known for its rocky coastlines, Celtic roots, frequent rains, and ancient dialect, which is akin to the Gaelic tongues of Wales and Ireland. Many French vacationers love the seacoast (rivaled only by the Côte d'Azur), for its sandy beaches, high cliffs, and relatively modest prices (by French standards, anyway). Highlights of the region are **Carnac** (home to ancient Celtic dolmens and burial mounds) and atmospheric fishing ports like Quimper, Quiberon, Quimperlé, and Concarneau. The region's most sophisticated resort, **La Baule,** lies near some of southern Brittany's best beaches. See chapter 9.

CHAMPAGNE   Every French monarch since A.D. 496 was crowned at Reims, and much of French history revolved around this holy site and the fertile hills ringing it. Joan of Arc was burned at the stake thanks partly to her efforts to lead her dauphin through enemy lines to **Reims.** Directly in the path of any invader wishing to occupy Paris, both Reims and the fertile Champagne district have been awash in more blood throughout the centuries, including the terrible World War I battles of Somme and Marne. There are industrial sites concentrated among patches of verdant forest, and the steep sides of valleys are sheathed in vineyards. The 78-mile road from Reims to Vertus, one of the three **Routes du Champagne,** takes in a trio of wine-growing regions that produce 80% of the bubbly used for celebrations around the world. See chapter 10.

THE ARDENNES & NORTHERN BEACHES   France's northern region is often neglected by North Americans (which is why we feature it only as a side trip from Reims in Champagne). In summer, French families arrive by the thousands to visit Channel beach resorts like **Le Touquet-Paris-Plage.** This district is heavily industrialized and (like neighboring Champagne) has always been horribly war torn. The region's best-known port, **Calais,** was a bitterly contested English stronghold on the French mainland for hundreds of years. Ironically, Calais functions today as the port of disembarkation for the ferries, hydrofoils, and Channel Tunnel arrivals from Britain. **Notre-Dame Cathedral in Amiens,** the medieval capital of Picardy, is a treasure, with a 140-foot-high nave—the highest in France. Other than Amiens, the town holding the most interest is **Laon,** 74 miles southeast; it's still surrounded by medieval ramparts, which are the northeast's most rewarding attraction. See chapter 10.

ALSACE-LORRAINE   Between Germany and the forests of the Vosges is the most Teutonic of France's provinces: Alsace, with cosmopolitan **Strasbourg** as capital. Celebrated for its cuisine, particularly its foie gras and *choucroute* (sauerkraut), this area is home to villages whose half-timbered designs will make you think of the Black Forest. If you travel the **Route de Vin (Wine Road)** you can visit historic towns like Colmar, Riquewihr, and Illhaeusern, all famous to those who love great food and wine. **Lorraine,** birthplace of Joan of Arc and site of the industrial center of Mulhouse, witnessed countless bloody battles during the world wars. Its capital, **Nancy,** is the proud guardian of a grand 18th-century plaza—place Stanislaus. The much-eroded peaks of the Vosges forest, the closest thing to a wilderness left in France, offer rewarding hiking. See chapter 11.

THE FRENCH ALPS   This area's resorts rival those of neighboring Switzerland and contain some incredible scenery: snowcapped peaks, glaciers, and alpine lakes. **Chamonix** is a world-famous ski resort facing **Mont Blanc,** Western Europe's highest mountain. However, **Courchevel** and **Megève** are more chic. During summer in the Alps you can enjoy such spa resorts as **Evian** and the calm and restful 19th-century resorts ringing **Lake Geneva.** See chapter 12.

BURGUNDY   Few trips will prove as rewarding as several leisurely days spent exploring Burgundy, with its splendid old cities like **Dijon.** Besides being famous for its cuisine (boeuf and escargots à la bourguignonne, for example), the district contains, along its Côte d'Or, hamlets whose names (Mercurey, Beaune, Puligny-Montrachet, Vougeot, and Nuits-St-Georges, among others) are synonymous with great wines. See chapter 13.

THE RHONE VALLEY   A fertile area of alpine foothills and sloping valleys in eastern and southeastern France, the upper Rhône Valley ranges from the cosmopolitan French suburbs of the Swiss city of Geneva to the northern borders of Provence. The district is thoroughly French, unflinchingly bourgeois, and dedicated to preserving the gastronomic and cultural traditions that have produced some of the most celebrated chefs in French history.

Only 2 hours by train from Paris, the region's cultural centerpiece, **Lyon,** is France's "second city." North of here, you can travel the Beaujolais trail or head for Bresse's ancient capital, **Bourg-en-Bresse,** which produces the world's finest poultry. You can explore the Rhône Valley en route from northern climes to Provence and the south. Try to visit the medieval villages of **Pérouges** and **Vienne,** 17 miles south of Lyon, the latter known for its Roman ruins. See chapter 14.

THE MASSIF CENTRAL   The rugged heartland of south-central France, this underpopulated district contains ancient cities, unspoiled scenery, and an abundance of black lava, from which many area buildings were created. According to Parisians, the Massif Central is provincial with a vengeance—and the locals work hard to keep it that way. The largest cities are historic **Clermont-Ferrand** and **Limoges**—the medieval capitals of the provinces of the Auvergne and the Limousin, respectively. **Bourges,** a gateway to the region and once capital of Aquitaine, has a beautiful Gothic cathedral. See chapter 15.

THE DORDOGNE & PERIGORD The land of foie gras and truffles is the site of some of Europe's oldest prehistoric settlements. For biking or just indulging in decadent gourmet meals, the region is among the top vacation spots in France. In the Périgord, traces of Cro-Magnon settlements are evidenced by the cave paintings at **Les Eyzies.** The Dordogne is the second-largest *département* (French equivalent of an American state). Some of France's most unusual châteaux were built in the valley of the Dordogne during the early Middle Ages. The region is, unfortunately, no longer undiscovered, as retirees from abroad have moved into the elegant stone manor houses dotting the banks of the many rivers. Highlights are the ancient towns of **Périgueux, Les Eyzies-de-Tayac, Sarlat-le-Canéda, Beynac-et-Cazenac,** and **Souillac.** See chapter 16.

THE ATLANTIC COAST Flat, fertile, and frequently ignored by North Americans, this region incorporates towns pivotal in French history (**Saintes, Poitiers, Angoulême,** and **La Rochelle**) and wine- and liquor-producing villages (**Cognac, Margaux, St-Emilion,** and **Sauternes**) whose names are celebrated around the world. **Bordeaux,** the district's largest city, has an economy firmly based on wine merchandising and boasts truly grand 18th-century architecture. See chapter 17.

THE BASQUE COUNTRY Since prehistoric times the rugged Pyrénées have formed a natural boundary between France and Spain. Sheltered within the mountain valleys flourished one of Europe's most unusual cultures: the Basques. In the 19th century, resorts like **Biarritz** and **St-Jean-de-Luz** attracted the French aristocracy—the empress Eugénie's palace at Biarritz is now a celebrated hotel. The **Parc National des Pyrénées** is crisscrossed with gorgeous hiking trails, and 4 million Catholics annually visit the pilgrimage city of Lourdes. In the isolated villages and towns of the Pyrénées, the old folkloric traditions, strongly permeated with Spanish influences, continue to thrive. See chapter 18.

LANGUEDOC-ROUSSILLON Languedoc may not be as chic as Provence, but it's also less frenetic and more affordable. **Roussillon** is the rock-strewn arid French answer to ancient Catalonia, just across the Spanish border. **The Camargue** is the name given to the steaming marshy delta formed by two arms of the Rhône River. Rich in bird life, it's famous for its flat expanses of tough grasses and for such fortified medieval sites as **Aigues-Mortes.** Also appealing are **Auch,** the capital of Gascony; **Toulouse,** the bustling pink capital of Languedoc; and the "red city" of **Albi,** birthplace of Toulouse-Lautrec. **Carcassonne,** a marvelously preserved walled city with fortifications begun around A.D. 500, is the region's highlight. See chapter 19.

PROVENCE One of France's most fabled regions flanks the Alps and the Italian border along its eastern end and incorporates a host of sites the rich and famous have long frequented. Premier destinations are **Aix-en-Provence,** associated with Cézanne; **Arles,** "the soul of Provence," captured so brilliantly by van Gogh; **Avignon,** the 14th-century capital of Christendom during the papal schism; and **Marseille,** a port city established by the ancient Phoenicians (in some ways more North African than French). Special Provence gems are the small villages, like **Les Baux, Gordes,** and **St-Rémy-de-Provence,** birthplace of Nostradamus. The strip of glittering coastal towns along Provence's southern edge is known as the **Côte d'Azur** (the French Riviera; see below). See chapter 20.

THE FRENCH RIVIERA (COTE D'AZUR) The fabled gold-plated Côte d'Azur has become hideously overbuilt and spoiled by tourism. Even so, the names of its resorts still evoke glamour and excitement: **Cannes, St-Tropez, Cap d'Antibes, St-Jean-Cap-Ferrat.** July and August are the most crowded, but spring and fall can be a delight. **Nice** is your nicest base for exploring the area. The principality of **Monaco,** the most fabled piece of real estate along the Côte d'Azur, occupies less than a square mile. Along the coast are some sandy beaches, but many are rocky or pebbly. Topless bathing is common, especially in St-Tropez, and some of the restaurants here are fabled citadels of conspicuous consumption. This is not just a place for sun and fun, however—dozens of artists and their patrons have littered the landscape with world-class galleries and art museums. See chapter 21.

2 France Today

In the spring of 1998, France ousted its Conservative parties, which amounted to a powerful endorsement for Prime Minister Lionel Jospin and his Socialist-led government. The triumph of Monsieur Jospin and his Communist and Green Allies threw a stunning blow to President Jacques Chirac's Neo-Gaullists and the center-right parties led by François Leotard, and certainly to Jeane-Marie Le Pen's often fanatical National Front.

The French, in essence and in spite of dire warnings, seem to have confirmed their old way of doing things. What they are saying, in effect, is they want no movement toward increasing job market flexibility and no basic redefinition of the vast system of social services, which represent a major drain on the French economy.

In spite of this resistance to change as expressed by the electorate, Jospin is still ever so gently moving France toward the millennium. Without breaking the budget or losing public favor, the prime minister has continued to pick his way through the traditional minefields of French politics—militant unions, a public wedded to generous benefits, and widespread resistance to any change. By 1998, France was poised—or at least within shouting distance—of the fiscal criteria needed for joining Europe's planned single currency. Jospin calls the pathway he is traveling "leftist realism."

Of course, everything in France isn't political. Cultural changes are in the air. African cuisine and ingredients are all the rage, and in Paris especially, people are flocking to tacky, untouristy arrondissements to find restaurants specializing in Senegalese fare. And although the French don't plan to build another Notre-Dame in this century, le Gothique c'est chic. This style influences everything from fashion to music, from advertising to novels.

Another change—and this one is major—sweeping across France is a return to the country. During the postwar years, there was a mass exodus to cities. But now the French are flocking, in droves, back to their lovely countryside to such remote areas as the Massif Central. Why? With the development of modern technology, the French can continue to work at their high-tech jobs while living on—say, a sheep farm in Provence.

3 History 101

EARLY GAUL   When the ancient Romans considered France part of their empire, their boundaries extended deep into the forests of the Paris basin and up to the edges of the Rhine. Part of Julius Caesar's early fame derived from his defeat of King Vercingetorix at Alésia in 52 B.C., a victory he was quick to publicize in one of the ancient world's literary masterpieces, *The Gallic Wars*. In that year the Roman colony of Lutetia (Paris) was established on an island in the Seine (Ile de la Cité).

Dateline

■ **121 B.C.** The Romans establish the province of Gallia Narbonensis to guard overland routes between Spain and Italy; its borders correspond roughly to today's Provence.

continues

- **58–51 B.C.** Julius Caesar conquers Gaul (north-central France).
- **52 B.C.** The Roman city of Lutetia, later Paris, is built on a defensible island in the Seine.
- **2nd century A.D.** Christianity arrives in Gaul.
- **485–511** Under Clovis I, the Franks defeat the Roman armies and establish the Merovingian dynasty.
- **511 on** Confusion and disorder; feudalism and the power of the Catholic church grow.
- **768** Charlemagne (768–814) becomes Frankish king and establishes the Carolingian dynasty; from Aix-la-Chapelle (Aachen) he rules lands from northern Italy to Bavaria to Paris.
- **800** Charlemagne is crowned Holy Roman Emperor in Rome.
- **814** Charlemagne dies and his empire breaks up.
- **1066** William of Normandy (the Conqueror) invades England; his Conquest is completed by 1087.
- **1140** St-Denis Cathedral, the first example of Gothic architecture, is completed.
- **1270** Louis IX (St. Louis), along with most of his army, dies in Tunis on the Eighth Crusade.
- **1309** The papal schism—Philip the Fair establishes the Avignon papacy, which lasts nearly 70 years; two popes struggle for domination.
- **1347–51** The bubonic plague (the Black Death) kills 33% of the population.
- **1431** The English burn Joan of Arc at the stake in Rouen for resisting their occupation of France.

continues

As the Roman Empire declined, its armies retreated to the flourishing colonies that had been established along a strip of the Mediterranean coast—among others, these included Orange, Montpellier, Nîmes, Narbonne, and Marseille, which retain some of the best Roman monuments in Europe.

As one of their legacies, the Roman armies left behind the Catholic church, which, for all its abuses, was the only real guardian of civilization during the anarchy following the Roman decline. A form of low Latin was the common language, and it slowly evolved into the archaic French that both delights and confuses today's medieval scholars.

The form of Christianity adopted by many of the chieftains was viewed as heretical by Rome. Consequently, when Clovis (king of northeastern Gaul's Franks and founder of the Merovingian dynasty) astutely converted to Catholicism, he won the approval of the pope, the political support of the powerful archbishop of Reims, and the loyalty of the many Gallic tribes who'd grown disenchanted with anarchy. (Clovis's baptism is viewed as the beginning of a collusion between the Catholic church and the French monarchy that flourished until the 1789 Revolution.) At the Battle of Soissons in 486, Clovis defeated the last vestiges of Roman power in Gaul. Other conquests that followed included expansions westward to the Seine, then to the Loire. After a battle in Dijon in 500, he became the nominal overlord of the king of Burgundy. Seven years later his armies drove the Visigoths into Spain, giving most of Aquitaine, in western France, to his newly founded Merovingian dynasty. Trying to make the best of an earlier humiliation, Anastasius, the Byzantium-based emperor of the Eastern Roman Empire, finally gave the kingdom of the Franks his legal sanction.

After Clovis's death in 511, his kingdom was split among his squabbling heirs. The Merovingian dynasty, however, managed to survive in fragmented form for another 250 years. During this period, the power of the bishops and the great lords grew, firmly entrenching the complex hierarchies and preoccupations of what we today know as feudalism. Although apologists for the Merovingians are quick to point out their achievements, the feudalistic quasi-anarchy of their tenuous reign has been (not altogether unfairly) identified by many historians as the Dark Ages.

THE CAROLINGIANS From the wreckage of the intrigue-ridden Merovingian court emerged a new dynasty: the Carolingians. One of their leaders,

Charles Martel, halted a Muslim invasion of northern Europe at Tours in 743 and left a much-expanded kingdom to his son, Pepin. The Carolingian empire eventually stretched from the Pyrénées to a point deep in the German forests, encompassing much of modern France, Germany, and northern Italy. The heir to this vast land was Charlemagne. Crowned emperor in Rome on Christmas Day in 800, he returned to his capital at Aix-la-Chapelle (Aachen) and created the Holy Roman Empire. Charlemagne's rule saw a revived interest in scholarship, art, and classical texts, defined by scholars as the Carolingian Renaissance.

Despite Charlemagne's magnetism, cultural rifts formed in his sprawling empire, most of which was eventually divided between two of his three squabbling heirs. Charles of Aquitaine annexed the western region; Louis of Bavaria took the east. Historians credit this division with the development of modern France and Germany as separate nations. Shortly after Charlemagne's death, his fragmented empire was invaded by Vikings from the north, Muslim Saracens from the south, and Hungarians from the east.

THE MIDDLE AGES When the Carolingian dynasty died out in 987, Hugh Capet, comte de Paris and duc de France, officially began the Middle Ages with the establishment of the Capetian dynasty. In 1154 the annulment of Eleanor of Aquitaine's marriage to Louis VII of France and subsequent marriage to Henry II of England placed the western half of France under English control, and vestiges of their power remained for centuries. Meanwhile, vast forests and swamps were cleared for harvesting (often by the Middle Ages' hardest-working ascetics, Cistercian monks), the population grew, great Gothic cathedrals were begun, and monastic life contributed to every level of a rapidly developing social order. Politically driven marriages among the ruling families more than doubled the size of the territory controlled from Paris, a city that was increasingly recognized as the country's capital. Philippe II (reigned 1179 to 1223) infiltrated more prominent families with his genes than anyone else in France, successfully marrying members of his family into the Valois, Artois, and Vermandois. He also managed to win Normandy and Anjou back from the English.

Louis IX (St. Louis) emerged as the 13th century's most memorable king, though he ceded most of the hard-earned military conquests of his predecessors back to the English. Somewhat of a religious fanatic,

- **1453** The French drive the English out of all of France except Calais; the Hundred Years War ends.
- **1515–47** France captures Calais after centuries of English rule.
- **1562–98** The Wars of Religion: Catholics fight Protestants; Henri IV converts to Catholicism and issues the Edict of Nantes, granting limited rights to Protestants.
- **1643–1715** The reign of Louis XIV, the Sun King; France develops Europe's most powerful army, but wars in Flanders and court extravagance sow seeds of decline.
- **1763** The Treaty of Paris effectively ends French power in North America.
- **1789–94** French Revolution: The Bastille is stormed on July 14, 1789; the Reign of Terror follows.
- **1793** Louis XVI and Marie Antoinette are guillotined.
- **1794** Robespierre and the leaders of the Terror are guillotined.
- **1799** Napoléon enters Paris and unites diverse factions; his military victories in northern Italy solidify his power in Paris.
- **1804** Napoléon crowns himself emperor in Notre-Dame de Paris.
- **1805–11** Napoléon and his armies successfully invade most of Europe.
- **1814–15** Napoléon abdicates after the failure of his Russian campaign; exiled to Elba, he returns; on June 18, 1815, finally defeated at Waterloo, he's exiled to St. Helena, where he dies in 1821.
- **1830–48** The reign of Louis-Philippe.

continues

■ **1848** A revolution topples Louis-Philippe; Napoléon III (nephew of Napoléon I) is elected president.

■ **1851–71** President Napoléon declares himself Emperor Napoléon III.

■ **1863** An exhibition of paintings marks the birth of Impressionism.

■ **1870–71** The Franco-Prussian War: Paris falls; France cedes Alsace-Lorraine but aggressively colonizes North Africa and Southeast Asia.

■ **1873** France loses Suez to the British; financial scandal wrecks an attempt to dredge the canal.

■ **1889** The Eiffel Tower built for Paris's Universal Exhibition and the Revolution's centennial; architectural critics howl with contempt.

■ **1914–18** World War I; French casualties exceed 5 million.

■ **1923** France occupies the Ruhr, Germany's industrial zone, demanding (and collecting) enormous war reparations.

■ **1929** France retreats from the Ruhr and the Rhineland and constructs the Maginot Line, dubbed "impregnable."

■ **1934** The Great Depression; a political crisis is spurred by clashes of left and right.

■ **1936** Germans march into the demilitarized Rhineland; France takes no action.

■ **1939** France and Britain guarantee to Poland, Romania, and Greece protection from aggressors; Germany invades Poland; France declares war.

■ **1940** Paris falls on June 14; Marshal Pétain's Vichy government collaborates with the Nazis; General de

continues

he died of illness (along with most of his army) in 1270 in a boat anchored off Tunis. The vainglorious and not-very-wise pretext for his trip was the Eighth Crusade. At the time of his death, Notre-Dame and the Sainte-Chapelle in Paris had been completed, and the arts of tapestry making and stone cutting were flourishing.

During the 1300s the struggle of French sovereignty against the claims of a rapacious Roman pope tempted Philip the Fair to encourage support for a pope based in Avignon. (The Roman pope, Boniface VIII, whom Philip publicly insulted and then assaulted in his home, is said to have died of the shock.) During one of medieval history's most bizarre episodes, two popes ruled simultaneously, one from Rome and one from Avignon. They competed fiercely for the spiritual and fiscal control of Christendom, until years of political intrigue turned the tables in favor of Rome and Avignon relinquished its claim in 1378.

The 14th century saw an increase in the wealth and power of the French kings, an increase in the general prosperity, and a decrease in the power of the feudal lords. The death of Louis X without an heir in 1316 prompted more than a decade of scheming and plotting before the eventual emergence of the Valois dynasty.

The Black Death began in the summer of 1348, killing an estimated 33% of Europe's population, decimating the population of Paris, and setting the stage for the exodus of the French monarchs to safer climes in such places as the Loire Valley. A financial crisis, coupled with a series of ruinous harvests, almost bankrupted the nation.

During the Hundred Years War, the English made sweeping inroads into France in an attempt to grab the throne. At their most powerful, they controlled almost all the north (Picardy and Normandy), Champagne, parts of the Loire Valley, and the huge western region called Guyenne. The peasant-born charismatic visionary Joan of Arc rallied the dispirited French troops as well as the timid dauphin (crown prince), whom she managed to have crowned as Charles VII in the cathedral at Reims. As threatening to the Catholic church as she was to the English, she was declared a heretic and burned at the stake in Rouen in 1431. Led by the newly crowned king, a barely cohesive France initiated reforms that strengthened its finances and vigor. After compromises among the quarreling factions, the French army drove the discontented English out, leaving them only the Norman port of Calais.

In the late 1400s Charles VIII married Brittany's last duchess, Anne, for a unification of France with its Celtic-speaking western outpost. In the early 1500s the endlessly fascinating François I, through war and diplomacy, strengthened the monarchy, rid it of its dependence on Italian bankers, coped with the intricate policies of the Renaissance, and husbanded the arts into a form of patronage that French monarchs continued to endorse for centuries.

Meanwhile, the growth of Protestantism and the unwillingness of the Catholic church to tolerate it led to civil strife. In 1572 Catherine de Médici reversed her policy of religious tolerance and ordered the St. Bartholomew's Day Massacre of hundreds of Protestants. Henri IV, tired of the bloodshed and fearful that a fanatically Catholic Spain would meddle in the religious conflicts, converted to Catholicism as a compromise in 1593. Just before being fatally stabbed by a half-crazed monk, he issued the Edict of Nantes in 1598, granting freedom of religion to Protestants in France.

THE PASSING OF FEUDALISM   By now France was a modern state, rid of all but a few of the vestiges of feudalism. In 1624 Louis XIII appointed a Catholic cardinal, the duc de Richelieu, his chief minister. Amassing enormous power, Richelieu virtually ruled the country until his death in 1642. His sole objective was investing the monarchy with total power—he committed a series of truly horrible acts trying to attain this goal and paved the way for the eventual absolutism of Louis XIV.

Although he ascended the throne when he was only 9, with the help of his Sicilian-born chief minister, Cardinal Mazarin, Louis XIV was the most powerful monarch Europe had seen since the Roman emperors. Through first a brilliant military campaign against Spain and then a judicious marriage to one of its royal daughters, he expanded France to include the southern provinces of Artois and Roussillon. Later, a series of diplomatic and military victories along the Flemish border expanded the country toward the north and east. The estimated population of France at this time was 20 million, as opposed to 8 million in England and 6 million in Spain. French colonies in Canada, the West Indies, and America (Louisiana) were stronger than ever. The mercantilism that Louis's brilliant finance minister, Colbert, implemented was one of the era's most important fiscal policies, hugely

Gaulle forms a government-in-exile in London to direct the maquis (French resistance fighters).

- **1944** On June 6 the Allies invade the Normandy beaches; other Allied troops invade from the south; Paris is liberated in August.
- **1946–54** War in Indochina; the French withdraw from Southeast Asia; North and South Vietnam created.
- **1954–58** The Algerian revolution and subsequent independence from France; refugees flood France; the Fourth Republic collapses.
- **1958** De Gaulle initiates the Fifth Republic, calling for a France independent from the United States and Europe.
- **1960** France tests its first atomic bomb.
- **1968** Students riot in Paris; de Gaulle resigns.
- **1981** François Mitterrand becomes the first Socialist president since World War II.
- **1986** The National Front articulates anti-immigrant rage, eventually gathering 10% of the popular vote.
- **1988** Mitterrand is reelected.
- **1989** The bicentennial of the French Revolution and the centennial of the Eiffel Tower.
- **1991** France joins its allies in a war against Iraq.
- **1993** Conservatives topple the Socialists, as Edouard Balladur becomes premier.
- **1994** The Channel Tunnel opens to link France with England.
- **1995** Jacques Chirac wins the French presidency on his third try and declares a war on unemployment; his

continues

popularity wanes and much unrest follows; terrorists bomb Paris several times.

- **1996** Thousands of Paris workers take to the streets, demanding a cut in the work week.
- **1997** Strict immigration laws are enforced, causing strife for many African and Arab immigrants and dividing the country; French voters rebuff Chirac, electing Socialist Lionel Jospin as his new prime minister.
- **1998** Socialists gain in local voting across France.

increasing France's power and wealth. The arts flourished, as did a sense of aristocratic style that's remembered with a bittersweet nostalgia today. Louis's palace of Versailles is the perfect monument to the most flamboyantly consumptive era in French history.

Louis's territorial ambitions so deeply threatened the other nations of Europe that, led by William of Orange, they united to hold him in check. France entered a series of expensive and demoralizing wars that, coupled with high taxes and bad harvests, stirred up much civil discontent. England was viewed as a threat both within Europe and in the global rush for lucrative colonies. The great Atlantic ports, especially Bordeaux, grew and prospered because of France's success in the West Indian slave and sugar trades. Despite the country's power, the total number of French colonies diminished thanks to the naval power of the English. The rise of Prussia as a militaristic neighbor posed an additional problem.

THE REVOLUTION & THE RISE OF NAPOLEON Meanwhile, the Enlightenment was training a new generation of thinkers for the struggle against absolutism, religious fanaticism, and superstition. Europe was never the same after the Revolution of 1789, though the ideas that engendered it had been brewing for more than 50 years. On August 10, 1792, troops from Marseille, aided by a Parisian mob, threw the dimwitted Louis XVI and his tactless Austrian-born queen, Marie Antoinette, into prison. After months of bloodshed and bickering among violently competing factions, the two thoroughly humiliated monarchs were executed.

France's problems got worse before they got better. In the ensuing bloodbaths, both moderates and radicals were guillotined in full view of a bloodthirsty crowd that included voyeurs like Dickens's Mme Defarge, who brought her knitting every day to place de la Révolution (later renamed place de la Concorde) to watch the beheadings. The drama surrounding the collapse of the ancien régime and the beheadings of Robespierre's Reign of Terror provides the most heroic and horrible anecdotes in the history of France. From all this emerged the Declaration of the Rights of Man, an enlightened document published in 1789; its influence has been cited as a model of democratic ideals ever since. The implications of the collapse of the French aristocracy shook the foundations of every monarchy in Europe.

Only the militaristic fervor of Napoléon Bonaparte could reunite France and bring an end to the revolutionary chaos. A political and military genius who appeared on the landscape at a time when the French were thoroughly sickened by the anarchy following their Revolution, he restored a national pride that had been severely tarnished. He also established a bureaucracy and a code of law that has been emulated in other legal systems around the world. In 1799, at the age of 30, he entered Paris and was crowned First Consul and Master of France. Soon after, a decisive victory in his northern Italian campaign solidified his power at home. A brilliant politician, he made peace through a compromise with the Vatican, quelling the atheistic spirit of the earliest days of the Revolution.

Napoléon's victories made him the envy of Europe. Beethoven dedicated his Eroica symphony to Napoléon—but later retracted the dedication when Napoléon committed what Beethoven considered atrocities. Just as he was poised on the verge of conquering all Europe, Napoléon's famous retreat from Moscow during the winter of 1812 reduced his formerly invincible army to tatters, as 400,000 Frenchmen died in the Russian snows. Napoléon was then defeated at Waterloo by the combined armies of the English, Dutch, and Prussians. Exiled to the British-held island of St. Helena in the South Atlantic, he died in 1821, probably the victim of an unknown poisoner.

THE BOURBONS & THE SECOND EMPIRE   In 1814, following the destruction of Napoléon and his dream, the Congress of Vienna redefined the map of Europe. The new geography was an approximation of the boundaries that had existed in 1792. The Bourbon monarchy was reestablished, with reduced powers for Louis XVIII, an archconservative, and a changing array of leaders who included the prince de Polignac and, later, Charles X. A renewal of the ancien régime's oppressions, however, didn't sit well in a France that had already spilled so much blood in favor of egalitarian causes.

In 1830, after censoring the press and dissolving Parliament, Louis XVIII was removed from power after yet more violent uprisings. Louis-Philippe, duc d'Orléans, was elected king under a liberalized constitution. His reign lasted for 18 years of calm prosperity during which England and France more or less collaborated on matters of foreign policy. The establishment of an independent Belgium and the French conquest of Algeria (1840–47) were to have resounding effects on French politics a century later. It was a time of wealth, grace, and expansion of the arts for most French people, though the industrialization of the north and east produced some of the 19th century's most horrific poverty.

A revolution in 1848, fueled by a financial crash and disgruntled workers in Paris, forced Louis-Philippe out of office. That year, Napoléon I's nephew, Napoléon III, was elected president. Appealing to the property-protecting instinct of a nation that hadn't forgotten the violent upheavals of less than a century before, he initiated a repressive right-wing government in which he was awarded the totalitarian status of emperor in 1851. Rebounding from the punishment they'd received during the Revolution and the minor role they'd played during the First Empire, the Second Empire's clergy enjoyed great power. Steel production was begun, and a railway system and Indochinese colonies were established. New technologies fostered new kinds of industry, and the bourgeoisie flourished. And the baron Georges-Eugène Haussmann radically altered Paris by laying out the grand boulevards the world knows today.

By 1866 an industrialized France began to see the Second Empire as more of a hindrance than an encouragement to its expansion. The dismal failure of colonizing Mexico and the increasing power of Austria and Prussia were setbacks to the empire's prestige. In 1870 the Prussians defeated Napoléon III at Sedan and held him prisoner with 100,000 of his soldiers. Paris was besieged by an enemy who only just failed to march its vastly superior armies through the capital.

After the Prussians withdrew, a violent revolt ushered in the Third Republic and its elected president, Marshal MacMahon, in 1873. Peace and prosperity slowly returned, France regained its glamour, a mania of building occurred, the impressionists made their visual statements, and writers like Flaubert redefined the French novel into what today is regarded as the most evocative in the world. As if as a symbol of this period, the Eiffel Tower was built as part of the 1889 Universal Exposition.

By 1890 a new corps of satirists (including Zola) had exposed the country's wretched living conditions, the cruelty of the country's vested interests, and the underlying hypocrisy of late 19th-century French society. The 1894 Dreyfus Affair exposed the corruption of French army officers who had destroyed the career and reputation of a Jewish colleague (Albert Dreyfus), falsely and deliberately punished—as a scapegoat—for treason. The ethnic tensions identified by Zola led to further divisiveness in the rest of the 20th century.

THE WORLD WARS   International rivalries, thwarted colonial ambitions, and conflicting alliances led to World War I, which, after decisive German victories for 2 years, degenerated into the mud-slogged horror of trench warfare. Mourning between 4 and 5 million casualties, Europe was inflicted with psychological scars that never healed. In 1917 the United States broke the European deadlock by entering the war. After the Allied victory, grave economic problems, plus the demoralization stemming from years of fighting, encouraged the growth of socialism and communism. The French government, led by a vindictive Georges Clemenceau, demanded every centime of reparations it could wring from a crushed Germany. The humiliation associated with this has often been cited as the origin of the German nation's almost obsessive determination to rise from the ashes of 1918 to a place in the sun.

The worldwide Great Depression had devastating repercussions in France. Poverty and widespread bankruptcies weakened the Third Republic to the point where successive coalition governments rose and fell with alarming regularity. The crises reached a crescendo on June 14, 1940, when Hitler's armies arrogantly marched down the Champs-Elysées, and newsreel cameras recorded French people openly weeping. Under the terms of the armistice, the north of France was occupied by the Nazis, and a puppet French government was established at Vichy under the authority of Marshal Pétain. The immediate collapse of the French army is viewed as one of the most significant humiliations in modern French history.

Pétain and his regime cooperated with the Nazis in unbearably shameful ways. Not the least of their errors included the deportation of more than 75,000 French Jews to German work camps. Pockets of resistance fighters (le maquis) waged small-scale guerrilla attacks against the Nazis throughout the course of the war and free-French forces continued to fight along with the Allies on battlegrounds like North Africa. Charles de Gaulle, the irascible giant whose personality is forever associated with the politics of his era, established himself as the head of the French government-in-exile, operating first from London and then from Algiers.

The scenario was radically altered on June 6, 1944, when the largest armada in history successfully established a bulkhead on the beaches of Normandy. Paris rose in rebellion even before the Allied armies arrived, and on August 26, 1944, Charles de Gaulle entered the capital as head of the government. The Fourth Republic was declared even as pockets of Nazi snipers continued to shoot from scattered rooftops throughout the city.

THE POSTWAR YEARS   Plagued by the bitter residue of colonial policies France had established during the 18th and 19th centuries, the Fourth Republic witnessed the rise and fall of 22 governments and 17 premiers. Many French soldiers died on battlefields as once-profitable colonies in North Africa and Indochina rebelled. It took 80,000 lives, for example, to put down a revolt in Madagascar. After suffering a bitter defeat in 1954, France ended the war in Indochina and freed its former colony. It also granted internal self-rule to Tunisia and (under slightly different circumstances) Morocco.

Algeria was to remain a greater problem. The advent of the 1958 Algerian revolution signaled the end of the much-maligned Fourth Republic. De Gaulle was called back from retirement to initiate a new constitution, the Fifth Republic, with a stronger set of executive controls. To nearly everyone's dissatisfaction, de Gaulle ended the Algerian war in 1962 by granting the country full independence. Screams of protest resounded long and loud, but the sun had set on most of France's far-flung empire. Internal disruption followed as vast numbers of *pieds-noirs* (French-born residents of Algeria recently stripped of their lands) flooded back into metropolitan France, often into makeshift refugee camps in Provence and Languedoc.

In 1968 major social unrest and a violent coalition hastily formed between the nation's students and blue-collar workers eventually led to the collapse of the government. De Gaulle resigned when his attempts to placate some of the marchers were defeated. The reins of power passed to his second-in-command, Georges Pompidou, and his successor, Valérie Giscard d'Estaing, both of whom continued de Gaulle's policies emphasizing economic development and protection of France as a cultural resource to the world.

THE 1980S & 1990S   In 1981 François Mitterrand was elected the first Socialist president of France since World War II (with a close vote of 51%). In almost immediate response, many wealthy French decided to transfer their assets out of the country, much to the delight of banks in Geneva, Monaco, the Cayman Islands, and Vienna. Though reviled by the rich and ridiculed for personal mannerisms that often seemed inspired by Louis XIV, Mitterrand was reelected in 1988. During his two terms he spent billions of francs on his grands projets (like the Louvre pyramid, Opéra Bastille, Cité de la Musique, and Grande Arche de La Défense), some of which are now beginning to fall apart or reveal serious weaknesses.

In 1992 France played a leading role in the development of the European Union (EU), 15 countries that will eventually abolish all trade barriers among themselves and, as of 1999, share a single currency, the euro. More recent developments include France's interest in developing a central European bank for the regulation of a shared intra-European currency, a ruling that some politicians have interpreted as another block in the foundation of a united Europe.

In April 1993 voters dumped the long-ruling Socialists and installed a new conservative government. Polls cited corruption scandals, rising unemployment, and urban insecurity as reasons for this. The Conservative premier Edouard Balladur had to "cohabit" the government with Mitterrand, whom he blamed for the country's growing economic problems. Diagnosed with terminal prostate cancer near the end of his second term, Mitterrand continued to represent France with dignity, despite his deterioration. The battle over who would succeed him was waged against Balladur with epic rancor by Jacques Chirac, tenacious survivor of many terms as mayor of Paris. Their public discord was among the most venomous since the days of Pétain.

On his third try, on May 7, 1995, Chirac won the presidency with 52% of the vote and immediately declared war on unemployment. Mitterrand turned over the reins of government on May 17. When Mitterrand died shortly thereafter, France embarked on a new era. Chirac's popularity soon faded in the wake of unrest caused by an 11.5% unemployment rate, an unpopular prime minister, a barrage of terrorist attacks by Algerian Muslims, and a stressed economy struggling to meet European Monetary Union entry requirements.

Chirac was hard-pressed to come up with creative answers to France's continuing high unemployment and chaired the government from a smoldering hot seat. He soon proved that the moniker bestowed on him, "Bulldozer," was apt: In an effort to boost his sagging popularity, he leveled his cabinet, ordering all 41 ministers to quit. The task of forming a new government was left to Prime Minister Alain Juppé, himself no stranger to intense public scrutiny after it was revealed that he'd used his position in 1993 as deputy mayor of Paris to procure his son a rent reduction.

A wave of terrorist attacks from July to September 1995 brought an unfamiliar wariness to Paris. Six bombs were planted, killing 7 people and injuring 115. In light of this, Parisians proved cautious if not fearful. Algerian Islamic militants, the suspected culprits, may have brought military guards to the Eiffel Tower, but they failed to throw France into panic.

France's recent history has also been marked by a return to the past. It returned to NATO following a 30-year absence. Its rejoining that military alliance signals an abandonment, or at least a deferral, of the belief that Europe would adopt a more independent defense structure after the Cold War, as espoused by France before the Bosnian conflict.

Throughout 1995 and early 1996, France infuriated everyone from the members of Greenpeace to the governments of Australia and New Zealand by resuming its long-dormant policy of exploding nuclear bombs on isolated Pacific atolls for testing purposes. This policy continued until public outcry, both in France and outside its borders, exerted massive pressure to end the tests.

In May 1996 thousands of Paris's workers took to the streets, disrupting passenger train service to demand a work week shorter than the usual 39 hours. They felt that this move would help France's staggering unemployment figures. Employer organizations are resisting this idea, claiming that even if the work week were cut to 35 hours, businesses wouldn't be able to take on many new employees.

The drama of 1996 climaxed with the heat of the summer, when the police took axes to the doors of the Paris church of St-Bernard de la Chapelle. Nearly 300 African immigrants were removed by force from this place of refuge and deported. Strikes and protests continued to plague the country, and Chirac's political horizon became dimmer still—with a 12% unemployment rate and crime on an alarming increase. Terrorist scares continued to flood the borders of France throughout 1997, forcing a highly visible armed police force, as part of a nationwide program known as Vigipirate, to take to the streets of major cities. One of the unusual offshoots of the Vigipirate program involved the closing of the crypts of many of France's medieval churches to visitors, partly in fear of a terrorist bomb attack on national historic treasures.

In the lastest power struggle between the Conservatives and the Socialists, in the spring of 1998, Conservatives were ousted in a majority of France's regional provinces, amounting to a powerful endorsement for Prime Minister Lionel Jospin's Socialist-led government.

4 Art & Architecture from Pre-Roman to Postmodern

The art and architecture produced in abundance on France's soil have contributed greatly to France's idenity. Annually, vast sums of money are earmarked for salvaging, cleaning, restoring, and documenting national treasures. Today many of the great buildings of France look as good as when they were first built.

The foundations of French art began with the Romans, who imported their monumental sense of symmetry and grandeur (and their engineering techniques) deep into the forests of northern France. But despite the strategic importance of Roman military bases like Lutetia (Paris), only the southernmost region was of any commercial or artistic merit. This region, through trade with the architecturally sophisticated Mediterranean, was quick to adopt the techniques common in the Roman world. Regarding architecture, it has been said that the Romans' triumphal arches, rhythmically massive aqueducts, and mausoleums fixed themselves in the French aesthetic for all time. Today some of the best-preserved ruins of the classical world are scattered though such Provençal towns as Nîmes, Orange, Saintes, and Arles.

ROMANESQUE   As Christianity made its way toward the Celtic tribes on the northern edges of Gaul, an abbreviated and naive kind of naturalism permeated the old Roman ideals, resulting in a crude, often-bulky aesthetic of geometric carvings and primitive masses. Some were influenced by Eastern motifs from Byzantium. Many purists consider Romanesque architecture a symbol of the growing power of the 11th- and 12th-century church, which in many areas was the only constant amid shifting feudal alliances. The earliest Romanesque buildings resembled thick-walled fortresses and often served as refuges during times of invasion. At first they were unembellished, relying on rounded arches and narrow windows for ornamentation.

Many critics think the echoing simplicity of the Cistercians—a reform-minded off-shoot of the Benedictines—to be among the era's more spiritually alluring styles. The abbeys Clairvaux (in the Troyes area in the Champagne country) and Fontenay (in Burgundy) are the best remaining examples. By the 1100s, notably in Poitou, the facades and sections of the interiors of some Romanesque churches were almost completely covered with sculptures whose forms emphasized the architecture rather than served as separate works of art. Though many more visible Romanesque sculptures are unyielding and lifeless, the capitals topping massive columns are often charming, the most natural representations that can be found.

The first French Romanesque church was built around 1002 in Dijon (**St-Bénigne Monastery**). The flowering of the style appeared in the vast ecclesiastical complex of Cluny in Burgundy, which was begun in 1089 and then destroyed by zealous townspeople just after the Revolution.

Contemporaneously with the 10th- and 11th-century construction of churches, the era produced secular fortresses whose crenellations and thick walls often concealed dank, drafty, cramped quarters where cooped-up occupants barely managed to stay sane during times of war. Often, when a fortress was destroyed during a pillage, the survivors rebuilt it in a more fashionable form. In this way, some of the greatest châteaux of France were built, altered, upgraded, and transformed into elegant palaces preserved today as symbols of the Renaissance.

GOTHIC   About 400 years before the great châteaux of the Loire Valley reached their present form, the architects of the royal abbey of St-Denis, outside Paris, completed the first section of a radically new architectural style—Gothic. The cathedrals of Noyon, begun a year later in 1145, and Laon, launched in 1155, almost immediately exemplified the new principles, as did Notre-Dame de Paris when construction was undertaken in 1163. Gothic churches usually included a choir, a ring-around ambulatory, radiating chapels, pointed arches, clustered (rather than monolithic) columns, and ceilings held aloft by ribbed vaulting. Most important is the presence of wide, soaring windows occupying the space that in a Romanesque church would be devoted to thick stone walls. This new design usually required the addition of exterior flying buttresses to keep the weight of the heavy roof and ceiling from pushing the walls apart.

It was at **Chartres,** 60 miles southwest of Paris, that an adaptation of earlier Gothic principles developed for the first time into a Flamboyant High Gothic when a section of the existing cathedral was destroyed in a fire. The tendency toward increased elevation was more fully developed until the cathedrals of Reims and Amiens reached heights so dizzying that medieval worshipers couldn't help but be awed by the might and majesty of God.

The ecclesiastical sculpture that ornamented the portals and facades of the Gothic church progressed from a static kind of stern rigidity to a more fluid, more relaxed, often coquettish kind of naturalism. By the 14th century, ecclesiastical and especially secular carvings attained a kind of international refinement and courtliness that was copied in aristocratic circles throughout Europe.

THE RENAISSANCE   It wasn't long, however, before the Renaissance helped the French realize that the glass-and-stone marvels erected to the glory of God were also fine examples of the skill and imagination of the humans who'd built them. When the

14th-century papal schism led to the recognition of Avignon, not Rome, as the legitimate seat of the papacy, a fortress that would also be a palace was required—hence the building of the **Palais des Papes.** No longer were aristocratic residences designed as gloomy, dank fortresses: Though defense was still a priority, the windows and doors were enlarged and interiors adorned with tapestries, paintings, elaborate religious artifacts (including triptychs), and music. Many of the new châteaux were inspired by Italian models—François I imported many designers, including Leonardo da Vinci, from Italy, whose influence changed French aesthetics forever; Chambord, the Renaissance king's hunting château, is a good example. Religious themes were abandoned as French painting modeled itself first after Flemish and then after northern Italian examples. To an increasing degree, artists began to distance themselves from church dictates.

BAROQUE The early 17th century witnessed the architectural burgeoning of Paris, whose skyline bristled with domes in the restrained baroque of the Italianate style. Louis XIV employed Le Vau, Perrault, both Mansarts, and Bruand for his buildings, with Le Nôtre in charge of the rigidly intelligent layouts of his gardens at Versailles. Meanwhile, court painters like Boucher depicted allegorical shepherdesses and cherubs at play, and Georges de la Tour used techniques of light and shadow (chiaroscuro) inspired by Caravaggio. The châteaux built during this era included the lavishly expensive **Vaux-le-Vicomte Clairvaux** (29 miles southeast of Paris), whose excesses led to the imprisonment of its owner, and the even more lavishly expensive royal residence of **Versailles,** whose excesses helped destroy the ancien régime.

NEOCLASSICISM Following the 1789 collapse of the monarchy, French architects returned to a dignified form of classicism that suited postrevolutionary ideals. Public parks in Metz, Bordeaux, Nancy, and Paris were laid out, sometimes requiring the demolition of acres of twisted medieval sections of cities. Styles inspired by the aesthetics of ancient Rome became the rage in painting, sculpture, and dress, though a brief fling with Egyptology followed the discovery of the Rosetta stone during Napoléon's campaign in Egypt. The revolutionary school of David came and went, and, within the new order, the artist Ingres strove for a kind of classical calm.

THE 19TH CENTURY Around 1850 a new school of eclecticism combined elements from scattered eras of the past into new, sometimes-inharmonious wholes. Between 1855 and 1869 Napoléon III and his chief architect, Baron Haussmann, demolished much of crumbling medieval Paris to lay out the wide avenues that today connect the various monuments in well-proportioned, broad vistas. New building techniques were developed, including the use of iron as the structural support of bridges, viaducts, and buildings such as the National Library, completed in 1860. Naturally, this opened the way for Eiffel to design and erect the most frequently slurred building of its day, the Eiffel Tower, for the 1889 Universal Exposition in Paris.

Among sculptors, the only authentic giant to emerge from the 19th century was Rodin. His human figures were vital, passionate, and lifelike, and he became known for such works as *The Thinker* and *The Kiss.*

Delacroix became the greatest name in French Romantic painting, showing amazing skill as a colorist. When landscape painting rose in prominence in the mid–19th century, **Corot,** of the Barbizon school, was considered one of the best. To many critics the first modern painter in France was **Manet;** he painted portraits and scenes of everyday life but could also create a scandal (*Déjeuner sur l'herbe*) by depicting nudes among dressed figures. Manet isn't to be confused with **Monet,** a great innovator known for his series of paintings of water lilies and of Rouen cathedral. Renoir became celebrated for his sensuously rounded nudes in pearl white, and **Degas** turned to ballet dancers and scenes of racing and the theater for his inspiration.

Outside all movements, but equally important, was **Toulouse-Lautrec.** Satiric but amusing, his style was exemplified by the posters and sketches of music-hall life he depicted.

THE 20TH CENTURY In the early 20th century the **Fauves** ("wild beasts") attracted the most attention, and the greatest of their lot was **Matisse,** who became known for his bright colors and flattened perspective.

Throughout the 20th century exquisite Beaux-Arts buildings continued to be erected throughout Paris, most at roughly the same height, giving it an evenly spaced skyline and rhythmically ornate facades that have caused it to be deemed the world's most beautiful city. The Art Nouveau movement added garlands of laurel and olive branches to the gray-white stone of elegant apartment buildings and hotels throughout France. In the 1920s and 1930s Art Deco's simplified elegance captivated sophisticated sensibilities. **Braque** defined cubism, and **Picasso** worked at his mission of turning the art world upside down. **Le Corbusier** developed his jutting, gently curved planes of concrete, opening the door for a new but often-less talented school of modern French architects.

Critics haven't been kind to the rapidly rusting exposed structural elements of Paris's notorious **Centre Pompidou,** which is under renovation until 2000. In the 1980s an obsolete rail station beside the Seine was transformed into the truly exciting **Musée d'Orsay,** and an expanse of dreary 19th-century slaughterhouses was transformed into a site of tourist worth by the addition of a hypermodern science museum. In the 1990s the **Opéra Bastille** brought new life to the decaying eastern edge of Le Marais but, predictably, sparked a controversy regarding its iconoclastic design. And the screams of outrage could be heard throughout France when I. M. Pei's glass pyramid was built as the postmodern centerpiece of one of the Louvre's most formal 17th-century courtyards.

Mitterrand inaugurated the **Grande Arche de La Défense** on France's bicentennial on July 14, 1989. This 35-story office complex shaped like a hollow cube is the endpoint of the voie triomphale (triumphal way) begun in 1664 at the Tuileries Gardens; its roof covers 2½ acres (it's estimated that Notre-Dame could fit into its hollow core). One of the latest additions to the architectural scene (opened in 1995) is the **Cité de la Musique,** designed by the architect Christian de Portzamparc as a complex of interconnected postcubist shapes.

Although the buildings of the Mitterrand presidency were "designed for eternity," critics are already sighting flaws in the late president's "chance for immortality" $5.8-billion architectural spending spree. Many of the Mitterrand buildings are suffering defects and mishaps—stone slabs have fallen from the Opéra Bastille's facade, netting has had to be placed under the Grand Arche to prevent fragments of it from falling and hitting pedestrians below, and rain gushes into the orchestra pit at the Cité de la Musique.

The great French architect Paul Chametov has said, "At the end of a decade [the 1980s] that was tipsy from competitions, drunk from media hype and driven mad by the expectations of a real-estate boom, we inherit an architecture that is only new on the day it is inaugurated."

President Jacques Chirac can hardly match the cultural monuments of his predecessor, falling slabs of marble or not. In 1996 he announced his building plans: the creation of a major new museum for African, Oceanic, and pre-Columbian art.

Assigned to the Passy Wing of the Palais de Chaillot in Paris's Trocadéro section, it will open (we hope) in late 2001, just months before the end of Chirac's 7-year term.

5 A Taste of France

As any French person will tell you, French food is the best in the world. That's as true today as it was during the 19th-century heyday of the master chef Escoffier. A demanding patriarch who codified the rules of French cooking, he ruled the kitchens of the Ritz in Paris, standardizing the complicated preparation and presentation of haute cuisine. Thanks to Escoffier and his legendary flare-ups and his French-born colleagues, whose kitchen tantrums have been the bane of many a socialite's life, the French chef for years has been considered a temperamental egomaniac, bearing singlehandedly the burden of diffusing French civilization into the kitchens of the Anglo-Saxon world.

The demands of these chefs, however, aren't as far-fetched as they might seem, considering the intense scrutiny that has surrounded every aspect of France's culinary arts since the start of the Industrial Revolution.

Until the early 1800s the majority of French citizens didn't eat well. Many diets consisted of turnips, millet, fruits, berries, unpasteurized dairy products, and whatever fish or game could be had. Cooking techniques and equipment were unsanitary and crude, and starvation was a constant threat. Fear of famine was one of the rallying cries of the Revolution—everyone knows Marie Antoinette's "Let them eat cake" response to cries that the poor couldn't afford bread. (However, to be fair to Marie, this comment has been taken out of context. At the time, bread flour was much more expensive than cake flour, so her words weren't as callous as they might seem.)

At the foundation of virtually every culinary theory ever developed in France is a deep-seated respect for the *cuisine des provinces* (also known as *cuisine campagnarde*). Ingredients usually included only what was produced locally, and the rich and hearty result was gradually developed over several generations of *mères cuisinières*. Springing from an agrarian society with a vivid sense of nature's cycles, the cuisine provided appropriate nourishment for bodies that had toiled through a day in the open air. Specific dishes and cooking methods were as varied as the climates, terrains, and crops of France's many regions.

CUISINE BOURGEOISE & HAUTE CUISINE Cuisine bourgeoise and its pretentious cousin, haute cuisine, were refinements of country cooking that developed from the increased prosperity brought on by 19th-century industrialization. As France grew more affluent, food and the rituals involved in its preparation and presentation became one of the hallmarks of culture. And as refrigerated trucks and railway cars carried meats, fish, and produce from one region to another, associations were formed and entire industries spawned, revolving around specific ingredients produced in specific districts. Like the country's wines (demarcated with "Appellation d'Origine Contrôlée"), lamb from the salt marshes of Pauillac, poultry from Bresse in Burgundy, and melons, strawberries, apples, and truffles from specific districts command premiums over roughly equivalent ingredients produced in less legendary neighborhoods.

France often names a method of preparation (or a particular dish) after its region of origin. Dishes described as *à la normande* are likely to be prepared with milk, cream, or cheese or with Calvados, in honor of the dairy products and apple brandy produced in abundance within Norman borders. Cassoulet (a stewed combination of white beans, duck, pork, onions, and carrots) will forever be associated with Toulouse, where the dish originated. And something cooked *à la bordelaise* has probably been flavored with ample doses of red bordeaux (along with bone marrow, shallots, tarragon, and meat juices).

Other than caviar (which the French consume in abundance but don't produce), the world's most elegant garnish is truffles, an underground fungus with a woodsy, oaky smell. Thousands of these are unearthed yearly from the Dordogne and Périgord forests, so if your menu proclaims a dish is *à la périgourdine,* you'll almost certainly pay a premium for the truffles and foie gras.

And what's all the fuss about foie gras? It comes from either a goose or a duck (the rose-hued goose liver is the greater delicacy). The much-abused goose, however, has a rough life, being force-fed about a kilogram (2.2 pounds) of corn every day in a process the French call *gavage*. In about 22 days the animal's liver is swollen to about 25 ounces (in many cases far more than that). When prepared by a Périgourdine housewife (some of whom sell the livers directly from their farmhouses to passing motorists) it's truly delicious. Foie gras is most often served with truffles; otherwise, it's called *au naturel.*

Bouillabaisse, a fish stew developed as a staple for fisherfolk along the Provence coast, has been elevated into one of the world's greatest dishes. Purists claim that key ingredients are *rascasse* (hogfish), a species found only in the Mediterranean; garlic-based aioli (a garlicky mayonnaise); and a medley of specific Provençal herbs—without these, the resulting stew simply isn't bouillabaisse.

Diners will find that a rebirth of *cuisine du terroir* (country cuisine) has returned to France with a vengeance. Chefs (especially the younger ones) are making creative statements, many as cerebral as they are sensual. Never has there been such an emphasis on fresh and authentic ingredients derived locally or from specific regions and provinces. Some chefs (including one we know in Bordeaux) have been known to shut down their restaurants for the day if they cannot find exactly what they want in the marketplace that morning.

The competition among chefs for patrons and prestige has heated up almost to the boiling point. And as the specific tastes and rituals associated with French food are disseminated around the globe, French-born chefs hired to prepare banquets as far away as Tokyo have been known to haul kegs of their own butter and cream halfway across the world as a guarantee that the flavors they create at the edge of the Pacific Rim are equivalent to those produced in the Ile de France.

CUISINE MODERNE & CUISINE MINCEUR   The anti-Escoffier revolution has been raging for so long that many early rebels are returning to the old style, as exemplified by *boeuf à la bourguignonne, blanquette de veau,* and *pot-au-feu.* Yet the unfashionable expression nouvelle cuisine (even if it isn't all that "new") remains a viable part of the dining scene. Unlike another revolution, the battle between haute and nouvelle cuisine didn't begin in Paris. The romantic in us would like to think it started when Michel Guérard's beautiful wife, Christine, murmured in his ear, "Vous savez, Michel, mon cher—if you would lose some weight, you'd look vraiment fantastique."

For a man who loves food as much as Guérard, that was a formidable challenge. However, he set to work and ultimately invented *cuisine minceur,* a way to cook good

Impressions

The French will only be united under the threat of danger. Nobody can simply bring together a country that has 265 kinds of cheese.

—Charles de Gaulle

French food without all the calories. You can sample it in Guérard's restaurant, Les Prés d'Eugénie, at Eugénie-les-Bains in the Landes, just east of the Basque country (see chapter 18). His *Cuisine Minceur* became a best-seller in North America (available now only in France), and the food critic Gael Greene hailed him as "the brilliant man who is France's most creative chef." Cuisine minceur is more of a diet cuisine than nouvelle or its later permutations. Yet the "new cuisine," like cuisine minceur, represents a major break with haute cuisine. Rich sauces are eliminated; cooking times that can destroy the best of fresh ingredients are considerably shortened. The aim is to release the natural flavor of food without covering it with layers of butter and cream. New flavor combinations in this widely expanding repertoire are often inspired.

Many chefs, including some of France's finest, dislike the word nouvelle when applied to cuisine. They call theirs *moderne,* which blends the finest dishes of the classic repertory with that of the nouvelle. Though widely defined, cuisine moderne basically means paying homage to the integrity of ingredients, certainly fresh ones, and working to bring out natural flavors and aromas.

6 By the Glass or Bottle: A Quick Lesson in French Wines

French cookery achieves perfection when accompanied by wine, which is considered an integral part of every meal. Certain rules about wine drinking have been long established, but no one except traditionalists seems to follow them anymore. For example, if you're having a roast, a steak, or game, a good burgundy might be your choice. If it's chicken, lamb, or veal, perhaps you might choose a red from Bordeaux; a full-bodied red is perfect with a cheese like Camembert, as is a blanc de blanc with oysters. A light rosé (beaujolais) can go with almost anything.

Let your own good taste and your budget determine your wine choice. Most wine stewards, called *sommeliers,* are there to help you, and only in the most dishonest of restaurants will they push you toward the most expensive selections. Of course, if you prefer only bottled water or beer, then be firm and order them without embarrassment. In fact, bottled water is a good idea at lunch if you're planning to drive later. Some restaurants include a beverage in their menu rates (*boisson compris*), but that's only in cheaper places. Some of the most satisfying wines we've drunk in France came from unlabeled house bottles or carafes, called *vin de la maison.* Unless you're a connoisseur, for the most part you needn't worry about labels and vintages.

You can rarely go wrong with a good burgundy or bordeaux, but you may want to be more experimental. That's when the sommelier (who's likely to be a woman) can help, particularly if you tell him or her your taste in wine (semidry or very dry, for example). State frankly how much you're willing to pay and what you plan to order for your meal. If you're dining with others, you may want to order two or three bottles, selecting a wine to suit each course. However, even the French at most informal meals (especially if there are only two people dining) select only one wine to go with everything from hors d'oeuvres to cheese.

WINE LABELS Since the late 19th century, French wine (at least French wine served in France) has been labeled. The general label is known as "Appellation d'Origine Contrôlée" (often abbreviated AC). The controls, for the most part, are designated by region. These simple, honest wines can be blended from grapes grown at any place in the region; some are composed of the vintages of different years.

The more specific the label, the greater the wine is (in most cases). For example, instead of a bordeaux, the wine might be labeled a Médoc, which is an intensely prestigious triangle of land extending some 50 miles north from Bordeaux. Wine labels can be narrowed down to a particular vine-growing property, such as a Château Haut-Brion, one of the greatest red wines of Bordeaux (this château produces only about 10,000 cases per year).

On some burgundies, you're likely to see the word *clos* (pronounced *clo*). Originally that meant a walled or otherwise enclosed vineyard, as in Clos de Beze, a celebrated Burgundian vineyard producing a superb red wine. *Cru* (pronounced *crew* and meaning "growth") suggests a wine of superior quality when it appears on a label as a vin de cru. Wines and vineyards are often divided into crus. A Grand Cru or Premier Cru should, by implication, be an even more superior wine.

Labels are only part of the story. It's the vintage that counts. Essentially, a vintage refers to a specific year's grape harvest and the wine made from those grapes. Therefore, any wine can be a vintage wine unless it was blended. Like people, there are good vintages and bad. The variation between wine produced in a "good year" and wine produced in a "bad year" can be major, even to the uninitiated palate.

Finally, **champagne** is the only wine that can be correctly served through all courses of a meal—but only to those who can afford its astronomical prices. (Did you know that only champagne made in France's Champagne region can by law be called champagne? True. A champagnelike wine made elsewhere in France cannot be called champagne and must be referred to as having been produced *à la méthode champenoise*. In America, each state has its own laws about this, so bubbly made in one state can be called champagne while bubbly made in another state cannot.) For more on bubbly, see the box "Champagne: The Fizz & the Fun" in chapter 10.

3

Planning Your Trip to France

This chapter is devoted to the where, when, and how of your trip. In the pages that follow, we've compiled everything you need to know to handle the practical details of planning your trip: what documents you'll need, how to use French currency, how to find the best airfare, when to go, and more.

1 Visitor Information & Entry Requirements

SOURCES OF INFORMATION

TOURIST OFFICES

IN THE UNITED STATES   Your best source of information—besides this guide, of course—is the **French Government Tourist Office,** 444 Madison Ave., 16th floor, New York, NY 10022; 676 N. Michigan Ave., Suite 3360, Chicago, IL 60611-2819; or 9454 Wilshire Blvd., Suite 715, Beverly Hills, CA 90212-2967. To request information at any of these offices, call the **France on Call** hot line at ☎ **202/659-7779.** For the office's Web site, see below.

IN CANADA   Contact the **Maison de la France/French Government Tourist Office,** 1981 av. McGill College, Suite 490, Montréal, H3A 2W9 (☎ **514/288-4264**).

IN THE UNITED KINGDOM   Contact the **Maison de la France/French Government Tourist Office,** 178 Piccadilly, London, W1V 0AL (☎ **0891/244-123;** fax 0171/493-6594).

IN AUSTRALIA   Contact the **French Tourist Bureau,** 25 Bligh St., Sydney, NSW 2000 (☎ **02/9231-5244;** fax 02/9221-8682).

IN IRELAND   Contact the **Maison de la France/French Government Tourist Office,** 35 Lower Abbey St., Dublin 1 (☎ **01/703-4046**).

IN NEW ZEALAND   There's no representative in New Zealand, so citizens should contact the Australian representative.

IN SOUTH AFRICA   The **French Government Tourist Office** is located in one of the suburbs of Johannesburg (☎ **011/880-8062**); address inquiries to P.O. Box 41022, Craig Hall 2024.

INFORMATION ON MONACO

Information on travel to Monaco (which retains some degree of autonomy from the rest of France) is available from the **Monaco Government Tourist and Convention Bureau,** 565 Fifth Ave., 23rd floor, New York, NY 10017 (☎ **212/286-3330;** fax 212/286-9890). Most of its facilities (along with its consulate) are in New York at the above address.

In London, the office is at 3/18 Chelsea Garden Market, The Chambers, Chelsea Harbour, London SW10 0XF (☎ **0171/352-9962;** fax 0171/352-2103).

Document requirements for travel to Monaco are exactly the same as those for travel to France, and there are virtually no border patrols or passport formalities at the Monégasque frontier.

INFORMATION ON THE WEB

- French Government Tourist Office: **www.fgtousa.org**
- Maison de la France: **www.franceguide.com**
- Relais & Châteaux: **www.integra.fr/relaischateaux**
- The Paris Pages: **www.paris.org**
- FranceScape: **www.france.com/francescape**
- WebMuseum: **sunsite.unc.edu/wm**

REQUIRED DOCUMENTS

PASSPORT   All foreign (non-French) nationals need a valid passport to enter France (check its expiration date).

VISA   The French government no longer requires visas for U.S. citizens, providing they're staying in France for fewer than 90 days. For longer stays, U.S. visitors must apply for a long-term visa, residence card, or temporary-stay visa. Each requires proof of income or a viable means of support in France and a legitimate purpose for remaining in the country. Applications are available from the **Consulate Section of the French Embassy,** 4101 Reservoir Rd. NW, Washington, DC 20007 (☎ **202/ 944-6000**), or from the **visa section of the French Consulate** at 10 E. 74th St., New York, NY 10021 (☎ **212/606-3689**). Visas are required for students planning to study in France even if the stay is for fewer than 90 days.

Visas are generally required for citizens of other countries, though Canadian, Swiss, and Japanese citizens and citizens of EU countries are exempt (but check with your nearest French consulate, as the situation can change overnight).

Citizens of Australia and South Africa need a visa to enter France. Australians must go to the French Consulate in Sydney for a visa. It's located at 31 Market St. (26th floor), Sydney, NSW 2000 (☎ **02/92-62-57-79**). South Africans in search of a visa should direct their attention to the French Consulate in Cape Town, which is located at 2 Dean St. (next to Queen Victoria Station), Cape Town 8001 (☎ **021/23-15-75;** fax 021/24-84-70).

DRIVER'S LICENSE   U.S. and Canadian driver's licenses are valid in France, but if you're going to tour other countries in Europe by car, you may want to invest in an **International Driver's License.** You're unlikely to be asked to produce one, but you can't count on it; the prudent traveler may want to be prepared for any chance encounters with police officers.

Apply at any branch of the **American Automobile Association (AAA).** You must be 18 years old and include two 2-by-2-inch photographs, a $10 fee, and your valid U.S. driver's license with the application. If the AAA doesn't have a branch in your hometown, send a photograph of your driver's license (front and back) with the fee and photos to AAA, 1000 AAA Dr., Heathrow, FL 32746-5063 (☎ **800/222-4357** or 407/444-7000; fax 407/444-4247). Always carry your original license with you to Europe, however.

In Canada, you can get the address of the **Canadian Automobile Association** closest to you by calling its national office at ☎ **613/247-0117.**

INTERNATIONAL INSURANCE CERTIFICATE   To drive in Europe, you must have an international insurance certificate, called a green card (carte verte). The car-rental agency will provide one if you're renting.

CUSTOMS

WHAT YOU CAN BRING INTO FRANCE   Customs restrictions for visitors entering France differ for citizens of the European Union and for citizens of non-EU countries. Non-EU nationals can bring in duty-free 200 cigarettes, 100 cigarillos, 50 cigars, or 250 grams of smoking tobacco. This amount is doubled if you live outside Europe. You can also bring in 2 liters of wine and 1 liter of alcohol over 22 proof and 2 liters of wine 22 proof or under. In addition, you can bring in 50 grams of perfume, a quarter liter of eau de toilette, 500 grams of coffee, and 200 grams of tea. Visitors ages 15 and over can bring in other goods totaling 1,200F ($216); for those 14 and under the limit is 600F ($108). (Customs officials tend to be lenient about general merchandise, realizing that the limits are unrealistically low.)

Visitors from European Union (EU) countries can bring in 300 cigarettes or 150 cigarillos or 75 cigars or 400 grams of smoking tobacco. You can also bring in 2 liters of wine and either 1 liter of alcohol over 38.80 proof or 2 liters of wine under 38.80 proof. In addition, visitors can bring in 75 grams of perfume, ⅜ liter of eau de toilette, 1,000 grams of coffee, and 80 grams of tea. Visitors 15 and over can bring in 4,200F ($756) of merchandise duty-free; those 14 and under can bring in 1,000F ($180) worth.

WHAT YOU CAN BRING HOME   Returning U.S. citizens who have been away for 48 hours or more are allowed to bring back, once every 30 days, $400 worth of merchandise duty-free. You'll be charged a flat rate of 10% duty on the next $1,000 worth of purchases. Be sure to have your receipts handy. On gifts, the duty-free limit is $100. You cannot bring fresh foodstuffs into the United States; tinned foods, how-ever, are allowed. For more information, contact the U.S. Customs Service, 1301 Con-stitution Ave. (P.O. Box 7407), Washington, DC 20044 (☎ **202/927 6724**) and request the free pamphlet *Know Before You Go.* It's on the web at www.customs.ustreas. gov/travel/kbygo.htm.

For a clear summary of Canadian rules, write for the booklet *I Declare,* issued by Revenue Canada, 2265 St. Laurent Blvd., Ottawa K1G 4KE (☎ **800/461-9999** or 613/993-0534). Canada allows its citizens a $500 exemption, and you're allowed to bring back duty-free 200 cigarettes, 2.2 pounds of tobacco, 40 imperial ounces of liquor, and 50 cigars. In addition, you're allowed to mail gifts to Canada from abroad at the rate of Can$60 a day, provided they're unsolicited and aren't alcohol or tobacco (write on the package "Unsolicited gift, under $60 value"). All valuables should be declared on the Y-38 form before departure from Canada, including serial numbers of, for example, expensive foreign cameras that you already own. *Note:* The $500 exemp-tion can be used only once a year and only after an absence of 7 days.

The duty-free allowance in Australia is A$400 or, for those under 18, A$200. Cit-izens can bring in 250 cigarettes or 250 grams of loose tobacco, and 1,125ml of alcohol. If you're returning with valuable goods you already own, such as foreign-made cameras, you should file form B263. A helpful brochure, available from Australian consulates or Customs offices, is *Know Before You Go.* For more information, contact Australian Customs Services, GPO Box 8, Sydney NSW 2001 (☎ **02/9213-2000**).

The duty-free allowance for New Zealand is NZ$700. Citizens over 17 can bring in 200 cigarettes, 50 cigars, or 250 grams of tobacco (or a mixture of all three if their combined weight doesn't exceed 250 grams); plus 4.5 liters of wine and beer, or 1.125 liters of liquor. New Zealand currency does not carry import or export restrictions. Fill out a certificate of export, listing the valuables you are taking out of the country; that way, you can bring them back without paying duty. Most questions are answered in a free pamphlet available at New Zealand consulates and Customs offices: *New Zealand Customs Guide for Travellers, Notice no. 4.* For more information, contact New Zealand Customs, 50 Anzac Ave., P.O. Box 29, Auckland (☎ **09/359-6655**).

2 Money

France is one of the world's most expensive destinations. But, to compensate, it often offers top-value food and lodging. Part of the problem is the value-added tax (VAT—called TVA in France), which tacks between 6% and 33% on top of everything.

It's expensive to rent and drive a car in France (gasoline is costly, too), and flying within France costs more than flying within the United States. Train travel is relatively inexpensive, however, especially if you purchase a rail pass. Inflation has stayed at 2% during the late 1990s.

Remember that prices in Paris and on the Riviera will be higher than those in the provinces. Three of the most touristed areas—Brittany, Normandy, and the Loire Valley—have reasonably priced hotels and scads of restaurants offering superb food at moderate prices.

CURRENCY   The basic unit of French currency is the franc (F), which consists of 100 centimes. Coins are issued in units of 5, 10, 20, and 50 centimes, plus 1, 2, 5, and 10 francs. Notes are denominated in 20, 50, 100, 200, 500, and 1,000 francs. The new 200F note honors Gustave Eiffel on the front.

All banks are equipped for foreign exchange, and you'll find exchange offices at the airports and airline terminals. Banks are open Monday through Friday from 9am to noon and 2 to 4pm. Major bank branches also open their exchange departments on Saturday from 9am to noon.

When converting your home currency into francs, be aware that rates may vary. Your hotel will offer the worst rate. In general, banks offer the best, but even they charge a commission, often $3, depending on the transaction. Whenever you can, stick to the big banks of France, like Crédit Lyonnais, which usually offer the best rates and charge the least commission. Always make sure you have enough francs for le week-end.

If you need a check denominated in French francs before your trip (for example, to pay a deposit on a hotel room), contact **Ruesch International,** 700 11th St. NW, 4th floor, Washington, DC 20001-4507 (☎ **800/424-2923**). Ruesch performs a wide variety of conversion-related services, usually for $3 per transaction. You can also inquire at a local bank.

CREDIT CARDS   Credit cards are useful in France. Both American Express and Diners Club are widely recognized. The French equivalent for Visa is Carte Bleue. A EuroCard sign on an establishment means that it accepts MasterCard.

Of course, you may make a purchase with a credit or charge card thinking it'll be at a certain rate, only to find that the U.S. dollar or British pound has declined by the

The French Franc

For American Readers At this writing, $1 = approximately 5.5F (or 1F = 18¢), and this was the rate of exchange used to calculate the dollar values given in this book.

For British Readers At this writing, £1 = approximately 10.18F (or 1F = 10p), and that was the rate of exchange used to calculate the pound values in the table below.

Note: Because the exchange rate fluctuates from time to time according to a complicated roster of political and economic factors, this table should be used only as a general guide.

F	US$	UK£	F	US$	UK£
1	0.18	0.10	75	13.50	7.50
2	0.36	0.20	100	18.00	10.00
3	0.54	0.30	125	22.50	12.50
4	0.72	0.40	150	27.00	15.00
5	0.90	0.50	175	31.50	17.50
6	1.08	0.60	200	36.00	20.00
7	1.26	0.70	225	40.50	22.50
8	1.44	0.80	250	45.00	25.00
9	1.62	0.90	275	49.50	27.50
10	1.80	1.00	300	54.00	30.00
15	2.70	1.50	350	63.00	35.00
20	3.60	2.00	400	72.00	40.00
25	4.50	2.50	500	90.00	50.00
50	9.00	5.00	1000	180.00	100.00

time your bill arrives and you're actually paying more than you bargained for. But those are the rules of the game. It also can work in your favor if the dollar or pound unexpectedly rises after you make a purchase.

Some ATMs in France accept U.S. bank cards like Visa and MasterCard. The exchange rates are often good and the convenience of obtaining cash on the road is without equal. Check with your credit-card company or bank before leaving home.

ATM NETWORKS Plus, Cirrus, and other networks connecting ATMs operate in France. If your bank card has been programmed with a Personal Identification Number (PIN), it's likely you can use your card at French ATMs to withdraw money as a cash advance on your credit card. Always determine the frequency limits for withdrawals and check to see if your PIN must be reprogrammed for use in France. For Cirrus locations abroad, call ☎ **800/424-7787**; for Plus usage abroad, dial ☎ **800/843-7587**. Note, however, that many banks have begun to impose a fee ranging from 50¢ to $3 every time you use the ATM in a different city. Your own bank may also charge you a fee for using ATMs from other banks.

TRAVELER'S CHECKS Most large banks sell traveler's checks, charging fees of 1% to 2% of the value of the checks, though some out-of-the-way banks assess as much as 7%. If your bank wants more than a 2% commission, call the traveler's check issuers directly for the address of outlets where this commission is less.

American Express (☎ 800/221-7282 in the U.S. and Canada) doesn't charge a commission to AAA members or holders of certain types of American Express cards. For questions or problems arising outside North America, contact any of the company's regional representatives. There's also **Citicorp** (☎ 800/645-6556 in the U.S. and Canada, or 813/623-1709, collect, from elsewhere). **Thomas Cook** (☎ 800/ 223-7373 in the U.S. and Canada) issues MasterCard traveler's checks. And **Interpayment Services** (☎ 800/221-2426 in the U.S. and Canada, or 212/858-8500, collect, from elsewhere) sells Visa checks issued by a consortium of member banks and the Thomas Cook organization.

Each of these agencies will refund your checks if they're lost or stolen, provided you have sufficient documentation. Of course, carry your documentation in a safe place—never along with your checks. When purchasing checks from one of the banks listed, ask about refund hot lines; American Express and Bank of America have the most offices around the world.

Sometimes you can purchase traveler's checks in the currency of the country you're visiting, thereby avoiding a conversion fee. American Express, for example, issues checks in French francs. Foreign banks may ask up to 5% to convert your checks into francs. Note, also, that you always get a better rate if you cash traveler's checks at a branch of the bank that issued them.

3 When to Go

July and August are the worst months—Parisians desert their city, leaving it to the crowds of tourists and the businesses that cater to them. Paris has an uncommonly long springtime, lasting through April, May, and June, and an equally extended fall, September through November. The weather, however, is temperate throughout the year.

The best time to come to Paris is off-season, in early spring or late autumn, when the tourist trade has trickled to a manageable flow and everything is easier to come by—from Métro seats to good-tempered waiters.

Hotels used to charge off-season rates during the cold, rainy period from November through February, when tourism slowed; now, however, they're often packed with business clients, trade fairs, and winter tour groups in those months, and there's less incentive for hoteliers to offer big reductions.

Airfares are less expensive in winter, when more promotions are also available. They rise in the spring and fall, peaking in the heavily trafficked summer months when tickets will cost the most.

Don't come to Paris in the first 2 weeks of October without a confirmed hotel reservation. The weather's fine, but the city is jammed for the annual motor show, when the French indulge their passion for cars.

WEATHER

France's weather varies considerably from region to region and sometimes from town to town as little as 12 miles apart. Despite its north latitude, Paris never gets very cold—snow is a rarity. The hands-down winner for wetness is Brittany, where Brest (known for the mold that adds flavor to its bleu cheeses—probably caused by the constant rainfall) receives a staggering amount of rain between October and December. The rain usually falls in a kind of steady, foggy drizzle and rarely lasts more than a day. May is the driest month.

Temperature Conversions

°C	−18°	−10	0	10	20	30	40
°F	0°	10	20	32	40	50	60	70	80	90	100

To convert degrees Fahrenheit to degrees Celsius, subtract 32 from °F, multiply by 5, then divide by 9 (example, 85°F − 32 x ⅝ = 29.4°C).

To convert degrees Celcius to degrees Fahrenheit, multiply °C by 9, divide by 5, and add 32 (example, 20°C x ⅝ + 32 = 68°F).

The Mediterranean coast of the south has the driest climate. When it does rain, it's usually heaviest in spring and autumn. (Surprisingly, Cannes sometimes receives more rainfall than Paris.) Summers are comfortably dry—beneficial to humans but deadly to much of the vegetation, which (unless it's irrigated) often dries and burns up in the parched months.

Provence dreads le mistral (an unrelenting, hot, dry, dusty wind), which most often blows in winter for a few days but can last for up to 2 weeks.

For up-to-the-minute weather forecasts, you can get updates from the **Weather Channel** by calling ☎ **900/WEATHER** in the United States (95¢ per minute). The 24-hour service reports on conditions in Paris and several other large cities throughout France.

HOLIDAYS

In France, holidays are known as *jours fériés*. Shops and many businesses (banks and some museums and restaurants) close on holidays, but hotels and emergency services remain open.

The main holidays—a mix of both secular and religious ones—include New Year's Day (January 1), Easter Sunday and Monday (April 12–13), Labor Day (May 1), Ascension Thursday (40 days after Easter, May 21), V-E Day in Europe (May 8), Whit Monday (May 19), Bastille Day (July 14), Assumption of the Blessed Virgin (August 15), All Saints' Day (November 1), Armistice Day (November 11), and Christmas (December 25).

FRANCE CALENDAR OF EVENTS

January
- **Monte Carlo Motor Rally.** The world's most venerable car race. Usually mid-January.
- **International Ready-to-Wear Fashion Shows (Le Salon International de Prêt-à-porter),** Parc des Expositions, Porte de Versailles, Paris 15e (Métro: Porte-de-Versailles). Various couture houses, such as Lanvin and Courrèges, present their own shows at their respective headquarters. Here you'll see what the public will be wearing in 6 months. Mid-January to mid-February.

February
- ✪ **Carnival of Nice.** Float processions, parades, confetti battles, boat races, street music and food, masked balls, and fireworks are all part of this ancient celebration. The climax follows the 113-year-old tradition of burning King Carnival in effigy, an event preceded by Les Batailles des Fleurs (Battles of the Flowers),

during which members of opposing teams pelt one another with flowers. Come with proof of a hotel reservation. For information or reservations, contact the Nice Convention and Visitors Bureau, 1 esplanade Kennedy (BP 4079), 06302 Nice CEDEX 4 (☎ **04-92-14-48-00;** fax 04-92-14-48-03). Mid-February to late March.

March

- **Foire du Trône,** on the Neuilly Lawn of the Bois de Vincennes, Paris. This mammoth amusement park operates daily from 2pm to midnight. Late March to June.

April

- **The 24-hours Le Mans Motorcycle Race.** For information, contact Automobile Club de l'ouest (☎ **02-43-40-24-24**).
- **Paris Marathon.** Runners from around the world compete. First weekend in April.
- **Son-et-Lumière (Sound-and-Light) Shows,** Loire Valley. April to September.

May

- **End of World War II,** Paris and Reims. Though the capitulation of the Nazis was signed on May 7, 1945, the celebration lasts several days in Paris, and with even more festivity in Reims. May 5 to 8.
- ✪ **Cannes Film Festival.** Movie madness transforms this city into a media circus, with daily melodramas acted out in cafes, on sidewalks, and in hotel lobbies. Great for voyeurs. This year marks the festival's 51st anniversary. Reserve early and make a deposit. Getting a table on the Carlton terrace is even more difficult than procuring a room. Admission to some of the prestigious films is by invitation only. There are box-office tickets for the less important films, which play 24 hours. For information, contact the **Direction du Festival International du Film,** 99 bd. Malesherbes, 75008 Paris (☎ **01-45-61-66-00;** fax 01-45-61-97-60). Two weeks before the festival, the event's administration moves en masse to the **Palais des Festivals,** esplanade Georges-Pompidou, 06400 Cannes (☎ **04-93-39-01-01**). May 12 to 23.
- **Les Grandes Eaux Musicales,** Versailles. This event features loudly broadcast music by French-born composers like Couperin, Charpentier, and Lully, as well as Mozart and Haydn, whose music was contemporaneous with the construction of the palace of Versailles. All the fountains in the parks around the palace are turned on, and people promenade through the gardens. The event is presented every Sunday from 3:30 to 5:30pm. Early May to early October.
- **Monaco Grand Prix.** Hundreds of cars race through the narrow streets and winding corniche roads in a surreal blend of high-tech machinery and medieval architecture. May 21 to 24.
- **French Open Tennis Championship,** Stade Roland-Garros, Paris. Late May to mid-June.

June

- **Le Prix du Jockey Club,** Hippodrome de Chantilly, Paris. For information on this and all other Paris equine events, call ☎ **01-49-10-20-30.** June 1 at 2pm.
- **Festival Juin,** Paris. A month of music, art exhibitions, and drama set for the most part in Paris's 16th arrondissement. For information, call ☎ **01-40-72-16-25.** Throughout June.
- **Festival de Musique de St-Denis,** Paris. Music is featured in the burial place of the French kings. For information, call ☎ **01-48-13-06-07.** Throughout June.

- **Le Prix Diane-Hermès,** Hippodrome de Chantilly, Paris. For information on this and all other Paris equine events, call ☎ **01-49-10-20-30.** June 8 at 2pm.
- **Cinéscénie de Puy du Fou,** son-et-lumière at the Château du Puy du Fou, Les Epesses (Poitou-Charentes). With a cast of 650 actors, dozens of horses, laser shows, and a soundtrack by famous actors, it celebrates the achievements of the Middle Ages. For information, call ☎ **02-51-64-11-11.** Early June to early September.
- **Paris Air Show,** Le Bourget Airport. Mid-June in odd-numbered years only (next in 1999).
- **The 24-Hour Le Mans Car Race.** For information, contact Automobile Club de l'ouest (tel. **02-43-40-24-24**). June 12 to 13.
- **Festival Chopin, Paris.** Everything you've ever wanted to hear from the Polish exile who lived most of his life in Paris. Piano recitals are held in the Orangerie du Parc de Bagatelle. For information, call ☎ **01-45-00-69-75.** June 16 to July 14.
- **Gay Pride Parade,** Paris. A week of expositions and parties climaxes in a massive parade patterned after those in New York and San Francisco. It begins at place de l'Odéon and proceeds to place de la Bastille, then is followed by the Grand Bal de Gay Pride at the Palais de Bercy, a major convention hall/sports arena. For information, contact Centre Gai et Lesbien, 3 rue Keller, 75011 Paris (☎ **01-43-57-21-47**). Mid-June.
- **Grand Prix de Paris,** Longchamp racetrack. Late June.
- **La Villette Jazz Festival.** One of the Paris region's most dynamic homages to the art of jazz incorporates 50 concerts in churches, auditoriums, and concert halls in all neighborhoods of the Paris suburb of La Villette. Past festivals have included Herbie Hancock, Shirley Horn, Michel Portal, and other artists from around Europe and the world. For information, call ☎ **01-40-03-75-03.** Late June to early July.
- **Les Nocturnes du Mont-St-Michel.** This is a sound-and-light tour through the maze of stairways and corridors of one of Europe's most impressive medieval monuments. Every evening from late June to mid-September.

July

- **Colmar International Music Festival,** Colmar. Different musical concerts are held in various public buildings of one of the most folkloric towns in Alsace. First 2 weeks of July.
- **St-Guilhem Music Season,** St-Guilhem le Désert (Languedoc). This festival of baroque organ and choral music is held in a medieval monastery. For information, call ☎ **04-67-63-14-99.** July to early August.
- **Le Tour de France.** The world's most famous (and most difficult) bicycle race catalyzes the ardor and patriotism of France. July 1 to 23.
- ✪ **Festival d'Avignon.** One of France's most prestigious theater events, this world-class festival has a reputation for exposing new talent to critical acclaim. The focus is usually on avant-garde works in theater, dance, and music by groups from around the world. Make hotel reservations early. For information, call ☎ **04-90-27-66-50** or fax 04-90-27-66-83. Edwards and Edwards can order tickets to many of the musical or theatrical events at the Avignon festival, as well as at other cultural events throughout France; contact them at 1270 Ave. of the Americas, Suite 2414, New York, NY 10020 (☎ **800/223-6108**). July 10 to August 2.
- ✪ **Festival d'Aix-en-Provence.** A musical event par excellence, featuring everything from Gregorian chant to melodies composed on computer synthesizers. The

audience sits on the sloping lawns of the 14th-century papal palace for operas and concerti. Local recitals are performed in the medieval cloister of the Cathédrale St-Sauveur. Make advance hotel reservations and bring written confirmation with you. Expect heat, crowds, and traffic. For information, contact the Festival International d'Art Lyrique et Academie Europeénne de Musique, Palais de l'Ancien Archevêche, 13100 Aix-en-Provence (☎ **04-42-17-34-00;** fax 04-42-96-12-61). Mid-July.

- **Les Chorégies d'Orange,** Orange. One of southern France's most important lyric festivals presents oratorios and choral works by master performers whose voices are amplified by the ancient acoustics of France's best-preserved Roman amphitheater. For information, call ☎ **04-90-34-24-24.** July 12 to August 4.

✪ **Bastille Day.** Celebrating the birth of modern-day France, the nation's festivities reach their peak in Paris with street fairs, pageants, fireworks, and feasts. In Paris, the day begins with a parade down the Champs-Elysées and ends with fireworks at Montmartre. No matter where you are, by the end of the day you'll hear Piaf warbling "La Foule" (The Crowd), the song that celebrated her passion for the stranger she met and later lost in a crowd on Bastille Day. July 14.

✪ **Grand Parade du Jazz (Nice Jazz Festival).** This is the biggest, flashiest, and most prestigious jazz festival in Europe, with world-class entertainers. Concerts begin in early afternoon and go on until late at night (sometimes all night in the clubs) on the Arènes de Cimiez, a hill above the city. Reserve hotel rooms way in advance. For information, contact the Grand Parade du Jazz, c/o Abela Regency Hotel, 223 promenade des Anglais, 06200 Nice (☎ **04-93-37-17-17**), or the Cultural Affairs Department of the city of Nice (☎ **04-93-13-25-90;** fax 04-93-80-53-64). Ten days in mid-July.

- **Paris Quartier d'Eté.** These 4 weeks of music evoke the style of the pop orchestral music featured on a village green in England. The setting is the Arènes de Lutèce or the Cour d'Honneur at the Sorbonne, both in the Latin Quarter. The dozen or so concerts are usually grander than the outdoorsy setting would imply and include performances by the Orchestre de Paris, the Orchestre National de France, and the Baroque Orchestra of the European Union. Spinoffs of this include plays and jazz concerts. For information, call ☎ **01-44-83-64-40** or fax 01-44-83-64-43. July 15 to August 15.

- **Le Grand Tour de France,** Paris. Europe's most visible bicycle race determines its winner at a finish line drawn across the Champs-Elysées. Late July.

August

- **Festival Musique en l'Ile,** Paris. A spectrum of classical music and oratorios are presented in four historic churches, including the Sainte-Chapelle. For information, call ☎ **01-44-62-70-90.** August to mid-September.

- **Festival Interceltique de Lorient,** Brittany. Traditional Celtic verse and lore are celebrated in the Celtic heart of France. The 150 concerts include 3,500 classical and folkloric musicians, dancers, singers, and painters from all over. Traditional Breton pardons (religious processions) take place in this once-independent maritime duchy. For information, call ☎ **02-97-21-24-29.** First 2 weeks of August.

✪ **Festival International de Folklore et Fête de la Vigne (Les Folkloriades),** Dijon, Beaune, and about 20 villages of the Côte d'Or. At the International Festival of Folklore and Wine in Dijon, dance troupes from around the world perform, parade, and participate in folkloric events in celebration of the famous wines of Burgundy. For information, contact the Festival de Musique et Danse Populares, 27 bd. de la Tremouille, 21025 Dijon (☎ **03-80-30-37-95;** fax 03-80-30-23-44). Late August and early September.

September
- **Festival d'Automne,** Paris. One of the most famous festivals in France, this is also one of the most eclectic, concentrating mainly on modern music, ballet, theater, and modern art. Tickets cost 100F to 300F ($18 to $54), depending on the venue. For details, call or write to the Festival d'Automne, 156 rue de Rivoli, 75001 Paris (☎ **01-53-45-17-00;** fax 01-53-45-17-01). During the festival itself, call ☎ **01-53-45-17-17** to reserve tickets for any of the events. Mid-September to just before Christmas.
- **International Ready-to-Wear Fashion Shows (Le Salon International de Prêt-à-porter),** Parc des Expositions, Porte de Versailles, Paris 15e (Métro: Porte-de-Versailles). Late September.

October
- **Perpignan Jazz Festival.** Musicians from everywhere jam in what many visitors consider Languedoc's most appealing season. For information, call ☎ **04-68-35-37-46.** Throughout October.
- **Festival d'Automne,** Paris. Throughout October.
- ✪ **Paris Auto Show,** Parc des Expositions, near the Porte de Versailles in western Paris. Glistening metal, glitzy attendees, lots of hype, and the latest models from world automakers: This is the showcase for European car design. Check *Pariscope* for details or contact the French Government Tourist Office (see "Visitor Information & Entry Requirements," earlier in this chapter). Ten days in early October.
- **Prix de l'Arc de Triomphe,** Paris. This is France's most prestigious horse race. Early October.

November
- **Festival d'Automne,** Paris. Throughout November.
- **Armistice Day,** nationwide. In Paris, the signing of the controversial document that ended World War I is celebrated with a military parade from the Arc de Triomphe to the Hôtel des Invalides. November 11.
- **Les Trois Glorieuses,** Clos-de-Vougeot, Beaune, and Meursault. The country's most important wine festival is celebrated in three Burgundian towns. Though you may not gain access to many of the gatherings, there are enough wine tastings and other amusements to keep you occupied. Festivities include wine auctions from some of the district's most historic cellars. Reserve early or visit as part of day trips from any of several nearby villages. Confirm information by contacting the Office de Tourisme de Beaune, rue de l'Hôtel-Dieu, 21200 Beaune (☎ **03-80-26-21-30**). Third week in November.
- **City of Paris's Festival of Sacred Art.** This dignified series of concerts is held in five of the oldest and most recognizable Paris churches. For information, call ☎ **01-44-70-64-10.** Late November to early December.

December
- **Festival d'Automne,** Paris. Through late December.
- **The Boat Fair (Le Salon International de la Navigation de Plaisance),** Parc des Expositions, Porte de Versailles, Paris. This is Europe's most visible exposition of what's afloat. Early December.
- **Christmas Fairs,** Alsace (especially Strasbourg). More than 60 Alsatian villages celebrate a traditional Christmas. The events in Strasbourg have continued for some 430 years. Other towns with noteworthy celebrations are Münster, Selestat, Riquewihr, Kaysersberg, Saverne, Wissembourg, and Than. Late November to December 24.

- **Fête de St-Sylvestre (New Year's Eve),** nationwide. In Paris, it's most boisterously celebrated in the Quartier Latin around the Sorbonne. At midnight, the city explodes. Strangers kiss strangers and boulevard St-Michel and the Champs-Elysées become virtual pedestrian malls. December 31.

4 Health & Insurance

STAYING HEALTHY   If you need a doctor, your hotel will locate one for you. You can also obtain a list of English-speaking doctors from the **International Association for Medical Assistance to Travelers (IAMAT):** in the United States at 417 Center St., Lewiston, NY 14092 (☎ **716/754-4883**); in Canada at 40 Regal Rd., Guelph, ON N1K 1B5 (☎ **519/836-0102**). Getting medical help is relatively easy. Don't be alarmed, even in rural areas. You can find competent doctors in all parts of the country.

INSURANCE   Insurance needs for the traveler abroad fall into three categories: health and accident, trip cancellation, and lost luggage.

First, review your present policies—you may already have adequate coverage between them and what's offered by your credit/charge-card companies. Many card companies insure their users in case of a travel accident, providing the ticket was purchased with their card. Sometimes fraternal organizations have policies protecting members in case of sickness or accidents abroad.

Incidentally, don't assume that Medicare is the answer to illness in France. It covers only U.S. citizens who travel south of the border to Mexico or north of the border to Canada.

Many homeowners' insurance policies cover theft of luggage during foreign travel and loss of documents—your Eurailpass, passport, or airline ticket, for instance. Coverage is usually limited to about $500 U.S. To submit a claim on your insurance, you'll need police reports or a statement from a medical authority that you did suffer the loss or experience the illness for which you're seeking compensation. Such claims, by their very nature, can be filed only when you return from France.

Some policies (and this is the type you should have) provide advances in cash or transfers of funds so you won't have to dip into your precious travel funds to settle medical bills.

If you've booked a charter flight, you'll probably have to pay a cancellation fee if you cancel a trip suddenly, even if the cancellation is caused by an unforeseen crisis. It's possible to get insurance against such a possibility. Some travel agencies provide this coverage, and often flight insurance against a canceled trip is written into the cost of tickets paid for by credit and charge cards from such companies as Visa and American Express. Many tour operators and insurance agents provide this type of insurance.

Access America, 6600 W. Broad St., Richmond, VA 23230 (☎ 800/284-8300), offers comprehensive travel insurance/assistance packages beginning at $34. **Wallach & Co.,** 107 W. Federal St. (P.O. Box 480), Middleburg, VA 20118-0480 (☎ 800/237-6615), offers a policy called Healthcare Abroad (MEDEX). It covers 10 to 120 days at $4 per day; the policy includes accident and sickness coverage to the tune of $250,000. Provisions for trip cancellation can also be written into the policy at a nominal cost. **Travel Guard International,** 1145 Clark St., Stevens Point, WI 54481 (☎ 800/826-1300), offers a comprehensive 7-day policy that covers basically everything, including emergency assistance, accidental death, trip cancellation /interruption, medical coverage abroad, and lost luggage.

5 Tips for Travelers with Special Needs

FOR TRAVELERS WITH DISABILITIES   Facilities for travelers with disabilities are certainly above average in Europe, and nearly all modern hotels in France now provide rooms designed for persons with disabilities. However, older hotels (unless they've been renovated) may not provide such important features as elevators, special toilet facilities, or ramps for wheelchair access.

The new high-speed TGV trains are wheelchair accessible; older trains have special compartments for wheelchair boarding. On the Paris Métro, those with disabilities are able to sit in wider seats provided for their comfort. Guide dogs ride free. Some stations don't have escalators or elevators, so these present problems.

There are agencies in the United States and France that can provide advance-planning information. Knowing in advance which hotels, restaurants, and attractions are wheelchair accessible can save you a lot of frustration—firsthand accounts by other travelers with disabilities are the best.

The **Association des Paralysés de France,** 17 bd. Auguste-Blanqui, 75013 Paris (☎ **01-40-78-69-00**), is a privately funded organization that provides documentation, moral support, and travel ideas for individuals who use wheelchairs. In addition to the central Paris office, it maintains an office in each of the 90 départements of France and can help find accessible hotels, transportation, sightseeing, house rentals, and (in some cases) companionship for paralyzed or partially paralyzed travelers. It's not, however, a travel agency.

The Travel Information Service of the **Industrial Rehab Program in Philadelphia** serves as a telephone resource for travelers with physical disabilities. Call ☎ **215/456-9600** (voice) or 215/456-9602 (TTY).

You can obtain *Air Transportation of Handicapped Persons* by writing to Free Advisory Circular No. AC12032, Distribution Unit, U.S. Department of Transportation, Publications Division, M-4332, Washington, DC 20590.

The **Society for the Advancement of Travel for the Handicapped,** 347 Fifth Ave., Suite 610, New York, NY 10016 (☎ **212/447-7284;** fax 212/725-8253), can provide information for people with disabilities and for the elderly, as well as listings of specialized tour operators. Yearly membership dues (which include quarterly issues of *Open World* magazine) are $45, or $30 for seniors and students.

One of the best organizations serving the needs of persons with disabilities (especially those assisted by wheelchairs and walkers) is **Flying Wheels Travel,** 143 W. Bridge (P.O. Box 382), Owatonna, MN 55060 (☎ **800/525-6790**), which offers various escorted tours and cruises internationally and private tours using a minivan with a lift.

For $25 annually, consider joining **Mobility International USA,** P.O. Box 10767, Eugene, OR 97440 (☎ **541/343-1284** voice and TDD; fax 541/343-6812). It answers questions about facilities at various destinations for persons with disabilities and offers discounts on videos, publications, and the programs it sponsors.

FOR GAY & LESBIAN TRAVELERS   Paris vies with London and Amsterdam as Europe's gay and lesbian capital. France is one of the world's most tolerant countries, and Paris, of course, is the center of French gay life, though gay and lesbian establishments exist throughout the country as well, especially on the Riviera.

Before going to France, men can order *Spartacus,* the international gay guide ($32.95), or *Paris Scene* ($10.95), published in London but available in the States. Also helpful is *Odysseus, the International Gay Travel Planner* ($27). Both lesbians and gays might want to pick up a copy of *Gay Travel A to Z* ($16).

Museum Passes

La Carte des Musées et Monuments (Museums and Monuments Pass) is available at any of the museums that honor it or at any branch of the Paris Tourist Office (see chapter 4). It offers free entrance to the permanent collections of 65 monuments and museums in Paris and the Ile de France. A 1-day pass is 70F ($12.60), a 3-day pass costs 140F ($25.20), and a 5-day pass goes for 200F ($36).

Anyone who admires the intricacies of medieval and Renaissance architecture and plans to visit a lot of the châteaux and monuments of France should consider buying a Laissez-Passer at 280F ($50.40) per year. Available in any branch of the Paris Tourist Office (see chapter 4) or at the ticket office of any of the hundreds of monuments that participate in the program, it allows free entrance to any building, site, or ruin administered by the Caisses des Monuments Historiques. The list encompasses sites of major interest (some in Paris, like the Sainte-Chapelle and the Conciergerie), as well as some that are much more esoteric.

Travelers to France's provinces can benefit from a cultural program offered by 13 cities with populations over 90,000. The Culture/Ville 3-day pass unlocks the door to various museums, monuments, and sights in Nice, Marseille, Besançon, Dijon, Lille, Lyon, Metz, Nancy, Nîmes, Toulouse, Orléans, St-Etienne, and Bordeaux. The all-inclusive price of 50F ($9) features either a guided or an audio tour in each city and entrance to one museum or one monument in each city; ask about this at each city's tourist office. For more information, contact the French Government Tourist Office at ☎ **202/659-7779** for the *Cities in France* brochure.

One of the most current guides is *Guide Gai/Gay Guide,* a bilingual guide to French-speaking Europe published in Paris ($16). These books and others are available from **A Different Light Book Store,** 151 W. 19th St., New York, NY 10011 (☎ 800/343-4002 or 212/989-4850), or **Giovanni's Room,** 1145 Pine St., Philadelphia, PA 19107 (☎ 215/923-2960; fax 215/923-0813).

Our World, 1104 N. Nova Rd., Suite 251, Daytona Beach, FL 32117 (☎ 904/441-5367; fax 904/441-5604), is a magazine devoted to gay and lesbian travel worldwide; it costs $35 for 10 issues. *Out & About,* 8 W. 19th St., Suite 401, New York, NY 10011 (☎ 800/929-2268; fax 800/929-2215), has been hailed for its "straight" reporting about gay travel. It profiles the best gay and gay-friendly hotels, gyms, clubs, and other places, with coverage ranging from Key West to Paris. It costs $49 per year for 10 information-packed issues. Aimed at the more upscale gay traveler, it has been praised by everybody from *Travel & Leisure* to the *New York Times.*

A company called **Our Family Abroad,** 40 W. 57th St., Suite 430, New York, NY 10019 (☎ 800/999-5500 or 212/459-1800), operates escorted tours that include about a dozen Europe itineraries. In California, a leading option for gay travel arrangements is **Above and Beyond,** 300 Townsend St., Suite 107, San Francisco, CA 94107 (☎ 800/397-2681 or 415/284-1666; fax 415/284-1660).

The **International Gay Travel Association (IGTA),** 4331 N. Federal, Suite 304, Ft. Lauderdale, FL 33308 (☎ 954/776-2626, or voice mail 800/448-8550), is an international network of travel-industry businesses and professionals who encourage gay/lesbian travel worldwide. With around 1,200 members, it offers quarterly newsletters, marketing mailings, and a membership directory that's updated quarterly. Membership often includes gay or lesbian businesses but is open to individuals for $125 yearly, plus a $100 administration fee for new members. Members are kept informed of gay and gay-friendly hoteliers, tour operators, and airline and cruise-line representatives, plus such ancillary businesses as the contacts at travel guide publishers and gay-related travel clubs.

FOR SENIORS   Many discounts are available in France for seniors—men and women who've reached the "third age," as the French say. For more information, contact the French Government Tourist Office (see "Visitor Information & Entry Requirements," earlier in this chapter).

At any rail station in the country, seniors (men and women age 60 and older—with proof of age) can obtain a **Carte Vermeil** (silver-gilt card). There are two types of Carte Vermeil: the Carte Vermeil Quatre Temps costs 146F ($26.30) and allows a 50% discount on four rail trips per year; a Carte Vermeil Plein Temps goes for 285F ($51.30) and is good for a 50% discount on unlimited rail travel throughout one year.

There are some restrictions on Carte Vermeil travel—it depends on what train you're using and when—and there's no Carte Vermeil discount on the Paris network of commuter trains. However, there are no restrictions on the T.G.V. network of trains. Holders of the Plein Temps card sometimes receive discounts of up to 30% on rail trips to many other countries in Western Europe. Carte Vermeil also delivers reduced prices on SNCF regional bus lines, as well as theater tickets in Paris and half-price admission at state-owned museums.

The French domestic airline **Air France** honors "third agers" by offering a 10% reduction on its regular nonexcursion tariffs. Restrictions do apply, however. Also, discounts of around 10% are offered to passengers age 62 and over on selected Air France international flights. Be sure to ask for the discount when booking, as some restrictions do apply.

The **American Association of Retired Persons (AARP),** 601 E St. NW, Washington, DC 20049 (☎ **202/434-AARP**), is the nation's leading organization for people 50 and older, offering members a wide range of special membership benefits, including *Modern Maturity* magazine and the monthly *Bulletin.*

Elderhostel, 75 Federal St., Boston, MA 02110-1941 (☎ **617/426-8056**), arranges numerous study programs around Europe, including France. Most courses, lasting about 3 weeks, represent great value since they include airfare, accommodations in student dormitories or modest inns, all meals, and tuition. The courses involve no homework, are ungraded, and often focus on the liberal arts. They're not luxury vacations, but they're fun and fulfilling. Participants must be 55 or older. Write or call for a free newsletter and a list of upcoming courses and destinations.

Mature Outlook, P.O. Box 9390, Des Moines, IA 50306 (☎ **800/336-6330**), is a travel organization for people over 50. Members are offered discounts at ITC-member hotels and receive a bimonthly magazine. Annual membership is $14.95 to $19.95, which entitles members to discounts and often free coupons for discounted merchandise from Sears.

SAGA International Holidays, 222 Berkeley St., Boston, MA 02116 (☎ **800/343-0273;** fax 617/375-5951), is well known for its inclusive tours and cruises for those 50 and older.

The **National Council of Senior Citizens,** 8403 Colesville Rd., Suite 1200, Silver Spring, MD 20910 (☎ **301/578-8800**), a nonprofit organization, offers a newsletter six times a year (partly devoted to travel tips) and discounts on hotel and auto rentals; annual dues are $13 per person or couple.

6 Special-Interest Vacations

BALLOONING   The world's largest hot-air-balloon operator is **Bombard Society,** 333 Pershing Way, West Palm Beach, FL 33401 (☎ **800/862-8537** or 561/ 837-6610; fax 561/837-6623). It maintains about three dozen hot-air balloons, some stationed in the Loire Valley and Burgundy. The 5-day/4-night tours—costing $5,494—incorporate food and wine tasting and include all meals, lodging in Relais & Châteaux hotels, sightseeing, rail transfers to and from Paris, and a daily balloon ride over vineyards and fields. Lunches are served in the best restaurants in the district; dinners are elegant picnics offered hunt-board style after a daily late-afternoon balloon ride.

   Bonaventura Balloon Co., 133 Wall Rd., Napa, CA 94558 (☎ **800/359-6272**), meets you in Paris and takes you via T.G.V. to Burgundy, where your balloon tour begins, carrying you over the most scenic parts of the region. Guests stay in a 14th-century mill converted into an inn and owned by a three-star chef. A 7-day trip is $2,395 per person, including a full day sightseeing in Paris, two balloon excursions, lodging, cooking classes, wine tasting, and at least one meal per day. The same trip with only one balloon excursion is $2,195 per person.

BARGE CRUISES   Before the advent of the railways, many of the crops, building supplies, raw materials, and finished products of France were barged through a series of rivers, canals, and estuaries. Many of these waterways are still graced with their old-fashioned locks and pumps, allowing shallow-draft barges easy access through the idyllic countryside. Many companies offer wonderful barging tours.

   French Country Waterways, P.O. Box 2195, Duxbury, MA 02331 (☎ **800/ 222-1236** or 781/934-2454), leads 1-week tours focusing on Burgundy and Champagne. For double occupany, the price ranges from $3,095 to $3,595. More unusual is **Le Boat,** 10 S. Franklin Turnpike, Suite 204-B, Ramsey, NJ 07446 (☎ **800/ 992-0291** or 201/236-2333; fax 201/236-1214), which focuses on regions of France not covered by the itineraries of many other barge operators. The company's two barges are luxury craft of a size and shape that fit through the relatively narrow canals and locks of the Camargue, Languedoc, and Provence. Each 6-night tour involves no more than 10 passengers in five cabins outfitted with mahogany and brass, plus meals prepared by a Cordon Bleu chef. Prices range from $1,900 per person off-season to $2,200 per person in summer. Itineraries include waterborne transit from Sete to Homps (a port near Carcassonne) and wine-country tours along the Garonne, through the Médoc region between Toulouse and Bordeaux.

   European Waterways, 140 E. 56th St., Suite 4C, New York, NY 10022 (☎ **800/ 217-4447** or 212/688-9489; fax 800/296-4554 or 212/688-3778), operates Great Island Voyages, a program featuring river cruise ships that ply Europe's historic rivers. The *Lafayette, Litote,* and *Escargot* traverse France's Burgundy region. Fares range from $1,600 to $3,500 per person (double occupancy) for a 1-week cruise. Bicycles are carried on board for sightseeing trips. This company also offers cruises in the Loire Valley and the south of France.

   The Crown Blue Line, c/o Maupintour, 1515 St. Andrews Dr., Lawrence, KS 66407 (☎ **800/255-4266**), acts as a clearinghouse for the chartering of at least 400 cruise craft, each with a shallow draft, that can slowly navigate the locks and channels of France's waterways. You choose from among 27 kinds of boats, each suitable for between two and about a dozen passengers. Rentals last for a week and can be arranged with a staff or without. Plan on cruising no more than 5 hours a day, then devoting the rest of your holiday to exploring the countryside, perhaps via bicycle. A

7-day rental of any of the vessels ranges from $1,290 to $4,620, depending on its capacity and the season.

With **Kemwel's Premier Selections,** 106 Calvert St., Harrison, NY 10528 (☎ **800/234-4000** or 914/835-5555; fax 914/835-8756), discover the secret corners of France as you wend your way along waterways on board a luxury hotel barge. Enjoy fine wines and cuisine, bicycling, walking, and exploring. Visit châteaux, old towns, and timeless villages. Its fleet can accommodate individuals as well as groups and offers a wide array of cruising areas, including Burgundy, Champagne, the Upper Loire, Alsace-Lorraine, and the south of France. Inclusive fares per person for 3 nights (double occupancy) begin at $1,160, with 6 nights beginning at $1,490.

BICYCLING TRIPS   A well-recommended company that has led cyclists through the provinces since 1979 is the California-based **Backroads,** 801 Cedar St., Berkeley, CA 94710 (☎ **800/462-2848** or 510/527-1555; fax 510/527-1444). Its well-organized tours of Brittany/Normandy, Burgundy, the Dordogne, the Loire Valley, and Provence last between 5 and 8 days and include stays in everything from Relais & Châteaux hotels to simple campgrounds, where staff members prepare most meals featuring local cuisine. All tours include an accompanying vehicle that provides drinks and assists in the event of breakdowns. Per-person rates range from $1,100 to $3,100, depending on the territory, the duration, and the degree of luxury.

Holland Bicycling Tours, Inc., P.O. Box 6485, Thousand Oaks, CA 91359 (☎ **800/852-3258;** fax 805/495-8601), is the North American representative of a Dutch company that leads 12-day bicycle tours through the Loire Valley and Normandy. Frequent stopovers manage to encompass many of the most glorious châteaux and palaces, tracing the Loire, Cher, and Indre rivers over mostly flat terrain. The price of the land portion (without airfare) of the Loire Valley tour is $1,950 per person; the Loire/Normandy tour is $1,850 per person (double occupancy, including all breakfasts and dinners, accommodations, bike rental, the services of a tour leader, and a tour van). The outfitter also offers a 10-day tour through Provence, past Roman ruins, van Gogh's sunflowers, and fields pungent with lavender, thyme, and basil. For the 10-day tour, the price is $1,750 per person, double occupancy.

Bridges Tours, 2855 Capital Dr., Eugene, OR 97403 (☎ 800/461-6760), offers several regional biking and walking tours. All tours feature groups of eight, escorts, van support, and stays at inns and small hotels, costing $200 or $300 per person per day. **Châteaux Bike Tours,** P.O. Box 5706, Denver, CO 80217 (☎ 800/678-2453), promotes luxury tours of France with small groups, van supports, two guides, and stays in châteaux. Tours (usually for 5 to 18 people) range from 5 to 9 days and cost $2,000 to $3,000 per person, double occupancy. **Classic Adventures,** P.O. Box 153, Hamlin, NY 14464 (☎ 800/777-8090), sponsors 1- and 2-week spring and fall tours of the Loire Valley, Burgundy, and the Dordogne. Accommodations are upscale, and all tours are van supported and escorted. The 7-day/6-night tours are $1,689 per person for the Loire Valley and $1,789 for Burgundy; an 11-day/10-night tour of the Dordogne is $2,389 per person.

Euro-Bike Tours, P.O. Box 990, DeKalb, IL 60115 (☎ 800/321-6060), offers 10-day tours in the Dordogne ($2,395 per person) and Provence ($2,495 per person), 6-day tours of Burgundy ($1,695 per person), and 8-day tours of the Loire Valley ($2,195). All are supported and escorted. Finally, **Uniquely Europe** (a subsidiary of Europe Express), 1940 116th Ave. NE, Bellevue, WA 98004 (☎ 800/426-3615), has biking and walking tours of Alsace, Burgundy, the Dordogne, Languedoc, the Loire Valley, Provence, and Tarn. A 7-day guided bike tour is $1,950 to $1,970 per person, double occupancy; a 7- or 8-day self-guided bike tour is $1,150 to $1,550 per person, double occupancy. Tours include van support, excellent accommodations, and most meals.

LANGUAGE SCHOOLS   The **Alliance Française,** 101 bd. Raspail, 75270 Paris, CEDEX 06 (☎ **01-45-44-38-28;** fax 01-45-44-25-95), is a state-approved nonprofit organization with a network of 1,100 establishments in 138 countries, offering French-language courses to some 350,000 students. The international school in Paris is open all year, and courses run on a month-to-month basis, ranging from 1,715F to 3,430F ($308.70 to $617.40). Write for information and application forms at least 1 month before your departure. In North America, the largest branch is the **Alliance Française,** 2819 Ordway St. NW, Washington, DC 20008 (☎ **800/6-FRANCE;** fax 202/362-1587).

A clearinghouse for information on French-language schools is **Lingua Service Worldwide,** 211 E. 43rd St., Suite 1303, New York, NY 10017 (☎ **800/ 394-LEARN** or 212/867-1225; fax 212/983-2590). Its programs cover not only Paris but also Aix-en-Provence, Antibes, Avignon, Bordeaux, Cannes, Juan-les-Pins, Megève, Montpellier, Nice, Strasbourg, and Tours. They range from $200 to $990 per week, depending on the city, the school, and the accommodations.

COOKING SCHOOLS   If you've always wanted to learn to cook à la française, you can take those all-important lessons from Maxime and Eliane Rochereau at their hotel/restaurant, **Le Castel de Bray-et-Monts,** Brehemont, 37130 Langeais (☎ **02-47-96-70-47;** fax 02-47-96-57-36). Before settling on the banks of the Loire, in the heart of châteaux country, the Rochereaux spent 15 years living and working in the United States—Maxime as chef de cuisine at Chicago's Ritz-Carlton and Palm Beach's Breakers, Eliane as a caterer for the Palm Beach jet set. In the charming vineyard village of Brehemont, Maxime now offers classes in classic French cooking at an 18th-century manor surrounded by a magnificent garden and stream. The price, including a week's accommodation and full board, is 6,800F ($1,224) per person, double occupancy. Maxime devotes mornings to the preparation of an intricate French meal (from aperitif to dessert), allowing students to observe the service rituals of a working restaurant. Afternoons are usually unscheduled, allowing time for you to explore the nearby châteaux of the Loire Valley. Courses are taught in English.

The famous/infamous Georges-Auguste Escoffier (1846–1935) taught the Edwardians how to eat. Today Le Ritz, once the site of many of Escoffier's meals, maintains the **Ritz-Escoffier Ecole de Gastronomie Française,** 15 place Vendôme, 75001 Paris (☎ **800/966-5758** in the U.S., or 01-43-16-30-50), offering demonstration classes of the master's techniques on Monday, Tuesday, and Thursday afternoons. These demonstrations cost 275F ($49.50) each. Courses, taught in French and English, start at 5,550F to 5,850F ($999 to $1,053) for 1 week, going up to 63,000F ($11,340) for 12 weeks.

Le Cordon Bleu, 8 rue Léon-Delhomme, 75015 Paris (☎ **800/457-CHEF** in the U.S., or 01-53-68-22-50), established in 1895, is the most famous French cooking school—this is where Julia Child learned to perfect her pâté brisée and mousse au chocolat. Bon appétit! Its best-known courses last 10 weeks, at the end of which certificates are issued. Many gourmet enthusiasts prefer a less intense immersion and opt for either a 4-day workshop or a 3-hour demonstration class. Enrollment in either of these is on a first-come, first-served basis; costs are 220F ($39.60) for a demonstration and around 4,590F ($826.20) for the 4-day workshop.

7   Flying to France from North America

Flying time to Paris from New York is about 7 hours; from Chicago, 9 hours; from Los Angeles, 11 hours; from Atlanta, 8 hours; from Miami, 8½ hours; and from Washington, D.C., 7½ hours.

Hardcore Paris hands consider its two airports—Orly and Charles de Gaulle—as almost even bets in terms of convenience to the city's center, though taxi rides from Orly might take a bit less time than those from de Gaulle. Orly, the older of the two, is 8 miles south of the center, whereas Charles de Gaulle is 14 miles northeast. In April 1996 the last of Air France's flights to Orly from North America was routed into Charles de Gaulle (Terminal 2C). Air France's U.S.-based competitors tend to focus on both airports in equal measure.

Most airlines divide their year into roughly seasonal slots, with the lowest fares between November 1 and March 13. Shoulder season, between the high and low seasons, is only slightly more expensive and includes mid-March to mid-June and all of October, which we think is the ideal time to visit France.

THE MAJOR AIRLINES

American Airlines (☎ 800/433-7300; www.americanair.com) offers daily flights to Paris from Dallas/Fort Worth, Chicago, Miami, Boston, and New York.

Continental Airlines (☎ 800/231-0856; www.flycontinental.com) provides non-stop flights to Paris from Newark and Houston. Flights from Newark depart daily, while flights from Houston depart four to seven times a week, depending on the season.

Delta Airlines (☎ 800/241-4141; www.delta-air.com) is one of the best choices for those flying to Paris from the southeastern United States or the Midwest. It's easy to connect with a flight to Atlanta, from which Delta offers a nonstop flight to Paris every evening. Delta also operates daily nonstop flights from both Cincinnati and New York. Note that Delta is the only airline offering nonstop service from New York to Nice.

TWA (☎ 800/221-2000; www2.twa.com) operates daily nonstop service to Paris from New York. In summer, several flights a week from Boston and Washington, D.C., go through New York; several times a week there are nonstop flights from St. Louis; and three times a week there are flights from Los Angeles, connecting in St. Louis or New York. In winter, flights from Los Angeles and Washington are suspended, and flights from St. Louis are direct, with brief touchdowns in New York or Boston en route.

US Airways (☎ 800/428-4322; www.usairways.com) offers daily nonstop service from Philadelphia to Paris.

The French national carrier, **Air France** (☎ 800/237-2747; www.airfrance.com), offers daily or several-times-a-week flights between Paris and such North American cities as Newark; Washington, D.C.; Miami; Chicago; New York; Houston; San Francisco; Los Angeles; Montréal; Toronto; and Mexico City. Flights to Paris from Los Angeles originate in Papeete, French Polynesia.

Canadians usually choose the daily **Air Canada** (☎ 800/776-3000 in North America; www.aircanada.ca/) nonstop flights to Paris from Toronto and Montréal. Two of Air Canada's flights from Toronto are shared with Air France and feature Air France aircraft.

GETTING THE BEST DEAL

Consolidators (or "bucket shops") act as clearinghouses for blocks of tickets that airlines discount and consign during normally slow periods of air travel. Tickets are usually priced 20% to 35% below the full fare.

Most flyers estimate their savings at $200 per ticket off the regular price. Nearly a third of the passengers reported savings of up to $300 off the regular price. But—and here's the hitch—many people reported no savings at all, as the airlines sometimes

CyberDeals for Net Surfers

It's possible to get some great deals on airfare, hotels, and car rentals via the Internet. So grab your mouse and start surfing—you could save a bundle on your trip. The Web sites we've highlighted below are worth checking out, especially since all services are free (but don't forget that time is money when you're online).

Microsoft Expedia (www.expedia.com)   The best part of this multipurpose travel site is the "Fare Tracker": You fill out a form on the screen indicating that you're interested in cheap flights to Paris from your hometown, and, once a week, they'll e-mail you the best airfare deals. The site's "Travel Agent" will also steer you to bargains on hotels and car rentals, and you can book everything, including flights, right online. This site is even useful once you're booked: Before you go, log on to Expedia for oodles of up-to-date travel information, including weather reports and foreign exchange rates.

Travelocity (www.travelocity.com)   This is one of the best travel sites out there. In addition to its "Personal Fare Watcher," which notifies you via e-mail of the lowest airfares for up to five different destinations, Travelocity will track the three lowest fares for any routes on any dates in minutes. You can book a flight right then and there, and if you need a rental car or hotel, Travelocity will find you the best deal via the SABRE computer reservations system (a huge database used by travel agents worldwide). Click on "Last Minute Deals" for the latest travel bargains.

Trip.Com (www.thetrip.com)   This site is really geared toward the business traveler, but vacationers can also use Trip.Com's valuable fare-finding engine, which will e-mail you every week with the best city-to-city airfare deals on your selected route or routes.

Discount Tickets (www.discount-tickets.com)   Operated by the ETN (European Travel Network), this site offers discounts on airfares, accommodations, car rentals, and tours.

E-Savers Programs   Several major airlines offer a free e-mail service known as E-Savers, via which each week they'll send you their best bargain airfares. Here's how it works: Once a week (usually Wednesday), subscribers receive a list of discounted flights to and from various destinations, both international and domestic. Now here's the catch: these fares are available only if you leave the very next Saturday (or sometimes Friday night) and return on the following Monday or Tuesday. It's really a service for the spontaneously inclined and travelers looking for a quick getaway. But the fares are cheap, so it's worth taking a look. If you have a preference for certain airlines (in other words, the ones you fly most frequently), sign up with them first.

Here's a list of airlines and their Web sites, where you can not only get on the e-mailing lists but also book flights directly:

- **American Airlines:** www.americanair.com
- **Continental Airlines:** www.flycontinental.com
- **TWA:** www.twa.com
- **Northwest Airlines:** www.nwa.com
- **US Airways:** www.usairways.com

Epicurious Travel (travel.epicurious.com), another good travel site, allows you to sign up for all of these airline e-mail lists at once.

match the consolidator ticket by announcing a promotional fare. The situation is a bit tricky and calls for some careful investigation to determine how much you're saving.

Bucket shops abound from coast to coast. Look for their ads in your local newspaper's travel section; they're usually very small and a single column in width. *Note:* Since dealing with unknown bucket shops might be a little risky, it's wise to call the Better Business Bureau in your area to see if complaints have been filed against the company from which you plan to purchase a ticket.

Here are some recommendations:

One of the biggest U.S. consolidators is **Travac,** 989 Sixth Ave., 16th floor, New York, NY 10018 (☎ **800/TRAV-800** in the U.S., or 212/563-3303), which offers discounted seats from throughout the United States to most cities in Europe on airlines like TWA, United, and Delta. Another Travac office is at 2601 E. Jefferson St., Orlando, FL 32803 (☎ **407/896-0014**).

In New York, try **TFI Tours International,** 34 W. 32nd St., 12th floor, New York, NY 10001 (☎ **800/745-8000** in the U.S. outside the New York City area or 212/736-1140 in New York City). This tour company offers service to 177 cities worldwide.

From anywhere, explore the possibilities of **Travel Avenue,** 10 S. Riverside Plaza, Suite 1404, Chicago, IL 60606 (☎ **800/333-3335** in the U.S.), a national agency. Its tickets are often cheaper than those at most shops, and it charges only a $25 fee on international tickets, rather than taking the usual 10% commission from an airline. Travel Avenue rebates most of that back to you—hence, the lower fares.

In Minnesota, a possibility is **TMI (Travel Management International),** 1129 E. Wayzata Blvd., Wayzata, MN 55391 (☎ **612/476-0005;** fax 612/476-1480), which offers a wide variety of discounts, including youth fares, student fares, and access to other kinds of air-related discounts.

1-800-FLY-4-LESS is a nationwide airline reservation and ticketing service that specializes in finding the lowest fares. For information on available consolidator airline tickets for last-minute travel, call ☎ **800/359-4537.** When fares are high and advance-planning time low, such a service is invaluable. Another reliable choice is **1-800-FLY-CHEAP. Council Travel** (☎ **800/226-8624**) caters especially to young travelers, but their bargain basement prices are available to people of all ages.

8 Package Tours

Package tours are not necessarily the same thing as escorted tours. They are simply a way of buying your airfare and accommodations at the same time—and they can save you a ton of money. In many cases, a package that includes airfare, hotel, and rental car will cost you less than just the hotel alone if you booked it yourself. That's because packages are sold in bulk to tour operators, who resell them to the public.

It pays to comparison shop among various packages, though. Some packages offer a better class of hotels than others; some provide the same hotels for lower prices. Some feature flights on scheduled airlines whereas others book charters. In some packages, your choices of accommodations and travel days may be limited. Some packages let you choose between escorted vacations and independent vacations; others allow you to add on just a few excursions or escorted day trips (also at prices lower than if you booked them yourself) without booking an entirely escorted tour. The time you spend shopping around will be well rewarded.

For package tours that offer adventure and activity, see "Special-Interest Vacations," earlier in this chapter.

Delta Airlines, through its tour division, **Delta Dream Vacations** (☎ **800/872-7786**), offers a full package (without airfare) to the Ile de France that includes 6 nights at a good hotel in Paris, with guided tours of the monuments, an excursion to Versailles, breakfasts, taxes, a 5-day public-transport pass, and a 3-day museum pass. It ranges from $999 to $1,799 per person, double occupancy, depending on the hotel you stay in. Also available are excursions to the Riviera, Geneva, and the rest of Europe at prices that are lower (sometimes significantly so) than if you'd arranged each component of the package yourself.

The French Experience, 370 Lexington Ave., Room 812, New York, NY 10017 (☎ **212/986-1115;** fax 212/986-3808), offers several fly/drive programs using different types and price categories of hotels. It also takes reservations for about 30 hotels in Paris, arranges short-term apartment rentals, and features prearranged package tours of various regions. Any of these can be adapted and altered to suit your individual needs. Package prices begin at around $600 per person.

American Express Vacations (as operated by Certified Vacations, Inc.), P.O. Box 1525, Fort Lauderdale, FL 33302 (☎ **800/446-6234** in the U.S. and Canada; fax 954/357-4682), is the world's most recognizable tour operator. Its offerings in France and the rest of Europe are more comprehensive than those of many other companies. Highlights include more than 40 "go-any-day" city packages (6 nights for $2,731 to $3,991, double occupancy, depending on season), 9 freelance vacations ($1,079 per person for land package only), and 18 escorted tours ($1,199 per person for land package only). If you have a clear idea of what you want and it's not already available, this operator can arrange an individualized itinerary.

One of Europe's largest operators, **Trafalgar Tours,** 11 E. 26th St., New York, NY 10010 (☎ **800/854-0103**), offers affordable packages with lodgings in middle-of-the-road hotels. Its Best of France is a 14-day trip starting and ending in Paris, with stops on the Riviera and in Lourdes, Nice, Monaco, and other cities. Most meals and twin-bed accommodations in first-class hotels are part of the package, which is $1,450 per person for the land package only. It also offers Treasures of France, a 9-day, four-city tour, also beginning and ending in Paris, with similar meal and accommodation offerings; it costs $925 per person for the land package only. Call your travel agent for more information (Trafalgar takes calls only from agents).

One of Trafalgar's leading competitors, known for offering roughly equivalent tours, is **Globus/Cosmos Tours,** 5301 S. Federal Circle, Littleton, CO 80123-2980 (☎ **800/338-7092**). Globus offers first-class escorted coach tours of various regions of France lasting from 8 to 16 days. Cosmos, a budget branch of Globus, offers escorted tours of about the same length. You must book tours through a travel agent, but you can call the 800 number for brochures.

Insight International Tours, 745 Atlantic Ave., Suite 720, Boston, MA 02111 (☎ **800/468-2825**), provides superior first-class, fully escorted coach grand tours of France as well as 1-week general tours of specific regions. Its 9-day trip to Paris and the Loire Valley costs $1,050 per person (land only), and its 17-day grand tour of France is $1,925 per person (land only). **Tauck Tours,** 276 Post Rd. W., Westport, CT 06880 (☎ **800/468-2855**), features a good general tour of France covering the Normandy landing beaches, the Bayeux Tapestry, and Mont-St-Michel among other places of historic interest in a 14-day trip beginning and ending in Paris. The price is $3,720 per person, double occupancy, without airfare.

9 Getting There from the United Kingdom

BY PLANE   From London, **Air France** (☎ **0181/742-6600;** www.airfrance.com) and **British Airways** (☎ **0345/222-111;** www.british-airways.com) fly regularly and frequently to Paris (trip time is 1 hour). Air France and British Airways alone operate up to 17 flights daily from Heathrow, one of the busiest air routes in Europe.

There are also direct flights to Paris from major cities like Edinburgh, Manchester, and Southampton. Some U.K. flights (check with a travel agent) will take you to a regional French city, if that's where you're going—thus letting you avoid a changeover in Paris. Destinations in France include Bordeaux, Clermont-Ferrand, Lyon, Marseille, Montpellier, Nantes, Nice, Quimper, and Toulouse.

Flying from England to France is often very expensive, even though the distance is short. That's why most Brits depend on a good travel agent to get them the lowest possible fares. Good values are offered by a number of companies, such as **Nouvelles Frontières,** 2–3 Woodstock St., London W1R 1HE (☎ **0171/629-7772**).

The newspapers are always full of classified ads touting "slashed" fares from London to other parts of the world. One good source is *Time Out* magazine. London's *Evening Standard* maintains a daily travel section, and the Sunday editions of virtually every newspaper in Britain run many ads. Though competition is fierce, a well-recommended company that consolidates bulk ticket purchases and passes the savings on to you is **Trailfinders** (☎ **0171/937-5400** in London). It offers access to tickets on such carriers as British Airways, KLM, and SAS.

BY TRAIN   Paris is one of Europe's busiest rail junctions, with trains arriving at and departing from its many stations every few minutes. If you're already in Europe, you may want to go to Paris by train. Even if you don't, the cost is relatively low—especially in comparison to renting a car.

The one-way fare from London to Paris by Eurostar is $199 in first class and $139 in second. See "By the Channel Tunnel," below.

Rail passes as well as individual rail tickets in Europe are available from most travel agents, at any **Rail Europe** office (☎ **800/677-8585** in the U.S.). You might also want to stop in at the **International Rail Centre,** Victoria Station, London SW1V 1JY (☎ **0990/848848**).

In London, an especially convenient place to buy rail tickets to virtually anywhere is **Wasteels Ltd.,** opposite Platform 2 in Victoria Station, London SW1V 1JY (☎ **0171/834-6744**). It provides railway-related services and information on the pros and cons of various types of fares and rail passes; its staff will probably spend more than the usual amount of time with you in planning your itinerary. Depending on circumstances, Wasteels sometimes charges a £5 (90¢) fee, but for the information provided the cost might be worth it.

BY BUS   Bus travel to Paris is available from London as well as from many other cities on the Continent. In the early 1990s the French government established strong incentives for long-haul buses to avoid driving into the center of Paris. The arrival and departure point for Europe's largest bus operators, **Eurolines France,** is at 28 av. du Général-de-Gaulle, 93541 Bagnolet (☎ **01-49-72-51-51**), a 35-minute Métro ride from central Paris, at the terminus of Métro line 3 (Métro: Gallieni), in the suburb of Bagnolet. Despite this inconvenience, many people prefer bus travel.

Because Eurolines doesn't have a U.S.-based sales agent, most people wait until they reach Europe to buy their tickets. Any European travel agent can arrange the purchase. If you're traveling to Paris from London, you can contact **Eurolines (U.K.) Ltd.,** 52 Grosvenor Gardens, Victoria, London, SW1, or call ☎ **0990/143-219** for information and credit-card sales.

BY FERRY   Services aboard ferryboats and hydrofoils operate day and night, in all seasons, with the exception of last-minute cancellations during particularly fierce storms. Many Channel crossings are carefully timed to coincide with the arrival/ departure of major trains (especially those between London and Paris). Trains let you off a short walk from the piers. Most ferries carry cars, trucks, and massive amounts of freight, but some hydrofoils take passengers only. The major routes include at least

A Note on British Customs

On January 1, 1993, the borders between European countries were relaxed as the European markets united. While you're traveling within the EU, this will have a big impact on what you can buy and take home with you for personal use.

If you buy your goods in a duty-free shop, the old rules still apply—you're allowed to bring home 200 cigarettes and 2 liters of table wine, plus 1 liter of spirits or 2 liters of fortified wine. But now you can buy your wine, spirits, or cigarettes in an ordinary shop in France or Belgium, for example, and bring home almost as much as you'd like. (Excise law does set theoretical limits.) If you're returning home from a non-EU country, the allowances are the standard ones from duty-free shops. You must declare any goods in excess of these allowances. British Customs tends to be strict and complicated in its requirements.

For details, get in touch with Her Majesty's Customs and Excise Office, Dorset House, Stamford Street, London SE1 9PY (☎ **0171/202-4510;** fax 0171/ 202-4131).

12 trips a day between Dover or Folkestone and Calais or Boulogne. Hovercraft and hydrofoils make the trip from Dover to Calais, the shortest distance across the Channel, in just 40 minutes during good weather, whereas the slower-moving ferries might take several hours, depending on weather conditions and tides. If you're bringing a car, it's important to make reservations, as space belowdecks is usually crowded. Timetables can vary depending on weather conditions and many other factors.

The leading operator of ferryboats across the channel is **P&O Channel Lines** (☎ **800/677-8585** for reservations in North America or 01301/212-121 in England). It operates car and passenger ferries between Portsmouth, England, and Cherbourg, France (three departures a day; 4¼ hours each way during daylight hours, 7 hours each way at night); between Portsmouth and Le Havre, France (three a day; 5½ hours each way). Most popular of all are the routes it operates between Dover and Calais, France (25 sailings a day; 75 minutes each way).

P&O's major competitor is **Stena Sealink** (☎ **800/677-8585** for reservations in North America or 01233/615-455 in England), which carries both passengers and vehicles on most of its routes. It offers conventional ferryboat service between Cherbourg and Southampton (one or two trips a day; 6 to 8 hours each way). Its conventional car-ferries between Calais and Dover are very popular; they depart 20 times a day in both directions and take 90 minutes to make the crossing. Typical fares between France and England are 25F ($4.50) one way for adults, 22F ($3.95) for seniors, and 15F ($2.70) for children.

As stated above, the shortest and by far the most popular route across the Channel is between Calais and Dover. **Hoverspeed** operates at least 12 hovercraft crossings daily; the trip takes 35 minutes. It also runs a SeaCat (a catamaran propelled by jet engines) that takes slightly longer to make the crossing between Boulogne and Folkestone; the SeaCats depart about four times a day on the 55-minute voyage. For reservations and information call Hoverspeed (☎ **800/677-8585** for reservations in North America or 01304/240-241 in England). Typical one-way fares are 25F ($4.50) per person.

If you plan to transport a rental car between England and France, check in advance with the rental company about license and insurance requirements and additional drop-off charges. And be aware that many car-rental companies, for insurance reasons,

---

A Weekend Trip to London

Regardless of how much you love Paris, too long a stint within the confines of the French capital might make you itch for the cultural familiarity of London, at least for a weekend. So if the allure of Gallic charm has begun to pale, know that transit between Paris and London is easier than ever.

Now the Eurostar train roars at high speeds through the **Chunnel,** reducing the travel time between Paris and London to a brief 3 hours, at prices that rival conventional train and ferryboat fares and at a level of convenience (direct transit between Paris's Gare du Nord and London's Waterloo Station) never before imagined. If you're willing to pay for it, you can opt for ultra-upscale service, enhanced cuisine, and such perks as limousine service to and from the station and your hotel.

Where should you lay your weary head during your weekend in London? The folks at Eurostar can even set that up for you as part of a rail-and-hotel package at a highly discounted rate. For as little as $299 per person, with a $30 per person supplement on Fridays and Saturdays, you can buy a package that includes rail transport, 2 nights (double occupancy) in a hotel, and an inner-city sightseeing tour. The price is hard to beat, and the sheer convenience of the routing makes the plan easier and faster than flying.

From North America, these packages can be arranged by calling the EuroStar division of RailEurope (☎ **800/EUROSTAR**). For details about hotel packages, contact EuroVacations (☎ **888/281-EURO**). Citizens of Australia, New Zealand, and South Africa should contact a local travel agent. If you're already in Paris, contact any travel agency or talk to your hotel concierge. Both should be able to arrange the same basic package, depending on seasonal promotions.

---

forbid transport of their vehicles over the water between England and France. Transport of a car each way begins at 650F ($117).

BY THE CHANNEL TUNNEL   A giant boost for cross-Channel commerce occurred in 1994, when Queen Elizabeth II and former French President François MitterRand jointly inaugurated the Channel Tunnel (the Chunnel), whose debut had been dreamed about since the military campaigns of Napoleon. The $15-billion tunnel, one of the great engineering feats of all time, is the first link between Britain and the Continent since the Ice Age.

Rail Europe (☎ **800/94-CHUNNEL**) sells tickets for the **Eurostar Express,** which offers twice-daily passenger service between London and both Paris and Brussels. One-way fares, with some restrictions, begin at $99 second-class and $139 first-class, with discounts for Eurail or Britrail passholders. Additional discounts are offered to travelers under 18 and bona-fide students. In London, make reservations for Eurostar at ☎ **0345/303-030,** in Paris call ☎ **01-33-31-58-03,** and in the United States call ☎ **800/677-8585.**

The Chunnel's **Le Shuttle** also accommodates passenger cars, charter buses, taxis, and motorcycles from Folkestone, England, to Calais, France. It operates 24 hours a day year-round, running every 15 minutes during peak travel times and at least once an hour at night. You can buy tickets at the tollbooth. With Le Shuttle, gone are weather-related delays, seasickness, and the need for advance reservations.

Before boarding Le Shuttle, motorists stop at a tollbooth and pass through Immigration for both countries at one time. They then drive onto a half-mile-long train and travel through an underground tunnel built beneath the seabed through a layer of impermeable chalk marl and sealed with a reinforced-concrete lining. During the ride, they stay in air-conditioned carriages, remain inside their cars, or step outside to stretch their legs. When the trip is completed, they simply drive off toward their destinations—in our case, to France. Travel time between the French and English highway systems is about 1 hour. Once on French soil, Britain-based drivers must, obviously, begin driving on the right-hand side of the road.

Stores selling duty-free goods, restaurants, and service stations are available to travelers on both sides of the Channel. A bilingual staff is on hand to assist travelers at both the French and the British terminals.

10 Getting Around France

BY TRAIN

With some 50 cities in France linked by the world's fastest trains, you can get from Paris to just about anywhere else in the country in just a few hours. With 24,000 miles of track and about 3,000 stations, SNCF (French National Railroads) is fabled throughout the world for its on-time performance. You can travel first or second class by day and in *couchette* or sleeper by night. Many trains carry dining facilities.

INFORMATION   If you plan much travel on European railroads, get the latest copy of the ***Thomas Cook European Timetable of Railroads.*** This comprehensive 500-plus-page book documents all Europe's mainline passenger rail services with detail and accuracy. It's available exclusively in North America from the **Forsyth Travel Library,** 226 Westchester Ave., White Plains, NY 10604 (☎ **800/367-7984**), at a cost of $27.95, plus $4.50 postage (priority airmail in the U.S. and $5 U.S. for shipments to Canada).

In the United States: For more information and to purchase rail passes (see below) before you leave, contact **Rail Europe** at 500 Mamaroneck Ave., Suite 314, Harrison, NY 10528 (☎ **800/677-8585;** fax 914/682-3712).

In Canada: Rail Europe offices are at 2087 Dundas St. E., Suite 105, Mississauga, ON L4X 1M2 (☎ **800/361-7245** or 905/602-4195; fax 905/602-4198).

In London: SNCF maintains offices at **French Railways,** 179 Piccadilly, London W1V 0BA (☎ **0171/803-3030;** fax 0171/491-9956).

In Paris: The SNCF administration maintains rail information lines for bookings and departures in both the U.S. and in Paris for English-speaking travelers (☎ **800/ 4-EURAIL** in the U.S., 08-36-35-35-39 in Paris). Information can also be obtained by visiting the nearest rail station, where staffs are on hand to assist with ticket sales and inquiries. Paris railway stations are Gare de l'Est, Gare du Nord, Gare St-Lazare, Gare Montparnasse, Gare d'Austerlitz, and Gare de Lyon.

FRENCH RAIL PASSES   Working cooperatively with SNCF, Air Inter Europe, and Avis, Rail Europe offers three flexible cost-saving rail passes that can reduce travel costs considerably.

The **France Railpass** provides unlimited rail transport throughout France for 3 days within 1 month, costing $195 in first class and $165 in second. You can purchase up to 6 more days for an extra $30 per person per day. Costs are even more reasonable for two adults traveling together: $156 per person for first class and $132 for second. Children 4 to 11 travel for half price.

The **France Rail 'n Drive Pass,** available only in North America, combines good value on both rail travel and Avis car rentals and is best used by arriving at a major rail depot, then striking out to explore the countryside by car. It includes the rail pass above, along with unlimited mileage on a car rental. Costs are lowest when two or more adults travel together. You can use it during 5 nonconsecutive days in 1 month, and it includes 3 days of travel on the train and 2 days' use of a rental car. If rental of the least expensive car is combined with first-class rail travel, the price is $189 per person; if rental of the least expensive car is combined with second-class travel, the charge is $174 per person. Cars can be upgraded for a supplemental fee. The above prices apply to two people traveling together; solo travelers pay from $259 for first class and $234 for second.

EURAILPASSES   For years, many in-the-know travelers have been taking advantage of one of Europe's greatest travel bargains: the Eurailpass, which permits unlimited first-class rail travel in any country in Western Europe except the British Isles (good in Ireland). Passes are for periods as short as 15 days or as long as 3 months and are strictly nontransferable.

The pass is sold only in North America. A Eurailpass is $538 for 15 days, $698 for 21 days, $864 for 1 month, $1,224 for 2 months, and $1,512 for 3 months. Children 3 and under travel free providing they don't occupy a seat (otherwise they're charged half fare); children 4 to 11 are charged half fare. If you're under 26, you can purchase a Eurail Youthpass, entitling you to unlimited second-class travel for 1 or 2 months, costing $605 and $857, respectively.

Seat reservations are required on some trains. Many of the trains have *couchettes* (sleeping cars), which cost extra. Obviously, the 2- or 3-month traveler gets the greatest economic advantages; the Eurailpass is ideal for such extensive trips. With the pass you can visit all of France's major sights, from Normandy to the Alps, then end your vacation in Norway, for example.

If you'll be traveling for two weeks or a month, you have to estimate rail distance before determining if such a pass is to your benefit. To obtain full advantage of the ticket for 15 days or a month, you'd have to spend a great deal of time on the train. Eurailpass holders are entitled to considerable reductions on certain buses and ferries as well.

Travel agents in all towns and railway agents in such major cities as New York, Montréal, and Los Angeles sell all these tickets. A Eurailpass is available at the North American offices of CIT Travel Service, the French National Railroads, the German Federal Railroads, and the Swiss Federal Railways.

The **Eurail Flexipass** allows you to visit Europe with more flexibility. It's valid in first class and offers the same privileges as the Eurailpass. However, it provides a number of individual travel days that you can use over a much longer period of consecutive days. That makes it possible to stay in one city and yet not lose a single day of travel. There are two passes: 10 days of travel in 2 months for $634, and 15 days of travel in 2 months for $836.

With many of the same qualifications and restrictions as the previously described Flexipass is a **Eurail Youth Flexipass.** Sold only to travelers under 26, it allows 10 days of travel within 2 months for $444, and 15 days of travel within 2 months for $585.

Miles & Kilometers

To convert kilometers to miles, multiply the number of kilometers by .62 (for example, 25km × .62 = 15.5 mi.). Note that this conversion can be used to convert speeds from kilometers per hour (kmph) to miles per hour (m.p.h.).

To convert miles to kilometers, multiply the number of miles by 1.61 (for example, 50 mi. × 1.61 = 80.5km).

BY CAR

The most charming châteaux and best country hotels always seem to lie away from the main cities and train stations. You'll find that renting a car is usually the best way to travel once you get to France, especially if you plan to explore in depth and not stick to the standard route, such as the Paris–Nice run.

Driving time in Europe is largely a matter of conjecture, urgency, and how much sightseeing you do along the way. Driving time from Geneva to Paris is 5½ hours minimum. Rouen to Paris requires 2½ hours; Nantes to Paris, 3½ hours; Lyon to Paris, 4 hours. The driving time from Marseille to Paris is a matter of national pride, and tall tales abound about how rapidly the French can do it. With the accelerator pressed to the floor, you might conceivably make it in 7 hours, but we always make a 2-day journey of it.

But frankly, Europe's rail networks are so well developed and so inexpensive, we recommend that you rent a car only for exploring areas little serviced by rail lines, such as Brittany, rural Burgundy, and the Dordogne.

RENTALS   Renting a car in France is easy. You'll need to present a passport, a valid driver's license, and a valid credit card. You'll also have to meet the minimum age requirement of the company. (For their least expensive cars, this is 21 at Hertz, 23 at Avis, and 25 at Budget. More expensive cars at any of the above-mentioned companies might require that you be at least 25.) It usually isn't obligatory, at least within France, but certain companies, especially the smaller ones, have at times asked for the presentation of an International Driver's License, even though this is becoming increasingly superfluous in Western Europe.

Note: The best deal is usually a weekly rental with unlimited mileage. All car-rental bills in France are subject to a whopping 20.6% government tax, among the highest in Europe. And though the rental company won't usually mind if you drive your car across the French border—into, say, Germany, Switzerland, Italy, or Spain—it's often expressly forbidden to transport your car on any ferryboat, including the dozens that ply the waters of the Channel to England.

Unless it's already factored into the rental agreement, an optional **collision-damage waiver (CDW)** carries an extra charge of 80F to 95F ($14.40 to $17.10) per day for the least expensive cars. Buying this will usually eliminate all but 1,500F ($270) of your responsibility in the event of accidental damage to the car. Because most newcomers aren't familiar with local driving customs and conditions, we highly recommend that you buy the CDW, though certain credit-card issuers will compensate you for any accident-related liability to a rented car if the imprint of their card appears on the original rental contract. At some of the companies the CDW won't protect you against the theft of a car, so if this is the case, ask about buying extra theft protection. This cost is around 37F ($6.65) extra per day.

Automatic transmission is considered a luxury in Europe, so if you want it you'll have to pay dearly.

Budget (☎ **800/472-3325** in the U.S. and Canada; www.budgetrentacar.com) maintains about 30 locations in Paris, with its largest branch at 81 av. Kléber, 16e (☎ **01-47-55-61-00;** Métro: Trocadéro). For rentals of more than 7 days, you can pick up a car (at least in most cases) in one French city and drop it off in another, but there are extra charges. Drop-offs in cities within an easy drive of the French border (including Geneva and Frankfurt) incur no extra charge; however, you can arrange drop-offs in other non-French cities for a reasonable surcharge.

Hertz (☎ **800/654-3001** in the U.S. and Canada; www.hertz.com) maintains about 15 locations in Paris, including offices at the city's airports. The main office is

Liters & Gallons

To convert liters to U.S. gallons, multiply the number of liters by .26 (for example, 50 liters × .26 = 13 U.S. gal.).

To convert U.S. gallons to liters, multiply the number of gallons by 3.79 (for example, 12 gal. × 3.79 = 45.48 liters).

at 27 rue St-Ferdinand, 17e (☎ **01-45-74-97-39;** Métro: Argentine). Be sure to ask about any promotional discounts.

Avis (☎ **800/331-2112** in the U.S. and Canada; www.avis.com) has offices at both Paris airports, as well as an inner-city headquarters at 5 rue Bixio, 7e (☎ **01-44-18-10-50;** Métro: Ecole-Militaire), near the Eiffel Tower.

National (☎ **800/227-3876** in the U.S. and Canada; www.nationalcar.com) is represented in Paris by Europcar, whose largest office is at 165 bis rue De Vaugirard (☎ **01-44-38-61-61;** Métro: St.-Sulpre). It has offices at both Paris airports and at about a dozen other locations. Any of its offices can rent you a car on the spot, but to qualify for the lowest rates it's best to reserve in advance from North America.

Two U.S.-based agencies that don't have Paris offices but act as booking agents for Paris-based agencies are **Kemwel Holiday Auto** (☎ **800/678-0678;** www.kemwel.com) and **Auto Europe** (☎ **800/223-5555;** www.autoeurope.com). These companies can make bookings in the U.S. only, so call before your trip.

GASOLINE Known in France as *essence,* gas is extraordinarily expensive for those used to North American prices. All but the least expensive cars usually require an octane rating that the French classify as essence super, the most expensive variety. At press time, essence super sold for about 6.70F ($1.20) per liter, which works out to around 24.52F ($4.40) per U.S. gallon. Depending on your car, you'll need either leaded (*avec plomb*) or unleaded (*sans plomb*), which costs just a fraction (about 25 centimes per liter) less than the version with lead. Depending on the capacity of your tank, filling a medium-size car will cost between $45 and $65.

Beware of the mixture of gasoline and oil sold in certain rural communities called *mélange* or *gasoil;* this mixture is for very old two-cycle engines.

Note: Sometimes you can drive for miles in rural France without encountering a gas station, so don't let your tank get dangerously low.

DRIVING RULES Everyone in the car, in both the front and the back seats, must wear seat belts. Children 11 and under must ride in the back seat. Drivers are supposed to yield to the car on their right, except where signs indicate otherwise, as at traffic circles.

If you violate the speed limits, expect a big fine. Those limits are about 130 kilometers per hour (80 m.p.h.) on expressways, about 100 kilometers per hour (60 m.p.h.) on major national highways, and 90 kilometers per hour (56 m.p.h.) on small country roads. In towns, don't exceed 60 kilometers per hour (37 m.p.h.).

MAPS For France as a whole, most motorists opt for the Michelin map 989. For regions, **Michelin** publishes a series of yellow maps that are quite good. Big travel-book stores in North America carry these maps, and they're commonly available in France (at lower prices). One useful feature of the Michelin map (in this age of congested traffic) is its designations of alternative routes de dégagement, which let you skirt big cities and avoid traffic-clogged highways.

BREAKDOWNS/ASSISTANCE A breakdown is called *une panne* in France, and it's just as frustrating here as anywhere else. Call the police at ☎ **17** anywhere in

France and they'll put you in touch with the nearest garage. Most local garages have towing services. If your breakdown occurs on an expressway, find the nearest roadside emergency phone box, pick up the phone, and put a call through. You'll immediately be connected to the nearest breakdown service facility.

BY PLANE

The French airline **Air France** was recently reorganized into a broader, more wide-ranging carrier with its acquisition of Air Inter Europe. Some 30 French cities and 8 other European cities are served, with plans for future routes to be added. Nonstop flights between cities on the mainland of France usually require about an hour each.

11 Tips on Accommodations

French hotels are government-rated by stars: from four-star luxury and four-star deluxe (no five stars) down through three-star (first-class), two-star (good-quality "tourist" hotel), and one-star (budget) hotels. In some of the lower categories, the rooms may not have private bathrooms; instead, many have what the French call a *cabinet de toilette* (hot and cold running water and a bidet), whereas others have only sinks. In such hotels, bathrooms are down the hall. Nearly all hotels in France have central heating, but, in some cases, you might wish the owners would turn it up a little on a cold night.

RELAIS & CHATEAUX   Now known worldwide, this organization of deluxe and first-class hostelries began in France for visitors seeking the ultimate in hotel living and dining, most often in a traditional atmosphere. Relais & Châteaux establishments (numbering about 150 in France) are former castles, abbeys, manor houses, and town houses that've been converted into hostelries or inns and elegant hotels. All have a limited number of rooms, so reservations are imperative. Sometimes these owner-run establishments have pools and tennis courts. The Relais part of the organization refers to inns called relais, meaning "posthouse." These tend to be less luxurious than the châteaux, but they're often quite charming. Top-quality restaurants are *relais gourmands.* Throughout this guide we've listed our favorite Relais & Châteaux, but there are many more.

For an illustrated catalog of these establishments, send $8 to **Relais & Châteaux,** 11 E. 44th St., Suite 704, New York, NY 10017 (for information on and reservations for individual Relais & Châteaux, call ☎ **800/860-4930** or 212/856-0115; fax 212/856-0193). Check out their Web site at www.integra.fr/relaischateaux.

BED & BREAKFASTS   Called *gîtes—chambres d'hôte* in France, these accommodations may be one or several bedrooms on a farm or in a village home. Many of them offer one main meal of the day as well (lunch or dinner).

There are at least 6,000 of these accommodations listed with **La Maison des Gîtes de France et du Tourisme Vert,** 59 rue St-Lazare, 75009 Paris (☎ **01-49-70-75-75**). Sometimes these B&Bs aren't as simple as you might think: instead of a bare-bones farm room, you might be housed in a mansion deep in the French countryside.

In the United States, a good source for this type of accommodation is **The French Experience,** 370 Lexington Ave., Room 812, New York, NY 10017 (☎ **212/986-1115;** fax 212/986-3808). It also rents furnished houses for as short a period as 1 week.

CONDOS, VILLAS, HOUSES & APARTMENTS   If you can stay for at least a week and don't mind cooking your own meals and cleaning house, you might want to rent a long-term accommodation. The local French Tourist Board might help you obtain a list of real-estate agencies that represent this type of rental (which tends to be especially popular at ski resorts). In France, one of the best groups of estate agents is the **Fédération Nationale des Agents Immobiliers,** 129 rue du Faubourg St-Honoré, 75008 Paris (☎ 01-44-20-77-00).

In the United States, **At Home Abroad,** 405 E. 56th St., Apt. 6H, New York, NY 10022-2466 (☎ 212/421-9165; fax 212/752-1591), specializes in villas on the French Riviera and in the Dordogne as well as places in the Provençal hill towns. Rentals are usually for 2 weeks. For a $25 registration fee (applicable to any rental), they'll send you photographs of the properties and a newsletter.

A worthwhile competitor is **Vacances en Campagne,** British Travel International, P.O. Box 299, Elkton, VA (☎ 800/327-6097; fax 540/298-2347). Its $4 directory contains information on more than 700 potential rentals across Europe, including France.

If you want to rent an apartment in Paris, the **Barclay International Group,** 150 E. 52nd St., New York, NY 10022 (☎ 800/845-6636 or 212/832-3777), can give you access to about 3,000 apartments and villas scattered throughout Paris (plus 39 other cities in France), ranging from modest modern units to the most stylish. Units rent from 1 night to up to 6 months; all have TVs and kitchenettes, and many have concierge staffs and lobby-level security. The least-expensive units cost around $89 per night, double occupancy. Incremental discounts are granted for a stay of 1 week or 3 weeks. Rentals must be prepaid in U.S. dollars or by a major U.S. credit or charge card.

Hometours International, Inc., P.O. Box 11503, Knoxville, TN 37939 (☎ 800/367-4668 or 423/690-8484), offers more than 400 moderately priced apartments, apartment hotels, and B&Bs in Paris. On the Riviera, you can rent beautiful villas, all with pools, at reasonable rates. For budget travelers, this organization offers a prepaid voucher program for the Campanile hotels, a chain of about 350 two-star family-run hotels throughout France. Rates begin as low as $70 per night double. This is an excellent alternative to B&B hotels, because all chain members provide a buffet breakfast for only 35F ($6.30) per person. B&B catalogs for $8 or apartment brochures for $4 are available from the address above.

HOTEL CHAINS   One good moderately priced choice is the **Mercure** chain—an organization of simple but clean and modern hotels offering attractive values throughout France. Even at the peak of the tourist season, a room at a Mercure in the heart of Paris rents for $85 to $150 per night. For more information on Mercure hotels and a copy of their 100-page directory, call **RESINTER** at ☎ 800/221-4542 in the United States.

Formule 1 (☎ 01-69-36-75-29) hotels are bare-bones and basic but clean and safe, offering rooms for up to three at around $30 per night. Built from prefabricated units, these air-conditioned, soundproofed hotels are shipped to a site and reassembled, often on the outskirts of cities like Paris (27 in the suburbs alone). In addition, there's a coterie of 150 of these low-budget hotels throughout the rest of France. (Formule 1, a member of the French hotel giant Accor, also owns the Motel 6 chain in the United States, to which Formule 1 bears a resemblance.)

While you can make a reservation at any member of the Accor group through the RESINTER number above, the chain finds that the low cost of Formule 1 makes it unprofitable and impractical to prereserve (from the States) rooms in the Formule chain. So you'll have to reserve your Formule 1 room on arrival in France. Be warned that Formule 1 properties have almost none of the Gallic charm for which some country inns are famous, but you can save money by planning your itinerary at Formule 1 properties. For a directory, write to Formule 1/ETAP Hotels, 6/8 rue du Bois-Briard, 91021 Evry CEDEX (☎ 01-69-36-75-00).

Other worthwhile economy bets, sometimes with a bit more charm, are the hotels and restaurants belonging to the **Fédération Nationale des Logis de France,** 83 av. d'Italie, 75013 Paris (☎ **01-45-84-70-00**). This is a marketing association of 3,828 hotels, usually simple country inns especially convenient for motorists, most rated one or two stars. The association publishes an annual directory. Copies are available for $23.95 from the French Government Tourist Office, 444 Madison Ave., 16th floor, New York, NY 10022 (☎ **212/838-7800**), and also from stores specializing in travel publications, including the Traveller's Bookstore, 22 W. 52nd St., New York, NY 10019 (☎ **800/755-8728** or 212/664-0995; fax 212/397-3984).

12 Tips on Shopping

France is the market basket of continental Europe—a jumble of products, colors, crafts, and cutting-edge style. Though its retail reputation has grown through fashion and style, the truth is that this is a country where shopping at the local produce market is a quasi-religious experience, where the dime stores are as much fun as (if not more fun than) the major department stores, and where many of the best things in life can be found in a *parapharmacie*—a newfangled concept that marries tons of drugstore/health-care/beauty products with a discount system.

Factory outlets are opening up *droit* and *gauche,* whereas the old factories continue to sell wares straight from their hometown (like Limoges), and the new factories have opened boutiquelike shops to hawk overruns to the public.

Add to all this a tradition of not only the finest antiques in the world but also heaps of fun junk and what locals call *brocante* and you have the makings of a spree even a nonshopper will love.

THE BEST BUYS IN FRANCE

BEAUTY PRODUCTS   There are scads of products and cures that locals are convinced will firm the bust, melt cellulite, fill in or eliminate wrinkles, take off weight, and make your hair healthier. Some of the cosmetic designer lines make a few products with these claims, but you'll find the bulk of this business in dime stores and pharmacies, where each of the major brands has between 30 and 50 products beginning below $10. Most of this stuff couldn't get FDA approval in the States or would be available only with a prescription. Do these products really work? You have to sample and try for yourself.

Regular designer makeup at retail may be the same price in France as in the States—or possibly more expensive in France. But at a "duty-free" (nonairport variety) store or a discounter where you can qualify for détaxe (see box, "How to Get Your VAT Refund") you'll see anywhere from 20% to 45% melt off your bill. It pays to save up and make a major purchase—or chip in with some friends. Go for the gold. Or the brun magenta. Paris offers more duty-free stores and bigger discounts on name-brand goods, but any city with a tourist business (Nice, Cannes, Monaco, Biarritz) will have at least one discounter. If you know you'll be qualifying for détaxe, ask at each parfumerie you visit until you find one that has the selection you need and the new détaxe program at 1,200F ($216) net.

CRAFTS   The main faïence cities are in the north, stretching from Rouen in the northeast to Quimper (for specific shops, see chapter 9) on the Atlantic coast. You'll find tiles in the south (check out Salernes), and Moustier Ste-Marie in Provence is known for a specific type of faïence with animals. Soap making is an art in the south of France, with soap makers dotting Marseille and Provence. L'Occitane, a Provençal brand, is now sold in its own boutiques in assorted Provence towns and in Paris.

You'll find copper cooking pots in northern France, especially in a Normandy village called Villedieu-les-Poêles, 22 miles south of St-Lô, not far from Mont-St-Michel. Copper-lined cookware has been manufactured here since the 1700s, and dozens of stores along the main street sell huge amounts of the stuff every year. To watch the artisans at work, stop by **Les Ateliers du Cuivre,** 54 rue du Général-Huard (☎ **02-33-51-31-85**). To buy, journey just outside town on the main road to Mauviel, the supplier to Williams-Sonoma and others. Northeastern France, near Strasbourg, is the home of Baccarat crystal, whereas Burgundy is known for its large hand-carved (and very heavy) pieces of furniture.

FASHION   You can find knockoffs of the latest trends all over France, at more-than-affordable prices, in the two major dime-store chains. Every major city has a Monoprix (owned by Galeries Lafayette) or Prisunic (owned by Au Printemps); some have both.

If you can't leave France without buying something from that icon Hermès, the sorry news is that you may find better deals outside France; London currently has a better price structure (depending on the rate of exchange for your dollar, of course). You'll qualify for a détaxe refund if you buy a scarf at Hermès, but you'll have to buy three ties or two ties and a pocket square to get a tax break.

Size Conversion Chart

Women's Clothing

American	6	8	10	12	14	16
French	36	38	40	42	44	46
British	8	10	12	14	16	18

Women's Shoes

American	5	6	7	8	9	10
French	36	37	38	39	40	41
British	4	5	6	7	8	9

Men's Suits

American	34	36	38	40	42	44	46	48
French	44	46	48	50	52	54	56	58
British	34	36	38	40	42	44	46	48

Men's Shirts

American	14½	15	15½	16	16½	17	17½	18
French	37	38	39	41	42	43	44	45
British	14½	15	15½	16	16½	17	17½	18

Men's Shoes

American	7	8	9	10	11	12	13
French	39½	41	42	43	44½	46	47
British	6	7	8	9	10	11	12

FOOD   You can bring into the United States cheeses that have aged more than 90 days—this basically means hard and moldy cheeses, not soft and runny ones. No fresh fruit or vegetables are allowed. You'll be safer with mustards; Dijon is brimming with choices, but any French grocery store will have a large selection of possibly a dozen choices of the Maille brand.

You can buy chocolates in grocery stores, but these are commercial chocolates. If you want to know what everyone's raving about, save up a few francs and head to the chocolatiers in Lyon or Paris, preferably in the cooler months, and begin your own taste test. Premium chocolates normally cost about 490F ($88.20) per kilo—that's

---

How to Get Your VAT Refund

French sales tax, or VAT (value-added tax), is now a hefty 20.6%, but you can get most of that back if you spend 1,200F ($216) or more at any participating retailer. Most stores participate, though discount perfume shops usually peg the minimum at 1,200F net, which actually works out to an equivalent pretax amount of 1,600F or 1,700F ($288 or $306). They then deduct the 20% discount so you're back where you started, at 1,200F. Since this sounds more complicated than it is, ask!

The name of the refund is *détaxe*, meaning exactly what it says. You never really get the full 20.6% back, but you can come close.

After you spend the required minimum amount, ask for your détaxe papers; fill out the forms before you arrive at the airport and allow at least half an hour for standing in line. All refunds are processed at the final point of departure from the EU, so if you're going to another EU country, you don't apply for the refund in France.

Mark the paperwork to request that your refund be applied to your credit card so you aren't stuck with a check in francs that you can't cash. Even if you made the purchase in cash, you can still get the refund put on a credit card. This ensures the best rate of exchange. While you can get cash in some airports, if you don't take the cash in French francs you'll lose money on the transaction.

If you're considering a major purchase, especially one that falls between 1,200F and 2,000F ($216 and $360), ask the store policy before you get too involved—or be willing to waive your right to the refund.

---

more than 2 pounds' worth. You should consume handmade fresh chocolate within 3 days. In Paris, the big outlets are **La Maison du Chocolat** and **Christian Constant** (see chapter 5).

KITCHENWARE   Innovative kitchen electrical machines are promoted all over France, but their electricity requirements aren't compatible with your household current in North America. However, the ubiquitous copper-lined casseroles and thick-walled roasters might last a lifetime once you recover from the shock of their prices. If you happen to be touring Normandy and want to pick up the best copper-lined saucepans available, head for the hamlet of Villedieu-les-Poêles (see "Crafts," above). You can buy used copperware at almost any flea market for $25 to $50 per pot and then clean it up yourself. Copper polish is sold at markets as well. In Paris, hit rue Montmartre in the 2nd arrondissement (not in Montmartre) for a choice of kitchen and restaurant suppliers that sell to the public.

PERFUME   Note that French perfume lasts longer than the U.S. counterpart of the same scent (it's made with potato alcohol, not grain alcohol) and that most new scents are launched in France before they come to the States. French perfume makers, especially the top-of-the-line designer names (like Chanel and Dior), are cracking down on the recent move toward discounting. Some stores will discount other brands and not these premium ones; some outlets will give a smaller discount on the big names.

Basically, if you don't qualify for détaxe (see "How to Get Your VAT Refund," above), you should be able to get a flat 20% discount in duty-free stores in Paris and in major cities in the provinces. The airport offers a 13% discount. Don't buy American brands of fragrance in Europe, even at a duty-free shop—they're more expensive than at home. If a store offers a 10% discount, ask what else you get for free—there could be lots of free samples and maybe a tote bag or promotional kit thrown in that the airport can't match.

PORCELAIN   For delicate porcelains, head for Limoges (in the Limousin), where zillions of factory shops sell local wares and a few seconds. Note that factory shops are always closed from noon to 2pm. In Limoges look for Bernardaud and Raynaud; in nearby Aixe-sur-Vienne there's the Ancienne Manufacture Royale de Limoges (see chapters 15 and 17).

For earthenware, or faïence, see "Crafts," above. If driving to the French provinces doesn't suit your itinerary, head for rue de Paradis in Paris, where you'll find several suppliers with massive displays from all the big French factories. Once you ship back to the States you'll eliminate any savings, but if you can carry a piece with you, you may save 20% to 25%.

WINE & CHAMPAGNE   Searching out unusual vintages from small vintners is great fun. Any wine outlet inventories an overwhelming choice of wines from Bordeaux, Burgundy, Alsace, the Rhône Valley, and Champagne. You'll find lots of sales outlets for exotic burgundies in and around Beaune, Brouilland, Montbard, and Gevrey-Chambertin, and any wine store in Dijon will be amply stocked. If bubbly is your thing, head for Epernay and Reims, where all sorts of champagnes are sold at decent prices—though prices may be no different from those in Paris or in the States, depending on promotions and the time of year (see chapter 10). While all the big maisons sell directly to visitors, they discount only a smidgen and then only for three bottles or for six bottles and no more. Prices in the local hypermarché in Reims or in any branch of the French wine-shop chain Nicolas may rival prices offered by the maisons.

Alsace, Provence, and the Bordeaux region retain thousands of cases of their local vintages for sale (at favorable prices). Bottles of unusual cognacs, often with labels scrawled in the shaky script of an old vintner, are for sale in out-of-the-way corners around southwestern France and in centre-ville Cognac.

If after-dinner liqueurs are your thing, in Normandy you'll find bottles of Calvados (the famous apple-based liqueur) everywhere in the region; out past Rouen you get into apple country and can taste your way to bed (or visit the apple museum if you can't drink and drive).

For information on customs and how much alcohol you can bring home with you, see "Customs" under "Visitor Information & Entry Requirements," above.

SHIPPING IT HOME
Shipping costs will possibly double your cost on goods; you'll also pay U.S. duties on the items if they're valued at more than $50. The good news is that détaxe is automatically applied to any item shipped to an American destination—no need to worry about the 1,200F minimum. However, some stores have a $100 minimum for shipping. You can also walk into any PT&T (post office) and mail home a Jiffy bag or small box of goodies. French do-it-yourself boxes can't be reopened once closed.

FAST FACTS: France

For information specifically about Paris, see "Fast Facts: Paris" in chapter 4.

Auto Clubs   The **Association Française des Auto Clubs,** 14 av. de la Grand-Armée, 17e (☎ **01-40-55-43-00;** Métro: Porte-Maillot), provides limited information to members of U.S. auto clubs like the AAA.

Business Hours   Business hours here are erratic, as befits a nation of individualists. Most banks are open Monday through Friday from 9:30am to 4:30pm.

Many, particularly in smaller towns or villages, take a lunch break at varying times. Hours are usually posted on the door. Most museums close 1 day a week (often Tuesday), and they're generally closed on national holidays. Usual hours are 9:30am to 5pm. Some museums, particularly the smaller and less-staffed ones, close for lunch from noon to 2pm. Most French museums are open on Saturday; many are closed Sunday morning but open Sunday afternoon. Again, refer to the individual museum listings.

Generally, offices are open Monday through Friday from 9am to 5pm, but always call first. In Paris or other big French cities, stores are open from 9 or 9:30am (often 10am) to 6 or 7pm without a break for lunch. Some shops, particularly those operated by foreigners, open at 8am and close at 8 or 9pm. In some small stores the lunch break can last 3 hours, beginning at 1pm. This is more common in the south than in the north.

Drugstores   If you need one during off-hours, have your concierge get in touch with the nearest **Commissariat de Police.** An agent there will have the address of a nearby pharmacy open 24 hours a day. French law requires that the pharmacies in any given neighborhood display the name and location of the one that remains open all night.

Electricity   In general, expect 200 volts, 50 cycles, though you'll encounter 110 and 115 volts in some older establishments. Adapters are needed to fit sockets. Many hotels have two-pin (in some cases, three-pin) sockets for electric razors. It's best to ask your hotel concierge before plugging in any appliance.

Embassies/Consulates   The **Embassy of Australia** is at 4 rue Jean-Rey, 75015 Paris (☎ 01-40-59-33-00; Métro: Bir-Hakeim), open Monday through Friday from 9:15am to 12:15pm. The Embassy of Canada is at 35 av. Montaigne, 75008 Paris (☎ 01-44-43-29-00; Métro: Franklin-D.-Roosevelt or Alma-Marceau), open Monday through Friday from 9am to noon and 2 to 5pm; the **Canadian Consulate** is at the same address. The **Embassy of the United Kingdom** is at 35 rue du Faubourg St-Honoré, 75383 Paris CEDEX 08 (☎ 01-44-51-31-00; Métro: Concorde or Madeleine), open Monday through Friday from 9:30am to 1pm and 2:30 to 6pm; the U.K. Consulate, 16 rue d'Anjou, 75008 Paris (☎ 01-44-51-31-00), is open Monday through Friday from 9:30am to 12:30pm and 2:30 to 5pm. The **Embassy of New Zealand** is at 7 ter rue Léonard-de-Vinci, 75116 Paris (☎ 01-45-00-24-11; Métro: Victor-Hugo), open Monday through Friday from 9am to 1pm and 2 to 5:30pm; summer hours (July and August) are Monday through Thursday from 8:30am to 1pm and 2 to 5:30pm and Friday from 8:30am to 2pm. The **South African Embassy** in Paris is located at 59 Quai d'Orsay, 7e (☎ **01-53-59-23-23;** Métro: Invalides). It's open Monday through Friday 9am to noon.

The **Embassy of the United States** is at 2 av. Gabriel, 75008 Paris (☎ **01-43-12-22-22;** Métro: Concorde), open Monday through Friday from 9am to 3pm. Passports are issued at its consulate at 2 rue St-Florentin (☎ **01-43-12-22-22;** Métro: Concorde). Getting a passport replaced costs about $55. In addition to its embassy and consulate in Paris, the United States maintains the following **consulates:** 12 bd. Paul-Peytral, 13286 Marseille (☎ **04-91-54-92-00**); and 15 av. d'Alsace, 67082 Strasbourg (☎ **03-88-35-31-04**).

Emergencies   In an emergency while at a hotel, contact the front desk. Most staffs are trained in dealing with a crisis and will call the police, summon an ambulance, or do whatever is necessary. But if the emergency involves something like a stolen wallet, go to the police station in person. Otherwise, you can get help anywhere in France by calling ☎ **17** for the police or ☎ **18** for the fire department (pompiers). For roadside emergencies, see "Getting Around France," earlier in this chapter.

Mail   Most post offices in France are open Monday through Friday from 8am to 7pm and Saturday from 8am to noon. Allow 5 to 8 days for your mail to reach North America. Airmail letters to North America cost 4.30F (75¢) for 20 grams or 8.20F ($1.50) for 40 grams. Letters to the U.K. cost 3F (55¢) for up to 20 grams. An airmail postcard to North America or Europe (outside France) costs 4.40F (80¢).

You can exchange money at post offices. Many hotels sell stamps, as do local post offices and cafes displaying a red TABAC sign outside.

Newspapers/Magazines   Most major cities carry copies of the *International Herald Tribune, USA Today,* and usually a major London paper or two. Nearly all big-city newsstands—at least in areas that cater to visitors—also sell *Time* and *Newsweek.*

The major newspapers are *Le Monde, Le Figaro,* and *La Libération.* The major French newsmagazines are *L'Express, Le Point,* and *Le Nouvel Observateur.*

Police   Call ☎ **17** anywhere in France.

Rest Rooms   If you're in dire need, duck into a cafe or brasserie to use the lavatory. It's customary to make some small purchase if you do so. Paris Métro stations and underground garages usually contain public rest rooms, but the degree of cleanliness varies. France still has some "hole-in-the-ground" toilets, so be warned.

Safety   Much of the country, particularly central France, the northeast, Normandy, and Brittany, remains relatively safe, even though no place in the world is crime-free. Those intending to visit the south of France, especially the Riviera, should exercise extreme caution—robberies and muggings here are commonplace. It's best to check your baggage into a hotel and then go sightseeing instead of leaving it unguarded in the trunk of a car, which can easily be broken into. Marseille is among the most dangerous French cities.

Taxes   Watch it: You could get burned. As a member of the European Union, France routinely imposes a value-added tax (VAT) on many goods and services. The standard VAT on merchandise is 20.6%, including clothing, appliances, liquor, leather goods, shoes, furs, jewelry, perfumes, cameras, and even caviar. Refunds are made for the tax on certain goods and merchandise, but not on services. The minimum purchase is 1,200F ($216) in the same store for nationals or residents of countries outside the EU. See the "How to Get Your VAT Refund" box earlier in this chapter for details.

How to Call France from Abroad

The international prefix when calling from the United States and Canada is **011.** The country code for France is 33. All phone numbers in France have 10 digits, and this includes the area code. For example, the phone number for the Hôtel Négresco—☎ 04-93-16-64-00—contains the area code for southeastern France (04). If you were anywhere in France, to call the Négresco all you'd have to dial is this 10-digit number. When calling from outside France, dial the international prefix for your country, the country code for France, and then the last nine digits of the number, dropping the 0 (zero) from the regional prefix.

Telephone   You'll find public phone booths in cafes, restaurants, Métro stations, post offices, airports, and train stations, and occasionally on the streets. Pay phones accept coins of ½ F, 1F, 2F, and 5F; the minimum charge is 2F (35¢). Pick up the receiver, insert the coin(s), and dial when you hear the tone, pushing the button when there's an answer.

The French also use a *télécarte,* a phone debit card, which you can purchase at rail stations, post offices, and other places. Sold in two versions, it allows you to use either 50 or 120 charge units (depending on the card) by inserting the card into the slot of most public phones. Depending on the type of card you buy, they cost 41 to 98F ($7.40 to $17.65).

If possible, avoid making calls from your hotel, as some French establishments double or triple the charges on you. When you're calling long distance within France, pick up the receiver, wait for the dial tone, and then dial the 10-digit number of the person or place you're calling. To make a direct international call, first dial 00, listen for the tone, then slowly dial the country code, the area code, and the local number. Common country codes include: USA and Canada, 1; Great Britain, 44; Ireland, 353; Australia, 61; New Zealand, 64; South Africa, 27. An easy and relatively inexpensive way to call home is USA Direct/AT&T WorldConnect. From within France, dial any of the following numbers: ☎ 0800/99-0011, -1011, -1111, -1211. Now follow the prompt, which will ask you to punch in the number of either your AT&T credit card or a MasterCard or Visa. Along with the USA, the countries which participate in the system— referred to as WorldConnect—include Canada, the U.K., Ireland, Australia, New Zealand, and South Africa. By punching in the number of the party you want in any of these countries, you'll avoid the surcharges imposed by the hotel operator. At any time, an AT&T operator will be available to help you with complications arising during this ritual.

For information, dial ☎ 12.

Time   The French equivalent of daylight saving time lasts from April to September, which puts it 1 hour ahead of French winter time. Depending on the time of year, France is 6 or 7 hours ahead of U.S. eastern standard time.

Tipping   This is practiced with flourish and style in France, and as a visitor you're expected to play the game. All bills, as required by law, are supposed to say *service compris,* which means that the tip has been included.

Here are some general guidelines: for hotel staff, tip 6 to 10F ($1.10 to $1.80) for every item of baggage the porter carries on arrival and departure, and 10F ($1.80) per day for the chambermaid. You're not obligated to tip the concierge (hall porter), doorman, or anyone else—unless you use his or her services. In cafes, waitstaff service is usually included. Porters have an official scale of charges—there's no real need to tip extra after their bill is presented unless they've performed some special service. Tip taxi drivers 10% to 15% of the amount on the meter. In theaters and restaurants, give cloakroom attendants at least 5F (90¢) per item. Give rest-room attendants about 2F (35¢) in nightclubs and such places. Give cinema and theater ushers about 2F (35¢). Tip the hairdresser about 15%, and don't forget to tip the person who gives you a shampoo or a manicure 10F ($1.80). For guides for group visits to museums and monuments, 5F to 10F (90¢ to $1.80) is a reasonable tip.

Water   Drinking water is generally safe, though it's been known to cause diarrhea. If you ask for water in a restaurant, it'll be served bottled (for which you'll pay) unless you specifically request tap water (*l'eau du robinet*).

4

Settling into Paris

Stroll along the river Seine and the broad tree-lined boulevards, stopping to browse through the chic shops and relax over coffee or wine at the sidewalk cafes; visit the world-renowned museums, monuments, and cathedrals; sample the legendary cuisine; attend an opera or a concert; and enjoy the red-hot nightlife. Despite the turmoil going on behind the scenes, Paris is still the City of Light—and it always manages to live up to its reputation as one of the world's most romantic cities.

Ernest Hemingway referred to the many splendors of Paris as a "moveable feast" and wrote, "There is never any ending to Paris, and the memory of each person who has lived in it differs from that of any other." It's this personal discovery of the city that has always been the most compelling reason for coming here.

1 Orientation

ARRIVING

BY PLANE Paris has two major international airports: Aéroport d'Orly, 8½ miles south, and Aéroport Roissy–Charles de Gaulle, 14¼ miles northeast of the city. A shuttle (75F/$13.50) operates between the two airports about every 30 minutes, taking 50 to 75 minutes to make the journey.

Charles de Gaulle Airport (Roissy) At Charles de Gaulle (☎ 01-48-62-22-80), foreign carriers use Aérogare 1 and Air France wings into Aérogare 2. From Aérogare 1 you take a moving walkway to the passport checkpoint and the Customs area. The two terminals are linked by a shuttle bus (*navette*).

The free shuttle bus connecting Aérogare 1 with Aérogare 2 also transports you to the **Roissy rail station,** from which fast RER trains leave every 15 minutes heading to such Métro stations as Gare du Nord, Châtelet, Luxembourg, Port-Royal, and Denfert-Rochereau. A typical fare from Roissy to any point in central Paris is 55F ($9.90).

You can also take an **Air France shuttle bus** to central Paris for 55F ($9.90). It stops at the Palais des Congrès (Port Maillot), then continues on to place Charles-de-Gaulle–Etoile, where subway lines can carry you farther along to any point in Paris. That ride, depending on traffic, takes between 45 and 55 minutes. The shuttle departs about every 12 minutes between 5:40am and 11pm.

Another option is the **Roissybus,** departing from the airport daily from 5:45am to 11pm and costing 45F ($8.10) for the 45- to 50-minute ride. Departures are about every 15 minutes, and the bus will take you near the corner of rue Scribe and place de l'Opéra in the heart of Paris.

A **taxi** from Roissy into the city will cost about 200F ($36), but from 8pm to 7am the fares are 40% higher. Long lines of both taxis and passengers form outside each of the airport's terminals and are surprisingly orderly.

Orly Airport   Orly (☎ 01-49-75-15-15) has two terminals—Orly Sud (south) for international flights and Orly Ouest (west) for domestic flights. They're linked by a free shuttle bus.

Air France buses leave from Exit E of Orly Sud and from Exit F of Orly Ouest every 12 minutes between 5:45am and 11pm, heading for Gare des Invalides for 40F ($7.20).

An alternative method for reaching central Paris is a free **shuttle bus** that leaves both of Orly's terminals about every 15 minutes for the nearby Métro and RER train station (Pont-de-Rungis/Aéroport-d'Orly), from which RER trains take 35 minutes for rides into the city center. A trip to Les Invalides, for example, is 57F ($10.25). (When you're returning to the airport, buses leave the Invalides terminal heading to Orly Sud or Orly Ouest every 15 minutes, taking about 30 minutes.)

A **taxi** from Orly to the center of Paris costs about 170F ($30.60), more at night. Don't take a meterless taxi from Orly Sud or Orly Ouest—it's much safer (and usually cheaper) to hire a metered cab from the lines, which are under the scrutiny of a police officer.

BY TRAIN   Paris has six major train stations: **Gare d'Austerlitz,** 55 quai d'Austerlitz, 13e (servicing the southwest with trains to and from the Loire Valley, the Bordeaux country, the Pyrénées, and Spain); **Gare de l'Est,** place du 11-Novembre-1918, 10e (servicing the east with trains to and from Strasbourg, Nancy, Reims, and beyond to Zurich, Basel, Luxembourg, and Austria); **Gare de Lyon,** 20 bd. Diderot, 12e (servicing the southeast with trains to and from the Côte d'Azur, Provence, and beyond to Geneva, Lausanne, and Italy); **Gare Montparnasse,** 17 bd. Vaugirard, 15e (servicing the west with trains to and from Brittany); **Gare du Nord,** 18 rue de Dunkerque, 15e (servicing the north with trains to and from London, Holland, Denmark, Belgium, and northern Germany); and **Gare St-Lazare,** 13 rue d'Amsterdam, 8e (servicing the northwest with trains to and from Normandy). Buses operate between the stations. Each of these stations has a Métro stop, making the whole city accessible. Taxis are also available at designated stands—look for the signs that say TÊTE DE STATION For general train information and to make reservations, call ☎ 08-36-35-35-35 from 7am to 8pm daily.

Note: The stations and the surrounding areas are usually seedy and frequented by pickpockets, hustlers, hookers, and drug addicts. Be alert, especially at night.

BY BUS   Most buses arrive at the **Gare Routière Internationale du Paris–Gallieni,** 28 av. du Général-de-Gaulle, in the suburb of Bagnolet (☎ 01-49-72-51-51; Métro: Gallieni).

BY CAR   Driving in Paris is definitely not recommended. Parking is difficult and traffic dense. If you do drive, remember that Paris is encircled by a ring road called the *périphérique.* Always obtain detailed directions to your destination, including the name of the exit on the périphérique (exits aren't numbered). Avoid rush hours.

Few hotels, except the luxury ones, have garages, but the staff will usually be able to direct you to one nearby.

Paris by Arrondissement

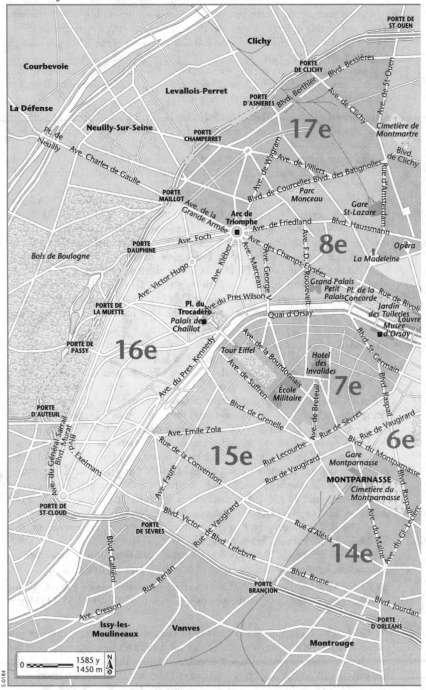

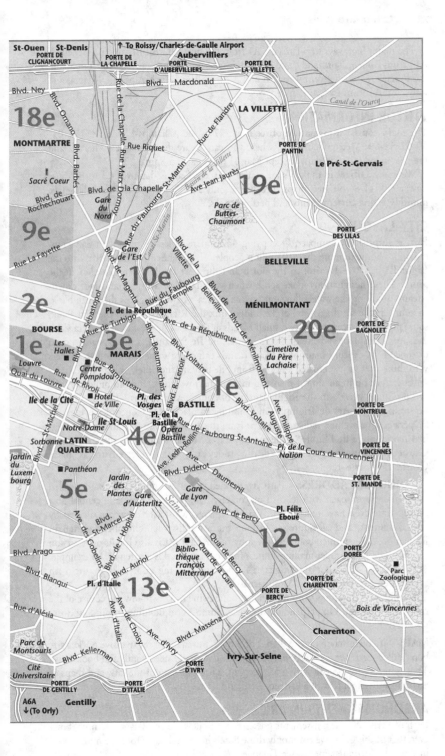

The major highways into Paris are A1 from the north (Great Britain and Benelux); A13 from Rouen, Normandy, and other points of northwest France; A10 from Spain, the Pyrénées, and the southwest; A6 and A7 from the French Alps, the Riviera, and Italy; and A4 from eastern France.

VISITOR INFORMATION

The **main tourist information office** is at 127 av. des Champs-Elysées, 8e (☎ **01-49-52-53-69;** Métro: George V), where you can secure details about both Paris and the provinces. It's open daily (except May 1) from 9am to 8pm.

Welcome Offices in the city's rail stations (except Gare St-Lazare) and at the Eiffel Tower will give you free maps, brochures, and *Paris Selection,* a French-language monthly listing current events and performances.

CITY LAYOUT

Paris is surprisingly compact. Occupying 432 square miles (6 more than San Francisco), it's home to more than 10 million people. The river Seine divides Paris into the **Right Bank (Rive Droite)** to the north and the **Left Bank (Rive Gauche)** to the south. These designations make sense when you stand on a bridge and face downstream, watching the waters flow out toward the sea—to your right is the north bank, to your left the south. A total of 32 bridges link the Right Bank and the Left Bank, some providing access to the two small islands at the heart of the city—**Ile de la Cité,** the city's birthplace and site of Notre-Dame, and **Ile St-Louis,** a moat-guarded oasis of sober 17th-century mansions. These islands can cause some confusion to walkers who think they've just crossed a bridge from one bank to the other, only to find themselves caught up in an almost-medieval maze of narrow streets and old buildings.

The "main street" on the Right Bank is, of course, **avenue des Champs-Elysées,** beginning at the Arc de Triomphe and running to place de la Concorde. Avenue de l'Opéra and 12 avenues radiate like a star from the Arc de Triomphe, giving it its original name, place de l'Etoile (*étoile* means "star"). It was renamed place Charles-de-Gaulle following the general's death; today it's often referred to as place Charles-de-Gaulle–Etoile.

FINDING AN ADDRESS   Paris is divided into 20 municipal wards called *arrondissements,* each with its own mayor, city hall, police station, and central post office; some even have remnants of market squares. Most city maps are divided by arrondissement, and all addresses include the arrondissement number (written in Roman or Arabic numerals and followed by "e" or "er"). Paris also has its own version of a zip code. The proper mailing address for a certain hotel is written as, for example, "75014 Paris." The last two digits, 14, indicate that the address is in the 14th arrondissement—in this case, Montparnasse.

Numbers on buildings running parallel to the Seine usually follow the course of the river—east to west. On perpendicular streets, numbers on buildings begin low closer to the river.

MAPS   If you're staying more than 2 or 3 days, purchase an inexpensive pocket-size book called *Paris par arrondissement,* available at all major newsstands and bookshops. These guides provide you with a Métro map, a foldout map of the city, and maps of each arrondissement, with all streets listed and keyed.

ARRONDISSEMENTS IN BRIEF

Each of Paris's 20 arrondissements possesses a unique style and flavor. Do note, however, that in this guide we cover only those hotels in central Paris; for accommodations in the outer arrondissements, see *Frommer's Paris '99.*

1er (Musée du Louvre/Les Halles)   One of the world's greatest art museums, the **Louvre** lures hordes to the 1st arrondissement. Here are many elegant addresses, rue de Rivoli, and the **Jeu de Paume** and **Orangerie** museums. Walk through the formal **Jardin des Tuileries,** laid out by Le Nôtre, Louis XIV's gardener. Pause to take in the classic beauty of **place Vendôme.** Jewelers and art dealers are plentiful, and the memories of Chopin are evoked at no. 12 on the square where he died. Zola's "belly of Paris" (Les Halles) is no longer the food-and-meat market but has become the **Forum des Halles,** a center of shopping, entertainment, and culture.

2e (La Bourse)   Home to the **Bourse (stock exchange),** this Right Bank district lies mainly between the grands boulevards and rue Etienne-Marcel. On weekdays the shouts of brokers echo across place de la Bourse until lunchtime, when they continue their hysteria in the district's restaurants. Much of the eastern end of the 2nd is devoted to the **garment district (Le Sentier),** where thousands of garments are sold to buyers from stores all over Europe. If you explore this district, you'll find gems amid the commercialism—none finer than the **Musée Cognacq-Jay,** at 25 bd. des Capucines, which features work by every artist from Watteau to Fragonard.

3e (Le Marais)   This district embraces much of **Le Marais (the Swamp),** one of the best loved of the old Right Bank neighborhoods. Allowed to fall into decay for decades, it has come back, though it'll never recapture its aristocratic heyday. Over the centuries kings have called Le Marais home, and its salons have echoed with the witty, often devastating remarks of Racine, Voltaire, Molière, and Mme de Sévigné. One of its chief draws today is the **Musée Picasso,** a great repository of 20th-century art. Le Marais is also the center of Paris's hot gay and lesbian scene. Rue des Rosiers with its Jewish restaurant remains as a memory of the hundreds of Jewish residents who used to reside in Le Marais.

4e (Ile de la Cité/Ile St-Louis & Beaubourg)   It seems as if the 4th has it all: not only the Ile de la Cité, with **Notre-Dame,** the **Sainte-Chapelle,** and the **Conciergerie,** but also the Ile St-Louis, with aristocratic town houses, courtyards, and antiques shops. Ile St-Louis, a former cow pasture and dueling ground, is home to 6,000 lucky Louisiens, its permanent residents. Of course, the whole area is touristy and overrun.

   The heart of medieval Paris, the 4th evokes memories of Danton and Robespierre, even of Charlotte Corday stabbing Marat in his bath. You get France's finest **bird and flower markets,** plus the **Centre Georges-Pompidou.** After all this pomp and glory, you can retreat to **place des Vosges,** a square of perfect harmony where Victor Hugo penned many masterpieces from 1832 to 1848.

5e (Latin Quarter)   The Quartier Latin is Paris's intellectual soul. Bookstores, schools, churches, smoky jazz clubs, student dives, Roman ruins, publishing houses, and chic boutiques characterize the district. With the founding of the **Sorbonne** in 1253, the quarter got its name because all the students and professors spoke Latin. As the traditional center of "bohemian Paris," it formed the setting for Henry Murger's novel *La Vie Bohème* (later the Puccini opera *La Bohème,* and even later the basis of the Broadway hit *Rent*).

   For sure, the old Latin Quarter is gone. Changing times have brought Greek, Moroccan, and Vietnamese immigrants, among others, hustling everything from couscous to fiery-hot spring rolls and souvlaki. The 5th borders the Seine, so you'll want to stroll along **quai de Montebello,** where vendors sell everything from antique Daumier prints to yellowing copies of Balzac's *Père Goriot.* The 5th also stretches to the **Panthéon,** the resting place of Rousseau, Zola, Hugo, Braille, Voltaire, and Jean Moulin, the Resistance leader who was tortured to death by the Gestapo. Now even Marie Curie rests here.

6e (St-Germain/Luxembourg)   This heartland of Paris publishing is, for some, the most colorful Left Bank quarter. You can see waves of earnest young artists emerging from the **Ecole des Beaux-Arts.** Strolling the boulevards of the 6th, including **St-Germain,** has its own rewards, but the secret of the district lies in discovering its narrow streets and hidden squares as well as the **Jardin du Luxembourg,** a classic French garden overlooked by Marie de Médici's Italianate **Palais du Luxembourg.** To be really authentic, you should stroll these streets with an unwrapped loaf of country sourdough bread from the wood-fired ovens of **Poilâne,** 8 rue du Cherche-Midi. Everywhere you turn you'll encounter famous historic and literary associations, none more so than on **rue Jacob,** where Racine, Wagner, Ingres, and Hemingway once lived at various times. Today's big name is likely to be filmmaker Spike Lee checking into his favorite, La Villa Hôtel, at 29 rue Jacob.

7e (Eiffel Tower/Musée d'Orsay)   Paris's most famous symbol, the **Eiffel Tower,** dominates the Left Bank 7th. The tower is now one of the most recognizable landmarks in the world, though many Parisians hated it when it was unveiled in 1889. Many imposing monuments are in the 7th, including the **Hôtel des Invalides,** which contains Napoléon's Tomb and the Musée de l'Armée (the world's greatest army musuem). But there's much hidden charm as well. Even visitors with no time to discover the 7th at least rush to the **Musée d'Orsay,** the world's premier showcase of 19th-century French art and culture.

8e (Champs-Elysées/Madeleine)   The 8th is the heart of the Right Bank and its prime showcase is **avenue des Champs-Elysées,** linking the **Arc de Triomphe** with the delicate Egyptian obelisk on **place de la Concorde.** Here you'll find the top fashion houses, the most elegant hotels, expensive restaurants and shops, and fashionably attired Parisians. By the 1980s it had become a garish strip, with too much traffic and too many fast-food joints. But in the 1990s the Gaulist mayor of Paris (now president of France), Jacques Chirac, launched a massive cleanup and improvement. The major change has been broadened sidewalks, with new rows of trees planted. The old glory is perhaps gone forever, but what an improvement!

The area is known for having either France's (perhaps the world's) best, grandest, and most impressive: the best restaurant (**Taillevent**), the sexiest strip joint (**Crazy Horse Saloon**), the most splendid square (**place de la Concorde**), the best rooftop cafe (at **La Samaritaine**), the grandest hotel (**Crillon**), the most impressive triumphal arch (**Arc de Triomphe**), the most expensive residential street (**avenue Matignon**), the oldest Métro station (**Franklin-D.-Roosevelt**), and the most ancient monument (**Obelisk of Luxor,** 3,300 years old). Also here is **La Madeleine** church, looking like a Greek temple.

9e (Opéra Garnier/Pigalle)   Everything from the Quartier de l'Opéra to the strip joints of Pigalle (the infamous "Pig Alley" for the GIs of World War II) falls within the 9th. The 9th was radically altered by Baron Haussmann's 19th-century urban redevelopment, and the grands boulevards here are among the most obvious of his labors. The 9th continues on, even if fickle fashion now prefers other addresses. Boulevard des Italiens is the site of the **Café de la Paix,** opened in 1856 and once the meeting place of Romantic poets like Théophile Gautier and Alfred de Musset. Later, de Gaulle, Dietrich, and 2 million Americans started showing up.

Another major attraction is the **Folies-Bergère,** where cancan dancers have been kicking since 1868 and such entertainers as Mistinguett, Piaf, and Chevalier have appeared, along with the American Josephine Baker. But more than anything, it was the **Opéra** (now the Opéra Garnier or Palais Garnier), once the haunt of the Phantom, that made the 9th the last hurrah of Second Empire opulence.

10e (Gare du Nord/Gare de l'Est)   Gare du Nord and Gare de l'Est, along with movie theaters, porno houses, and dreary commercial zones, make the 10th one of the least desirable arrondissements for tourists to spend their time. We always try to avoid the 10th, except for two longtime favorite restaurants: **Brasserie Flo,** 7 cour des Petites-Ecuries (go for *la formidable choucroute*—a heap of sauerkraut garnished with everything), and **Julien,** 16 rue du Faubourg St-Denis (called the poor man's Maxim's because of its belle époque interior and moderate prices).

11e (Opéra Bastille)   For many years this quarter seemed to sink lower and lower. However, the 1989 opening of the **Opéra Bastille** gave it a new lease on life. The "people's opera house" now stands on the landmark **place de la Bastille,** where on July 14, 1789, 633 Parisians stormed the fortress, seized the ammunition depot, and released the few remaining prisoners.

Even when the district wasn't fashionable, visitors flocked to the most famous brasserie in Paris, **Bofinger,** 5–7 rue de la Bastille, to sample its Alsatian choucroute. (Technically Bofinger lies in the 4th arrondissement, but it has always been associated with place de la Bastille.) What charms exist in the 11th? Whatever is here has to be sought out, including the **Marché place d'Aligre,** a secondhand market in the Middle Eastern food market. Everything is cheap, and though you must search hard for treasures, you'll often find them.

12e (Bois de Vincennes/Gare de Lyon)   Few out-of-towners came here until a French chef opened **Au Trou Gascon.** Then the whole world started showing up. The major attraction is the **Bois de Vincennes,** a sprawling park on the eastern periphery of Paris. It has been a longtime favorite of families who enjoy its zoos and museums, its royal château and boating lakes, and the Parc Floral de Paris, whose springtime rhododendrons and autumn dahlias are among the city's major lures. The dreary **Gare de Lyon** lies in the 12th, but going here is worthwhile even if you don't have to take a train. The attraction is **Le Train Bleue,** the station's restaurant, whose ceiling frescoes and Art Nouveau decor are classified as national artistic treasures—and the food's good, too. The 12th, once a depressing neighborhood, is moving toward a multi-million-dollar resuscitation, including new housing, shops, gardens, and restaurants.

13e (Gare d'Austerlitz)   Centering around the grimy Gare d'Austerlitz, the 13th might have its fans, though we've yet to meet one. British snobs who flitted in and out of the train station were among the first foreign visitors, and they in essence wrote the 13th off as a "dreary working-class district." Certainly there remain more fashionable places to be seen, but there's at least one reason to go here: the **Manufacture des Gobelins,** 42 av. des Gobelins—this is the tapestry factory that made the word *Gobelins* world famous.

14e (Montparnasse)   The northern end of this district is **Montparnasse,** home of the Lost Generation. One of its major monuments, helping set the tone of the neighborhood, is the Rodin statue of Balzac at the junction of boulevard Montparnasse and boulevard Raspail. At this corner are famous **literary cafes** like La Rotonde, Le Sélect, La Dôme, and La Coupole. Perhaps only Gertrude Stein didn't come here (she loathed cafes), but all the other American expatriates, including Hemingway and Fitzgerald, arrived for a drink or four. At 27 rue de Fleurus, Stein and Toklas collected their paintings and entertained T. S. Eliot and Matisse. At its southern end, the 14th contains residential neighborhoods filled with well-designed apartment buildings, many constructed between 1910 and 1940.

15e (Gare Montparnasse/Institut Pasteur)   A mostly residential district beginning at Gare Montparnasse, the 15th stretches to the Seine. It's the largest arrondissement, but attracts few visitors and has few attractions, except for the **Parc des Expositions** and the **Institut Pasteur.**

16e (Trocadéro/Bois de Boulogne)   Highlights of the 16th are the **Bois de Boulogne, Jardins du Trocadéro, Musée de Balzac, Musée Guimet** (famous for its Asian collections), and the **Cimetière de Passy,** resting place of Manet, Talleyrand, Giraudoux, and Debussy. One of the largest arrondissements, it's known for its well-heeled bourgeoisie, upscale rents, and posh residential boulevards. Prosperous and suitably conservative addresses include **avenue d'Iéna** and **avenue Victor-Hugo;** also prestigious is **avenue Foch,** the widest boulevard, with homes that at various periods were maintained by Onassis, the shah of Iran, Debussy, and Prince Rainier of Monaco. The 16th also includes the best place in Paris to view the Eiffel Tower from afar: **place du Trocadéro.**

17e (Parc Monceau/Place Clichy)   Flanking the northern periphery of Paris, the 17th is one of the most spread out arrondissements, incorporating the northern edge of glamorous place de Charles-de-Gaulle–Etoile in the west, the conservatively bourgeois place Wagram at its center, and the relatively tawdry place Clichy in the east. Highlights are **Parc Monceau,** the **Palais des Congrès** (which will be of interest only if you're attending a convention or special exhibit), and the **Porte Maillot Air Terminal,** no grand distinction. More exciting than any of those are two great restaurants: **Guy Savoy** and **Michel Rostang** (see "Dining," below).

18e (Montmartre)   The 18th is the most famous outer arrondissement, embracing **Montmartre** and associated with such legendary names as the **Moulin Rouge, Sacré-Coeur,** and **place du Tertre** (a tourist trap if there ever was one). Utrillo was its native son, Renoir lived here, and Toulouse-Lautrec adopted the area as his own. Today place Blanche is known for its prostitutes, and Montmartre is filled with honky-tonks, souvenir shops, and terrible restaurants. Go for the attractions and mémoires. The **Marché aux Puces de Clignancourt** flea market is another landmark.

19e (La Villette)   Visitors come here to what was once the village of La Villette to see the much-publicized angular **Cité des Sciences et de l'Industrie,** a spectacular science museum/park built on a site that for years was devoted to slaughterhouses. Mostly residential, the district is one of the most ethnic in Paris, home of workers from all parts of the former Empire. A highlight is **Les Buttes Chaumont,** a park where kids can enjoy puppet shows and donkey rides.

20e (Père-Lachaise Cemetery)   This district's greatest landmark is the **Père-Lachaise Cemetery,** resting place of Piaf, Proust, Wilde, Duncan, Stein and Toklas, Bernhardt, Colette, Jim Morrison, and many others. Nostalgia buffs sometimes visit Piaf's former neighborhood, Ménilmontant-Belleville, but it has been almost totally bulldozed and rebuilt. The district is now home to many Muslims and hundreds of members of Paris's Sephardic Jewish community, many of whom fled from Algeria or Tunisia. With turbaned men selling dates and grains on the street, this arrondissement seems more North African than French.

2 Getting Around

Paris is a city for strollers whose greatest joy is rambling through unexpected alleys and squares. If you have a choice, try to make it on your own two feet whenever possible. How else can you rub elbows (literally) with Parisians and experience the real Paris?

BY METRO (SUBWAY)   Easy to use, the Métro (☎ 08-36-68-77-14) is the most efficient and fastest means of transportation in Paris. Each line is numbered, and the

Discount Transportation Passes

You can purchase a **Paris-Visite,** a pass valid for 3 or 5 days on the public transport system, including the Métro, buses, and RER (Réseau Express Régional) trains. (The RER has both first- and second-class compartments, and the pass lets you travel in first class.) As a bonus, the funicular ride to the top of Montmartre is included. The cost is 120F ($21.60) for 3 days or 170F ($30.60) for 5 days. The card is available at RATP (Régie Autonome des Transports Parisiens) offices, the tourist office, and the main Métro stations; call ☎ **08-36-68-77-14** for information.

There are other discount passes as well, though most are available only to French residents with government ID cards and proof of taxpayer status. One available to temporary visitors is **Mobilis,** which allows unlimited travel on all bus, subway, and RER lines during a 1-day period for 30F ($5.40). Ask for it at any Métro station.

final destination of each line is clearly marked on subway maps, in the underground passageways, and on the train cars.

The Métro runs daily from 5:30am to around 1:15am. It's reasonably safe at any hour, but beware of pickpockets.

To familiarize yourself with Paris's Métro system before you leave, check out the map on the inside back cover of this book. Most stations display a map of the Métro at the entrance. To make sure you catch the correct train, find your destination, then follow the rail line it's on to the end of the route and note the name of the final destination—this final stop is the direction. To find your train in the station, follow the signs labeled with your direction in the passageways until you see it labeled on a train.

Transfer stations are known as *correspondances*—some require long walks; Châtelet is the most difficult—but most trips will require only one transfer. When transfering, follow the bright-orange CORRESPONDANCE signs until you reach the proper platform. Don't follow a SORTIE ("Exit") sign or you'll have to pay another fare to resume your journey.

Many of the larger stations have easy-to-use maps with pushbutton indicators that light up your route when you press the button for your destination.

On the urban lines, it costs the same to travel to any point: 8F ($1.45). On the Sceaux, Boissy-St-Léger, and St-Germain-en-Laye lines serving the suburbs, fares are based on distance. A *carnet* is the best buy—10 tickets for 48F ($8.65).

At the turnstile entrances to the station, insert your ticket and pass through. At some exits tickets are also checked, so hold on to it. There are occasional ticket checks on trains and platforms and in passageways, too.

BY BUS   Buses are much slower than the Métro and the majority run only from 7am to 8:30pm (a few operate until 12:30am, and 10 operate during early-morning hours). Service is limited on Sunday and holidays. Bus and Métro fares are the same, and you can use the same carnet tickets on both. Most bus rides require one ticket, but there are some destinations requiring two (never more than two within the city limits).

At certain bus stops, signs list the destinations and numbers of the buses serving that point. Destinations are usually listed north to south and east to west. Most stops along the way are also posted on the sides of the buses. During rush hours you may have to take a ticket from a dispensing machine, indicating your position in the line at the bus stop.

If you intend to use the buses a lot, pick up an RATP bus map at the office on place de la Madeleine, 8e, or at the tourist offices at RATP headquarters, 53 bis quai des

Grands-Augustins, 6e. For detailed recorded information in English on bus and Métro routes, call ☎ **08-36-68-41-14.**

The same organzation that runs the Métro and the buses, the **RATP** (☎ **01-44-68-20-20**), also offers the **Balabus,** big-windowed orange-and-white motor coaches that, unfortunately, run only during limited hours—from April 15 to September, it runs only on Sunday and national holidays from noon to 9pm. Itineraries run in both directions between Gare de Lyon and the Grande Arche de La Défense, encompassing some of the city's most beautiful vistas. It's a great deal—three Métro tickets (24F/$4.30)) will carry you the entire route. You'll recognize the bus and the route it follows by the *Bb* symbol emblazoned on each bus's side and on signs posted beside the route it follows.

BY TAXI   It's impossible to secure one at rush hour, so don't even try. Taxi drivers are strongly organized into an effective lobby to keep their number limited to 15,000.

Watch out for the common rip-offs. Always check the meter to make sure you're not paying the previous passenger's fare. Beware of cabs without meters, which often wait outside nightclubs for tipsy patrons, or settle the tab in advance. You can hail regular cabs on the street when their signs read LIBRE. Taxis are easier to find at the many stands near Métro stations.

The flag drops at 13F ($2.35), and from 7am to 7pm you pay 3.36F (60¢) per kilometer. From 7pm to 7am, expect to pay 5.45F ($1) per kilometer. On airport trips you're not required to pay for the driver's empty return ride.

You're allowed several small pieces of luggage free if they're transported inside and don't weigh more than 5 kilograms (11 pounds). Heavier suitcases carried in the trunk cost 6F to 10F ($1.10 to $1.80) apiece. Tip 12% to 15%—the latter usually elicits a *merci.* For radio cabs, call ☎ **01-45-85-85-85,** 01-42-70-41-41, or 01-42-70-00-42—note that you'll be charged from the point where the taxi begins the drive to pick you up.

BY BOAT   The **Batobus** (☎ **01-44-11-33-44**) are 150-passenger ferryboats with big windows. Every day between May and September, they operate along the Seine, stopping at five points of interest: from west to east, the **Eiffel Tower, Musée d'Orsay,** the **Louvre, Notre-Dame,** and the **Hôtel de Ville** (from east to west, the order is reversed). Transit from one stop to another is 12F ($2.15), and departures are about every 30 minutes from 10am to 7pm. Unlike on the Bâteaux-Mouches (see chapter 5), there's no recorded commentary. The Batobus isn't really a sightseeing tour (though the views are panoramic and sometimes inspiring); instead, it offers a way to move from one attraction to another.

FAST FACTS: Paris

For additional practical information, see "Fast Facts: France" in chapter 3.

American Express   With a grand Paris office, American Express, 11 rue Scribe, 9e (☎ **01-47-77-70-00;** Métro: Opéra, Chaussée-d'Antin, or Havre-Caumartin; RER: Auber), is extremely busy with customers buying and cashing traveler's checks (not the best rates for exchange transactions), picking up mail, and solving travel problems. It's open Monday through Friday from 9am to 6pm; the bank is also open Saturday (from 9am to 5:30pm), but the mail-pickup window is closed. A less busy office is at 38 av. de Wagram, 8e (☎ **01-42-27-58-80;** Métro: Ternes), open Monday through Friday from 9am to 5pm.

Area Code   There isn't one as North Americans think of it. All French telephone numbers now consist of 10 digits, the first two of which are sort of like an area code. If you're calling anywhere in France from inside France, just dial all 10 digits—no additional codes are needed. If you're calling from the United States, drop the initial 0 (zero). For more, see "Fast Facts: France" in chapter 3.

Currency Exchange American Express can fill most banking needs. Most banks in Paris are open Monday through Friday from 9am to 4:30pm, but only a few are open Saturday; ask at your hotel for the location of the one nearest you. For the best exchange rate, cash your traveler's checks at banks or foreign-exchange offices, not at shops and hotels. Most post offices will also change traveler's checks or convert currency. Currency exchanges are also found at Paris airports and train stations and along most of the major boulevards like the Champs-Elysées. A small commission is charged.

Some exchange places charge favorable rates to lure you into their stores. For example, **Paris Vision,** 214 rue de Rivoli, 1er (☎ 01-42-86-09-33; Métro: Tuileries), maintains a minibank in the back of a travel agency, open daily from 9am to 2:30pm and 3:30 to 6pm (closes at 4:30pm on Sunday). Its exchange rates are only a fraction less favorable than those offered for very large blocks of money as listed by the Paris stock exchange.

Dentists For emergency dental service, call ☎ **01-43-37-51-00** Monday through Friday from 8pm to midnight and Saturday and Sunday from 9:30am to midnight. The **American Hospital,** 63 bd. Victor-Hugo, Neuilly (☎ **01-46-41-25-41;** Métro: Pont-de-Levallois or Pont-de-Neuilly; Bus: 82), operates a 24-hour English/French clinic on the premises.

Doctors Some large hotels have a doctor on staff. If yours doesn't, try the **American Hospital,** 63 bd. Victor-Hugo, Neuilly (☎ **01-46-41-25-41;** Métro: Pont-de-Levallois or Pont-de-Neuilly; Bus: 82), which operates a 24-hour emergency service. The direct line to its emergency service is ☎ **01-47-47-70-15.** Blue Cross and other American insurance are accepted by their bilingual staff.

Drugstores After regular hours, have your concierge contact the Commissariat de Police for the nearest 24-hour pharmacy. French law requires one pharmacy in any given neighborhood to stay open 24 hours. You'll find the address posted on the doors or windows of all other drugstores. One of the most central all-nighters is **Pharmacy "les Champs,"** 84 av. des Champs-Elysées, 8e (☎ **01-45-62-02-41;** Métro: George-V).

Embassies/Consulates See "Fast Facts: France" in chapter 3.

Emergencies For the police, call ☎ **17;** to report a fire, call ☎ **18.** For an ambulance, call the fire department at ☎ **01-45-78-74-52;** a fire vehicle rushes cases to the nearest emergency room. **S.A.M.U.** is an independently operated, privately owned ambulance company; call ☎ **15.** In nonemergency situations, you can reach the police at 9 bd. du Palais, 4e (☎ **01-53-71-53-71** or 01-53-73-53-73; Métro: Cité).

Hospitals See "Doctors," above.

Newspapers/Magazines English-language newspapers, including *Time, Newsweek, USA Today,* and the *International Herald Tribune* (published Monday through Saturday) are available at nearly every newsstand. They're generally open daily from 8am to 9pm.

The major French newspapers are *Le Monde, Le Figaro,* and *La Libération.* The major French newsmagazines are *L'Express, Le Point,* and *Le Nouvel Observateur.* To find out what's going on in the city, check out *Paris Scope.*

Police In an emergency, call ☎ **17.** For nonemergency situations, the principal Préfecture is at 9 bd. du Palais, 4e (☎ **01-53-71-53-71;** Métro: Cité).

Safety   Beware of child pickpockets, who roam Paris preying on visitors around such sites as the Louvre, the Eiffel Tower, Notre-Dame, and Montmartre and especially like to pick pockets in the Métro, often blocking the entrance and exit to the escalator. A band of these young thieves can clean out your pockets even while you try to fend them off. They'll get very close, sometimes ask for a handout, and deftly help themselves to your money, passport, or whatever. Women should hang on to their purses with both hands. Gendarmes advise visitors to carry umbrellas and keep anyone who looks like a pickpocket an umbrella's length away.

Taxes   France's VAT (value-added tax) should already be included in the cost of all items you buy. See the box "How to Get Your VAT Refund" in chapter 3.

Transit Information   For information on public transportation, stop in at the **Services Touristiques de la RATP** at 53 bis quai des Grands-Augustins, 6e (Métro: St-Michel), or call ☎ **01-43-46-14-14** for recorded information, in French, about stoppages, subway or bus breakdowns, or exceptionally heavy traffic on any particular bus or Métro line.

Weather   Call ☎ **08-36-68-02-75** at 2.23F (40¢) per minute.

3 Paris Accommodations

Although Paris hotels—at least to most of the world—remain paralyzing in price, there is some good news. Scores of lackluster, cheap Paris lodgings, where the wallpaper seemingly wasn't rehung since the twilight of the Napoleonic era, have emerged as newly renovated establishments in the moderate to inexpensive price range. The most outstanding example of this is in the **7th arrondissement,** a normally pricey district of Paris that has emerged with several good-value hotels blossoming from establishments that couldn't be recommended until now. They're not cheap like a Day's Inn along the highway in central Florida, but they're not $750 a night like some swanky palaces in the City of Light either. Of course, we don't assume that everybody is poor, so we've also included a range of the deluxe places for those who'd like to live like the Sultan of Brunei. Even though there are some 80,000 hotel rooms in Paris, you should still reserve well in advance.

By now the Paris "season" has almost ceased to exist. Most visitors, at least those from North America, come in July and August. Since many French are on vacation then and trade fairs and conventions come to a halt, there are usually plenty of rooms, even though these months have traditionally been the peak season for European travel. In most hotels, February is just as busy as April or September because of the volume of business travelers and the increasing number of tourists who've learned to take advantage of the off-season discount airfares.

Hot weather doesn't last long in Paris, so most hotels, except the deluxe ones, don't provide air-conditioning. If you're trapped in a Paris garret on a hot summer night, you may have to sweat it out. To avoid the noise problem when you have to open windows, request a room in the back when making a reservation.

Most hotels offer a continental breakfast of coffee, tea, or hot chocolate; a freshly baked croissant and roll; and limited quantities of butter and jam or jelly. Though nowhere near as filling as a traditional English or American breakfast, it does have the advantage of being quick to prepare—it'll be at your door a few moments after you call down for it and can be served at almost any hour. The word "breakfast" in the following entries refers to this continental version.

Note: Service and value-added tax are included in the rates below unless otherwise specified. Also, unless otherwise specified, all rooms come with a private bathroom.

RIGHT BANK: 1ST ARRONDISSEMENT (LOUVRE/LES HALLES)
VERY EXPENSIVE

✪ **Costes.** 239 rue St-Honoré, 75001 Paris. ☎ **01-42-44-5050.** Fax 01-42-44-50-01. 86 units. A/C MINIBAR TV TEL. 2,000–2,750F ($360–$495) double; 3,250–3,750F ($585–$675) suite. AE, DC, MC, V. Métro: Tuileries or Concorde.

Its grand style, and a location close to the headquarters of some of the most upscale shops in Paris, seems to attract goodly numbers of high-style fashion types, some of whom work in the nearby editorial offices of *Harper's Bazaar.* The five-story, town house–style premises functioned as a *maison bourgeoise* for many generations, presenting a severely dignified facade to the prestigious neighborhood around it. In 1996, it was richly accessorized with the jewel-toned colors, heavy swag curtains, and lavish accessories of the late 19th-century (the Napoléon III) style. Today, everything about it evokes the rich, ornate days of France's Gilded Age, especially the bedrooms. Although small, they're cozy, ornate, and evocative of the late 19th century in virtually all of their accoutrements and decor.

Dining: Don't overlook a possibility of a meal at this hotel's restaurant. Four dining rooms, each with a different decorative theme, and each overlooking the building's Italianate-style inner courtyard, are chockablock with chinoiserie, dried and framed flowers, and 19th-century art. Open daily, nonstop from noon to 1am, the dining rooms feature menu items such as grilled scallops and a grilled version of steak tartare that includes all the spicy accessories of its original (raw) version.

Amenities: Car-rental desk, concierge, room service, dry cleaning, laundry service, baby-sitting, gym with steam room, sauna, indoor pool, and masseurs/masseuses.

Hôtel du Louvre. Place André-Malraux, 75001 Paris. ☎ **800/777-4182** in the U.S., 800/673-1286 in Canada, or 01-44-58-38-38. Fax 01-44-58-38-01. 195 units. A/C MINIBAR TV TEL. 1,650–2,100F ($297–$378) double; from 2,800F ($504) suite. Ask about midwinter discounts. AE, DC, MC, V. Métro: Louvre.

When this hotel was inaugurated in 1855 by Napoléon III, French journalists described it as "a palace of the people, rising adjacent to the palace of kings." In 1897 Camille Pissarro moved into one of its rooms, using the view to inspire many of his Parisian landscapes. Between the Musée du Louvre and the Palais Royal, the hotel has a decor of soaring marble, bronze, and gilt. The rooms are quintessentially Parisian— cozy, soundproofed, and filled with souvenirs of the belle époque. Many of its smaller rooms received a thorough renovation in 1996.

Dining/Diversions: Le Bar "Defender" is a cozy hideaway, with mahogany trim, Scottish overtones, and a collection of single-malt whiskeys; a pianist plays after dusk. There's also the French Empire Brasserie du Louvre, whose tables extend to the terrace in fine weather.

Amenities: Concierge, 24-hour room service, baby-sitting, laundry, valet, business center.

Hôtel Regina. 2 place des Pyramides, 75001 Paris. ☎ **01-42-60-31-10.** Fax 01-40-15-95-16. www.reginotel.com. E-mail: helene@reginotel.com. 135 units. A/C MINIBAR TV TEL. 1,950–2,250F ($351–$405) double; from 2,750F ($495) suite. AE, DC, MC, V. Métro: Pyramides or Tuileries.

Until a radical renovation upgraded its old-fashioned grandeur in 1995, this hotel slumbered in central Paris, adjacent to rue de Rivoli's equestrian statue of Joan of Arc. The management has poured lots of francs into the renovation, retaining the patina

Paris Accommodations

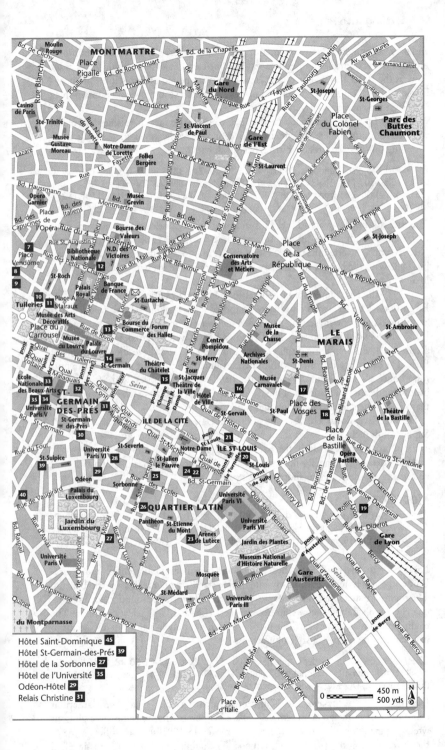

Hôtel Saint-Dominique 45
Hôtel St-Germain-des-Prés 39
Hôtel de la Sorbonne 27
Hôtel de l'Université 35
Odéon-Hôtel 29
Relais Christine 31

and beeswax of the Art Nouveau interior and adding historically appropriate improvements. Rooms overlooking the Tuileries, in some cases, enjoy panoramic views as far away as the Eiffel Tower. The public areas have every period of Louis furniture imaginable, Oriental carpets, 18th-century paintings, and bowls of flowers. Fountains play in a flagstone-covered courtyard.

Dining: In the well-managed Le Pluvinel, conservative French cuisine is served in an Art Deco atmosphere. Pluvinel is closed on weekends, when there's only a less appealing but more affordable bistro-style snack bar.

✪ **Le Ritz.** 15 place Vendôme, 75001 Paris. ☎ **800/241-3333** in the U.S. and Canada, or 01-43-16-30-30. Fax 01-43-16-31-78. 187 units. A/C MINIBAR TV TEL. 3,400–4,300F ($612–$774) double; from 6,000F ($1,080) suite. AE, DC, MC, V. Parking 150F ($27). Métro: Opéra.

The Ritz is Europe's greatest hotel This enduring symbol of elegance stands on one of Paris's most beautiful and historic squares. César Ritz, the "little shepherd boy from Niederwald," converted the private Hôtel de Lazun into a luxury hotel that he opened in 1898. With the help of the culinary master Escoffier, he made the Ritz a miracle of luxury living.

In 1979 the Ritz family sold the hotel to the Egyptian businessman Mohamed Al Fayed (Dodi's father), who refurbished it and added a cooking school. (Dodi Fayed and Princess Diana were staying here when they set out on their fateful drive through Paris, which ended in such tragedy.) Two town houses were annexed, joined by a long arcade lined with miniature display cases representing 125 of the leading boutiques of Paris. The salons are furnished with museum-caliber antiques: gilt pieces, ornate mirrors, Louis XV and Louis XVI furniture, hand-woven tapestries, and 10-foot-high bronze candelabras. The decor of the bathrooms is impeccably French, with wood and marble, antique chests, and crystal lighting.

Dining/Diversions: The Espadon grill room is one of the finest in Paris. The Ritz Supper Club includes a bar, a salon with a fireplace, a restaurant, and a dance floor. You can order drinks in either the Bar Vendôme or the Bar Hemingway.

Amenities: Concierge, 24-hour room service, laundry, valet, health club (with pool and massage parlor), florist, shops, squash court.

MODERATE

✪ **Hôtel Britannique.** 20 av. Victoria, 75001 Paris. ☎ **01-42-33-74-59.** Fax 01-42-33-82-65. www.hotel-britannique.fr. E-mail: mailbox@hotel-britannique.fr. 40 units. MINIBAR TV TEL. 610–995F ($109.80–$179.10) double. AE, DC, MC, V. Parking 100F ($18). Métro: Châtelet.

Located in the heart of Paris, near Les Halles, the Pompidou Centre, and Notre-Dame, the newly renovated, newly rated three-star Britannique is a terrific bargain. The rooms are small, but they are spick-and-span, comfortable, soundproof, and adequately equipped, and the satellite receiver gets U.S. and U.K. televison shows. The reading room is a cozy retreat. The place is British not only in name but also seems to have cultivated an English style of graciousness.

✪ **Hôtel Mansart.** 5 rue des Capucines, 75001 Paris. ☎ **01-42-61-50-28.** Fax 01-49-27-97-44. E-mail: espranc@micronet.fr. 57 units. 580–880F ($104.40–$158.40) double; 1,550F ($279) suite. AE, DC, MC, V. Métro: Opéra or Madeleine.

Designed by its namesake, the 17th-century architect Jules Hardouin-Mansart, it composes part of the grand ensemble of place Vendôme. After operating as a glorious wreck for many decades, it was radically renovated in 1991 and now offers some of the lowest rates in this pricey neighborhood. The public areas contain Louis-inspired reproductions and startling floor-to-ceiling geometric designs inspired by inlaid

ⓘ Family-Friendly Hotels

Hôtel de Fleurie *(see p. 97)*   In the heart of St-Germain-des-Prés, this has long been a family favorite. You can rent its *chambres familiales*—two connecting rooms with two large beds. Children 12 and under stay free in their parents' room.

Hôtel du Louvre *(see p. 87)*   This hotel has welcomed families to Paris since 1855. It's well situated near the Louvre and the Palais Royal and offers generally spacious rooms, many large enough to accommodate families. Baby-sitting can be arranged.

Timhôtel Louvre *(see below)*   This is especially great for families, as it offers some rooms with four beds, and since children 12 and under stay free in their parents' room, this can be a great deal.

marble floors (or formal gardens) of the French Renaissance. The guest rooms are subtly formal and comfortable, though only half a dozen of the suites and most expensive rooms actually overlook the famous square. Breakfast, the only meal offered, is served one floor above lobby level.

Relais du Louvre. 19 rue des Prêtres, 75001 Paris. ☎ **01-40-41-96-42.** Fax 01-40-41-96-44. 20 units. MINIBAR TV TEL. 850–980F ($153–$176.40) double; from 1,300F ($234) suite. AE, MC, V. Parking 70F ($12.60). Métro: Louvre or Pont-Neuf.

One of the neighborhood's most up-to-date hotels opened in 1991, midway between the wings at the eastern end of the Musée du Louvre. The Relais has a lot more atmosphere, glamour, and history than its major competitor, the Britannique—between 1800 and 1941, the upper floors of this historical gem housed the printing presses that recorded the goings-on in Paris's House of Representatives; and its street level held the Café Momus, favored by Voltaire, Hugo, and intellectuals of the day; Puccini set one of the pivotal scenes of *La Bohème* in that legendary cafe. The guest rooms are painted in bold colors, with modern conveniences, soundproof windows, and reproductions of antique furniture.

Timhôtel Louvre. 4 rue Croix des Petits-Champs, 75001 Paris. ☎ **01-42-60-34-86.** Fax 01-42-60-10-39. E-mail: pascalgauthier@compuserve.com. 56 units. TV TEL. 550F ($99) double. Métro: Palais-Royal.

This hotel and its sibling, the Timhôtel Bourse, are mirror images of each other, at least inside; they're part of a new breed of two-star business-oriented hotels that are cropping up around France. These Timhôtels share the same manager and the same temperament, and though the rooms at Timhôtel Bourse are larger than those here, the Louvre branch is irresistibly close to the museum. The ambience is bland and standardized but modern and comfortable, with tiled bathrooms, monochromatic guest rooms, and wall-to-wall carpeting. Breakfasts are served rather anonymously from self-service cafeterias.

Timhôtel Bourse is at 3 rue de la Banque, 75002 Paris (☎ **01-42-61-53-90;** fax 01-42-60-05-39; Métro: Bourse). It has 46 units and charges the same price as above.

RIGHT BANK: 3RD ARRONDISSEMENT (LE MARAIS)
VERY EXPENSIVE

✪ **Pavillon de la Reine.** 28 place des Vosges, 75003 Paris. ☎ **01-40-29-19-19.** Fax 01-40-29-19-20. 62 units. A/C MINIBAR TV TEL. 1,850–2,100F ($333–$378) double; 2,000–2,400F ($360-$432) duplex; 2,300–3,800F ($414–$684) suite. AE, DC, MC, V. Free parking. Métro: Bastille.

Built in 1986, this cream-colored neoclassical villa blends in perfectly with the rest of the neighborhood. You enter through an arcade that opens onto a small formal garden. The Louis XIII decor evokes the heyday of place des Vosges, while the mixture of wing chairs with flame-stitched upholstery and iron-banded Spanish antiques creates a rustic feel. Each guest room is unique; some are duplexes with sleeping lofts above cozy salons. All have a warm decor of weathered beams, reproductions of famous oil paintings, and marble bathrooms.

Amenities: A receptionist/concierge can arrange massage and tickets for shows, concerts, and theater; limited 24-hour room service.

INEXPENSIVE

Hôtel des Chevaliers. 30 rue de Turenne, 75003 Paris. ☎ **01-42-72-73-47.** Fax 01-42-72-54-10. 24 units. MINIBAR TV TEL. 572–622F ($102.95–$111.95) double; 778F ($140.05) triple. Métro: Chemin-Vert or St-Paul.

Half a block from the northwestern edge of place des Vosges, this carefully renovated hotel occupies a dramatic corner building whose 17th-century vestiges have been elevated into high art. These include the remnants of a stone-sided well in the cellar, a sweeping stone barrel vault that covers the breakfast area, half-timbering that's artfully exposed in the stairwell, and Louis XIII accessories that'll remind you of the hotel's origins. Each room is comfortable and clean, with a safe and simple, modern built-in furniture.

RIGHT BANK: 4TH ARRONDISSEMENT (ILE DE LA CITE/ILE ST-LOUIS)
MODERATE

✪ **Hôtel de Lutèce.** 65 rue St-Louis-en-l'Ile, 75004 Paris. ☎ **01-43-26-23-52.** Fax 01-43-29-60-25. www.france-hotel-guide.com/h.75004lutèce.htm. 23 units. A/C TV TEL. 850F ($153) double; 990F ($178.20) triple. AE, V. Métro: Pont-Marie or Cité.

This hotel feels like a country house in Brittany. The lounge, with its old fireplace, is graciously furnished with antiques and contemporary paintings. Each of the individualized guest rooms boasts antiques, adding to a refined atmosphere that attracts celebrities, like the duke and duchess of Bedford. The hotel is comparable in style and amenities to the Deux-Iles (same ownership).

Hôtel des Deux-Iles. 59 rue St-Louis-en-l'Ile, 75004 Paris. ☎ **01-43-26-13-35.** Fax 01-43-29-60-25. 17 units. TV TEL. 860F ($154.80) double. AE, DC, MC, V. Métro: Pont-Marie.

This much-restored 17th-century town house was an inexpensive hotel until 1976, when the owner/decorator Roland Buffat added an elaborate decor with lots of bamboo and reed furniture and French provincial touches. The result is an unpretentious but charming hotel with a great location. A garden of plants and flowers off the lobby leads to a basement breakfast room with a fireplace.

RIGHT BANK: 8TH ARRONDISSEMENT (CHAMPS-ELYSEES/MADELEINE)
VERY EXPENSIVE

Hôtel Balzac. 6 rue Balzac, 75008 Paris. ☎ **800/457-4000** in the U.S. and Canada, or 01-44-35-18-00. Fax 01-44-35-18-05. E-mail: liz.tabet@wanadoo.fr. 70 units. A/C MINIBAR TV TEL. 2,001–2,200F ($360.20–$396) double; from 3,200F ($576) suite. AE, DC, MC, V. Parking 150F ($27). Métro: George-V.

If you liken the Crillon and the Ritz to a Rolls-Royce, you could say that the Balzac is like a Bentley. Elegant and discreet, it boasts a well-trained formal staff and comfortable accommodations with modern furniture. The hint of opulence is unmatched by many other hotels in its neighborhood near the upper end of the Champs-Elysées. The hotel opened in 1986 in a belle époque mansion, then was redecorated in 1994 by the famed English designer Nina Campbell. Each room is soundproofed and conceived as a well-upholstered hideaway.

Dining: In November 1996 a prominent spot near the hotel's elegant lobby was rented to the Restaurant Pierre Gagnaire (see "Dining," later in this chapter). Its namesake is a promising culinary newcomer to Paris whose three-star cuisine has impressed critics throughout France.

Amenities: Concierge, 24-hour room service, dry cleaning, express laundry.

✪ **Hôtel de Crillon.** 10 place de la Concorde, 75008 Paris. ☎ **800/241-3333** in the U.S. and Canada, or 01-44-71-15-00. Fax 01-44-71-15-02. E-mail: crillon@crillon-paris.com. 163 units. A/C MINIBAR TV TEL. 3,200–4,200F ($576–$756) double; from 4,900F ($882) suite. AE, DC, MC, V. Parking 150F ($27). Métro: Concorde.

One of Europe's greatest hotels, the Crillon sits across from the U.S. Embassy. The 200-year-old building, once the palace of the duc de Crillon, has been a hotel since the early 1900s and is now owned by Jean Taittinger of the champagne family. Inside are many preserved architectural details as well as museum-quality antiques and reproductions. The salons boast 17th- and 18th-century tapestries, gilt-and-brocade furniture, chandeliers, fine sculpture, and Louis XVI chests and chairs. The large guest rooms are classically furnished, featuring bathrooms lined with travertine or pink marble.

Dining: You can dine at the elegant Les Ambassadeurs or the more informal L'Obélisque, where menu choices are less experimental. Les Ambassadeurs offers a businessperson's lunch Monday through Friday only. The *menu dégustation* is served at lunch on weekends and every evening.

Amenities: Room service (24 hours), secretarial/translation service, laundry, valet, meeting and conference rooms, garden-style courtyard with restaurant service, shops.

✪ **Hôtel Plaza Athénée.** 27 av. Montaigne, 75008 Paris. ☎ **800/448-8355** in the U.S. and Canada, or 01-53-67-66-65. Fax 01-53-67-64-66. 247 units. A/C MINIBAR TV TEL. 3,200–4,650F ($576–$837) double; from 6,500F ($1,170) suite. AE, MC, V. Parking 150F ($27). Métro: Franklin-D.-Roosevelt or Alma Marceau.

Plaza Athénée, halfway between the Champs-Elysées and the Seine, is a landmark of discretion and style. About half the celebrities visiting Paris have been pampered here. The finest public room is the Montaigne Salon, paneled in grained wood and dominated by a marble fireplace. The best guest rooms overlook a courtyard with awnings and parasol-shaded tables; they have ample closet space, and their large tiled bathrooms have double basins and a shower.

Dining/Diversions: La Régence is a pink, peach, and gold room of handsome period furniture. The food is superb—try the lobster soufflé. For lunch, Grill Relais Plaza is the meeting place of dress designers and personalities from the worlds of publishing, cinema, and art. The Bar Anglais is a favorite spot for a late-night drink.

Amenities: Concierge, 24-hour room service, laundry, Reuters telex with international stock quotes, conference rooms, beauty salon, massage, fitness club.

EXPENSIVE

Hôtel Concorde St-Lazare. 108 rue St-Lazare, 75008 Paris. ☎ **800/888-4747** in the U.S. outside New York State and Canada, 212/752-3900 in New York State, 0171/630-1704 in London, or 01-40-08-44-44. Fax 01-42-93-01-20. www.concordestlazare-paris.com. E-mail: stlazare@concordestlazare-paris.com. 300 units. A/C MINIBAR TV TEL. 1,300–1,900F ($234–$342) double; from 3,500F ($630) suite. AE, DC, MC, V. Parking 110F ($19.80). Métro: St-Lazare.

This hotel, built in 1889 to accommodate visitors who flocked to the Universal Expedition, is across from the St-Lazare rail station and the best in the area. In the 1990s the St-Lazare's main lobby (a carefully protected historic monument) was restored under the supervision of the Concorde chain. The guest rooms were elevated to modern standards of comfort, redecorated, and soundproofed.

Dining/Diversions: The hotel has a gilt-and-russet room that's devoted to French billiards—the only room of its kind in any Paris hotel. An American bar, Le Golden Black, bears the fashion designer Sonia Rykiel's signature decor of black lacquer with touches of gold and amber. The Café Terminus offers daily brasserie service from noon to 11pm. Bistrot 108 serves provincial dishes with great vintages that you can order by the glass.

Amenities: Concierge, 24-hour room service, baby-sitting, laundry, valet.

MODERATE

Hôtel Queen Mary. 9 rue Greffulhe, 75008 Paris. ☎ **01-42-66-40-50.** Fax 01-42-66-94-92. E-mail: hotelqueenmary@wanadoo.fr. 36 units. A/C MINIBAR TV TEL. 755–945F ($135.90–$170.10) double; 1,300F ($234) suite. AE, DC, MC, V. Métro: Madeleine or Havre-Caumartin.

Meticulously renovated both inside and out, this hotel was built around the turn of the century. It's graced with an iron-and-glass canopy, ornate wrought iron, and the kind of detailing you might expect in more expensive hotels. The public rooms have touches of greenery and reproductions of mid-19th-century antiques; each guest room has an upholstered headboard and mahogany furnishings, plus a carafe of sherry.

INEXPENSIVE

Hôtel Opal. 19 rue Tronchet, 75008 Paris. ☎ **01-42-65-77-97.** Fax 01-49-24-06-58. E-mail: hotelopal@francemultimedia.fr. 36 units. A/C MINIBAR TV TEL. 590–660F ($106.20–$118.80) double. Extra bed 100F ($18). AE, DC, V. Parking 120F ($21.60) nearby. Métro: Madeleine.

This rejuvenated hotel is a real find in the heart of Paris, behind the Madeleine and near the Opéra Garnier. The guest rooms are somewhat cramped but very clean and comfortable, and many of them are air-conditioned. Those on the top floor are reached by a narrow staircase; some have skylights. The reception desk will make arrangements for parking at a nearby garage.

LEFT BANK: 5TH ARRONDISSEMENT (LATIN QUARTER)
MODERATE

Grand Hôtel St-Michel. 19 rue Cujas, 75005 Paris. ☎ **01-46-33-33-02.** Fax 01-40-46-96-33. 45 units. MINIBAR TV TEL. 690–790F ($124.20–$142.20) double, 1,290F ($232.20) suite. AE, DC, MC, V. Métro: Cluny–La Sorbonne. RER: Luxembourg or St-Michel.

Built in the 19th century, this hotel is larger and more businesslike than many of the nearby, smaller town house–style inns. It basks in the reflected glow of the Brazilian dissident Georges Amado, whose memoirs (released in 1996) recorded his 2-year literary sojourn in one of the rooms. In 1997 the hotel completed a renovation and thus moved from two- to three-star status. The architectural changes enlarged some rooms, lowering their ceilings and adding such modern amenities as minibars, but retained old-fashioned touches like wrought-iron balconies (fifth floor only). Rooms on the sixth (uppermost) floor have interesting views over the rooftops. Guests enjoy a copious breakfast buffet.

Hôtel Abbatial St-Germain. 46 bd. St-Germain, 75005 Paris. ☎ **01-46-34-02-12.** Fax 01-43-25-47-73. 43 units. A/C MINIBAR TV TEL. 600–820F ($108–$147.60) double. AE, MC, V. Métro: Maubert-Mutualité.

The origins of this hotel are so old that interior renovations have revealed such 17th-century touches as dovecotes and massive oaken beams. In the early 1990s a radical restoration brought the six stories of rooms up to modern, smallish, but comfortable standards. The public areas are especially appealing. The guest rooms are furnished in faux Louis XVI, each with a different color scheme. All windows are double-glazed, and the fifth- and sixth-floor rooms enjoy views over Notre-Dame. Breakfast is served beneath the vaulted ceilings of the stone-sided cellar.

Hôtel Agora St-Germain. 42 rue des Bernardins, 75005 Paris. ☎ **01-46-34-13-00.** Fax 01-46-34-75-05. 39 units. A/C MINIBAR TV TEL. 720F ($129.60) double; 960F ($172.80) triple. AE, DC, MC, V. Parking 120F ($21.60). Métro: Maubert-Mutualité.

One of the best of the neighborhood's moderately priced choices, this hotel occupies a building constructed in the early 1600s, probably to house a group of guardsmen protecting the brother of the king at his nearby lodgings. Located in the heart of the artistic and historic section, this hotel offers compact soundproofed guest rooms, each comfortably furnished and equipped with an alarm clock, a hair dryer, and a safe-deposit box. Room service is provided daily from 7:30 to 10:30am.

Hôtel-Résidence St-Christophe. 17 rue Lacépède, 75005 Paris. ☎ **01-43-31-81-54.** Fax 01-43-31-12-54. 30 units. MINIBAR TV TEL. 650F ($117) double. AE, DC, MC, V. Parking 100F ($18). Métro: Place-Monge.

This hotel, in one of the Latin Quarter's undiscovered though charming districts, has a gracious English-speaking staff. Millions of francs after a renovation in 1987, which combined a derelict hotel and butcher shop, the St-Christophe is inviting and comfortable, with Louis XV–style furniture and wall-to-wall carpeting. All the rooms were renovated in 1998. Breakfast is the only meal served, but the staff offers advice about neighborhood bistros.

INEXPENSIVE

Hôtel de la Sorbonne. 6 rue Victor-Cousin, 75005 Paris. ☎ **01-43-54-58-08.** Fax 01-40-51-05-18. 37 units. TV TEL. 460–490F ($82.80–$88.20) double; 570F ($114) triple. MC, V. Métro: Cluny–La Sorbonne. RER: Luxembourg.

Near the Jardin du Luxembourg, this hotel enjoys one of the most dramatic positions in the Quarter. On a street from the 1400s, between the Panthéon and rue Souflot, the hotel is aptly named, as it's in front of the famous university. You're welcomed with a certain French style and grace at this family-type place, which features an observatory with hanging and flowering plants. Though smallish, the rooms are traditionally furnished and contain extras like hair dryers. Breakfast is served in a small room with an African statue overseeing the service.

✪ **Hôtel Le Home Latin.** 15–17 rue du Sommerard, 75005 Paris. ☎ **01-43-26-25-21.** Fax 01-43-29-87-04. 55 units. TV TEL. 495–565F ($89.10–$101.70) double. AE, V. Métro: St-Michel or Maubert-Mutualité.

This is one of the most famous budget hotels in Paris, known since the 1970s for clean and simple lodgings. The Home Latin originally consisted of two separate side-by-side buildings, which were united in the 1970s. Renovations in 1992 made the rooms blandly functional; some of them have small balconies overlooking the street. The rooms facing the courtyard are quieter than those fronting the street, and the elevator doesn't reach beyond the fifth floor. To make up for the stair climb, the sixth floor's chambres mansardées offer a romantic location under the eaves and panoramic views over the rooftops.

Gay-Friendly Hotels

In Paris gay-friendly hotels (at least to a degree) aren't hard to find—the following are especially welcoming.

Hôtel Central, 33 rue Vieille-du-Temple, 75004 Paris (☎ **01-48-87-99-33;** fax 01-42-77-06-27; Métro: Hôtel-de-Ville), is the most prominent gay hotel in Paris. The seven rooms (one with bathroom) are on the second, third, and fourth floors of this 18th-century building, which contains one of the top gay bars in Le Marais. Women are welcome but rare. Rates are 535F ($96.30) double with or without bathroom. MC, V.

Renovated in 1996, **Le Saint-Hubert,** 27 rue Traversière, 75012 Paris (☎ **01-43-43-39-16;** fax 01-43-43-35-32; Métro: Gare-de-Lyon), occupies a five-story 19th-century town house (no elevator) on a quiet but unremarkable residential street. The eastern edge of Le Marais, with all its gay bars, is a 10-minute walk west. The 15 rooms are cozy and comfortable, those on the upper floors less expensive because of the climb. Rates are 315F to 345F ($56.70 to $62.10) double. MC, V.

LEFT BANK: 6TH ARRONDISSEMENT (ST-GERMAINE/LUXEMBOURG)
VERY EXPENSIVE

Relais Christine. 3 rue Christine, 75006 Paris. ☎ **01-40-51-60-80.** Fax 01-40-51-60-81. 51 units. A/C MINIBAR TV TEL. 1,700–1,900F ($306–$342) double; 2,400–3,300F ($432–$594) duplex suite. AE, DC, MC, V. Free parking. Métro: Odéon.

Relais Christine welcomes you into what was a 16th-century Augustinian cloister. You enter from a narrow cobblestone street into a symmetrical courtyard, which leads into an elegant reception area with baroque sculpture and Renaissance antiques. Each guest room is uniquely decorated with wooden beams, a marble bathroom, and Louis XIII–style furnishings.

Dining: Off the reception area is a paneled sitting room/bar area ringed with 19th-century portraits and comfortable leather chairs. The breakfast room is in a vaulted cellar; the ancient well and massive central stone column are part of the cloister's former kitchen.

Amenities: Room service (24 hours), laundry, baby-sitting.

EXPENSIVE

✪ **Hôtel de l'Abbaye St-Germain.** 10 rue Cassette, 75006 Paris. ☎ **01-45-44-38-11.** Fax 01-45-48-07-86. www.hotel-abbaye.4in.com. E-mail: hotel.abbaye@wanadoo.fr. 46 units. A/C TV TEL. 1,000–1,600F ($180–$288) double; 1,950F ($351) suite. Rates include continental breakfast. AE, MC, V. Métro: St-Sulpice.

Built early in the 18th century as a convent for the Eglise St-Germain, this place later became a cheap youth hostel, which was transformed into a charming boutique hotel in 1985. The brightly colored rooms have traditional furniture and touches of sophisticated flair. In front is a small garden, and in back is a verdant courtyard featuring a fountain, raised flower beds, and masses of ivy and climbing vines. The public areas include a trio of salons and a bar. If you don't mind the expense, note that one of the most charming rooms has a terrace overlooking the upper floors of neighboring buildings.

Dining: Breakfast is the only meal served, although the hotel has limited room service from 7am to midnight.

Amenities: Access to nearby health club, car-rental desk, concierge, dry cleaning/laundry.

✪ **L'Hôtel.** 13 rue des Beaux-Arts, 75006 Paris. ☎ **01-44-41-99-00.** Fax 01-43-25-64-81. 26 units. A/C MINIBAR TV TEL. 800–2,500F ($144–$450) double; from 2,800F ($504) suite. AE, DC, MC, V. Parking 125F ($22.50). Métro: St-Germain-des-Prés.

This boutique hotel is unique on the Left Bank. In the 19th century it was a fleabag called the Hôtel d'Alsace, and its major distinction was that Oscar Wilde, broke and in despair, died here. However, today's guests aren't anywhere near poverty row: through the lobby march many show-business and fashion celebrities. L'Hôtel was the creation of the late French actor Guy-Louis Duboucheron, who established an atmosphere of super-sophistication. You'll feel like a movie star while bathing in your tub of rosy-pink marble. Throughout is an eclectic collection of antiques that includes Louis XV and Louis XVI, Empire, and Directoire pieces.

Dining: Breakfast is served in a winter garden, which in the evening becomes a tavern offering intimate dinners. Le Bélier is a luxurious restaurant.

Amenities: Concierge, 24-hour room service, baby-sitting, laundry, valet.

MODERATE

Hôtel Aviatic. 105 rue de Vaugirard, 75006 Paris. ☎ **01-45-44-38-21.** Fax 01-45-49-35-83. E-mail: parishotel@aol.com. 43 units. MINIBAR TV TEL. 740–1,150F ($133.20–$207) double. AE, DC, MC, V. Parking 120F ($21.60). Métro: Montparnasse-Bienvenue.

This family-run hotel is a bit of old Paris, with a modest inner courtyard and a vine-covered lattice on the walls. The reception lounge, with marble columns, brass chandeliers, antiques, and a petit salon, provides an attractive setting. It doesn't have the decorative flair of some of the other 6th arrondissement hotels we've listed but does offer good comfort and a warm ambience. Completely remodeled, it's in an interesting section of Montparnasse, surrounded by cafes frequented by artists, writers, and jazz musicians. The staff speaks English.

✪ **Hôtel de Fleurie.** 32–34 rue Grégoire-de-Tours, 75006 Paris. ☎ **01-53-73-70-00.** Fax 01-53-73-70-20. www.hotel-de-fleurie.tm.fr. E-mail: bonjour@hotel-de-fleurie.tm.fr. 29 units. A/C MINIBAR TV TEL. 900–1,200F ($162–$216) double; 1,450–1,560F ($261–$280.80) family room. Children 12 and under stay free in parents' room. AE, DC, MC, V. Métro: Odéon.

Just off boulevard St-Germain on a colorful little street, the Fleurie is one of the best of the "new" old hotels. Restored to its former glory in 1988, the facade, studded with statuary spotlit by night, recaptures the 17th-century elegance. The stone walls have been exposed in the reception salon, where you check in at a refectory desk. An elevator takes you to the well-furnished modern rooms, each with a safe; a spiral staircase leads down to the breakfast room. This has long been a family favorite because of its *chambres familiales*—connecting rooms with two large beds.

Hôtel Le Clos Médicis. 56 rue Monsieur-le-Prince, 75006 Paris. ☎ **01-43-29-10-80.** Fax 01-43-54-26-90. 38 units. A/C MINIBAR TV TEL. 790–990F ($142.20–$178.20) double; 1,200F ($216) duplex suite. AE, DC, MC, V. Métro: Odéon. RER: Luxembourg.

In 1994 this hotel opened on the premises of what had been a private home in 1860 and most recently had been a bookstore and a run-down boardinghouse. You'll find a verdant garden with lattices and exposed stone walls, a lobby with modern spotlights and simple furniture, and a multilingual staff. Its location, adjacent to the Jardin du Luxembourg, is one of the place's major advantages. The warmly colored guest rooms are comfortable. Breakfast is the only meal served.

Hôtel St-Germain-des-Prés. 36 rue Bonaparte, 75006 Paris. ☎ **01-43-26-00-19.** Fax 01-40-46-83-63. 30 units. MINIBAR TV TEL. 750–970F ($135–$174.60) double; from 1,700F ($306) suite. Rates include breakfast. MC, V. Métro: St-Germain-des-Prés.

Most of this hotel's attraction comes from its enviable location in the Latin Quarter—behind a well-known Left Bank street near many shops. Janet Flanner, the legendary correspondent for *The New Yorker* in the 1920s, lived here for a while. Each room is small but charming, with antique ceiling beams and a safe, and each received an extensive renovation in 1994. The public areas are severely elegant, with dentil moldings, Louis XIII furnishings, and original stonework. Air-conditioning is available in most of the rooms.

Odéon-Hôtel. 3 rue de l'Odéon, 75006 Paris. ☎ **01-43-25-90-67.** Fax 01-43-25-55-98. 33 units. A/C TV TEL. 912–1,412F ($164.15–$254.15) double. AE, DC, MC, V. Métro: Odéon.

Near boulevard St-Germain, but reminiscent of a modernized Norman country inn, this hotel offers charming rustic touches such as exposed beams, rough stone walls, high crooked ceilings, and tapestries mixed with contemporary fabrics, mirrored ceilings, and black leather furnishings. After modern plumbing was added, each room was individually designed.

INEXPENSIVE

Hôtel du Globe. 15 rue des Quatre-Vents, 75006 Paris. ☎ **01-46-33-62-69.** Fax 01-46-33-62-69. 15 units. TV TEL. 390–495F ($70.20–$89.10) double. V. Closed 3 weeks in Aug. Métro: Mabillon, Odéon, or St-Sulpice.

This 17th-century building occupies an evocative street in one of Paris's oldest neighborhoods. Inside, you'll find most of the original stonework and dozens of the original timbers and beams. Each room is decorated with individual flair in an old-fashioned style. The accommodations with a tub are almost twice as large as the rooms with a shower stall, so for the extra expense you'll get a lot more than just an improvement in the plumbing. There's no elevator (you have to lug your suitcases up a very narrow, antique staircase) and no breakfast area (trays are brought to your room). The largest and most desirable rooms are nos. 1, 12 (with a baldaquin-style bed), 14, 15, and 16. The room without bathroom is a single at 255F ($45.90).

LEFT BANK: 7TH ARRONDISSEMENT (EIFFEL TOWER/MUSEE D'ORSAY)
VERY EXPENSIVE

✪ **Hôtel Montalembert.** 3 rue de Montalembert, 75007 Paris. ☎ **800/447-7462** in the U.S. and Canada, or 01-45-49-68-68. Fax 01-45-49-69-49. www.montalembert.com. E-mail: welcome@hotel-montalembert.fr. 56 units. A/C MINIBAR TV TEL. 1,695–2,200F ($305.10–$396) double; 2,750F ($495) junior suite; 4,300F ($774) suite. AE, DC, MC, V. Parking 120F ($21.60). Métro: Rue-du-Bac.

Unusually elegant for the Left Bank, the Montalembert was built in 1926 in the Beaux-Arts style. In 1989 the hotel, much in need of renovation, was bought by the Hong Kong–based Leo group, whose directors hired one of France's premier architectural designers, Christian Liaigre. The hotel reopened in 1992 with smashing restorations. You'll find a sophisticated modern interpretation that borrows elements of Bauhaus and postmodern design in honey beiges, creams, and golds. Half the guest rooms follow the style established in the public rooms; the other half are stylishly but conservatively decorated in Louis-Philippe style.

Dining/Diversions: The Restaurant Montalembert is favored by area artists, writers, publishers, and antiques dealers. The stylish dining room provides excellent service and exceptionally good food. The hotel also has a fully stocked bar and 24-hour room service.

Amenities: The hotel has an "I can arrange anything" concierge; rooms contain VCRs and safes. Guests receive privileges at a nearby health club.

MODERATE

Hôtel de l'Académie. 32 rue des Saints-Pères, 75007 Paris. ☎ **800/246-0041** in the U.S. and Canada, or 01-45-49-80-00. Fax 01-45-49-80-10. 34 units. A/C MINIBAR TV TEL. 490–1,290F ($88.20–$232.20) double. AE, DC, MC, V. Parking 150F ($27). Métro: St-Germain-des-Prés.

The exterior walls and old ceiling beams are all that remain of this 17th-century residence of the private guards of the duc de Rohan. In 1983 the hotel was completely renovated to include an elegant reception area. The comfortably up-to-date guest rooms have Directoire beds, an Ile-de-France decor, and views over the 18th- and 19th-century buildings of the neighborhood. The staff speaks English.

✪ **Hôtel de l'Université.** 22 rue de l'Université, 75007 Paris. ☎ **01-42-61-09-39.** Fax 01-42-60-40-84. www.paris-hotel.tm.fr/fr/saintgermain.04/univerisite.html. 27 units. A/C TV TEL. 850–1,300F ($153–$234) double. AE, MC, V. Métro: St-Germain-des-Prés.

Long favored by the well-heeled parents of North American students studying in Paris, this hotel enjoys a location in a discreetly upscale neighborhood. It's the love child of Mme Bergmann, who has renovated this 300-year-old town house and filled it with fine antiques. Number 54 is a favorite room, with a rattan bed, period pieces, and a marble bathroom. Opening onto a courtyard, no. 35 is another charmer, with a fireplace. The most expensive accommodation, at 1,300F ($234), has a small terrace overlooking the surrounding rooftops. The bistro-style breakfast room opens onto a courtyard with a fountain. Everything is personal here.

Hôtel du Quai-Voltaire. 19 quai Voltaire, 75007 Paris. ☎ **01-42-61-50-91.** Fax 01-42-61-62-26. 33 units. TV TEL. 650–700F ($117–$126) double; 850F ($153) triple. AE, DC, MC, V. Parking 110F ($19.80) nearby. Métro: Musée d'Orsay.

Built in the 1600s as an abbey, then transformed into a hotel in 1856, the Quai-Voltaire is best known for its illustrious guests, who've included Wilde, Baudelaire, and Wagner, who occupied Rooms 47, 56, and 55, respectively. Pissarro painted *Le Pont Royal* from a suite on the fourth floor that no longer exists. Many rooms in this modest inn have been renovated, and most overlook the bookstalls and boats of the Seine. You can have drinks in the bar or small salon, and simple meals (like omelets and salads) can be prepared for those who prefer to eat in.

INEXPENSIVE

Grand Hôtel L'Eveque. 29 rue Cler, 75007 Paris. ☎ **01-47-05-49-15.** Fax 01-45-50-49-36. 50 units. TV TEL. 350–383F ($63–$68.95) double. AE, MC, V. Métro: Ecole Militaire.

Built in the 1930s, with pastel-colored bedrooms that retain a vague inspiration from the Art Deco era, this five-story hotel was recommended on one of the TV travel documentaries of travel guru Rick Steves. As such, it's loaded with English-speaking clients, many of whom appreciate its location close to the Eiffel Tower. Each bedroom contains a small lockbox for valuables, just enough space to be comfortable, and double-insulated windows that overlook either a courtyard in back or the street in front. There's an elevator and a one-star format that's utterly unpretentious.

Hôtel de l'Empereur. 2 rue Chevert, 75007 Paris. ☎ **01-45-55-88-02.** Fax 01-45-51-88-54. 38 units. MINIBAR TV TEL. 470–500F ($84.60–$90) double. AE, DC, MC, V. Parking 110–150F ($19.80–$27) per day in public parking lot across the street. Métro: Latour-Maubourg.

The name of this six-story hotel derives from Napoléon I, whose body lies in state within a porphyry sarcophagus at Les Invalides, across the street. There's an elevator to haul you and your luggage to one of the smallish but attractively decorated bedrooms, where a style that's vaguely English in its inspiration can shelter you for as long as you like. This might be longer than you had expected, thanks to the hotel's relatively low costs and convenient location. There's no restaurant or bar on the premises, but the hotel maintains a dialogue with a nearby restaurant that will agree to send platters of food to any of the bedrooms on request. Originally constructed in the early 1700s, the building has functioned as a hotel since the 1930s and enjoys a loyal following.

Hôtel de Nevers. 83 rue du Bac, 75007 Paris. ☎ **01-45-44-61-30.** Fax 01-42-22-29-47. 11 units. MINIBAR TV TEL. 400–470F ($72–$84.60) double. No credit cards. Métro: Rue-du-Bac.

This is one of the most historic choices in an old neighborhood. Between 1627 and 1790 it was a convent for the Soeurs de la Recollette; they were disbanded by the Revolution. (Look for the religious plaque on the stone wall opposite the reception desk.) The building, brought to its present level of modernization in 1983, is presently classé, which means that any restoration must respect the original architecture. That precludes an elevator, so you'll have to climb the never-ending but beautiful white staircase. The rooms, cozy and pleasant, contain a combination of antique and reproduced furniture. Rooms 10 and 11 are especially sought-after because of their terraces overlooking either a corner of rue du Bac or a rear courtyard.

Hôtel du Champ de Mars. 7 rue du Champ de Mars, 75007 Paris. ☎ **01-45-51-52-30.** Fax 01-45-51-64-36. 25 units. TV TEL. 360–390F ($64.80–$70.20) double. AE, DC, MC, V. Parking 100–150F ($18–$27) in nearby public parking lot. Métro: Ecole Militaire.

Favored by families, many of whom arrive with children, this hotel rises five floors above a position close to the park that flanks the base of the Eiffel Tower. Built during the mid–20th century, it offers clean and simple bedrooms that, although cramped, are frilly and pretty enough to be referred to as "coquettish" by the manager, who remains proud of their fancy detailings. The most memorable of the public areas is a stone-sided breakfast room, which features the only meal served in the hotel.

Hôtel Lindbergh. 5 rue Chomel, 75007 Paris. ☎ **01-45-48-35-53.** Fax 01-45-49-31-48. www.hotellindbergh.com. E-mail: linhotel@club-internet.fr. 26 units. TV TEL. 450–620F ($81–$111.60) double; 550–720F ($99–$129.60) triple or quad. AE, DC, MC, V. Parking 70F ($12.60). Métro: Sèvres-Babylone or St-Sulpice.

Constructed between 1880 and 1881, this building was made into a hotel shortly after its namesake (Charles Lindbergh) electrified Paris with his solo flight across the Atlantic in 1927. Between then and the hotel's renovation in 1995, it looked as if little had changed. Today, however, the hotel sits behind a modern facade, has streamlined and simple but comfortable rooms, and lies about a 3-minute walk from St-Germain-des-Prés. Breakfast is the only meal served, but the staff will point out worthy restaurants nearby—one is an inexpensive but well-managed bistro, Le Cigale, a few buildings away.

Hôtel Saint-Dominique. 62 rue Saint-Dominique, 75007 Paris. ☎ **01-47-05-51-44.** Fax 01-47-05-81-28. 34 units. MINIBAR TV TEL. 520–560F ($93.60–$100.80) double. AE, DC, MC, V. Métro: Latour-Maubourg or Invalides.

Part of the charm of this establishment derives from its division into three separate buildings that are connected through an open-air courtyard. With the fifth, second, and first floors, respectively, each building contains a collection of cozy bedrooms that are nostalgically outfitted with French provincial fabrics and patterns. None is particularly large, but each is safe, warm, simply decorated, and comfortable.

4 Dining

Our best piece of advice—even if your budget is lean—is to splurge on one grand classic French meal. (You'll need to make reservations weeks or even months in advance.) A meal at a place such as **La Tour d'Argent, Taillevent, Alain Ducasse,** or **Violin d'Ingres** will be a memory you'll always carry.

THE DINING SCENE   Three-star dining remains extremely expensive in Paris, with appetizers sometimes priced at $50 and dinners easily costing $175 per person in the top Michelin-starred dining rooms. But you can get around that high price tag in many places by ordering a fixed-price menu, perhaps for $90, or patronizing one of the not so celebrated but equally stellar dining rooms—**Pierre Gagnaire,** for example, instead of the almost legendary Alain Ducasse.

One question we're often asked is if you can dine badly in Paris. The answer is an emphatic yes—and increasingly so. We repeatedly get complaints from visitors who cite haughty service and mediocre food dispensed at outrageous prices. Often these complaints are about places catering almost solely to tourists. We'll help you avoid them by sharing our favorite discoveries. Considering the prices charged, view your culinary pursuit as an investment. While others are fighting it out for a table at one of the less-than-wonderful places along the Champs-Elysées, you might be seeking finer fare at some well-recommended choice farther afield.

Changes are in the Paris air. In the past, suits and ties were a given, and women always wore a smart dress or suit. Well, you can kiss your suits *au revoir*—these days, except in first-class and luxe places, dress has become more relaxed. Relaxed doesn't mean sloppy jeans and jogging attire, however. Parisians still value style, even when dressing informally.

And note that it's now considered provincial to request *l'addition* (the bill). Chic Parisians ask for *la note.*

Restaurants are still required by law to post their menus outside, so peruse them carefully. The prix-fixe menu still remains a solid choice if you want to have some idea of what your bill will be when it's presented by the waiter (whom, by the way, you should call *monsieur,* not *garçon*).

Part of the fun of a trip to Paris is enjoying the experience of an old-fashioned, family-run bistro. And just when you thought bistros were dying off, new wave chefs are moving in, hoping to revive them with excellent food at affordable prices. A trend that developed in the early 1990s—that of the "baby bistro"—continues into the late 1990s. These babies are reasonably priced spinoffs from some of Paris's ultra-deluxe restaurants. We've recommended some of the best of them, including **Jacques Cagna's Rôtisserie d'en Face.**

WHAT'S NEW & HOT   If Paris has a king chef today—the equivalent of Escoffier of yesterday—it is none other than Alain Ducasse. As a first for the Michelin guide, it has awarded one chef six stars in 1998, three for his citadel of haute cuisine in Paris and three for his other establishment, the swanky Louis XV in the Hôtel de Paris in Monte Carlo.

At the height of his celebrity, the brilliant chef Joël Robuchon, creator of cuisine actuelle, retired. In his wake, it seems that everybody who ever worked in one of his kitchens, including a dishwasher, has now opened a restaurant in some faraway place like North Yorkshire, England. These far-scattered chefs are now coasting on Robuchon's reputation, offering dishes "in the style of Robuchon."

The direct heir apparent to Robuchon is Benoit Guichard, who was the great chef's own chef de cuisine. The culinary colonel is no longer carrying out the general's

Paris Dining

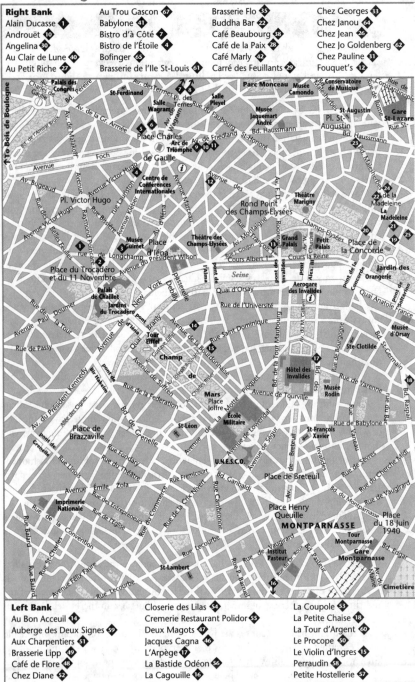

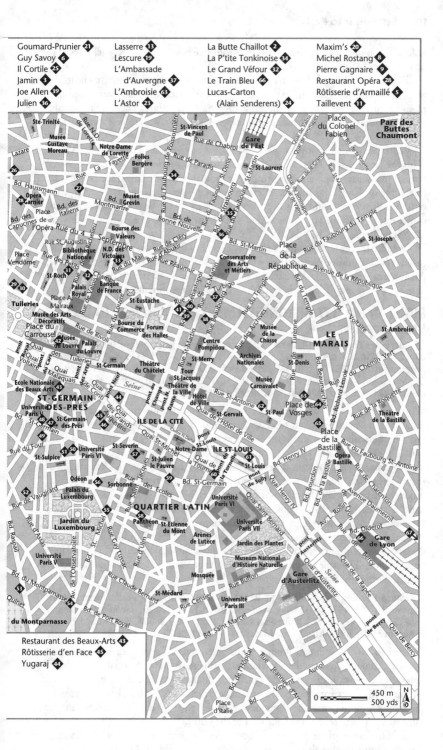

Goumard-Prunier **21**
Guy Savoy **6**
Il Cortile **25**
Jamin **3**
Joe Allen **39**
Julien **36**

Lasserre **13**
Lescure **19**
L'Ambassade
  d'Auvergne **37**
L'Ambroisie **63**
L'Astor **23**

La Butte Chaillot **2**
La P'tite Tonkinoise **34**
Le Grand Véfour **32**
Le Train Bleu **66**
Lucas-Carton
  (Alain Senderens) **24**

Maxim's **20**
Michel Rostang **8**
Pierre Gagnaire **9**
Restaurant Opéra **28**
Rôtisserie d'Armaillé **5**
Taillevent **11**

Restaurant des Beaux-Arts **43**
Rôtisserie d'en Face **45**
Yugaraj **44**

103

orders, for young Guichard has reopened **Jamin** (see below), where Robuchon rose to fame in the 1980s.

Pierre Gagnaire (see below) arrived in Paris fresh from his disappointment in the town of St-Etienne. There he rose to a three-Michelin-star diety but was forced into receivership in 1996. Some of the most discriminating diners flock nightly to the **Hôtel Balzac** to sample what has been called Gagnaire's "I dare you" approach to cuisine.

What's perhaps the hottest news is the arrival of Christian Constant's **Le Violin d'Ingres** (see below). There's talk that M. Constant will be the "new Robuchon," though many Paris chefs are vying ruthlessly for that position. This is the perfect year to splurge on Constant's sublime offerings before he becomes too firmly entrenched on the culinary scene and his prices skyrocket. We love the way Monsieur Constant comes out to welcome you at the end of a meal, inviting you to return as if this were his private home.

These are the great chefs with the great cuisine. But if you want to go where it's chic, make it **The Buddha Bar** (see below). The food is somewhere between French and Asian, but many of the fashionable guests are hardly concerned with that, as they are here to be seen and to spot others on the see-and-be-seen circuit.

RIGHT BANK: 1ST ARRONDISSEMENT (LOUVRE/LES HALLES)
VERY EXPENSIVE

✪ **Carré des Feuillants.** 14 rue de Castiglione (near place Vendôme and the Tuileries). ☎ **01-42-86-82-82.** Reservations required. Main courses 205–285F ($36.90–$51.30); fixed-price menus 285–385F ($51.30–$69.30) at lunch, 680–850F ($122.40–$153) at dinner. AE, DC, MC, V. Mon–Fri noon–2:30pm, Mon–Sat 7:30–10:30pm. Closed the first 3 weeks in Aug. Métro: Tuileries, Concorde, Opéra, or Madeleine. FRENCH.

When leading chef Alain Dutournier converted this 17th-century convent into a restaurant, it was an overnight success. The interior is like a turn-of-the-century bourgeois house with several small salons opening onto a skylit courtyard, across from which is a glass-enclosed kitchen. Dutournier used to call his style of cooking *cuisine du moment;* he feels the term is now a bit dated but hasn't come up with a replacement. He prefers a light, healthful cuisine, working with farmers who supply fresh produce. His beef comes from one of France's oldest breeds, the *race bazadaise,* and his lamb is raised in Pauillac. Winning raves are his chestnut soup with white truffles, suckling veal with a blanquette of wild mushrooms, red snapper roasted on a fondue of lettuce, and gâteau of Jerusalem artichokes with foie gras and truffles. His signature dessert is almond-pistachio cream cake with pistachio ice cream and a mandarin-orange confit. The wine list is exciting, including several little-known wines and a fabulous collection of armagnacs.

Goumard-Prunier. 9 rue Duphot. ☎ **01-42-60-36-07.** Reservations recommended. Main courses 210–380F ($37.80–$68.40); fixed-price lunch 390F ($70.20); menu gastronomique 780F ($140.40). AE, DC, MC, V. Tues–Sat 12:30–2:30pm and 7:30–10:30pm. Closed 2 weeks in Aug and Mon in Oct–Mar. Métro: Madeleine or Concorde. SEAFOOD.

Opened in 1872, Goumard-Prunier is the forerunner of the staid, bourgeois, and famous Prunier found in the 16th arrondissement. A most unusual collection of Lalique crystal fish is displayed in "aquariums" lining the walls. (Even more unusual are the men's and women's rest rooms, now classified as historical monuments by the French government. The commodes were designed by the Art Nouveau master cabinetmaker Majorelle around the turn of the century.)

You'll find some of the freshest and best seafood in Paris here—it's usually flown in directly from Brittany. Examples are a craquant of crayfish in its own herb salad, a salad of baby red mullet with onions and tomatoes in the Catalán style, Breton lobster grilled or poached, and filet of grilled turbot on a bed of artichokes with tarragon. In all these dishes nothing (no excess butter, spices, or salt) is allowed to interfere with the natural flavor of the sea. Be prepared for some very unusual food here—the staff will help translate the menu items for you.

✪ **Le Grand Véfour.** 17 rue de Beaujolais. ☎ **01-42-96-56-27.** Reservations required. Main courses 230–380F ($41.40–$68.40); fixed-price menus 345–780F ($62.10–$140.40) at lunch, 750F ($135) at dinner. AE, DC, MC, V. Mon–Fri 12:30–2:15pm and 7:30–10:15pm. Métro: Louvre. FRENCH.

This has been a restaurant since the reign of Louis XV—the name has changed, however. The exact date of its opening as the Café de Chartres isn't known, but this place is more than 200 years old. In 1812 it was named after its owner, Jean Véfour, a former chef to a member of the royal family. Napoléon, Danton, Hugo, Colette, and Cocteau have dined here—as the brass plaques on the tables testify. Jean Taittinger of the champagne family (owner of the Hôtel de Crillon) purchased the restaurant and meticulously restored it to its former glory.

Dining here is a great gastronomic experience. Specialties, served on Limoges china, are pigeon Prince Rainier III, noisettes of lamb with star anise, and Breton lobster. The desserts are often grand, like the gourmandises au chocolat, a richness of chocolate served with chocolate sorbet. The dining room is under the watchful eye of the peerless maître d', Christian David.

EXPENSIVE

Chez Pauline. 5 rue Villedo. ☎ **01-42-96-20-70.** Reservations recommended. Main courses 120–155F ($21.60–$27.90); fixed-price menu 220F ($39.60). AE, DC, MC, V. Mon–Fri 12:15–2:30pm and 7:30–10:30pm, Sat 7:30–10:30pm. Métro: Pyramides. BURGUNDIAN/FRENCH.

Many of its loyal fans say that this is a less expensive, less majestic version of Le Grand Véfour. The setting is grand enough to impress a business client and lighthearted enough to attract an impressive roster of VIPs. You'll be ushered to a table on one of two levels, amid polished mirrors, red-leather banquettes, and the memorabilia of long-ago Paris. The emphasis is on the cuisine of central France, especially Burgundy, as shown by the liberal use of wines in time-honored favorites like foie gras; hot oysters; stews swimming with savory herbs and morsels of duck, wild boar, and venison; and boeuf bourguignon. Looking for a way to combine wine with your food in an inseparable way? Sample the terrine of wild hare in an aspic of Pouilly.

MODERATE

Joe Allen. 30 rue Pierre-Lescot. ☎ **01-42-36-70-13.** Reservations recommended for dinner. Main courses 75–140F ($13.50–$25.20). AE, MC, V. Daily noon–1am. Métro: Etienne-Marcel. AMERICAN.

Joe Allen long ago invaded Les Halles with his hamburger. Though the New York restaurateur admits "it's a silly idea," it works. After he set the place up, most of his work went into creating the American burger, easily the best in Paris. While listening to the jukebox, you can order savory black-bean soup, spicy chili, juicy sirloin steak, barbecued spareribs, or apple pie. Try the spinach salad topped with creamy roquefort dressing and sprinkled with crunchy bacon bits and fresh mushrooms. Joe Allen is getting more sophisticated, catering to modern tastes with dishes like grilled salmon with coconut rice and sun-dried tomatoes.

Joe claims that his saloon is the only place in Paris that serves authentic New York cheesecake or real pecan pie. Thanks to French chocolate, he feels that his brownies are better than those in the States. Giving the brownies tough competition are the

California chocolate-mousse pie, strawberries Romanoff, and coconut-cream pie. Thanksgiving dinner is becoming a tradition (you'll need a reservation way in advance). On a regular night, if you haven't made a reservation for dinner, expect to wait at the New York bar for at least 30 minutes.

Il Cortile. In the Hotel Castille, 37 rue Cambon. ☎ **01-40-15-97-64.** Reservations recommended. Main courses 100–150F ($18–$27). AE, DC, MC, V. Mon–Fri noon–2:30pm and 7:30–10:30pm. Métro: Concorde or Madeleine. ITALIAN.

Flanking the verdant courtyard of a small, discreetly elegant hotel, in a district known for its fashion powerhouses and grandiose architecture, this is a much-talked about restaurant whose Italian food is the best in Paris. Its culinary inspiration is French wunderkind Alain Ducasse, whose penchant for fresh and innovative gastronomy is the most debated and talked-about culinary phenomenon in Paris. There are two conservatively modern, beige-and-yellow dining rooms, plus a small courtyard (the Italian staff here refers to it as a "*cortile*") where tables spill over during clement weather. The cuisine is fresh, inventive, and seasonal. There's an emphasis on items from the north of Italy, as shown by a special promotion of wines of Tuscany and the Piedmont. Look for *farfalle* pasta with squid ink and fresh shellfish, fettuccine with pistou, grilled swordfish with grilled and skewered vegetables, and an award-winning version of guinea fowl. Spit-roasted, and served with artfully shaped slices of the bird's gizzard, heart, and liver, it is served with polenta. Service is virtually flawless: you'll get the feeling that many members of the Italian-speaking staff consider their roles as semiofficial ambassadors of goodwill to the Parisians and thus behave with the courtliness and humor of life on a very grand scale.

INEXPENSIVE

Angelina. 226 rue de Rivoli. ☎ **01-42-60-82-00.** Reservations accepted for lunch, not for teatime. Pot of tea for one 35F ($6.30); sandwiches and salads 35–58F ($6.30–$10.45); plats du jour 85–95F ($15.30–$17.10). AE, V. Daily 9am–7pm (lunch served 11:45am–3pm). Métro: Tuileries. TEA/LIGHT FARE.

In the high-rent district near the Hôtel Inter-Continental, this *salon de thé* combines glitter and bourgeois respectability. The carpets are red, the ceilings are high, and the gilded accessories have the right amount of patina. For a view (over tea and delicate sandwiches) of the lionesses of the world of haute couture, this place has no equal. Overwrought waitresses bearing silver trays serve light platters, pastries, drinks, and tea or coffee at tiny marble-top tables. Lunch usually offers a salad and a plat du jour like chicken salad, sole meunière, or poached salmon. The house specialty, designed to go well with a cup of tea, is a Mont Blanc, a combination of chestnut cream and meringue. There are two drawbacks, however: The tearoom is in a section of rue de Ravoli that's getting scuzzy, and the service tends to be a bit snooty.

Café Richelieu. In the Louvre's Richelieu Wing, 34–36 quai du Louvre. ☎ **01-47-03-99-68.** Reservations recommended for meals. Café au lait 22F ($3.95); pastries 16–35F ($2.90–$6.30); salads, sandwiches, and platters 30–51F ($5.40–$9.20). To enter the cafe, you must pay the museum admission. AE, DC, MC, V. Wed 9am–9:30pm, Thurs–Mon 9am–5:30pm. Métro: Palais-Royal–Musée-du-Louvre. INTERNATIONAL.

While in the Louvre, consider stopping for a pick-me-up in the most unusual museum restaurant in Europe. Housed in three grandiose rooms of the premises formerly occupied by the French finance minister, the Richelieu boasts lavish 19th-century adornments and a view over the forecourt's glass pyramid. It's defined as a *café de haute gamme* (upscale cafe), not a restaurant, and the menu is limited to coffee, pastries (by the legendary pastry maker Lenôtre), salads, sandwiches, and simple platters. Far more

A Dining Tip

If a full meal in one of the top spots in Paris is far beyond your means, you can still get a peek into this world by dropping into the bar at **Alain Ducasse** and ordering one of the best arrays of tapas in town (Madrid, eat your heart out). Of course, you'll have to put up with a lot of the increasingly fashionable cigar smoke. And note that **Pierre Gagnaire** features a highly touted plat du jour, costing 150F ($27), at lunch in his bar.

interesting, however, is the arch, witty chitchat you'll overhear in this setting rife with art politics, cultural pride, and bureaucratic intrigue. The carpets, tables, chairs, and computer-generated artworks are modern contrasts (by designer Jean-Michel Wilmotte and photographer Francis Giacobetti) to the building.

✪ **Lescure.** 7 rue de Mondovi. ☎ **01-42-60-18-91.** Reservations not accepted. Main courses 26–84F ($4.70–$15.10); four-course fixed-price menu 100F ($18). V. Mon–Fri noon–2:15pm and 7–11pm. Closed 3 weeks in Aug. Métro: Concorde. FRENCH.

This minibistro is a major find—it's one of the few reasonably priced restaurants near place de la Concorde. It's animated, fun, irreverent, and very appealing. You'll get a lot for your franc here. The tables on the sidewalk are tiny, and there isn't much room inside, but what this place does have is rustic charm. The kitchen is wide open, and the aroma of drying bay leaves, salami, and garlic pigtails hanging from the ceiling fills the room. Expect *cuisine bourgeoise*—nothing too innovative, just substantial, hearty fare. Perhaps begin with *pâté en croûte* (pâté encased in pastry). Main-course house specialties include *confit de canard* (duckling) and cabbage stuffed with salmon. A favorite dessert is one of the chef's fruit tarts.

RIGHT BANK: 2ND ARRONDISSEMENT (LA BOURSE)
MODERATE/EXPENSIVE

Babylone. 34 rue Tiquetonne. ☎ **01-42-33-48-35.** Main courses 70–120F ($12.60–$21.60). V. Daily 8pm–8am. Métro: Etienne-Marcel or Sentier. WEST INDIAN/AFRICAN.

This place honors the French Caribbean island of Guadeloupe, with culinary special-ties of accras of codfish and Créole boudin (blood sausage) that usually prefaces such main courses as fricassée of shrimp or chicken or a colombo (stew) of baby goat. Look for African masks, touches of zebra skin, and photos of the divas and celebrities (like Stevie Wonder and Jesse Jackson) who have dined here. Some (Diana Ross) you might know; others are sports stars and fashion models better known in France. Don't even think of coming here before dark. After 2am or so, the focus shifts away from the hearty Caribbean soul food toward reggae, jazz, and cocktails.

Chez Georges. 1 rue du Mail. ☎ **01-42-60-07-11.** Reservations required. Main courses 100–165F ($18–$29.70). AE, MC, V. Mon–Sat noon–2:15pm and 7–9:45pm. Closed 3 weeks in Aug. Métro: Bourse. FRENCH.

This bistro is something of a local landmark, opened in 1964 near the Bourse. The place has been run by three generations of the Broillet family—George, the patriarch, founded it, and his son, Bernard, manages it today. Naturally, at lunch it's packed with stock-exchange members. The owners serve what they call *la cuisine typiquement bourgeoise*—"food from our grandmère in the provinces." Waiters bring around bowls of appetizers, such as celery rémoulade, to get you started. You can follow with *pot-au-feu* (beef simmered with vegetables), classic cassoulet, or beef braised in red wine. A delight is filet of sole with a sauce made from Pouilly wine and crème fraîche. Beaujolais goes great with this hearty food.

INEXPENSIVE

Au Clair de Lune. 27 rue Française. ☎ **01-42-33-59-10.** Reservations recommended. Main courses 55–70F ($9.90–$12.60); fixed-price menu 62F ($11.15). AE, DC, MC, V. Daily noon–2:30pm and 7:30–11pm. Métro: Etienne-Marcel or Sentier. ALGERIAN/FRENCH.

This neighborhood staple has flourished in the heart of the wholesale garment district since the 1930s, when Algeria was a distinct part of the French-speaking world. Today you'll dine in a long, narrow room whose walls are hung with colorful Berber carpets and whose patrons are likely to include many shop workers from the nearby wholesale clothiers. There's always the Algerian staple of couscous on the menu, as well as an array of such oft-changing daily specials as *blanquette de veau* (veal stew), shoulder or rack of lamb, grilled or pan-fried fish, and roast chicken. The portions are large, so bring your appetite. The wines are from throughout France and North Africa.

RIGHT BANK: 3RD ARRONDISSEMENT (LE MARAIS)
MODERATE

L'Ambassade d'Auvergne. 22 rue de Grenier St-Lazare. ☎ **01-42-72-31-22.** Reservations recommended. Main courses 88–120F ($15.85–$21.60). AE, MC, V. Daily noon–2pm and 7:30–10pm. Métro: Rambuteau. AUVERGNE/FRENCH.

You enter this rustic tavern through a busy bar, with heavy oak beams, hanging hams, and ceramic plates. More than any other Paris restaurant, this favorite showcases the culinary generosity of France's most isolated and slow-to-change region. Consider ordering the 300F ($54) *grand menu dégustation d'Auvergne*—a copious medley of the region's traditional dishes presented in a way that might otherwise have been experienced only at a wedding or family celebration. Both red and white wines from the region are included, along with a collection of *cochonailles* (pork by-products, including sausages and cured ham); the potato, garlic, and cheese medley known as *aligot;* and a savory *pot-au-feu* (beef simmered with vegetables) in the antique style. For dessert there are verveine-flavored ice creams, wine-flavored sorbets, and pastries.

INEXPENSIVE

Chez Janou. 2 rue Roger-Verlomme. ☎ **01-42-72-28-41.** Reservations recommended. Main courses 55–90F ($9.90–$16.20). No credit cards. Daily noon–3pm and 7:30pm–midnight. Métro: Chemin-Vert. PROVENÇAL.

On one of the narrow 17th-century streets behind place des Vosges, this unpretentious bistro operates from a pair of cramped but cozy dining rooms filled with memorabilia from Provence. It includes a covered terrace. Service is brusque and usually somewhat hectic. The menu items include such dishes as *gambas* (large shrimp) with pastis sauce, *brouillade des pleurotes* (baked eggs with oyster mushrooms), *velouté* of frogs' legs, fondue of ratatouille, lamb cutlets, and a simple but savory version of *daube provençale,* which is sometimes compared to pot roast.

RIGHT BANK: 4TH ARRONDISSEMENT (ILE DE LA CITE/ILE ST-LOUIS)
VERY EXPENSIVE

✪ **L'Ambroisie.** 9 place des Vosges. ☎ **01-42-78-51-45.** Reservations required. Main courses 290–500F ($52.20–$90). AE, MC, V. Tues–Sat noon–1:30pm and 8–9:30pm. Métro: St-Paul. FRENCH.

Bernard Pacaud trained at the prestigious Vivarois before deciding to strike out on his own, first on the Left Bank and now at this ideal location in Le Marais. The restaurant occupies an early 17th-century town house built for the duc de Luynes. You'll dine in either of two rooms with high ceilings and a decor vaguely inspired by an Italian palazzo; in summer there's outdoor seating as well. The dishes change seasonally but may include fricassée of Breton lobster with a civet/red-wine sauce; filet of turbot braised with celery and celeriac, served with a julienne of black truffles; and one of our favorites, Bresse chicken roasted with black truffles and truffled vegetables. An award-winning dessert is the bitter-cocoa soufflé.

MODERATE

Bofinger. 5–7 rue de la Bastille. ☎ **01-42-72-87-82.** Reservations recommended. Main courses 76–144F ($13.70–$25.90); fixed-price menu 169F ($30.40). AE, DC, MC, V. Mon–Fri noon–3pm and 6:30pm–1am, Sat–Sun noon–1am. Métro: Bastille. FRENCH/ALSATIAN.

This is Paris's oldest Alsatian brasserie, tracing its origins back to 1864, and its decor is such a part of the Paris landscape that it has been classified a historic landmark. At night, many operagoers venture here for beer and sauerkraut. The brasserie offers excellent Alsatian fare in hearty portions. In 1996 the restaurant was acquired by Les Restaurants de Jean Bucher, losing its independent status but gaining a new lease on life—now affiliated with La Coupole, Julien, and Brasserie Flo, the menu has been updated, retaining only the most popular dishes (such as sauerkraut and sole meunière). Recent additions have included roast leg of lamb with a fondant of artichoke hearts and a purée of parsley, grilled turbot with a brandade of fennel, and filet of stingray with chives and burnt-butter sauce. Shellfish, including lots of fresh oysters and langoustines, is available in season.

Brasserie de l'Ile St-Louis. 55 quai de Bourbon. ☎ **01-43-54-02-59.** Reservations not accepted. Main courses 88–115F ($15.85–$20.70). MC, V. Thurs–Tues noon–midnight. Métro: Pont-Marie. FRENCH/ALSATIAN.

This is the kind of retro-chic brasserie where celebrities sometimes turn up for informal meals and rendezvous. Little about the patina and paneled decor has changed since the 1880s, so the atmosphere can't be matched in more modern nearby competitors. Menu items are flavorful and well prepared, with absolutely no concern for cutting-edge fads and trends. Examples are an always-popular version of Alsatian sauerkraut, cassoulet in the Toulouse style, stingray with a nut-and-butter sauce, calf's liver, and a succulent version of jarret of pork with a warm apple marmalade.

INEXPENSIVE

Chez Jo Goldenberg. 7 rue des Rosiers. ☎ **01-48-87-20-16.** Reservations recommended. Main courses 70–90F ($12.60–$16.20). AE, DC, MC, V. Daily noon–1am. Métro: St-Paul. JEWISH/CENTRAL EUROPEAN.

On the "Street of the Rosebushes" this is the best-known restaurant. Albert Goldenberg, the doyen of Jewish restaurateurs in Paris, long ago moved to a restaurant in choicer surroundings (at 69 av. de Wagram, 17e), but his brother, Joseph, has remained here. Dining is on two levels, one reserved for nonsmokers. Look for the collection of samovars and the white fantail pigeon in a wicker cage. Interesting paintings and strolling musicians add to the ambience. The *carpe farcie* (stuffed carp) is a preferred selection, but the beef goulash is also good. We like the eggplant moussaka and the pastrami. The menu also offers Israeli wines, but M. Goldenberg admits that they're not as good as French wine.

RIGHT BANK: 8TH ARRONDISSEMENT (CHAMPS-ELYSEES/MADELEINE)
VERY EXPENSIVE

Buddha Bar. 8 rue Boissy d'Anglas. ☎ **01-53-05-90-00.** Reservations recommended. Main courses 100–210F ($18–$37.80). AE, MC, V. Daily 7:30pm–12:30am, with seatings arranged 7:30–8:30pm and 11pm–12:30am. Métro: Concorde. FRENCH/PACIFIC RIM.

This place is hot, hot, and hot, and it's truly the restaurant of the moment in Paris. Its location on a chic street near the Champs-Elysées, and its allegiance to a fashionable fusion of French with Asian and Californian cuisine almost guarantee a clientele that seems slavishly devoted to the whims of fashion and trend. That might actually enhance your appreciation of a cutting-edge culinary theme that combines Japanese sashimi, Vietnamese spring rolls, lacquered duck, sautéed shrimp with a black-bean sauce, sweet-and-sour spareribs, and crackling squab à l'orange. Many come here just for a drink in the carefully lacquered, hip-looking bar, which is set upstairs from the street-level dining room. In the twin dining rooms dominated by a plaster-and-fiberglass copy of a tranquil and meditating Buddha, and flanked by walls that are lavishly ornamented with Asian castings and carvings, you can revel in one of the most sophisticated cross-cultural medleys in Paris.

Lasserre. 17 av. Franklin-D.-Roosevelt. ☎ **01-43-59-53-43.** Reservations required. Main courses 140–160F ($25.20–$28.80) at lunch, 240–280F ($43.20–$50.40) at dinner. AE, MC, V. Tues–Sat 12:30–2:30pm, Mon–Sat 7:30–10:30pm. Closed Aug. Métro: Franklin-D.-Roosevelt. FRENCH.

This deluxe restaurant was a simple bistro before World War II. Then came René Lasserre, and today it's one of the few remaining examples of *le grand restaurant à la française*. Behind the front doors are two private dining rooms with a "disappearing wall," plus a reception lounge with Louis XVI furnishings and brocaded walls. You ascend to the second landing in an elevator lined with brocaded silk, where you are seated on a Louis XV salon chair at an exquisite table set with porcelain, gold-edged crystal glasses, a silver bird, a ceramic dove, and a silver candelabra. The ceiling is pulled back in fair weather to reveal the sky.

The appetizers are among the finest in Paris, including a salad of truffles, a three-meat terrine, and Belon oysters flavored with chablis. The fish selections include the signature filet of sole Club de la Casserole (poached filets served in puff pastry with asparagus tips and asparagus-flavored cream sauce). When you taste the meat and poultry dishes, such as veal kidneys flambée or pigeon André Malraux, you'll think Escoffier is still alive. The best of the spectacular desserts are soufflé Grand Marnier and a selection of three freshly made sorbets of the season. The cellar, with 180,000 bottles of wine, is among Paris's most remarkable.

✪ **L'Astor.** In the Hôtel Astor, 11 rue d'Astorg. ☎ **01-53-05-05-20.** Reservations recommended. Main courses 100–500F ($18–$90). AE, DC, MC, V. Mon–Fri noon–2pm and 7:30–10pm. Métro: St-Augustin. FRENCH.

Have you ever wondered what happens to great French chefs after they retire? If they're lucky (and well funded) enough, they become "culinary consultants," dropping in two or three times a week to keep an eye on what's happening. That's what happened when Joël Robuchon retired from his citadel on avenue Raymond-Poincaré. His replacement is the well-respected Eric Lecerf, a formidable force who maintains better than anyone else Robuchon's culinary tours de force. The setting, which moved into this hotel dining room early in 1996, is a gray-and-white enclave with a stained-glass ceiling in the Art Deco style.

Expect a double-tiered menu: items created by Lecerf (roasted and braised rack of lamb, a galette of scallops with sea urchins) cost 100F to 180F ($18 to $32.40). Those invented by Robuchon (truffle tarte, Bresse chicken with truffles and macaroni, gelée of caviar with cauliflower cream sauce) cost 250F to 500F ($45 to $90).

Lucas-Carton (Alain Senderens). 9 place de la Madeleine. ☎ **01-42-65-22-90.** Fax 01-42-65-06-23. Reservations required several days ahead for lunch, several weeks ahead for dinner. Main courses 240–700F ($43.20–$126); fixed-price lunch 395F ($71.10). AE, DC, MC, V. Mon–Fri noon–2:30pm, Mon–Sat 8–10:15pm. Closed 3 weeks in Aug and 3 weeks in Dec. Métro: Madeleine. FRENCH.

This landmark was designed by an Englishman, Lucas, and a talented French chef, François Carton. Since Alain Senderens has taken over, he has added some welcome modern touches. The two dining rooms downstairs and private rooms upstairs are decorated with mirrors, fragrant bouquets, and paneling that has been polished weekly since 1900. Every dish is influenced by Senderens's creative flair. Menu items change seasonally and include ravioli aux truffes (truffles), foie gras with cabbage, duckling Apicius (roasted with honey and spices), and a delectable millefeuille with vanilla sauce. Senderens's latest sensation is *poularde demi-deuil*—a Bresse hen whose flesh has been scored with black truffles; he says that the resulting black-and-white flesh is "in partial mourning," and it's accompanied by saffron-flavored rice.

Maxim's. 3 rue Royale. ☎ **01-42-65-27-94.** Reservations required. Main courses 225–300F ($40.50–$54) at lunch, 265–460F ($47.70–$82.80) at dinner. AE, DC, MC, V. Mon–Sat 12:30–2pm and 7:30–10pm. Métro: Concorde. FRENCH.

Maxim's is the world's most legendary restaurant and even has clones in cities like New York, Beijing, and Tokyo. It preserves the era of belle époque decor and was a favorite of Edward VII, then the prince of Wales. It was the setting for *The Merry Widow,* so you can be sure the orchestra will play that tune at least once each evening. Much later, Louis Jourdan took Leslie Caron to the restaurant in the musical *Gigi.* Today rich tourists from around the world are likely to occupy once-fabled tables where Onassis wooed Callas. The clothing industry giant Pierre Cardin took over the restaurant in 1981. Although not always available, billi-bi soup (made with mussels, white wine, cream, chopped onions, celery, parsley, and coarsely ground pepper) is a classic opener. Another favorite is sole Albert, flavored with chopped herbs and bread crumbs, plus a large glass of vermouth. For dessert, try the tarte Tatin.

✪ **Pierre Gagnaire.** In the Hôtel Balzac, 6 rue Balzac. ☎ **01-44-35-18-25.** Fax 01-44-35-18-37. Reservations imperative (difficult to make). Fixed-price menus 480–860F ($86.40–$154.80) at lunch, 560–860F ($100.80–$154.80) at dinner. AE, DC, MC, V. Mon–Fri 12:30–2:15pm, Sun–Fri 8:15–10pm. Métro: George-V. FRENCH.

In the town of St-Etienne, Pierre Gagnaire rose to greatness and won coveted three-Michelin-star fame. However, his restaurant went into receivership. When he popped up in Paris, operating on the premises of the Hôtel Balzac, all of Paris tried to make its way to Gagnaire's closely guarded door. The chef is hot, but this shy man, who prefers to remain in the kitchen instead of appearing on TV, is hard to reach. In many cases, his reception doesn't even answer the phone from eager callers wanting a reservation. They're often told by an answering machine to fax a "request" for a table. If you do get through, you'll find it worth the effort.

Gagnaire's menus are seasonally adjusted to take advantage of France's bounty, and he blends flavors and textures in ways that are dazzling. One critic wrote, "Picasso stretched the limits of painting; Gagnaire does it with cooking." Begin, perhaps, with a first course of tiny Provençal artichokes and raw, paper-thin black truffles bathed in a cream of Jerusalem artichokes. After that, try anything, especially the turbot wrapped in herb leaves and served with a side dish of celeriac lasagne or the bundles of rolled farm chicken roasted in goose fat and braised in an aromatic medley of spices, onions, and carrots. Another standout is smoked bacon in a casserole with pan-roasted rabbit kidneys and sea snails, with a bean purée flavored with Chinese peppercorns. It's hard to match that.

✪ **Taillevent.** 15 rue Lamennais. ☎ **01-44-95-15-01.** Fax 01-42-25-95-18. Reservations required weeks, even months, in advance. Main courses 295–500F ($53.10–$90). AE, DC, MC, V. Mon–Fri noon–2:30pm and 7–10pm. Closed Aug. Métro: George-V. FRENCH.

Dine in grand 18th-century style in this town house just off the Champs-Elysées. In 1946, when owner Jean Claude Vrinat's father opened the doors, he established one of Paris's outstanding restaurants. The competition is great, but this is the number one dining choice in Paris. The wines are superb, and the service is impeccable. Under chef Philippe Legendre, the menus are deftly balanced between traditional and modern cuisine. You might begin with aspic de foie gras (liver and veal sweetbreads in aspic with slivers of carrots and truffles). Main-dish specialties are cassolette de langoustines (casserole of prawns) and *agneau aux trois cuissons* (feet, breast, and tenderloin of lamb with various sauces). A star dessert is the *fondant aux deux parfumes* (an almond-toffee Bavarian cream covered with chocolate).

MODERATE

Androuët. 6 rue Arsène-Houssaye. ☎ **01-42-89-95-00.** Reservations required. Main courses 100–180F ($18–$32.40); fixed-price menus 140–300F ($25.20–$54); dégustation de fromages 270F ($48.60). AE, DC, MC, V. Mon–Fri noon–3pm and Mon–Sat 7:30–11pm. Métro: Charles-de-Gaulle–Etoile. FRENCH.

This is one of the world's most unusual restaurants, as cheese is the basic ingredient in most dishes. It all began in 1909, when the founder, M. Androuët, started inviting favored guests down to his cellar to sample cheese and good wine. The idea caught on. Today Androuët isn't merely chic—it's an institution. To accommodate its continued and growing popularity, it moved to new headquarters in spring 1997. Cheese experts, of course, flock here; we've heard one claim that he could tell what the goat ate by the cheese made from its milk. For a first course, the ravioles de chèvre frais (ravioli stuffed with fresh goat cheese) is wonderful. A good main dish is *filet de boeuf cotentin* (beef filet with roquefort sauce, flambéed with Calvados). True cheese lovers order the *dégustation de fromages affinés dans nos caves* (a sampling of cheese). There are as many as 120 varieties.

RIGHT BANK: 9TH ARRONDISSEMENT (OPERA GARNIER/PIGALLE)
VERY EXPENSIVE

Restaurant Opéra. In the Grand Hôtel Inter-Continental, place de l'Opéra. ☎ **01-40-07-30-10.** Reservations recommended. Main courses 113–315F ($20.35–$56.70); fixed-price menus 245–355F ($44.10–$63.90). AE, DC, MC, V. Mon–Fri noon–2pm and 7:30–10:30pm. Métro: Opéra. FRENCH.

Dine here with the ghosts of Dalí, Josephine Baker, Dietrich, Chevalier, Callas, and Chagall, who often came here while working on the famous ceiling of the nearby Opéra Garnier. On August 25, 1944, de Gaulle placed this restaurant's first food order in a newly freed Paris—a cold plate to go. Today you can enjoy a before-dinner drink in the ornate bar before heading for a table in what some diners compare to a gilded jewel box. Appetizers may include lobster bisque with champagne or deep-fried frogs' legs with tomato and cauliflower in the Greek style. The most sumptuous main courses are sweetbreads cooked in walnut butter, filet of John Dory with celery, and rack of veal (divided into veal chops and prepared only for two), garnished with wild mushrooms and small new potatoes. Chocoholics will find Nirvana with the Tour Chocolat.

MODERATE

✪ **Au Petit Riche.** 25 rue Le Peletier. ☎ **01-47-70-68-68.** Reservations recommended. Main courses 90–140F ($16.20–$25.20); fixed-price menus 160F ($28.80) at lunch, 135–175F ($24.30–$31.50) at dinner. AE, DC, MC, V. Mon–Sat noon–2:30pm and 7pm–12:15am. Métro: Le Peletier or Richelieu-Drouot. LOIRE VALLEY (ANJOU).

When it opened in 1865, this bistro was conceived as the food outlet for the grandly ornate Café Riche next door. Today, all that remains is the bistro, serving simple but well-prepared bistro food and a sense of nostalgia for another time. You'll be ushered to one of five "compartments," each of which was crafted for maximum intimacy, with red velour banquettes, ceilings painted with allegorical themes, and accents of brass and frosted glass. The wine list favors Loire Valley vintages that go well with such dishes as *rillettes* and *rillons* (potted fish or meat, especially pork) in a Vouvray wine aspic, poached fish with a buttery white-wine sauce, seasonal game like civet of rabbit, roast pork with lentils, and duck breast roasted with green peppercorns.

Chez Jean. 8 rue St-Lazare. ☎ **01-48-78-62-73.** Reservations recommended. Main courses 175–200F ($31.50–$36); fixed-price menu 175F ($31.50). MC, V. Daily noon–2pm and 7:30–10:30pm. Métro: Notre-Dame de Lorette, Opéra, or Cadet.

There's been a brasserie of one sort or another on this site since 1900, and some specialties here remain intact from the days of Clemenceau. You'll dine in one of two rooms, amid well-oiled panels and carefully polished copper, feasting on menu items that include some of grandmother's favorites. More modern dishes include risotto with lobster and squid ink, scallops with a fricassée of endive, a "nougat" of oxtails with a balsamic-flavored vinaigrette, a combination of mussels and fennel, and a pavé of duckling served with honey sauce and a fricassée of exotic mushrooms. The menu changes virtually every day, a fact that attracts lots of fans who consider its food a lot more sophisticated than what's featured within many other brasseries.

RIGHT BANK: 10TH ARRONDISSEMENT (GARE DU NORD/GARE DE L'EST)
MODERATE

Brasserie Flo. 7 cour des Petites-Ecuries. ☎ **01-47-70-13-59.** Reservations recommended. Main courses 70–140F ($12.60–$25.20); fixed-price menu 123F ($22.15) at lunch, 169F ($30.40) at dinner, 128F ($23.05) at late supper (after 10pm). AE, DC, MC, V. Daily noon–3pm and 7pm–1:30am. Métro: Château-d'Eau or Strasbourg–St-Denis. ALSATIAN.

This restaurant, in a remote area, is a bit hard to find, but once you arrive (after walking through passageway after passageway), you'll see that fin-de-siècle Paris lives on. The restaurant was opened in 1860, and the decor has changed very little. The thing to order is the delicious formidable choucroute, but don't expect just a heap of sauerkraut—the mound is surrounded by ham, bacon, and sausages. It's bountiful in the best tradition of Alsace. The onion soup is always delectable and full of rich flavor, as is the guinea hen with lentils. Look for the plats du jour, ranging from roast pigeon to fricassée of veal with sorrel.

Julien. 16 rue du Faubourg St-Denis. ☎ **01-47-70-12-06.** Reservations required. Main courses 80–130F ($14.40–$23.40); fixed-price lunch and late supper (after 10pm) 128F ($23.05). AE, DC, MC, V. Daily noon–3pm and 7pm–1:30am. Métro: Strasbourg–St-Denis. FRENCH.

This is one of the most sumptuous restaurants in Paris. The building was conceived in 1889 for the Universal Exposition yet didn't open until 1903. Until 1976 it was a famous working-class eatery and has now been restored to its former elegance. The food is *cuisine bourgeoise* but without the heavy sauces. The perfectly prepared appetizers include smoked salmon rillettes (minced), duckling foie gras, and snails à la bourguignon. Among the main courses are a cassoulet of Gascony, salmon with sorrel, and chateaubriand béarnaise. The wine list is extensive and reasonably priced.

✪ **La P'tite Tonkinoise**. 56 rue du Faubourg-Poissonière. ☎ **01-42-46-85-98.** Reservations recommended. Main courses 85–140F ($15.30–$25.20); fixed-price lunch 133F ($23.95). AE, DC, MC, V. Mon–Fri noon–2pm, Mon–Sat 7:30–10:15pm. Closed Aug. Métro: Poissonière or Bonne-Nouvelle. VIETNAMESE.

Paris has hundreds of Vietnamese restaurants, and this is our favorite. Named after the diminutive matriarch who has run this place since 1972, La P'tite Tonkinoise provides an exceptional opportunity to learn more about Tonkin (the 19th-century Asian province later renamed North Vietnam) and its culture and cuisine. The decor mimics a Vietnamese hut, with walls almost completely sheathed in bamboo. The dining room can accommodate only about 30 at a time. Menu items, usually based on seafood, chicken, or pork, are less spicy than you might expect. A perennial favorite (served only Friday and Saturday) is my sao, stir-fried vegetables served on a crispy rice cake and garnished with shrimp.

RIGHT BANK: 12TH ARRONDISSEMENT (BOIS DE VINCENNES/GARE DE LYON)
VERY EXPENSIVE

Au Trou Gascon. 40 rue Taine. ☎ **01-43-44-34-26.** Reservations required. Main courses 130–160F ($23.40–$28.80); fixed-price menu 200F ($36) at lunch, 320F ($57.60) at dinner. AE, DC, MC, V. Mon–Fri noon–2pm and 7:30–10pm, Sat 7:30–10pm. Closed Aug. Métro: Daumesnil. GASCONY.

Alain Dutournier launched his career in southwestern Gascony, working in the kitchen with his mother and grandmother. His parents mortgaged the inn they owned to allow him to open a turn-of-the-century bistro in an unchic part of the 12th arrondissement, where word soon spread that he was a true artist. Today he has opened another restaurant. The owner's wife, Nicole, is here to greet you, and Dutournier has distinguished himself with an extensive cellar (more than 800 varieties) containing several little-known wines along with an array of armagnacs. Here you get the true cuisine of Gascony: cassoulet, wild salmon with smoked bacon, foie gras, and Gascon ham farmer's style. We suggest that you order the roasted chicken from the Chalosse region of Landes, served in its own drippings.

MODERATE/EXPENSIVE

Le Train Bleu. In the Gare de Lyon, 20 bd. Diderot. ☎ **01-43-43-09-06.** Reservations recommended. Main courses 95–165F ($17.10–$29.70); fixed-price menu (including wine) 250F ($45). AE, DC, MC, V. Daily 11:30am–3pm and 7–11pm (last orders). Métro: Gare-de-Lyon. FRENCH.

Though the food is quite standard and a bit overpriced, the setting makes it worthwhile. To reach this restaurant, climb the ornate double staircase that faces the Gare de Lyon's grimy platforms. Both the restaurant and the station were built with the Grand Palais, Petit Palais, and pont Alexandre III for the 1900 World Exhibition. The architects designed a restaurant whose decor is now classified as a national artistic treasure. Opened in 1901 and renovated and cleaned at great expense in 1992, it displays an army of bronze statues, a frescoed ceiling, mosaics, mirrors, and old-fashioned banquettes. Each of the 41 murals celebrates the distant corners of the French-speaking world—the depictions of Marseille, Algiers, and the North African port of Sousse are particularly appealing. The service is attentive and efficient in case you must catch a train. The staff brings steaming platters of brill soufflé, escargots in chablis sauce, steak tartare, loin of lamb provençal, and rib of beef for two.

RIGHT BANK: 16TH ARRONDISSEMENT (TROCADERO/BOIS DE BOULOGNE)
VERY EXPENSIVE

✪ **Alain Ducasse.** 59 av. Raymond-Poincaré. ☎ **01-47-27-12-27.** Fax 01-47-27-31-22. Reservations required, 6 weeks in advance. Main courses 325–490F ($58.50–$88.20); fixed-price menus 490F ($88.20) at lunch, 920–1,450F ($165.60–$261) at dinner. AE, DC, MC, V. Mon–Fri noon–1:45pm and 7:30–10pm. Métro: Trocadéro. FRENCH/MEDITERRANEAN.

The celebrated Monte Carlo chef has taken Paris by storm since taking over the reigns here from the great Joël Robuchon (now consultant at L'Astor). This six-star Michelin chef (three for Paris, three for Monte Carlo) divides his time between Paris and Monaco. Why so many stars? Ducasse brilliantly refines and defines produce from every region of France in this restored four-story mansion. On the ground floor is a bar stocked with rare brandies and fine cigars. Taking advantage of his southern roots, Ducasse includes typically Mediterranean dishes on his menu. He serves fish from the French coasts and vegetables from all over France. Though many dishes are light, Ducasse isn't afraid of lard, as in his thick, oozingly delicious slabs of pork grilled to a crisp. He has kept a single Robuchon dish as a tribute: the famed caviar in aspic with cauliflower cream. The food remains sober in presentation, true, precise, and authentic in flavor. Ducasse told us, "The tasting of a dish must leave a remembrance. If nothing remains in the memory of a single guest, I have fooled myself."

The wine list is based on the fine existing cellar left by Robuchon and noted for its classic composition, extensiveness, and high quality. Ducasse has added many new acquisitions from the vineyards of France but has also opened his cellar to young wine growers, including those from Germany, Switzerland, Spain, and Italy.

✪ **Jamin.** 32 rue de Longchamp. ☎ **01-45-53-00-07.** Fax: 01-45-53-00-15. Reservations imperative. Main courses 120–185F ($21.60–$33.30); fixed-price menus 280–375F ($50.40–$67.50) at lunch, 375F ($67.50) at dinner. AE, DC, MC, V. Mon–Fri noon–2pm and 7:30–10:15pm. Métro: Trocadéro. FRENCH.

In the 1980s the great Joël Robuchon became a sensation here. Nowadays, Benoit Guichard, longtime second in command, is in charge. Clearly inspired by his master, he is also an imaginative and inventive chef in his own right. Guichard has chosen pale-green panels and pink banquettes for a soothing backdrop to his short but well-chosen menu. Classic technique and an homage to tradition characterize the cuisine, with offerings like pan-fried veal flank steak with drop-dead potatoes laced with Cantal cheese. You might start with ocean-fresh Brittany langoustines married to spaghetti-sized strips of ginger-laced squid. The beef shoulder is so tender it obviously is braised for hours. Unafraid of meat by-products, this chef has created a "sonnet to the sow," where he earthily blends the robust cheeks and tail of the animal with golden pan-fried potatoes. His wife, Marjorie, is on hand, as is his dream team of chefs. Finish off with a tarte Tatin that deserves an award.

MODERATE

La Butte Chaillot. 110 bis av. Kléber. ☎ **01-47-27-88-88.** Reservations recommended. Main courses 98–118F ($17.65–$21.25). AE, MC, V. Daily noon–2:30pm and 7pm–midnight. Métro: Trocadéro. FRENCH.

This "baby bistro" showcases the cuisine of high priest Guy Savoy. It draws lots of corporate types from the affluent surrounding neighborhood, who congregate in the congested but posh dining areas. Menu items change weekly (sometimes daily), depending on whatever is in season, and are carefully and artfully packaged. Examples are a sophisticated medley of terrines, codfish steak with herbs, a salad of snails and herbed potatoes, grilled filet of rascasse (scorpion fish) with ginger and lemon, succulent rack of lamb, and *raviolis du Royans aux herbes fines* (cheese ravioli with herbs).

RIGHT BANK: 17TH ARRONDISSEMENT (PARC MONCEAU/PLACE CLICHY)
VERY EXPENSIVE

✪ **Guy Savoy.** 18 rue Troyon. ☎ **01-43-80-40-61.** Fax 01-46-22-43-09. Reservations required a week in advance. Main courses 280–350F ($50.40–$63); menu dégustation 880F ($158.40). AE, MC, V. Mon–Fri noon–2:30pm and 7:30–10:30pm, Sat 7–10:30pm. Métro: Charles-de-Gaulle–Etoile. FRENCH.

Guy Savoy is among Europe's hottest chefs, and both the restaurant and the cuisine bear his signature style. His cooking almost always takes its inspiration from the market. Save your appetite and order his nine-course menu dégustation. Perhaps you'll get red mullet and wild asparagus; cassoulet of snails with tarragon; or chicken quenelles (a sort of dumpling) with chicken livers and cream, garnished with black truffles. Depending on when you visit, you may have the pleasure of tasting Savoy's masterfully prepared mallard, venison, or game birds. He's fascinated with mushrooms and has been known to serve as many as a dozen types, especially in autumn. One of his most delectable dishes is fresh oysters in a frozen aspic of their own juices.

✪ **Michel Rostang.** 20 rue Rennequin. ☎ **01-47-63-40-77.** Reservations required. Main courses 235–320F ($42.30–$57.60); fixed-price menus 325–800F ($58.50–$144). AE, MC, V. Mon–Fri 12:30–2:30pm, Mon–Sat 7:30–10:30pm. Closed 2 weeks in Aug. Métro: Ternes. FRENCH.

Michel Rostang is a creative fifth-generation chef from one of France's most distinguished cooking families. From Grenoble, he eventually came to the 17th arrondissement, where the world soon came to dine at what he modestly calls his "boutique restaurant" seating up to 70. Menu choices may include ravioli filled with goat cheese and sprinkled with chervil bought fresh from the market, as well as Bresse chicken, the finest in France. From October to March he prepares quail eggs with sea urchins. On occasion he also concocts a delicate fricassée of sole or duckling cooked in its own blood. One dish worth the trek across town is a galette of artichokes with fresh truffles and duckling foie gras, served in a cream sauce that has been reduced and flavored with vinegar. Wines from the Rhône are available, including Châteauneuf du Pape and Hermitage.

EXPENSIVE

Bistro d'à Côté. 10 rue Flaubert. ☎ **01-42-67-05-81.** Reservations recommended. Main courses 140–180F ($25.20–$32.40). AE, MC, V. Daily 12:30–2pm and 7:30–11pm. Métro: Ternes. FRENCH.

This is one of four baby bistros scattered across Paris, each of which features a pared-down, less expensive version of the haute gastronomy developed by the superstar Michel Rostang. As this branch is next door to the temple where Michel Rostang reigns, it's the most interesting. You'll enter a nostalgically decorated dining area ringed with unusual porcelain and antique copies of Michelin guides, some of which date from 1900. The place is stylishly informal and chic, with a simple menu that's enhanced by daily chalkboard specials. Tantalizing items include ravioli stuffed with

In case you want to be welcomed there.

We're here to see that you're always welcomed at establishments everywhere. That's why millions of people carry the American Express® Card—for peace of mind, confidence, and security, around the world or just around the corner.

do more®

AMERICAN EXPRESS

Cards

In case you're running low.

We're here to help with more than 118,000 Express Cash locations around the world. In order to enroll, just call American Express before you start your vacation.

do more

AMERICAN EXPRESS

Express Cash

And just in case.

We're here with American Express® Travelers Cheques and Cheques *for Two.*® They're the safest way to carry money on your vacation and the surest way to get a refund, practically anywhere, anytime.

Another way we help you...

do more

AMERICAN EXPRESS

Travelers Cheques

ⓘ Family-Friendly Restaurants

Crémerie-Restaurant Polidor *(see p. 121)* One of the most popular restaurants on the Left Bank, this reasonably priced dining room is so family-friendly it even calls its food *cuisine familiale*. This might be the best place to introduce your child to French cuisine.

Joe Allen *(see p. 105)* Joe Allen delivers everything from chili to chocolate-mousse pie. This place in Les Halles serves real American cuisine, including the best hamburgers in Paris.

pulverized lobster, roasted Bresse chicken accompanied by a salad of chicken thighs and herbs, and a rable de lievre (rabbit stew) en cocotte.

MODERATE

Bistro de l'Etoile. 19 rue Lauriston. ☎ **01-40-67-11-16.** Reservations recommended. Main courses 89–105F ($16–$18.90); fixed-price lunch 165F ($29.70). AE, MC, V. Mon–Fri noon–2:30pm and Mon–Sat 7:30pm–midnight. AE, MC, V. Métro: Charles-de-Gaulle–Etoile. FRENCH.

This is the most interesting of three baby bistros, all with the same name, clustered around place Charles-de-Gaulle. Each benefits from sponsorship by the superstar Guy Savoy, who inspires affordable versions of the haute cuisine featured in his nearby restaurant. The setting is a warmly contemporary dining room in butterscotch and caramel. Menu items include a mijotée of cheeks of pork with sage as well as codfish studded with lard and prepared with coconut-lime sauce. An interesting starter is a sampler of three of Savoy's creations: a cup of lentil cream soup, a fondant of celery, and a pan-fried slice of foie gras. Expect some odd terms on the dessert menu, which only a chef can fully describe. An example is spice bread baked like pain perdu, garnished with banana sorbet and pineapple sauce.

Rôtisserie d'Armaillé. 6 rue d'Armaillé. ☎ **01-42-27-19-20.** Reservations recommended. Fixed-price menus 165–218F ($29.70–$39.25). AE, DC, MC, V. Mon–Fri noon–2:30pm and Mon–Sat 7:30–11pm. Métro: Charles-de-Gaulle–Etoile. FRENCH.

The impresario behind this baby bistro is Jacques Cagna, who originally established his star role in the Latin Quarter long ago. This chic place, ringed with light wood paneling and banquettes with patterns of pink and green, bristles with businesspeople and the residents and shoppers of this grand neighborhood, which surrounds the place d'Etoile. You have only two options at both lunch and dinner—the 218F meal or the less-expensive 165F meal. Menu choices include flan of wild mushrooms with red-wine sauce, terrine of foie gras, a salad of sweetbreads and crayfish, scorpion fish (rascasse) en papillote, and rack of lamb accented with parsley and sage. The artwork features bucolic depictions of the cows, pigs, and lambs that are likely to be among the menu's grilled steaks and chops.

LEFT BANK: 5TH ARRONDISSEMENT (LATIN QUARTER)
VERY EXPENSIVE

✪ **La Tour d'Argent.** 15–17 quai de la Tournelle. ☎ **01-43-54-23-31.** Fax 01-44-07-12-04. Reservations required, far in advance. Main courses 200–400F ($36–$72); fixed-price lunch 350F ($63). AE, DC, MC, V. Tues–Sun noon–2:30pm and 8–10:30pm. Métro: Maubert-Mutualité or Pont-Marie. CLASSIC FRENCH.

The penthouse Tour d'Argent is a national institution, boasting a panoramic view over the Seine and the apse of Notre-Dame. Although this restaurant's position as the best in Paris has long been taken over by Taillevent and others, dining here remains a major theatrical event. Since the 16th century there has always been a restaurant on this spot. It became famous when it was owned by Frédéric Delair, who purchased the wine cellar of the Café Anglais and began issuing certificates to diners who ordered the house specialty, pressed duck (*caneton*). Today La Tour d'Argent is under the direction of the debonair Claude Terrail.

The cuisine is classically French. New diners often order the duck—it's sensational. Other selections are filet de sole cardinal and filet Tour d'Argent. Begin with the potage (soup) Claudius Burdel made with sorrel, egg yolks, fresh cream, chicken broth, and butter whipped together. For dessert, the *pêches flambées* (flambéed peaches) is marvelous.

EXPENSIVE

Auberge des Deux Signes. 46 rue Galande. ☎ **01-43-25-46-56.** Reservations required for dinner. Main courses 136–192F ($24.50–$34.55); fixed-price menu 150F ($27) at lunch, 230F ($41.40) at dinner. AE, DC, MC, V. Mon–Fri 12:30–2pm, Mon–Sat 7:30–10:30pm. Closed Aug. Métro: Maubert-Mutualité or St-Michel. FRENCH/AUVERGNE.

The Auvergne-born Georges Dhulster has taken over this medieval building, which once served as the Chapel of St-Blaise, and many visitors come here in the evening to enjoy the view of floodlit Notre-Dame and St-Julien-le-Pauvre (without having to pay La Tour d'Argent's prices). Try for a table upstairs, with a view of the garden. The cuisine is Auvergne with a twist and we recommend the veal medallions with morels, beef from the Aurillac in central France, and goose confit with flap mushrooms. Be prepared, at times, to wait for a table (even if you have a reservation).

INEXPENSIVE

✪ **Perraudin.** 157 rue St-Jacques. ☎ **01-46-33-15-75.** Reservations not accepted. Main courses 59F ($10.60); fixed-price lunch 63F ($11.35). No credit cards. Tues–Fri noon–2:15pm, Mon–Sat 7:30–10:15pm. Métro: Cluny–La Sorbonne. RER: Luxembourg. FRENCH.

Everything about this place—decor, cuisine, low prices, and service rituals—attempts to duplicate the bustling Parisian bistros at the turn of the century. The walls look as if they've been marinated in tea for about a year; marble-top tables, old mirrors, and posters of Parisian vaudeville of the cancan years complete the picture. You don't make reservations: instead, diners usually drink a glass of kir at the zinc-top bar as they wait. (Tables turn over quickly.) Marie-Christine K'vella and her brother offer old-fashioned dishes that include roast leg of lamb with dauphinois potatoes, beef bourguignon, grilled salmon with sage sauce, and blanquette of veal in white sauce. Any of these might be preceded with onion tart, pumpkin soup, snails, or any of several pâtés or terrines.

✪ **Petite Hostellerie.** 35 rue de la Harpe (a side street running north of bd. St-Germain, just east of bd. St-Michel). ☎ **01-43-54-47-12.** Fixed-price menus 55–70F ($9.90–$12.60) at lunch, 59–89F ($10.60–$16) at dinner. AE, DC, MC, V. Tues–Sat noon–2pm, Mon–Sat 7–11pm. Closed Aug 3–23. Métro: St-Michel or Cluny–La Sorbonne. FRENCH.

This place has two dining rooms: a usually crowded ground-floor one and a larger (seating 100) upstairs one with attractive 18th-century woodwork. Since 1902 diners have been coming here for the cozy ambience and decor, decent French country cooking, polite service, and excellent prices. The fixed-price dinner menu might feature favorites like *coq au vin* (chicken in wine), *canard* (duckling) *à l'orange*, and *entrecôte à la moutarde* (steak with mustard sauce). Start with onion soup or stuffed mussels and finish with cheese or salad and *pêches Melba* (peach Melba) or *tarte aux pommes* (apple tart).

LEFT BANK: 6TH ARRONDISSEMENT (ST-GERMAINE/LUXEMBOURG)

VERY EXPENSIVE

✪ **Jacques Cagna.** 14 rue des Grands-Augustins. ☎ **01-43-26-49-39.** Reservations required. Main courses 230–389F ($41.40–$70); fixed-price menu 240F ($43.20) at lunch, 470F ($84.60) at dinner. AE, DC, MC, V. Mon–Fri noon–2pm, Mon–Sat 7:30–10:30pm. Closed 3 weeks in Aug. Métro: St-Michel. FRENCH.

In a 17th-century town house, Jacques Cagna is a place where both the patrons and the food are among the grandest in Paris. Its pinkish-beige interior is filled with massive timbers and 17th-century Dutch paintings. A specialty is the Aberdeen Angus beef, aged for 3 weeks, which Cagna imbues with a rich shallot-flavored sauce. Each dish is sublime: rack of veal with ginger-and-lime sauce, breast of duck with burgundy sauce, line-caught sea bass with caviar in a potato shell, and fried scallops with celery and potatoes in truffle sauce. The menu changes according to the season and the inspiration of the chef. If you're lucky, he'll offer his carpaccio of sea bream with a rémoulade of celery garnished with caviar.

EXPENSIVE

Closerie des Lilas. 171 bd. du Montparnasse. ☎ **01-40-51-34-50.** Reservations required. Main courses 190–250F ($34.20–$45) in the restaurant, 90–130F ($16.20–$23.40) in the brasserie. AE, DC, V. Restaurant, daily noon–3pm and 7:30pm–midnight; brasserie, daily 11:30am–1am. Métro: Port-Royal or Vavin. FRENCH.

The number of famous people who've dined here watching the fallen leaves blow along the Montparnasse streets is almost countless: Stein and Toklas, Ingres, Henry James, Chateaubriand, Lenin and Trotsky, Proust, Sartre and de Beauvoir, and Whistler. Since getting a seat in the *bateau* (brasserie) section is difficult, you can while away the hours waiting at the bar and ordering the best champagne julep in the world. Once seated in the brasserie, you can select dishes like poached haddock and steak tartare. In the chic restaurant, the cooking is classic. Try the escargots (snails) façon Closerie for openers. Of the main-course selections, the *rognons de veau à la moutarde* (veal kidneys with mustard) and ribs of veal in cider sauce are highly recommended. Both sections are on the street level—the brasserie faces boulevard du Montparnasse, while the restaurant looks out onto boulevard du Port-Royal.

MODERATE

Aux Charpentiers. 10 rue Mabillon. ☎ **01-43-26-30-05.** Reservations required. Main courses 71–185F ($12.80–$33.30); fixed-price menu 120F ($21.60) at lunch, 158F ($28.45) at dinner. AE, DC, MC, V. Daily noon–3pm and 7:30–11:30pm. Métro: Mabillon. FRENCH.

Aux Charpentiers used to be the rendezvous of master carpenters, whose guild was next door. Nowadays it's full of young couples on dates. Although not especially imaginative, the food is well prepared in the best tradition of *cuisine bourgeoise*. Appetizers include pâté of duck and rabbit terrine. Especially recommended as a main course is the roast duck with olives. Each day a different plat du jour is offered, with time-tested French home cooking: *Pot-au-feu* (beef simmered with vegetables) and *petit salé of pork* (derived from boiling salted pork, then reheating it with richly seasoned lentils) are among the main dishes. The chef suggests the platters of fresh fish. There's a large choice of Bordeaux wines direct from the châteaux. The reactions of readers to this restaurant have been mixed over the years, ranging from "How dare you send me to that dive!" to "We took all our meals here—and how good they were!"

✪ **Chez Diane.** 25 rue Servandoni. ☎ **01-46-33-12-06.** Reservations recommended for groups of 4 or more. Main courses 90–130F ($16.20–$23.40); fixed-price menu 150F ($27). V. Mon–Fri noon–2pm, Mon–Sat 8–11:30pm. Métro: St-Sulpice. FRENCH.

Although its prices say "simple bistro," this place serves a surprisingly chic and sophis-ticated cuisine. This is a result of the care and dedication of Didier and Diane Derrieux. Designed to accommodate only 40 diners at a time, the site is illuminated with Venetian glass chandeliers and paved with floor tiles manufactured near Aix-en-Provence. The menu changes seasonally and with the inspiration of the owners. Examples are Toulouse-inspired cassoulet of fish with emulsified-butter sauce, minced salmon prepared as a terrine with green peppercorns, and a light-textured adaptation of a dish every French-born diner remembers, *hachis Parmentier* (elegant meat loaf lightened with parsley, chopped onions, and herbs). The fish dishes are likely to include turbot with béarnaise sauce and stingray with caper-flavored butter sauce.

La Bastide Odéon. 7 rue Corneille. ☎ **01-43-26-03-65.** Reservations recommended. Fixed-price menus 150–190F ($27–$34.20). MC, V. Tues–Sat 12:30–2:15pm and 7:30–11pm. Métro: Odéon. RER: Luxembourg. PROVENÇAL.

This brasserie has recently developed into a star. The decor evokes the sunny climes of southern France with its pale-yellow walls, heavy oaken tables, and bouquets of dried wheat and flowers. Chef Gilles Ajuelos prepares a market-based Provençal cuisine that varies according to his inspiration and the available ingredients. The simplest first courses seem the most satisfying, like a platter of sardines and seared sweet peppers with olive oil and pine nuts, grilled eggplant layered with herbs and olive oil, and roast rabbit stuffed with eggplant and served with olive toast and balsamic vinegar. Main courses include wild duckling with pepper sauce, stuffed suckling pig with a gratin of polenta and parmesan, and lambs' feet and giblets prepared in the age-old Provençal style. Pastas (creamy tagliatelle with clams and parsley is especially savory) can be pre-pared as a starter or a main course. A dessert winner is warm almond pie with prune-and-armagnac ice cream.

Le Procope. 13 rue de l'Ancienne-Comédie. ☎ **01-40-46-79-00.** Reservations recom-mended. Main courses 82–148F ($14.75–$26.65); fixed-price menu 109F ($19.60) 11:30am–8pm, 170F ($30.60) all day, 125F ($22.50) after 11pm. AE, DC, MC, V. Daily 11:30am–1am. Métro: Odéon. FRENCH.

Paris's oldest cafe, Le Procope was opened in 1686 by a Sicilian named Francesco Pro-copio dei Coltelli. The art of coffee drinking was popularized here, brought from Italy. Along the walls are portraits of former patrons—Franklin, Rousseau, Robespierre, Danton, Marat, Bonaparte, and Balzac, among others. The cafe is more of a restau-rant today than it was originally. There are two levels for dining: the spacious upstairs section and the more intimate street-level room. Fresh oysters and shellfish are served from a refrigerated display. Well-chosen French classics include baby duckling with spices, "drunken chicken," and "green coffee." The fare isn't in any way remarkable, but few places have the nostalgia of this venerated cafe. Its major drawback is that it's too touristy and famous for its own good.

✪ Rôtisserie d'en Face. 2 rue Christine. ☎ **01-43-26-40-98.** Reservations recommended. Fixed-price menu 210F ($37.80). AE, MC, V. Mon–Fri noon–2:30pm and 7–11pm, Sat 7–11pm. Métro: St-Michel. FRENCH.

This is the most packed baby bistro in Paris, operated by Jacques Cagna, whose vastly more expensive eponymous restaurant is across the street. And this place has earned its popularity, because the food, though simply prepared, is very good, using high-quality ingredients. The place features a postmodern decor with high-tech lighting and black lacquer chairs. Menu items include several types of ravioli, a pâté of duck-ling en croûte with foie gras, *friture d'éperlans* (tiny fried freshwater fish), smoked Scot-tish salmon with spinach, and several types of fresh fish and grilled meats. Pork cheeks is based on an old-fashioned recipe passed down to Cagna from his mother. The Barbary duckling in red-wine sauce is incomparable.

Yugaraj. 14 rue Dauphine. ☎ **01-43-26-44-91.** Reservations recommended. Main courses 98–120F ($17.65–$21.60); fixed-price menus 130–220F ($23.40–$39.60) at lunch, 170–220F ($30.60–$39.60) at dinner. AE, DC, MC, V. Tues–Sun noon–2:15pm, daily 7–11pm. Métro: Odéon. INDIAN.

In an old but not particularly historic Latin Quarter building, this restaurant serves moderately priced, flavorful food based on the recipes of northern and (to a lesser degree) southern India. Here you can sample the spicy, aromatic tandoori dishes that are all the rage in France. Seafood specialties are usually concocted from warm-water fish from the Seychelles and include species with names like thiof (an Indian Ocean whitefish), capitaine, and bourgeois, prepared Calcutta style, with tomatoes, onions, cumin, coriander, ginger, and garlic. The flavors are spicy and earthy, rich with mint and sometimes touches of yogurt.

INEXPENSIVE

✪ **Crémerie-Restaurant Polidor.** 41 rue Monsieur-le-Prince. ☎ **01-43-26-95-34.** Reservations not accepted. Main courses 40–69F ($7.20–$12.40); fixed-price menu 55F ($9.90) at lunch Mon–Fri, 100F ($18) at dinner Mon–Fri. No credit cards. Daily noon–2:30pm, Mon–Sat 7pm–12:30am, Sun 7–11pm. Métro: Odéon. FRENCH.

This little bistro serves *cuisine familiale.* Frequented by students and artists, it opened in 1930 and has changed none since then. The restaurant's name still contains the word *crémerie,* referring to its specialty: frosted crème desserts. This has become one of the Left Bank's most established literary bistros; it was André Gide's favorite. Lace curtains and brass hat racks, drawers in the back where repeat customers lock up their cloth napkins, and clay water pitchers on the tables create an old-fashioned atmosphere. Overworked but smiling waitresses serve grandmother's favorite dishes, such as pumpkin soup, snails from Burgundy, rib of beef with onions, rabbit with mustard sauce, and veal in white sauce. The desserts include raspberry and lemon tarts.

Restaurant des Beaux-Arts. 11 rue Bonaparte. ☎ **01-43-26-92-64.** Reservations recommended. Main courses 65–100F ($11.70–$18); fixed-price menu (including wine) 85F ($15.30). V. Daily noon–2:15pm and 7–10:45pm. Métro: St-Germain-des-Prés. FRENCH.

This is Paris's most famous budget restaurant. Does it please everyone? No. Have there been complaints about bad food and service? Some. But is it packed daily? That's for sure. So it must be doing something right, because thousands of hungry diners have come for its low prices, large portions, and robust stick-to-the-ribs dishes, all featured on a fixed-price menu. Tables are upstairs, but if you can get a place on the main floor you can see the steaming pots in the open kitchen. Typical platters are boeuf bourguignon, *navarin d'agneau* (lamb chops cooked with carrots, onions, and tomatoes), *lapin sauce moutarde* (rabbit leg with mustard sauce), codfish filet with garlic sauce, and fish soup—plus that dish the French always like, *blanquette de veau* (veal with white sauce).

LEFT BANK: 7TH ARRONDISSEMENT (EIFFEL TOWER/MUSEE D'ORSAY)
VERY EXPENSIVE

✪ **L'Arpège.** 84 rue de Varenne. ☎ **01-47-05-09-06.** Reservations required. Main courses 240–320F ($43.20–$57.60); fixed-price lunch 390F ($70.20); menu dégustation 790F ($142.20). AE, DC, V. Mon–Fri noon–2pm and 7:30–10pm, Sun 7:30–10pm. Métro: Varenne. FRENCH.

Three-star L'Arpège is where Alain Passard prepares his divine specialties. It's in a prosperous residential neighborhood, on the site of what for years was the world-famous L'Archestrate, where Passard once worked in the kitchens. Amid a cultivated decor of etched glass, burnished steel, and monochromatic paintings, you can enjoy specialties that've been heralded as truly innovative: some of his latest creations are Breton lobster in sweet-and-sour rosemary sauce, scallops prepared with cauliflower and lime-flavored grape sauce, and pan-fried duck with juniper-and-lime sauce, followed by the restaurant's signature dessert, a candied tomato stuffed with 12 kinds of dried and fresh fruit and served with anise-flavored ice cream. The wine list is something to write home about.

EXPENSIVE

✪ **Le Violin d'Ingres.** 135 rue St-Dominique. ☎ **01-45-55-15-05.** Reservations required 3–4 days in advance. Main courses 120–165F ($21.60–$29.70); fixed-price menu 240F ($43.20) at lunch, 290F ($52.20) at dinner. AE, MC, V. Tues–Sat noon–2:30pm and 7–10:30pm. Métro: Ecole Militaire. FRENCH.

This is it—the restaurant that quickly became Paris's pièce de résistance. Chef/owner Christian Constant is the man of the moment. Those who are fortunate enough to dine in Violin's warm atmosphere of rose-colored wood, soft cream walls, and elegant chintz fabrics rave about the cleverly artistic dishes. They range from a starter of pan-fried foie gras with gingerbread-and-spinach salad to elegant main courses like lobster ravioli with crushed vine-ripened tomatoes, roast veal in a creamy milk sauce with tender spring vegetables, and rotisseried leg of lamb rubbed with fresh garlic and thyme. One memorable dish is a delicate slice of sea bass enfolded in a crust of tiny croûtons, topped with almonds and set on a bed of sweet spinach and encircled by a ravigote of capers and a blancmange of red mullet. Even his familiar dishes seem new at each tasting. The repertoire goes from classicism to novelty. Constant keeps a well-chosen selection of wine to accompany his satisfying meals. The service is all about discreet charm.

MODERATE

Au Bon Acceuil. 14 rue de Monttessuy. ☎ **01-47-05-46-11.** Reservations required. Main courses 135–150F ($24.30–$27); fixed-price menu 130F ($23.40) at lunch, 160F ($28.80) at dinner. MC, V. Mon–Fri noon–2pm, Mon–Sat 7:30–10:30pm. Métro: Alma-Marceau. FRENCH.

When it opened in 1870, Au Bon Acceuil was configured as a neighborhod bistro with a superb view of the then-controversial Eiffel Tower. Today, it maintains all the accoutrements and accessories of its original decor, with a cachet of glamour that isn't matched by many other bistros in Paris. Look for a pair of old-fashioned dining rooms, each with panels, and stone columns that are carved into leafy patterns that emulate the twisting strands of a grapevine. And although you won't see the Eiffel Tower from inside the restaurant, the head-on view you'll get from the street outside, and the terrace in front of the restaurant, will almost knock you over the head. The food is consistently reliable, full of flavor, robust, and based on the freshest of ingredients. Menu items include filet of beef *périgourdine* garnished with foie gras, gigotin of monkfish; and a carte that changes virtually every day based on the availability of raw materials and the inspiration of the chef.

La Petite Chaise. 36–38 rue de Grenelle. ☎ **01-42-22-13-35.** Reservations required. Fixed-price menus 110–180F ($19.80–$32.40). AE, V. Daily noon–2pm and 7–11pm. Métro: Sèvres-Babylone. FRENCH.

This is the oldest restaurant in Paris, established by the baron de la Chaise in 1680 as an inn at the edge of what was then a large hunting preserve. (The baron, according to the restaurant's lore, maintained a series of upstairs bedrooms for mid-afternoon dalliances.) Very Parisian, the "Little Chair" invites you into a world of cramped but attractive tables, old wood paneling, and ornate wall sconces. The only option is a cost-conscious four-course fixed-price menu with a large choice of dishes. Samplings from the menu may be salad of strips of duck breast on a bed of fresh lettuce, filet of beef prepared with green peppercorns, and a trio of poached fish with steamed vegetables served in a sauce of fish and vegetable stock and cream.

LEFT BANK: 14TH ARRONDISSMENT (GARE MONTPARNESSE)
MODERATE

La Cagouille. 10–12 place Brancusi. ☎ **01-43-22-09-01.** Reservations recommended. Fixed-price menus 150–250F ($27–$45). Main courses 95–200F ($17.10–$36). AE, MC, V. Daily noon–2:30pm and 5–10:30pm. Métro: Gaité. FRENCH/ CHARENTAIS.

Don't expect to get or receive meat at this temple of seafood—the burly and genteel owner, Gérard Allamandou, refuses to allow it to appear on his menu. Everything about this place is a testimonial to a modernized version of the culinary arts of La Charente, the sandy, flat district that hugs the Atlantic south of Bordeaux. Within a trio of deliberately simple, oak-sheathed dining rooms, where the main decorative appeal derives from marble-topped tables and a minimum of accessories, you can enjoy seafood that's prepared as simply and naturally as possible. The beauty here lies in the utter simplicity and a strict allegiance to fresh ingredients, many of which arrive directly from the Atlantic coasts only a few hours before they are cooked—you won't find any heavy sauces here. Allamandou's preferred fish is red mullet, which might appear sautéed in a bland oil or baked in rock salt from the Ile de Ré, or any of several other all-natural dishes that are served with the same lack of pretention as the methods used to cook them. The name of the place derives from the regional symbol of La Charente: the sea snail, whose preparation here is elevated to a fine culinary art. Look for a vast assemblage of all-French, mostly white wines, and at least 150 types of cognac.

5 The Top Cafes

To a Parisian, a cafe is a club/tavern/snack bar. Whatever your pleasure—reading a newspaper, meeting a lover or a friend, doing your homework, writing your memoirs, nibbling at a hard-boiled egg, or drinking yourself into oblivion—you can do it all at a French cafe. In addition to Le Procope and Café Richelieu (with separate entries earlier in this chapter), here are Paris's top cafes:

Brasserie Lipp, 151 bd. St-Germain, 6e (☎ **01-45-48-53-91;** Métro: St-Germain-des-Prés), has an upstairs dining room, but it's more fashionable to sit in the backroom. For breakfast, order the traditional black coffee and croissants. At lunch or dinner, the house specialty is pork and *choucroute* (sauerkraut)—the best in Paris. Open daily from 9am to 1am, although restaurant service is available only from noon to 1am—it's fashionable to arrive late.

Across from the Centre Pompidou, the avant-garde **Café Beaubourg,** 100 rue St-Martin, 4e (☎ **01-48-87-63-96;** Métro: Rambuteau or Hôtel-de-Ville), boasts soaring concrete columns and a minimalist decor by the architect Christian de Portzamparc. In summer, tables are set on the sprawling terrace, providing a panoramic view of the neighborhood's goings-on. Open Sunday through Thursday from 8am to 1am and Friday and Saturday from 8am to 2am.

Sartre, the granddaddy of existentialism, often came to **Café de Flore,** 172 bd. St-Germain, 6e (☎ **01-45-48-55-26;** Métro: St-Germain-des-Prés), during the war.

Wearing a leather jacket and beret, he sat at his table and wrote his trilogy, *Les Chemins de la liberté* (The Roads to Freedom). The cafe is still going strong, though the celebrities have moved on. Open daily from 7am to 1:30am.

Café de la Paix, place de l'Opéra, 9e (☎ **01-40-07-30-20;** Métro: Opéra), has been a popular American enclave since the U.S. troops marched through Paris in their victory parade after World War II. No one can remember de Gaulle dining here, but a messenger arrived and ordered a "tinned" ham for the general's first supper when he returned after the Liberation. Open daily from noon to midnight.

Café Marly, 93 rue de Rivoli, 1er (☎ **01-49-26-06-60;** Métro: Palais-Royal–Musée-du-Louvre), occupies the Louvre's historic cour Napoléon. It's accessible only from a point close to the pyramid and has become a favorite refuge for Parisians escaping the roar of traffic. Anyone is welcome to sit for just a café au lait whenever meals aren't being served (noon to 3pm and 8 to 11pm). Menu items, served in three Louis-Philippe-style rooms, include club sandwiches, oysters and shellfish, steak au poivre (pepper steak), and upscale bistro food. In summer, outdoor tables overlook the majestic courtyard. Open daily from 8am to 2am.

At **La Coupole,** 102 bd. Montparnasse, 14e (☎ **01-43-20-14-20;** Métro: Vavin), the patrons range from artists' models to young men dressed like Rasputin. Perhaps order a coffee or cognac VSOP at one of the sidewalk tables. The dining room looks like a railway station and serves food that is sometimes good, sometimes indifferent. But patrons don't really come here for the cuisine; it's more on the see-and-be-seen circuit. Try the sole meunière, *carré d'agneau* (lamb), or cassoulet. A buffet breakfast is served Monday through Friday from 7:30 to 10:30am. Open daily from 7:30am to 2am.

The legendary **Deux Magots,** 6 place St-Germain-des-Prés, 6e (☎ **01-45-48-55-25;** Métro: St-Germain-des-Prés), is still the hangout for sophisticated neighborhood residents and a favorite for visitors in the summer. Inside are two large Oriental statues that give the cafe its name. Open daily from 7:30am to 1:30am.

Fouquet's, 99 av. des Champs-Elysées, 8e (☎ **01-47-23-70-60;** Métro: George-V), is the premier cafe on the Champs-Elysées. The outside tables are separated from the sidewalk by a barricade of potted flowers. Inside is an elegant grill room with leather banquettes and rattan furniture, private banquet rooms, and a restaurant. The cafe and grill room are open daily from 9am to 2am; the restaurant is open daily from noon to 3pm.

Exploring Paris 5

Paris is one of those cities where taking in the street life—shopping, strolling, and hanging out—should claim as much of your time as sightseeing in churches and museums. A gourmet picnic in the Bois de Boulogne, a sunrise pilgrimage to the Seine, an afternoon of bartering at the flea market—Paris bewitches you with these kinds of experiences. For all the Louvre's beauty, you'll probably remember the Latin Quarter's crooked alleyways better than the 370th oil painting of your visit.

The best way to discover Paris is on foot—and it won't cost you a franc to explore the streets of the City of Light. Walk along the grand avenue des Champs-Elysées, tour the quays of the Seine, wander around Ile de la Cité and Ile St-Louis, browse the countless shops and stalls, wander through the famous squares and parks. Each turn will open a new vista. If you're an early riser, a stroll through Paris at dawn can be enthralling as you see the city coming to life: Shopfronts are washed clean for the new day, cafes begin serving hot coffee and warm croissants, and vegetable and fruit vendors start setting up their stalls and arranging their produce.

Paris is also a shopper's city—with everything from tony boutiques to colorful street markets. We've covered the best of the best in this chapter.

And for sheer variety, there's nothing like Parisian nightlife. Nowhere else will you find such a huge and mixed bag of nightclubs, bars, dance clubs, cabarets, jazz dives, music halls, and honky-tonks. (For Paris's cafe scene, see chapter 4.)

ORGANIZED TOURS

Before plunging into more detailed sightseeing on your own, you might like to take the most popular get-acquainted tour in Paris: **Cityrama,** 147–149 rue St-Honoré, 1er (☎ **01-44-55-61-00;** Métro: Palais-Royal–Musée-du-Louvre). On a double-decker bus with enough windows for Versailles, you're taken on a leisurely 2-hour ride through the city. Since you don't go inside any attractions, you must settle for a look at the outside of such places as Notre-Dame and the Eiffel Tower, but it'll help you get a feel for the city if this is your first visit. The language barrier is overcome by the individual earphones distributed with commentary in 10 languages. Tours depart daily at 9:30, 10:30, and 11:30am and 1:30, 2:30, 3:30, and 4:30pm. A 2-hour orientation tour is 150F ($27). A morning tour with interior visits to Notre-Dame and the Louvre is 295F ($53.10). Half-day tours

A Tribute to Diana

Place de l'Alma (Métro: Alma-Marceau) has been turned into a memorial to the late Diana, Princess of Wales, who was killed in an auto accident on August 31, 1997, in the nearby underpass. The bronze flame in the center of the concrete island, a replica of the flame in the Statue of Liberty, was a 1989 gift by the *International Herald Tribune* to honor Franco-American friendship. Since pedestrians cannot go into the tunnel, many place bouquets and messages around the flame, which has come to represent the princess.

to Versailles at 195 to 320F ($35.10 to $57.60) and half-day tours to Chartres at 270F ($48.60) represent good value and remove at least some of the hassle associated with visiting those monuments. A joint ticket that includes both Versailles and Chartres costs 485F ($87.30). Another Cityrama offering, a tour of the nighttime illuminations, leaves daily at 10pm in summer or at 9pm in winter and costs 150F ($27); however, it tends to be tame and touristy.

The same entity that maintains Paris's network of Métros and buses, the **RATP** (☎ 08-36-68-77-14), operates the **Balabus,** with a fleet of orange-and-white big-windowed motorcoaches whose one drawback is their limited operating hours—only on Sunday from noon to 9pm and the afternoons of some national holidays. Itineraries run in both directions between Gare de Lyon and the Grand Arche de La Défense. Three Métro tickets will carry you along the entire route. You'll recognize the bus, and the route it follows, by the *Bb* symbol emblazoned across its side and along signs posted beside the route it follows.

A boat tour on the Seine provides sweeping views of the riverbanks and some of the best vistas of Notre-Dame. Many of the boats have open sundecks, bars, and restaurants. **Bateaux-Mouche cruises** (☎ 01-42-25-96-10 for reservations or 01-40-76-99-99 for schedules; Métro: Alma-Marceau) depart from the Right Bank of the Seine, adjacent to pont de l'Alma, and last 1¼ hours. Tours depart daily at 30-minute intervals between 11am and 10:30pm and at 15-minute intervals in good weather. Fares are 40F ($7.20) for adults and 20F ($3.60) for children. Lunch cruises cost 300F ($54) Monday through Saturday; a deluxe dinner cruise goes for 500F to 650F ($90 to $117), depending on the menu you select.

The **Batobus** (☎ 01-44-11-33-44) are 150-passenger ferryboats with big windows suitable for viewing the passing riverfronts. Daily between April and September, they operate east-west along the Seine, stopping at six points en route. Departures occur at 30-minute intervals between 10am and 7pm daily. (The boats don't run between October and March.) In either direction, the stops include the Eiffel Tower, Musée d'Orsay, points on both the Left Bank and the Right Bank opposite the Louvre, Notre-Dame, and the Hôtel de Ville. These ferries weren't conceived as sightseeing vehicles, and unlike on the bateaux-mouches, which are run by a separate outfit, there's no recorded commentary. Fares between any two stops are 12F ($2.15) per person, though frankly we consider the Batobus an expensive way to cross a river that's already crisscrossed with an impressive network of bridges. More appealing is to pay 65F ($11.70) per adult or 25F ($4.50) per child 11 and under (children under 3 ride free) for a day ticket that allows you to enter and exit from the boats as many times as you like (and ride as long as you like) during any single day. The views are panoramic and majestic, and the boat allows you to move from one history-rich neighborhood to another without heading into the bowels of the Métro or braving the roaring street traffic.

1 The Top Museums

For a list of museum passes good in Paris and elsewhere in France, see the "Museum Passes" box on p. 49.

✪ **Musée du Louvre.** 34–36 quai du Louvre, 1er (entrance: Pyramid/cour Napoléon). ☎ **01-40-20-53-17** or 01-40-20-51-51 for recorded information, or 01-49-87-54-54 for advance credit-card orders. Admission 45F ($8.10) before 3pm, 26F ($4.70) after 3pm and all day Sun, free for children 17 and under; free for everyone the first Sun of every month. Mon and Wed 9am–9:45pm (Mon, short tour only), Thurs–Sun 9am–6pm. 90-minute English-language tours Mon, Wed–Sat at 11am, 2pm, and 3:45pm and Sun 11:30am, 38F ($6.85) adults, 22F ($3.95) children 13–18, free for children 12 and under with museum ticket. Métro: Palais-Royal–Musée-du-Louvre.

The Louvre is the world's largest palace and one of the world's largest and greatest museums—and now it's more beautiful than ever since the facade has been thoroughly cleaned. You'll have to resign yourself to missing certain masterpieces here because you won't have the time or stamina to see everything; the Louvre's collection is truly staggering. People on one of those "Paris-in-a-day" tours try to break track records to glimpse the two most famous ladies here: the *Mona Lisa* and the *Venus de Milo.* Those with an extra 5 minutes go in pursuit of *Winged Victory,* that headless statue discovered at Samothrace and dating from about 200 B.C.

To enter the Louvre, you pass through the controversial 71-foot **I. M. Pei glass pyramid** in the courtyard. Commissioned by Mitterrand and completed in 1989, it received mixed reviews. The pyramid allows sunlight to shine on an underground reception area and shelters shops and restaurants that stretch beneath the Jardin du Carrousel. The renovation also increases the Louvre's gallery space by an astonishing 80% and provides underground garages for the tour buses that used to jam rue de Rivoli. If you don't want to wait in line for tickets at the entrance of the pyramid or use the new automatic ticket machines, you can now order tickets over the phone (see above) by giving your credit/charge-card number; you can have them mailed to you or can pick them up at any FNAC location in Paris.

Those with little time should go on one of the **guided tours** (in English), which last about 1½ hours. These tours start under the pyramid at the station marked ACCEIL DES GROUPES.

The collections are divided into seven departments: Asian antiquities; Egyptian antiquities; Greek, Estruscan, and Roman antiquities; sculpture; paintings; prints and drawings; and objets d'art. The $1.2 billion Grand Louvre Project is expected to be entirely completed in 1999. For up-to-the-minute data on what is open or about to open, you can check out the Louvre's Web site at **www.louvre.fr**. In December 1997, President Jacques Chirac inaugurated 107,000 square feet of gallery space, most of it in the eastern Sully wing and including a new presentation of the Louvre's vast collection of Egyptian antiquities. This innovation means 60 percent more space for the world of the pharaohs, a culture that has fascinated the French since Napoléon's occupation of Egypt in 1798.

New areas also now open include freshly restored and newly occupied rooms of Greek, Etruscan, and Roman antiquities. The Grand Galerie, a 600-foot hall opening onto the Seine, is dedicated to mostly Italian paintings from the 1400s to the 1700s, including works by Raphael and Leonardo da Vinci.

The **Richelieu Wing,** inaugurated in 1993, houses the museum's collection of northern European and French paintings, along with decorative arts, French sculpture, Oriental antiquities (a rich collection of Islamic art), and the grand salons of Napoléon III. Originally constructed from 1852 to 1857, this wing has been virtually rebuilt,

✪ Frommer's Favorite Paris Experiences

Strolling Along the Seine. Painters like Turner and Monet have fallen under the Seine's spell. Lovers still walk hand in hand alongside it, and vendors on its banks still peddle everything from postcards to 100-year-old pornography. Some energetic types walk the full 7-mile stretch of the river, but you may want to confine your stroll to central Paris, passing the Louvre, Notre-Dame, and pont Neuf.

Window Shopping Along the Faubourg St-Honoré. In the 1700s this was home to the wealthiest of Parisians; today it's home to the stores that cater to them. Even if you don't purchase anything, you'll enjoy some great window shopping with all the big names, like Hermès, Larouche, Lacroix, Lanvin, Courrèges, Cardin, Saint Laurent, and Lagerfeld.

An Afternoon of Cafe-Sitting. The Parisian cafe is an integral part of life. Even if it means skipping a museum, spend some time at a cafe. Whether you have one small coffee or the most expensive cognac in the house, nobody will hurry you, and you can see how the French really live. See our recommendations in chapter 4.

Taking Afternoon Tea à la Française. Skip London's cucumber-and-watercress sandwiches and get down to the business of rich, luscious desserts like Mont Blanc, that creamy purée of sweetened chestnuts. Try the grandest Parisian tea salon of them all: **Angelina,** 226 rue de Rivoli, 1er (see chapter 4). A close rival is the **Salon de Thé Bernardaud,** 11 rue Royale, 8e (☎ 01-42-66-22-55; Métro: Concorde), run by the Limoges-based manufacturer of fine porcelain. Teatime here is unique: A staff member presents you with five porcelain patterns and you choose the one in which you'd like your tea served.

Attending an Opera or a Ballet. In 1989 the acoustically perfect Opéra Bastille was inaugurated to compete with the grande dame of Paris's musical scene, the Opéra Garnier, which then was reserved for dance only and eventually closed for renovations. Now the Garnier has reopened, and opera has returned to its rococo splendor. A night here will take you back to the Second Empire, beneath a ceiling

---

adding some 230,000 square feet of exhibition space. In its 165 rooms, plus three covered courtyards, some 12,000 works of art are displayed. Of the Greek and Roman antiquities, the most notable (aside from *Venus* and *Winged Victory*) are **fragments of the Parthenon's frieze.**

Of course we love Mona and Venus, but our eternal passion burns for Jacques-Louis David's *Portrait of Madame Récamier,* depicting Napoléon's opponent at age 23; on her comfortable sofa, she reclines in the style of classical antiquity. Other favorites of ours are *Ship of Fools* by Hieronymous Bosch, tucked in the Flemish galleries (no one can depict folly and greed more vividly than Bosch); *Four Seasons* by Nicolas Poussin, the canonical work of French classicism; Eugène Delacroix's *Liberty Leading the People,* perhaps the ultimate endorsement of revolution (Louis-Philippe purchased the painting and hid it during his reign); and Paolo Veronese's gigantic *Wedding Feast at Cana,* showing (if nothing else) how stunning colors can be when applied by a master.

When you tire of strolling the galleries, you might like a pick-me-up at the Richelieu Wing's Café Richelieu (see chapter 4) or Café Marly. Boasting Napoléon III opulence, the Marly offers a perfect oasis. Perhaps try a café crème, a club sandwich, a decadent pastry, or something from the upscale bistro menu.

by Chagall. Whether for a performance of Bizet or Tharp, check out these two major Paris landmarks. Dress with pomp and circumstance.

Going to the Races. Paris has eight racetracks, some within the city boundaries. The most famous (and classiest) is **Longchamp,** in the Bois de Boulogne, 16e. The site of the Prix de l'Arc de Triomphe and Grand Prix, Longchamp is the world's longest racetrack. If it's a major social event, you'll have to dress up, of course—with a fabulous hat if you're a woman. Take the Métro to Porte d'Auteuil, then a special bus from there to the track. *Paris-Turf,* the racing paper, has details about racing times and special events.

Discovering Hidden Montmartre. This is the most touristy part of Paris. But far removed from the area's top draw, Sacré-Coeur, another neighborhood unfolds—that of the true Montmartrois. Wander on any of the backstreets away from the souvenir shops. Arm yourself with a good map and seek out such streets as rue Lepic (refresh yourself at the Lux Bar at no. 12), rue Constance, rue Tholozé (with its view over the rooftops of Paris), lively rue des Abbesses, and rue Germain-Pilon. None of these is famous, none receives hordes of visitors, but each is flanked with buildings whose detailing shows the pride and care that permeates Paris's architecture. You'll discover dozens of other streets on your own.

Checking Out the Marchés. A daily Parisian ritual is ambling through one of the open-air markets to purchase fresh food to be consumed that day—some ripe and properly creamy Camembert or a pumpkin-gold cantaloupe at its peak when consumed before sundown. You can partake of this tradition and gather supplies for a picnic in one of the city's parks. The vendors arrange their wares into a mosaic of vibrant colors. Sanguine, an Italian citrus whose juice is the color of an orange sunset; ruby-red peppers; golden yellow bananas from Martinique—all dazzle the eye. Our favorite market is on rue Montorgeuil, beginning at rue Rambuteau, 1er (Métro: Les-Halles). See "Paris Shopping" at the end of this chapter for other markets to check out.

In the northwest wing of the Louvre's Pavillon de Marsan is the **Musée des Arts Décoratifs** (☎ 01-44-55-57-50). See "The Champs-Elysees: The Grand Promenade of Paris," below, for complete details.

✪ **Musée d'Orsay.** 1 rue de Bellechasse or 62 rue de Lille, 7e. ☎ **01-40-49-48-14.** Admission 40F ($7.20) adults, 24F ($4.80) ages 18–24, free for children 17 and under; admission charges reduced by 10F ($1.80) on Sun. Tues–Wed and Fri–Sat 10am–6pm, Thurs 10am–9:45pm, Sun 9am–6pm. June 20–Sept 20, opens at 9am. Métro: Solférino. RER: Musée-d'Orsay.

The handsome neoclassical Gare d'Orsay train station has been transformed into one of world's greatest art museums. It contains an important collection devoted to the pivotal years from 1848 to 1914. Across the Seine from the Louvre and the Tuileries, this museum is a repository of works by the Impressionists as well as lesser-known groups like the Symbolists, Pointillists, Realists, and late Romantics. Artists represented include van Gogh, Manet, Monet, Degas, and Renoir. It houses thousands of sculptures and paintings spread across 80 galleries, plus belle époque furniture, photographs, objets d'art, architectural models, and even a cinema.

One of Renoir's most joyous paintings is here: *Moulin de la Galette* (1876). Another celebrated work is by the American James McNeill Whistler—*Arrangement in Gray and Black: Portrait of the Painter's Mother.* The most famous piece in the museum is Manet's 1863 *Déjeuner sur l'herbe* (Picnic on the Grass), which created a scandal when it was first exhibited; it depicts a nude woman nonchalantly picnicking with two fully clothed men in a forest. Two years later his *Olympia*, lounging on her bed wearing nothing but a flower in her hair and high-heeled shoes, met the same response.

✪ **Musée Picasso.** In the Hôtel Salé, 5 rue de Thorigny, 3e. ☎ **01-42-71-25-21.** Admission 30F ($5.40) adults, 20F ($3.60) ages 18–25 and seniors over 60, free for children 17 and under. Apr–Sept, Wed–Mon 9:30am–6pm; Oct–Mar, Wed–Mon 9:30am–5pm. Métro: St-Paul, Filles-du-Calvaire, or Chemin-Vert.

When it opened in the beautifully restored Hôtel Salé (salt mansion, built in 1656 for Aubert de Fontenay, who collected the dreaded salt tax), a state-owned property in the Marais, the press hailed it as a "museum for Picasso's Picassos," meaning those he chose not to sell. Far superior to a similar museum in Barcelona, this museum offers an unparalleled view of the artist's long and varied career and his different periods, including his fabled gaunt blue figures and harlequins. Almost overnight the museum became (and continues to be) one of Paris's most popular attractions. The world's greatest Picasso collection, acquired by the state in lieu of $50 million in inheritance taxes, consists of 203 paintings, 158 sculptures, 16 collages, 19 bas-reliefs, 88 ceramics, and more than 1,500 sketches and 1,600 engravings, plus 30 notebooks. These works span some 75 years of Picasso's life and changing styles.

The range of paintings includes a remarkable 1901 self-portrait and embraces such masterpieces as *Le Baiser* (The Kiss), painted at Mougins in 1969. Another masterpiece is *Reclining Nude and the Man with a Guitar*. It's easy to stroll through seeking your own favorite work—ours is the delightfully wicked *Jeune garçon à la langouste* (Young Man with a Lobster), painted in Paris in 1941. The museum also owns several intriguing studies for *Les Demoiselles d'Avignon*, the painting that launched Cubism in 1907.

✪ **Musée National Auguste Rodin.** In the Hôtel Biron, 77 rue de Varenne, 7e. ☎ **01-44-18-61-10.** Admission 28F ($5.05) adults, 18F ($3.25) ages 18–26 and seniors 60 and over, free for children 17 and under. Apr–Sept, Tues–Sun 9:30am–5:45pm; Oct–Mar, Tues–Sun 9:30am–4:45pm. Métro: Varenne.

This beautiful house and its gardens are a repository of the work of Auguste Rodin (1840–1917), the undisputed master of French 19th-century sculpture (even though his works were first thought obscene). After his death the government purchased Rodin's gray-stone 18th-century mansion in Faubourg St-Germain, where he had his studio from 1910 until 1917. The rose gardens were restored to their original splendor, making a perfect setting for Rodin's most memorable works.

In the courtyard are three world-famous creations: *The Gate of Hell, The Thinker,* and *The Burghers of Calais*. Rodin's first major public commission, *The Burghers* commemorated the heroism of six burghers who in 1347 offered themselves as hostages to Edward III in return for his ending the siege of their port. The best-known work, *The Thinker,* in Rodin's own words, "thinks with every muscle of his arms, back, and legs, with his clenched fist and gripping toes." Inside the mansion, the sculptures, plaster casts, reproductions, originals, and sketches reveal the freshness and vitality of that remarkable man. Many of his works appear to be emerging from marble into life. Everybody is drawn to *The Kiss* (of which one critic wrote, "the passion is timeless"). Upstairs are two versions of the celebrated and condemned nude of Balzac, his bulky torso rising from a tree trunk. Included are many versions of his *Monument to Balzac*

A Time-Saving Tip

Museums require that you check shopping bags and book bags, and sometimes lines for these can be longer than the ticket and admission lines. If you value your time, leave these bags behind or do your shopping afterward. Ask if a museum has more than one coat line; if so, avoid the main one and go to the less-frequented ones.

(a large one stands in the garden), Rodin's last major work. Generally overlooked is a room devoted to Camille Claudel, Rodin's mistress and a towering artist in her own right. His pupil, model, and lover, she created such works as *Maturity, Clotho,* and (donated in 1995) the *Waltz* and the *Gossips.*

The little alley behind the mansion winds its way down to a pond with fountains and flower beds, even sandpits for children. It's one of the most idyllic hidden spots of Paris.

Centre Pompidou. Place Georges-Pompidou. ☎ **01-44-78-12-33.** Admission 30F ($5.40) adults, 20F ($3.60) ages 18–25, free for children 17 and under. Atelier Brancusi, 20F ($3.60). Two-in-one ticket (Galerie Sud and Atelier Brancusi), 40F ($7.20) adults, 30F ($5.40) ages 18–25, free 17 and under. Mon and Wed–Fri noon–10pm, Sat–Sun 10am–10pm. Métro: Rambuteau, Hôtel-de-Ville, Châtelet, or Les Halles.

Although the world-famous Museum of Modern Art remains closed for renovations until December 31, 1999, parts of it are limping along.

The museum remains partially open to the public, with exhibitions, meetings, and performances available both inside and outside the building. Inside, documentation spaces and the Atelier Brancusi remain open, as well as access to the fifth-floor panorama of Paris. The "Tepe," set up on the square out front, provides free access to multimedia information on the center and its activities, as well as artistic activity in general. Here you can learn about numerous Pompidou exhibitions presented in other locations in Paris as well as elsewhere in France. The public information library of the museum has been temporarily transferred to a building nearby at 11 rue Brantôme.

The **Atelier Brancusi** houses 137 sculptures, 87 pedestals, 41 drawings, 2 paintings, and more than 1,600 glass photographic plate and original prints. Born in Romania in 1876, Constantin Brancusi was a major figure in the history of modern sculpture. He lived in Paris from 1904 until his death in 1957, and he created the greater part of his work in the studios he occupied at 8 and 11 impasse Ronsin in the 15th arrondissement. His atelier—willed to the French state—was reconstructed at the Pompidou Center and opened in 1997.

Galerie Sud, accessible via rue Saint Merri on the south side of the Pompidou Center, is a showcase for temporary exhibitions—it's devoted to David Hockney in 1999.

Cité des Sciences et de l'Industrie. La Villette, 30 av. Corentin-Cariou, 19e. ☎ **01-40-05-12-12.** Exhibitions (including the *Argonaut* submarine), 50F ($9) Sun–Fri, 35F ($6.30) Sat, free for children 7 and under; Géode, 57F ($10.25) adults; Cinaxe, 33F ($5.95); three-in-one ticket, 92F ($16.55); Cité des Enfants, 25F ($4.50). Tues–Sat 10am–6pm, Sun 10am–7pm. Closed May 1 and Dec 25. Métro: Porte-de-la-Villette.

In 1986 this opened as the world's most expensive ($642 million) science complex, designed to "modernize mentalities" as a first step in the process of modernizing society. The place is so vast, with so many options, that a single visit will give you only an idea of its scope. Some exhibits are couched in an overlay of Gallic humor, including seismographic activity as presented in the comic-strip adventures of a jungle explorer. The silver-skinned Géode (a geodesic dome) shows the closest thing to a

Paris Attractions

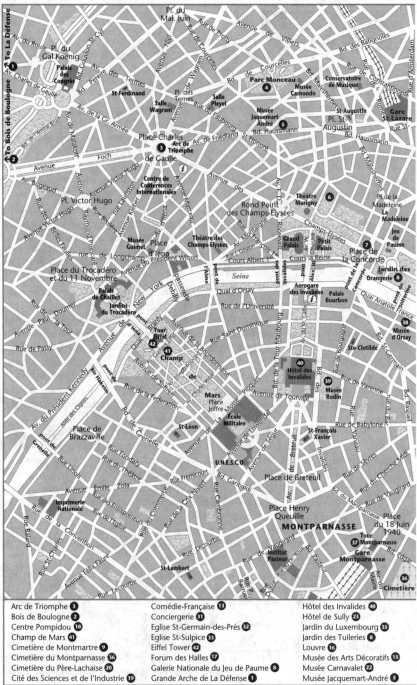

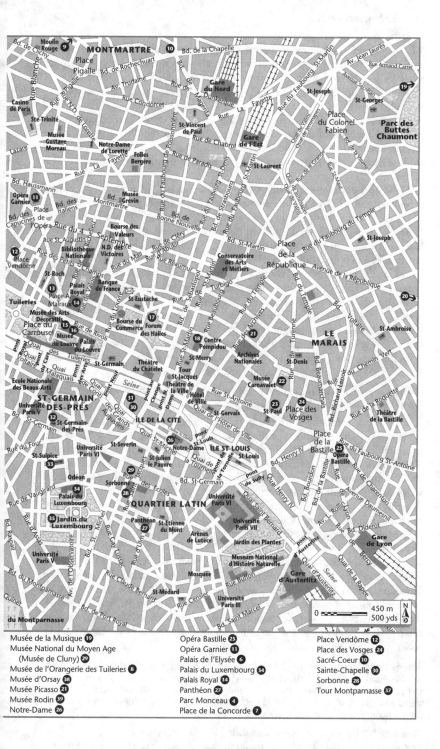

Musée de la Musique **19**
Musée National du Moyen Age
   (Musée de Cluny) **29**
Musée de l'Orangerie des Tuileries **8**
Musée d'Orsay **38**
Musée Picasso **21**
Musée Rodin **39**
Notre-Dame **26**

Opéra Bastille **25**
Opéra Garnier **11**
Palais de l'Elysée **6**
Palais du Luxembourg **34**
Palais Royal **14**
Panthéon **27**
Parc Monceau **4**
Place de la Concorde **7**

Place Vendôme **12**
Place des Vosges **24**
Sacré-Coeur **10**
Sainte-Chapelle **30**
Sorbonne **28**
Tour Montparnasse **37**

3-D cinema in Europe on the inner surfaces of its curved walls. It's a 112-foot sphere with a 370-seat theater. Explora, a permanent exhibit, is spread over the three upper levels; its displays revolve around four themes: the universe, life, matter, and communication. The Cité also has a multimedia library and a planetarium. An "inventorium" is for children.

At Cinaxe, sophisticated stereo systems and larger-than-normal screens combine to enhance the sensations of the scenes being presented in the film. The experience includes several 10-minute episodes, representing what you'd see, for example, in an airplane flying low over mountains or if you were positioned on the nose cone of a rocket.

The *Argonaut* is a submarine that was originally built in 1905 as part of a scientific experiment and is today a historic machine and a forerunner of the giant nuclear subs whose construction was partially based on ideas developed here. It was disarmed in 1982 and would have been demolished but for its purchase by the Musée de la Villette. Today, it's a somewhat nationalistic source of pride, although it's firmly mounted on concrete and is never submerged.

La Cité des Enfants is divided into two sections: one for ages 3 to 5, the other for ages 6 to 12. This is an adventure playground, with water sports, a butterfly greenhouse, robots, an ant farm, interactive TVs, and even a Techno Cité where kids are given an explanation of the workings of computers and other machines. There are also visual exhibits on such subjects as electricity.

The Cité is in La Villette park, Paris's largest city park, with 136 acres of greenery—twice the size of the Tuileries. Here you'll find a belvedere, a video workshop for children, and information about exhibitions and events, along with a cafe and restaurant.

Musée Jacquemart-André. 158 bd. Haussmann, 8e. ☎ **01-42-89-04-91.** Admission 47F ($8.45). Daily 10am–6pm. Métro: Miromesnil or St-Philippe-du-Roule.

This is the best decorative-arts museum in Paris, though it's no place to take the kids (unless they've confessed they want to be decorators). Give it at least 2½ hours. The museum derives from the André family, prominent Protestants in the 19th century. The family's last scion, Edouard André, spent most of his life as an officer in the French army stationed abroad, returning later in his life to marry Nélie Jacquemart, a well-known portraitist of government figures and members of the aristocracy. Together they compiled a collection of rare French 18th-century decorative art and European paintings in an 1850s town house, which they continually upgraded and redecorated according to the fashions of their time.

In 1912 Mme André willed the house and its collections to the Institut de France, which paid for extensive renovations and enlargements that were completed in 1996. The collection's pride are works by Bellini, Carpaccio, and Uccelo, complemented by Houdon busts, Gobelin tapestries, Savonnerie carpets, della Robbia terra-cottas, an awesome collection of antiques, and works by Rembrandt (*The Pilgrim of Emmaus*), van Dyck, Tiepolo, Rubens, Watteau, Fragonard, and Boucher. Take a break from all the gilded-age opulence with a cup of tea, a salad, or a tart in Mme André's dining room, with 18th-century tapestries.

Musée de la Musique. In the Cité de la Musique, 221 av. Jean-Jaurès, 19e. ☎ **01-44-84-45-00.** Admission 35F ($6.30) adults, 25F ($4.50) students and seniors 60 and over, 10F ($1.80) children 17 and under. Visits with commentary, 60F ($10.80) adults, 45F ($8.10) students and seniors 60 and over, 20F ($3.60) children 17 and under. Tues–Thurs noon–6pm, Fri–Sat noon–9:30pm, Sun 10am–6pm. Métro: Porte-de-Pantin.

Contained in the stone-and-glass Cité de la Musique, this museum serves as a tribute and testament to the rich musical tradition that has been passed down through the world's many ages and cultures. You can view 4,500 instruments, primarily from the 17th century to the present, as well as paintings, engravings, and sculptures that all relate to musical history. One especially appealing section of mandolins, lutes, and zithers evokes music from 400 years ago. It's all here: Cornets disguised as snakes, antique music boxes, and even a postwar electric guitar that Elvis might have collected. As part of the permanent collection, models of the world's great concert halls and interactive display areas give you a chance to hear and better understand the art and technology of musical heritage.

2 Ile de la Cité: Where Paris Was Born

Medieval Paris, that architectural blending of grotesquerie and Gothic beauty, began on this island in the Seine. Explore as much of it as you can, but if you're in a hurry, try to visit at least Notre-Dame, the Sainte-Chapelle, and the Conciergerie.

✪ **Cathédrale Notre-Dame.** 6 place du parvis Notre-Dame, 4e. ☎ **01-42-34-56-10.** Admission: Cathedral, free; towers, treasury, or crypt, each 32F ($5.75) adults, 21F ($3.80) ages 12–24 and seniors 60 and over, free for children 11 and under. Cathedral, daily 8am–7pm (closed Sat 12:30–2pm); towers, daily 10am–5pm; museum, Wed and Sat–Sun 2:30–6pm; treasury and crypt Mon–Sat 9:30am–5:30pm. Six masses are celebrated on Sun, four on Mon–Sat. Métro: Cité or St-Michel. RER: St-Michel.

This cathedral ranks near the top as one of the world's most famous houses of worship. For six centuries it has stood as a fabled Gothic masterpiece of the Middle Ages. Although many may disagree, we feel that Notre-Dame is more interesting outside than in. You'll have to walk around the entire structure to appreciate more fully this "vast symphony of stone" with its classic flying buttresses. Better yet, cross the bridge to the Left Bank and view it from the quay. Talk about a Kodak moment!

From square parvis, you can view the trio of 13th-century sculpted portals. On the left, the Portal of the Virgin depicts the signs of the zodiac and the Virgin's coronation. The restored central Portal of the Last Judgment is divided into three levels: The first shows Vices and Virtues; the second, Christ and his Apostles; the third, Christ in triumph after the Resurrection. On the right is the Portal of Ste. Anne, depicting such scenes as the Virgin enthroned with Child. It's Notre-Dame's most perfect piece of sculpture. Over the central portal is a remarkable rose window, 31 feet in diameter, forming a showcase for a statue of the Virgin and Child. Equally interesting (yet often missed) is the Cloister Portal (around on the left), with its dour-faced 13th-century Virgin, a unique survivor of the many that originally adorned the facade. (Unfortunately, the Child she's holding is decapitated.)

If possible, view the interior at sunset. Of the three giant medallions that warm the austere cathedral, the north rose window in the transept, from the mid–13th century, is best. The interior is typical Gothic, with slender, graceful columns. The carved-stone choir screen from the early 14th century depicts biblical scenes like the Last Supper. Near the altar stands the highly venerated 14th-century Virgin and Child. Behind glass in the treasury is a display of vestments and gold objects, including crowns. Notre-Dame is especially proud of its relic of the True Cross and the Crown of Thorns.

To visit those grimy gargoyles immortalized by Victor Hugo (where Quasimodo lurked and yearned), you have to scale steps leading to the twin square towers, rising to a height of 225 feet. Once here, you can closely inspect those devils (some sticking out their tongues), hobgoblins, and birds of prey.

Approached through a garden behind Notre-Dame is the **Memorial des Martyrs Français de la Déportation,** jutting out on the tip of the Ile de la Cité. This memorial honors the French martyrs of World War II, who were deported to camps like

Auschwitz and Buchenwald. In blood-red are the words (in French): "Forgive, but don't forget." It's open Monday through Friday from 8:30am to 9:45pm, Saturday and Sunday from 9am to 9:45pm. Admission is free.

✪ Sainte-Chapelle. In the Palais de Justice, 4 bd. du Palais, 1er. ☎ **01-53-73-78-50.** Admission 32F ($5.75) adults, 21F ($3.80) students and children 13–25, free for children 12 and under. Apr–Sept daily 9:30am–6:30pm; Oct–Mar daily 10am–5pm. Métro: Cité, St-Michel, or Châtelet–Les-Halles. RER: St-Michel.

Go here if for no other reason than to see one of the world's greatest examples of Flamboyant Gothic architecture—"the pearl among them all," as Proust called it—and brilliantly colored stained-glass windows with a lacelike delicacy, a triumph of transparency. The reds are so red and the blues so blue that there's a phrase in Paris, "wine the color of Sainte-Chapelle's windows." Sainte-Chapelle is Paris's second most important monument of the Middle Ages (after Notre-Dame), erected to enshrine relics from the First Crusade. These included what were believed to have been the Crown of Thorns, two pieces from the True Cross, and even the Roman lance that pierced the side of Christ. St. Louis (Louis IX) acquired the relics from the emperor of Constantinople and is said to have paid heavily for them, raising money through unscrupulous means.

Viewed on a bright day, the 15 stained-glass windows vividly depicting Bible scenes seem to glow ruby red and Chartres blue. The walls consist almost entirely of the glass. Built in only 5 years, beginning in 1246, the chapel has two levels. You enter through the lower chapel, supported by flying buttresses and ornamented with fleurs-de-lis. The lower chapel was used by the servants of the palace, the upper chamber by the king and his courtiers; the latter is reached by ascending a narrow spiral staircase. At the top you're sure to ooh and aah at the sight.

Conciergerie. 1 quai de l'Horloge, 1er. ☎ **01-53-73-78-50.** Admission 32F ($5.75) adults, 21F ($3.80) ages 12–25, free for children 11 and under. Apr–Sept daily 9:30am–6:30pm; Oct–Mar daily 10am–5pm. Métro: Cité, Châtelet, or St-Michel. RER: St-Michel.

The Conciergerie is the most sinister building in France. Though it had a long, regal history before the Revolution, it's visited today chiefly by those wishing to bask in the Reign of Terror's horrors. The Conciergerie conjures images of the days when tumbrils pulled up daily to haul off the fresh supply of victims to the guillotine.

You approach the Conciergerie through its landmark twin towers, the Tour d'Argent and Tour de César, though the 14th-century vaulted Guard Room is the actual entrance. Also from the 14th century—and even more interesting—is the vast, dark, foreboding Salle des Gens d'Armes (People at Arms), chillingly transformed from the days when the king used it as a banqueting hall.

Few of the prisoners in the Conciergerie's history endured the tortures of Ravaillac, who assassinated Henry IV in 1610. He got the full treatment—pincers in the flesh as well as hot lead and boiling oil poured on him like bathwater. This was also where Marie Antoinette, in failing health and in shock, was brought to await her trial and eventual beheading.

ANOTHER ISLAND IN THE STREAM: ILE ST-LOUIS

As you walk across the iron footbridge from the rear of Notre-Dame, you descend into a world of tree-shaded quays, aristocratic town houses and courtyards, restaurants, and antiques shops.

The Ile St-Louis (Métro: Sully-Morland or Pont-Marie), the sibling island of the Ile de la Cité, is primarily residential; its denizens fiercely guard their heritage, privileges, and special position. It was originally two "islets," one named Island of the Heifers,

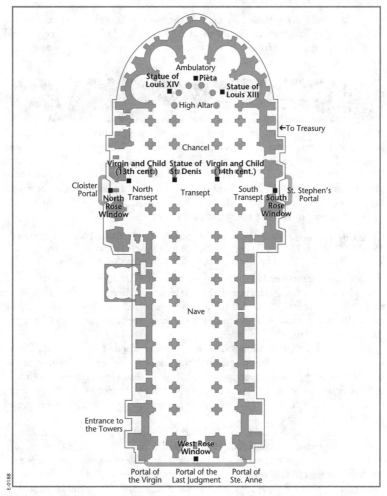

Statue of Louis XIV · Pièta · Ambulatory · Statue of Louis XIII

High Altar

←To Treasury

Chancel

Virgin and Child (13th cent.) · Statue of St. Denis · Virgin and Child (14th cent.)

Cloister Portal · North Rose Window · North Transept · Transept · South Transept · South Rose Window · St. Stephen's Portal

Nave

Entrance to the Towers

West Rose Window

Portal of the Virgin · Portal of the Last Judgment · Portal of Ste. Anne

E-0188

until the two islands were ordered joined by Louis XIII. The number of famous people who have occupied these patrician mansions is now legend. Plaques on the facades make it easier to identify them: Madame Curie, for example, lived at 36 quai de Bethune, near pont de la Tournelle, from 1912 until her death in 1934.

The most exciting mansion is the **Hôtel de Lauzun,** built in 1657, at 17 quai d'Anjou; it's named after a 17th-century rogue, the duc de Lauzun, famous lover and on-again/off-again favorite of Louis XIV. The French poet Charles Baudelaire lived here in the 19th century with his "Black Venus," Jeanne Duval. Baudelaire attracted such artists as Delacroix and Courbet to his apartment, which was often filled with the aroma of hashish. Occupying another apartment was the novelist Théophile Gautier ("art for art's sake"), who's remembered today chiefly for his *Mademoiselle de Maupin.*

Voltaire lived in the **Hôtel Lambert,** 2 quai d'Anjou, with his mistress, Emilie de Breteuil, the marquise du Châteley, who had an "understanding" husband. The mansion was built by Louis Le Vau in 1645 for Nicolas Lambert de Thorigny, the president of the Chambre des Comptes. For a century the hotel was the home of the royal family of Poland, the Czartoryskis, who entertained Chopin, among others.

Farther along, at no. 9 quai d'Anjou, is the house where Honoré Daumier, the painter/sculptor/lithographer, lived between 1846 and 1863. From here he satirized the petite bourgeoisie. His caricature of Louis-Philippe netted him a 6-month jail sentence.

3 The Champs-Elysées: The Grand Promenade of Paris

In late 1995, after two hard, dusty, and hyperexpensive years of construction, several important improvements in Paris's most prominent triumphal promenade were unveiled. The *contre-allées* (side lanes that had always been clogged with parked cars) had been removed, new lighting added, the pedestrian sidewalks widened, new trees planted, and underground parking garages added to relieve what had been the neighborhood's curse—far too many parked cars. Now the Grand Promenade truly is grand again . . . except for all those garish fast-food places.

✪ **Arc de Triomphe.** Place Charles-de-Gaulle–Etoile, 8e. ☎ **01-43-80-31-31.** Admission 35F ($6.30) adults, 23F ($4.15) ages 12–25, free for children 11 and under. Apr–Sept daily 9:30am–10pm; Oct–Mar daily 10am–10:30pm. Métro: Charles-de-Gaulle–Etoile.

Situated at the western end of the Champs-Elysées, the Arc de Triomphe is the largest triumphal arch in the world, about 163 feet high and 147 feet wide. To reach it, don't try crossing the square, the busiest traffic hub in Paris (death is certain!). Instead, take the underground passage. With a dozen streets radiating from the "Star," the traffic circle is vehicular roulette.

The triumphal arch has witnessed some of France's proudest moments—and some of its more humiliating defeats, notably those of 1871 and 1940. The memory of German troops marching under the arch that had come to symbolize France's glory is still painful to the French. And who could forget the 1940 newsreel of the Frenchman standing on the Champs-Elysées openly weeping as the Nazi stormtroopers goose-stepped through Paris?

Commissioned by Napoléon in 1806 to commemorate his Grande Armée's victories, the arch wasn't completed until 1836, under Louis-Philippe. Four years later Napoléon's remains—brought from his grave on St. Helena—passed under the arch on their journey to his tomb at the Hôtel des Invalides. Since then it has become the focal point for state funerals. It's also the site of the tomb of the unknown soldier, where an eternal flame is kept burning.

Of the sculptures decorating the monument, the best known is Rude's *Marseillaise,* also called *The Departure of the Volunteers.* J. P. Cortot's *Triumph of Napoléon in 1810,* and the *Resistance of 1814* and *Peace of 1815,* both by Etex, also adorn the facade. The arch is engraved with the names of hundreds of generals (those underlined died in battle) who commanded troops in Napoléonic victories.

You can take an elevator or climb the stairway to the top. Up there is an exhibition hall, with lithographs and photos depicting the arch throughout its history. From the observation deck you have a panoramic view of the Champs-Elysées as well as such landmarks as the Louvre, Eiffel Tower, and Sacré-Coeur.

Galerie Nationale du Jeu de Paume. In the Jardin des Tuileries at place de la Concorde, 8e. ☎ **01-47-03-12-50.** Admission 38F ($6.85) adults, 28F ($5.05) students, free for visitors 18 and under. Tues noon–9:30pm, Wed–Fri noon–7pm, Sat–Sun 10am–7pm. Métro: Concorde.

Jeu de Paume, in the northeast corner of the Tuileries, was ordered constructed by Napoléon III as a court on which to play *jeu de paume,* a precursor to tennis. For years

Where the Royal Heads Rolled

In the east, avenue des Champs-Elysées begins at **place de la Concorde,** an octagonal traffic hub ordered built in 1757 to honor Louis XV—it's one of the world's grandest squares. The statue of the king was torn down in 1792 and the name of the square changed to place de la Révolution. Floodlit at night, it's dominated now by an **Egyptian obelisk** from Luxor, the oldest man-made object in Paris; it was carved circa 1200 B.C. and presented to France in 1829 by the viceroy of Egypt.

During the Reign of Terror, Dr. Guillotin's splendid little invention was erected on this spot, where it claimed thousands of lives—everybody from Louis XVI, who died bravely, to Mme du Barry, who went kicking and screaming all the way. Before the leering crowds, Marie Antoinette, Robespierre, Danton, Mlle Roland, and Charlotte Corday lost their heads here. (You can still lose your life on place de la Concorde—if you try to chance the frantic traffic and cross over.)

For a spectacular sight, look down the Champs-Elysées—the view is framed by Coustou's Marly horses, which once graced the gardens at Louis XIV's Château de Marly (these are copies—the originals are in the Louvre). On the opposite side, the gateway to the Tuileries is flanked by Coysevox's winged horses. On each side of the obelisk are two fountains with bronze-tailed mermaids and bare-breasted sea nymphs. Gray-beige statues ring the square, honoring the cities of France. To symbolize that city's fall to Germany in 1871, the statue of Strasbourg was covered with a black drape that wasn't lifted until the end of World War I. Two of the palaces on place de la Concorde are today the Ministry of the Marine and the deluxe Hôtel de Crillon. They were designed in the 1760s by Jacques-Ange Gabriel.

it was one of Paris's treasured addresses, displaying some of the finest works of the Impressionists. To the regret of many, the collection was hauled off to the Musée d'Orsay in 1986. Following a $12.6-million face-lift, the Second Empire building has been transformed into a new art gallery with state-of-the-art display facilities and a video screening room. There's no permanent collection; every 2 or 3 months a new show is mounted. Sometimes the works of little-known contemporary artists are on display; at other times the exhibition features established artists like Jean Dubuffet.

✪ **Musée de l'Orangerie des Tuileries.** In the Jardin des Tuileries, place de la Concorde, 1er. ☎ **01-42-97-48-16.** Admission 30F ($5.40) adults, 20F ($3.60) ages 18–24, free for children 17 and under. Wed–Mon 9:45am–5pm. Métro: Concorde.

This gem of a museum has an outstanding collection of art and one acclaimed masterwork—Claude Monet's exquisite *Nymphéas* (1915–27), a light-filtered tangle of lily pads and water. The work panels the walls of two oval rooms on the ground floor; the artist himself supervised the installation. Creating his effects with hundreds of minute brushstrokes (one 19th-century critic called them "tongue lickings"), Monet achieved the unity and harmony of his Rouen cathedral series. See his lilies and feel for yourself the melancholy he experienced so many years ago. Monet continued to paint his water landscapes right up until he died in 1926, though he was greatly hampered by failing eyesight.

The renovated building also contains the Walter-Guillaume collection, which houses more than 24 Renoirs, including *Young Girl at a Piano.* Cézanne is represented by 14 works, notably *The Red Rock,* and Matisse by 11 paintings. The star of

Rousseau's nine works is *The Wedding,* and of the dozen Picassos the most brilliant is *The Female Bathers.*

✪ **Jardin des Tuileries.** Bordering place de la Concorde. ☎ **01-44-50-75-01.** Métro: Tuileries.

These spectacular, statue-studded gardens are as much a part of Paris as the Seine. They were designed by Le Nôtre, Louis XIV's gardener and planner of the Versailles grounds. About 100 years before that, Catherine de Médici ordered a palace built here, connected to the Louvre; other occupants have included Louis XVI (after he left Versailles) and Napoléon. Twice attacked by enraged Parisians, it was finally burned to the ground in 1871 and never rebuilt. The gardens, however, remain. In orderly French manner, the trees are arranged according to designs and even the paths are arrow-straight. Breaking the sense of order and formality are bubbling fountains.

Seemingly half of Paris can be found in the Tuileries on a warm spring day, listening to the chirping birds and admiring the daffodils and tulips. As you walk toward the Louvre, you'll enter the **Jardin du Carrousel,** dominated by the **Arc de Triomphe du Carrousel,** at the Cour du Carrousel. Pierced with three walkways and supported by marble columns, the monument honors Napoléon's Grande Armée, celebrating its victory at Austerlitz on December 5, 1805. The arch is surmounted by statuary, a chariot, and four bronze horses.

Musée des Arts Décoratifs. In the Palais du Louvre, 107 rue de Rivoli, 1er. ☎ **01-44-55-57-50.** Admission 30F ($5.40) adults, 20F ($3.60) ages 18–25, free for children 17 and under. Tues and Thurs–Fri 11am–6pm, Wed 11am–9pm, Sat–Sun 10am–6pm. Métro: Palais-Royal or Tuileries.

In the northwest wing of the Louvre's Pavillon de Marsan, this museum holds a treasury of furnishings, fabrics, wallpaper, objets d'art, and other items displaying living styles from the Middle Ages to the present. Notable on the first floor are the 1920s Art Deco boudoir, bath, and bedroom done for couturière Jeanne Lanvin by the designer Rateau, plus a prestigious collection of the works donated by Jean Dubuffet. Decorative art from the Middle Ages to the Renaissance is housed on the second floor; rich collections from the 17th, 18th, and 19th centuries occupy the third and fourth floors. The fifth floor has specialized centers, such as wallpaper and drawings, and documentary centers detailing fashion, textiles, toys, crafts, and glass trends.

OTHER SIGHTS NEARBY

Palais de l'Elysée. Rue du Faubourg St-Honoré, 8e. Métro: Miromesnil.

The "French White House" occupies a block along fashionable Faubourg St-Honoré and since 1873 has been occupied by the president of France (though when Mitterrand was alive he decided to remain at his private home on rue de Bièvre). You can admire the palace from the outside (from a point about a block away) but can't enter without an official invitation. Built in 1718 for the comte d'Evreux, it had many owners before it was purchased by the Republic. It was once owned by Mme de Pompadour; when she "had the supreme delicacy to die discreetly at the age of 43," she bequeathed it to the king. After her divorce from Napoléon, Joséphine lived here. A grand dining hall was built for Napoléon III, and an orangerie (now a winter garden) was constructed for the duchesse du Berry.

Palais Royal. Rue St-Honoré, on place du Palais-Royal, 1er. Métro: Louvre.

At the demolished Café Foy in the Palais Royal, the outraged Camille Desmoulins once jumped up on a table and shouted for the mob "to fight to the death." The date was July 13, 1789. The renown of the Palais Royal goes back even farther. The gardens were planted in 1634 for Cardinal Richelieu, who presented them to Louis

XIII. In time the property became the residence of the ducs d'Orléans. Philippe-Egalité, a cousin of Louis XVI, built his apartments on the grounds and subsequently rented them to prostitutes. By the 20th century those same apartments were rented by such artists as Cocteau and Colette. (A plaque at 9 rue Beaujolais marks the entrance to her apartment, which she inhabited until her death in 1954.) Today the Palais Royal contains apartments, some discreet shops, and a few great restaurants (such as Le Grand Véfour; see chapter 4). Note sculptor Daniel Buren's prison-striped columns, added to the garden in 1986, and Pol Bury's steel-ball sculptures decorating the fountains.

Place Vendôme. 8e. Métro: Opéra.

Always aristocratic and often royal, place Vendôme enjoyed its golden age during the Second Empire. Fashion designers—the great ones, such as Worth—introduced the crinoline here. Louis Napoléon lived here, wooing his future empress, Eugénie de Montijo, at the Hôtel du Rhin. In its halcyon days, Strauss waltzes echoed across the plaza. In time, however, they were replaced by cannon fire. The square is dominated by a column crowned by Napoléon. There was a statue of the Sun King here until the Revolution, when it was replaced briefly by *Liberty.*

Then came Napoléon, who ordered that a sort of Trajan's Column be erected in honor of his victory at Austerlitz. It was made of bronze melted from captured Russian and Austrian cannons. After Napoléon's downfall, the statue was replaced by one of Henri IV, everybody's favorite king and every woman's favorite man. Later Napoléon surmounted it again, this time in uniform and without the pose of a Caesar.

The Communards of 1871, who detested royalty and the false promises of emperors, pulled down the statue. Courbet is said to have led the raid. For his part in the drama, he was jailed and fined the cost of restoring the statue. He couldn't pay it, of course, and was forced into exile in Switzerland. Eventually, the statue of Napoléon, wrapped in a Roman toga, finally won out.

La Grande Arche de La Défense. 1 place du parvis de La Défense, 18e. ☎ **01-49-07-27-57.** Admission 40F ($7.20) adults, 32F ($5.75) children 4–18, free for children 5 and under. Daily 10am–6pm. RER: La Défense.

Designed as the architectural centerpiece of the sprawling futuristic suburb of La Défense, this massive steel-and-masonry arch rises 35 stories. It was built with the blessing of the late François Mitterrand and ringed with soaring office buildings and a circular avenue (*périphérique*), patterned after the one surrounding the more famous Arc de Triomphe. This deliberately overscaled archway is one of the latest major landmarks to dot the Paris skyline, along with the Cité de la Musique in the city's northwestern section. High enough to shelter Notre-Dame below its canopy, the monument was designed as an extension of the panorama that connects the Louvre, Arc de Triomphe du Carrousel, Champs-Elysées, Arc de Triomphe, avenue de la Grande-Armée, and place du Porte-Maillot into a magnificent straight line. An elevator carries you to an observation platform from which you can see the carefully conceived geometry of the street plan.

Note that the netting you'll see has been placed there to catch any falling fragments of the arch. Watch your head.

4 The Eiffel Tower & Environs

From place du Trocadéro, you can step between the two curved wings of the Palais de Chaillot and gaze out on a panoramic view. At your feet lie the Jardins du Trocadéro, centered by fountains. Directly in front, pont d'Iéna spans the Seine, leading to the iron immensity of the Tour Eiffel. And beyond, stretching as far as your eye can see, is the **Champ-de-Mars,** once a military parade ground but now a garden with arches, grottoes, lakes, and cascades.

Also easily combined with these sights is the Musée Rodin; see "The Top Museums," earlier in this chapter, for complete details.

✪ **Tour Eiffel.** In the Champ-de-Mars, 7e. ☎ **01-44-11-23-23.** Admission: First landing, 20F ($3.60); second landing, 42F ($7.55); third landing, 59F ($10.60); stairs to second landing, 14F ($2.50). June–Aug daily 9am–midnight; Sept–May daily 9:30am–11pm (stairs close at 6:30pm). Métro: Trocadéro, Ecole-Militaire, or Bir-Hakeim. RER: Champ-de-Mars/Tour-Eiffel.

Except for the Leaning Tower of Pisa, this is the single most recognizable structure in the world—it's the symbol of Paris. Weighing 7,000 tons but exerting about the same pressure on the ground as an average-size person sitting in a chair, the tower was never meant to be permanent. It was built for the Universal Exhibition of 1889 by Gustave-Alexandre Eiffel, the engineer whose fame rested mainly on his iron bridges. (Incidentally, he also designed the framework for the Statue of Liberty.)

The tower, including its 55-foot TV antenna, is 1,056 feet tall. On a clear day you can see it from some 40 miles away. An open-framework construction, the tower ushered in the almost-unlimited possibilities of steel construction, paving the way for the 20th century's skyscrapers. Skeptics said it couldn't be built, and Eiffel actually wanted to make it soar higher. For years it remained the tallest man-made structure on earth, until such skyscrapers as the Empire State Building usurped the record. The advent of wireless communication in the early 1890s preserved the tower from destruction.

You can visit the tower in three stages: Taking the elevator to the first landing, you have a view over the rooftops of Paris. Here you'll find a cinema museum and restaurants and a bar open year-round. The second landing provides a panoramic look at the city (on this level is Le Jules Verne restaurant, a great place for lunch or dinner; see below). The third landing offers the most panoramic view, allowing you to identify monuments and buildings. On the ground level, in the eastern and western pillars, you can visit the 1899 elevator machinery when the tower is open.

To get to **Le Jules Verne** (☎ **01-45-55-61-44**), you take a private south foundation elevator. You can enjoy an aperitif in the relaxing piano bar, then take a seat at one of the dining room's tables, all of which provide an inspiring view. The menu changes seasonally, offering fish and meat dishes that range from filet of turbot with seaweed and buttered sea urchins to veal chops with truffled vegetables. Reservations are recommended.

Hôtel des Invalides (Napoléon's Tomb). Place des Invalides, 7e. ☎ **01-44-42-37-72.** Admission to Musée de l'Armée, Napoléon's Tomb, and Musée des Plans-Reliefs 37F ($6.65) adults, 27F ($4.85) children 12–18, free for children 11 and under. Apr–Sept daily 10am–6pm (Napoléon's Tomb, to 7pm June–Sept); Oct–Mar daily 10am–5pm. Closed Jan 1, May 1, Nov 1, and Dec 25. Métro: Latour-Maubourg, Varenne, or Invalides.

The glory of the French military lives on in the Musée de l'Armée, the world's greatest army museum. It was the Sun King who decided to build the "hotel" to house soldiers who had been disabled by war. It wasn't entirely a benevolent gesture, since these veterans had been injured, crippled, or blinded while fighting Louis's battles. In 1670 this massive building program was launched. Eventually the structure was crowned by a Jules Hardouin-Mansart gilded dome.

The best way to approach the Invalides is by walking from the Right Bank across the turn-of-the-century pont Alexandre-III. Among the collections (begun by a French inspector in 1794) are Viking swords, Burgundian bacinets, 14th-century blunderbusses, Balkan khandjars, American Browning machine guns, war pitchforks, salamander-engraved Renaissance serpentines, musketoons, and grenadiers. As a sardonic touch, there's even General Daumesnil's wooden leg. Outstanding are the suits of armor—especially in the Arsenal—worn by kings and dignitaries, including Louis XIV. The famous "armor suit of the lion" was made for François I. The showcases of swords are among the finest in the world.

Crossing the Cour d'Honneur (Court of Honor), you'll come to Eglise du Dôme, designed by Hardouin-Mansart for Louis XIV. He began work on the church in 1677, though he died before its completion. The dome is Paris's second-tallest monument. In the Napoléon Chapel is the hearse used at the emperor's funeral on May 9, 1821.

To accommodate the Tomb of Napoléon—made of red porphyry, with a green granite base—the architect Visconti had to redesign the high altar in 1842. First buried at St. Helena, Napoléon's remains were returned to Paris in 1840 and then locked inside six coffins. Legends abound that not all those parts were buried with Napoléon, notably his penis and his heart. According to Napoleonic scholars, the two doctors who dissected the emperor placed all his body parts in an urn positioned between his legs. Scholars deny the truth of these legends about the missing parts, though one wealthy gentleman in Connecticut frequently exhibits a penis preserved in alcohol, claiming that it was once attached to the emperor. Surrounding the tomb are a dozen amazonlike figures representing his victories. Almost lampooning the smallness of the man, everything is made awesome: You'd think a real giant were buried here, not a symbolic one. The statue of Napoléon in his coronation robes stands 8½ feet tall.

5 Montparnasse

For the Lost Generation, life centered around the literary cafes here. Hangouts like the Dôme, Coupole, Rotonde, and Sélect became legendary. Artists, especially U.S. expatriates, turned their backs on touristy Montmartre. Picasso, Modigliani, and Man Ray came this way, and Hemingway was a popular figure. So was Fitzgerald when he was poor (when he was in the chips, he hung out at Le Ritz). Faulkner, Isadora Duncan, Miró, Joyce, Ford Madox Ford, and even Trotsky came here.

The life of Montparnasse still centers around its cafes and nightclubs, many only a shadow of what they used to be. Its heart is at the crossroads of boulevards Raspail and du Montparnasse, one of the settings of *The Sun Also Rises*. Rodin's controversial statue of Balzac swathed in a large cape stands guard over the prostitutes who cluster around the pedestal. Balzac seems to be the only one in Montparnasse who doesn't feel the impact of time and change.

Musée Bourdelle. 18 rue Antoine-Bourdelle, 15e. ☎ **01-49-54-73-73.** Admission 27F ($4.85) adults, 19F ($3.40) students and children. Tues–Sun 10am–5:40pm. Métro: Falguière.

Here you can see works by the prime student of Rodin, Antoine Bourdelle (1861–1929). The museum displays the artist's drawings, paintings, and sculptures and lets you wander at will through his studio, garden, and house. The most notable exhibits are the 21 studies he did of Beethoven. The original plaster casts of some of his greatest works are also on display. Though some of the exhibits are badly captioned, you'll still feel the impact of Bourdelle's genius.

Tour Montparnasse. ☎ **01-45-38-52-56.** Admission 44F ($7.90) adults, 38F ($6.85) seniors, 34F ($6.10) students, 28F ($5.05) children 5–14, free for children 4 and under. Apr–Sept daily 9:30am–11:30pm; Oct–Mar Mon–Fri 9:30am–10:30pm. Métro: Montparnasse-Bienvenue.

Towering over the entire arrondissement is the Tour Montparnasse, rising 688 feet—like the Eiffel Tower, a landmark on the Paris skyline. Completed in 1973, it was immediately denounced by some critics as "bringing Manhattan to Paris." The city soon passed an ordinance outlawing any further structures of this size in the heart of Paris. Today, the tower houses a mammoth underground shopping mall and even a train station. You can ride an elevator up to the 56th floor, then climb three flights to the rooftop terrace. At viewing tables at the top you can pick out all the landmarks, from Sacré-Coeur and Notre-Dame to the new Défense area in the distance. A bar and restaurant are on the 56th floor.

Cimetière du Montparnasse. 3 bd. Edgar-Quinet, 14e. ☎ **01-44-10-86-50.** Mon–Fri 8am–6pm, Sat 8:30am–6pm, Sun 9am–6pm (closes at 5:30pm Nov–Mar). Métro: Edgar-Quinet.

In the shadow of the Tour Montparnasse lies this burial ground of yesterday's celebrities, sadly debris-littered and badly maintained. A map (available to the left of the main gateway) will direct you to the most famous occupants: the shared gravesite of Simone de Beauvoir and Jean-Paul Sartre. Others buried here include Samuel Beckett, Guy de Maupassant, Alfred Dreyfus, the auto tycoon André Citroën, Camille Saint-Saëns, and Man Ray.

6 St-Germain-des-Prés

This was the postwar home of existentialism, associated with Jean-Paul Sartre, Simone de Beauvoir, Albert Camus, and an intellectual, bohemian crowd that gathered at the Café de Flore, the Brasserie Lipp, and Les Deux-Magots. Among them, the black-clad poet Juliette Greco was known as *la muse de St-Germain-des-Prés,* and to Sartre she was the woman with "millions of poems in her throat." Her long hair and uniform of black slacks, black turtleneck sweater, and sandals launched a fashion trend adopted by young women from Paris to California.

In the 1950s new names appeared—like Françoise Sagan, Gore Vidal, and James Baldwin—but by the 1960s the tourists had become just as firmly entrenched at the cafes. Today St-Germain-des-Prés retains a bohemian street life, full of interesting bookshops, art galleries, *caveaux* (basement) nightclubs, bistros, and coffeehouses.

Eglise St-Germain-des-Prés. 3 place St-Germain-des-Prés, 6e. ☎ **01-43-25-41-71.** Free admission. Daily 8am–7:30pm. Métro: St-Germain-des-Prés.

Outside it's a handsome early-17th-century town house; inside it's one of Paris's oldest churches, dating from the 6th century when a Benedictine abbey was founded on the site. Unfortunately, the marble columns in the triforium are all that remain from that period. Restoration of the Chapelle St-Symphorien—the site of a pantheon for Merovingian kings, at the entrance of the church—began in 1981. During that work, unknown Romanesque paintings were discovered on the chapel's triumphal arch. The Romanesque tower, topped by a 19th-century spire, is the most enduring landmark in the village of St-Germain-des-Prés. Its church bells, however, are hardly noticed by the patrons of Deux-Magots across the way.

The Normans nearly destroyed the abbey at least four times. The present building has a Romanesque nave and a Gothic choir with fine capitals. Among the people interred at the church are Descartes (well, his heart at least) and Jean-Casimir, the king of Poland who abdicated his throne.

When you leave the church, turn right onto rue de l'Abbaye and have a look at the 17th-century Palais Abbatial, a pink palace.

Eglise St-Sulpice. Rue St-Sulpice, 6e. ☎ **01-46-33-21-78.** Free admission. Daily 7:30am–7:30pm. Métro: St-Sulpice.

A Church-Concert Tip

Eglise St-Germain-des-Prés stages the most wonderful concerts on the Left Bank, featuring fantastic acoustics and a marvelous medieval atmosphere. The church was built to accommodate an age without microphones, and the sound effects will thrill you. For more information, call ☎ **01-43-25-41-71.** Performances take place on Tuesday and Thursday; arrive about 45 minutes early if you'd like a front-row seat.

Pause first on the quiet rue St-Sulpice. The 1844 fountain by Visconti displays the sculpted likenesses of four bishops of the Louis XIV era: Fenelon, Massillon, Bossuet, and Flechier. Work on the church itself, at one time Paris's largest, began in 1646 as part of the Catholic revival then occurring in France. Although the body of the church was completed in 1745, work on the bell towers continued until 1780, when one was finished, the other left incomplete. One of the most notable treasures inside is Servandoni's rococo Chapelle de la Vierge (Chapel of the Madonna), which contains a Pigalle statue of the Virgin. The church houses one of the world's largest organs; it has 6,700 pipes and has been played by such musicians as Charles-Marie Widor and Marcel Dupré.

The main draw at St-Sulpice is the Delacroix frescoes in the Chapel of the Angels (the first on your right as you enter). Seek out his muscular Jacob wrestling (or is he dancing?) with an angel. On the ceiling, St. Michael has his own troubles with the devil, and yet another mural depicts Heliodorus being driven from the temple. Painted in the final years of his life, the frescoes were a high point in the baffling career of Delacroix.

7 The Latin Quarter

This is the Left Bank precinct of the **University of Paris** (often called the Sorbonne), where students meet and fall in love over coffee and croissants. Rabelais called it the *Quartier Latin* because of the students and professors who spoke Latin in the classrooms and on the streets. The sector teems with belly dancers, exotic restaurants (from Vietnamese to Balkan), sidewalk cafes, bookstalls, and *caveaux* (basement nightclubs).

A good starting point is **place St-Michel** (Métro: Pont-St-Michel), where Balzac used to get water from the fountain when he was a youth. This center was the scene of much Resistance fighting in the summer of 1944. The quarter centers around **boulevard St-Michel** ("Boul Mich"), to the south.

Musée National du Moyen Age (Musée de Cluny). 6 place Paul-Painlevé, 5e. ☎ **01-53-73-78-00.** Admission 30F ($5.40) adults, 20F ($3.60) ages 18–25, free for children 17 and under. Wed–Mon 9:15am–5:45pm. Métro: Cluny–La Sorbonne.

There are two reasons to come here: The museum houses the world's finest collection of art from the Middle Ages, including jewelry and tapestries; and it's all displayed in a well-preserved manor house built atop Roman baths. In the cobblestone Cour d'Honneur you can admire the Flamboyant Gothic building with its clinging vines, turreted walls, gargoyles, and dormers with seashell motifs. Along with the Hôtel de Sens in the Marais, this is all that remains in Paris of domestic medieval architecture.

Originally, the Cluny was the mansion of a 15th-century abbot. By 1515 it was the residence of Mary Tudor, the teenage widow of Louis XII and the daughter of Henry VII of England and Elizabeth of York. Seized during the Revolution, it was rented in 1833 to Alexandre du Sommerard, who adorned it with medieval works of art. On his death in 1842, both the building and the collection were bought back by the government.

Most people come primarily to see the **Unicorn Tapestries,** the world's most out-standing tapestries. A beautiful princess and her handmaiden, beasts of prey, and just plain pets—all the romance of the age of chivalry lives on in these remarkable yet mys-terious tapestries. They were discovered only a century ago in the Château de Boussac in the Auvergne. Five seem to deal with the senses (one depicts a unicorn looking into a mirror held by a dour-faced maiden). The sixth shows a woman under an elaborate tent, her pet dog resting on an embroidered cushion beside her. The lovable unicorn and its friendly companion, a lion, hold back the flaps. The red and green background forms a rich carpet of spring flowers, fruit-laden trees, birds, rabbits, donkeys, dogs, goats, lambs, and monkeys.

Downstairs are the ruins of the Roman baths, dating from around A.D. 200. You wander through a display of Gallic and Roman sculptures and an interesting marble bathtub engraved with lions.

La Sorbonne. Bd. St-Michel. Métro: St-Michel.

The University of Paris—everybody calls it the Sorbonne—is one of the most famous institutions in the world. Founded in the 13th century, it had become the most pres-tigious university in the West by the 14th century, drawing such professors as Thomas Aquinas. Reorganized by Napoléon in 1806, the Sorbonne is today the premier uni-versity of France. At first glance from place de la Sorbonne, it may seem architecturally undistinguished; it was rather indiscriminately reconstructed at the turn of the cen-tury. Not so the **Eglise de la Sorbonne,** however, built in 1635 by Le Mercier at the exact center of the Sorbonne. It contains the marble tomb of Cardinal Richelieu, a work by Girardon based on a Le Brun design. At his feet is the remarkable statue *Science in Tears.*

Panthéon. Place du Panthéon, 5e. ☎ **01-44-32-18-00.** Admission 32F ($5.75) adults, 21F ($3.80) ages 12–25, free for children 11 and under. Apr–Sept daily 9:30am–6:30pm; Oct–Mar daily 10am–6:15pm. (Last entrance 45 minutes before closing.) Métro: Cardinal-Lemoine or Maubert-Mutualité.

Some of the most famous men in the history of France (Victor Hugo, for one) are buried here in austere grandeur, on the crest of the mount of Ste-Geneviève. In 1744 Louis XV made a vow that if he recovered from a mysterious illness, he would build a church to replace the decayed Abbaye de Ste-Geneviève. He recovered—and Mme de Pompadour's brother hired Soufflot for the job. He designed the church in the form of a Greek cross, with a dome reminiscent of St. Paul's Cathedral in London. When Soufflot died, his pupil Rondelet carried out the work, completing the structure 9 years after his master's death.

Following the Revolution, the church was converted into a "Temple of Fame"—ultimately a pantheon for the great men of France. The body of Mirabeau was buried here, though his remains were later removed. Likewise, Marat was only a temporary tenant. However, Voltaire's body was exhumed and placed here—and allowed to remain. In the 19th century the building changed roles so many times—first a church, then a pantheon, again a church—that it was hard to keep its function straight. After Victor Hugo was buried here it became a pantheon once more. Other notable men entombed within include Jean-Jacques Rousseau, Soufflot, Emile Zola, and Louis Braille.

In spring 1995, the ashes of the scientist Marie Curie were entombed at the Pan-théon, "the first lady so honored in our history for her own merits," in the words of the late François Mitterrand. Madame Curie had once been denied membership in the all-male Academy of Sciences. Another woman, Sophie Bertholet, was buried here first, but only alongside her chemist husband, Marcellin, and not as a personal honor to her.

Most recently, the ashes of André Malraux were transferred here because he "lived [his] dreams and made them live in us," according to President Jacques Chirac. As Charles de Gaulle's culture minister, Malraux decreed that the arts should be part of the lives of all French people—not just Paris's elite.

The finest frescoes, the Puvis de Chavannes, are at the end of the left wall before you enter the crypt. One illustrates Ste. Geneviève bringing supplies to relieve the victims of the famine. The best depicts her white-draped head looking out over moonlit medieval Paris, the city whose patroness she became.

8   Les Halles

For eight centuries Les Halles was the major wholesale fruit, meat, and vegetable market of Paris. The smock-clad vendors, the carcasses of beef, the baskets of the most appetizing vegetables in the world—all that belongs to the past. Today the action has moved to the modern steel-and-glass structure at Rungis, a suburb near Orly. Here today is **Les Forum des Halles** (Métro: Les Halles; RER: Châtelet–Les Halles), which opened in 1979. This large complex, much of it underground, houses dozens of shops, plus several restaurants and movie theaters.

For many visitors, a night on the town still ends in the wee hours with the traditional bowl of onion soup at Les Halles, usually at **Au Pied de Cochon** ("Pig's Foot") or **Au Chien Qui Fume** ("Smoking Dog").

There's still much to see in Les Halles, beginning with the **Eglise St-Eustache,** 2 rue du Jour, 1er (☎ **01-42-36-31-05;** Métro: Les Halles), with another entrance on rue Rambuteau. In the old days, cabbage vendors came here to pray for their produce. The Gothic-Renaissance church dates from the mid-16th century yet wasn't completed until 1637. It has been known for its organ recitals ever since Liszt played here in 1866. Inside is the black marble tomb of Jean-Baptiste Colbert, the minister of state under Louis XIV. A marble statue of the statesman rests on top of his tomb, which is flanked by Coysevox's *Abundance* (a horn of flowers) and J. B. Tuby's *Fidelity.* The church is open daily from 9am to 7:30pm; mass is at 11am Sunday, and there's also an organ concert Sunday at 5:30pm.

9   Le Marais

When Paris began to overflow the confines of the Ile de la Cité in the 13th century, the citizenry settled in the Marais, the marsh that used to be flooded regularly by the high-rising Seine. By the 17th century the Marais had reached the pinnacle of fashion, becoming the center of aristocratic Paris. At that time, most of its great *hôtels particuliers* (mansions)—many now restored or being spruced up today—were built by the finest craftsmen in France.

In the 18th and 19th centuries, the fashionable deserted the Marais in favor of the expanding Faubourg St-Germain and Faubourg St-Honoré. Industry eventually took over the quarter, and the once-elegant hôtels were turned into tenements. There was talk of demolishing this blighted sector, but in 1962 the alarmed Comité de Sauvegarde du Marais banded together and saved the district. The regeneration of the neighborhood was sparked by the Pompidou Center.

No longer "the Swamp" (its English name), the Marais in the 3rd and 4th arrondissements is trendy once again, filled with tiny twisting streets, bars for both gays and straights, and cutting-edge designer shops.

In **place de la Bastille** on July 14, 1789, a mob of Parisians attacked the Bastille and thus sparked the French Revolution. Nothing remains of the historic Bastille, built in 1369, for it was torn down. Many prisoners—some sentenced by Louis XIV for "witchcraft"—were kept within its walls, the best known being the "Man in the Iron Mask." When the fortress was stormed, only seven prisoners were discovered (the marquis de Sade had been transferred to the madhouse 10 days earlier). Authorities had discussed razing it anyway, so the attack was more symbolic than anything else. What it signified, however, and what it started will never be forgotten. Bastille Day is celebrated with great festivity every July 14. In the center of the square is the **Colonne de Juillet** (July Column), which doesn't commemorate the Revolution; rather, it honors the victims of the 1830 July Revolution, which put Louis-Philippe on the throne. The tower is crowned by the God of Liberty, a winged nude with a star emerging from his head.

Not far away, ✪ **place des Vosges,** 4e (Métro: St-Paul or Chemin-Vert), is Paris's oldest square and once its most fashionable. Situated in the heart of the Marais, it was called the Palais Royal in the days of Henri IV, who planned to live here—but his assassin, Ravaillac, had other intentions for him. Henry II was killed while jousting on the square in 1559, in the shadow of the Hôtel des Tournelles. His widow, Catherine de Médici, had the place torn down. Place des Vosges, once a major dueling ground, was one of Europe's first planned squares. Its grand siècle redbrick houses are ornamented with white stone, and its covered arcades allowed people to shop at all times, even in the rain—quite an innovation at the time. In the 18th century chestnut trees were added, sparking a controversy that continues to this day: Critics say that the addition spoils the perspective.

As you stroll the Marais, you might want to seek out the following hôtels: The **Hôtel de Rohan,** 87 rue Vieille-du-Temple (☎ **01-40-27-60-09**), was once occupied by the fourth Cardinal Rohan, who was involved in the scandal that framed Marie Antoinette for buying a priceless diamond necklace. The first Cardinal Rohan, the original occupant, was reputed to be the son of Louis XIV. The main attraction is the amusing 18th-century Salon des Singes (Monkey Room). In the courtyard is a stunning bas-relief of a nude Apollo and four horses against exploding sunbursts. The hotel can be visited only during special exhibitions announced in Paris newspapers.

At 47 rue Vieille-du-Temple is the **Hôtel des Ambassadeurs de Hollande,** where Beaumarchais wrote *The Marriage of Figaro.* It's one of the most splendid mansions in the area—and was never occupied by the Dutch embassy. It's not open to the public.

Although the facade of the 17th-century **Hôtel de Beauvais,** 68 rue François-Miron, was badly damaged during the Revolution, it remains one of the most charming in Paris. A plaque commemorates the fact that Mozart inhabited the mansion in 1763. To visit inside, speak to the Association du Paris Historique, on the ground floor of the building, any afternoon.

Hôtel de Sens, a landmark at 1 rue de Figuier (☎ **01-42-78-14-60**), was built from the 1470s to 1519 for the archbishops of Sens. Along with the Hôtel de Cluny on the Left Bank, it's the only domestic architecture remaining from the 15th century. Long after the archbishops had departed in 1605, it was occupied by the scandalous Queen Margot, wife of Henri IV. Her "younger and more virile" new lover slew the discarded one as she looked on in amusement. Today the mansion houses the Bibliothèque Forney. In the courtyard is ornate stone decoration—the gate is open Tuesday through Friday from 1:30 to 8:15pm and Saturday from 10am to 8:15pm.

Work began on the **Hôtel de Bethune-Sully,** 62 rue St-Antoine (☎ **01-44-61-20-00**), in 1625. In 1634 it was acquired by the duc de Sully, who had been Henri IV's minister of finance before the king was assassinated in 1610. After a straitlaced life,

AT&T

AT&T Direct℠ Service

Steps to follow for easy calling worldwide:

1. Just dial the AT&T Access Number for the country you are calling from.
2. Dial the phone number you're calling.
3. Dial your card number.

AT&T Access Numbers

Argentina	0-800-54-288	Costa Rica	0-800-0-114-114
Australia ▲	1-800-881-011	Czech Rep. ▲	00-42-000-101
Austria ○	022-903-011	Ecuador ▲	999-119
Bahamas	1-800-872-2881	Egypt•(Cairo)†	510-0200
Belgium •	0-800-100-10	France	0-800-99-0011
Brazil	000-8010	Germany	0130-0010
Canada	1 800 CALL ATT	Greece•	00-800-1311
China, PRC ▲	10811	Guam	1 800 CALL ATT
Colombia	980-11-0010	Guatemala ○✕	99-99-190

AT&T

AT&T Direct℠ Service

Steps to follow for easy calling worldwide:

1. Just dial the AT&T Access Number for the country you are calling from.
2. Dial the phone number you're calling.
3. Dial your card number.

AT&T Access Numbers

Argentina	0-800-54-288	Costa Rica	0-900-0-114-114
Australia ▲	1-800-881-011	Czech Rep. ▲	00-42-000-101
Austria ○	022-903-011	Ecuador ▲	999-119
Bahamas	1-800-872-2881	Egypt•(Cairo)†	510-0200
Belgium •	0-800-100-10	France	0-800-99-0011
Brazil	000-8010	Germany	0130-0010
Canada	1 800 CALL ATT	Greece•	00-800-1311
China, PRC ▲	10811	Guam	1 800 CALL ATT
Colombia	980-11-0010	Guatemala ○✕	99-99-190

AT&T Access Numbers

Honduras	800-0-123	Panama		109
Hong Kong	800-96-1111	Philippines●		105-11
Ireland✓	1-800-550-000	Saudi Arabia○		1-800-10
Israel	1-800-94-94-949	Singapore		800-0111-111
Italy●	172-1011	Spain		900-99-00-11
Jamaica○	1-800-872-2881	Sweden		020-795-611
Japan●▲	0039-111	Switzerland●		0-800-89-0011
Japan●▲	0066-55-111	Taiwan		0080-10288-0
Korea, Republic●	0072-911	Thailand◖		001-999-111-11
Mexico▽◊	01-800-288-2872	U.K.▲✧		0800-89-0011
Netherlands●	0800-022-9111	U.K.▲✧		0500-89-0011
New Zealand	000-911	Venezuela		800-11-120

For access numbers not listed ask any operator for **AT&T Direct™** Service.
In the U.S. call 1-800-331-1140 for a wallet card listing all worldwide
AT&T Access Numbers.

Visit our Web site at: www.att.com/traveler

Bold faced countries permit country-to-country calling outside the U.S.

- ● Public phones require coin or card deposit.
- ✕ Available from select hotels
- ◖ Dial "02" first, outside of Cairo
- ▲ May not be available from every phone/public phone
- ◊ Calling available to most countries
- ○ Public phones require local coin payment during call.
- ✧ When calling from public phones, use phones marked "Ladatel"
- ✦ Collect calling only.
- ✓ Use U.K. access number in N. Ireland.
- ∨ When calling from public phones, use phones marked "Lenso"
  If call does not complete, use 0800-013-0011
- ↓ When calling from public phones, use phones marked "Ladatel"
  If call does not complete, use 001-800-462-4240

When placing an international call *from* the U.S.
dial 1 800 CALL ATT

© 5/98 AT&T

AT&T Access Numbers

Honduras	800-00-123	Panama		109
Hong Kong	800-96-1111	Philippines●		105-11
Ireland✓	1-800-550-000	Saudi Arabia○		1-800-10
Israel	1-800-94-94-949	Singapore		800-0111-111
Italy●	172-1011	Spain		900-99-00-11
Jamaica○	1-800-872-2881	Sweden		020-795-611
Japan●▲	0039-111	Switzerland●		0-800-89-0011
Japan●▲	0066-55-111	Taiwan		0080-10288-0
Korea, Republic●	0072-911	Thailand◖		001-999-111-11
Mexico▽◊	01-800-288-2872	U.K.▲✧		0800-89-0011
Netherlands●	0800-022-9111	U.K.▲✧		0500-89-0011
New Zealand	000-911	Venezuela		800-11-120

For access numbers not listed ask any operator for **AT&T Direct™** Service.
In the U.S. call 1-800-331-1140 for a wallet card listing all worldwide
AT&T Access Numbers.

Visit our Web site at: www.att.com/traveler

Bold faced countries permit country-to-country calling outside the U.S.

- ● Public phones require coin or card deposit.
- ✕ Available from select hotels
- ◖ Dial "02" first, outside of Cairo
- ▲ May not be available from every phone/public phone
- ◊ Calling available to most countries
- ○ Public phones require local coin payment during call.
- ✧ When calling from public phones, use phones marked "Ladatel"
- ✦ Collect calling only.
- ✓ Use U.K. access number in N. Ireland.
- ∨ When calling from public phones, use phones marked "Lenso"
  If call does not complete, use 0800-013-0011
- ↓ When calling from public phones, use phones marked "Ladatel"
  If call does not complete, use 001-800-462-4240

When placing an international call *from* the U.S.
dial 1 800 CALL ATT

© 5/98 AT&T

(say yes)

You pop the question in Paris, you better have an **AT&T Direct**® Service wallet guide in your pocket. It's a list of access numbers you need to call home fast and clear from around the world, using an AT&T Calling Card or credit card.

So you can give everyone back home a ring.

For a list of **AT&T Access Numbers,** take the attached wallet guide.

It's all within your reach.

For
Travelers
who want more than
the Official Line

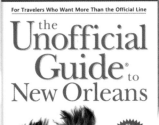

Macmillan Publishing USA

Sully broke loose in his later years, adorning himself with diamonds and garish rings—and a young bride who had a preference for very young men. The hôtel was acquired by the government after World War II and now contains the National Office of Historical Monuments and Sites. Recently restored, the relief-studded facade is especially appealing. There's daily admittance to the courtyard and the garden that opens onto place des Vosges.

The most characteristic street in the district is **rue des Rosiers (Street of the Rosebushes),** one of the most colorful of the streets remaining from the old Jewish quarter. The Star of David shines here, Hebrew letters flash (in neon), couscous is sold from the shops run by Moroccan or Algerian Jews, bearded old men sit in doorways, restaurants serve strictly kosher meals, and signs appeal for Jewish liberation.

Shoppers will delight in such places as **Marais Plus,** 20 rue des Francs-Bourgeois (☎ 01-48-87-01-40), at the corner of rue Elzévir and rue des Francs-Bourgeois. This very artsy gift shop has a cozy tearoom at the rear. At **Hier, Aujourd'hui, and Demain,** 14 rue de Bretagne (☎ 01-42-77-69-02), you'll fall in love with 1930s Art Deco. For copies of 17th-century maps and engravings, head for **Jardin de Flore,** 24 Place des Vosges (☎ 01-42-77-61-90). These shops are just suggestions to get you going; you'll discover dozens more on your own as you wander the district.

Musée Carnavalet. 23 rue de Sévigné, 3e. ☎ **01-42-72-21-13.** Admission 35F ($6.30) adults, 25F ($4.50) ages 25 and under and seniors over 60. Tues–Sun 10am–5:40pm. Métro: St-Paul or Chemin-Vert.

The history of Paris comes alive here in intimately personal terms—right down to the chessmen Louis XVI used to distract himself in the days before he went to the guillotine. A renowned Renaissance palace, the hôtel was built in 1544 by Pierre Lescot and Jean Goujon and later acquired by Mme de Carnavalet. The great François Mansart transformed it between 1655 and 1661. It's probably best known because one of history's most famous letter writers, Mme de Sévigné, moved here in 1677. Fanatically devoted to her daughter (until she had to live with her), she poured out nearly every detail of her life in letters, virtually ignoring her son; a native of the Marais, she died at her daughter's château in 1696. It wasn't until 1866 that the city acquired the mansion and turned it into a museum.

10 Montmartre

From the 1880s to just before World War I, Montmartre enjoyed its golden age as the world's best-known art colony, where *la vie de bohème* reigned supreme. Following World War I, the pseudoartists flocked here in droves, with camera-snapping tourists hot on their heels. The real artists had long gone to such places as Montparnasse.

Before its discovery and subsequent chic, Montmartre was a sleepy farming community, with windmills dotting the landscape. Those who find the trek up to Paris's highest elevations too much of a climb may prefer to ride **Le Petit Train de Montmartre,** a miniature train that passes all the major landmarks; it seats 55 passengers and offers English commentary. Board at place du Tertre (at the Eglise St-Pierre) or place Blanche (near the Moulin Rouge). From June to September, trains run daily from 10am to midnight; off-season, daily from 10am to 6pm. For information, contact Promotrain, 131 rue de Clignancourt, 18e (☎ 01-42-62-24-00).

The simplest way to reach Montmartre is to take the Métro to Anvers, then walk up rue du Steinkerque to the funicular, which runs to the precincts of Sacré-Coeur every day from 5:30am to 12:30am. Except for Sacré-Coeur (see below), Montmartre has only minor attractions; it's the historic architecture and the atmosphere that are compelling.

Specific attractions to look for include the **Bateau-Lavoir (Boat Warehouse),** place Emile-Goudeau. Although gutted by fire in 1970, it has been reconstructed. Picasso once lived here and, in the winter of 1905 to 1906, painted one of the world's most famous portraits, *The Third Rose* (Gertrude Stein).

Espace Montmartre Salvadore-Dalí, 11 rue Poulbot (☎ **01-42-64-40-10**), presents Dalí's phantasmagorical world with 330 original works, including his 1956 *Don Quixote* lithograph. It's open daily from 10am to 6pm, charging 35F ($6.30) for adults and 25F ($4.50) for children.

One of the most famous churches here is the **Eglise St-Pierre,** rue du Mont-Cenis, originally a Benedictine abbey. The church was consecrated in 1147; two of the columns in the choir stall are the remains of a Roman temple. Among the sculptured works, note the nun with the head of a pig, a symbol of sensual vice. At the entrance are three bronze doors sculpted by Gismondi in 1980: The middle door depicts the life of St. Peter; the left is dedicated to St. Denis, first bishop of Paris; and the right is dedicated to the Holy Virgin.

Musée de Vieux Montmartre, 12 rue Cortot (☎ **01-46-06-61-11**), exhibits a wide collection of mementos. This 17th-century house was once occupied by Dufy, van Gogh, Renoir, and Suzanne Valadon and her son, Utrillo. It's open Tuesday through Sunday from 11am to 6pm. Admission is 25F ($4.50) for adults and 20F ($3.60) for children 10 and under.

✪ **Basilique du Sacré-Coeur.** Place St-Pierre, 18e. ☎ **01-53-41-89-00.** Admission: basilica, free; dome, 15F ($2.70) adults, 8F ($1.45) ages 6–25; crypt, 15F ($2.70) adults, 5F (90¢) ages 6–25; joint ticket for both, 30F ($5.40). Basilica, daily 6:45am–11pm. Dome and crypt, Apr–Sept daily 9:15am–7pm; Oct–Mar daily 9:15am–5:45pm. Métro: Abbesses; then take the elevator to the surface and follow the signs to the funiculaire, which takes you up to the church for the price of one Métro ticket.

Montmartre's crowning achievement is Sacré-Coeur, though the view of Paris from its precincts takes precedence over the basilica itself. Like other Parisian landmarks, it has always been the subject of much controversy. One Parisian called it "a lunatic's confectionery dream." Zola declared it "the basilica of the ridiculous." Sacré-Coeur's supporters included the Jewish poet Max Jacob and the artist Maurice Utrillo. Utrillo never tired of drawing and painting it, and he and Jacob came here regularly to pray.

Its gleaming white domes and *campanile* (bell tower) tower over Paris like a Byzantine church of the 12th century. But it's not that old: After France's defeat by the Prussians in 1870, the basilica was planned as an offering to cure the country's misfortunes; rich and poor alike contributed the money to build it. Construction began in 1873, but the church wasn't consecrated until 1919. The interior of the basilica is brilliantly decorated with mosaics, the most striking of which are the ceiling depiction of Christ and the mural of the Passion found at the back of the altar. The crypt contains a relic of what some of the devout believe is a piece of the sacred heart of Christ—hence the church's name.

On a clear day the vista from the dome can extend for 35 miles. You can also walk around the inner dome of the church, peering down like a pigeon (a few will likely be there to keep you company).

Cimetière de Montmartre. 20 av. Rachel (west of the Butte Montmartre and north of bd. de Clichy), 18e. ☎ **01-43-87-64-24.** Mon–Fri 8am–6pm, Sat 8:30am–6pm, Sun 8am–7pm (closes at 5:30pm in winter). Métro: La Fourche.

Interred at this resting place of famous composers, writers, and artists is everybody from the novelist Alexandre Dumas to the Russian dancer Vaslav Nijinsky. The great Stendhal was buried here, as were Hector Berlioz, Heinrich Heine, Edgar Degas,

Jacques Offenbach, and even François Truffaut. We like to pay our respects at the tomb of Alphonsine Plessis, the courtesan on whom Dumas based his Marguerite Gautier in *La Dame aux camélias*. Emile Zola was interred here, but his corpse was exhumed and taken to the Panthéon in 1908. In the tragic year of 1871, the cemetery became the site of the mass burials of victims of the Siege and the Commune.

11 Parks, Gardens & Cemeteries

See section 3, "The Champs-Elysees: The Grand Promenade of Paris," for details on the **Tulieries**. **Cimetière du Montparnasse** is covered earlier in section 5, "Montparnasse," and the **Cimetière de Montmartre** can be found in section 10, "Montmartre."

✪ **Jardin du Luxembourg.** 6e. Métro: Odéon. RER: Luxembourg.

Hemingway told a friend that the Jardin du Luxembourg "kept us from starvation." He related that in his poverty-stricken days in Paris, he wheeled a baby carriage through the gardens because it was known "for the classiness of its pigeons." When the gendarme left to get a glass of wine, the writer would eye his victim, then lure it with corn and snatch it. "We got a little tired of pigeon that year," he confessed, "but they filled many a void."

Before it became a feeding ground for struggling artists in the 1920s, the Luxembourg Gardens knew greater days. They are the finest formal gardens on the Left Bank (some say in all of Paris). Marie de Médici, the much-neglected wife and later widow of the roving Henri IV, ordered the **Palais du Luxembourg** built on this site in 1612. She planned to live here with her "witch" friend, Leonora Galigaï. A Florentine by birth, the regent wanted to create another Pitti Palace, or so she ordered the architect, Salomon de Brosse. She wasn't entirely successful, although the overall effect is most often described as Italianate.

The queen didn't get to enjoy the Luxembourg Palace for very long after it was finished. She was forced into exile by her son, Louis XIII, after he discovered that she was plotting to overthrow him. She died in Cologne in poverty, quite a comedown from the luxury she'd known in the Luxembourg. (Incidentally, the 21 paintings she commissioned from Rubens that glorified her life were intended for her palace but are now in the Louvre.) For 45F ($8.10) you can visit the palace the first Sunday of each month at 10:15am. However, you must call ☎ **01-44-61-20-89** to make a reservation. There is no information number for the park itself.

But the main draw here is not the palace but the gardens. For the most part, they're in the classic French style: well groomed and formally laid out, the trees planted in designs. The large central water basin is encircled by urns and statuary—one statue honors Ste. Geneviève, the patroness of Paris, depicted with pigtails reaching to her thighs. Come here to soak in the atmosphere, and bring the kids if you have any. You can sail a toy boat, ride a pony, or attend a Grand Guignol puppet show on occasion. Best of all, play boules with a group of elderly men who aren't afraid of looking like a French cliché from 1928, complete with black berets and Gauloises.

✪ **Bois de Boulogne.** Porte-Dauphine, 16e. ☎ **01-40-67-90-82.** Métro: Les-Sablons, Porte-Maillot, or Porte-Dauphine.

This is one of the most spectacular parks in Europe. Horse-drawn carriages traverse it, but you can also take your car through. Better still, stroll its many hidden pathways. If you had a week to spare, you could spend it all in the Bois de Boulogne and still not see everything.

Porte-Dauphine is the main entrance, but you can take the Métro to Porte-Maillot as well. West of Paris, the park was once a forest kept for royal hunts. In the late 19th

Royal Remains at St-Denis

In the 12th century, Abbot Suger placed an inscription on the bronze doors of St-Denis: "Marvel not at the gold and expense, but at the craftsmanship of the work." The first Gothic building in France that can be dated precisely, St-Denis was the "spiritual defender of the State" during the reign of Louis VI ("The Fat"). The massive façade with its crenelated parapet on the top similar to the fortifications of a castle, has a rose window. The stained-glass windows, in stunning colors—mauve, purple, blue, and rose—were restored in the 19th century.

St-Denis, the first bishop of Paris, became the patron saint of the French monarchy. Royal burials began here in the sixth century and continued until the Revolution. The sculptures designed for tombs—some two stories high—span the country's artistic development from the Middle Ages to the Renaissance. The guided tour (in French only) takes you through the crypt. Francois I was entombed at St-Denis. His funeral statue is nude, although he demurely covers himself with his hand. Other kings and queens here include Louis XII and Anne of Brittany, as well as Henri II and Catherine de Medici. However, the Revolutionaries stormed through, smashing many marble faces and dumping royal remains in a lime-filled ditch in the garden. Royal remains were reburied under the main altar during the 19th century. The basilica stands today in a dreary northern suburb of Paris, but it's easily reached by the Metro. Free organ concerts are presented here on Sunday at 11:15am.

The Basilique St-Denis is located at Place de l'Hotel-de-Ville, 2 rue de Strasbourg, ☎ 01-48-09-83-54. Admission is 32F ($6.40) for adults and 21F ($4.20) for seniors and students, free for visitors 11 and under. It's open daily from April through September, and Monday through Saturday during the rest of the year. The closest Metro is St-Denis Basilique.

century it was very much in vogue: Carriages bearing elegant Parisian damsels with their foppish escorts rumbled along avenue Foch. Nowadays, it's more likely to attract middle-class picnickers.

When Napoléon III gave the grounds to the city in 1852, they were developed by Baron Haussmann. Separating Lac Inférieur from Lac Supérieur is the Carrefour des Cascades (you can stroll under its waterfall). The Lower Lake contains two islands connected by a footbridge. From the east bank, you can take a boat to these idyllic grounds, perhaps stopping at the cafe-restaurant on one of them. Restaurants in the Bois are numerous, elegant, and expensive. The Pré-Catelan contains a deluxe restaurant of the same name and a Shakespearean theater in a garden said to have been planted with trees mentioned in the bard's plays.

The **Jardin d'Acclimation,** at the northern edge of the Bois de Boulogne, is for children, with a small zoo, an amusement park, and a narrow-gauge railway. Two racetracks, **Longchamp** and **Auteuil,** are also in the park. The annual Grand Prix is run in June at Longchamp (site of a medieval abbey). The most fashionable Parisians turn out, the women attired in their finest haute couture and hats to die for. To the north of Longchamp is the Grand Cascade, the artificial waterfall of the Bois de Boulogne.

In the 60-acre **Bagatelle Park,** the comte d'Artois (later Charles X), brother-in-law of Marie Antoinette, made a wager with her that he could erect a small palace in less than 3 months. He hired nearly 1,000 craftsmen and irritated the local populace by requisitioning all shipments of stone and plaster arriving through the west gates of

Paris. He hired ébenistes, painters, and the Scottish landscape architect Thomas Blaikie—and he won his bet. If you're in Paris in late April, go to the Bagatelle to look at the tulips, if for no other reason. In late May one of the finest and best-known rose collections in all of Europe is in full bloom. If you can, visit also in September, when the light is less harsh than summer, or even in February when, stripped of much of its greenery, the park's true shape can be seen. *Note:* Beware of muggers and knife-carrying prostitutes at night.

Parc Monceau. 8e. ☎ **01-42-27-39-56.** Métro: Monceau or Villiers.

An American expatriate once said that all babies in Parc Monceau were respectable. Whether or not babies like the park, their mothers and nurses seem fond of wheeling their carriages through it. Much of the park is ringed with 18th- and 19th-century mansions, some evoking Proust's *Remembrance of Things Past.* The park was opened to the public during Napoléon III's Second Empire. It was built in 1778 by the duc d'Orléans, or Philippe-Egalité, as he became known. Carmontelle designed the park for the duke, who was at the time the richest man in France.

Parc Monceau was laid out with an Egyptian-style obelisk, a medieval dungeon, a thatched alpine farmhouse, a Chinese pagoda, a Roman temple, an enchanted grotto, various chinoiseries, and a waterfall. These fairy-tale touches have largely disappeared except for a pyramid and an oval *naumachie* fringed by a colonnade. Many of the former fantasies have been replaced by solid statuary and monuments, one honoring Chopin. In spring, the red tulips and magnolias alone are worth the airfare to Paris.

✪ **Cimetière du Père-Lachaise.** 16 rue de Repos, 20e. ☎ **01-43-70-70-33.** Mon–Fri 8am–6pm, Sat 8:30am–6pm, Sun 9am–6pm (closes at 5:30pm from Nov to early Mar). Métro: Père-Lachaise.

When it comes to name-dropping, this cemetery knows no peer—it's been called the "grandest address in Paris." Everybody from Sarah Bernhardt to Oscar Wilde (his tomb by Epstein) was buried here. So were Balzac, Delacroix, and Bizet. The body of Colette was taken here in 1954 (legend has it that cats replenish the red roses always found on her black granite slab), and in time, the "little sparrow," Edith Piaf, would follow. The lover of George Sand, the poet Alfred de Musset, was buried here under a weeping willow. Napoléon's marshals Ney and Masséna were entombed here, as were Chopin and Molière. Marcel Proust's black tombstone rarely lacks a tiny bunch of violets; alas, Proust wished to be buried with his friend/lover, the composer Maurice Ravel, but their families wouldn't allow it.

Some tombs are sentimental favorites: that of American rock star Jim Morrison reportedly draws the most visitors—and causes the most disruption. The great dancer Isadora Duncan came to rest in a "pigeonhole" in the Columbarium, where bodies have been cremated and then "filed." If you search hard enough, you can find the tombs of star-crossed Abélard and Héloïse, the ill-fated lovers of the 12th century. At Père-Lachaise, they've found peace at last. Other famous lovers also rest here: One stone is marked GERTRUDE STEIN on one side, ALICE B. TOKLAS on the other.

Spreading over more than 110 acres, Père-Lachaise was acquired by the city in 1804. Nineteenth-century French sculpture abounds, each family trying to outdo the others in ornamentation and cherubic ostentation. Some French socialists still pay tribute at the Mur des Fédérés, the anonymous gravesite of the Communards who were executed on May 28, 1871. The French who died in the Resistance or in Nazi concentration camps are also honored by several monuments.

Note: A free map is available at the newsstand across from the main entrance; it will help you find the well-known gravesites.

12 Paris Underground

Les Catacombs. 1 place Denfert-Rochereau, 14e. ☎ **01-43-22-47-63**. Admission 27F ($4.85) adults, 19F ($3.40) ages 7–18 and over 60, free for ages 6 and under. Tues–Fri 2–4pm, Sat–Sun 9–11am and 2–4pm. Métro: Denfert-Rochereau.

Every year an estimated 50,000 tourists explore some 1,000 yards of tunnel in these dank Catacombs to look at six million ghoulishly arranged skull-and-crossbones skeletons. First opened to the public in 1810, this "empire of the dead" is now illuminated with overhead electric lights througout its entire length.

In the Middle Ages the Catacombs were originally quarries, but in 1785 city officials decided to use them as a burial ground. The bones of several million persons were moved here from their previous resting places, since the overcrowded cemeteries were considered health menaces. In 1830 the prefect of Paris closed the Catacombs to the viewing public, considering them obscene and indecent. He maintained that he could not understand the morbid curiosity of civilized people who wanted to gaze upon the bones of the dead. Later, in World War II, the Catacombs were the headquarters of the French Resistance.

The Sewers of Paris (Les Egouts). Pont de l'Alma, 7e. ☎ **01-53-68-27-81.** Admission 25F ($4.50) adults, 20F ($3.60) students and seniors over 60, 15F ($2.70) ages 5–12, free for children 4 and under. May–Oct Sat–Wed 11am–5pm; Oct–April Sat–Wed 11am–4pm. Closed 3 weeks in Jan for maintenance. Métro: Alma-Marceau. RER: Pont de l'Alma.

Some sociologists assert that the sophistication of a society can be judged by the way it disposes of waste. If that's true, Paris receives good marks for its mostly invisible network of sewers. Victor Hugo is credited with making these sewers famous in *Les Misérables*. "All dripping with slime, his soul filled with a strange light," Jean Valjean makes his desperate flight through the sewers of Paris. Hugo also wrote, "Paris has beneath it another Paris, a Paris of sewers, which has its own streets, squares, lanes, arteries, and circulation."

In the early Middle Ages, drinking water was taken directly from the Seine, while wastewater was poured onto fields or thrown onto the then-unpaved streets, transforming the urban landscape into a sea of rather smelly mud.

Around 1200, the streets of Paris were paved with cobblestones, with open sewers running down the center of each. These open sewers helped spread the Black Death, which devastated the city. In 1370, a vaulted sewer was built in the rue Montmartre, draining effluents directly into a tributary of the Seine. During the reign of Louis XIV improvements were made, but the state of waste disposal in Paris remained deplorable.

During the early 1800s, under the reign of Napoléon I, 18½ miles of underground sewer were added beneath the Parisian landscape. By 1850, as the Industrial Revolution made the manufacture of iron pipe and steam-digging equipment more practical, Baron Haussmann developed a system that used separate underground channels for both drinking water and sewage. By 1878, it was 360 miles long. Beginning in 1894, under the guidance of Belgrand, the network was enlarged, and new laws required that discharge of all waste and storm water runoff be funneled into the sewers. Between 1914 and 1977, an additional 600 miles of sewers were added beneath the pavements of a burgeoning Paris.

Today, the city known for its gastronomy boasts some memorable statistics regarding its waste disposal: The network of sewers, one of the world's best, is 1,300 miles long. Within its cavities, it contains freshwater mains, compressed-air pipes, telephone cables, and pneumatic tubes. Every day, 1.2 million cubic meters of wastewater are collected and processed by a plant in the Parisian suburb of Achères. One of the largest in Europe, it's capable of treating more than two million cubic meters of sewage per day.

The *égouts* of the city, as well as telephone and telegraph pneumatic tubes, are constructed around four principal tunnels, one 18 feet wide and 15 feet high. It's like an underground city, with the street names clearly labeled. Further, each branch pipe bears the number of the building to which it is connected. These underground passages are truly mammoth, containing pipes bringing in drinking water and compressed air as well as telephone and telegraph lines.

Tours of the sewers begin at Pont de l'Alma on the Left Bank, where a stairway leads into the bowels of the city. However, you often have to wait in line as much as half an hour. Visiting times might change in bad weather, as a storm can make the sewers dangerous. The tour consists of a movie on sewer history, a visit to a small museum, and a short trip through the maze.

13 Shopping

Shopping is the local pastime of the Parisians; some would even say it reflects the city's very soul. The City of Light is one of the rare places in the world where you don't go anywhere in particular to shop—instead, shopping surrounds you on almost every street. Each walk you take immerses you in uniquely French styles. The windows, stores, people (and yes, even their dogs) brim with energy, creativity, and a sense of visual expression found in few other cities.

You don't have to buy anything to appreciate shopping in Paris—just soak up the art form the French have made of rampant consumerism. Peer in the *vitrines* (display windows), absorb cutting-edge ideas, witness new trends—and take home with you a whole new education in style.

BUSINESS HOURS

Shops are usually open Monday through Saturday from 10am to 7pm, but the hours vary greatly, and Paris doesn't run at full throttle on Monday mornings. Small shops sometimes take a 2-hour lunch break and may not open until after lunch on Mondays. Aside from Monday, while most stores open at 10am weekdays and Saturday, some stores prefer to open at 9:30am or even 11am. Thursday is the best day for late-night shopping, with stores open until 9 or 10pm.

Sunday shopping is currently limited to tourist areas and flea markets, though there's growing demand for full-scale Sunday hours, à la the United States and the United Kingdom. The big department stores are now open for the five Sundays before Christmas; otherwise they're dead on *dimanche.*

The Carrousel du Louvre, an underground mall adjacent to the Louvre, is open and hopping on Sundays but closed on Mondays. The tourist shops that line rue de Rivoli across from the Louvre are all open on Sundays, as are the antiques villages, assorted flea markets, and several good food markets in the streets. The Virgin Megastore on the Champs-Elysées pays a fine in order to stay open on Sunday. It's *the* teen hangout.

GREAT SHOPPING AREAS

1er & 8e These two *quartiers* adjoin each other and form the heart of Paris's best Right Bank shopping neighborhood. This area includes the famed **rue du Faubourg St-Honoré,** where the big designer houses are, and **avenue des Champs-Elysées,** where the mass-market and teen scenes are hot. At one end of the 1er is the **Palais Royal**—one of the city's best shopping secrets, where an arcade of boutiques flanks the garden of the former palace.

At the other side of town, at the end of the 8e, lies **avenue Montaigne,** 2 blocks of the fanciest shops in the world, where you simply float from big name to big name; in a few hours you can see everything from **Louis Vuitton** at no. 54 (☎ 01-45-62-47-00) to **Inès de la Fressange** (Chanel model turned retailer) at no. 14 (☎ 01-47-23-08-94). **Ferragamo** (☎ 01-47-23-36-37) is housed at no. 45, one of the most beautiful apartment buildings in Paris. In addition, you'll find fabulous perfumes at no. 34, **Parfums Caron** (☎ 01-47-23-40-82), which was founded in 1904.

2e   Right behind the Palais Royal lies the **Garment District** (Sentier), as well as a few very upscale shopping secrets like **place des Victoires.** This area also hosts a few old-fashioned *passages,* alleys filled with tiny stores such as **Galerie Vivienne** on rue Vivienne.

3e & 4e   The difference between these two arrondissements gets fuzzy, especially around **place des Vosges,** center stage of the Marais. Even so, they offer several dramatically different shopping experiences.

On the surface, the shopping includes the real-people stretch of **rue de Rivoli** (which becomes **rue St-Antoine**). Two department stores are in this area: **La Samaritaine,** 19 rue de la Monnaie (☎ 01-40-41-20-20), occupies four architecturally noteworthy buildings erected between 1870 and 1927. **BHV** (Bazar de l'Hôtel de Ville), which opened in 1856, has seven floors loaded with merchandise; it lies adjacent to Paris's City Hall at 52–64 rue de Rivoli (☎ 01-42-74-90-00).

Meanwhile, hidden away in the Marais is a medieval warren of tiny, twisting streets chockablock with cutting-edge designers and up-to-the-minute fashions and trends. Start by walking around place des Vosges for art galleries, designer shops, and fabulous little finds, then dive in and get lost in the area leading to the Musée Picasso.

Finally, the 4e is also home of **place de la Bastille,** an up-and-coming area for artists and galleries where the newest entry on the retail scene, the **Viaduc des Arts** (which actually stretches into the 12e), is situated.

6e & 7e   Whereas the 6e is one of the most famous shopping districts in Paris—it's the soul of the Left Bank—much of the really good stuff is hidden in the zone that becomes the wealthy residential 7e. **Rue du Bac,** stretching from the 6e to the 7e in a few blocks, stands for all that wealth and glamour can buy. The street is jammed with art galleries, home-decorating stores, and gourmet-food shops.

9e   To add to the fun of shopping the Right Bank, 9e sneaks in behind 1er, so if you choose not to walk toward the Champs-Elysées and the 8e, you can instead head to the city's big department stores, built in a row along **boulevard Haussmann** in the 9e. Here you'll find not only the two big French icons, **Au Printemps** and **Galeries Lafayette,** but also a large branch of Britain's **Marks & Spencer.**

SHOPPING A TO Z

ANTIQUES   Directly across from the Louvre, within the premises of what was conceived during the regime of Baron Haussmann as a department store, ✪ **Le Louvre des Antiquaires,** 2 place du Palais-Royal, 1er (☎ **01-42-97-27-00;** Métro: Palais-Royal), is the largest repository of antiques and antiques dealers in central Paris. More than 250 dealers display their wares on three floors. The place specializes in precious objets and small-scale furniture of the type that might have been favored by Mme de Pompadour. You may find 30 matching Baccarat crystal champagne flutes from the 1930s, a Sèvres tea service dated 1773, or a small signed Jean Fouquet pin of gold and diamonds. Too stuffy? No problem. There's always the 1940 Rolex with the aubergine crocodile strap.

Village St-Paul, 23–27 rue St-Paul, 4e (no phone; Métro: St-Paul), isn't an antiques center but a cluster of individual dealers in their own hole-in-the-wall hideout; the rest of the street, stretching from the river to the Marais, is lined with dealers, most of which are closed on Sundays. The Village St-Paul, however, *is* open on Sunday, and hopping. Inside the courtyards and alleys are every dreamer's visions of hidden Paris: many dealers in a courtyard selling furniture and other decorative items in French provincial and, to a much lesser extent, formal styles.

ART ✪ **Galerie Adrien Maeght,** 42 rue du Bac, 7e (☎ 01-45-48-45-15; Métro: Rue-du-Bac), is among the most famous names in galleries, selling contemporary art on a very fancy Left Bank street. In addition to major works of art, they sell posters beginning at 30F ($5.40), signed and numbered lithographs from 500F ($90), and books on art and artists.

The **Viaduc des Arts,** 9–147 av. Daumesnil (between rue de Lyon and av. Diderot), 12e (☎ 01-44-75-80-66; Métro: Bastille, Ledru-Rollin, Reuilly-Diderot, or Gare-de-Lyon), occupies a long, 2-block stretch from the Bastille Opera to the Gare de Lyon, and features art galleries and artisans in individual boutiques created within the arches of an old train viaduct. As you can tell from the number of Métro stops that serve the address, you can start at one end and work your way to the other, or even start in the middle.

BOOKS The most famous bookstore on the Left Bank was **Shakespeare and Company,** on rue de l'Odéon, home to the legendary Sylvia Beach, "mother confessor to the Lost Generation." Hemingway, Fitzgerald, and Gertrude Stein were all frequent patrons. Anaïs Nin, the diarist noted for her description of struggling American artists in 1930s Paris, also often stopped in. At one point she helped her companion, Henry Miller, publish *Tropic of Cancer,* a book so notorious in its day that returning Americans trying to slip a copy through Customs often had it confiscated as pornography. (When times were hard, Nin herself wrote pornography for a dollar a page.) Long ago, the shop moved to 37 rue de la Bûcherie, 5e (☎ 01-43-26-96-50; Métro: St-Michel), where expatriates swap books and literary gossip.

Tea and Tattered Pages, 24 rue Mayet, 6e (☎ 01-40-65-94-35; Métro: Duroc), is one of the largest stores in Paris specializing in used English-language books. Fiction titles on the street level seem to contain an inordinate number of mysteries and crime/suspense titles. Nonfiction, with both biography and some semiantique travel guides, is arranged by subject in the cellar.

Scattered over two floors of tightly packed inventory, **The Village Voice Bookshop,** 6 rue Princesse, 6e (☎ 01-46-33-36-47; Métro: Mabillon), specializes in new English-language books from English and American publishers, so it's a favorite among expat Yankees and Brits. The location is near some of the Left Bank gathering places described in Gertrude Stein's *The Autobiography of Alice B. Toklas.* Look for copies of that biography or crime/mystery title you left back home, or even copies of whatever Frommer's guides you might need to continue your journeys around Europe.

W. H. Smith France, 248 rue de Rivoli, 1er (☎ 01-44-77-88-99; Métro: Concorde), is the French flagship of a chain of English-language bookstores and is France's largest store devoted to English and American books, magazines, and periodicals. You can get the *Times* of London and the Sunday *New York Times,* available every Monday afternoon. There's a fine selection of maps and travel guides, including titles by Frommer's.

CHILDREN'S CLOTHES, SHOES & TOYS **Au Nain Bleu,** 406 rue St-Honoré, 8e (☎ 01-42-60-39-01; Métro: Concorde), is the world's fanciest toy store. But don't panic; in addition to the expensive stuff, there are rows of penny candy–style cheaper toys in jars on the first floor.

Bonpoint, 15 rue Royale, 8e (☎ 01-47-42-52-63; Métro: Concorde), is part of a well-known chain that helps parents transform their darlings into models of well-tailored conspicuous consumption. Though you'll find some garments for real life, the primary allure of the place lies in its tailored, traditional—and very expensive—garments designed by the "Coco Chanel of the children's garment industry," Marie-France Cohen, the company's resident designer. The shop sells clothes for boys and girls ages 1 day to 16 years.

The prices are a whole lot lower at **Dipaki,** 18 rue Vignon, 9e (☎ 01-42-66-24-74; Métro: Madeleine), which carries selections for toddlers to 12-year-olds. Kids will love the fashions, which are wearable, washable, and affordable. It's only a short walk from place de la Madeleine.

Natalys, 92 av. des Champs-Elysées, 8e (☎ 01-43-59-17-65; Métro: Franklin-D.-Roosevelt), is part of a French chain with about 15 stores in Paris and many elsewhere. It's an upscale mass-marketer of maternity clothes and garments for kids 1 day to 6 years old. The styles have just enough French panache without going over the top in design or price. There's also a wide inventory of strollers, cribs, bassinettes, and car seats. You'll find the place midway between Planet Hollywood and the Lido.

CHINA & CRYSTAL   Purveyor to kings and presidents of France since 1764, ✪ **Baccarat,** 30 bis rue de Paradis, 10e (☎ 01-47-70-64-30; Métro: Gare-de-l'Est), and 11 place de la Madeleine, 8e (☎ 01-42-65-36-26; Métro: Madeleine), produces world-renowned full-lead crystal in dinnerware, jewelry, chandeliers, and even statuary. The rue Paradis address is the more historic of the two, while the Madeleine branch is more glamorous but less well stocked; prices are equivalent in both stores. The Madeleine showroom also stocks porcelain and crystal from other manufacturers like Christofle, but the rue Paradis shop carries Baccarat products only.

Lalique, 11 rue Royale, 8e (☎ 01-53-05-12-12; Métro: Concorde), famous for its clear- and frosted-glass sculpture, Art Deco crystal, and unique perfume bottles, has recently branched out into sales of other types of merchandise—like silk scarves meant to compete with Hermès and leather belts with Lalique buckles.

And then there's ✪ **Limoges-Unic & Madronet,** at 34 and 58 rue de Paradis, 10e (☎ 01-47-70-54-49 or 01-47-70-61-49; Métro: Gare-de-l'Est). In two shops of more or less equal size, a 3-minute walk from each other on the same street, you'll find Limoges china brands and anything else you might need for the table—glass, crystal, and silver. It pays to drop into both stores before making a purchase, as their inventories vary slightly according to the season and the whims of the buyers. They'll ship your purchases, but it will severely cut into your savings.

CHOCOLATE   Some of Paris's most sinfully delicious chocolates can be found at **Christian Constant,** 37 rue d'Assas, 6e (☎ 01-53-63-15-15; Métro: Saint-Placide), arranged in rows that reflect an awesome range of flavors and scents that the French refer to as *parfums.* Of Paris's chocolate dealers, Constant is most often named tops in town. Particularly appealing are his combinations of chocolate meringue, chocolate mousse, and bitter chocolate known as *feuilles d'automne* (autumn leaves).

Racks and racks of chocolates are priced individually or by the kilo at **Maison du Chocolat,** 225 rue du Faubourg St-Honoré, 8e (☎ 01-42-27-39-44; Métro: Ternes), though it'll cost you nearly or over 500F ($90) for a kilo. Note the similarity to Hermès when it comes to the wrapping and ribbon (and prices). The chocolate pastries are affordable; the store even has its own chocolate milk! There are five other branches around Paris.

CRAFTS   One of the few regional handcrafts stores in Paris worth going out of your way to find, ✪ **La Tuile à Loup,** 35 rue Daubenton, 5e (☎ **01-47-07-28-90;** Métro: Censier-Daubenton), carries beautiful pottery and faïence from many regions of France. Look for figures of Breton folk on the faïence of Quimper as well as garlands of fruits, leaves, and flowers from the *terre vernissée* (varnished earth, a charming way to define stoneware) from Normandy, Savoy, Alsace, and Provence. Prices begin at 10F ($1.80) for a sachet of Provençal lavender and climb as high as 4,000F ($720) for a bulky but undeniably beautiful wall plaque. There's also a bookstore filled with titles on French provincial handcrafts.

DEPARTMENT & DIME STORES   After you've admired the superb architecture of one of Europe's most famous department stores, step inside ✪ **Au Printemps,** 64 bd. Haussmann, 9e (☎ **01-42-82-50-00;** Métro: Havre-Caumartin; RER: Auber), for a view of all it offers. Inside the main building is Printemps de la Mode, which occupies the bulk of the structure, and an affiliated housewares shop, Printemps de la Maison. Don't be fooled by the rows of fragrances in display cases near the entrance—upstairs are floors of wares of every conceivable sort, especially clothing. An affiliated store, under the same management but across the street, is **Brummel,** the menswear division. Directly behind the main store is a branch of **Prisunic,** Printemps's workaday but serviceable dime store, which contains a grocery. Be sure to check out the magnificent stained-glass dome, built in 1923, through which kaleidoscopic light cascades into the 6th-floor cafe. English-speaking interpreters are stationed throughout the store and at the Welcome Desk in the basement of the main building. *Note:* Foreign visitors who show their passport will receive a flat 10% discount.

A two-part department store, **Bon Marché,** 22 and 28 rue de Sèvres, 7e (☎ **01-44-39-80-00;** Métro: Sèvres-Babylone), is on the Left Bank in the midst of all the chic boutiques. Number 28 houses a gourmet grocery store; no. 22 is a source for all your general shopping needs.

Named after the great and still controversial French writer, ✪ **Colette,** 213 rue St-Honoré, 1er (☎ **01-55-35-33-90;** Métro: Palais-Royal), is Paris's new store of the moment, a splendid and swank citadel for à la mode fashion that has made the elegant but staid rue St-Honoré less stuffy. For cutting-edge design, this is the place to go; you'll see fashions by young talents like Marni and Lucien Pellat-Fimet, home furnishings by such designers as Tom Dixon, and even zany Japanese accessories. We'll let you in on a secret: Even if you don't buy any of the merchandise, patronize the tea salon downstairs, with its freshly made quiches, salads, and cakes. In addition, there are three dozen brands of bottled water—take your pick.

At **Galeries Lafayette,** 40 bd. Haussmann, 9e (☎ **01-42-82-34-56;** Métro: Chaussée-d'Antin; RER: Auber), take a minute to stand under "The Dome"—a stained-glass cupola that towers above the arcaded store. Built in 1912, Galeries Lafayette is now divided into several stores: Galfa men's store, Lafayette Sports, and two other general-merchandise stores, both known simply as "GL." Next door is a branch of the dime store **Monoprix,** which the chain also owns. Above Monoprix is one of the fanciest grocery stores in town, **Gourmet Lafayette,** with prices half those at Fauchon.

FASHION: CUTTING-EDGE CHIC   **Azzadine Alaïa,** 7 rue de Moussy, 4e (☎ **01-42-72-19-19;** Métro: Hôtel-de-Ville), showcases the collection of the darling of French fashion in the 1970s. Alaïa revived body consciousness and put the ooh-la-la in Paris chic; he specializes in tailored evening dresses. If you can't afford the current collection, try the stock shop around the corner at 18 rue de Verrerie (same phone), where last year's leftovers are sold at serious discounts.

Jean-Charles de Castelbajac, 6 place St-Sulpice, 6e (☎ **01-46-33-87-32**; Métro: Odéon or St-Sulpice), is the bad boy of French fashion, known for flamboyant yet amusing gear in primary colors, often with big bold sayings scribbled across the clothes. His store is in a cluster of designer shops that's great for gawking.

Lolita Lempicka, 14 rue du Faubourg St-Honoré, 8e (☎ **01-49-24-94-01**; Métro: Concorde), formerly of the hidden Marais and the underground fashion scene, went mainstream in the mid-1990s when she established herself on what is arguably the most prestigious shopping street in France. Her style? Very, very feminine, with diaphanous evening dresses of silk mousseline, form-fitting tailored vests, and clingy skirts, many accented with touches of lace.

FASHION FLAGSHIPS   If you can't have the sun, the moon, and the stars, at least buy something with Coco Chanel's initials on it, created in either drop-dead chic or tongue-in-chic wicked fun by Karl Lagerfeld, who's laughing all the way to the bank—the Right Bank. The ✪ **Chanel** boutique is at 31 rue Cambon, 1er (☎ **01-42-86-28-00**; Métro: Concorde or Tuileries), and 42 av. Montaigne, 8e (☎ **01-47-23-74-12**; Métro: Franklin-D.-Roosevelt).

During the decade (1947–57) that he directed his empire, **Christian Dior,** 11 rue François-1er, 8e (☎ **01-40-73-54-44**; Métro: Franklin-D.-Roosevelt), was the only couturier whose name was known throughout the Western Hemisphere. The house continues to thrive since its reorganization into a small-scale version of a department store. Departments are devoted to men's, women's, and children's clothing; gift items; makeup and perfume; and so on. Unlike some of the other big-name fashion houses, Dior is very approachable.

One of the most instantly recognizable accessories in France is a lavishly opulent silk scarf or tie from ✪ **Hermès,** 24 rue du Faubourg St-Honoré, 8e (☎ **01-40-17-47-17**; Métro: Concorde). You'll find them in abundance, along with virtually everything else (bags, purses, suitcases) endorsed by the legendary saddlemaker, at the flagship branch, which occupies sunflooded premises on the most prestigious shopping street in France. It also carries beach towels and accessories, dinner plates, clothing for men and women, a large collection of Hermès fragrances, and even a saddle shop.

Hervé Leger, 29 rue du Faubourg St-Honoré, 8e (☎ **01-44-51-57-17**; Métro: Concorde), creator of the Band Aid Dress (*la robe à bande*), a tightly wrapped concoction of stretch materials and color, has opened his own shop for those with curves to flaunt. Fashionable colors change with the seasons (black or red for winter, pastels for spring), and clothes can come in either covered-midriff or bare-midriff styles, and are sold at prices that begin at 500F ($90).

✪ **Louis Vuitton,** 6 place St-Germain-des-Prés, 6e (☎ **01-45-49-62-32**; Métro: St-Germain-des-Prés), is the most interestingly decorated branch of Vuitton in Paris. Antiques and fine hardwoods evoke the grand age of travel, when steamships and railway cars hauled the affluent off to uncharted destinations. It stocks a wide inventory of purses, suitcases, and trunks with the traditional monogram, plus new lines of Vuitton leathergoods crafted from beige-colored cowhide—without any monograms—whose patina darkens with age and the rigors of international travel. The store also sells writing instruments as well as a Carnet du Voyage, a do-it-yourself scrapbook graced with watercolors and space in which to jot down your own memories.

FASHION: DISCOUNT & RESALE   **Anna Lowe,** 104 rue du Faubourg St-Honoré, 8e (☎ **01-42-66-11-32**; Métro: Miromesnil), is one of the premier boutiques for the discriminating woman who wishes to purchase a little Chanel or perhaps a Versace . . . at a discount, *bien sur.* Many clothes are runway samples; some have been gently worn. It's next door to stores where the ready-to-wear is much more expensive.

The twin shops of **Catherine Baril (Dépôts-Vent de Passy),** 14 (women) and 25 (men) rue de la Tour, 16e (☎ 01-45-20-95-21 for women and 01-45-27-11-46 for men; Métro: Passy), are located just a few storefronts from each other. Opened in 1982 by its namesake (who still works on the premises), it buys the used suits, gowns, and dresses of style-setters who either outgrew or grew tired of their garments. The items are separated by designer and size, then resold at deep discounts. Though some merchandise is outdated from its cutting-edge debut season, you'll nonetheless find an occasional garment with classic lines that will remain in style for years. Inventories for women include Chanel, Yves Saint Laurent, Hermès, Jil Sander, and Donna Karan. Articles for men include selections from Hugo Boss and Ralph Lauren.

Mouton à Cinq Pattes, 19 rue Gregoire-de-Tours, 6e (☎ **01-43-29-73-56;** Métro: Odéon), sells designer clothes at a fraction of the cost. The labels are cut out, so you can't point them out to your friends while bragging about your Parisian purchases. You can, however, show off expertly tailored, top-of-the-line fashions you didn't have to sell your car for. The stock of men's, women's, and children's clothing changes frequently. You'll probably want to avoid this place on Saturdays, unless you like watching frantic shoppers compete for the best items.

Promod, 67 rue de Sèvres, 6e (☎ **01-45-49-42-92;** Métro: Sèvres-Babylone), is a member of a citywide chain (more than 20 in Paris); it's crammed with women's clothing that manages to be whimsical, stylish, and inexpensive. Examples are well-made T-shirts, sweaters, clingy skirts or billowy slacks with coordinated vests, and jeans. There are also shoes of all possible degrees of sensibility, faux pearls, purses, and accessories.

The inventory at **Réciproque,** 88–123 rue de la Pompe (between av. Victor-Hugo and av. Georges-Mandel), 16e (☎ **01-47-04-30-28;** Métro: Pompe), is scattered over five buildings on rue de la Pompe in a prosperous residential neighborhood. Everything it carries is used, clustered into sections devoted to Chanel, Versace, Lacroix, Mosquino, Hermès, and Mugler. Women will find gowns, business suits, sportswear, and shoes. Men should go to no. 101; the other buildings are for women's apparel. Although everything here has already been worn, in some cases that means only on runways or during photo shoots.

FOOD At the place de la Madeleine stands one of the most popular sights in the city—not La Madeleine church but ✪ **Fauchon,** 26 place de la Madeleine, 8e (☎ **01-47-42-60-11;** Métro: Madeleine), which offers a wider choice of upscale gourmet products than anyplace else in the world. Distinct areas are devoted to candy, pastries, and bread; fresh fruits and veggies; dry and canned goods; fresh fish and meats; awe-inspiring take-away food that simply requires reheating before a grand dinner party; and wine. If you're hungry (and who wouldn't be after a promenade around Fauchon?), you won't have to resort to munching an apple or opening a package of cookies. There are five restaurants on the premises, ranging from the grand (Le 30) to the simple (Brasserie Fauchon).

Fauchon's main competitor, **Hédiard,** 21 place de la Madeleine, 8e (☎ **01-43-12-88-77;** Métro: Madeleine), opened in 1854. It was recently renovated and transformed into a series of salons filled with almost Disneyesque displays meant to give the store the look of a turn-of-the-century spice emporium. Upstairs is the solidly reliable Restaurant de l'Epicerie.

More intimate than its larger competitors, **Albert Ménès,** 41 bd. Malesherbes, 8e (☎ **01-42-66-95-63;** Métro: St-Augustin or Madeleine), serves the Parisian upper crust with jams, confiture, sugared almonds, teas, and assorted packed gourmet foodstuffs, many from small-scale producers from the provinces. Virtually everything can be shipped or, even better, packed for easy transport. A specialty food basket for the holidays (and saints days) is a status treat and can be made in virtually any price range.

Le Maison du Miel, "The House of Honey," at 24 rue Vignon, 9e (☎ 01-47-42-26-70; Métro: Madeleine, Havre-Caumartin, or Opéra), has been a family tradition since before World War I. The entire store is devoted to products made from honey: honey oil, honey soap, regional varieties of nougat, and certainly various honeys to eat. It's around the corner from Fauchon and worth the walk.

JEWELRY   Well-dressed women around the world wear fabulous gemstones from ✪ Van Cleef & Arpels, 22 place Vendôme, 1er (☎ 01-53-45-45-45; Métro: Opéra or Tuileries). Though virtually anything is available for a price, one of the firm's distinctive specialties is yellow diamonds whose color resembles amber but whose fire is unmistakably brilliant. Floral motifs, cunningly set into platinum or gold with vibrant hues, are also a trademark.

Can't afford those diamonds? Check out **Agatha,** 97 rue de Rennes, 6e (☎ 01-45-48-81-30; Métro: Rue-de-Rennes), where everything is imitation. Look for ropes of pearls in the style popularized long ago by Chanel, glittering baubles patterned after something that might have belonged to the late duchess of Windsor, or simple bangles that go with shorts and sneakers for a day on a yacht. Lots of worthwhile pieces sell for under 1,000F ($180).

LEATHER   A cult hero in France yet virtually unknown elsewhere, **Didier Lamarthe,** 219 rue St-Honoré, 1er (☎ 01-42-96-09-90; Métro: Tuileries), is famous for his handbags and small leather goods in funky fashion shades like melon or mint. Sure, he does more conservative colors like navy and black, but if you want the world to know you've been to Paris and that you're totally *branché* (plugged in), spring for one of the more risqué shades.

Longchamp, 390 rue St-Honoré, 1er (☎ 01-42-60-00-00; Métro: Concorde), is known for high-quality leather and strong everyday durables that come in basic as well as fashion shades. Except for a handful of men's accessories (briefcases, belts, and ties), most of the inventory is designed for women. Most of the leatherware comes in four colors: black, brown, navy blue, and "Longchamp green," which has been likened to the shade in a dense woodland glade in midsummer. Their best bet is a series of nylon handbags with leather handles; they fold for storage or travel and unfold for shopping.

LINGERIE   The undergarments sold and manufactured by **Cadolle,** 14 rue Cambon, 1er (☎ 01-42-60-94-94; Métro: Concorde), are among the world's most comfortable and opulent. Herminie Cadolle invented the brassiere from premises nearby in 1889, and in 1911 she moved to this location near the former headquarters of Coco Chanel, whose "emaciated" styles she thoroughly disliked. Today the store is managed by her charming great-granddaughters. What's new here? The magic word is corsets, preferably in black, worn with long skirts or slacks and without blouses or jackets, that emphasize the curvaceous lines of full-figured women to their best advantage. Fashioned from everything from velvet to embroidered satins, they're almost guaranteed to turn heads day or night.

At **Comme des Femmes,** 31 rue St-Placide, 6e (☎ 01-45-48-97-33; Métro: St-Placide), you'll find items from every major manufacturer in France—like Antinea, Bolero, Lise Charmel, Aubade, Ligne Rien, and Barbara—and including a selection of brassieres priced from 100 to 600F ($18 to $108). In addition to the perennially popular ivory and white, hot colors now are black, red, brown, and yellow in winter and pastels in spring and summer.

MALLS At **Carrousel du Louvre,** 99 rue de Rivoli, 1er (no phone; Métro: Palais-Royal–Musée-du-Louvre), you can combine a convenient location, a fun food court, handy boutiques, and plenty of museum gift shops with a touch of culture. Always mobbed with locals and visitors, this is one of the few venues allowed to stay open on Sundays. The easiest way to get here is to enter straight from rue de Rivoli and take the escalator down one level for the food court and two levels for the boutiques. There's a Virgin Megastore, the Body Shop, and several big-name boutiques, like Courrèges and Lalique. Check out Diane Claire for the fanciest souvenirs of Paris you've ever seen. A branch of the French Government Tourist Office is next door to Virgin.

Forget about the street address of **Forum des Halles,** 1–7 rue Pierre-Lescot, 1er (no phone; Métro: Etienne-Marcel or Châtelet–Les-Halles). This mall fills an entire city block where the great old produce market, Les Halles, once stood. Now it's a vast crater of modern metal with layers of boutiques built around a courtyard. There's one of everything here—but the feel is sterile, without a hint of the famous French joie de vivre. It's near the Centre Pompidou if you're in a rush and need access to a lot of stores in a hurry.

MARKETS Artists love to paint the **Marché aux Fleurs,** place Louis-Lépine, on Ile de la Cité, 4e (Métro: Cité); photographers love to click away. The stalls are ablaze with color, each a showcase of flowers (most of which escaped the fate of being hauled to the perfume factories of Grasse in the French Riviera). The Flower Market is along the Seine, behind the Tribunal de Commerce. On Sundays, this is a bird market.

Paris's most famous flea market is actually a grouping of more than a dozen flea markets. ✪ **Marché aux Puces de Clignancourt,** av. de la Porte de Clignancourt (Métro: Porte-de-Clignancourt; then turn left, cross bd. Ney, and walk north on av. de la Porte de Clignancourt), is a complex of 2,500 to 3,000 open stalls and shops on the fringes of Paris, selling everything from antiques to junk, from new to vintage clothing.

The first clues showing you're here are the stalls of cheap clothing along avenue de la Porte de Clignancourt. As you proceed, various streets will tempt you. Hold off until you get to rue des Rosiers, then turn left. Vendors start bringing out their offerings around 9am and begin taking them in around 6pm. Hours are a tad flexible, depending on weather and crowds. Monday is traditionally the best day for bargain seekers, as there is smaller attendance at the market and a greater desire on the part of the merchants to sell.

First-timers at the flea market always ask two things: "Will I get any real bargains here?" and "Will I get fleeced?" It's all comparative. Obviously, the best buys have been skimmed by dealers (who often have a prearrangement to have items held for them). And it's true that the same merchandise displayed here will sell for less out in the provinces. But from the point of view of the visitor who has only a few days to spend in Paris—and only half a day for shopping—the flea market is worth the experience. Vintage French postcards, old buttons, and bistroware are quite affordable; each market has its own personality and an aura of Parisian glamour that can't be found elsewhere.

Most of the markets have toilets; some have a central office to arrange shipping. Cafes, pizza joints, and even a few real restaurants are scattered throughout. Beware of pickpockets and troublemakers.

Then there's the **Marché aux Puces de la Porte de Vanves,** av. Georges-Lafenestre, 14e (Métro: Porte-de-Vanves). More a giant yard sale than anything serious, this weekend event sprawls along two streets and is actually Paris's best flea market—dealers swear by it. There's little in terms of formal antiques and few large pieces of furniture. You'll do better if you collect old linens, used Hermès scarves, toys, ephemera, costume jewelry, perfume bottles, or bad art. Asking prices tend to be high as dealers prefer to sell to nontourists. On Sundays, there's a food market one street over.

Marché Buci, rue de Buci, 6e (Métro: St-Germain-des-Prés), is a traditional French food market held at the intersection of two streets. It's only one block long, but what a block! Seasonal fruits and vegetables dance across tabletops while chickens spin in the rotisserie. One stall is devoted to big bunches of fresh flowers. Avoid Monday mornings, since very little is open then.

MUSIC If you're feeling nostalgic for the French popular song of yesterday and today, **Crocodisc,** 40–42 rue des Ecoles, 5e (☎ **01-43-54-47-95;** Métro: Maubert-Mutualité), sells it, in vinyl, cassette, or CD format. You can find virtually every cutting-edge musician in Europe, as well as the chansons of everyone from Mistinguett to Aznavour to Piaf. In brief, if you're looking for the oldies but goodies you used to listen to during parties held by your high school French club, this place will almost certainly stock it.

The chain called **FNAC,** with a branch at 136 rue de Rennes, 6e (☎ **01-49-54-30-00;** Métro: St-Placide), is a mecca for anyone looking for computers, CDs, records and tapes, photography equipment, TVs, and stereo systems. It's known for its wide selection and competitive prices; recordings made by every artist of consequence in Europe and the Americas are readily available. The ticket service sells tickets for most of the entertainment venues and concerts in the city. There are eight other locations in Paris.

The showcase **Virgin Megastore,** 52–60 av. des Champs-Elysées, 8e (☎ **01-49-53-50-00;** Métro: Franklin-D.-Roosevelt), is one of the anchors that helped rejuvenate the Champs-Elysées. Built in a landmark building on the famed strip, it's Paris's largest music store. In addition to the music store, which carries every French and North American release imaginable, the building houses a bookstore and cafe. A ticket-buying service can reserve tickets for you to plays, concerts, and sporting events. Even if you're not interested in purchasing anything, you might want to stop by to see where Parisian teens spend their time and money. Other branches are in the Carrousel du Louvre (see "Malls," above), at both airports, and in Gare Montparnasse.

PERFUME, COSMETICS & TOILETRIES Just about every working woman around place de la Madeleine shops at **Catherine,** 7 rue Castiglione, 1er (☎ **01-42-60-48-17;** Métro: Concorde)—they appreciate its deep discounts and absolute lack of pretensions. It resembles a high-volume pharmacy more than a chichi boutique; bottles and *flacons* of perfume move in and out of the expanded premises very fast. You get a 30% discount on most brands of makeup and perfume and a 20% discount on brands like Chanel and Dior.

Parfumerie du Havre, 9 place de la Madeleine, 8e (☎ **01-42-66-52-20;** Métro: Madeleine), offers good discounts off suggested retail, but the amount varies with the brand—10% on Chanel but up to 30% on some others, such as Gucci. There are tons of fragrances and a few designer accessories (ties, belts, handbags, costume jewelry) in this chic shop that since 1995 has been linked to one of France's largest discount perfume chains. Prices are marked with the discount already applied, so it's hard to figure out how much you're actually saving.

Though you can buy its scents in any duty-free or discount parfumerie, we advise you to visit the source of some of the world's most famous perfumes: **Caron,** 34 av. Montaigne, 8e (☎ **01-47-23-40-82;** Métro: Franklin-D.-Roosevelt). Established in 1904, it gained a reputation as the choice of temptresses both demure and debauched; the store is small but stylish, boasting old-fashioned glass beakers filled with fragrances. Caron's Fleurs de Rocaille was the featured perfume in the movie *Scent of a Woman,* in which the blind protagonist (Al Pacino) could identify its scent on the woman he eventually falls in love with.

A specialist in products for skin and hair, **Annick Goutal,** 14 rue de Castiglione, 1er (☎ **01-42-60-52-82;** Métro: Tuileries), or 12 place St-Sulpice, 6e (same phone; Métro: St-Sulpice), sells everything a person would need to stay young-looking—or at least try. Though the products appear in hotel rooms across France, you might want to pop in for access to herbalized and aromatized shampoos, liquid soaps, bubble bath, oils, and creams and unguents.

At the rear of a small courtyard, halfway between place de la Madeleine and the Champs-Elysées, is **Makeup Forever,** 5 rue de la Boetie, 8e (☎ **01-42-66-01-60;** Métro: St-Augustin). Established in the 1980s, its products were quickly endorsed by professional stylists; since then, its allure has only increased among retail clients. The company's purse-sized makeup case, at about 100F ($18), as well as virtually anything with the brand name, has become a mini–status symbol for French yuppies and fashionable types.

At **Octée,** 53 rue Bonaparte, 6e (☎ **01-46-33-18-77;** Métro: St-Germain-des-Prés or St-Sulpice), the collection of fragrances is color-coded to your personality, skin type, and mood. Confused about which family of scents best corresponds to you? Consider the florals (rose, jasmine, gardenia, or iris), the orientals (sandalwoods and cedars), the aerial plants (orchid scents), and such gastronomic scents as vanilla and chocolate. Prices are surprisingly reasonable, with any scent priced at 185F ($33.30) for a purse-sized vial. Though most of the scents were conceived for women, a limited number are meant for men, the most popular of which is Black Cedar.

Sephora, 70 av. des Champs-Elysées, 8e (☎ **01-53-93-22-50;** Métro: Franklin-D.-Roosevelt), is the world's largest store devoted to perfumes and skin-care products. Look for rows of men's and women's scents arranged on opposite sides of a very long room, as well as sections devoted to books on all aspects of the perfume maker's art. Booths are staffed by professional "noses," who prove their skill hundreds of times a day. A less dramatic branch is at 50 rue de Passy, 16e (☎ **01-45-20-03-15;** Métro: Passy).

SHOES   The collection of shoes at **Maud Frizon,** 83 rue des Sts-Pères, 6e (☎ **01-45-49-20-59;** Métro: Sèvres-Babylone), is among the city's most inventive and sexiest. Don't come here looking for sensible shoes to go with your tweeds. Footwear is likely to be available in shades like pink, orange, and several variations of green, as well as black and brown. In most cases, very, very feminine.

Cheap and cheerful, with an inventory that includes all kinds of women's shoes, **Shoe-Bizz,** 42 rue du Dragon, 6e (☎ **01-45-44-93-50;** Métro: St-Sulpice or Sèvres-Babylone), is an all-gray showroom where the most expensive pair costs around 750F ($135) and many others average about 400F ($72). Though most of the shoes are made in Italy, everything bears the name of either Shoe-Bizz or some France-based designer. There's also a selection of footwear for men by designers like Kenzo and Roberto Botticelli.

Acclaimed as one of the most creative designers of women's shoes in Paris, **Stéphane Kélian,** 23 bd. de la Madeleine, 1er (☎ **01-42-96-01-84;** Métro: Madeleine), attracts formidably chic women from all over the city. Look for stylish, sexy shoes, often with stiletto heels or bulky platforms. A selection of about a dozen styles for men is also available.

TABLEWARE & MORE   Don't get the **Conran Shop,** 117 rue du Bac, 7e (☎ **01-42-84-10-01;** Métro: Sèvres-Babylone), and Habitat confused, even though they look similar and were associated at their beginnings with the same entrepreneur. The

Habitat shops in Paris are okay, but the Conran Shop is a small piece of heaven, filled with color and style and all sorts of things to touch and take home. Despite its British origins, the place is geared to French tastes in home and garden decor. Look for lighting fixtures, fabrics, furniture, garden furniture, and everything you might need for country living à la française.

Looking for the perfect table accessories to make your dinner party unique? **Geneviève Lethu,** 95 rue de Rennes, 6e (☎ **01-45-44-40-35;** Métro: St-Germain-des-Prés), a Provençal designer, has shops all over France, with several in Paris, all selling her clever and colorful designs that seem to reflect what happens when Pottery Barn style goes French Mediterranean. Prices are moderate. Her goods, filled with energy, style, and charm, are also sold in the major department stores.

WINES   Les Caves Taillevent, 199 rue du Faubourg St-Honoré, 8e (☎ **01-45-61-14-09;** Métro: Charles-de-Gaulle–Etoile), is a temple to the art of making fine French wine. Associated with one of Paris's grandest restaurants, Taillevent, which is nearby, it occupies the street level and cellar of an antique building in a neighborhood awash with memories of the French empire. Stored here are more than half a million bottles of wine—some at around 25F ($4.50); others, rare vintages at 20,000F ($3,600). When was the last time you bought a $4,000 bottle of wine?

14 Paris After Dark

THE PERFORMING ARTS

Announcements of shows, concerts, and operas are plastered on kiosks all over town. You can find listings of what's playing in *Pariscope,* a weekly entertainment guide, or the English-language *Boulevard,* a bimonthly magazine. Performances start later in Paris than in London or New York City—anywhere from 8 to 9pm—and Parisians tend to dine after the theater. (But you may not want to follow suit, since many of the less expensive restaurants close as early as 9pm.)

There are many ticket agencies in Paris, but most are found near the Right Bank hotels. *Avoid them if possible.* You can buy the cheapest tickets at the theater box office. Remember to tip the usher who shows you to your seat in a theater or movie house 3F (55¢).

For information on and tickets to just about any show and entertainment in Paris (also Dijon, Lyon, and Nice), **Edwards & Edwards** has a New York office if you'd like to make arrangements before you go. It's at 1270 Ave. of the Americas, Suite 2414, New York, NY 10020 (☎ **800/223-6108** or 914/328-2150). It also has an office in Paris at 19 rue des Mathurins, 9e (☎ **01-42-65-39-21;** Métro: Havre-Caumartin). A personal visit isn't necessary; Edwards & Edwards will mail tickets to your home, fax confirmation, or leave tickets at the box office in Paris. There's a markup of 20% (excluding opera and ballet) over box-office price, plus a U.S. handling charge of $8. Hotel and theater packages are also available.

Several agencies sell tickets for cultural events and plays at discounts of up to 50%. One is the **Kiosque Théâtre,** 15 place de la Madeleine, 8e (no phone; Métro: Madeleine), offering leftover tickets for about half price on the day of performance. Tickets for evening performances are sold Tuesday through Friday from noon to 7pm and Saturday from 11am to 4pm. If you'd like to attend a matinee, buy your ticket Saturday or Sunday from 11am to 4pm.

For discounts of 20% to 40% on tickets for festivals, concerts, and the theater, try one of two locations of the **FNAC** department-store chain: 136 rue de Rennes, 6e (☎ **01-49-54-30-00;** Métro: Montparnasse-Bienvenue), or in the Forum des Halles, 1–7 rue Pierre-Lescot, 1er (☎ **01-40-41-40-00;** Métro: Châtelet–Les-Halles).

THE TOP VENUES

The ✪ **Opéra Garnier,** place de l'Opéra, 9e (☎ **01-40-01-17-89;** Métro: Opéra), is the premier stage for dance and once again for opera. Because of the competition from the Opéra Bastille, the original opera has made great efforts to present more up-to-date works, including choreography by Jerome Robbins, Twyla Tharp, and George Balanchine. This rococo wonder was designed as a contest entry by the young architect Charles Garnier in the heyday of the empire. The facade is adorned with marble and sculpture, including *The Dance* by Carpeaux. The world's great orchestral, operatic, and ballet companies have performed here. Months of painstaking restorations have returned the Garnier to its former glory: Its boxes and walls are once again lined with flowing red and blue damask, the gilt gleams, the ceiling (painted by Marc Chagall) has been cleaned, and an air-conditioning system has been added. The box office is open Monday through Saturday from 11am to 6:30pm.

The controversial building known as the ✪ **Opéra Bastille,** place de la Bastille, 120 rue de Lyon (☎ **01-43-43-96-96;** Métro: Bastille), was designed by the Canadian architect Carlos Ott, with curtains created by the Japanese fashion designer Issey Miyake. The showplace was inaugurated in July 1989 (for the Revolution's bicentennial), and on March 17, 1990, the curtain rose on Hector Berlioz's *Les Troyens.* Since its much-publicized opening, the opera house has presented masterworks like Mozart's *Marriage of Figaro* and Tchaikovsky's *Queen of Spades.* The main hall is the largest of any French opera house, with 2,700 seats, but music critics have lambasted the acoustics. The building contains two additional concert halls, including an intimate room with only 250 seats, usually used for chamber music. Both traditional opera performances and symphony concerts are presented here. There are sometimes free concerts on French holidays; call before your visit.

For the best orchestra performances in France, try **Maison de Radio France,** 116 av. du Président-Kennedy, 16e (☎ **01-42-30-15-16;** Métro: Passy-Ranelagh), which offers top-notch concerts with guest conductors. It's the home of the Orchestre Philharmonique de Radio France and the Orchestre National de France. The box office is open Monday through Saturday from 11am to 6pm.

The Art Deco **Théâtre des Champs-Elysées,** 15 av. Montaigne, 8e (☎ **01-49-52-50-50;** Métro: Alma-Marceau), which attracts the haute-couture crowd, hosts both national and international orchestras as well as opera and ballet. If Brooke Astor were your date, you'd take her here, perhaps to a performance of the visiting Vienna Philharmonic. The box office is open Monday through Saturday from 11am to 7pm. Events are held year-round, except in August.

Théâtre Musical de Paris (Théâtre du Châtelet), 1 place du Châtelet, 1er (☎ **01-40-28-28-40;** Métro: Châtelet), occupies a neoclassical building near the Hôtel de Ville. Built in 1862 on the site of an ancient Roman stadium, it's largely subsidized by the government of Paris and known for its superb acoustics. Opera, classical music, and occasional dance recitals are performed here year-round, except in July and August. It's currently closed for extensive renovations and slated to reopen in September 1999.

Designed as part of the architectural complex facing the Eiffel Tower, **Théâtre National de Chaillot,** 1 place du Trocadéro, 16e (☎ **01-53-65-30-00;** Métro: Trocadéro), is one of the city's largest concert halls, hosting a variety of cultural events from dance to drama that are announced on billboards out front. The box office is open Monday through Saturday from 11am to 7pm and Sunday from 11am to 5pm.

Of the half-dozen *grands travaux* conceived by the Mitterrand administration, **Cité de la Musique,** 221 av. Jean-Jaurès, 19e (☎ **01-44-84-45-00,** or 01-44-84-44-84 for tickets and information; Métro: Porte-de-Pantin), has been the most widely applauded and the most innovative. At the city's northeastern edge in what used to be a run-down and depressing neighborhood, the $120-million stone-and-glass structure, designed by the noted architect Christian de Portzamparc, incorporates a network of concert halls, a library/research center for the study of all kinds of music from around the world, and a museum (see "The Top Museums," earlier in this chapter). The complex hosts a rich variety of concerts, ranging from Renaissance to 20th-century programs.

Even those with only a modest understanding of French can still delight in a sparkling production of Molière at the **Comédie-Française,** 2 rue de Richelieu, 1er (☎ **01-44-58-15-15;** Métro: Palais-Royal–Musée-du-Louvre), established to keep the classics alive and promote important contemporary authors. The box office is open daily from 11am to 6pm, but the hall is dark from July 21 to September 5. In 1993 a Left Bank annex was launched, the **Comédie-Française–Théâtre du Vieux-Colombier,** 21 rue du Vieux-Colombier, 4e (☎ **01-44-39-87-00**). Although its repertoire can vary, it's known for presenting some of the most serious French dramas in town.

MUSIC HALLS

Le Bataclan. 50 bd. Voltaire, 11e. ☎ **01-47-00-39-12.** Tickets 120–150F ($21.60–$27). Métro: Oberkampf.

Few other Paris nightspots contain such a bizarre amalgam of old and new. In a working-class neighborhood far off the beaten path, it was built in the mid–19th century as a music hall and later flourished during the reign of Napoléon III. Today Le Bataclan boasts original wrought iron and ornate plaster, reproductions of Toulouse-Lautrec works, and a nostalgia for the belle époque, even though it rocks almost every night with a changing roster of blues, jazz, and electronic *artistes.* (Emmylou Harris performed here during our most recent visit.) Concerts usually begin around 8pm and end before 11pm.

Olympia. 28 bd. des Capucines, 9e. ☎ **01-47-42-25-49.** Tickets 150–300F ($27–$54). Métro: Opéra or Madeleine.

Charles Aznavour and other big names make frequent appearances in this cavernous hall. The late Yves Montand performed once—and the performance was sold out 4 months in advance. Today you're more likely to catch Gloria Estefan. A typical lineup might include an English rock group, showy Italian acrobats, a well-known French singer, a dance troupe, an American juggler/comedy team (doing much of their work in English), plus the featured star. A witty emcee and an onstage band provide a smooth transition between acts.

CHANSONNIERS

The *chansonniers* (literally "songwriters") provide a bombastic musical satire of the day's events. This combination of parody and burlesque is a time-honored Gallic amusement and a Parisian institution. Songs are often created on the spot, inspired by the "disaster of the day."

Au Caveau de la Bolée. 25 rue de l'Hirondelle, 6e. ☎ **01-43-54-62-20.** Fixed-price dinner 260F ($46.80) Mon–Fri, 300F ($54) Sat. Cover 150F ($27) Mon–Sat if you don't order dinner. Métro: St-Michel.

To enter this bawdy boîte, you descend into the catacombs of the early 14th-century Abbey of St-André, once a famous literary cafe that attracted such personages as Verlaine and Oscar Wilde, who downed (or drowned in) glass after glass of absinthe here. The singing is loud and bawdy, just the way the young student regulars like it. Occasionally the audience sings along. You'll enjoy this place a lot more if your French is pretty good, but even if it's not, there are enough visuals (magic acts and performances by singers) to amuse. A fixed-price dinner, served Monday through Saturday at 8:30pm, is followed by at least four entertainers, usually comedians. The cabaret starts at 10:30pm, and in lieu of paying admission, you can order dinner. If you've already eaten, you can just order a drink.

✪ **Au Lapin Agile.** 22 rue des Saules, 18e. ☎ **01-46-06-85-87.** Cover (including the first drink) 130F ($23.40). Tues–Sun 9pm–2am. Métro: Lamarck.

Picasso and Utrillo once patronized this little cottage near the top of Montmartre, formerly known as the Café des Assassins. It has been painted by numerous artists, including Utrillo, and was used as a setting for a Steve Martin play. For many decades it has been the heartbeat of French folk music. You'll sit at carved wooden tables in a dimly lit room with walls covered by bohemian memorabilia, listening to French folk tunes, love ballads, army songs, sea chanteys, and music-hall ditties. You're encouraged to sing along, even if it's only the "oui, oui, oui—non, non, non" refrain of "Les Chevaliers de la Table Ronde." The best sing-alongs are on weeknights after tourist season ends.

NIGHTCLUBS & CABARETS

These places are all decidedly expensive, but they provide some of the most lavish, spectacular floor shows anywhere.

Chez Michou. 80 rue des Martyrs, 18e. ☎ **01-46-06-16-04.** Reservations required for dinner. Dinner and show (including aperitif, wine, and coffee) 550F ($99); show only (at bar) 200F ($36). Métro: Pigalle.

The setting is blue, the emcee wears blue, and the spotlights shining on the stage bathe the cross-dressing performers in a celestial blue light. The creative force behind all this is Michou, veteran impresario whose 20-odd belles bear names like Hortensia and DuDuche, and lip-synch their way through revivals of songs by real females such as Whitney Houston, Diana Ross, and Tina Turner and such French luminaries as Mireille Mathieu, Sylvie Vartan, "Dorothée," and the immortal Brigitte Bardot.

✪ **Crazy Horse Saloon.** 12 av. George-V, 8e. ☎ **01-47-23-32-32.** Cover (including 2 drinks) 450–560F ($81–$100.80); dinner spectacle 750F ($150). Métro: George-V or Alma-Marceau.

Le Crazy has been hailed as the best nude revue in the universe. Founded in 1951, it's a French parody of a western saloon; its strippers were the first in France to toss their G-strings to the winds, throwing up their hands for the big revelation. Despite the incredibly steep prices (100F/$18 for a drink!), the place is always packed with out-of-towners; the very professional (and highly erotic) performers seem to justify the cost. Between the acts, vaudeville skits are performed.

Folies-Bergère. 32 rue Richer, 9e. ☎ **01-44-79-98-98.** Cover 100–350F ($18–$63); dinner and show 460–510F ($82.80–$91.80). Métro: Rue-Montmartre or Cadet.

The Folies-Bergère is a Paris institution; foreigners have been flocking here for excitement since 1886. Josephine Baker, the nude African-American singer who used to throw bananas into the audience, became "the toast of Paris" here. According to legend, the first G.I. to reach Paris at the 1944 Liberation asked for directions to the club.

   Don't expect the naughty and slyly permissive skin-and-glitter revue that used to be the trademark of this place. In 1993, that all ended with a radical restoration of the theater and a reopening under new management. The site now functions as a conventional 1,600-seat theater, presenting musical revues filled with a sense of nostalgia for old Paris. You're likely to witness an intriguing, often charming, but not particularly erotic repertoire of songs, mostly in French but sometimes in English, interspersed with the banter of an emcee. A restaurant serves bland fixed-price dinners in an ante-room to the theater. The experience probably isn't worth the staggering cost, but for many a first-timer, a visit to Paris without going to the Folies-Bergère would be no visit at all.

✪ **Lido de Paris.** 116 bis av. des Champs-Elysées, 8e. ☎ **800/227-4884** in the U.S., or 01-40-76-56-10. Cover (including a half bottle of champagne) for 10pm or midnight show 550F ($99); 8pm dinner dance (including a half bottle of champagne) and 10pm show 795–995F ($143.10–$179.10). Métro: George-V.

As it heads for the millennium, the Lido has changed its feathers and modernized its shows; today it competes with the best Las Vegas has to offer. Its $15-million current production, *C'est Magique,* reflects a dramatic reworking of the classic Parisian cabaret show, with eye-popping special effects, water technology using more than 60,000 gallons per minute, and bold new themes, even an acrobatic aerial ballet. The show, the most expensive ever produced in Europe, uses 70 performers, $4 million in costumes, and a $2-million lighting design with lasers. There's even an ice rink and swimming pool that magically appear and disappear. The 45 Bluebell Girls, those legendary sensual showgirls, are still here, however. Now that celebrated chef Paul Bocuse is the consultant for the culinary offerings, the cuisine is better than ever.

Moulin Rouge. Place Blanche, 18e. ☎ **01-53-09-82-82.** Cover (including champagne) 550F ($99); dinner and show 750F ($135). Métro: Blanche.

Toulouse-Lautrec, who put this place on the map about a century ago, wouldn't recognize it today. The windmill is still here and so is the cancan, but the rest has become a superslick, gimmick-ridden variety show with a heavy emphasis on undraped females. You'll see young women in swings and on stairs and young women naked except for a satirical take on the bewigged grandeur of 18th-century Versailles, who cavort amid a handful of (fully clothed) men. Up to 60 artists participate in shows that include animal acts, comic jugglers, and singing trios. These are just a smattering of the acts usually found on the daily bill—it's all expertly staged, but any connection with the old, notorious Moulin Rouge is purely coincidental. In our view, this is becoming more of a tourist trap; the high prices aren't justified unless you simply must stop in for nostalgic purposes.

Villa d'Este. 4 rue Arsène-Houssaye, 8e. ☎ **01-42-56-14-65.** Cover (including first drink) 190F ($34.20); dinner (including wine) and show 250–720F ($45–$129.60). Métro: Charles-de-Gaulle–Etoile.

In the past this club booked Amalia Rodrigues, Portugal's leading fadista, and the French chanteuse Juliette Greco. Today you're more likely to hear the French singer François de Guelte or other top talent from Europe and America. Villa d'Este has been around for a long time, and the quality of its offerings remains high. You'll probably hear some of the greatest hits of such beloved French performers as Piaf, Aznavour, Brassens, and Brel.

LE COOL JAZZ

The great jazz revival that long ago swept America is still going strong here, with Dixieland or Chicago rhythms being pounded out in dozens of jazz cellars, mostly called *caveaux.* Most clubs are crowded on the Left Bank near the Seine, between rue Bonaparte and rue St-Jacques, which makes things easy for seekers of syncopation.

For the latest details, see *Jazz Hot, Jazz Magazine,* or *Pariscope.*

Jazz Club La Villa. In the Hôtel La Villa, 29 rue Jacob, 6e. ☎ **01-43-26-60-00.** Cover (including first drink) 120–150F ($21.60–$27). Closed Aug. Métro: St-Germain-des-Prés.

This club is unusual because it lies in the red-velour cellar of a small but chic four-star hotel in the Latin Quarter. It's quite upscale, sometimes booking famous artists such as Shirley Horn. Music ranges from beebop to modern jazz.

✪ **Le Bilboquet/Club St-Germain.** 13 rue St-Benoît, 6e. ☎ **01-45-48-81-84.** No cover. Métro: St-Germain-des-Prés.

This restaurant/jazz club/piano bar offers some of the best music in Paris. The film *Paris Blues* was shot here. Jazz is played on the upper level in the restaurant, Le Bilboquet, a wood-paneled room with a copper ceiling, brass-trimmed sunken bar, and Victorian candelabra. The menu is limited but classic French, and a dinner will run you 250F to 300F ($45 to $54). Under separate management is the downstairs disco, Club St-Germain, which charges no cover (but drinks cost a staggering 100F/$18). You can walk from one club to the other but have to buy a new drink each time you change venues.

New Morning. 7–9 rue des Petites-Ecuries, 10e. ☎ **01-45-23-51-41.** Cover 100–140F ($18–$25.20). Métro: Château-d'Eau.

Jazz maniacs come here to drink, talk, and dance at this enduring club. It's sometimes a scene, recently attracting such guests as Spike Lee and The Artist Formerly Known As Prince. The place is especially popular with jazz groups from Central and South Africa.

Slow Club. 130 rue de Rivoli, 1er. ☎ **01-42-33-84-30.** Cover 60F ($10.80) Tues–Thurs, 75F ($13.50) Fri–Sat and holidays. Students 53F ($9.55) Mon–Fri. Métro: Châtelet.

One of the most famous jazz cellars in Europe, the Slow Club features the well-known French jazz band of Claude Luter, who played 10 years with the late Sidney Bechet. The hip crowd tends to be in their 30s.

DANCE CLUBS

The area around the Eglise St-Germain-des-Prés is full of dance clubs. They come and go so quickly that last year's Disco Inferno could be a hardware store by the time you get there—but new ones will spring up to take the place of the old. For the most up-to-date information, see *Time Out, Pariscope,* or *L'Officiel des Spectacles.*

Bus Palladium. 6 rue Fontaine, 9e. ☎ **01-53-21-07-33.** Cover for men, none Wed–Thurs, 100F ($18) Tues and Fri–Sat; for women, none Tues–Thurs, 100F ($18) Fri–Sat. Métro: Blanche or Pigalle.

Housed in a single room with a very long bar, this temple to rock has varnished hardwoods and fabric-covered walls that absorb only some of the reverberations of the nonstop recorded music. Rock music provides the soundtrack for a serious mating game among heterosexuals ages 25 to 35. Drinks are a hefty 80F ($14.40), though women drink free on Tuesdays.

La Balajo. 9 rue de Lappe, 11e. ☎ **01-47-00-07-87.** Cover (including first drink) 100F ($18) Thurs–Sat evenings, 50F ($9) Sun afternoon. Métro: Bastille.

Established in 1936, this dance club is best remembered as the place where Edith Piaf first won the hearts of thousands of Parisian music lovers. Today Le Balajo is hardly as fashionable, though it continues its big-band traditions on Sunday afternoons, when a group of patrons aged 45 and up dance to an eclectic mix of World War II–era swing and bebop. Thursday to Saturday nights, the focus is on disco and, to a lesser degree, reggae, salsa, rock, and rap.

La Java. 105 rue du Faubourg du Temple, 11e. ☎ **01-42-02-20-52.** Cover 80F ($14.40) Thurs, 60–90F ($10.80–$16.20) Fri, 80F ($14.40) Sat, 40F ($7.20) Sun. Métro: Belleville.

Once this bal-musette dance hall was one of the most frequented in Paris, and the great Piaf and even Maurice Chevalier made their names here. Today, you can still dance the waltz here on what one critic called "Retro fetish night," or perhaps even tango on a Sunday afternoon. Other nights feature Brazilian and Latin themes—we even spotted a young Carmen Miranda wanna-be in drag.

Le New Riverside. 7 rue Grégoire-de-Tours, 6e. ☎ **01-43-54-46-33.** Cover (including first drink) 90F ($18) for men at all times, for women only after midnight Fri–Sat. Métro: St-Michel or Odéon.

This battered Left Bank cellar club attracts droves of jaded veteran club-goers, who appreciate the indestructible premises and the classic rock from the '70s (particularly The Doors). Expect a crowd aged 25 to 40; women, especially when unaccompanied, are almost always admitted free. If fond thoughts of Woodstock fill you with nostalgia, this is the place to meet like-minded French folks.

Le Saint. 7 rue St-Severin, 5e. ☎ **01-43-25-50-04.** Cover (including first drink) 60–90F ($10.80–$16.20). Métro: St-Michel.

Occupying three medieval cellars deep within Paris's densest concentration of university facilities, this place attracts a crowd in their 20s and 30s who dance (to music from both the U.S. and Europe), drink, and generally soak up the Left Bank student-dive scene. Vacationers will enjoy this fun spot, and its "Young Love Beside the Seine" vibe can be a hoot.

Les Bains. 7 rue du Bourg-l'Abbé, 3e. ☎ **01-48-87-01-80.** Cover (including first drink) 100F ($20). Métro: Réaumur.

This chic spot has been pronounced "in" and "out" many times, but lately it's very in, attracting a good-looking local crowd and growing a bit more gay.

Les Coulisses. 5 rue du Mont-Cenis (place du Tertre), 18e. ☎ **01-42-62-89-99.** Cover 100F ($18) Fri–Sat; no cover for people who eat in the restaurant. Métro: Abbesses.

There are more tourist traps in Montmartre than anywhere else in Paris, but this fairly new club has some legitimacy, providing a good spot for drinking and dancing in the heart of the district. Its premises combine a basement-level dance club, a first-floor bar, and a restaurant on the second floor. The decor changes all the time, but management usually sticks to baroque and medieval themes. The club stays open until dawn.

Les Etoiles. 61 rue du Château-d'Eau, 10e. ☎ **01-47-70-60-56.** Cover with dinner 120F ($21.60). Métro: Château-d'Eau.

Since 1856, this old-fashioned music hall has reverberated with the sounds of performers at work and patrons at play. Its newest incarnation is a restaurant discotheque where the music is exclusively salsa and the food Cubano. Expect simple but hearty portions of fried fish, shredded pork or beef, rice, beans, and flan as bands from Venezuela play salsa to a crowd that already knows or quickly learns how to dance to South American rhythms.

Rex Club. 5 bd. Poissonière, 2e. ☎ **01-42-36-83-98.** Cover (including first drink) 70–80F ($12.60–$14.40). Métro: Bonne-Nouvelle.

During its "tea dance" sessions, this place attracts patrons ages 40 to 65 with recorded tangos and waltzes and occasional flirtations with 1970s disco. It really gets bizarre after 11:30pm, when the echoing blue-and-orange space pulsates with techno music and a young, international (sometimes mood-altered) crowd. A revolving host of DJs is on hand.

WINE BARS

Many Parisians now prefer the wine bar to the traditional cafe or bistro. The food is often better and the ambience more inviting.

✪ **Au Sauvignon.** 80 rue des Sts-Pères, 7e. ☎ **01-45-48-49-02.** Closed Aug. Métro: Sèvres-Babylone.

This tiny spot has tables overflowing onto a covered terrace and a decor featuring old ceramic tiles and frescoes done by Left Bank artists. Wines range from the cheapest beaujolais to the most expensive Puligny-Montrachet. A glass of wine costs 17F to 30F ($3.05 to $5.40), with an additional charge of 2F (35¢) to consume it at a table. To go with your wine, choose an Auvergne specialty, like goat cheese or a terrine. The fresh Poilane bread is ideal with the ham, pâté, or goat cheese.

Les Bacchantes. 21 rue Caumartin, 9e. ☎ **01-42-65-25-35.** Métro: Havre-Caumartin.

This place prides itself on offering more wines by the glass—at least 50—than any other wine bar in Paris; prices range from 13F to 25F ($2.30 to $4.50). It also does a hefty restaurant trade in well-prepared *cuisine bourgeoise.* Its cozy, rustic setting—with massive exposed beams, old-fashioned paneling, and chalkboards announcing both the vintages and the platters—attracts dozens of theater-goers before and after performances at the nearby Théâtre Olympia, as well as anyone interested in carefully chosen vintages from esoteric or smale-scale wine makers. Wines derive mainly from France, but you'll also find examples from neighboring countries of Europe.

Juveniles. 47 rue de Richelieu, 1er. ☎ **01-42-97-46-49.** Métro: Palais-Royal.

This is a spin-off of one of Paris's most successful wine bars, Willi's, which is nearby. Louder, less formal, less restrained, and (at least to wine lovers) more provocative than its older sibling, it prides itself on experimenting with a wide roster of wines. There's no stuffiness at this British-owned spot, where high-quality but less well-known wines from Spain, France, California, and Australia go for between 15F and 50F ($2.70 and $9) a glass. Anything you like, including bottles of the "wine of the week," can be hauled away uncorked from a wine boutique on the premises. And if you get hungry, savory tapas-style platters are available for 30F to 40F ($5.40 to $7.20).

✪ **Willi's Wine Bar.** 13 rue des Petits-Champs, 1er. ☎ **01-42-61-05-09.** Métro: Bourse, Louvre, or Palais-Royal.

Journalists and stockbrokers patronize this increasingly popular wine bar in the center of the financial district. About 250 kinds of wine are offered, including a dozen "wine specials" you can taste by the glass for 20F to 60F ($3.60 to $10.80). Lunch is the busiest time—on quiet evenings you can better enjoy the warm ambience and 16th-century beams. Daily specials are likely to include lamb brochette with cumin or lyonnaise sausage in truffled vinaigrette, plus a spectacular dessert like chocolate terrine. The fixed-price dinner is 185F ($33.30).

BARS & PUBS

Académie de la Bière. 88 bis bd. du Port-Royal, 5e. ☎ **01-43-54-66-65.** Métro: Port-Royal.

The decor is paneled and rustic, an appropriate foil for an "academy" whose curriculum includes access to more than 150 kinds of microbrewed beer. More than half of the dozen on tap are from small breweries in Belgium that deserve to be better known. Mugs or bottles cost 22F to 65F ($3.95 to $11.70) each, depending on how esoteric they are. Getting hungry? Snack-style food is available, including platters of mussels, assorted cheeses, and sausages with mustard.

After-Dark Diversions: Dives, Drag & More

On a Paris night the cheapest entertainment, especially if you're young, is "the show" staged at the southeasterly tip of the Ile de la Cité, behind the Notre-Dame. Like a Gallic version of the Sundowner Festival in Key West, Florida, it attracts anyone who has ever wanted to try his or her hand at performance art. The entertainment is strictly spontaneous, usually including magicians, fire-eaters, jugglers, mimes, and music-makers from all over the world, performing against the backdrop of the illuminated cathedral. Completely unchoreographed, the setting provides one of the greatest places in Paris to meet other young people.

What's the least formal way to quench the thirst you'll develop during your participation in the be-in? Wander over to the **Café-Brasserie St-Regis,** 6 rue Jean-du-Bellay, 4e (☎ **01-43-54-59-41;** Métro: Musée-du-Louvre), for a take-away drink. It's on the Ile St-Louis, across from pont St-Louis. If you want to linger inside, you can order a plat du jour for around 57F ($10.25) or a coffee at the bar. But if you're looking for maximum mobility, order a beer to go (*une bière à emporter*) in a plastic cup, priced at 13F ($2.35), and take it with you on a stroll around the island. The little cafe is open daily from 7am to 2am.

For another memorable way to see spontaneous Paris in action, take a walk along the Seine after 10pm. Follow the graveled pathway down to the Seine from the Left Bank side of the Pont de Sully, close to the Institut du Monde Arabe, and walk to the right, away from the cathedral of Notre-Dame. Joggers come here, saxophone players entertain, and many Parisians show up to dance everything from the cancan to the jitterbug. These dance parties are impromptu and depend on the weather, of course.

Looking for a dive to hang out in until the Métro starts running again at 5am? Try **Sous-Bock Tavern,** 49 rue St-Honoré, 1er (☎ **01-40-26-46-61;** Métro: Pont-Neuf), at the corner of rue du pont-Neuf. A crowd of young beer drinkers gathers here to sample some 400 varieties. If you want a shot of whiskey to accompany your brew, you face a choice of 180 varieties. The tavern is open Monday through Saturday from 11am to 5am and Sunday from 3pm to 5am. The dish to order here is a platter of mussels—curried, with white wine, or with cream sauce. They go well with the brasserie-style french fries.

When it's time to check out some of the best drag in Paris far afield from the tourist circuit, head for **Le Piano Show,** 20 rue de la Verrerie, 4e (☎ **01-42-72-23-81;** Métro: Hôtel-de-Ville). Only four *artistes* perform in this somewhat bedraggled cabaret that attracts a predominantly gay crowd: All are stylish and

Bar Anglais. In the Hôtel Plaza-Athénée, 25 av. Montaigne, 8e. ☎ **01-53-67-66-65.** Métro: Alma-Marceau.

As its name implies, this terribly upscale bar, located in one of Paris's most opulent hotels, has a woodsy, leathery, and vintage Anglo-Saxon decor, though the service is definitely French and the drinks international. Every evening between 10:30pm and 1:30am, a pianist and singer entertain the prosperous clientele in a medley of languages.

Bar du Crillon. In the Hôtel de Crillon, 10 place de la Concorde, 8e. ☎ **01-44-71-15-00.** Métro: Concorde.

Though some visitors consider the Bar du Crillon too stuffy and self-consciously elegant, the social and literary history of this bar is remarkable. Hemingway set a fetchingly attired (with décolletage for miles)—and male. Variety acts change monthly, but impersonations of those dear to the French include Edith Piaf and Melina Mercouri but also the obligatory Streisand and Minnelli. The spectacle is preceded by a mandatory 189F to 249F ($34 to $44.80) dinner; after that, drinks cost 85F ($15.30). Open daily, with dinner beginning at 8:30pm and the show at 10:30pm.

Remember Marlon Brando in *Last Tango in Paris?* Relive it at **Le Tango,** 13 rue au Maire, 3e (☎ **01-42-72-17-78;** Métro: Arts-et-Métiers). It's a dive with bordello decor, but you can tango and dance to various salsa and zouk music originating from the French Caribbean to Africa. The club attracts those in their 20s and 30s. The cover ranges from 40F to 60F ($7.20 to $10.80).

Experience the best Brazilian samba and African music in Paris at **Chez Félix,** 23 rue Moffetard, 5e (☎ **01-47-07-68-78;** Métro: Monge), where the people-watching can be even more fun than dancing. Featuring a cutting-edge blend of music from Cuba, Brazil, and the Antilles, it's often filled with colorful Latin expatriates and is a gathering place for Paris's late-night hard-core party crowd. The cover is 100F ($18); a first drink costs 50F ($9).

What's one of the most fun and trendy things to do in Paris today? Put on your red dancing shoes and head for **La Guinguette Pirate,** quai de la Gare, 13e (☎ **01-44-24-89-89;** Métro: Quai-de-la-Gare), a Chinese junk moored off the banks of the Seine. This is the 1990s version of the fabled *guinguette* (river-bordering cafe). Some of the best jazz, zouk, and live salsa is waiting to enthrall you.

Much hipper than that is **What's Up?,** 15 rue Daval, 11e (☎ **01-48-05-88-33;** Métro: Bastille), where the young existentialistes of today flock. The later you go, the more fashionable. Some of the city's aspiring artists, writers, and painters, along with designers and models, show up.

Looking for a sophisticated, laid-back venue without the high-energy exhibitionism of more cutting-edge nightclubs? Consider a drink at the **Sans-Sens,** 49 rue du Faubourg St-Antoine, 4e (☎ **01-44-75-78-78;** Métro: Bastille), where the dialogue attests to the unifying power of jazz and humor. Expect the children of prominent Parisians to mingle freely at this multiracial playground. Set within a richly upholstered, red-velvet duplex, many of the most important dialogues seem to occur on the stairway or the back-room couches where the margaritas slide quickly down many a silk-scarved throat. The later it gets, the sexier the scene. No cover.

climactic scene of *The Sun Also Rises* here, and over the years it has attracted a crowd of diplomats from the nearby U.S. Embassy as well as visiting heiresses, stars, starlets, and wanna-bes. Under its new owner, the Concorde Group, the bar has been redecorated by Sonia Rykiel. Another option down the hall is the Edwardian-style **Jardin d'Hiver,** where, amid potted palms and upscale accessories, you can order tea, cocktails, or coffee.

✪ **Bar Hemingway/Bar Vendôme.** In Le Ritz, 15 place Vendôme, 1er. ☎ **01-43-16-30-30.** Métro: Opéra.

In 1944 during the Liberation of Paris, Ernest Hemingway made history by ordering a drink at the Ritz Bar while gunfire from retreating Nazi soldiers was still audible in the streets. Today, basking in the literary glow, the Ritz commemorates this event with bookish memorabilia, rows of newspapers, and stiff drinks. Look for the bar's entrance, and homages to other writers such as Proust, near the hotel's rue Cambon entrance. If you develop a thirst in the daytime, when the Bar Hemingway isn't open, head for the Bar Vendôme, which is near the hotel's main (place Vendôme) entrance. The setting there is just as cozy and woodsy, albeit a bit more grand.

The China Club. 50 rue de Charenton, 12e. ☎ **01-43-43-82-02.** Métro: Bastille.

Designed to recall France's 19th-century colonies in Asia (on the ground floor) and England's empire in India (upstairs), the China Club offers a chance to chitchat or flirt with the singles who crowd into the street-level bar, then escape to a quieter setting upstairs. You'll see regulars from the worlds of fashion and the arts, along with post-show celebrants from the nearby Opéra Bastille. There's a Chinese restaurant on the street level; a scattering of books, newspapers, and chessboards upstairs; and a more animated (and occasionally raucous) bar in the cellar.

✪ **Harry's New York Bar.** 5 rue Daunou, 2e. ☎ **01-42-61-71-14.** Métro: Opéra or Pyramides.

Sank roo doe noo, as the ads tell you to instruct your cabdriver, is the most famous bar in Europe—quite possibly in the world. Opened on Thanksgiving Day 1911 by a bearded Hemingway precursor named MacElhone, it's sacred to Papa disciples as the spot where heroic members of the World War I ambulance corps drank themselves silly and as Ernest's favorite place for Parisian imbibing. The site is legendary for other reasons as well: White lady and sidecar cocktails were invented here in 1919 and 1931, respectively, and it's also the alleged birthplace of the Bloody Mary and the headquarters of a loosely organized fraternity of drinkers known as the International Bar Flies (IBF). Harry's has stayed in the family: MacElhone's bilingual grandson, Duncan, now owns and runs it.

The place's historic core is the street-level bar, where CEOs and office workers loosen their ties on more or less equal footing. Daytime crowds draw from the neighborhood's insurance, banking, and travel industries; evening crowds include pre- and post-theater groupies and night owls who aren't bothered by the gritty setting and deliberately unflattering lighting. A softer, somewhat less macho ambience reigns in the cellar, where a pianist provides music every night from 10pm to 2am.

Le Bétel. In L'Hotel, 13 rue des Beaux-Arts, 6e. ☎ **01-43-25-27-22.** Métro: St-Germain-des-Prés.

Located in one of the golden nugget hotels of the Left Bank, this is the city's most romantic bar. Oscar Wilde checked out long ago, but the odd celebrity still shows up: We were once 15 minutes into a conversation before realizing we were speaking to the great French actress Jeanne Moreau. Drinks are expertly mixed, the place is sleek and chic, and conversations are held at a discreet murmur. There's no better place to take her (or him) for a romantic rendezvous.

Le Forum. 4 bd. Malesherbes, 8e. ☎ **01-42-65-37-86.** Métro: Madeleine.

Its regulars, who include international business travelers, compare this place to a private club in London—probably due to the carefully polished oak paneling and ornate stucco as well as the list of single-malt whiskeys, among the most comprehensive in town. Cocktails, anyone? The drink menu lists more than 150 choices. Order champagne by the glass, or perhaps a martini.

Pub St-Germain-des-Prés. 17 rue de l'Ancienne-Comédie, 6e. ☎ **01-43-29-38-70.** Métro: Odéon.

With nine rooms and 650 seats, this is the largest pub in France, offering 500 brands of beer, 26 of them on draft. The deliberately tacky decor, which has seen a lot of beer swilled and spilled since its installation, consists of leather booths, faded gilt-framed mirrors, hanging lamps, and a stuffed parrot in a gilded cage. It gets *really* fun between 10:30pm and 4am, when live rock turns everything louder, sudsier, and more raucous.

GAY & LESBIAN CLUBS

Gay life is centered around Les Halles and Le Marais, with the greatest concentration of gay and lesbian clubs, restaurants, bars, and shops between the Hôtel-de-Ville and Rambuteau Métro stops. Gay dance clubs come and go so fast that even the magazines devoted somewhat to their pursuit—*3 Keller* and *Exit,* both distributed free in the gay bars and bookstores—have a hard time keeping up. *Lesbia,* a monthly national lesbian magazine, focuses on women's issues.

✪ **Banana Café.** 13 rue de la Ferronnerie, 1er. ☎ **01-42-33-35-31.** Métro: Châtelet-Les-Halles.

This is the most popular gay bar in the Marais, a required stop for gay Europeans (mostly male) visiting or doing business in Paris. Occupying two floors of a 19th-century building, it has walls the color of an overripe banana, dim lighting, and a well-publicized policy of raising drink prices after 10pm, when the joint becomes really interesting. On theme nights such as Valentine's Day, expect the entire premises to be plastered with pink crêpe paper. There's a street-level bar and a dance floor in the cellar that features a live pianist and recorded music. On many nights, go-go dancers perform in the cellar.

Bar Hotel Central. 33 rue Vieille-du-Temple, 4e. ☎ **01-48-87-99-33.** Métro: Hôtel-de-Ville.

Bar Hotel Central is one of the leading bars for men in the Hôtel-de-Ville area. The club has opened a small hotel upstairs. Both the bar and its hotel are in a 300-year-old building in the heart of the Marais. The hotel caters mostly to gay men, less frequently to lesbians.

La Champmeslé. 4 rue Chabanais, 2e. ☎ **01-42-96-85-20.** Métro: Pyramides or Bourse.

With dim lighting, background music, and comfortable banquettes, La Champmeslé offers a cozy meeting place for women, and to a much, much lesser extent (about 5%), "well-behaved" men. Paris's leading women's bar is housed in a 300-year-old building with exposed stone, ceiling beams, and 1950s-style furnishings. Every Thursday night one of the premier lesbian events in Paris, a cabaret, begins at 10pm (with the same cover and drink prices as on any other day), and every month there's a well-attended exhibition of paintings by mostly lesbian artists. Josy is your sophisticated hostess.

Le Bar. 5 rue de la Ferronerie, 1er. ☎ **01-40-41-00-10.** Métro: Châtelet.

Covering the street level and cellar of a sprawling building in a neighborhood known for its serious pickup scene, this is the largest gay bar in Paris. You'll find three bars on the premises, a mostly blue decor with lots of sinuous lines, and an ambience that's more sexually charged and explicit in the cellar than on the street level. The average age of most patrons is around 32, and the majority are gay and male.

Le Pulp. 25 bd. Poissonnière, 2e. ☎ **01-40-26-01-93.** Métro: Rue-Montmartre.

This is one of the most popular (and most fun) lesbian discos in Paris, welcoming women of all ages. After a change in management, the club's seedy past is now a distant memory; today this replica of a late 19th-century French music hall is trendy and chic, with all types of cutting-edge music. It's best to show up before midnight. What to do if you're a gay male who wants to hang out with the girls? Head for the side entrance, where a "separate but equal facility" called Le Scorpion welcomes gay guys into a roughly equivalent place that, alas, never manages to be as much fun as Le Queen.

✪ **Le Queen.** 102 av. des Champs-Elysées, 8e. ☎ **01-53-89-08-90.** No cover Tues–Thurs and Sun, 50F ($9) Mon, 100F ($18) Fri–Sat. Métro: Franklin-D.-Roosevelt.

Should you miss gay life à la New York, follow the flashing purple sign on the "main street" of Paris, near the corner of avenue George-V. This place is often mobbed, primarily by gay men and, to a much lesser degree, chic women who work in the fashion and film industries. Look for drag shows, muscle shows, striptease from danseurs who gyrate atop the bars, and everything from Monday '70s-style disco nights to Tuesday-night foam parties (only in summer), when cascades of mousse descend onto the dance floor. Go very, very late, as the place is open daily from midnight to 6 or 7am.

6

Side Trips from Paris: Versailles, Chartres & the Best of Ile de France

The Château de Versailles, the Cathédrale Notre-Dame de Chartres, and the Palais de Fontainebleau draw countless tour buses. They're the stars of the Ile de France and need no selling from us. However, the lesser-known but stunning spots in this greenbelt around Paris may not be as familiar to you.

Many people know of this region through the paintings of Corot, Renoir, Degas, Monet, and Cézanne. Here you'll find everything from Romanesque ruins, Gothic cathedrals, and feudal castles to splendid 18th-century châteaux, enormous forests like Fontainebleau and Chantilly, sleepy villages, and even an African game reserve. To top it off, there's Disneyland Paris if your kids just have to see Mickey and Minnie with a Gallic twist.

Everything described in this chapter can be seen on a day trip from Paris or as an overnight excursion.

1 Versailles

13 miles SW of Paris, 44 miles NE of Chartres

Back in the grand siècle, all you needed was a sword, a hat, and a bribe for the guard at the gate. Providing you didn't look as if you had smallpox, you'd be admitted to the precincts of the Château de Versailles, where you could stroll through salon after glittering salon—watching the Sun King at his banquet table, gossiping, dancing, plotting, flirting. Louis XIV was accorded about as much privacy as an institution.

Today Versailles needs Louis XIV and his fat treasury to return. You wouldn't believe it to look at the glittering Hall of Mirrors, but Versailles is down-at-the-heels. It suffers from a lack of funds, which translates into a shortage of security forces. At Versailles today you get to see only half its treasures; the rest are closed to the public, including the Musée de France, with its 6,000 paintings and 2,000 statues. Some 3.2 million visitors arrive annually, and on average they spend 2 hours here.

ESSENTIALS

GETTING THERE Catch RER **train** line C at Paris's Gare-d'Austerlitz, St-Michel, Musée-d'Orsay, Invalides, Pont-de-l'Alma, Champ-de-Mars, or Javel station and take it to the Versailles Rive Gauche station, from which there's a shuttle bus to the château. The 14F to 21F ($2.50 to $3.80) trip takes about 40 minutes; **Eurailpass**

The Ile de France

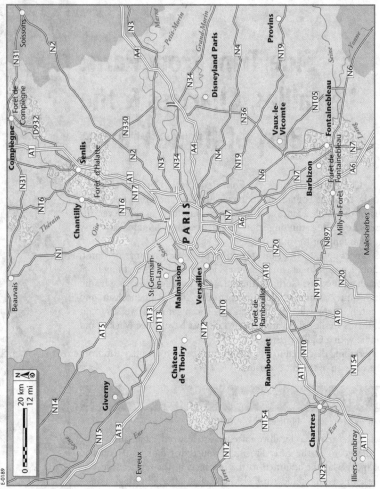

holders travel free. A regular train also leaves from Gare Montparnasse for the Versailles Rive Gauche RER station.

If you go **by Métro,** get off at the Pont-de-Sèvres stop and transfer to bus no. 171. The trip takes 35 minutes. To get here from Paris, it's cheaper to pay with three Métro tickets from a carnet. You'll be let off near the gates of the palace.

If you're **driving,** exit the périphérique on N10 (or avenue du Général-Leclerc), which will take you straight to Versailles; park on place d'Armes in front of the château.

VISITOR INFORMATION   The **Office de Tourisme** is at 7 rue des Réservoirs (☎ **01-39-50-36-22;** fax 01-39-50-68-07).

VERSAILLES EVENTS   The tourist office offers the **Grand Fête de Nuit de Versailles (Son-et-Lumière),** an evening of fireworks and illuminated fountains, several times during summer. Two hundred actors portray Louis XIV and his court over 7 nights: June 27, July 4, 18, and 25, August 29, and September 5 and 12. For the 1¼-hour show you sit on bleachers clustered at the boulevard de la Reine entrance to the Basin of Neptune. The gates open 1½ hours before show time. In June and July

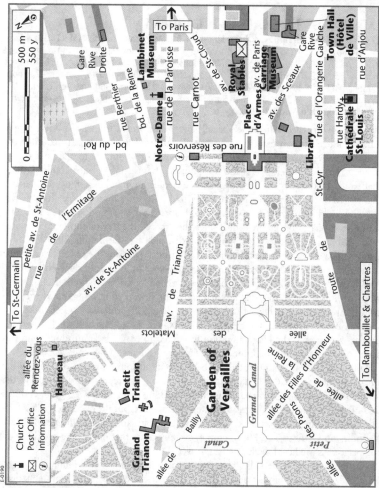

shows are at 10:30pm; and at 9:30pm in August and September. For information about these shows, call ☎ **01-30-83-78-88.**

The best front seats cost 250F ($45); standing room on the *promenoir* is 70F ($12.60); children 9 and under enter free in the standing room on the promenoir, but don't expect great seats, kids. You can buy tickets in advance at the tourist office (see "Visitor Information" above) beginning in April or by fax, phone, or mail from 9am to 7pm. You can also buy them in Paris at some travel agents. If you've just arrived in Versailles, you can take a chance and purchase tickets all day long at the tourist office and before the show at boulevard de la Reine.

Every Sunday from May 4 to October 12, a less elaborate spectacle is staged. Called the **Les Grandes Eaux Musicales,** it features loud broadcast music by French-born composers (Couperin, Charpentier, Delalande) and others (Mozart and Haydn) whose music was contemporaneous with court life in Versailles. All the fountains are illuminated in their effusive grandeur. The show takes place from 3:30 to 6pm, with the finale at the Neptune Basin beginning at 5:30pm. The 28F ($5.05) price admits you to both events; free for children 9 and under.

EXPLORING THE CHATEAU & GARDENS

✪ **Château de Versailles.** ☎ **01-30-84-74-00.** Admission: palace, 45F ($8.10) adults, 35F ($6.30) adults after 3:30pm and for ages 18–25, free for seniors 60 and over; Grand Trianon, 25F ($4.50) adults, 15F ($2.70) adults after 3:30pm and for ages 18–25; Petit Trianon, 15F ($2.70) adults, 10F ($1.80) adults after 3:30pm and for ages 18–25; both Trianons, 30F ($5.40) adults, 20F ($3.60) ages 18–25. Everything free for children 17 and under. May 2–Sept 30 Tues–Sun 9am–6:30pm; Oct 1–May 1 Tues–Sun 9am–5:30pm. Grounds daily dawn–dusk.

Within 50 years the Château de Versailles was transformed from Louis XIII's simple hunting lodge into an extravagant palace. Begun in 1661, the construction of the château involved 32,000 to 45,000 workmen, some of whom had to drain marshes—often at the cost of their lives—and move forests. Louis XIV set out to build a palace that would be the envy of all Europe, and he created a symbol of pomp and opulence that was to be copied, yet never quite duplicated, all over Europe and even in America.

So he could keep an eye on the nobles of France (and with good reason), Louis XIV summoned them to live at his court. Here he amused them with constant entertainment and lavish banquets. To some he awarded such tasks as holding the hem of his ermine-lined robe. While the aristocrats frivolously played away their lives, often in silly intrigues and games, the peasants on the estates sowed the seeds of the Revolution.

When Louis XIV died in 1715, he was succeeded by his great-grandson, Louis XV, who continued the outrageous pomp, though he is said to have predicted the outcome: "Après moi, le déluge" (After me, the deluge). His wife, Marie Leczinska, was shocked by the blatant immorality at Versailles. When her husband tired of her, she lived as a nun, and the king's attention wandered to Mme de Pompadour, who was accused of running up a debt for France far beyond that of a full-scale war.

Louis XVI found his grandfather's behavior scandalous—in fact, on gaining the throne he ordered that the "stairway of indiscretion" (secret stairs leading up to the king's bedchamber) be removed. This dull, weak king (who did have good intentions) and his queen, Marie Antoinette, were well liked at first, but the queen's excessive frivolity and wild spending soon led to her downfall. Louis and Marie Antoinette were at Versailles on October 6, 1789, when they were notified that mobs were marching on the palace. As predicted, le déluge had arrived.

Napoléon stayed at Versailles but never seemed fond of it. Louis-Philippe (reigned 1830–48) prevented the destruction of the palace by converting it into a museum dedicated to the glory of France. To do that, he had to surrender some of his own not-so-hard-earned currency. Many years later John D. Rockefeller contributed heavily toward the restoration of Versailles, and work continues to this day.

The six magnificent **Grands Appartements** are in the Louis XIV style, each named after the allegorical painting on the room's ceiling. The best known and largest is the **Hercules Salon,** with a ceiling painted by François Lemoine, depicting the Apotheosis of Hercules. In the **Mercury Salon** (with a ceiling by Jean-Baptiste Champaigne), the body of Louis XIV was put on display in 1715; his 72-year reign was one of the longest in history.

The most famous room at Versailles is the 236-foot-long **Hall of Mirrors.** Begun by Mansart in 1678 in the Louis XIV style, it was decorated by Le Brun with 17 large arched windows matched by corresponding beveled mirrors in simulated arcades. On June 28, 1919, the treaty ending World War I was signed in this corridor. Ironically, the German Empire was also proclaimed here in 1871.

The royal apartments were for show, but Louis XV and Louis XVI retired to the **Petits Appartements** to escape the demands of court etiquette. Louis XV died in his bedchamber in 1774, a victim of smallpox. In a second-floor apartment, which you can visit only with a guide, he stashed away first Mme de Pompadour and then Mme

Peaches & Peas Fit for a King

Between 1682 and 1789, Versailles housed a royal entourage whose population, except for 8 years during the minority of Louis XV, remained constant at 3,000. To feed them, the sprawling kitchens employed a permanent staff of 2,000. Without benefit of running water or electricity, they labored over the banquets that became day-to-day rituals at the most glorious court since the collapse of ancient Rome.

The fruits and vegetables that arrayed the royal tables were produced on-site, in *Les Potagers du Roi* (the King's Kitchen Gardens). Surprisingly, the gardens have survived and can be found a 10-minute walk south of the château's main entrance, at 6 rue du Hardy, behind an industrial-looking gate. Here, 23 acres of fertile earth are arranged into parterres and terraces as formal as the legendary showcases devoted, during the royal tenure, to flowers, fountains, and statuary.

Meals at Versailles were quite a ritual. The king almost always dined in state, alone, at a table visible to hundreds of observers and, in some cases, other diners, who sat in order of rank. Fortunately for gastronomic historians, there are many detailed accounts of what Louis XIV enjoyed and how much he consumed: Addicted to salads, he ate prodigious amounts of basil, purslane, mint, and wood sorrel. He loved melons, figs, and pears. With him apples weren't particularly popular, but he found peaches so desirable that he rarely waited to cut and peel them, preferring to let the juices flow liberally down his royal chin. The culinary rage, however, was peas—imported from Genoa for the first time in 1660. According to Mme de Maintenon, Louis XIV's second wife, the entire court was obsessed with "impatience to eat them."

Today Les Potagers du Roi are maintained by about half a dozen gardeners under the direction of the Ecole Nationale du Paysage. It manages to intersperse the fruits and vegetables once favored by the monarchs with experimental breeds and hundreds of splendidly espaliered fruit trees.

du Barry. Attempts have been made to return the Queen's Apartments to their appearance in the days of Marie Antoinette, when she played her harpsichord in front of specially invited guests.

Her king, Louis XVI, had an impressive **Library,** designed by Jacques-Ange Gabriel, which was sumptuous. Its panels are delicately carved, and the room has been restored and refurnished. The **Clock Room** contains Passement's astronomical clock, encased in gilded bronze. Twenty years in the making, it was completed in 1753. The clock is supposed to keep time until the year 9999. At the age of 7 Mozart played in this room for the court.

Gabriel designed the **Opéra** for Louis XV in 1748, though it wasn't completed until 1770. In its heyday it took 3,000 candles to light the place. With gold-and-white harmony, Hardouin-Mansart built the **Royal Chapel** in 1699, dying before its completion. Louis XVI, when still the dauphin (crown prince), married Marie Antoinette here in 1770. At this arranged marriage, both the bride and the groom were teenagers.

Spread across 250 acres, the **Gardens of Versailles** were laid out by the great landscape artist André Le Nôtre. At the peak of their glory, 1,400 fountains spewed forth. *The Buffet* is an exceptional one, having been designed by Mansart. One fountain depicts Apollo in his chariot pulled by four horses, surrounded by tritons emerging from the water to light the world. Le Nôtre created a Garden of Eden using ornamental lakes and canals, geometrically designed flower beds, and avenues bordered with statuary. On the mile-long Grand Canal, Louis XV—imagining he was in Venice—used to take gondola rides with his favorite of the moment.

A long walk across the park will take you to the **Grand Trianon,** in pink-and-white marble, designed by Hardouin-Mansart for Louis XIV in 1687. Traditionally it has been a place where France has lodged important guests, though de Gaulle wanted to turn it into a weekend retreat. Nixon once slept here in the room where Mme de Pompadour died. Mme de Maintenon also slept here, as did Napoléon. The original furnishings are gone, of course, with mostly Empire pieces there today.

Gabriel, the designer of place de la Concorde in Paris, built the **Petit Trianon** in 1768 for Louis XV. Louis used it for his trysts with Mme du Barry. In time, Marie Antoinette adopted it as her favorite residence, a place to escape the rigid life at the main palace. Many of the current furnishings, including a few in her rather modest bedchamber, belonged to the ill-fated queen.

WHERE TO STAY
EXPENSIVE

✪ **Hôtel Trianon Palace.** 1 bd. de la Reine, 78000 Versailles. ☎ **01-30-84-38-00.** Fax 01-39-49-00-77. www.westin.com. 200 units. MINIBAR TV TEL. 1,200–2,000F ($216–$360) double; 2,700–7,500F ($486–$1,350) suite. AE, DC, DISC, MC, V.

In 1919 this was the headquarters of the peace conference where Woodrow Wilson, Lloyd George, Georges Clemenceau, and other world leaders gathered. This hotel dwarfs all the competition in town, especially the new Sofitel Château de Versailles. A classically designed palace with stately charm, it's set in a 5-acre garden bordering those of the Trianons at Versailles. Japanese owners have restored the place to the tune of $60 million. You can stay in either the palace or the new Hôtel Trianon, separated from the palace by a garden and connected to it by an underground tunnel. Though many of the dignified rooms are old-fashioned, others (in the new wing) are modern. They're decorated traditionally with subdued colors, antiques, and fine reproductions. The Japanese suites are the ultimate in luxury.

Dining/Diversions: Breakfast is served in the sumptuous Salle Clemenceau, where the Treaty of Versailles was negotiated. Chef Gérard Vié, the finest in Versailles, operates his world-class Les Trois Marchés (see "Dining," below) glass veranda overlooking the park. You can dine less expensively by ordering a menu du jour in the Brasserie La Fontaine, in the Trianon Hotel. A Japanese restaurant overlooks a zen garden. After 6pm daily you can relax and listen to good music, occasionally with featured jazz performers, in the Marie-Antoinette Piano Bar.

Amenities: Room service (24 hours), baby-sitting, laundry, health club, indoor pool, tennis courts. The hotel has joined with Givenchy, one of the top names in French beauty care, to create an outstanding spa, with many treatments and services available.

INEXPENSIVE

Hôtel Paris. 14 av. de Paris, 78000 Versailles. ☎ **01-39-50-56-00.** Fax 01-39-50-21-83. 38 units, 32 with bathroom. TV TEL. 200F ($36) double without bathroom, 340–380F ($61.20–$68.40) double with bathroom. AE, DC, MC, V.

This is the best deal in town. The Paris is a somewhat nondescript wood-and-stucco hotel that was built late in the 19th century and has been modernized into a clean, well-maintained, if not particularly exciting design. The price is hard to beat, especially because of its great location, a 15-minute walk west of the château. Even the cheapest rooms have showers and sinks (no toilets), and those at 340F ($61.20) represent the best value, since they have toilets, sinks, and showers. (If you upgrade to the 380F ($68.40) rate, all you'll get in terms of improvement is a bathtub instead of a shower stall.) The staff is helpful.

Novotel Versailles Le Chesnay. 4 bd. St-Antoine, 78150 Le Chesnay. ☎ **01-39-54-96-96.** Fax 01-39-54-94-40. 105 units. A/C MINIBAR TV TEL. 580F ($104.40) double. Children 15 and under stay free in parents' room. AE, DC, MC, V. Parking 50F ($9).

A 15-minute walk north from one of the side wings of the château, this hotel, built in 1988 as part of a nationwide chain, has a modern facade with columns and large windows. It's a good price and a convenient choice. The rooms are practical and all are identical; four are equipped for persons with disabilities. There's also a restaurant and a bar, but the food, though plentiful, is mediocre.

Relais Mercure Versailles Château. 19 rue Philippe-de-Dangeau, 78000 Versailles. ☎ **800/221-4542** for reservations in the U.S. and Canada, or 01-39-50-44-10. Fax 01-39-50-65-11. 60 units. TV TEL. 385–395F ($69.30–$71.10) double. AE, DC, MC, V. Parking 40F ($7.20).

In 1994 the interior of an 18th-century Mansard-style building a 10-minute walk from the château was completely gutted, leaving only the awesomely thick walls. Inserted in its place was the town's newest middle-bracket hotel. The result is a stately stone-and-slate exterior and an interior providing all the modern comforts of one of France's most successful chain hotels. The service is brisk and efficient, very much what you'd expect. Breakfast is the only meal served.

WHERE TO DINE
VERY EXPENSIVE

✪ **Les Trois Marchés.** In the Hôtel Trianon Palace, 1 bd. de la Reine. ☎ **01-30-84-38-40.** Reservations required. Main courses 220–350F ($39.60–$63); fixed-price menus 500–700F ($90–$126); menu affaires (lunch Tues–Fri) 300F ($54). AE, DC, MC, V. Daily noon–2pm and 7:30–10pm. Closed Aug. CUISINE BOURGEOISE.

The food here is of the highest order—and so are the prices. Chef Gérard Vié, known for the inventiveness of his cuisine bourgeoise, serves the finest food in Versailles. His soaring greenhouse-inspired dining room is remarkable for its generous expanses of glass and its intimate size (only 55 seats). In summer the front terrace is adorned with a canopy and extra tables, as well as formal flower and vegetable beds. Begin with the delectable lobster salad flavored with fresh herbs and served with an onion soufflé, the foie gras of duckling, or the delightful citrus-flavored scallop bisque. You'll endorse the claim that the chef is a great innovator when you taste his main courses, especially his pigeon roasted and flavored with rosé and accompanied with celeriac and truffles and his filet of sea bass with a "cake" of eggplant. The best dessert? Opt for the signature assortment. Note that some people have found the staff a bit too stiff and patronizing.

MODERATE

La Flottille. In the Parc du Château. ☎ **01-39-51-41-58.** Reservations recommended. Restaurant, main courses 98–110F ($17.65–$19.80); fixed-price menu 132F ($23.75). Brasserie, snacks 50F ($9). AE, MC, V. Restaurant daily noon–3:30pm; brasserie daily 8:30am–7pm for coffee, ice cream, and snacks. FRENCH.

This place was built around 1896 as a bar for the laborers who maintained the gardens surrounding the château. Today, as the only restaurant inside the park, it occupies an enviable position at the head of the Grand Canal, with a sweeping view over some of Europe's most famous landscaping. Tables for lunch are placed outside in warm weather, and there's also a charming pavilion-inspired dining room. A brasserie/snack bar serves sandwiches, omelets, crêpes, salads, and ice cream. At lunch most people prefer the dining room, where unpretentious menu specialties are *assiette La Flottille* (several kinds of raw marinated fish with olive oil and anise), filet of beef in sauce *périgourdine* (with truffles), and medallion of *lotte* (anglerfish) cooked in cider.

Le Potager du Roy. 1 rue du Maréchal-Joffre. ☎ **01-39-50-35-34.** Reservations required. Main courses 80–190F ($14.40–$34.20); fixed-price menus 130F ($23.40) at lunch, 130–175F ($23.40–$31.50) at dinner. AE, MC, V. Tues–Sat noon–2:30pm and 7:30–10:30pm. FRENCH.

Philippe Letourneur has emerged as a formidably talented chef after spending years perfecting a distinctive cuisine and now adding novelty to the oft-jaded dining scene in Versailles. Latourner rotates, or reinvents his skillfully prepared menu, with the seasons. Examples are foie gras with a vegetable-flavored vinaigrette, ragoût of macaroni with a persillade of snails, roasted codfish with creamed spinach and croutons, and supreme of turbot braised with fresh endives and herbs. Looking for something unusual and more earthy? Try the fondant of pork jowls with a confit of fresh vegetables.

✪ **Le Quai No. 1.** 1 av. de St-Cloud. ☎ **01-39-50-42-26.** Reservations required. Main courses 70–180F ($12.60–$32.40); fixed-price menus (without wine) 120–168F ($21.60–$30.25). MC, V. Tues–Sun noon–2:30pm, Tues–Sat 7:30–11pm. SEAFOOD/ FRENCH.

Megachef Gérard Vié, along with his on-site manager and owner Dominique de Ravel, serves an elegant cuisine at this mostly seafood restaurant, a longtime favorite overlooking the château's western facade. The dining room is decorated with lithographs and wood paneling; there's also a summer terrace. Though the cuisine isn't opulent, it's charming, very French, and reasonable in price and dependable in presentation. The fixed-price menus make Le Quai a dining bargain in high-priced Versailles. Specialties are seafood sauerkraut, seafood paella, bouillabaisse, and home-smoked salmon. The chef recommends the *plateau de fruits de mer,* a plate of the "fruits of the sea." Carnivores appreciate the three meat-based main courses, the best of which are magrêt of duckling dressed with aged vinegar and navarin of lamb. Care and imagination go into the cuisine, and the service is professional and polite.

Le Rescatore. 27 av. de St-Cloud (2nd floor). ☎ **01-39-25-06-34.** Reservations recommended. Main courses 110–180F ($19.80–$32.40); fixed-price menu 180F ($32.40). AE, MC, V. Mon–Fri 12:30–2pm, Mon–Sat 7:30–10pm. Closed Aug. SEAFOOD.

The decor includes exposed ceiling beams, high ceilings, Louis XIV furnishings, and tall French doors overlooking a busy avenue. Chef Frank Ruaz's specialties merge the Creole cuisine of New Orleans with French seafood. Many dishes are available throughout the year, including cannelloni of scallops with morels and fresh spinach and ravioli stuffed with lobster. Others—such as the bass roasted with sage or the half-cooked lobster prepared with cognac, a fricassée of mushrooms, and shallots—change with the seasons and whatever is available.

2 The Forest of Rambouillet

34 miles SW of Paris, 26 miles NE of Chartres

Georges Pompidou used to visit the château here, as did Louis XVI and Charles de Gaulle. Dating from 1375, it's surrounded by a park in one of the most famous forests in France, with more than 47,000 acres of greenery stretching from the valley of the Eure to the high valley of Chevreuse, the latter rich in medieval and royal abbeys. The lakes, deer, and even wild boar are some of the attractions of this beautiful area.

ESSENTIALS

GETTING THERE   **Trains** depart from Paris's Gare Montparnasse every 20 minutes throughout the day. One-way passage costs 41F to 61F ($7.40 to $11) for a ride of about 35 minutes. For train information and schedules, contact **La Gare de Rambouillet,** place Prud'homme (☎ **01-53-90-20-20**).

VISITOR INFORMATION   The **Office de Tourisme** is at the Hôtel de Ville, place de la Libération (☎ **01-34-83-21-21**).

SEEING THE CHATEAU

Château de Rambouillet, Parc du Château. ☎ **01-34-83-00-25.** Admission 32F ($5.75) adults, 21F ($3.80) students 12–25, free for children 11 and under. Apr–Sept Wed–Mon 10–11:30am and 2–5:30pm; Oct–Mar Wed–Mon 10am–11:30am and 2–4:30pm.

This is one of the royal châteaux of France, though it offers no serious competition to Fontainebleau or Versailles. François I, the Chevalier King, died of a fever at Rambouillet in 1547 at the age of 52. When the château was later occupied by the comte de Toulouse, Rambouillet was often visited by Louis XV, who was amused (in more ways than one) by the comte's witty and high-spirited wife. Louis XVI acquired the château, but his wife, Marie Antoinette, was bored with the place and called it "the toad." In his surprisingly modest boudoir are four panels representing the continents.

Napoléon's second wife, Marie-Louise, came here in 1814, after leaving him. She was on her way to Vienna with the exiled king of Rome, her son, Napoléon II. A sad Napoléon slept here shortly before leaving on the long voyage into exile at St. Helena.

In 1830 Charles X, Louis XVI's brother, abdicated after the July Revolution. Following that, Rambouillet became privately owned. At one time it was a fashionable restaurant, attracting Parisians, who could also go for rides in gondolas. Napoléon III, however, returned it to the Crown. In 1897 it was designated as a residence for the presidents of the Republic. Superb woodwork is used throughout, and the walls are adorned with tapestries, many dating from the era of Louis XV.

Today it's used as a vacation retreat by the president. When the president is not in residence, the rooms of the château can be visited on a self-guided tour. And although there are no guided tours of the 30,000-acre Rambouillet forest, you can pick up a map at the tourist office and go hiking, biking, or driving through it.

WHERE TO STAY

Climat de France. Lieu-Dit la Louvière, rue de la Louvière, 78120 Rambouillet. ☎ **01-34-85-62-62.** Fax 01-30-59-23-57. 67 units. TV TEL. 280–305F ($50.40–$54.90) double. AE, DC, MC, V. Exit from N10 at the Dampierre Chevreuse exit.

Built in 1988 and rated two stars, this stone-fronted building sits in the famous forest about half a mile north of the town center. Offering comfortable if not distinguished rooms, this is an affordable chain hotel that appeals to business travelers. It has a heated outdoor pool and a restaurant serving fixed-price menus, including ones for children.

WHERE TO DINE

La Poste. 101 av. du Général-de-Gaulle. ☎ **01-34-83-03-01.** Reservations recommended Sat–Sun. Main courses 70–120F ($12.60–$21.60); fixed-price menus 74F ($13.30) at lunch (Tues–Fri only), 103–190F ($18.55–$34.20) at lunch or dinner. AE, MC, V. Tues–Sun noon–2pm, Tues–Sat 7–10pm. FRENCH.

On a street corner in the town's historic center, across from the Sous-Préfecture de Police, this restaurant has been serving food since the mid–19th century, when it was a coaching inn. The two dining rooms have rustic beams and old-fashioned accents that complement the flavorful but old-fashioned food, such as homemade terrines of foie gras and freshly made pastries. Main courses of note are fricassée of chicken with crayfish and noisettes of lamb prepared "in the style of roebuck" with copious amounts of red wine and herbs. A particularly flavorful dish is filet of beef with a Périgueux sauce of madeira and foie gras.

3 The Glorious Cathedral of Chartres

60 miles SW of Paris, 47 miles NW of Orléans

Many observers feel that medieval architecture reached its pinnacle in the world-renowned cathedral at Chartres. Come to see its architecture, its sculpture, and—most of all—its stained glass, which gave the world a new color, Chartres blue.

The ancient town of Chartres also played a role in more modern history, particularly World War II. There's even a monument to Jean Moulin, the great Resistance hero and friend of de Gaulle. Under torture, he refused to sign a document stating that French troops committed atrocities. The Gestapo killed him in 1943 (today he's buried in the Panthéon in Paris). From the cathedral, head down rue du Cheval-Blanc until it becomes rue Jean-Moulin (the monument is up ahead on your right). Other street names also commemorate the World War II Resistance, including boulevard de le Résistance.

ESSENTIALS

From Paris's Gare Montparnasse, **trains** run directly to Chartres, taking less than an hour. If you're **driving,** take A10/A11 southwest from the périphérique and follow the signs to Le Mans and Chartres (the Chartres exit is clearly marked).

The **Office de Tourisme** is on place de la Cathédrale (☎ **02-37-21-50-00**).

SEEING THE CATHEDRAL & EXPLORING THE TOWN

THE TOWN   If time remains after you see the cathedral, you may want to explore the medieval cobblestone streets of the *Vieux Quartiers* (Old Town). Next door to the cathedral is the **Musée des Beaux-Arts de Chartres,** 29 Cloître Notre-Dame (☎ **02-37-36-41-39**), open Wednesday through Monday from 10am to noon and 2 to 5pm Oct 31 to May 2; 10am to noon and 2 to 6pm the rest of the year. Admission is 10F ($1.80) for adults and 5F (90¢) for children. Installed in a former episcopal palace, the building at times competes with its exhibitions. One part dates from the 15th century and encompasses a courtyard. The permanent collection of paintings covers mainly the 16th to the 20th century, offering the works of old masters like Zurbarán, Watteau, and Brosamer. Of particular interest is David Ténier's *Le Concert.*

At the foot of the cathedral, the lanes contain gabled houses. Humped bridges span the Eure River. From the Bouju Bridge, you can see the lofty spires in the background. Try to find **rue Chantault,** which boasts houses with colorful facades; one is eight centuries old.

Shopping in Town   Your best shopping bet in Chartres is **place des Epars.** This pedestrian area is home to most of the apparel shops, even some haute couture boutiques. Along rue Noël-Balay is a small **mall** with about 15 shops you might find interesting, especially if it's raining. Many of the shops selling regional items are along the narrow streets that fan southeast from the cathedral.

A Free Concert

If you visit Chartres on a Sunday afternoon, note that the church features free hour-long organ concerts every Sunday beginning at 4:45pm, when the filtered light makes the cathedral's western windows come thrillingly alive.

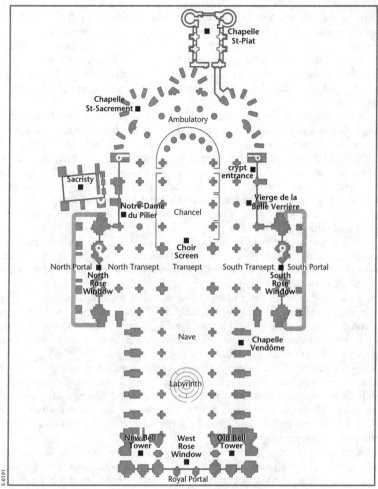

At **Galerie du Virtrail,** 17 Cloître Notre-Dame (☎ **02-37-36-10-03**), you'll find a huge selection of stained glass for sale—all illuminated in its radiant glory by natural light or light boxes. These works of art come in every size and style. **Lassaussois Antiquités,** 17 rue des Changes (☎ **02-37-21-37-74**), specializes in antique objets d'art and contemporary furnishings. If antique lace is your passion, stop by **Ariane,** 39 rue des Changes (☎ **02-37-21-20-68**), which also sells handmade sweaters, elegant linens, and children's clothing.

✪ **Cathédrale Notre-Dame de Chartres.** 16 Cloître Notre-Dame. ☎ **02-37-21-56-33.** Free admission to cathedral (see below for tour, crypt, and tower charges). Easter–Oct daily 7:30am–7:30pm (closes at 7pm the rest of the year).

Reportedly, Rodin once sat for hours on the edge of the sidewalk, admiring this cathedral's Romanesque sculpture. His opinion: Chartres is the French Acropolis. When it began to rain, a kind soul offered him an umbrella—which he declined, so transfixed was he by the magic of this place.

The cathedral's origins are uncertain; some have suggested that it grew up over an ancient Druid site that had later become a Roman temple. It is known that as early as the 4th century there was a Christian basilica here. A fire in 1194 destroyed most of what had then become a Romanesque cathedral, but it spared the western facade and crypt. The cathedral you see today dates principally from the 13th century, when it was rebuilt with the combined efforts and contributions of kings, princes, churchmen, and pilgrims from all over Europe. One of the world's greatest High Gothic cathedrals, it was the first to use flying buttresses.

French sculpture in the 12th century broke into full bloom when the Royal Portal was added. A landmark in Romanesque art, the sculptured bodies are elongated, often formalized beyond reality, in their long, flowing robes. But the faces are amazingly (for the time) lifelike, occasionally betraying Mona Lisa smiles. In the central tympanum, Christ is shown at the Second Coming, with his descent depicted on the right, his ascent on the left. Before entering, stop to admire the Royal Portal and then walk around to both the North Portal and the South Portal, each dating from the 13th century. They depict such biblical scenes as the expulsion of Adam and Eve from the Garden of Eden.

Inside is a celebrated choir screen (parclose screen); work on it began in the 16th century and lasted until 1714. The niches, 40 in all, contain statues illustrating scenes from the life of the Madonna and Christ—everything from the massacre of the innocents to the coronation of the Virgin.

But few rushed visitors ever notice the screen: They're too transfixed by the light from the stained glass. Covering an expanse of more than 3,000 square yards, the glass is without peer in the world and is truly mystical. It was spared in both world wars because of a decision to remove it painstakingly piece by piece. Most of the stained glass dates from the 12th and 13th centuries.

See the windows in the morning, at noon, in the afternoon, at sunset—whenever and as often as you can. They constantly change like the images of a kaleidoscope. It's difficult to single out one panel or window of special merit; however, an exceptional one is the 12th-century *Vierge de la Belle Verrière* (Virgin of the Beautiful Window) on the south side. Of course, there are three fiery rose windows, but you couldn't miss those even if you tried.

The nave—the widest in France—still contains its ancient labyrinth. The wooden *Notre-Dame du Pilier* (Our Lady of the Pillar), to the left of the choir, dates from the 14th century. The crypt was built over two centuries, beginning in the 9th. Enshrined within is *Notre-Dame de Sous Terre* (Our Lady of the Crypt), a 1976 Madonna that replaced one destroyed during the Revolution.

Try to get a tour conducted by **Malcolm Miller,** an Englishman who has spent three decades studying the cathedral and giving tours in English. His rare blend of scholarship, enthusiasm, and humor will help you understand and appreciate the cathedral. He usually conducts 75-minute tours at noon and 2:45pm Monday through Saturday for a fee of 30F ($5.40) per person. Tours are cancelled in the event of pilgrimages, religious celebrations, and large-scale funerals. French-language tours at 28F ($5.05) are conducted at 10:30am and 3pm from Easter to October and at 2pm the rest of the year.

If you're fit enough, don't miss the opportunity, especially in summer, to climb to the top of the tower. Open the same hours as the cathedral, except for a lunch closing between noon and 2pm, it costs 28F ($5.05) for adults and 15F ($2.70) for students. You can visit the crypt, gloomy and somber but rich with medieval history, only as part of a French-language tour conducted whenever there's enough demand. The cost is 11F ($2) per person.

After your visit, stroll through the episcopal gardens and enjoy yet another view of this remarkable cathedral.

To Taste a Madeleine

And suddenly the memory returns. The taste was that of the little crumb of madeleine which on Sunday mornings at Combray (because on those mornings I did not go out before church-time), when I went to say good day to her in her bedroom, my aunt Léonie used to give me, dipping it first in her own cup of real or of lime-flower tea.

—Marcel Proust, *Remembrance of Things Past*

Illiers-Combray, a small town 54 miles southwest of Paris and 15 miles southwest of Chartres, was once known simply as Illiers. Then Proust groupies started to come and signs were posted: ILLIERS, ILLIERS, LE COMBRAY DE MARCEL PROUST. Illiers was and is a real town, but Marcel Proust in his imagination made it world famous as Combray in his masterpiece, *A la recherche du temps perdu* (*Remembrance of Things Past*). So today the town is known as Illiers-Combray.

It was the taste of a luscious little madeleine that launched Proust on his immortal recollection. To this day hundreds of his readers from all over the world flock to the pastry shops in Illiers-Combray to eat a madeleine or two dipped in lime-flower tea. Following the Proustian labyrinth, you can explore the gardens, streets, and houses he wrote about so richly and had frequently visited until he was 13. The town is epitomized by its **Eglise St-Jacques,** where Proust as a boy placed hawthorn on the altar.

Some members of Proust's family have lived in Illiers for centuries. His grandfather, François, was born here on rue du Cheval-Blanc. At 11 place du Marché, just opposite the church, he ran a small candle shop. His daughter, Elisabeth, married Jules Amiot, who ran a shop a few doors away. Down from Paris, young Marcel would visit his aunt at 4 rue du St-Esprit, which has been renamed rue du Docteur-Proust, honoring Marcel's grandfather.

The **Maison de Tante Léonie,** 4 rue du Docteur-Proust (☎ **02-37-24-30-97**), is a museum, charging 30F ($5.40) for admission. In the novel this was Aunt Léonie's home; filled with antimacassars, it's typical of the solid bourgeois comfort of its day. Upstairs you can visit the bedroom where the young Marcel slept; today it contains souvenirs of key episodes in the novel. You can visit the house Tuesday through Sunday for tours conducted at 2:30 and 4pm.

In the center of town, a sign will guide you to further Proustian sights.

WHERE TO STAY

Grand Monarque Best Western. 22 place des Epars, 28005 Chartres. ☎ **800/528-1234** in the U.S., or 02-37-21-00-72. Fax 02-37-36-34-18. 44 units. MINIBAR TV TEL. 585–700F ($105.30–$126) double; 1,160F ($208.80) suite. Rates include continental breakfast. AE, DC, MC, V. Parking 45F ($8.10).

The leading hotel of Chartres is housed in a classical building enclosing a courtyard. Functioning as an inn almost since its original construction, and greatly expanded over the centuries, it still attracts guests who enjoy its old-world charm—such as Art Nouveau stained glass and Louis XV chairs in the dining room. The guest rooms are decorated with reproductions of antiques; most have sitting areas. The hotel also has an old-fashioned, unremarkable restaurant.

Hôtel Châtelet. 6–8 av. Jehan-de-Beauce, 28000 Chartres. ☎ **02-37-21-78-00.** Fax 02-37-36-23-01. 48 units. TV TEL. 420–480 F ($75.60–$86.40) double. Extra person 60F ($10.80). AE, DC, MC, V.

Though this 1982 hotel is part of a chain, it has many traditional touches, and the rooms are inviting, with reproductions of Louis XV and Louis XVI furniture. Most accommodations face a garden and many windows open out to a panoramic cathedral view. In chilly weather, guests gather around the log fire. Breakfast is the only meal served, but there are numerous restaurants nearby.

Hôtel de la Poste. 3 rue du Général-Koenig, 28003 Chartres. ☎ **02-37-21-04-27.** Fax 02-37-36-42-17. 58 units. TV TEL. 300–320F ($54–$57.60) double. AE, DC, MC, V. Parking 39F ($7).

A Logis de France, this modest hotel offers one of the best values in Chartres—even though it's short on charm. It's in the center of town, across from the main post office. The rooms are soundproofed and comfortably furnished and have wall-to-wall carpeting. The surprise here is the good food served at affordable prices, everything backed up by one of the town's finest wine cellars. The curse of the hotel is bookings by group tours.

WHERE TO DINE

Note that the restaurant at the **Hôtel de la Poste** (see above) serves good, reasonably priced food.

Le Buisson Ardent. 10 rue au Lait. ☎ **01-02-37-34-04-66.** Reservations recommended. Main courses 98–122F ($17.65–$21.95); fixed-price menus 128–228F ($23.05–$41.05). MC, V. Daily 12:30–2pm, Mon–Sat 7:30–9:30pm. FRENCH.

In a charming 300-year-old house in the most historic section of town, this restaurant is one floor above street level in the shadow of the cathedral. From its location you might expect it to be a tourist trap, but it isn't, and it steadfastly refuses to follow many of the fads that sweep through restaurants in nearby Paris. The fixed-price menus change every 3 weeks and, like the à la carte dishes, are based on strictly fresh meats, produce, and fish. Best-sellers are escalope of warm foie gras with apples and Calvados and *émincée* of roasted pigeon with lemon juice and a galette of potatoes and fresh vegetables. A dessert specialty is crispy hot apples with sorbet and Calvados-flavored butter sauce.

CHARTRES AFTER DARK

For a formal evening of theater or modern dance, try the **Théâtre Municipal,** 1 place Ravenne (☎ **02-37-18-27-27**), which offers presentations from September to May. From time to time you can catch a jazz or rock concert here as well. **Forum de la Madeleine,** 1 Mail Jean-de-Dunois (☎ **02-37-35-08-83**), presents lighter fare and usually has a busier performance season.

For a relaxing drink, try **La Bodega,** 20 place des Halles (☎ **02-37-36-05-05**). It has one of the best selections of beer in town, with a Cuban/salsa atmosphere and live entertainment on weekends. For dancing the night away, go to **Le Privilège,** 1 place St-Pierre (☎ **02-37-35-52-02**), where you'll find a wide range of dance music from zouk to funk and even disco. For ballroom dancing, the place is the elegant **Le Venitien,** 43 rue Gabriel-Péri (☎ **02-37-21-13-35**), with a polished parquet dance floor big enough for 150 party-goers. Here you can enjoy anything from a waltz to a tango, even a little disco every now and then. A restaurant in the back hosts dinner dances on Saturday.

4 Barbizon: The School of Rousseau

35 miles SE of Paris, 6 miles NW of Fontainebleau

In the 19th century the Barbizon school of painting gained world renown. On the edge of the Forest of Fontainebleau, the village was a refuge for artists like Rousseau,

Millet, and Corot, many of whom couldn't find acceptance in the more conservative Paris salons. In Barbizon they turned to nature for inspiration and painted more realistic pastoral scenes, without nude nymphs and dancing fauns. These artists attracted a school of lesser painters, including Daubigny and Diaz. Charles Jacques, Decamps, Paul Huet, Troyon, and many others followed. Today Barbizon attracts fashionable Parisians—often off the record—for le week-end. Some complain about its outrageous prices, but others just enjoy Barbizon's sunshine and clean air. Even with hordes of art galleries and souvenir shops, the town still retains much of its traditional atmosphere.

ESSENTIALS
You can take the **train** from Paris to Fontainebleau (below), then continue on to Barbizon via a connecting bus. Buses, however, don't run in summer. For information and schedules, call ☎ **01-64-23-71-11.**

The **Office de Tourisme** is at 55 Grande-Rue (☎ **01-60-66-41-87**).

BARBIZON MUSEUMS
Musée Ganne. 92 Grande-Rue. ☎ **01-60-66-22-27.** Admission 25F ($4,50). Apr–Sept Wed–Mon 10am–12:30pm and 2–6pm; to 5:30pm Oct–Mar Wed–Mon 10am–12:30pm and 2–5:30pm.

The inn that housed most of the Barbizon artists during their late 19th-century sojourns here was L'Auberge du Père-Gannes. In the mid-1990s through collaboration with Paris's Musée d'Orsay, it was transformed into the Musée Ganne, a showcase for Rousseau, the founder of the Barbizon school, who began painting landscapes directly from nature (novel at the time) and settled in Barbizon in the 1840s.

Maison et Atelier de Jean-François Millet. 27 Grande-Rue. ☎ **01-60-66-21-55.** Free admission. Wed–Mon 10am–12:30pm and 2–5:30pm.

This museum stands adjacent to the Hostellerie Les Pléiades recommended below. Its premises are devoted to the best-known Barbizon painter, who settled here in 1849. Millet painted religious, classical, and especially peasant subjects. See his etching of *The Man with the Hoe,* as well as some of his original furnishings.

WHERE TO STAY
✪ **Hostellerie du Bas-Bréau.** 22 Grande-Rue, 77630 Barbizon. ☎ **01-60-66-40-05.** Fax 01-60-69-22-89. www.integra.ft/relaischateaux/basbreau. E-mail: basbreau@relaischateaux.fr. 20 units. TV TEL. 900–1,500F ($162–$270) double; 1,700–2,800F ($306–$504) suite. AE, DC, V.

Dwarfing all the local competition, this member of Relais & Châteaux is one of France's great old inns, set amid shade trees and courtyards. In the 1830s many famous artists and writers stayed here, notably Robert Louis Stevenson, who scattered anecdotes of the inn throughout his novels. When Napoléon III and his empress, Eugénie, came here for a day in 1868 to purchase some paintings from the Barbizon school, the inn became known as Hôtel de l'Exposition. It's furnished in lustrous provincial antiques and fantastic reproductions. In the colder months, guests gather around the brick fireplace in the living room. The guest rooms are furnished in part with antiques. The rear building's rooms open directly onto semiprivate terraces.

Dining: Whether in an old-world dining room or the courtyard, you can enjoy specialties like filet of the choicest and tenderest cuts of beef, followed by cold raspberry soufflé. In summer you can order good-tasting fish dishes flavored with herbs from the hotel's own garden. During the brisk autumn you'll find wild game on the menu, none finer than the specialty of the house: pâté chaud de grouse (a gamey Scottish grouse pâté wrapped in puff pastry and coated with a clear brown sauce).

Hostellerie La Clé d'Or. 73 Grande-Rue, 77360 Barbizon. ☎ **01-60-66-40-96.** Fax 01-60-66-42-71. 17 units. MINIBAR TV TEL. 400–500F ($72–$90) double; 700–850F ($126–$153) suite. AE, DC, MC, V.

Encircled by a stone wall, the grounds of this 100-year-old hotel include a large garden and an intimate stone terrace full of plants that flower in a wash of pinks and yellows during spring and summer. The terrace leads directly to many of the rooms, which are all modern but mainly quite small, with upholstered chairs and simple tables. Other rooms provide a bit more architectural flair and sport A-frame ceilings with exposed heavy wooden beams. Note that in some rooms a color-coordinated curtain of sorts has been used in lieu of a bathroom door. The hotel has a cozy English-style bar where you can relax with a drink before or after dinner, and a fixed-price menu is always available at the on-site French restaurant.

Hostellerie Les Pléiades. 21 Grande-Rue, 77630 Barbizon. ☎ **01-60-66-40-25.** Fax 01-60-66-41-68. 23 units. TV TEL. 320–550F ($57.60–$99) double. AE, DC, MC, V.

Les Pléiades combines antique decor with modern comforts in the former home of the landscape painter Charles Daubigny. It's the seat of a conference held 4 or 5 times a year, to which important politicians, artists, and writers are invited. The place is run and directed by the town's local historian, Roger S. Karampournis, and his wife, Yolande.

Dining: Before Karampournis bought the place 14 years ago, he was a dishwasher near the fish piers in Boston and later managed several PX operations for U.S. soldiers in Europe. Today he's one of the best-known chefs in Barbizon, preparing French food with flair and style. Examples are galette of pigeon with foie gras, house-style lobster in puff pastry, and carpaccio of smoked duckling.

WHERE TO DINE

We also recommend the restaurants at the **Hostellerie du Bas-Bréau** and **Hostellerie Les Pléiades** (see "Where to Stay," above).

Le Relais. 2 av. Charles-de-Gaulle. ☎ **01-60-66-40-28.** Reservations recommended on weekends. Main courses 86–110F ($15.50–$19.80); fixed-price menus 105–200F ($18.90–$36) Mon–Fri only, 150–200F ($27–$36) otherwise. MC, V. Thurs–Tues noon–2:15pm, Thurs–Mon 7:30–9:30pm. Closed 1 week at Christmas and the last week of Aug. FRENCH.

Many people prefer dining at this down-to-earth, comfortable restaurant than at the more pricey inns, such as the Bas-Bréau. Consistently offering excellent value, Le Relais is a corner tavern in a building boasting 300-year-old walls, with a provincial dining room centering around a small fireplace. In sunny weather, tables are set in the rear yard, with a trellis, an arbor, and trees. Typical menu choices are quenelle (a kind of dumpling) de brochet, roast quail with prunes, breast of duckling with cherries, and grilled beef.

5 Fontainebleau—Refuge of Kings

37 miles S of Paris, 46 miles NE of Orléans

Napoléon called the Palais de Fontainebleau the house of the centuries. Much of French history has taken place behind its walls, perhaps none more memorable than when Napoléon stood on the horseshoe-shaped exterior staircase and bade farewell to his army before his departure to exile on Elba. That scene has been the subject of countless paintings, including Vernet's *Les Adieux.*

Set in 50,000 acres of fabulous forest, Fontainebleau today remains a country retreat for Parisians, even for those who have seen the château a dozen times. Visitors

Fontainebleau

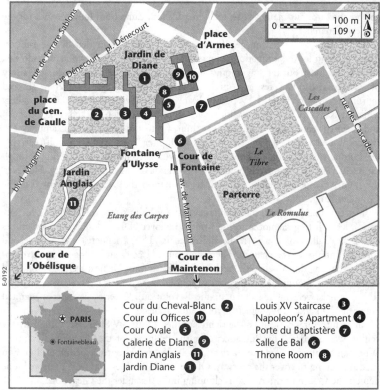

Cour du Cheval-Blanc ②		Louis XV Staircase ③	
Cour du Offices ⑩		Napoleon's Apartment ④	
Cour Ovale ⑤		Porte du Baptistère ⑦	
Galerie de Diane ⑨		Salle de Bal ⑥	
Jardin Anglais ⑪		Throne Room ⑧	
Jardin Diane ①			

come to enjoy the grounds for horseback riding, picnicking, and hiking. Not as crowded with tourists, it's more peaceful here than Versailles.

ESSENTIALS

Trains to Fontainebleau depart from Paris's Gare de Lyon, and the trip takes 35 to 60 minutes. The Fontainebleau station is just outside the town in Avon, a suburb of Paris; a local bus makes the 2-mile trip to the château every 10 to 15 minutes Monday through Saturday and every 30 minutes on Sunday.

By car, from the périphérique, take A6 south from Paris, exit onto N191, and follow the signs.

The **Office de Tourisme** is at 4 rue Royale in Fontainebleau (☎ **01-60-74-99-99**).

SEEING THE CHATEAU & GARDENS

✪ **Musée National du Château de Fontainebleau.** ☎ **01-60-71-50-70.** Combination ticket including the grands appartements, the Napoleonic Rooms, and the Chinese Museum 35F ($6.30) adults, 23F ($4.15) students 18–25. Ticket to petits appartements 16F ($2.90) adults, 12F ($2.15) students 18–25. Free for children 17 and under. July–Aug Wed–Mon 9:30am–6pm; Sept–June Wed–Mon 9:30am–12:30pm and 2–5pm.

Napoléon joined in the grand parade of French rulers who used the Palais de Fontainebleau as a resort, hunting in its magnificent forest. Under François I (reigned 1515–47) the hunting lodge here was enlarged into a royal palace (as at Versailles under Louis XIV), much in the Italian Renaissance style the king admired. The style got botched up, but many artists, including Cellini, came from Italy to work for the French monarch.

Under François I's patronage, the School of Fontainebleau (led by the painters Rosso Fiorentino and Primaticcio) increased in prestige. These two artists adorned one of the most outstanding rooms at Fontainebleau: the 210-foot-long **Gallery of François I.** (The restorers under Louis-Philippe didn't completely succeed in ruining it.) Surrounded by pomp, François I walked the length of his gallery while artisans tried to tempt him with their wares, job seekers asked favors, and scented courtesans tried to lure him from the duchesse d'Etampes. The stucco-framed panels depict such scenes as Jupiter (portrayed as a bull) carrying off Europa, the Nymph of Fontaine-bleau (with a lecherous dog peering through the reeds), and the monarch holding a pomegranate, a symbol of unity. However, the frames compete with the pictures. Everywhere is the salamander, symbol of the Chevalier King.

If it's true that François I built Fontainebleau for his mistress, then Henri II, his successor, left a fitting memorial to the woman he loved, Diane de Poitiers. Sometimes called the Gallery of Henri II, the **Ballroom** is in the Mannerist style, the second splendid interior of the château. The monograms H & D are interlaced in the decoration (the king didn't believe in keeping his affection for Diane a secret). At one end of the room is a monumental fireplace supported by two bronze satyrs, made in 1966 (the originals were melted down in the Revolution). A series of frescoes, painted between 1550 and 1558, depicts mythological subjects.

An architectural curiosity is the richly adorned **Louis XV Staircase.** Originally the ceiling was decorated by Primaticcio for the bedroom of the duchesse d'Etampes. When an architect added the stairway, he simply ripped out her bedroom floor and used the ceiling to cover the stairway. Of the Italian frescoes that were preserved, one depicts the Queen of the Amazons climbing into Alexander the Great's bed.

Fontainebleau found renewed glory under Napoléon. You can wander around much of the palace on your own, visiting sites that evoke his 19th-century imperial heyday. They include the **throne room,** the room where he abdicated his rulership of France (the abdication document displayed is a copy), his offices, his monumental bedroom (look for his symbol, a bee), and his bathroom. Some of the smaller rooms, especially those containing his personal mementos and artifacts, are accessible by guided tour only. The furnishings in the grand apartments of Napoléon and Joséphine are marvelous.

Musée Chinois or Chinese Museum holds the Empress Eugénie's private collection of stunning Chinese treasures, including Far Eastern porcelain, jade, and crystal.

After your long trek through the palace, visit the gardens and, especially, the carp pond; the gardens, however, are only a prelude to the Forest of Fontainebleau and not nearly as spectacular as those surrounding Versailles.

WHERE TO STAY

✪ **Hôtel de l'Aigle-Noir (The Black Eagle).** 27 place Napoléon-Bonaparte, 77300 Fontainebleau. ☎ **01-60-74-60-00.** Fax 01-60-74-60-01. 56 units. A/C MINIBAR TV TEL. Mon–Thurs 1,050F ($189) double; from 1,200F ($216) suite. Fri–Sun 790F ($142.20) double; from 1,050F ($189) suite. AE, DC, MC, V. Parking 55F ($9.90).

Once the home of Cardinal de Retz, this mansion opposite the château was built with a formal courtyard entrance, using a high iron grille and pillars crowned by black eagles. It was converted into a hotel in 1720 and has recently been remodeled, making it the finest lodgings in Fontainebleau, far superior in amenities and style to the Napoléon. The rooms are decorated with Louis XVI, Empire, or Restoration-era antiques or reproductions. Have a drink in the Napoléon III–style piano bar before dinner; Le Beauharnais restaurant serves wonderful food (see below). Facilities include indoor pool, gymnasium, sauna, and underground garage.

Hôtel de Londres. 1 place du Général-de-Gaulle, 77300 Fontainebleau. ☎ **01-64-22-20-21.** Fax 01-60-72-39-16. 12 units. TV TEL. 550–650F ($99–$117) double. AE, DC, MC, V. Parking 25F ($4.50).

Attractive and modestly priced, this hotel is conveniently across from the palace. It dates from the Second Empire but has been substantially modernized over the years. In the mid-1990s half the hotel was restored. Ask for one of the beautifully decorated renovated rooms, as they tend to be larger, with new bathrooms and soundproofed windows. Much of the old furniture from 1830 remains, however. A reader from Pasadena wrote: "Ten being perfect, we would rate Londres a 20. Where else can one sit in one's room, day or night, and gaze endlessly at the Farewell Court or the Horseshoe Staircase that welcomed Thomas Jefferson and others?"

Hôtel Napoléon. 9 rue Grande, 77300 Fontainebleau. ☎ **01-60-39-50-50.** Fax 01-64-22-20-87. www.concorde-hotels.com. 57 units. MINIBAR TV TEL. 590–800F ($106.20–$144) double; 990F ($178.20) suite. AE, DC, MC, V. Parking 50F ($9).

This classically designed hotel—the number-two choice in Fontainebleau—is a short walk from the château. The lobby has Oriental rugs, big arched windows overlooking the street, and a garden tearoom. An inviting bar off the reception area has an ornate oval ceiling, Louis-Philippe chairs, and a neoclassical fireplace. The rooms are filled with reproductions of antiques and eye-catching flowered headboards. All are comfortable, but those facing the courtyard are larger and more tranquil.

Dining: Since the Napoléon is so close to the château, many visitors dine in its first-class restaurant, **La Table des Maréchaux**—the food is among the finest served in Fontainebleau.

✪ **Hôtel-Restaurant Legris et Parc.** 36 rue Paul-Séramy, 77300 Fontainebleau. ☎ **01-64-22-24-24.** Fax 01-64-22-22-05. 35 units. TV TEL. 390–570F ($70.20–$102.60) double; 600F ($108) suite. AE, CB, DC, MC, V.

This is our favorite hotel bargain, on a country lane just steps from the château. Part of the facade is Art Nouveau, unusual for Fontainebleau, and another wing is much older. The classical lobby contains elegant reproduction furniture, marble floors, a few antiques, and gold-and-blue fabric-covered walls. Some of the cozy rooms are freshly painted and papered, with a scattering of 17th-century timbers dating from the original construction. A restaurant is across the courtyard from the lobby. In summer, lunch and dinner are served in the garden.

WHERE TO DINE

La Table des Maréchaux in the Hôtel Napoléon (see above) is a superb choice.

Le Beauharnais. In the Hôtel de l'Aigle-Noir, 27 place Napoléon-Bonaparte. ☎ **01-60-74-60-00.** Reservations required. Main courses 140–280F ($25.20–$50.40); fixed-price menus 180–450F ($32.40–$81). AE, DC, MC, V. Daily noon–2pm and 7:30–9:30pm. Closed Dec 23–30. FRENCH.

This is the most beautiful restaurant in town, occupying a former courtyard; the refined interior boasts Empire-style furniture and potted palms. Try to avoid it if a conference is in town, as its usually fine atmosphere often becomes raucous and service falls off considerably. Some dishes have been truly memorable, namely the salmon mariné with cucumbers and caviar-filled blinis. Other specialties are foie gras of duckling in an aspic of yellow wine, served with exotic lettuce; blanquette of crayfish with asparagus; and a rack of lamb in the style of "Matignon" with celery and truffles. The desserts are sumptuous.

Le Caveau des Ducs. 24 rue de Ferrare. ☎ **01-64-22-05-05.** Reservations recommended. Main courses 90–125F ($16.20–$22.50); fixed-price menus 125–240F ($22.50–$43.20). AE, MC, V. Daily noon–2pm and 7–10pm. FRENCH.

Deep underground, beneath a series of 17th-century stone vaults built by the same masons who laid the cobblestones of rue de Ferrare upstairs, this reasonably priced restaurant occupies what once was a storage cellar for the nearby château. The decor is traditional, with lots of wood and flickering candles, and the staff helpful. The restaurant isn't in the same league as Le Beauharnais: It offers much simpler food, though the setting is more dramatic. Menu items include staples like snails in garlic butter, roast leg of lamb with garlic-and-rosemary sauce, and virtually everything that can be concocted from the body of a duck (terrines, magrêt, and confits). The filet of rumpsteak is quite tasty, especially when served with brie sauce, as are the platters of sole, crayfish tails, and salmon on a bed of pasta.

Le François-1er. 3 rue Royale. ☎ **01-64-22-24-68.** Reservations required. Main courses 85–110F ($15.30–$19.80); fixed-price menus 120–150F ($21.60–$27). AE, DC, MC, V. Mon–Sat 12:30–2pm and 7:30–9:30pm, Sun 12:30–2pm. FRENCH.

The premier dining choice for Fontainebleau has Louis XIII decor and walls that the owners think are about 200 years old. If weather permits, sit on the terrace overlooking the château and the cour des Adieux. In game season, the menu includes hare, roebuck, duck liver, and partridge. Other choices may be cold salmon with *cèpes* (flap mushrooms), *rognon de veau* (veal kidneys) with mustard sauce, and a salad of baby scallops with crayfish. The cuisine is meticulous, with an undeniable flair. The *magrêt de canard* (duck) flavored with cassis is delicious. The only reader who has written us with a complaint said he found it all too stuffy. Closed on Sunday night.

6 Vaux-le-Vicomte: Life Before Versailles

29 miles SE of Paris, 12 miles NE of Fontainebleau

Though it's so close to Paris, it's tough to reach Vaux-le-Vicomte without a car. Once you get here, allow 2 hours to see the château. **By car,** take N-6 southeast from Paris to Melun, which is 3¾ miles west of the château. **By train,** you'll need to take the 45-minute ride from Gare de Lyon to Melun first, then take one of the taxis lining up at the railway station for the jaunt to Vaux-le-Vicomte.

SEEING THE CHATEAU

✪ **Château de Vaux-le-Vicomte.** 77950 Maincy. ☎ **01-64-14-41-90.** Admission 56F ($10.10) adults, 46F ($8.30) children 6–15, free for children 5 and under. Apr–Oct daily 10am–6pm. Additionally, on a schedule that varies with the school holidays, most of Mar and Nov 1–11 daily 11am–5pm. Otherwise closed Nov–Mar.

The chateau was built in 1656 for Nicolas Fouquet, Louis XIV's ill-fated finance minister. Louis wasn't at all pleased that Fouquet was able to live so extravagantly here, hosting banquets that rivaled the king's. Then Louis discovered that Fouquet had embezzled funds from the country's treasury, and the king was not amused. Fouquet was swiftly arrested, then Louis hired the same artists and architects who had built Vaux-le-Vicomte to begin the grand task of creating Versailles. If you visit both you'll see the striking similarities between the two.

The view of the château from the main gate reveals the splendor of 17th-century France. On the south side, a majestic staircase sweeps toward the formal gardens, designed by Le Nôtre. The grand canal, flanked by waterfalls, divides the lush greenery. The château's interior, now a private residence, is completely furnished and decorated with 17th-century pieces. The great entrance hall leads to 12 state rooms, including the oval rotunda. Many of the rooms are hung with Gobelin tapestries and decorated with painted ceiling and wall panels by Le Brun, with sculpture by Girardon. A self-guided tour of the interior includes Fouquet's personal suite, the huge basement with its wine cellar, the servants' dining room, and the copper-filled kitchen.

A **Musée d'Equipages** (Carriage Museum) is housed in the stables. The carriages are of three types: country, town, and sports and hunting. Some 25 perfectly restored 18th- and 19th-century carriages are on exhibit, with mannequin horses and people. Hours are the same as that of the château itself, and entrance is included in the price of admission to the château.

From May to mid-October, **candlelight evenings** are held every Saturday from 8 to 11pm, when you can visit the château by the light of more than 1,000 candles. On those evenings, L'Ecureuil (below) and the Carriage Museum stay open to midnight. On the second and last Saturday of each month, the fountains of the 13 main pools bubble from 3 to 6pm.

WHERE TO DINE

Auberge de Crisenoy. Grande Rue, Crisenoy. ☎ **01-64-38-83-06.** Reservations recommended. Main courses 80–135F ($14.40–$24.30); fixed-price menus 162–220F ($29.15–$39.60). AE. Thurs–Tues noon–3pm and 7:30–9:30pm. From Vaux-le-Vicomte, follow N36 toward Meaux for 1½ miles. FRENCH.

Though it's near Vaux-le-Vicomte, this auberge does more business with locals from Melun than with tourists. Behind the solid stone walls of a former private home, the two dining rooms (on separate floors) overlook a garden. The menu items are based on modern interpretations of French classics, like oysters in puff pastry with asparagus coulis, warm foie gras with a purée of figs, and a well-seasoned cassolette of crayfish with spinach and mussels, served in a copper pot placed directly on the table.

7 Disneyland Paris

20 miles E of Paris

After provoking some of the most enthusiastic and controversial reactions in recent French history, the multimillion-dollar Euro Disney Resort opened in 1992 as one of the world's most lavish theme parks. Conceived on a scale rivaling that of Versailles, the project didn't begin auspiciously: European journalists delighted in belittling it and accused it of everything from cultural imperialism to the death knell of French culture. But after goodly amounts of public relations and financial juggling, the resort is now on track. As Disneyland (renamed from Euro Disney) faces the millennium, it has become France's number-one tourist attraction, with 50 million annual visitors. Disney surpasses the Eiffel Tower and the Louvre in the number of visitors and accounts for 4% of the French tourism industry's foreign currency sales. Figures reveal that 40% of the visitors are French, half of them from Paris. Disneyland Paris looks, tastes, and feels like its parents in California and Florida—except for the $10 cheeseburgers "*avec pommes frites.*"

Situated on a 5,000-acre site (about one-fifth the size of Paris) in the suburb of Marne-la-Vallée, with a European flair, the park incorporates the most successful elements of its Disney predecessors.

ESSENTIALS

GETTING THERE   By Train   The resort is linked to the RER commuter express rail network (Line A), which maintains a stop within walking distance of the theme park. Board the RER at such inner-city Paris stops as Charles-de-Gaulle–Etoile, Châtelet–Les Halles, or Nation. Get off at Line A's last stop, Marne-la-Vallée/Chessy, 45 minutes from central Paris. The fare is 38F ($6.85) one-way or 76F ($13.70) round-trip. Trains run daily, every 10 to 20 minutes from 5:30am to midnight.

Each hotel in the resort is connected by shuttle bus with Orly and Charles de Gaulle airports. Buses depart from both at intervals of 30 to 45 minutes, depending on the time of day and day of the year. One-way transport to the park from either airport costs 80F ($14.40) per person.

By Car   Take A4 east from Paris and get off at Exit 14, where it's marked PARC EURO DISNEYLAND. Guest parking at any of the thousands of spaces begins at 40F ($7.20) per day. A series of interconnected moving sidewalks speeds up pedestrian transit from the parking areas to the entrance to the park. Parking is free for guests of any of the hotels in the resort.

VISITOR INFORMATION   All the hotels we recommend offer general information about the theme park. For details about Disney and for reservations at any of the resort hotels, call ☎ **01-60-30-60-53** (in English) or 01-60-30-60-30 (in French). For general information about Disneyland Paris and specific details about the many other attractions and monuments in the Ile de France and the rest of the country, contact the **Maison du Tourism,** Disney Village (B.P. 77705), Marne-la-Vallée CEDEX 4 (☎ **01-60-43-33-33**).

SPENDING A DAY AT DISNEY

Admission (depending on season): 1 day, 160 to 200F ($28.80 to $36) for adults and 130 to 155F ($23.40 to $27.90) for children 3 to 11; 2 days, 305 to 380F ($54.90 to $68.40) for adults and 250 to 295F ($45 to $53.10) for children; children 2 and under enter free. Peak season is mid-June to mid-September as well as Christmas and Easter weeks. Entrance to Village Disney is free, though there's usually a cover charge to enter the dance clubs.

Open: July and August, daily from 9am to 11pm; September through June, Monday to Friday from 10am to 6pm and Saturday and Sunday from 9am to 8pm. Opening and closing hours vary with the weather and the season. It's usually good to phone the information office (see above).

Tours: Guided tours can be arranged for 50F ($9) for adults, 35F ($6.30) for children 3 to 11, and free for children 2 and under. Lasting 3½ hours and including 20 or more people, the tours offer an opportunity for a complete visit. In view of the well-marked paths leading through the park and the availability of printed information in virtually any language, guided tours are not recommended.

Disneyland Paris is a total vacation destination. Clustered into one enormous unit, the Disneyland Park includes five "lands" of entertainment, six massive well-designed hotels, a campground, an entertainment center (Festival Disney), a 27-hole golf course, and dozens of restaurants, shows, and shops.

Visitors from all over Europe stroll amid an abundance of flower beds, trees, reflecting ponds, fountains, and a large artificial lake flanked with hotels (see below). An army of smiling employees and Disney characters—many of whom are multilingual, including Buffalo Bill, Mickey and Minnie Mouse, and the French-born Caribbean pirate Jean Laffite—are on hand to greet and delight the thousands of children.

Main Street, U.S.A., is replete with horse-drawn carriages and street-corner barbershop quartets. Steam-powered railway cars embark from the Main Street Station for a trip through a Grand Canyon diorama to **Frontierland,** with its paddlewheel steamers reminiscent of Mark Twain's Mississippi River. Other attractions are a petting zoo called the Critter Corral at the Cottonwood Creek Ranch and the Lucky Nugget Saloon, whose inspiration comes from the gold-rush era; ironically, the steps and costumes of the cancan show originated in the cabarets of turn-of-the-century Paris.

The park's steam trains chug past **Adventureland**—with its swashbuckling 18th-century pirates, tree house of the Swiss Family Robinson, and reenacted *Arabian Nights* legends—to **Fantasyland.** Here you'll find the park's symbol, the **Sleeping Beauty Castle** (*Le Château de la Belle au Bois Dormant*), whose soaring pinnacles and turrets are an idealized (and spectacular) interpretation of the châteaux of France. Parading in its shadow are time-tested but Europeanized versions of *Blanche neige et les sept nains* (Snow White and the Seven Dwarfs), Peter Pan, Dumbo, Alice (from Wonderland), the Mad Hatter's Teacups, and Sir Lancelot's Magic Carousel.

Visions of the future are exhibited at **Discoveryland,** whose tributes to human invention and imagination are drawn from the works of Leonardo da Vinci, Jules Verne, H. G. Wells, the modern masters of science fiction, and the *Star Wars* series.

As Disney continues to churn out animated blockbusters, look for all their newest stars to appear in the theme park. You'll see characters from *Aladdin, The Lion King, Pocahontas,* and *Toy Story.*

In addition to the theme park, Disney maintains the **Village Disney** entertainment center. Illuminated inside by a spectacular gridwork of lights suspended 60 feet above ground, the complex contains dance clubs, shops, restaurants (one of which offers a dinner spectacle, Buffalo Bill's Wild West Show), bars for adults trying to escape their children for a while, a French Government Tourist Office, a post office, and a marina.

WHERE TO STAY

The resort contains six hotels, each evoking a different theme but all sharing a reservations service. For more information in North America, call ☎ **407/934-7639.** For information or reservations in France, contact the **Central Reservations Office,** Euro Disney S.C.A. (B.P. 105), F-77777 Marne-la-Vallée CEDEX 4 (☎ **01-60-30-60-30**). In correspondence, Euro Disney Resort (not Disneyland Paris) remains the official designation. For travelers with internet access, all Disneyland Paris hotels can be reached through one Web site: www.disneylandparis.com.

✪ **Disneyland Hotel.** Euro Disney Resort, B.P. 105, F-77777 Marne-la-Vallée CEDEX 4. ☎ **01-60-45-65-00.** Fax 01-60-45-65-33. 500 units. A/C MINIBAR TV TEL. 1,550–2,250F ($279–$405) room for 1–4; from 3,850F ($693) suite. AE, CB, DC, DISC, MC, V.

The flagship hotel of the resort, positioned at the entrance, this place resembles a massive Victorian resort hotel, with red-tile turrets and jutting balconies. The guest rooms are plushly and conservatively furnished and contain private safes. On the "Castle Club" floor, free newspapers, all-day beverages, and access to a well-equipped private lounge are provided.

Dining/Diversions: The hotel has three restaurants (**The California Grill** is recommended under "Dining" below) and two bars.

Amenities: Room service; laundry; baby-sitting; health club with indoor/outdoor pool, whirlpool, and sauna.

Hotel Cheyenne and Hotel Santa Fe. Euro Disney Resort, B.P. 115, F-77777 Marne-la-Vallée CEDEX 4. ☎ **01-60-45-62-00** for the Cheyenne or **01-60-45-78-00** for the Santa Fe. Fax 01-60-45-62-33 for the Cheyenne or 01-60-45-78-33 for the Santa Fe. 2,000 units. TV TEL. 435–780F ($78.30–$140.40) room for 1–4 in Hotel Santa Fe; 535–925F ($96.30–$166.50) room for 1–4 in Hotel Cheyenne. AE, DC, DISC, MC, V.

Adjacent to each other, these are the least expensive places to stay at the resort (except for the campgrounds). They're near a re-creation of Texas's Rio Grande and evoke the Old West. The Cheyenne accommodates visitors in 14 two-story buildings along Desperado Street, whereas the Santa Fe, sporting a desert theme, encompasses four "nature trails" winding among 42 adobe-style pueblos. The guest rooms are basic. The only drawback for parents is the lack of a pool. Tex-Mex specialties are offered at La Cantina (Santa Fe), and barbecue and smokehouse specialties predominate at the Chuck Wagon Café (Cheyenne).

Newport Bay Club. Euro Disney Resort, B.P. 105, F-77777 Marne-la-Vallée CEDEX 4. ☎ **01-60-45-55-00.** Fax 01-60-45-55-33. 1,098 units. A/C MINIBAR TV TEL. 830–1,180F ($149.40–$212.40) room for 1–4; from 1,600F ($288) suite. AE, DC, MC, V.

This hotel is designed with a central cupola, jutting balconies, a large front porch with comfortable rocking chairs, and a color scheme of blue and cream inspired by a harborfront New England hotel. It's ringed by verdant lawns. Each nautically decorated room receives closed-circuit movies. The upscale Yacht Club and less formal Cape Cod are the dining choices. Facilities include a lakeside promenade, a croquet lawn, a glassed-in pool pavilion, an outdoor pool, and a health club with sun beds and a sauna.

WHERE TO DINE

There are at least 45 restaurants and snack bars in the resort, each trying to please thousands of European and North American palates. Here are two recommendations:

Auberge de Cendrillon. In Fantasyland. ☎ **01-64-74-24-02.** Reservations recommended. Main courses 110–130F ($19.80–$23.40); fixed-price menus 175–210F ($31.50–$37.80). AE, DC, DISC, MC, V. Thurs–Mon 11:30am to 90 minutes before the park closes. FRENCH.

The most visible and whimsical French restaurant at the resort is a fairy-tale version of Cinderella's sumptuous country inn, with a glass couch in the center. A master of ceremonies, in a plumed tricorne hat and an embroidered tunic and lace ruffles, welcomes you. Try the warm goat-cheese salad with lardons or the smoked-salmon platter for an appetizer. If you don't choose one of the fixed-price meals, you can order from the limited but excellent à la carte menu. Perhaps you'll settle happily for poultry in puff pastry, loin of lamb roasted with mustard, or sautéed medallions of veal. The only drawback to this place is its location in the theme park, limiting its accessibility to its seasonal schedules. Lunches are usually easier to arrange than dinners.

The California Grill. In the Disneyland Hotel. ☎ **01-60-45-65-00.** Reservations required. Main courses 58–205F ($10.45–$36.90); children's menus from 75F ($13.50). AE, DC, DISC, MC, V. Sun–Fri 7–11pm, Sat 6–11pm. CALIFORNIAN.

Focusing on the lighter recipes for which the Golden State is famous, this airy and elegant restaurant features specialties like poached oysters with leeks and salmon, grilled tuna with white beans and soy sauce, and grilled shrimp with spicy rice. Main courses are likely to feature goat-cheese tortellini with grilled vegetables, grilled veal chops with morel-flavored cream sauce, and glazed veal loin with asparagus and fresh chives. The most expensive item is a roasted rib of beef with traditional rib-sticking garnishes. A number of children's dishes are named after everybody from Peter Pan to Goofy (skip the Tom Thumb). The Napa Feast, the more elegant of the two fixed-price menus, begins with home-cured smoked salmon, follows with roast rack of lamb scented with fresh thyme, and ends with crème brûlée. Children (one per adult) dine free every Saturday between 6 and 7pm when accompanied by an adult. If you're looking for a quieter meal, go here as late as your hunger pangs will allow.

8 Provins: City of Roses

50 miles SE of Paris, 30 miles E of Melun

Feudal Provins, the "city of roses," is one of this region's most interesting towns. Historic, romantic, and beautiful, Provins soared to the pinnacle of its power and prosperity in the Middle Ages, then fell to ruin in the Hundred Years War. Given its proximity to Paris, it's surprising that Provins today remains so relatively little known by foreigners.

Once it was the third town of France, after Paris and Rouen, and its Champagne Fair rivaled that of Troyes. But it sits high and dry today with its memories. The city is also known for its Damask Rose, brought back from the Crusades by Thibault IV. When the duke of Lancaster, through marriage, became the comte de Provins, he included the rose in his coat-of-arms. A century and a half later the red rose of Lancaster confronted the white rose of York in the War of the Roses.

ESSENTIALS

Trains depart from Paris's Gare de l'Est six times a day. Each way requires 80 minutes, but a bit longer if a transfer is required en route in the town of Longueville.

The **Maison du Visiteur** (tourist office) is on chemin de Villecran (☎ **01-64-60-26-26**), adjacent to the entrance to the medieval ramparts.

EXPLORING THE TOWN

With its towers and bastions, Provins was surrounded in the 13th century by ramparts that protected it from the vast plains of Brie. The once-mighty fortifications are so well preserved that scholars refer to Provins as the "Carcassonne of the North." The best site for viewing these ramparts is the **Porte Jouy,** on the Upper Town's northwestern edge, at the terminus of rue de Jouy. A staircase rises to the top. Though the ramparts no longer make a full circuit of the town, you can still promenade along the top, enjoying a composite of military, secular, and ecclesiastical architecture from the Middle Ages. Entrance is free, and you can climb anytime you want.

Ville Haute (Upper Town) is perched on a promontory, and **Ville Basse** (Lower Town) is crossed by two rivers, the Durteint and the Voulzie, the latter an effluent of the Seine.

Tour César. Rue de la Pie. ☎ **01-64-60-26-26.** Admission 17F ($3.05) adults, 10F ($1.80) children 5–12, free for children 4 and under. Nov 3–Apr 3 daily 2–5pm; Apr 4–Nov 2 daily 2–6pm.

This 12th-century tower is the pride of the town. Since the 17th century it has functioned as the bell tower for the nearby Eglise St-Quiriace. When a fire destroyed the bell tower of St-Quiriace in the 17th century, the church was rebuilt with a vaguely baroque-looking dome, according to the fashion of the time, and the role of the bell tower was transferred to the Tour César.

The adjoining **Eglise St-Quiriace** was constructed in the 12th and 13th centuries, then rebuilt in the 17th. It contains a majestic, primitive Gothic choir and a modern dome. Joan of Arc stopped here on her way to Orléans. The church is open day and night. For information, call the tourist office. Admission is free.

Grange-aux-Dîmes. Rue St-Jean. ☎ **01-64-60-26-26.** Admission to exhibition 22F ($3.95) adults, 14F ($2.50) children. June 7–Aug Mon–Fri 11am–6pm, Sat–Sun and holidays 10am–7pm; Mar 29–June 6 and Sept–Nov 2 Mon–Fri 2–6pm, Sat–Sun 11am–6pm; Nov 3–Jan 4 Sat–Sun and holidays 2–5pm.

This historic building was used first as a covered marketplace for the medieval merchants who sold their goods here, then as lodgings for the merchants who traveled from far away. Later it was a warehouse for the tithes (*dîmes*) the Catholic church extracted from the corps of its faithful. In 1995 a permanent exhibition was added: *Provins aux Temps des Foires de Champagne* (Provins During the Trade Fairs of Champagne).

Les Souterrains de Provins (The Tunnels of Provins). Tours begin from the Hôtel-Dieu (Town Hall) on rue de Jouy. The tourist office (see above) will provide information. Guided tour 22 F ($3.95) adults, 14F ($2.50) children. Spring and autumn tours Sat–Sun and holidays 11am–6pm, Mon–Fri one tour at 2:30pm. June–Aug tours Mon–Fri 2–6pm, Sat–Sun 11am–6pm. Winter tours Sat–Sun and holidays at 3 and 4pm.

The city is home to a mysterious network of underground passageways that no one in town fully understands today. Possible explanations of why they were dug, between the 12th and the 13th century, include the following: A particular type of mineral was extracted from the porous soil for the treatment of the textiles manufactured during that era; the tunnels were used to escape enemy forces during sieges; they were used to conceal treasures; or they were used as a secret meeting place for Freemasons. A guided tour of the labyrinth begins and ends at the Hôtel-Dieu and requires 45 minutes.

WHERE TO DINE

Le Médiéval. 6 place Honoré-de-Balzac. ☎ **01-64-00-01-19.** Reservations recommended. Main courses 75–145F ($13.50–$26.10); fixed-price menus 98–178F ($17.65–$32.05). AE, CB, V. Tues–Sun noon–2:30pm, Tues–Sat 7–9pm. FRENCH.

In a turn-of-the-century building in the Ville Basse's commercial center, this is a worthwhile restaurant that has served thousands of meals during its long life. There are two dining rooms, one outfitted with big windows like a greenhouse, the other more confined and cozy. Menu items are based on solid, flavorful (though not particularly imaginative) combinations of tried-and-true French cuisine. Examples are sole meunière, grilled shrimp with basil butter, and roast beef stuffed with foie gras.

9 Malmaison: Love Nest of Joséphine

10 miles W of Paris, 3 miles NW of St-Cloud

In the 9th century the Normans landed in this area and devasated the countryside, hence the name of this suburb of Paris, which translates to "bad house." History abounds at the country retreat, the Château de Malmaison.

EXPLORING THE CHATEAU

Musée National du Château de Malmaison. Av. du Château. ☎ **01-41-29-05-55.** Admission to Malmaison, which includes entrance to Bois Préau (if it's open), 30F ($5.40) Mon and Wed–Sat, 20F ($3.60) Sun, free for children 17 and under and students. May–Oct Malmaison open Mon and Wed–Fri 9:30am–noon and 1:30–5pm, Sat–Sun 10am–5:30pm; Bois Préau open only Thurs–Sun 12:30–6pm. Nov–Apr, both châteaux close half an hour earlier. Tours available weekdays at 10am, 2pm, and 3:30pm; every 15 minutes on Sat. Take the RER A-1 line from place Charles-de-Gaulle–Etoile to La Défense. Transfer to bus no. 258 for the 6-mile ride to the château (stop Rueil-Malmaison).

This site boasts lots of history. Construction on the château, used as a country retreat far removed from the Tuileries or Compiègne (other Napoleonic residences), began in 1622. It was purchased in 1799 by Joséphine Bonaparte, Napoléon's wife, who had it restored and fashionably decorated as a love nest. She then enlarged the estate (but not the château). Popular references to Malmaison as having been a lepers' sanitarium are unfounded.

Today Malmaison is filled with mementos from Napoléon's euphoric early days as a general shortly after the Revolution and during his rise to power as first consul of

France. The veranda and council room were obviously inspired by the tent he occupied on his military campaigns and are filled with Empire furnishings. His study and desk are exhibited in the library. Marie-Louise, his second wife, took Napoléon's books with her when she left France; however, these books were purchased by an English couple who presented them to the museum here. Most of the furnishings are originals; some came from the Tuileries and St-Cloud. Napoléon always attached a sentimental importance to Malmaison, and he spent a week here before his departure for St. Helena.

Many of the portraits and sculpture immortalize a Napoleonic deity—for example, David's equestrian portrait of the emperor and also a flattering portrait of Joséphine by Gérard.

In 1809, following her divorce because she couldn't bear Napoléon an heir, Joséphine retired here and was passionately devoted to her roses until her death in 1814 at the age of 51. The roses in the garden today are a fitting memorial. The bed in which Joséphine died is exhibited, as is her toilette kit, including her toothbrush.

Also here is the small **Château de Bois-Préau** (follow the signs through the park, a 5-minute walk from the main building). Built in 1700 and acquired by Josephine in 1810, it's smaller, darker, sadder, and less architecturally distinguished than Malmaison. The château (more of a villa since its reconstruction in 1854) is a museum/shrine to the emperor's exile on the isolated Atlantic outpost of St. Helena, after his fall from grace. (In case you're interested: Napoléon wore boxer shorts.) For better coverage of the years between his rise to power (as exhibited at Malmaison) and his disgrace and death on St. Helena, see the Napoleonic museum in Fontainebleau (above).

10 The Remarkable Zoo of Château de Thoiry

25 miles W of Paris

✪ **Château et Parc Zoologique de Thoiry.** 78770 Thoiry-en-Yvelines. ☎ **01-34-87-52-25.** Admission: château, 38F ($6.85) adults, 30F ($5.40) children 3–12, free for children 2 and under; reserve or gardens, 100F ($18) adults, 79F ($14.20) children 3–12, free for children 2 and under. Park, Apr–Oct Mon–Sat 10am–6pm, Sun 10am–6:30pm; Nov–Mar daily 10am–5pm. Château, Apr–Oct daily 2–6pm; Nov–Mar daily 2–5pm. Take the Autoroute de l'Ouest (A13) toward Dreux, exiting at Bois-d'Arcy. Then get on N12, following the signs on D11 to Thoiry.

This is a major attraction that in one year drew more visitors than the Louvre or Versailles. The 16th-century château, owned by the vicomte de La Panouse family (now run by son Paul and his wife, Annabelle), displays two unpublished Chopin waltzes, antique furniture, and more than 343 handwritten letters of French or European kings, as well as the original financial records of France from 1745 to 1750. But these aren't as much a draw as the Parc Zoologique.

The château's grounds have been turned into a game reserve with elephants, giraffes, zebras, monkeys, rhinoceroses, alligators, lions, tigers, kangaroos, bears, and wolves—more than 1,000 animals and birds roam at liberty. The reserve and park cover 300 acres, though the estate is on 1,200 acres.

In the French gardens you can see llamas, Asian deer and sheep, and many types of birds, including flamingos and cranes. In the tiger park a promenade has been designed above the tigers. In addition, in the basement of the château is a vivarium. Paul and Annabelle are also restoring the 300 acres of 17th-, 18th-, and 19th-century gardens as well as creating new ones.

To see the animal farm you can drive your own car, providing it isn't a convertible (an uncovered car may be dangerous). Anticipating troubles, the owners carry thousands of francs' worth of insurance. The park is most crowded on weekends, but if you want to avoid the crush, visit on Saturday or Sunday morning.

11 Giverny: In the Footsteps of Monet

50 miles NW of Paris

On the border between Normandy and the Ile de France, the Claude Monet Foundation is where the great painter lived for 43 years. The restored house and its gardens are open to the public.

ESSENTIALS

If you're going **by train,** take the Paris-Rouen line (Paris-St-Lazare) to the Vernon station. A taxi can take you the 3 miles to Giverny. Bus tours are operated from Paris by American Express and Cityrama.

If you're **driving,** take the Autoroute de l'Ouest (Port de St-Cloud) toward Rouen. Leave the autoroute at Bonnières, then cross the Seine on the Bonnières Bridge. From here, a direct road with signs will bring you to Giverny. Expect about an hour of driving, and try to avoid weekends.

Another way is to leave the highway at the Bonnières exit and go toward Vernon. Once here, cross the bridge over the Seine and follow the signs to Giverny or Gasny (Giverny is before Gasny). This is easier than going through Bonnières, where there aren't many signs.

MEETING MONET

✪ **Claude Monet Foundation.** Rue Claude-Monet. ☎ **02-32-51-28-21.** RESERVATIONS IMPERATIVE. Admission 35F ($6.30) adults, 25F ($4.50) children. Gardens only, 25F ($4.50). Mar 28–Nov 20 Tues–Sun 10am–6pm. Closed rest of year.

Born in 1840, the French impressionist was a brilliant innovator, excelling in presenting the effects of light at different times of the day. In fact, some critics claim that he "invented light." His series of paintings of Rouen cathedral and of the water lilies, which one critic called "vertical interpretations of horizontal lines," are just a few of his masterpieces.

Monet came to Giverny in 1883. While taking a small railway linking Vetheuil to Vernon, he discovered the village at a point where the Epte stream joined the Seine. Many of his friends used to visit him here at Le Pressoir, including Clemenceau, Cézanne, Rodin, Renoir, Degas, and Sisley. When Monet died in 1926, his son, Michel, inherited the house but left it abandoned until it decayed into ruins. The gardens became almost a jungle, inhabited by river rats. In 1966 Michel died and left it to the Académie des Beaux-Arts. It wasn't until 1977 that Gerald van der Kemp, who restored Versailles, decided to work on Giverny. A large part of it was restored with gifts from U.S. benefactors, especially the late Lila Acheson Wallace, former head of *Reader's Digest,* who contributed $1 million.

You can stroll through the garden and view the thousands of flowers, including the *nymphéas.* The Japanese bridge, hung with wisteria, leads to a dreamy setting of weeping willows and rhododendrons. Monet's studio barge was installed on the pond.

WHERE TO DINE

Auberge du Vieux Moulin. 21 rue de la Falaise. ☎ **02-32-51-46-15.** Main courses 70–110F ($12.60–$19.80); fixed-price menus 98–178F ($17.65–$32.05). MC, V. Tues–Sun noon–3pm and 7:30–10pm. Closed Jan. FRENCH.

This is a convenient lunch stop for visitors to the Monet house, in a stone building with a pair of flowering terraces. The Boudeau family maintains a series of cozy dining rooms filled with original Impressionist paintings. Since you can walk here from the museum in about 5 minutes, leave your car in the museum lot. Specialties include escalope of salmon with sorrel sauce and aiguillettes of duckling with peaches. The kitchen doesn't pretend that the food is anything more than good, hearty country fare with a dash of panache. The charm of the staff helps a lot, too.

12 Senlis

32 miles S of Paris, 62 miles S of Amiens

Today sleepy Senlis, which some Parisians treat as a suburb of Paris, remains a quiet township surrounded by forests. No history has been made here in a long time, but its memories are many and regal. Barbarians no longer threaten its walls as they did in the 3rd century; and gone, too, are all those kings of France, from Clovis to Louis XIV, who either passed through or took up temporary residence here. You can tie a visit to this northern French town in with a trek to nearby Chantilly (below). Today the core of Vieux Senlis is an archaeological garden that attracts visitors from all over the world.

ESSENTIALS

Take a **train** from Paris's Gare du Nord to Chantilly; then a 20-minute bus ride will bring you to Senlis.

The **Office de Tourisme** is on place parvis Notre-Dame (☎ 03-44-53-06-40).

SEEING THE SIGHTS

Cathédrale Notre-Dame de Senlis. Place parvis Notre-Dame in the town center. Admission is free. Daily 8am–7pm. Notre-Dame has a graceful 13th-century spire that towers 256 feet and dominates the countryside for miles around. The severe western facade contrasts with the Flamboyant Gothic southern portal. A fire swept over the structure in 1504 and much rebuilding followed, so the original effect is lost. A 19th-century decorative overlay was applied to the original Gothic structure, which was begun in 1153. Before entering, walk around to the western porch to see the sculptures. Depicted in stone is an unusual calendar of the seasons, along with scenes showing the ascension of the Virgin and the entombment. The builders of the main portal imitated the work at Chartres. In the forecourt are memorials to Joan of Arc and Marshal Foch.

Château Royal et Parc and Musée de la Vénerie (Hunting Museum). ☎ 03-44-53-00-80, ext. 1315. Admission 15F ($2.70) adults, free for children 16 and under. Wed 2–5pm, Thurs–Mon 10am–noon and 2–5pm. Closed mid-Dec to Jan.

A short walk away from the Cathédrale, you'll find the Château Royal et Parc. Built on the ruins of a Roman palace, the castle followed the outline of the Gallo-Roman walls, some of the most important in France owing to their state of preservation. Once inhabited by such monarchs as Henri II and Catherine de Médici, the château (now in ruins) encloses a complex of buildings. Of the 28 towers originally constructed against the Gallo-Roman walls, only 16 remain. One ruin houses the King's Chamber, the boudoir of French monarchs since the time of Clovis. In the complex is the Prieuré St-Mauritius, a priory that not only honors a saint but also was founded by one, Louis IX.

The Musée de la Vénerie (Hunting Museum), in the Château Royal, is housed in an 18th-century prior's building in the middle of the garden and displays hunting-related works of art from the 15th century to the present—paintings, drawings, engravings, old hunting suits, arms, horns, and trophies.

WHERE TO STAY

Hostellerie de la Porte Bellon. 51 rue Bellon, 60300 Senlis. ☎ 03-44-53-03-05. Fax 03-44-53-29-94. 19 units, all with shower or tub, 10 with toilet; 1 suite. MINIBAR TV TEL. 210F ($37.80) double without toilet; 280–380F ($50.40–$68.40) double with toilet; 990F ($178.20) suite. Closed Dec 21–Jan 5. MC, V.

This hotel/restaurant is on a quiet cobblestone street with an adjacent parking lot. The 300-year-old building was a former abbey and is designed with three floors of big windows, shutters, and flower boxes filled with pansies. Five rooms are cramped, with only small showers, and are suitable only for those without much luggage. The ground floor contains a bar area. The adjacent restaurant is accented with flowered wallpaper, charmingly rustic accessories, and a massive fireplace.

WHERE TO DINE

The restaurant at the **Hostellerie de la Porte Bellon** (see above) is open to the public.

Vieille Auberge. 8 rue Long Filet. ☎ 03-44-60-95-50. Reservations recommended Fri–Sat. Main courses 80–110F ($14.40–$19.80); fixed-price menus 109F and 155F ($19.60 and $27.90). AE, MC, V. Daily noon–2pm; Mon–Sat 7–10pm. FRENCH.

This is the town's best restaurant. Each dining room, with its stone walls and heavy tables, has been coordinated with simple fabrics and candlelight to create a refined rustic ambience. During warm months, a small terrace functions as another dining area. The attentive staff takes an unmistakable pride in serving classically French dishes, which may include such favorites as monkfish tournedos in a piquant pepper sauce, filet of beef in a country wine sauce and accompanied by a vegetable crêpe, and duck filet with fois gras and whole-grain mustard sauce. Even though the cuisine isn't worth a special drive from Paris, the restaurant is nevertheless memorable for its atmosphere and perfectly prepared dishes.

13 Compiègne

50 miles N of Paris, 20 miles NE of Senlis

A visit to this Oise River valley town is usually tied in with an excursion to Senlis. The most famous dance step of all time was photographed in a forest about 4 miles from town: Hitler's "jig of joy" on June 22, 1940, which heralded the ultimate humiliation of France and shocked the world.

Like Senlis, this is another town north of Paris that still lives for its memories—not all of them pleasant. Many Parisians (who don't already live here and commute to Paris) visit not for the attractions (which they may have seen years ago) but for the 35,000-acre **Forest of Compiègne.** With its majestic avenues and ponds, it merits exploration, especially the colorful little villages of St-Jean-aux-Bois and Vieux-Moulin.

ESSENTIALS

There are frequent **rail** connections from the Gare du Nord in Paris. The ride takes 50 minutes. The station is across the river from the town center. If you're **driving,** take the northern Paris-Lille motorway (A1 or the less convenient E15) for 50 miles.

The **Office de Tourisme** is on place Hôtel-de-Ville (☎ 03-44-40-01-00).

SEEING THE SIGHTS

An imposing statue of Joan of Arc, who was taken prisoner at Compiègne by the Burgundians on May 23, 1430, before she was turned over to the English, stands in the town square.

Musée National du Château de Compiègne. Place du Palais. ☎ **03-44-38-47-00.** Admission (including the museums) 35F ($6.30) adults, 23F ($4.15) students, free for children under 18. Apr 1–Sept 30 Wed–Mon 9:15am–6:15pm; Oct 1–Mar 31 Wed–Mon 9:15am–5:45pm.

In the town's heyday, royalty and the two Bonaparte emperors flocked here. But this wasn't always a place of pagentry. Louis XIV once said: "In Versailles, I live in the style befitting a monarch. In Fontainebleau, more like a prince. At Compiègne, like a peasant." But the Sun King returned again and again. His successor, Louis XV, started rebuilding the château, based on plans by Gabriel. The king died before work was completed, but Louis XVI and Marie Antoinette continued to expand it.

Napoléon's second wife, Marie-Louise, arrived at Compiègne to marry him, and in a dining room, which you can visit only on the guided tour, she had her first meal with the emperor. Accounts maintain that she was paralyzed with fear of this older man (Napoléon was in his 40s, she was 19). After dinner, he seduced her and is said to have only increased her fears.

It wasn't until the Second Empire that Compiègne reached its pinnacle of success. Under Napoléon III and Eugénie, the autumnal hunting season was the occasion for gala balls and parties, some, according to accounts, lasting 10 days without a break. It was the "golden age": Women in elegant hooped gowns danced with their escorts to Strauss waltzes, Offenbach's operas echoed through the chambers and salons, and Eugénie, who fancied herself an actress, performed in the palace theater for her guests.

On the guided tour you'll see the gold-and-scarlet Empire Room, where Napoléon I spent many a troubled night. His library, known for its secret door, is also on the tour. In the Queen's Chamber, the "horn of plenty" bed was used by Marie-Louise. The furniture is by Jacob, and the saccharine nude on the ceiling by Girodet. Dubois decorated the charming Salon of Flowers, and the largest room, the Ball Gallery, was adorned by Girodet. In the park, Napoléon ordered the gardeners to create a green bower to remind Marie-Louise of the one at Schönbrunn in Vienna, where she grew up.

Various wings of the château contain a handful of museums, entrance to which is included in the château admission. They include the **Musée National de la Voiture (National Automobile Museum),** which exhibits about 150 vehicles: everything from Ben Hur chariots to bicycles to a Citroën "chain-track" vehicle. About 10 of the vehicles are gas-powered antique autos; another 40 are exotic forms of horse-drawn carriages. For insights into the decorative arts of France's Industrial Revolution years, visit the **Musée du Second-Empire,** which has a fine collection of paintings, sculpture, and furniture, including works by Carpeaux; and the **Musée de l'Impératrice,** with souvenirs and memorabilia from the imperial family.

Musée de la Figurine Historique (Museum of Historical Figurines). Place de l'Hôtel-de-Ville. ☎ **03-44-40-72-55.** Admission 12F ($2.15) adults, 6F ($1.10) children. Mar–Oct Tues–Sat 9am–noon and 2–6pm, Sun 2–6pm (closes earlier off-season).

One of Compiègne's finest monuments is the Flamboyant Gothic **Hôtel de Ville.** Built from 1499 to 1503, with a landmark belfry that's visible from far away, it houses a unique museum of great interest to students of the wars that have raged across northern France. The Musuem of Historical Figurines offers a unique collection of about 100,000 tin soldiers, from a Louis XIV trumpeter to a soldier from World War II. The Battle of Waterloo, staged in miniature form on a landscape with thousands of figurines, is depicted in all its gore.

Château de Pierrefonds. In the Forêt de Compiègne. ☎ **03-44-42-72-72.** Admission 32F ($5.75) adults, 21F ($3.80) children. May–Aug daily 10am–5:15pm; Sept–Apr daily 10am–12:30pm and 2–5:15pm.

While flitting through the forest, call at this splendid 12th-century château-fortress that once belonged to Napoléon. It has a picture-postcard look with its round towers with pointy tops, and there's even a moat. Artifacts from the Middle Ages fill the interior. Save time for a stroll through the little village with its half-timbered houses after a visit to the château.

Wagon de l'Armistice (Wagon du Maréchal-Foch). Route de Soissons. ☎ **03-44-85-14-18.** Admission 10F ($1.80) adults, 6F ($1.10) children 7–14, free for children 6 and under. Apr to mid-Oct Wed–Mon 9am–12:15pm and 2–6:15pm; mid-Oct to Mar Wed–Mon 9am–11:45am and 2–5:30pm.

At the peak of his power, in one of the most ironic twists of fate in European history, Hitler forced the vanquished French to capitulate in the same rail coach where German officials signed the Armistice on November 11, 1918. The coach was transported to Berlin and then to Ordüff in the Thuringe Forest, where it was burned in April 1945. In Compiègne you can visit a replica, the Wagon de l'Armistice. The museum is complemented by two rooms with many newspapers, photos, and maps from November 1918 and June 1940. Three-dimensional slides showing scenes from the Great War are projected.

WHERE TO STAY

The **Rôtisserie du Chat Qui Tourne** (see below) also rents rooms.

Au Relais Napoléon. Av. de l'Europe, 60200 Compiègne. ☎ **03-44-20-11-11.** Fax 03-44-20-41-60. 49 units. TV TEL. 415F ($74.70) double. AE, DC, MC, V. Head west on av. Berthelot, which becomes av. de l'Europe, a 10-minute trip.

This modern hotel outside of town is near sports complexes and the border of the forest, surrounded by a sunny terrace, green lawns, and even a small vineyard. The interior is First Empire style, with honeycomb ceilings, tiled floors, and dark woodwork. The medium-size guest rooms offer a relaxing ambience with rich colored walls, reproduction furniture, and firm mattresses. The elegant bar is open 24 hours, and an air-conditioned restaurant provides both fixed-price menus and à la carte selections.

Hostellerie du Royal-Lieu. 9 rue de Senlis, 60200 Compiègne. ☎ **03-44-20-10-24.** Fax 03-44-86-82-27. 23 units. TV TEL. 475F ($85.50) double; 625F ($112.50) suite. AE, DC, DISC, MC, V. Follow the signs southwest toward Senlis until you reach rue de Senlis, a 5-minute drive from the town center.

Monsieur and Madame Bonechi have carefully decorated the rooms in this rambling two-story hotel about 1¼ miles from town. They have names like Madame Pompadour, Madame Butterfly, and La Goulue; less fancifully named rooms are done in a scattering of different "Louis" periods or Empire style. Both the rooms and the restaurant's terrace look out over an immaculate garden. Meals in the elegantly rustic dining room may include four-fish stew with red butter, scallops with endive, and filet of beef with morels in cream sauce or with foie gras. Dessert soufflés are available if you order them 30 minutes in advance.

WHERE TO DINE

Note that the restaurants in both hotels above are open to the public.

Rôtisserie du Chat Qui Tourne. In the Hôtel de France, 17 rue Eugène-Floquet. 60200 Compiègne. ☎ **03-44-40-02-74.** Reservations recommended. Main courses 85–185F ($15.30–$33.30); fixed-price menus 150–260F ($27–$46.80). MC, V. Daily noon–2:15pm and 7:15–9:15pm. FRENCH.

The name, "Inn of the Cat That Turns the Spit," dates from 1665. The bar and a traditional country inn–style dining room are downstairs. Madame Robert, the proprietor, believes in judicious cooking and careful seasoning and prices her table d'hôte menus to appeal to a wide range of budgets. The menu gastronomique is likely to include terrine de canard (duck), then trout meunière, followed by poulet rôti (roast chicken) à la broche, and finally a dessert.

Madame Robert also rents 20 clean rooms, each with bathroom, TV, and phone. Doubles are 165F to 390F ($29.70 to $70.20).

14 Chantilly—A Day at the Races

26 miles N of Paris, 31 miles SE of Beauvais

This is a resort town for Parisians who want a quick getaway for le week-end. Known for its frothy whipped cream and black lace, it also draws visitors to its racetrack and château. The first two Sundays in June are the highlight of the turf season, bringing out an exceedingly fashionable crowd.

ESSENTIALS

Trains depart frequently for Chantilly from the Gare du Nord in Paris; the ride takes about an hour.

The **Office de Tourisme** is at 60 av. du Maréchal-Joffre (☎ **03-44-57-08-58**).

TOURING THE CHATEAU & MUSEUMS

✪ **Château de Chantilly/Musée Condé.** ☎ **03-44-62-62-62.** Admission 39F ($7) adults, 34F ($6.10) children 12–18, 12F ($2.15) children 3–11. Mar–Oct Wed–Mon 10am–6pm; Nov–Feb Wed–Mon 10:30am–12:45pm and 2–5pm.

Once the seat of the Condé, the Château de Chantilly and the Musée Condé (within the château) are on an artificial carp-stocked lake. You approach via the same forested drive that Louis XIV, with hundreds of guests, rode along for a banquet prepared by Vatel, one of the best-known French chefs. (One day when the fish didn't arrive on time, Vatel committed suicide.) The château is French Renaissance, with gables and domed towers, but part was rebuilt in the 19th century. It's skirted by a romantic forest once filled with stag and boar.

In 1886 the château's owner, the duc d'Aumale, bequeathed the park and palace to the Institut de France, along with his fabulous art collection and library. The château houses sumptuous furnishings as well as works by artists like Memling, van Dyck, Botticelli, Poussin, Watteau, Ingres, Delacroix, Corot, Rubens, and Vernet. See especially Raphael's *Madonna of Lorette, Virgin of the House d'Orléans,* and *Three Graces* (sometimes called the *Three Ages of Woman*). The foremost French painter of the 15th century, Jean Fouquet, is represented here by a series of about 40 miniatures. A copy of the rose diamond that received worldwide attention when it was stolen in 1926 is on display in the jewel collection. One of the most celebrated Condé library acquisitions is *Les Très Riches Heures du Duc de Berry,* a 15th-century illuminated manuscript illustrating the months of the year.

The château was built about 1560 by Jean Bullant for one of the members of the Montmorency family. The stables (see below), a hallmark of French 18th-century architecture, were constructed to house 240 horses, with adjacent kennels for 500 hounds. If you have time, take a walk in the garden laid out by Le Nôtre. A hamlet of rustic cottages and the Maison de Sylvie, a graceful building constructed in 1604 and rebuilt by Maria-Felice Orsini, are in the park.

Musée Vivant du Cheval. 7 rue du Connétable. ☎ **03-44-57-40-40.** Admission 50F ($9). July–Aug Tues 2–5:30pm, Wed–Mon 10:30am–5:30pm; May–June daily 10:30am–5:30pm; Apr and Sept–Oct Wed–Mon 10:30am–5:30pm; Nov–Mar Wed–Mon 2–5pm. Equestrian displays: Apr–Oct daily 11:30am, 3:30pm, and 5:15pm; the rest of the year one display at 3:30pm.

This museum occupies the restored *Grandes Ecuries,* the stables built between 1719 and 1735 for Louis-Henri, prince de Bourbon and prince de Condé, who occupied the château. Besides being fond of horses, he believed in reincarnation and expected to come back as a horse in his next life; therefore, he built the stables fit for a king.

The stables and an adjoining kennel fell into ruins over a couple of centuries, but they've now been restored as a museum of the living horse, with thoroughbreds housed alongside old breeds of draft horses, Arabs and Hispano-Arabs, and farm horses. Yves Bienaimé, the certified riding instructor who established the museum, presents exhibitions tracing the horse's association with humans, as well as a blacksmith shop and displays of saddles, equipment for the care of horses, and horse-race memorabilia.

The three daily **equestrian displays** (from April to October) last about half an hour and explain how the horse is ridden and trained. A wonderful restaurant on the premises, Le Carrousel Gourmand (☎ **03-44-57-19-77**), features the specialties of Picardy.

WHERE TO STAY

Château de Chaumontel. 21 rue André-Vassord-Chaumontel, 95270 Chaumontel. ☎ **01-34-71-00-30.** Fax 01-34-71-26-97. www.chateau-chamontel.com. E-mail: rigard@club-internet.fr. 20 units. TV TEL. 940F ($169.20) double; 1,140–1,240F ($205.20–$223.20) suite. AE, MC, V. Take N16 south for 4 miles.

Northeast of Luzarches and south of Chantilly is this hotel/restaurant from the late 16th century. It has had many aristocratic owners and was once the hunting lodge of the prince de Condé, who lived at Chantilly. In 1956 it was turned into a hotel, with well-furnished rooms. Surrounded by a moat and a verdant landscape dotted with wildflowers, the château is about as evocative a site as any in this region. The rustic dining room serves excellent food, offering specialties like crabs' legs, filet mignon, and eggplant and caviar.

Château de la Tour. Chemin de la Chaussée, 60270 Chantilly-Gouvieux. ☎ **03-44-62-38-38.** Fax 03-44-57-31-97. 41 units. MINIBAR TV TEL. 690–930F ($124.20–$167.40) double. AE, DC, MC, V.

This turn-of-the-century château and its 12-acre park was built as a weekend getaway by a wealthy Parisian banking family. During World War II it became the home of the German l'Etat Major, and in 1946 it was transformed into a luxury hotel. The likes of Edith Piaf, Tino Rossi, and Jean Gabin would meet and mingle with friends in the restaurant. Today many celebrities and sports personalities still frequent the château. In 1990 a new wing was added, giving you the opportunity to choose rooms with a modern flavor or a more traditional ambience. In either case, all rooms are large and have hardwood floors, high ceilings, and first-class furnishings. You can also enjoy haute French cuisine in the grand dining room with parquet floors and two wood-burning fireplaces. Other amenities are a tennis court, a pool, a fitness room, and even mountain-bike rentals.

Hôtel du Parc. 36 av. du Maréchal-Joffre, 60500 Chantilly. ☎ **03-44-58-20-00.** Fax 03-44-57-31-10. 58 units. TV TEL. 460F ($82.80) double. AE, DC, MC, V.

This modern hotel is in the center of town, close to a host of restaurants and sights. The contemporary-styled spacious lobby, dominated by sharp angles of mirror and chrome, gives way to a more inviting English-style bar with plenty of dark wood and leather. The medium-size guest rooms have built-in furnishings and sliding glass doors opening onto private balconies. There's no hotel restaurant, but nearby you'll find any number of good places.

WHERE TO DINE

The restaurant at the **Château de la Tour** (see above) is open to the public.

Le Tiperrary. 6 av. du Maréchal-Joffre. ☎ **03-44-57-00-48.** Reservations recommended. Main courses 90–150F ($16.20–$27); fixed-price menus 98F ($17.65) at lunch, 160–250F ($28.80–$45) at dinner. AE, DC, MC, V. Tues–Sun noon–2pm, Tues–Sat 7–9:30pm. FRENCH.

The owners welcome you to their traditional restaurant in a 19th-century town house. There are also cafe tables outdoors, where you can enjoy an aperitif. To begin, try the specialty: ravioli stuffed with snails and shrimp. Other dishes likely to be featured are scallops sautéed in endive-flavored cream sauce, rabbit à la Marseillaise (with concassé of tomatoes and garlic), or fricassée of sweetbreads flavored with port. Some choices are pleasing in their simplicity and others are overdressed.

7

The Loire Valley

Bordered by vineyards, the winding Loire Valley cuts through the land of castles deep in France's heart. Crusaders returning to their medieval quarters here brought news of the opulence of the East, and soon they began rethinking their surroundings. Later, word came from neighboring Italy of a great artistic flowering led by Leonardo da Vinci and Michelangelo. So when royalty and nobility built châteaux throughout this valley during the French Renaissance, sumptuousness was uppermost in their minds. An era of excessive pomp reigned until Henri IV moved his court to Paris, marking the Loire's decline.

The Loire is blessed with abundant attractions—ranging from medieval, Renaissance, and classical châteaux to Romanesque and Gothic churches to treasures like the Apocalypse Tapestries. There's even the castle that inspired the fairy tale *Sleeping Beauty.*

REGIONAL CUISINE Patricia Wells, author of *The Food Lover's Guide to France,* has said that the Loire's cuisine reminds her "of the daffodil days of spring and blue skies of summer." Particularly superb are rose-fleshed salmon caught in the Loire River, often served with sorrel. The region's rivers are stocked with other fish as well, including pike, carp, shad, and mullet.

Various types of *rillettes* (potted pork) begin most meals. Gourmets highly prize *pâté d'alouettes* (lark pâté) and *matelote d'anguille* (stewed eel). From the mushroom-rich Sologne emerges wild boar, along with deer, miniature quail, hare, pheasant, and mallard duck. Two popular poultry dishes are chicken casserole in red-wine sauce and spit-roasted capon.

The valley's Atlantic side produces an astonishing variety of grapes, used to make wines ranging from dry to lusciously sweet and from still to sparkling and fruity. The best whites are Vouvray (ideal with Loire salmon) and Montlouis. Red Anjou wines, including Rouge de Cabernet and Saumur-Champigny, have a slight raspberry flavor. Dry Sancerre wines, with plenty of backbone, are wonderful with the Loire's fabled goat cheese and whitewater fish.

1 Châteaudun

64 miles SW of Paris, 27 miles SW of Chartres

The first château you'll come to is the **Château de Châteaudun,** place Jean-de-Dunois (☎ **02-37-94-02-90**). Austere and foreboding, it rises on a stonebound table over a tributary of the Loire.

The Loire Valley

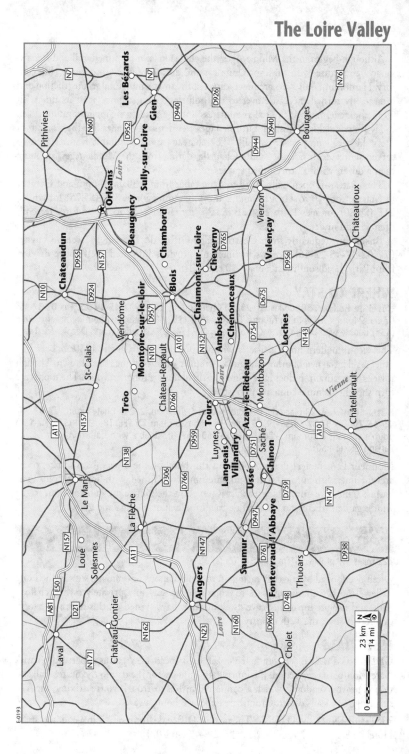

Although begun in the Middle Ages, the château is a mix of medieval and Renaissance architecture, with towering chimneys and dormers. After a fire in the 18th century, Hardouin, Louis XV's architect, directed the town's near-total reconstruction and indiscreetly turned the castle over to the homeless, who stripped it of its finery. In 1935 the government acquired the fortress and launched a major restoration. Even today it's not richly furnished, but fine tapestries depicting scenes like the worship of the golden calf now cover its walls. The château's most admirable features are two carved staircases. Inside the Sainte-Chapelle, dating from the Middle Ages, are more than a dozen 15th-century robed statues.

The château is open daily, April to September from 9:30am to 6pm and October to March from 10 to 11:30am and 2 to 5pm. Admission is 32F ($5.75) for adults, 21F ($3.80) for ages 18 to 25, 18F ($3.25) for children 12 to 18, and free for children 11 and under.

Buses run frequently from Chartres. The **Office de Tourisme,** 1 rue de Luynes (☎ **02-37-45-22-46**), keeps schedules and provides information. If you're **driving** from Paris, head southwest along A10 and N10.

WHERE TO STAY

Hôtel de Beauce. 50 rue Jallans, 28200 Châteaudun. ☎ **02-37-45-14-75.** Fax 02-37-45-87-53. 24 units, 18 with bathroom. TV TEL. 180F ($32.40) double without bathroom, 300F ($54) double with bathroom. MC, V. Parking 26F ($4.70). Closed Sun and Dec 20–Jan 14.

This clean, modern hotel is utterly without pretense. Built in the 1950s, it's set in a quiet residential neighborhood about a 2-minute walk from the edge of town. Though it lacks a restaurant, it does have a small cocktail lounge for guests only. The rooms are furnished in a simple contemporary style.

Hôtel St-Michel. 28 place du 18-Octobre and 5 rue Péan, 28200 Châteaudun. ☎ **02-37-45-15-70.** Fax 02-37-45-83-39. 19 units, 15 with bathroom. TV TEL. 185–200F ($33.30–$36) double without bathroom, 220–330F ($39.60–$59.40) double with bathroom. AE, DC, V. Parking 25F ($4.50).

Monsieur Lemenesteel Pierre, who owns this hotel on the town's main square, operates the finest inn in town. The rooms are simply furnished, with hot- and cold-water basins; eight have minibars. Breakfast is served in the lounge, in your room, or in the winter garden (there's no restaurant). Facilities include a sauna and gym.

2 Trôo

122 miles SW of Paris, 31 miles NE of Tours

Often overlooked by travelers racing on to more famous or dramatic sites in the Loire Valley, Trôo is a charming place to stop. You can stay in a privately owned château here, and explore intriguing cave dwellings that have existed on this hill in one form or another since the 12th century.

ESSENTIALS

GETTING THERE   About half a dozen high-speed TGV **trains** depart from Paris's Gare Montparnasse every day, requiring 45 minutes for the trip to the nearest rail station in nearby Vendôme, which is connected by bus to Trôo. If you're **driving,** the A10 superhighway leads directly from Paris, about 2 hours away.

VISITOR INFORMATION   The nearest **Office de Tourisme** is in Vendôme at the Hôtel de Saillant, 47 rue Poterie (☎ 02-54-77-05-07).

EXPLORING THE TOWN

Perched high over the southern bank of the Loire, Trô o boasts enough panoramic overviews to keep a shutterbug busy for hours. As you wander through the town, aim for **rue Haute,** a medieval cobblestone road stretching from place de la Mairie to the Château de la Voûte. This road takes you through the Loire Valley's densest concentration of *maisons troglodytes.* The town contains about 200 of them, and though there are others in the valley and (to a lesser degree) in other parts of France, no other site has cave houses perched on the side of a steep rocky hillside. Most of the facades, usually crafted of chiseled blocks of the *pierre de tuffeau* used for such nearby châteaux as Chambord, include 18th-century-style vaulted arcades and hints of neoclassicism. (*Pierre de tuffeau* is a soft beige limestone valued for its ability to cleave and be cut cleanly.)

The interiors extend as much as 150 feet into the mountain and maintain a relatively constant temperature, thanks to the insulating effects of the local geology. Over the generations, irregularities in the floors and walls have been leveled out to make the spaces more habitable. The more comfortable and better-maintained caves in some cases are used as secondary homes (*résidences secondaires*) for urbanites escaping Paris. The draftier, damper ones are sometimes used to store wines, and the really wet and murky ones are perfect for growing mushrooms.

Capping the hillside that supports the village is the settlement's most visible and historic church, the 12th-century **Collegiale St-Martin.** Most of it is in the Romanesque style, with some Gothic-style later additions. A few steps away is the **Butte de Trô o,** a stone-sided, much-eroded bastion that served as a military stronghold for the ancient Gauls. The view over the valley is panoramic.

WHERE TO STAY

Le Cheval Blanc (see "Where to Dine," below) also rents rooms.

✪ **Château de la Voûte.** 41800 Trô o. ☎ and fax **02-54-72-52-52.** 5 units. 380–480F ($68.40–$86.40) double; 480–580F ($86.40–$104.40) suite. Rates include breakfast. No credit cards. No children under 10.

The most elegant and aristocratic lodging in the region is this stately home, whose earlier occupants have included Henri IV and the famous antagonists Diane de Poitiers and Catherine de Médici. It was built in the 1200s, with a symmetrical *pierre de tuffeau* facade erected in the 18th century. Don't expect all the perks and services of a conventional hotel, as you'll be occupying a rented room in an upscale and genteel private home. And your charming and affable hosts, Claude Venon and Jacques Clays, prefer not to accept children under 10—the elaborate upholsteries, parquet floors, and expensive carpets will simply not handle the wear and tear. At least part of the building's street level is off-limits. The guest rooms, however, are outfitted like elegant salons, with sitting areas and many personalized, often antique touches. Breakfast is the only meal served (either in your room or in the garden), though Claude and Jacques are eager to oblige with nearby dining recommendations. The panoramic terrace affords a view over the Loire, whose banks adjoin the 8-acre park surrounding the château, and the gardens, forests, and *maisons troglodytes* of Trô o are within a short and invigorating ramble.

WHERE TO DINE

Barring an excursion to nearby Montoire-sur-le-Loir for a meal at Le Cheval Rouge, your choices for dining are limited.

Le Cheval Blanc. Rue Auguste-Arnault, 41800 Trôo. ☎ **02-54-72-58-22.** Fax 02-54-72-55-44. Reservations recommended. Main courses 90–110F ($16.20–$19.80); fixed-price menus 110F ($19.80) Mon–Fri, 165–400F ($29.70–$72) Tues–Sat. AE, MC, V. Wed–Sat noon–2pm, Tues–Sat 7:30–9pm. Closed Nov. FRENCH.

Trôo's most refined restaurant, accented with old ceiling beams and a fireplace that blazes in winter, sits at the base of the hill on which the rest of the town is located, adjacent to the Château de la Voûte. Menu items include filet of John Dory with vanilla sauce and carpaccio of scallops with truffle-flavored vinegar and three kinds of ground peppercorns. The most popular dessert is a soufflé flavored with liqueur distilled from white Alsatian wine.

In 1990 Michel and Yveline Coyault, the chefs and directors, added a second story, creating 9 cozy guest rooms with bathroom, TV, and phone. They rent at 250F to 400F ($45 to $72) for a double, depending on the view and season.

OFF THE BEATEN TRACK: A SIDE TRIP TO MONTOIRE-SUR-LE-LOIR

Far off the beaten track for those visiting the Loire and Loir valleys, Montoire-sur-le-Loir is a village with a population of 4,300 and a setting that has changed little since the early 20th century. It's 4 miles southwest of Trôo (follow A10 to reach it), 30 miles from Tours, and 31 miles from Blois (midway between the two towns). Though Montoire has one of the most infamous railway stations in France (see below), it's defunct and no longer in use. Consequently, you'll have to drive or take a train to the station in nearby Vendôme, which is a 10- to 15-minute taxi ride away (taxis are lined up at the rail station and will take you to Montoire for around 60F/$10.80), though taxis from Montoire back to Vendôme are undependable at best).

The Montoire-sur-le-Loir **Office de Tourisme** is at place Clémenceau (☎ 02-54-85-23-30).

During the early Middle Ages, this village was an important stop for pilgrims on their way to Santiago de Compostela in northwestern Spain. That's around the time that the Chapelle St-Gilles was built, and that's what everyone comes here to see. In the 1500s the village became the personal possession of the Bourbon family, who later became the rulers of France.

The town made news around the world on October 22, 1940. Adolf Hitler used a closed railway car at the town's station, surrounded by crack Nazi troops and airplane protection, for a meeting with members of the collaborationist (later Vichy) government. Why Montoire? Partly because of a rail tunnel nearby into which Hitler's train could shelter itself in the event of an air attack. As we stated above, this station is now closed.

The best way to get your bearings is to stand on the town's only bridge, **pont de Montoire,** for a view of the tree-lined banks of the Loir (a tributary of the bigger Loire). Less than a block east of the bridge is **place Clémenceau,** the commercial center of this very small town. Less than a block west is the town's most important monument, the 11th-century ✪ **Chapelle St-Gilles,** rue St-Gilles, known for its Romanesque frescoes depicting various portrayals of Christ (the earliest were painted around 1125) and its severely dignified stonework. To enter, walk uphill less than 300 yards to the administrative headquarters (the sign will say CHAPPELL ST-GILLES) at 33 bis rue St-Oustrille and get the keys (one to the wooden gate, one to the chapel's front door) from Mme Chereau (☎ 02-54-85-03-70), the longtime caretaker. (Please note that on Tuesdays the keys are available at the Café de la paix (☎ 02-54-85-10-48) on place Clémenceau. Once you enter the gate, you'll come upon fruit trees and greenery, with no other tourists vying for room to see. It will be just you and the Middle Ages. Ronsard, France's best-known lyrical poet at the time, was a prior here when this was a Benedictine priory.

You can visit the chapel daily between 8:30am and 7pm. The cost is 12F ($2.15) for adults and 8F ($1.45) for students and children under 18.

Notice the ruined fortress, **Château de Montoire,** on the hill above the chapel. Once a prized possession for whoever controlled this area, it's closed to sightseers and remains only as a brooding reminder of France's feudal age.

If you have time, less than a mile from Montoire is the hamlet of **Lavardin** (take D108 west). Though there's little to see other than a semiruined château that's almost always closed for renovations, you'll find charming, well-tended houses and architecture that has changed little since around 1850. You'll feel as though you've walked into a postcard photo. On Lavardin's outskirts, housed in a limestone cave, is **Le Caveau** (☎ **02-54-85-31-11**), a reliable lunch stop open from June to September. Since its hours depend on the whims of the owners, call first to make a reservation.

WHERE TO STAY & DINE

Le Cheval Rouge. Place du Maréchal-Foch, 41800 Montoire-sur-le-Loir. ☎ **02-54-85-07-05.** Fax 02-54-85-17-42. Fixed-price menus 128–245F ($23.05–$44.10). AE, MC, V. Thurs–Tues noon–4pm, Thurs–Mon 7:30–9pm. FRENCH.

Built in 1870 and frequently enlarged and upgraded since, Le Cheval Rouge is a *restaurant avec chambres,* so more emphasis is placed on the cuisine than on the relatively simple rooms. Menu items include a fresh foie gras of duckling and Loire Valley whitefish (*sandre*) or turbot in a beurre blanc (white-butter) sauce. Salmon is smoked on the premises and always makes for a succulent appetizer.

There are 15 comfortable guest rooms, all with phones and bathrooms and 9 with TVs. Doubles rent for 220F to 245F ($39.60 to $44.10), a great bargain considering the many more expensive contenders nearby.

3 Tours

144 miles SW of Paris, 70 miles SW of Orléans

Though it doesn't boast a major château, Tours, at the junction of the Loire and Cher rivers, is the traditional center for exploring the valley. The devout en route to Santiago de Compostela in northwest Spain once stopped off here to pay homage at the tomb of St. Martin, the Apostle of Gaul, who was bishop of Tours in the 4th century. One of the most significant conflicts in world history, the 732 Battle of Tours, checked the Arab advance into Gaul.

Tours, with a population of 130,000, is a major city, known for its fine food and wine. Because many of its buildings were bombed in World War II, ugly 20th-century apartment towers have taken the place of stately châteaux. However, since Tours is at the doorstep of some of the most magnificent châteaux in France, it makes a good base from which to explore. Most Loire Valley towns are rather sleepy, but Tours is where the action is centered, as you'll see by its noisy streets and cafes. One-quarter of the residents are students, who add a vibrant, active touch to a soulless commercial enclave.

ESSENTIALS

Tours is a 55-minute TGV **train** ride from Paris's Montparnasse. Nearly 10 trains per day make this run, costing 289F to 406F ($52 to $73.10) one-way. Trains arrive at place du Maréchal-Leclerc, 3 rue Edouard-Vaillant (☎ **02-47-20-50-50** for information and schedules). If you're **driving,** take highway A10 to Orléans, and continue on to Tours.

The **Office de Tourisme** is at 78 rue Bernard-Palissy (☎ **08-36-35-35-39**).

EXPLORING THE CITY

The heart of town is **place Jean-Jaurès.** The principal street (the valley's Champs-Elysées) is **rue Nationale,** running north to the Loire River. Head along rue du Commerce and rue du Grand-Marché to reach **Vieux Tours/Vieille Ville (Old Town).**

In the pedestrian area of **rue de Bordeaux,** starting essentially to the right of the magnificent train station (when you're facing the station) and running to rue Nationale, you'll find dozens of mall-type shops and department stores selling clothes, shoes, jewelry, leather goods, and the like. Up rue Nationale toward the river are more stores, a little more upscale when it comes to clothing, as well as a small modern mall with chain boutiques. Rue Nationale continues all the way across the river, but turn left on **rue du Commerce** toward the old town center. You'll want to explore this district's small streets and courtyards for regional specialties, books, toys, and craft items. A hotbed for antiques is on the other side of rue Nationale, heading toward the cathedral along **rue de la Scellerie.** If you like to search through secondhand items, place des Victoires is the place to be every Wednesday and Saturday from 8am to noon for an **open-air flea market.**

Cathédrale St-Gatien. 5 place de la Cathédrale. ☎ **02-47-71-21-00.** Free admission. Daily 9am–7pm.

This cathedral, which honors a 3rd-century evangelist, has a Flamboyant Gothic facade flanked by towers with bases from the 12th century, though the lanterns are Renaissance. The choir is from the 13th century, with new additions built each century through the 16th. Sheltered inside is the handsome 16th-century tomb of Charles VIII and Anne de Bretagne's two children. Some of the glorious stained-glass windows are from the 13th century.

Musée des Beaux-Arts. 18 place François-Sicard. ☎ **02-47-05-68-73.** Admission 30F ($5.40) adults, 15F ($2.70) children. Wed–Mon 9am–12:45pm and 2–6pm.

This fine provincial museum is housed in the Palais des Archevêques, which would be worth a visit just to see its lovely rooms and gardens. However, there are old masters as well, including works by Degas, Delacroix, Rembrandt, and Boucher. The impressive sculpture collection includes works by Houdon and Bourdelle. You can tour the gardens for free daily from 8am to 8pm.

Musée de l'Historial de la Touraine. Château Royal, 25 av. André-Malraux. ☎ **02-47-61-02-95.** Admission 35F ($6.30) adults, 20F ($3.60) children 7–15, free for children 6 and under. July–Aug daily 9am–6:30pm; May 16–June and Sept–Oct daily 9am–noon and 2–6pm; Nov–Mar 15 daily 2–5:30pm.

This museum traces the tormented tides of change that have swept over the Loire Valley. It depicts the region's history in 31 moderately kitschy but forcefully evocative scenes with 165 wax figures. They follow 1,500 years of interaction between locals and such personalities as Charlemagne and his queen, Luitgarde; St. Martin and assorted bishops; Clovis, king of the Visigoths; and Joan of Arc. Other scenes simulate the grisly death of Henry V and the hangings of the Huguenots during the Wars of Religion.

WHERE TO STAY

The most sumptuous rooms, as well as the finest cuisine, are found at the **Parc de Belmont** (see "Where to Dine," below).

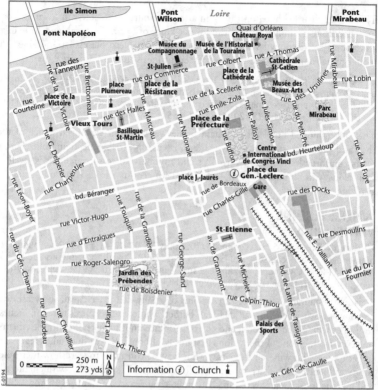

Hôtel Alliance. 292 av. de Grammont, 37200 Tours. ☎ **02-47-28-00-80.** Fax 02-47-27-77-61. 125 units. A/C MINIBAR TV TEL. 450F ($81) double; from 600F ($108) suite. AE, DC, MC, V. Bus: 1, 2, 5, or 9. Head for place Jean-Jaurès, then take av. Grammont south, following the signs that say TOURS SUD.

Located about a mile south of the town center, this is a large, modern hotel, despite an exterior designed to appear much older. A member of a respected nationwide chain of three-star hotels, it's decorated in grand siècle style and boasts a reception area with chandeliers and marble columns. The rooms are painted in pleasing tones of soft oranges or greens and contain a blend of modern pieces and antique reproductions. There's plenty of open space, a French garden, and a pool. The hotel has a distinguished restaurant with a terrace, and breakfast and drinks are served in a sitting area.

Hôtel du Manoir. 2 rue Traversière, 37000 Tours. ☎ **02-47-05-37-37.** Fax 02-47-05-16-00. 20 units. TV TEL. 270–290F ($48.60–$52.20) double. DC, MC, V.

On a quiet street near the train station and many shops and restaurants, this 19th-century residence has recently been renovated to provide guests with a comfortable stay. The cheerful reception area, with its marble tile and rich woodwork, is a good indication of the quality of the guest rooms. Though small to average in size, all units have big windows that let in lots of light, affording views of the residential neighborhood or the hotel's courtyard. Most have simple furnishings, but a few showcase decorative touches like wall sconces, antique armoires, and custom bed linens.

Hôtel de l'Univers. 5 bd. Heurteloup, 37000 Tours. ☎ **02-47-05-37-12.** Fax 02-47-61-51-80. 85 units. TV TEL. 780F ($140.40) double. AE, DC, MC, V. Parking 50F ($9).

This highly regarded hotel on the main artery of Tours is the oldest in town and has hosted Edison, Hemingway, and the former kings of Spain, Portugal, and Romania. The rooms are decorated with both modern and Art Deco pieces. La Touraine, the main dining room (open daily), serves excellent meals from a fixed-price menu.

Le Central. 21 rue Berthelot, 37000 Tours. ☎ **02-47-05-46-44.** Fax 02-47-66-10-26. 40 units, 2 with sink and bidet only, 38 with bathroom (tub or shower). TEL. 180F ($32.40) double with sink and bidet only, 350F ($63) double with shower, 400F ($72) double with tub. AE, DC, MC, V. Parking 40F ($7.20). Bus: 1, 4, or 5.

This old-fashioned hotel off the main boulevard is within walking distance of the river and cathedral, surrounded by gardens, lawns, and trees. The Tremouilles family offers comfortable rooms (38 with TVs and minibars) at reasonable rates, as well as two salons with reproductions of 18th- and 19th-century pieces. A parking garage is available.

WHERE TO DINE
VERY EXPENSIVE

✪ **Pare de Belmont.** 57 rue Groison, 37100 Tours. ☎ **02-47-41-41-11.** Reservations recommended. Main courses 200–320F ($36–$57.60); fixed-price menus 380–780F ($68.40–$140.40). AE, DC, MC, V. Apr–Oct Tues–Sun noon–2pm, daily 7:30–10pm; Nov–Mar Tues–Sun noon–2pm, Tues–Sat 7:30–10pm. FRENCH.

This fine restaurant housed in three rooms of a 19th-century château showcases the creations of two-Michelin-star chef Jean Bardet, who considers meals here "an orchestration of wines, alcohol, food, and cigars." You need not partake of all four elements, however, to enjoy one of the region's best meals, although Bardet does take great pains to get to know his wines and cigars. In this way, he continues to learn how their roles subtly influence each of his dishes, including favorites like wild duck with chanterelle and gigrolle mushrooms served in chanterelle-cream sauce and stew of Breton lobster and shellfish seasoned with fresh ginger and lime. The dining rooms, with black-and-gold Napoléon III furnishings, look out onto the surrounding 7½ acres of English gardens and park. Fireplaces warm the rooms in cooler months, and fresh flowers are a staple year-round.

The rest of the château has been transformed into a truly luxury-class hotel and is the domain of Bardet's wife, Sophie. The spacious guest rooms are individually decorated and invite relaxation with their soft pastel walls, high ceilings, cozy fireplaces, and antique furnishings. Some even have private balconies that look out onto the gardens. A double ranges from 750F to 1,050F ($135 to $189); suites begin at 1,500F ($270).

EXPENSIVE

✪ **La Roche le Roy.** 55 rte. St-Avertin. ☎ **02-47-27-22-00.** Reservations recommended. Main courses 110–160F ($19.80–$28.80); fixed-price menus 160–350F ($28.80–$63) at lunch, 200–350F ($36–$63) at dinner. AE, MC, V. Tues–Fri and Sun 12:15–1:45pm, Tues–Sat 7:15–10pm. Closed the first 3 weeks in Aug. Follow the signs pointing to St-Avertin-Vierzon; the restaurant is beside that road, on the southern periphery of Tours. FRENCH.

One of the hottest chefs in town, Alain Couturier blends new and old culinary techniques at this restaurant in a 15th-century manor 2 miles south of the town center. Couturier's repertoire includes scalloped foie gras with lentils, fresh cod with saffron cream, and pan-fried scallops with a truffle vinaigrette. His masterpiece is suprême of pigeon with "roughly textured" sauce. For dessert, try his mélange of seasonal fruit with sabayon made from Vouvray Valley wine.

MODERATE

La Rôtisserie Tourangelle. 23 rue du Commerce. ☎ **02-47-05-71-21.** Reservations required. Main courses 98–185F ($17.65–$33.30); fixed-price menus 95–195F ($17.10–$35.10). AE, DC, MC, V. Tues–Sat 12:15–1:45pm and 7:30–9:45pm, Sun noon–1:30pm. Bus: 1, 4, or 5. FRENCH.

This local favorite offers solidly reliable traditional food and a staff that refuses to be hurried. In summer you can dine on a terrace overlooking a garden, but there's not much to see. It's better to concentrate on the changing menu, which may include homemade foie gras, snails in red-wine sauce, and a local whitefish (*sandre*) caught in the Loire. Regional ingredients mix well with the local wines, as exemplified by pike-perch with sabayon and magrêt de canard (duck) served with a "jam" of red Chinon wine. Dessert might be strawberry parfait with raspberry coulis. Our only criticism: The service could be a little better.

Les Tuffeaux. 19 rue Lavoisier. ☎ **02-47-47-19-89.** Reservations required. Main courses 85–98F ($15.30–$17.65); fixed-price menus 110F ($19.80) Mon–Fri, 110–200F ($19.80–$36) Mon–Sat. AE, MC, V. Tues–Sat noon–1:45pm, Mon–Sat 7–9:30pm. Bus: 1, 4, or 5. FRENCH.

This 18th-century house contains one of the best restaurants in Tours, although the cuisine at La Rôtisserie Tourangelle (see above) has a slight edge. A meal might consist of thyme-flavored langoustines soup, suprême of pike-perch, filet of sole with asparagus, roast pigeon with pink grapefruit, and sumptuous desserts. Though the 110F ($19.80) fixed-price menu isn't available on Saturday, try this bargain meal on any other night, as it's the best value in town. Chef Gildas Marsollier faithfully prepares the classics but also experiments with dishes like lamb sweetbreads with asparagus and filet of sea bass with *salsify* (a tubular vegetable).

INEXPENSIVE

Le Relais Buré. 1 place de la Résistance. ☎ **02-47-05-67-74.** Reservations not required. Main courses 65–120F ($11.70–$21.60); fixed-price menu (Mon–Fri only) 98F ($17.65). AE, DC, MC, V. Daily noon–3pm and 7pm–midnight. Bus: 1, 4, or 5. FRENCH.

A 5-minute walk east of the center of Tours, this loud and likable upscale brasserie specializes in shellfish and regional recipes. It has a busy bar and a front terrace, with tables scattered inside on the street level and mezzanine. Menu items include six well-flavored versions of sauerkraut (including the traditional version and a more imaginative variation with seafood), a wide choice of grilled meats (like peppery steak au poivre), and a jarret of pork. Begin your meal with foie gras or smoked salmon, both prepared in-house, and end with one of the tempting array of desserts. If the cassolette of scallops appears as a special offering of the day, go for it.

NEARBY ACCOMMODATIONS & DINING

✪ **Château d'Artigny.** Rte. d'Azay-le-Rideau, 37250 Montbazon. ☎ **02-47-34-30-30.** Fax 02-47-34-30-39. E-mail: chartartigny@relaischateaux.fr. 27 units. TV TEL. 1,340–1,670F ($241.20–$300.60) double; from 2,900F ($522) suite. Half board 1,020–1,890F ($183.60–$340.20) per person extra. AE, MC, V. Closed Nov 24–Jan 10. From Tours, take N10 south for 7 miles to Montbazon, then take D17 a mile southeast.

This château was built for the perfume king François Coty, who lived and entertained lavishly here. The drawing room and corridors are classically furnished with fine antiques, Louis XV–style chairs, and bronze statuary. The grounds contain acres of private park and a large formal garden with reflecting pool. The guest rooms are furnished in various periods, with many antiques. Weekend soirees and musical evenings are popular, and superb cuisine is served in the gilded dining room.

Château de Beaulieu. 67 rue de Beaulieu, 37300 Joué-les-Tours. ☎ **02-47-53-20-26.** Fax 02-47-53-84-20. 19 units. A/C MINIBAR TV TEL. 450–750F ($81–$135) double. Half board 850–1,180F ($153–$212.40). AE, MC, V. Take D86 from Tours, then D207 for Beaulieu, 4½ miles southwest of Tours.

At this secluded 18th-century country estate's restaurant and three-star hotel, you can experience the lifestyle of another era. Beyond the formal entrance, a double curving stairway leads to the reception hall. The rooms have mahogany and chestnut furniture, decorative fireplaces, and good plumbing. Nine are in the château (we recommend these); the others, a bit more sterile, are housed in a recently constructed pavilion nearby.

Dining: The owner, Jean-Pierre Lozay, is an excellent chef, so at least try to visit for a meal. The dining room's French windows open onto views of the gardens. Fixed-price menus run 195F to 480F ($35.10 to $86.40), and à la carte meals feature traditional French specialties. Reservations are recommended.

Amenities: A park with public pool (open from July to September) and four tennis courts are across the road; a terrace also overlooks the garden.

TOURS AFTER DARK

Long a student town, Tours has a lively young population that demands a hip night scene. Even during summer, when most students have fled the city, the younger crowd still rules the hot spots. **Place Plumereau** (often shortened to "place Plume"), a large square of medieval buildings, now houses a riot of restaurants and bars. During the warmer months, the square explodes with tables and umbrellas, which quickly fill with people who like to look and be looked at—this is definitely the cruisy place to begin an evening out.

The most interesting clubs in and around place Plumereau include **Blues Rock Café,** 24 rue de la Monnaire (☎ 02-47-61-57-97), with its classically American memorabilia and young crowd. In the triple-decker bar building of **Le Pharoan, Louis XIV,** and **Duke Ellington,** place Plumereau (☎ 02-47-05-77-17), the basement level gyrates to techno, the Louis XIV street level offers a more middle-of-the-road bar scene, and the top level operates a cool blues and jazz club. And perhaps the hottest place in town is **L'Excalibur,** 35 rue Briçonnet (☎ 02-47-64-76-78), with its disco beat and ultramodern video system.

If you're young, gay, and like to dance, check out **Club 71 la Gamme,** 71 rue Courtline (☎ 02-47-37-01-54). You'll want to drive here or walk in a group, as it's on a rather dark street in the middle of a questionable neighborhood. Inside, though, is a lively disco with a local male crowd that really packs the place on weekends. The dance floor, at the far end of the club, has plenty of mirrors, flashing lights, and smoke.

4 Loches

160 miles SW of Paris, 25 miles SE of Tours

Forever linked to legendary beauty Agnès Sorel, Loches is the *cité médiévale* of the valley, situated in the hills on the banks of the Indre. Known as the acropolis of the Loire, the château and its satellite buildings form a complex called the ✪ **Cité Royale.** The House of Anjou, from which the Plantagenets descended, owned the castle from 886 to 1205. The kings of France occupied it from the mid-13th century until Charles IX became king in 1560.

Château de Loches, 5 place Charles-VII (☎ **02-47-59-01-32**), is remembered for the *belle des belles* (beauty of beauties), Agnès Sorel. Inside is her tomb, where two angels guard her velvet cushion. In 1777 the tomb was opened, but all that remained of the dazzling 15th-century beauty were a set of dentures and some locks of hair. Maid of honor to Isabelle de Lorraine, she was singled out by Charles VII to be his mistress and had great influence on the king until her mysterious death. Afterward, Fouquet painted her as a practically topless Virgin Mary, with a disgruntled Charles VII looking on. (The original masterpiece is in Antwerp, but the château has a copy.) The château also contains the oratory of Anne de Bretagne, decorated with sculpted ermine tails. One of its most outstanding treasures is *The Passion* triptych (1485) from the Fouquet school.

You can visit the apartments without a guide daily, July to mid-September from 9am to 7pm, mid-March to June and mid- to the end of September from 9am to noon and 2 to 6pm, and October to mid-March from 9am to noon and 2 to 5pm. The dungeon opens 30 minutes after the castle and closes 1 hour after the castle. One ticket for both costs 30F ($5.40) for adults, 20F ($3.60) for seniors, and 17F ($3.05) for children.

The château presents a *son-et-lumière* (sound-and-light) show depicting the exploits of Joan of Arc on the second and fourth Friday and Saturday in July at 10:30pm and on every Friday and Saturday in August at 10pm. Shows begin promptly and last 1½ hours, with tickets costing 70F ($12.60) for adults and 40F ($7.20) for children 5 to 12; children 4 and under enter free.

You can visit the ancient **keep** (*donjon*), reached along the mail du Donjon, of the comtes d'Anjou during the same hours as the château. The **Round Tower** of Louis XI contains rooms formerly used for torture; a favorite method involved suspending the victim in an iron cage. In the 15th century the duke of Milan, Ludovico Sforza, was imprisoned in the Martelet, and he painted frescoes on the walls to pass the time; he died here in 1508.

Nearby, the Romanesque **Collegiale St-Ours** (Collegiate Church of St. Ours), 1 rue Thomas-Pactius (☎ 02-47-59-07-98), spans the 10th to the 15th centuries. Its portal is richly decorated with sculpted figures, unfortunately damaged but still attractive. Monumental stone pyramids (*dubes*) surmount the nave; the carving on the west door is exceptional. The church is open daily, April to October from 9am to 7pm.

Finally, you may want to walk the **ramparts** and enjoy the view of the town, including a 15th-century gate and Renaissance inns.

Four **buses** run here daily from Tours, costing 43F ($7.75) for the one-way, 50-minute trip. If you **drive** from Tours, take N143 southeast to Loches.

The **Office de Tourisme** is near the bus station on place Wermelskirchen (☎ 02-47-59-07-98).

WHERE TO STAY & DINE

✪ **Grand Hôtel de France.** 6 rue Picois, 37600 Loches. ☎ **02-47-59-00-32.** Fax 02-47-59-28-66. 19 units. TV TEL. 250–380F ($45–$68.40) double. DC, V. Parking 25F ($4.50). Closed Jan 5–Feb 13.

Charmingly French and on a par with the George-Sand (see below), this hotel has many rooms overlooking an inner courtyard. The rates are low for the area, and English is spoken. Enjoy your meals in the petite dining room with paneling and crystal, or under parasols in the courtyard. Three excellent fixed-price meals are offered: 84F ($15.10), 110F ($19.80), and 160F ($28.80). The restaurant is open daily in July and August but is closed Sunday nights and Mondays the rest of the year.

Hôtel George-Sand. 39 rue Quintefol, 37600 Loches. ☎ **02-47-59-39-74.** Fax 02-47-91-55-75. 20 units. TV TEL. 260–550F ($46.80–$99) double; 650F ($117) suite. MC, V.

Loaded with faithful reproductions of medieval tapestries, this tastefully decorated inn, a 5-minute walk from the town center and a few steps from the base of the château, dates from the 15th century. George Sand used to stash her luggage here before trekking up the hill to visit her lover, Chopin, who resided in the town's château. The inn, owned by M. and Mme Fortin, was completely renovated in 1995. Several of the rooms look out over a tributary of the Indre; the quieter ones are at the rear.

Dining: This Logis de France hotel has a restaurant with a view of the Indre. A la carte dishes feature Touraine cuisine, including fondue of goat with confit of leeks, filet of pike-perch (a river fish) in beurre blanc sauce, and breast of duck George Sand. The food is very good, and all breads and pastries are baked fresh on the premises daily.

5 Villandry

157 miles SW of Paris, 20 miles NE of Chinon, 11 miles W of Tours, 5 miles E of Azay-le-Rideau

The extravagant 16th-century-style gardens of the Renaissance ✪ **Château de Villandry,** 37510 Villandry (☎ **02-47-50-02-09**), are celebrated throughout the Touraine. Forming a trio of superimposed cloisters with a water garden on the highest level, the gardens were purchased in a decaying state and restored by the Spanish doctor/scientist Joachim Carvallo, the present owner's grandfather.

The grounds contain 10½ miles of boxwood sculpture, which the gardeners must cut to style in only 2 weeks each September. Every square of the gardens is like a geometric mosaic. The borders represent the many faces of love: tender, tragic (represented by daggers), and crazy (evoked by a labyrinth that doesn't go anywhere). Pink tulips and dahlias suggest sweet love; red, tragic; and yellow, unfaithful. Crazy love is symbolized by all colors. The vine arbors, citrus hedges, and shady walks keep six men busy full-time. One garden contains all the common French vegetables except the potato, which wasn't known in France in the 16th century.

Originally, a feudal castle stood at Villandry, but in 1536 Jean Lebreton, François I's chancellor, built the present château, whose buildings form a U and are surrounded by a two-sided moat. Near the gardens is a terrace from which you can see the small village and its 12th-century church.

Admission to the gardens including a tour of the château costs 45F ($8.10). A separate visit to the gardens, without a guide, costs 32F ($5.75). The château is open from mid-February to mid-November, and guided tours in French only (English leaflets are available) are conducted daily from 9am to 6:30pm. The gardens are open daily from 9am to sunset.

Unfortunately, Villandry doesn't have bus service from Tours. Rent a **bike** and ride along the Cher, or **drive,** following D7 from Tours.

WHERE TO STAY & DINE

Le Cheval Rouge. Villandry, 37510 Joué-les-Tours. ☎ **02-47-50-02-07.** Fax 02-47-50-08-77. Reservations recommended. Fixed-price menus 95–250F ($17.10–$45). MC, V. Tues–Sun noon–2pm and 7:30–9pm. Closed late Jan to early Mar and Mon unless it's a holiday. FRENCH.

In spite of the uptight management and stiff welcome, this is the major lunch choice near the château. Many of the famous gardens of the château are visible from the dining-room windows, and the Cher flows 100 yards away. Specialties include lobster Thermidor and medallions of veal with morels. The food is competent enough, but chances are this won't be one of your most memorable meals in the Loire.

This inn also rents 20 comfortable rooms, 18 with bathroom. A double goes for 200F to 250F ($36 to $45), a triple for 400F ($72).

6 Langeais

161 miles SW of Paris, 16 miles W of Tours

Château de Langeais, 37130 Langeais (☎ **02-47-96-72-60**), is a true medieval fortress, a formidable gray pile that dominates the town. It's one of the few châteaux actually on the Loire. The facade is forbidding, but once you cross the drawbridge and go inside, you'll find the apartments so richly decorated that the severe effect is softened. The castle dates from the 9th century, when the dreaded Black Falcon erected the first dungeon in Europe, the ruins of which remain to this day. The present structure was built in 1465. The interior is well preserved and furnished thanks to Jacques Siegfried, who not only restored it over 20 years but also bequeathed it to the Institut de France in 1904.

On December 6, 1491, Anne de Bretagne "arrived at Langeais carried in a litter decked with gold cloth, dressed in a gown of black trimmed with sable. Her wedding gown of gold cloth was ornamented with 160 sables." Her marriage to Charles VIII was to be Langeais's golden hour. Their symbols—scallops, fleurs-de-lis, and ermine—set the motif for the Guard Room, while seven tapestries known as the Valiant Knights cover the walls of the Wedding Chamber.

In a bedchamber known sardonically as "the Crucifixion," the 15th-century black-oak four-poster bed is reputed to be one of the earliest known. The room takes its odd name from a tapestry of the Virgin and St. John standing on flower-bedecked ground. A rare Flemish tapestry hangs in the Monsieur's Room. The Chapel Hall was built by joining two stories under a ceiling of Gothic arches. In the Luini Room is a large 1522 fresco by that artist, removed from a chapel on Lake Maggiore, Italy; it depicts St. Francis of Assisi and St. Elizabeth of Hungary with Mary and Joseph. The Byzantine Virgin in the Drawing Room is thought to be an early work of Cimabue, the Florentine artist. Finally, the Tapestry of the Thousand Flowers is an ageless celebration of spring, a joyous riot of growth, a symbol of life's renewal.

The château is open daily, July 15 to August from 9am to 9pm, April 1 to July 14 and September 1 to 30 from 9am to 6:30pm, October 1 to November 2 from 9am to 12:30pm and 2 to 6:30pm, and November 3 to March 31 from 9am to noon and 2 to 5pm (closed Christmas). Admission is 40F ($7.20) for adults, 20F ($3.60) for children, and 35F ($6.30) for seniors.

Eighteen **trains** per day make a stop here en route from either Tours or Saumur. For train schedules and information, call ☎ **08-36-35-35-39.** If you **drive** from Tours, take N152 southwest to Langeais.

The **Bureau du Tourisme** is at place du 14 Julliet (☎ **02-47-96-58-22**).

WHERE TO STAY & DINE

Hosten et Restaurant Langeais (Logis de France). 2 rue Gambetta, 37130 Langeais. ☎ **02-47-96-82-12.** Fax 02-47-96-56-72. 11 units. 280–450F ($50.40–$81) double; 550F ($99) suite. AE, MC, V. Closed Jan 11–Feb 8.

This country inn offers an informal atmosphere and excellent food. The restaurant is expensive (and has received many honors), but the hotel charges reasonable rates for its well-furnished, comfortable rooms. Guests dine indoors or at tables set in the open courtyard under umbrellas and flowering trees. The *menu de prestige* includes escalope of salmon with sorrel and *homard* (lobster) *Cardinal.* The desserts may include soufflé au Grand-Marnier and *charlotte au coulis de framboises* (raspberries). A meal costs 125F to 245F ($22.50 to $44.10). The restaurant is open for lunch Wednesday through Monday and for dinner Wednesday through Sunday.

La Duchesse Anne. 10 rue de Tours, 37130 Langeais. ☎ **02-47-96-82-03.** 15 units. TV TEL. 294–310F ($52.90–$55.80) double. MC, V.

On the eastern outskirts of town, this hotel was conceived in the 18th century as a coaching inn, providing food and shelter for people and horses. What used to be a covered carriageway is now an entry for cars, piercing the white facade with a tunnellike aperture that leads to a courtyard. The clean rooms are simply furnished but comfortable. Garden tables are set out for dining, and there's a holding tank for the fresh trout that's one of the house specialties. The cuisine reflects the traditions of the Loire Valley and includes flavorful but not experimental dishes such as fresh salmon with beurre blanc sauce or guinea fowl with Bourgueil wine sauce. Fixed-price meals range from 78F to 210F ($14.05 to $37.80). From March to October, the restaurant is open for lunch and dinner daily; the rest of the year, it's closed Sunday night and all day Monday.

7 Azay-le-Rideau

162 miles SW of Paris, 13 miles SW of Tours

Its machicolated towers and blue-slate roof pierced with dormers shimmer in the moat, creating a reflection like one in a Monet painting. But the defensive medieval look is all for show: the Renaissance ✪ **Château d'Azay-le-Rideau,** 37190 Azay-le-Rideau (☎ **02-47-45-42-04**), was created as a residence at an idyllic spot on the Indre River. Gilles Berthelot, François I's finance minister, commissioned the castle while his spendthrift wife, Philippa, supervised its construction. So elegant was the creation that the Chevalier King grew immensely jealous. In time Berthelot was forced to flee, and the château reverted to the king. He didn't live here, however, but granted it to "friends of the Crown." It became the property of the state in 1905.

Before entering, circle the château and note the perfect proportions of the crowning achievement of the Renaissance in the Touraine. Check out its most fancifully ornate feature, the bay enclosing a grand stairway with a straight flight of steps. The Renaissance interior is a virtual museum.

From the second-floor Royal Chamber, look out at the gardens. This bedroom, also known as the Green Room, is believed to have sheltered Louis XIII. The adjoining Red Chamber contains a portrait gallery that includes a *Lady in Red* and Diane de Poitiers (Henri II's favorite) in her bath.

The château is open daily, July to August from 9am to 7pm, April to June and September to October from 9:30am to 6pm, and November to March from 9:30am to 12:30pm and 2 to 5:30pm. Admission is 32F ($5.75) for adults and 21F ($3.80) for children.

The château presents a nightly *son-et-lumière* (sound-and-light) show from May to July at 10:30pm, in August at 10pm, and in September at 9:30pm. Shows begin promptly, with tickets costing 60F ($10.80) for adults and 35F ($6.30) for children.

Just 4½ miles from Azay-le-Rideau, you can visit the **hometown of Honoré de Balzac,** where he wrote *The Lily of the Valley.* The **Château de Saché** (☎ **02-47-26-86-50**) houses a Balzac museum, with his bedroom preserved as it was when he lived here. A collection of Balzac's scribblings, first editions, etchings, letters, political cartoons, and even a copy of Rodin's famous sculpture of the controversial writer are on display. The castle is open from July to August, daily from 10am to 6:30pm; March 15 to May 14 and in September, daily from 9:30am to noon and 2 to 6pm; May 15 to June 30, daily from 10am to 6pm; February to March 14 and in October and November, daily from 9:30am to noon and 2 to 5pm. Admission is 23F ($4.15) for adults, 17F ($3.05) for children 7 to 18, and free for children 6 and under. From Azay-le-Rideau, take D17 east.

Seven **trains** or **buses** run daily from Tours or Chinon (trip time: 30 minutes), costing 27F ($4.85) one-way. If you're **driving** from Tours, take D759 southwest to Azay-le-Rideau.

The **Syndicat d'Initiative** (tourist office) is on place de l'Europe (☎ 02-47-45-44-40).

WHERE TO STAY

Le Grand Monarque. 3 place de la République, 37190 Azay-le-Rideau. ☎ 02-47-45-40-08. Fax 02-47-45-46-25. 26 units. TV TEL. 440–650F ($79.20–$117) double. AE, MC, V. Closed Dec 15–Jan 31.

The exterior of this hotel, conveniently located less than 500 feet from the château, is covered by a coat of lush ivy that seems to protect the interior from the shallow modern world. As you enter the rustic French manor house with its heavy limestone walls and dark exposed ceiling beams, you'll feel transported back to a different era. The large guest rooms are accented with deep-red tones and outfitted with antique furnishings. You can enjoy a casual evening in the lounge area or in the hotel restaurant's warm dining room, whose fireplace you'd expect to see in the château across the way. During warmer months, guests can also dine out on the private courtyard terrace.

WHERE TO DINE

We also recommend the restaurant at **Le Grand Monarque** (see above).

L'Aigle d'Or. 10 av. Adélaïde-Riché. ☎ 02-47-45-24-58. Reservations recommended. Main courses 72–110F ($12.95–$19.80); fixed-price menus 100F ($18) at lunch, 150–280F ($27–$50.40) at dinner. MC, V. Thurs–Tues noon–2pm and 7:30–9pm. Closed Feb, Dec 10–25, and Sun and Tues nights off-season. FRENCH.

This longtime favorite of visitors to the château offers an often charming welcome, professional service, and the best food in Azay. The cuisine has notably improved, beginning with the selection of appetizers, which range from foie gras to a mousseline of scallops with a crayfish coulis. Main dishes often feature fresh fish from the Loire with regional wine, filet of beef cooked in Chinon wine, and tender pigeon decorated with celeriac and truffles. The desserts are prepared fresh daily.

8 Chinon

176 miles SW of Paris, 30 miles SW of Tours, 19 miles SW of Langeais

Remember in the film *Joan of Arc* when Ingrid Bergman sought out the dauphin as he tried to conceal himself among his courtiers? The action took place in real life at the Château de Chinon, one of the oldest fortress-châteaux in France. Charles VII, mockingly known as the King of Bourges, centered his government at Chinon from 1429 to 1450. In 1429, with the English besieging Orléans, the Maid of Orléans, that "messenger from God," prevailed upon the weak dauphin to give her an army. The rest is history. The seat of French power stayed at Chinon until the end of the Hundred Years War.

Today Chinon remains a tranquil little village known mainly for the delightful red wine produced here. After you visit the attractions, we recommend taking a long walk along the Vienne River; definitely stop to taste the wine at one of Chinon's terraced cafes.

ESSENTIALS

GETTING THERE   Three **trains** arrive daily from Tours (trip time: 1 hour), costing 46F to 70F ($8.30 to $12.60) one-way. For tickets and train information, call ☎ 08-36-35-35-39 in Tours. If you're **driving** from Tours, take D759 southwest through Azay-le-Rideau to Chinon.

VISITOR INFORMATION   The **Office de Tourisme** is at 12 rue Voltaire (☎ 02-47-93-17-85).

SPECIAL EVENTS   The best time to visit is the first weekend in August, for the celebrated **Marché Médiéval** (☎ 02-47-93-17-85 for information). This fair, marked by overtones of both the Middle Ages and the Renaissance, celebrates native son Rabelais with presentations of early music along with arts and crafts. The food is bountiful, and the wine flows freely as the whole town devotes itself to revelry.

SEEING THE TOWN & CHATEAU

Situated on the banks of the Vienne, the town of Chinon consists of winding streets and turreted houses, many built in the 15th and 16th centuries in the heyday of the court. For the best view, drive across the river and turn right onto **quai Danton.** From that vantage point you'll have the best perspective, seeing the castle in relation to the village and the river. The gables and towers make Chinon look like a toy village. The most typical street is **rue Voltaire,** lined with 15th- and 16th-century town houses. At no. 44, Richard the Lion-Hearted died on April 6, 1199, from a mortal wound suffered during the siege of Chalus in Limousin. The **Grand Carroi,** in the heart of Chinon, served as the crossroads of the Middle Ages.

In between châteaux visits and vineyard tastings, you may want to pop in to **Fleurisson Production,** 5 rue de l'Olive (☎ 02-47-93-21-79). Expect a French twist to their grapes—they make not vino but jam (*confiture de vin*). Ask about purchasing products at the vineyard.

As for wine, Chinon is famous for the reds and whites that crop up on prestigious wine lists around the world. These are sold in supermarkets and wine shops throughout the region, but the two most interesting stores are maintained by families who have been in the business longer than anyone can remember. At **Caves Plouzeau,** 94 rue Haute-St-Maurice (☎ 02-47-93-16-34), the 12th-century cellars were dug to provide building blocks for the foundations of the nearby château. The present management dates from 1929, and bottles of red or white are 30F to 45F ($5.40 to $8.10). You're welcome to climb down to the massive cellars, whose presence in the center of urban Chinon are a medieval oddity even by French standards. It's open for wine sales and visits Tuesday through Saturday from 9:30am to noon and 2pm to 6pm and Sunday from 10am to 2pm.

The cellars at ✪ **Couly-Dutheil,** 12 rue Diderot (☎ 02-47-97-20-20), are suitably medieval, many carved into the rock undulating through the area's forests. This company produces largely Chinon wines (mostly reds), though they're justifiably proud of the Borgeuil and St-Nicolas de Borgeuil, whose popularity in the North American market has grown in recent years. Tours of the caves and a dégustation des vins require an advance phone call and cost 20F ($3.60) per person. Visits are conducted Monday through Friday from 8am to noon and 2 to 5:45pm.

Château de Chinon. ☎ **02-47-93-13-45.** Admission 27F ($4.85) adults, 18F ($3.25) children. July–Aug daily 9am–7pm; Mar 15–June and Sept daily 9am–6pm; Oct daily 9am–5pm; Nov 1–Mar 14 daily 9am–noon and 2–5pm.

The château consists of three separate strongholds; once badly ruined, today two of the buildings, Château du Milieu and Château du Coudray, have been partially restored (except they're still missing roofs). Château de Milieu dates from the 11th to the 15th centuries and contains the keep and clock tower, which houses a museum of Joan of Arc. Separated from Château de Milieu by a moat, Château du Coudray contains the Tour du Coudray, where Joan of Arc once stayed. In the 14th century, the Knights Templar were imprisoned here (they're responsible for the graffiti) before meeting their violent deaths. Some of the grim walls from other dilapidated edifices remain, although many of the buildings—including the Great Hall where Joan of Arc sought out the dauphin—have been torn down; among the most destructive owners were the heirs of Cardinal Richelieu. Also gone is Château St-Georges, which was built by Henry II of England, who died here in 1189.

Musée de la Devinière. La Devinière, on D117 near N751. ☎ **02-47-95-91-18.** Admission 23F ($4.15) adults, 17F ($3.05) seniors 60 and over, 15F ($2.70) children and students 11–25, free for children 10 and under. Tickets for theatrical performances 50F ($9). May–Sept daily 10am–7pm; mid-Mar to Apr daily 9:30am–12:30pm and 2–6pm; Oct to mid-Mar daily 9:30am–12:30pm and 2–5pm.

The most famous son of Chinon, Renaissance writer François Rabelais, was born at La Devinière, which is now the small Musée de la Devinière. Here you can wander the sparsely furnished rooms of the country house where Rabelais spent his childhood. The ground-floor rooms house literary works, prints, and documents of Rabelais and his contemporaries, thoroughly retracing the Rabelaisian era. Upstairs, you can see his parents' bedroom with the infant Rabelais's room just beside it. Throughout the year, the museum hosts special events such as shows by local artists, displays of 16th-century clothing, and (in the courtyard at night) performances that bring to life some of Rabelais's own works.

WHERE TO STAY

Chris' Hôtel. 12 place Jeanne-d'Arc, 37500 Chinon. ☎ **02-47-93-36-92.** Fax 02-47-98-48-92. 33 units. TV TEL. 260–380F ($46.80–$68.40) double. AE, DC, MC, V.

This well-run hotel is housed in a 19th-century building near the town's historic district. Many rooms offer views of the castle and river; most are furnished in Louis XV style, and all have modern amenities. Breakfast is the only meal served.

Hostellerie Gargantua. 73 rue Voltaire, 37500 Chinon. ☎ **02-47-93-04-71.** 7 units, 6 with bathroom. TEL. 160F ($28.80) double without bathroom, 380–540F ($68.40–$97.20) double with bathroom. MC, V. Closed Nov 11–Mar 1. Parking 20F ($3.60).

This 15th-century mansion features a terrace with a château view. Try to stop here for at least a meal, served formally in a stylish medieval hall; on weekends the staff dons medieval attire. You can sample Loire sandre prepared with Chinon wine or magrêt of duckling with dried pears and smoked lard, followed by a medley of seasonal red fruits in puff pastry. We're not as fond of the food here as we once were, but it's still recommendable.

Hôtel Diderot. 4 rue Buffon, 37500 Chinon. ☎ **02-47-93-18-87.** Fax 02-47-93-37-10. 27 units. TEL. 300–400F ($54–$72) double. AE, DC, MC, V.

This sprawling aristocratic house from the 1700s has a calm elegance about it. With its high black-slate roof and white limestone walls, the hotel still maintains a regal air. The friendly staff helps you settle into the large guest rooms, which feature hardwood floors, exposed beams, and antique furniture. A sense of the past is preserved in the rough-hewn exposed beams and supports, the 18th-century staircase, and the 15th-century fireplace in the dining room, where breakfast is served. As an added bonus, you have use of a private garden and patio.

WHERE TO DINE

✪ **Au Plaisir Gourmand.** 2 rue Parmentier. ☎ **02-47-93-20-48.** Reservations required. Main courses 95–130F ($17.10–$23.40); fixed-price menus 175–245F ($31.50–$44.10). AE, V. Tues–Sun noon–2pm, Tues–Sat 7:30–9:30pm. Closed Feb. FRENCH.

The area's premier restaurant is owned by Jean-Claude Rigollet, who used to direct the chefs at the fabled Templiers in Les Bézards. His restaurant, at the foot of the château in the old section of town, offers an intimate dining room with a limited number of tables in a charming 18th-century building. Menu items might include roast rabbit in aspic with foie-gras sauce or sandre in beurre blanc sauce. For dessert, try prunes stuffed in puff pastry. Fine wines (especially those from Chinon) accompany the chef's refined, subtle cuisine, and only the finest and freshest produce is used.

NEARBY ACCOMMODATIONS & DINING

✪ **Château de Marcay.** Marcay, 37500 Chinon. ☎ **02-47-93-03-47.** Fax 02-47-93-45-33. www.relaischateaux.fr/marcay. E-mail: marcay@club-internet.fr. 34 units. TV TEL. 495–1,360F ($89.10–$244.80) double; 1,325–1,660F ($238.50–$298.80) suite. Extra bed 160F ($28.80). AE, DC, MC, V. Closed for 6 weeks from late Jan to early Mar. Take D116 for 4½ miles southwest of Chinon.

This Relais & Châteaux began in the 1100s as a fortress and changed to its present form during the Renaissance. Remarkably, it remained untouched during the region's civil wars. The centerpiece of the wine-producing hamlet of Marçay, it's sumptuously decorated throughout. The main building houses the more opulent lodgings, while a handful of less expensive, less dramatic rooms are located in a nondescript annex a short walk away. Menu specialties change with the season, and the chef works hard to maintain high standards. There's a panoramic view from the garden terrace and dining room, where the decor is elegantly rustic.

Manoir de la Giraudière. Beaumont-en-Veron, 37420 Avoine. ☎ **02-47-58-40-36.** Fax 02-47-58-46-06. www.hotel-france.com. E-mail: manoir@lenet.fr. 25 units. TV TEL. 200–390F ($36–$70.20) double; 490–590F ($88.20–$106.20) suite. AE, MC, V. Head 3 miles west of Chinon along D749 toward Bourgueil.

Built during the mid-1600s, this elegant manor house resembles a small château because of its use of *tuffeau* (the beige-colored stone used to build the residences of many of the French monarchs). Set in a 6-acre park surrounded by hundreds of acres of fields and forests, this two-star choice offers classic decor and modern comforts. Air-conditioning isn't necessary because of the very thick walls that act as natural insulation against the heat and cold. Note the 17th-century *pigeonnière* (dovecote) that doubles as a salon during warm weather. The hotel's restaurant closes in January; otherwise, it's open daily except Tuesday and Wednesday at lunch. The fixed-price menus range from 115F to 230F ($20.70 to $41.40) and feature dishes like crêpinette of pig's foot with braised cabbage and juniper-berry sauce, a "duet" of local freshwater fish with sage, and an eggplant "caviar" with essence of fresh green peppers.

9 Ussé

183 miles SW of Paris, 9 miles NE of Chinon

At the edge of the hauntingly dark forest of Chinon, **Château d'Ussé** (☎ **02-47-95-54-05**) was the inspiration for Perrault's legend of *The Sleeping Beauty* (*La Belle au bois dormant*). Conceived as a medieval fortress, the complex of steeples, turrets, towers, chimneys, and dormers was erected at the dawn of the Renaissance on a hill overlooking the Indre River. Two powerful families—the Bueil and the d'Espinay—lived here in the 15th and 16th centuries. The terraces, laden with orange trees, were laid out in the 18th century. When the need for a fortified château had passed, the north wing was demolished, opening up a greater view.

The château was later owned by the duc de Duras and then by Mme de la Roche-jacquelin; its present owner, the marquis de Blacas, has opened many rooms to the public. The guided tour begins in the Renaissance chapel, with its sculptured portal and handsome stalls. You then proceed to the royal apartments, which are furnished with tapestries and antiques like a four-poster bed draped in red damask. One gallery displays an extensive collection of swords and rifles. A spiral stairway leads to a tower with a panoramic view of the river and a waxwork Sleeping Beauty waiting for her prince to come.

The château is open mid-February through March and October to mid-November, daily from 10am to noon and 2 to 5:30pm; April to June and September from 9am to noon and 2 to 6:45pm; July and August from 9am to 6:30pm; closed mid-November to mid-February. Admission is 59F ($10.60) for adults and 19F ($3.40) for children. The château is best visited by car or on an organized bus tour from Tours. If you're **driving** from Tours or Villandry, follow D7 to Ussé.

10 Fontevraud-l'Abbaye

189 miles SW of Paris, 10 miles SE of Saumur

You'll find the Plantagenet dynasty of England buried in the **Abbaye Royale de Fontevraud** (☎ **02-41-51-71-41**). Why here? These monarchs, whose male line ended in 1485, were also the comtes d'Anjou, and they left instructions that they be buried in their native soil.

In the 12th-century Romanesque church—boasting four Byzantine domes—are the remains of two English kings or princes, including Henry II of England, the first Plantagenet king, and his wife, Eleanor of Aquitaine, the most famous woman of the Middle Ages. Her crusading son, Richard the Lion-Hearted, was also entombed here. The Plantagenet line ended with the death of Richard III at the 1485 Battle of Bosworth. The tombs fared badly in the Revolution as mobs invaded the church, desecrating the sarcophagi and scattering their contents on the floor.

More interesting than the tombs, however, is the octagonal **Tour d'Evraud,** the last remaining Romanesque kitchen in France. A group of apsides, crowned by conically roofed turrets, surrounds the tower. A pyramid tops the conglomeration, capped by an open-air lantern tower pierced with lancets.

The abbey was founded in 1099 by Robert d'Arbrissel, who spent much of his life as a recluse. His abbey was like a public-welfare commune, liberal in its admission policies. One part, for example, was occupied by aristocratic ladies, many banished from court, including discarded mistresses of kings. The four youngest daughters of Louis XV were educated there as well.

The abbey is open daily, June 1 to September 21 from 9am to 6:30pm, September 22 to October from 9:30am to 12:30pm and 2 to 5:30pm, November to April 4 from 9:30am to noon and 2 to 5pm, and April 5 to May 31 from 9:30am to noon and 2 to 6pm. Admission is 32F ($5.75) adults, 21F ($3.80) ages 12 to 25, free for ages 11 and under.

Four **buses** run daily from Saumur, costing 12F ($2.15) for the 30-minute, one-way trip. If you're **driving,** take N147 about 2½ miles from the village of Montsoreau.

The **Office de Tourisme** is at the Chapelle Ste-Catherine (☎ **02-41-51-79-45**), open May 15 to September 30.

WHERE TO STAY

Hostellerie du Prieuré St-Lazare. 49590 Fontevraud-l'Abbaye. ☎ **02-41-51-73-16.** Fax 02-41-51-75-50. E-mail: prieure.stlazare@wanadoo.fr. 52 units. MINIBAR TV TEL. 360–480F ($64.80–$86.40) double; 640F ($115.20) triple. Closed Nov 15–Mar 15. AE, MC, V.

This is one of the most unusual hotels in Europe, set on 11th-century foundations within the perimeter of the legendary Abbaye Royale, in what functioned long ago as cells for penitent monks. As part of the continuing restoration of the abbey, one of its four-story wings was transformed into a conference center in the 1970s. In 1990, those facilities were turned over to a private management company and operated as a hotel. The guest rooms are well maintained and monastically simple, with white walls, modern furniture, and exposed sections of cream-colored tuffeau, the easy-to-carve rock that was used to build the abbey during the early Middle Ages.

Dining: On the premises is Le Cloître, a restaurant housed in a panoramic enclosure of the 11th-century medieval cloister. Fixed-price menus at 90F to 200F ($16.20 to $36) are served every day at lunch and dinner.

WHERE TO DINE

Another choice is the restaurant at the **Hostellerie du Prieuré St-Lazare** (see above).

✪ **La Licorne.** Allée Ste-Catherine. ☎ **02-41-51-72-49.** Reservations required. Main courses 85–130F ($15.30–$23.40); fixed-price menus 130–350F ($23.40–$63). AE, DC, MC, V. Apr to mid-Sept daily noon–1:30pm and 7–9pm; mid-Sept to Mar Tues–Sun noon–1:30pm, Tues–Sat 7–9pm. FRENCH.

For the perfect combination of medieval history and culinary sensuality, visit the nearby abbey, then dine at this 30-seat restaurant set on a linden-lined pedestrian walkway stretching between the abbey and a nearby parish church. Its symmetrical proportions and neoclassical pilasters, built in the 1700s just before what the owners refer to as "La Révolution," evoke the ancien régime at its most graceful and opulent. In summer, guests dine in the garden or in the elegantly rustic dining room. Chef Jean-Michel Bezille's menu almost always includes filet of beef flavored with smoked pork and shallots, crayfish-stuffed ravioli with morel sauce, filet of salmon with vanilla sauce, and luscious desserts like warm chocolate tart with pears and lemon-butter sauce.

11 Saumur

186 miles SW of Paris, 33 miles SE of Angers

Saumur is set in a region of vineyards, where the Loire separates to encircle an island; it makes one of the best bases for exploring the western Loire Valley. A small but thriving town, it doesn't entirely live off its past: Saumur produces some 100,000 tons per year of the mushrooms the French so adore. Balzac left us this advice: "Taste a mushroom and delight in the essential strangeness of the place." The cool tunnels for the *champignons* also provide the ideal resting place for the celebrated sparkling wines of the region. By all means, enjoy them at a local cafe.

ESSENTIALS

Trains run frequently between Tours and Nantes, with stopovers at Saumur. Twelve trains per day arrive from Tours (trip time: 45 minutes), costing 57F to 84F ($10.25 to $15.10) one-way; 11 trains per day also pull in from Angers (trip time: 30 minutes), costing 42F to 63F ($7.55 to $11.35) one-way. The train station is on the north side of town. Most major points of interest, including the château, are on the south bank. From the station, take bus A into town. If you're **driving** from Tours, take N152 southwest to Saumur.

The **Office de Tourisme** is on place de la Bilange (☎ **02-41-40-20-60**).

EXPLORING THE AREA

Of all the Loire cities, Saumur is the most French bourgeois, even today, and perhaps that's why Balzac used it for his classic characterization of a smug little town in his *Eugénie Grandet*. Saumur is famous as the birthplace of the couturière Coco Chanel. Founded in 1768, its Cavalry School and riding club, the Black Cadre, are world renowned. Its horsemen are among the finest in Europe—to see a rider carry out a *curvet* is a thrill.

The area surrounding the town has become especially famous for its delicate sparkling wines. In the center of Saumur, you can wander up and down the many aisles of **La Maison du Vin,** 25 rue Beaurepaire (☎ **02-41-51-16-40**), choosing from a large stock direct from the many surrounding vineyards.

An alternative is to travel east of Saumur to the village of St-Hilaire, where you'll find a host of vineyards. One of the better ones is **Veuve Amiot,** 21 rue Jean-Ackerman (☎ **02-41-83-14-14**), where you can tour the wine cellars, taste different vintages and varieties, and even buy bottles and gift boxes right in the showroom.

Château de Saumur. 49400 Saumur. ☎ **02-41-40-24-40.** Admission 37F ($6.65) adults, 26F ($4.70) children. June–Sept daily 9am–6pm; Apr–May daily 9:30am–noon and 2–5:30pm; Oct–Mar Wed–Mon 9:30am–noon and 2–5:30pm. Closed Christmas and New Year's Day.

In the famous *Les Très Riches Heures du Duc de Berry* at the Château de Chantilly, the 15th-century painting depicts Saumur as a fairy-tale castle of bell turrets and gilded weathercocks. These adornments are largely gone, however, leaving a stark and foreboding fortress towering from a promontory over the Loire. Under Napoléon, the castle became a prison, then eventually a barracks and munitions depot. The town of Saumur acquired it in 1908 and began restoration efforts. It now houses an interesting regional museum, the **Musée des Arts Décoratifs,** noted for its 16th- to 18th-century ceramics collection. The series of 13th-century enamel crucifixes from Limoges is remarkable. There's also the **Musée du Cheval,** which is devoted to the history of the horse through the ages, complete with stirrups, antique saddles, and spurs.

WHERE TO STAY

✪ **Hostellerie du Prieuré.** Chênehutte-les-Tuffeaux, 49350 Gennes. ☎ **02-41-67-90-14.** Fax 02-41-67-92-24. E-mail: prieure@wanadoo.fr. 35 units. MINIBAR TV TEL. 700–1,350F ($126–$243) double; 1,600F ($288) suite. AE, DC, MC, V. Closed Jan 5–Mar 5. Take D751 4 miles west of Saumur.

This 12th-century priory (now a Relais & Châteaux), set in a 60-acre park a few miles from town, has a steep roof, dormer windows, and a large peaked tower. It offers graciously comfortable rooms; two of the most beautiful are in a 10th-century chapel. The least expensive (and less desirable) rooms are in a simple outlying pavilion. The Grand Salon features an ornately carved stone fireplace, crystal chandeliers, oak furniture, and a bar with a fleur-de-lis motif.

Dining: The dining room boasts one of the finest views of the Loire, spanning 40 miles—truly beautiful at sunset. The *rognons de veau sautés à la moutarde* (sautéed veal kidneys in mustard sauce) is heavenly. The chef wisely recommends filet of beef "Maine Anjou."

Amenities: Miniature-golf course and heated pool.

Hôtel Anne d'Anjou. 32 quai Mayaud, 49400 Saumur. ☎ **02-41-67-30-30.** Fax 02-41-67-51-00. 50 units. TV TEL. 425–540F ($76.50–$97.20) double. AE, DC, MC, V. Parking 50F ($9).

This 18th-century building was constructed as a family home; its magnificent stair-well below a trompe-l'oeil ceiling has been designated a historic monument. The rooms in the back overlook the château, while the front faces the Loire. Five units still have their original decor, ranging from Louis XVI to Empire. Former guests have included the actor Jean Marais, the late Ginger Rogers, and Prince Albert of Monaco. The hotel also operates one of the most prestigious restaurants in Saumur, Les Menestrels.

Hôtel St-Pierre. Rue Haute-Saint-Pierre, 49400 Saumur. ☎ **02-41-50-33-00.** Fax 02-41-50-38-68. 15 units. MINIBAR TV TEL. 540–800F ($97.20–$144) double. AE, DC, DISC, MC, V.

Nestled among tiny winding roads and built against the Eglise St-Pierre, this hotel overflows with character, boasting such features as finely upholstered antiques, half-timbered walls, beamed ceilings, stained-glass windows, massive stone fireplaces, and spiral staircases. Guest rooms are individually decorated in the same rich style; even the bathroom walls showcase custom tile designs. The intimate breakfast room opens onto a small garden terrace.

Le Clos des Bénédictins. 2 rue des Lilas, St-Hilaire–St-Florent, 49400 Saumur. ☎ **02-41-67-28-48.** Fax 02-41-67-13-71. E-mail: clos@club-internet.fr. 23 units. TV TEL. 315–580F ($56.70–$104.40) double; 720–850F ($129.60–$153) suite. AE, MC, V.

This hotel boasts a host of amenities, including modern rooms, a large pool, a land-scaped courtyard, and plenty of green parkland dotted with benches, tables, and chairs. The medium-size guest rooms are standard, with contemporary built-in furni-ture; the best have private balconies overlooking the Loire Valley. An adjoining small restaurant, with candelabras on each table and panoramic views, serves decent meals that tend to have an international appeal.

Le Roi René. 94 av. du Général-de-Gaulle, 49400 Saumur. ☎ **02-41-67-45-30.** Fax 02-41-67-74-59. 39 units. TV TEL. 250–310F ($45–$55.80) double; 385–410F ($69.30–$73.80) triple; 485F ($87.30) quad. AE, MC, V. Parking 30F ($5.40). Closed late Nov to Dec 23.

Erected around 1900 and bombed into rubble during World War II, this river front hotel was rebuilt in the 1950s using the same honey-colored stone used in its original construction. A serviceable but unexciting choice, it offers conservative but comfortably furnished rooms, each with double-paned windows, as well as a hard-working and thoughtful staff. The on-premises restaurant has large bay windows over-looking the river and fixed-price menus ranging from 80F to 170F ($14.40 to $30.60). The restaurant, but not the hotel, is closed from mid-November to mid-March.

WHERE TO DINE

One of Saumur's great restaurants is **Les Menestrels,** in the Hôtel Anne d'Anjou (see above).

Les Délices du Château. Les Feuquières, Château de Saumur. ☎ **02-41-67-65-60.** Reser-vations required. Main courses 95–160F ($17.10–$28.80); fixed-price menus 130F ($23.40) at lunch, 175–285F ($31.50–$51.30) at lunch and dinner. AE, DC, MC, V. Daily noon–2:30pm and 7–10pm. Closed mid-Dec to Jan 1, Sun dinner Oct–Apr. FRENCH.

Saumur's finest restaurant, housed in a restored 12th-century house on the grounds of the town's massive château, offers panoramic views of the city and the Loire from its flowery terrace. Assisted by a youthful and impeccably trained staff, the outstanding chef, Pierre Millon, offers classic cuisine with a personal touch. Try the filet of beef sautéed with duck liver and essence of truffles, sautéed crayfish with mushroom sauce, or the signature dish: *sandre* encased in a shell of puréed potatoes and served with a coulis of a local wine (Saumur Champigny).

12 Angers

179 miles SW of Paris, 55 miles E of Nantes

Once the capital of Anjou, Angers straddles the Maine River at the western end of the Loire Valley. Though it suffered extensive damage in World War II, it has been considerably restored, somehow blending provincial charm with a suggestion of sophistication. The bustling regional center is often used as a base for exploring the château district to the west. With its skyscrapers and industrial complexes, it hardly suggests a sleepy Loire town; its preponderance of young people, including some 25,000 college students, keeps this vital city of 225,000 jumping until late at night.

ESSENTIALS

GETTING THERE   From Saumur, 12 **trains** per day leave for the 30-minute trip to Angers, with a one-way ticket costing 42F to 63F ($7.55 to $11.35); from Tours, seven trains per day leave for the 1-hour trip, with a one-way cost of 85F to 127F ($15.30 to $22.85). Twelve trains per day also leave Paris's Gare d'Austerlitz for the 2¾-hour trip, costing 237F to 438F ($42.65 to $78.85) one-way. The train station at place de la Gare is a convenient walk from the château. For train information and schedules, call ☎ **08-36-35-35-39.** If you're **driving** to Angers, take N152 southwest to Saumur, turning west on D952.

VISITOR INFORMATION   The **Office de Tourisme** is on place du Président-Kennedy (☎ **02-41-23-51-11**).

SEEING THE SIGHTS

If you have some time for shopping, wander to the pedestrian zone in the center of town. The boutiques and small shops here sell everything from clothes and shoes to jewelry and books. For regional specialty items, head to **La Maison du Vin,** 5 place du Président-Kennedy (☎ **02-41-88-81-13**), where you can learn about the area's many vineyards, taste their wares, and buy a bottle or two for gifts or an afternoon picnic. Another libation that's unique to Angers is Cointreau. **La Distillerie Cointreau,** rue Croix-Blanche in nearby St-Barthélémy d'Anjou (☎ **02-41-43-25-21**), has a showroom where you can sample and stock up on this citrusy liqueur.

Château d'Angers. ☎ **02-41-87-43-47.** Admission 35F ($6.30) adults, 23F ($4.15) seniors, 6F ($1.10) children 7–17, free for children 6 and under. June–Sept 15 daily 9am–7pm; Sept 16–May daily 9:30am–12:30pm and 2–6pm.

The moated Château d'Angers, dating from the 9th century, was once the home of the comtes d'Anjou. The notorious Black Falcon lived here, and in time the Plantagenets also took up residence. From 1230 to 1238, the outer walls and 17 massive towers were built, creating a formidable fortress well prepared to withstand invaders. The château was favored by Good King René, during whose reign a brilliant court life flourished here until he was forced to surrender Anjou to Louis XI. Louis XIV turned the château into a prison, dispatching his finance minister, Fouquet, to a cell here. In the 19th century, the castle again became a prison, and during World War II it was used by the Nazis as a munitions depot, which was bombed by Allied planes in 1944.

Visit the castle if only to see the ✪ **Apocalypse Tapestries,** one of the masterpieces of art from the Middle Ages. This series of tapestries wasn't always so highly regarded—they once served as a canopy for orange trees, protecting the fruit from unfavorable weather; they were also used to cover the damaged walls of a church. Made by Poisson beginning in 1375 for Louis I of Anjou, they were purchased for only a nominal sum in the 19th century. The series of 77 pieces, illustrating the book of St. John, stretch a distance of 335 feet. One scene is called *La Grande prostituée,* and another shows Babylon invaded by demons; yet another depicts a peace scene of two multiheaded monsters holding up a fleur-de-lis.

After seeing the tapestries, you can tour the fortress, including the courtyard of the nobles, prison cells, ramparts, windmill tower, 15th-century chapel, and royal apartments.

Cathédrale St-Maurice. Place Freppel. ☎ **02-41-87-58-45.** Free admission, but donation appreciated. Daily 8:30am–7pm, sometimes longer for special events.

The cathedral dates mostly from the 12th and 13th centuries; the main tower, however, is from the 16th century. The statues on the portal represent everybody from the Queen of Sheba to David at the harp. *Christ Enthroned* is depicted on the tympanum; the symbols, such as the lion for St. Mark, represent the Evangelists. The stained-glass windows from the 12th through the 16th centuries have made the cathedral famous. The oldest one illustrates the martyrdom of St. Vincent (the most unusual is of the former St. Christopher with the head of a dog). All of the Apocalypse Tapestries were once shown here; now only a few remain, with the majority on display in the nearby château. The 12th-century nave, considered a landmark in cathedral architecture, is a clear, coherent plan that's a work of harmonious beauty, the start of the Plantagenet architecture. If you're interested in a guided tour (offered in English in July and August), call the church's presbytery (see the number above). Tours are conducted erratically, often by an associate of the church itself, and usually with much charm and humor.

WHERE TO STAY

Hôtel d'Anjou. 1 bd. Foch, 49100 Angers. ☎ **02-41-88-24-82.** Fax 02-41-87-22-21. 53 units. MINIBAR TV TEL. 370–670F ($66.60–$120.60) double. AE, DC, MC, V. Parking 48F ($8.65).

This four-story hotel, on the main boulevard next to a large park, is clearly the best choice—but still offers reasonable rates. The management claims that it opts to retain its three-star status, even though its size and comfort levels match those of four-star hotels in regions nearby. Room decor and size vary widely by price: The most expensive ones have upholstered walls, antiques or convincing reproductions, and carefully coordinated colors and fabrics; the less expensive rooms are comfortable but a lot more prosaic.

Dining: La Salamandre is the best restaurant in town, charging 130F to 210F ($23.40 to $37.80) for fixed-price menus; you'll dine amid carefully maintained paneling, a valuable antique tapestry, and a wood-burning fireplace inspired by the Renaissance and designed "in the style of François 1er." Meals, served Monday through Saturday from noon to 3pm and 7:30 to 10pm, offer regional specialties and fresh Loire Valley fish.

Hôtel de France. 8 place de la Gare, 49100 Angers. ☎ **02-41-88-49-42.** Fax 02-41-86-76-70. 55 units. MINIBAR TV TEL. 395–495F ($71.10–$89.10) double. AE, DC, MC, V. Parking 40F ($7.20).

One of the most respected in town, this 19th-century hotel has been run by the Bouyers since 1893. It's the preferred choice near the railway station. The rooms are soundproofed, but only four are air-conditioned (it can get hot on a summer night). The restaurant, Les Plantagenets, serves reliable fixed-price meals.

Hôtel du Mail. 8–10 rue des Ursules, 49100 Angers. ☎ **02-41-25-05-25.** Fax 02-41-86-91-20. 27 units. MINIBAR TV TEL. 270–330F ($48.60–$59.40) double. AE, DC, MC, V.

"The attraction of this hotel is, of course, its peaceful, relaxing atmosphere, but above all else its soul shines through," say owners M. and Mme Dupuis. This becomes apparent the moment you set eyes on the stately three-story 17th-century mansion. The owners have gone to great lengths to restore the large guest rooms, each individually decorated. You can enjoy breakfast in either the spacious dining room with its hardwood floors or the garden courtyard under the lime trees.

WHERE TO DINE

Hôtel d'Anjou (see above) boasts the town's best restaurant.

Le Toussaint. 7–9 place du Président-Kennedy. ☎ **02-41-87-46-20.** Reservations recommended. Main courses 85–150F ($15.30–$27); fixed-price menus 98–250F ($17.65–$45). AE, MC, V. Tues–Sun noon–2pm, Tues–Sat 7:30–9:30pm. FRENCH.

This restaurant is housed in a late-19th-century building constructed from the same white stone (*pierre de tuffeau*) as the town's famous château, which it overlooks. The larger of the two dining rooms is one floor above street level. The chef uses only fresh ingredients, many from the region, as part of a culinary repertoire that changes with the seasons. Favorites include fried Loire Valley fish (either *sandre* or *l'alose*, the latter available only between April and June) usually served with beurre blanc sauce, *pied de porc farci et truffé* (stuffed and truffled pig's foot), and an array of freshly made desserts flavored with Cointreau, a liqueur of the region. In any season, look for an array of pâtés (pork and duck) made on the premises by the owners, the Bignon family.

Provence Caffè. 9 place du Ralliement. ☎ **02-41-87-44-15.** Reservations recommended. Main courses 78F ($14.05); fixed-price menus 94–149F ($16.90–$26.80). AE, MC, V. Mon–Sat noon–2pm and 7–10pm. PROVENÇAL.

This restaurant opened in 1994; ever since, it has celebrated the herbs, spices, and seafood of Provence here in the colder and foggier climes of the Loire Valley. The decor features bundles of herbs, bright colors, and souvenirs of the Mediterranean, and the ambience is unstuffy and sunny. Menu items include risotto, either with asparagus and basil or with snails, a bourride of monkfish, and a ballotine of chicken with ratatouille.

ANGERS AFTER DARK

If you head to place du Ralliement and its fountain or rue St-Laud with its many bars and cafes, you'll find yourself in the center of Angers's nightlife. But for a great night of beer drinking with your friends, go to **Le Kent,** 7 place Ste-Croix (☎ **02-41-87-88-55**), where you can choose from some 50 varieties of beer and 70 brands of whiskey. If you prefer quantity to quality when it comes to beer, stop by **Le Spirit Factory,** 14 rue Bressigny (☎ **02-41-88-50-10**). Just walk in and order *un mètre,* and for 94F ($16.90), you'll be served a meter-long wooden feeding trough filled with beer. For those of you who have never had the pleasure of drinking a meter of beer before, here's a bit of etiquette—fill your drinking glass using the spout on the end of the trough and don't try to slurp your beer from the top, as that's *trop gauche,* even for this place.

13 Amboise

136 miles SW of Paris, 22 miles E of Tours

On the banks of the Loire, Amboise is located in the center of vineyards known as Touraine-Amboise. Unlike commercial Tours, this is still a real Renaissance town. That's the good news. The bad news: Because the town is so beautiful, it's overrun by buses filled with tour groups, especially in summer. Many townspeople still talk about the purchase of a small nearby château by Mick Jagger, granddaddy of rock. Before Mick moved in to get his satisfaction, there was Leonardo da Vinci, the quintessential Renaissance man, who spent his last years in this city.

ESSENTIALS

GETTING THERE   Amboise lies on the main Paris–Blois–Tours rail line, with 14 **trains** per day arriving from both Tours and Blois. The trip from Tours takes only 20 minutes and costs 28F to 41F ($5.05 to $7.40) one-way; the trip from Blois lasts just 15 minutes, at a cost of 33F to 49F ($5.95 to $8.80) one-way. Five trains arrive daily from Paris (trip time: 2½ hours), costing 142F to 213F ($25.55 to $38.35) one-way. For train information and schedules, call ☎ **08-36-35-35-39.**

Tourisme Verney, operating out of Tours (☎ **02-47-37-81-81**), runs five **buses** a day here, taking about half an hour and costing 28F ($5.05) one-way. If you're **driving** from Tours, take N152 east to D31. Turn south on D31 to Amboise.

VISITOR INFORMATION   The **Office de Tourisme** is on quai du Général-de-Gaulle (☎ **02-47-57-09-28**).

SEEING THE SIGHTS

✪ **Château d'Amboise.** ☎ **02-47-57-14-47.** Admission 37F ($6.65) adults, 24F ($4.30) students, 15F ($2.70) children. July–Aug daily 9am–7pm; Apr–June daily 9am–6:30pm; Sept–Oct daily 9am–6pm; Nov–Mar daily 9am–noon and 2–5pm.

This 15th-century chateau, which dominates the town, was the first in France to reflect the Italian Renaissance. A combination of both Gothic and Renaissance styles, it is mainly associated with Charles VIII, who built it on a rocky spur separating the valleys of the Loire and the Amasse.

You enter via a ramp that opens onto a panoramic terrace fronting the river. At one time, this terrace was surrounded by buildings; fêtes were staged in the enclosed courtyard. The castle fell into decline during the Revolution, and today only a quarter or even less remains of this once-sprawling edifice. You first come to the Flamboyant Gothic Chapelle de St-Hubert, distinguished by its lacelike tracery. It allegedly contains Leonardo's remains; actually the great artist was buried in the castle's Collegiate Church, which was destroyed between 1806 and 1810. Excavations conducted during the Second Empire unearthed bones that were "identified" as Leonardo's.

Today, tapestries cover the walls of the château's grandly furnished rooms. The *Logis du Roi* (king's apartment) escaped destruction and can be visited. It was built against the Tour des Minimes ou des Cavaliers and was known for its ramp that horsemen could ride up. The other notable tower is the Heurtault, which is broader than the Minimes, with thicker walls.

Clos-Lucé. 2 rue de Clos-Lucé. ☎ **02-47-57-62-88.** Admission 38F ($6.85) adults, 29F ($5.20) children. Jan 2–31 daily 10am–5pm; Feb 1–Mar 22 and Nov 13–31 daily 9am–6pm; Mar 23–June 30 and Sept 1–Nov 12 daily 9am–7pm; July and Aug daily 9am–8pm. Closed Dec.

This 15th-century brick-and-stone manor was once an oratory for Anne de Bretagne. In it, François I installed "the great master in all forms of art and science," Leonardo himself. Venerated by the Chevalier King, Leonardo lived here for 3 years, until his death in 1519. (Those paintings of Leonardo dying in François's arms are probably symbolic; the king was supposedly out of town at the time.) The manor's rooms are well furnished, some with reproductions from Leonardo's time.

WHERE TO STAY

Belle-Vue. 12 quai Charles-Guinot, 37400 Amboise. ☎ **02-47-57-02-26.** Fax 02-47-30-51-23. 32 units. TV TEL. 280–350F ($50.40–$63) double. MC, V. Closed Dec–Mar 15.

This modest inn lies at the bridge crossing the Loire at the foot of the château. It features rows of French doors and outdoor tables on two levels, shaded by umbrellas in summer. The interior lounges are well maintained; modernized guest rooms are comfortably furnished with traditional French pieces. Try to stay here and not in the annex across the river. Breakfast is the only meal served.

Hostellerie du Château-de-Pray. Route de Chargé (D751), 37400 Amboise. ☎ **02-47-57-23-67.** Fax 02-47-57-32-50. 19 units. TEL. 490–850F ($88.20–$153) double; 870F ($156.60) suite. Half board 215F ($38.70) per person extra. AE, DC, V. Closed Jan 2–27.

From its position above parterres surveying the Loire in a park about a mile east of the town center, this château resembles a tower-flanked castle on the Rhine. Inside you'll find antlers, hunting trophies, antiques, and a paneled drawing room with a fireplace and a collection of antique oils. The guest rooms in the main building are stylishly conservative and comfortable (try to avoid the four rooms in the annex).

Dining: Open to nonguests, the hotel restaurant offers fixed-price menus of excellent quality. In summer, diners can sit on a terrace overlooking formal gardens. The menu might include grilled salmon with beurre blanc (white butter), lobster cannelloni, or roast rabbit with wine sauce.

✪ **Le Choiseul.** 36 quai Charles-Guinot, 37400 Amboise. ☎ **02-47-30-45-45.** Fax 02-47-30-46-10. E-mail: choiseul@wanadoo.fr. 32 units. MINIBAR TV TEL. 890–1,350F ($160.20–$243) double; 1,450–1,800F ($261–$324) suite. MC, V. Closed Nov 26–Jan 15.

This Relais & Châteaux is Amboise's finest hotel, with a nearly impeccable 18th-century pedigree. Named after its original owner, the duc de Choiseul (finance minister to Louis XV), the hotel encompasses its namesake's original house and two other old buildings. The grandest rooms are in what was built as a convent for an obscure French sect (Les Minimes). All rooms are luxurious; although recently modernized, they have retained their old-world charm. Sixteen are air-conditioned.

Dining: The formal dining room, the best in town, offers views of the Loire and of flowering garden terraces; nonguests who phone ahead are welcome. It's open daily from noon to 2pm and 7 to 9:30pm. Fixed-price menus range from 290F to 500F ($52.20 to $90). The cuisine, presented with seamless style, utilizes only the freshest and highest-quality products; even the bread is homemade. The service is impeccable, and the wine list is the best in the area.

Amenities: Outdoor pool, tennis court within a 5- or 10-minute walk, Ping-Pong table.

WHERE TO DINE

The finest dining choice is **Le Choiseul** (see above).

Le Manoir St-Thomas. Place Richelieu. ☎ **02-47-57-22-52.** Reservations required. Fixed-price menus 175–295F ($31.50–$53.10). AE, DC, MC, V. Tues–Sun noon–2:30pm and 7:15–9:30pm. Closed Jan 15–Mar 15 and Sun evenings in winter. FRENCH.

The best food in town outside Le Choiseul is served at this Renaissance house, set in a pleasant garden in the shadow of the château. The dining room is richly decorated with a polychrome ceiling and massive stone fireplace. Owner/chef François Le Coz's specialties include truffles with foie gras, lamb filet with pork, and red mullet filet with cream of sweet-pepper sauce. The tender saddle of hare is perfectly flavored.

14 Chenonceaux

139 miles SW of Paris, 16 miles E of Tours

A Renaissance masterpiece, the ✪ **Château de Chenonceau** (☎ **02-47-23-90-07**) is best known for the *dames de Chenonceau* who once occupied it. (Note that the town is spelled with a final "x," but the château isn't.)

In 1547, Henri II gave Chenonceau to his mistress, Diane de Poitiers, 20 years his senior. For a time this remarkable woman was virtually queen of France, infuriating Henri's dour wife, Catherine de Médici. Diane's critics accused her of using magic to preserve her celebrated beauty and to keep Henri's attentions from waning. Apparently Henri's love for Diane continued unabated, although she was in her 60s when he died in a jousting tournament in 1559.

Upon Henri's death, Catherine became regent of France (her eldest son was still a child) and wasted no time in forcing Diane to return the jewelry Henri had given her and abandon her beloved Chenonceau. Catherine added her own touches to Chenonceau, building a two-story gallery across the bridge—obviously inspired by her native Florence.

Many of the château's walls are covered with Gobelin tapestries, including one depicting a woman pouring water over the back of an angry dragon. The chapel contains a delicate marble *Virgin and Child* by Murillo as well as portraits of Catherine de Médici in her traditional black and white, looking like Whistler's mother. There's even a portrait of the stern Catherine in the former bedroom of her rival, Diane de Poitiers, obviously disapproving of the action that took place here between Diane and Henri II. In François I's Renaissance bedchamber, the most interesting portrait is that of Diane as the huntress Diana.

The history of Chenonceau is related in 15 tableaux in the wax museum, which charges 15F ($2.70) admission. Diane de Poitiers, who, among other accomplishments, introduced the artichoke to France, is depicted in three tableaux. One portrays Catherine de Médici tossing out her husband's mistress.

The château is open daily, March 16 to September 15 from 9am to 7pm, September 16 to 30 from 9am to 7:30pm, March 1 to 15 and October 1 to 15 from 9am to 6pm, February 16 to 28 and October 16 to 31 from 9am to 5:30pm, February 1 to 15 and November 1 to 15 from 9am to 5pm, and November 16 to January 31 from 9am to 4:30pm. Admission is 45F ($8.10) for adults, 35F ($6.30) for children 7 to 15, and free for children 6 and under.

The château presents a *son-et-lumière* (sound-and-light) show called *In the Days of the Dames of Chenonceau* from July to August every night at 10:15pm. Shows begin promptly, with tickets costing 45F ($8.10) for adults and 30F ($5.40) for children 7 to 15; children 6 and under enter free.

ESSENTIALS

GETTING THERE   There are four daily **trains** from Tours to Chenonceaux (trip time: 45 minutes), costing 34F to 51F ($6.10 to $9.20) one-way. The train deposits you half a mile from the château; from there, you can either walk or take a taxi.

A six-passenger barge, the ***Nymphéa,*** makes 6-night trips from May to October from St-Aignan on the Cher to the Château de Chenonceau and Château de Cheverny, then past the Château de Plessis and Château de Montrichard, and finally to the Château de Gue-Pean before returning to St-Aignan. Tickets are 2,090F to 2,590F ($376.20 to $466.20) per person, double occupancy, depending on the season. For information, call ☎ **800/217-4447.** If you're **driving** from Tours, take N76 east to Chenonceaux.

VISITOR INFORMATION   The **Syndicat d'Initiative** (tourist office) is at 13 bis rue du Château (☎ **02-47-23-94-45**), open Easter to September.

WHERE TO STAY

La Renaudière. 24 rue du Dr.-Bretonneau, 37150 Chenonceaux. ☎ **02-47-23-90-04.** Fax 02-47-23-90-51. 15 units. TEL. 280–440F ($50.40–$79.20) double. Rates include breakfast. AE, MC, V. Closed Nov 15–Mar 15.

This gem of an inn, set on extensive grounds, is located at the exit of the village, a few steps from the château. Built as a private home for Dr. Bretonneau, a local doctor of taste and style, it has been successfully converted to receive guests. Rooms are decorated in traditional French provincial style, cozy and comfortable.

Even if you're not a guest, the inn is also a good dining choice. Many of its recipes are based on old-time Loire favorites that have been updated for modern tastes—such as medallions of monkfish flavored with vanilla as well as *pigeon en cocotte*. Fixed-price menus cost 98F ($17.65), 129F ($23.20), and 189F ($34).

✪ **La Roseraie.** 7 rue du Dr.-Bretonneau, 37150 Chenonceaux. ☎ **02-47-23-90-09.** Fax 02-47-23-91-59. 16 units. TV TEL. 280–480F ($50.40–$86.40) double; from 900F ($162) suite. Feb–Mar and mid-Oct through Nov rates include breakfast; Dec–Jan, Apr to mid-Oct breakfast 38F ($6.85). AE, DC, MC, V. Closed Dec and Jan.

You'll find the most charming hotel in Chenonceaux on the main street, across from the post office, in a late-19th-century building covered with streams of clinging ivy-like vines. Until its decline after the death of its longtime owner in 1955, the French government used it as a stop during the official visits of such VIPs as Harry Truman, Winston Churchill, and Franklin D. Roosevelt. In 1993, after decades of neglect, its fortunes were reversed by the hotelier Laurent Fiorito, who radically upgraded its guest rooms, bathrooms, and gardens and reinstated the tradition of carefully supervised cuisine. There's a heated pool on the property.

Dining: The restaurant serves some of the finest meals in town at lunch and dinner daily. Fixed-price menus range from 98F to 160F ($17.65 to $28.80) and include such specialties as foie gras maison and a delicious version of rumpsteak prepared with cassis.

WHERE TO DINE

Note that **La Renaudière** and **La Roseraie** (see above) boast very good restaurants.

Au Gâteau Breton. 16 rue du Dr.-Bretonneau. ☎ **02-47-23-90-14.** Reservations required July–Aug. Fixed-price menus 57–102F ($10.25–$18.35). MC, V. June–Sept Mon–Sat noon–3pm and 7–10pm; Oct–May Mon–Sat noon–2:30pm and 7–9:30pm. FRENCH.

After the World War II bombardments of L'Orient, an industrial port in Brittany, destroyed his home, a successful restaurateur relocated to Chenonceaux. Ever since, even with other owners, this place has retained its name—despite the fact that its cuisine is more French than exclusively Breton. A short walk from the town's château, this is a refreshing place for dinner or tea, especially in summer, when the terrace provides a close-up view of the garden. Gravel paths run among beds of pink geraniums and lilacs, and bright canopies and umbrellas offer shade. The chef offers home cooking that's sometimes enhanced with the fruit-based liqueurs (cherry, strawberry, and other flavors) made at the nearby Fraise d'Or distillery. Specialties include small chitterling sausages of Tours, chicken with armagnac sauce, and blood sausage with apples, a highly touted local favorite.

15 Chaumont-sur-Loire

124 miles SW of Paris, 25 miles E of Tours

On the morning when Diane de Poitiers crossed the drawbridge, the ✪ **Château de Chaumont** (☎ 02-54-51-26-26) looked fiercely grim, with its battlements and pepper-pot turrets crowning the towers. Henri II, her lover, had recently died. The king had given her Chenonceau, but his angry widow, Catherine de Médici, forced her to trade her favorite château for Chaumont. Inside, portraits reveal that Diane truly deserved her reputation as forever beautiful. Another portrait—of Catherine looking like a devout nun—invites unfavorable comparisons.

Chaumont (Burning Mount) was built during the reign of Louis XII by Charles d'Amboise. Overlooking the Loire, it's approached by a long walk up from the village through a tree-studded park. It was privately owned until the state acquired it in 1938. The castle spans the period between the Middle Ages and the Renaissance, and its prize exhibit is a rare collection of medallions by Nini, an Italian artist. A guest of the château for a while, he made medallion portraits of kings, queens, and nobles—even Benjamin Franklin, who once visited. In the bedroom once occupied by Catherine de Médici, you can see a rare portrait, painted when she was young. The superstitious Catherine always kept her astrologer, Cosimo Ruggieri, at her beck and call, housing him in one of the tower rooms (a portrait of him remains). He reportedly foretold the disasters awaiting her sons, including Henri III. In Ruggieri's room, an unusual tapestry depicts Medusa with a flying horse escaping from her head.

The château is open mid-March to September daily from 9:30am to 6pm; February to mid-March and October to December daily from 10am to 4:30pm (closed January). Admission is 32F ($5.75) for adults, 21F ($3.80) for children 12 and over, and free for children 11 and under.

From Blois, Chaumont is served by 15 **trains** per day (trip time: 15 minutes), costing 17F to 26F ($3.05 to $4.70) one-way. Fifteen trains also arrive from Tours (trip time: 25 min.), costing 42F to 63F ($7.55 to $11.35) one-way. The train station is north of the château in Onzain, a pleasant 1½-mile walk. If you're **driving** from Tours, take N152 east from Blois and follow N152 southwest to Chaumont-sur-Loire.

The **Office de Tourisme** is on rue du Maréchal-Leclerc (☎ **02-54-20-91-73**).

WHERE TO STAY & DINE

Domaine des Hauts de Loire. Route d'Herbault, 41150 Onzain. ☎ **02-54-20-72-57.** Fax 02-54-20-77-32. 35 units. MINIBAR TV TEL. 680–1,450F ($122.40–$261) double; 1,650–2,250F ($297–$405) suite. AE, DC, MC, V. From Chaumont, cross pont de Chaumont and follow rte. d'Herbault through the hamlet of Onzain.

Less than 2 miles from the château, on the opposite side of the Loire, this Relais & Châteaux is a stately manor house built by the prosperous owner of a Paris-based newspaper in 1840. It's the most appealing stop in the neighborhood, with a roster of Louis-Philippe–style guest rooms. About half the accommodations are in a half-timbered annex that, originally a stable, was adapted to its present use in the 1960s.

Dining: The stately dining room once hosted the parties of one of France's most influential newspaper owners; it's now open to nonguests who phone in advance and serves well-prepared food that knowledgeable locals often drive many miles to enjoy. Fixed-price menus for 295F to 380F ($53.10 to $68.40) include congealed oysters on a layered sheet of sardines, roasted filet of Loire Valley whitefish (*sandre*) with parsley-flavored cream sauce and cabbage stuffed with a compote of snails, and the ultimate Loire Valley main course, filet of smoked eel prepared with Vouvray wine. The restaurant is open daily for lunch and dinner.

16 Blois

112 miles SW of Paris, 37 miles NE of Tours

A wound in battle earned him the name *Balafré* (Scarface), but he was quite a ladies' man. In fact, on the cold misty morning of December 23, 1588, the duc de Guise had just left a warm bed and the arms of one of Catherine de Médici's lovely "flying squadron" girls (ladies-in-waiting and courtesans skilled at political intrigue). His archrival, Henri III, had summoned him. The king's minions were about. That was nothing unusual—Henri was always surrounded by attractive young men these days.

Then it happened: The guards moved menacingly toward him with daggers. Wounded, the duke was still strong enough to knock a few down. He made for the door, where more guards awaited him. Staggering, he fell to the floor in a pool of his own blood. Only then did Henri emerge from behind the curtains. "Mon Dieu," he's reputed to have exclaimed, "he's taller dead than alive!" The body couldn't be shown: The duke was too popular. Quartered, it was burned in a fireplace. Then Henri's mother, Catherine de Médici, was told the "good news."

ESSENTIALS

GETTING THERE   The Paris-Austerlitz line via Orléans delivers six **trains** per day from Paris (trip time: 1 hour), costing 166F to 222F ($29.90 to $39.95) one-way. From Tours, five trains arrive per day (trip time: 1 hour), at a cost of 77F to 100F ($13.85 to $18) one-way, and from Amboise, 10 trains arrive per day (trip time: 20 minutes), costing 40F to 62F ($7.20 to $11.15) one-way. For train information and schedules, call ☎ **08-36-35-35-39.** If you're **driving** from Tours, take N152 east to Blois.

VISITOR INFORMATION   The **Office de Tourisme** is in the Pavillon Anne-de-Bretagne, 3 av. Jean-Laigret (☎ **02-54-74-06-49**).

EXPLORING THE TOWN & THE CHATEAU

If you have time for shopping, head for the area around rue St-Martin and rue du Commerce. Shops here offer high-end items like quality clothing, perfumes, shoes, and jewelry. For contemporary art, watercolors, and oils, visit **Art Cadre,** 18 rue Denis-Papin (☎ 02-54-74-80-10). If you're in the market for a one-of-a-kind piece of jewelry or want to have something created to suit your tastes, go to the master jeweler **Ph. Denies,** 3 rue St-Martin (☎ 02-54-74-78-24). But if you prefer antique jewelry, stop by **Antebellum,** 12 rue St-Lubin (☎ 02-54-78-38-78), and browse through its selection of precious and semiprecious stone jewelry set in gold and silver. For something a little less serious, stop at **Le Paradis des Enfants,** 2 rue des Trois-Clefs (☎ 02-54-78-09-68), where you'll find toys in every shape and size imaginable.

✪ **Château de Blois.** ☎ **02-54-78-06-62.** Admission 35F ($6.30) adults, 25F ($4.50) students 6–20, free for children under 6. July–Aug daily 9am–7:30pm; mid-Mar to June and Sept daily 9am–6pm; mid-Oct to mid-Mar daily 9am–noon and 2–5pm.

The murder of the duc de Guise is only one of the memories evoked by the Château de Blois, begun in the 13th century by the comtes de Blois. Charles d'Orléans (son of Louis d'Orléans, assassinated by the Burgundians in 1407) lived at Blois after his release from 25 years of English captivity. He had married Mary of Cleves and brought a "court of letters" to Blois. In his 70s, Charles became the father of the future Louis XII, who was to marry Anne de Bretagne. Blois was then launched in its new role as a royal château. In time it was to be called the second capital of France, with Blois the city of kings.

However, Blois soon became a palace of banishment. Louis XIII got rid of his interfering mother, Marie de Médici, by sending her here; but this plump matron escaped by sliding into the moat down a mound of dirt left by the builders. In 1626, the king sent his conspiring brother, Gaston d'Orléans, here; he stayed.

If you stand in the courtyard, you'll find that the château is like an illustrated storybook of French architecture. The Hall of the Estates-General is a beautiful 13th-century work; the Charles d'Orléans gallery was actually built by Louis XII from 1498 to 1501, as was the Louis XII wing. The Gaston d'Orléans wing was constructed by Mansart between 1635 and 1637. Most remarkable is the François I wing, a French Renaissance masterpiece, containing a spiral staircase with elaborately ornamented balustrades and the king's symbol, the salamander. In the Louis XII wing, seek out paintings by Antoine Caron, Henri III's court painter, depicting Thomas More's persecution.

The château presents a *son-et-lumière* (sound-and-light) show in French from mid-May to mid-September, nightly at 10:30pm. Shows begin promptly, with tickets costing 60F ($10.80) for adults and 30F ($5.40) for ages 6 to 20; children 5 and under enter free.

WHERE TO STAY

Note that some of the best rooms in town are found at **Le Médicis** (see "Where to Dine," below).

Holiday Inn Garden Court. 26 av. Maunoury, 41000 Blois. ☎ **800/465-4329** in the U.S., or 02-54-55-44-88. Fax 02-54-74-57-97. 78 units. MINIBAR TV TEL. 495F ($89.10) double. Children 12 and under stay free in parents' room. AE, DC, MC, V. Bus: 1.

This leading three-star hotel has all the modern amenities as well as a respect for traditional charm. The rooms are furnished with contemporary flair. There's a good restaurant, where meals are moderately priced and children's meals are available. The hotel is more predictable and reliable than exciting.

Hôtel Le Savoie. 6–8 rue du Dr.-Ducoux, 41000 Blois. ☎ **02-54-74-32-21.** Fax 02-54-74-29-58. 26 units. TV TEL. 230–280F ($41.40–$50.40) double. AE, MC, V.

This modern hotel has made every effort to keep itself inviting. It all begins with the courteous staff, who greet you the moment you enter the long, narrow reception area. Though the guest rooms tend to be small, they're nonetheless quiet and relaxing. The hotel lounge area offers an ambience that falls somewhere between rustic French and the Brady Bunch, creating the perfect spot to meet friends and traveling companions. In the morning, a breakfast buffet is set up in the bright dining room with its wall of windows looking out onto the surrounding residences.

Mercure Centre. 28 quai St-Jean, 41000 Blois. ☎ **02-54-56-66-66.** Fax 02-54-56-67-00. 84 units, 12 duplex suites. A/C MINIBAR TV TEL. 495F ($89.10) double; 600F ($108) suite. AE, DC, MC, V. Parking 35F ($6.30).

This is the best-located hotel in Blois, beside the quays of the Loire, a 5-minute walk from the château. With three stories of reinforced concrete and big windows, it contains larger-than-expected rooms filled with contemporary furniture and soothing colors. The greenhouse-style lobby leads into a pleasant restaurant where meals are served daily. The duplex suites all feature private terraces and views of the river.

WHERE TO DINE

Le Médicis. 2 allée François-1er, 41000 Blois. ☎ **02-54-43-94-04.** Fax 02-54-42-04-05. Reservations required. Main courses 90–145F ($16.20–$26.10); fixed-price menus 100–420F ($18–$75.60). AE, DC, MC, V. Daily 12:30–2pm and 7–10pm. Closed Jan 1–15. FRENCH.

Christian and Annick Garanger maintain the most sophisticated inn in Blois—ideal for a gourmet meal or an overnight stop. Fresh fish is the chef's specialty. Typical main courses are asparagus in mousseline sauce and scampi ravioli with saffron sauce. Dessert brings chocolate in many manifestations. Some dishes aren't recommended for those with high cholesterol.

In addition, the Garangers rent 12 elegant rooms, each with bathroom. Doubles cost 450F to 550F ($81 to $99), and the suite goes for 700F ($126).

✪ **Rendezvous des Pêcheurs.** 27 rue du Foix. ☎ **02-54-74-67-48.** Reservations recommended. Main courses 98–140F ($17.65–$25.20); fixed-price menu 145F ($26.10). MC, V. Tues–Sat 12:30–2pm, Mon–Sat 7:30–10pm. Closed 1 week in Feb and 3 weeks in Aug. FRENCH.

This restaurant occupies a small 16th-century house near the Eglise St-Nicolas, a 5-minute walk south of the château, beside the quays of the Loire. Don't come expecting lots of red meat, though, as chef Eric Reithler prepares only two meat dishes (pigeon and veal kidneys), which appear alongside a much longer roster of popular seafood dishes. Some dishes may seem deceptively simple, but the result is usually a taste sensation. The menu changes daily according to the availability of fish in the markets; sea urchins raw from the shell is a favorite. Other savory specialties include crisp-skinned stingray filet with wild herbs and foie gras, or filet of sea bass roasted with shellfish and lardons that are caramelized in Loire Valley red wine.

BLOIS AFTER DARK

Although Blois doesn't offer the many distractions you'll find in France's larger towns, you'll still have a healthy selection of clubs to choose from. For flashing lights, steady beats, and occasional sweaty bodies rubbing against you, throw on something casual and head for any of the several dance clubs around, like **Le Joker,** 42 rue Foulerie (☎ **02-54-78-75-34**), and **Le Nonstop,** rue de la Chaîne (☎ **02-64-78-17-73**). If you prefer the pub scene, saunter on down to the fun and friendly **Pub Mancini,** 1 rue du Puits-Châtel (☎ **02-54-78-04-36**), with its 100 brands of beer and 40 brands of whiskey; **Riverside,** 3 rue Henri-Drussy (☎ **02-54-78-33-79**); or **L'Estaminet,** 25 rue St-Lubin (☎ **02-54-74-37-45**).

17 Cheverny

119 miles SW of Paris, 12 miles SE of Blois

The upper crust still heads to the Sologne area for the hunt, just as if the 17th century had never ended. However, 20th-century realities—like formidable taxes—can't be entirely avoided, so the **Château de Cheverny** (☎ **02-54-79-96-29**) must open some of its rooms for visitors. At least that keeps the tax collector at bay and the hounds fed in winter.

The town of Cheverny is best reached by **car** along D765 southeast of Blois or on an organized **bus** tour from nearby Blois.

Unlike most of the Loire châteaux, Cheverny is actually occupied by the descendants of the original owner, the vicomte de Sigalas. The family's lineage can be traced back to Henri Hurault, the son of the chancellor of Henri III and Henri IV, who built the first château here in 1634. Upon finding his wife, Françoise, carrying on with a page, he killed the page and offered his spouse two choices: She could swallow poison or have his sword plunged into her heart. She elected the less bloody method. Perhaps to erase the memory, he had the castle torn down and the present one built for his second wife. Designed in classic Louis XIII style, it boasts square pavilions flanking the central pile.

Inside, you'll be impressed by the antique furnishings, tapestries, decorations, and objets d'art. A 17th-century French artist, Jean Mosnier, decorated the fireplace with motifs from the legend of Adonis. The Guards' Room contains a collection of medieval armor; also on display is a Gobelin tapestry depicting the abduction of Helen of Troy. In the king's bedchamber, another Gobelin tapestry traces the trials of Ulysses. Most impressive, however, is a stone stairway of carved fruit and flowers.

The château is open daily, June to mid-September from 9:15am to 6:45pm, April and May from 9:15am to noon and 2:15 to 6:30pm, March and mid-September to October from 9:30am to noon and 2:15 to 5:30pm, and November to February from 9:30am to noon and 2:15 to 5pm. Admission is 21F ($3.80) for adults and 17F ($3.05) for children.

WHERE TO STAY & DINE

Hôtel St-Hubert. Rue Nationale, 41700 Cour-Cheverny. ☎ **02-54-79-96-60.** Fax 02-54-79-21-17. Main courses 60–160F ($10.80–$28.80); fixed-price menus 98–280F ($17.65–$50.40). MC, V. Thurs–Tues 12:15–2pm and 7:30–9pm. Closed Jan 5–Feb 15 and Wed nights off-season. FRENCH.

About 800 yards from the château, this roadside inn was built in the provincial style in the 1950s, using age-old techniques and a local stone (*le bourré*) that grows whiter with its exposure to the sun. The kindly owner/chef, Jean-Claude Pillaut, is the secret of the St-Hubert's success, thanks to his talent, hard work, and refusal to use anything but fresh ingredients, most of them local. The least expensive menu may include terrine of quail, pike-perch (*sandre*) with beurre blanc (white butter), a selection of cheese, and a homemade fruit tart. The most expensive may offer lobster or fresh spring asparagus, an aiguillette of duckling prepared with grapes, or wild boar with a creamy house signature sauce. Game is featured in season. The chef recommends the filet of beef Rossini, a flavorful blend of prime beef filet and foie gras.

Les Trois Marchands. Place de l'Eglise, 41700 Cour-Cheverny. ☎ **02-54-79-96-44.** Fax 02-54-79-25-60. Fixed-price menus 115–240F ($20.70–$43.20). AE, DC, MC, V. Tues–Sun noon–2pm and 7:30–9pm. Closed Feb–Mar 15. FRENCH.

This much-renovated coaching inn, more comfortable than the St-Hubert, has been handed down for many generations from father to son. Today the three-story building sports awnings, a mansard roof, a glassed-in courtyard, and sidewalk tables with umbrellas. In the attractive tavern-style dining room, the menu almost always includes frogs' legs with fines herbes, fish cooked in a salt crust, fresh asparagus in mousseline sauce, and a panaché of sweetbreads and kidneys prepared with port wine. The less formal Bistro des Gourmets features fixed-price meals for 70F to 120F ($12.60 to $21.60).

The inn also rents 35 well-furnished, comfortable rooms, 20 with bathroom. A double with bathroom is 260F to 350F ($46.80 to $63); a double without goes for 180F ($32.40). Breakfast costs 40F ($7.20). Free parking.

18 Valençay

145 miles SW of Paris, 35 miles S of Blois

One of the Loire's handsomest Renaissance châteaux, the **Château de Valençay** (☎ **02-54-00-10-66**) was acquired in 1803 by Talleyrand on the orders of Napoléon, who wanted his shrewd minister of foreign affairs to receive dignitaries in style. In 1838, Talleyrand was buried at Valençay, and the château passed on to his nephew, Louis de Talleyrand-Périgord. Valençay was built in 1550 by the d'Estampes family. The dungeon and great west tower are of this period, as is the main body of the building, but other wings were added in the 17th and 18th centuries. The effect is grandiose—almost too much so—with domes, chimneys, and turrets.

The private apartments are open to the public; they're sumptuously furnished, mostly in the Empire style but with Louis XV and Louis XVI trappings as well. A star-footed table in the main drawing room is said to have been the one on which the Final Agreement of the Congress of Vienna was signed in June 1815 (Talleyrand represented France).

Visits to Valençay usually last about 45 minutes longer than those to other châteaux in the valley. The Musée de Talleyrand that used to stand on the premises is now closed, but some of the collection is displayed in the new rooms of the castle. In the park is a museum of 60 antique cars (ca. 1890 to 1950). After your visit to the main buildings, you can walk through the garden and deer park. On the grounds are many exotic birds, including flamingos.

Admission to the castle, car museum, and park is 45F ($8.10) for adults, 35F ($6.30) for students, and 25F ($4.50) for children 17 and under. It's open in July and August daily from 9:30am to 7:30pm; April to November 1 daily from 9:30am to 6pm; November 2 through February Saturday and Sunday from 2 to 5pm; and in March Monday through Friday from 2 to 5pm.

There are frequent **SNCF rail connections** from Blois. For train information and schedules, call ☎ **08-36-35-35-39.** If you're **driving** from Tours, take N76 east, turning south on D956 to Valencay. From Blois, follow D956 south.

The **Office de Tourisme** is on route de Blois (☎ **02-54-00-04-42**).

WHERE TO STAY & DINE

✪ **Hôtel d'Espagne.** 9 rue du Château, 36600 Valençay. ☎ **02-54-00-00-02.** Fax 02-54-00-12-63. 14 units. TV TEL. 450–600F ($81–$108) double; 800–900F ($144–$162) suite. AE, DC, MC, V. Closed Jan–Feb. Parking 25F ($5).

This former coaching inn has a wide-arched entrance leading to a U-shaped building whose stone walls ring a flagstone-covered courtyard. Monsieur and Madame Fourré and their family provide an old-world ambience and a first-class kitchen; the family has maintained a smooth operation since 1875. The unique guest rooms are each named after an ancestral manor house in the region. Yours might feature authentic Empire, Louis XV, or Louis XVI decor.

Dining: Lunch is served in the dining room or gardens Tuesday through Sunday; specialties are noisettes of lamb in tarragon and sweetbreads with morels. The fixed-price menu in the simple bistro (open daily for lunch and dinner in summer, Saturday and Sunday only in winter) is 100F ($18), and main courses in the more formal restaurant (open daily from June to September; closed Monday off-season) are 160F to 250F ($28.80 to $45). Most restaurant meals are à la carte and cost around 350F ($63), with wine.

19 Chambord

118 miles SW of Paris, 11 miles E of Blois

When François I used to say, "Come on up to my place," he meant the ✪ **Château de Chambord,** 41250 Bracieux (☎ **02-54-50-40-40**), not Fontainebleau or Blois. Some 2,000 construction workers began to piece together "the pile" in 1519. What emerged after 20 years was the pinnacle of the French Renaissance, the largest château in the Loire Valley. It was ready for the visit of Charles V of Germany, who was welcomed by nymphets in transparent veils gently tossing wildflowers in his path. French monarchs like Henri II and Catherine de Médici, Louis XIII, and Henri III came and went from Chambord, but none developed an affection for it to match François I's. The state acquired Chambord in 1932.

The château is set in a park of more than 13,000 acres, enclosed by a wall stretching some 20 miles. Looking out of a window in one of the 440 rooms, François is said to have carved these words on a pane with a diamond ring: "A woman is a creature of change; to trust her is to play the fool." Chambord's facade is dominated by four monumental towers. The keep has a spectacular terrace from which the ladies of the court used to watch the return of their men from the hunt.

The three-story keep also encloses a corkscrew staircase, superimposed so that one person may descend at one end and a second ascend at the other without ever meeting. The apartments of Louis XIV, including his redecorated bedchamber, are also in the keep.

The château is open daily, in July and August from 9:30am to 7:15pm, April to June and September from 9:30am to 6:15pm, and October to March from 9:30am to 5:15pm. Admission is 40F ($7.20) for adults, 25F ($4.50) for children 12 to 17, and free for children 11 and under. The château is illuminated every evening throughout the year for 4 hours beginning at nightfall. One of the highlights of a visit here is returning at night to watch the illuminations.

It's best to **drive** to Chambord. Take the D951 northeast from Blois to Mènars, turning onto the rural road to Chambord. You can also rent a **bicycle** in Blois and cycle the 11 miles to Chambord, or take one of the organized tours to Chambord leaving from Blois in summer.

The **Office de Tourisme** is on place St-Michel (☎ 02-54-20-34-86).

WHERE TO STAY & DINE

Hôtel du Grand-St-Michel. 103 place St-Michel, 41250 Chambord, Bracieux. ☎ **02-54-20-31-31.** Fax 02-54-20-36-40. 39 units. TV TEL. 290–450F ($52.20–$81) double. MC, V. Closed Nov 14–Dec 20.

This inn, across from the château, is about the only one in town. Try for a front room overlooking the château, which is dramatic when floodlit at night. The rooms are plain but comfortable, with provincial decor. The staff is rather blasé and inarticulate, even in French. Most visitors arrive for lunch, which in summer is served on an awning-shaded terrace. Fixed-price menus are 135F ($24.30). The regional dishes rarely match the Loire wines.

20 Beaugency

93 miles SW of Paris, 53 miles NE of Tours

Situated on the right bank of the Loire, the town of Beaugency boasts a 14th-century bridge that's unusual because each of its 26 arches is in a different style. The heart of this ancient Loire Valley town is an archaeological garden called the City of the Lords, named after the counts who enjoyed great power in the Middle Ages. A major event in medieval Europe took place here: the 1152 annulment of the marriage of Eleanor of Aquitaine to Louis VII. Eleanor sought an annulment on the grounds of consanguinity: They were cousins in the fourth degree and so forbidden to marry. This remarkable woman later became queen consort of Henry II of England, bringing southwestern France as her dowry. She was also the mother of Richard the Lion-Hearted.

The 15th-century **Château Dunois,** 2 place Dunois (☎ 02-38-44-55-23), contains a folklore museum of the Orléans district. The collection includes antique toys, hairpieces, furniture, costumes, paintings, and sculpture found in the district. The museum is open Wednesday through Monday from 10am to noon and 2 to 5pm (to 6:30pm in summer). Admission is 25F ($4.50) for adults, 15F ($2.70) for children 6 to 17, and 10F ($1.80) for children 5 and under. Near the château is the Voûte St-George (St. George's Vault), a gate of the former castle of the Lords of Beaugency, which opened from the fortress onto the Rû Valley and the lower part of town.

Eglise Notre-Dame would have been a good example of 12th-century Romanesque architecture if Gothic touches hadn't been added. Originally, it was attached to a Benedictine abbey. Nearby is the Tour St-Firmin, all that remains of a church that once stood on place St-Firmin. A trio of bells is sheltered in this tower, whose spire rises 180 feet. From here you'll have a panoramic view of the river valley.

In the archaeological garden, the **Hôtel-Dieu** (hospital) is one of the oldest buildings in Beaugency, dating to the 11th century. The Eglise St-Etienne, also from the

11th century, is one of the oldest churches of France, and the Tour César is a fine example of the period's military art.

About 20 **trains** per day run between Beaugency and either Blois or Orléans; each trip takes 20 minutes and costs 29F to 63F ($5.20 to $11.35) one-way. From Orléans there are about eight **buses** a day making the trip to Beaugency. If you're **driving** from Blois to Beaugency, take D951 northeast.

The **Office de Tourisme** is at 3 place du Dr.-Hyvernaud (☎ **02-38-44-54-42**).

WHERE TO STAY & DINE

Abbaye de Beaugency. 2 quai de l'Abbaye, 45190 Beaugency. ☎ **02-38-44-67-35.** Fax 02-38-44-87-92. 17 units. TV TEL. 510–570F ($91.80–$102.60) double. AE, DC, MC, V.

This three-star hotel offers the finest and most historic accommodations in Beaugency, dwarfing the competition. Built in 1640 as an Augustinian monastery, it retains the stone window and door frames of its original construction. Functioning as a hotel since 1935, it occupies a small tract of land beside the Loire, within view of the town's oldest bridge. The large, sunny guest rooms were recently renovated, and the bathrooms are spacious and modern. The restaurant is known for classics like whitefish with mushroom cream sauce, and game is a specialty in season. Fixed-price menus begin at 190F ($34.20).

La Tonnellerie. 12 rue des Eaux-Bleues, Tavers, 45190 Beaugency. ☎ **02-38-44-68-15.** Fax 02-38-44-10-01. 20 units. TEL. 475–990F ($85.50–$178.20) double; from 730–1,240F ($131.40–$223.20) apartment or suite. AE, MC, V. Take A10, exit at Beaugency, then N152 to Beaugency/Tavers.

This longtime favorite offers comfortable, soothingly traditional rooms in a pleasant old house with garden and pool. The inn is also known for its food, with foie gras, duck, and monkfish among the specialties, plus a good choice of Loire Valley wines. The Pouey family can arrange visits to the château, a game of golf, hiking, cycling, or a trip to a winery.

21 Orléans

74 miles SW of Paris, 45 miles SE of Chartres

After suffering heavy damage in World War II, many Orléans neighborhoods were rebuilt in dull postwar styles, so visitors who hope to see how it looked when the Maid of Orléans was here are likely to be disappointed. There are still many rewarding sights, though, and a jazz festival held the first week of July significantly livens the place up. Today, this city of 200,000 has lost a lot of its former importance to Tours, but signs of urban restoration bring hope for the city's future.

Ten **trains** per day arrive from Paris's Gare d'Austerlitz (trip time: 1¼ hours); there are also a dozen connections from Tours (trip time: 1¼ hours). The one-way fare from Paris is 90F to 135F ($16.20 to $24.30); from Tours it's 89F to 134F ($16 to $24.10). If you're **driving** to Orléans, it's easiest from either Paris or Tours, since Orléans lies on the road between the two cities. From Paris, take A10 south; from Tours, take A10 north.

The **Office de Tourisme** is on place Albert-1er (☎ **02-38-24-05-05**).

EXPLORING THE TOWN

Orléans is the chief town of Loiret, on the Loire, and beneficiary of countless associations with the French aristocracy—even giving its name to ducs and duchesses who influenced the course of the nation's history. Joan of Arc relieved the city in 1429 from attacks by the Burgundians and the English. That deliverance is celebrated every year on May 8, the anniversary of her victory. An **equestrian statue of Jeanne d'Arc** stands in place du Martroi, which was created by Foyatier in 1855. From the square, you can drive down rue Royal (rebuilt in 18th-century style) across pont George-V (erected in 1760). After crossing the bridge, you'll have a good view of the town. A simple cross marks the site of the Fort des Tourelles, which Joan of Arc and her men captured.

If you're looking for a unique gift indigenous to the area, go to **La Chocolaterie Royale,** 53 rue Royale (☎ 02-38-53-93-43), where you'll find jars of *cotignac,* an apricot-colored jelly made from quince. While in the store, you can also stock up on fine handmade chocolate.

Near rue Royale is **place du Châtelet,** with its many boutiques, including a Galeries Lafayette. Look for fashionable clothing, jewelry, books, and leather goods. For antiques, walk along **rue de Bourgogne,** where you'll find a host of dealers offering everything from objets d'art to furniture.

Cathédrale Ste-Croix. Place Ste-Croix. ☎ **02-38-77-87-50.** Free admission, but you should tip the guide. Daily 10am–noon and 2–5pm (to 6pm May–Sept). Guided visits, in French only, can be arranged by the tourist office for 25F ($4.50) per person. July–Sept tours at 3, 4, and 5pm; Oct–June usually Sat only at 3:30 and 4:30pm (hours are erratic).

Begun in 1287 in the High Gothic period, the cathedral was burned by the Huguenots in 1568. The first stone on the present building was laid by Henri IV in 1601, and work continued until 1829. The cathedral boasts an excellent 17th-century organ and some magnificent woodwork from the early 18th century in its chancel, the masterpiece of Jules Hardouin-Mansart and other artists of Louis XIV. You'll need a guide to tour the chancel and the crypt and to see the treasury with its Byzantine enamels, goldwork from the 15th and 16th centuries, and Limoges enamels.

Hôtel Groslot. Place de l'Etape (northwest of the cathedral). ☎ **02-38-79-22-22.** Free admission.

This Renaissance mansion was begun in 1550 and embellished in the 19th century. François II (first husband of Mary Queen of Scots) lived in it during the fall of 1560 and died here on December 5. Between the Revolution and the mid-1970s, it functioned as Orléans's town hall (*Mairie*) until it was replaced with something less dramatic but more functional. Despite that, marriage ceremonies, performed by the town's civil magistrates, still occur here. Romance is nothing new to this building: It was here that Charles IX met his lovely Marie Touchet. The statue of Joan of Arc praying (at the foot of the flight of steps) was the work of Louis-Philippe's daughter, Princesse Marie d'Orléans. In the garden you can see the remains of the 15th-century Chapelle St-Jacques.

Eglise St-Aignan. Place St-Aignan. July–Sept Sun–Fri 9am–7pm, Sat 5–9pm; Oct–June Sun–Fri 10am–noon and 2–6pm, Sat 4:30–6pm.

One of the most frequently altered churches in the Loire Valley, this was consecrated in 1509 in the form you see today. It's noted for possessing one of France's earliest vaulted hall crypts, complete with polychromed capitals. Scholars of pre-Romanesque art view the place with passionate interest, for its 10th- and 11th-century aesthetic are exceptionally rare. Above ground, the church's Renaissance-era choir and transept remain, but the nave was burned by the Protestants during the Wars of Religion. In a gilded carved-wood shrine are the remains of the church's patron saint.

Musée des Beaux-Arts. 1 rue Fernand-Rabier. ☎ **02-38-53-39-22.** Admission 18F ($3.25) adults, 9F ($1.60) children. Thurs–Sat 10am–6pm, Wed 10am–8pm, Tues and Sun 11am–6pm.

This is primarily a picture gallery of French and (to a lesser degree) Dutch and Flemish works from the 16th to the late 19th centuries. Some of the works once hung in

Orléans

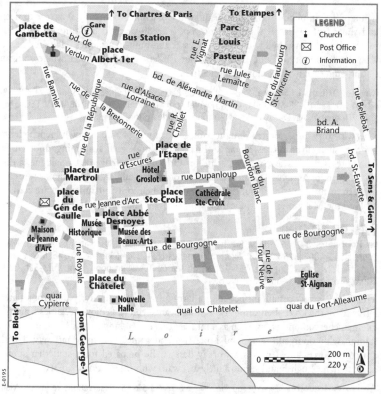

Cardinal Richelieu's château. The collection includes busts by Pigalle and a fine array of portraits, including one of Mme de Pompadour. Among non-French works, the undisputed star is a lovely Velásquez commemorating the Apostle St. Thomas.

WHERE TO STAY

Hôtel d'Arc. 37 rue de la République, 45000 Orléans. ☎ **02-38-53-10-94.** Fax 02-38-81-77-47. 35 units. MINIBAR TV TEL. 390F ($70.20) double. AE, DC, MC, V.

This hotel, with its ornate Art Deco facade, sits in the middle of the historic town center and is close to just about everything. Most rooms are of average size, with functional, built-in furnishings. Whereas most rooms are peaceful, avoid those that face rue de la République, as they tend to be somewhat noisy. Although the hotel has no restaurant, it does serve breakfast in an ornate room with a carved marble fireplace.

Hôtel Mercure Orléans. 44–46 quai Barentin, 45000 Orléans. ☎ **02-38-62-17-39.** Fax 02-38-53-95-34. 102 units. A/C MINIBAR TV TEL. 555F ($99.90) double. AE, DC, MC, V.

Along the river, adjacent to pont Joffre, this modern eight-floor bandbox structure is within walking distance of place du Martroi and its Joan of Arc statue. Though rather impersonal and preferred by the many businesspeople traveling the length of the Loire Valley, it offers the best and most comfortable rooms in the city. There's a heated pool, and a restaurant/bar, Le Gourmandin, serves straightforward French and Loire Valley specialties, with fixed-price menus at 95F to 140F ($17.10 to $25.20).

Hôtel St-Martin. 52 bd. Alexandre-Martin, 45000 Orléans. ☎ **02-38-62-47-47.** Fax 02-38-81-13-28. 22 units. TEL. 245–300F ($44.10–$54) double. AE, DC, V.

If you prefer simplicity over opulence and think of a hotel room only as a place to sleep and shower, then this is the place for you. The 80-year-old building has spacious rooms, sparsely furnished with firm mattresses and built-in armoires. Half are blessed with windows that look out onto the private garden behind the hotel, where you can sit and enjoy a refreshing nonalcoholic drink.

Novotel Orléans La Source. 2 rue Honoré-de-Balzac, 45100 Orléans La Source. ☎ **02-38-63-04-28.** Fax 02-38-69-24-04. www.novotel.com. 119 units. A/C MINIBAR TV TEL. 515F ($92.70) double. AE, DC, V. Follow N20 south of Orléans for 7 miles.

This two-story hotel, set in a verdant park, is a member of a well-known French chain. It offers such diversions as *pétanque* (French bowling), golf, swimming, and tennis. The hotel is 9 miles south of the center of Orléans at the edge of La Sologne, a district known for its natural beauty. The guest rooms are standardized, with no-nonsense modern furnishings that include a writing desk. The rooms and amenities are comparable to the Mercure's, but its location works only if you have a car.

WHERE TO DINE

La Poutrière. 8–10 rue de la Brèche. ☎ **02-38-66-02-30.** Reservations required. Main courses 140–400F ($25.20–$72); fixed-price menus 189–259F ($34–$46.60). AE, MC, V. July–Aug 27 daily noon–2pm and 7:30–10pm; off-season Tues–Sun noon–2pm, Tues–Sat 7:30–10pm. Closed Dec 24–Jan 10. FRENCH.

This 18th-century restaurant occupies a farmhouse on the relatively underpopulated left bank of the Loire. Beneath heavy ceiling beams, you can enjoy specialties from the talented chef Simon Lebras, such as a lobster "cake," veal kidneys with sauterne sauce, salmon with Bourgueil wine, and Loire fish and game. The apple tart served with apricot-flavored sorbet makes a worthy dessert. Be prepared for a staff that speaks absolutely no English and seems a little awkward with international guests.

✪ **Les Antiquaires.** 2–4 rue au Lin. ☎ **02-38-53-52-35.** Reservations required. Main courses 92–165F ($16.55–$29.70); fixed-price menus 200–320F ($36–$57.60). AE, DC, MC, V. Tues–Sat noon–2:30pm and 7:30–10pm. Closed Apr 13–21, 3 weeks in Aug, and Dec 24–Jan 1. FRENCH.

This rustically elegant mansion on a small street near the river was built during the time of Joan of Arc. Chef/owner Michel Pipet creates a virtually flawless cuisine based on conservative French staples, with occasional modern touches; it has a definite edge over that of its major rival, La Poutrière. If you're lucky enough to arrive in autumn or winter, savor the Loire Valley's abundance of wild game in dishes like noisettes of roe deer prepared with small cherries or an estouffade of wild boar with red-wine sauce. From February to March, try wild Loire Valley salmon with *beurre maître d'hôtel* (parsley, lemon, and butter). For dessert, enjoy a warm soufflé prepared with Grand Marnier sauce or fresh limes.

ORLEANS AFTER DARK

You'll find most of the after-dark action in this town in the bars along rue de Bourgogne and the handful of places that spill over onto rue Bannier. A trendy young crowd dances and drinks the night away at the **George V,** Les Halles Châtelet (☎ **02-38-53-08-79**). A few streets over is one of the better jazz clubs, **Paxton's Head,** 264 rue de Bourgogne (☎ **02-38-81-23-29**), with a down-home English pub feel. The mid-20s crowd enjoys live blues music on the weekends at **Le Caveau des Trois Maries,** 2 rue des Trois-Maries (☎ **02-38-54-68-68**); housed in a 13th-century building, it looks like a church on the inside with its stone walls and vaulted ceilings. If you like to drink beer and shoot pool or billiards, head for **Bar Darlington,** 3 rue du Colombier (☎ **02-38-54-67-98**), where there's a real easygoing ambience.

8

Normandy & Mont-St-Michel

Ten centuries have passed since the Vikings invaded the province of Normandy. The early Scandinavians might have come to ravish the land, but they stayed to cultivate it. The Normans produced great soldiers, none more famous than William the Conqueror, who defeated the forces of King Harold at Battle Abbey in 1066. The English and the French continued to do battle on and off for 700 years—a rivalry that climaxed at the 1815 Battle of Waterloo.

Much of Normandy was later ravaged in the 1944 invasion that began on a June morning when airborne troops parachuted down into Ste-Mère-Eglise and Bénouville-sur-Orne. The largest armada ever assembled was responsible for a momentous saga: the reconquest of continental Europe from the Nazis. Today many come to Normandy just to see the D-Day beachheads.

Some of this province may remind you of a Millet landscape, with cattle grazing sleepily in verdant fields and wood-framed houses alongside modern buildings. Not far from the Seine you'll come on the hamlet where Monet painted his water lilies. Here and there you can still find stained-glass windows and Gothic architecture that miraculously survived the bombardments; however, many great buildings were leveled to the ground. And Normandy's wide beaches may attract families, but in August the Deauville sands draw the chicest of the chic from Europe and North America.

REGIONAL CUISINE   Normandy is the land of the three Cs: cider, Calvados, and Camembert. Butter, cream, and other dairy products with such accompaniments as pear or apple cider and fiery apple brandy make up a large part of the diet. Norman cream is velvety in texture and ivory in color. The region's sauce normande might be called a plain white sauce anywhere else, but here it takes on added allure because of its richer taste.

Certain Norman towns and regions are associated with certain dishes—tripe in the mode of Caen, sole from Dieppe, duck from Rouen, and soufflélike omelets from Mont-St-Michel. Auge Valley chicken, though not as highly praised as that of Bresse, also has a place in the diet. Locals adore andouillet (tripe sausage) from Vire, mussels from Isigny, oysters from Courseulles, cockles from Honfleur, and lobsters from La Hague. Highly prized lamb (pré salé) is raised on the salt meadows of Normandy.

The supple, fragrant cow's-milk Camembert, sold in a wooden box since 1880, is joined by other cheeses of the area, including

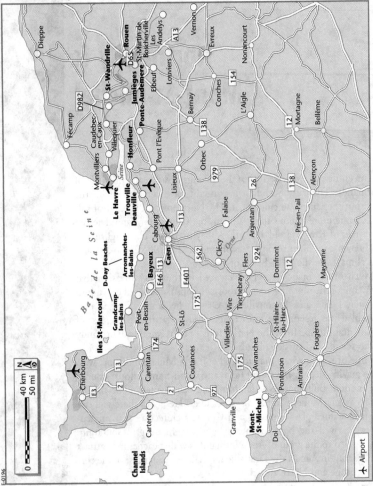

Pont-L'Evêque. Brillat-Savarin, with a high fat content of 75%, was invented in the 1930s by the cheese merchant Henri Androuët.

Normans consume cider at nearly every meal. *Bon bère* is the term for true cider, and sometimes it's so strong that it must be diluted with water. It takes 12 to 15 years to bring Calvados to taste perfection (in America Calvados may be called apple jack). Many a Norman finishes a meal with black coffee and a glass of this strong drink, which is also used to flavor main courses.

1 Rouen

84 miles NW of Paris, 55 E of Le Havre

The capital of Normandy, Rouen is the north's second most important center. It's also a hub of commerce, the fifth-largest port in France. Rouen is a bustling, vibrant place, bursting with activity generated by an explosion of industrial businesses connected to the port and a lively scene generated by students at nearby universities and art schools.

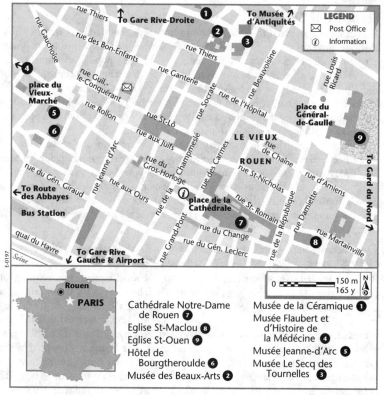

LEGEND
⊠ Post Office
ⓘ Information

Cathédrale Notre-Dame de Rouen ❼
Eglise St-Maclou ❽
Eglise St-Ouen ❾
Hôtel de Bourgtheroulde ❻
Musée des Beaux-Arts ❷

Musée de la Céramique ❶
Musée Flaubert et d'Histoire de la Médécine ❹
Musée Jeanne-d'Arc ❺
Musée Le Secq des Tournelles ❸

Today it's a city of half a million people holding memories of its former occupants, including the writers Pierre Corneille and Gustave Flaubert, along with Claude Monet, who endlessly painted the Cathédrale de Notre-Dame here, and even Joan of Arc ("Oh, Rouen, art thou then my final resting place?").

Victor Hugo called Rouen "the city of a hundred spires." Half of it was destroyed during World War II, mostly by Allied bombers, and many Rouennais were killed. During the reconstruction of the old quarters, some of the almost-forgotten crafts of the Middle Ages were revived. On the Seine, the city is rich in historic associations: William the Conqueror died here in 1087, and Joan of Arc was burned at the stake on place du Vieux-Marché in 1431.

The Seine, as in Paris, splits Rouen into a *Rive Gauche* (Left Bank) and *Rive Droite* (Right Bank). The old city is on the right bank.

ESSENTIALS

GETTING THERE From Paris's Gare St-Lazare, **trains** leave for Rouen about once every hour (trip time: 70 minutes), costing 102–152F ($18.35–$27.35) one-way. The rail station is at rue Jeanne d'Arc. For train information and schedules, call ☎ **02-35-98-50-50.** When **driving** from Paris, take A13 northwest to Rouen (trip time: 1½ hours).

VISITOR INFORMATION The **Office de Tourisme** is at 25 place de la Cathédrale (☎ **02-32-08-32-40**).

SEEING THE SIGHTS

A lane running between the cathedral and place du Vieux-Marché is **rue du Gros-Horloge** (Street of the Great Clock). Now a pedestrian mall, it's named for an ornate gilt Renaissance clock mounted on an arch, Rouen's most popular monument. The arch bridges the street and is connected to a Louis XV fountain with a bevy of cherubs and a belltower. At night the bells still toll a curfew. If you purchase a ticket at the Musée des Beaux-Arts (see below), you can visit the belfry to see the iron clockworks and the bells. It's open only Easter to mid-September, Wednesday from 2 to 6pm and Thursday to Monday from 10am to noon and 2 to 6pm.

Place du Vieux-Marché (Old Marketplace) is where Joan of Arc was executed for heresy. Tied to a stake, she was burned alive on a pyre set by the English on May 30, 1431. Kissing a cross while being chained, she's reported to have called out "Jesus!" as the fire was set. Her ashes were gathered and tossed into the Seine. A modern church displaying stained-glass windows from St-Vincent sits in the center of a monumental complex in the square; beside it a bronze cross marks the position of St. Joan's stake.

✪ **Cathédrale Notre-Dame de Rouen.** Place de la Cathédrale. Free admission. Mon–Sat 8am–7pm, Sun 7:30am–6pm. Closed during mass and on bank holidays.

Rouen's cathedral was immortalized by Monet in a series of Impressionist paintings of the three-portal facade with its galaxy of statues. The main door, Porte Central, is embellished with sculptures (some decapitated) depicting the Tree of Jesus. It's flanked by the 12th-century Porte St-Jean and Porte St-Etienne. Consecrated in 1063, the cathedral, a symphony of lacy stonework, was last reconstructed after the bombings of World War II. Two soaring towers distinguish it: Tour de Beurre was financed by the faithful willing to pay in exchange for the privilege of eating butter during Lent and is a masterpiece of the Flamboyant Gothic style. Containing a carillon of 56 bells, the three-story Tour Lanterne (Lantern Tower)—built in 1877 and utilizing 740 tons of iron and bronze—rises to almost 500 feet.

The cathedral's interior is fairly uniform. The nave has 11 bays and a sexpartite vault, and the choir is a masterpiece of harmony, with a delicate triforium and 14 soaring pillars. The Booksellers' Stairway, in the north wing of the transept, is adorned with a large rose window with stained glass that dates in part from the 1500s. The 13th-century chancel is beautiful, with relatively simple lines. Especially interesting is the **Chapelle de la Vierge,** adorned with the Renaissance tombs of the cardinals d'Amboise as well as Jean de Brézé. Also entombed inside was the heart of Richard the Lion-Hearted, a token of his affection for the people of Rouen.

Behind the cathedral is the **Palais de l'Archevêché** (Archbishop's Palace), which was bombed in the war. Now it stands naked against the sky. The broken arches and rosette windows witnessed the trial of Joan of Arc in 1431, and her rehabilitation was proclaimed here in 1456.

Eglise St-Maclou. Behind the cathedral, at 3 rue Dutuit. ☎ **02-35-71-71-72.** Mon–Sat 10am–noon and 2–6pm, Sun 3–6pm. Closed Jan 1, May 1, July 14, and Nov 11.

It was built in the Flamboyant Gothic style, with a step-gabled porch and handsome cloisters, and is known for the remarkable 16th-century panels on its doors. Our favorite (to the left) is the *Portail des Fontaines* (Portal of the Fonts). The church was constructed in 1200, rebuilt in 1432, and finally consecrated in 1521, though its lantern tower is from the 19th century. It sits on a square of old Norman crooked-timbered buildings. Inside, pictures dating from June 4, 1944, document St-Maclou's destruction.

A Spectacular Drive Along the Route des Abbayes

Beginning at Rouen, the Seine winds through black forests and lush green countryside along the Route des Abbayes, eventually ending at Le Havre. As you make your way past the ruins of monasteries and châteaux, you'll agree that this is one of the most evocative and memorable routes in France.

Ten minutes after leaving Rouen (via D982), you arrive at the 11th-century **Abbaye St-George**, in St-Martin de Boscherville. From here, go along D982 and D65 around the Seine for 12 miles to Jumièges. One of France's most beautiful ruins, **Abbaye de Jumièges** was founded by St. Philbert in the 7th century and rebuilt in the 10th century. The abbey church was consecrated in 1067 by the archbishop of Rouen in the presence of William the Conqueror. The 100-foot-high nave is complete, and the porch is surrounded by two towers 150 feet high.

Another 10 miles along the right bank of the Seine leads to St-Wandrille, 33 miles northwest of Rouen (reached via D982 from Jumièges). **Abbaye de St-Wandrille** was founded in 649. Over the centuries the abbey has suffered various attacks, including from the Vikings, and today nothing remains of the 7th-century monastery. A huge 18th-century blue gate frames the entrance, and inside you can visit cloisters from the 14th to the 16th century.

From St-Wandrille, continue for 2 miles or so to **Caudebec-en-Caux,** set in an amphitheater along the Seine. Nearly destroyed in World War II, it has a Gothic church from the 15th century that was spared in the war bombings. Henri IV considered it the handsomest chapel in his kingdom. On its west side is a trio of Flamboyant Gothic doorways, crowned by a rose window.

Drive west around the north bank of the Seine to **Villequier,** a tranquil village with a château. It was here that Victor Hugo lost his daughter, along with her husband, in a seasonal tidal wave. You can visit the **Musée Victor-Hugo,** on quai Victor-Hugo (☎ 02-35-56-78-31). It has the manuscript of his poem "Contemplations," a lament. It's open Wednesday to Monday, March to October from 10am to 12:30pm and 2 to 6pm and November to February from 10am to 12:30pm and 2 to 5:30pm.

Some 33 miles to the west, along D81 and N182, you reach **Le Havre,** France's major Atlantic port. The city was the target of more than 170 bombings during World War II, but its recovery was amazing. From here you can take boat tours to Trouville and Deauville, a pair of lovely, chic resorts.

Eglise St-Ouen. Place du Général-de-Gaulle. Mar 15–Oct Wed–Mon 10am–12:30pm and 2–6pm; Jan 16–Mar 14 and Nov–Dec 14 Wed and Sat–Sun 10am–12:30pm and 2–4:30pm. Closed Dec 15–Jan 15.

This church is the outgrowth of a 7th-century Benedictine abbey. Flanked by four turrets, its 375-foot octagonal lantern tower is called "the ducal crown of Normandy." One of the best-known Gothic buildings in France, the church represents the work of 5 centuries. Its nave is from the 15th century, its choir from the 14th (but with 18th-century railings), and its remarkable stained glass from the 14th to the 16th. On May 23, 1431, Joan of Arc was taken to the cemetery here, where officials sentenced her to be burned at the stake unless she recanted. She signed an abjuration, thus condemning herself to life imprisonment, but that sentence was later revoked.

Hôtel de Bourgtheroulde. 15 place de la Pucelle (Square of the Maid). ☎ **02-35-08-64-00.** Courtyard visits Mon–Fri 8am–12:30pm and 1:30–5:15pm. Closed Sat and Sun except for special exhibitions. Call for details.

One of the most frequently showcased Gothic buildings of Rouen, this building functions today as the headquarters of a local bank, Crédit Industrielle de Normandie (C.I.N.). Built in the 15th century by William the Red, then enlarged during the Renaissance, it's noteworthy for an interior courtyard, which is the only part you can visit regularly. In the courtyard, whose ageless architecture warrants a brief visit, look back at the octagonal stair tower. The left gallery is entirely Renaissance.

Musée des Beaux-Arts. Place Verdel. ☎ **02-35-71-28-40.** Admission 20F ($3.60) adults, 13F ($2.35) students and children 11 and under. Wed–Mon 10am–6pm.

This is one of France's most important provincial museums, with portraits by David, plus works by Delacroix and Ingres (seek out his *La Belle Zélie*). A Gérard David retable, *La Vierge et les saints* (The Virgin and the Saints), is a masterpiece. One salon is devoted to Géricault, including a portrait of Delacroix. Other works are by Veronese, Velásquez, Caravaggio, Rubens, Poussin, Fragonard, and Corot, and several paintings by Impressionists like Monet, including several versions of his Rouen Cathedral.

Musée de la Céramique. 1 rue Faucon. ☎ **02-35-07-31-74.** Admission 15F ($2.70) adults, 10F ($1.80) children. Thurs–Mon 10am–noon and 2–6pm.

One of the greatest treasures here is the 17th-century Rouen faïence, which pioneered a special red in 1670. The exhibits provide a showcase for the talents of Masseot Abaquesne, the premier French artist in faïence and of the specific Rouen-style production (1650–1780). An exceptional showcase is devoted to chinoiserie from 1699 to 1745.

Musée Le Secq des Tournelles (Wrought Ironworks Museum). Rue Jacques-Villon. ☎ **02-35-71-28-40.** Admission 35F ($6.30). Wed–Mon 10am–6pm.

Housed in the 15th-century Eglise St-Laurent, the museum showcases an art form (wrought iron) for which the Normans have been famous for centuries. Its collection ranges from what the press once called "forthright masculine forging to lacy feminine filigree, from Roman keys to the needlepoint balustrade that graced Mme de Pompadour's country mansion." A Parisian aristocrat, Le Secq des Tournelles, began the collection in 1870. So passionately was he devoted to it that his wife divorced him, charging alienation of affection. Donated to the city of Rouen, the collection now has some 14,000 pieces.

Musée Flaubert et d'Histoire de la Médécine. In the Hôtel-Dieu, 51 rue de Lecat. ☎ **02-35-15-59-95.** Admission 12F ($2.15) adults, free for students and children. Tues–Sat 10am–noon and 2–6pm. Closed holidays.

Gustave Flaubert, author of *Madame Bovary*, was born in the director's quarters of Rouen's public hospital (his father was the director). Flaubert spent his first 25 years in the city, and the room where he was born in 1821 is still intact. In addition, family furniture and medical paraphernalia are displayed. Only a glass door separated the Flauberts from the ward and its moaning patients.

Musée Jeanne-d'Arc. 33 place du Vieux-Marché. ☎ **02-35-88-02-70.** Admission 24F ($4.30) adults, 12F ($2.15) children and students. May–Sept 15 daily 9:30am–7pm, rest of the year daily 10am–noon and 2–6:30pm.

The life and martyrdom of Joan of Arc, France's national heroine, are traced here. In a vaulted cellar are dioramas and waxworks as well as commentary in four languages, depicting the main stages of her life—from Domrémy, where she was born, to her burning at the stake on the square near the museum's entrance. The site also contains a research library on her life and the politics of her era.

SHOPPING IN ROUEN

Rouen was once one of France's major producers of the fine decorative ceramic ware known as *faïence de Rouen*. Examples of both antique and contemporary faïence still abound, and it's worth picking up one or two pieces for your home or even as gifts. For contemporary faïence, your best bet is the shop of **Michel Carpentier,** 26 rue St-Romain (☎ **02-35-88-77-47**), where his artisans carry on the tradition of making faïence de Rouen.

Another Rouen specialty to keep on the lookout for when exploring area antiques shops is *coffret de Rouen*. These little hand-painted wooden boxes were all the rage during the 18th and 19th centuries, and the original versions continue to be popular—but watch out for modern forgeries.

Rouen has also become an antiques capital, and the best hunting ground is in Vieux Rouen (the Old Town) along **rue Eau-de-Robec, place Barthélémy, rue Damiette,** and **rue St-Romain.** The first Saturday of every month you can find an **antiques fair** on rue Eau-de-Robec. The city also has two **flea markets,** one on Saturday and Sunday at place St-Mare and the other every Thursday at place des Emmurés. Medium- and large-scale antiques auctions take place throughout the year at the **Salles des Ventes,** 25 rue du Général-Giraud (☎ **02-35-71-13-50**) and 20 rue de la Croix-de-Fer (☎ **02-35-98-73-49**).

Other antiques shops worth visiting are **M. Bertran,** 108 rue Molière (☎ **02-35-98-24-06**), with a good selection of 18th- and 19th-century paintings; **E. Bertran,** 110 rue Molière (☎ **02-35-70-79-96**), with its collection of antique books dating back to the 1400s; **Antic St-Maclou,** 178 rue Martainville (☎ **02-35-89-52-61**), a 20-year-old shop specializing in estate jewelry and silver; **P. Chasset,** 12 rue de la Croix-de-Fer (☎ **02-35-70-59-97**), where you'll find toys and gaming cards from the 1700s and 1800s as well as bottles and glassware. You'll find watercolors by local artists, as well as antique Norman and English engravings, at **Atelier St-Romain,** 28 rue St-Romain (☎ **02-35-88-76-17**).

Lovers of chocolate will find a veritable paradise at **La Chocolatière,** 18 rue Guillaume-le-Conquérant (☎ **02-35-71-00-79**). If hats are your thing, head for **Monique,** 58 rue St-Romain (☎ **02-35-98-07-03**). Here hats run the gamut from funky to refined and elegant—and you won't be paying Parisian prices.

WHERE TO STAY

Hôtel de Bordeaux. 9 place de la République, 76000 Rouen. ☎ **02-35-71-93-58.** Fax 02-35-71-92-15. 48 units. TV TEL. 290–330F ($52.20–$59.40) double. AE, DC, MC, V.

Practically on the banks of the Seine, this hotel provides medium-size rooms that have the standard built-in furnishings but are accented with calming earth tones. All look out onto views of either the town's medieval rooftops or the cathedral. Accommodations on the upper floors get the bonus of a river view. The hotel has an intimate breakfast room that can, at times, overflow with an assortment of healthy green plants. In reception/sitting area, with its mahogany furniture, guests congregate before setting out on a day of adventure, shopping, and sightseeing.

✪ **Hôtel Cardinal.** 1 place de la Cathédrale, 76000 Rouen. ☎ **02-35-70-24-42.** Fax 02-35-89-75-14. 20 units. TV TEL. 270–380F ($48.60–$68.40) double. MC, V. Parking 30F ($5.40) nearby.

You couldn't find a more ideally located hotel as affordable as this one. It's right across from the cathedral (imagine waking up to the view of this ancient majesty and surrounding half-timbered buildings each morning) and in the middle of a part of town known for antiques stores, art galleries, and fine dining. With this much to do, you won't mind the hotel's simplicity. The rooms are business-class plain—with built-in furnishings and color schemes in whites and beiges. The small breakfast room takes advantage of natural sun shining through the multicolored windows.

Hôtel de la Cathédrale. 12 rue St-Romain, 76000 Rouen. ☎ **02-35-71-57-95.** 24 units. TV TEL. 300–355F ($54–$63.90) double. MC, V. Parking 25F ($4.50) nearby. Bus: 1, 3, 5, 7, or 10.

Built around a timbered courtyard, the hotel is on a pedestrian street midway between the cathedral and the Eglise St-Maclou, opposite the Archbishop's Palace where Joan of Arc was tried. The recently remodeled rooms are well maintained and tastefully furnished, accessible by both stairs and an elevator. Breakfast is the only meal served.

Hôtel de Dieppe. Place Bernard-Tissot, 76000 Rouen. ☎ **800/528-1234** in the U.S. and Canada, or 02-35-71-96-00. Fax 02-35-89-65-21. 41 units. TV TEL. 51–610F ($91.80–$109.80) double. AE, DC, MC, V. Bus: 1, 3, 5, 7, or 10.

This Best Western across from the train station has been run by the Gueret family since 1880. Though modernized, it's still a traditional French inn. The only problem might be the noise, but the double-glazed windows help; after 10pm the last train from Paris arrives and the area quiets down. The rooms are done in either period or contemporary styling and are fairly compact. In the adjoining rôtisserie, Le Quatre Saisons, you can enjoy dishes such as duckling *à la presse* and sole poached in red wine.

Hôtel Le Viking. 21 quai du Havre, 76000 Rouen. ☎ **02-35-70-34-95.** Fax 02-35-89-97-12. 37 units. TV TEL. 285–330F ($51.30–$59.40) double. Rates include breakfast. AE, DC, V. Parking 45F ($9). Bus: 1, 3, 5, 7, or 10.

On a riverbank overlooking the Seine, this seven-story hotel is in a white-sided concrete building. The traffic noise can be bad at times, but the front rooms open onto charming river views. In July and August reserve well in advance, since it's usually packed. The accommodations are a little small but still comfortable. Breakfast is the only meal served.

Mercure Centre. Rue de la Croix-de-Fer, 76000 Rouen. ☎ **02-35-52-69-52.** Fax 02-35-89-41-46. 125 units. A/C MINIBAR TV TEL. 440–530F ($79.20–$95.40) double; 850–950F ($153–$171) suite. AE, DC, MC, V. Parking 50F ($9). Métro: Place-Foch.

In a town of lackluster hotels, the Mercure is a fine choice for an overnight, although hardly romantically appealing. The functionally designed rooms, all almost exactly identical to those in hundreds of other Mercure hotels across Europe, are clean and well maintained, though perhaps a tad small. There's a bar on the premises, but breakfast is the only meal served.

WHERE TO DINE

✪ **Gill.** 9 quai de la Bourse. ☎ **02-35-71-16-14.** Reservations recommended. Main courses 145–195F ($26.10–$35.10); fixed-price menus 199–460F ($35.80–$82.80). AE, DC, MC, V. May–Sept Mon–Sat noon–2:15pm and 7–9:45pm; Oct–Apr Tues–Sat noon–2:15pm, Tues–Sun 7–9:45pm. Métro: Théâtre-des-Arts. FRENCH.

The most talked about and best place in town is located just beside the traffic of the Seine's quays. The uncluttered modern decor with high-tech accessories is an appropriate backdrop for the sophisticated cuisine of Gilles Tournadre, who believes in exemplary ingredients and innovation within a classic context. Who can resist the ravioli stuffed with foie gras and served in a bouillon sprinkled with fresh truffles? And what about a terrine of artichoke flavored with fresh truffles, roasted white turbot with fresh asparagus flavored with Parmesan, or filet of sea bass with smoked salmon in red-wine sauce? The lobster fricassée with fresh mushrooms "from the woods" is another winning selection. Save room for the Calvados soufflé. It's a winner!

Maison Dufour. 67 bis rue St-Nicholas. ☎ **02-35-71-90-62.** Reservations required. Main courses 80–160F ($14.40–$28.80); fixed-price menus 150–230F ($27–$41.40). AE, MC, V. Tues–Sun noon–2pm, Tues–Sat 7–9:30pm. Métro: Théâtre-des-Arts. NORMAN.

One of Normandy's best-preserved 15th-century inns has flourished under four generations of the Dufour family since 1906. The three street-level dining rooms are decorated with copper pots, wood carvings, and engravings. The food, reflecting Normandy's culinary traditions, is so outstanding it's hard to single out specialties. However, the home-smoked salmon, *canard* (duckling) *rouennais,* John Dory in cider sauce, and sole normande are exemplary. The most appropriate dessert is a Calvados-flavored soufflé or a thin but wide slice of apple tart.

Pascaline. 5 rue de la Poterne. ☎ **02-35-89-67-44.** Reservations recommended. Main courses 59–77F ($10.60–$13.85); fixed-price menus 79–99F ($14.20–$17.80); fixed-price lunch (Mon–Fri only) 59F ($10.60). V. Daily noon–2:30pm and 7:30–11:30pm. Métro: Place-Foch. FRENCH.

This informal bistro with a turn-of-the-century decor is often filled with regulars, though it's not as atmospheric or charming as the Brasserie de la Grande Poste. The cheapest fixed-price menus represent some of the best bargains in town. Menu items include seafood dishes like pavé of monkfish with roughly textured mustard sauce, a savory pot-au-feu maison, tenderloin steaks, and cassoulet toulousain. Don't come for refined cuisine—instead, you can expect hearty and time-tested old favorites.

ROUEN AFTER DARK

The citizens of Rouen usually start their nights on the town at a pub or cafe. The better ones frequented by 25- to 45-year-olds are the always-crowded **Café Leffe,** 36 place des Carmes (☎ **02-35-71-93-30**); and **La Taverne St-Amand,** 11 rue St-Amand (☎ **02-35-88-51-34**), with a friendly environment perfect for enjoying a mug or two of the best Irish, Belgian, and German beers around. Many students call the **Underground Pub,** 26 rue des Champs-Maillets (☎ **02-35-98-44-84**), their home away from home. This place has both a street-level bar and an underground bar outfitted in wood and British bric-a-brac.

WINE BAR   If beer drinking doesn't turn you on, try **Le Petit Zine,** 20 place du Vieux-Marché (☎ **02-35-89-39-69**). This bistro-style wine bar, with its early 1900s retro decor, has one of the best wine selections in town. Of course, you can order Norman cider as well.

DISCO   At **Le Diosque,** 43 bd. de Verdun (☎ **02-35-88-54-50**), plenty of young twentysomethings rule the dance floor. Paying a cover of 90F ($16.20) will get you into the hard-edged techno music and psychedelic light action.

GAY & LESBIAN BARS   **Le Kox,** 138 rue Beauvoisine (☎ **02-35-07-71-97**), attracts a très cool crowd of mostly gay males from their 20s to their 40s who prefer the James Dean look of jeans and t-shirts. There's a full bar and lots of distractions, like pinball machines, video screens, billiards, and dartboards. **L'Opium,** 2 rue Malherbe (☎ **02-35-03-29-36**), open only on Friday, Saturday, and Sunday nights, is where the hip young gay and lesbian crowd comes to be seen and dance. The cover is 50F ($9). The modern **Le Traxx,** 4 bis bd. Ferdinand-de-Lesseps (☎ **02-35-10-12-02**), attracts its share of young, well-connected gays and lesbians. It's known for killer light shows, intense techno, and a wild crowd until the wee hours. Here you'll pay 50F ($9) to get in.

MUSIC   Rouen also has its cultural side. **Théâtre des Arts,** 7 rue du Dr.-Rambert (☎ **02-35-71-41-36**), has a very busy schedule of classical and contemporary operas. A variety of musical concerts are hosted at the **Eglise St-Maclou,** 3 rue Dutuit, and the **Eglise St-Ouen,** place du Général-de-Gaulle. You can obtain current concert schedules from the Office de Tourisme (above).

2 Honfleur

125 miles NW of Paris, 39 miles NE of Caen

At the mouth of the Seine, opposite Le Havre, Honfleur is one of Normandy's most charming fishing ports. Having miraculously escaped damage in World War II, the port today looks like an antique, although it's a working one. Thanks to the pont de Normande suspension bridge, which links it directly to Le Havre, greater and greater hordes are now flocking here. Honfleur is actually 500 years older than Le Havre, dating from the 11th century. Early in the 17th century, colonists set out for Québec in Canada. The township has long been favored by artists, including Daubigny, Corot, and Monet.

ESSENTIALS

Three **Bus Verts** per day connect Caen and Honfleur (trip time: 2 hours), costing 82F ($14.75) one-way. Call ☎ **02-31-44-77-44** for information and schedules. If you're **driving** in from Pont l'Evêque to the south, D579 leads to the major boulevard, rue de la République. Follow it until the end for the town center (driving time from Paris: 2½ hours).

The **Office de Tourisme** is on place Arthur-Boudin (☎ **02-31-89-23-30**).

SEEING THE TOWN

From place de la Porte-de-Rouen you can begin your tour of the town, which should take about an hour. Stroll along the **Vieux Bassin,** the old harbor, which has fishing boats and slate-roofed narrow houses. The former governor's house, **Lieutenance,** on the north side of the basin, dates from the 16th century. Nearby is the **Eglise Ste-Catherine,** built by shipbuilders entirely of timber in the 15th century. The church's belfry stands on the other side of the street and is also of wood.

Musée Eugène-Boudin, place Erik-Satie (☎ **02-31-89-54-00**), has a good collection of the painters who flocked to this port when Impressionism was born. The largest collection is of the pastels and paintings of Boudin, of course. It's open March 15 to September, Wednesday to Monday from 10am to noon and 2 to 6pm; October to March 14, Monday and Wednesday to Friday from 2:30 to 5pm and Saturday and Sunday from 10am to noon and 2 to 5pm. Admission is 25F ($4.50).

WHERE TO STAY

Restaurant/Hôtel L'Absinthe (see below) also rents rooms.

Castel Albertine. 19 cours Albert-Manuel, 14600 Honfleur. ☎ **02-31-98-85-56.** Fax 02-31-98-83-18. 26 units. TV TEL. 50–600F ($90-$108) double; 800F ($144) suite. AE, DC, MC, V.

Great care was taken to maintain the character of this stately home of Albert Sorel, a 19th-century historian/scholar, during its renaissance into a handsome, welcoming hotel. Its reception area is a unique greenhouse room linking the main house to its modern built-to-look-old addition—one that retains the architectural integrity of the estate. All the individually decorated rooms have antique reproduction furnishings, soft colors, and floor-to-ceiling windows that open up on views of gardens and century-old trees. The airy dining room with its light pine hardwood floor, tables, and chairs is bathed in sun in the morning. You can also enjoy the hotel's Finnish sauna with its multijet shower.

✪ **Hostellerie Lechat.** 3 place Ste-Catherine, 14600 Honfleur. ☎ 02-31-14-49-49. Fax 02-31-89-28-61. 23 units. TV TEL. 410–480F ($73.80–$86.40) double; 800F ($144) suite. AE, DC, MC, V. Closed Jan–Feb 15. Bus: 20 or 50.

Near (but not directly adjacent to) the port, this hotel has parts dating from the 16th century and an undeniable sense of old-fashioned coziness. The comfortably furnished rooms, though modest, are fine for an overnight stop.

Dining: The rustic restaurant offers an array of seafood, like sole, salmon, and turbot, plus lobster and oysters. The chef also does some superb terrines. The restaurant is closed on Wednesday evening and all day Thursday. During January, it's open only on Saturday night, presumably to profit from the stream of Parisians seeking weekend getaways.

✪ **La Ferme St-Simeon.** Route Adolphe-Marais, 14600 Honfleur. ☎ **02-31-89-23-61.** Fax 02-31-89-48-48. 34 units. MINIBAR TV TEL. 790–3,510F ($142.20–$631.80) double; 4,400–5,400F ($792–$972) suite. AE, V.

An old cider press is the focal point in front of this 17th-century wood-and-slate house, which has become one of Normandy's most elegant inns. The shimmering water of the English Channel drew artists to this hilltop inn, said to be where Impressionism was born in the 19th century. Much of the hotel has terra-cotta floors, carved wood, and copper and faïence touches. The guest rooms are decorated in an 18th-century style.

Dining: Food is served in the restaurant or on the terrace, with a view of the Seine estuary and Le Havre. The classic yet simple cuisine is superb: try the chausson of lobster, fricassée of rice and kidneys, or sole normande.

Amenities: Heated indoor pool, sauna, solarium, fitness center, whirlpool.

WHERE TO DINE

✪ **L'Assiette Gourmande.** 2 quai des Passagers. ☎ **02-31-89-24-88.** Reservations required. Main courses 140–195F ($25.20–$35.10); fixed-price menus 160–415F ($28.80–$74.70). AE, DC, MC, V. Tues–Sun noon–2:15pm and 7–9:45pm. FRENCH.

Beside the medieval port, this is the town's finest restaurant. On the street level of the Cheval Blanc hotel, with which it's not associated, it's the domain of Gérard and Anne-Marie Bonnefoy, who serve delectable dishes such as omelet au gratin studded with lobster chunks, escalope of warm foie gras with lentil-flavored cream sauce, roasted crayfish with a marinade of two vegetables, and roasted turbot with essence of chicken. Be sure to leave room for the *petit gâteau moelleux au chocolate* (very moist, deliberately overcooked chocolate-fudge cake).

Restaurant/Hôtel L'Absinthe. 10 quai de la Quarantaine, 14600 Honfleur. ☎ **02-31-89-39-00.** Reservations required. Main courses 155–300F ($27.90–$54); fixed-price menus 169–340F ($30.40–$61.20). AE, DC, MC, V. Daily 12:15–2:15pm and 7:15–9:15pm. Bus: 20 or 50. FRENCH.

This tavern—named for the drink preferred by many 19th-century writers in Honfleur—is known by practically everyone in town for its beautiful decor, extravagant portions, and well-prepared savory cuisine. It has two dining rooms—one from the 17th century, one from the 15th. Owner Antoine Ceffrey and chef Michel Cassou will probably make an appearance in the dining rooms before the end of your meal. Menu choices may be veal kidneys with Calvados, baked turbot with pepper sauce, and attractive desserts like assorted fresh fruit with essence of raspberries.

If the food is so good that you can't bear to leave, you'll be happy to know that the restaurant also rents six simple but comfortable rooms and one suite, all with satellite TV and phone. A double is 500F to 700F ($90 to $126), and the suite is 1,200F ($216). Parking is available for 30F ($5.40).

3 Deauville

128 miles NW of Paris, 29 miles NE of Caen

Deauville has been associated with the rich and famous since it was founded as an upscale resort in 1859 by the duc de Morny, Napoléon III's half-brother. In 1913 it entered sartorial history when Coco Chanel launched her career here by opening a boutique selling tiny hats that challenged the current fashion of huge-brimmed hats loaded with flowers and fruit. (Coco's point of view: "How can the mind breathe under those things?")

ESSENTIALS

GETTING THERE There are four **rail** connections from Paris's Gare St-Lazare (trip time: 2½ hours), costing 122F to 215F ($21.95–$38.70) one-way. The rail depot is between Trouville and Deauville, south of the town. **Bus Verts du Calvados** (☎ **02-31-88-95-36**) serves the lower Normandy coast from Caen to Le Havre. When **driving** from Paris (trip time: 2½ hours), take A13 west to Pont L'Evêque. From here follow D579 to D180 traveling east to Deauville.

VISITOR INFORMATION The **Office de Tourisme** is on place Mairie (☎ **02-31-14-40-00**).

SPECIAL EVENTS For a week in early September the **Deauville Film Festival** honors movies made in the United States only. Actors, producers, directors, and writers flock here and briefly eclipse the high rollers at the casinos and the horse-race/polo crowd.

EXPLORING THE RESORT

The tradition for elegance Coco Chanel helped perpetuate is still a part of Deauville, as well as a part of its smaller and less prestigious neighbor, Trouville, on the opposite bank of the Toques (see below). Don't expect flashiness—in its own way, restrained and ever-so-polite Deauville is the most British seaside resort in France.

However, in its heart Deauville is more French than English and more Parisian than French. It has even been dubbed Paris's 21st arrondissement in the same way that the Hamptons have been called New York City's sixth borough. Don't come here looking for medieval France. The aura is Edwardian and even healthy and recuperative. The crowds tend to be more urban and hip than the folk at resorts, say, near La Rochelle or in the remote stretches of Brittany. None of this comes cheaply—Deauville is stylish and not (by anyone's definition of the word) inexpensive.

With its golf courses, casinos, deluxe hotels, La Touques and Clairefontaine race-tracks, regattas, yachting harbor, polo grounds, and tennis courts, Deauville is still a formidable contender for the business of the smart set. Looking for a particularly charming place to stroll through the town? Head for **rue Eugène-Colas, place Morny** (named in honor of the resort's founding patriarch), and **rue des Villas** (lined with expansive and expensive holiday homes built by the well-heeled during France's gilded age).

BEACHES Expect to spend time on Deauville's boardwalk, **Les Planches,** a wooden plank promenade running parallel to the beach; its edges are lined with formal Beaux-Arts or half-timbered Norman-inspired architecture. In summer, especially August, parasols dot the beach, and oiled bodies stretch out and seemingly cover every inch of sand.

The resort's only beach is **Plage de Deauville,** a long strip of sand that's part of Plage Fleurie. Flowers don't actually grow from the sand, but its name was part of a successful 19th-century marketing ploy developed by entrepreneurs to attract Parisians and even, to a lesser extent, the English. Allegedly, its borders harbored some fragile flowers long before the mobs of sunbathers, high tides, and building sprees buried them forever, but today, if they bloom at all, they appear during April and May, when most people aren't likely to be here.

If you're looking for a specifically gay beach, you'll have to drive 24 miles from Deauville toward Caen, to **Merville-France-Ville,** but considering how permissive most Deauville fans are, many gays feel perfectly comfortable remaining here.

GOLF　On Mont Canisy, Deauville's **New-Golf Club** (☎ **02-31-14-24-24,** see below) offers a tranquil country setting tinged by the sea's salty tang. The par-71 18-hole course rolls through 6,490 yards of rapid greens and difficult roughs, with sweeping views of the Auge valley and the sea, and the par-36 9-hole course runs 3,315 yards through a typically lush wooded setting. In addition, there's an indoor driving range, a putting green, a practice bunker, available instruction from three professionals, and a clubhouse with not only a bar and restaurant but also an exclusive line of golfing gear. A franchise of the Lucien Barrière chain of resorts, hotels, and casinos, the facility includes a palatial Norman-style hotel (see below). Greens fees for hotel residents are 350F ($63) on Saturday and Sunday and 25F ($45) Monday through Friday. Nonguests pay a supplement of 10% above those rates.

HORSE RACES　Take a break from the sun and sand to watch the horse races, but only from late June to early September. There's at least one racing event held every afternoon, either a race at 2pm or a polo match at 3pm. The venues are the **Hippodrome de Deauville La Touques,** boulevard Mauger (☎ **02-31-14-20-00**), in the heart of town, near the Mairie de Deauville (Town Hall); or the **Hippodrome de Deauville Clairefontaine,** route de Clairefontaine (☎ **02-31-88-66-80**), a bit farther afield but still within the city limits.

SHOPPING　This seaside town has a pedestrian shopping area between the polo field and the port and centers around rue Mirabeau, rue Albert-Fracasse, and the west end of avenue de la République. At **La Ferme Normande,** 13 rue Breney (☎ **02-31-88-17-86**), or **La Cave de Deauville,** 48 rue Mirabeau (☎ **02-31-87-35-36**), you'll be able to find a great selection of apple ciders, Calvados apple brandy, and the aperitif known as pommeau—the very drinks that are part of Normandy's rich heritage.

WHERE TO STAY
EXPENSIVE

Hôtel du Golf. At New-Golf Club, Mont Canisy, St-Arnoult 14800 Deauville. ☎ **02-31-14-24-00.** Fax 02-31-14-24-01. 178 units. MINIBAR TV TEL. 850–1,700F ($153–$306) double; 1,600–3,000F ($288–$540) suite. AE, DC, MC, V. Closed Nov–Mar 15. From Deauville, take D278 south for 1½ miles.

Sports fans—especially golfers—gravitate to this colossal Norman inn that was created by the Lucien Barrière chain in the late 1980s. It's one of the few hotels in Normandy with its own adjoining golf course. If golf isn't your thing, however, perhaps consider the Normandy and Le Royal instead. The accommodations here come in a wide range of sizes, many with traditional pieces; some have balconies. The older rooms aren't as good as the more recently renovated ones; those in back open onto the links, but those in front have better views of the Channel.

Dining: A glass-enclosed dining room encircles a veranda, offering views of the Channel. The food doesn't rate a trip here but is competently prepared in the international style. Poolside barbecues are a summer feature.

Amenities: Heated pool, sauna, three tennis courts, 27-hole golf course, room service, laundry.

✪ **Hôtel Normandy.** 38 rue Jean-Mermoz, 14800 Deauville. ☎ **02-31-98-66-22.** Fax 02-31-98-66-23. 303 units. MINIBAR TV TEL. 1,100–2,200F ($198–$396) double; from 2,000F ($360) suite. AE, DC, MC, V. Parking 100F ($18) in garage, free outside.

Resembling a Norman village, with turrets, gables, and windows piercing sloping roofs, this year-round hotel is near the casino, in a park of well-manicured shrubs and flowers. It's Deauville's best, though some discriminating people prefer Le Royal. The interior is as warm and comfortable as a rambling country house, with chandeliers and Oriental carpeting. Activities center around the main rotunda, encircled by a marble colonnade. The rooms are in a constant state of refurbishment, each with double-glazed windows and mirrored closets. The fourth-floor units under sloping ceilings are the most cramped.

Dining: Guests gather in the paneled piano bar before selecting one of three restaurants: a gourmet enclave, the main dining room, or La Fermette, a restaurant dedicated to younger guests.

Amenities: Heated indoor pool, sauna, fitness room, steam room, tennis courts, miniature-golf course, room service, laundry, safes, nursery.

✪ **Le Royal.** Bd. Eugène-Cornuché, 14800 Deauville. ☎ **02-31-98-66-33.** Fax 02-31-98-66-34. 249 units. MINIBAR TV TEL. 1,010–2,300F ($181.80–$414) double; from 2,000F ($360) suite. AE, DC, MC, V. Closed Nov–Mar.

Le Royal adjoins the casino and fronts a block-wide park between itself and the Channel. An ideal place for a holiday, it rises like a regal palace, with columns and exposed timbers. The accommodations range from sumptuous suites to cozy little nooks. More than two dozen rooms were recently renovated, with designer fabrics and thick rugs; others seem to languish back in the 1970s. The rooms on the upper floors open onto the most panoramic views.

Dining: L'Etrier is the chic choice for dining, and Sunday is caviar night. The chef often creates innovative dishes. There's also terrace dining in summer.

Amenities: Heated outdoor pool, beach, sauna, two recreation rooms, bicycle rental, health club, room service, valet parking.

MODERATE TO INEXPENSIVE

L'Augeval. 15 av. Hocquart-de-Turtot, 14800 Deauville. ☎ **02-31-81-13-18.** Fax 02-31-81-00-40. 32 units. MINIBAR TV TEL. 420–850F ($75.60–$153) double; 880–1,400F ($158.40–$252) suite. AE, DC, MC, V.

Across from the racetrack and mere blocks from the beach and casino, this rare gem provides you with a great mix of city flair and country charm. This three-story brick-and-stone former private villa was built in the early 1900s and sits in the middle of well-kept lawns and gardens. You can walk out the back of the hotel and take a dip in the heated pool or have a drink on the garden patio. The guest rooms range from medium-size to spacious and are outfitted with overstuffed armchairs and sofas. Some even have bubble baths. The public areas include a bar and dining room, both with tall stone and brick vaulted ceilings, plus an exercise room.

✪ **Hôtel Ibis.** 9 quai de la Marine, 14800 Deauville. ☎ **02-31-14-50-00.** Fax 02-31-14-50-05. 95 units. TV TEL. 325–455F ($58.50–$81.90) double; 605–745F ($108.90–$134.10) duplex suite for two to five. AE, DC, MC, V. Parking 40F ($7.20).

Built in the mid-1980s as part of a nationwide chain, the Ibis is scenically located and offers some of the best values of any hotel in Deauville. The modern building overlooks the harbor; the rooms are comfortable but done in a rather dull chain style. The restaurant offers a traditional French menu.

Hôtel Le Trophée. 81 rue du Général-Leclerc, 14800 Deauville. ☎ **02-31-88-45-86.** Fax 02-31-88-07-94. 24 units. MINIBAR TV TEL. 340–680F ($61.20–$122.40) double; 680–980F ($122.40–$176.40) suite. AE, DC, MC, V.

This modern replica of a half-timbered medieval building is in the middle of Deauville, 500 feet from the beach. The rooms, with nondescript contemporary furniture, are on the small side but do have private balconies overlooking the shopping streets. The roof of the hotel has been converted into a sun terrace and provides a bird's-eye view of the town as well as a more private tanning area than the beach. The intimate restaurant serves breakfast and three fixed-price menus as well as daily specials. If you plan on taking one or more of your meals here, eat at least one under the stars in the patio courtyard garden.

WHERE TO DINE

Chez Miocque. 81 rue Eugène-Colas. ☎ **02-31-88-09-52.** Reservations recommended. Main courses 100–150F ($18–$27). MC, V. May–Oct daily 9am–midnight, mid-Feb to Apr and Nov–Dec Wed–Mon noon–3pm and 7pm–midnight. Closed Jan 1 to mid-Feb. FRENCH.

Irreverent and hip, this cafe near the casino and the resort's boutiques does a bustling business at its sidewalk tables. The owner, known simply as Jack, speaks English and will welcome you for lunch or dinner or provide a convivial bar-type setting if you just want to stop in for a drink. You get hearty brasserie-style food, including succulent lamb stew with spring vegetables, filet of skate with cream-based caper sauce, mussels in white-wine sauce, and steaks. The portions are filling, and the atmosphere can be lively.

✪ **Le Ciro's.** Promenade des Planches. ☎ **02-31-14-31-31.** Reservations required. Main courses 90–350F ($16.20–$63). AE, DC, MC, V. Daily noon–2:30pm, Sun–Thurs 7:15–9:30pm, Fri–Sat 7:15–10pm. FRENCH/SEAFOOD.

Hot on the resort's social scene, Le Ciro's serves Deauville's best seafood—expensive but worth it. As you enter, you can make your lobster selection from the bubbling tank; the kitchen stocks a wide range of delectable oysters and mussels. If you want a bit of everything, ask for the *plateau de fruits de mer,* with lobster and various oysters and clams. The most expensive item is grilled lobster. For an elaborate appetizer, we recommend foie gras of duckling or lobster salad with truffles. Crunchy Dublin Bay prawns in orange-flavored butter are typical of the fresh seafood. Classics like grilled beef filet with béarnaise and grilled lamb cutlets are offered. The collection of Bordeaux wine is exceptional.

✪ **Le Spinnaker.** 52 rue Mirabeau. ☎ **02-31-88-24-40.** Reservations required. Main courses 140–170F ($25.20–$30.60); fixed-price menus 160–250F ($28.80–$45). AE, MC, V. Thurs–Mon 12:30–2:30 and 7:30–10pm. Closed Jan. NORMAN.

Directed by the owner/chef, Pascal Angenard, this charming restaurant in a half-timbered building features regional cuisine and is filled with English chintz and white napery. The menu specialties are ultrafresh and richly satisfying, like terrine of foie gras with four spices, roast lobster with cider vinegar and cream-enriched potatoes, slow-cooked baby veal flank, and a succulent tart with hot apples. Pascal recommends the roast turbot flavored with shallots. A fine array of wines can accompany your meal. There are nights when a dish here or there might not always be sublime, but usually most are excellent.

DEAUVILLE AFTER DARK

Opened in 1912, the **Casino de Deauville,** rue Edmond-Blanc (☎ **02-31-14-31-14**), is one of France's premier casinos. Its original belle époque core has been expanded with a theater, a nightclub, three restaurants (two French and one Italian), and an extensive collection of slot machines (*machines à sous*). Jackets (but not ties) are required for men after 8pm. In July and August the main body of the casino is open Monday to Thursday from 4pm to 3am and Saturday and Sunday from 4pm to 4am (the area with the slot machines opens at 10am). Off-season, the room with slot machines opens at 11am, and the entire casino is open Monday to Thursday from 4pm to 2am, Saturday and Sunday from 4pm to 4am. The most interesting nights here are Friday and Saturday, when all the restaurants and the cabaret theater are open. The theater presents glittering, moderately titillating shows at 10:30pm on Friday and Saturday. Entrance is 120F ($21.60) per person.

Two popular dance clubs are the **Y Club,** 14 bis rue Désiré-le-Hoc (☎ **02-31-88-30-91**), with its high-energy dance scene, and the **Deauville Melody Club,** 13 rue Albert-Fracasse (☎ **02-31-88-34-83**), where the energy level is a little less intense but by no means sleepy. If you want to say you've played miniature golf in France, stop by for a round at **Bar du Golf Miniature,** boulevard de la Mer (☎ **02-31-98-40-56**), with its sophisticated little bar alongside that attracts a varied crowd. On Friday nights a DJ spins the tunes.

4 Trouville

128 miles NW of Paris, 27 miles NE of Caen

Across the Touques River from its more fashionable (and more expensive) rival, Deauville, Trouville feels like a fisher's port, something like the more charming and evocative Honfleur but with fewer boutiques and art galleries. Don't expect the grand Beaux-Arts atmosphere of Deauville—Trouville is much more low-key. It's also less dependent on resort francs than its neighbor, for when the sea bathers leave the splendid sands to return to Paris or wherever, Trouville lives on—its resident population of fishers sees to that.

ESSENTIALS

GETTING THERE   There are **rail connections** from Gare St-Lazare in Paris to Trouville (see the Deauville section earlier in this chapter). **Bus Verts du Calvados** serves the coast from Caen to Le Havre, and **Bus Inter Normandie** serves the region from Caen to Rouen. If you're traveling **by car,** from Deauville, simply travel west along D180 to Trouville.

VISITOR INFORMATION   The **Office de Tourisme** is at 32 quai Fernand-Moureaux (☎ 02-31-14-60-70).

EXPLORING THE TOWN

It was at Trouville that the novel concept of immersing one's carefully clad body in the sea first became popular. In the heyday of Napoléon III, boulevardiers used to bring wife and family to Trouville and stash their mistresses in the then-fledgling Deauville.

Our recommendation? Stamp around Trouville, enjoying its low-key charm, and when you tire of it, join the caravan of traffic that heads across the river to the bright lights and glamour of Deauville (see above).

The main **shopping streets** are quai Fernand-Moureaux, rue des Bains, and rue du Général-de-Gaulle. You'll find a wide, though typical, selection of shops here, ranging from small boutiques to larger department stores that carry anything from clothing and lingerie to jewelry and leather goods. More upscale shopping exists in the neighboring town of Deauville.

Les Planches is a rambling stretch of seafront boardwalk dotted with concessions on one side and a view of the sea on the other. Expect lots of flesh sprawled on the sands before you in midsummer in various states of undress—this is France. There's only one beach, **Plage de Trouville,** though when you've tired of it, you'll only have to cross the river to Plage de Deauville. On the seafront promenade is the **Piscine Olympique** (☎ 02-31-88-89-81), a large indoor seawater pool that's open daily from 10am to 7pm. Admission is 34F ($6.10).

WHERE TO STAY

Hôtel Carmen. 24 rue Carnot, 14360 Trouville. ☎ **02-31-88-35-43.** Fax 02-31-88-08-03. 16 units, 15 with bathroom. MINIBAR TV TEL. 500F ($90) double without bathroom; 620–660F ($111.60–$118.80) double with bathroom. Rates include half board. AE, DC, MC, V.

This Logis de France consists of two connected late-18th-century villas, one designed by a cousin of Georges Bizet. The management prefers that you take the half-board plan (breakfast and dinner). It's run by the Bude family, whom some guests find a bit bourgeois. The rooms are simply furnished, some overlooking a flower-filled courtyard. The restaurant is open daily.

Le Beach Hotel. 1 quai Albert-1er, 14360 Trouville. ☎ **02-31-98-12-00.** Fax 02-31-87-30-29. 118 units. TV TEL. 490F ($88.20) double; from 880F ($158.40) suite. AE, DC, MC, V. Closed Jan 5–30.

This hotel emerges out of the lackluster lot as the resort's top accommodation, only 150 feet from the beach, facing Trouville harbor. Although a poor relation to the palace hotels of Deauville, it offers grand comfort at a more affordable price. Its average-size rooms have modern furniture and fabrics with sunny tropical island colors, plus ocean views. You can mingle in the bar and sample the excellent Norman and international cuisine in the hotel's restaurant, which features fixed-price menus. You can even sip a fruity drink with a little umbrella in it while sunning on the deck or taking a dip in the pool.

WHERE TO DINE

La Petite Auberge. 7 rue Carnot. ☎ **02-31-88-11-07.** Reservations required. Fixed-price menus 128F ($23.05), 182F ($32.75), and 198F ($35.65). AE, MC, V. Daily noon–2:30pm and 7–10pm. Closed Wed Sept–June. FRENCH.

If you want something inexpensive without sacrificing quality, head to this Norman bistro a block from the casino. Try the *soupe de poissons* (fish soup), one of the finest along the Flower Coast, or the seafood pot-au-feu, featuring filet of sole, scallops, monkfish, and salmon beautifully simmered together. You can also order grilled beef and stuffed rabbit braised in cider. Since there are only 30 seats, reservations are vital in summer.

✪ **Les Vapeurs.** 160 bd. Fernand-Moureaux. ☎ **02-31-88-15-24.** Reservations recommended. Main courses 70–170F ($12.60–$30.60). AE, MC, V. Daily 12:30pm–1am. FRENCH/SEAFOOD.

This Art Deco brasserie, one of the most popular on the Norman coast, is frequented by Parisians on le week-end. This has been called the Brasserie Lipp of Normandy. The windows face the port, and in warm weather you can dine at sidewalk tables. Seafood is the specialty, and a wide range of shrimp, mussels laced with cream, crinkle-shelled oysters, and fish is served. Sauerkraut is also popular. Patrons here seem to have a good time and enjoy the food.

TROUVILLE AFTER DARK

If the casino in Deauville seems a little too stuffy for your tastes, you'll feel more comfortable at its sibling in Trouville, **Louisiane Follies,** place du Maréchal-Foch (☎ **02-31-87-75-00**). Here you can try your hand at Lady Luck in a more New Orleans–style environment, with areas that add to the city-of-sin feel, like a blues/jazz bar and a takeoff on Bourbon Street. Patrons can also relax in **L'Embellie** nightclub located in the casino. The dress code at this casino isn't too strict or formal—but no tennis shoes allowed.

5 Caen

148 miles NW of Paris, 74 miles SE of Cherbourg

On the banks of the Orne, the port of Caen suffered great damage in the Allied invasion of Normandy in 1944. Nearly three-quarters of its buildings, 10,000 in all, were destroyed, though the twin abbeys founded by William the Conqueror and his wife, Mathilda, were spared. The city today is essentially modern and has many broad avenues and new apartment buildings. Completely different from Deauville and Trouville, this capital of Lower Normandy is bustling, traffic congested, and commercial. The resident student population of 30,000 and the hordes of international travelers have made this city more cosmopolitan than ever, and it's a major rail and ferry junction.

ESSENTIALS

GETTING THERE   From Paris's Gare St-Lazare, 13 **trains** per day arrive in Caen (trip time: 2½ hours), costing 152F to 228 F ($27.35 to $41.05) one-way. There are also six trains from Rouen (trip time: 1¾ hours), costing 113F to 170F ($20.35 to $30.60) one-way. When **driving** from Paris, travel west along A13 to Caen (driving time: 2½ hours).

VISITOR INFORMATION   The **Office de Tourisme** is on place St-Pierre in the 16th-century Hôtel d'Escoville (☎ **02-31-27-14-14**).

EXPLORING THE CITY

Caen has several good boutique-lined shopping streets, like **boulevard du Maréch al-Leclerc, rue St-Pierre,** and **rue de Strasbourg. Antiques** hunters should check out the shops along rue Ecuyère and rue Commerçantes, as well as the antiques show held at the **Parc aux Expositions,** rue Joseph-Philippon (☎ **02-31-29-99-99**), each year during early June. The **markets** at place St-Sauveur on Friday mornings and place Courtonne on Sunday mornings also sell various secondhand articles.

For antique reproduction furniture that can be built to meet your specific needs, visit **La Reine Matilde,** 47 rue St-Jean (☎ **02-31-85-45-52**); it also sells decorative items, including a wide selection of bed linens and curtains. If you need to pick up some gift items, **Le Chocolatier Hotot,** 13 rue St-Pierre (☎ **02-31-86-31-90**), has a cornucopia of chocolate products as well as local jams and jellies; or you may want to stop by **Folklore,** 7 rue de Geole (☎ **02-31-86-34-13**), where you can find many regional items, like pottery, ciders, faïence, and decorative plates.

For objets and paintings, check out **L'Agnel,** 25 bd. du Maréchal-Leclerc (☎ **02-31-86-13-35**), specializing in reproductions of the masters of painting and photography, or **L'Atelier,** 33 rue Montoir-Poissonnerie (☎ **02-31-44-49-38**), which showcases many local artisans.

Abbaye aux Dames. Place de la Reine-Mathilde. ☎ **02-31-06-98-98.** Free admission. Daily 2–6pm. Free guided tour of choir, transept, and crypt (in French) daily at 2:30 and 4pm.

Founded by Mathilda, the abbey embraces Eglise de la Trinité, which is flanked by Romanesque towers. Destroyed in the Hundred Years War, its spires weren't rebuilt. In the 12th-century choir is the tomb of Queen Mathilda; note the ribbed vaulting.

Abbaye aux Hommes. Esplanade Jean-Marie-Louvel. ☎ **02-31-30-42-01.** Tours (in French) daily at 9:30 and 11am and 2:30 and 4pm, for 10F ($1.80).

Founded by William and Mathilda, the abbey is adjacent to the Eglise St-Etienne, which you enter on place Monseigneur-des-Hameaux. During the height of the Allied invasion, denizens of Caen flocked to St-Etienne for protection. The church is dominated by twin 276-foot Romanesque towers, and its 15th-century spires helped earn Caen the appellation of "a city of spires." A marble slab inside the high altar commemorates the site of William's tomb. The Huguenots destroyed the tomb in an uprising in 1562, save for a hipbone that was recovered. However, during the Revolution the last of William's dust was scattered to the wind. The hand-carved wooden doors and elaborately sculpted wrought-iron staircase are exceptional. From the cloisters you get a good view of the two towers of St-Etienne. Part of the former abbey houses municipal offices.

Caen Memorial. Esplanade Dwight-Eisenhower. ☎ **02-31-06-06-44.** Admission 69F ($12.40) adults, 61F ($11) children and seniors over 60; free to World War II veterans, war disabled, war widows, and children 9 and under accompanied by an adult. Daily 9am–7pm (to 9pm in summer). Closed Christmas, Jan 1–18, and 24–-25.

The memorial stands 10 minutes from the Pegasus Bridge and 15 minutes from the landing beaches. The museum presents a journey through history from 1918 to the present, recalling the unfolding and the meaning of World War II. It's also an ideal place to relax with walks through International Park; to have brunch, tea, a cold buffet, or a drink in the restaurant; or to browse through the boutique for that special souvenir.

WHERE TO STAY

Note that **Le Dauphin** (see below) also offers accommodations.

Holiday Inn. Place du Maréchal-Foch, 14000 Caen. ☎ **800/465-4329** in the U.S., or 02-31-27-57-57. Fax 02-31-27-57-58. www.holiday-inn.com. 92 units. TV TEL. 380–580F ($68.40–$104.40) double. AE, DC, MC, V. Bus: 1, 3, 4, 10, or 11.

Across from the racecourse and opposite an angel-capped monument to a military hero, this hotel was built before World War II but was enlarged and modernized in 1991 when it adopted the Holiday Inn logo. Today it's the best hotel in town, with a flavor that's French and international. The Holiday Inn offers a cozy bar favored by Americans visiting the D-Day beaches, plus a restaurant, Le Rabelais, where fixed-price menus feature meals the 16th-century writer and Chinon native—and restaurant's namesake—might have enjoyed in his day. The guest rooms are predictable, comfortable, and well maintained.

Hôtel Bristol. 31 rue du 11-Novembre, 14000 Caen. ☎ **02-31-84-59-76.** Fax 02-31-52-29-28. 20 units. TV TEL. 230–260F ($41.40–$46.80) double. V. Bus: 12.

Built shortly after the devastating bombings of World War II and renovated in 1992, this hotel is on a block of modern apartments and shops, not far from the park. Consider the Bristol more as a bare-bones stopover hotel than as a charming inn. The price is fair, however. A continental breakfast is the only meal served.

Hôtel de France. 10 rue de la Gare, 14000 Caen. ☎ **02-31-52-16-99.** Fax 02-31-83-23-16. 47 units. TV TEL. 250–300F ($45–$54) double. MC, V.

The exterior of this six-story brick building is plain but still reflects a bit of charm. Maybe it's the window boxes outside every room or the French door–style windows that swing open to let breezes in. The rooms are functional with simple furnishings, but many make a definite statement with their strong colors that often border on the garish—deep fuchsia with metallic blues, for example. The public areas create a provincial charm—the bar with its calm carnation-colored walls and soft blue-gray fabrics and the reception area with wood paneling and fresh flowers on the tables. This hotel is a favorite with tour groups (often World War II veterans) and offers a restaurant that opens solely to serve these groups.

✪ **Hôtel des Quatrans.** 17 rue Gémare, 14300 Caen. ☎. **02-31-86-25-57.** Fax 02-31-85-27-80. 32 units. TV TEL. 250–300F ($45–$54) double. V. Free parking. Bus: 2 or 7.

This agreeable and unpretentious hotel was built after the devastations of World War II, and thanks to renovations that occur at 10-year intervals, it remains one of Caen's best bargains. Don't expect luxury: The rooms are simply furnished and offer basic amenities. Breakfast is the only meal served.

Hôtel Royal. 1 place de la République, 14000 Caen. ☎ **02-31-86-55-33.** Fax 02-31-79-89-44. 42 units. TV TEL. 270–320F ($48.60–$57.60) double. AE, MC, V.

The original Hôtel Royal was built in 1794 but destroyed 150 years later during a World War II bombing raid. The new hotel was built several years later on the site of the original, and today it's surrounded by a busy commercial area of shops and restaurants as well as more tranquil pedestrian streets. The last renovation, about 8 years ago, brought all the rooms up to an acceptable level of comfort, though space is a bit cramped. The public areas include a standard restaurant, open for breakfast and dinner, and a small lobby/sitting area that has an austere look but opens onto place de la République.

ACCOMMODATIONS NEARBY

Relais Château d'Audrieu. 14250 Audrieu. ☎ **02-31-80-21-52.** Fax 02-31-80-24-73. E-mail: chateaudaudrieu@caen.pacwan.net. 30 units. TV TEL. 1,450–1,900F ($261–$342) double; 2,200F ($396) suite. AE, MC, V. Closed Dec 15–Jan. From Caen, take N13 for 11 miles, then D158 for 2 miles to Audrieu.

This château in a 50-acre park offers some of the most luxurious accommodations near Caen. It was built of local stone (*pierre de Caen*) at the beginning of the 18th century. During the Allied invasion of Normandy, the house and its grounds sat in the midst of some of the fiercest fighting, so many of the trees in the surrounding park bear gashes and wounds from the millions of bullets and pieces of shrapnel that were unleashed on all sides. The château functioned as a private home until 1976, when it was transformed into this stately hotel. The rooms are lovely and well appointed, usually with antiques, each with a carefully planned unique style.

Dining: Dinner here may include bouillon of duckling with cider or croustade of oysters with beet-flavored vinaigrette. Fixed-price menus range from 240F to 430F ($43.20 to $77.40). The restaurant, but not the hotel, is closed on Monday.

WHERE TO DINE

✪ **La Bourride.** 15–17 rue du Vaugueux. ☎ **02-31-93-50-76.** Reservations required. Main courses 143–180F ($25.75–$32.40) at lunch, 340–490F ($61.20–$88.20) at dinner. AE, DC, V. Tues–Sat noon–2pm and 7:15–10pm. Closed Jan 4–24 and Aug 18–Sept 3. Bus: 1, 3, 4, 10, or 11. NORMAN.

This restaurant serves Caen's best food. As the name implies, a *bourride* is served, concocted from five kinds of fish, delicately seasoned and simmered under the expert eye of Michel Bruneau. The place occupies a beautiful 17th-century house near the château, and its dining room has thick stone walls and a magnificent Renaissance fireplace. The service includes tactful advice on wines to accompany any of the specialties, such as foie gras of Norman duckling and roast lamb with onion confit. The desserts, which contain seasonal fruits, are excellent, like the Calvados sorbet.

Le Dauphin. 29 rue Gémare, 14300 Caen.☎ **02-31-86-22-26.** Fax 02-31-86-35-14. Reservations required. Main courses 65–150F ($11.70–$27); fixed-price menus 100–310F ($18–$55.80). AE, DC, MC, V. Sun–Fri noon–2:30pm, daily 7–9:30pm. Hotel and restaurant closed 2 weeks in winter; restaurant also July 15–Aug 8. FRENCH.

This restaurant was originally a medieval priory. The menu is wisely limited, and all ingredients are market fresh; alas, the chef/owner, Robert Chabredier, doesn't measure up to Bruneau at La Bourride. However, interesting items appear on the menu, like ragoût of lobster with fresh pasta, sweetbreads forester style, and oysters stuffed with leeks and asparagus.

Le Dauphin also offers 22 well-furnished guest rooms with bathroom, costing 440F ($79.20) for a double and 610F ($109.80) for a suite.

Les Echevins. 35 rte. de Trouville. ☎ **02-31-84-10-17.** Reservations required. Main courses 89–175F ($16–$31.50); fixed-price menus 165–349F ($29.70–$62.80). AE, DC, MC, V. Daily noon–2:30pm and 7:30–9:30pm. Closed July 31–Aug 27. From the town center, follow the signs for the Deauville–Cabourg rd. and take it less than a mile east. FRENCH.

This restaurant occupies what was built as a private home in 1884. It has four dining rooms with original paneling, a lounge bar, and a pleasant garden. The owner/chef, Patrick Regnier, prepares meals with big-city flair and fresh ingredients. His most succulent specialty is *marmite caennaise,* a savory stewpot filled with filets of John Dory, turbot, sole, salmon, and scallops, all melded with a blanquette of fish, bouillabaisse-style rouille, basmati rice, and garlicky crootons. Other worthy choices, usually available in any season, are turbot with morels, filet of beef, and a salad of scallops flavored with fresh basil. The desserts are appropriately Norman and feature soufflés flavored with apple brandy (Calvados).

A NEARBY CHOICE

✪ **Le Manoir d'Hastings.** Av. Côte-de-Nacre, 14970 Bénouville. ☎ **02-31-44-62-43.** Fax 02-31-44-76-18. Reservations required. Main courses 79–140F ($14.20–$25.20); fixed-price menus 125–240F ($22.50–$43.20) at lunch, 170–260F ($30.60–$46.80) at dinner. AE, DC, MC, V. Daily 12:30–2pm and 7–9:30pm. Closed Sun dinner and Mon in Sept–Mar. From Caen, follow the signs north for Ouistreham, then go 6½ miles after turning off onto RD35, following the signs to Bayeux and Bénouville; the manor is next to the village church. FRENCH.

One of Normandy's most famous and charming inns (and a magnet for Parisians seeking a rustically elegant weekend getaway), this restaurant occupies a converted 17th-century priory with an enclosed Norman garden. The owners, José and Carole Aparicio, focus much of their attention on the sophisticated cuisine moderne that emerges with panache from their kitchens. Many dishes are twists on traditional Norman favorites, like cider-cooked lobster with Nantua sauce, delicately flavored sea bass, and filet of monkfish poached in port. Beef filets are stuffed with foie gras and scallops braised in an old-fashioned apple-based liqueur, Pommeau. For dessert, try the tarte normande flambéed with Calvados.

The manor also offers 15 handsome rooms in a stone-sided annex. Each has a garden view, bathroom, TV, minibar, and phone. A double goes for 660F to 800 F ($118.80 to $144). The hotel lies very close to Pegasus Bridge, one of the first strategic targets liberated by Allied soldiers after the invasion of Normandy in 1944.

CAEN AFTER DARK

Take a walk down rue de Bras, rue St-Pierre, and the north end of rue Vaugueux to take a look at the action. If you want to connect with the hip 18-to-35 crowd, go to **Berlin West,** rue des Croissiers (☎ **02-31-85-10-10**). This is a French version of the trendy cyber cafe, a classic rock club, and a booming techno free-for-all. Live concerts and art showings round out the mix. Another dance club is **Joy's/Le Paradis,** 10 rue de Strasbourg (☎ **02-31-85-40-40**), with a frenetic crowd and a techno beat.

A couple of the better pubs/bars are **Pub Concorde,** 7 rue Montoir-Poissonnerie (☎ **02-31-93-61-29**), with more than 150 beers to choose from, and **Le Dakota,** 54 rue de Bernières (☎ **02-31-50-05-25**). **Café des Beaux-Arts,** 88 rue de Geôle (☎ **02-31-86-43-21**), has become the hang-out-and-hang-about place where you can talk, play pinball, and listen to jazz, reggae, and salsa. There's no attitude here, just good music and fun people.

6　Bayeux

166 miles NW of Paris, 16 miles NW of Caen

The ducs de Normandie sent their sons to this Viking settlement to learn the Norse language. Bayeux has changed a lot since, but miraculously it was spared from bombardment in 1944. This was the first French town liberated, and the citizens of Bayeux gave de Gaulle an enthusiastic welcome when he arrived on June 14. Today the sleepy town is filled with timbered houses, stone mansions, and cobblestone streets.

Visitors wanting to explore sites associated with "the longest day" flood the town today, as many memorials, along with beaches, are only 6 to 12 miles away. The cozy little streets are lined with shops, many selling World War II memorabilia, and more postcards and T-shirts than you'll ever need.

ESSENTIALS

GETTING THERE　Seven **trains** per day arrive from Paris (trip time: 2½ hours), costing 166F to 249F ($29.90 to $44.80) one-way; 13 trains from Caen pull in daily (trip time: 20 minutes), costing 31F to 46F ($5.60 to $8.30) one-way. When **driving** to Bayeux from Paris (driving time: 3 hours), simply take E46 west from Caen.

VISITOR INFORMATION　The **Office de Tourisme** is at pont St-Jean (☎ **02-31-51-28-28**).

SPECIAL EVENTS　The town goes wild with **Fêtes Médiévales** the first weekend in July, when Bayeux has 2 complete days of lunacy and revelry, filling the streets with wine and song outside the cathedral.

SEEING THE SIGHTS

✪ **Musée de la Tapisserie de Bayeux.** Centre Guillaume-le-Conquérant, 13 rue de Nesmond. ☎ **02-31-51-25-50.** Admission 38F ($6.85) adults, 15F ($2.70) students, free for children 9 and under. May 1–Sept 15 daily 9am–6:15pm, Sept 16–Apr 30 daily 9:30am–11:45pm and 2–5:15pm.

Here you'll find the Bayeux tapestry—the most famous tapestry in the world. Actually, it's an embroidery on a band of linen, 231 feet long and 20 inches wide, depicting some 58 scenes in 8 colors. Contrary to legend, it wasn't made by Queen Mathilda but was probably commissioned in Kent and created by unknown embroiderers between 1066 and 1077. The first recorded mention of the embroidery was in 1476, when it was explained that it was used to decorate the nave of the Cathédrale Notre-Dame de Bayeux.

Housed in a Plexiglas case, the embroidery tells the story of the conquest of England by William the Conqueror, including such scenes as the coronation of Harold as the Saxon king of England, Harold returning from his journey to Normandy, the surrender of Dinan, Harold being told of the apparition of a comet (a portent of misfortune), William dressed for war, and the death of Harold. The decorative borders include scenes from *Aesop's Fables*.

Admission to this museum also gets you into two less significant museums, the **Musée Baron Gérard** and the **Musée de l'Art Sacré,** each within 200 yards of the main attraction. Both share the same phone and hours as the Musée de la Tapisserie and exhibit local examples of regional lacework, religious statues, and religious and secular paintings.

Cathédrale Notre-Dame de Bayeux. In the center of city. ☎ **02-31-92-01-85.** Free admission. Daily 9am–6pm (to 7pm in July–Aug).

The cathedral was consecrated in 1077 and partially destroyed in 1105. Left from that church, its Romanesque towers rise on the western side, and the central tower is from the 15th century, with an even later top. The nave is a fine example of Norman Romanesque style. Rich in sculpture, the 13th-century choir, a perfect example of Norman Gothic style, has handsome Renaissance stalls. The crypt was built in the 11th century and then sealed. Its existence remained unknown until 1412.

Musée Memorial de la Bataille de Normandie. Bd. Fabian-Ware. ☎ **02-31-92-93-41.** Admission 30F ($5.40) adults, 15F ($2.70) children. May–Sept 15 daily 9:30am–6:30pm, Sept 16–Apr daily 10am–12:30pm and 2–6pm. Closed last 2 weeks in Jan.

Across from the cemetery, this museum deals exclusively with the military and human history of the Battle of Normandy (June 6 to August 22, 1944). Inside are 440 feet of window and film displays, plus a diorama. Wax soldiers in their uniforms, along with the tanks and guns used to win the battle, are exhibited.

WHERE TO STAY

Family Home. 39 rue du Général-de-Dais, 14400 Bayeux. ☎ **02-31-92-15-22.** Fax 02-31-92-55-72. 13 units. 250F ($45) double. Rates include breakfast. AE, MC, V.

In the town center, this 16th-century presbytery, now a private home, encompasses four interconnected buildings. The rooms are furnished with Norman antiques, and you can cook your own meals in the kitchen. Madame Lefèvre also serves copious and varied meals of Normandy specialties at a long communal table for 65 F ($11.70), including wine and service charge. The wine served is a smooth Anjou produced by Mme Lefèvre's family at their own vineyards.

Hôtel d'Argouges. 21 rue St-Patrice, 14402 Bayeux. ☎ **02-31-92-88-86.** Fax 02-31-92-69-16. 25 units. MINIBAR TV TEL. 280–440F ($50.40–$79.20) double. AE, DC, MC, V.

Monsieur and Madame Auregan have handsomely restored this 18th-century hotel. In fair weather you can enjoy sipping drinks in the garden. The rooms are comfortable, all with hair dryers. Breakfast is the only meal served; however, five restaurants line the plaza outside.

Hôtel Churchill. 14 rue St-Jean, 14404 Bayeux. ☎ **02-31-21-31-80.** Fax 02-31-21-41-66. 32 units. TV TEL. 360–460F ($64.80–$82.80) double; 520–680F ($93.60–$122.40) suite. AE, DC, MC, V. Closed Nov 15–Mar 15.

Built in 1850, this hotel sits in the heart of the old town on a quiet pedestrian street near lots of boutiques, restaurants, and historic sites. The rooms are somewhat cramped but thoughtfully appointed with refined and delicate Louis XVI reproductions. They're enhanced by large windows that look out onto panoramic views of black slate rooftops and Bayeux's 11th-century cathedral. The hotel wraps around a private courtyard that has been turned into a glassed-in patio dining room for its restaurant— a cheery environment in which to wake up over morning coffee and croissants. Evening meals filled with Norman specialties are also served here.

Hôtel de Luxembourg. 25 rue Bouchers, 14403 Bayeux. ☎ **800/528-1234** in the U.S. and Canada, or 02-31-92-00-04. Fax 02-31-92-54-26. 22 units. MINIBAR TV TEL. 470–540F ($84.60–$97.20) double; from 1,200F ($216) suite. Half board 370F ($66.60) per person extra. AE, MC, V.

After Le Lion d'Or (below), this Best Western is the area's finest hotel. The completely restored interior has terrazzo floors and a decor combining neoclassical and Art Deco. The Luxembourg contains a richly decorated bar, an elegant restaurant, and an elevator. Fixed-price menus run 130F to 280F ($23.40 to $50.40).

Le Lion d'Or. 71 rue St-Jean, 14400 Bayeux. ☎ **02-31-92-06-90.** Fax 02-31-22-15-64. 27 units. MINIBAR TV TEL. 380–480F ($68.40–$86.40) double; 600–900F ($108–$162) suite. AE, DC, MC, V. Closed Dec 20–Jan 20.

This old-world hotel, the best in town, has an open courtyard with lush flower boxes decorating the facade. The personalized guest rooms are set back from the street. One meal is required of overnight guests, and the traditional cuisine is inspired by the region's bounty, like homemade Normandy sausage, mushroom-stuffed chicken with creamy Pommeau sauce, and sole filet with cider-butter sauce. Of course, Normandy cheese or warm apple tart with creamy Calvados sauce perfectly tops off a meal. There are lots of reasonably priced wines. Fixed-price menus cost 100F ($18) for lunch (Monday through Saturday) or 180F to 230F ($32.40 to $41.40) for dinner.

7 The D-Day Beaches

Arromanches-les-Bains: 169 miles NW of Paris, 6½ miles NW of Bayeux; Grandcamp-Maisy (near Omaha Beach): 186 miles NW of Paris, 35 miles NW of Caen

From June 6 to July 18, "the longest day" was very long indeed. The greatest armada ever known—soldiers and sailors, warships, landing craft, tugboats, jeeps, whatever— assembled along the southern coast of England in late spring 1944. At 9:15pm on June 5, the BBC announced to the French Resistance that the invasion was imminent, signaling the underground to start dynamiting the railways. Before midnight, Allied planes began bombing the Norman coast fortifications. By 1:30am on June 6, members of the 101st Airborne were parachuting to the ground on German-occupied French soil. At 6:30am the Americans began landing on the beaches, code-named Utah and Omaha. An hour later British and Canadian forces made beachheads at Juno, Gold, and Sword.

The Nazis had mocked Churchill's promise in 1943 to liberate France "before the fall of the autumn leaves." When the invasion did come, it was swift, sudden, and a surprise to the formidable "Atlantic wall." Today aging veterans from Canada, the United States, and Britain walk with their children and grandchildren across the beaches where "Czech hedgehogs," "Belgian grills," pillboxes, and "Rommel asparagus" once stood.

ESSENTIALS

GETTING THERE Bus service from Bayeux is a bit uneven and sometimes involves long delays. **Bus Verts** (☎ **02-31-92-02-92**) heads for Port-en-Bessin and points west along the coast, and no. 74 buses offer service to Arromanches and other points in the east. It's best to explore the coast by car and not have to depend on public transportation. When **motoring** to the beaches from Paris, expect a lengthy drive (3 hours). Take A-13 west to Caen, continuing west on E46 to Bayeux. From Bayeux, travel north along D6 until you reach the coast at Port-en-Bessin, a junction of D514. D514 runs along the coastline, with D-Day sites generally west of Port-en-Bessin. Parking is not a problem, as there are designated areas all along the roadway, most of them free. The best days to visit are during the week, as weekends (especially in summer) can be a bit overcrowded with tourists and sunbathers alike.

VISITOR INFORMATION   The **Office de Tourisme** is at 4 rue du Maréchal-Joffre, Arromanches-les-Bains (☎ **02-31-21-47-56**), open April to September.

RELIVING THE LONGEST DAY

Start out your exploration of the D-Day beaches at the modest seaside resort of **Arromanches-les-Bains.** In June 1944 it was a fishing port, until it was taken by the 50th British Division. Towed across the English Channel, a mammoth prefabricated port known as Winston was installed to supply the Allied forces. "Victory could not have been achieved without it," said Eisenhower. The wreckage of that artificial harbor—known as Mulberry—lies right off the beach, la plage du débarquement. The **Musée du Débarquement,** place du 6-Juin (☎ **02-31-22-34-31**), features relief maps, working models, a cinema, and photographs, plus a diorama of the landing, with an English commentary. Admission is 30F ($5.40) for adults and 17F ($3.05) for students and children. It's open daily: February 2 to March 29, 9:30am to 5pm; March 30 to May 3, 9am to 6pm; May 4 to August 31, 9am to 7pm; September 1 to November 1, 9am to 6pm; November 2 to December 23, 9:30am to 5pm. Closed Dec. 24 to February 1. The museum does not open on Sundays until 10am, except June through August.

Moving along the coast, you arrive at **Omaha Beach,** where you can still see the war wreckage. "Hanging on by their toenails," the men of the 1st and 29th American Divisions occupied the beach that June day. The code-name Omaha became famous throughout the world, though up to then the beaches had been called St-Laurent, Vierville-sur-Mer, and Colleville. A monument commemorates the heroism of the invaders. Covering some 173 acres at Omaha Beach, the **Normandy American Cemetery** (☎ **02-31-51-62-00**) is filled with Latin crosses and Stars of David in Lasa marble. The remains of 9,386 American military dead were buried here on territory now owned by the United States, a gift from the French nation. The cemetery is open daily: summer from 9am to 6pm and winter from 9am to 5pm.

Farther along the coast you'll see the jagged lime cliffs of the **Pointe du Hoc.** A cross honors a group of American Rangers led by Lt.-Col. James Rudder, who scaled the cliffs using hooks to get at the pillboxes. The scars of war are more visible here than at any other point along the beach. Much farther along the Cotentin Peninsula is **Utah Beach,** where the 4th U.S. Infantry Division landed at 6:30am. The landing force was nearly 2 miles south of its intended destination, but, fortunately, Nazi defenses were weak at this point. By midday the infantry had completely cleared the beach. A U.S. monument commemorates their heroism.

Nearby you can visit **Ste-Mère-Eglise,** which not many people had heard of until the night of June 5 and 6, when paratroopers dropped from the sky above the town. They were from the 82nd U.S. Airborne Division, under the command of Gen. Matthew B. Ridgeway. Members of the 101st U.S. Airborne Division, commanded by Gen. M. B. Taylor, were also involved. Also in Ste-Mère-Eglise is Kilometer "0" on the Liberty Highway, marking the first of the milestones the American armies reached on their way to Metz and Bastogne.

More fervently than residents of any other region of France, Normans spent most of the summer of 1994 celebrating the 50th anniversary of D-Day. Representatives of 11 nations participated in the countless ceremonies, the most visible of which was held on Omaha Beach on June 6, when President Clinton, Queen Elizabeth II, and President Mitterrand shared the spotlight. Less elaborate observances were held in 1995 commemorating the 50th anniversary of the end of World War II in Europe.

WHERE TO STAY & DINE

Hôtel Duguesclin. 4 quai Crampon, 14450 Grandcamp-Maisy. ☎ **02-31-22-64-22.** Fax 02-31-22-34-79. Reservations recommended. Main courses 70–120F ($12.60–$21.60); fixed-price menus 65–180F ($11.70–$32.40). AE, MC, V. Daily noon–2pm and 7–9pm. Closed Jan 15–Feb 6. FRENCH.

We recommend this three-story Norman inn, built in 1932 and repaired after the ravages of World War II, for lunch or even for an overnight. The fish soup, grilled scallops, and Norman sole (if available) are excellent. Everything tastes better with the dining room's country bread and Norman butter.

The hotel rents 31 simple but comfortable rooms, 25 with bathroom and all with TV. A double without bathroom is 125F to 175F ($22.50 to $31.50), and a double with bathroom goes for 250F to 290F ($45 to $52.20).

La Marée. 5 quai Chéron. ☎ **02-31-21-41-00.** Reservations required. Main courses 85–148F ($15.30–$26.65); fixed-price menus 98–249F ($17.65–$44.80). AE, DC, MC, V. Daily 12:30–2:30pm and 7–9:30pm. Closed Dec and Jan. NORMAN.

At the port, this small restaurant in a 1920s building is ideal for seafood devotees. The fish, always fresh and savory, is often bought from the boats that gathered the harvest. First try the fresh oysters, then perhaps the medley of monkfish, morels, and sweetbreads cooked in the same dish. Meals are served in the rustic dining room or on the terrace.

8 Mont-St-Michel

201 miles W of Paris, 80 miles SW of Caen, 47 miles E of Dinan, 30 miles E of St-Malo

One of Europe's great attractions, ✪ **Mont-St-Michel** is surrounded by massive walls measuring more than half a mile in circumference. Connected to the shore by a causeway, it crowns a rocky islet at the border between Normandy and Brittany. The rock is 260 feet high.

ESSENTIALS

GETTING THERE You can reach Mont-St-Michel **by train** from Paris's Gare Montparnasse; take the train to Dol and transfer to Pontorson, the closest rail station. From Rennes, there's **bus service**, Les Couriers Bretons, to Mont-St-Michel that connects with the **TGV** from Paris's Gare Montparnasse, enabling you to visit from Paris in 1 day. Bus schedules vary; call ☎ **02-99-56-79-09** for exact information and times. When **driving** to Mont-St-Michel, the best route is to go from Caen along N175 southwest to Pontorson, then take E3 north to Mont-St-Michel (driving time from Paris: 4½ hours).

VISITOR INFORMATION The **Office de Tourisme** is in the Corps de Garde des Bourgeois (the Old Guard Room of the Bourgeois), at the left of the town gates (☎ **02-33-60-14-30**). The office closes the last week of January and the first week of February.

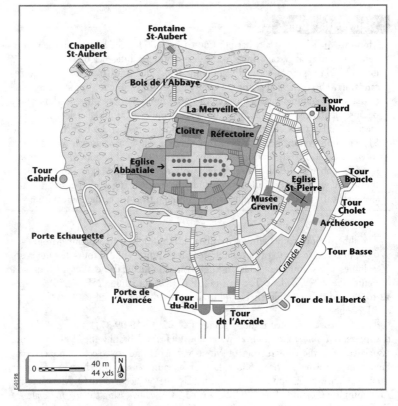

EXPLORING MONT-ST-MICHEL

You'll have a steep climb up Grande Rue, lined with 15th- and 16th-century houses, to reach the **abbey** (☎ 02-33-60-14-14). Those who make it to the top can begin their exploration of the Marvel of the West. In the 8th century an oratory was founded on the spot by St. Aubert, the bishop of Avranches. It was replaced by a Benedictine monastery, founded in 966 by Richard I. That met with destruction by fire in 1203. Large parts of the abbey were financed by Philip Augustus in the 13th century.

Ramparts encircle the church and a three-tiered ensemble of 13th-century buildings called **La Merveille** that rise dramatically to the pointed spire of the abbey church. This terraced complex is one of Europe's most important Gothic monuments, a citadel from which the concept of an independent France was nurtured during the darkest years of the English occupation of Aquitaine.

On the second terrace of La Merveille, midway up the rock, is one of Mont-St-Michel's largest and most beautiful rooms, a 13th-century banquet hall known as the **Salle des Chevaliers.**

Crowning the mountain's summit is the **Eglise Abbatiale** (not to be confused with the less important Eglise St-Pierre lower down on the mountain). Begun in the 11th century, the abbey church consists of a Romanesque nave and transept, plus a choir in the Flamboyant Gothic style. The rectangular refectory is from 1212, the cloisters with their columns of pink granite from 1225.

Sign of the Tides

Mont-St-Michel historically has been noted for its tides, the highest on the Continent, measuring at certain times of the year a 50-foot difference between high and low tide. Unsuspecting visitors wandering across the sands (notorious for quicksands) have been trapped as the sea rushes toward the mont at a speed comparable to that of a galloping horse. However, the bay around the abbey has silted, not only because of the causeway (*le digue*) but also because of various barriers and dikes erected. Today tides engulf the island less and less frequently. France will spend $110 million over the next few years replacing the mile-long causeway with a bridge so water can lap freely around the mont. Parking lots will be moved farther away from the abbey, and ecology experts will work to encourage bird and marine life in the air and water. Bridge construction and other engineering works began on a massive scale early in 1998 and will continue through the turn of the millennium.

The abbey is open daily (with mass daily at 12:15pm): May to September from 9am to 5:30pm and October to April from 9:30am to 4:30pm. Guided tours, leaving every 15 minutes, last 45 minutes. Tours in English are conducted daily. After the tour, you can enter the abbey gardens. The cost is 40F ($7.20) for adults, 25F ($4.50) for ages 12 to 25, and free for children 11 and under. Everything is closed January 1, May 1, and December 25.

The **Archeoscope,** chemin de la Ronde (☎ **02-33-48-09-37**), is a small theater that presents *L'Eau et La Lumière* (Water and Light), celebrating the legend and lore associated with the construction of Mont-St-Michel and its role as a preserver of French medieval nationalism. Shows last for 30 minutes and are shown every hour from 9:30am to 5:30pm. More unusual is the adjacent **Musée Maritime et Archéologique,** Grande Rue (☎ **02-33-60-14-09**), showcasing the marine crafts of civilizations throughout history and the world, information on the ecology of the local tidal flats, and illustrations of the French government's plans to reactivate the tidal cleansing of the nearby marshes. Finally, the **Musée Grevin** (Musée Historique de Mont-St-Michel), chemin de la Ronde (☎ **02-33-60-07-01**), traces the history of the abbey. Admission to each of these is 45F ($8.10), but a combined ticket is 75F ($13.50). Each is open daily from 9:30am to 6pm. Note that locals regard these "attractions" as tourist traps.

WHERE TO STAY

Hôtel du Mouton-Blanc. Grande Rue, 50116 Mont-St-Michel. ☎ **02-33-60-14-08.** Fax 02-33-60-05-62. 22 units, 20 with bathroom. TEL. 200F ($36) double without bathroom; 390–450F ($70.20–$81) double with bathroom. AE, MC, V.

In a trio of buildings, parts of which date from the 14th century, this inn stands halfway between the sea and the basilica and has been accepting guests since the 1700s. The lower floors contain the restaurant; the simple double rooms are upstairs. Tables are set in a Norman-style dining room accented with stone and roughly textured wood and on a terrace overlooking the sea. As in most restaurants here, omelets are offered, along with fruits de mer, mussels in cream sauce, several preparations of lobster, and roast pork in cider sauce.

Les Terrasses Poulard. Grande Rue, 50116 Mont-St-Michel. ☎ **02-33-60-14-09.** Fax 02-33-60-37-31. 29 units. MINIBAR TV TEL. 200–900F ($36–$162) double. AE, DC, MC, V.

This inn was formed when two village houses—one medieval, the other built in the 1800s—were united. Today the hotel is one of the best in town, with an

English-speaking staff. The rates depend on the view: of the pedestrian traffic on the main street, the village, or the medieval ramparts. The largest and most expensive rooms have fireplaces. The restaurant, which is open every day throughout the year for lunch and dinner, offers a sweeping view over the bay to accompany its seafood and regional Norman specialties.

WHERE TO DINE

La Mère Poulard. Grande Rue, 50116 Mont-St-Michel. ☎ **02-33-60-14-01.** Reservations recommended. Main courses 90–180F ($16.20–$32.40); fixed-price meals 175–350F ($31.50–$63). AE, DC, MC, V. Daily noon–10pm. NORMAN.

This country inn is a shrine to those who revere the omelet that Annette Poulard created in 1888 when the hotel was founded. Her secret has been passed on to the inn's operators: The beaten eggs are cooked over an oak hearth fire in a long-handled copper skillet (they sell these skillets if you'd like one to take home). The frothy mixture really creates more of an open-fire soufflé than an omelet. Other specialties are lamb (agneau du pré salé) raised on the saltwater marshes near the foundations of the abbey and an array of fish, including lobster.

The inn, which is better described as a guest house, rents 27 rooms with TV, phone, minibar, and hair dryer; however, we recommend that you opt for one of the two hotels above and come here strictly for the omelet. A double ranges from 250F to 1,600F ($45 to $288).

NEARBY ACCOMMODATIONS & DINING

La Verte Campagne. Hameau Chevalier par Trelly, 50660 Quettreville. ☎ **02-33-47-65-33.** Fax 02-33-47-38-03. 7 units, 2 with shower only, 2 with tub. TEL. 220F ($39.60) double without bathroom; 260F ($46.80) double with shower only; 380F ($68.40) double with tub. V. Free parking. Closed Jan 20–30 and Dec 1–8. Take D7 north from Avranches to Lengronne and follow the signs 2½ miles north from Trelly.

Charming, wholesome, rustic, and noted for its cuisine, this 1717 Norman farmhouse lies in an isolated position about 30 miles north of Mont-St-Michel, where you'll be welcomed by Mme Bernou and her cats. The farmhouse has been sumptuously decorated with antiques and lots of brass. If you're spending the night, ask for the double room (no. 7) that has red carpeting, curtains, bedcover, and vanity—all in harmony with the pink "Vichy" pattern.

Dining: In the restaurant, fixed-price menus cost 140F to 350F ($25.20 to $63); à la carte meals begin at 225F ($40.50). Specialties are chicken and lamb raised on the property, magrêt of duckling with walnut-butter sauce, and saffron-flavored monkfish. Hours are 12:30 to 1:30pm and 7:30 to 9pm; no meals are served Sunday night or Monday in winter or Monday lunch in summer. Nonguests are welcome but should phone ahead for a table.

9 Brittany

In this ancient northwestern province, many Bretons stubbornly cling to their traditions. Deep in l'Argoat (the interior), many older folks quietly live in stone farmhouses, just as their grandparents did, and on special occasions the women still wear the trademark starched-lace headdresses. The Breton language is still spoken, but it's better understood by the Welsh and Cornish than by the French. Sadly, it may die out altogether, despite attempts by folklore groups to keep it alive.

Nearly every village and hamlet has its own *pardon,* a religious festival that sometimes attracts thousands of pilgrims in traditional dress. The best-known ones are on May 19 at Treguier (honoring St. Yves), on the second Sunday in July at Locronan (honoring St. Ronan), on July 26 at St-Anne-d'Auray (honoring the "mothers of Bretons"), and on September 8 at Le Folgoet (honoring *ar foll coat*—"idiot of the forest").

Traditionally, the province is divided into Haute-Bretagne and Basse-Bretagne. The rocky coastline, some 750 miles long, is studded with promontories, coves, and beaches. Like the prow of a ship, Brittany projects into the sea. The interior, however, is a land of sleepy hamlets, stone farmhouses, and moors covered with yellow broom and purple heather. We suggest that first-time visitors to the craggy peninsula stick to the coast, where you can see salt-meadow sheep grazing on pastureland whipped by sea breezes. If you're coming from Mont-St-Michel in Normandy, you can easily use St-Malo, Dinan, or Dinard as a base. Visitors coming from the château country of the Loire can explore the south Brittany coastline.

REGIONAL CUISINE Breton cuisine derives its excellence from the flavors and freshness of its ingredients rather than from the skill of its preparation. Seafood is abundant: Oysters, shellfish, barnacles, and crabs from the Breton coastline are famous throughout France. Many are served raw, especially Belon oysters, as appetizers (on a bed of seaweed with lemon/onion sauce and white wine).

Other regional specialties are *homard* (lobster) in cream sauce, grilled, or *à l'armoricaine;* salmon en brochet; trout and *l'alose,* excellent with one of the Loire's fruity whites; and lamb and mutton, raised on the salt marshes. *Gigot à la bretonne* (leg of lamb), traditionally served with white beans, is one of France's great dishes. The ducklings of Nantes and chickens of Rennes are succulent, as are the strawberries of Plougastel.

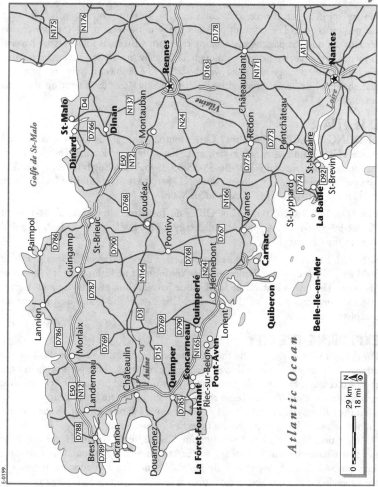

Brittany is closely associated with crêpes, those delectable thin pancakes served plain, sweet, or salted and often filled with jam, cheese, ham, salad, or eggs. Most villages have their own crêperie, some of which sell crêpes right on the street.

The only famous wine produced in Brittany is muscadet, cultivated near Nantes, an excellent complement to seafood.

1 St-Malo

257 miles W of Paris, 43 miles W of Rennes, 8 miles E of Dinard

Built on a granite rock in the Channel, St-Malo is joined to the mainland by a causeway. It's popular with the English, especially those from the Channel Islands, and, with its warm brown sands, makes a modest claim to be a swimming resort. The peninsula curves like a boomerang around a natural harbor whose interior has been subdivided into several smaller basins. The walled city, one of the most impressive examples of civil architecture in Brittany, radiates outward from the town's château and its spiritual centerpiece, the Cathédrale St-Vincent, both of which lie near the peninsula's tip. The curse of St-Malo today is the swarms of tour buses that descend upon it, the passengers engulfing the narrow streets as souvenirs are hawked to them. There's charm here, even though it's "merely the mock," having been virtually rebuilt after damage caused by World War II. The problem is trying to appreciate that charm while being trampled by millions of other travelers intent on the same pursuit.

ESSENTIALS

GETTING THERE　From Paris's Gare Montparnasse, about nine **trains** per day, each a TGV (Train à Grande Vitesse), make the journey via Rennes. For train information and schedules, call ☎ **08-36-35-35-39.** If you're **driving** from Paris, take A13 west to Caen, continuing southwest along N175 to the town of Miniac Morvan. From there, travel north on N137 directly to St. Malo.

VISITOR INFORMATION　The **Office de Tourisme** is on esplanade St-Vincent (☎ **02-99-56-64-48**). A passport is necessary for the hydrofoil or car-ferry trips and tours to the Channel Islands.

SPECIAL EVENTS　One of the most important Breton *pardons* (festivals) is held at St-Malo in February: the **Pardon of the Newfoundland Fishing Fleet** (*Pardon de St-Ouen*). The town's **Festival de la Musique Sacrée,** from mid-July to mid-August, offers evening concerts from time to time. Check with the Office de Tourisme for complete details.

EXPLORING THE CITY

For the best view of the bay and the islets at the mouth of the Rance, walk along the ramparts. These walls were built over a period of centuries, some parts of them from the 14th century. However, they were mainly reconstructed in the 17th century, then restored in the 19th. You can begin at the 15th-century **Porte St-Vincent.**

At the harbor, you can book tours of the **Channel Islands.** Hydrofoils leave for the English island of Jersey (a passport is necessary, of course).

At low tide, you can take a 25-minute stroll to the **Ile du Grand-Bé,** the site of the tomb of Chateaubriand, "deserted by others and completely surrounded by storms." The tomb—marked by a cross—is simple, unlike the man it honors, but the view of the Emerald Coast from here makes up for it.

Called the Bastille of the West, **Château de St-Malo,** Porte St-Vincent (☎ **02-99-40-71-58**), and its towers shelter a museum with souvenirs of Duguay-Trouin and Surcouf, the most famous of the St-Malo privateers. **Musée de St-Malo** is in the *donjon* (keep). You can visit Tuesday through Sunday from 10am to noon and 2 to 6pm. Admission is 26F ($4.70) for adults and 13F ($2.35) for children 18 and under. Guided tours are available on an as-needed basis, in July and August only.

After the castle/ramparts tour, you may have time to explore the cobblestone plazas, flagstone courtyards, narrow streets, fish market, and tall gabled houses.

St-Malo's **Cathédrale St-Vincent,** 12 rue St-Benoît (☎ **02-99-40-82-31**), is known for its 1160 nave vault. It's of the Angevin or Plantagenet style, elegantly marking the transition between Romanesque and Gothic. The cathedral also has a Renaissance west facade, with additions from the 18th century and a 15th-century tower. The 14th-century choir is surmounted by a triforium with trefoiled arches and flanked by chapels. It's open daily from 8am to 7pm.

As you drive along the coast, you'll find long stretches of sand interspersed with rocky outcroppings that suggest fortresses protecting the rest of Brittany from Atlantic storms. You can swim virtually wherever you like (beware of undertows in these storm-tossed waters!), but if you're staying in St-Malo, the two best beaches are **Plage du Bon Secours,** near the northern tip of the Vieille Ville, and **La Grande Plage,** a longer stretch of tawny sand that begins at the eastern perimeter of the Vieille Ville.

If you're in St-Malo on Tuesday or Friday morning and want to experience a great Breton **market,** walk down to the ramparts around 9am. You can't miss the activity, the bustle, and the hawking of country-fresh produce, clothing (both new and old), and dozens of other items, including handcrafts.

For **boutique shopping,** head for rue St-Vincent, rue Porcon, rue Broussaus, and rue de Dinan. Here you'll find everything from the trendy to the trashy. In particular, check out **Vêtements Marin-Marine,** 5 Grand' Rue (☎ **02-99-40-90-32**), for quality men's and women's fashions that include, of course, those great Breton wool sweaters, one of the town's best buys. For last-minute souvenir shopping, stop by **Aux Délices Malouins,** 12 rue St-Vincent (☎ **02-99-40-55-22**).

WHERE TO STAY

Hôtel Central. 6 Grand' Rue, 35400 St-Malo. ☎ **02-99-40-87-70.** Fax 02-99-40-47-57. 46 units. MINIBAR TV TEL. 580–680F ($104.40–$122.40) double; 880F ($158.40) suite. Half board 170F ($30.60) per person extra. AE, DC, MC, V. Parking 45F ($8.10).

On a street near the harbor, this hotel is the best of a fairly lackluster lot but is just as provincial as its staff. The structure you see today was rebuilt of granite blocks after the bombings of World War II, like much of the neighborhood surrounding it. Don't expect old-time touches; the furnishings are all contemporary. One of the most compelling reasons to stay here is the food: La Frégate restaurant serves wonderful seafood. Before dinner, enjoy a drink in the cozy bar.

Hôtel de France et de Chateaubriand. Place Chateaubriand, 35412 St-Malo. ☎ **02-99-56-66-52.** Fax 02-99-40-10-04. 80 units. TV TEL. 400–550F ($72–$99) double. AE, DC, MC, V.

This hotel, within the walls of old St-Malo, is a masterpiece of Napoléon III architecture. Guest rooms run from comfortably cozy to spacious and feature such details as cove moldings, ornate plaster ceiling reliefs, and chandeliers. All contain period reproductions, and most have panoramic ocean views. In the chic bar, with gold-trimmed Corinthian columns, you can chat over drinks, play billiards, and listen to the baby grand. A restaurant with four sumptuous dining rooms serves breakfast, lunch, and dinner. Two less formal dining alternatives are the sunny courtyard terrace and the sidewalk cafe tables in front of the hotel.

Hôtel de la Cité. Place Vauban, 35412 St-Malo. ☎ **02-99-40-55-40.** Fax 02-99-40-10-04. 41 units. TV TEL. 492F–570F ($88.55–$102.60) double; 810–1,000F ($145.80–$180) suite. AE, DC, MC, V.

Among the town's leading inns, this new establishment fools the eye because it was built in 18th-century style following the plan of the building that once stood here. The contemporary interior, however, is no match for the richly embellished facade. Like most modern chain hotels, it offers solid comforts but is short on style. The rooms are well laid out, however, ranging from rather cramped to most spacious. Those on the top floor do break away from the norm with their angled ceilings. As a saving grace, many rooms open onto views of the often turbulent ocean. The hotel also has an elegant breakfast room and a small bar.

WHERE TO DINE

✪ **A la Duchesse Anne.** 5 place Guy-La-Chambre. ☎ **02-99-40-85-33.** Reservations required. Main courses 90–130F ($16.20–$23.40). V. Thurs–Tues 12:15–1:30pm and 7:15–9:15pm. Closed Dec–Jan. FRENCH.

This leading restaurant, built into the ramparts, offers summer dining under a large canopy amid hydrangeas. Try the fish specialties—the fish soup with chunks of fresh seafood, spiced and cooked in an iron pot, is excellent, as are the Cancale oysters. Main courses include grilled turbot with beurre blanc and pepper steak. The equally tempting desserts may include the *fantaisie du chocolat*, several chocolate-based desserts artfully arranged on a platter. Year after year, this choice delivers the finest food in town.

Le Chalut. 8 rue de la Corne-de-Cerf. ☎ **02-99-56-71-58.** Reservations required. Main courses 100–130F ($18–$23.40); fixed-price menus 9–-300F ($17.10–$54). AE, V. Tues–Sun 12:15–1:30pm, Tues–Sat 7:15–9:30pm (also Sun night in summer). FRENCH.

The decor here is nautical, with green and blue throughout. Chef Jean-Philippe Foucat's flavorful cuisine, based on fresh ingredients, includes braised sweetbreads with baby vegetables in tarragon sauce, terrine of scallops, and John Dory with smoked lobster seasoned with fresh coriander. For dessert, try the gâteau of bitter chocolate with almond paste or the feuilleté of red seasonal berries. The only complaint we've heard is that the place is touristy, but that's the curse of St-Malo in general.

ST-MALO AFTER DARK

For a full evening of dinner, dancing, and gambling, experience the **Casino,** 2 chausée du Sillon (☎ **02-99-40-64-09**). Here you can take in a show, enjoy a dinner concert, and even trip the light fantastic at the casino's disco, City's Club. The dress code is informally elegant. Admission is 75F ($13.50), including one drink.

La Belle Epoque, 11 rue de Dinan (☎ **02-99-40-82-23**), attracts a 20-and-over crowd with its inviting setting, complete with a fireplace that heats things up on cooler nights. Play a game of darts, study the exhibits of local artists' work, or listen to one of the regular jazz or rock performances while enjoying a drink.

If you're out on a pub crawl, hunt for **Le O'Flaherty's,** 18 rue des Cordiers (☎ **02-99-56-87-54**), where you can experience a real Irish pub with a French twist. They serve at least 6 different draft beers and more than 40 brands of whiskey.

2 Dinard

259 miles W of Paris, 14 miles N of Dinan

Dinard (not to be confused with its Breton neighbor, Dinan) sits on a rocky promontory at the top of the Rance River, opposite St-Malo (see above). Ferries ply the waters between the two resorts. Turn-of-the-century Victorian-Gothic villas, many now hotels, overlook the sea, and gardens and parks abound. Dinard today seems to have passed its prime, though a number of modern buildings dot the landscape. The old is still best here, and for a look at what the Edwardians admired, go down the pointe de la Vicomte at the resort's southern tip or stroll along the promenade. You'll expect to see Maurice Chevalier in top hat and cane appear at any moment.

One of France's best-known resorts, Dinard offers safe, well-sheltered bathing and bracingly healthful sea air in La Manche ("The Sleeve," the term given centuries ago to a body of water claimed by the British as the English Channel). During Queen Victoria's time, this town became popular with the Channel-crossing English, who wanted a continental holiday that was "not too foreign."

ESSENTIALS

GETTING THERE   SNCF **trains** don't travel as far as Dinard, forcing rail travelers to get off at St-Malo, then continue on any of about a dozen **buses** that depart from the rail station there for the 20-minute ride to Dinard. For bus information, call Compagnie T.I.V. (☎ **02-99-40-83-33**). Buses arrive from many large cities in Brittany, including Rennes et St-Malo. Between May and September, a **ferry** makes one daily trip from Dinan. A **taxi** ride to Dinard from St-Malo is a great option, costing 90F ($16.20) during the day and 110F ($19.80) after 7pm. For taxi information, call ☎ **02-99-81-30-30**. If you **drive,** simply take D186 west from St-Malo to Dinard.

VISITOR INFORMATION   The **Office de Tourisme** is at 2 bd. Féart (☎ **02-99-46-94-12**).

SPECIAL EVENTS   From June to September there's *musique-et-lumière* along the floodlit seafront promenade du Clair-de-Lune.

ENJOYING THE RESORT

Dinard's main beach is **Plage de l'Ecluse** or **La Grande Plage,** the strip of sand between the seaward-jutting peninsulas that define the edges of the old town. Favored by families and holidaymakers, it's crowded on hot days. Smaller and somewhat more isolated, and accessible after a 20-minute hike east from Dinard that'll take you through the village of St-Enogat, is **Plage de St-Enogat.** There's also **Plage du Prieuré,** a 10-minute walk from the center; you may or may not like the many trees that shade the sand. Because there's such a difference in elevation between high and low tides here, the municipality has built swimming pool–style basins along all three beaches as a means of catching seawater during high tides. Most people, however, trek along the salt flats during low tides to bathe in the sea.

Looking for a bona-fide pool that's covered, heated, filled with sea water, and open year-round? Head for the **Piscine Olympique,** boulevard du Président-Wilson (☎ **02-99-46-22-77**). Entrance is 25F ($4.50). From July to September 15, it's open Monday through Saturday from 10am to 1pm and 3 to 8pm, and on Sunday to 7pm. The rest of the year, it runs on a schedule that varies according to the agendas of local school groups and swim teams.

About 5 miles from Dinard is a par-68, 18-hole golf course, **Le Dinard Golf,** at St-Briac (☎ **02-99-88-32-07**), one of the finest in Brittany. It's set on sandy, windy terrain studded with tough grasses and durable trees and shrubs. You'll have to reserve your tee-off time in advance and present a membership card from a golf course in your hometown. Greens fees are 220F to 300F ($39.60 to $54) per person, depending on the season. A limited number of clubs can be rented, but it's wiser to bring your own.

For the usual selection of shops and boutiques selling men's and women's clothes, antiques, shoes, and jewelry, concentrate on **rue du Maréchal-Leclerc, rue Revavasseur,** and **boulevard du Président-Wilson.** Your best bet is the **Galerie Line Boutique,** 13 bd. du Président-Wilson (☎ **02-99-46-11-21**). The art gallery scene offers you a chance to pick up some unique pieces at affordable prices. The owner of the **Atelier du Prince Noir,** 70 av. George-V (☎ **02-99-46-29-99**), travels the country seeking talented artists for exhibitions in her gallery. In this 15th-century medieval house you'll find a wide range of paintings and sculptures from some of the most talented artists in France. The gallery is closed from October to April.

WHERE TO STAY

Note that **Altaïr** and **Le Prieuré** (see "Where to Dine," below) also rent rooms.

Grand Hôtel de Dinard. 46 av. George-V, 35801 Dinard. ☎ **02-99-88-26-26.** Fax 02-99-88-26-27. 66 units. MINIBAR TV TEL. 680–1,080F ($122.40–$194.40) double; from 1,580F ($284.40) suite. AE, DC, MC, V. Closed late Oct to late Mar.

Dinard's largest hotel, a member of the nationwide Lucien Barrière chain, was built in 1859. Its location, just a 2-minute walk from the town center, commands an excellent view of the harbor. It rises in two wings, with three and four stories, respectively, that are separated from each other by a heated outdoor pool. Most rooms have balconies and are furnished with traditional pieces.

Dining: The inviting bar is a popular spot before and after dinner. Fine meals, with generous portions, are offered in the dignified in-house restaurant, the George V.

✪ **Hôtel de la Reine-Hortense.** 19 rue de la Malouine, 35800 Dinard. ☎ **02-99-46-54-31.** Fax 02-99-88-15-88. 10 units. TV TEL. 490–980F ($88.20–$176.40) double; 1,500–1,800F ($270–$324) suite. AE, DC, MC, V.

This hotel on the beach was built in 1860 as a retreat for one of the Russian-born courtiers of Holland-based Queen Hortense de Beauharnais, daughter of Joséphine de Beauharnais (who went on to marry Napoléon I) and mother of Napoléon III. It offers glamorously outfitted public salons and many guest rooms decorated in either Louis XV or Napoléon III style. One high-ceilinged room even has Hortense's silver-plated bathtub, dating from the early 19th century. Breakfast is the only meal served.

Under the same management as the Hortense, the 6-room **Castel Eugénie** next door charges the same rates. About a decade old, it's well appointed and comfortable.

Hôtel des Dunes. 5 rue Georges-Clemenceau, 35800 Dinard. ☎ **02-99-46-12-72.** Fax 02-99-88-14-90. 38 units. TV TEL. 290–315F ($52.20–$56.70) double. Half board 265–275F ($47.70–$49.50) per person extra. AE, DC, MC, V. Closed mid-Nov to Mar.

High on a cliff, this turn-of-the-century hotel evokes Edwardian days with its French windows and balustraded balconies. It offers comfortable rooms and garden furniture out on the front terrace. A dining room/lounge, open to nonguests who reserve a table in advance, overlooks the terrace and charges 95F to 130F ($17.10 to $23.40) for fixed-price menus. The only drawback to an otherwise worthy setting is the lack of sea view from any of the rooms, but with the reasonable rates and other advantages, no one seems to mind.

Hôtel Printania. 5 av. George-V, 35800 Dinard. ☎ **02-99-46-13-07.** Fax 02-99-46-26-32. 59 units. TV TEL. 350–400F ($63–$72) double. Half board 260–340F ($46.80–$61.20) per person extra. AE, MC, V. Closed Nov 20–Mar 23.

On August 15, 1944, this Breton hotel was damaged in a bombing raid, but the debris was removed in time for the Allied victory. The Printania draws many repeat guests, among them writers and artists. The main villa boasts terraces and a glassed-in veranda with potted palms, while the sitting room has carved-oak furniture, old clocks, and provincial chairs. The old-fashioned guest rooms contain antiques and Breton decorations. Dinner here combines superb cookery with a view of the coast; the restaurant specializes in seafood and various shellfish, and the waitresses wear traditional Breton costumes.

WHERE TO DINE

Another choice is the restaurant at the **Hôtel des Dunes** (see above).

Altaïr. 18 bd. Féart, 64200 Dinard. ☎ **02-99-46-13-58.** Fax 02-99-88-20-49. Reservations recommended. Main courses 95–150F ($17.10–$27); fixed-price menus 88–200F ($15.85–$36). AE, DC, MC, V. Daily noon–2pm and 7–9:30pm. Closed Sun dinner and Mon in winter. FRENCH.

Patrick Leménager, who operates the intimate Altaïr, serves excellent cuisine that includes sea scallops in puff pastry with coriander sauce, fresh salmon with herbs, and duck breast with apple-and-honey sauce, followed by gratin of red fruits. The portions are generous, and most prices are a good value for the area. In warm weather, you may dine alfresco on the terrace.

The Altaïr also rents 21 standard rooms with bathroom and TV. A double is 220F to 330F ($39.60 to $59.40) per person, including half board.

Le Prieuré. 1 place du Général-de-Gaulle, 35800 Dinard. ☎ **02-99-46-13-74.** Reservations recommended. Main courses 70–110F ($12.60–$19.80); fixed-price menus 90–175F ($16.20–$31.50). MC, V. Tues–Sun 12:30–2pm, Tues–Sat 7:30–9pm. Closed Jan and Sept 22–28. SEAFOOD.

Diners at this family-style seafood restaurant are greeted by a lively room full of seafaring bric-a-brac. Come here with a hearty appetite and you'll be rewarded with dishes like sautéed sole in beurre blanc with baby potatoes, grilled salmon with a stir-fry of seasonal vegetables, and even a beef filet topped with a rich black-pepper sauce. Desserts like the ever-popular crème caramel and the commendable wine list round out the menu.

Le Prieuré also rents 4 small double guest rooms for 260F ($46.80). Each is simply outfitted with the bare essentials of bed, armoire, a chair or two, and a phone.

DINARD AFTER DARK

Like many of Brittany's seaside towns, Dinard has a **Municipal Casino,** boulevard du Président-Wilson (☎ **02-99-16-30-30**). It's liveliest from Easter to late October, when all its facilities, including a room for roulette and blackjack, are open; the rest of the year, only the slot machines are in operation. Regardless of season, the hours are Sunday through Thursday from 11am to 2am and Friday and Saturday from 11am to 3am. Admission is free, and the management encourages men to wear ties, especially in the roulette and blackjack areas. Also on the premises is La Brasserie de la Mer, open April to October, Wednesday through Monday from noon to 2:30pm and 7pm to midnight.

In the evenings from June to September, the **promenade du Clair-de-Lune** attracts a huge crowd of strollers for the *musique-et-lunière,* when the buildings and flowers along the promenade are illuminated and musical groups of just about every ilk—from rock to blues to jazz—perform.

3 Dinan

246 miles W of Paris, 32 miles NW of Rennes

Once a stronghold of the ducs de Bretagne, Dinan is one of the best-preserved towns of Brittany, characterized by houses built on stilts over the sidewalks. The 18th-century granite dwellings provide sharp contrast to the medieval timbered houses in this walled town with a once-fortified château. Dinan today remains one of Brittany's prettiest towns, with a tranquil population of 14,000—it's not overrun like St-Malo.

ESSENTIALS

GETTING THERE   Four **trains** per day arrive from Paris via Rennes (trip time: 3½ hours). From St-Malo (see above), 5 trains per day arrive, with a change at Dol (trip time: 1¼ hours). For train information and schedules, call ☎ **08-36-35-35-39.** **Ferry** service is offered daily from Dinard and St-Malo. If you're **driving** from Dinard, take D766 south to Dinan.

VISITOR INFORMATION   The **Office de Tourisme** is at 6 rue de l'Horloge (☎ **02-96-39-75-40**).

SPECIAL EVENTS   The most activity you'll ever see here is during the first weekend in September for the 3-day **Fêtes des Remparts.** Duels from the Age of

Chivalry are staged, and locals don their apparel from the Middle Ages for riotous fun in the streets. The festival takes place every odd-numbered year; on even-numbered years it occurs in Dinan's sister city, Québec, Canada.

EXPLORING THE TOWN

For a panoramic view of the valley, head for the **Jardin Anglais** (English Garden), a terraced garden that huddles up to the ramparts. A Gothic-style bridge spans the Rance River; it was damaged in World War II but has since been restored. Dinan's most typical street is the sloping **rue du Jerzual,** flanked with some buildings dating from the 15th century. The street ends at the **Porte du Jerzual,** an ancient gate. **Rue du Petit-Fours** contains a number of 15th-century *maisons.*

Dominating the old city's medieval ramparts, **Château de Dinan,** rue du Château (☎ **02-96-39-45-20**), contains a 14th-century keep and a 15th-century tower, built to withstand lengthy sieges. Within the stones you'll see the space for the portcullis and the drawbridge. Inside you can view an exhibition of the architecture and art of the city, including locally carved sculpture from the 12th to the 15th centuries. Admission is 25F ($4.50) for adults and 10F ($1.80) for children. The castle is open in summer, daily from 10am to 5:45pm; in spring and fall, daily from 10am to noon and 2 to 5:45pm; and in winter, Wednesday through Monday from 1:30 to 5pm.

The old city's **Tour de l'Horloge** (clock tower), on rue de l'Horloge, now classified a historic monument, boasts a clock made in 1498 and a great bell donated by Anne de Bretagne in 1507. You'll have a panoramic view of medieval Dinan from the 75-foot belfry. Admission is 16F ($2.90) for adults and 10F ($1.80) for children, and the belfry is open daily from 10am to 7pm, June to September.

The heart of Bertrand du Guesclin, who defended the town when the duke of Lancaster threatened it in 1359, was entombed in a place of honor in the **Basilique St-Sauveur,** place St-Sauveur; note the basilica's Romanesque portals and ornamented chapels. It's open daily from 8am to 6pm.

This town is a great place to find any number of arts and crafts made by local artisans. Walk along **rue du Jerzual** to discover a host of galleries and boutiques selling jewelry, objets d'art made out of glass and wood, hand-painted silks, and leather products. For some real finds, stop by the studio of **M. Charabot,** 8 rue du Jerzual (☎ **02-96-39-47-93**), where you'll encounter fluidly graceful hand-blown glassware; and the galleries of either **J. P. Poiron,** 31 rue du Jerzual (☎ **02-96-39-33-95**), or **M. Roinel,** 19 rue du Petit-Fort (☎ **02-96-85-40-52**), to pick up one-of-a-kind sculptures created out of materials such as marble, metal, and sandstone.

WHERE TO STAY

Hôtel Arvor. 5 rue Pavie, 22100 Dinan. ☎ **02-96-39-21-22.** Fax 02-96-39-83-09. 23 units. TV TEL. 280–380F ($50.40–$68.40) double. AE, MC, V.

In 1992, M. Pierre took over the run-down premises of what used to be a Jacobin convent in the 14th century; after demolishing all but the four exterior walls, he transformed it into one of the most inviting little hotels in town. It's located in the oldest neighborhood, in a labyrinth of narrow cobblestone streets. Breakfast is the only meal served, but many inviting places to eat are a short walk away. The clean and comfortable rooms are a good value but retain none of the building's original medieval characteristics.

✪ **Hôtel d'Avaugour.** 1 place du Champs-Clos, 22100 Dinan. ☎ **02-96-39-07-49.** Fax 02-96-85-43-04. 27 units. MINIBAR TV TEL. 350–700F ($63–$126) double. Rates include buffet breakfast. AE, DC, MC, V.

It's hard to believe that what was once a gutted old building has been transformed into Dinan's best, most up-to-date hotel. The rooms boast new fabrics inspired by traditional French 18th-century design and furniture reflecting the heritage of Dinan. Half of the units overlook the square; the others face the rear garden. The stylish front lounge utilizes natural stone and modern furnishings. The Restaurant d'Avaugour, in the garden overlooking the ramparts, is open daily year-round; its chef, Jean-François, prepares excellent food. A summer restaurant, in a former guards' room in a 15th-century tower at the rear of the garden, specializes in meats grilled in a wood-burning fireplace. A buffet lunch is available for 50F ($9).

WHERE TO DINE

Note that the restaurant in the **Hôtel d'Avagour** (see above) is open to nonguests.

✪ **Chez La Mère Pourcel.** 3 place des Merciers. ☎ **02-96-39-03-80.** Reservations recommended. Main courses 100–150F ($18–$27); fixed-price menus 97F ($17.45) at lunch Tues–Fri, 162–370F ($29.15–$66.60) at dinner. AE, DC, MC, V. Daily noon–2pm and 7:15–10pm. Closed Feb; Sun dinner and Mon in Mar–June and Sept–Jan. FRENCH.

This restaurant enjoys an outstanding reputation for regional food. Most diners prefer the à la carte menu, with choices like consommé with ham- and duckling-stuffed ravioli and mushrooms from the forest with lobster and green butter. For a main course, try Breton lobster, pastry-encased pigeon, or chicken suprême with foie gras. The sumptuous desserts include cold chocolate soufflé. The extensive wine carte, alas, is too expensive for most budgets.

La Caravelle. 14 place Duclos. ☎ **02-96-39-00-11.** Reservations required. Main courses 130–250F ($23.40–$45); fixed-price menus 130–245F ($23.40–$44.10). AE, MC, V. Daily noon–2pm and 7–9:30pm. Closed Nov 12–Dec 3 and Wed Dec–July. FRENCH.

We used to hail Jean-Claude Marmion as the most inventive chef in Dinan. He still serves wonderful food, and his 130F ($23.40) menu is the town's best value, but some of the magic has gone now that he prepares only time-tested dishes. Specialties are warm oysters with shallots, John Dory with green-mustard and red-pepper/cream sauce, and veal kidneys in cider. In season, Marmion prepares fine game dishes like jugged hare and rabbit. When the first of the spring turnips come in, he uses them with a veal filet often served with onion compote.

DINAN AFTER DARK

Head for **rue de la Sois** and you'll find plenty of bars and clubs where you can let your whimsy be your guide. **Petit Marcel,** 20 rue Haute-Voie (☎ 02-96-39-06-95), is a busy cafe/bar that caters to those in their 20s; you can grab a bite to eat and a beer while soaking up the atmosphere. For a more folksy experience, set out for **La Truye Qui File,** 14 rue de la Cordonnerie (☎ 02-98-39-72-29), and don't be surprised to hear everybody in the place breaking out in song as the proprietor saddles up to a table and starts crooning away.

4 Quimper

342 miles W of Paris, 127 miles NW of Rennes

The town that pottery built, Quimper, at the meeting of the Odet and Steir rivers, is the historic capital of Brittany's most traditional region, La Cornouaille. Today its faïence decorates tables from Europe to America. Skilled artisans have been turning out Quimper ware since the 17th century, using bold provincial designs. You can tour one of the ateliers during your stay; inquire at the tourist office (see below). Today's

Quimper is rather smug and bourgeois, home to some 65,000 Quimperois, who walk narrow streets miraculously spared from World War II damage.

ESSENTIALS

GETTING THERE   Two or three regular **trains** from Paris arrive daily (trip time: 7½ hours). The speedier TGV has 12 trains per day from Paris (trip time: 4 to 5 hours). Fifteen trains also arrive from Rennes (trip time: 3 hours). For train information and schedules, call ☎ **08-36-35-35-39.** If you **drive** to Quimper, the best route is from Rennes, taking E50/N12 west to just outside the town of Montauban and continuing west along N164 to the town of Châteaulin in western France. From Châteaulin, head south along E60 to Quimper.

VISITOR INFORMATION   The **Office de Tourisme** is on place de la Résistance (☎ **02-98-53-04-05**).

SPECIAL EVENTS   In late July, the **Celtic Festival de Cornouaille** adds a traditional flavor to the nightlife scene with Celtic and Breton concerts held throughout the city. For detailed information, contact the Office de Tourisme.

EXPLORING THE TOWN

In some quarters, Quimper still maintains its old-world atmosphere, with charming footbridges spanning the rivers. At place St-Corentin, is the landmark **Cathédrale St-Corentin** (tel. **02-98-95-06-19**), characterized by two towers that climb 250 feet. The cathedral was built between the 13th and the 15th centuries; the spires weren't added until the 19th. Inside, note the exceptional 15th-century stained glass. The cathédrale is currently under renovation until December 1999, but remains open to the public. It's open daily from 9am to 6:30pm.

Also on the square is the **Musée des Beaux-Arts,** 40 place St-Corentin (☎ **02-98-95-45-20**), with a collection that includes Rubens, Boucher, Fragonard, Oudry, and Corot, plus an exceptional exhibit from the Pont-Aven school (Bernard, Sérusier, Lacombe, Maufra, Denis). Admission is 25F ($4.50) for adults and 15F ($2.70) for children. The gallery is open in July and August, daily from 10am to 7pm; September to June, Wednesday through Monday from 10am to noon and 2 to 6pm.

When artisans from Rouen and other parts of France settled in Quimper, the city became forever associated with ceramics. The most typical are white ceramics painted in blue and yellow with Breton figures, fruits, and flowers. Quimper ware is featured in virtually every shop in town. The best shopping streets are **rue Kereron** and **rue du Parc,** where you'll find all kinds of quintessentially Breton products, including pottery, dolls and puppets, clothing made from regional cloth and wool, jewelry, metal and wooden crafts, lace, and even those beautiful Breton costumes.

For Breton pottery and fine pieces of the faïence that was once heavily produced in the area, visit **H. B. Henrio,** rue Haute (☎ 02-98-90-09-36), or **Maison à Breton,** 16 bis rue du Parc (☎ 02-98-95-34-13). At **François le Villec,** 4 rue du Roi-Gradlon (☎ 02-98-95-31-54), you'll find quality tablecloths as well as other household linens. With 16 years of experience and more than 1,200 square feet of showroom, **Le Grenier,** 60 rue du President Sadate (☎ 02-98-52-04-60), is a treasure trove of antique furniture, bibelots, and paintings.

WHERE TO STAY

La Tour d'Auverge. 13 rue des Réguaires, 29000 Quimper. ☎ **02-98-95-08-70.** Fax 02-98-95-17-31. 41 units, 38 with bathroom. TV TEL. 515–550F ($92.70–$99) double with bathroom. AE, DC, MC, V.

An Idyll on an Ile

Ile de Bréhat is home to some 500 hearty people who live most of the year isolated from others—until the summer crowds arrive to see their lovely island. The tiny island (actually two islands, Ile Nord and Ile Sud, linked by a bridge) is in the Golfe de St-Malo, north of Paimpol. A visit to Bréhat is an offbeat adventure, even to the French.

Walking is the primary activity here, and it's possible to stroll the marked footpaths around the islands in a day. Cars aren't allowed, except those used by the police and fire departments. Some tractor-driven carts carry visitors on a 5-mile circuit of Bréhat, charging 28F ($5.05) for the 45-minute jaunt. A number of places rent bikes, but one isn't necessary.

The rich flora here astonishes many visitors, who get off the ferry expecting a windswept Channel island—only to discover a place more evocative of a Mediterranean climate. Flower gardens are in full summer bloom, though both the gardens and houses appear tiny because of the scarcity of land. At the highest point, Chapelle St-Michel, you'll be rewarded with a panoramic view.

If you need information, there's a little summer tourist office at Le Bourg, place du Bourg (☎ **02-96-20-04-15**).

To reach the island, take D789 3 miles north of Paimpol, where the peninsula ends dramatically at the pink-granite Pointe de l'Arcouest. A CAT bus from Paimpol (about 5 to 10 per day) makes the 15-minute run to the point for a one-way fare of 12F ($2.15). Once here, catch one of the ferries operated by **Les Vedettes de Bréhat** (☎ **02-96-55-79-50** for schedules), which will take you to the Ile de Bréhat from April to September—at other times, it's too cold. Ferries depart about every 30 minutes, costing 40F ($7.20) round-trip. Once at Bréhat, you can take a 45-minute cruise of this idyllic Breton retreat (65F/$11.70). Visitors in April, May, June, and September will find the island pleasantly less crowded.

Although they're small and overlook a not particularly picturesque area in the town center, about 200 yards from the cathedral, the rooms here represent good value for Quimper. Each double has a private bathroom (3 of the bargain singles don't). The present owner's grandparents bought the hotel in 1927, and one part or another has been renovated every year since.

Dining: One of main attractions here is the kitchen's Breton cuisine. Menu items may include tian of monkfish with Basmati rice and vegetable "caviar," saddle of rabbit with mustard sauce, and croustillant of crayfish and scallops with tarragon sauce.

Novotel. 17 rue Dupoher, pont de Poulguinan, 29000 Quimper. ☎ **02-98-90-46-26.** Fax 02-98-53-01-96. www.novotel.com. 92 units. A/C MINIBAR TV TEL. 470–490F ($84.60–$88.20) double. Two children ages 15 and under can stay free in parents' room and get a free breakfast. AE, DC, MC, V. From the town center, follow the signs to Route Pont-l'Abbé.

In a garden about a mile southwest of the town center, the Novotel, despite its blandness, is your best choice here. Built in the early 1980s, it boasts a Breton-style slate roof that would be the envy of any homeowner. It's ideal for motoring families (the pool is a magnet in summer) and is the best business-oriented hotel in the region. Each of its chain hotel–style rooms has lots of space, plus a writing desk and single and double beds. The food here is prepared competently—and that's it.

WHERE TO DINE

Another good dining choice is the restaurant at **La Tour d'Auvergne** (see above).

✪ **Le Capucin Gourmand.** 29 rue des Réguaires. ☎ **02-98-95-43-12.** Reservations required in summer. Main courses 90–145F ($16.20–$26.10); fixed-price menus 95–360F ($17.10–$64.80). AE, DC, V. Mon–Sat 12:15–2pm, daily 7:15–10pm. FRENCH.

This popular restaurant, run by Jacques Pichon, offers the area's finest dining. Delightful appetizers may include foie gras in a terrine, a dozen Breton oysters, or a succulent plate of ravioli filled with basil-flavored lobster. For your entree, opt for a blanquette of turbot with langoustines and artichokes or filet of sole with fresh basil. Breton lamb appears frequently, usually roasted and served in a made-from-scratch sauce, perhaps flavored with leeks. The chef's secret involves giving familiar dishes a new twist by adding an unexpected ingredient or two.

NEARBY ACCOMMODATIONS & DINING

In an orchard district 8 miles from Quimper, the sleepy village of **La Forêt-Fouesnant** produces the best cider in the province and is home to one of Brittany's finest manor houses. Take N783 and turn off at the clearly marked sign.

✪ **Manoir du Stang.** 29940 La Forêt-Fouesnant. ☎ **02-98-56-97-37.** 26 units. TEL. 580–920F ($104.40–$165.60) double. No credit cards. Closed Sept 20–May 10. Drive a mile north of the village center and follow the signs from N783; access is by private road.

To get to this 16th-century ivy-covered manor, you travel down a tree-lined avenue and under a stone tower gate into a courtyard. On your right is a formal garden; raised stone terraces lead to 25 acres of rolling woodland. This is the domain of M. and Mme Guy Hubert, who provide gracious living in period rooms. Guests stay either in the main building or in the even older but less desirable annex with a circular stone staircase. Your room is likely to be furnished with silk and fine antiques, and a maid in a lacy Breton cap will bring your breakfast tray each morning. The restaurant's specialties are grilled lobster with tarragon, côte of beef with green peppercorns, fruits de mer (seafood), and oysters house style.

QUIMPER AFTER DARK

A trip down **rue Ste-Catherine** will lead to some of the best nightspots. The steadfastly Celtic bar, the **Céili Pub,** 4 rue Aristide-Briand (☎ 02-98-95-17-61), was recently renovated and has lots of polished wood, regional music, and happy people—join in a game of darts with any of the regulars. **St. Andrew's Pub,** 11 place Styvel (☎ 02-98-53-34-49), with its wood-and-leather interior and 44 varities of beer, attracts a large number of Brits and Americans.

The young and stylish flock to **Les Naïdes Discothèque,** boulevard Créac'h Gwen (☎ 02-98-53-32-30), where you can dance to the latest tunes (there's sometimes a 60F/$10.80 cover). **Le Coffee Shop,** 26 rue du Frout (☎ 02-98-95-43-30), has a cool gay and lesbian crowd that unwinds to disco and techno; there's no cover here.

5 Concarneau

335 miles W of Paris, 58 miles SE of Brest

This port is a favorite of painters, who never tire of capturing on canvas the subtleties of the fishing fleet in the harbor. It's also our favorite of the coast communities—primarily because it doesn't depend on tourists for its livelihood. In fact, its canneries today produce nearly three-quarters of all the tunny fish consumed in France. Walk along the quays here, especially in the late evening, and watch the rustic Breton fishers unload their catch; later, join them for a pint of potent cider in the taverns.

ESSENTIALS

GETTING THERE   Local rail service is limited to freight. If you're **driving**, the town is 13 miles southeast of Quimper along D783. A Caoudal **bus** (☎ **02-98-56-96-72**) runs from Quimper to Concarneau (trip time: 40 minutes), and another runs from Resporden to Concarneau (trip time: 20 minutes).

VISITOR INFORMATION   The **Office de Tourisme** is on quai d'Aiguillon (☎ **02-98-97-01-44**).

EXPLORING THE AREA

The town is built on three sides of a natural harbor whose innermost sheltered section is the **Nouveau Port.** In the center of the harbor, connected to its westernmost edge by a bridge, is the heavily fortified **Ville-Close,** an ancient hamlet surrounded by ramparts, some from the 14th century. From the quay, cross the bridge and descend into the town. Admittedly, souvenir shops have taken over, but don't let that spoil it for you. You can easily spend an hour wandering the winding alleys, gazing up at the towers, peering at the stone houses, and pausing in the secluded squares. For a splendid view of the port, walk the ramparts—it's free. Walks are possible mid-April to mid-June, daily from 10am to 6:30pm; and mid-June to mid-September, daily from 10am to 9:30pm.

Also in the old town is a fishing museum, **Musée de la Pêche,** rue Vauban (☎ **02-98-97-10-20**). Its 17th-century building contains ship models and exhibits tracing the development of the fishing industry throughout the world; you can also view the preserved ship *Hemerica.* Admission is 30F ($5.40) for adults and 20F ($3.60) for children. Hours are daily, in July and August from 9:30am to 7:30pm and September to June from 10am to noon and 2 to 6pm; the museum is closed the first 3 weeks in January.

Concarneau's largest and most beautiful beach, popular with families, is **Plage des Sables Blancs,** near the historic core. Within a 10-minute walk is **Plage de Cornouaille** and two small beaches, **Plage des Dames** and **Plage de Rodel,** where you'll find fewer families with children. The wide-open **Plage du Cabellou,** 3 miles west of town, is less congested than the others.

Excursions on the sea can be diverting between June and September—and downright treacherous the rest of the year, when storms that brewed in the central Atlantic are unleashed onto the battered coastline. During clement midsummer periods, you can arrange deep-sea fishing with the captain of the **Santa Maria** (☎ **02-98-50-69-01**). For **boat excursions** to anywhere along the coastline, contact Vedettes Glenn (☎ **02-98-97-10-31**) or Vedettes de l'Odet (☎ **02-99-57-00-58** or 02-99-50-72-12).

WHERE TO STAY

Grand Hôtel. 1 av. Pierre-Guéguen, 29186 Concarneau. ☎ **02-98-97-00-28.** Fax 02-98-97-00-89. 33 units, 18 with bathroom. TEL. 168–190F ($30.25–$34.20) double without bathroom, 260–350F ($46.80–$63) double with bathroom. V. Closed late Oct–Mar 27.

This is the best budget choice in the center of the port. Across from the Ville-Close, the Grand overlooks the fishing fleet and marketplace and has open stalls selling fresh vegetables, fruit, fish, and even clothing. The rooms are simple but suitable for at least a stopover. Breakfast is the only meal served.

WHERE TO DINE

La Coquille. 1 rue du Moros, at Nouveau Port. ☎ **02-98-97-08-52.** Reservations required Sat–Sun and in summer. Main courses 100–190F ($18–$34.20); fixed-price menus 150–280F ($27–$50.40). AE, DC, MC, V. Tues–Sun 12:30–1:30pm, Tues–Sat 7:30–9:30pm. Closed Jan. FRENCH.

This 30-year-old restaurant occupies one end of a stone-sided harborfront building; guests dine in a trio of rooms with exposed stone walls and ceiling beams. La Coquille serves primarily seafood, particularly lobster. Much of the food is prepared simply because the fish is always so fresh and succulent. The service is bistro style (no great compliment), with a cheerful, somewhat old-fashioned kind of panache that's enhanced by the harbor view.

NEARBY ACCOMMODATIONS & DINING

On the outskirts of the once-fortified town of **Hennebont,** 35 miles west of Concarneau, is the most delightful hotel in all of southern Brittany.

✪ **Château de Locguénolé.** Route de Port-Louis, 56700 Hennebont. ☎ **02-97-76-29-04.** Fax 02-97-76-82-35. www.relaischateaux.fr. E-mail: locguenole@relaischateaux.fr. 20 units, 4 suites. MINIBAR TV TEL. 660–1,800F ($118.80–$324) double; 1,300–2,200F ($234–$396) suite. AE, DC, MC, V. Closed Jan 2–Feb 8. From Hennebont, follow the prominent signs to the château, 3 miles south.

This country estate in a 250-acre private park has been owned by the same family for more than 500 years. Now a Relais & Châteaux, with views over rugged coastline and an inlet, it's filled with antiques, tapestries, and paintings. The rooms vary widely in size and furnishings, but each has harmonious colors and, season permitting, sprays of flowers. The converted maids' rooms are smaller than the others yet still charming; some units are in a converted Breton cottage.

Dining: Even if you can't stay here, consider taking a meal in the dining hall. Specialties are filet of beef with foie gras, *suprême de barbue* (brill) with cider and leeks, and grilled salmon. Fixed-price menus range from 190F to 480F ($34.20 to $86.40).

Amenities: Outdoor pool heated from May to October, sauna and steam bath, free use of mountain bikes.

6 Pont-Aven

324 miles W of Paris, 20 miles SE of Quimper, 10 miles S of Concarneau

Paul Gauguin loved this peaceful village with its little white houses along the gently flowing Aven. In the late 19th century, many painters followed him here, including Maurice Denis, Sérusier, and Emile Bernard. The artistic theories and techniques developed here at the time have been known ever since as the School of Pont-Aven.

Before leaving for Tahiti, Gauguin painted *The Golden Christ* and *The Beautiful Angela* here. You can admire the crucifix that inspired *The Golden Christ* in the **Chapelle de Trémalo,** less than a mile southeast from the town center. Every year, the Société de Peinture organizes an exhibition of paintings, usually in the chapel, by other members of the School of Pont-Aven.

From Quimperlé, **drive** west along D783 toward Concarneau. Because the SNCF **rail lines** stop at Quimperlé, rail passengers take a bus (one of up to 6 per day) for the 15-minute ride to Pont-Aven, for a cost of 20F ($3.60) each way. For train information, call either the Pont-Aven tourist office (see below) or ☎ **08-36-35-35-39.**

The **Office de Tourisme** is on place de l'Hôtel-de-Ville (☎ **02-98-06-04-70**).

WHERE TO STAY & DINE

✪ **Le Moulin de Rosmadec.** 29123 Pont-Aven. ☎ **02-98-06-00-22.** Fax 02-98-06-18-00. Reservations recommended. Main courses 130–170F ($23.40–$30.60); fixed-price menus 160–295F ($28.80–$53.10); *menu tradition* (with oysters and lobster) 398F ($71.65). MC, V. Thurs–Tues 12:30–2pm and 7:30–9pm. Closed Feb, Nov 15–Dec 1, and Sun night in winter. FRENCH.

For a charming setting, nothing in Brittany compares to this 15th-century reconstructed stone mill. Meals are served in a bilevel dining room with antique furniture or, in good weather, on a flower-filled "island" terrace. The owners, M. and Mme Sebilleau, serve carefully prepared food, with specialties like trout with almonds, sole suprême with champagne, and duck breast with cassis. The fish dishes are especially sublime.

The Moulin also rents 4 comfortable rooms, at 470F ($84.60) for a double.

7 La Baule

281 miles SW of Paris, 49 miles NW of Nantes

Founded during the Victorian seaside craze, La Baule remains as inviting as the Gulf Stream that warms the waters of its 5-mile crescent of white-sand beach. Occupying the Côte d'Amour (Coast of Love), it competes with Biarritz today as the Atlantic coast's most fashionable resort. But La Baule is still essentially French, drawing only a nominal number of foreigners.

The gambler François André founded the casino and major resort hotels here. Pines grow on the dunes, and villas on the outskirts draw the wealthy chic from late June to mid-September; if you arrive at any other time you might have La Baule all to yourself. While the movie stars and flashy rich go to Deauville or Cannes, La Baule draws a more middle-class crowd; however, the more reserved wealthy still come here—as the yachts in the harbor testify.

The town itself is north of a popular stretch of beachfront. The two main boulevards run roughly parallel through the long, narrow town; the one closer to the ocean changes its name six times—at its most famous point, it's called boulevard de l'Océan.

Other than a rock outcropping much weathered by Atlantic storms, the beaches here are clean and sandy bottomed, providing safe swimming and lots of options for admiring flesh in all states of fitness and differing degrees of preservation.

Avenue du Général-de-Gaulle and avenue Louis-Lajarrige have the best collection of shops and boutiques. Beside the casino on esplanade de Françoise-André, you'll hit the shopping jackpot—a minimall with 40 or so French chain stores and boutiques.

ESSENTIALS

GETTING THERE   The **train** trip from Nantes is about an hour. Get off at the most central inner-city station, La Baule-Escoublac, or the more easterly and remote La Baule-Les Pins. For train information and schedules, call ☎ **08-36-35-35-39.** If you're **driving** from Nantes, take N165 northwest to Savenay, continuing west along D773 to La Baule.

VISITOR INFORMATION   The **Office de Tourisme** is at 8 place de la Victoire (☎ **02-40-24-34-44**).

WHERE TO STAY
VERY EXPENSIVE

✪ **Castel Marie-Louise.** 1 av. Andrieu, 44504 La Baule. ☎ **02-40-11-48-38.** Fax 02-40-11-48-35. www.relaischateaux.fr/marielouise. E-mail: marielouise@relaischateaux.fr. 29 units. MINIBAR TV TEL. 810–1,240F ($145.80–$223.20) per person. Rates include breakfast. Half board 340F ($61.20) extra. AE, DC, MC, V. Closed mid-Jan to mid-Feb.

This turn-of-the-century Breton manor offers grand living in an oceanfront pine park. The public rooms are furnished in French provincial style, with tapestries of stylized animals. Most upper-floor guest rooms come with a balcony; two are in a tower. Their furnishings reflect several styles: Louis XV, Directoire, and rustic.

Dining: The excellent chef is reason enough to stay here, and even if you aren't a guest you may want to stop in for a meal of regional-based fare that dares to be different. Specialties are lobster and home-smoked salmon. You might want to begin with Breton oysters.

Amenities: Water sports, tennis. Golf (guests receive a 30% discount) is a 15-minute drive away. Nearby is the Thalgo La Baule Thalassotherapy Centre, with gym, sauna, solarium, and steam room.

MODERATE TO INEXPENSIVE

Hôtel Alexandra. 3 bd. René-Dubois, 44500 La Baule. ☎ **02-40-60-30-06.** Fax 02-40-24-57-09. 36 units. TV TEL. 490–690F ($88.20–$124.20) double. Half board 1,050–1,300F ($189–$234) extra for 2. AE, DC, MC, V. Closed Oct–Feb.

Built in 1966 adjacent to the beach, the Alexandra boasts eight floors of modern rooms with balconies. There's an open-air terrace with umbrellas and sidewalk tables, plus planters of flowers and greenery. The ninth-floor solarium is a popular spot for drinks and coffee. Although the dining room has a view of the ocean and the lounge is intimate, the breezy, spacious rooms are the best feature.

Hôtel Bellevue-Plage. 27 bd. de l'Océan, 44500 La Baule. ☎ **02-40-60-28-55.** Fax 02-40-60-10-18. www.hotel-bellevue-plage.fr. E-mail: hotel@hotel-bellevue-plage.fr. 35 units. TV TEL. 360–845F ($64.80–$152.10) double. AE, DC, MC, V. Closed mid-Nov to mid-Feb.

This hotel, which many prefer to the Alexandra, is more reliable than exciting, with a tranquil position in the center of the shoreline curving around the bay. Frequent renovations have removed many of the original Art Deco features, leaving a modern, somewhat banal decor that's appropriate for a beach hotel. Guests gravitate to the rooftop solarium and the restaurant with its sweeping view. The rooms have been frequently renovated and contain soundproofed windows. The staff behaves correctly, albeit in ways that some consider anonymous and somewhat detached. You'll find a beach, sailboats for rent, and access to spa facilities.

Hôtel La Palmeraie. 7 allée des Cormorans, 44500 La Baule. ☎ **02-40-60-24-41.** Fax 02-40-42-73-71. 23 units. TV TEL. 350–500F ($63–$90) double. Half board (required July–Aug) 330–390F ($59.40–$70.20) per person extra. AE, DC, MC, V. Closed Oct–Apr 6.

In high-priced La Baule, this is a charmer. Built in the 1930s and renovated in the 1990s, it's named after eight large palms that thrive in the garden, thanks to the mild climate. Decorated in festive pink and white, La Palmeraie is near a beach and luxuriant with flowers in summer. The rooms are attractively decorated, often with English-style pieces. The only drawback: The soundproofed rooms aren't all that soundproof. Half board is obligatory in July and August; the food, however, is hardly in the league of that at the first-class hotels. The management and staff are helpful and even friendly.

WHERE TO DINE

Another fine dining choice is the restaurant at the **Castel Marie-Louise** (see above).

La Marcanderie. 5 av. d'Agen. ☎ **02-40-24-03-12.** Reservations required. Main courses 80–180F ($14.40–$32.40); fixed-price menus 145–320F ($26.10–$57.60). AE, MC, V. Daily noon–2pm and 7:30–10pm. Closed Sun dinner and Mon in Sept–June; Mon lunch in July–Aug. FRENCH.

In 1989, the award-winning chef Jean-Luc Giraud transformed a ratty-looking stable into La Baule's finest restaurant. Since then, hundreds of locals, up to 50 at a time, have dined here. There's something two-fisted and attractively gutsy about this place. Sometimes, particularly if the restaurant is full, you'll have to wait quite a while between courses. The savory and satisfying cuisine utilizes only the finest ingredients. Try the marmite of shellfish Montgolfier (the puff pastry on top swells like the hot-air balloon of the famous brothers with the same name), served with caramelized scalloped potatoes. The grilled turbot is flavored with Giraud's variation of a Choron sauce, with butter, shallots, tarragon, vinegar, and a secret process that's unique to his kitchens.

LA BAULE AFTER DARK

The highlight is the **Casino,** esplanade de François-André (☎ **02-40-11-48-28**), which is rather fashionable but can't compete with Deauville's. Entrance is free, and men should wear jackets.

A cruise down avenue du Général-de-Gaulle or avenue Mar-de-Latitre-de-Tassigny will turn up any number of interesting pubs and bars, including **Safari,** 157 av. du Général-de-Gaulle (☎ **02-40-24-14-46**); **Le Sailor,** 305 av. Mar-de-Lattre-de-Tassigny (☎ **02-40-60-24-49**); and **Antidote,** 104 av. du Général-de-Gaulle (☎ **02-40-11-04-03**).

8 Carnac

302 miles SW of Paris, 23 miles SE of Lorient, 62 miles SE of Quimper

In May and June, the fields here are resplendent with golden broom. Aside from being a seaside resort, Carnac is home to the most important prehistoric find in northern France: the hundreds of huge stones in the ✪ **Field of Megaliths,** whose arrangement and placement remain a mystery. At Carnac Ville, **Musée de Préhistoire,** 10 place de la Chapelle (☎ **02-97-52-22-04**), displays collections from 450,000 B.C. to the 8th century. Admission is 30F ($5.40) for adults and 15F ($2.70) for children 10 to 18, free for children 9 and under. The museum is open June 15 to September 15, daily from 10am to 6:30pm; September 16 to June 14, Wednesday through Monday from 10am to noon to 2 to 6pm; and October to May, Wednesday through Monday from 10am to noon and 2 to 5pm.

Even if Carnac didn't possess these prehistoric monuments, its pine-studded sand dunes would be worth the trip. Protected by the Quiberon Peninsula, **Carnac-Plage** is a family resort beside the ocean and alongside the waterfront boulevard de la Plage.

The center of Carnac is about half a mile from the sea. From the main square, rue du Tumulus leads north from the center of town to the **Tumulus St-Michel,** a Celtic burial chamber three-quarters of a mile from the center. Visitation has been halted until 2003 for an archaeological dig.

Carnac has two **shopping** areas: one along the beachfront called Carnac-Plage and the other about 1½ miles inland in Carnac proper. Along the beachfront, you'll run into your fair share of touristy souvenir shops, but venture down avenue des Druids and avenue de l'Atlantique for more specialized galleries and antiques stores. Other good areas are rue St-Cornély and place de l'Eglise, with a host of clothing and shoe stores, antiques dealers, and jewelry and fine gift items.

For a real treat, visit **L'Enfant d'Armor,** 2 place de l'Eglise (☎ **02-97-52-06-87**), which offers a vast array of regional Breton embroidery. **Kryso,** 10 rue St-Cornély (☎ **02-97-52-28-31**), sells unique creations of jewelry that combine silver and semiprecious and precious stones, as well as mother-of-pearl. They can also design pieces to meet your particular tastes. Finally, go to **Clémentine,** avenue de l'Atlantique (☎ **02-97-52-96-34**), if you're in the market for fine-quality French household linens and dishware.

ESSENTIALS

GETTING THERE Public transport links are possible but inconvenient. Nine **TIM buses** (call ☎ **02-97-47-29-64** in Vannes or 02-97-24-26-20 in Auray for schedules) run to Carnac from Quiberon (trip time: 30 minutes). There are also at least 9 TIM buses from Auray to Carnac (trip time: 30 minutes). The **SNCF rail network** will take you as far as Plouharnel, and from here you can catch one of seven buses per day (trip time: 5 minutes). For train information and schedules, call ☎ **08-36-35-35-39.** If you're **driving** from Lorient, take N165 east to Auray, turning south on D768 to Carnac.

VISITOR INFORMATION The **Office de Tourisme,** on avenue des Druides (☎ **02-97-52-13-52**), is open all year.

WHERE TO STAY & DINE

Hôtel Lann-Roz. 36 av. de la Poste, 56340 Carnac. ☎ **02-97-52-10-48.** Fax 02-97-52-24-36. 14 units. TV TEL. 480–680F ($86.40–$122.40) double. Rates include half board. Closed Jan 3–Feb 3.

Within walking distance of the water, this oasis for the budget-minded is surrounded by a garden and lawns. Lann-Roz is managed by the friendly Mme Le Calvez, who will invite you to have a drink on the veranda. In the typical Breton dining room, the chef serves generous portions of regional food. Fixed-price meals begin at 95F ($17.10), and you don't have to be a guest to dine here.

Hôtel Le Diana. 21 bd. de la Plage, 56340 Carnac. ☎ **02-97-52-05-38.** Fax 02-97-52-87-91. 33 units. MINIBAR TV TEL. 590–1,820F ($106.20–$327.60) double; 1,100–2,250F ($198–$405) suite. AE, DC, MC, V. Closed Oct 4–Easter.

Located on the most popular beach, the Diana is the most reliable and comfortable hotel at Carnac and better than its chief rival, the nearby Novotel. On the terrace, you can sip drinks and watch the crashing waves. The spacious, contemporary guest rooms contain balconies facing the sea. The hotel restaurant also faces the sea and serves standard seafood fare.

Hôtel Les Alignements. 45 rue St-Cornély, 56340 Carnac. ☎ **02-97-52-06-30.** Fax 02-97-52-76-56. 27 units. TV TEL. 230–325F ($41.40–$58.50) double. AE, MC, V. Hotel closed Oct–Easter.

This four-story hotel, about 200 yards from the famous megaliths, looks onto a garden. Inside, everything's clean and efficient. Some rooms have balconies or loggias; those facing the street offer double windows to filter the noise. Nonguests are welcome to dine in the rustic restaurant, where the 95F ($17.10) fixed-price menu is the best value in Carnac. Unlike the hotel, the restaurant remains open year-round.

CARNAC AFTER DARK

Sleepy Carnac doesn't wake up much at night, but a few places are worth checking out. The **Whiskey Club,** 8 av. des Druides (☎ **02-97-52-10-52**), operates in an old stone house with two floors devoted to entertainment—the first offers an atmosphere conducive to casual conversation over drinks, whereas the second offers dancing and loud music. **Les Chandelles,** avenue de l'Atlantique (☎ **02-97-52-90-98**), manages to pull together a young, flashy crowd. The club plays mainly disco and charges a 50F ($9) cover. As is the case with most discos in France, no jeans or sneakers are allowed. The professional crowd gathers at **Petit Bedon,** 106 av. des Druides (☎ **02-97-52-11-62**). With its exotic mixture of African and Mexican decor, this is the place for dancing to the classic rock of the 1960s. Though there's no cover here, a beer will set you back a hefty 40F ($7.20).

Exploring the Wild Coast

If you take D768 south from Carnac and follow it onto the peninsula (formerly an island) connected to the mainland by a narrow strip of alluvial deposits, you'll come to the port of **Quiberon,** with its white-sand beach. You'll probably see the rugged Breton fishers hauling in their sardine catch.

This entire coast—the **Côte Sauvage,** or Wild Coast—is dramatic and rugged; the ocean breaks with fury against the reefs. Northern winds, especially in winter, lash across the dunes, shaving the short pines that grow here. On the landward side, however, the beach is calm and relatively protected.

Ten miles west of Brittany's tormented shoreline is **Belle-Ile-en-Mer,** an outpost of sand, rock, and twisted vegetation that the French love for summer holidays. Depending on the season, 4 to 12 ferries depart daily for this island from Port Maria in Quiberon (☎ **02-97-31-80-01**). The trip takes 45 minutes and costs 105F ($18.90) round-trip for adults, 64F ($11.50) round-trip for children. In summer, you must reserve space on board for your car. The ferry docks at **Le Palais,** a fortified 16th-century port that serves as the island's chief window to the rest of France. Storm-wracked and eerie, the local topography contains rocky cliffs; a reef-fringed west coast; the **Grotte de l'Apothicairerie,** a cave whose name derives from pendulous stalactites shaped like apothecary jars; and a general sense of isolation, despite a scattering of hotels and seasonal restaurants. A drive around the island's periphery is about 35 miles, each rife with bracing Atlantic sights, breezes, and smells.

In the days before he was jailed for embezzlement, the Sun King's finance minister, Nicolas Fouquet, the inspirational force behind Vaux-le-Vicomte, erected a château on this island. Much later the "Divine Sarah" Bernhardt spent many pleasant summers here in a 17th-century fortress that was "always swarming with guests."

You'll find excellent accommodations in **Port de Goulphar,** one of the most charming spots on Belle-Ile. It's on the southern shore, on a narrow inlet framed by cliffs. Certainly the standout, and the only four-star hotel on the island, is the Relais & Chateaux **Castel Clara,** Port de Goulphar, 56360 Bangor (☎ **02-97-31-84-21;** fax 02-97-31-51-69; www.relaischateaux.fr/castelclara; e-mail: castelclara@relaischateaux.fr). Containing 32 units and set 2 miles from the center of Bangor, it was built in the early 1970s in a bay-windowed style that permits maximum visibility of the rugged terrain and seascapes nearby. Few other places along the coast provide such a sense of isolated peace accompanied by ideal service and first-class cuisine.

The rooms are monochromatic, comfortable, and well furnished, with TV, phone, and balcony facing the sea. The chef takes pride in his achievements, and the menu is a good showcase for his talents, particularly the seafood. Sea bass, for example, might be steamed over seaweed, then served with a beurre blanc sauce. The hotel also offers a large terrace with a solarium around a heated seawater pool. Depending on the season, rates for two occupants (including half board) range from 1,440F to 2,170F ($259.20 to $390.60) for a double and from 2,805F to 3,830F ($504.90 to $689.40) for a suite. Family-style apartments without kitchens, which are a lot less elegant than the rooms and suites but have space for up to four occupants, begin at 1,820F ($327.60). American Express, MasterCard, and Visa are accepted. The hotel is closed November 15 to February 15.

9 Nantes

239 miles SW of Paris, 202 miles N of Bordeaux

Nantes is Brittany's largest town, although in spirit it seems to belong more to the Loire Valley's châteaux country. The mouth of the Loire is 30 miles away, and here it divides into several branches. A commercial/industrial city, Nantes is a busy port that suffered great damage in World War II. It's best known for the Edict of Nantes, issued by Henri IV in 1598, guaranteeing religious freedom to Protestants (it was later revoked). Many famous people, from Molière to Stendhal, have lived here. But Nantes hardly lives off its illustrious past. Now home to dozens of high-tech industries, it has some 30,000 college students and a bustling population of half a million who welcome you as you make a stop between Brittany and points south or east in the Loire Valley.

Built on the largest of three islands in the Loire, the city expanded in the Middle Ages to the northern edge of the river, where its center lies today. The most prominent building is the Château des Ducs de Bretagne, which rises several hundred feet from a wide boulevard, the main artery of Nantes: quai de la Fosse. At one end of this boulevard is the train station; at the other are the promenades beside the Loire.

ESSENTIALS

GETTING THERE   About 20 **trains** leave Paris, usually from Gare Montparnasse, for Nantes every day (trip time: between 2¼ and 5½ hours, depending on the number of stops). The world's fastest train (300 m.p.h.), the TGV Atlantique from Paris to Rennes and Nantes, is the best connection. Trains also make the 3- to 4-hour trip from Bordeaux about 10 times a day. For train information and schedules, call ☎ **08-36-35-35-39.** If you're **driving,** take A11 highway from Paris to Nantes.

VISITOR INFORMATION   The **Office de Tourisme** is at place du Commerce (☎ **02-40-20-60-00**).

EXPLORING THE CITY

Nantes overflows with shops and boutiques. The principal shopping streets are **rue du Calvaire, rue Crebillon, rue Boileau, rue d'Orléans, rue de la Marne, rue de Verdun,** and **passage Pommeraye.** Most of these encompass the shopping districts around place Graslin, place Royale, the château, and the cathedral. One of the prime areas for antiques is around place Aristide-Briand and rue Mercoeur.

The more interesting antiques dealers here are **Antique Bijoux,** 21 rue Mercoeur (☎ 02-40-35-60-84), specializing in antique and secondhand jewelry; **Jean-Yves Coue,** 7 rue Mercoeur (☎ 02-40-08-29-95), dealing in antique primitive art; and **L'Ecritoire Antiquités,** 12 rue Jean-Jaurès (☎ 02-40-47-78-18), offering 18th- and 19th-century furniture and decorative pieces like historic mantels. **Trouvailles,** 4 rue Léon-Blum (☎ 02-40-20-08-80), carries perfume atomizers along with Art Deco and Art Nouveau objects; and **Antiquités Cibot,** 7 rue Voltaire (☎ 02-40-73-84-37), offers a variety of sculptures, bronzes, paintings, and primitive art.

For other unique gifts, check out the stores of two talented master artists: **Maison Devineau,** 2 place Ste-Croix (☎ 02-40-47-19-59), which brings the art of wax-working to a new level, "growing" bushels of fruits and vegetables from liquid wax; and **Georges Gautier,** 9 rue de la Fosse (☎ 02-40-48-23-19), where you'll find the town's best chocolates.

Cathédrale St-Pierre. Place St-Pierre. ☎ **02-40-47-84-64.** Free admission. Summer daily 8:45am–6:45pm; off-season daily 8:45am–5:30pm.

Cathédrale St-Pierre **6**
Château des Ducs de Bretagne **5**
Grand Théâtre **4**
Manoir de la Touche **2**

Musée des Beaux-Arts de Nantes **7**
Musée Jules Verne de Nantes **1**
Musée Thomas Dobrée **3**

✝ Church ✉ Post Office ⓘ Information

Begun in 1434, this cathedral wasn't finished until the end of the 19th century, yet it remained harmonious architecturally—a rare feat. Two square towers dominate the facade, but the 335-foot-long interior is more impressive. Its pièce de résistance, however, is Michel Colomb's Renaissance tomb of François II, duc de Bretagne, and his second wife, Marguerite de Foix. Another impressive work is the tomb of Gen. Juchault de Lamoricière, a native of Nantes and a great African campaigner; the sculptor Paul Dubois completed the tomb in 1879. After a 1972 fire destroyed the roof (rebuilt in 1975), the interior was restored. The white walls and pillars contrast with the rich colors of the stained-glass windows. The crypt, from the 11th century, shelters a museum of religions, although at press time it remains closed to the public due to terrorist threats.

Château des Ducs de Bretagne. 4 place Marc-Elder. ☎ **02-40-41-56-56.** Admission 20F ($3.60) adults, 10F ($1.80) students, free for children 17 and under. July–Aug daily 10am–noon and 2–6pm (closed Tues rest of the year).

Between the cathedral and the Loire is Nantes' second major sight, where the Edict of Nantes was discussed and signed. The castle was constructed in the 9th or 10th century, enlarged in the 13th century, destroyed, and then rebuilt into more or less its present shape by François II in 1466. His daughter, Anne de Bretagne, continued the work. The castle is flanked by large towers and a bastion and contains a formally symmetrical section (the Grand Gouvernement) built during the 17th and 18th centuries. The duchesse du Berry, royal courtesan, was imprisoned here, as was Gilles de Retz ("Bluebeard"), one of France's most notorious mass murderers.

The castle's rich collections are being shaped into a museum of the history of Nantes from the 17th century to the present day. Currently, special exhibitions are staged at the château pending completion of the museum. One exhibit, running from June to September 1999, traces the Turner tour of the Loire valley in 1826 through the artist's drawings, watercolors, and gouaches.

Musée des Beaux-Arts de Nantes. 10 rue Georges-Clemenceau, east of place du Maréchal-Foch. ☎ **02-40-41-65-65.** Admission 20F ($3.60) adults; 10F ($1.80) students, children, and seniors. Free Sun. Mon, Wed–Thurs, and Sat 10am–6pm; Fri 10am–9pm; Sun 11am–6pm.

One of western France's most interesting provincial galleries, its upper floors contain an unusually fine collection of sculptures and paintings from the 12th to the late 19th centuries. The street level is devoted to mostly French modern or contemporary art created since 1900, with special emphasis on painters from the 1950s and 1960s.

Musée Thomas-Dobrée. 18 rue Voltaire. ☎ **02-40-71-03-50.** Admission 20F ($3.60) adults; 10F ($1.80) children, students, and seniors. Tues–Sun 10am–noon and 1:30–5:30pm.

This 19th-century mansion built by an important collector stands besides the 15th-century manor of Jean V, where the bishops of Nantes occasionally lived. Both are now museums, containing a varied collection gathered by M. Dobrée, including prehistoric and medieval antiquities, Flemish paintings from the 15th century, many ecclesiastical relics, and the Dobrée family jewels. The museum also displays paintings by such masters as Dürer.

Musée Jules Verne de Nantes. 3 rue de l'Hermitage. ☎ **02-40-69-72-52.** Admission 8F ($1.45) adults, 4F ($0.70) children and seniors. Mon and Wed–Sat 10am–noon and 2–5pm.

The novelist Jules Verne (*Journey to the Center of the Earth, Around the World in Eighty Days*) was born in Nantes in 1828, and literary fans seek out his house at 4 rue de Clisson in the Ile-Feydeau. This museum is filled with memorabilia and objects inspired by his writings, from inkspots to a "magic" lantern with glass slides.

WHERE TO STAY

Hôtel Graslin. 1 rue Piron, 44000 Nantes. ☎ **02-40-69-72-91.** Fax 02-40-69-04-44. 47 units. TV TEL. 290–360F ($52.20–$64.80) double. AE, DC, MC, V.

In the center of town, Graslin is on a steep old street near the harbor. The managers, M. and Mme Rochehave, have given it many homelike touches, so it now offers more for the money than almost any other hotel in its price category. The comfortable rooms, each with a safe, are decorated functionally; 8 contain minibars.

✪ **Hôtel Nantes.** 6 rue Henri-IV, 44000 Nantes. ☎ **02-40-29-30-31.** Fax 02-40-29-00-95. 31 units. MINIBAR TV TEL. 390F ($70.20) double. AE, DC, MC, V.

Within sight of the château and the cathedral, this hotel is, for the price, a perfect base in Nantes. The place is neat and modern but still manages to maintain an inviting atmosphere. The rooms range from medium to large in size and boast firm beds, rich colors, and contemporary furnishings. Some accommodations even have their own private balconies looking out over the château, whereas others open onto a small garden and terrace. You'll find a paneled sitting area with overstuffed couches and chairs next to the reception desk, as well as a softly lit breakfast room with terrace views.

Mercure Beaulieu. Ile-Beaulieu, 44200 Nantes-Beaulieu. ☎ **02-40-95-95-95.** Fax 02-40-48-23-83. www.mercure.com. 100 units. A/C MINIBAR TV TEL. 515–850F ($92.70–$153) double. AE, DC, MC, V. Follow the blue NOVOTEL signs from any of the major traffic arteries in the city to a point 2 miles north of the town center.

Situated on an island surrounded by the Loire, the Mercure offers well-furnished, soundproofed chambers. If you prefer contemporary comforts to historic charm, you'll be satisfied by the up-to-date amenities and the alert, hardworking staff who know how to welcome international guests. The restaurant/bar, Le Tilbury, offers a wide choice of seafood dishes. Facilities include a heated outdoor pool and tennis courts.

WHERE TO DINE

La Cigale. 4 place Graslin. ☎ **02-51-84-94-94.** Reservations recommended. Main courses 80–90 ($14.40–$16.20); fixed-price menus 75F ($13.50) for 2 courses, 135F ($24.30) for 3 courses. MC, V. Daily 11:45am–12:30am. Bus: 11 or 34. FRENCH/SEAFOOD.

This is Nantes's most historic and charming brasserie, decorated in a gracefully sprawling belle époque style that has changed little since the place opened in 1895 across from the landmark Théâtre Graslin. Menu items might include heaping platters of fresh shellfish, *confit des cuisses de canard* (duckling), an array of grilled steaks, and fresh scallops with green peppers and emulsified butter. It's usually quite loud, and the staff members tend to be overworked.

L'Atlantide. Centre des Salorges, 16 quai Ernest-Renaud. ☎ **02-40-73-23-23.** Reservations required. Main courses 98–155F ($17.65–$27.90); fixed-price menus 144–270F ($25.90–$48.60) at lunch, 200–320F ($36–$57.60) at dinner. AE, MC, V. Mon–Fri noon–2:30pm, Mon–Sat 7–10:30pm. Closed May 17–22 and Aug 3–31. FRENCH.

On the fourth floor of the complex that houses the city's chamber of commerce, this panoramic restaurant serves the finest cuisine. The world-renowned designer Jean-Pierre Wilmotte caused a stir when he did the room, but it's the innovative cooking of Pierre Lecoutre that draws patrons in. Monsieur Lecoutre deals only with market-fresh ingredients and isn't afraid to use spices from far-flung corners of the world. Menu items, steeped in the traditions of both the Loire Valley and the Breton coast, may include a galette of eels with a tomato-flavored butter sauce, Breton sole with oyster sauce, and grilled baby pigeon with a roughly textured compote of onions and spices. The cellar is known for some of the finest bottles from the Loire, especially rich in muscadets.

Villa Mon Rêve. Route des Bords-de-Loire. ☎ **02-40-03-55-50.** Reservations recommended. Main courses 118–248F ($21.25–$44.65). AE, DC, MC, V. Daily noon–2pm and 7–9pm. Closed 2 weeks in early Nov. Take D751 5 miles east of Nantes. FRENCH.

This restaurant, housed in a stone-sided, late-l9th-century villa built by a prosperous producer of fruits and vegetables, is set in a 1-acre garden awash in summer with rose beds. Chef Gérard Ryngel and his wife, Cécile, took over Mon Rêve in 1979. Monsieur Ryngel's repertoire includes both regional specialties and his own creations: wild duck with Bourgeuil wine sauce, an unusual combination of veal sweetbreads with crayfish, gazpacho studded with chunks of lobster, and frogs' legs with local white wine. The vast wine list features more than 40 locally produced wines.

NANTES AFTER DARK

When the sun goes down, this town turns into one big party. Head over to **place du Bouffay** and **place du Pilori,** where you'll find lots of atmospheric cafes and pubs, many with live music and plenty of fun people. A younger crowd rules **rue Scribe** like Louis XIV throwing a party at Versailles.

To beat that unshakable urge to check your e-mail before committing to an evening of fun, stop by **CyberHouse,** 8 quai de Versailles (☎ 02-40-12-11-84); you'll pay 1F (20¢) per minute to hook up to the Internet and 11F ($2) to drink a beer. Afterward, catch some live blues, jazz, or rock at **Le Verlaine,** 3 quai de la Fosse (☎ 02-51-88-90-47); the very busy **Le Pub Univers,** 16 rue Jean-Jacques-Rousseau

(☎ 02-40-73-49-55); or the **Nashville Music Café,** 17 rue Jean-Jacques-Rousseau (☎ 02-40-69-19-18), a veritable shrine to Elvis with its very own Cadillac-seat couches. A great piano bar complete with dance floor and occasional jazz concerts is **Le Tie Break,** 1 rue des Petites-Ecuries (☎ 02-40-47-77-00).

The pump-it-up dance scene has a huge following of everyone from students to seniors. **Balapapa,** 24 quai François-Mitterrand (☎ 02-40-48-40-29), has a real cabaret feel in both its dance rooms. It plays an eclectic mix ranging from big band to funk and attracts a crowd just as diverse. The cover is 90F ($16.20). The over-30 crowd heads to the vintage 1970s disco **L'Evasion,** 3 rue de l'Emery (☎ 02-40-47-99-84). Other discos that keep their dance floors packed are **New's,** place Emile-Zola (☎ 02-40-58-01-04); **Le Royal Club Privé,** 7 rue des Salorges (☎ 02-40-69-11-10); and **Walton's Club,** 23 rue de Rieux (☎ 02-40-12-01-13). Don't wear blue jeans to any of these places, and be prepared to pay between 45F and 70F ($8.10 and $12.60) to get in.

The perennial favorite with gays and lesbians is **Le Plein Sud,** 2 rue Prémion (☎ 02-40-47-06-03), where people come to meet and talk in a friendly atmosphere that welcomes everything from leather to lace. Two gay bars that don't have the same draw but are nevertheless worth a look are **L'Amazone,** 4 rue des Chapeliers (☎ 02-40-35-61-88), in a turn-of-the-century house with a rustic atmosphere; and **Le Second Soufflé,** 1 rue Kervégan (☎ 02-40-20-14-20), where there's a more equal representation of the sexes. **Le Temps d'Aimer,** 14 rue Alexandre-Fourny (☎ 02-40-89-48-60), though not exclusively gay, does provide a carefree atmosphere that lets you be yourself while dancing the night away. This medium-size disco with its small dance floor attracts a pretty sophisticated crowd—no sneakers or jeans. The most you'll pay to get in is 70F ($12.60).

The Champagne Country

In about 3 days, you can take the the Autoroute de l'Est (N3) from Paris and explore a region of beautiful cathedrals, historic battlefields, fantastic food, and world-famous vineyards, topping your tour with a heady glass or two of bubbly. On one of the three Routes du Champagne, you can drive first to the wine-producing center of Epernay, then on to Reims, some 90 miles northeast of Paris. After visiting Reims and its cathedral, you can leave on Route 31 east, heading toward Verdun, of World War I fame.

REGIONAL CUISINE   Champagne's wine overshadows its cuisine, though several culinary specialties are unique to the district. Most are simple, hearty recipes developed over the centuries in country homes, using pork, beef, fish, and the area's fresh vegetables.

The tang and bite of the sparkling wines dissolve—in the most appetizing of ways—some of the flavorful grease and oils that are part of the local charcuteries and pâtés. Specialties include pork or sheep *andouillettes* (chitterlings) from Bar-sur-Aube and Bar-sur-Seine, pig's trotters from Ste-Menehould, and an endless variety of pâtés made from offal—which many North Americans would never consider eating. A *matelote* is a fish stew, generally prepared with freshwater fish and red or white wine. The matelotes here usually employ champagne and carp, pike, and trout.

Most of the area's cheeses are made from cows' milk. The most famous are the *maroilles,* aged collectively (so their skins turn a terra-cotta red) in communal cellars. Some maroilles are sprinkled with tarragon, pepper, and paprika and aged 2 months to produce the strong, aromatic Boulette d'Avesnes, which the French consume with beer. One cheese enjoying popularity in North America is Brie de Melun or Brie de Meaux—the best varieties are made in Champagne, preferably near Meaux.

The largest champagne producer here is Moët et Chandon, though there are excellent smaller vintners like Krug, Roederer, Böllinger, and Veuve Clicquot. Some of the still (nonsparkling) wines from the region, including blanc de blancs, are famous as well.

1 La Ferté-sous-Jouarre

41 miles E of Paris, 51 miles SW of Reims

In the village of Jouarre, 2 miles south of Ferté-sous-Jouarre, you can visit a 12th-century Benedictine abbey and explore one of the oldest

Champagne

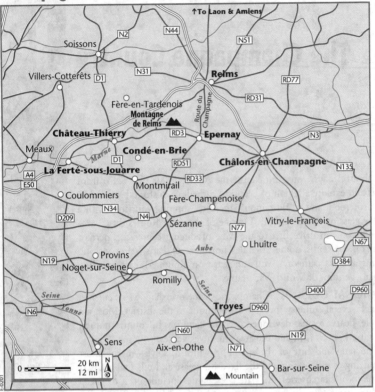

crypts in France. At the **Tour de l'Abbaye de Jouarre,** 6 rue Montmorin (☎ 01-60-22-64-54), those interested in medieval history will appreciate the preserved documents referring to the Royal Abbey of Jouarre as well as the stones in the Merovingian crypt, which evoke the 7th century. There's also a collection of prehistoric artifacts, remnants of the Roman occupation, and sculptural fragments. The crypt and towers are open May 1 to October 30, Wednesday through Monday from 9am to noon and 2 to 6pm; November 1 to April, Wednesday through Monday from 9am to noon and 2 to 5pm. Admission to the crypt and tower is 30F ($5.40); to the crypt only, it's 20F ($3.60), and to the tower only, 15F ($2.70).

About 10 **trains** per day make the 55-minute run from Paris's Gare de l'Est, stopping at Ferté-sous-Jouarre. From there, it's a brief taxi ride 2 miles south to Jouarre and its abbey. If you're **driving,** take N3 along the Marne.

The **Syndicat d'Initiative** (tourist office) is at 26 place de l'Hôtel-de-Ville (☎ 01-60-22-63-43) in Ferté-sous-Jouarre.

WHERE TO DINE

✪ **Auberge de Condé.** 1 av. de Montmirail. ☎ **01-60-22-00-07.** Reservations required. Main courses 145–195F ($26.10–$35.10); fixed-price menus 210–460F ($37.80–$82.80). AE, DC, MC, V. Wed–Mon noon–2pm, Wed–Sun 7–9:30pm. FRENCH.

This is one of the best restaurants in "the ring around Paris," a mile and a half from the abbey. The old-fashioned inn has lots of provincial character but serves delectable food worthy of its two-star rating. The manager/chef, Pascal Tingaud, is the grandson of the famous founder, Emile Tingaud. Perhaps begin with a semiliquified foie gras marinated in red wine; then try salade Alexis, an original recipe of the founder that combines lobster and green beans. Another specialty is ragoût of Bresse chicken with Breton lobster in a lobster cream sauce. The grand traditional cooking is accompanied by the best champagne.

2 Château-Thierry

56 miles E of Paris, 6 miles SW of Reims

An industrial town on the Marne's right bank, Château-Thierry contains the ruins of a castle believed to have been constructed for the Frankish king Thierry IV. Château-Thierry gained fame for being the farthest point reached by the German offensive in the summer of 1918. Under heavy bombardment, French forces were aided by the Second and Third Divisions of the American Expeditionary Force. The Battlefields of the Marne are a mile west of town; here, thousands of Allied soldiers who died fighting in World War I are buried. Atop Hill 204 stands a monument honoring American troops who lost their lives.

Château-Thierry is also where the poet/fable writer Jean de la Fontaine (1621–95) was born, in a stone-sided house built in 1452. Today it contains one of France's most oft-visited literary shrines, the **Musée Jean-de-la-Fontaine,** 12 rue Jean de la Fontaine (☎ **03-23-69-05-60**). Located a few steps from place de l'Hôtel-de-Ville, it contains a collection of his mementos, including many editions of his works from the Charles-Henri Genot collection, plus paintings and engravings from the 17th to the 20th centuries. Copies of his fables (allegorical barnyard stories depicting the foibles of humans) and *contes* (short stories that are usually a lot racier than his fables) are for sale in the museum bookshop. Hours are Wednesday through Monday from 10am to noon and 2:30 to 6:30pm (to 6pm from October to June). Admission is 19F ($3.40) for adults and 12F ($2.15) for children.

If you're interested in World War I relics, head 5 miles northwest of Château-Thierry to the **Bois de Belleau** (Belleau Wood). The Battle of Belleau Wood marked the second clash between American and German troops in World War I and demonstrated the bravery of the U.S. soldiers in modern warfare. After a bitter 2-week struggle, the woods were taken by the Second Division of the U.S. Expeditionary Force under Maj.-Gen. Omar Bundy. Though the Germans suffered many losses and some 1,650 prisoners were taken, U.S. casualties were appalling: nearly 7,585 soldiers and 285 officers were wounded, killed, or missing in action.

In 1923 the battleground was dedicated as a memorial to the men who gave their lives here. The **American cemetery** contains 2,288 graves. You'll also see a chapel that was damaged in World War II.

There are frequent local **trains** from Paris and Reims. For information and schedules, call ☎ **08-36-35-35-39.** If you're **driving,** take A4 southwest from Reims.

The **Office de Tourisme** is at 11 rue Vallée (☎ **03-23-83-10-14**).

WHERE TO STAY

Hôtel Ile-de-France. Route de Soissons, 02400 Château-Thierry. ☎ **03-23-69-10-12.** Fax 03-23-83-49-70. 50 units. TV TEL. 390F ($70.20) double. AE, DC, MC, V.

This elegant modern hotel is the leading choice in the area, which has a rather poor selection. Set in a park overlooking the green Marne Valley, near the ruins of the town's château, the four-story structure boasts balconies and dormers, a view of the town, and well-maintained rooms furnished in contemporary style. The restaurant is competent, but not particularly noteworthy. Fixed-price menus range from 98F to 245F ($17.65 to $44.10).

WHERE TO DINE

Auberge Jean-de-la-Fontaine. 10 rue des Filoirs. ☎ **03-23-83-63-89.** Reservations required. Main courses 60–95F ($10.80–$17.10); fixed-price menu (including aperitif, champagne, and coffee) 200F ($36). AE, DC, V. Tues–Sun 12:30–2pm, Tues–Sat 7:30–9:30pm. Closed Jan 5–18 and July 28–Aug 18. FRENCH.

This restaurant is filled with engravings dedicated to the fables of Jean de la Fontaine. The menu changes every 3 weeks but may include dishes like homemade smoked salmon (smoked with the beechwood common to the area), duck terrine and leek with a vinaigrette sauce, or even curry-flavored mussels in a sauce of cream and mushrooms. Fish selections include steamed bass filet and rockfish suprême pot-roasted and flavored with sesame seeds. A typical regional dish might be chicken fricassée flavored with champagne.

3 Condé-en-Brie

55 miles E of Paris, 15 miles W of Epernay

West of Epernay, **Château de Condé** (☎ **03-23-82-42-25**) was inherited in 1814 by the comte de Sade and remained in his family until 1983. The Sade name was besmirched by the infamous marquis, an innovative writer (*Justine, Juliette, The 120 Days of Sodom*) whose sexual practices as described in his works gave us the word *sadism.*

If you're traveling between Château-Thierry and Epernay on N3, head south at Dormans and follow the signs to Condé-en-Brie.

The castle was built in the late 12th century by Enguerran of Coucy. A part of the old keep still remains—two big rooms with great chimneys and thick walls. The castle was reconstructed in the Renaissance style at the beginning of the 16th century by Cardinal de Bourbon, a member of the royal family. His nephew, Louis de Bourbon, called himself the prince de Condé, most likely because he had many fond childhood memories of the place. After sustaining damage in the early 18th century, the château was rebuilt yet again—this time for the marquis de La Faye. The Italian architect Servandoni invited artists like Boucher and Watteau to do frescoes and paintings, which you can still see today. Servandoni decorated the largest room, making it a theater hall for music and entertainment. The present castle is an exceptional ensemble, with its paintings, woodwork, chimneys, and so-called Versailles floor.

In 1994 the new owners, the de Rocheforts, discovered several Watteau paintings concealed behind mirrors installed during the 18th century. Now, at the push of a button, the mirrors open to reveal the previously hidden treasures.

Admission is 32F ($5.75) for adults and 17F ($3.05) for children 14 and under. The castle is open for tours from June to August, daily at 2:30, 3:30, and 5:30pm. In May and September, it's open on Sundays and bank holidays at the same hours.

4 Reims

89 miles E of Paris, 28 miles NW of Châlons-en-Champagne

Reims (pronounced *Rahns*), an ancient Roman city, was important at the time Caesar conquered Gaul. French kings have traditionally come here to be crowned, and it's said that the French nation was born here in A.D. 498. Joan of Arc escorted Charles VII here in 1429, kissing the silly man's feet. But don't let this ancient background mislead you: As you approach Reims you'll pass through prefabricated suburbs that look like apartment-house blocks in Eastern Europe. There are gems in Reims, including the cathedral, of course, but you must seek them out.

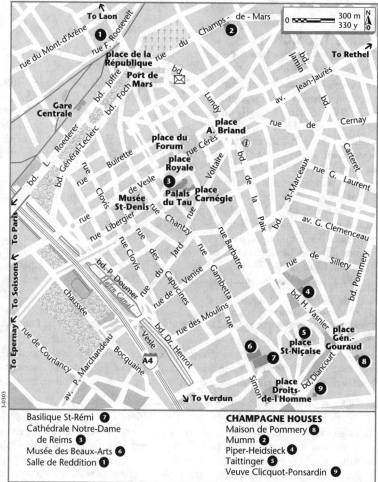

Basilique St-Rémi **7**
Cathédrale Notre-Dame
de Reims **3**
Musée des Beaux-Arts **6**
Salle de Reddition **1**

CHAMPAGNE HOUSES
Maison de Pommery **8**
Mumm **2**
Piper-Heidsieck **4**
Taittinger **5**
Veuve Clicquot-Ponsardin **9**

Most visitors come to Reims because it's the center of a wine-growing district whose bubbly is present at celebrations all over the world. The city today, with a population of 185,000, is filled with swank restaurants, ritzy champagne houses, large squares, and long tree-lined avenues. The champagne bottled here is the lightest and subtlest in flavor of the world's wines. Make an effort to linger, exploring the vineyards and wine cellars, the Gothic monuments, and the battlefields (the Germans occupied Reims in 1870, 1914, and 1940).

ESSENTIALS

GETTING THERE **Trains** depart from Paris every 2 hours (trip time: 1½ hours). There are also 5 trains per day from Strasbourg (trip time: 4 hours). For train information and schedules, call ☎ **08-36-35-35-39.** If you're **driving** from Paris to Reims, take A4 east.

VISITOR INFORMATION The **Office de Tourisme** is at 2 rue Guillaume-de-Machault (☎ **03-26-77-45-25**).

SEEING THE SIGHTS

✪ **Cathédrale Notre-Dame de Reims.** Place du Cardinal-Luçon. ☎ **03-26-47-49-37.** Free admission. Mon–Sat 7am–7:30pm, Sun 8:30am–7pm.

This is one of the world's most famous cathedrals. After World War I, its restoration was funded largely by U.S. contributions from John D. Rockefeller; mercifully, it escaped World War II relatively unharmed. Built on the site of a church that burned to the ground in 1211, it was intended as a sanctuary where French kings would be anointed—St. Rémi, the bishop of Reims, baptized Clovis, the pagan king of the Franks, here in 496. All of the kings of France from Louis the Pious (son of Charles the Great) in 815 to Charles X in 1825 were crowned here.

Laden with statuettes, its three western facade portals are spectacular. A rose window is above the central portal, which is dedicated to the Virgin. The right portal portrays the Apocalypse and the Last Judgment; the left, Martyrs and Saints. At the western facade's northern door is a smiling angel. Lit by lancet windows, the immense nave has many bays. Beside the cathedral is the treasury with a 12th-century chalice for the communion of French monarchs and a talisman supposedly containing a relic of the True Cross that Charlemagne is said to have worn. From the interior of the cathedral, you can visit Palais du Tau, the ancient residence of the bishop of Reims, now a museum.

Salle de Reddition. 12 rue Franklin-D.-Roosevelt. ☎ **03-26-47-84-19.** Admission 10F ($1.80). Apr–Nov Wed–Mon 10am–noon and 2–6pm. Closed May 1 and July 14. At other times of the year, visits can be arranged by advance reservation with the Musée des Beaux Arts (☎ 03-26-47-28-44).

On May 7, 1945, the Germans surrendered to General Eisenhower in this structure, which was once a little schoolhouse near the railroad tracks. The walls of the room are lined with maps of the rail routes, exactly as they were on the day of surrender.

Basilique St-Rémi. 53 rue St-Simon. ☎ **03-26-85-23-36.** Admission 10F ($1.80) adults, free for children and students. Sat–Sun 2–7pm, Mon–Fri 2–6:30pm.

Although sometimes unfavorably compared to the cathedral, the Basilique St-Rémi is a classic. The abbey/museum is housed in the grandiose former royal abbey of St. Rémi, who was once the guardian of the holy ampula used to anoint the kings of France. The extensive collections cover the history of Reims, regional archaeology, and aspects of military history. The architect Louis Duroché designed the majestic ornamental front of the main quadrangle as well as the Grand Staircase (1778), where you can admire one of the official portraits of the young Louis XV in his coronation robes. It also contains a grand Romanesque nave leading to a magnificent choir crowned with massive pointed arches. The nave, the transepts, one of the towers, and the aisles date from the 11th century; the portal of the south transept is in flamboyant early-16th-century style. Some of the stained glass in the apse is from the 13th century. The tomb of St. Rémi is elaborately carved with Renaissance figures and columns.

Musée des Beaux-Arts. 8 rue Chanzy. ☎ **03-26-47-28-44.** Admission 10F ($1.80) adults, free for children and students. Wed–Mon 10am–noon and 2–6pm. Closed Jan 1, May 1, July 14, Nov 1 and 11, and Dec 25.

Housed in the 18th-century buildings belonging to the old Abbaye St-Denis, this fine provincial art gallery contains more than a dozen portraits of German princes of the Reformation by both "the Elder" and "the Younger" Cranach; the museum has owned this remarkable collection since it opened in 1795. You can see the *Toiles Peintes* (light painting on rough linen) that date from the 15th and 16th centuries and depict the *Passion du Christ* and *Vengeance du Christ*. Paintings and fine furniture from the 17th and 18th centuries are in the Salles Diancourt and Jamot-Neveux. There's an excellent series of 26 of Corot's tree-shaded walks.

EXPLORING THE CHAMPAGNE CELLARS

Many of the vast ✪ **champagne cellars** of Reims extend for miles through chalky deposits. In fact, during the German siege of 1914 and throughout the war, people lived in them and even published a daily paper there. Although the cellars are open all year, they're most interesting during the fall grape harvest. After that, the wine is fermented in vats in the caves, then is bottled with a small amount of sugar and natural yeast. The yeast feeds on the sugar and causes a second fermentation to take place—thus producing those fabulous bubbles. The wine growers wait until the sparkle has "taken," as they say, before they remove the bottles to racks or pulpits. For about 3 months, *remueurs* are paid just to turn them a fraction every day, which brings the impurities (dead yeast cells and other matter) toward the cork. Eventually these sediments are removed and the wine is given its proper dosage (sugar dissolved in wine), depending on the desired sweetness. The process takes 4 or 5 years and is carried out in caves that are usually 100 feet deep and kept at a constant 50°F.

Maison de Pommery. Place du Général-Gouraud. ☎ **03-26-61-62-56.** Admission 30F ($5.40), free for children 15 and under. Apr–Oct daily 10am–5:30pm; Nov–Mar Mon–Fri 10am–5pm.

Among the most visited cellars are those under the Gothic-style buildings and spacious gardens of the Maison de Pommery. A magnificent 116-step stairway leads to a maze of galleries dug into the chalk that are more than 11 miles long and about 100 feet below ground. Various stages of champagne making are shown.

Mumm. 34 rue du Champ-de-Mars. ☎ **03-26-49-59-70.** Tours in English 20F ($3.60), free for children and students. Mar–Oct daily 9–11am and 2–5pm; Nov–Feb Mon–Fri 9–11am and 2–5pm, Sat–Sun and holidays 2–5pm.

A visit here includes a video show and a cellar tour; a small museum exhibits casks and the ancient tools of a vintner. Champagne is available for purchase in the gift shop.

Piper-Heidsieck. 51 bd. Henri-Vasnier. ☎ **03-26-84-43-44.** Admission 35F ($6.30). Daily 9–11:45am and 2–5:15pm. Closed Tues and Wed Dec–Feb.

One of the oldest champagne houses in the world, this firm was established in 1785. Here you explore the cellars in an electric-powered car (six occupants at a time) known as *une nacelle* and enjoy a tasting at the end of the tour.

Taittinger. 9 place St-Niçaise. ☎ **03-26-85-84-33.** Admission 20F ($3.60). Mar–Nov Mon–Fri 9:30am–noon and 2–4:30pm, Sat–Sun 9–11am and 2–5pm; Dec–Feb Mon–Fri 9:30am–noon and 2–4:30pm.

Taittinger is a grand marque of French champagne, one of the few whose ownership is controlled by members of the family that founded it in 1930. It's one of the most visitor-friendly of the champagne houses. The Romanesque cellars were dug from the site of Gallo-Roman chalk mines in use between the 4th and 13th centuries. Tours—including a film presentation, a guided cellar visit, and a surprisingly rich set of anecdotes about Reims, the champagne-making process, and Taittinger family lore—last about an hour.

Veuve Clicquot–Ponsardin. 1 place des Droits-de-l'Homme. ☎ **03-26-89-54-44.** Free admission. Apr–Oct Mon–Sat, Nov–Mar Mon–Fri (call for an appointment).

You can visit part of the 16 miles of underground galleries on guided tours at Veuve Clicquot–Ponsardin. The highlight is the screening of a film about one of Champagne's grande dames, the Veuve Clicquot (Widow Clicquot).

Champagne: The Fizz & the Fun

The love of that effervescent mystery called champagne is certainly nothing new. During the Renaissance, the only thing François I of France and Henry VIII of England could agree on was a preference for bubbly. Napoléon carted along cases of the stuff to his battlefronts. Casanova used it to liven up his legendary seductions, Mme Pompadour employed it to tempt the Sun King, and Tallyrand imported cases of it to the Congress of Vienna for a different sort of seduction—procuring more favorable peace terms.

We all owe a toast or two to Dom Pérignon, that Benedictine monk (1638–1715) who initiated the technique of adding cane sugar and natural yeast to the still wine to cause it, after years of fermentation, to foam. Without a complicated series of additives, double fermentations, cooling at precise temperatures, and turnings and twistings, champagne would be a nonsparkling wine. But without the fizz, where would be the fun?

The best champagne grapes are grown in a network of vineyards that meander like narrow ribbons along the bottomlands south of Reims. French vintners consider the best regions the Côte des Blancs, Montagne de Reims, and Vallée de la Marne; these are also the names for the three Routes du Champagne, signposted wine roads extending through the area.

The association of this bubbling wine with glamour, romance, and celebration is a triumph of marketing. Off the record, Burgundy's vintners will remind oenophiles that it takes a lot more work, with a greater chance of failure from uncontrollable variables, to produce a great bottle of still red than a jeroboam of sparkling Veuve Clicquot.

Nonetheless, the fascination with real champagne remains fervent, as shown by the spectacular increase in worldwide consumption of the stuff since Leslie Caron and Louis Jourdan sang about "The Night They Invented Champagne" in the 1958 movie *Gigi*.

And now a word about the word *champagne*. Since the days of the grand époque, when dandies drank bubbly out of ladies' slippers and beauties bathed in the stuff, the misuse of that word has aroused the wrath of even such venerable personages as the Veuve Clicquot herself. Only champagne made in France's Champagne region can by law be called champagne. Bubbly made in any other area of France (or the world) must be categorized as having been produced via the *méthode champenoise*. In the U.S., each state has its own laws about this—in one state you can call your bubbly champagne and in another you cannot. But don't dare try that in France, as you'll face lengthy litigation. Just ask Yves Saint Laurent, who once had the effrontery to name a new perfume he'd invented Champagne.

SHOPPING

The main shopping district is conveniently located around the cathedral. Nearby streets to shop are the very long **rue de Vesle** and **cours Langlet.**

Of course, you'll definitely want to include bottles of champagne on your shopping list. Many people opt to visit one of the major champagne houses in town, including **Maison de Pommery,** place du Général-Gourand (☎ **03-26-61-62-55**); others get in their car and drive along the **Routes du Champagne,** three signposted wine roads that cover the region. This is where you'll find more of the smaller champagne makers. When you're making the rounds along these roads, be aware that most champagne houses prefer you to take their tour and not just stop in their shops. If you do take the tour, you'll at least get a glass of bubbly at the end. When purchasing here, be aware that the bottles are priced individually, but you can get discounts if you buy three or six bottles at a time. However, if you're looking for a good deal, you may want to buy at stores in town like **Le Marché aux Vins,** 3 place Léon-Bourgeois (☎ **03-26-40-12-12**), where you can choose from a very large selection of not only local champagnes but also other wines. For complete information on the champagne houses in and around Reims, contact the Office de Tourisme.

Another specialty here is the light and delicious little cookie known as *biscuit de Reims.* Two of the best places to find them are **La Maison Fossier,** 25 cours Langlet (☎ **03-26-47-59-84**), and **Boutique Nominee,** place du Parvis (☎ **03-26-40-43-85**). For chocolate and candied specialties, try **La Petite Friande,** 15 cours Langlet (☎ **03-26-47-50-44**), where you can purchase liqueur-filled chocolate champagne bubbles and corks.

If you want to comb the flea markets and antiques stores while in town, **Parc des Expositions,** route de Châlons-en-Champagne, hosts a flea market the first Sunday of each month, except during August. On the first weekend of April there's a huge "Euro" flea market, with more than 500 vendors, in the same location. The organization responsible for these events is **Artcom/Puces de Reims,** 82 rue Jacquart (☎ **03-26-02-04-06**).

WHERE TO STAY
VERY EXPENSIVE

✪ **Boyer-les-Crayères.** 64 bd. Henri-Vasnier, 51100 Reims. ☎ **03-26-82-80-80.** Fax 03-26-82-65-52. www.integra.fr/relaischateaux/crayeres. 19 units. A/C MINIBAR TV TEL. 1,290–1,900F ($232.20–$342) double; from 2,000F ($360) suite. AE, DC, MC, V. Closed Dec 22–Jan 12.

This hotel occupies one of the finest châteaux in eastern France, and there's no better place to stay or dine in Champagne. Set in a 14-acre park, it boasts 18-foot ceilings, burnished paneling, and luxurious furnishings. The rooms, with terraces and all the amenities, are individually decorated and usually available when a champagne mogul isn't in residence.

Dining: The hotel's restaurant is one of the greatest in the area. World-famous chef Gérard Boyer imbues each dish with his culinary imprint. One of his masterpieces is *salade du Père-Maurice,* with green beans, artichoke hearts, lemon, foie gras, truffles, and lobster. Reservations are required a few days in advance for weekday dinners, at least a month in advance for weekend dinners.

Amenities: A masseur or hairdresser can be sent to your room.

EXPENSIVE

Les Templiers. 22 rue des Templiers, 51100 Reims. ☎ **03-26-88-55-08.** Fax 03-26-47-80-60. 17 units. A/C MINIBAR TV TEL. 950–1,400F ($171–$252) double; 1,800F ($324) suite. AE, DC, MC, V. Bus: G or H.

This hotel, just a short walk from the cathedral, may be small, but it's your best inner-city bet. A restored 1800s mock-Gothic house, the place exhibits taste and sensitivity, with antiques, ornate ceilings, and hand-carved woodwork creating an inviting ambience. The rooms continue the 19th-century allure with color-coordinated fabrics and bold print wallcoverings. Breakfast, the only meal served, can be taken in your room or beside an indoor pool.

MODERATE TO INEXPENSIVE

Best Western Hôtel de la Paix. 9 rue Buirette, 51100 Reims. ☎ **800/528-1234** in the U.S., or 03-26-40-04-08. Fax 03-26-47-75-04. www.bestwestern.com. 106 units. MINIBAR TV TEL. 430–650F ($77.40–$117) double; 680F ($122.40) junior suite for 2–3. AE, DC, MC, V. Parking 45F ($8.10). Bus: G or H.

Conveniently located between the train station and the cathedral, this is probably the only modern hotel in France that owns a medieval chapel (built for Benedictine nuns in the 1200s) overlooking its garden and pool. Constructed in 1946, it has been massively enlarged since then into the pleasant chain-hotel format you'll see today. The rooms are contemporary and well maintained, and many are air-conditioned. The hotel's Taverne du Maître Kanter serves excellent meals daily between noon and midnight. The cuisine might incude sauerkrauts, fish, grills, oysters, and casseroles.

Grand Hôtel du Nord. 75 place Drouet-d'Erlon, 51100 Reims. ☎ **03-26-47-39-03.** Fax 03-26-40-92-26. 50 units. MINIBAR TV TEL. 285–320F ($51.30–$57.60) double. AE, DC, MC, V. Parking 30F ($5.40). Bus: G or H. Take A4 (A26) motorway and exit at Reims-Centre.

This old-fashioned hotel offers comfortably decorated rooms. Two steps from the drab entrance, the liveliness of place Drouet-d'Erlon unfolds with its many boutiques, cafe terraces, and cinemas. You're also near the cathedral, the basilica, and various museums.

Grand Hôtel L'Univers. 41 bd. Foch, 51100 Reims. ☎ **03-26-88-68-08.** Fax 03-26-40-95-61. 42 units. TV TEL. 310–325F ($55.80–$58.50) double. AE, MC, V.

In the heart of Reims and across from the train station, this five-story modern hotel has small to average-size rooms outfitted in a basic manner, with a simple desk and chair along with a firm bed. Since this area can get rather noisy, all the rooms fortunately have double-pane windows to block out the street "ambience." You can have breakfast in the American-style bar or dinner in the hotel's small but elegant restaurant, which specializes in traditional French cuisine and offers fixed-price menus. The hotel was recently awarded two-star status.

L'Assiette Champenoise. 40 av. Paul-Vaillant-Couturier, 51430 Tinqueux. ☎ **03-26-84-64-64.** Fax 03-26-04-15-69. 62 units. MINIBAR TV TEL. 545–770F ($98.10-$138.60) double; 1,100F ($198) suite. AE, DC, MC, V. From Reims, take A4 west toward Paris and exit at "Sortie 22-Tinqueux"; av. Paul-Vaillant-Couturier will lead you directly to Tinqueux.

About 4 miles from Reims, this is the second-best hotel/restaurant in the area. Built in the 1970s among century-old trees, it occupies part of what was once a private Norman estate. Rooms are attractively furnished and well maintained in a combination of French traditional and modern style. On the premises you'll find an indoor pool and outdoor terrace.

Many people come here just to enjoy the cooking of Jean-Pierre Lallement, who is assisted by his wife, Colette. In their artfully rustic dining room, the cuisine covers a medley of conservative classics prepared in some cases with an innovative twist. Try the veal kidneys and sweetbreads with star anise, John Dory with a ragoût of vegetables, or grilled duck liver with fondue of tomatoes. Homemade foie gras is always a reliable starter. Fixed-price menus range from 295F to 495F ($53.10 to $89.10).

Mercure Reims Cathédrale. 31 bd. Paul-Doumer, 51100 Reims. ☎ **03-26-84-49-49.** Fax 03-26-84-49-84. 122 units. A/C MINIBAR TV TEL. 510F ($91.80) double; 670–950F ($120.60–$171) suite. AE, DC, MC, V. Parking 40F ($7.20).

This hotel, a member of a national chain, sits on the banks of the Marne Canal, a 5-minute walk from the town center. It's near the entrance to the autoroute, so it's easy to find. The good-size rooms have all the modern conveniences, and some have views of a scenic waterway. Les Ombrages restaurant serves French specialties nightly to 10pm.

WHERE TO DINE

Boyer-les-Crayères and **L'Assiette Champenoise** (see above) both contain excellent restaurants.

Le Chardonnay. 194 av. d'Epernay. ☎ **03-26-06-08-60.** Reservations recommended. Main courses 90–160F ($16.20–$28.80); fixed-price menus 140–480F ($25.20–$86.40); "Menu champagne" for 2 (including a bottle of a "champagne de marque") 790F ($142.20). AE, DC, MC, V. Sun–Fri noon–2:30pm, Mon–Sat 7:30–10pm. Drive 4 miles south of Reims's center, following the signs to Epernay. FRENCH.

This cozy enterprise serves superb cuisine in a much-restored turn-of-the-century building managed by members of the Lange family. You're likely to be greeted by either Delphine or Chantal, the daughter-mother team that oversees the dining room and serves the succulent cuisine of Jean-Jacques. In a conservatively modern venue that includes a view over a flowering courtyard, you can enjoy cuisine that's remarkably consistent from week to week, with sauces often based on a generous use of local wines. Examples include duck filet with cherries, beef ribs with a sauce based on hearty Bouzy wine, and John Dory served with a sauce concocted from hibiscus blossoms.

Le Vigneron. Place Paul-Jamot. ☎ **03-26-79-86-86.** Reservations recommended. Main courses 80–160F ($14.40–$28.80); fixed-price menus 160–390F ($28.80–$70.20). DC, MC, V. Mon–Fri 11:30am–2:30pm, Mon–Sat 5:30–10pm. Closed Aug 1–15 and Dec 23–Jan 2. CHAMPENOISE.

At this sophisticated, low-key restaurant, the cuisine is firmly rooted in the traditions of Champagne: Much of the cuisine is laced with one or another of the region's delectable wines. Wine experts grab the carte even before glancing at the menu. With 650 choices, it includes some museum-quality vintages, such as a Pol Roger 1892 (not for sale at any price) and a Veuve Clicquot 1923. Hervé Liegent and the charming staff offer such specialties as a filet of trout from the Marne, prepared with crayfish sauce, and poached eggs with a sauce made with mariolles (a mild locally fermented cheese). A superb dessert is the *biscuits roses de Reims* served with a liqueur (*marc*) distilled from sparkling champagne. Try to step into the restaurant's small-scale museum, maintained in honor of the vintner's art, before you leave.

NEARBY ACCOMMODATIONS & DINING

For the most superb restaurant in the environs, head for the Château de Fère on D967. About 1½ miles north of this hamlet are the ruins of a 12th-century fortified castle—also called the Château de Fère. Take N31 northwest of Reims, pass through Fismes, then turn southwest onto N367.

✪ **Château de Fère.** Route de Fismes (D967), 02130 Fère-en-Tardenois. ☎ **03-23-82-21-13.** Fax 03-23-82-37-81. Reservations required. Main courses 90–340F ($16.20–$61.20); fixed-price menus 180F ($32.40) at lunch Mon–Fri, 290–480F ($52.20–$86.40) at lunch (weekends) and dinner. AE, DC, MC, V. Daily noon–2:30 and 7:15–9pm. Closed mid-Jan to mid-Feb. FRENCH.

Set in a park, this fabulous restaurant occupies a restored 16th-century crenellated château with turrets. The only restaurant in Champagne that's superior to it in cuisine is Boyer-les-Crayères. In summer, begin your repast in the sunny garden, sipping an aperitif or a glass of champagne with juice from freshly crushed raspberries. The owners oversee every detail and serve imaginative meals, with specialties like champagne-cooked turbot, paupiette of truffles and calves' kidneys, and *dégustation des trois mignons* (a platter of beef, lamb, and veal). The desserts are mouth-watering, but we prefer to order the *boulette d'Avesnes,* a cone of cheese flecked with herbs and crushed peppercorns and coated with paprika.

Also available here are 19 luxuriously furnished guest rooms and 6 suites, each with bathroom, minibar, TV, and phone. The doubles cost 850F to 1,200F ($153 to $216); the suites, 1,150F to 1,950F ($207 to $351).

REIMS AFTER DARK

The best place to start is place Drouet-d'Erlon, with its radiating streets that are home to Reims's premier clubs. This is a university town, so for the most part students rule the night. Just follow them to the best venues.

For a beer, head to **The Glue Pot,** 49 place Drouet-d'Erlon (☎ 03-26-47-36-46), with its heavy dose of noise and rowdy students; **Au Bureau,** 80 place Drouet-d'Erlon (☎ 03-26-40-33-06), where a mixed-age crowd congregates in a typically Irish pub that has more than 120 brands of beer; or the exotic **Au Lion de Belfort,** 37 place Drouet-d'Erlon (☎ 03-26-47-48-17), where stuffed heads of hippos, elephants, and the like keep watch over the young patrons.

The best dance floors in town are **Le Boss,** 17 rue Lesage (☎ 03-26-88-33-83), where techno is king and disco is dead; and **Le Tigre,** 2 bis av. Georges-Clemenceau (☎ 03-26-82-64-00), with its decor of old French cars placed like artwork against the brick walls and mirrors. The fave of young gays and lesbians is **Les Lilas Club,** 75 rue des Courcelles (☎ 03-26-47-02-81). A private alcove, decorated with Greek statues and red carpet, separates its two dance rooms. Everybody wears jeans; cover to any of these dance clubs is between 40F and 60F ($7.20 and $10.80).

Another activity that always draws a crowd is the free laser show on the exterior walls of the cathedral on Saturday nights in July and August. The Office de Tourisme has all the details. If you want to enjoy an evening of stage performance, **Comédie de Reims,** chaussée Bocquaine (☎ 03-26-48-49-00), has a varied and full schedule, with tickets costing 120F ($21.60).

5 Laon & Amiens: Side Trips from Reims

North Americans tend to overlook France's northern region, but savvy travelers know that this pristine area offers restful alternatives to the densely populated tourist meccas of Paris and the Riviera. The landscape of this low-lying region, adjacent to Belgium's border, will be familiar to admirers of Matisse, who found much inspiration here. Amiens and Laon are the area's major draws.

From Reims, **Laon** would be a logical first stop, particularly for those traveling by rail who will have to transfer here anyway en route to Amiens. This site is the north's most intriguing due to its history and setting. Over the years, it has witnessed much tur-bulence from its perch on an isolated ridge 328 feet above the plain and the Ardon River.

Amiens, on the Somme River, has subsisted as a textile center since medieval days. It was once the ancient capital of Picardy, and its old town is a warren of jumbled streets and intersecting canals. Today, Amiens is renowned for its Gothic cathedral, one of the finest in France.

The champagne country is a trove of gems awaiting discovery for those who would like to explore more than Amiens and Laon. The heavily forested **Ardennes** attracts lovers of nature and French poetry alike. Rimbaud lived and wrote here; other writers such as Victor Hugo, George Sand, and Alexandre Dumas also expounded on its beauty in their writings. The sandy beaches of **Le Touquet-Paris-Plage** are the most fashionable and best equipped of the many resorts along the Channel. A mini–Monte

Carlo, it was dubbed the "playground of kings" in the days before World War II. Many other stops merit a look if you have the time.

LAON

28 miles NW of Reims, 74 miles SE of Amiens, 86 miles NE of Paris

Arguably the single most intriguing town in the north of France, Laon is perched on an isolated ridge that rises 328 feet above the plain and the Ardon River. The capital of the département of Aisne, Laon has had a long, turbulent history, due in large part to its remarkable site.

Trains arrive from Paris's Gare du Nord at least 15 times a day, requiring between 1½ and 2 hours for the trip. Other trains arrive from Reims 7 times a day, taking about 45 minutes. For train information and schedules, call ☎ **08-36-35-35-39.** If you're **driving** from Reims, go 28 miles on A26 north directly to Laon.

The **Office de Tourisme** is on place du Parvis (☎ **03-23-20-28-62**).

SEEING THE SIGHTS

The Romans, recognizing Laon's strategic value early on, had it fortified. It was later besieged by Vandals, Burgundians, Franks, and many others. German troops entered Laon in 1870 and again in the summer of 1914, holding it until the end of World War I. The town is still surrounded by medieval ramparts, regarded by many as the single most rewarding attraction in the north. They appear to have survived intact from the Middle Ages and provide a ready-made itinerary for touring Laon. They aren't structurally sound enough to be climbed on) so must be admired from below.

You don't have to huff and puff as you head from Laon's Basse Ville to its Haute Ville, thanks to a cable-operated tram, **Poma 2000** (☎ **03-23-79-07-59**), that shuttles passengers up and down the rocky hill at 3-minute intervals. It departs from the rail station on place de la Gare and ascends to the Hôtel-de-Ville on place du Général-Leclerc. The tram operates Monday through Saturday from 7am to 8pm. The cost is 6.50F ($1.15) one-way and 8.50F ($1.55) round-trip.

Cathédrale Notre-Dame de Laon. 8 rue du Cloître, off place Aubry. ☎ **03-23-20-26-54.** Free admission. Daily 8:30am–6:30pm.

Most visitors head first to this famous cathedral with the huge carved oxen on its facade. Having escaped World War I relatively unharmed, it stands on the same spot where an ancient basilica stood until it was destroyed by fire in 1111. The structure has six towers, four of which are complete. Inside is stained glass, some panels dating from the 13th century, and an 18th-century choir grille.

After visiting the cathedral, stroll down the pedestrians-only **rue Châtelaine,** Laon's major shopping street.

Musée Archéologique Municipal. 32 rue George-Ermant. ☎ **03-23-20-19-87.** Admission 20F ($3.60) adults, free for children 17 and under. Wed–Mon 10am–noon and 2–6pm (to 5pm Oct–Apr).

This museum was founded in 1861 and remained rather sleepy until 1937, when a collection of 1,700 artifacts (mainly from Greece, Rome, Egypt, Cyprus, and Asia Minor) was added, as well as a collection of French painting and sculpture.

WHERE TO STAY & DINE

Hostellerie St-Vincent. 29 av. Charles-de-Gaulle, 02000 Laon. ☎ **03-23-23-42-43.** Fax 03-23-79-22-55. 47 units. TV TEL. 295F ($53.10) double. AE, DC, MC, V.

At the edge of the city, near the point where the road from Reims (A26) enters the Basse Ville, this simple two-star hotel is the most modern and comfortable in town, with basic but comfortable guest rooms. The restaurant is noted for its good food, served in a setting accented by lots of plants and a serpentine staircase that acts as the focal point of the dining room. Fixed-price menus range from 90F to 120F ($16.20 to $21.60). Meals are served from noon to 2:30pm and 7 to 9:30pm; closed Saturday at lunch and Sunday night.

Hôtel de la Bannière de France. 11 rue Franklin-D.-Roosevelt, 02000 Laon. ☎ **03-23-23-21-44.** Fax 03-23-23-31-56. www.leisureplanet.com. 18 units. TV TEL. 360–375F ($64.80–$67.50) double. AE, DC, MC, V. Parking 35F ($6.30). Closed May 1 and Dec 20–Jan 20.

This revered hotel, built in 1685, is located in the most historic part of Laon, Haute Ville. Despite its antique-looking facade, its interior has been completely modernized, though an attempt was made to maintain the ambience of a traditional French hotel. The rooms are small but comfortably furnished and cozy.

Dining: The personality of the owner, Mme Paul Lefevre, is most obvious in the traditional restaurant, open daily from noon to 2pm and 7 to 9:30pm. The flavorful menu items include trout poached in champagne, sole *à la normande,* and a delicious version of chocolate profiteroles.

AMIENS

68 miles NW of Reims, 75 miles N of Paris, 71 miles SW of Lille

A major textile center since medieval days, Amiens was the ancient capital of Picardy, set on the south bank of the Somme, where it divides into a complex series of canals and irrigation networks. Its old town—a jumble of narrow streets crisscrossed by canals—is run-down and seedy but still worth exploring. The city's focal point is its world-famous Gothic cathedral, one of France's finest. The edge of the modern town begins several blocks south of the cathedral, around the Tour Perret.

Reaching Amiens by **train** from Reims requires a transfer in Laon (which you can explore before continuing on; see above) or Tergnier. Trains are relatively infrequent—only three a day—and take 80 minutes to 3 hours, depending on the schedule.

Many visitors come here straight from Paris, for Amiens sits astride the main rail lines connecting Paris's Gare du Nord with Lille. Depending on the season, four or five trains a day make the trip, taking 65 minutes each way. The rail station in Amiens is at place Alphonse-Fiquet, a 10-minute walk from the old town. For train information and schedules, call ☎ **08-36-35-35-39.**

If you're **driving,** take A26 north 28 miles to Laon, then travel west on N44 to N32, which becomes D934 en route to Amiens. The distance traveled is 68 miles; however, the trek may take you more than 1½ hours because of the country roads you'll be traversing after you exit A26. Amiens is adjacent to the main autoroute (A1) connecting Paris with Lille. Driving time from Paris is about 90 minutes. Drivers coming from the northern suburbs of Paris usually prefer to take a different autoroute, A16, which opened in 1995 and passes near Amiens on its way to Lille.

The **Office de Tourisme** is at 6 bis rue Dusevel (☎ **03-22-71-60-50**).

EXPLORING AMIENS

Julius Caesar himself praised the fertility of the fields around Amiens. During the Middle Ages, **Les Hortillonnages,** an expanse of almost 600 acres at the eastern edge of the historic core, was set aside for the cultivation of pears, carrots, turnips, and all kinds of herbs and vegetables. Irrigated by a web of canals fed by the Somme, the district is still a commercial garden, producing ample amounts of foodstuffs. Not too long ago, the harvest was floated on barges and in shallow-bottomed boats to the Quai Bélu, near the cathedral, for sale to consumers. Although today the produce is hauled from the fields into the town center by truck and not by boat, the ritual retains its medieval name, the **Marché sur l'Eau.** The tradition continues every Thursday and

Saturday from 8 to 11am, when the river's quays are transformed into a huge outdoor vegetable market.

A few paces north of the cathedral, straddling both banks of the Somme, is a cluster of carefully restored 13th- and 14th-century houses arranged within a labyrinth of narrow cobblestone streets. Known as the **Quartier St-Leu,** this is a neighborhood of gift shops, antiques shops, art galleries, boutiques, and cafes.

☼ **Cathédrale Notre-Dame d'Amiens.** Place Notre-Dame. ☎ **03-22-71-60-50.** Free admission. Apr–Sept daily 8:30am–7pm; Oct daily 8:30am–5pm; Nov–Mar daily 8:30am–noon and 2–5pm.

At 469 feet long, this cathedral is the largest church in France. It was begun in 1220 to the plans of Robert de Luzarches and completed around 1270. Its original purpose was to house the head of St. John the Baptist, brought back from the Crusades in 1206. Two unequal towers were added later—the south one in 1366, the north one in 1402. The renowned architect Viollet-le-Duc restored the cathedral in the 1850s.

The Amiens cathedral is the crowning example of French Gothic architecture. In John Ruskin's rhapsodical *Bible of Amiens* (1884), which Proust translated into French, he extolled the door arches. The three portals of the west front are lavishly decorated, important examples of Gothic cathedral sculpture. The portals are surmounted by two galleries. The upper one contains 22 statues of kings, and the large rose window is from the 16th century.

Inside are beautifully carved stalls and a Flamboyant Gothic choir screen. These stalls with some 3,500 figures were made by local artisans in the early 16th century. The interior is held up by 126 slender pillars, the zenith of the High Gothic in the north of France. The cathedral, like St. Paul's in London, somehow managed to escape destruction in World War II, and the architecture of Europe is richer because of it. In 1996 the *Portail de la Mère-Dieu* (Portal of the Mother of God), to the right of the cathedral's main entrance as you look over the facade, was restored at enormous expense.

Musée de Picardie. 48 rue de la République. ☎ **03-22-97-14-00.** Admission 20F ($3.60) adults, 12F ($2.15) children. Tues–Sun 10am–12:30pm and 2–6pm.

This museum occupies a building constructed from 1855 to 1867. The palace of the Napoleonic dynasty, inaugurated by Napoléon III, is divided into three sections, including one devoted to archaeology. Other sections include exhibits on the Roman occupation of Gaul, the Merovingian era, ancient Greece, and Egypt. One collection documents the Middle Ages with ivories, enamels, art objects, and sculpture. The sculpture and painting collection traces the European schools from the 16th to the 20th centuries, with works by El Greco, Quentin-Lautour, Guardi, and Tiepolo. Fragonard's *Les Lavandières* is his most beautiful work here.

La Maison de Jules Verne. 2 rue Charles-Dubois. ☎ **03-22-45-09-12.** Admission 15F ($2.70) adults, 5F (90¢) children.

Amiens was the home of Jules Verne (1828–1905), author of *20,000 Leagues Under the Sea* and *Journey to the Center of the Earth,* who wrote many of his novels here. Most of the interior is devoted to a research center that documents his life and literary achievements, and admission for members of the general public is not encouraged. If you have a consuming interest in Jules Verne and the early years of the science-fiction genre, visit Monday through Friday from 9am to noon and 2 to 6pm, Saturday from 2 to 6pm.

Jules Verne is buried in Amiens, and you may want to visit him at the **Cimetière de la Madeleine,** rue St-Maurice, about half a mile northwest of the town center. His Beaux-Arts tomb bears a representation of Verne as if physically rising from the dead. The cemetery is open daily from 9am to 7pm.

WHERE TO STAY

Note that **Le Prieuré** (see below) also rents rooms.

Hôtel Le Carlton. 42 rue de Noyon, 80000 Amiens. ☎ **03-22-97-72-22.** Fax 03-22-97-72-00. 25 units. TV TEL. 380–620F ($68.40–$111.60) double; 1,000F ($180) suite. AE, DC, MC, V.

From a glance at this hotel's Napoléon III architecture, you'll immediately see that this is Amiens's stellar choice. Though it's geared toward business travelers, the rooms are luxurious, with rich furniture and murals of turn-of-the-century city-scapes. The public areas include a reception area, English bar, and deluxe brasserie-style restaurant. All have the same masculine yet elegant style of polished dark woods and deep hunter-green and burgundy walls. Menus range from 80F to 145F ($14.40 to $26.10).

Relais Mercure. 16 place au Feurre, 8000 Amiens. ☎ **03-22-91-46-17.** Fax 03-33-91-86-57. 47 units. MINIBAR TV TEL. 460–500F ($82.80–$90) double. Free parking.

Radically renovated and upgraded in 1998, and based on an 18th-century core that was originally conceived as a coaching inn, this hotel lies directly opposite the main facade of Amien's most legendary building, the cathedral. It was purchased by France's biggest hotel conglomerate in 1997. Despite the meticulous preservation of its stately facade and some of the antique beams in many of its bedrooms, its interior was upgraded and given a clean, unfussy, modern look. The pricier rooms contain cramped but cozy sitting areas; the less expensive units are smaller and more functional. Some have windows overlooking the cathedral. Overall, the place provides good value, an unbeatable location, and the cost-consciousness of the Accor group. A woodsy-looking pub on the premises serves coffee and drinks but no food. Other than breakfast, no meals of any kind are served.

WHERE TO DINE

Le Prieuré. 17 rue Porion, 8000 Amiens. ☎ **03-22-92-27-67.** Reservations recommended. Main courses 65–150F ($11.70–$27); fixed-price menus 100–220F ($18–$39.60). AE, DC, MC, V. Tues–Sun noon–2:30pm, Tues–Sat 7–9pm. Closed 2 weeks in Nov. FRENCH.

This place, occupying a much-restored 18th-century building, has absolutely no pretentions. Your tablemates are as likely to be celebrating the end of a successful soccer match as a demure wedding anniversary. The menu items are well flavored, with grills, stews, racks of lamb, and fish served in generous quantities.

On the premises are 22 simple but clean rooms, each with TV and phone; a double costs 200F to 420F ($36 to $75.60).

Les Marissons. 68 rue des Marissons. ☎ **03-22-92-96-66.** Reservations recommended. Main courses 125–158F ($22.50–$28.45); fixed-price menus 110–255F ($19.80–$45.90). AE, DC, MC, V. Mon–Fri noon–2pm, Mon–Sat 7–10pm. FRENCH.

Two or three places around town match the quality of the food here, but none of them offers such a charming antique setting. Adjacent to one of the city's oldest bridges (pont de la Dodane), it occupies a heavily timbered 15th-century building. The cuisine is elegantly and flavorfully presented by chef Antoine Benoit and is defined as a celebration of Picardy. Menu specialties are pâté made from local ducklings, roast lamb *pré-salé* from the salt marshes off the English Channel, scallops baked in their shells, and succulent sea bass prepared whole and presented with morels. In summer you can dine on the terrace in the garden.

AMIENS AFTER DARK

Try the **Riverside Café,** place du Don (☎ **03-22-92-50-30**), with its movie posters and photos of 1960s American icons filling the walls and an active young crowd filling the seats; or the **Café Expo Vents et Marées,** 48 rue du Don (☎ **03-22-92-99-79**), where you can absorb the fusion of rock, alcohol, and comic strips—exhibits of original art boards from France's most famous strips. You'll find the largest number of nightspots around quai Bélu.

If you're big on musical events, head for a place next to the train station: **Le Grand Wazoo,** 5 rue Vulfran-Warmé (☎ **03-22-91-64-91**). Named in honor of Frank Zappa, this cool club with its exotic Arab decor draws a mixed crowd intent on listening to local musicians as well as groups famous throughout the continent. Concerts are generally scheduled on Fridays and Saturdays and range from techno and reggae to punk rock. Tickets cost about 30F ($5.40).

While you're checking out the nightlife along the canal area, stop in the old medieval house that's home to the traditional wine bar **La Queue de Vache** (the Cow's Tail), 51 quai Bélu (☎ **03-22-91-91-15**), where you'll be gregariously welcomed and immediately drawn into the heady atmosphere of half-timbered walls, fireplaces, live jazz, and (on occasion) accordion music. It's the ideal setting in which to drink good French wine and sample rich, chewy country breads along with aromatic French cheeses.

For dancing, your best bet is **Le Nemo,** 9 rue des Francs-Mûriers (☎ **03-22-97-96-71**), with its spacious interior and majestic frescoes of dolphins and marine life. The mainly young, hip crowd pays as much as 70F ($12.60) to dive in here.

6 Epernay

87 miles E of Paris, 16 miles S of Reims

On the left bank of the Marne, Epernay rivals Reims as a center for champagne. Although home to only one-sixth of Reims's population, Epernay today produces nearly as much champagne as its larger sibling. It boasts an estimated 200 miles or more of cellars and tunnels, a veritable rabbit warren, for storing champagne. These caves are vast vaults cut into the chalk rock on which the town is built. Represented in Epernay are such champagne companies as Moët et Chandon (the largest), Pol Roger, Mercier, and de Castellane.

Epernay's main boulevards are the elegant residential avenue de Champagne, rue Mercier, and rue de Reims, all radiating from place de la République. Two important squares in the narrow streets of the commercial district are place Hughes-Plomb and place des Arcades.

Epernay has been either destroyed or burned nearly two dozen times, as it lay in the path of invading armies, particularly from Germany. Few of its old buildings are left. However, check out avenue de Champagne for its neoclassical villas and Victorian town houses.

ESSENTIALS

GETTING THERE   Thirteen **trains** per day arrive from Paris (trip time: 1¼ hours); there are also 13 trains per day from Reims (trip time: 20 minutes). For train information and schedules, call ☎ **08-36-35-35-39.** The major bus link is **SDTM Trans-Champagne** (☎ **03-26-65-17-07** in Epernay for schedules), operating 4 buses per day Monday through Saturday between Châlons-en-Champagne and Epernay (trip time: 1 hour); a one-way fare is 33.50F ($6.05). If you're **driving** to Epernay from Reims, head south along E51.

VISITOR INFORMATION   The **Office de Tourisme** is at 7 av. de Champagne (☎ **03-26-53-33-00**).

EXPLORING THE TOWN

Boutiques and shops abound in the pedestrian district of **place des Arcades** and **rue du Général-Leclerc, rue St-Martin,** and **rue Port Lucas.** Here you'll find art galleries, gift shops, and stores selling clothes, antiques, books, and regional food items.

Of course, you may want to stock up on some vintages. You can go to the individual houses along avenue de Champagne—places like **Moët et Chandon,** 18 av. de Champagne (☎ 03-26-51-20-20), and **Mercier,** 73 av. de Champagne (☎ 03-26-51-22-22)—or try one of the champagne stores that represent a variety of houses. Two are **La Cave Salvatori,** 11 rue Flodoard (☎ 03-26-55-32-32), and **La Boutique Achille Princier,** 9 rue Jean-Chandon-Moët (☎ 03-26-54-04-06).

For champagne gift items like flutes and corks as well as linens and table decorations, visit **La Boutique de Sophie,** 33 rue du Général-Leclerc (☎ 03-26-54-48-56); **La Boutique Fromm,** 33 rue St-Thibault (☎ 03-26-55-25-64); and **Camaieu,** 12 rue du Professeur-Langevin (☎ 03-26-51-83-83). For regional antiques from the 18th and 19th centuries, try **Bonne Epoque,** 106 av. Foch (☎ 03-26-54-11-39).

Moët et Chandon Champagne Cellars. 18 av. de Champagne. ☎ **03-26-51-20-20.** Admission 35F ($6.30). Daily 9:30am–noon and 2–5pm. Closed national holidays.

An expert staff member gives guided tours in English, describing the champagne-making process and filling you in on champagne lore: Napoléon, a friend of Jean-Rémy Moët, used to stop by here for thousands of bottles on his way to the battlefront. The only time he didn't take a supply with him was at Waterloo—and look what happened there. At the end of the tour you're given a complimentary glass of bubbly. No appointment is necessary, except for large groups.

Mercier. 70 av. de Champagne. ☎ **03-26-51-22-22.** Admission 20F ($3.60). Mon–Sat 9:30–11:30am and 2–4:30pm, Sun 9:30–11:30am and 2–5pm. Closed Tues–Wed in Dec–Feb.

Since Mercier is near Moët et Chandon, you can visit them both on the same day. In the middle of the vineyard, Mercier conducts tours in English of its 11 miles of tunnels from laser-guided trains. The caves contain one of the world's largest wooden barrels, with a capacity of more than 200,000 bottles. No appointment is necessary if there are fewer than 10 in your group.

Musée Municipal. 13 av. de Champagne. ☎ **03-26-51-90-31.** Admission 10F ($1.80). May–Nov Wed–Mon 10am–noon and 2-6pm.

Housed in the 19th-century Château Perrier, this museum explores the region's life through the tools with which locals earned their living—from agricultural implements to wine presses, even old champagne bottles. Only group tours of at least 10 people are possible and must be reserved in advance by correspondence.

Abbaye d'Hautvillers. On D386, signposted just north of Epernay. ☎ **03-26-51-20-00.** Free admission. Open by appointment only.

The abbey, owned and maintained by Moët et Chandon, is one of its most prized architectural treasures; it contains the tomb of the monk Dom Pérignon (cellar master at the abbey from 1670 to 1715). The abbey has been rebuilt several times since it was founded in the 12th century. When the monks were evicted during the Revolution, the abbey was purchased by the Moët family; today, it's once again a church.

WHERE TO STAY

Note that **Les Berceaux** (see below) also rents rooms.

Best Western Hôtel de Champagne. 30 rue Eugène-Mercier, 51200 Epernay. ☎ **800/528-1234** in the U.S., or 03-26-53-10-60. Fax 03-26-51-94-63. www.bestwestern.com. 33 units. TV TEL. 410–550F ($73.80–$99) double. AE, MC, DC, V.

Brothers, brothers, come quickly! I am drinking stars!

—Dom Pérignon

Built in the 1970s about 200 yards from the Moët et Chandon showroom, near place de la République, this simple inn is one of the best of a modest lot in the town itself. It offers reasonably priced, well-maintained rooms; some are outfitted in modern style, others look vaguely inspired by Louis XV. A generous buffet breakfast is served every morning, and parking is available on the grounds.

✪ **Royal Champagne.** 51160 Champillon Belevue. ☎ **03-26-52-87-11.** Fax 03-26-52-89-69. E-mail: royalchampagne@wanadoo.fr. 32 units. MINIBAR TV TEL. 870–1,300F ($156.60–$234) double; 1,500–1,800F ($270–$324) suite. AE, DC, MC, V. Drive 4 miles from Epernay toward Reims on the Route du Vignoble (N2051); the hotel is in the hamlet of Champillon.

Constructed around what was originally built in the 1700s as a relay station for the French postal system, this historic hotel is a member of the prestigious Relais & Châteaux chain. The establishment's historic core contains the reception, bar, and dining facilities; guest rooms are in town house–style accommodations set edge to edge overlooking the nearby vineyards. The units are artfully rustic and very comfortable, exemplifying the coziness of wine country living.

Dining: The food is exceptional, with specialties like lobster ragoût, salt cod with mousseline of truffles, and roast lamb with garlic. The chef is known for classic dishes with an innovative twist. The fixed-price menus cost 275F and 375F ($49.50 and $67.50); expect to spend 500F ($90) for an entire à la carte meal.

WHERE TO DINE

Les Berceaux. 13 rue Berceaux, 51200 Epernay. ☎ **03-26-55-28-84.** Fax 03-26-55-10-36. Reservations recommended. Main courses 120–170F ($21.60–$30.60); fixed-price menus 190–260F ($34.20–$46.80). AE, DC, MC, V. Daily noon–2:30pm Tues–Sat 7–9:30pm. CHAMPENOIS.

Owners Patrick Michelon and Mathilde Gagnon serve generous portions of flavorful and relatively conservative Champenois cuisine. Monsieur Michelon has much experience as a chef at several prestigious restaurants in other parts of France. The menus change seasonally but always feature fresh produce (from the region whenever possible) and superior cuts of fish, meat, and game in season. Local wines are showcased and include a respectable assortment of champagnes. You're welcome to taste a glass of wine or champagne at The Wine Bar.

Les Berceaux, only a 5-minute walk from the famous houses of champagne, also rents 29 well-furnished rooms; a double with bathroom is 390F ($70.20).

EPERNAY AFTER DARK

Start out with a stop at the chic cafe/bar **Le Progrès,** 5 place de la République (☎ **03-26-55-22-72**). This popular place lets you loosen up before the real festivities get under way. **Le Tap-Too,** 5 rue du Près Dimanche (☎ **03-26-51-56-10**), attracts all ages and types to its four dance halls and six bars together in one big warehouse. For live concerts and the occasional lighthearted theatrical performance, head over to the two-story American-style bar/pub **La Marmite Swing,** 160 av. Foch (☎ **03-26-54-17-72**). Most acts take the stage on Friday and Saturday evenings, but the place continues to sizzle during the rest of the week as high-energy partiers work the crowd against a backdrop of techno and rock. For performance nights, expect to pay a cover upward of 60F ($10.80).

7 Troyes

102 miles SE of Paris, 94 miles NW of Dijon

The capital of the southern champagne country, Troyes (*twah* or *twrah*) is filled with Renaissance architectural glories. The comtes de Champagne acquired the town in the 10th century. The historic core of the city is called Bouchon de Champagne, meaning "champagne cork," to which it bears a faint resemblance. However, don't come here for champagne caves—there aren't any.

The town was rebuilt in the Renaissance style after a 1524 fire wiped out much of it, but it was destroyed again in World War II. By 1745 Troyes had become the capital of the knitware industry. The old city lies on the River Seine, but it's the capital of the département of Aube, named for the River Aube.

ESSENTIALS

GETTING THERE Because French rail lines radiate from Paris, you might have to transfer in the capital if you're coming from Reims or Lille. Once you're in Paris, however, service is frequent and fast from Gare de l'Est, a total of 12 trains per day. For **train** information and schedules, call ☎ **08-36-35-35-39.** If you're **driving** from Paris to Troyes, head southeast along N19.

VISITOR INFORMATION The **Office de Tourisme** is at 16 bd. Carnot (☎ **03-25-82-62-70**).

SEEING THE SIGHTS

Rue Urbain-IV leads to the principal plaza of Troyes, **place du Maréchal-Foch,** named for the famed World War I general. Here you can enjoy coffee and crêpes at numerous cafes and restaurants while you admire the Hôtel de Ville (town hall); dating from 1624, it's one of the region's few Louis XIII–style buildings.

The city has at least nine churches that merit exploration (the tourist office will provide a map). Church visiting hours are daily from 10am to noon and 2 to 5pm (to 6pm in July and August). Every Thursday, Friday, and Saturday between June and September, a free *son-et-lumière* is conducted in three of the churches (Ste-Madeleine, St-Urbain, and St-Pantaléon, in that order). The show begins at 10pm, lasts about 90 minutes (depending on how long participants take to straggle from one building to another), and is replete with anecdotes and a sense of the pageantry of the French Middle Ages.

Cathédrale St-Pierre et St-Paul. 1 place St-Pierre. ☎ **03-25-76-98-18.** Sept 16–June daily 10am–noon and 2–5pm; July–Sept 15 daily 9am–7pm.

Begin at place de la Libération, where you'll have a view of this Gothic church built primarily in the 13th and 17th centuries. The architecture is remarkably elegant, and the detail in the tall stained-glass windows and two rose windows provides a particularly striking example of the skill of 13th-century artists. Above the richly decorated facade rises the 200-foot Tour St-Pierre. The sumptuous treasury includes enamel work, relics, and alms boxes from the comtes de Champagne and others. The facade is lit by floodlights at night. In the crypt is a historically significant treasury.

Eglise Ste-Madeleine. Rue de la Madeleine. ☎ **03-25-73-82-90.**

This is the city's oldest church, from the mid–12th century. It was built in the late Roman and early Gothic style, with many changes made in the 1500s. The tower is from the 16th and 17th centuries. A charnel house dates from 1525, and its triple-arched rood screen, unique in France, was carved by Jean Galide; it's a fine example of stone tracery. Its stained-glass windows are among the most beautiful examples left from the Champagne school of artisans.

Basilique St-Urbain. Rue Clemenceau. ☎ **03-25-73-37-13.** Closed Sept 16–June.

Called the Parthenon of Champagne because of its superb design, the church was founded by Troyes-born Pope Urban IV; construction began in the 13th century. The bold architecture with pillars and tapered mullion windows, harmonious proportions, and elegant sculptures makes this Troyes's greatest monument. The exterior is decorated with sculpted gargoyles.

Eglise St-Jean. Rue Champeaux. ☎ **03-25-73-06-96.**

This church is noted for its landmark clock tower. In 1420, the marriage of Catherine de France to Henry V of England took place here after the signing of the Treaty of Troyes. (Incidentally, the treaty led to an English invasion and the Hundred Years War.)

Eglise St-Pantaléon. Rue de Vauluisant. ☎ **03-25-73-06-99.**

Built between the 1500s and the 1700s, this structure is younger than the impressive collection of sculptures it contains. These are among the most unusual and sought-after pieces of once-polychromed stone sculpture in the district, depicting a lavish array of Virgins, Christs, cunning merchants, and carpenters.

Musée d'Art Moderne. Place St-Pierre (to the right of the cathedral). ☎ **03-25-76-26-80.** Admission 40F ($7.20); free on Wed. Wed–Mon 11am–6pm.

Housed in a restored bishop's palace from the 16th and 17th centuries, this magnificent modern-art collection, from the Pierre and Denise Lévy donation, is one of the largest private art collections ever given to France. The museum owns 350 paintings, 1,300 drawings and sketches, and more than 100 sculptures. Works by a host of masters—Gauguin, Matisse, Modigliani, Picasso, Cézanne, Degas, and Bonnard—are on display. Note in particular the works by the Fauves (the movement that followed Impressionism).

Musée des Beaux-Arts et d'Archéologie. 1 rue Chrétien-de-Troyes. ☎ **03-25-76-21-68.** Admission 30F ($5.40) adults, 10F ($1.80) children. Wed–Mon 10am–noon and 2–6pm.

Situated on the far side of the cathedral square, this is actually two museums, housed in the former Abbaye St-Loup; you can still see part of the cloisters today. One section is devoted to a large archaeology and natural-history museum, with an outstanding bronze Gallo-Roman statue of Apollo, a collection of Merovingian weapons, gold and garnet jewelry from Attila's time, and medieval sculpture from the 12th to the 15th centuries. Another section displays paintings from the 15th to the 20th centuries, including works by Boucher, Fragonard, David, and Watteau.

Pharmacie Musée de l'Hôtel-Dieu. Quai des Comtes de Champagne. ☎ **03-25-80-98-97.** Admission 20F ($3.60). Wed–Mon 10am–noon and 2–6pm.

The magnificent Hôtel-Dieu (hospital) of Troyes, founded in the 12th century by the comtes de Champagne, has been converted into a university, but it's still possible to visit this part of it. It's now a museum, one of the most unusual apothecary dispensaries in France. The laboratory contains ancient documents, a collection of pewter in all shapes and sizes, and such items as reliquaries from the 16th century. Painted wooden boxes and pots still hold herbs and other medicines.

SHOPPING

In the old town along **rue de la Cité,** is an array of antiques shops and galleries. Next, hit **rue Zola,** with its shops selling clothing, shoes, books, and regional gastronomic specialties.

While in town, look into the exclusive **Espace Art de la Table,** 26 rue de la République (☎ 03-25-73-31-25), for fine crystal and table settings; **Mortier d'Or,** 27 rue des Quinze Vingts (☎ 03-25-73-05-17), for local gastronomic products, including a selection of champagnes, andouilettes, and the sweet liqueur known as *prunelle de champagne;* or the refined **Palais du Chocolate,** 2 rue de la Monnaie (☎ 03-25-73-35-73), for a delectable light lunch and melt-in-your-mouth hand-made chocolates.

Looking for factory-outlet shopping and hefty savings? Try the two shopping centers just outside town with their 200 or so stores. **Marques Avenue,** 114 bd. de Dijon (☎ 03-25-82-00-72), is about 2 miles south of town in St-Julien-les-Villas. The other, approximately 2½ miles north of town in Pont-St-Marie, is **McArthur Glen,** voie du Bois (☎ 03-25-70-47-10).

Because Troyes was once the site of the knitting factories in France, it also has a free-standing outlet business. In fact, there are gobs of outlets all over town and, like the malls, in suburbs of Troyes like St-Julien-les-Villas. Try **Rodier,** 55 bd. du Quatorze-Juillet, Troyes (☎ 03-25-73-49-87), for knits from the famous maker of men's and women's ready-to-wear; **Tartine et Chocolat,** 3 rue Salomon-Rachi, Troyes (☎ 03-25-80-89-57), for well-styled kiddie clothes; and **Benetton,** rue Marc-Verdier, Pont-Ste-Marie (☎ 03-25-81-48-05), for the usual, which is made in France as well as in Italy.

WHERE TO STAY

Grand Hôtel/Patiotel. 4 av. Joffre, 10000 Troyes. ☎ **03-25-79-90-90.** Fax 03-25-78-48-93. 104 units. TV TEL. Grand Hôtel, 370F ($66.60) double; 750–950F ($135–$171) suite. Patiotel, 275F ($49.50) double. MC, V. Parking 50F ($9).

The core of this hotel/restaurant complex was built on a downtown street corner near the rail station in the 1930s and gained a reputation for comfort and respectability. In 1987, a U-shaped wing was added, and the budget Patiotel, with much less desirable rooms, opened. Today the Grand Hôtel and its less-expensive sibling share a lobby, breakfast room, covered pool, and garden but maintain completely different rates.

The rooms at the Grand are conservatively traditional, with minibars. Those at the Patiotel are modern and somewhat cramped, but all have windows opening onto the garden.

Dining: On the premises are five restaurants. The most elegant is Le Champagne, serving fixed-price meals that rival the price of a room at Patiotel. Less expensive are Le Jardin de la Louisiane, Le Grill Aquarius, Le Croco (a brasserie), and La Taverne de l'Ecailler (a pleasant place for unpretentious food).

Hôtel de la Poste. 35 rue Emile-Zola, 10000 Troyes. ☎ **800/528-1234** in the U.S., or 03-25-73-05-05. Fax 03-25-73-80-76. 40 units. MINIBAR TV TEL. 530–590F ($95.40–$106.20) double; 900F ($162) suite. AE, DC, MC, V.

This four-star hotel offers not only comfortable accommodations but also some of the city's finest dining. The rooms have sleek modern styling but, as an homage to the past, often have exposed ceiling beams as well.

Dining/Diversions: In addition to a modern bar, the hotel has two restaurants open Monday through Saturday; Les Gourmets features seafood prepared on a spit roaster, and Le Carpaccio is an Italian brasserie.

✪ **Les Champ des Oiseaux.** 20 rue Linard-Gonthier, 10000 Troyes. ☎ **03-25-80-58-50.** Fax 03-25-80-98-34. 15 units. TV TEL. 450–820F ($81–$147.60) double; 750–850F ($135–$153) suite. AE, DC, MC, V. Parking 50F ($9).

This hotel, dating back to 1465, is in the heart of the old town near the cathedral. The stone and half-timbered exterior gives way to a spectacularly restored interior straight out of the movie *Le Retour de Martin Guerre*. The rooms are of various sizes and offer unique touches—one may have a gloriously wide bay window, another a private alcove with a large double bed. All have hardwood floors, exposed beams, sloping ceilings, and antique furnishings. Windows look out on the private courtyard and garden, and guests can gather around the large open fireplace in the reception area or escape to the intimate library.

WHERE TO DINE

The restaurants at the **Hôtel de la Poste** (see above) are two other good choices.

Le Bourgogne. 40 rue du Général-de-Gaulle. ☎ **03-25-73-02-67.** Reservations required. Main courses 95–130F ($17.10–$23.40); fixed-price menu 175F ($31.50). MC, V. Mon–Sat 12:15–1:30pm, Tues–Sat 7:15–9:15pm. Closed Aug 3–26. FRENCH.

The owners, the Dubois brothers, are from Bresse, which has the finest poultry in France. Their refined cuisine is made with very fresh ingredients, and their wine cellar boasts several treasures. Specialties are duck liver with raspberry vinaigrette, grilled turbot in white butter, and sweetbreads Florentine style in puff pastry.

Le Valentino. Cour de la Rencontre. ☎ **03-25-73-14-14.** Main courses 90–160F ($16.20–$28.80); fixed-price menus 110–270F ($19.80–$48.60). AE, DC, V. Sun–Fri noon–2pm, Tues–Sat 7–10pm. Closed Jan 1–21. FRENCH.

Chef Alain Vattier operates a distinguished Art Deco dining room across from the town hall. He serves his *cuisine du marché* (based on market-fresh ingredients) on two terraces. Among the town's restaurateurs, M. Vattier is the seafood expert, and he attends the fish market every morning. Try his lobster with butter sauce flavored with orange juice or salmon cut into raviolilike pieces and served with caviar and shallot-flavored butter sauce. One food critic deplored his habit of adding "chi-chi touches" to the plates, but that seems like such a minor quibble about this original and well-balanced cuisine.

TROYES AFTER DARK

If you've already been down rue Zola while shopping, you surely noticed the many pubs and pool halls lining the street. You can hop from one place to another until something (or someone) grabs you. Particular bars of interest are **Le Tricasse,** 16 rue Paillor-de-Montabert (☎ **03-25-73-14-80**), with its French version of Gen-Xers mingling in a warm-paneled interior; and the **Bar Montabert,** 24 rue Paillot-de-Montabert (☎ **03-25-73-58-04**), a rowdy, pubby place with lots of traditional bar games, good beer, and fun people.

The Egyptian-themed disco **Planet Macumba,** place Claude-Huez (☎ **03-25-73-85-76**), blasts techno and funk all night long onto its three dance floors packed with young chic locals and their raging hormones. For a more mature dance scene, stop in **Le Caveau,** in front of the train station at 2 Cour de la Gare (☎ **03-25-78-22-35**). It's not as glitzy and has only two dance floors, but it still pulls people in—especially those who want to avoid the teenybopper scene. Admission to the discos is 10F ($1.80).

11 Alsace-Lorraine

The provinces of Alsace and Lorraine, with ancient capitals at Strasbourg and Nancy, respectively, have been much disputed by Germany and France. Alsace has been called "the least French of French provinces," more reminiscent of the Black Forest across the Rhine. In fact, it became German from 1870 until after World War I and then was ruled by Hitler from 1940 to 1944. But now both provinces are under French control, though they're somewhat independent.

In the Vosges mountains you can follow **La Route des Crêtes** (Crest Road) or skirt along the foothills, visiting the wine towns of Alsace. In its cities and cathedrals, the castle-dotted landscape evokes memories of a great past and (in battle monuments or scars) sometimes military glory or defeat. Lorraine is Joan of Arc country, and many of its towns still suggest their heritage from the Middle Ages.

REGIONAL CUISINE The ample use of pork and goose fat in Alsatian dishes gives the cuisine a distinctive flavor. Alsace is a leader in the production of pâtés, with more than 40 varieties, so you really must visit a local *charcuterie* (delicatessen) for a sampling. Don't miss the richly flavorful pâté de foie gras (goose-liver pâté).

In Lorraine, the joyful excesses of cholesterol are even more exaggerated. In addition to butter and loads of cream, local chefs use large quantities of salted lard. Even local pot-au-feu (known as *une potes*) replaces beef with salted lard and locally made pork sausages.

Other regional specialties are *choucroute* (sauerkraut) with sausages; salted ham, pork chops, or (in deluxe versions) truffles; chicken with Riesling; trout in cream, with Riesling, or simply fried (*au bleu*); Alsatian *kouglof* (made with almonds, dried raisins, sugar, milk, flour, and eggs); and a simple tart made with flour, milk, and sugar called *un ramequin*.

The most famous Alsatian beer is Kronenbourg, which you'll find in thousands of bars throughout France. There are more than 90 varieties of Alsatian wines, traditionally drunk from slender flutes whose glass is sometimes colored blue or green. The most celebrated Alsatian varieties are Riesling, gewürztraminer (traminer), pinot blanc, pinot gris, sylvaner, and muscat ottonel.

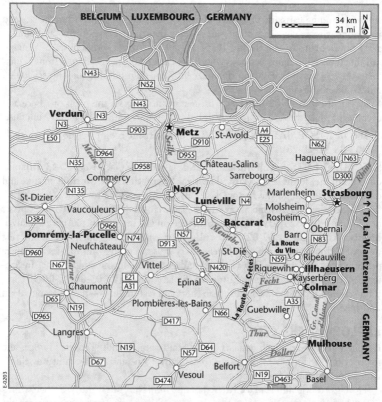

1 Strasbourg

303 miles SE of Paris, 135 miles SW of Frankfurt

The capital of Alsace, Strasbourg is one of France's greatest cities and is also the birth-place of pâté de foie gras. And it was in Strasbourg that Rouget de Lisle first sang "La Marseillaise" (the French national anthem).

Strasbourg is not only a great university city but also one of France's most impor-tant ports, being only 2 miles west of the Rhine. In addition to being host to the Council of Europe, Strasbourg is the meeting place of the European Parliament, which convenes at the Palais de l'Europe.

In 1871 Strasbourg was absorbed by Germany and made the capital of the imperial territory of Alsace-Lorraine, but it reverted to France in 1918. One street is a perfect illustration of the city's identity crisis: More than a century ago it was avenue Napoléon. In 1871 it became Kaiser-Wilhelmstrasse, then turned into boulevard de la République in 1918. In 1940 it became Adolf-Hitler-Strasse, then ended up as avenue du Général-de-Gaulle in 1945.

One of the most happening cities of France, Strasbourg today is the seat of the Uni-versity of Strasbourg, once attended by the likes of Goethe, Napoléon, and Pasteur. Today some 40,000 students follow in their footsteps.

ESSENTIALS

GETTING THERE The **Strasbourg-Entzheim Airport** (☎ 03-88-64-67-67), 9 miles southwest of the center, receives daily flights from many major European cities—including Paris and Frankfurt. Shuttle buses connect the airport to the city and run Monday to Friday every 30 minutes during the day and on Saturday and Sunday every time a plane arrives; the fare is 25F ($4.50) one-way. Strasbourg is a major **rail** junction. Nine trains per day arrive from Paris (trip time: 4 hours); from Nancy, there are 13 trains per day (trip time: 1½ hr.). For train information and schedules, call ☎ **08-36-35-35-39.**

By **car,** the giant N83 highway, with many lanes, crosses the plain of Alsace and becomes at times the A35 expressway. It links Strasbourg with Colmar and Mulhouse.

VISITOR INFORMATION   The **Office de Tourisme** is on place de la Cathédrale (☎ **03-88-52-28-28**).

SPECIAL EVENTS   **Wolf Music,** 24 rue de la Mésange (☎ **03-88-32-43-10**), puts on two summer festivals: the classical **Festival International de Musique** in June and the **Festival de Jazz** in the first week of July. Both feature performances by internationally acclaimed artists and always draw a large crowd despite the hefty ticket prices of 130F to 420F ($23.40 to $75.60); tickets go on sale in mid-April. Another festival, **Musica** (☎ **03-88-21-02-02**), takes place from the end of September to the first week of October and combines contemporary music concerts with movies and opera performances. Tickets are 80F ($14.40) and go on sale in the end of June. In September the **Forum du Cinema European,** 9 place Kléber (☎ **03-88-75-06-95**), features screenings of an array of European short and feature films—tickets go on sale in mid-July.

EXPLORING THE CITY

Despite war damage, much remains of Old Strasbourg, including covered bridges and towers from its former fortifications, plus many 15th- and 17th-century dwellings with painted wooden fronts and carved beams.

The city's traffic hub is **place Kléber,** dating from the 15th century. Sit here with a tankard of Alsatian beer and slowly get to know Strasbourg. The bronze statue in the center is of J. B. Kléber, born in Strasbourg in 1753; he became one of Napoléon's most noted generals and was buried under the monument. Apparently his presence offended the Nazis, who removed the statue in 1940. However, this Alsatian bronze was restored to its proper place in 1945 at the Liberation.

Next, take rue des Grandes-Arcades to **place Gutenberg,** one of the city's oldest squares and formerly a *marché aux herbes.* The central statue (1840) by David d'Angers is of Gutenberg, who perfected his printing press in Strasbourg in the winter of 1436–37. The former town hall, now the **Hôtel du Commerce,** was built in 1582 and is one of the most significant Renaissance buildings in all Alsace.

La Petite France is the most interesting quarter of Strasbourg. Its 16th-century houses are mirrored in the waters of the Ill. In "Little France," old roofs with gray tiles have sheltered families for ages, and the cross-beamed facades with their roughly carved rafters are in typical Alsatian style. Rue du Bain-aux-Plantes is of particular interest. An island in the middle of the river is cut by four canals—for a good view, walk along rue des Moulins, branching off from rue du Bain-aux-Plantes.

One of the most romantic ways to spend your time in Strasbourg is to take an excursion on the **Ill River,** leaving from the Palais de Rohan near the cathedral. Daytime outings operate year-round, but night excursions are offered only from May to October. The 75-minute cruise is 40F ($7.20) for adults and 20F ($3.60) for children and includes a prerecorded running commentary on the history of the region. Information is provided by the **Strasbourg-Fluvial,** 15 rue de Nantes (☎ **03-88-84-13-13**).

Strasbourg

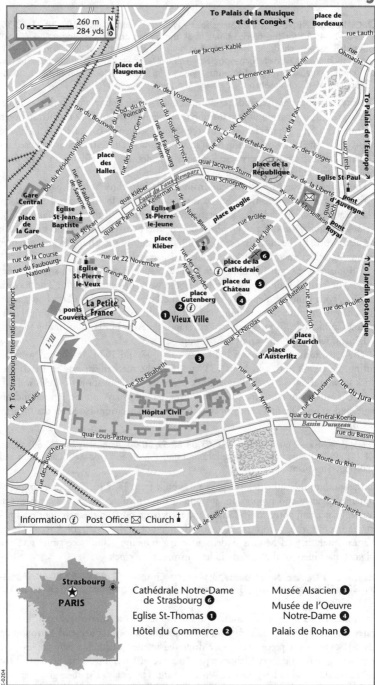

To Palais de la Musique et des Congès ↖

place de Bordeaux

rue Lauth

rue Jacques-Kablé

bd. Clemenceau

rue Oberlin

rue Ohmacht

place de Haugenau

av. des Vosges

rue du G.-de-Castelnau

To Palais de l'Europe ↗

rue du Travail

Bd. du Pr. Poincare

rue du Bouxwiller

rue du Fossé-des-Treize

rue du Faubourg de Pierre

rue du Fossé-des-Treize

rue du G.- Maréchal-Foch

av. de la Paix

av. des Vosges

rue des Bonnes-Cens

place des Halles

quai Jacques-Sturm

place de la République

Eglise St-Paul

Pont d'Auvergne

Gare Central

bd. du Président-Wilson

rue du Faubourg de Savnerne

quai Kléber

Fossé du Faux Rempart

quai Schoepflin

av. de la Liberté

Pont Royal

rue Koch

quai Kellermann

quai St-Jean

quai de Paris

Eglise St-Pierre-le-Jeune

rue de la Nuée-Bleu

place Broglie

rue Brûlée

av. de la Marseillaise

place de la Gare

Eglise St-Jean-Baptiste

rue Déserté

rue de la Course

rue du Faubourg-National

Eglise St-Pierre-le-Veux

rue de 22 Novembre

Grand' Rue

place Kléber

rue des Grandes Arcades

rue des Juifs

place de la Cathédrale ⓘ

place du Château ❺

place Gutenberg ❷ ⓘ

❻

❶ Vieux Ville

❹

rue des Bateliers

rue de Zurich

rue des Poules

To Jardin Botanique

La Petite France

ponts Couverts

L'Ill

❸

quai St-Nicolas

place de Zurich

place d'Austerlitz

rue Ste-Elisabeth

rue de la 1er Armée

rue de Lausanne

rue du Jura

rue de Saales

Hôpital Civil

quai du Général-Koenig

Bassin Dusuzeau

rue du Bassin

quai Louis-Pasteur

Route du Rhin

rue des Bouchers

rue de Belfort

av. Jean-Jaurès

0 — 260 m / 284 yds   N

Information ⓘ   Post Office ✉   Church ✝

Strasbourg ★   PARIS

Cathédrale Notre-Dame de Strasbourg ❻

Eglise St-Thomas ❶

Hôtel du Commerce ❷

Musée Alsacien ❸

Musée de l'Oeuvre Notre-Dame ❹

Palais de Rohan ❺

E-0204

335

✪ **Cathédrale Notre-Dame de Strasbourg.** Place de la Cathédrale. ☎ **03-88-21-43-34,** or 03-88-21-43-30 for the precise times of all the masses and offices. Tower 20F ($3.60) adults, 10F ($1.80) children. Tower July–Aug daily 8:30am–7pm; Apr–June and Sept daily 9am–5:30pm; Mar–Oct daily 9am–5pm; Nov–Feb daily 9am–4:30pm. (You may have to wait to climb the tower.) Close-up views of the clock available noon–12:30pm for 5F (90¢); tickets on sale daily in the south portal at 11:30am.

The city's crowning glory stands proudly, an outstanding example of Gothic architecture, representing a harmonious transition from the Romanesque. Construction began on it in 1176. The pyramidal tower in rose-colored stone was completed in 1439 and at 469 feet is the tallest one dating from medieval times. This cathedral is still used for Roman Catholic worship services. Religious ceremonies, particularly on feast days, meld perfectly with the historic majesty of this place.

Four large counterforts divide the main facade into three vertical parts and two horizontal galleries. Note the great **rose window,** which looks like real stone lace. The facade is rich in sculptural decoration: On the portal of the south transept, the *Coronation and Death of the Virgin* in one of the two tympana is the finest such medieval work. In the north transept, see also the facade of the **Chapelle St-Laurence,** a stunning achievement of the late Gothic German style.

A Romanesque **crypt** lies under the chancel, which is covered with square stonework. The central stained-glass window is the work of Max Ingrand. The **nave** is majestic, with windows depicting emperors and kings on the north Strasbourg aisle. Five chapels are grouped around the transept, including one built in 1500 in the Flamboyant Gothic style. In the south transept stands the **Angel Pillar,** illustrating the Last Judgment, with angels lowering their trumpets.

The **astronomical clock** was built between 1547 and 1574. It stopped working during the Revolution, and from 1838 to 1842 the mechanism was replaced. The clock is wound once a week. People flock to see its 12:30pm show of allegorical figures. On Sunday Apollo drives his sun horses, on Thursday you see Jupiter and his eagle, and so on. The main body of the clock has a planetarium based on the theories of Copernicus.

Palais de Rohan. 2 place du Château. ☎ **03-88-52-50-00.** Admission 20F ($3.60) adults, 10F ($1.80) students, free for children 15 and under. Mon and Wed–Sat 10am–noon and 1:30–6pm, Sun 10am–5pm.

To the south of the cathedral, the palace was built from 1732 to 1742, an example of supreme elegance and proportion. It's one of the crowning design achievements in eastern France and noted for its facades and rococo interior. On the first floor is a fine-arts museum, with works by Rubens, Rembrandt, van Dyck, El Greco, Goya, Watteau, Renoir, and Monet. A decorative-arts museum exhibits ceramics and the original machinery of the cathedral's first astronomical clock.

Musée de l'Oeuvre Notre-Dame. 3 place du Château. ☎ **03-88-52-50-00.** Admission 20F ($3.60) adults, 10F ($1.80) children. Tues–Sat 10am–noon and 1:30–6pm, Sun 10am–5pm.

The museum occupies a collection of ancient houses with wooden galleries. It illustrates the art of the Middle Ages and Renaissance in Strasbourg and surrounding Alsace. Some of the pieces were once displayed in the cathedral, where copies have been substituted. The most celebrated prize is a circa-1070 stained-glass head of Christ from a window said to have been at Wissembourg. There's also a stained-glass window depicting an emperor from around 1200. The medieval sculpture is of great interest, as are the works of Strasbourg goldsmiths from the 16th and 17th centuries. The winding staircase and interior are in the pure Renaissance style. The 13th-century hall contains the loveliest sculptures from the cathedral, including the wise and foolish virgins from 1280.

Musée Alsacien. 23 quai St-Nicolas. ☎ **03-88-35-55-36.** Admission 20F ($3.60) adults, 10F ($1.80) students, free for children and seniors. Mon and Wed–Sat 10am–noon and 1:30–6pm, Sun 10am–5pm.

This occupies three mansions from the 16th and 17th centuries and is like a living textbook of the folklore and customs of Alsace, containing arts, crafts, and tools of the old province.

Eglise St-Thomas. Rue Martin-Luther (along rue St-Thomas, near pont St-Thomas). ☎ **03-88-32-14-46.** Free admission. Mar–Oct daily 10am–6pm (to 5pm in winter).

Built between 1230 and 1330, this Protestant church boasts five naves. It contains the mausoleum of Maréchal de Saxe, a masterpiece of French art by Pigalle (1777).

SHOPPING

Strasbourg overflows with antiques shops, artisans, craftspeople, and beer makers.

Every well-accessorized home in Alsace stocks at least some of the napkins, aprons, tablecloths, and tea and bath towels of the Beauvillé textile mills, one of eastern France's largest producers. One of its premier outlets is **Nappes d'Alsace,** 6 rue Mercière (☎ **03-88-22-69-29**). Very close to the cathedral, this store has one of the widest selections of textiles in town.

Bastian, 22–24 place de la Cathédrale (☎ **03-88-32-45-93**), specializes in the 18th- and 19th-century ceramic tureens that Alsace produced with charm and abundance. Look for ragoût pots with the form of a cabbage, a trout, a boar's head, or a turkey, brightly painted in appetizing colors. There's also a selection of Louis XV and Louis XVI furniture, crafted in the region during the 18th and 19th centuries, that follows Parisian models from the same era.

Bastian's main competitor is **Antiquités de l'Ill, 23 quai des Bateliers** (☎ **03-88-36-96-84**), in a Renaissance-style 17th-century building across from the Palais de Rohan. Standout items are polychromed Alsatian antiques (especially 18th- and 19th-century armoires and chests of drawers), Louis- and Directoire-style furnishings, and statues and antique paintings.

More affordable and accessible is **Arts et Collections d'Alsace,** 18 quai des Bateliers (☎ **03-88-14-03-77**). This outlet sells copies of articles found exclusively in Alsatian museums or prestigious private collections. Look for articles in wood, glass, stone, and ceramics. A name you're likely to encounter is Soufflenheim, a provincial rococo pattern named after the Alsatian village where the style originated.

If you're looking for ceramics and pottery, consider an excursion 17 miles north to this village. Ceramics and pottery have been staples of the economy here since the bronze age, and Soufflenheim contains at least 15 factory outlets selling cake molds, tureens, saucers and cups, and dinnerware sets, usually in rustic patterns of enduring charm. One of the most prominent of the outlets belongs to local manufacturer **Gérard Wehrling,** 64 rue de Haguenau (☎ **03-88-86-65-25**). Selling directly to visitors, it's known for pottery that can withstand the rigors of modern ovens, microwaves, and freezers. Expect to pay about 300F ($54) for a large casserole.

And if you're driving around, you may want to check out the nearby villages of Obernai, Illhauesern, Ribeauville, and Schiltigheim (the last is beer-drinking territory; the others offer country wares, antiques, warrenlike old-fashioned streets, and pure charm).

WHERE TO STAY
VERY EXPENSIVE

Hilton International Strasbourg. Av. Herrenschmidt, 67000 Strasbourg. ☎ **800/ 445-8667** in the U.S. and Canada, or 03-88-37-10-10. Fax 03-88-36-83-27. www.hilton.com or www.travelweb.com/hiltnint.html. 246 units. A/C MINIBAR TV TEL. 1,200–1,600 F ($216–$288) double; from 5,700F ($1,026) suite. AE, MC, V. Parking 65F ($11.70). Take the Strasbourg-Centre exit from the autoroute and follow signs to the Wacken, Palais des Congrès, and Palais de l'Europe.

The seven-story Hilton International is quite luxurious. The steel-and-glass hotel stands over a university complex and is opposite the Palais de la Musique et des Congrès. Five kinds of Iberian marble were used in the decor—much of it chosen to resemble the ruddy sandstone of the famous cathedral, visible from the hotel. The guest rooms contain tasteful artwork and spacious marble-trimmed bathrooms; some are suitable for nonsmokers or persons with disabilities.

Dining/Diversions: Live music and guests ranging from heads of state to international visitors make the hotel's Bugatti Bar the town's social center. The moderately priced Le Jardin du Tivoli offers a buffet at all three meals. Some evenings are devoted to special themes, like seafood, Italian, or vegetarian. There's also a brasserie and a buffet.

Amenities: Room service (24 hours), laundry, dry cleaning, boutique, interpretive/ secretarial facilities.

✪ Le Régent Petite France. 5 rue des Moulins, 67000 Strasbourg. ☎ **800/223-5652** in the U.S. and Canada, or 03-88-76-43-43. Fax 03-88-76-43-76. 72 units. 1,090–1,490F ($196.20–$268.20) double; 1,850–2,300F ($333–$414) suite. AE, DC, MC, V.

Opened in 1992, this is the first serious challenger in years to the Hilton, and many guests check in here for its more comfortable rooms and more intriguing atmosphere. This site on the banks of the Ill was once an ice factory, and many of its old steam machines were wisely kept in place as artifacts of a vanished era. The large marble lobby sets the design note, with summery ice-cream colors, potted palms, and paintings. Guest rooms come in various sizes, the best of which are quite spacious and open onto river views. The staff is one of the finest in Strasbourg.

Dining: The river-view restaurant serves fine Alsatian cuisine.

Amenities: Jacuzzi, sauna, concierge, room service, dry cleaning/laundry, fitness club.

EXPENSIVE

Hôtel Beaucour. 5 rue Bouchers, 67000 Strasbourg. ☎ **03-88-76-72-00.** Fax 03-88-76-72-60. 56 units. A/C MINIBAR TV TEL. 780F ($140.40) double; from 950F ($171) suite. AE, DC, MC, V. Parking 45F ($8.10).

This three-star hotel is geared mainly to business travelers, but anyone will find it ideal. At the end of a private street a few blocks east of the cathedral, it occupies a 17th-century building with lots of timbered ceilings and is the city's most tranquil hotel. Both the rooms and the suites harmoniously blend modern and traditional furnishings; every room has a whirlpool tub, a fax hookup, and computer connections. The best rooms are the three Alsatian suites. The hotel maintains an affiliation with three restaurants a short walk away.

Amenities: The concierge, who seems to know all the city's secrets, will gladly make reservations for you.

✪ Le Régent Contades. 8 av. de la Liberté, 67000 Strasbourg. ☎ **03-88-15-05-05.** Fax 03-88-15-05-15. 45 units. A/C MINIBAR TV TEL. 820–2,000F ($147.60–$360) double. AE, DC, MC, V.

Our favorite choice in Strasbourg outshines its competition, except for Le Régent Petite France, its main rival. Le Régent Contades is a glorified B&B, housed in a regal three-story structure with dormers, close to both the cathedral and the Rhine. Diplomats often guard it as a secret address—but the secret is out. The hostelry is stylish and fashionable and has an intelligent and helpful staff. The guest rooms are alluring, furnished with classic style. The most spacious are in a new wing offering 14 accommodations.

Dining: Breakfast is the only meal served, though 24-hour room service is available.
Amenities: Sauna and solarium.

MODERATE

Hôtel de l'Europe. 38–40 rue du Fosse-des-Tanneurs, 67000 Strasbourg. ☎ **03-88-32-17-88.** Fax 03-88-75-65-45. www.strasbourg.com/hotel-europe. E-mail: hoteleurope@tpgnet.net. 60 units. MINIBAR TV TEL. 610–950F ($109.80–$171) double. AE, DC, MC, V. Parking 70F ($12.60).

Behind a half-timbered facade a 3-minute walk west of the cathedral, this is one of the best-located three-star hotels in town. Its roots go back to the 15th century, when it functioned as a coaching inn, and it was later enlarged with the annexation of an 18th-century house next door. It's frequently renovated and today offers an elevator and all the electronic gadgets you might want. It's comfortable and unpretentious. About a third of the rooms are air-conditioned. They run the gamut from glossily modern to a half-timbered fantasy directly under the roof (no. 404), where steeply angled beams evoke the original construction. There's no in-house restaurant, but room service is available 24 hours.

✪ **Hôtel des Rohan.** 17–19 rue du Maroquin, 67000 Strasbourg. ☎ **03-88-32-85-11.** Fax 03-88-75-65-37. www.hotel-rohan.com. E-mail: info@hotel-rohan.com. 36 units. TV TEL. 595–795F ($107.10–$143.10) double. AE, DC, MC, V.

In the pedestrian-only zone, 50 yards from the cathedral, this is one of the city's best values, with nearby underground parking. The hotel is within walking distance of the Palais des Rohan, from which it takes its name. It offers a choice of elegantly furnished rooms, the cheapest of which are small and have a French bed called a *matrimonial,* which is a standard double bed. Large and more classic rooms have either a large double bed or twin beds. Twenty-four of the rooms are air-conditioned.

Hôtel Monopole-Métropole. 16 rue Kuhn, 67000 Strasbourg. ☎ **800/528-1234** in the U.S., or 03-88-14-39-14. Fax 03-88-32-82-55. www.strasbourg.com/best-western. 90 units. A/C MINIBAR TV TEL. 550–750F ($99–$135) double. AE, DC, MC, V. Parking 50F ($9).

The Monopole-Métropole is on a quiet street corner near the train station and has a modern lobby with a scattering of antiques, among them a 17th-century carved armoire and a bronze statue of a night watchman. An extension of the salon displays oil portraits of 18th-century Alsatian personalities and glass cases with pewter tankards and brass candlesticks. Breakfast (the only meal served) is presented in the high-ceilinged Alsatian-style dining room. Each guest room is unique—many contain Louis-Philippe antiques. Léon and Monique Siegel are the proprietors; members of their family have owned this place since 1919.

INEXPENSIVE

Hôtel de l'Ill. 8 rue des Bateliers, 67000 Strasbourg. ☎ **03-88-36-20-01.** Fax 03-88-35-30-03. 27 units. TV TEL. 245–370F ($44.10–$66.60) double. MC, V. Bus: 10 direct from the train station.

A 5-minute walk from the cathedral, this two-star hotel is a good value for Strasbourg. An inviting little place, it offers comfortably furnished and quiet rooms. Each is in either a modern or an Alsatian traditional style (smoking and no-smoking rooms are available). Those at the rear contain a private terrace or balcony, opening onto a view of neighboring gardens. Breakfast is served in a room with a cuckoo clock, decorated in Laura Ashley style.

Hôtel des Princes. 33 rue Geiler, Conseil de l'Europe, 67000 Strasbourg. ☎ **03-88-61-55-19.** Fax 03-88-41-10-92. www.perso.hol.fr/hdprince. 43 units. TEL. 410–550F ($73.80–$99) double. AE, V. Bus: 20.

A 15-minute walk from the center of town, the Hôtel des Princes has received a three-star government rating and is one of the best values in the city. The management is helpful, and the rooms are furnished comfortably but simply. A continental breakfast is the only meal served.

WHERE TO DINE
VERY EXPENSIVE

✪ **Au Crocodile.** 10 rue de l'Outre. ☎ **03-88-32-13-02.** Reservations required. Main courses 185–295F ($33.30–$53.10); fixed-price menus 295F ($53.10) at lunch, 420–650F ($75.60–$117) at dinner. AE, DC, MC, V. Tues–Sat noon–1:45pm and 7–9:30pm. Closed the last 3 weeks of July and Dec 24–Jan 1. ALSATIAN.

A beautifully skylit restaurant, Au Crocodile serves some of the most inventive food in Strasbourg. If we awarded more than one star, we'd give this one three. There are only two restaurants in this entire region of France to equal it: Buerehiesel (below) and the Auberge de l'Ill (see section 3 in this chapter). Chef Emile Jung offers a wide array of dishes, like salmon-and-eel terrine with tarragon and cucumber and cauliflower *à la grecque*, pike-perch filet with timbale of chicken livers and crayfish tails, and truffled goose liver with vegetables and potatoes. His menu continues to be charged with energy and inventiveness. Our major problem with the place comes only when the bill (or *la note*, as the French say) does, especially when you indulge in those high-priced wines.

✪ **Buerehiesel.** 4 parc de l'Orangerie. ☎ **03-88-45-56-65.** Reservations required. Main courses 190–290F ($34.20–$52.20); fixed-price menus 340–690F ($61.20–$124.20). AE, DC, MC, V. Thurs–Mon noon–2:30pm and 7:30–10pm. Closed Feb 16–27, Aug 10–26, and Dec 22–Jan 5. FRENCH.

Also known as Chez Westermann, Buerehiesel is famous for Antoine Westermann's *cuisine moderne,* as well as for the restaurant's prime location—in l'Orangerie, a beautiful park at the end of the allée de la Robertsau that was planned by the landscape artist Le Nôtre, who gave it to Joséphine. Main courses might include sole and lobster *à la nage* (cooked in court bouillon and flavored with herbs), *salmis de pigeon au Bourgogne,* whole Bresse chicken with truffles, and braised sweetbreads with truffles. We cannot praise the cuisine too highly: Distantly remembered recipes are brought down from the attic and recycled here in innovative and exciting ways. Even though the place elevates stuffiness to an art form, the movers and shakers of the European Union seem to lap it up.

EXPENSIVE

Maison des Tanneurs. 42 rue du Bain-aux-Plantes. ☎ **03-88-32-79-70.** Reservations required. Main courses 120–170F ($21.60–$30.60); fixed-price menus 245–285F ($44.10–$51.30). AE, DC, MC, V. Tues–Sat noon–2:15pm and 7:15–10pm (also open for Sun lunch in summer). Closed July 21–Aug 12 and Dec 23–Jan 15. ALSATIAN.

With an overworked staff that rushes sometimes frantically from one task to another, this restaurant stands on a typical street in the Petite France quarter. Flowers and Alsatian antiques create a warm atmosphere, and the dining terrace opens onto the canal.

It has been called La Maison de la Choucroute, as the sauerkraut-and-pork platter is a specialty, the finest in the area. But the chef prepares many other dishes as well, including an extravagant parfait of foie gras with fresh truffles. Main courses we recommend are crayfish tails in court bouillon, guinea fowl with green peppercorns served on a bed of sauerkraut, and coq au Riesling (chicken cooked in white wine and served with noodles).

Maison Kammerzell. 16 place de la Cathédrale. ☎ **03-88-32-42-14.** Reservations required. Main courses 85–120F ($15.30–$21.60); fixed-price menus 195–295F ($35.10–$53.10). AE, DC, MC, V. Daily noon–3pm and 7–11:30pm. ALSATIAN.

The gingerbread Maison Kammerzell is a sightseeing attraction as well as a fantastic restaurant. The carved-wood framework was constructed during the Renaissance; the overhanging stories were built in 1589. We suggest *la choucroute formidable* (for two), the Alsatian specialty prepared with goose fat and Riesling wine, as well as Strasbourg sausages and smoked breast of pork. The owner, Guy-Pierre Baumann, also offers guinea hen with mushrooms, medallion of young wild boar, filet of beef Vigneronne with vegetables, and other regional dishes.

MODERATE

L'Arsenal. 11 rue de l'Abreuvoir. ☎ **03-88-35-03-69.** Reservations required. Main courses 78–150F ($14.05–$27); fixed-price menus 140F and 250F ($25.20 and $45). AE, DC, V. Mon–Fri noon–2pm, Mon–Sat 7:15–9:30pm. Closed 8 days in Feb and Aug 1–21. ALSATIAN.

This pleasant Alsatian restaurant is in a historic building and often counts European Parliament members among its patrons. The inventive regional menu changes often but may feature young rabbit and goose liver in jelly, veal escalope and calf's feet in red-wine sauce, or carp and salmon on sauerkraut. A specialty of the house is kouglhof with escargots—normally this pastry is sweet, but the chef here makes it salted with snails.

INEXPENSIVE

✪ **Brasserie de l'Ancienne Douane.** 6 rue de la Douane. ☎ **03-88-15-78-78.** Reservations recommended. Main courses 79–135F ($14.20–$24.30); fixed-price menus 90–160F ($16.20–$28.80); children's menu 49F ($8.80). AE, DC, MC, V. Daily 11:30am–11pm. Closed Jan 8–22. ALSATIAN.

This is the largest and most colorful dining spot in Strasbourg. Established as part of a historic renovation, it offers 600 seats indoors and 200 seats on a terrace. From the outside, along a street in the oldest part of town, you'll see the arcades of the lower floor and the small windows of the stone facade. The high-ceilinged rooms are somewhat formal, with Teutonic chairs and heavily timbered ceilings. Among the Alsatian specialties are the well-known "sauerkraut of the Customs officers" and the foie gras of Strasbourg; chicken in Riesling with Alsatian noodles; onion pie; and ham knuckle with potato salad and horseradish also are popular.

NEARBY DINING

Instead of dining in Strasbourg, many visitors drive north for 7½ miles to the village of La Wantzenau, which has very good restaurants. From Strasbourg, travel northeast on D468, which runs along the west bank of the Rhine.

✪ **A la Barrière.** 3 rte. de Strasbourg. ☎ **03-88-96-20-23.** Reservations required. Main courses 85–175F ($15.30–$31.50); fixed-price menu 250F ($45). AE, DC, MC, V. Thurs–Tues noon–2:30pm, Thurs–Mon 7–9:30pm. Closed Feb and Aug 7–30. FRENCH.

This restaurant is a 5-minute walk from the center of La Wantzenau. In a restrained Art Deco interior, Claude Sutter, former pupil of the recently retired master chef and original founder, prepares a sophisticated cuisine. The menu might include filet of sole with scallops and scampi in ginger sauce, roast rack of lamb with a potato casserole, white ocean fish with celery and tomatoes, and salmon steaks with sorrel. In autumn the game dishes (especially pheasant and venison) are excellent.

STRASBOURG AFTER DARK

For family fun in July and August, head to La Petite France and its ponts Converts around 9 or 10pm for *Les Nuits de Strass*—a water-show spectacular with fountains, lasers, music, and entertainers. Another bastion of outdoor entertainment is **place de la Cathédrale,** where you can find an astonishing assortment of street performers and artists. For a chance to see folk-dancing troupes from the world over, go to the **Palais des Rohan** around 8:30pm in summer. Performance dates vary, so check with the Office de Tourisme (see "Essentials," above) for a precise schedule.

For opera and ballet, try the **Opéra du Rhin,** 19 place Broglie (☎ 03-88-75-48-01), with tickets at 70 to 300 F ($12.60 to $54). The **Orchestre Philharmonique de Strasbourg** gives concerts at the Palais de la Musique et des Congrès, place de Bordeaux (☎ **03-88-15-09-09** for tickets or 03-88-15-09-00 for more information). Tickets cost 135F to 245F ($24.30 to $44.10). The **Théâtre National de Strasbourg** also has a busy schedule. Its venue is at 1 av. de la Marseillaise (☎ **03-88-24-88-24**), with tickets costing 140F ($25.20) October to May. And from May to September, short organ and trumpet **concerts** are given each evening at 9pm in the cathedral. Tickets are 40F ($7.20).

For the **club scene,** head over to the streets surrounding place de la Cathédrale: rue des Frères, rue des Soeurs, and rue de la Croix. For jazz and blues, your best bets are **Gayot Piano Jazz,** 18 rue des Frères (☎ 03-88-36-31-88), with occasional guest performers; and the more refined though still sultry **Le Bistro Piano Bar,** 30 rue des Tonneliers (☎ **03-88-23-02-71**), with a jazz piano player and free concerts Wednesday, Friday, and Saturday. **Café des Anges,** 5 rue Ste-Catherine (☎ **03-88-37-12-67**), provides an underground dance floor converted from an old wine cellar as well as a ground-level bar/concert area that hosts anything from rock and jazz to reggae. The dance club never has a cover charge, but for concerts expect to pay between 25F and 50F ($4.50 and $9).

The trendiest dance clubs are the small **Le Rock's Academy,** 56 rue Jeu-des-Enfants (☎ **03-88-32-21-43**), where you can expect to be overrun by an extremely young crowd, most of whom haven't even hit 18 yet; and **The Best of Music,** 25 rue des Tonneliers (☎ **03-88-32-61-50**), with a below-street-level dance floor that features any type of music but disco. The place stays packed with a stylish crowd between 20 and 35. Cover charges at the two dance clubs range between 30F and 60F ($5.40 and $10.80).

Gays and lesbians should head for either of the leading gay discos: **Le Warning,** 3 rue Klein (☎ **03-88-37-99-33**), and its more opulent competitor, **Monte Carl',** 1 quai Turkheim (☎ **03-88-22-35-02**), which attracts greater numbers of gay women.

2 La Route du Vin (Wine Road)

From Strasbourg, motorists heading south for 42 miles to Colmar can take the N83 direct route. However, if you've got time, the famous *Route du Vin* (Wine Road) makes a rewarding experience. For 60 miles the road passes through charming villages, many illuminated on summer nights for your viewing pleasure. Along the way are country inns if you'd like to sample some of the wine, take a leisurely lunch or dinner, or rent a room for the night.

The Wine Road runs along the Vosges foothills, with medieval towers and feudal ruins evoking faded pageantry. Of course, the slopes are covered with vines, as there's an estimated 50,000 acres of vineyards along this road, sometimes reaching a height of 1,450 feet. Some 30,000 families earn their living tending the grapes. The best time to go is for the vintage in September and October.

The traditional route starts at Marlenheim.

MARLENHEIM

This agreeable wine town—noted for its Vorlauf red wine—is 13 miles due west of Strasbourg on N4. You might want to visit it even if you can't take the drive the full length of the Wine Road, as it offers an excellent inn.

WHERE TO STAY & DINE

✪ **Hostellerie du Cerf.** 30 rue du Général-de-Gaulle, 67520 Marlenheim. ☎ **03-88-87-73-73.** Fax 03-88-87-68-08. 17 units. TEL. 385–850F ($69.30–$153) double; 650F ($117) suite. AE, DC, MC, V. Parking 10F ($1.80).

In the heart of this medieval village, occupying a half-timbered building at least 300 years old, this hotel offers pleasantly furnished rooms adjoining an excellent restaurant.

Dining: Robert Husser and his son, Michel, will feed you specialties like fresh foie gras, cassoulet of lobster, ballotine of quail (autumn only) with sweetbreads, oysters cooked in court bouillon and flavored with herbs, and roast turbot with vegetables. One of the most charming offerings is an all-Alsatian fixed-price meal for 395F ($71.10). Other fixed-price meals begin at 295F ($53.10) at lunch during the week. Regular fixed-price menus are 395F to 550F ($71.10 to $99). The restaurant is closed on Tuesday and Wednesday; on other days, the service hours are noon to 2:15pm and 7 to 9:30pm.

WANGEN

One of the many jewels along the route, Wangen (18.6 miles from Strasbourg) contains a city gate crowned by a tower and twisting narrow streets. It's one of the most typical of the Alsatian wine towns. The road from Wangen winds down to Molsheim.

MOLSHEIM

One of the 10 free cities of Alsace, called the "Decapolis," Molsheim (15½ miles from Strasbourg) retains its old ramparts and a Gothic/Renaissance church built from 1614 to 1619. Its *Alte Metzig* (town hall) was erected by the Guild of Butchers and is a most interesting sight, with its turret, gargoyles, loggia, and a belfry housing a clock with allegorical figures striking the hour.

ROSHEIM

Nestled behind medieval fortifications, this old wine-producing town (19¼ miles from Strasbourg)—another of the 10 free Alsatian cities—has a 12th-century Romanesque house and the Eglise St-Pierre et St-Paul, also Romanesque, from two centuries later; it's dominated by an octagonal tower. Medieval walls and gate towers evoke its past.

OBERNAI

The patron saint of Alsace, Obernai, was born here. Located 20 miles from Strasbourg, and with old timbered houses and a colorful marketplace, **place du Marché,** this is one of the most interesting stopovers on the Wine Route. The market is staged Thursday from 8am to noon; go early. **Place de l'Etoile** is decked out in flowers, and

La Formidable Choucroute

There's no single recipe and no universal preparation, even in Alsace, but *choucroute garnie à l'alsacienne* is the dish most often associated with the province. Best consumed when the leaves start falling, it's a hearty dish intended to fortify hardworking bodies against the coming winter. You'll know autumn is at hand when in restaurant windows you see signs announcing NOUVELLE CHOUCROUTE—the season's first batch of cabbage marinated for weeks in herbs and salt brine, with hints of crunchiness and acidity permeating the healthful fibers. Added zest comes from juniper berries, caraway seeds, freshly ground pepper, bouquet garni, bacon fat, and (in truly classic versions) a dollop or two of goose fat.

Choucroute and its perfect accompaniment, Riesling, are both products of Alsace. Potatoes and cabbage are produced locally and can be stored in barrels in a cool cellar through a long cropless winter. Since the Middle Ages, local farmers have produced vast amounts of pork products, some traditionally smoked over fir or cherrywood fires to impart the earthy taste that permeates the shredded cabbage. The sanitized version you'll likely encounter in restaurants will include only the choicest cuts of pork (a variety of chops, sausages, knuckles, and offal keeps even the most jaded diner from growing bored). Earthier, more traditional versions that many Alsatians are likely to remember from their childhoods include pork brains, entrails, feet, ears, tail, and pork-liver dumplings. Regardless of the ingredients, many diners find the result nothing less than *formidable*.

So how does a connoisseur identify the best choucroute? A worthy version is easy to digest, is free of excess grease and/or acidity, and doesn't float on a lake of juices. The dish should be cooked carefully so the potatoes don't turn to mush; and the meat and marinated cabbage should gracefully blend so they coordinate with the flavors of an Alsatian Riesling. (Enjoying it with a hearty glass or two of beer is a dignified alternative, but if you opt for other types of liquid accompaniments you're likely to be labeled an infidel.)

How can you tell whether the sauerkraut you're eating is authentically strasbourgeoise or the rip-off version served in Germany? The difference is in the sausage, which any charcutier within 40 miles of either side of the Rhine could identify as *vraiment alsacien* (frankfurters best consumed with beer and mustard).

Riesling is the king of Alsatian wine, with its exquisitely perfumed bouquet. Other regional wines are chasselas, knipperle, sylvaner, pinot blanc (one of the oldest), muscat, pinot gris, pinot auxerrois, traminer, and gewürztraminer.

the 1523 Hôtel de Ville has a delightful loggia (inside you can see the council chamber). An old watchtower, the **Tour de la Chapelle,** is from the 13th and 16th centuries. The town's six-pail **fountain** is one of the most spectacular in Alsace. The **Office de Tourisme** is at place du Beffroi (☎ **03-88-95-64-13**).

WHERE TO STAY & DINE

Le Parc. 169 rte. d'Ottrott, 67210 Obernai. ☎ **03-88-95-50-08.** Fax 03-88-95-37-29. 57 units. TV TEL. 590–990F ($106.20–$178.20) double; 990–1,400F ($178.20–$252) suite. AE, MC, V. Closed June 29–July 11 and Dec 8–Jan 6.

This contemporary hotel, most recently renovated in 1996, offers wonderful dining and many of the facilities you'd find in a health spa, with a decorative motif and architectural style of traditional Alsacian. Surrounded by a verdant park, it has well-furnished, spacious rooms that are often used by harried city dwellers seeking rest and recuperation.

Dining: There's a well-recommended restaurant with three dining rooms. The food depends on what's available in the local markets and may include monkfish with mushrooms, duckling with apples and *cèpes* (flap mushrooms), salad of foie gras, salmon in red-wine sauce, and rich fruit desserts. Fixed-price menus are 365F ($65.70). The dining rooms are closed Sunday night and Monday; sometime during the lifetime of this edition, the management will add an informal brasserie serving mostly Alsatian specialties.

Amenities: Hot tub, sauna, steam room, indoor and outdoor pools, fitness center.

BARR

The grapes for some of the finest Alsatian wines, sylvaner and gewürztraminer, are harvested here. The castles of Landsberg and Andlau stand high above the town. Barr (23 miles from Strasbourg) has many pleasant old timbered houses and a charming **place de l'Hôtel-de-Ville** with a town hall from 1640.

MITTELBERGHEIM

Perched like a stork on a housetop, this is a special village. Its place de l'Hôtel-de-Ville is bordered by houses in the Renaissance style.

WHERE TO STAY & DINE

Winstub Gilg. 1 rte. du Vin, Mittelbergheim, 67140 Barr. ☎ **03-88-08-91-37.** Fax 03-88-08-45-17. 15 units. TV TEL. 250–400F ($45–$72) double. AE, DC, MC, V.

This is an excellent inn. Though parts of the building date from 1614, its architectural showpiece is a two-story stone staircase, classified a historic monument, which was carved by the medieval stonemasons who worked on the cathedral at Strasbourg. The rooms are attractively furnished.

Dining: Chef Georges Gilg attracts a loyal following with regional specialties like onion tart, sauerkraut, and foie gras in brioche. His main courses include stewed kidneys and sweetbreads and duck with oranges. In season, he's likely to offer roast pheasant with grapes and filet of roebuck. Fixed-price menus run 125F to 350F ($22.50 to $63). The restaurant is closed Tuesday night and Wednesday and from June 23 to July 9.

ANDLAU

This gardenlike resort, located 26 miles from Strasbourg, was once the site of an abbey dating from 887, founded by the disgraced wife of Emperor Charles the Fat. It has now faded into history, but a church remains that dates from the 12th century. In the tympanum are noteworthy Romanesque carvings.

WHERE TO DINE

Au Boeuf Rouge. 6 rue du Dr.-Stoltz. ☎ **03-88-08-96-26.** Reservations recommended. Main courses 85–147F ($15.30–$26.45); fixed-price menus 98–175F ($17.65–$31.50). AE, DC, MC, V. Fri–Wed 11am–3pm, Fri–Tues 6:30–9:30pm. Closed Jan 3–26 and June 19–July 6. FRENCH.

Once a 16th-century postal relay station, this structure is now occupied by a ground-floor rustic dining room and bar, owned by the Kieffer family for 100 years. It offers classic specialties like homemade terrines, gamecock, fresh fish, a wide array of meats, and a tempting dessert cart. This place doesn't offer the most innovative cookery on the wine trail, but it's reliable and consistent. The chef knows how to impress most palates without reverting to ostentation. There's also a wine stube on site. From March to October, you can dine out on the terrace in front of the restaurant in the traditional Parisian cafe style.

DAMBACH

In the midst of its well-known vineyards, Dambach (30 miles from Strasbourg) is one of the delights of the Wine Route. Its timbered houses are gabled with galleries, and many contain oriels. Wrought-iron shop signs still tell you if a place is a bakery or a butcher. The town has ramparts and three fortified gates. A short drive from the town leads to the **Chapelle St-Sebastian,** with a 15th-century ossuary.

Going through Chatenois, you reach Sélestat.

SELESTAT

Located 32 miles from Strasbourg, this was once a free city, a center of the Renaissance, and the seat of a great school. Towered battlements enclose the town. The **Bibliothèque Humaniste,** 1 rue de la Bibliothèque (☎ 03-88-92-03-24), houses a rare collection of manuscripts, including Sainte-Foy's *Book of Miracles.* It's open Monday to Friday from 9am to noon and 2 to 6pm and Saturday from 9am to noon (July and August Saturay and Sunday 2 to 5pm); admission is 20F ($3.60) for adults and 10F ($1.80) for children.

The Gothic **Eglise St-George** has some fine stained glass and a gilded and painted stone pulpit. You should also try to visit the 12th-century **Eglise Ste-Foy,** built of red sandstone in the Romanesque style. One of the town's most noteworthy Renaissance buildings is the **Maison de Stephan Ziegler.**

The **Office de Tourisme** is in La Commanderie, boulevard du Général-Leclerc (☎ 03-88-58-87-20).

Château Haut-Koenigsbourg. 67600 Orschwiller. ☎ 03-88-82-50-60. Admission 40F ($7.20) adults, 25F ($4.50) per person for groups, 25F ($4.50) people 12 to 25, free for children 11 and under. June and Sept daily 9am–6pm; Apr–May daily 9am–noon and 1–6pm; Mar and Oct daily 9am–noon and 1–5:30pm; Feb 6–28 and Nov–Jan 4 daily 9am–noon and 1–4:30pm; July–Aug 9am–6:30pm.

From Sélestat you can take a detour about 2,500 feet up on an isolated peak to a 15th-century castle, which is the largest in Alsace and treats you to an eagle's-nest view. It once belonged to the Hohenstaufens. During the Thirty Years War the Swedes dismantled it, but it was rebuilt in 1901 after it was presented to Kaiser Wilhelm II.

WHERE TO DINE

✪ **La Couronne.** 45 rue de Sélestat-Baldenheim. ☎ 03-88-85-32-22. Reservations required. Main courses 90–160F ($16.20–$28.80); fixed-price menus 250–410F ($45–$73.80). AE, MC, V. Tues–Sun noon–2pm, Tues–Sat 7–9pm. Closed first week in Jan and last 2 weeks in July. From Sélestat, go 5½ miles east on D21; when the road forks, go to the right, taking D209 to the village of Baldenheim. FRENCH.

This family-run place serves dishes reflecting the bounty of Alsace, prepared with considerable finesse. A flower-filled vestibule near the entrance leads to a trio of pleasant dining rooms. Menu choices may include noisettes of roebuck (midsummer to Christmas), frogs' legs in garlic, omble chevalier (the elusive whitefish from Lake Geneva) with sauerkraut and cumin-laced potatoes, and traditional sandre.

BERGHEIM

Renowned for its wines, this town (54 miles from Strasbourg) has kept part of its 15th-century fortifications. You can see timbered Alsatian houses and a Gothic church.

RIBEAUVILLE

At the foot of vine-clad hills, the town (53 miles from Strasbourg) is charming, with old shop signs, pierced balconies, turrets, and flower-decorated houses. See its Renaissance fountain and **Hôtel de Ville,** on place de la Mairie, which has a collection of silver-gilt medieval and Renaissance tankards known as hanaps. (These are showcased only from May to September, Tuesday to Friday at 10am, 11am, 1:45pm, and 2:30pm, as part of free guided tours.) Also of interest is the **Tour des Bouchers,** a "butchers' tower" of the 13th and 16th centuries, whose interior is closed to the public. The town is noted for its Riesling and traminer wines. In September, a "Day of the Strolling Fiddlers" fair is held here.

The **Office de Tourisme** is at 1 Grand' Rue (☎ **03-89-73-62-22**).

WHERE TO STAY & DINE

✪ **Clos St-Vincent.** Rte. de Bergheim, 68150 Ribeauvillé. ☎ **03-89-73-67-65.** Fax 03-89-73-32-20. 15 units. 750–900F ($135–$162) double; from 1,100F ($198) suite. Rates include breakfast. MC, V.

This hotel is one of the most elegant dining and lodging choices along Route du Vin. Most of the individually decorated rooms have a balcony or terrace, but you get much more than a lovely view of the Haut-Rhin vineyards and summer roses.

Dining: Bertrand Chapotin's food is exceptional: hot duck liver with nuts, turbot with sorrel, roebuck (in season) in hot sauce, and veal kidneys in pinot noir. Of course, the wines are smooth, especially the Riesling and gewürztraminer, which seem to be most popular. The fixed-price menu is 255F ($45.90).

RIQUEWIHR

This town (51 miles from Strasbourg), surrounded by some of the finest vineyards in Alsace, appears much as it did in the 16th century. With well-preserved walls and towers and great wine presses and old wells, it's one of the most rewarding targets along the route. You can see many Gothic and Renaissance houses, with wooden balconies, voluted gables, and elaborately carved doors and windows. Its most interesting are **Maison Liebrich,** from 1535; **Maison Preiss-Zimmer,** from 1686; and **Maison Kiener,** from 1574. Try to peer into some of the galleried courtyards, where time seems frozen. **Tour de Dolder** (Dolder Belfry Tower), straddling an arch through which you can pass, is from 1291. Nearby, the pentagonal **Tour des Voleurs** (Tower of Thieves, often called "the robbers' tower") contains a torture chamber. The château of the duke of Wurtembrg, from 1539 (now called the **Musée d'Histoire des P.T.T. d'Alsace** or Alsace Postal History Museum) (☎ **03-89-49-08-40**), offers a museum devoted to postal and telecommunications history.

The **Office de Tourisme** is at 2 rue de la Première-Armée (☎ **03-89-49-08-40**).

WHERE TO DINE

✪ **Auberge du Schoenenbourg.** 2 rue de la Piscine. ☎ **03-89-47-92-28.** Reservations required. Main courses 138–170F ($24.85–$30.60); fixed-price menus 190F ($34.20) Mon–Fri, 250–410F ($45-$73.80) Sat–Sun. AE, MC, V. Fri–Tues noon–2pm, Thurs–Tues 7–9:30pm. Closed Jan 8–Feb 8. FRENCH.

We highly recommend the food served here. You'll dine in a garden completely surrounded by vineyards at the edge of the village. The cuisine of François Kiener offers a delectable array of tantalizingly prepared fare—foie gras maison, of course, but salmon soufflé with sabayon truffles is an elegant surprise. Perhaps try the panache of fish with sorrel or ravioli of snails with poppy seeds.

KIENTZHEIM

Located 8½ miles from Strasbourg and known for its wine, Kientzheim is one of the three towns to explore in this valley of vineyards, ranking along with Kaysersberg and Ammerschwihr. Two castles, timber-framed houses, and walls from the Middle Ages make it an appealing stop. After you've passed through, it's just a short drive to Kayersberg.

KAYSERSBERG

Once a free city of the empire, Kaysersberg (51 miles from Strasbourg) lies at the mouth of the Weiss Valley, between two vine-covered slopes; it's crowned by a feudal castle ruined in the Thirty Years War. Kaysersberg rivals Riquewihr as one of the most visited towns along the Wine Route. From one of the many ornately carved bridges, you can see the city's medieval fortifications stretching along the top of one of the nearby hills. Many of the houses are Gothic and Renaissance, and most have prominent half-timbering, lots of wrought-iron accents, small leaded windows, and multiple designs carved into the reddish sandstone that seems to have been the principal building material.

In the cafes you'll hear a combination of French and Alsatian. The language is usually determined by the age of the speaker—the older ones remain faithful to the dialect of their grandparents. Dr. Albert Schweitzer was born here in 1875, and his house is near the fortified bridge over the Weiss: You can visit the **Centre Culturel Albert-Schweitzer** (Albert Schweitzer Cultural Center) June to October, daily from 9am to noon and 2 to 6pm.

The **Office de Tourisme** is at 37 rue Général-de-Gaulle (☎ **03-89-78-22-78**).

WHERE TO STAY & DINE

Au Lion d'Or. 66 rue du Général-de-Gaulle. ☎ **03-89-47-11-16.** Reservations required. Main courses 75–150F ($13.50–$27); fixed-price menus 98–240F ($17.65–$43.20). AE, MC, V. Thurs–Tues noon–2:30pm and 6:30–9:30pm. Closed Jan; Thurs lunch in Dec–Apr. FRENCH.

This restaurant boasts an exceptionally beautiful decor. A carved lion's head is set into the oak door leading into the restaurant, with a beamed ceiling, stone detailing, brass chandeliers, and a massive fireplace. If you eat at an outdoor table, you'll have a view of one of Alsace's prettiest streets. The food, a medley of typical Alsatian dishes, is reliable and quite fine—it's true to the flavors of the region.

✪ **Chambard.** 9–13 rue du Général-de-Gaulle, 68240 Kaysersberg. ☎ **03-89-47-10-17.** Fax 03-89-47-35-03. Reservations required. Main courses 140–220F ($25.20–$39.60); fixed-price menus 250–450F ($45–$81). AE, MC, V. Wed–Sun noon–2pm and 7–9:30pm. Closed Jan 1–7 and Mar 1–21. FRENCH.

The regional cuisine here is so good it's well worth planning your wine tour to include a stopover. Chambard is the domain of Pierre Irrmann, a chef of unusual versatility and imagination. You'll recognize the restaurant—the finest in town—by the gilded wrought-iron sign above the cobblestones. Inside you'll find a rustic ambience, with exposed stone and polished wood. Try M. Irrmann's foie gras, turbot in ginger, or chicken sautéed with Riesling.

The Chambard offers a 20-room hotel annex built in 1981 to match the other buildings on the street. It has a massive Renaissance fireplace that was transported from another building. A double is 650F to 750F ($117 to $135).

ROUFFACH

One vineyard worth exploring is **Clos St-Landelin,** Route du Vin, at the intersection of RN83 (route de Soultzmatt, 54 miles from Strasbourg, ☎ **03-89-78-58-00**),

10½ miles south of Colmar. Rouffach is sheltered by one of the highest of the Vosges mountains, Grand-Ballon, which stops the winds that bring rain. That makes for a dry climate and a special grape. A clerical estate from the 6th century until the Revolution and celebrated over the centuries for the quality of wine it produces, Clos St-Landelin covers 40 acres at the southern end of the Vorbourg Grand Gru area. Its steep slopes call for terrace cultivation.

Ironically, the soil that produces these famous wines is anything but fertile. Loaded with pebbles and high in alkalines, sand, and limestone, it produces low-yield, scraggly vines whose fruit (depending on where the vines are planted and how they're exposed to the sun) is used to make superb Rieslings, gewürtztraminers, and pinot noirs. Since 1648 the Muré family has owned the vineyards, which today sprawl across 62 acres. In their cellar is the oldest wine press in Alsace, from the 13th century. They welcome visitors and speak English.

AMMERSCHWIHR

This is a good stop to cap off your Wine Road tour, near the outskirts of Colmar (49 miles from Strasbourg). Once a free city of the empire, Ammerschwihr was almost destroyed in 1944 battles but has been reconstructed in the traditional style. More and more travelers stop off here to sample the wine, especially Käferkopf. Check out its trio of gate towers, 16th-century parish church, and remains of early fortifications.

WHERE TO STAY & DINE

A l'Arbre Vert. 7 rue des Cigognes, 68770 Ammerschwihr. ☎ **03-89-47-12-23.** Fax 03-89-78-27-21. www.alsanet.com.arb-vrt. 17 units. TV TEL. 380F ($68.40) double. Half board 290–370F ($52.20–$66.60) per person extra. AE, DC, MC, V. Restaurant closed Tues year-round and Nov 11–27; closed Mon dinner in winter.

If you don't want to go on to Colmar, A l'Arbre Vert is a charming place to stay. Its public rooms are delightfully decorated, though the guest rooms are rather plain. The inn also serves very good Alsatian specialties in its restaurant, where you can dine even if you aren't staying at the hotel. Fixed-price meals go for 105F to 230F ($18.90 to $41.40).

✪ **Aux Armes de France.** 1 Grand' Rue, 68770 Ammerschwihr. ☎ **03-89-47-10-12.** Fax 03-89-47-38-12. Reservations required. Main courses 180–230F ($32.40–$41.40); fixed-price menus 360–460F ($64.80–$82.80); menu dégustation 510F ($91.80). AE, DC, DISC, MC, V. Fri–Tues noon–2pm, Thurs–Tues 7–9pm. FRENCH.

Although you can rent a room here (doubles go for 360F to 460 F/$64.80 to $82.80), the real reason to come is the cuisine—this is the most superb restaurant along the Wine Road. In a flower-filled setting, brothers Philippe and François Gaertner receive many French and German gourmets. A specialty is fresh foie gras served in its own golden aspic. Main courses include classics with imaginative variations: for example, roebuck (in season) in hot sauce and lobster fricassée with cream and truffles.

3 Colmar

273 miles SE of Paris, 87 miles SE of Nancy, 44 miles SW of Strasbourg

One of the most attractive towns in Alsace, Colmar is filled with many medieval and early Renaissance buildings, with half-timbered structures, sculptured gables, and gracious loggias. Tiny gardens and wash houses surround many of the homes. Its old quarter looks more German than French, filled with streets of unexpected twists and turns. As a gateway to the Rhine country, Colmar is a major stopover south from Strasbourg—it's the third-largest town in Alsace, near the vine-covered slopes of the southern Vosges.

Colmar today has been so well restored that it's now Alsace's most beautiful city, far more so than Strasbourg. By walking its streets you'll find it hard to tell that Colmar was hard hit in two world wars.

ESSENTIALS

GETTING THERE   Railway lines link Colmar to Nancy, Strasbourg, and Mulhouse, as well as to Germany via Freiburg, across the Rhine. Nine trains per day arrive from Paris (trip time: 6 hours). For train information and schedules, call **08-36-35-35-39.**

If you're **driving,** take N83 from Strasbourg (trip time: 1 hour).

Because of Colmar's narrow streets, we suggest that you park northeast of the rail station, in the Champ-de-Mars, before walking a few blocks east to the heart of the old city.

VISITOR INFORMATION   The Office de Tourisme is at 4 rue des Unterlinden (☎ **03-89-20-68-92**).

For information about winery visits, contact the **CIVA (Alsace Wine Committee),** Maison du Vin d'Alsace, 12 av. de la Foire-aux-Vins (☎ **03-89-20-16-20**). The CIVA office is usually open Monday to Friday from 9am to noon and 2 to 5pm. Make your arrangements far in advance.

SPECIAL EVENTS   Alsacien folk dances take place on Tuesday at 8:30pm on place de l'Ancienne-Douane from mid-May to mid-September. If you want to listen to classical music, try the **Festival International de Musique de Colmar** during the first 2 weeks in July, when 22 concerts are held in various venues around the city. Les Mardis de la Collégiale at place de la Cathedrale offers **organ and instrumental concerts** every Tuesday at 8:30pm from the end of July to mid-September. And **L'Eté Musical** presents instrumental classical concerts each Thursday during August at the Eglise St-Pierre. Tickets for any of these range from 50F to 200F ($9 to $36), and you can get complete information at the Office de Tourisme.

SEEING THE SIGHTS

Colmar boasts lots of historic houses, many of them half-timbered and, at least in summer, accented with geranium-draped window boxes. One of the most beautiful is the **Maison Pfister,** 11 rue des Marchands at the corner of rue Mercière, a civic building erected in 1537 with wooden balconies. On the ground floor is a wine boutique owned by a major Alsace wine grower, **Mure,** proprietor of the vineyard Clos St-Landelin. (A cursory glance of its exterior may be all you'll get, as this isn't a public maison.)

If you take pont St-Pierre over the Lauch River, you'll have an excellent view of Old Colmar and can explore the section known as **Petite Venice** because it's filled with canals.

SHOPPING   If you're up for a little shopping, head for the old town of Colmar, in particular rue de Clefs, Grand Rue, rue des Têtes, and rue des Marchands.

Antiques abound in Colmar, and you'll find a large grouping of stores in the old town, especially along rue des Marchands. Shops that deserve particular attention are **Fontaine,** 26 rue des Marchands (☎ **03-89-23-95-87**), offering among other items collections of metal and wood toys; **Gelsmar Dany,** 32 rue des Marchands (☎ **03-89-23-30-41**), specializing in antique furniture; and **Antiquités Guy Caffard,** 56 rue des Marchands (☎ **03-89-41-31-78**), with its mishmash of furniture, currency, postcards, books, toys, bibelots, and the like. For reproductions of objects found in Strasbourg's Alsacien Museum, such as glassware, jewelry, fabrics, and pottery, go to **Arts et Collections d'Alsace,** 1 rue des Tanneurs (☎ **03-89-24-09-78**).

WINERIES   Since Colmar is one of the gateways into the wine-producing Rhine country, local wine is one of the best purchases you can make. If you don't have the time to head out to the vineyards along the Wine Road, stop in at **Cave du Musée,** 11 rue Kléber (☎ **03-89-23-85-29**), for one of the largest selections of wines and liqueurs from the region as well as the rest of France.

However, if you have a car, you can drive to one of the most historic vineyards in Alsace-Lorraine. ✪ **Domaines Schlumberger,** at Guebwiller (where it's signposted), lies 16 miles southwest of Colmar. The cellars, established by the Schlumberger family beginning in 1810, are an unusual combination of early 19th-century brickwork and modern stainless steel. A visit here will go far in enhancing your understand of the subtle differences between wines produced by the seven varieties of grape cultivated in Alsace. Each of these—including Rieslings, gewürztraminers, muscats, sylvaners, and pinots (blancs, gris, noir)—is produced with enduring success by the Schlumberger vineyards. Though views of the vineyards and the tasting rooms are given without an appointment, tours of the cellars are conducted whenever a staff member isn't too busy to provide one. A phone call or a fax in advance (☎ **03-89-74-85-75**) is necessary.

✪ **Musée d'Unterlinden (Under the Linden Trees).** Place d'Unterlinden. ☎ **03-89-41-89-23.** Admission 32F ($5.75) adults, 27F ($4.85) seniors and students, 2F ($3.60) children 12–17, free for children 11 and under. Apr–Oct daily 9am–6pm; Nov–Mar Wed–Mon 9am–noon and 2–5pm. Closed on national holidays.

Housed in a former Dominican convent (1232) that was the chief seat of Rhenish mysticism in the 14th and 15th centuries, this was converted to a museum around 1850, and it's been a treasure house of the art and history of Alsace ever since.

The jewel of its collection is the **Issenheim Altarpiece,** created by the Würzburg-born Matthias Grünewald, "the most furious of realists." His colors glow and his fantasy will overwhelm you. One of the most exciting works in the history of German art, it's an immense altar screen with two-sided folding wing pieces—designed to show first the Crucifixion, then the Incarnation, framed by the Annunciation and the Resurrection. The carved altar screen depicts St. Anthony visiting the hermit St. Paul; it also reveals the Temptation of St. Anthony, the most beguiling part of a work that contains some ghastly misshapen birds, weird monsters, and loathsome animals. The demon of the plague, for example, is depicted with a swollen belly and purple skin, his body blotched with boils, a diabolical grin on his horrible face.

The museum has other attractions as well, including the magnificent altarpiece of Jean d'Orlier by Martin Schongauer (ca. 1470), a large collection of religious wood carvings and stained glass from the 14th to the 18th century, and Gallo-Roman lapidary collections, including funeral slabs. Its armory collection includes ancient arms from the Romanesque to the Renaissance, featuring halberds and crossbows.

Eglise St-Martin. Place de la Cathédrale. ☎ **03-89-41-27-20.** Free admission. Daily 9am–noon and 2:30–6pm. Closed to casual visitors during mass.

In the heart of Old Colmar is a collegiate church begun in 1230 on the site of a Romanesque church. It has a notable choir erected by William of Marburg in 1350 and is crowned by a steeple rising to a height of 232 feet.

Eglise des Dominicains. Place des Dominicains. ☎ **03-89-24-46-57.** Admission 8F ($1.45) adults, 6F ($1.10) students, free for children. Apr–Sept daily 10am–6pm.

This church contains one of the most famous artistic treasures of Colmar: Martin Schongauer's painting *Virgin of the Rosebush,* all gold, red, and white, with fluttering birds. Look for it in the choir.

Musée Bartholdi. 30 rue des Marchands. ☎ **03-89-41-90-60.** Admission 20F ($3.60) adults, 15F ($2.70) children 12–18, free for children 11 and under. Daily 10am–noon and 2–6pm. Closed Jan–Feb.

Because of the fame of the Statue of Liberty in New York City, interest continues in the sculptor Frédéric-Auguste Bartholdi, who was born in Colmar in 1834. In this small memento-filled museum, there are Statue of Liberty rooms containing plans and scale models, as well as documents in connection with its construction and other works regarding U.S. history. The Paris apartment of Bartholdi, with furniture and memorabilia, has been reconstructed here. The museum supplements its exhibits with water and oil paintings of Egyptian scenes this diversified talent captured during his travels in 1856.

WHERE TO STAY

Rooms are also available in the **Hôtel des Têtes** (see below).

✪ **Hostellerie le Maréchal.** 4–5 place des Six-Montagnes-Noires, 68000 Colmar. ☎ **03-89-41-60-32.** Fax 03-89-24-59-40. 30 units. MINIBAR TV TEL. 600–1,200F ($108–$216) double; 1,500F ($270) suite. AE, MC, V.

This hotel, the most tranquil in town, was formed when three 16th-century houses were joined. You climb a wide staircase to reach the rooms, most of which are air-conditioned. In the east wing is a small partially timbered room with a sloping ceiling. There's a winter restaurant with a welcoming fireplace; in summer the restaurant is moved to another part of the complex, so you have a water view. You can feast on stuffed quail, good beef and veal dishes, and lamb Provençal—accompanied by Tokay and Alsatian wines.

Hôtel Bristol. 7 place de la Gare, 68000 Colmar. ☎ **03-89-23-59-59.** Fax 03-89-23-92-26. E-mail: BestWestern.com/Best.html. 70 units. MINIBAR TV TEL. 500–750F ($90–$135) double. AE, DC, V.

This red sandstone hotel is the traditional first-class choice. Right at the train station, it provides well-maintained rooms with both modern and provincial decor. Though the location is noisy, the housekeeping is superior and the welcome helpful and intelligent.

The Bristol boasts a restaurant worthy of a star, ✪ **Rendez-vous de Chasse,** in an elegant setting with a monumental fireplace. Specialties are terrine of duckling with foie gras, roast pike-perch, and young rabbit with turnips and prunes. A specialty is boned pigs' trotters, which tastes far better than it sounds.

Le Colombier. 7 rue Turenne, 68000 Colmar. ☎ **03-89-23-96-00.** Fax 03-89-23-97-27. 24 units. A/C MINIBAR TV TEL. 560–960F ($100.80–$172.80) double; 1,200–1,400F ($216–$252) suite. AE, DC, MC, V.

In 1994, after a 2-year renovation, what had been a 14th-century half-timbered ruin was transformed into an appealing combination of old and new whose main elements (massive wall and ceiling beams, a corkscrew-shaped staircase that's the focal point of the street level) evoke medieval Colmar. Otherwise, the furnishings are streamlined and the staff is engaging and helpful. This three-star hotel is worthy of four-star status, and but for the fact that it doesn't have a restaurant (breakfast is the only meal served), it would certainly attain that status. With the exception of the cozy room beneath the steeply pitched pinnacle of the roofline, the guest rooms are high-ceilinged and come in a variety of sizes and shapes that were determined by the original layout. Each contains a safe. Some overlook the canals of the Petite Venise neighborhood that surrounds it, whereas others open onto a half-timbered courtyard.

WHERE TO DINE

✪ **Au Fer Rouge.** 52 Grand' Rue. ☎ **03-89-41-37-24.** Reservations required. Main courses 185–245F ($33.30–$44.10); fixed-price menus 295–370F ($53.10–$66.60); menu dégustation 495F ($89.10). AE, DC, MC, V. Mon–Sat noon–2:15pm and 7:15–10pm. Closed Jan. FRENCH.

In a black-and-white half-timbered building on a cobblestone square in Colmar's historic core, Au Fer Rouge has stained- and bottle-glass windows and window boxes that overflow with geraniums in summer. Inside, carved oak beams and brass and copper decorations provide a setting straight out of a Teutonic folktale. The owner, Patrick Fulgraff, has departed from the typical Alsatian fare in favor of more inventive styles. His specialties are noisettes of lamb with tarragon, quail with shredded cabbage and truffles, roast suckling pig, and wild duck cooked in its own juice, with apples and cinnamon in puff pastry for dessert. The chef rises and falls in popularity as food critics award toques one year, then take one away the next. However, M. Fulgraff retains his Michelin star—deservedly so.

✪ **Maison des Têtes.** In the Hôtel des Têtes, 19 rue des Têtes, 68000 Colmar. ☎ **03-89-24-43-43.** Reservations required. Main courses 99–145F ($17.80–$26.10); fixed-price menus 165–220F ($29.70–$39.60); menu dégustation 330F ($59.40). AE, DC, MC, V. Tues–Sat noon–2pm and 7–9:30pm, Sun noon–2pm. FRENCH.

This Colmar monument, named for the sculptured heads on its stone facade, is reached via a covered cobblestone drive and an open courtyard. The dining rooms are decorated with aged-wood beams and paneling, Art Nouveau lighting fixtures, and stained-glass and leaded windows. The food is excellent, including traditional foie gras with truffles, choucroute (sauerkraut), seasonal roebuck with morels, and fresh trout or Rhine salmon braised in Riesling. The Alsatian wines are sublime.

Hôtel des Têtes offers 18 nicely furnished rooms, all with minibar, TV, phone, coffee-making facilities, and hair dryer and some with Jacuzzi. The rates are 550F to 950F ($99 to $171) for a double; the one suite is 1,250F ($225).

NEARBY ACCOMMODATIONS & DINING

Gourmets flock to Illhaeusern, 11 miles from Colmar, east of the N83 highway, for one important reason—to dine at the Auberge de l'Ill, one of France's greatest restaurants. The signs for the restaurant, beside the main highway, are difficult to miss.

✪ **Auberge de l'Ill.** Rte. de Collonges, 68970 Illhaeusern. ☎ **03-89-71-89-00.** Fax 03-89-71-82-83. Reservations required, sometimes 6 weeks in advance on summer weekends. Main courses 145–300F ($26.10–$54); fixed-price menu 720F ($129.60). AE, DC, MC, V. Wed–Sun noon–2pm and 7–9pm. Open Mon for lunch in summer. Closed Feb. FRENCH.

Run by the Haeberlin brothers in what used to be their family's 19th-century farmhouse, Auberge de l'Ill combines the finest-quality Alsatian specialties with cuisine moderne and classic offerings. You can take your aperitif or coffee under the weeping willows in a beautiful garden, with a river view. The house is furnished with antiques, polished silver hollowware, and Buffet paintings. Chef Paul Haeberlin takes dishes of Alsatian origin and makes them into grande cuisine—*matelotes* (small glazed onions) in Riesling, eel stewed in Riesling, and an inventive foie gras. His partridge, pheasant, and duckling are among the best in Europe. Two unsurpassed choices that may be offered are his braised slices of pheasant and partridge served with a winey game sauce, chestnuts, wild mushrooms, and Breton cornmeal and his salmon soufflé. Some dishes require 24-hour notice, so inquire when you make reservations.

You can spend the night at the restaurant's air-conditioned **Hôtel de Berges** (☎ **03-89-71-87-87;** fax 03-89-71-87-88) in a delightfully furnished room (11 in all) overlooking the Ill. A double costs 1,300F to 1,500F ($234 to $270).

COLMAR AFTER DARK

Head for the smoky and seductive **Haricot Rouge,** 6 place de la Cathédrale (☎ **03-89-41-74-13**), where rock concerts pull people in; or the local version of the Hard Rock Café known as **Rock Café,** 6 rue des Trois-Epis (☎ **03-89-24-05-36**). Both places attract a cool crowd flaunting a little bit of a rough edge. For a softer atmosphere, try the piano bar **Louisiana Club,** 3A rue Berthe-Molly (☎ **03-89-24-94-18**), where you can groove to authentic blues and jazz. If you can imagine a French version of a country/western bar, mosey on down to the **Country Bar,** 9 rte. d'Ingersheim (☎ **03-89-41-48-47**), with its barnyard country dance floor and ample supply of big belt buckles, cowboy boots, and ten-gallon hats.

4 La Route des Crêtes

From Basel to Mainz, a distance of some 150 miles, the Vosges mountain range stretches along the west side of the Rhine Valley, bearing a great similarity to the Black Forest of Germany. Many German and French families spend their summer vacation exploring the Vosges. However, those with less time may want to settle for a quick look at these ancient mountains that once formed the boundary between France and Germany. The Vosges are filled with tall hardwood and fir trees and traversed by a network of twisting roads with hairpin curves. Deep in these mountain forests is the closest that France comes to having a wilderness.

You can explore the mountains by heading west from Strasbourg, but you can take a more interesting route from Colmar. From that ancient Alsatian town, you can explore some of the highest of the southern Vosges with their remarkable beauty. La Route des Crêtes (Crest Road) begins at **Col du Bonhomme,** to the west of Colmar. It was devised by the French High Command during World War I to carry supplies over the mountainous front. From Col du Bonhomme you can strike out along this magnificent road, once the object of such bitter fighting but today a series of panoramic vistas, including one of the Black Forest.

By **Col de la Schlucht** you'll have climbed 4,905 feet. Schlucht is a winter/summer resort, one of the most beautiful spots in the Vosges—with a panoramic view of the Valley of Münster and the slopes of Hohneck. As you skirt the edge of this glacier-carved valley, you'll be in the midst of a land of pine groves with a necklace of lakes. You may want to turn off the main road and go exploring in several directions, the scenery is that tempting. But if you're still on the Crest Road, you can circle **Hohneck,** one of the highest peaks at 5,300 feet, dominating the Wildenstein Dam of the Bresse winter-sports station.

At **Markstein** you'll come into another pleasant summer/winter resort. From here, take N430 and then D10 to **Münster,** where the savory cheese is made. You go via the Petit-Ballon, a landscape of forest and mountain meadows with lots of grazing cows. Finally, at **Grand-Ballon** you'll have attained the highest point you can reach by car in the Vosges, 4,662 feet. From here you can get out of your car and go for a walk. If it's a clear day, you'll be able to see the Jura, with the French Alps beyond, and can gaze on a lovely panorama of the Black Forest.

WHERE TO STAY & DINE IN MUNSTER

Au Chêne Voltaire. Rte. du Chêne-Voltaire, at Luttenbach, 68140 Münster. ☎ **03-89-77-31-74.** Fax 03-89-77-45-71. 19 units, 15 with bathroom. TEL. 245F ($44.10) double without bathroom. 265F ($47.70) double with bathroom. AE, DC, MC. Take D10 less than 1½ miles southwest from the center of Münster.

This chalet-style inn, built in 1939 and renovated many times since, lies in an isolated section of the forest. The modern but no-frills rooms are in a separate building from the rustic core that contains the popular restaurant. The hotel isn't a destination in and of itself; it's just good to keep in mind if you need to rest for the night before pressing on your way in the morning.

You can dine here even if you're not staying at the hotel, ordering any of the fixed-price menus that range from 105F to 185F ($18.90 to $33.30). Facilities include a sauna and a solarium.

5 Lunéville & Baccarat

Lunéville: 208 miles SE of Paris, 22 miles SE of Nancy; Baccarat: 223 miles SE of Paris, 37 miles SE of Nancy

If crystal chandeliers and decanters, along with wineglasses, evoke glamour and glitter for you and you've come this deep into Lorraine, you might spend one of the most enjoyable days of your trip here by visiting Lunéville and Baccarat.

GETTING THERE

The towns are connected with Nancy and Strasbourg by local **train** service. Two trains per day arrive from Paris (trip time: 3½ hours); there's one train per day from Strasbourg (trip time: 1½ hours); and 13 from Nancy (trip time: 30 minutes). For train information and schedules, call ☎ **08-36-35-35-39.** Once in Lunéville, you'll find that trains to Baccarat run every hour or two daily from 6:30am to 10pm (trip time: 20 minutes). When **motoring** to Lunéville and Baccarat, you can drive the N4 east straight from Paris, through Nancy to Lunéville. From Lunéville, take the N59 southeast into the nearby town of Baccarat.

LUNEVILLE

Lunéville was a walled town in medieval days. After a decline brought on by war, plague, and famine, it rose again under Ducs Léopold and Stanislas. Lunéville contains factories that produce some of France's best-known porcelain, whose painted patterns are noted for their vivid colors and whimsical designs. For much of the early 18th century this town was the residence of Léopold, duc de Lorraine, who so admired (and wanted to flatter) Louis XIV that he built the Château de Lunéville, a near replica of the one at Versailles, particularly the chapel.

The **Office de Tourisme** is at the Château (☎ **03-83-74-06-55**).

ATTRACTIONS   **Musée du Château,** in the Château de Lunéville (☎ **03-83-76-23-57**), is rich in old porcelain, drawings, and paintings, plus military weapons. The museum occupies only part of the château, which for the most part is in need of repair and off-limits. It's open Wednesday to Monday from 10am to noon and 2 to 6pm (to 5pm in winter). Admission is 10F ($1.80) for adults, 5F (90¢) for students, and free for children 18 and under.

The baroque **Eglise St-Jacques,** on place St-Jacques (☎ **03-83-73-04-12**), contains a 15th-century pietà of polychrome stone, wood panels, stalls, a pulpit, a porch with a Régence-style ornament carved in it, an 18th-century organ, and an organ case richly adorned with pipes hidden in ornamental columns. The church is open daily from 9am to 5:30pm.

SHOPPING   Porcelain shops everywhere sell modern examples of the famed dinnerware, which—if you can pack it properly—can become a treasured souvenir. Here are two of the best: **Aux Belles Choses,** 42 rue d'Alsace (☎ **03-83-74-05-14**), is a small boutique selling a choice but limited selection of porcelain and gift items. Larger and much better stocked is the factory outlet, **Le Magasin des Faïenceries,** 1 rue Keller et Guerin (☎ **03-83-74-07-58**). Both can insure and ship your purchases.

WHERE TO STAY

Hôtel des Pages. 5 quai des Petits-Bosquets, 54300 Lunéville. ☎ **03-83-74-11-42.** Fax 03-83-73-46-63. 30 units. TV TEL. 260–300F ($46.80–$54) double. AE, MC, V.

This three-story centrally located hotel, in a quiet district near the château, has well-equipped rooms designed to give you a good night's sleep. In the restaurant, Le Petit Comptoir, excellent-value fixed-price menus feature good regional fare at 38F to 120F ($6.85 to $21.60).

Hôtel Oasis. 3 av. Voltaire, 54300 Lunéville. ☎ **03-83-74-11-42.** Fax 03-83-73-46-63. 32 units. TV TEL. 290F ($52.20) double. AE, V.

A 10-minute walk from the town center, this hotel opened in 1990 and has since been the best in town (though the competition isn't exactly stiff). The rooms are spacious and tastefully decorated. There's a lounge, a bar, a breakfast room, and a pool, which is just 50 yards away.

WHERE TO DINE

✪ **Château d'Adomenil.** Rehainviller, 54300 Lunéville. ☎ **03-83-74-04-81.** Fax 03-83-74-21-78. Reservations required. Main courses 150–175F ($27–$31.50); fixed-price menus 250–465F ($45–$83.70). AE, DC, MC, V. Wed–Sun noon–2pm, Mon–Sat 7–9:30pm. Closed Nov 2–Apr 1. Follow av. Georges-Pompidou from the town center for 2½ miles south; the château is signposted along the way. FRENCH.

Château d'Adomenil is set on 16 acres of parkland containing a 17th-century wine press. While there are 12 rooms for rent—a double costs 750 to 1,100F ($135 to $198)—most people come here to dine. You might begin with cocktails and miniquiches Lorraine in the oak-beamed salon. Dinner is served in an elegant room with a view of the expansive lawns, reflecting pools (and a swimming pool), and peacocks. The outstanding owner/chef, Michel Million, will often help guide you by suggesting delectable fare like quail wrapped in cabbage leaves, lobster in court bouillon with saffron, filet of lamb en croûte with thyme, and chanterelle-stuffed pigeon. His wife, Bernadette, cheerfully greets you and sees that you receive impeccable service.

BACCARAT

This small town owes its fame to Baccarat crystal. The company, founded in 1764, was originally a glass manufacturer called La Verrerie Sainte-Anne. In 1817, however, it switched to crystal and became known as the Compagnie des Cristalleries de Baccarat.

The **Syndicat d'Initiative** (tourist office), at place des Arcades (☎ **03-83-75-13-37**), is open only from June to September.

In addition to displaying some of the factory's oldest and most noteworthy pieces, **Musée du Cristal** (☎ **03-83-76-60-06**) has a video in English about crystal manufacturing. You'll learn how lead, potassium, and silica combine to form crystal. The museum is open daily: April to November 1 from 9:30am to 12:30pm and 2 to 6:30pm, and November 2 to March from 10am to noon and 2 to 6pm.

A Baccarat shop, simply called **Baccarat,** 2 rue des Cristalleriës (☎ **03-83-76-60-01**), on the square near the museum is housed in a futuristic rectangular building whose walls are made almost entirely of glass. It's loaded with crystal for sale.

WHERE TO STAY & DINE

Hôtel de la Renaissance. 31 rue des Cristalleries, 54120 Baccarat. ☎ **03-83-75-11-31.** Fax 03-83-75-21-09. 16 units. TEL. 260–310F ($46.80–$55.80) double. AE, MC, V.

This provincial hotel caters to visitors and businesspeople in town. The rooms are functional but well kept, and most were upgraded in 1996. This place does have one drawback, unless you find the serenade of 16-wheelers soothing: A truck route passes under it, and, though the windows are soundproofed, guests in the heat of summer may find that keeping the windows closed is too steep a price to pay for quiet.

The hotel restaurant presents a solid roster of French-inspired specialties, offering fixed-price menus at 89F to 180F ($16 to $32.40) at lunch and dinner, plus a 60F ($10.80) fixed-price lunch. It's open daily in summer; from October to March, it closes on Monday and Friday night.

6 Nancy

230 miles SE of Paris, 92 miles W of Strasbourg

Nancy, in the northeastern corner of France, was the capital of old Lorraine. The city was built around a fortified castle on a rock in the swampland near the Meurthe River. The important canal a few blocks east of the historic center connects the Marne to the Rhine.

The city is serenely beautiful, with a historic tradition, a cuisine, and an architecture all its own. It was once the rival of Paris as a center for Art Nouveau. Nancy has a triple face: the medieval alleys and towers around the old Palais Ducal where Charles II received Joan of Arc, the rococo golden gates and frivolous fountains, and the spreading dull modern sections with their university and industry.

With a population of 100,000, Nancy remains the hub of commerce and politics in Lorraine. The seat of the third-largest scientific university in France, it's a center of mining, engineering, metallurgy, and finance. Its 30,000 students, who have a passion for *le cool jazz,* keep Nancy jumping at night.

ESSENTIALS

GETTING THERE   **Trains** from Strasbourg arrive every 30 minutes (trip time: 1 hour); trains from Paris's Gare de l'Est pull in about every hour (trip time: 3 hours). For train information and schedules, call ☎ **08-36-35-35-39.** When **driving** to Nancy from Paris, follow N4 east (trip time: 4 hours).

VISITOR INFORMATION   The **Office de Tourisme** is at 14 place Stanislas (☎ **03-83-35-22-41**).

SPECIAL EVENTS   Serious jazz lovers come to town during the middle of October to attend the best music festival in Nancy, **Jazz Pulsations.** Just head over to the Parc de la Pépinière around sundown, when festivities crank up and continue well into the early morning. The Office de Tourisme (see above) has complete information.

SEEING THE SIGHTS

The most monumental square in eastern France and the heart of Nancy is ✪ **place Stanislaus,** named for Stanislaus Leczinski, the last of the ducs de Lorraine, ex-king of Poland, and father-in-law of Louis XV. His 18th-century building programs transformed Nancy into one of Europe's most palatial cities. The square stands between Nancy's two most notable neighborhoods—the **Ville Vieille,** which occupies the medieval core in the northwest, centered around the cathedral, Grande-Rue, and the labyrinth of narrow meandering streets that funnel into it; and the **Ville Neuve,** in the southeast. Built in the 16th and 17th centuries, when streets were laid out in generally straight lines, Ville Neuve is centered around rue St-Jean.

Place Stanislas was laid out from 1752 to 1760 to the designs of Emmanuel Héré. Its ironwork gates are magnificent. Grilles stand at each corner, and two enclose fountains, the Neptune and the Amphitrite. The most imposing building on the square is the **Hôtel de Ville** (town hall); try to see its inner staircase and 80-foot forged-iron balustrade with a single-piece handrail, the masterpiece of Jean Lamour, who designed the square's screens and fountains. On the eastern side is the Musée des Beaux-Arts.

The **Arc de Triomphe,** constructed by Stanislas from 1754 to 1756 to honor Louis XV, brings you to the long rectangular place de la Carrière, a tree-lined promenade leading to the **Palais du Gouvernement,** built in 1760. This governmental palace adjoins the **Palais Ducal,** built in 1502 in the Gothic style with Flamboyant balconies; the much-restored palace contains the Musée Historique Lorrain. Alongside the Ducal Palace is the **Eglise des Cordeliers** with its round chapel. And the **Musée de l'Ecole de Nancy** attracts Art Nouveau devotees from all over the world.

Musée des Beaux-Arts. 3 place Stanislas. ☎ **03-83-85-30-72.** Admission 20F ($3.60). Mon 2–6pm, Wed–Sun 10:30am–6pm.

Built in the 1700s, this is an outstanding regional art museum, encompassing the Collection Galilée, works displayed in Paris between 1919 and 1930. Its gardens have been razed to make way for an annex that has increased the exhibition space. Its collection boasts a Manet portrait of the wife of Napoléon III's dentist—remarkable because of its brilliance and intensity, as well as because Manet portraits are rare. There are also works by Delacroix, Utrillo, Modigliani, Boucher, and Rubens. The Italians, like Perugino, Caravaggio, Ribera, and Tintoretto, are also represented.

✪ **Musée Historique Lorrain.** In the Palais Ducal, 64 Grande-Rue. ☎ **03-83-32-18-74.** Admission 20F ($3.60) adults, 15F ($2.70) children. May–Sept daily 10am–6pm; Oct–Apr Wed–Mon 10am–noon and 2–5pm.

This is one of France's great museums, covering the art and history of the Lorraine region from prehistoric times. The first floor devotes an entire room to the work of Jacques Callot, the noted engraver who was born in Nancy in 1592. Galerie des Cerfs displays intricately woven tapestries. You'll also find a vast collection of 17th-century Lorraine masterpieces by J. Bellange, J. Callot, G. de la Tour, and C. Deruet, from when the duchy was known as a cultural center. The museum also has a room portraying eastern France's Jewish history.

Musée de l'Ecole de Nancy. 38 rue Sergent-Blandan. ☎ **03-83-40-14-86.** Admission 20F ($3.60), free for children 9 and under. Mon 2–6pm, Wed–Sun 10:30am–6pm. Guided tours available Fri, Sat, and Sun for 50F ($9) extra.

Housed appropriately in a stunning turn-of-the-century building is a museum displaying the works of Emile Gallé, the greatest artist of the Nancy style. See, in particular, Gallé's celebrated "Dawn and Dusk" bed and our favorite, the well-known "mushroom lamp." Works by Eugène Vallin, another outstanding artist, are also on display.

Eglise des Cordeliers. 66 Grande-Rue. ☎ **03-83-32-18-74.** Admission 20F ($3.60), 15F ($2.70) per person for groups. May–Sept Wed–Mon 10am–6pm; Oct–Apr Wed–Mon 10am–noon and 2–5pm.

This church, with a round chapel based on a design for Florence's Medici, contains the burial monuments of the ducs de Lorraine. The most notable are those of René II (1509), attributed to Mansuy Gauvain, and his second wife, Philippa of Gueldres, by Ligier Richier. The octagonal ducal chapel (1607) holds the baroque sarcophagi. The convent houses the **Musée des Arts et Traditions Populaires,** which has antiques, porcelain, and reconstructed interiors of regional maisons.

SHOPPING

For glitz and glamour, your first stops should be along **rue Gambetta** and **rue des Dominicains,** where exclusive boutiques carry the best names in fashion and perfume.

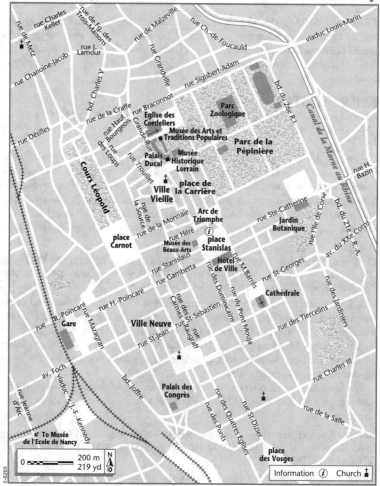

Along **rue St-Sebastien** and **rue St-Dizier** you'll run across more down-to-earth shops selling clothes, shoes, jewelry, and leather goods at more affordable prices. The old town is home to small boutiques that sell antiques, arts and crafts, books, and bric-a-brac, as well as some clothing and jewelry.

For chic women's clothing and accessories, including the finest in handbags and shoes, try **Vanessa,** 14 place St-Epvre (☎ **03-83-32-85-88**), or **Signatures,** 39 rue St-Jean (☎ **03-83-32-93-30**). From the sophisticated to the trendy, men of class, or their partners who want them to dress the part, seek out **Alto Stratus,** 34 rue des Dominicains (☎ **03-83-30-17-33**), and **Ecee Omo,** 2 bis rue d'Amerval (☎ **03-83-32-12-82**).

Many of Nancy's antiques shops specialize in Art Nouveau. Visit **Jean Claude Jantzen,** 13 rue Stanislas (☎ **03-83-35-20-79**), for the best pieces. If you'd like a more modern objet d'art, consider **Galerie Ovadia,** 14 Grande-Rue (☎ **03-83-37-93-32**), with its offerings by contemporary masters of painting, sculpture, and intensely colorful mixed-media collages; and **Galerie Art International,** 17 rue d'Amerval (☎ **03-83-35-06-83**), where you can choose from lilac crystal, brightly colored vases and boxes known as Emaux de Longwy, and an assortment of lamps. **Daum Glassworks Showroom,** 17 rue des Cristalleries (☎ **03-83-30-80-28**), offers exquisite crystal, especially items of the world-famous transparent-colored pâte de verre.

WHERE TO STAY

Albert-1er-Astoria. 3 rue de l'Armée-Patton, 54000 Nancy. ☎ **03-83-40-31-24.** Fax 03-83-28-47-78. 85 units. TV TEL. 295–380F ($53.10–$68.40) double. AE, DC, MC, V. Parking 35F ($6.30).

In 1997 the size of this once-sprawling hotel was reduced from 126 to 85 rooms when the more luxurious part of its premises was sold as private apartments. Today, having endured a reduction in standards from three- to two-star status, it offers comfortable if not exactly plush rooms, an interior garden, and an English bar called L'Astor. Across from the railway station, the well-equipped hotel is run in a businesslike manner. Guests stay here mainly for the price and central location. Breakfast is the only meal served.

✪ **Grand Hôtel de la Reine.** 2 place Stanislas, 54000 Nancy. ☎ **800/777-4182** in the U.S. and Canada, or 03-83-35-03-01. Fax 03-83-32-86-04. www.concordehotels.fr. 55 units. 600–850F ($108–$153) double; from 1,200F ($216) suite. AE, DC, MC, V. Parking 50F ($9).

This 18th-century mansion was built simultaneously with the monumental square that contains it and so figures prominently in the town's historic framework. The hotel is one of the showplaces of the upscale Concorde chain, operators of such bastions of luxury as Paris's Hôtel de Crillon. The Louis XV–style guest rooms boast draped testers over the beds, Venetian-style chandeliers, and gilt-framed mirrors. The salons are decorated with antique wainscoting.

The Stanislas restaurant serves both classic and modern dishes as part of fixed-price meals ranging from 180F to 360F ($32.40 to $64.80), and the waiters are formal and considerate.

Mercure Altea Thiers. 11 rue Raymond-Poincaré, 54000 Nancy. ☎ **03-83-39-75-75.** Fax 03-83-32-78-17. 192 units. MINIBAR TV TEL. 525–635F ($94.50–$114.30) double; 1,000F ($180) suite. AE, DC, MC, V.

Rising above every other building in Nancy, this streamlined seven-story hotel caters to both business travelers and visitors. Functional and efficient, with a hardworking staff, it's a top choice for Nancy but lacks the style of the Grand Hôtel de la Reine. The rooms are outfitted in the chain-format style that nonetheless offers comfort, predictability, and warmth.

Two restaurants on the premises are the upscale choice, La Toison d'Or, and a less formal, somewhat more raucous brasserie, Le Rendez-Vous. Both offer cuisine inspired by Lorraine and the rest of France.

WHERE TO DINE

✪ **La Table de Mengin.** 27 rue des Ponts. ☎ **03-83-35-17-25.** Reservations imperative. Main courses 115–145F ($20.70–$26.10); fixed-price menus 130–350F ($23.40–$63). AE, DC, V. Tues–Sat noon–2:30pm, Mon–Sat 7:30–9:30pm. SEAFOOD/FRENCH.

Nancy's finest restaurant lies behind a facade of chiseled stone from the 15th century, in the heart of the city. The dining room has a soothing decor, and the staff is the city's best trained. Jean-Luc Mengin is all the rave, and when it comes to fish and seafood, he has no serious contenders in eastern France. The dining room is luxurious and contemporary, and the atmosphere is made all the more inviting by the chef's wife,

Danièle Mengin, a sommeliere who almost never fails to please with her suggestions. After trying the filet of red snapper with a tapenade of black olives and mashed potatoes, the John Dory with larded potatoes and bacon, and the sole in tomato coulis, we agree that the chef does indeed work a kind of magic on what might be rather prosaic dishes. The service is flawless and the wine list well chosen. Not interested in things that swim? Try his version of lasagne *d'encornets* (lasagne with foie gras) or his pot-au-feu of Bresse chicken with horseradish.

✪ **Le Capucin Gourmand.** 31 rue Gambetta. ☎ **03-83-35-26-98.** Reservations required. Main courses 135–145F ($24.30–$26.10); fixed-price menus 180–550F ($32.40–$99). MC, V. Tues–Sat noon–2pm and 7:30–10pm. Closed 1 week in Feb and 3 weeks in Aug. FRENCH.

Chef Gérard Veissière treats you to excellent service and regional cuisine. In homage to Nancy's Art Nouveau tradition, the restaurant, in a 1920s-era house, integrates Gallé and Daum glass with Louis Majorelle furniture. The chef's specialty is foie gras maison, and he recommends *nage océane* (fish cocktail) flavored with saffron, gratin of lobster with fresh tagliatelle, or aiguillettes of duckling with sweet-and-sour sauce. The 180F ($32.40) fixed-price menu is one of the city's dining bargains.

Restaurant Le Foy. 1 place Stanislas. ☎ **03-83-32-21-44.** Reservations recommended. Main courses 80–110F ($14.40–$19.80); fixed-price menus 160–180F ($28.80–$32.40). AE, MC, V. Mon–Tues and Thurs–Sun noon–2pm, Mon–Tues and Thurs–Sat 7–9:30pm. Closed Feb and July 15–Aug 9. FRENCH.

This restaurant occupies the second floor of a building that's part of the 18th-century borders of place Stanislaus. Outfitted with exposed timbers and Louis XIII furnishings, it sits above, but is completely independent of, a simple brasserie/cafe (Café Foy) that occupies the building's street level but serves much less appealing food. Menu items are prepared by two generations of the Zenden family and include a stylish roster of such dishes as roasted rabbit with violet-flavored mustard sauce, fried crayfish with a concasse of tomatoes, and a local freshwater fish (sandre) baked in a potato crust. Try a dessert that's both unusual and heavenly: honey mousse cake prepared with brandy.

NANCY AFTER DARK

As night approaches, most of the student population heads to the old town. The hottest rock club is the loud and packed **Planet Rock,** 22 rue St-Dizier (☎ **03-83-32-83-42**). **Le Blue Note,** 3 rue des Michottes (☎ **03-83-30-31-18**), has a room reserved for weekly rock performances, a laid-back piano bar, a fireplace room with comfy armchairs, and an upbeat and rowdy beer hall. A cover of 60F ($10.80) is charged on concert nights.

For a pub experience, go to the **Be Happy Bar,** 23 rue Gustave-Simon (☎ **03-83-35-56-41**), with its 12 brands of beer on tap. It's new, it's got an English flavor, and it's full of colorful characters playing games and guzzling beer well into the night. The most popular dance clubs are **Les Caves du Roi,** 9 place Stanislas (☎ **03-83-35-24-14**), with its industrial techno crowd flailing around in the chrome-and-metallic space; and the wine-cellar-turned-rock-dance-club called **Métro,** 1 rue du Général-Hoche (☎ **03-83-40-25-13**). Covers at both of these dance clubs range from 20F to 50F ($3.60 to $9), depending on the night and the entertainment.

7 Domrémy-la-Pucelle

275 miles SE of Paris, 6½ miles NW of Neufchâteau

A pilgrimage center attracting tourists from all over the world, Domrémy is a plain village that would have slumbered in obscurity except for the fact that Joan of Arc was born here in 1412. Here she heard the voices and saw the visions that led her to play out her historic role as the heroine of France.

A residence traditionally considered her family's house, near the church, is known as **Maison Natale de Jeanne d'Arc,** 2 rue de la Basilique (☎ **03-29-06-95-86**). Here you can see the bleak chamber where she was born. A museum beside the house shows a film depicting St. Joan's life. You can visit the house Wednesday to Monday: April to September from 9am to 12:30pm and 2 to 7pm and October to March from 9:30am to noon and 2 to 5pm. Admission is 6F ($1.10) for adults, 3F (55¢) for children 10 to 14, and free for children 9 and under.

Adjacent to the museum, on rue Principale, is **Eglise St-Rémi,** a much-reconstructed building whose 12th-century origins have mostly been masked by more recent repairs. All that remains from the age of Joan of Arc is a baptismal font and some stonework. Above the village, on a slope of the Bois-Chenu, is a monument steeped in turn-of-the-century French nationalism, the **Basilique du Bois-Chenu,** which was begun in 1881 and consecrated in 1926.

To get here: By car, take N4 southeast of Paris to Toul, from there A31 south toward Neufchâteau/Charmes. Then N74 southwest (signposted in the direction of Neufchâteau). At Neufchâteau follow D164 northwest to Coussey. From here, take D53 into Domremy. There is no train station in Domrémy—you must take one of four **trains** daily going to either Nancy or Toul where bus and rail connections can be made to Neufchâteau. From here, there are three buses running daily to Domrémy. The cost of a one-way ticket is 11F ($2.00). You can also take a taxi for 80F to 90F ($14.40 to $16.20) (☎ **03-29-06-12-13**).

8 Verdun

162 miles E of Paris, 41 miles W of Metz

Built on both banks of the Meuse and intersected by a complicated series of canals, Verdun has an old section, the Ville Haute on the east bank, which includes the cathedral and episcopal palace. Today stone houses clustered on narrow cobblestone streets give Verdun a medieval appearance.

But most visitors come to see the famous World War I battlefields, 2 miles east of the town, off N3 toward Metz.

ESSENTIALS

GETTING THERE   Four **trains** (sometimes fewer) arrive daily from Paris's Gare de l'Est, after a change at Châlons-en-Champagne. Several daily trains also arrive from Metz, after a change at Conflans. For train information and schedules, call ☎ **08-36-35-35-39.**

Driving is easy, since Verdun is several miles north of the Paris–Strasbourg autoroute (A4).

VISITOR INFORMATION   The **Office de Tourisme,** place de la Nation (☎ **03-29-86-14-18**), is closed on bank holidays only.

TOURING THE BATTLEFIELDS

At this garrison town in eastern France, Maréchal Pétain said, "They shall not pass!"— and they didn't. Verdun is where the Allies held out against a massive assault by the German army in World War I. Near the end of the war, 600,000 to 800,000 French and German soldiers died battling over a few miles on the muddy Meuse between Paris and the Rhine. Two monuments commemorate these tragic events: Rodin's *Defense* and Boucher's *To Victory and the Dead.*

A tour of the battlefields is called the *Circuit des Forts,* covering the main fortifications. On the Meuse's right bank, this is a good 20-mile run, taking in **Fort Vaux,** where Raynal staged a heroic defense after sending his last message by carrier pigeon. After passing a vast **French cemetery** of 16,000 graves, an endless field of crosses, you arrive at the **Ossuaire de Douaumont,** where the bones of those literally blown to bits were embedded. Nearby at the mostly underground **Fort de Douaumont,** the "hell of Verdun" was unleashed. From the roof you can look out at a vast field of corroded tops of "pillboxes." Then you proceed to the **Tranchée des Baïonettes** (Trench of Bayonets). Bayonets of French soldiers instantly entombed by a shell-burst form this unique memorial.

The other tour, *Circuit Rive Gauche,* is about a 60-mile run and takes in the **Butte de Montfaucon,** a hill on which Americans erected a memorial tower, and the **Cimetière Américain at Romagne,** with some 15,000 graves.

Because of inadequate public transportation, only visitors with cars should attempt to make these circuits.

WHERE TO STAY & DINE

Château des Monthairons. Rte. D34, 55320 Dieue-sur-Meuse. ☎ **03-29-87-78-55.** Fax 03-29-87-73-49. www.bplorraine/chateaumonthairons. E-mail: chateaumonthairons@ bplorraine.fr. 18 units. MINIBAR TV TEL. 510–840F ($91.80–$151.20) double; 990–1,040F ($178.20–$187.20) suite. AE, DC, MC, V. Drive 7½ miles south of Verdun on D334.

This hotel, operated by the Thouvenin family, occupies an 1857 château crafted of chiseled blocks of pale stone. The grounds contain a pair of 15th-century chapels, a nesting ground for herons, and opportunities for canoeing and fishing.

In summer the dining room serves meals Tuesday to Sunday from noon to 4pm and 7:30 to 9:30pm; closed Sunday night to Tuesday at dinner from November to March 15. Fixed-price menus are 165F to 310F ($29.70 to $55.80) and include pigeon soufflé with truffles, scallops with basil-cream sauce, and roast lobster with risotto and Thai herbs.

Le Coq Hardi. 8 av. de la Victoire, 55100 Verdun. ☎ **03-29-86-36-36.** Fax 03-29-86-09-21. 35 units. TV TEL. 450–670F ($81–120.60) double; from 1,200F ($216) suite. AE, MC, V. Parking 65F ($11.70).

This is our favorite hotel in town, composed of four connected 18th-century houses near the Meuse. The interior contains church pews and antiques and a Renaissance fireplace. Most of the well-maintained rooms have been decorated in regional style.

This hotel serves the best food in town in a dining room with a painted ceiling, Louis XIII chairs, and two deactivated World War I bombshells at its entrance. Menu specialties are salade Coq Hardi with green mustard and pine nuts, Challons duck, cassolette of snails in champagne, and foie gras from Landes. Fixed-price menus range from 198F to 310F ($35.65 to $55.80).

12

The French Alps

No part of France has more dramatic scenery than the Alps, for the western ramparts of these mountains and their foothills are truly majestic. From the Mediterranean in the south to the Rhine in the north, they stretch along the southeastern flank of France. The skiing here has no equal in Europe, not even in Switzerland. Some of the resorts are legendary, like Chamonix-Mont Blanc, the historic capital of alpine skiing, with its 12-mile Vallée Blanche run. Mont Blanc, at 15,780 snowy feet, is the highest mountain in Western Europe.

Most of this chapter covers the area known as the Savoy (Savoie), taking in the French lake district, including the largest alpine lake, which the French share with Switzerland. The French call it Lac Léman, but it's known as Lake Geneva in English.

From January to March, skiers flock to Chamonix-Mont Blanc, Megève, Val di'Isère, and Courchevel 1850; from July to September, spa fans head to Evian-les-Bains and Aix-les-Bains. Grenoble, the capital of the French Alps, is the gateway. It's just 30 minutes by car from the Grenoble-St-Geoirs airport, 40 minutes from the Lyon-Satolas international airport, and 90 minutes from Geneva's Cointrin airport. The city is also connected with the Paris-Lyon-Marseille motorway on the west and to the Chambéry-Geneva motorway on the east.

REGIONAL CUISINE The cuisine of the Savoy is robust and straightforward, well suited to the lack of cereals and grains and to the active lifestyle of the people. Most indicative are the recipes that depend on the region's superb raw ingredients: fresh produce, eggs, fish, meats, and—most important—cheese and milk.

Cheesemaking, a process developed over thousands of years as a means of preserving the proteins and nutrients of milk, was carefully fine-tuned in the Savoy (where cows and goats thrived on the grasses of the alpine meadows). The region's most famous cheese is a form of especially savory Gruyère known as beaufort, which, though similar to Emmenthal "Swiss" cheese, has hardly any holes. Aged for up to 2 years, it's at its best when made from milk produced between June and September, when the aroma of herbs and flowers is especially pungent. Another famous cheese is reblochon, a slightly bitter semihard cheese that gourmets insist must be fermented at high altitude to achieve its full flavor. Another name for reblochon, in Savoyard dialect, is *tôme* (cheese) *de Savoie*.

Those who appreciate the pungent taste of goats'-milk cheese search out the most famous Savoyard chèvre: St-Marcellin or (as its devoted

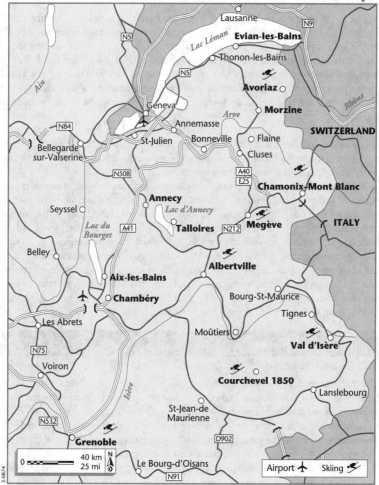

aficionados call it) petit St-Marcellin. Once made solely from the milk of alpine goats, it's now based on a combination of cows' and goats' milk; its exterior is firm and supple, but its interior runs with sweet creamy goodness. You'll note the presence of a cheese fondue on almost every menu of the region.

The Savoy and its neighbor, the Dauphine, are most famous for the ways cheese and milk are used to augment the flavors of other dishes. There's much confusion in the non-French world about the meaning of *au gratin*. A concept developed in some of the most rugged countryside here (the isolated Vercors southwest of Grenoble), it refers to the crusty top (not the ingredients) formed when certain ingredients are baked in a certain type of flat (usually oval) dish. "Au gratin" might be the most famous culinary concept to come out of the region and is seen today on menus throughout the world. It usually implies the addition of cheese: a gratin dauphinoise, for example, is a baked casserole of sliced potatoes, usually with onions, cream, cheese, and sometimes eggs. A *gratin Savoyard* substitutes beef bouillon for the cream, omits the eggs, and sometimes adds cheese.

The freshwater lakes and streams of the Savoy have always yielded a healthy catch, like trout, carp, grayling, pike, eel, perch, and a famous regional delicacy found only in the cold alpine lakes of France and Switzerland, omble chevalier. In one recipe for the thousands of unnamed tiny fish, too small to filet, they're seasoned, batter-fried, and usually served with a white Savoyard wine. As for vegetables, the traditional greens were those that endured a long growing season amid the alpine snows. Most notable was the spikey-leafed cardoon, whose firm flesh inspired many methods of preparation.

The region's smoked hams, pâtés, and sausages (sometimes served with red lentils) are delicious, and the rich chocolate confections whipped up in elegant bakeries reflect the tastes of citizens who can permit themselves the extra calories—at this high altitude, outdoor activities make calories easy to burn.

As for wines and spirits, the gentle foothills benefiting from southern exposure have produced good wines, although—with one exception—nothing like the world-famous vintages of Burgundy or Bordeaux. The most famous red is the Montmélian, similar to a beaujolais. The best-known white is a sparkling Seyssel, whose best vintages have been favorably compared with champagne. As in many mountain regions of Europe, the Alps produce potent eaux-de-vie, which should usually be consumed to top off a full evening meal. Most celebrated is Gentian, flavored with a blue alpine wildflower, and the famous Chartreuse, whose herbal green tint has been used for centuries as an adjective to describe a certain color. The local Marc de Savoie is a deceivingly potent residue from the brandy-distillation process guaranteed to give you a hangover.

1 Evian-les-Bains

358 miles SW of Paris, 26 miles NE of Geneva

On the château-dotted southern shore of Lac Léman, Evian-les-Bains is one of the leading spa resorts in eastern France. Its lakeside promenade lined with trees and sweeping lawns has been fashionable since the 19th century. The waters of Evian became famous in the 18th century, and the first spa buildings were erected in 1839. Bottled Evian, one of the great French table waters, is considered beneficial for everything from baby's formula and salt-free diets to treating gout and arthritis.

Back in the days when Marcel Proust came here to enjoy the belle époque grandeur of the town, Evian was the haunt of the very rich. The hotel where Proust stayed, the Splendid, is no longer here, but he fashioned his "Balbec baths" after those of Evian. Today the spa, with its long lakefront promenade and elegant casino, attracts a broader range of clients—it's not just for the rich anymore.

In addition to its **spa buildings,** Evian offers an imposing **Ville des Congrès** (convention hall), earning the resort the title of "city of conventions." In summer the **Nautical Center** on the lake is a popular attraction; it has a 328-foot pool with a diving stage, solarium, restaurant, bar, and children's paddling pool.

The major excursion from Evian is a boat trip on Lake Geneva offered by the **Compagnie Générale de Navigation,** a Lausanne-based outfit whose agent in Evian is the Office du Baigneur, place du Port (☎ **04-50-70-73-20**). Either contact them directly or head for the Office de Tourisme (see below) to pick up a schedule of prices and hours—in summer, night cruises are also offered. If you want to see it all, you can tour both the Haut-Lac and the Grand-Lac. The quickest and most heavily booked of all trips is the crossing from Evian to Ouchy-Lausanne, Switzerland, on the north side.

Crescent-shaped **Lake Geneva** is the largest lake in central Europe (the name Lac Léman was revived in the 18th century). Taking in an area of approximately 225 square miles, the lake is formed by the Rhône and is noted for its unusual blueness.

Driving the Route des Grandes Alpes

Evian could be a starting point for the 460-mile drive to Nice along the Route des Grandes Alpes, one of Europe's great drives, linking Lake Geneva with the Riviera and crossing 35 passes along the way. Leaping from valley to valley, it's open from end to end only during summer (many passes are closed in winter).

It's possible to make the drive in 2 days, but what would be the point? The charm of this journey involves stopping at scenic highlights along the way, including Morzine, Chamonix, Megève, and Val d'Isère. The most dramatic pass is the Galibier Pass (Col du Galibier) at 8,686 feet, marking the dividing line between the northern and southern parts of the French Alps.

En route to Nice you'll pass through such towns as St-Veran, at 6,530 feet the highest community in Europe; Entrevaux, once a fortress town marking the dividing line between Upper Provence and the Alps; and Touet-sur-Var, a village filled with tall narrow houses constructed directly against the towering rocky slope.

ESSENTIALS

GETTING THERE   Evian-les-Bains is easily reached from Geneva by **train.** In Geneva, the Gare des Eaux-Vives, on the eastern edge of the city on avenue de la Gare des Eaux-Vives, serves Evian-les Bains. For train information and schedules, call ☎ 022/731-64-50. Evian can also be reached from Geneva by one of the popular **ferries** (CGN) that depart from quai du Mont-Blanc at the foot of the rue des Alpes or from Le Jardin Anglais. From May 24 to September 21, one ferry a day departs Geneva daily at 9am, arriving in Evian at 11:40am. The return from Evian is at 5:50pm daily, with an arrival in Geneva at 8:45pm. A first-class one-way ticket costs 156F ($28.10), a second-class ticket, 116F ($20.90). For ferry information and schedules, call ☎ 022/732-39-16. If you're **driving** from Geneva, take N5 heading east along the southern rim of the lake. If you're driving down from Paris, take the A6 south. Before Macon, signs point to the turnoff for Thonon-Evian. At Thonon, N5 leads to Evian. Anticipate 5½ hours for trip time, although this can vary greatly depending on traffic conditions.

VISITOR INFORMATION   The **Office de Tourisme** is on place d'Allinges (☎ 04-50-75-04-26).

TAKING THE WATERS AT EVIAN

The clear, cold waters at Evian, legendary for their health and beauty-inducing benefits, attract a distinguished clientele of visitors who possess both the time and money to appreciate them.

For the most luxurious way to immerse yourself in the resort's hydro-rituals, check into either of these two hotels, both of which maintain (private) spa facilities that are open only to well-heeled residents: **Hotel Royal,** Rive Sud du Lac de Genève (☎ 04-50-26-85-00), and **Hotel Ermitage,** route Abondance (☎ 04-50-26-85-00), offer the most expensive packages, and are adept at pampering the bodies, souls, and egos of their world-class patrons.

More reasonably priced are the spa facilities at the **Espace Thermal Evian,** place de la Libération, BP 21, Evian CEDEX. (☎ 04-50-75-02-30). Their spa treatments are on a more democratic basis, and they do not restrict who can gain access. In some instances, clients pay lower rates yet receive treatments conceived and managed by the same supervisory organization. The hotel spas are more likely to place an emphasis on beauty regimes and stress therapies, but the public facilities at Espace Thermal contain a broader range of services that feature preventive measures for alleviating potential medical problems as well.

The origins of this public facility date from around 1900, although the modern facilities you see today date from the mid-1980s. Positioned adjacent to Débarcadère, just uphill from the edge of the lake, you'll find all the facilities you might need for tanning, massage, and skin and beauty care (but no facilities for overnight guests).

For the best way to indulge, pay 330F ($59.40) for a *journée thermale,* which provides access to exercise rooms and classes, saunas, steam baths, floods of water from the Evian springs, and two massage sessions. You can also spend up to 1,000F ($180) extra per day on additional massage, health, and beauty regimes, depending on your time and inclination. The facilities are open daily from 9am to 8:30pm, with a 1-hour break between 1:30 and 2:30pm.

WHERE TO STAY

Note that the **Hôtel-Restaurant Le Bourgogne** (see below) also rents rooms.

EXPENSIVE

✪ **Hôtel de la Verniaz et ses Chalets.** Av. Verniaz, à Neuvecelle, 74500 Evian-les-Bains. ☎ **04-50-75-04-90.** Fax 04-50-70-78-92. E-mail: verniaz@relaischateaux.fr. 35 units, 5 chalets. MINIBAR TV TEL. 600–1,300F ($108–$234) double; 1,800–2,600F ($324–$468) suite; 1,100–1,500F ($198–$270) chalet. AE, DC, MC, V. Closed mid-Nov to mid-Feb.

This glamorous country house stands on a hillside with a panoramic view of woods, water, and the Alps. The well-furnished rooms, complete with amenities, are in either the main house or one of the separate chalets; the chalets have their own gardens and more privacy, but they do cost a fortune.

Dining: Since guests stay here on half board, they're usually delighted at the care that goes into the food. The chefs turn out dishes for the discriminating palate, including omble chevalier, that fabled fish of Lake Geneva, served with a mousseline sauce, or herb-flavored alpine lamb.

✪ **Hôtel Les Prés Fleuris.** Rte. de Thollon, 74500 Evian-les-Bains. ☎ **04-50-75-29-14.** Fax 04-50-70-77-75. 12 units. MINIBAR TV TEL. 850–1,000F ($153–$180) double; 1,100–1,400F ($198–$252) junior suite. AE, MC, V. Closed Oct to mid-May.

Beside a high-altitude alpine lake 5 miles east of Evian, this Relais & Châteaux occupies a white villa that evolved from a farmhouse built in 1842. In summer, flower boxes are affixed to the windows and balconies, and the glass walls capitalize on the view. Each room is richly furnished, often with antiques or reproductions. Tables and wrought-iron chairs are set under the trees for meals in fair weather.

Dining: M. and Mme Roger Frossard serve exceptional food, using deluxe ingredients such as delectable Bresse chicken, whose flavor M. Frossard enhances with fresh herbs. His fricassée of meadow mushrooms is sublime. Nonguests must make reservations, as this is a popular place, with even better cuisine than La Verniaz et ses Chalets (though the service might be a bit off-putting).

INEXPENSIVE

Hôtel Les Cygnes. Grande-Rive, 74500 Evian-les-Bains. ☎ **04-50-75-01-01.** 38 units, 23 with shower only, 15 with bathtub. TEL. 225F ($40.50) double with shower only; 375F ($67.50) double with bathtub. Rates include breakfast. AE, DC, MC, V. Closed Sept–June.

This is one of the bargains at the spa. The Norman-style villa is characterized by dormer windows, a conical tower, a beam-and-plaster facade, a mansard roof, an entrance courtyard surrounded by flowers and shrubs, and a waterside terrace. The guest rooms are simply but comfortably furnished. This family-run hotel makes a convenient base from which to explore Lake Geneva.

WHERE TO DINE

The restaurant at the **Hôtel Les Prés Fleuris** (see above) is a marvelous dining choice.

Hôtel-Restaurant Le Bourgogne. Place Charles-Cottet, 74500 Evian-les-Bains. ☎ **04-50-75-01-05.** Fax 04-50-75-04-05. Reservations required. Restaurant, main courses 90–110F ($16.20–$19.80); fixed-price menus 145–250F ($26.10–$45). Brasserie, fixed-price menus 69–98F ($12.40–$17.65). AE, DC, MC, V. Restaurant, Wed–Mon noon–2pm and 7:30–9:30pm; brasserie, daily noon–2pm and 7:30–10pm. Closed Nov 15–Dec 15. FRENCH.

Come here if you want a delectable meal, impeccable service, an attractive setting, and excellent wine—regional wines featured are Crépy and Rousette. Menu choices in the restaurant (which is more formal and attentive than the brasserie) are likely to include the inevitable house version of foie gras, beef in peppercorn poivrade sauce, émincé of duckling with caramelized peaches, and a poached version of the local whitefish (omble chevalier) with whiskey sauce. Items in the brasserie are flavorful and unpretentious, like robust portions of cassoulets, magrêts of duckling, and steaks.

The inn also offers 31 comfortable rooms, costing 395F to 520F ($71.10 to $93.60).

✪ **La Toque Royale.** In the Casino Royal, domaine du Royal Club Evian, on the south bank of Lake Geneva. ☎ **04-50-26-87-10.** Reservations required. Main courses 170–250F ($30.60–$45); fixed-price menus 250–480F ($45–$86.40). AE, DC, MC, V. Mon–Sat 7:30–10pm. SAVOYARD.

The gourmet restaurant of the Domaine du Royal Club Evian, overlooking the lake, is the most elegant place to dine in town. The refined atmosphere creates an appropriate setting for the tasty gourmet cuisine: scallops with flap mushrooms, the tenderest lamb in the Alps, the succulent omble chevalier, and filet of veal with morels. The kitchen also concocts the most delicious desserts in town.

EVIAN-LES-BAINS AFTER DARK

In the town center is the **Casino Royal Evian,** domaine du Royal Club Evian, on the south bank of Lake Geneva (☎ **04-50-26-87-87**), patronized heavily by the Swiss from across the lake. Charging 70F ($12.60) admission, it offers blackjack, baccarat, and roulette, among other games, and has its own disco (Le Flash) that's open nightly from June to September, Friday and Saturday nights from October to May. Hours are 11pm to 3am, and admission is 60F ($10.80). The casino's slot machine area offers more than 250 slot, roller, and video-poker machines and one of the largest machines in the world, the "Jumbo." The Jackpot Bar is open until the casino closes.

2 Annecy

334 miles SE of Paris, 35 miles SE of Geneva, 85 miles E of Lyon

On Lac d'Annecy, the jewel of the Savoy Alps, the resort of Annecy makes the best base for touring the Haute-Savoie, of which it's the capital. The former seat of the comtes de Genève, and before that a Gallo-Roman town, Annecy opens onto one of the best views of lakes and mountains in the French Alps. Since the 1980s, this has become a booming urban center with a savvy city government that has prompted industry yet preserved its natural setting as well. In summer, its lakefront promenade is crowded and active.

ESSENTIALS

GETTING THERE   Annecy is near a network of highways, so many people travel here by car. If you're **driving** to Annecy from Paris, follow the same directions as for Evian (see above)—except when you come to Bellegarde-sur-Valserine, cut southeast along N508. Annecy also has **railway** and **bus** service from Geneva, Grenoble, and Lyon. Nine trains per day arrive from Grenoble (trip time: 2 hours); about 10 trains pull in daily from Paris (trip time: 3½ hours). For train information and schedules, call ☎ **08-36-35-35-39.** There's also a nearby **airport** in the hamlet of Meythet that accepts flights from Paris.

VISITOR INFORMATION   The **Office de Tourisme** is at 1 rue Jean-Jaurès (☎ 04-50-45-00-33).

SEEING THE SIGHTS

Built around the river Thiou, Annecy has been called the Venice of the Alps because of the canals that cut through the old part of town, **Vieil Annecy.** You can explore the arcaded streets of the old town, where Jean-Jacques Rousseau arrived in 1728.

After seeing Annecy, consider a trek to the **Gorges du Fier,** a dramatic river gorge 6 miles west. To reach it, take either a train or a bus from in front of Annecy's rail station, getting off at the hamlet of Poisy. For the latest schedules, go to the Office de Tourisme (see above). Then walk the remaining 2 miles along a well-marked trail. This striking gorge is one of the most interesting sights in the French Alps. A gangway takes you through a winding gully, varying from 10 to 30 feet wide. The gully was cut by the torrent through the rock and over breathtaking depths; you'll hear the roar of the river at the bottom. Emerging from this labyrinth, you'll be greeted by a huge expanse of boulders. You can visit the gorge from June 15 to September 10, daily from 9am to 7pm; March 15 to June 14 and September 11 to October 15, daily from 9am to noon and 2 to 6pm. A hike through its well-signposted depths takes less than an hour and costs 25F ($4.50) for adults and 16F ($2.90) for children. Call ☎ **04-50-46-23-07** for more information.

You can also take a cruise on the ice-blue lake for which the town is famous. Tours of **Lac d'Annecy,** from Easter to the end of September, usually last 1 to 2 hours. A tour that makes stops at every significant village around the lake's edge lasts 1¾ hours and costs 70F ($12.60) per person. During July and August, there are three of these boat tours per day, allowing you to get off at whatever port you want, explore the town and environs, and pick up the next boat for a return before nightfall to Annecy. Inquire at the Office de Tourisme (see above) about various possibilities, or call the **Compagnie des Bateaux du Lac d'Annecy** (☎ 04-50-51-08-40) for more information.

Château d'Annecy. ☎ **04-50-33-87-30.** Admission 30F ($5.40) adults, 10F ($1.80) students and children 11–16, free for children 10 and under. June–Sept daily 10am–6pm; Oct–May Wed–Mon 10am–noon and 2–6pm.

This forbidding gray-stone monument, whose 12th-century pinnacle is known as the Queen's Tower, dominates the resort. It was in this castle that the comtes de Genève took refuge from their enemies in the 13th century. The château contains a museum of regional artifacts that include alpine furniture, religious art, oil paintings, and modern art. A section is devoted to the geology and marine life of the region's deep, cold lakes.

Château de Montrottier. 74330 Lovagny. ☎ **04-50-46-23-02.** Admission 28F ($5.05) adults, 18F ($3.25) children and students. Wed–Mon 9:30–11:30am and 2–5:30pm. Closed Oct 16–Mar 14.

Within walking distance of the gorges is the 13th- and 14th-century Château de Montrottier. A once-feudal citadel that was partially protected by the surrounding rugged geology, its tower offers a panoramic view of Mont Blanc. Inside, a small museum showcases pottery, Asian costumes, armor, tapestries, and antiques, as well as some bronze bas-reliefs from the 16th century.

WHERE TO STAY

Note that the **Auberge de l'Eridan** (see below) also rents rooms.

Au Faisan Doré. 34 av. d'Albigny, 74000 Annecy. ☎ **04-50-23-02-46.** Fax 04-50-23-11-10. 40 units. TV TEL. 320–460F ($57.60–$82.80) per person double. Rates include half board. MC, V. Parking 50F ($9). Closed Dec 17–Feb 1.

Near the casino at the end of a tree-lined lakefront boulevard, this hotel is only 2 minutes on foot from the lake and Imperial Park. Owned and run by the Clavel family since 1919, it earned three stars in 1992; it's a member of the Logis de France, a value-oriented choice catering to the family trade. The public and private rooms follow the decor of the Haute Savoy. Each guest room is cozy and comfortable but not extravagant. The chef serves three fixed-price menus in the adjacent restaurant.

Demeure de Chavoire. 71 rte. d'Annecy, 74290 Veyrier-du-Lac. ☎ **04-50-60-04-38.** Fax 04-50-60-05-36. 13 units. MINIBAR TV TEL. 750–1,000F ($135–$180) double; 1,200–1,600F ($216–$288) suite. AE, DC, MC, V. From Annecy, follow the signs to Chavoires and Talloires.

One of the most charming accommodations in the area is at Chavoires, about 2 miles west of Annecy. It's intimate and cozy, brightly decorated with well-chosen Savoy antiques. Large doors lead to the gardens overlooking the lake. The rooms have names rather than numbers, and each is uniquely decorated. Thoughtful extras such as fruit in the rooms make this a deserving selection—plus it's more tranquil than the hotels in the center of Annecy. The helpful staff will direct you to nearby restaurants.

Hôtel du Nord. 24 rue Sommeiller, 74000 Annecy. ☎ **04-50-45-08-78.** Fax 04-50-51-22-04. www.clarine.com. 32 units. TV TEL. 258–278F ($46.45–$50.05) double. AE, MC, V.

A two-star hotel in the center of Annecy, the continually renovated du Nord is one of the better bargains here—just minutes from the train station and Lac d'Annecy. The staff is extremely helpful and speaks English. You'll appreciate the cleanliness and modernity of the soundproofed rooms; some are air-conditioned as well. Breakfast is the only meal served, but the staff will direct you to nearby reasonably priced restaurants.

WHERE TO DINE

✪ **Auberge de l'Eridan.** 13 vieille rte. des Pensières, 74290 Veyrier-du-Lac. ☎ **04-50-60-24-00.** Fax 04-50-60-23-63. Reservations required. Main courses 250–395F ($45–$71.10); fixed-price menus 595–995F ($107.10–$179.10). AE, DC, MC, V. Daily noon–1:30pm, Mon–Sat 7:30–9:30pm. Closed Dec 6–Jan 15; Mon and Sun dinner from Sept 2 to mid-June. From Annecy's lakefront boulevard, follow the signs to Veyrier-du-Lac, Chavoires, and Talloires. FRENCH.

Famous throughout France because of the excellent and unusual cuisine of the owner, Marc Veyrat-Durebex, this world-class restaurant occupies a romanticized version of a château at the edge of the lake in the village of Veyrier-du-Lac, about a mile from Annecy. Guests dine in a posh room with ceiling frescoes. Menu choices include ravioli of vegetables flavored with rare alpine herbs gathered by M. Veyrat-Durebex and his team in the mountains. Also recommended are pike-perch sausage, crayfish poached with bitter almonds, and poached sea bass with caviar.

The Auberge also rents traditionally furnished rooms, charging 1,550F to 3,250F ($279 to $585) for a double, with suites going for 3,250F to 3,650F ($585 to $657).

Le Belvédère. 7 chemin du Belvédère, 7400 Annecy. ☎ **04-50-45-04-90.** Fax 04-50-45-67-25. Reservations recommended. Main courses 120–150F ($21.60–$27); fixed-price menus 170–330F ($30.60–$59.40). AE, MC, V. Tues–Sun 12:30–2:15pm, Tues–Sat 8–9:30pm. From downtown Annecy, follow the signs leading uphill to Le Semnoz. FRENCH/SEAFOOD.

This is one of the most appealing reasonably priced restaurants in town, run by hard-working owners/chefs Jean-Louis and Michelle Aubeneau since 1969. On a belvedere above Annecy, about a mile west of the town center, it provides views that extend up to 5 miles over mountains and lakes. Menu items stress fish in many variations, prepared with finesse and something approaching devotion. Examples are a soup of scallops with strips of fresh vegetables, grilled turbot with a sauce made from violet-flavored mustard, and filet of sole stuffed with a mousseline of scallops. Other than some token dishes (like guinea fowl with Indian spices), little meat is served.

The restaurant maintains 10 guest rooms, much more simple and less opulent than the restaurant. (They're often used spontaneously by diners who discover they've had too much wine at dinner and prefer not to drive home.) Each has a phone. The 6 rooms with bathroom are 230F ($41.40) for one or two occupants; the 4 rooms without bathroom are 190F ($34.20).

ANNECY AFTER DARK

In the old town, you'll find an assortment of bars, cafes, pubs, and (in warmer months) street dances, fairs, and even carnivals. A calmer alternative is an evening of theater or dance at the **Théâtre d'Annecy,** 1 rue Jean-Jaurès (☎ 04-50-33-44-11), where tickets average 125F ($22.50).

If a long day of activities has left you thirsty, try **Le Roi Arthur,** 14 rue Perrière (☎ 04-50-51-27-06), where you can mingle with the twentysomething, out-to-have-a-good-time crowd. A traditional Irish pub, **Le Captain Pub,** 11 rue Pont-Morenc (☎ 04-50-45-79-80), has a selection of hearty dark ales on tap. Alternatively, **Le Vieux Necy,** 3 rue Filaterie (☎ 04-50-45-01-57), attracts a younger, more boisterous crowd.

The best piano bar is **Le Duo,** 104 av. Jenève (☎ 04-50-57-01-46), an ideal spot for quiet conversation. **Comedy Café,** 13 rue Royale Galerie des Sorbiers (☎ 04-50-52-82-83), is the sole gay nightspot in town. This bar/cabaret is a wild fusion of dance bar, pool hall, and piano bar, with plenty of young men on the prowl. It's a fun place that really gets crazy with drag shows on Fridays and Saturdays.

Among dance clubs, the lively **Le Pop Plage,** 30 av. d'Albigny (☎ 04-50-23-12-86), pulls in an older, more sophisticated crowd than the **Discothèque l'Esprit,** 37 av. Chavoire (☎ 04-50-23-33-43), which is a haven for teenyboppers. Both places are bastions of techno and rock and can charge a cover of as much as 100F ($18) on Fridays and Saturdays. Le Pop Plage is open in summer only.

For the most elegant evening on the town, head for the swank **Casino de l'Impérial,** 32 av. d'Albigny (☎ 04-50-09-30-00), part of the belle époque Impérial Palace hotel on a peninsula jutting out into Lake Annecy.

3 Talloires

342 miles SE of Paris, 20 miles N of Albertville, 8 miles S of Annecy

The charming village of Talloires is old enough to appear on lists of territories once controlled by Lothar II, great-grandson of Charlemagne—it dates back to 866. Chalk cliffs surround a pleasant bay, and at the lower end a wooden promontory encloses a small port. An 18-hole golf course and water sports like skiing, boating, swimming, and fishing make this a favorite spot with French vacationers. Talloires is also a great stop for gourmet types, boasting one of France's great restaurants, Auberge du Père-Bise, and a Benedictine abbey founded in the 11th century but now transformed into the deluxe Hôtel de l'Abbaye.

From Annecy (see above), you can reach Talloires by **driving** south along N508 (on the eastern shore of Lac d'Annecy) for 8 miles.

The **Office de Tourisme** is on rue André-Theuriet (☎ **04-50-60-70-64**).

WHERE TO STAY

Auberge du Père-Bise and **Villa des Fleurs** (see "Where to Dine," below) also rent luxurious rooms.

Hôtel de l'Abbaye. Rte. du Port, 74290 Talloires. ☎ **04-50-60-77-33.** Fax 04-50-60-78-81. E-mail: abbaye@alp.pink.com. 30 units. TV TEL. 675–1,280F ($121.50–$230.40) double; 1,230–1,485F ($221.40–$267.30) suite. Half board 600–870F ($108–$156.60) per person extra double, 855–975F ($153.90–$175.50) per person extra suite. AE, DC, MC, V. Closed Nov–Mar 15.

This place was built in the 1500s as a Benedictine monastery but has functioned as a hotel almost continuously since the Revolution. A Relais & Châteaux, with close-up views of the lake, it makes for a memorable stop even though it doesn't equal the cuisine or the luxury of the Auberge du Père-Bise (then again, it's a lot more affordable). The secluded hotel is rich with beamed ceilings, antique portraits, leather chairs, formal French gardens, and richly carved balustrades. The great corridors lead to converted guest rooms—no two alike; suspended wooden balconies lead to a second level of rooms. The tasteful, well-chosen furnishings include all the Louis periods as well as Directoire and Empire. In summer, the restaurant expands onto a lakefront terrace shaded by trees.

WHERE TO DINE

✪ **Auberge du Père-Bise.** Rte. du Port, Bord du Lac, 74290 Talloires. ☎ **04-50-60-72-01.** Fax 04-50-60-73-05. Reservations required. Main courses 180–450F ($32.40–$81); fixed-price menus 490–820F ($88.20–$147.60). AE, DC, MC, V. May–Oct daily noon–2pm and 7–9pm. Closed Tues and lunch on Wed Feb 13–Apr and Nov 1–15; closed altogether Nov 15–Feb 12. FRENCH.

Since the 1950s, when billionaires and starlets were drawn here like iron filings to a magnet, Auberge du Père-Bise has radiated style and charm. A chalet built beside the lake in 1901 and renovated many times since (most recently in 1996), it's one of France's most acclaimed—and astronomically expensive—restaurants. Today it's directed by Sophie Bise, granddaughter of the patriarch who established it. The elegant dining room has sparkling silverware and bowls of flowers, but in fair weather you can dine under a vine-covered pergola and enjoy the view of mountains and lake. The kitchen excels at traditional dishes like mousse of goose foie gras, delicate young lamb, and gratin of crayfish tails.

The inn also offers 31 guest rooms and 3 suites, each with a minibar, TV, and phone; they cost 1,100F to 2,200F ($198 to $396) for a double, 2,500F to 3,000F ($450 to $540) for a suite. Because this place is so popular and intimate, it's wise to make reservations at least 2 months in advance, especially in summer.

Villa des Fleurs. Rte. du Port, 74290 Talloires. ☎ **04-50-60-71-14.** Fax 04-50-60-74-06. Reservations required. Main courses 115–165F ($20.70–$29.70); fixed-price menus 150–290F ($27–$52.20). AE, V. Tues–Sun noon–2pm and 5–9pm. Closed Nov 15–Dec 15 and Mon Nov–May. FRENCH.

This attractive *restaurant avec chambres* should be better known, as it's the best place in Talloires in this price range. The proprietors, Marie-France and Charles Jaegler, serve wonderfully prepared meals, which often include salade landaise with foie gras and filet of fera, a fish that lives only in Lac Annecy. The dining room overlooks the water.

Eight simply furnished rooms are available for rent, each with minibar, phone, and Victorian-era decor. Doubles cost 490F ($88.20) and are at the top of a winding staircase—there's no elevator.

4 Aix-les-Bains

332 miles SE of Paris, 21 miles SW of Annecy, 10 miles N of Chambéry

On the eastern edge of Lac du Bourget, modern Aix-les-Bains is the most fashionable (and largest) spa in eastern France. The hot springs, which offered comfort to the Romans, are said to be useful for treating rheumatism.

ESSENTIALS

GETTING THERE Some 20 **trains** per day arrive from Paris (trip time: 3½ hours); 10 trains pull in from Annecy (trip time: 30 minutes). For information and schedules, call ☎ **08-36-35-35-39.** If you're **driving** to Aix-les-Bains from Annecy (see above), follow RN 201.

VISITOR INFORMATION The **Office de Tourisme et Syndicat d'Initiative** is on place Maurice Mollard (☎ **04-79-35-05-92**).

SEEING THE SIGHTS

The spa is well equipped for visitors: It contains flower gardens, a casino (the Palais de Savoie), a racecourse, a golf course, and Lac du Bourget, which has a beach. **Thermes Nationaux** lie in the center of town, more than 2 miles from the lakeshore, near the casino, the Temple of Diana, and the Hôtel de Ville (town hall). Closer to the lake, a long string of flower beds and ornamental shrubs border the town's famous waterside promenades, where you can take a lovely stroll.

Regular steamer service takes you on a 4-hour **boat ride on Lac du Bourget**—a beautiful trip. For information about departure times (which change seasonally), consult the Les Bateaux d'Aix (☎ **04-79-63-45-00**). Boats depart from the landing stage at Grand Port. You can also take a bus ride from Aix to the small town of Revard, at 5,080 feet, where you'll be rewarded with a panoramic view of Mont Blanc. For bus information, contact Trans Savoir (☎ **04-79-35-21-74**).

Abbaye d'Hautecombe. 73310 St-Pierre de Curtille. ☎ **04-79-54-26-12.** Tours are free, but donations welcome. 30-minute guided tours, in English and French, depart at 6-minute intervals Wed–Mon 10–11:30am and 2–5pm, Sun 10:30–11:30am and 2–5pm. You can reach the abbey by car or boat, with two to five steamers leaving daily Easter–Sept. To board, go to the landing stage at Aix-les-Bains. The price is 56F ($10.10) for the 2½-hour trip. See Les Bateaux d'Aix above for steamer information.

This is the spiritual centerpiece of the French Alps and the mausoleum of many of the princes of the House of Savoy. It was built by a succession of monks from the Cîteaux, Cistercian, and Benedictine orders beginning in the 1100s and stands on a promontory jutting into the western edge of Le Bourget lake, almost directly across the water from Aix-les-Bains. Before the 1500s, at least 40 members of the royal family of the Savoy were buried here.

After years of neglect, the church was reconstructed and lavishly embellished during the 19th century by Charles-Felix, king of Sardinia, in what is called the Troubadour

Gothic style. The fervently religious ecumenical community occupying the abbey organizes seminars, welcomes short- or medium-term devotees, and perpetuates the tradition of worship maintained on this site since the 12th century. Sincere pilgrims are welcome to attend morning mass Monday through Friday at 8am, communion Monday through Saturday at noon and Sunday at 9:15am, and Vespers daily at 7pm. The abbey is open to casual visitors during the hours given above for tours.

Musée Faure. 10 bd. des Côtes. ☎ **04-79-61-06-57.** Admission 20F ($3.60). Mon and Wed–Fri 9:30am–noon and 1:30–6pm, Sat–Sun 9:30am–noon and 2–6:45pm.

This is the town's most interesting museum, with a modern-art collection that includes sculptures by Rodin and works by Degas, Corot, and Cézanne. It's situated on a hill overlooking the lake and the town.

Thermes Nationaux d'Aix-les-Bains. Place Maurice-Mollard. ☎ **04-79-35-38-50.** Tours 20F ($3.60), given May–Oct Tues–Sat at 3pm (closed holidays).

The original structure for the Thermes Nationaux d'Aix-les-Bains was begun in 1857 by Victor Emmanuel II; the New Baths, launched in 1934, were expanded and renovated in 1972. To visit, go to the caretaker at the entrance opposite the Hôtel de Ville, the former château of the marquises of Aix in the 16th century. Before you enter the baths, you can visit the thermal caves. In the center of the spa are two Roman remains—a Temple of Diana and the 30-foot-tall triumphal Arch of Campanus.

WHERE TO STAY

Hôtel-Restaurant Davat and **Lille** (see "Where to Dine," below) also rent rooms.

Hostellerie Le Manoir. 37 rue Georges-1er, 73100 Aix-les-Bains. ☎ **04-79-61-44-00.** Fax 04-79-35-67-67. 73 units. TV TEL. 395–695F ($71.10–$125.10) double. AE, DC, MC, V. Closed Dec 25–Jan 1.

In 1968 the present owners took a structure that had functioned for years as a stable and transformed it into a white-sided hotel with many modern conveniences. Today you'll find an architecturally interesting site that includes shutters, an overhanging roof, and paths weaving through turn-of-the-century gardens with outdoor furniture placed under shade trees. You can order breakfast or dinner, weather permitting, on a terrace bordering the garden. Most of the public rooms, as well as the guest rooms, open onto terraces. The decor is traditional, with antique and provincial furniture. Facilities include an indoor pool, a Turkish bath, and a sauna.

Hôtel Ariana. Av. de Marlioz, à Marlioz, 73100 Aix-les-Bains. Tel. **04-79-61-79-79.** Fax 04-79-61-79-00. E-mail: hotels@aix-marlige.com. 60 units. MINIBAR TV TEL. 430–625F ($77.40–$112.50) double. AE, DC, MC, V.

The Ariana caters to a spa-oriented crowd that enjoys taking quiet walks through the surrounding park. The stylized loggia-dotted glass exterior opens into an Art Deco interior highlighted by contrasting metal, wood, and fabrics, plus plenty of white marble and antique reproductions. Tunnellike glass walkways connect it to the hotel's main core; facilities include two indoor pools, a sauna, and a health center. The guest rooms are quite comfortable, though small. Café Adelaïde functions as both a cafe and a restaurant, offering fine classic dishes.

WHERE TO DINE

Hôtel-Restaurant Davat. Au Grand Port, 73100 Aix-les-Bains. ☎ **04-79-63-40-40.** Reservations required. Main courses 75–120F ($13.50–$21.60); fixed-price menus 90–225F ($16.20–$40.50). AE, MC, V. Mon noon–1:30pm, Tues–Wed and Fri–Sun noon–1:30pm and 7–9:30pm. Closed Nov–Mar. FRENCH.

You'll enjoy the traditional cooking, gracious service, and selection of regional wines here. This is not only a leading restaurant but also an excellent moderately priced place to stay, where the chief attraction is the beautiful flower garden. The 20 rooms are simply furnished and begin at 280F ($50.40) for a double, which includes breakfast.

Lille. Au Grand Port, 73100 Aix-les-Bains. ☎ **04-79-63-40-00.** Fax 04-79-34-00-30. Reservations required. Main courses 80–150F ($14.40–$27); fixed-price menus 98–250F ($17.65–$45). AE, DC, MC, V. Thurs–Mon noon–2pm and 7:30–9pm. FRENCH.

Near the landing stages where the Lac du Bourget steamers depart is the best restaurant in Aix-les-Bains, housed in what was once a 19th-century private villa. Four generations of the Lille family have welcomed guests to this lakeside retreat. Appetizers include a roster of terrines made from pork, duck, rabbit, veal, and various kinds of liver. Main courses feature skillfully prepared versions of omble chevalier (the famous whitefish from Lake Geneva), either meunière style or with champagne-flavored cream sauce. Also look for Bresse chicken with a succulent gratin dauphinois.

Eighteen simply furnished rooms are available for rent; doubles begin at 360F ($64.80).

5 Grenoble

352 miles SE of Paris, 34 miles S of Chambéry, 64 miles SE of Lyon

Because this city, the ancient capital of the Dauphine, is the commercial, intellectual, and tourist center of the Alps, it's a major stop for travelers (including those driving between the Riviera and Geneva). A sports capital in both winter and summer, it also attracts many foreign students—its university has the largest summer-session program in Europe.

Founded in 1339, the University of Grenoble today has a student body of some 40,000 and is the heart of intellectual life in the region. With an overall population of some 400,000, this town is also home to four other universities with a large influx of English and American students, giving it a cosmopolitan air. Many residents are employed at a major nuclear research station on the banks of the Drac, and the Hewlett-Packard aircraft company also has its headquarters here.

ESSENTIALS

GETTING THERE   An important rail and bus junction, Grenoble is easily accessible from Paris and all the cities in this chapter. About 11 **trains** per day arrive from Paris (trip time: 3 hours); trains arrive almost every hour from Chambéry (trip time: 30 minutes). For train information and schedules, call ☎ **08-36-35-35-39.** Grenoble's **airport** (☎ 04-76-65-48-48) is 24½ miles northwest of the city center. If you're **driving,** take A6 from Paris to Lyon, then continue the rest of the way along A48 into Grenoble. Depending on conditions, the entire drive should take from 6 to 7 hours.

VISITOR INFORMATION   Designed by the architect A. Wogenscky and constructed in 1968, the **Maison de la Culture,** 14 rue de la République (☎ 04-76-51-33-71), lies in the new quarter of Malherbe. At the **Office de Tourisme** (☎ 04-76-42-41-41), you can pick up a calendar listing the month's events, which range from Impressionist exhibits to cinema showings, from orchestral concerts to dance. The center is open Tuesday through Saturday from 1 to 7pm (closed part of August).

SEEING THE SIGHTS

Grenoble lies near the junction of the Isère and Drac rivers. Most of the city is on the south bank of the Isère, though its most impressive monument, the **Fort de la**

Bastille, stands in relative isolation on a rocky hilltop on the north bank (a cable car will carry you from the south bank's quai Stéphane-Jay across the river to the top of the fort). The center of Grenoble's historic section is the **Palais de Justice** and **place St-André.** The more modern part of town is southeast, centered around the contemporary **Hôtel de Ville** (town hall) and the nearby **Tour Perret.**

Begin at **place Grenette,** a lively square filled with flowers in late spring and early summer, where you can enjoy a drink or an espresso. This square enjoys many associations with Grenoble-born Stendhal, who wrote such masterpieces as *The Red and the Black* and *The Charterhouse of Parma.* It was here that Antoine Berthet, supposedly the model for Stendhal's Julien Grel, was executed for attempted murder in 1827.

Next, enjoy a ride on the **Téléférique de la Bastille** (☎ **04-76-44-33-65**), high-swinging cable cars that take you over the Isère. It operates in July and August, Monday from 11am to 12:30am and Tuesday through Sunday from 9am to 12:30am; June 14 to 30 and September 1 to 13, Monday from 11am to midnight and Tuesday through Sunday from 9am to midnight; March 21 to June 13 and September 14 to October 31, Monday from 11am to 7:30pm, Tuesday through Saturday from 9am to midnight, and Sunday from 9am to 7:30pm; and November 1 to March 20, Monday from 11am to 6:30pm and Tuesday through Sunday from 10:30am to 6:30pm (closed Jan 5 to Jan 23). A round-trip ticket costs 34F ($6.10). From the belvedere where you land, you'll have a panoramic view of the city and surrounding mountains. You can return on foot if you want to walk. Signs point the way to Parc de la Bastille and Parc Guy-Pape and eventually lead you to the Jardin des Dauphins, open daily in summer from 9am to 7:30pm.

If you prefer, from the Belvédère de Grenoble you can take the **Télésiège Bastille-Mont-Jalla** for an even loftier view. To board the car in Grenoble, head for the Gare de Départ on quai Stéphane-Jay, facing the Jardin de Ville.

Musée de Peinture et de Sculpture. 5 place de Lavalette. ☎ **04-76-63-44-44.** Admission 25F ($4.50) adults; 15F ($2.70) children, students, and seniors. Wed 11am–10pm and Thurs–Mon 11am–7pm.

Founded in 1796, this is one of the country's oldest art museums. It was the first French museum to focus on modern art, a fact appreciated by Picasso, who donated his *Femme Lisant* in 1921. Flemish and Italian Renaissance works are displayed, although it's the Impressionist paintings that generate the most interest. Note in particular Matisse's *Intérieur aux aubergines* and Léger's *Le Remorqueur.* Ernst, Klee, Bonnard, Monet, Rouault—they're all here.

Musée Dauphinois. 30 rue Maurice-Gignoux. ☎ **04-76-85-19-01.** Admission 20F ($3.60) adults, 10F ($1.80) children 10–16, free for children 9 and under. May–Oct Wed–Mon 10am–7pm; Nov–Apr Wed–Mon 10am–6pm. Closed Jan 1, May 1, and Dec 25.

Housed in a 17th-century convent and enhanced by the cloister, gardens, and baroque chapel, the museum lies across the Isère in the Ste-Marie-d'en-Haut section of town. A collection of ethnographic and historic mementos of the Dauphine is displayed, along with folk arts and crafts.

A SIDE TRIP FROM GRENOBLE IN PURSUIT OF CHARTREUSE

Local monks are the custodians of the secret formula for the liqueur known as Chartreuse, which Maréchal d'Estrées gave them in 1605. It was an elixir involving the distillation of 130 herbs, believed to have been originated by an anonymous alchemist.

Eventually the formula found its way to **La Grande Chartreuse** (charterhouse), founded in 1084 about 20 miles north of Grenoble. The monastery is no longer open to the public, but you're allowed to visit the **Musée de la Correrie,** 38380 St-Pierre-de-Chartreuse (☎ **04-76-88-60-45**), housed in a 15th-century building at the head of the valley about 1½ miles from the monastery. Admission to the museum costs 15F ($2.70) for adults and 8F ($1.45) for children; it's open in July and August, daily from 9:30am to noon and 1:30 to 6pm; in May, June, and September, daily from 9:30am to noon and 2 to 6pm; and in April and October, daily from 10am to noon and 2 to 6pm. This unusual museum provides a glimpse into a monk's life; the sound you'll hear is chanting.

Even more interesting is a trip to **Voiron,** about 20 miles away, where you can visit the **Caves de la Grande Chautreuse,** 10 bd. Edgar-Kofler (☎ **04-76-05-81-77**), the distillery where the famed Chartreuse is made. Free tours are possible in July and August, daily from 8am to 6:30pm; Easter to June and in September and October, daily from 8:30 to 11:30am and 2 to 6:30pm; and November to Easter, Monday through Friday from 8:30 to 11:30am and 2 to 5:30pm. Dressed in chartreuse green, a guide will show you the copper stills and take you to the cellar, filled with gargantuan oak casks in which the liqueur matures for several years. At the end of the tour, you'll get a free taste of the yellow or fiery green Chartreuse or of one of the new products. You can also purchase bottles at a shop on the premises. It's said that only three monks and the father procurator have access to the formula.

Before you head out into the Massif de la Chartreuse, where the monastery and distillery lie, obtain a good detailed map from the tourist office in Grenoble.

WHERE TO STAY

Hôtel d'Angleterre. 5 place Victor-Hugo, 38000 Grenoble. ☎ **04-76-87-37-21.** Fax 04-76-50-94-10. www.neptune.fr/hotel-grenoble/hotel-d-angleterre. E-mail: service.reception@dial.oleane.com. 66 units. A/C MINIBAR TV TEL. 490–690F ($88.20–$124.20) double. AE, DC, MC, V.

This hotel, located in the center of Grenoble, has tall windows and wrought-iron balconies; it opens onto a pleasant square with huge chestnut trees. Inside, the stylish salons boast wood-grained walls and ceilings and tropical plants. The guest rooms have contemporary styling, and some look out on the Vercors Massif. Breakfast is the only meal served.

Hôtel Lesdiguières. 122 cours de la Libération, 38000 Grenoble. ☎ **04-76-96-55-36.** Fax 04-76-48-10-13. 36 units. TV TEL. 400F ($72) double. AE, DC, MC, V. Parking 40F ($7.20). Closed Sat–Sun and all school holidays.

This imposing gray-brown stucco building, surrounded by a spacious lawn, is a training ground for the local hotel school, so the receptionist, porters, and restaurant staff are all members of the most recent graduating class. Inside, you'll find well-furnished guest rooms and sunny public areas filled with Louis XIII chairs and Oriental rugs. A stay here can have its own brand of charm—the staff probably works harder to impress than their more jaded counterparts elsewhere. The drawbacks are weekend closings and shutdowns during school holidays, most notably from early July to late September.

Hôtel Trianon. 3 rue Pierre-Arthaud, 38000 Grenoble. ☎ **04-76-46-21-62.** Fax 04-76-46-37-56. 38 units. TV TEL. 264–399F ($47.50–$71.80) double. AE, DC, MC, V. Parking 35F ($6.30).

Few other hotels in town have as effectively masked a banal 1950s design with such a dose of historic decorative styles. Trianon caters to lots of business travelers during the week; it's a comfortable, well-managed hotel that survives on more than just tourism. The rates are reduced on weekends, when business is slower. The rooms are somewhat cramped but cozy, furnished with just about every Louis style; a handful are done in a "shepherd" style that evokes a folkloric grange in the Alps. You'll find this popular two-star hotel a short walk south of the pedestrians-only district in the town center, near a well-known school, the Lycée Champollion.

WHERE TO DINE

Le Berlioz. 4 rue Strasbourg. ☎ **04-76-56-22-39.** Reservations required. Main courses 68–140F ($12.25–$25.20); fixed-price menus 120–260F ($21.60–$46.80). AE, DC, DISC, MC, V. Mon–Fri noon–2pm, Mon–Sat 7:30–10:30pm. Closed Aug. FRENCH.

Talented chef Françoise Legras, who has won much local acclaim, offers a gourmet tour of France by featuring a different menu with regional specialties every month. Try, for example, the fresh codfish with green cabbage and smoked lard, side of beef with baby vegetables in wine sauce, or, if featured, the roast duck in spicy honey sauce—a real winner.

Poularde Bressane. 12 place Paul-Mistral. ☎ **04-76-87-08-90.** Reservations required. Fixed-price menus 145–220F ($26.10–$39.60). AE, MC, V. Mon–Fri noon–2pm, Mon–Sat 7:30–9:45pm. Closed July 21–Aug 26. FRENCH.

At the finest restaurant in Grenoble, you'll enjoy superb and intelligent cuisine in an elegant setting. The chef, Jean-Charles Piccinini, describes his food as a subtly modern derivation of traditional cuisine. In honor of the restaurant's namesake, fatted hen is the major specialty. The chef's fish pâté is excellent, as is his foie gras, ravioli of fresh lobster, and poached filet of sea bass accented with olive oil and aromatic herbs. More adventurous palates try the sweetbreads in puff pastry. The menu is very much a *cuisine du marché*, based on what's available in the market that day. The desserts are delectable, many freshly prepared when you order.

GRENOBLE AFTER DARK

To get things started, all you have to do is walk to **place St-André, place aux Herbes,** or **place de Gordes.** On a good night, these squares overflow with young people, whose energy level builds in anticipation of an irrepressible explosion of dancing and serious partying.

You may want to pace yourself, though, starting out on the sedate side at the **Cybernet Café,** 3 rue Bayard (☎ 04-76-51-73-18). Here you'll find an unusual mix of soft candlelight and flea-market finds like car parts, signs, and bedposts, all interspersed between state-of-the-art computers. You'll pay 30F ($5.40) for 30 minutes of time online. Then you might check out **La Soupe aux Choux,** 7 rte. de Lyon (☎ 04-76-87-05-67), for an evening of jazz and blue haze. Two popular sports pubs that host a wild crowd of students are **Le Couche Tard,** 1 rue Palais (☎ 04-76-44-18-79), and **The London Pub,** 11 rue Brocherie (☎ 04-76-44-41-90). **L'Entre-Pôt,** 8 rue Auguste-Gemin (☎ 04-76-48-21-48), is a die-hard rock club famous in town for its live concerts.

For a great outdoor party, check out **Le Saxo,** 5 place d'Agier (☎ 04-76-51-06-01). Its big patio, with killer speakers blasting out techno and rock well into the early morning, has the feeling of a college frat party. If you're really pumped up and need to cut loose on the dance floor, bop on over to **Le Mae Vas,** 1 rue Lamartine (☎ 04-76-87-23-48), where the young rule the scene. The cover is 50F ($10).

The town's most popular gay bars are **Le Happy Bar,** 9 rue Etienne-Marcel (☎ 04-76-46-83-67), sporting a mixed gay and straight crowd; and **Bar l'Acqua,** 3 rue Etienne-Marcel (☎ 04-76-17-01-73). A restaurant frequented by gays is **La Créperie,** place de Metz (☎ 04-76-87-55-89).

6 Courchevel 1850

393 miles SE of Paris, 32 miles SE of Albertville, 60 miles SE of Chambéry

Courchevel has been called a resort of "high taste, high fashion, and high profile," a chic spot where multimillion-dollar chalets sit perched on pristine pine-covered slopes. Skiers and geographers know of it as part of Les Trois Vallées, sometimes called "the skiing supermarket of France." The resort, with 1,400 acres of ski runs, employs as many workers in summer as in winter, simply to manicure and maintain the top-notch ski conditions. Courchevel 1850 has excellent resorts and superb hotels—with price tags to match, so it largely draws the super-rich. Persons on average budgets should avoid the place and head for more reasonably priced resorts in winter, especially Chamonix (see below).

Courchevel maintains three ski schools with an average staff of 450 instructors, a labyrinth of chairlifts, and more than 200 ski runs, which are excellent in the intermediate and advanced categories. Also in Les Trois Vallées are the less well known resorts of Méribel, Les Menuires, and Val Thorens, which you should avoid unless you direly need to save money. Courchevel consists of four planned ski towns, each marked by its elevation in meters. Thus there's less fashionable Courchevel 1300 (Le Prez), Courchevel 1550, and Courchevel 1650. Crowning them all is Courchevel 1850.

Courchevel 1850 is the most attractive ski mecca in the French Alps, a position once held by Megève. It's also the focal point of a chair-hoist network crisscrossing the region. At the center of one of the largest ski areas in the world, Courchevel was built at the base of a soaring alpine amphitheater whose deep snowfalls last longer than those at most other resorts because it faces the north winds. Expect reliable snow conditions throughout the winter, perfectly groomed runs, vertical cliffs, and enough safe runs to appease the intermediate skier as well. The glacier skiing alone draws experts from around the world. The whole complex of Les Trois Vallées is one vast ski circus.

A 1-day ski pass for Courchevel alone costs 184F ($33.10), but a 1-day pass to the facilities of Les Trois Vallées goes for 220F ($39.60). A 3-day pass costs 516F ($92.90) for Courchevel or 634F ($114.10) for Les Trois Vallées.

ESSENTIALS

GETTING THERE Courchevel 1850 is the last stop on a steep alpine road that dead-ends at the village center, and it sometimes makes for perilous driving during winter snowstorms—but roads are kept open all year. To go any higher, you'll have to take a cable car from the center of town. Most visitors drive here (you'll need snow tires and chains), but some buses link the city to railway junctions farther down the mountain. If you're **driving** from Paris, you can take A6 to Lyon, then A42 to Chambéry, then A430 to Albertville. At Albertville, get on N90 to Moutiers, then follow the narrow roads 915 and 75 into Courchevel.

The nearest **train** station is in Moutiers Salins. From here you can catch one of 5 buses leaving Monday through Friday or 15 per day on Saturday and Sunday. These buses will take you along the final lap of the journey into Courchevel. From Paris, five trains per day connect the capital with Moutiers. The TGV, a high-speed train, covers the distance from Paris to Chambéry in about 3 hours. In Chambéry, you must transfer to another train going to Moutiers (and then by bus, as mentioned, into Courchevel).

The nearest **airport** is at Geneva, to which Courchevel is connected by three buses Monday through Friday and eight buses Saturday and Sunday. It's a 4-hour ride, costing 355F ($63.90) one-way. If you land at the airport at Lyon, there are four buses a day running to Courchevel; the 4-hour trip costs 350F ($63) one-way. The nearest airport is the much smaller one at Chambéry. From here, there are two buses on Saturday only, taking 3 hours and costing 400F ($72) one-way.

VISITOR INFORMATION   The **Office de Tourisme** is at La Croisette (☎ **04-79-08-00-29**).

WHERE TO STAY

✪ **Hôtel Bellecôte.** Rte. de Bellecôte, 73120 Courchevel 1850. ☎ **04-79-08-10-19.** Fax 04-79-08-17-16. 58 units. MINIBAR TV TEL. 1,120–1,680F ($201.60–$302.40) per person double; 2,150–2,800F ($387–$504) per person suite. AE, DC, MC, V. Rates include half board. Closed Apr 15–Dec 20.

Beside the Jardin Alpin, this seven-story chalet is known for its collection of unusual antiques. Bored with traditional alpine motifs, founder Roger Toussaint scoured the bazaars of Afghanistan and the Himalayas for an array of fascinating objects that lend exotic warmth to the wood-sheathed walls and ceilings. (After his sale of the property, the antiques fortunately remained in place.) Each room contains plush accessories as well as Far or Middle Eastern carved wooden objects.

Dining: Full meals in the elegant dining room include cassolette of sweetbreads with flap mushrooms, frogs' legs Provençal, and chicken with morels. The impressive luncheon buffet table has a dazzling array of seafood, like crayfish and urchins, followed by sauerkraut with pork. The most flavorful fondant au chocolat in the Alps is served here. Lunch and dinner are offered daily.

Amenities: Indoor pool, direct access to the slopes, fitness center, hairdresser, and ski-rental shop.

✪ **La Sivolière.** Quartier Les Chenus, 73120 Courchevel 1850. ☎ **04-79-08-08-33.** Fax 04-79-08-15-73. 32 units. TV TEL. 1,350–1,950F ($243–$351) double; 2,950F ($531) suite. AE, MC, V. Parking 90F ($16.20). Closed May to late Nov.

The secret of La Sivolière's success is the owner, Madeleine Cattelin, who has a rich knowledge of and appreciation for her native Savoy. It was constructed in the 1970s by her husband, a building contractor, who used lots of pinewood boards and artfully rustic lichen-covered boulders. It's set near a small forest (*une sivolière*) in a sunny position near the ski slopes. Each guest room contains tasteful furnishings, a sense of alpine warmth, and all the modern conveniences.

Dining: You're invited to enjoy a richly laden afternoon tea table. There's no formal menu in the dining rooms; you're likely to get such dishes as filet of John Dory with watercress sauce and sea bass with essence of zucchini. Lunch and dinner are served daily; nonguests should make reservations.

Amenities: Free access to sauna, steambath, and exercise room.

Le Chabichou. Quartier Les Chenus, 73120 Courchevel 1850. ☎ **04-79-08-00-55.** Fax 04-79-08-33-58. www.courchevel.com/chabichou. E-mail: chabi@chorchevel.com. 40 units. TV TEL. Winter 875–1,900F ($157.50–$342) per person. Summer 770–950F ($138.60–$171) per person. Rates include half board. AE, DC, MC, V. Closed Apr 27–June 25 and Sept 15–Dec 21.

Within easy walking distance of many bars and clubs, this is one of the town's finest hotels, boasting a superb restaurant (see below). Most of the rooms in this gingerbread-trimmed chalet are large and well furnished; their daring modern design might not appeal to everyone, however. The owners would like guests to appreciate their rooms as much as their cuisine, but that's not the case. Facilities include sauna, Jacuzzi, and exercise room.

Le Dahu. Près de la Station (near the bus station), 73120 Courchevel 1850. ☎ **04-79-08-01-18.** Fax 04-79-08-11-98. 38 units. TV TEL. 710–840F ($127.80–$151.20) per person double. Rates include half board. MC, V. Closed mid-Apr to mid-Dec.

This is one of the resort's best bargains, offering clean and comfortable guest rooms, a charming salon, a bar, and a restaurant. Built in the mid-1950s and radically renovated in 1988, the hotel is named after a mythical alpine goat whose capture by visitors is jokingly encouraged by local guides. The social center is one flight above the reception, where there's stylish furniture and a long bar. The restaurant serves lunch and dinner daily; nonguests who make reservations are welcome. Your host is the very charming and amusing Mme Régine Pugliese.

Les Ducs de Savoie. Au Jardin Alpin, 73120 Courchevel 1850. ☎ **04-79-08-03-00.** Fax 04-79-08-16-30. www.nova.fr/alpazur. E-mail: 101564.1050@compuserve.com. 70 units. TEL. 700–1,500F ($126–$270) per person. Rates include half board. V. Parking 70F ($12.60). Closed Apr 13–Dec 20.

This hotel, one of the largest at Courchevel, has elaborately scrolled pinewood and often rows of icicles hanging from the protruding eaves. There's a covered garage, plus an indoor pool with walls intricately chiseled from mountain flagstones. The hotel has spacious, pleasant rooms, each with a terrace. It lies a few feet from the Téléski of the Jardin Alpin, and you can ski directly to the hotel's vestibule at the end of the day.

Dining/Diversions: In the lobby bar, the stone base deliberately retains its mountain lichens. Fireplaces add to the conviviality of the good food, drinks, and lively conversation.

WHERE TO DINE

✪ **Chalet des Pierres.** Au Jardin Alpin. ☎ **04-79-08-18-61.** Reservations required. Main courses 79–200F ($14.20–$36); fixed-price dinners 295–400F ($53.10–$72). AE, MC, V. Daily 11:45am–5pm, Wed–Sat 7:30–10pm. Closed late Apr to mid-Dec. FRENCH/SAVOYARD.

This one is the best of the several lunch restaurants scattered over the ski slopes. Accented with weathered planking and warmed with open hearths, it sits in the middle of the Verdon slope, a few paces from the whizzing path of skiers. Lunch is served on a sun terrace, but most visitors gravitate to the rustic two-story interior, where blazing fireplaces, hunting trophies, and a hip international crowd contribute to the charm of the place. Meals often include an array of air-dried alpine meat and sausages, the best *pommes frites* (french fries) in Courchevel, pepper steak, rack of lamb, and plats du jour (plates of the day).

La Bergerie. Quartier Nogentile. ☎ **04-79-08-24-70.** Reservations required. Main courses 70–150F ($12.60–$27); plat du jour (lunch) 105F ($18.90). AE, V. Restaurant, daily noon–3pm and 8–10pm; bar and cafe, daily 10am–midnight. Closed late Apr to mid-Dec. FRENCH.

Its uneven flagstone steps, stacks of carefully split firewood, and roughly weathered pine logs and planks testify to La Bergerie's 1830s origins as a shepherd's hut. A low-ceilinged dining room on the ground floor contains a dance floor and live entertainment. The ambience is warm, charming, and outdoorsy. Typical and well-prepared menu items are scallops in shallot butter, fondue bourguignonne, and raclette from cheese imported from small-scale producers in Switzerland. An especially refined platter that usually meets with success is paté of salmon that's smoked, poached, and grilled, then served with lemon-and-caviar crème fraîche.

✪ **Le Bateau Ivre.** In the Hôtel Pomme-de-Pin, quartier Les Chenus. ☎ **04-79-08-36-88.** Reservations required. Main courses 150–190F ($27–$34.20); fixed-price menus 250–560F ($45–$100.80) at lunch, 350–510F ($63–$91.80) at dinner. AE, DC, MC, V. Daily 12:30–2:15pm and 7:30–10pm. Closed Apr–Dec 20. FRENCH.

This restaurant, one of the greatest in the French Alps, is on the sixth floor of a hotel that's poised in the upper reaches of the resort and consequently offers a panoramic view over the town and slopes. Its fine reputation is the result of the dedicated efforts of the Jacob family, who prepare such dishes as polenta and escalopes of foie gras in vinaigrette and fricassée of lobster and truffles; especially delectable is succulent rack of lamb with black olives and artichokes, John Dory with red pepper oil, and scallops scented with gentiane, an alpine flower.

✪ **Le Chabichou.** Quartier Les Chenus. ☎ **04-79-08-00-55.** Reservations required. Main courses 120–280F ($21.60–$50.40); fixed-price menus 200–620F ($36–$111.60). AE, DC, MC, V. Daily noon–2pm and 8–10pm. Closed Apr 20–June 21 and Sept 15–Dec 1. FRENCH.

The best restaurant in town aside from the Bateau Ivre (see above), Le Chabichou is on the lobby level of the hotel of the same name. Michel and Maryse Rochedy acquired a reputation for their delectable cuisine at their similarly named (but no longer existing) restaurant in St-Tropez. Big windows here showcase a view of the snow. The menu lists a number of superlative dishes, like oyster soup with wild mushrooms, magrêt of duckling with honey sauce, alpine curry, and a parmentier of confit of duckling with caramelized potatoes.

COURCHEVEL AFTER DARK

As a chic but seasonal resort, Courchevel offers nightlife that roars into the wee hours during midwinter but is reduced to a pale shadow of itself as the snows begin to melt. You'll never have to walk far from the center to sample the fun, as the area around **La Croisette** (departure point for most of the ski lifts) contains lots of restaurants, bars, and dance clubs that come and go constantly. Here are two nightspots that have survived for a while:

Les Caves de Courchevel, Porte de Courchevel (☎ **04-79-08-12-74**), attracts an upscale crowd. A mock Tyrolean facade of weathered wood hides a club evoking a medieval cloister, with stone arches and columns. Full meals in the restaurant, open nightly from 11pm to 4am, begin at 250F ($45). It's open December to April only, daily from 6pm to 6am.

La Grange, rue Park-City (☎ **04-79-08-37-99**), is an informal spot for music and dancing. If a spectacle is being staged on the night of your visit, the doors may open earlier. Drinks start at a hefty 100F ($18)! It's open December to April 15 only, daily from 11pm to 4am.

7 Megève

372 miles SE of Paris, 45 miles SE of Geneva

Megève is famous as a summer resort set amid pine forests, foothills, and mountain streams. But it's even better known in winter as a charming, cosmopolitan ski resort, with more than 180 miles of downhill runs plus nearly 50 miles of cross-country trails.

The old village, with its turreted houses gathered around a 17th-century church, suggests what Megève looked like at the turn of the century. After 1920, however, the new town came along and started attracting people who like to go to the mountains for fun—especially skiers. People who have made Megève their winter home have included several prominent members of the Rothschild family, the most visible of whom, Mme Nadine de Rothschild, has an interest in the well-known Mont d'Arbois hotel. Hubert de Givenchy claims that the big draw of Megève is its *"parfum d'authenticité,"* from its scent of wood smoke to the sounds of heels and hooves clopping on cobblestones.

The interesting center contains **place de l'Eglise** and its famous hotel, the **Mont-Blanc,** south of the main arteries that cut through the valley. Rita Hayworth and Prince Aly Kahn were photographed at this hotel, nuzzling over glasses of marc in the 1950s. Some of the resort's hotels and one of its most important cable-car depots are in the village of **Mont d'Arbois,** about a mile east of the center of Megève, at the end of a steep, narrow, and winding road. (In winter it's unwise to drive up that road without chains on your snow tires.)

Tennis, horseback riding, and cable railways add to the attractions, with wide views of the Mont Blanc area from the top of each ski lift. The range of amusements includes a casino, nightclubs, dance clubs, and shows. Megève has more diversions than almost any of the French winter-sports resorts and is a social center of international status.

ESSENTIALS

GETTING THERE   You can fly into Geneva's **Cointrin Airport** (☎ 022/717-71-11), from which there's bus service 4 times a day direct from the airport to Megève. The 90-minute transit costs 190F ($34.20) per person. For information, contact Megève's tourist office (see below) or **Borini & Cie** (☎ 04-50-21-18-24).

Many visitors come by **train,** but you'll have to get off at the hamlet of Sallanches, 8 miles away. (Beware that although another hamlet, Bellegarde, lies about the same distance from Megève as Sallanches, bus service from Bellegarde to Megève was discontinued in 1996.) From Sallanches, about 10 buses every day make the trip to Megève for a price of 30F ($5.40) each way. Your journey from Paris to Megève will be faster on Saturday or Sunday, when the high-speed TGV travels directly to Sallanches, with stops en route, taking about 5½ hours. Monday through Friday, the TGV goes only as far as Annecy, after which travelers transfer onto conventional (slower) trains for the continuation of their trip into Sallanches. Trip time is around 7½ hours. For train information, contact Megève's tourist office (below) or the SNCF at ☎ 08-36-35-35-39.

If you're **driving** to Megève from Paris, take A6 southeast to Mâcon, connecting to the A40 east to St-Gervais, following N212 south straight into Megève. Be alert: Winter driving conditions can be perilous.

VISITOR INFORMATION   The **Office de Tourisme** is on rue Monseigneur-Conseil (☎ 04-50-21-27-28).

ACTIVE PURSUITS ON THE SLOPES & BEYOND

You can take a chair hoist to **Mont d'Arbois,** at 6,000 feet, where a panorama unfolds for you, including not only Mont Blanc but also the Fis and Aravis massifs. Cable service operates from July 1 to October 1 every half hour from 9am to 6pm. To reach the station, take route du Mont-d'Arbois from the resort's center, going past the golf course. The mountain was developed in the 1920s by members of the Rothschild family, whose search for solitude led them to this scenic outpost. Today Mont d'Arbois is a pocket of poshness in an already posh resort.

From 11am to 6am the center of the old village of Megève is closed to traffic, except for pedestrians and sledges. You can shop at your leisure—some 200 tradespeople await, ranging from a cobbler to an antiques dealer, plus many boutiques.

The Ski School, 176 rue de la Poste (☎ 04-50-21-00-97), is one of Europe's foremost, with 197 instructors for adults and 32 for children. Collective courses include the complete French skiing method, modern ski techniques, monosurf-acrobatic skiing, cross-country skiing, and ski touring. The school is open from December 20 to the end of April, daily from 9am to 7pm.

Two Megève Highlights

If you have the stamina, take the 9-mile footpath called the **Way of the Cross,** which begins at the edge of town and links more than a dozen country rustic chapels from the mid–19th century. Nothing is more memorable in Megève than the annual **Foire de la Croix,** a fair on the first Saturday of September, marking the return of the herds from the high alpine pastures. You can also taste the rich farmers' bounty at dozens of stands at the fair. It's been a tradition here since 1282.

Much improvement has been made in recent years in sports facilities, including a Chamois gondola, which takes skiers to the mountain from the center of town; the Rocharbois cable car, linking the two major ski areas of Mont d'Arbois and Rochebrune; and the addition of a gondola and chairlift at the Rochebrune massif. Skiing here appeals to both intermediates and experts. A 3-day ski pass costs 453F ($81.55).

The **Megève Palais des Sports et des Congrès** (Sports Palace and Assembly Hall), route du Jaillet (☎ **04-50-21-15-71**), was built in 1968 as the town's showcase for ice sports, swimming, tennis, conventions, political meetings, concerts, and shows and gala festivals. It contains two pools with a solarium, saunas, an indoor Olympic-size skating rink open throughout summer, a curling track, a body-building room, a bar, a restaurant, a gymnasium, tennis courts, an auditorium, conference rooms, and an exhibition gallery. Hours change with the seasons and any special competitions occurring inside, though in most cases it's open daily from 10am to noon and 2:30 to 7:30pm. Annual closings occur during May and November.

WHERE TO STAY
VERY EXPENSIVE

Chalet du Mont-d'Arbois. Rte. du Mont-d'Arbois, 74120 Megève. ☎ **04-50-21-25-03.** Fax 04-50-21-24-79. www.silicone.fr/arbois. E-mail: arbois@silicone.fr. 20 units. TV TEL. Winter 1,650–2,200F ($297–$396) double. Off-season 1,100–1,650F ($198–$297) double. Rates include breakfast. Half board 200F ($36) per person extra. AE, DC, MC, V. Closed Apr 9–June 15 and Sept 15–Dec 15.

Built in 1928 by a Rothschild matriarch, in a design emulating Switzerland's fanciful chalets, this is the most opulent and stylish small-scale resort on the mountain. Its beautiful guest rooms are worthy of a Relais & Châteaux. The public rooms are the grandest in Megève, with roaring fireplaces, beamed ceilings, alpine antiques, and silver-plated replicas of alert deer. During part of the season, the hotel might be filled with friends of Mme Nadine de Rothschild, a novelist/autobiographer whose advice on how a woman should treat her husband became a best-seller in France.

✪ **Le Fer à Cheval.** 36 rte. du Crêt-d'Arbois, 74120 Megève. ☎ **04-50-21-30-39.** Fax 04-50-93-07-60. 41 units. TV TEL. 1,160–1,520F ($208.80–$273.60) double; 1,600–1,800F ($288–$324) suite for two. Rates include half board. AE, MC, V. Closed Apr 8–June and Sept 10–Dec 15.

This is the finest hotel in the center of the village, filled with skiers in winter and travelers wishing to escape into the mountains in summer. The rooms are beautifully maintained and have traditional styling.

Dining: Even if you don't stay here you can enjoy the restaurant, decked out with wood to evoke an old-fashioned Savoy atmosphere. Guests often gather for tea around a wood-and-stone fireplace, where they can also enjoy good-tasting alpine meals.

Amenities: In summer a pool draws guests to the beautiful garden, and the sauna and Jacuzzi are winter lures.

✪ **Les Fermes de Marie.** Chemin de Riante Colline, 74120 Megève. ☎ **04-50-93-03-10.** Fax 04-50-93-09-84. www.skifrance.fr/~fermesdemarie. 60 units, 5 chalets. Winter, 1,400–3,000F ($252–$540) double; from 3,000F ($540) suite or chalet for 2. Off-season, 1,300–1,900F ($234–$342) double; from 2,000F ($360) suite or chalet for 2. Rates include half board. AE, MC, V.

In 1989 the Sibuet family opened a hotel with a style that had not been seen before in Megève. The remnants of at least 20 antique barns and crumbling chalets were assembled, then discreetly modernized in a desirable location at the eastern edge of the resort. The result is a compound of appealing, comfortable buildings loaded with atmosphere and eccentricities. The folkloric theme extends to the guest rooms, which look like attractive alpine cabins.

Dining: The hotel contains three restaurants: Le Gastronomique, dining site for most guests on half-board plans; Le Restaurant du Fromage, which serves fondues; and La Rôtisserie, a baronial enclave with lots of rustic glamour.

Amenities: Spa, indoor pool.

INEXPENSIVE

✪ **Hôtel Gai Soleil.** Rue du Crêt-du-Midi, 74120 Megève. ☎ **04-50-21-00-70.** Fax 04-50-58-74-50. 21 units. TV TEL. 280–450F ($50.40–$81) double. Reductions of 20%–50% for children, depending on age. AE, DC, MC, V. Parking 25F ($4.50).

This choice boasts a charming setting at the base of hills at the eastern edge of town, midway between Megève's center and the Rochbrune slopes. Its design was inspired by a Swiss chalet, except for the broad staircase that sweeps down to the front. In back there's a heated outdoor pool; within is a cozy, warm, and colorful interior with lots of exposed wood and well-upholstered comfort. Your hosts, Bernard and Joëlle Demonchy, work hard to make guests comfortable. The cozy, clean rooms are highlighted with varnished pine; however, they're not very large and aren't accessible via elevator. Fixed-price menus, featuring traditional Savoyard cuisine, cost around 130F ($23.40).

Le Rond Point d'Arbois. 111 rte. du Mont-d'Arbois, 74120 Megève. ☎ **04-50-21-17-50.** Fax 04-50-58-90-24. 13 units. TV TEL. 300–345F ($54–$62.10) per person double. Rates include half board. MC, V. Free parking on street; 85F ($15.30) for 24 hours in nearby underground garage. Closed May and 2 weeks in Nov. At the edge of town, at the bottom of the road that meanders uphill to the ski slopes of the Mont d'Arbois.

In many ways this hotel, built between the world wars, is more evocative than many of its modern competitors. It's not about glamour; rather, it's a welcoming two-star family-run place with functional but comfortable guest rooms. About half of the guests opt for the reasonably priced half-board plan, served in a simple but cozy setting near a lounge with a blazing fireplace. The cuisine is old-fashioned and hearty, featuring high-altitude Savoyard specialties.

WHERE TO DINE

You might also like to try the restaurant at **Le Fer à Cheval** (see above).

Chalet du Mont-d'Arbois. Rte. du Mont-d'Arbois. ☎ **04-50-21-25-03.** Reservations required. Main courses 90–180F ($16.20–$32.40); fixed-price menu 190F ($34.20). MC, V. Daily noon–2pm and 7:30–10pm. Closed Apr 8–June 14 and Oct to mid-Dec. FRENCH.

Richly decorated, this restaurant in the above-recommended hotel is one floor below lobby level and has a wood-burning grill. Accumulated mementos of the restaurant's owners, the Rothschilds, are part of the decor. As might be expected from a family connected with some of the greatest vineyards of France, the wine list is overwhelming. Some menu items have been named after the Rothschild image, like *vol-au-vent financière* (puff pastry with madeira sauce and truffle sauce); another special dish is spit-roasted Bresse chicken, the best at Megève.

Le Prieuré. Place de l'Eglise. ☎ **04-50-21-01-79.** Reservations required. Main courses 95–280F ($17.10–$50.40); fixed-price menus 119–193F ($21.40–$34.75). AE, DC, V. Daily noon–10:30pm. Closed June 15–July 1, Nov, and Mon off-season. FRENCH.

Le Prieuré offers traditional French cooking, with specialties like foie gras de canard and salad made from crab, mussels, and lake fish. An excellent appetizer is fresh melon with locally cured ham, which can be followed by grilled bass filet with fennel or magrêt of duckling flavored with peaches. For dessert, try the tasty apple pie. The restaurant is frequently cited as one of the best dining choices outside the hotels.

Les Enfants Terribles. In the Hôtel du Mont-Blanc, place de l'Eglise. ☎ 04-50-58-76-69. Reservations required. Main courses 60–140F ($10.80–$25.20); fixed-price menu 149F ($26.80) in winter, 125F ($22.50) in summer. AE, DC, MC, V. Daily noon–3pm and 7–11pm. Closed 3 weeks in May and 3 weeks in Oct. FRENCH.

In the bar adjoining this acclaimed restaurant, Jean Cocteau painted wall frescoes that gave the place its name. Today, though far from being the most glamorous restaurant in town, it's one of the more fun, ripe with the shenanigans of young vacationers and snow bunnies. Warmly outfitted with wood panels and rustic artifacts, it serves generous portions of dishes that include escalope of veal Savoyard, sole meunière, and filet of beef with a sauce "Enfants Terrible" (mustard, ground black pepper, and flambéed cognac). Is this place no longer chic since its 1995 overhaul, as locals once predicted? Probably not—it operates completely independently of the stylish hotel that contains it. Nonetheless, stop in for nostalgia of the naughty old days of France and judge for yourself.

MEGEVE AFTER DARK

This town is a hotbed of intimate clubs and bars for après-ski fun. The absolute ultimate is a little jazz club by the name of **Club de Jazz des 5 Rues,** rue du Comte-de-Capré (☎ **04-50-21-24-36**), the popular rendezvous for such jazz notables as Claude Luter and Claude Bolling; unfortunately, it's open only during the peak winter season. However, if you're out and about looking to spot the rich and famous, head for the **Casino,** 115 av. Charles-Feige (☎ **04-50-93-01-83**), or its piano bar, **Palo Alto,** av. Charles-Feige (☎ **04-50-93-01-83**), where you might run into members of the French jet set. For the 18- to 25-year-old dance scene, stop by the underground disco **Le Pallas,** route du Mont-d'Arbois (☎ **04-50-91-82-70**), where a steep 90F ($16.20) cover gains you entrance to this techno/rock hotspot.

8 Chamonix-Mont Blanc

381 miles SE of Paris, 58 miles E of Annecy

At an altitude of 3,422 feet, Chamonix is the historic capital of alpine skiing. If you're not a millionaire, this is the resort to choose—not super-priced Courchevel 1850. Site of the first winter Olympic Games in 1924, Chamonix huddles in a valley almost at the junction of France, Italy, and Switzerland. Dedicated skiers all over the world know of its 12-mile Vallée Blanche run, one of Europe's most rugged and certainly its longest. Thrill seekers also flock here for mountain climbing and hang gliding.

A charming old-fashioned mountain town, Chamonix has a most thrilling backdrop—✪ **Mont Blanc,** Western Europe's highest mountain at 15,780 feet. When two Englishmen, Windham and Pococke, first visited Chamonix in 1740, they were thrilled with its location and later wrote a travel book that advertised the village around the world. When their guide was published, it was believed that no human foot had yet trod on Mont Blanc. On August 7, 1786, Jacques Balmat became the first man to climb the mountain, destroying the myth that no one could spend a night up there and survive. In the old quarter of town a memorial to this brave pioneer stands in front of the village church.

With the opening of the 7-mile **Mont Blanc Tunnel** (☎ 04-50-53-06-15), Chamonix became a major stop along one of Europe's busiest highways. By going underground, the tunnel provides the easiest way to get past the mountains to Italy; motorists now stop here even if they aren't interested in winter skiing or summer mountain climbing. Toll rates depend on the distance between the axles of your vehicle: it's 145F ($26.10) one-way for a small car and 195F ($35.10) for a big car or caravan trailer. Round-trip tickets are 180F and 240F ($32.40 and $43.20), respectively. Round-trip tickets are sold at considerable discount compared to the price of two one-way tickets, but be warned that the return portion of those tickets must be used within 3 days of purchase.

Because of its exceptional equipment, including gondolas, cable cars, and chairlifts, Chamonix is one of the major sports resorts of Europe, attracting an international crowd.

Chamonix sprawls in a narrow strip along both banks of the Arve River. Its casino, its rail and bus stations, and most of its restaurants and nightlife are in the town center. Cable cars reach into the mountains from the town's edge. Locals refer to Les Praz, Les Bossons, Les Moussoux, and Les Pélerins as satellite villages within Greater Chamonix, though technically Chamonix refers to only a carefully delineated section around place de l'Eglise.

ESSENTIALS

GETTING THERE   Most (but not all) **trains** coming from other parts of France or Switzerland require a transfer in such nearby villages as St-Gervais (in France) or Martigny (in Switzerland). Through either of those towns, passengers are routed here from Aix-les-Bains, Annecy, Lyon, and Chambéry and, farther afield, Paris and Geneva. There are 2 connections from Paris every 24 hours (trip time: 8 hours); from Lyon, there are 6 rail links per day (trip time: 4 hours). For more information and schedules for trains throughout France, call ☎ 08-36-35-35-39.

In any season there's at least one daily **bus** from Annecy and Grenoble.

If you're **driving,** you probably won't have to worry about road conditions: Since Chamonix lies on a main road link between Italy and the Mont Blanc Tunnel, conditions are excellent throughout the year. Even after a severe snowstorm, roads are quickly swept clean of heavy snow. Motorists from Paris can follow A6 toward Lyon, taking the A40 toward Geneva. Before Geneva, turn south along A40 leading into Chamonix.

GETTING AROUND   Within Chamonix, a local network of small-scale buses (*navettes,* usually brightly painted in yellow and blue) make frequent runs from strategic points within the town to many of the téléphériques and villages up and down the valley. Transit on any of them is usually included in the price of any lift ticket, but for nonskiers and summer visitors the cost is 7.50F ($1.35) for each 3-mile sector you travel. For information, contact **Chamonix-Bus** at ☎ 04-50-53-05-55.

VISITOR INFORMATION   Chamonix's **Office de Tourisme** is on place du Triangle-de-l'Amitié (☎ 04-50-53-00-24).

SPECIAL EVENTS   If you're here from mid-July to August, you may want to attend the classical and jazz concerts during the **Semaines Musicales du Mont-Blanc.**

Concerts take place every Tuesday and Wednesday at 9pm at the Grande Salle du Majestic, allée du Majestic. Tickets cost 80F and 120F ($14.40 and $21.60) and are available along with program schedules from the Office de Tourisme.

EXPLORING THE ALPS

With the highest mountain in western Europe as a backdrop, this is an area for the highly skilled skier. Regrettably, none of the five main ski areas spread along the valley floor are connected by lifts, and lines at the most popular areas are the longest in the alpine world. Weather and snow conditions create crevasses and avalanches that may close whole ski sections for days, even threatening parts of the resort itself.

Skiing is not actually on Mont Blanc but on the shoulders and slopes across the valley facing this giant mountain. Vertical drops can be spectacular—with lift-serviced hills rising to as much as 10,500 feet in one instance. Glacier skiing begins at 12,465 feet. This is not for the beginner or timid intermediate skiers, who should head for the satellite resorts of Les Houches or Le Tour. World-class skiers come here to face the daunting challenges of the high snows of Brévant, La Flégère, and especially Les Grands Monets, that fierce north-facing wall of snow that stretches about three city blocks wide.

A 1-day ski pass costs 150F ($27) and a 3-day pass costs 450F ($81), to be used mainly in the Brévant area. However, the Chamski Pass—good for at least 5 major areas—costs 230F ($41.40) for 1 day or 560F ($100.80) for 3 days and is a better investment than the cheaper but more limited offering.

The belvederes you can reach from Chamonix by cable car or mountain railway are famous. For information about these rides, contact the **Société Touristique du Mont-Blanc,** 100 Parking de l'Aiguille du Midi, 74400 Chamonix (tel. **04-50-53-30-80**).

In the heart of town, you can board a cable car heading for the **Aiguille du Midi** and on to Italy—a harrowing journey. The first stage, a 9-minute run to the Plan des Aiguilles at an altitude of 7,544 feet, isn't so alarming. But the second stage, to an altitude of 12,602 feet, the Aiguille du Midi station, may make your heart leap, especially when the car rises 2,000 feet between towers. At the summit, you'll be 1,110 yards from Mont Blanc's peak. The belvedere affords a commanding view of the Aiguilles of Chamonix and Vallée Blanche, the largest glacier in Europe (9.3 miles long and 3.7 miles wide). You also have a 125-mile view of the Jura and the French, Swiss, and Italian Alps.

You leave the tram station along a chasm-spanning narrow bridge leading to the third cable car and the glacial fields that lie beyond. Or you can end your journey at Aiguille du Midi and return to Chamonix. Generally the cable cars operate all year: in summer, daily from 6am to 5pm, leaving at least every 10 minutes; in winter, daily from 8am to 4pm, leaving every 10 minutes. The first stage, to Plan des Aiguilles, costs 76F to 82F ($13.70 to $14.75) round-trip, increasing to 184F to 194F ($33.10 to $34.90) per person for a round-trip to Aiguille du Midi.

You then cross over high mountains and pass jagged needles of rock and ice bathed in dazzling light. The final trip to **Pointe Helbronner** in Italy—at 11,355 feet—requires a passport if you want to leave the station and descend on two more cable cars to the village of Courmayeur. From here you can go to nearby Entrèves to dine at La Maison de Filippo, called a "chalet of gluttony." The round-trip from Chamonix to Pointe Helbronner is 270F to 290F ($48.60 to $52.20); the cable car operates from mid-May to mid-October only.

Another aerial cableway takes you up to **Brévent,** at 8,284 feet. From here you'll have a first-rate (frontal) view of Mont Blanc and the Aiguilles de Chamonix. The trip takes about 1½ hours round-trip. Cable cars operate from December 16 to October, from 8am to 5pm. Summer departures are at least every half hour. A round-trip costs 80F ($14.40).

Yet another aerial journey takes you to **Le Montenvers** (☎ 04-50-53-12-54), at 6,276 feet. From the belvedere at the end of the cable-car run you'll have a view of the 4-mile-long *mer de glace* (sea of ice, or glacier). Aiguille du Dru is a rock climb notorious for its difficulty. The trip takes 1½ hours, including a return by rail. Departures are 8am to 6pm in summer, until 4:30pm off-season. The round-trip fare is 78F ($14.05) per person, and service is usually from May to November.

You can also visit a cave hollowed out of the mer de glace; a cable car connects it with the upper resort of Montenvers, and the trip takes just 3 minutes. Train, cable car, and visit to the cave costs 105F ($18.90).

WHERE TO STAY

Au Bon Coin. 80 av. de l'Aiguille-du-Midi, 74400 Chamonix. ☎ **04-50-53-15-67.** Fax 04-50-53-51-51. 20 units, 16 with bathroom. TEL. 312F ($56.15) double without bathroom, 452F ($81.35) double with bathroom. Rates include continental breakfast. MC, V. Closed May–June and Oct-Dec 18.

This two-star hotel is very French alpine. It has comfortable modern rooms, often with views of the mountainside—in autumn the colors are spectacular. The accommodations also feature terraces where you can soak up the sun, even in winter. The chalet is tranquil, and the owner provides free private parking as well as a garden.

Chalet Hôtel Le Chantel. 391 rte. des Pecles, 74400 Chamonix. ☎ **04-50-53-02-54.** Fax 04-50-53-54-52. 7 units. TEL. 418–508F ($75.25–$91.45) double. Rates include breakfast. V.

Within a 30-minute walk west from the city hall, this white-stucco hotel evokes a Swiss chalet with its dark-stained wood, balconies, and mountain panoramas. It benefits from the care and attention of its owners, Peter and Françoise Schmid, who have added decorative touches akin to what you'd expect in a private home. The cozy guest rooms are paneled with lovely knotty-pine wood. Breakfast is the only meal served.

Hôtel Albert-1er et de Milan. 119 impasse Montenvers, 74400 Chamonix. ☎ **04-50-53-05-09.** Fax 04-50-55-95-48. www.silicone.fr/hotalber. E-mail: hotalberta@silicone.fr. 41 units. MINIBAR TV TEL. 850–2,800F ($153–$504) double; 988–1,665F ($177.85–$299.70) per person half board. AE, DC, MC, V. Closed May 5–15 and Oct 22–Dec 6.

This hotel is an enlarged alpine chalet, ringed by a garden and private residences. Each of the well-furnished rooms offers a mountain view; several also feature private balconies. Facilities include outdoor pool, tennis court, sauna, and Jacuzzi. In the mid-1990s, the owners of this hotel erected a satellite hotel nearby, but the newer accommodations are completely separate and less desirable. Despite the newcomer's more modern style, we still prefer the original, older establishment.

You can dine in one of three elegant rooms, outfitted with Oriental carpets and 18th-century chests. (See below for a complete review of the restaurant.) A copper-topped bar is in the lobby.

Hôtel de l'Arve. 60 impasse des Anémones, 74400 Chamonix. ☎ **04-50-53-02-31.** Fax 04-50-53-56-92. 39 units, 35 with bathroom. 258–354F ($46.45–$63.70) double without bathroom, 294–452F ($52.90–$81.35) double with bathroom. Half board 85F ($15.30) per person extra. MC, V. Closed Nov–Dec 20.

Originally a cafe around the turn of the century, this place expanded into a comfortable, unpretentious two-star hotel. Most of its stucco-fronted facade dates from the 1960s, and the interior is a simple kind of setting where furniture and accessories are well chosen, childproof, and much used. It's a simple place that offers warmth and comfort, a friendly welcome, an appreciation for the great outdoors, and lovely views from many of the rooms over the rocky banks of the Arve, which flows nearby. The setting is particularly convenient, just a 5-minute walk from the town hall.

WHERE TO DINE

Bartavel. 26 cours du Bartavel (impasse du Vox). ☎ **04-50-53-26-51.** Pizzas 40–55F ($7.20–$9.90); main courses 38–70F ($6.85–$12.60). AE, DC, MC, V. Daily noon–midnight. ITALIAN.

Decorated much like a tavern you'd expect to find in Italy, this pizzeria is the domain of Treviso-born Valerio Commazzetto, who prepares 20 kinds of pizza and a wide range of pastas, plus a medley of rib-sticking platters designed to go well with cold air and high altitudes. Menu items include grilled steaks and chops, escalopes milanese or pizzaiola, and an array of simple desserts. The cooking is like Mamma's back in old Italy. Beer and wine flow liberally, and Bartavel attracts a good share of outdoor enthusiasts, who appreciate its copious portions and reasonable prices.

Le Chaudron. 79 rue des Moulins. ☎ **04-50-53-40-34.** Reservations recommended. Main courses 80–130F ($14.40–$23.40); fixed-price menu 140F ($25.20). AE, MC, V. Daily 7pm–midnight. Closed June and Oct–Nov. FRENCH.

Chef Pierre Osterberger cooks right in front of you, and you're sure to appreciate his specialties, which include house-style sweetbreads, several robust beef dishes, and fondues, as well as many salads and desserts. There are a lot of fancier places in town, but for good value, honest cooking, and fine mountain ingredients, Le Chaudron emerges near the top of our list. The cellar is filled with well-chosen wines, including Château Mouton-Rothschild and Château Latour.

Restaurant Albert 1er et Milan. 119 impasse du Montenvers. ☎ **04-50-53-05-09.** Reservations recommended. Main courses 150–220F ($27–$39.60). Set menus 190–470F ($34.20–$84.60). AE, DC, MC, V. Thurs-Tues 12:30–2pm and daily 7:30–9:30pm. FRENCH.

Although the hotel complex that contains this establishment features other newer eateries, this is the culinary star. You'll dine in one of a trio of cozily decorated dining rooms, which have bay windows opening onto views of Mont Blanc and walls accented with rustic artifacts and antique farm implements. Begin with master chef Pierre Carrier's broth (*fumet*) of wild mushrooms garnished with ravioli stuffed with foie gras. Appealing entrees include sweet onions cooked in rock salt, locally smoked salmon prepared with a caviar-flavored cream sauce, and a savory blanquette of lamb studded with fresh morels. Try the classic honey ice cream with a raspberry coulis—there's nothing more succulent on the dessert menu. In summer, dine al fresco in the garden.

Restaurant Matafan. In the Hôtel Mont-Blanc, 62 allée du Majéstic. ☎ **04-50-53-05-64.** Reservations required. Main courses 110–140F ($19.80–$25.20); fixed-price menus 140–360F ($25.20–$64.80). AE, DC, MC, V. Daily noon–2pm and 7–10pm. Closed Oct 15–Dec 15. FRENCH.

This stellar restaurant has a decor of soft pastels and hand-woven tapestries, arranged around a central pentagonal fireplace. Specialties change seasonally but may include omble chevalier (lake fish) meunière, rack of lamb roasted with herbs (for two), and sinful desserts. Many of the dishes are inspired by Savoy cooking but with a refined touch. The excellent cellar contains more than 500 wines, many reasonably priced. In summer you can lunch next to the pool in the garden.

CHAMONIX AFTER DARK

Nightlife in Chamonix runs the gamut from the classical and sublime to the campy and riotous. You'll find the highest concentration of bars and pubs along **rue des**

Moulins and **rue Paccard,** including the sexy, high-energy disco **Le Refuge,** 269 rue Paccard (☎ **04-50-53-00-94**), where a 60F ($10.80) cover gets you in the door; and the British bastion, **Mill Street Bar,** 123 rue des Moulins (☎ **04-50-55-80-92**), with its tables spilling onto the sidewalk and English-language après-ski stories floating about. The **Casino,** 12 place H.-B.-de-Saussure (☎ **04-50-53-07-65**), offers evenings of chance at the slot machines and roulette and blackjack tables.

9 Morzine & Avoriaz

370 miles SE of Paris, 25 miles S of Evian

Morzine and Avoriaz are the last stops on an ascending road from Lake Geneva to a dead end near the Swiss border. Most visitors drive to Morzine, but bus service from Geneva stops near the center of town. To reach Avoriaz by car, drive along a 9-mile winding road northeast from Morzine or take a téléphérique from the station 3 miles east of the center of Morzine. Since cars are usually not allowed on Avoriaz's innermost streets, many visitors prefer to park at the base of the téléphérique and enjoy the alpine views during their ascent.

MORZINE

The tourist capital of the Haut-Chablais district, Morzine offers attractions like sleigh rides, beautiful pine forests, ice shows, and more than a dozen cabarets. For years it was known as a summer resort, but now it's also an acclaimed winter ski center. From Morzine, you can visit Lac de Montriond, at an altitude of 3,490 feet. An 18-mile tour of this famous lake takes about 2 hours.

The **Office de Tourisme** is on place Crusaz (☎ **04-50-74-72-72**).

WHERE TO STAY

Hôtel des Champs-Fleuris. Rte. du Téléphérique, 74110 Morzine. ☎ **04-50-79-14-44.** Fax 04-50-79-27-75. www.cyberaccess.fr/user/hotel-champs-fleuris. E-mail: champsff.@ cyberaccess.fr. 45 units. TEL. 430–630F ($77.40–$113.40) per person double; 600–800F ($108–$144) per person suite. Rates include half board. V. Free parking. Closed Apr 9–June 25 and Sept 10–Dec 18.

Proud of its role as the third hotel built in Morzine, this establishment is as popular in summer as it is in winter. Against a backdrop of forested mountains, it rises a few paces from T-lifts and gondolas. You can enjoy the view of the slopes from a setting marked by lots of exposed wood softened with earth-toned carpeting and curtains. In summer, hill climbers appreciate the walking trails that begin nearby. There's also a heated pool near the garden, plus an indoor weightlifting room with an adjacent sauna, bar, billiards room, cafe, and restaurant. Though unexceptional, the rooms are modern and comfortable, and the family that runs the place is both helpful and charming.

Hôtel Le Carlina. Av. Joux-Plane, 74110 Morzine. ☎ **04-50-79-01-03.** Fax 04-50-75-94-11. 18 units. TEL. 400–450F ($72–$81) double; 700F ($126) suite. AE, DC, MC, V. Closed May and June and Sept 10–25.

The interior of this informal village chalet, built in the 1950s and renovated many times since, is rustic, with several lounges containing open fireplaces. Its guest rooms are pleasantly decorated and comfortable. In summer you can enjoy refreshments on a street-level terrace with umbrella-shaded tables. The fixed-price menus, 110F ($19.80) at lunch and 150F ($27) at dinner, are inexpensive and heartily recommended.

Hôtel Le Dahu. Chemin du Mas-Metout, Avoriaz, 74110 Morzine. ☎ **04-50-75-92-92.** Fax 04-50-75-92-50. www.portesdusoleil.com/dahu. E-mail: ledahu@portesdusoleil.com. 44 units. TV TEL. 500–830F ($90–$149.40) double; 900–1,230F ($162–$221.40) duplex suite for 2–5. MC, V. Closed Apr–June 14 and Sept 16–Dec 15.

Ski bunnies find no better choice than this well-run inn offering panoramic views of the village and the Alps. It has a faithful list of regulars, drawn not only to its handsomely decorated rooms but also to its cuisine. Slightly outside the town center, the hotel offers a sauna and the best-equipped fitness center in town, along with a Jacuzzi, workout equipment, and two pools. The staff offers free shuttle service to the lifts.

Dining: The fare in the wood-paneled restaurant features innovative food that utilizes quality ingredients, with heavy use of Savoie cheese. Le Dahu has one of the liveliest atmospheres in town for après-ski. The staff is both helpful and attentive.

AVORIAZ

One of the most modern and sophisticated ski centers in the Alps has been developed at Avoriaz. Set at around 8,250 feet above sea level, considerably higher than the older, more traditional-looking resort of Morzine, at 3,300 feet, it's part of more than 390 miles of ski trails that extend over a sweeping panorama of France and, in some cases, over the frontier into Switzerland. More than 70 mechanical lifts interconnect the region's 12 hamlets and resorts, of which Morzine and Avoriaz are the best known. Within the district, slopes are designated as suitable for beginners, intermediates, and died-in-the-wool speed demons, with skiable snow that blankets the region between mid-December and sometime in mid-April, depending on weather conditions.

Should you opt for accommodations in Morzine or Avoriaz? Connoisseurs usually claim that it doesn't matter, because of the easy connections between the two. Although travel by car involves a drive of around 9 curving miles, there's direct access via a 3-mile stretch of cable car (*Le Téléphérique Super-Morzine*), which makes frequent trips between the two resorts.

Astride a series of peaks and valleys called **Portes du Soleil** (Gates of the Sun), Avoriaz is most easily reached by cable car, and in the village the only transportation is by foot, skis, or horse-drawn sleigh. Even if you don't want to stay in one of the hotels here, you may want to take a cable car up for a look and perhaps a meal.

The village of Avoriaz is architecturally interesting; this planned ski-resort community was set above the **Vallée des Ardoisières** (Valley of the Slate Quarries) and designed to blend in with the mountain landscape. Especially notable are the stepped rooflines and geometric balconies on the cylindrical buildings, designed to reflect the sharp lines of the cliffs.

The local ski school, an accredited branch of the **French Ski School Federation,** has around 100 experienced instructors, many of whom are proficient in English. Both downhill and cross-country skiing are offered, as well as snowshoeing and indoor activities like aerobic dancing and squash. This family-oriented ski resort also features the **Village des Enfants,** where children as young as 3 are taught to ski.

By cable car or bubble car you can also go to **Le Pléney,** at 5,367 feet and enjoy a view from its belvedere looking out on Mont Blanc. Through the Dranse Gap, a vista of Lake Geneva unfolds.

The **Office de Tourisme** (☎ **04-50-74-02-11**) is at the last stop on the road before the real mountains begin.

WHERE TO STAY

Hôtel des Dromonts. Avoriaz 1800, 74110 Morzine. ☎ **04-50-74-08-11.** Fax 04-50-74-02-79. 40 units. TV TEL. 1,000–1,400F ($180–$252) double. Rates include breakfast. Half board 650–880F ($117–$158.40) per person extra. AE, DC, MC, V. Parking 40F ($7.20) outside, 80F ($14.40) inside. Closed Apr 14–Dec 15.

This hotel occupies most, but not all, of a dramatically cantilevered building in the heart of the resort. Managed by a well-trained English-speaking staff, it includes at least 10 private condominiums, some boutiques, and two restaurants (one Savoyard, one upscale French), all managed by separate financial entities. Because all the guest rooms benefit from a southern exposure, most of them are bright and sunny, with modern design and natural wood. The hotel is usually filled with a young crowd, and ski runs and lifts begin right at the door.

10 Val d'Isère

413 miles SE of Paris, 73 miles E of Albertville, 81 miles E of Chambéry

Set in an open valley, and originally conceived as a hunting station for the ducs de Savoie, Val d'Isère (6,068 feet above sea level) has grown into the centerpiece for some of Europe's most spectacular skiing. Less snobbish and exhibitionist than Courchevel and less old-fashioned than Megève, it's a youthful, rather brash resort where virtually everyone comes to enjoy active, outdoor pursuits. Its fans compare it favorably to Chamonix, which—despite the allure of nearby Mont Blanc and some superb (mostly expert) skiing—seems to be burdened with longer lift lines and a less accessible layout of its network of ski lifts and slopes. In 1992 Val d'Isère hosted most of the men's downhill racing events for the winter Olympics, which were headquartered at Albertville.

ESSENTIALS

GETTING THERE & GETTING AROUND   Most visitors traveling by **car** use Albertville, accessible by superhighway from Paris, as the gateway to Val d'Isère. From Albertville, follow the signs to Moutiers. From Moutiers, take R.N. 202 to Bourg-St-Maurice (36 miles) and continue for another 19 miles to Val d'Isère. The meandering R.N. 202 is panoramic and breathtaking—for both its views and its lack, along some sections, of guard rails that might prevent your car from plunging over the side of a cliff. During snowfalls, chains on your tires are required. When you get to the resort, we strongly advise you to park your car and not use it again until you're ready to leave. Parking problems here are legendary, and without chains you'll risk getting stuck during snowfalls. You can walk to virtually anywhere in town faster than you can drive.

Almost two dozen red-and-white Train Rouge **shuttle buses,** each with a capacity of 100 people and their equipment, connect the hamlets at either end of the valley (Daille and Fornet) to the center of Val d'Isère. The central terminus is the Rond-Point des Pistes. Transit is free. During summer, service is available only during July and August.

Convenient nearby **airports** include Cointrin outside Geneva (☎ 022/717-71-11), Lyon-Satolas (☎ 04-72-22-72-21), and Chambéry (☎ 04-79-54-49-54). Bus and limo service is available from any of those airports via Cars Martin (☎ 04-79-06-00-42).

The nearest **railway station** is at Bourg-St-Maurice (☎ 04-79-07-10-10), an alpine village 19 miles west of Val d'Isère. For train information and schedules, call ☎ 08-36-35-35-39. From here, buses maintained by Cars Martin (☎ 04-79-07-04-49) depart between 4 and 10 times a day, depending on the season. If that's inconvenient, you can take a taxi from Bourg-St-Maurice for a one-way fare of about 350F

($63) for up to four passengers. (Call Altitude Taxis at ☎ **04-79-41-14-15** or arrange
the pickup in advance with your hotel.)

VISITOR INFORMATION   The resort's **Office de Tourisme,** B.P. 228, 73150 Val
d'Isère (☎ **04-79-06-06-60**), is a font of information on outdoor activities.

The widest spectrum of information on sports in town is available from the **Sports
Department,** B.P. 61, 73152 Val d'Isère (☎ **04-79-06-03-49**).

FUN ON & OFF THE SLOPES

As recently as 1930, Val d'Isère was little more than a French-speaking mountain village near the Italian frontier, with a church and a handful of slate and stone houses
that were accessible to the rest of the world only via mule track. Today the town is a
mass of urban sprawl whose boundaries are defined by high avalanche-prone walls that
rise steeply up to altitudes where snow is common even during spring and autumn. It's
bisected by a gravel-bottomed mountain stream, La Tarentaise. The resort's developed
(some say overdeveloped) sections sprawl along either side of the highest road in
Europe, R.N. 202.

Don't expect a pristine-looking alpine village, like the picture-perfect Swiss resort of
Zermatt. In Val d'Isère, traffic roars through the town center. Clusters of cheap restaurants, crêperies, and more than 125 stores and outlets line either side of the road. Since
1983, however, some of the worst of the town's architectural sins have been corrected,
thanks to tighter building codes and greater emphasis on traditional chalet-style architecture. Access to this plateau, less than 6 miles from the most savage stretch of the
Italian border, is inconvenient and time-consuming. Parking is a nightmare during
busy seasons, and the medieval cluster of stone farm buildings and a 13th-century
church that comprised the original hamlet were long ago pushed into the background
in the region's sometimes hysterical rush to modernize. But despite the commercialism
and the big stakes that Savoyard investors have poured into the resort, the town hums
with the sense that its visitors are really here to enjoy skiing. And few other European
resorts can boast as logical a layout for a far-flung network of ski slopes.

Much of the town is permeated with memories of the 1968 Olympic champion
Jean-Claude Killy, a hometown boy who made good and whose endorsements have
given Val d'Isère additional weaponry in its competition with other resorts in the
alpine world.

Val d'Isère is the focal point for a network of satellite resorts scattered around the
nearby valleys, including the architecturally uninspired Tignes (6,888 feet above sea
level), whose layout is divided into at least four resort-style villages. The most stylish
and prosperous of these is Val Claret; less fortunate and successful are Tignes le Lac,
Tignes les Boisses, and Tignes les Brévières.

Guarding one entrance to Val d'Isère is La Daille (a resort of mostly high-rise
condos and time-shares) and guarding the other is the medieval hamlet of Le Fornet
(best known as the departure point for gondolas leading over a mountain ridge to the
Pissaillas Glacier and another network of ski trails, the Système de Solaise). All these
satellites, however, lack the cachet and diversity of Val d'Isère's nightlife and dining.
Public transport via the Train Rouge can pick you up and deposit you at the departure
point to the terminus of virtually any ski lift or trail in the region.

The best time to visit is midwinter, despite the resort's efforts to promote itself as a
summer destination. Though snow in summer melts on the rock faces around town,
exposing the gray bedrock, icy granules remain skiable year-round on the Pissaillas.
The glacier is accessible via the Fornet cable car, on the northwestern (uppermost)
edges of town. The tourist office considers the ski conditions safe and suitable only

between June 28 and August 17. A lift ticket costs 151F ($27.20) for half a day, 217F ($39.05) for a full day, and 400F ($72) for 2 days. Note that these prices do not include insurance. Access to the glacier from Val Disole requires two cable-car transfers. For information, contact **Ski Lifts,** B.P. 269, 73155 Val d'Isère (☎ 04-79-06-00-35). Officially, the resort is closed to all winter activities from May 5 to November 25.

Val d'Isère is legendary for its "death-defying" chutes and its off-piste walls. These slopes, of course, are for the experts, but the intermediate skier of moderate skills will also find open snowfields. The best place for intermediates is Tignes, with its wide variety of runs, including the Grande Motte at 11,150 feet. Skiers find enough variety here to stay 2 weeks and never repeat the slopes that stretch from the Pissaillas Glacier far above Val d'Isère to Tignes Les Brévières four valleys away.

There are only a few marked expert runs; it's the more accessible off-piste areas that lure experts from all over Europe and the U.S. Most of these runs can be reached after short traverses from the Bellevarde, Solaiwse, and Fornet cable cars in Val d'Isère and the Grande Motte cable car in Val Claret.

At least a dozen **ski schools** flourish during winter. One of the largest and busiest is the Ecole de Ski Français (French National Ski School), B.P. 265, 73155 Val d'Isère (☎ **04-79-06-02-34**), with 260 ski guides and teachers. Somewhat more personalized is Snow Fun, B.P. 287, 73150 Val d'Isère (☎ **04-79-41-11-81**), with 60 guides. Purists usually gravitate to Top Ski, galerie des Cimes (B.P. 41), 73153 Val d'Isère (☎ **04-79-06-14-80**), a small but choice outfit with 12 extremely well-trained guides who cater exclusively to alpine connoisseurs who want to ski off-piste (away from the officially recognized and maintained ski trails).

WHERE TO STAY

The staff at **Val Hôtel,** B.P. 73, 73153 Val d'Isère (☎ **04-79-06-18-90;** fax 04-79-06-11-88), the resort's central reservations network, can reserve accommodations for you.

Hôtel Altitude. Rte. de la Balme, 73150 Val d'Isère. ☎ **04-79-06-12-55.** Fax 04-79-41-11-09. E-mail: altitude-valdisere@laposte.fr. 40 units. TV TEL. Winter 1,240–1,300F ($223.20–$234) double. Summer 720–1,020F ($129.60–$183.60) double. Rates include half board. MC, V. Closed May 6–June 30 and Sept 9–Dec 5.

This frequently renovated and oft-modernized chalet was built in the 1970s in true Savoyard style. Because of the similarity of their names, it's frequently confused with the four-star Hôtel Latitude nearby. The three-star Altitude is comfortable and cozy, a short walk south of the town center so you'll be able to escape the madding crowd. Many of the guests return year after year.

Dining: On the premises is Le Restaurant, with well-prepared, straightforward food, several open fireplaces, and a bar.

Amenities: The hotel has the benefit of remaining open in summer, when an outdoor pool and sundeck supplement the sauna and steam bath that are open year-round.

✪ **Hôtel Christiania.** B.P. 48, 73152 Val d'Isère. ☎ **04-79-06-08-25.** Fax 04-79-41-11-10. 70 units. TV TEL. 1,674–2,434F ($301.30–$438.10) double; 2,834–3,414F ($510.10–$614.50) suite. Rates include half board. Full board 160F ($28.80) per person extra. AE, MC, V. Closed May–Dec 5.

A stylishly designed chalet, this hotel opened in 1949 but was demolished and almost completely rebuilt in 1991. Today it's the best-recommended hotel in a town filled with worthy contenders. Homage to its original design appears at unexpected moments, most obviously in the *Sputnik*-style furniture a decorator incorporated into a sunken lobby that's otherwise ringed with exposed stone, varnished pine, and blazing fireplaces. The guest rooms are deliberately cozy, with lots of pine trim and alpine touches.

Dining: Le Christiania restaurant welcomes guests and nonguests. It's open only from early December to late April, daily for lunch and dinner.

Amenities: Room service (24 hours), baby-sitting, concierge. State-of-the-art fitness center with indoor pool, sauna, Turkish baths, exercise areas, massage facilities.

Hôtel Mercure Village. B.P. 45, 73152 Val d'Isère. ☎ **04-79-06-12-93.** Fax 04-79-41-11-12. 45 units. TV TEL. Winter 680–1,160F ($122.40–$208.80) double; 810–1,440F ($145.80–$259.20) suite for 2. Summer 580F ($104.40) double; 800F ($160) suite for 2. Rates include breakfast. AE, DC, MC, V. Parking 65F ($11.70). Closed May 6–June 15.

The success of this hotel is based on its relatively reasonable rates and its deliberate lack of the ostentation and glitter that permeate many of Val d'Isère's properties. Don't judge its charm by its rather uninspired four-story chalet-style exterior: The hotel was rebuilt in 1991 from an older, rather ugly core, but inside are enough alpine touches to evoke a bit of nostalgia. In the public areas are pinewood paneling and flowered curtains. The guest rooms are simpler and rather angular but still feature touches of varnished pine. The hotel is in the town center, with easy access to the chairlifts and the nightlife.

Dining: Well-prepared meals are served in generous portions in the rustic La Spatule, specializing in Savoyard cuisine. Those who opt for half-board plans use Le Potager, a room that's more formal and appealing than what you'd find in most members of the Mercure chain. Room service is available during regular meal hours in the two restaurants.

WHERE TO DINE

La Grande Ourse. Sur le Front de Neige, adjacent to the church. ☎ **04-79-06-00-19.** Reservations recommended at dinner. Main courses 90–160F ($16.20–$28.80) at dinner; fixed-price menu 120F ($21.60) at lunch, 195F ($35.10) at dinner. AE, V. Daily noon–3pm and 7:30–9:30pm. Closed May 5–Nov 30. SAVOYARD.

This restaurant isn't as formal and Parisian as Le New Solaise (see below), and during the crowded lunch hour its prices are a great deal. At nighttime, however, its real charm emerges as it transforms into a glamorous candlelit restaurant with a blazing fireplace and plenty of Savoyard charm. It was built in 1937 by an important painter, Jean Fautrier, who's almost unknown outside France. The place's name derives from a mural he painted of the zodiac, part of which features a large female bear. Menu items at lunch include grilled meats, pastas, salads, and simple but fortifying dishes of the day. Evening menus offer more sophisticated fare, like roast rack of lamb with herbs, Italian carpaccio, Savoyard fondue with three cheeses, and escalope of foie gras with purple artichokes. Dessert may be a tarte fine with apples or a Gallic version of a North American brownie.

La Vieille Maison. Vieux Village, La Daille. ☎ **04-79-06-11-76.** Reservations recommended. Main courses 76–105F ($13.70–$18.90). AE, MC, V. Daily 7–10pm. Closed May–June and Sept–Nov. SAVOYARD.

Amid cozy but relatively new buildings in the satellite hamlet of La Daille, this former farmhouse is one of the valley's oldest chalets. Constructed 300 years ago, it has lots of exposed stone, not particularly comfortable chairs, and a staff that tends to be blasé. Menu items are based on traditional Savoyard themes, specializing in hearty cold-weather dishes like fondues and raclettes, many of which are prepared only for a minimum of two to four diners. Other choices are filet mignon with lemon and sour cream and the signature specialty, Vieille Maison–style veal that's stuffed with ham and slathered with cheese au gratin. Hands-on chefs sometimes opt for La Viande à l'Auze—a super-hot slab of rock is placed directly on your table so you can sizzle your beef strips yourself.

Le New Solaise. Galerie du Solaise. ☎ **04-79-06-08-10.** Reservations recommended. Main courses 75–130F ($13.50–$23.40). AE, MC. Daily 7pm–midnight. Closed May–Nov. FRENCH/SAVOYARD.

In 1996 an English-born investor bought what had been one of the resort's most gas-tronomically sophisticated restaurants, lowered its prices to relatively affordable levels, and inaugurated a new moderately priced renaissance of well-prepared favorites. At the end of a covered gallery in the heart of the resort, the venue is modern but with enough exposed wood to feel cozy and warm; its bar is hopping every night from 5pm until sometime after midnight. Menu items include fresh marinated salmon prepared with dill, braised leeks in a delicately herbed vinaigrette, and melted Saint-Marcellin cheese (a local cows'-milk cheese) on a bed of spinach.

A NEARBY PLACE TO STAY & DINE

The unpretentious rail and highway junction of **Albertville** lies within **La Vallée de la Tarantaise,** a sinuous valley that climbs upward along a distance of 53 miles along Route 90. Route 90 extends from low-lying Albertville (at around 1,200 feet above sea level) and eventually branches into **La Vallée d'Isère,** whose focal point is the resort of Val d'Isère. Most visitors travel between the two points by car, although about five trains a day go uphill between Albertville and Bourg-St-Maurice. At Bourg-St-Maurice, a bus, whose departure is timed to coincide with the arrival of trains, con-tinues for another 18 miles uphill to Val d'Isère. Train passengers should expect total transit time of between 60 and 90 minutes, depending on the day of the week, and a one-way fare of 100F ($18).

✪ **Hôtel Million.** 8 place de la Liberté, 73200 Albertville. ☎ **04-79-32-25-15.** Fax 04-79-32-25-36. Reservations recommended. Main courses 140–200F ($25.20–$36); fixed-price menus 190–500F ($34.20–$90). AE, DC, MC, V. Tues–Sun noon–2pm, Tues–Sat 7:45–9:30pm. FRENCH.

Set back from the main road through town, the Hôtel Million was established in 1770 by an ancestor of Philippe Million, the current owner and chef whose cuisine did much to put Albertville on the gourmet map. It's housed in a white building with strong horizontal lines and gables on a flagstone-covered square; the anterooms have authentic 19th-century decor, while the spacious dining room itself has high ceilings and conservatively classic furnishings. Some of the traditional dishes featured on the menu derive from popular Savoy tastes of the 19th century, in particular the frogs' legs, freshwater fish from Lake Annecy, and freshwater crayfish. Other choices include a filet of fera (a white fish found in Alpine lakes) served with chanterelles and herb-flavored butter, Bresse chicken prepared with a coulis of truffles, and roasted rack of veal served with a fricassée of artichokes.

Although the establishment is best known for its restaurant, which attracts both gastonomes and sports enthusiasts, it also contains 26 attractive and unpretentious guest rooms. Outfitted in rustic alpine style, each contains a private bathroom, TV, and phone, and thanks to the hotel's construction about a century ago, more space than you might imagine. Friday and Saturday nights between December and April are the most expensive, when doubles rent for 550F to 600F ($99 to $108) a night. The rest of the year, doubles range from 350F to 400F ($63 to $72). Parking is free.

VAL D'ISERE AFTER DARK

The resort has its share of bars that come and go every season with the arrival and departure of the snow. Most are in the town's pedestrian zone or adjacent to **rue Principale.** One of the most reliable bars is **L'Aventure** (☎ 04-79-06-20-82). If you want to go dancing, there are only two discos, both mobbed in winter and dead during spring and autumn: **Dick's Tea Bar** (☎ 04-79-06-14-87), which also opens half-heartedly during July and August but only on evenings when business might justify the effort, and **Club 21** (☎ 04-79-06-04-93), open only in winter. Admission to both is around 70F ($12.60) and includes the first drink.

13 Burgundy

Vineyard castles and ancient churches mark the landscape of Burgundy, which is the land of the good life for those who savor fine cuisine and wines served in historic surroundings. Burgundy was once an incredibly powerful independent province, its famed Valois dukes spreading their might across all of Europe from 1363 to 1477. To maintain its shaky independence, Burgundy faced many struggles, notably under Charles the Bold, who was always in conflict with Louis XI. When Charles died in 1477, Louis invaded and annexed the duchy. Nonetheless, the Habsburgs still maintained their claims to it. Even after its reunion with France, Burgundy knew no peace, as it suffered many more upheavals, such as its ravaging in the Franco-Spanish wars beginning in 1636. Peace came in 1678.

At the time of the Revolution, Burgundy disappeared as a political entity, and it was subdivided into the départements of France, Yonne, Saône-et-Loire, and Côte-d'Or. The ducs de Bourgogne are but a dim memory now, but they left a legacy of vintage red and white wines to please and excite the palate. The six major wine-growing regions of Burgundy are Chablis, Côte de Nuits, Côte de Beaune, Côte de Chalon, Mâconnais, and Nivernais.

REGIONAL CUISINE   For centuries the cuisine of Burgundy has been appreciated for the freshness and variety of its ingredients and the skill and finesse of its native chefs. Many Roman historians, Charles VI, Escoffier, and Brillat-Savarin (who was born in the Burgundian town of Bugey) have praised the food and/or wine of Burgundy. There's something about the mild climate, adequate rainfall, and nutrient-rich soil that produces some of the most excellent beef (especially of the rare Charolais breed), mushrooms, grapes, fish, wild game, snails, fruit, and vegetables in Europe. The cuisine seems to have been invented for healthy appetites, and the typical Bourguignon/Bourguignonne has been defined as someone who's both a gourmet and a gourmand.

Any sauce created with a dose of wine added to it (at least in Burgundy) is called *une meurette,* and there are lots listed as accompaniments to main courses on menus in the province. These meurettes, whether bound with butter and flour or strongly spiced with quantities of herbs and (occasionally) the blood of the slaughtered animal, are enormously flavorful and seem to make whatever wine you happen to be drinking taste even better. In the same vein, any cut of meat

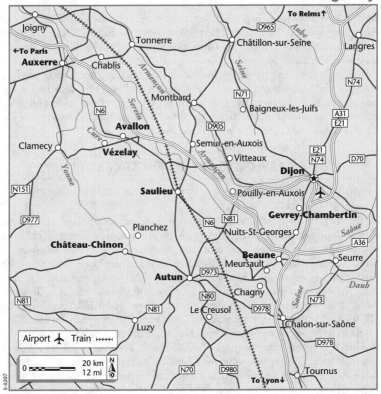

prepared *à la bourguignonne* is usually braised and then served with a sauce concocted from wine (usually red), onions, mushrooms, and (except if it's served with fish) lardons.

One major specialty is a succulent species of snail, cooked in the shell and flavored with garlic and butter. Other recipes handed down for generations are *coq au vin* (flavored with red wine, brandy, some of the pulverized liver of the animal, and blood) and chicken or ham cooked *en sauce* (made traditionally with white wine and cream) or *au sang* (with blood sauce, lard, and baby onions).

The region also produces fine cheese, which is sold in wine bars across Europe, most visibly the goat cheese *crottin de chavignol*, made in the district of Sancerre along with the superb white wine of the same name—the cheese and the wine accompany each other splendidly. Another is the blue-veined Gex, which has a flavor similar to Roquefort, and all of the famous Epoisses cheeses, made in the Yonne valley.

Almost everyone appreciates the flavor of Dijon mustard, called the "king of French condiments," made with ground mustard seeds and slightly fermented wine or vinegar. Any menu item followed by the adjective *dijonnaise* will have a sauce containing a liberal dose of that mustard. It's estimated that Dijon produces nearly three-quarters of the mustard consumed in France.

And, of course, there are Burgundy's wines. Consisting of only 2% of all the wines produced in France (only one-third the production of all the wines of Bordeaux), they include vintages sought the world over. The best are those from the Côte d'Or, a narrow strip of gravel-studded soil usually divided into family-owned plots of fewer than 40 acres, which lies between Dijon and Santenay. In the Côte d'Or, the two major categories are the Côte de Nuits and the Côte de Beaune. Other burgundy categories are Gevrey-Chambertin, Chambolle-Musigny, Nuits-St-Georges, Beaune, Meursault, Chassagne-Montrachet, Santenay, and Pommard.

Dr. Lavalle, a noted wine expert, has said of these wines: "They have an exquisite finesse of the bouquet and a flavour at once hot and delicate which lasts a few moments and leaves a sweet and fragrant after-taste, ruby color of perfect limpidity and beneficient action on the digestive organs—such are the high qualities of the wines of the Côte d'Or, the first wines in the world."

EXPLORING THE REGION BY CAR

Burgundy is perhaps the finest region in France to tour by car. Here's a suggested way to link together the best of the region.

DAY 1   Begin at Burgundy's northwestern edge, in **Chablis.** Capital of the vineyards of Basse Bourgogne (Lower Burgundy), Chablis is surrounded by vineyards. The town is more famous for its wine than for its monuments, but it does contain two interesting churches: the 12th-century Eglise St-Martin and the Eglise St-Pierre, which retains little of its original Romanesque design. Chablis is really not worth an overnight stop, though 9 miles to the east along D965, in the hamlet of **Tonnere,** is one of the best restaurants in the province: **L'Abbaye St-Michel,** route St-Michel (☎ **03-86-55-05-99**). In a 10th-century monastery, it's open daily for lunch and dinner, and the owners rent 9 comfortable rooms; many visitors, however, prefer this as a lunch stopover. Menus begin at 220F ($39.60). Then backtrack for about 15 miles east along D965 (passing through Chablis en route) to Auxerre.

Scene of many pivotal moments in French history, **Auxerre** is the site of one of France's most impressive churches, the Gothic **Cathédrale St-Etienne.** If you're looking for truly fine dining, drive north for 17 miles to the hamlet of **Joigny** for **A la Côte St-Jacques** (see section 1 in this chapter). Return to Auxerre for the night or stay over in Joigny if you wish.

DAY 2   Drive south from Auxerre along N151 for 32 miles to the hilltop hamlet of **Vézelay**—if there's any Romanesque church in France that's a must-see, this town's is it. Pray for your loved ones or the dead, depending on your beliefs, or marvel at the severe majesty of a pilgrimage site consecrated to Mary Magdalen. Ordinances encourage you to park at the bottom of the village and climb the sloping cobblestone main street. A luxurious ending to your day is at the base of the hill on which the famous church sits: **L'Espérance,** St-Père-sous-Vézelay (☎ **03-86-33-39-10**), is one of the best restaurants in the world. It's closed all day Tuesday, and Monday and Wednesday at lunch, however, so you may want to plan your itinerary accordingly.

You have the option now of spending the night in Vézelay, driving 6 miles east on D951 to the densely forested town of **Avallon,** or continuing south for 35 miles on well-signposted country roads to **Château-Chinon.** Wherever you opt to spend the night, plan on an early-morning departure the following day.

DAY 3   From Château-Chinon, drive east 20 miles on D978 to visit one of the oldest towns in France, **Autun.** En route, perhaps take a detour: heading east on D978 toward Autun, turn right (south) at the town of Arleuf, going right onto D500. At a fork, turn right to Glux and then follow the arrows to Mont Beuvray via D18. You reach the summit through D274. After 2 miles of climbing you'll be at **Oppidum of Bibracte,** home of the Eduens, a Gallic tribe. At this altitude of 2,800 feet, Vercingetorix organized the Gauls to fight Caesar's legions in A.D. 52. From here you'll have a splendid view of Autun and Mont St-Vincent. If the weather is clear, you can see the Jura and snowy Mont Blanc. Leave Mont Beuvray via D274 and continue northeast to Autun.

At Autun, you'll find a historic town loaded with ruins left by the ancient Romans, as well as a hilltop cathedral built in 1120 to hold the remains of St. Lazarus. Spend the night here.

DAY 4   Start your day early, prepared for brief tours of various châteaux, feudal fortresses, vineyards, and other historic sites. Your route will be loaded with appealing detours, so be as flexible as possible as you negotiate your way through a labyrinth of well-marked country roads leading toward Beaune.

Leave Autun on D973. After 6 miles, turn left onto D326 toward Sully. Here you'll find the **Château de Sully,** once known as the Fontainebleau of Burgundy; it's closed to the public, but a view from the outside might satisfy you. The gardens are open from Easter to September, daily from 8am to 6pm. Leave Sully, following the road signs to the small village of Nolay. Three miles past Nolay you'll reach the **Château de La Rochepot** (☎ **03-80-21-71-37**), a medieval-style fortress built during the Renaissance. It's open daily: April 1 to June 30 from 10 to 11:30am and 2 to 5:30pm, July 1 to August 31 from 10am to noon and 2 to 6pm, September from 10 to 11:30am and 2 to 5:30pm, and in October from 10 to 11:30am and 2 to 4:30pm. Closed November 1 to March 30. Admission is 32F ($5.75) for adults and 14F ($2.50) for children.

Now head toward Beaune on D973, passing near some of the best-known **vineyards:** Chassagne-Montrachet, Puligny-Montrachet, Meursault, Auxey Duresses, Volnay, and Pommard. En route, perhaps stop at a restaurant whose setting is as interesting as its food. **Chagny,** 27 miles east of Autun and 11 miles southwest of Beaune, rarely attracts sightseers, though gourmands from all over stop in for a meal at **Lameloise,** 36 place d'Armes (☎ **03-85-87-08-85**). It offers choices like lamb filet in a rice crêpe, Bresse pigeon cooked in a bladder, hot lemon soufflé, and one of the broadest spectrums of burgundies anywhere in France. Reservations are required. Closed Wednesday and Thursday at lunch.

Continue north to Beaune on D973, which will soon change to N74. You'll pass villages like Aloxe-Corton, where Charlemagne once owned vineyards, and Comblanchien. In Vougeot you can visit the **Château du Clos-de-Vougeot** (☎ **03-80-62-86-09**), surrounded by France's most celebrated vineyards. The Renaissance château is associated with the Brotherhood of the Knights of Tastevin, an organization revived in 1934 along medieval lines; it maintains a 12th-century cellar, open for visits April to September, daily from 9am to 7pm (off-season, daily from 9 to 11:30am and 2 to 5:30pm). Admission is 20F ($3.60).

Leave N74 for D122, which will take you through the scenic hamlet of Chambolle Musigny, then to Morey St-Denis and the site of your overnight stay, historic **Gevrey-Chambertin.** It marks the beginning of the Côte de Nuits district, source of some of the world's most prestigious wines.

DAYS 5–8   Continue north the remaining short distance to **Dijon,** home to some of the region's most spectacular architecture.

If you have the time, use Dijon as a base and make excursions to any sites you missed during the first half of your tour. Consider lunch trips to Aubigny or Saulieu, 20 and 40 miles west of Dijon, respectively (see section 8 in this chapter).

Other places to fan out from Dijon include:

Leave Dijon on A6, heading toward Paris. You'll be traveling along a good road in the Vallée de l'Ouche, alongside the Burgundy Canal. At pont de Pany, on the outskirts of Sombernon, exit onto a local highway (D905) and continue northwest. On your left lies the artificial lake of Grosbois. The scenery is typical of agricultural France, with isolated farms, woods, and pastures.

You pass through Vitteaux and just before the next village, Posanges, stands a feudal château. You can't visit it, but it's worth a picture. Continue on D905 for a few miles until you come to a railroad crossing. On your left is another old castle, now part of a private farm. The next village you reach along D905 is Pouillenay. Follow the signs for a short detour to the hamlet of **Flavigny-sur-Ozerain.** Park your car outside the walls and walk through the old streets.

Leave Flavigny and follow the signs for a few miles on country roads to **Alise-Ste-Reine,** the site of the camp of Alesia, where Caesar wiped out a concentration of Gallic soldiers. Here, Millet sculpted a bronze statue of Vercingetorix. You can explore the excavated ruins of a Roman-Gallic town and visit the **Musée Alesia,** rue de l'Hôpital (☎ **03-80-96-10-95**); it's open June 30 to September 7, daily from 9am to 7pm; March 21 to June 29 and September 8 to November 4, daily from 10am to 6pm (closed November 5 to March 20). Admission is 28F ($5.05) for adults and 18F ($3.25) for children. Alise-Ste-Reine honors a Christian girl who was decapitated for refusing to marry a Roman governor, Olibrius. As late as the 17th century, a fountain at the site of the beheading was said to have curative powers.

After Alise-Ste-Reine, you can head back to the village of Les Laumes, a railroad center. Before entering the village, make a U-turn to the right and take N454 to Baigneux-les-Juifs. After the village of Grésigny, on your left is a farm-fortress surrounded by water.

One mile farther, turn right toward the **Château de Bussy-Rabutin.** Roger de Rabutin, cousin of Mme de Sévigné, ridiculed Louis XIV's court, for which he spent 6 years in the Bastille. The château, with two round towers, has survived mostly intact, including the interior decoration. The gardens and park are attributed to Le Nôtre. It's open Wednesday to Monday: April to September from 9am to noon and 2 to 6pm and October to March from 10am to noon and 2 to 5pm.

Going back to Grésigny, turn right before the farm-fortress, then go left. Outside the village, turn right again toward Menetreux Le Pitois. You're now off the main road and into the real countryside. Once back on D905, head on to **Montbard,** hometown of George-Louis Leclerc, comte de Buffon, one of the 18th century's greatest naturalists and author of *L'Histoire naturelle,* a 44-volume encyclopedia. The scientist's home is on display, as well as a minimuseum of his life and work. The town is also the site of a pleasant hotel/restaurant, the **Hôtel de l'Ecu,** 7 rue Auguste-Carré (☎ **03-80-92-11-66**), where moderately priced meals are prepared in what was during the 1700s a postal relay station.

Continue east for another 6 miles to Marmagne, then turn left on D32 and head toward the **Abbaye de Fontenay** (☎ **03-80-92-15-00**). Isolated in a valley, Fontenay is one of Europe's most unspoiled 12th-century Cistercian abbeys. It was classified as a site of "Universal Heritage" by UNESCO in 1981 and is open daily from 9am to noon and 2 to 6pm (to 5pm in winter). Admission is 40F ($7.20) for adults and 20F ($3.60) for children and students.

1 Auxerre

103 miles SE of Paris, 92 miles NW of Dijon

Auxerre was founded by the Gauls and enlarged by the Romans. On a hill overlooking the Yonne River, it's the capital of Lower Burgundy and the center of vineyards, some of which produce chablis. Joan of Arc spent several days here in 1429. Napoléon met Maréchal Ney here on March 17, 1815, on the former emperor's return from Elba. Louis XVIII had sent Ney to stop Napoléon, but Ney embraced him and turned his army against the king. For that gesture, Ney was later shot in Paris.

The handsome city of Auxerre is a sleepy, dreamy kind of place today, as you'll agree if you spend an afternoon with the Auxerrois reading a paper in a cafe. Its population of 42,000 live with memories of their past and will often admit that not a lot is happening around here these days—and that's how they'd like to keep it.

ESSENTIALS

GETTING THERE   Many of the **trains** traveling between Paris and Lyon stop at Auxerre: 12 per day from Paris (trip time: 2 hours) and 9 per day from Lyon (trip time: 2 hours). For train information and schedules, call ☎ **08-36-35-35-39.**

Many visitors **drive** here, since Auxerre is near A6/E1 (Autoroute du Soleil).

VISITOR INFORMATION   The **Office de Tourisme** is at 1–2 quai de la République (☎ **03-86-52-06-19**).

TOURING THE CATHEDRAL

The railway station lies at the eastern edge of town, about a mile from the historic center. Most of Auxerre is on the opposite (western) bank of the Yonne River. Its heart is between place du Maréchal-Leclerc (where you'll find the Hôtel de Ville) and the Cathédrale St-Etienne.

Cathédrale St-Etienne. ☎ **03-86-52-23-29.** Admission to crypt and treasury, 20F ($3.60). Sept–May Mon–Sat 9am–noon and 2–6pm; June Mon–Sat 9am–6pm; July–Aug Mon–Sat 2–5pm, Sun 2–6pm.

Pay a visit to the Flamboyant Gothic Cathédrale St-Etienne, begun in the 13th century but not completed until the 16th. The front facade is remarkable, with sculptured portals. The stained glass is famous, some of it the original from the 13th century. In the crypt, all that remains of the Romanesque church that stood on this site, you can see 11th-century frescoes.

Every Sunday in July and August you can attend an organ concert from 5 to 6pm; admission is free. And daily June to August from 10 to 11:10pm and in September from 9:30 to 10:40pm there's a sound-and-light show here depicting the history of the church. It's presented in English, French, and German for 30F ($5.40) for adults, free for children 13 and under.

WHERE TO STAY

Hôtel Le Maxime. 2 quai de la Marine, 89000 Auxerre. ☎ **03-86-52-14-19.** Fax 03-86-52-21-70. 25 units. TV TEL. 480F ($86.40) double. AE, DC, MC, V. Parking 15F ($2.70).

This family-run hotel (with elevator) was extensively renovated—actually almost rebuilt—in 1970, about a century after its construction. It contains attractive rooms, many with views of the river Yonne or the old city. Most retain their original wall and ceiling beams. You can take breakfast in your room or in the quiet salon, amid Oriental rugs, polished paneling, and a sense of the gentility of an earlier era.

Hôtel Le Normandie. 41 bd. Vauban, 89000 Auxerre. ☎ **03-86-52-57-80.** Fax 03-86-51-54-33. www.unimedia.fr/arcantus. 47 units. TV TEL. 290–370F ($52.20–$66.60) double. AE, DC, MC, V. Parking 26F ($4.70).

This centrally located hotel offers traditional hospitality, combining antique furnishings with modern amenities. The tranquil and comfortably furnished rooms open onto garden views. There's overnight parking for 30 cars, plus a complete gymnasium, sauna, bar, terrace, and room service with hot and cold dishes anytime.

✪ **Le Parc des Maréchaux.** 6 av. Foch, 89000 Auxerre. ☎ **03-86-51-43-77.** Fax 03-86-51-31-72. 25 units. TV TEL. 370–490F ($66.60–$88.20) double; 450–490F ($81–$88.20) triple or quad. AE, DC, MC, V.

Colette: An Unlikely Literary Heroine

"C'est Colette! C'est un miracle!"

That's what her fans had to say, and Colette's fans included the poet Stephen Koch (he claimed that she was the only writer who got it right when writing about sex), Proust, Updike, Woolf, Gide, and her beloved friend Cocteau. Auden compared her favorably to Tolstoy.

Born in 1873 to a one-legged, once-bankrupt tax collector from Provence and raised in the obscure Burgundian village of St-Sauveur-en-Puisaye, Sidonie Gabrielle Colette was an unlikely literary heroine. As a schoolgirl, Colette fell for a would-be writer twice her age—known as Willy, pseudonym of Henri Gauthier-Villars—and married him at age 20. He exposed her to the murky world of Paris society and imposed a rigid writing discipline, frequently locking her in a room until she finished a designated number of pages. Those pages were eventually compiled into four novellas known as the Claudine series. Published at yearly intervals between 1900 and 1903 under her husband's pseudonym, each was based on the experiences of a *libertine ingenue,* with an acute preoccupation for evoking the sounds, tastes, textures, colors, and interaction of that era's beautiful people. They began to explore a theme that Colette returned to again and again, with exquisite sensitivity: the pleasures and pains of love, permeated with a mix of naïveté and cunning.

In 1910 she divorced Willy and did a stint as a vaudeville entertainer in a Paris music hall. By late in that year she was writing for *Le Matin,* whose editor in chief was Henri de Jouvenel, whom she married in 1912. That partnership produced a daughter, Colette de Jouvenel (or Bel Gazou, "beautiful warbler," as her mother called her), and lasted until 1925. Then Colette met and married her third and final husband, Maurice Goudeket.

Two of Colette's most enduring works are *Chéri* (1920), the story of a semi-crazed youthful survivor of World War I who initiates a love affair with an older woman, and *Gigi* (1944), about a young girl reared to become a Parisian courtesan by two sophisticated and aging sisters. This work gained even more popularity when Hollywood made it into a musical starring Leslie Caron and Louis Jourdan.

The former country girl's official awards eventually included membership in the Belgian Royal Academy (1935), France's Académie Goncourt (elected a

An absolute gem that completely outshines the competition, this was a private residence in the 19th century, set on its own extensive grounds. It lies on the outskirts of town surrounded by century-old trees and is the most secluded choice in the area. The guest rooms are "christened" with the names of the marshals of France; though each enjoys a distinctive decor, the predominant style is Empire. Unlike in many of these old places, the bathrooms here are modern and functional. There's a breakfast room, plus a Victorian-style bar.

WHERE TO DINE

Le Jardin Gourmand. 56 bd. Vauban. ☎ **03-86-51-53-52.** Reservations required. Main courses 80–150F ($14.40–$27); fixed-price menus 150–280F ($27–$50.40). AE, MC, V. Thurs–Mon noon–2pm and 7:30–9:30pm. Closed Feb 16–Mar 3 and Aug 31–Sept 15. FRENCH.

Le Jardin Gourmand serves *cuisine moderne du marché,* using the freshest ingredients from the markets. Try such good-tasting dishes as mousseline of haddock and special oysters brought in from Normandy. Pierre Boussereau is the experienced and subtle member in 1945, elected president in 1949), and the French Légion d'Honneur (elected a member in 1920, elected Grand Officer in 1953)—honors that until then had rarely been granted to women.

Literary fans around the world mourned the passing of Colette in 1954. In Paris they shouted "Gigi!" or "Chéri!" as her body traveled from an elaborate ceremony in the courtyard of the Palais Royal to the Cemetière du Père-Lachaise, to be buried with honors near Oscar Wilde and other literary icons.

Today you can pay homage to Colette by journeying to the village of St-Sauveur-en-Puisaye, where you can visit the **Musée Colette** (☎ **03-86-45-61-95**). It's open April to October, Wednesday to Monday from 10am to 6pm; November to March, Saturday and Sunday from 2 to 6pm. Admission is 25F ($4.50) for adults or 10F ($1.80) for scholars, students, and children.

Colette fans from around the world—led by her daughter and only child—helped establish the museum. Her daughter died in 1981, long before the shrine opened in 1995. Photographs in the museum serve as a guidebook to Colette's life. Pictured are Colette with her trio of husbands and even her lesbian lover, the marquise de Belboeuf. (Colette came out of the closet long before it was fashionable to do so.) One photograph depicts her going up in a balloon over Paris for *Le Matin.* She's seen with many of the leading legends of her day, including Sarah Bernhardt.

One room is a trompe-l'oeil copy of Colette's apartment in the Palais Royal (not open to the public) in Paris. You can also watch a 50-minute 1951 film of Colette in which she appears with Cocteau.

What comes as a surprise is that at a tearoom here you can order, among other items, *fra,* that salt cheese tart so beloved by Colette. Colette's other favorite Burgundian pastries are made fresh daily and served here, including a pastry called *gâteau à six cornes* culled from a recipe of Colette's.

To reach the village, take the Autoroute du Soleil (A6) south from Paris heading toward Lyon but exit at Joigny. From here, follow the signs for Toucy, where you go in the direction of Orléans-St-Fargeau. At the Toucy exit, St-Sauveur-en-Puisayne is signposted. If you're already in Auxerre, take D965 to Toucy.

chef at this restaurant, which offers garden and terrace seating. The wine list boasts 300 wines, including 50 types of chablis and some reasonably priced local burgundies.

NEARBY ACCOMMODATIONS & DINING

✪ **A la Côte St-Jacques.** 14 Faubourg de Paris (N6), 89300 Joigny. ☎ **03-86-62-09-70.** Fax 03-86-91-49-70. Reservations required. Main courses 250–350F ($45–$63); fixed-price menus 340–540F ($56.80–$90.20) at lunch, 780–880F ($130.25–$146.95) at dinner. AE, DC, MC, V. Daily 12:15–2:45pm and 7:15–9:45pm. From Auxerre, head north on N6 (toward Sens) for 17 miles. FRENCH.

Jean-Michel Lorain and his wife, Brigitte, are the directors of this top-echelon Relais & Châteaux. The 300-year-old foundation and 19th-century design contribute to the atmosphere in what is one of the region's most luxurious hotels and restaurants. In addition to the main building, there's a luxurious annex across the N6 highway that's connected to it via an underground tunnel fashioned from rocks salvaged from old buildings nearby. In one of the elegant dining rooms you can enjoy specialties like Brittany oysters in delicately potted sealoaf, sea perch lightly smoked with Sevruga caviar, and suckling pig with pearl barley and sweet-and-sour new carrots, as well as an incredible array of desserts. The cuisine sounds a trifle heavy but actually is light and delightful.

The hotel rents 20 beautiful rooms and 9 suites, each with air-conditioning, TV, minibar, and phone. There's also a heated pool, tennis courts, and a sauna. Doubles are 500F to 1,380F ($90 to $248.40); suites, 1,580F to 2,500F ($284.40 to $450).

2 Vézelay

135 miles SE of Paris, 32 miles S of Auxerre

Vézelay, a living museum of French antiquity, stands frozen in time. For many, the town is the high point of their trip through Burgundy. Because it contained what was believed to be the tomb of St. Mary Magdalene, that "beloved and pardoned sinner," it was once one of the great pilgrimage sites of the Christian world.

Today the medieval charm of Vézelay is widely known throughout France, and the town is virtually overrun with visitors in summer. The hordes are especially thick on July 22, the official day of homage to La Madeleine.

ESSENTIALS

GETTING THERE   **Trains** travel from Auxerre to nearby Sermizelles, where a bus makes the run to Vézelay. For train information and schedules, call ☎ **08-36-35-35-39. Bus service** to Vézelay is Monday to Friday at 10am and also at 3:20pm in July and August. When **driving** from Paris to Vézelay, travel A6 south to Auxerre, continuing south along N151 to Clamency, turning east along D951 to Vézelay.

VISITOR INFORMATION   The **Office de Tourisme** is on rue St-Pierre (☎ **03-86-33-23-69**), open daily April to September and Friday to Wednesday October to March.

EXPLORING THE TOWN

On a hill 360 feet above the countryside, Vézelay is known for its ramparts and houses with sculptured doorways, corbeled staircases, and mullioned windows. The site was originally an abbey founded by Girart de Roussillon, a comte de Bourgogne (troubadours were fond of singing of his exploits). It was consecrated in 878 by Pope John VIII.

On March 31, 1146, St. Bernard preached the Second Crusade there; in 1190 the town was the rendezvous point for the Third Crusade, drawing such personages as Richard the Lion-Hearted and King Philippe-Auguste of France. Later, St. Louis of France came here several times on pilgrimages.

Park outside the town hall and walk through the medieval streets lined with 15th-, 16th-, and 18th-century houses, past flower-filled gardens.

Most of Vézelay's shops line either side of **rue St-Etienne** and **rue St-Pierre.** You'll find an assortment of stores selling religious books and statuary, including **Jerusalem,** 78 rue St-Pierre (☎ **03-86-33-37-43**), and **Le Magasin du Pélerin,** place de la Basilique (☎ **03-86-33-29-14**). For one-of-a-kind pieces by local craftspeople and artists, go to **Atelier Marie-Noëlle,** 69 rue St-Pierre (☎ **03-86-33-26-02**), offering rich, colorful weavings and silk decorations; **Galerie Leiber,** 14 rue St-Etienne (☎ **03-86-33-33-90**), which specializes in handmade jewelry using semiprecious and precious stones in both heavy and delicate settings of silver and gold; and **Jacques d'Aubres,** rue St-Etienne (☎ **03-86-33-22-32**), with his unique textiles as well as stone and metal sculptures. You may also want to pick up a bottle or two of Vézelay wine at **Caves Guyard,** 32 rue St-Etienne (☎ **03-86-33-33-29**), or **La Vézelienne,** route de Nanchèvres in St-Père-sous-Vézelay (☎ **03-86-33-29-62**).

Basilique Ste-Madeleine. ☎ **03-86-33-26-73.** July–Aug daily 7am–6pm; Sept–June daily sunrise to sunset.

Built in the 12th century, France's largest and most famous Romanesque church, this basilica is only 10 yards shorter than Notre-Dame de Paris. You enter the narthex, a vestibule of large dimensions, about 4,000 square feet. Raise your eyes to the famous doorway depicting Christ giving the apostles the Holy Spirit. From the Romanesque nave, with its alternately white and gray stone of the traverse arches, you discover the light Gothic chancel. It's possible to visit the Carolingian crypt, where the tomb of Mary Magdalene formerly rested (today it contains some of her relics). There's a panoramic view from the back terrace.

WHERE TO STAY

L'Espérance (see "Where to Dine," below) rents luxurious rooms.

Le Compostelle. Place du Champ-de-Foire, 89450 Vézelay. ☎ **03-86-33-28-63.** Fax 03-86-33-34-34. 18 units. TV TEL. 270–330F ($48.60–$59.40) double. AE, V. Closed Jan.

This unpretentious and pleasant hotel occupies a late-19th-century building that was radically renovated in 1991. It's in the center of town, midway up the hill leading to the basilica, evoking in some ways a country house in England. It's the best of the simpler and more affordable inns in town. Despite the building's modernization, many of the old ceiling beams were left intact. Breakfast is the only meal served.

Poste et Lion d'Or. Place du Champ-de-Foire, 89450 Vézelay. ☎ **03-86-33-21-23.** Fax 03-86-32-30-92. 39 units. TEL. 400–600F ($72–$108) double. AE, MC, V. Parking 35F ($6.30). Closed Nov 11–Apr 1.

A local historic monument on the main square, at the bottom of the hill that rises to the basilica, this was built in the 17th century as a postal station. With a terrace and small garden, the Poste et Lion d'Or is a first-class place with surprisingly reasonable rates. Other than L'Espérance, which is in the countryside, it's the finest address in town, but only slightly better than Le Pontot.

The food is exceptional—especially the escargots de Bourgogne in chablis and stuffed trout with herbs. Fixed-price menus cost 118F to 240F ($21.25 to $43.20). It's classic Burgundian—nothing experimental here. The restaurant is closed Tuesday at lunch and all day Monday.

Résidence-Hôtel Le Pontot. Place du Pontot, 89450 Vézelay. ☎ **03-86-33-24-40.** Fax 03-86-33-30-05. 11 units. TEL. 600–950F ($108–$171) double; 950–1,200F ($171–$216) suite. DC, MC, V. Parking 50F ($9). Closed Nov–Easter.

Near the basilica, this tastefully renovated medieval structure is Vézelay's other leading hotel. The rooms are decorated in a romantic French style—at times not to everyone's taste but a lovely attempt at creating a cozy, homelike environment. It has a charming walled garden for breakfast and bar service but no restaurant. English is spoken.

WHERE TO DINE

L'Espérance. St-Père-sous-Vézelay, 89450 Vézelay. ☎ **03-86-33-39-10.** Fax 03-86-33-26-15. Reservations required. Main courses 200–500F ($36–$90); fixed-price lunch (Mon–Fri) 360F ($64.80); fixed-price menus 350–860F ($63–$154.80). AE, DC, MC, V. Thurs–Mon noon–2pm and 7:30–9:30pm. Closed Feb. Take D957 1¼ miles south of Vézelay. FRENCH.

L'Espérance is the most celebrated restaurant in Burgundy, one of the best in the world. Marc and Françoise Meneau began with what had been a family bakery in a stone farmhouse. Marc is the self-taught son of a village harness maker; Françoise helped decorate the exquisite public rooms, the elegant marble guest rooms, and the dining room with its flagstone floors, Oriental rugs, high windows, and garden view. The complex consists of a main building (with the restaurant) and three outbuildings (with 34 rooms and 6 suites). In the restaurant you're offered superb fare like ambrosia of poultry with truffles and foie gras. As for dessert, you'll beg them for their recipe for orange soufflé pie.

Double rooms cost 500–1,300F ($90–$234); suites run 1,700–2,500F ($306–$450).

3 Avallon

133 miles SE of Paris, 32 miles SE of Auxerre

This old fortified town is shielded behind its ancient ramparts, upon which you can stroll. A medieval atmosphere still permeates Avallon, and you'll find many 15th- and 16th-century houses. At the town gate on Grande Rue Aristide-Briand is a clock tower from 1460. The Romanesque **Eglise St-Lazarus** dates from the 12th century and has two interesting doorways. The church is said to have received the head of St. Lazarus in 1000, thus turning Avallon into a pilgrimage site. Today Avallon is mainly visited for its fabulous food, as reflected by our following recommendations.

ESSENTIALS

GETTING THERE   Avallon is connected by **rail** to Paris and the rest of France by about half a dozen daily trains. Ten trains arrive daily from Paris (trip time: 3 hours), and 8 trains pull in from Dijon daily (trip time: 3 hours). For train information and schedules, call ☎ **08-36-35-35-39.** To reach Avallon by **car,** travel south from Paris along A6 to Auxerre, driving southeast along D944 from Auxerre. From Vézelay, go east on D951.

VISITOR INFORMATION   The **Office de Tourisme** is at 4–6 rue Bocquillot (☎ **03-86-34-14-19**).

WHERE TO STAY & DINE

✪ **Château de Vault-de-Lugny.** A Vault-de-Lugny, 89200 Avallon. ☎ **03-86-34-07-86.** Fax 03-86-34-16-36. www.ila-chateau.com/lugny. E-mail: lugny@transeo.fr. 13 units. TV TEL. 800–1,300F ($144–$234) double; 1,600–2,500F ($288–$450) suite. Rates include breakfast. AE, MC, V. Closed Nov 13–Mar 15. Take D957 from Avallon; turn right in Pontaubert (after the church) and follow the signs to the château; Vault-de-Lugny is about 2 miles away.

At this château halfway between Avallon and Vézelay, Matherat Audan and his daughter, Elisabeth, welcome you. This 16th-century château is encircled by a moat, and on the grounds are a fortress tower and peacocks. Personal service is a hallmark (two staff members to every guest). The rooms and suites are often sumptuous, with half-tester or canopied beds and antique furnishings and fireplaces. You can order cocktails in an ornate salon, then proceed to dinner by candlelight.

Market-fresh ingredients are the hallmark of the cuisine. A special bourguignon meal is offered nightly, consisting, perhaps, of typical dishes of the region, including a homemade beef terrine in aspic jelly, snails with butter and garlic, a regional beef stew, and cheese and a *carte des desserts.* A more elaborate menu gourmand is also offered nightly—perhaps fresh scampi roasted with green beans and artichoke hearts, duck foie gras, homemade ravioli, fresh turbot or sole, and prime beef steak with pepper sauce or else a traditional coq au vin (chicken in wine), followed by cheese and dessert.

Moulin des Ruats. Vallée du Cousin, 89200 Avallon. ☎ **03-86-34-97-00.** Fax 03-86-31-65-47. 24 units. TEL. 370–650F ($66.60–$117) double. AE, DC, MC, V. Closed Nov 15–Feb 5 and Mon and Tues lunch. Take D427 2 miles outside town.

On the banks of the Cousin, this country inn is enchanting, with rooms that are simultaneously rustic and modern.

The elegant restaurant, with a terrace, serves freshwater fish. In addition to the excellent menu, the hostelry offers a fine wine list. The restaurant is outstanding, certainly more impressive than the hotel it's in. The meals are discreetly balanced, and everything has a certain zest and flavor. Specialties include escargots (snails) in Burgundy wine, a pavé of rumpsteak in shallot butter, and a duo of salmon and hogfish with a coulis of crayfish. You might also try magret of roast duck with an olive sauce or medallions of veal. Foie gras appears frequently on the menu.

4 Autun

182 miles SE of Paris, 53 miles SW of Dijon, 30 miles W of Beaune, 37 miles SE of Auxerre

Deep in burgundy country, Autun is one of the oldest towns in France, and in the days of the Roman Empire it was called "the other Rome." Some relics still stand, including the remains of a theater, the Théâtre Romain, the largest in Gaul, holding some 15,000 spectators. It was nearly 500 feet in diameter. Outside the town you can see the quadrangular tower of the Temple de Janus rising incongruously 80 feet over the plain.

Today Autun is a thriving provincial town of some 20,000 people, though as it's off the beaten track, the hordes go elsewhere. But it has its memories, even of Napoléon, who studied here in 1779 at the military academy (today the Lycée Bonaparte).

ESSENTIALS

GETTING THERE Autun has **shuttle** connections to Montchanin-le-Creusot, where one **train** per day arrives from Paris. Four trains pull in from Lyon. The shuttles don't run every day or with every arrival. For train information, call the Montchanin-le-Creusot station (☎ **03-85-77-83-34**) or the national information line (☎ **08-36-35-35-39**), and for bus information, call the bus station in Autun (☎ **03-85-52-30-02**).

If you're **driving,** take D3 from St-Léger-sous-Beuvray.

VISITOR INFORMATION The **Office de Tourisme** is at 4 av. Charles-de-Gaulle (☎ **03-85-86-80-38**).

EXPLORING THE TOWN

Once Autun was an important link on the road from Lyon to Boulogne, as reflected by the **Porte d'Arroux,** with two large archways now used for cars and two smaller ones for pedestrians—it's in the northwest section, rising 55 feet. Also exceptional is the **Porte St-André** (St. Andrew's Gate), about a quarter of a mile northwest of the Roman theater. Rising 65 feet, it, too, has four doorways and is surmounted by a gallery of 10 arcades.

Cathédrale St-Lazare. Place St-Louis. ☎ **03-85-52-12-37.** Free admission. Daily 9am–5pm.

On the highest point in Autun, the cathedral was built in 1120 to house the relics of St. Lazarus. On the facade, the tympanum in the central portal depicts the *Last Judgment*—a triumph of Romanesque sculpture. Inside, a painting by Ingres depicts the martyrdom of St. Symphorien, who was killed in Autun. In the 1860s, Viollet-le-Duc, the architect who restored (sometimes with controversial results) some of the major monuments of France, had to double the size of some of the columns supporting the cathedral's roof to avoid a collapse of the structure. New capitals matching the Romanesque style of the original building were crafted for placement atop the new columns. The original capitals, however, are now on display, more or less at eye level, in the Salle Capitulaire, one flight above street level. Especially noteworthy are *La Reveil des Mages* (The Awakening of the Magi) and *La Fuite en Egypte* (The Flight into Egypt).

Musée Rolin. 3 rue des Bancs. ☎ **03-85-52-09-76.** Admission 18F ($3.25) adults, 9F ($1.60) children. Apr–Sept Wed–Mon 9:30am–noon and 1:30–6pm; Oct Mon and Wed–Sat 10am–noon and 2–5pm, Sun 2:30–5pm; Nov–Mar Mon and Wed–Sat 10am–noon and 2–6pm, Sun 2:30–5pm.

This 15th-century mansion was built for Nicolas Rolin (b. 1380), who became a famous lawyer in his day. An easy walk from the cathedral, the museum displays a fine collection of Burgundian Romanesque sculpture, as well as paintings and archaeological mementos. From the original Rolin collection are exhibited the *Nativity* by the Maître de Moulins, along with a statue that's a masterpiece of 15th-century work, *Our Lady of Autun* (La Vierge d'Autun, also known as La Vierge Bulliot after the benefactor who donated the original statue back to the cathedral in 1948).

NEARBY ATTRACTIONS

After visiting Autun, and if you have a car, you can pay a visit to one of Burgundy's finest wineries. ✪ **Domaine Protheau,** Château d'Etoyes, lies at Mercurey, which is linked to Autun by D798, a 25-mile drive. The 150 acres of grapevines straddle at least two appellations contrôlées, so you'll have a chance to immerse yourself in the subtle differences among reds (both pinot noirs and burgundies), whites, and rosés produced under the auspices of both Rully and Mercurey. The headquarters of the organization, founded in the 1740s, is a château built in the late 1700s and early 1800s. Free tours of the sprawling cellars and explanations of the various vintages it produces are offered, in French and halting English, daily from 9am to 6pm. (Skip touring on Monday mornings, when operations are slower.) A dégustation des vins and the opportunity to haul a bottle or two away with you are included in every visit.

Two miles away, you can visit the **Château Féodale de Rully** (☎ **03-85-87-20-42**; fax 03-85-87-32-06), a 12th-century stronghold of the comtes de Ternay; it's open daily from 10am to noon and 2 to 6pm. An appointment is necessary—groups are preferred, though exceptions are sometimes made for individuals. The cost is 35F ($6.30) per person.

WHERE TO STAY & DINE

Hostellerie du Vieux Moulin. Porte d'Arroux, 71400 Autun. ☎ **03-85-52-10-90.** Fax 03-85-86-32-15. 16 units. TEL. 240–370F ($43.20–$66.60) double. AE, MC, V. Closed Dec–Feb.

This fine hotel, a 10-minute walk north of the town center, contains Autun's best restaurant. At the edge of the Arroux River, within the stone walls of what was built in the 1870s as a grain mill, it boasts a warm ambience, a scattering of 19th-century regional antiques, and simple but clean rooms.

Dining: In summer you can sit at a table overlooking the garden and the stream that abuts it. Fixed-price menus range from 150 to 250 F ($27 to $45). Menu items include filet of local whitefish (sandre) with basil-flavored cream sauce, Charolais beef simmered in red wine, and tournedos Tallyrand (the namesake was a local bishop, not the politician, and the dish is flavored with shallots and red wine). An appropriate starter? Consider escargots en meurette—snails simmered in red wine. Naturally, a wide roster of red burgundies can accompany your meal. From June to September, the dining room is open daily from noon to 2pm and 7:30 to 9pm. The rest of the year, it's closed Sunday night and all day Monday.

Hôtel des Ursulines. 14 rue Rivault, 71400 Autun. ☎ **03-85-86-58-58.** Fax 03-85-86-23-07. 38 units. A/C MINIBAR TV TEL. 400–585F ($72–$105.30) double; 500–820F ($90–$147.60) suite. AE, DC, MC, V.

The best hotel in Autun, the Ursulines (in a former convent) offers attractively decorated rooms with views of the countryside and the distant Morvan mountains. The hotel is also known for its cuisine, pleasing to both the eye and the palate. The results are sometimes more interesting than the menu suggests. The wine list needs expanding.

5 Beaune

196 miles SE of Paris, 24 miles SW of Dijon

This is the capital of the burgundy wine country and also one of the best-preserved medieval cities in the district, with a girdle of ramparts. Its history goes back more than 2,000 years. Beaune was a Gallic sanctuary, then later a Roman town. Until the 14th century it was the residence of the ducs de Bourgogne. When the last duke, Charles the Bold, died in 1477, Beaune was annexed by Louis XI. Visited today for its art, architecture, wines, and Burgundian cuisine, Beaune is a thriving town of some 20,000.

ESSENTIALS

GETTING THERE   Beaune has good railway connections with Dijon, Lyon, and Paris. From Paris, there are 4 **TGV trains** per day (trip time: 2 hours); from Lyon, 7 trains arrive per day (trip time: 1½ hours); and from Dijon, 22 trains per day (trip time: 25 minutes). For train information and schedules, call ☎ **08-36-35-35-39.**

If you're **driving,** note that Beaune is a few miles from the junction of four super-highways that fan out—A6, A31, A36, and N6.

VISITOR INFORMATION   The **Office de Tourisme** is on rue de l'Hôtel-Dieu (☎ 03-80-26-21-30).

SPECIAL EVENTS   The town comes to life on the third Saturday, Sunday, and Monday in November when wine buyers and oenophiles from all over the world descend on the medieval old town for a 3-day festival and wine auction called **Les Trois Glorieuses.** The town is packed with wineries offering free *dégustations*—and also packed with tourists visiting the labyrinth of caves or wine cellars. With all that free drink, visitors crowding the streets on summer nights are more than a bit tipsy. It's a fun, sometimes funky, and always colorful event that really puts you in the spirit to buy a lot of wine.

EXPLORING THE TOWN

SHOPPING   The best commercial shopping streets are **rue de Lorraine, rue d'Alsace, rue Mauffoux,** and **place de la Madeleine.** For smaller boutiques, stroll down the pedestrian **rue Carnot** and **rue Monge.** For antiques, concentrate your efforts around **place de la Halle.**

FOR WINE LOVERS   Beaune is one of the best towns in the region for sampling and buying famous Burgundy wines. In one of the town's more extraordinary wine cellars, you can tour, taste, and buy these hearty wines. **Marché aux Vins,** rue Nicolas-Rolin (☎ 03-80-25-08-20), is housed in a 14th-century church. Its cellars are set in and among the ancient tombs, under the floor of the church, and hold 18 wines.

Another cellar, **Caves Patriarche Père et Fils,** 7 rue du Collège (☎ **03-80-24-53-78**), is under the former Convent of the Visitandines with individual cellars from the 13th, 16th, and 17th centuries. You can choose from 13 wines here. The tour and tasting at either cellar is 50F ($10).

Musée du Vin de Bourgogne. Rue d'Enfer. ☎ **03-80-22-08-19.** Admission 25F ($4.50) adults, 15F ($2.70) children, free for children 11 and under. Daily 9:30am–6pm. Closed Thurs in Dec–Mar.

Housed in the former mansion of the ducs de Bourgogne, the Musée du Vin de Bourgogne traces the evolution of the region's wine making. The collection of tools, objets d'art, and documents is contained in 15th- and 16th-century rooms. A collection of wine presses is displayed in a 14th-century press house.

OTHER ATTRACTIONS   North of the Hôtel-Dieu, the **Collégiale Notre-Dame** is an 1120 Burgundian Romanesque church. Some remarkable tapestries illustrating scenes from the life of Mary are displayed in the sanctuary. You can view them from Easter to Christmas.

Musée de l'Hôtel-Dieu. ☎ **03-80-24-45-00.** Admission 32F ($5.75) adults, 25F ($4.50) children. Apr–Nov 16 daily 9am–6:30pm; Nov 17–Mar daily 9–11:30am and 2–5:30pm.

The perfectly preserved 15th-century Hôtel-Dieu is one of the world's richest working hospices, since its vineyards produce renowned wines like Aloxe-Corton and Meursault. The Gothic building also houses the Musée de l'Hôtel-Dieu, displaying Flemish-Burgundian art, such as Roger van der Weyden's 1443 polyptych *The Last Judgment.* In the Chambre des Pauvres (Room of the Poor) you'll find painted, broken-barrel, timbered vaulting, with mostly authentic furnishings.

Musée des Beaux-Arts et Musée Marey. In the Hôtel de Ville (town hall). ☎ **03-80-24-56-92.** Free admission if you've paid for admission to the Musée du Vin (above). Daily 2–6pm. Closed Nov–Mar (except open on the 3rd weekend in Nov).

This museum contains a rich Gallo-Roman archaeological section. The main gallery of paintings has works from the 16th to the 19th century, like Flemish primitives and many paintings by Felix Ziem, a precursor of the Impressionist school. Sculptures from the Middle Ages and the Renaissance are also displayed. A larger part of the museum honors the Beaune physiologist Etienne Jules Marey, who discovered the principles of the cinema long before 1895.

WHERE TO STAY

✪ **Hostellerie de Bretonnière.** 43 Faubourg Bretonnière, 21200 Beaune. ☎ **03-80-22-15-77.** Fax 03-80-22-72-54. 25 units. TEL. 295–425F ($53.10–$76.50) double. AE, DC, MC, V.

This is the best bargain in town: It's well run, with clean and quiet rooms. The accommodations in the rear are the cheapest and most tranquil, though most visitors prefer those overlooking the garden. There's no restaurant, but a continental breakfast is available.

Hôtel de la Poste. 1 bd. Georges-Clemenceau, 21200 Beaune. ☎ **03-80-22-08-11.** Fax 03-80-24-19-71. E-mail: francoise.stratigos@wanadoo.fr. 30 units. TEL. 680–1,000F ($122.40–$180) double; 1,200–1,500F ($216–$270) suite. AE, DC, MC, V. Parking 50F ($9).

Outside the town fortifications, this traditional hotel has been completely renovated. The rooms overlook either the ramparts or the vineyards; some have brass beds, TV, and air-conditioning. Many are just too petite, however.

   Dining: Menu specialties at the hotel's restaurant, La Saint-Christophe, include chicken fricassée with tarragon and sole in court bouillon with white butter. The restaurant is closed Saturday at lunch. The bar and restaurant are in the belle époque style.

✪ **Hôtel Le Cep.** 27 rue Maufoux, 21206 Beaune. ☎ **03-80-22-35-48.** Fax 03-80-22-76-80. www.slh.com/hotelcep. E-mail: gcbernard@wanadoo.fr. 53 units. A/C TV TEL. 800–1,200F ($144–$216) double; 1,500F ($270) suite for 2. AE, DC, V.

The chic address for oenophiles visiting Beaune is this mansion in the town center, fit enough for the ducs de Bourgogne should they miraculously return. All the charm, grace, and style of Burgundy is reflected in this once-private residence. Each room is individually decorated and named after a Grand Cru wine of the Côte-d'Or vineyards. Our favorites are the Chambre Montrachet and the Chambre Meloisey. Beaune's loveliest courtyard is here, with arcades and sculptured Renaissance stone medallions. A magnificent tower housing one of the city's most beautiful stone staircases rises from here.

A former wine cellar, Le Cellier is the venue for breakfast (the only meal served) under a vaulted stone ceiling. Beaune's finest restaurant, Bernard Morillon (see below), is next door.

WHERE TO DINE

✪ **Bernard Morillon.** 31 rue Maufoux. ☎ **03-80-24-12-06.** Reservations recommended. Main courses 145–230F ($26.10–$41.40); fixed-price menus 180–480F ($32.40–$86.40). AE, DC, DISC, MC, V. Tues 7:30–10pm, Wed–Sun noon–2pm and 7–10pm. Closed Jan 2–22 and Apr 10–17. FRENCH.

You'll dine here in a Directoire/Louis XV room on specialties like gratin of crayfish tails, an unusual version of pigeonneau made with fish served with a fumet of red wine, sweetbreads with saffron seasoning, and deboned Bresse pigeon stuffed with foie gras and truffles. Bernard Morillon has a distinctive style and his food always pleases. The desserts are sumptuous. To find a better restaurant, you'll have to journey outside town to the Hostellerie de Levernois.

Relais de Saulx. 6 rue Louis-Very. ☎ **03-80-22-01-35.** Reservations required for large groups. Main courses 150–170F ($27–$30.60); fixed-price menus 170–215F ($30.60–$38.70). MC, V. Tues–Sat noon–2pm, Mon–Sat 7–9:30pm. Closed Dec. FRENCH.

In a 200-year-old stone-trimmed building named after one of the ancient and noble families of the Beaune region, Relais de Saulx is decorated with heavy timbers, oil paintings, and all the accessories you'd expect from one of the region's most respected restaurants. Chef Jean-Louis Monnoir, assisted by his wife, Christiane, prepares a sophisticated combination of traditional bourguignon cuisine and up-to-date adaptations. Ongoing staples are Bresse chicken with morels, rack of lamb studded with rosemary and mountain herbs, cabbages braised with snails, lobster garnished with a sauce derived from the carapaces of shellfish, and roast pigeon whose sauce and garnishes vary according to the season (like baby asparagus tips in springtime and a wine-dark game sauce in winter). Monnoir's presentation is excellent and sometimes flavors elicit gasps of delight. The skillfully compiled wine list includes many unusual local vintages.

NEARBY ACCOMMODATIONS & DINING

✪ **Hostellerie de Levernois.** Rte. de Verdun-sur-le-Doubs, Levernois, 21200 Beaune. ☎ **03-80-24-73-58.** Fax 03-80-22-78-00. E-mail: levernois@relaischateaux.fr. Reservations required. Main courses 150–300F ($27–$54); fixed-price menus 395–535F ($71.10–$96.30). AE, DC, MC, V. Thurs–Mon noon–2pm, Wed–Mon 7–9:30pm. Take D970 south of Beaune for 2 miles, following the signs for Lons le Saunier. FRENCH.

Jean Crotet and his sons, Christophe and Guillaume, offer grand cuisine in a setting that's based on a stone-sided maison bourgeoise from the 1800s; it was enlarged between 1989 and 1994 with a series of newer annexes. All of it is set in an 8-acre park. Two of the ongoing distinctive trademarks are salmon smoked on the grounds and a delicious version of snails in puff pastry with a purée of watercress. Three kinds of fish arranged on the same platter, drenched with a garlic-tinged cream sauce, as well as hare filet with pepper sauce, make worthy and memorable main courses. There isn't a major emphasis on virtuoso techniques, just a powerful knowledge of first-class ingredients and what to do with them.

The inn rents 15 beautiful rooms—each with TV and phone—and one suite, all in a recently constructed pavilion. Doubles are 950F to 1,100F ($171 to $198); the suite is 1,700F ($306).

BEAUNE AFTER DARK

Your best bets for a good time out on the town are the local nightclubs and discos. To hear some solid jazz and rock and maybe even flirt with some of the locals, step over to the **Cotton Bar,** 164 rte. de Dijon (☎ **03-80-24-69-48**), which fills up early with a 30-plus crowd that seems to complete the retro ambience. Or if you're more in the mood for a little piano bar and karaoke in a pub atmosphere, try **Why Not,** 74 rue de Faubourg-Madeleine (☎ **03-80-22-64-74**). For a more jolting, electric evening, head over to **Opéra-Night,** rue du Beaumarché (☎ **03-80-24-10-11**), with its booming house music, immense dance floor, strobe lights, and mirrors revealing every angle imaginable. This is one of the hottest places in town, so expect to pay a 50F ($9) cover.

6 Gevrey-Chambertin

194 miles SE of Paris, 17 miles NE of Beaune, 8 miles SW of Dijon

This town was immortalized by the writer Gaston Roupnel. Typical of the villages of the Côte d'Or, Gevrey added Chambertin to its name to honor its most famous vineyard.

On the top of the village stands the **Château de Gevrey-Chambertin** (☎ **03-80-34-36-13**), a fortress built in around the 10th century, as you can see by the architecture with its square towers, five arches, and no portcullis and by the placement of the drawbridge. The ladder was probably used by the villagers to go up to the big room to be protected. They built a corkscrew staircase in the 13th century. You can see the rooms of the big tower, which has many windows, used by the soldiers as an observation tower. At the bottom are also windows from which the soldiers shot with their bows and arrows. In one of the cellars you'll see the curious shape of the arches. Here you can taste and buy wine. Between April 15 and November 15, half-hour guided tours are given in English, daily from 10am (11am on Sunday) to noon and 2 to 6pm; from November 16 to April 14, hours are 10am to noon and 2 to 5pm. Admission is 20F ($3.60) for adults, 10F ($1.80) for children 7 to 12, and free for children 6 and under.

The village church with its Romanesque doorway dates from the 14th century.

ESSENTIALS

GETTING THERE South of Burgundy is the Côte d'Or (golden slope), a famous wine-growing district. Leave Dijon via D122 (grandly called the Route des Grands-Crus) and follow it south until the junction with N74 at Vougeot. Along the way the most notable wine-producing town you'll go through is Gevrey-Chambertin.

VISITOR INFORMATION The **Office de Tourisme,** 1 bis rue Gaston Roupnel (☎ **03-80-34-38-40**), is open May to October only.

WHERE TO STAY

Arts et Terroirs. 28 rte. de Dijon, 21220 Gevrey-Chambertin. ☎ **03-80-34-30-76.** Fax 03-80-34-11-79. 16 units. TV TEL. 330–580F ($59.40–$104.40) double. AE, DC, MC, V.

A radical renovation of an 18th-century manor, built of pinkish-beige stone on the northern outskirts of the village, this hotel is flanked by a small but pleasant garden and many acres of vineyards associated with the home's former owners. The rooms (on the ground floor or a flight above street level) are cozy and comfortable, each in a different traditional style that includes Napoléon III and Louis XVI. Breakfast is the only meal served, but you'll appreciate the wine bar open during the day and evening, where local Gevrey-Chambertin is sold by the glass. Also for sale are local jams, preserves, honey, and bottles of the regional vintage.

Hôtel Les Grands Crus. Rte. des Grands-Crus, 21220 Gevrey-Chambertin. ☎ **03-80-34-34-15.** Fax 03-80-51-89-07. 24 units. TEL. 380–470F ($68.40–$84.60) double. MC, V. Closed Dec–Feb 27.

This charming hotel, near a tiny 12th-century château, is run by the helpful Mme Farnier, who speaks English. The rooms, some of which have Louis XV furnishings, provide views of vineyards and a 12th-century church. The hotel doesn't have a restaurant but serves a continental breakfast; however, regional wines are available. The small accommodations on the second floor are a budget traveler's dream.

WHERE TO DINE

La Rôtisserie du Chambertin. Rue Chambertin. ☎ **03-80-34-33-20.** Reservations required. Main courses 65–130F ($11.70–$23.40); fixed-price menus 250–410F ($45–$73.80). MC, V. Tues–Sun noon–1:30pm, Tues–Sat 7–9pm. Closed 3 weeks in Feb and 2 weeks in Aug. FRENCH.

The entrance to this popular regional restaurant is marked only with the menu. You must first pass through a museum devoted to the history of barrel making, in honor of the owner's great-grandfather, who was the town cooper on this very spot. When you arrive, be sure to take advantage of the inn's wines. Chambertin has been called "the wine for moments of great decision." That's why Napoléon always took it on his campaigns—even to Moscow. Although the wine list isn't monumental, it includes the best of recent vintages. The chef prepares regional classics, some so universally well received that they haven't changed in years. Examples are coq au vin, sandre prepared with the yellow wine of the Jura region, and chicken cooked with a local cows'-milk cheese known as l'Ami du Chambertin.

✪ Les Millésimes. 25 rue de l'Eglise (at rue de Meixville). ☎ **03-80-51-84-24.** Reservations required. Main courses 140–210F ($25.20–$37.80); fixed-price menus 325–600F ($58.50–$108). V. Wed 7:30–9:30pm, Thurs–Mon 12:30–2pm and 7–9:30pm. Closed Dec 22–Jan 25. FRENCH.

Monique Sangoy is the charming matriarch who directs a large staff and four of her children in this outstanding restaurant in the courtyard of what used to be a 17th-century warehouse for local wines. Until 1976 the site produced its own wine—look for the winepress now an ornament in the salon. The success of the place also depends on the Sangoy offspring, Laurent and Denis (the chefs), Didier (the wine steward, whose 50,000 bottles of wine won three annual awards from *Wine Spectator*, beginning in 1993), and Sophie, who'll likely greet you at the door. House specialties are formulated to accompany the superb vintages that are de rigueur here. They're likely to include a petite salade of foie gras, lobster, and mushrooms; sea bass cooked in salt crust with Gevry-Chambertin wine; and confit of shallots and Burgundian snails. Equally delicious is a rack of lamb prepared in a bread crust in a style that evokes beef

Wellington. For dessert, consider a soufflé served with a fruit syrup. The place attracts both local gastronomes and the visiting wine chic from Paris and the rest of the world. The cuisine is refined, of the highest quality, and enjoyable.

7 Dijon

194 miles SE of Paris, 199 miles NE of Lyon

Dijon is known overseas mainly for its mustard. In the center of the Côte d'Or, it's the ancient capital of Burgundy. In this town good food is always accompanied by great wine. Between meals you can enjoy Dijon's art and architecture.

The first impression, especially if you arrive at the rail station, is misleading. You'll think Dijon today is a dreary modern city. Not so. Press on to the medieval core only a few blocks away. Many old streets and buildings have been restored. The present mayor was the minister of environment in the Pompidou government, and he thinks he's still back at his old job, wildly planting trees everywhere.

ESSENTIALS

GETTING THERE Dijon has excellent air, rail, bus, and highway connections to the rest of Europe. A total of 25 **trains** arrive from Paris each day (trip time: 1¾ hours). Trains arrive from Lyon every hour (trip time: 2 hours). For train information and schedules, call ☎ **08-36-35-35-39.** To reach Dijon from Paris **by car,** follow A6 southwest to the town of Pouilly-Saulieu, turning west on N81 to Dijon. From Troyes, follow A5 southwest.

VISITOR INFORMATION The **Office de Tourisme** is on place Darcy (☎ **03-80-44-11-44**).

SPECIAL EVENTS During the first part of September, the streets of Dijon go through a lively renaissance when **Estivade** comes to town. This festival uses the city's streets as a stage for folk dances, music, and theatrical art that never fails to be a big hit. The Office de Tourisme has complete details.

SEEING THE SIGHTS

One of the most historic buildings in this ancient province is the **Palais des Ducs et des Etats de Bourgogne,** which symbolizes perfectly the proudly independent (or semi-independent, depending on the era) status of this fertile region. Capped with an elaborate tile roof, it's a solid complex built in stages from the 1300s to the 1800s, all of it arranged around a trio of spacious courtyards. The oldest section, only part of which you can visit (see below), is the **Ancien Palais des Ducs de Bourgogne,** erected in the 12th century and rebuilt in the 14th. The newer section is the **Palais des Etats de Bourgogne,** constructed between the 17th and 18th centuries as a meeting place for the equivalent of a Burgundian parliament (it struggled unsuccessfully to retain the duchy's semi-independent status against encroachments from the French monarchy). Today, as the palace is Dijon's La Mairie (Town Hall), all of its newer section and a substantial part of its older section are reserved for the municipal government and can't be visited. However, there's a fine museum in the building that we highly recommend, the **Musée des Beaux-Arts** (see below).

A mile from the center of town on N5 stands the **Chartreuse de Champmol,** the Carthusian monastery built by Philip the Bold as a burial place; it's now a psychiatric hospital. Much of it was destroyed during the Revolution, but you can see the Moses Fountain in the gardens designed by Sluter at the end of the 14th century. The Gothic entrance is superb.

Ancien Palais des Ducs de Bourgogne ❸
Musée Archéologique ❶
Musée des Beaux-Arts ❺
Musée Magnin ❹
Musée Perrin de Puycousin ❷
Palais des Etats de Bourgogne ❸

Musée Archeologique, 5 rue du Dr-Maret (☎ **03-80-30-88-54**), contains the rather dusty findings unearthed from Dijon's many archaeological digs. **Musée Perrin de Puycousin,** 15–17 rue Ste-Anne (☎ **03-80-44-12-69**), houses the **Musée d'Arts Sacrés,** devoted to sacred art objects that were culled from various churches, and the **Musée de la Vie Bourguignonne,** focusing on folkloric costumes, farm implements, and even some of the 19th- and early-20th-century storefronts removed from Dijon's commercial center. All of these secondary museums charge 12F ($2.15) and are open from 10am to noon and 2 to 6pm (closed Tuesday).

Musée des Beaux-Arts. In the Palais des Ducs et des Etats de Bourgogne, cour de Bar. ☎ **03-80-74-52-09.** Admission 18F ($3.25) adults, 9F ($1.60) seniors, free for students and children 17 and under; free for everyone on Sun. Wed–Mon 10am–6pm.

The part of the older palace that you can visit contains one of France's oldest and richest museums. It boasts exceptional sculpture, ducal kitchens from the mid-1400s (with great chimneypieces), a collection of European paintings from the 14th to the 19th century, and modern French paintings and sculptures. Take special note of the Salle des Gardes, the banqueting hall of the old palace built by Philip the Good. The tomb of Philip the Bold was created between 1385 and 1411 and is one of the best in France—a reclining figure rests on a slab of black marble, surrounded by 41 mourners.

Musée Magnin. 4 rue des Bons-Enfants. ☎ **03-80-67-11-10.** Admission 18F ($3.25). Tues–Sun 10am–noon and 2–6pm.

Built in the 19th century as the opulent home of an arts-conscious member of the grande bourgeoisie, it was willed, along with all its contents, to the city of Dijon as a museum following the death of the family's last descendant. It contains an eclectic display of 19th-century antiques and art objects, as well as a collection of paintings accumulated by, or painted by, the former owners.

SHOPPING

Your shopping list might include robust regional wines, Dijon mustard, antiques, and the black-currant cordial called cassis (try a splash in champagne for a Kir Royale). The best streets to hone in on are **rue de la Liberté, rue du Bourg, rue Bosseut,** and **rue Verrerie,** the latter for antiques.

Dijon hosts a flea market, **Le Broe du Forum,** the last Sunday of every month at the Forum, rue du Général-Delaborde (☎ **03-80-74-31-23**), beginning at 9am and running through the afternoon. There's also a market at **Les Halles Centrales** every Tuesday and Friday from 8am to noon and all day Saturday. On the outside of the covered market are booths set up with household merchandise and clothes as well as the occasional antique. The inside of the market is devoted to produce and food items.

For the ideal picnic lunch, begin at the mustard shop of **Grey Poupon,** 32 rue de la Liberté (☎ **03-80-30-41-02**), to purchase a supply of that world-famous condiment; head over to **Au Pain d'Autrefois,** 47 rue du Bourg (☎ **03-80-30-47-92**), for a baguette or round of your favorite chewy French country bread; move onto **La Boucherie Nouvelle,** 27 rue Pasteur (☎ **03-80-66-37-10**), to choose one of its many selections of mouth-watering deli meats; follow with a visit to the **Crémerie Porcheret,** 18 rue Bannelier (☎ **03-80-30-21-05**), to pick up several varieties of regional cheeses, including the heavenly citeaux, made by a group of brothers at a nearby monastery; then finish off at one of the three locations of **Mulot et Petitjean,** 1 place Notre-Dame, 16 rue de la Liberté, or 13 place Bossuet (☎ **03-80-30-07-10**), where you can pick up a bottle of wine and a gingerbread for dessert. Another excellent source for wines is **Nicot,** rue J.-J.-Rousseau (☎ **03-80-73-29-88**).

For antiques, try **Monique Buisson,** 21 rue Verrerie (☎ **03-80-30-31-19**), where you'll find a good collection of regional furniture from the 1700s; **Dubard,** 25 bis rue Verrerie (☎ **03-80-30-50-81**), carrying 18th-century decorative antiques as well as contemporary upholstery fabrics; and **Au Vieux Dijon,** 8 rue Verrerie (☎ **03-80-31-89-08**), with its assortment of 18th- and 19th-century vases, bibelots, and more refined examples of Burgundian furniture. Other recommended stops are **Galerie 6,** 6 rue Auguste-Comte (☎ **03-80-71-68-46**), offering a wide selection of antique paintings from the 1600s to the 1800s; and **Occasions,** 29 rue Auguste-Comte (☎ **03-80-73-55-13**), where you can browse through a multitude of mainly English antiques from the 1800s as well as handmade Oriental rugs, both old and new.

WHERE TO STAY

La Toison d'Or (see below) also rents rooms.

Hostellerie du Chapeau-Rouge. 5 rue Michelet, 21000 Dijon. ☎ **800/528-1234** in the U.S and Canada, or 03-80-30-28-10. Fax 03-80-30-33-89. www. bestwestern.com. 32 units. MINIBAR TV TEL. 650–950F ($117–$171) double; 1,100F ($198) suite. AE, DC, MC, V. Parking 16F ($2.90).

This Dijon landmark, with an acclaimed restaurant, is the town's best address. The hotel is filled with 19th-century antiques and has rooms with modern conveniences and comfortable furnishings; 10 are air-conditioned. Some of the bathrooms have Jacuzzis.

Dining: Since no other hotel restaurant here serves comparable food, you may want to visit even if you're not a guest. The hotel has a supercharged chef who serves Burgundian favorites but has broken new ground with mouth-watering fare, the specialties depending on what's good in any given season.

Hôtel Ibis Central. 3 place Grangier, 21000 Dijon. ☎ **03-80-30-44-00.** Fax 03-80-30-77-12. 90 units. TV TEL. 360–395F ($64.80–71.10) double. AE, DC, MC, V. Parking 45F ($8.10).

On a busy downtown square, this hotel was built in 1930 and renovated by the Ibis chain into a streamlined design in the late 1980s. It doesn't have the atmosphere and charm of some Dijon hotels, but we recommend it for its economy and its simple but businesslike and comfortable rooms.

Dining: The Central Grill Rôtisserie offers candlelit dinners and a panoramic view of Dijon (closed Sunday).

Hôtel Sofitel-La Cloche. 14 place Darcy, 21000 Dijon. ☎ **03-80-30-12-32.** Fax 03-80-30-04-15. E-mail: lacloche@axnet.fr. 68 units. A/C MINIBAR TV TEL. 780–1,100F ($140.40–$198) double; 1,500–1,800F ($270–$324) suite. AE, DC, MC, V.

This 15th-century historic monument is in the center of town. The sophisticated interior features Oriental rugs and a pink-and-gray marble floor. The lobby bar is one of the most elegant places in town, with a view of the garden shared by an adjoining glassed-in tearoom. The hotel has been renovated in neoclassical style, and, though of chain format, the rooms are among the most elegant and comfortable in town.

✪ **Hôtel Wilson.** Place Wilson. ☎ **03-80-66-82-50.** Fax 03-80-36-41-54. 27 units. TV TEL. 490F ($88.20) double. AE, MC, V.

Our favorite nest in Dijon, opening onto a very pleasant square, is this *ancien relais de poste* from the 17th century. The coaching inn has been tastefully restored. Although it has been completely modernized with traditional Burgundian wood furniture, many of the old wooden and time-darkened ceiling beams have been exposed, adding a hard-to-come-by charm. In spite of the age of this inn, it has modern bathrooms kept in state-of-the-art condition. A bonus is the neighboring restaurant, Thiebert, which serves a delectable French cuisine and is known for its wine cellar, which is especially rich in burgundies.

WHERE TO DINE

The **Hostellerie du Chapeau-Rouge** (see above) boasts a marvelous restaurant.

La Toison d'Or. 18 rue Ste-Anne, 21000 Dijon. ☎ **03-80-30-73-52.** Fax 03-80-30-95-51. Reservations required. Main courses 90–170F ($16.20–$30.60); fixed-price menus 160–260F ($28.80–$46.80). AE, DC, MC, V. Mon–Sat noon–1:30pm, Mon–Sat 7–9:30pm. FRENCH.

This elegantly rustic restaurant, in a building supposedly from the 1500s, offers traditional food that's hearty and satisfying but doesn't attempt cutting-edge grandeur. On entering, you'll be offered a tour (in English) of the adjoining museum, where testimonials to wine making and medieval life include grisly depictions of medieval slayings and Carolingian tortures, as well as a look at everything connected to local wine making. Amid stone walls, Oriental rugs, and Louis XIII chairs, you'll enjoy specialties like poached eggs with lardons and onions in wine sauce, fricassée of guinea fowl with fresh pasta, snails with pasta and fresh basil, and a cold main course that the staff believes isn't offered anywhere else in the region—compôte of marinated rabbit in a sauce made from the after-dinner digéstif, marc de bourgogne. Daniel Boyer is the chef.

A simple and modern 27-room hotel is associated with this restaurant, Hôtel Philippe-le-Bon (same address and phone), where doubles, each with bathroom, TV, and phone, rent for 350F ($70).

✪ **Le Pré aux Clercs.** 13 place de la Libération. ☎ **03-80-38-05-05.** Reservations required. Main courses 120–200F ($21.60–$36); fixed-price menus 260–500F ($46.80–$90) at lunch, 230–360F ($41.40–$64.80) at dinner. AE, MC, V. Tues–Sun noon–2pm, Tues–Sat 7:30–9:30pm. BURGUNDIAN/FRENCH.

In an 18th-century house across from the Palais des Ducs, this is one of Burgundy's finest restaurants. Its chef/owner, Jean-Pierre Billoux, assisted by his wife, Marie Françoise, prepares deceptively simple meals that have won acclaim. Menu items might include a roast chicken steeped in liquefied almonds, terrine of pigeon, a "gâteau" of guinea fowl with artichokes and capers, or thick-sliced filet of sole on a bed of tomato-infused polenta. Some recently sampled and more innovative dishes are John Dory with thyme oil and confit of fennel and a *paillasson* (potato galette) layered with crayfish tails. The array of wines will be a joy to any connoisseur.

NEARBY DINING

✪ **Joël Perreaut's Restaurant des Gourmets.** 8 rue Puits-de-Têt, 21160 Marsannay-la-Côte. ☎ **03-80-52-16-32.** Reservations required. Main courses 128–215F ($23.05–$38.70); fixed-price menus 150–260F ($27–$46.80); menu dégustation 410F ($73.80). AE, DC, MC, V. Tues–Sun 12:15–2pm, Tues–Sat 7–9:30pm. Closed last week of Jan and first week of Feb, and the last 2 weeks of Aug. Drive 6 miles south of Dijon on R.N. 17, following the signs for Beaune and then Marsannay-la-Côte. FRENCH.

This restaurant is ample justification for journeying outside Dijon to a charming stone village. After Joël and Nicole Perreaut added an annex, modern kitchens, and a dining room, the place became well known as one of Burgundy's best restaurants. Forget the questionable decor and concentrate on the cuisine, enjoying such excellent dishes as Burgundy snails, filet of John Dory in balsamic-vinegar sauce, and filet of roast pigeon. The roast lamb is marvelous. Joël Perreaut is a remarkable chef, and the service is always polite.

DIJON AFTER DARK

Begin at one of the many cafes or brasseries lining **place Zola, rue des Godrans, place du Théâtre,** or **place Darcy,** including the **Concorde,** 2 place Darcy (☎ 03-80-30-69-43); **Brasserie du Théâtre,** 1 bis place du Théâtre (☎ 03-80-67-13-59); and **La Comédie,** 3 place du Théâtre (☎ 03-80-67-11-22). All quickly fill up with young people who like to start the evening with a drink and a cruisy look at others.

For a 30s-and-40s crowd who like to mingle in the low-key atmosphere of a piano bar, try **Hunky Dory,** 5 av. Foch (☎ 03-80-53-17-24); **Le Messire,** 3 rue Jules-Mercier (☎ 03-80-30-16-40); or the two-floored **Le Cintra,** 13 av. Foch (☎ 03-80-43-65-89), with its piano bar up above and a cramped little disco down below. If the warm, welcoming, boisterous (and often sloshed) atmosphere of an Irish pub is what you're needing, head over to **Le Kilkenny,** 1 rue Auguste-Perdrix (☎ 03-80-30-02-48). Or for a more British spin, try **Le Brighton,** 33 rue Auguste-Comte (☎ 03-80-73-59-32), where you'll find a south-of-the-border dance club downstairs. The best jazz is at the **Jazz Rock Café,** 2 rue des Perrirères (☎ 03-80-41-36-11), with its live concerts performed in an intimate space barely big enough for eight tables.

L'Atmosphère Internationale, 14 rue Audra (☎ 03-80-30-52-03), attracts a young crowd made up mainly of students who like to cut loose on the dance floor to the sound of rock and techno. You'll pay 30F ($5.40) to get in. Other high-octane dance floors are at **L'An Fer,** 8 rue Pierre-Marceau (☎ 03-80-71-32-44) or

03-80-70-03-69), with its 60F ($10.80) cover charge, gay/straight crowd, and Métro station decor complete with billboards; and **Le Grizzli,** 131 av. Gustave-Eiffel (☎ **03-80-43-19-91**), where guys always pay the 40F ($7.20) cover, but women get in free on Friday.

The opera season in Dijon is from the middle of October through May. Contact the **Théâtre de Dijon,** place du Théâtre (☎ **03-80-67-20-21**), for information on opera, operettas, and concerts. The **Nouveau Théâtre de Bourgogne,** rue Danton (☎ **03-80-30-12-12**), also offers a variety of stage presentations. Tickets for both theaters range between 110F to 250F ($19.80 to $45).

8 Saulieu

155 miles SE of Paris, 47 miles NW of Beaune

The town is fairly interesting, but its food placed it on the international map. On the boundaries of Morvan and Auxois, Saulieu has enjoyed a reputation for cooking since the 17th century. Even Mme de Sévigné praised it in her letters. So did Rabelais.

The main sight is the **Basilique St-Andoche,** on place de la Fontaine, which has some interesting decorated capitals. In the art museum, the **Musée François-Pompon,** place de la Fontaine at rue Sallier (☎ **03-80-64-19-51**), you can see many works by François Pompon, the well-known sculptor of animals. His bull, his masterpiece, stands on a plaza off N6 at the entrance to Saulieu. The museum is open Wednesday to Monday from 10am to 12:30pm and 2 to 5pm (to 6pm in summer). Admission is 20F ($3.60) for adults, 15F ($2.70) for children 12 to 16, and free for children 9 and under.

ESSENTIALS

GETTING THERE   Saulieu has a **rail** station (northeast of the town center) linked to the French railway network. For train information and schedules, call ☎ **08-36-35-35-39.** If you're **driving,** take N80 from Montbard or N6 from Paris to Lyon.

VISITOR INFORMATION   The **Maison du Tourisme** is at 24 rue d'Argentine (☎ **03-80-64-00-21**).

WHERE TO STAY & DINE

✪ **Hôtel de la Côte d'Or.** 2 rue d'Argentine, 21210 Saulieu. ☎ **03-80-90-53-53.** Fax 03-80-64-08-92. www.integra.fr/relaischateau/loiseau. E-mail: loiseau@relaischateaux.fr. 22 units. 980–1,900F ($176.40–$342) double; from 2,400F ($432) suite. AE, CB, DC, MC, V.

This former stagecoach stop is an excellent choice—one of the best-known restaurants in France. If you want to stay overnight, you'll find guest rooms with everything from Empire to Louis XV decor. Your bed will be comfortable, but it's likely to be 200 years old.

Dining: Chef Alexandre Dumaine, the man who made this a world-famous restaurant, is long gone, but the inventive Bernard Loiseau works hard to maintain his standards. (According to most critics, Loiseau has surpassed all previous standards, becoming one of Europe's culinary stars.) The cooking is less traditional, leaning away from heavy sauces to *cuisine légère.* The emphasis is on bringing out maximum taste with no excess fat or sugar. All the great burgundies are on the wine list. Fixed-price menus are 580 to 890F ($104.40 to $160.20), with a fixed-price lunch during the week at 420F ($75.60)

Hôtel de la Poste. 1 rue Grillot, 21210 Saulieu. ☎ **03-80-64-05-67.** Fax 03-80-64-10-82. 48 units. A/C MINIBAR TV TEL. 335–585F ($60.30–$105.30) double. AE, DC, MC, V.

Originally a 17th-century postal relay station, Hôtel de la Poste has been completely renovated by Guy Virlouvet. The rooms are comfortable, with conservative and traditional furniture, and sometimes have courtyard views.

Dining: In the dining room, where antique timbers have been artfully exposed, specialties include escalope of sea perch with baby vegetables, shrimp with saffron and asparagus tips, filet of Charolais beef with marrow sauce, and kidneys in a sauce of aged mustard. Menus, served to guests and nonguests alike, cost 98 to 188F ($17.65 to $33.85). Service is daily from noon to 2:30pm and 7 to 10:30pm.

NEARBY ACCOMMODATIONS & DINING

Auberge du Vieux Moulin. Porte de la Bourgogne, Aubigney, 70140 Pesmes. ☎ **03-84-31-61-61.** Fax 03-84-31-62-38. Reservations recommended. Main courses 115–145F ($20.70–$26.10); fixed-price menus 100–400F ($18–$72). AE, CB, DC, V. Daily noon–2pm and 7:30–9pm. Closed Dec 15–Feb 15. From Dijon, take D70 northeast toward Gray for 27 miles. FRENCH.

The town of Aubigney has little to recommend save for the Auberge du Vieux Moulin. The property has been in the Mirbey family since the end of the 18th century, and you'll find elegant antiques, gilt-rimmed mirrors, and sparkling table settings. Elisabeth Mirbey is one of France's outstanding *dames cuisinières*, and she (with two other chefs) was the first woman to prepare a meal in the Elysée Palace, where President Mitterrand and Françoise Sagan enjoyed her crêpes. The menu has a regional section that includes chicken suprême in a sauce flavored with Savagnin and cassolette of Burgundy snails. The terrines are excellent, as are the duckling, veal kidneys, rabbit, and sweetbreads. The homemade desserts are light and delectable.

The auberge is also a good place to stay if you prefer to be away from the crowds of Dijon. There are 7 rooms, all with bathroom. A double is 385F ($69.30).

The Rhône Valley 14

The Rhône is as mighty as the Saône is peaceful, and these two great rivers form a part of the French countryside that travelers often head through only briefly, glimpsing it out of their car windows as they rush south to the Riviera on the thundering Mediterranean Express. But this land of mountains and rivers, linked by a good road network, invites more exploration than that: it's beaujolais country, home to the city of Lyon, a fabulous stop for gourmets, and boasts Roman ruins, charming villages, castles, and even the Grand Canyon of France.

It was from the Rhône Valley that Greco-Roman architecture and art made their way to the Loire Valley, the château country, and finally to Paris. The district abounds in time-mellowed inns and gourmet restaurants, offering a cuisine that's among the finest in the world.

REGIONAL CUISINE   Lyon and environs are the gastronomic capital of France. Excellent ingredients are readily available nearby—the best chicken and beef in France (from Bresse and Charolais, respectively), freshwater fish from the high lakes of the Savoy, and game from the dense forests.

Regional specialties are *quenelles de brochet* (pulverized brochet—a local whitefish—fashioned into cigar-shaped cylinders, served with white butter); Lyonnaise sausages; many preparations of chicken, especially garnished with truffles; and a full array of pâtés and terrines, often made from wild game. One excellent dish is *pommes de terres lyonnaises* (sautéed potatoes with onions).

As for wines, some of the vineyards along the Rhône are the oldest in France, established by the ancient Greeks. The better wines are sold under the names of the specific villages that produce them: Côtes-du-Rhône Ardèche, Côtes-du-Rhône Gigondas, Tavel, Châteauneuf-du-Pape, Muscat de Baumes-de-Venise, Condrieu, and Beaujolais. Among them, beaujolais is the premier young wine of France. It's intended for early consumption—the annual release of a year's vintage is truly a national event.

1 Bourg-en-Bresse

264 miles SE of Paris, 38 miles NE of Lyon

The ancient capital of Bress, this farming/business center lies on the border between Burgundy and the Jura and offers fabulous food.

ESSENTIALS

GETTING THERE   Bourg-en-Bresse is easily accessible by **train** from Paris, Lyon, and Dijon. Fifteen TGV trains arrive from Paris's Gare de Lyon each day (trip time: 2 hours) and from Lyon, 10 trains arrive per day (trip time: 70 minutes). From Dijon, 5 trains arrive per day (trip time: 2 hours). For train information and schedules, call ☎ **08-36-35-35-39.** If you're **driving** from Lyon, take A42 or N83 for the 35- to 45-minute trip; if you're leaving from Dijon, follow A31 to Mâcon and then switch to A40 for the approximately 2-hour drive.

VISITOR INFORMATION   The **Office de Tourisme** is at 6 av. Alsace-Lorraine (☎ **04-74-22-49-40**).

SEEING THE SIGHTS

If you have time, visit the **Eglise Notre-Dame,** off place Carriat. Begun in 1505, it contains some finely carved 16th-century stalls. If you'd like to wander around town, check out the **15th-century houses** on rue du Palais and rue Gambetta,.

✪ **Eglise de Brou.** 63 bd. de Brou. ☎ **04-74-22-83-83.** Admission to church, cloisters, and museum 35F ($6.30) adults, 23F ($4.15) ages 12–25, free for children 11 and under. Apr–Sept daily 9am–12:30pm and 2–6:30pm; Oct–Mar daily 9am–noon and 2–5pm. Closed Jan 1, May 1, Nov 1 and 11, and Dec 25.

Art lovers will want to stop at the Eglise de Brou to see its magnificent royal tombs. One of the great artistic treasures of France, this Flamboyant Gothic monastery was built between 1506 and 1532 (the three cloisters between 1506 and 1512, the church between 1513 and 1532) for Margaret of Austria, the ill-fated daughter of Emperor Maximilian. Over the ornate Renaissance doorway, the tympanum depicts Margaret and her "handsome duke," Philibert, who died when he caught cold on a hunting expedition. The initials of Philibert (sometimes known as "the Fair") and Margaret are linked by loveknots. The nave and its double aisles are admirable. Look for the ornate rood screen, decorated with basket-handle arching. Ask a guide for a tour of the choir, which is rich in decorative detail; the 74 choir stalls were made of oak in just 2 years by Flemish sculptors and local craftsmen.

The tombs form the church's treasure. The Carrara marble statues are of Philibert, who died in 1504, and Margaret, who remained faithful to his memory until her death in 1530. Another tomb is that of Marguerite de Bourbon, mother of Philibert and grandmother of François I, who died in 1483. See also the stained-glass windows inspired by a Dürer engraving and an alabaster retable depicting *The Seven Joys of the Madonna.*

WHERE TO STAY

Hôtel du Prieuré. 49–51 bd. de Brou, 01000 Bourg-en-Bresse. ☎ **04-74-22-44-60.** Fax 04-74-22-71-07. 15 units. TV TEL. 400–550F ($72–$99) double; 720F ($129.60) suite. AE, DC, V. Parking 60F ($10.80).

Owned by sisters Mmes Alby and Guerrin, this is the town's most gracious hotel. Its angled exterior is surrounded by an acre of carefully planned gardens and 400-year-old stone walls. The place is especially alluring in spring, when forsythia, lilacs, roses, and Japanese cherries fill the air with perfume. Most guest rooms are large and tranquil, each outfitted in Louis XV, Louis XVI, or French country rustic style.

Le Logis de Brou. 132 bd. de Brou, 01000 Bourg-en-Bresse. ☎ **04-74-22-11-55.** Fax 04-74-22-37-30. 30 units. TV TEL. 300–380F ($54–$68.40) double. AE, DC, V. Parking 50F ($9).

This is actually a much better hotel than its boxlike exterior suggests. The four-story building—fully refurbished and soundproofed—has landscaped grounds and is near

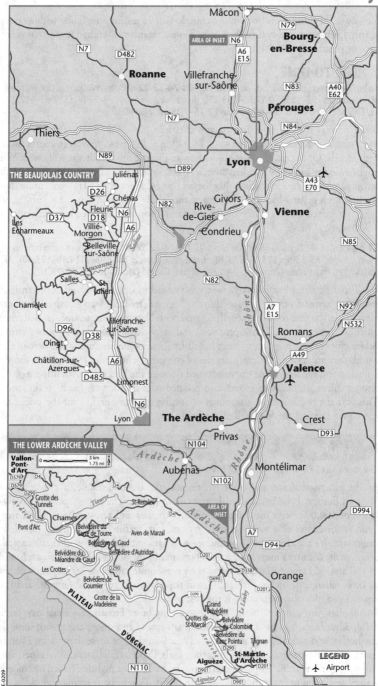

The Rhône Valley

Mâcon

N79

Bourg-
en-Bresse

AREA OF INSET · N6
A6
E15

N7 · D482

Roanne · Villefranche-
sur-Saône

N83 · A40
E62

Pérouges

N7 · N84

Thiers

N89 · D89 · Lyon · A43
E70

THE BEAUJOLAIS COUNTRY

Juliénas

D26 · Chénas · N82 · Givors · Vienne

Fleurie · N6 · Rive-
de-Gier · Condrieu · N85

Les
Écharmeaux · D37 · D18 · A6 · Villié-
Morgon

Belleville-
sur-Saône · N82

Salles · St-
Julien

A7
E15 · N92

Chamelet · N532

Villefranche-
sur-Saône · Romans

D96 · D38 · A49

Oingt

Châtillon-sur-
Azergues · A6 · Valence

D485 · Limonest

N6 · The Ardèche · Crest

Lyon · N104 · Privas · D93

THE LOWER ARDÈCHE VALLEY

Vallon-
Pont-
d'Arc

0 ___ 3 km
0 ___ 1.75 mi · Ardèche · Aubenas · N102 · Montélimar

D579
D579 · D4

D290 · Grotte des
Tunnels · D4 · St-Remèze · D4 · AREA OF
INSET

Chames · D490 · A7 · D994

Pont d'Arc · Belvédère du
Serre de Tourre · Aven de Marzal · D94

Belvédère de Gaud

Belvédère du
Méandre de Gaud · Belvédère d'Autridge · Orange

Les Crottes · D290 · D590 · D201

Belvédère de
Gournier · D690 · D358

PLATEAU · Grotte de la
Madeleine · D201

D290 · Grand
Belvédère

D'ORGNAC · Grottes de
St-Marcel · Belvédère
du Colombier

Belvédère du
Ranc Pointu · Tignan

D290

St-Martin-
d'Ardèche

Aiguèze · D201

N110 · D901

D901

LEGEND

✈ Airport

E-0209

427

the busy road running in front of the church. Guests register in a lobby with a raised hearth. Each comfortably furnished guest room contains well-crafted reproductions of antique furniture.

WHERE TO DINE

Auberge Bressane. 166 bd. de Brou. ☎ **04-74-22-22-68.** Reservations recommended. Main courses 98–185F ($17.65–$33.30); fixed-price menus 98–290F ($17.65–$52.20). AE, DC, MC, V. Daily noon–1:30pm and 7:15–9:45pm. FRENCH.

Bresse poultry is the best in France, and chef Jean-Pierre Vullin specializes in succulent *volaille de Bresse,* served five ways, including a delectable version in cream sauce with morels. Of course, the chef knows how to prepare other dishes equally well: You might enjoy a gâteau of chicken liver, crayfish gratin, or sea bass with fresh basil, accompanied by regional wines like Seyssel and Montagnieu. This restaurant has recently been getting bad press because of the "chilly staff"; on our latest visit, however, we arrived with a party of friends from Lyon and received a very gracious welcome.

✪ **Au Chalet de Brou.** 168 bd. de Brou. ☎ **04-74-22-26-28.** Reservations recommended. Main courses 75–130F ($13.50–$23.40); fixed-price menus 80–130F ($14.40–$23.40). AE, MC, V. Sat–Thurs noon–2pm, Sat–Wed 7–9:30pm. Closed Dec 23–Jan 23. FRENCH.

You'll find flavorful but relatively inexpensive food in this small-scale, unpretentious restaurant across from the village church. Regional traditions and fresh ingredients meet in platters that include quenelles of pike with Nantua sauce, terrines crafted from artichoke hearts or local pork products, and crêpes with mussels and butter sauce. Bresse chickens are a specialty here; hailed by gastronomes as among the best in the world, they are served in varying degrees of complexity. You might want yours simply grilled so you can appreciate the unadorned flavor of the bird in its own drippings. It's also succulent stuffed with morels and drizzled with chardonnay-laced cream sauce. This isn't the region's most glamorous or cutting-edge restaurant, but the prices are more than fair and the food is well prepared.

2 Lyon

268 miles SE of Paris, 193 miles N of Marseille

At the junction of the turbulent Rhône and the tranquil Saône, a crossroads of Western Europe, Lyon is the third-largest city in France. The city proper has a population of 400,000, with more than a million others spread across a large urban area. Lyon is the center of a vast industrial region, with textile manufacturing especially important. It's a leader in book publishing and banking and is the world's silk capital. Some of the country's most highly rated restaurants, including Paul Bocuse, are found in and around Lyon. In fact, it's called the gastronomic capital of France. Such dishes as Lyon sausage, quenelles (fish balls), and tripe lyonnais are world famous, and the region's succulent Bresse poultry is the best in France.

Although you can dine better here than in any other French provincial city, there are disadvantages. You have to cope with urban sprawl and smog, along with some of the hottest and most humid summers in France. In spite of these drawbacks, Lyon is much more relaxed and a lot friendlier than Paris. Parks in full bloom, skyscrapers and sidewalk cafes, a great transport system, concert halls, and a nightlife fueled by student energy await you in Lyon today, along with talented chefs, both young and old.

Lyon

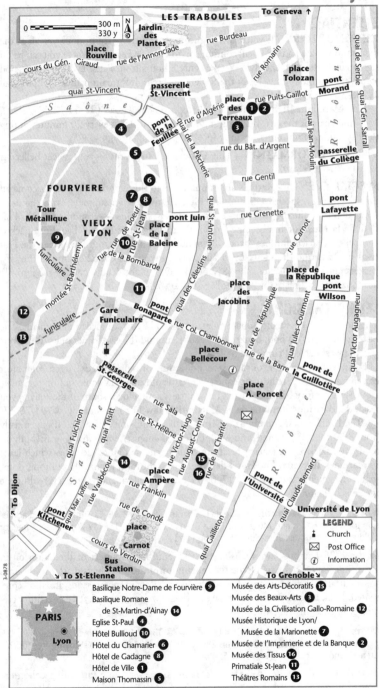

LES TRABOULES

To Geneva ↑

0 ——— 300 m
330 y

N

Jardin
des
Plantes

place
Rouville

cours du Gén. Giraud

rue de l'Annonciade

rue Burdeau

rue Romarin

place
Tolozan

pont
Morand

quai St-Vincent

passerelle
St-Vincent

S a ô n e

quai de Serbie

quai Gén. Sarrail

R h ô n e

rue Puits-Gaillot

place
des
Terreaux

1
2

rue d'Algérie

pont
de la
Feuillée

quai de la Pêcherie

rue du Bât. d'Argent

quai Jean-Moulin

passerelle
du Collège

4

5

FOURVIERE

6

rue Gentil

Tour
Métallique

7 8

VIEUX
LYON

rue de Boeuf

rue St-Jean

pont Juin

place
de la
Baleine

rue Grenette

rue Carnot

pont
Lafayette

9

10

rue de la Bombarde

quai St-Antoine

11

montée St-Barthélemy

funiculaire

12

Gare
Funiculaire

pont
Bonaparte

quai des Célestins

place
des
Jacobins

place de
la République

pont
Wilson

13

funiculaire

rue Col. Chambonnet

rue de République

quai Jules-Courmont

place
Bellecour

i

rue de la Barre

la Guillotière

pont de

quai Victor Augagneur

passerelle
St-Georges

place
A. Poncet

⊠

rue Sala

rue St-Hélène

rue Victor-Hugo

rue August-Comte

rue de la Charité

quai Fulchiron

quai Tilsitt

15

16

pont de
l'Université

R h ô n e

quai Claude-Bernard

Université de Lyon

14

place
Ampère

rue Franklin

LEGEND

⚓ Church
⊠ Post Office
ⓘ Information

To Dijon ←

quai Vaubécour

rue Mar. Joffre

rue de Condé

quai Cailleton

pont
Kitchener

place
Carnot

cours de Verdun

Bus
Station

↙ To St-Etienne

To Grenoble ↘

3-0878

PARIS

★

Lyon

Basilique Notre-Dame de Fourvière 9
Basilique Romane
    de St-Martin-d'Ainay 14
Eglise St-Paul 4
Hôtel Bullioud 10
Hôtel du Chamarier 6
Hôtel de Gadagne 8
Hôtel de Ville 1
Maison Thomassin 5

Musée des Arts-Décoratifs 15
Musée des Beaux-Arts 3
Musée de la Civilisation Gallo-Romaine 12
Musée Historique de Lyon/
    Musée de la Marionette 7
Musée de l'Imprimerie et de la Banque 2
Musée des Tissus 16
Primatiale St-Jean 11
Théâtres Romains 13

ESSENTIALS

GETTING THERE   If you're arriving from the north by **train,** don't get off at the first station, Gare La Part-Dieu; continue on to Gare de Perrache, where you can begin sightseeing. The high-speed TGV takes only 2 hours from Paris. Lyon makes a good stopover en route to the Alps or the Riviera. For train information and schedules, call ☎ **08-36-35-35-39.**

It's a 45-minute **flight** from Paris to Aéroport Lyon-Satolas (☎ **04-72-22-72-21**), 15½ miles east of the city. Buses run into the center of Lyon every 20 minutes during the day, taking 45 minutes for the trip.

VISITOR INFORMATION   The **Office de Tourisme** is on place Bellecour (☎ **04-72-77-69-69**).

SPECIAL EVENTS   Festivals are so numerous in this city that they can become an everyday event, especially in summer. Music festivals reign supreme, with the most popular one occurring on France's National Day of Music—around June 21. This **Fête de la Musique** has become famous for turning the streets of Lyon into packed performance spaces for local bands. From mid-November to mid-December, the **Festival de Musique du Vieux-Lyon** takes place in various churches around the city. Tickets range from 70F to 220F ($12.60 to $39.60). For details, contact the festival's headquarters at 5 place du Petit-Collège (☎ **04-78-38-09-09**).

SEEING THE SIGHTS

The city sprawls over many square miles, divided, like Paris, into arrondissements. The historic heart lies on both banks of the Saône, around the east bank's **place Bellecour** and the west bank's **Primatiale St-Jean.**

Begin your tour of Lyon at **place Bellecour,** one of France's largest and most charming squares. A handsome equestrian statue of Louis XIV looks out on the encircling 18th-century buildings. Going down rue Victor-Hugo, south of the square, you reach the **Basilique Romane de St-Martin-d'Ainay,** 11 rue Bourgelat (☎ **04-78-37-48-97**), Lyon's oldest church, dating from 1107. Admission is free, and it's open daily from 8:30 to 11:30am and 3 to 6:30pm (closed August), and closing at 6:15pm on Saturdays. Back at the square, head north along rue de l'Hôtel-de-Ville, which leads to **place des Terreaux.** The **Hôtel de Ville,** one of the most beautiful in Europe, dominates the square. It dates from 1746; the outside is dark and rather severe, but the inside is brilliant.

Musée des Arts-Décoratifs. 30 rue de la Charité. ☎ **04-78-38-42-00.** Combined admission for this museum and Musée des Tissus 28F ($5.05) adults, 15F ($2.70) students, free for children 17 and under. Tues–Sun 10am–noon and 2–5:30pm.

In the 1739 Lacroix-Laval mansion built by Soufflot (architect of the Panthéon in Paris), the Musée des Arts-Décoratifs contains furniture and objets d'art, mostly from the 17th and 18th centuries. The medieval and Renaissance periods are also represented. Look for a rare five-octave clavecin by Donzelague, the great 18th-century creator of musical instruments.

Musée des Tissus. 34 rue de la Charité. ☎ **04-78-38-42-00.** Combined admission for this museum and Musée des Arts-Décoratifs 28F ($5.05) adults, 15F ($2.70) students, free for children 17 and under. Tues–Sun 10am–5:30pm.

Next door to the Musée des Arts-Décoratifs is an even more interesting collection, housed in the 1730 Palais de Villeroy. On view are priceless fabrics from all over the world, spanning 2,000 years. Some of the finest fabrics made in Lyon from the 18th century to the present are displayed. The 15th- and 16th-century textiles embroidered with religious motifs are noteworthy, as are the 17th-century Persian carpets. Seek out the partridge-motif brocade for Marie Antoinette's bedchamber at Versailles, as well as a brocaded satin woven for Queen Victoria of 150 colors with birds of paradise and orchids.

Musée des Beaux-Arts. 20 place des Terreaux. ☎ **04-72-10-17-40.** Admission 25F ($4.50) adults, 13F ($2.35) students, free for children 17 and under. Wed–Sun 10:30am–6pm.

On the south side of the square stands the Palais des Arts (also called the Musée de St-Pierre). This former Benedictine abbey was built between 1659 and 1685 in the Italian baroque style. Today it contains the Musée des Beaux-Arts, with its outstanding collection of paintings and sculpture. You enter via a charming courtyard graced with statuary and shade trees. The ground floor houses a display of Quattrocento (14th-century) paintings. The collection also includes Etruscan, Egyptian, Phoenician, Sumerian, and Persian art. See, in particular, Perugino's altarpiece. The top floor is devoted to works by artists ranging from Veronese, Tintoretto, and Rubens to Braque, Bonnard, and Picasso, with one of France's richest 19th-century collections. Be sure to see Joseph Chinard's bust of Mme Récamier, the captivating Lyon beauty who charmed Napoleonic Paris by merely reclining, and the Fantin-Latour masterpiece *Reading.*

Musée de l'Imprimerie et de la Banque. 13 rue de la Poulaillerie. ☎ **04-78-37-65-98.** Admission 25F ($4.50) adults, 12.50F ($2.25) students, free for children. Wed–Sun 9:30am–noon and 2–6pm.

Occupying a 15th-century mansion, this museum is devoted to Lyon's role in the world of printing. Exhibits include a page from a Gutenberg Bible, 17th- to 20th-century presses, 16th- to 19th-century woodcuts, and many engravings. This is one of the most important printing museums in Europe, ranking with those at Mainz and Antwerp. It has a collection of books dating from "all epochs," including incunabula, books printed before Easter 1500.

EXPLORING VIEUX LYON

From place Bellecour, walk across pont Bonaparte to the right bank of the Saône River, catch bus no. 1 or 31, or take the Métro to reach ✪ **Vieux Lyon.** Covering about a square mile, Old Lyon contains an amazing collection of medieval and Renaissance buildings. Many of these houses were built five stories high by thriving merchants to show off their new wealth. After years as a slum, the area is now fashionable, attracting antiques dealers, artisans, weavers, sculptors, and painters, who never seem to tire of depicting scenes along the characteristic **rue du Boeuf,** one of the most interesting streets for walking and exploring.

Your first stop should be the **Primatiale St-Jean** (see below). South of the cathedral is the **Manécanterie,** 70 rue St-Jean (☎ **04-78-92-82-29**), noted for its 12th-century Romanesque facade and its role as a dormitory beginning in the 11th century. The boys who sang in the medieval choir lived here, making it the oldest residence in Lyon. The only time you can ever hope to visit its interior is during mass, celebrated at 7pm every day.

North of the cathedral is the most historically and architecturally evocative neighborhood of Old Lyon, with narrow streets, spiral stairs, hanging gardens, soaring towers, and unusual courtyards whose balconies seem to sit precariously atop medieval pilings or columns.

While in Vieux Lyon, try to see the exceptional Gothic arcades of the 16th-century **Maison Thomassin,** place du Change, and the 16th-century **Hôtel du Chamarier,** 37 rue St-Jean, where Mme de Sévigné lived. You can admire but not enter these buildings. The neighborhood also contains the awesomely old **Eglise St-Paul,** 3 place Gerson (☎ **04-78-28-34-45**), consecrated in A.D. 549. A rebuilding began in 1084 after its destruction by the Saracens. Its distinctive octagonal lantern tower was completed in the 1100s and the rest of its premises in the 13th century. You can visit it Monday through Saturday from noon to 6pm and Sunday from 2 to 6pm. Admission is free.

Primatiale St-Jean. Place St-Jean. ☎ **04-78-42-11-04.** Free admission. Daily 8am–noon and 2–7pm, Sat–Sun 2–5pm.

The cathedral was built between the 12th and the 15th centuries. Its apse is a masterpiece of Lyonnais Romanesque. The exceptional stained-glass windows are from the 12th to the 15th centuries. A highlight is the Flamboyant Gothic chapel of the Bourbons. On the front portals are medallions depicting the signs of the zodiac, the Creation, and the life of St. John. The cathedral's 16th-century Swiss astronomical clock is intricate and beautiful; it announces the hour daily at noon, 2pm, and 3pm in grand style—a rooster crows and angels herald the event. The treasury, on the right side of the cathedral, was closed for renovation at press time but might (or might not, depending on bomb scares in France) be open at the time of your visit.

Musée Historique de Lyon. 1 place du Petit-Collège. ☎ **04-78-42-03-61.** Admission (including Musée de la Marionette) 25F ($4.50) adults, 13F ($2.35) students, free 17 and under. Both museums, Wed–Mon 10:45am–6pm.

In the Hôtel de Gadagne, an early-16th-century residence, you'll find the Musée Historique de Lyon, with interesting Romanesque sculptures on the ground floor. Other exhibits are 18th-century Lyonnais furniture and pottery, antique ceramics from the town of Nevers, a pewter collection, and numerous paintings and engravings of Lyon vistas.

In the same building is the **Musée de la Marionette** (same phone), which has three puppets by Laurent Mourguet, creator of Guignol, the best known of all French marionette characters. The museum also has marionettes from other parts of France (including Amiens, Lille, and Aix-en-Provence) and important collections from around the world.

CLIMBING FOURVIÈRE HILL

Rising to the west of Vieux Lyon on the west bank of the Saône is **Colline de Fourvière (Fourvière Hill).** This richly wooded hill—on which numerous convents, colleges, hospitals, two Roman theaters, and a superb Gallo-Roman museum have been established—affords a panoramic vista of Lyon, with its many bridges across two rivers, the rooftops of the medieval town, and (in clear weather) a view of the countryside extending to the snow-capped Alps.

Enthroned on its summit is the gaudy 19th-century **Basilique Notre-Dame de Fourvière,** 8 place de Fourvière (☎ **04-78-25-13-01**), rising fortresslike with four octagonal towers and crenellated walls. Its interior is covered with richly colored mosaics; adjoining is an ancient chapel. The belfry is surmounted by a gilded statue of the Virgin. Admission is free, and it's open daily from 7am to 6:30pm.

Jardin du Rosaire extends on the hillside between the basilica and the 13th-century **Primatiale St-Jean.** They're open daily between 7am and 7pm and provide a pleasant walk. You'll see a vast shelter for up to 200 pilgrims. An elevator takes you to the top of the towers and two funiculars service the hill.

In a park south of the basilica are the excavated **Théâtres Romains,** Montée de Fourvière, a Roman theater/odeum at 6 rue de l'Antiquaille. The theater is the most ancient in France, built by order of Augustus in 17–15 B.C. and greatly expanded during the reign of Hadrian. The odeum, reserved for musical performances, apparently was once sumptuously decorated. Its orchestra floor, for example, contains mosaics of such materials as brightly colored marble and porphyry. The third building in the sanctuary was dedicated in A.D. 160 to the goddess Cybele, or Sibella, whose cult originated in Asia Minor. All that remains are the foundations, though they seem to dominate the theater (175 feet by 284 feet).

An altar dedicated to a bull cult and a monumental marble statue of the goddess are shown in the **Musée de la Civilisation Gallo-Romaine,** 17 rue Cléberg (☎ 04-72-38-81-90), a few steps from the archaeological site. The museum's collection of Gallo-Roman artifacts is the finest in France outside Paris. The site is open Wednesday through Sunday from 9:30am to noon and 2 to 6pm. Admission costs 20 F ($3.60) for adults, free for children 12 and under. Guides are available on Sundays and holidays from 3 to 6pm. Performances are given at both theaters in summer.

NEARBY ATTRACTIONS

One of Lyon's grandest archaeological sites, which regrettably you can view only from the outside, is **Amphithéâtre des Trois-Gauls,** rue du Jardin-des-Plantes, Croix-Rousse (no phone), in Lyon's 4th arrondissement, near the city's northern perimeter. At the time of its construction, it was the centerpiece of Condate, an ancient Gallic village, near the junction of the Rhône and Saône, that predated the arrival of the Roman legions by several centuries. According to scattered historic accounts, delegates from 60 tribes from throughout Gaul met here in the earliest known example of a French parliamentary system. Based on those dimly remembered events, the 2,000th anniversary of France, its bimillennium, was celebrated in Lyon in 1989.

On the opposite side of the Rhône, you'll have the chance to explore Lyon's largest public park and garden, the 260-acre **Parc de la Tête d'Or** (☎ 04-78-89-53-52). Its largest (but by no means only) entrance is on boulevard des Belges. It opened in 1857 with all the fountains, pedestrian walkways, and ornamental statues you'd expect from Lyon's showcase park. Surrounded by wealthy residential neighborhoods, the park has a lake, illuminated fountains, a little zoo, a botanical garden with greenhouses, and a rose garden with some 100,000 plants.

At **Rochetaillée-sur-Saône,** 7 miles north of Lyon on D433, the **Musée Français de l'Automobile "Henri Malartre"** is housed in the Château de Rochetaillée, 645 chemin du Musée (☎ 04-78-22-18-80). Established by a wealthy benefactor (Henri Malartre) and taken over as a public museum by the city of Lyon in 1960, the collection includes 100 cars dating back to 1890, 65 motorcycles from 1903 and after, and 40 cycles dating back to 1848. The château is surrounded by a large park. Admission to the museum and château is 35F ($6.30), free for children 18 and under. Both are open daily from 9am to 5pm.

SHOPPING

Since this is the third-largest city in France, you'll find a full array of shopping options. For small boutiques, art galleries, and local artists' studios and workshops, head to **Vieux Lyon** and the area around **rue Mercière** and **quai St-Antoine.** For antiques, concentrate around **rue Auguste-Comte** as it approaches place Bellecour. And consider venturing to the **Cité des Antiquaires,** 117 bd. Stalingrad (☎ 04-72-44-91-98), with more than 100 antiques dealers.

Lyon remains a bastion for fashion—everything from the cutting edge to the classically elegant. Most of the upscale boutiques are on the Presque'île along **rue Victor-Hugo** and **rue de la République.** You might also explore the perpendicular and parallel streets, like **rue Emile-Zola.**

For ultrachic couture, try **George Rech,** 59 rue du Président-Herriot (☎ 04-78-37-82-90). There's also the large *centre commercial* **(mall),** 17 rue du Dr.-Boudent

(☎ **04-72-60-60-62**), with more than 200 shops. Though not the major silk center of yesteryear, Lyon still hangs on to several silk manufacturers; and for a good selection of silk scarves, ties, sashes, and squares, try **La Maison des Canuts,** 10–12 rue d'Ivry (☎ **04-78-28-62-04**), as well as the famous Parisian supplier **Hermès,** 56 rue du Président-Herriot (☎ **04-78-42-25-14**), in a store that, alas, still doesn't offer discounts—not even to employees.

For a thoroughly Lyonais gift, keep your eye out for **marionettes de Lyon.** These expertly crafted puppets are sold at various stores and workshops around town, including **Atelier de Guignol,** 4 place du Change (☎ **04-78-29-33-37**), and **A Noëlle,** 22 rue St-Jean (☎ **04-78-37-21-31**).

Bernachon, 42 cours Franklin-Roosevelt (☎ **04-78-52-23-65**), is home to Lyon's best chocolates and pastries. Here you'll find 30 varieties of bite-size pastries known as minigâteaux, 30 varieties of petits fours, and even dark, rich chocolates lightly dusted with 24-karat gold. Also at the Bernachon store is a small restaurant/tearoom called **Bernachon Passion.** Just down the way, at 46 cours Franklin-Roosevelt, is **Bocuse & Bernachon** (☎ **04-72-74-46-19**), which takes the quality behind the Bernachon name and combines it with the Lyonnais gourmet heavyweight of Paul Bocuse for the finest in gourmet takeout specialties.

WHERE TO STAY

Alain Chapel (see "Where to Dine," below) also rents rooms.

VERY EXPENSIVE

✪ **Cour des Loges.** 2468 rue du Boeuf, 69005 Vieux Lyon. ☎ **04-72-77-44-44.** Fax 04-72-40-93-61. 63 units. A/C MINIBAR TV TEL. 1,200–1,800F ($216–$324) double; 2,000–3,000F ($360–$540) suite. AE, DC, MC, V. Parking 120F ($21.60). Métro: St-Jean.

This four-star luxury hotel in Old Lyon occupies several houses from the 14th to the 17th centuries. It offers beautifully furnished rooms and suites, each containing a TV with foreign channels and a VCR. Most units face gardens, the square, or a large sunlit lobby. The staff is courteous, highly efficient, and the most savvy in Lyon.

Dining: The restaurant serves excellent food in an elegant setting; there are also lounges and a wine cellar.

Amenities: Roman-style indoor pool, Jacuzzi, dry sauna, terraced gardens, private garage, valet, 24-hour room service.

MODERATE

Best Western Hôtel des Beaux-Arts. 75 rue du Président-Herriot, 69002 Lyon. ☎ **800/ 528-1234** in the U.S., or 04-78-38-09-50. Fax 04-78-42-19-19. www.bestwestern.com. 75 units. A/C TV TEL. 510–670F ($91.80–$120.60) double; 710–790F ($127.80–$142.20) suite. AE, DC, V. Métro: Cordelier.

This has long been one of the leading moderately priced choices in central Lyon. The lobby evokes the 1930s more than the rooms, which, although comfortable, are for the most part outfitted in businesslike modern style. Many were renovated in 1996. Since this is a noisy part of the city, double glazing on the windows helps shut out traffic sounds; the quieter rooms are in the rear. A large breakfast is the only meal served, though you may prefer having croissants and coffee at one of the cafes along place Bellecour.

✪ **Grand Hôtel Château Perrache.** 12 cours de Verdun, 69002 Lyon. ☎ **800/MERCURE** or 04-72-77-15-00. Fax 04-78-37-06-56. 117 units. A/C MINIBAR TV TEL. 515–870F ($92.70–$156.60) double. AE, DC, MC, V. Métro: Perrache.

This hotel near the Perrache train station offers some of Lyon's best rooms, with plush fabrics and inviting colors. The hotel is a monument to Art Nouveau and even has a winter garden. Les Belles Saisons, the house restaurant, does more than just cater to the tired business traveler who doesn't want to leave the premises at night. Its finely honed cuisine is often innovative and features continental and regional dishes.

Hôtel Globe et Cécil. 21 rue Gasparin, 69002 Lyon. ☎ **04-78-42-58-95.** Fax 04-72-41-99-06. 58 units. TV TEL. 550F ($99) double. AE, DC, MC, V. Parking 65F ($11.70). Métro: Bellecour.

Near place Bellecour, this hotel is a good value for Lyon, not only because of its location but also because of its attentive staff. The rooms are comfortable, attractively furnished, and individually decorated. Breakfast is the only meal served, but many dining places are nearby.

INEXPENSIVE

✪ **Hôtel Bayard.** 23 place Bellecour, 69002 Lyon. ☎ **04-78-37-39-64.** Fax 04-72-40-95-51. 15 units. TV TEL. 307–397F ($55.25–$71.45) double. AE, DC, MC, V. Métro: Bellecour.

This town house is on the landmark place Bellecour. Don't be put off by the entrance, down a narrow hallway on the second floor. Inside you'll find special accommodations, each with a different name, price, and decor. This place is a real find, considering its rates.

Hôtel Bellecordière. 18 rue Bellecordière, 69002 Lyon. ☎ **04-78-42-27-78.** Fax 04-72-40-92-27. 45 units. TV TEL. 280–320F ($50.40–$57.60) double. AE, MC, V. Métro: Bellecour.

A savvy gourmet traveler we know always stays at this nondescript two-star hotel, preferring to spend her money on Lyon's restaurants. The small accommodations are no-frills, although each is reasonably comfortable. Breakfast is the only meal served, but many worthwhile restaurants are nearby.

Le Résidence. 18 rue Victor-Hugo, 69002 Lyon. ☎ **04-78-42-63-28.** Fax 04-78-42-85-76. 65 units. TV TEL. 330F ($59.40) double. AE, DC, V. Métro: Bellecour.

Long a favorite with budget travelers, this hotel is at the corner of a pedestrian zone in the center of Lyon. Beyond an ornate 19th-century facade, the rooms are comfortably but not spectacularly furnished. For the price, however, they offer one of the best values in this rather overpriced city. Breakfast is the only meal served, but many fine restaurants are literally outside the door, as is some of the finest shopping. Many members of the staff speak English and are filled with helpful advice.

WHERE TO DINE

The food in Lyon is among the finest in the world—and can be very expensive. However, we've found that a person of moderate means can often afford the most reasonable fixed-price menus even in the city's priciest choices.

VERY EXPENSIVE

✪ **Alain Chapel.** N83 Mionnay, 01390 St-André-de-Corcy. ☎ **04-78-91-82-02.** Fax 04-78-91-82-37. Reservations required. Main courses 200–330F ($36–$59.40); fixed-price lunch 380F ($68.40) Wed–Fri only; fixed-price menus 595–795F ($107.10–$143.10). AE, DC, MC, V. Tues 7:30–10:30pm, Wed–Sun 12:30–1:30pm and 7:30–9:30pm. Closed Jan. Take N83 12½ miles north of Lyon. FRENCH.

This Relais Gourmand occupies a 19th-century postal station that has evolved after years of architectural improvements into a comfortable, conservatively stylish place. Alain Chapel was one of the world's premier chefs, and after his death many people claimed that the stellar reputation of his restaurant would tarnish; but under Philippe Jousse (who trained under Chapel), that hasn't been the case. Jousse, assisted by M. Chapel's widow, continues to maintain the image of Lyon as a gastronomic capital, with perhaps a bit less emphasis on the media hype and cutting-edge glamour of his predecessor.

Menu items change with the seasons but are likely to include lobster salad or velvety eel pâté in puff pastry with two butter sauces. Delectable main courses feature pan-fried skillet of fresh mushrooms and *poulette de Bresse en vessie*—truffled chicken poached and sewn into a pig's bladder (to retain its juices), baked, and served with a cream sauce with a bit of foie gras. Fresh vegetables such as turnips, parsnips, and carrots cooked al dente accompany many of the main courses. Looking for maximum flavor in the simplest of dishes? Consider roast rack of veal or fried veal kidneys served in their own juices.

Also offered are 14 beautiful rooms, priced at 600F to 800F ($108 to $144) for a double.

✪ **La Mère Brazier.** 12 rue Royale. ☎ **04-78-28-15-49.** Reservations required. Main courses 95–220F ($17.10–$39.60); fixed-price menus 250F and 300F ($45 and $54); business menu (Mon–Fri) 170F ($30.60). AE, DC, MC, V. Mon–Fri noon–2pm, Mon–Sat 7:30–10pm. Closed Aug. Métro: Hôtel-de-Ville. FRENCH.

This restaurant near pont Morand has grown from a 1921 lunch spot for silk workers to an internationally known gourmet restaurant that draws connoisseurs. It's managed by Carmen and Jacotte Brazier—the daughter-in-law and one of the granddaughters of the founding mother, Mme Brazier. The simple decor and wood paneling make an attractive setting for a leisurely lunch or an outstanding supper. Here you can order some excellent regional dishes, accompanied by such local wines as Mâcon, Juliénas, Morgon, and Chiroubles. Appetizers include artichoke hearts stuffed with foie gras as well as smoked Nordic salmon. Specialties are *volaille demi-deuil* (boiled chicken with truffles under the skin, served with vegetables, rice, and bouillon) and superbly smooth *quenelles de brochet* (pike). More extravagant fare includes lobster Belle Aurore or à la nage. The service is solicitous.

Léon de Lyon. 1 rue Pleney. ☎ **04-78-28-11-33.** Reservations required. Main courses 150–480F ($27–$86.40); fixed-price lunch menu 290F ($52.20); fixed-price menus 560–720F ($100.80–$129.60). AE, DC, MC, V. Mon–Sat noon–2pm and 7:30–10pm. Closed Aug 10–17. Métro: Hôtel-de-Ville. FRENCH.

Upstairs in what was once a private home, tables are placed in a series of small rooms decorated with culinary artifacts. The atmosphere may be traditional and typical, but the food isn't. The owner, Jean-Paul Lacombe, has been called a daring challenger to the top chefs of Lyon, serving both regional and modern cuisine with innovative flair. His brilliant use of Lyonnais offal might scare off the timid but will please the dedicated gastronome. Offerings might include pheasant soup with foie gras and red beans, pike quenelles (fish balls), or lobster with asparagus. Seasonal offerings include snails bubbling in butter. More challenging fare includes terrine of sweetbreads with spinach and even Bresse chicken with truffles. His sorbets made with fresh fruits are a perfect ending.

✪ **Paul Bocuse.** Pont de Collonges, Collonges-au-Mont-d'Or. ☎ **04-72-42-90-90.** Reservations required as far in advance as possible. Main courses 170–295F ($30.60–$53.10); fixed-price menus 510–740F ($91.80–$133.20). AE, DC, MC, V. Daily noon–2pm and 7–10pm. Take N433 5½ miles north of Lyon. LYONNAISE.

Paul Bocuse is one of the world's most famous contemporary chefs, and his restaurant is on the banks of the Saône at Collonges-au-Mont-d'Or. He specializes in regional cuisine, though long ago he was the leading exponent of nouvelle cuisine (which he later called "a joke"). Since Bocuse (now in his 70s) is gone at least part of the time, the chefs he leaves behind must carry on with the mass production (for up to 180

Bravo Bocuse

A resurgence in interest in chef Paul Bocuse swept across Lyon in 1994 when he bought the ✪ **Brasserie Le Nord,** 18 rue Neuve (☎ **04-72-10-69-69**), a turn-of-the-century brasserie the master once worked in as a teenager. Menu prices here—about 180F ($32.40) per person for a meal with wine and coffee—signaled that the last of the truly great chefs had finally decided to go for the mass market. And we're definitely not complaining! It's the most popular restaurant in town, particularly with the bankers and merchants who seem to pack the place at lunch. A short while after, Bocuse opened a twin of Le Nord, **Brasserie Le Sud,** place Antonin-Poncet (☎ **04-72-77-80-00**), specializing in the cuisine of the French-speaking Mediterranean.

At least some of the success of these brasseries stems from the Bocuse name, for he is the most prominent and enduring grand chef in France. His almost mythical restaurant in Lyon's suburb of Collanges-au-Mont-d'Or has earned a trio of Michelin stars (the top rating) every year since 1965 (see our review, below). Less secure chefs might tremble at the thought of the public scrutiny this involves, fearing that the laurels thrown by culinary critics will be ripped away later. But Bocuse, with his irrepressible ego, seems to thrill year after year to the notion that he's without parallel.

So will the master be here when you drop in his brasserie? Not necessarily. He may not even be found at Collanges-au-Mont-d'Or—or even in Lyon. Since creating some of the most award-winning dishes in Europe (black truffle soup, filet of sea bass en croûte, chicken cooked in a pig's bladder), Bocuse has launched his own line of vacuum-packed foods, endorsed a string of bakeries in Japan, purchased a beaujolais vineyard, become interested in the French Pavilion at Walt Disney World's Epcot Center in Florida, and helped develop a collection of CDs (Matins et Câlins) designed to soothe the grumpy after effects of too much wine and foie gras. He's in demand everywhere from Chicago to Tokyo, and virtually every agent in Hollywood salivates at the thought of getting him to endorse anything and everything—from T-shirts to slotted spoons.

His team, however, quickly assures the press and diners alike that although "temporarily absent," M. Bocuse is present "in spirit." And in this case the spirit, as priests have affirmed for many years, is invariably stronger than the flesh.

---

diners at a time) of the signature dishes the master created and on which there isn't a lot of variation.

In one of the three dining rooms lined with oil paintings, perhaps begin with the famous black truffle soup, then try one of the most enduring dishes in the Bocuse repertoire—the perfumey Bresse chicken cooked in a pig's bladder. Newer options include sea bass with a lobster mousse and Choron sauce, red snapper in a crusty potato shell, and roast pigeon in puff pastry with baby cabbage leaves and foie gras.

If you want to take more away with you than just a satisfied appetite, a boutique on the premises sells Bocuse's preferred versions of wine, cognac (vintage Bocuse X.O.), jams and jellies, coffees and teas, and cookbooks. Most prominently display his image and logo.

Note: You can't miss this place. In the mid-1990s, tired of the conventional facades that shelter most French restaurants, M. Bocuse commissioned a local artist to paint the history of French cuisine, in cartoon form, on the outside of his restaurant. The tale begins in the 1700s and proceeds through the years to its "defining moment" as interpreted in a depiction of Bocuse himself.

MODERATE

Café des Fédérations. 8 rue Major-Martin. ☎ **04-78-28-26-00.** Reservations recommended. Fixed-price menu 145F ($26.10). V. Mon–Fri 10am–11pm. Closed Aug. Métro: Hôtel-de-Ville. FRENCH.

This is the city's best bistro, operated with panache by Yves Rivoiron. A sawdust-covered tile floor and long sausages hanging from the ceiling set the tone, and the traditional food completes the picture. The host will help you choose from dishes like sliced pork sausages with boiled potatoes and watercress; tripe marinated, breaded, and grilled; and blood sausage with sautéed apples. End with some of the excellent cheeses or a fruit tart.

La Tassée. 20 rue de la Charité. ☎ **04-72-77-79-00.** Reservations not required. Main courses 75–150F ($13.50–$27); fixed-price menus 110–270F ($19.80–$48.60). AE, DC, V. Mon–Sat noon–2:30pm and 7–10:30pm. Métro: Bellecour. FRENCH.

The chef here isn't interested in fancy frills, but believes in serving good food at prices most people can afford. Huge portions are dished out, and you might be offered anything from strips of tripe with onions to game or sole. On a recent visit, we arrived just when the beaujolais nouveau had come in. It's a thin, sharp wine, bearing little resemblance to the real beaujolais—but its arrival is a major event. The dining room boasts noteworthy 19th-century frescoes.

Le Bistrot de Lyon. 64 rue Mercière. ☎ **04-78-37-00-62.** Reservations not required. Main courses 51–115F ($9.20–$20.70); fixed-price menus 115–215F ($20.70–$38.70). AE, MC, V. Daily noon–2:30pm and 7pm–1:30am. Métro: Cordeliers. FRENCH.

This place stays hopping until the wee hours of the morning. It stands on a street of bistros, with several wine bars mixed in. The setting is elegant and traditional, with marble-topped tables. You might want to stick to classic Lyonnais fare, like poached eggs in red-wine sauce and pot-au-feu, a stew with fresh vegetables. Another classic is chicken with heaps of fresh pasta. This is a great place to people watch.

✪ Philippe B. 42 rue Pierre-Corneille. ☎ **04-78-52-19-13.** Reservations recommended. Main courses 90–105F ($16.20–$18.90); fixed-price menus 135–225F ($24.30–$40.50). AE, DC, MC, V. Mon–Fri noon–2pm, Mon–Sat 7–9:30pm. Closed Aug. Métro: Avenue-Foch. LYONNAISE.

In 1996 a youthful survivor of apprenticeships under four of France's premier chefs (including Bocuse and Ducasse) took over the premises of an existing restaurant in Lyon's 6th arrondissement and went to work. The result is a trio of dining rooms featuring delectable and traditional versions of Lyonnais cuisine at surprisingly reasonable prices. Menus change with the seasons but may include roasted monkfish with asparagus tips and a lemon-flavored *velouté*, curried sweetbreads of lamb with an eggplant caviar, and *d'Allobroges* (local) chicken roasted with garlic and rosemary.

LYON AFTER DARK

This cosmopolitan hub of entertainment and culture offers many options. At a newsstand, buy a copy of the weekly guide *Lyon-Poche*, which lists all the cultural happenings around town from bars and theaters to classical concerts.

For the theater or opera buff, Lyon's **Théâtre des Célestins,** 4 rue Charles-Dulliln (☎ 04-72-77-40-00), is the premier venue for comedy and drama, and the **Opéra,** place de la Comédie (☎ 04-72-00-45-45), always has a lively and diverse season.

For the best pubs in town, go to the **Smoking Dog,** 16 rue Lainerie (☎ 04-78-28-38-27), a happy neighborhood bar with a mixed-age crowd; or **The Barrel House,**

13 rue Ste-Catherine (☎ 04-78-29-20-40), filled with a younger, English-speaking crowd bent on drinking themselves under the table and having a good time in the process.

Rock-and-rollers head over to the old train station to one of the newest clubs, **Bar Live,** 13 place J.-Ferry (☎ 04-72-74-04-41), with its up-and-coming yuppies. Another club to check out is **Navire Night,** 3 rue Terme (☎ 04-78-30-02-01), where you can hear original rock from the 1950s and 1960s. For a wild night of dancing, head for **Palace Mobile,** 2 rue René-Leynaud (☎ 04-78-27-88-80), where part of the fun is switching from ballroom to techno in a single beat; or **L'Empire,** 30 bd. Eugène-Deruelle (☎ 04-78-95-12-93), with its brash techno crew. Cover charges to these clubs range from 60F to 100F ($10.80 to $18). For jazz enthusiasts, give a listen to what has become a Lyon jazz and blues tradition, **Le Hot Club,** 26 rue Lanterne (☎ 04-78-39-54-74).

Surprisingly, in a town this size there are no exclusively gay and lesbian discos; the closest thing is a gay-friendly dance club called **Le Mylord,** 112 quai Pierre-Scize (☎ 04-78-28-96-69), with its smoke machines, flashing lights, mirrors, and average cover of 60F ($10.80). It's a fun and safe place to let your hair down and burn off some calories. The macho leather crowd hangs out at **Bar des Traboules,** 86 Grande Rue de la Croix-Rousse (☎ 04-78-29-20-09). Other bars are **Le Verre à Soi,** 25 rue des Capucins (☎ 04-78-28-92-44), with a mixed gay and lesbian crowd; **Le Broadway,** 9 rue Terraille (☎ 04-78-39-50-54), with an older crowd of men and women who enjoy a theme night every 2 weeks or so; and the popular **Le Bar du Centre,** 3 rue Simon-Maupin (☎ 04-78-37-40-18), where a guy can relax, have a drink, and strike up a conversation with what one of the bartenders called "the hottest men in Lyon."

3 Pérouges

288 miles SE of Paris, 22 miles NE of Lyon

The Middle Ages live on. Saved from demolition by a courageous mayor in 1909 and preserved by the government, this village of craftspeople often attracts movie crews; *The Three Musketeers,* starring Michael York, and *Monsieur Vincent* (1948) were filmed here. The town sits on what has been called an "isolated throne," atop a hill northeast of Lyon.

Follow rue du Prince, once the main business street, to place du Tilleul, at the center of which is an ***Arbre de la Liberté*** (Tree of Liberty) planted in 1792 to honor the Revolution. Nearby is the **Musée du Vieux-Pérouges,** place de la Halle (☎ **04-74-61-00-88**), displaying such artifacts as hand looms. Between Easter and November 1, it's open daily from 10am to noon and 2 to 6pm; the rest of the year, it's open only on Saturdays and Sundays (same hours). Admission is 15F ($2.70). This price includes the museum, the Arbre de la Liberté, and the Maison des Princes de Savoie. In the 13th century, weaving was the principal industry here, and linen merchants sold their wares in the Gothic gallery.

Wander at your leisure through the village, soaking in the atmosphere. The finest house is on rue du Prince—the 14th-century **Maison des Princes de Savoie**—and you can visit its watchtower; also ask to be shown the garden planted with "flowers of love." You can visit from Easter to November 1, daily from 10am to noon and 2 to 6pm; the rest of the year, it's open on Saturdays and Sundays only (same hours). Admission is inclusive of the other museums. In the eastern sector of **rue des Rondes** are many stone houses of former hand weavers. The stone hooks on the facades were for newly woven pieces of linen.

It's easiest to drive to Pérouges, though the signs for the town, especially at night, are confusing. Remember as you drive that it lies northeast of Lyon, off route 84, near Meximieux.

The **Syndicat d'Initiative** (tourist office) is in the Hostellerie du Vieux-Pérouges, place des Tilleuls (☎ **04-74-61-00-88**).

WHERE TO STAY & DINE

✪ **Hostellerie du Vieux-Pérouges.** Place des Tilleuls, 01800 Pérouges. ☎ **04-74-61-00-88.** Fax 04-74-34-77-90. 28 units. TV TEL. 720–1,050F ($129.60–$189) double. MC, V. Free parking.

This is a treasure in a lavishly restored group of 13th-century timbered buildings. Georges Thibaut runs a museum-caliber inn furnished with polished antiques, cupboards with pewter plates, iron lanterns hanging from medieval beams, glistening refectory dining tables, and stone fireplaces.

Dining: The restaurant is run in association with Le Manoir, where guests are accommodated. The food is exceptional, especially when it's served with the local sparkling wine, Montagnieu, which has been compared to Asti-Spumante. Specialties are *terrine truffée Brillat-Savarin, écrevisses* (crayfish) *pérougiennes,* and *galette pérougienne à la crème* (a dessert crêpe). After dinner, ask for a unique liqueur made from a recipe from the Middle Ages: Ypocras. Fixed-price meals cost 190F to 430F ($34.20 to $77.40).

4 Roanne

242 miles SE of Paris, 54 miles NW of Lyon

This industrial town on the left bank of the Loire is often visited from Lyon or Vichy because it contains one of France's greatest three-star restaurants, the Hôtel-Restaurant Troisgros (see below).

There's also a worthwhile museum. In a stately neoclassic mansion built at the end of the 18th century, **Musée Joseph-Déchelette,** 22 rue Anatole-France (☎ **04-77-70-00-90**), offers an exceptional display of Italian and French earthenware from the 16th, 17th, 18th, and 20th centuries, as well as earthenware produced in Roanne from the 16th to the 19th centuries. This is the most important privately endowed museum in this part of France. Admission is 20F ($3.60); hours are Wednesday through Monday from 10am to noon and 2 to 6pm.

There are train and bus connections from nearby cities, notably Lyon; the train is a lot more convenient. For **train** information and schedules, call ☎ **08-36-35-35-39.** By train, Roanne lies 3 hours from Paris but only 1 hour from Lyon. If you're **driving** from Lyon, simply follow N7 northwest to Roanne. If you're driving from Paris, follow A6 south to the town of Nemours, continuing southwest along N7.

The **Office de Tourisme** is on cours de la République (☎ **04-77-71-51-77**).

WHERE TO STAY & DINE

✪ **Hôtel-Restaurant Troisgros.** Place de la Gare, 42300 Roanne. ☎ **04-77-71-66-97.** Fax 04-77-70-39-77. Reservations required. Main courses 200–300F ($36–$54); fixed-price menus 620–750F ($111.60–$135). AE, DC, MC, V. Thurs–Mon noon–1:30pm, Wed–Mon 7:30–9:30pm. Closed Feb and Aug 1–15. FRENCH.

Decorated with contemporary art, the restaurant in this railway-station hotel is one of the best in France. The prices are astronomical, but you're paying for acclaimed cuisine, beautiful service, and quality ingredients. Brothers Pierre and Michel Troisgros are the chefs. Their menu is a virtual celebration of the bounty of the countryside, with appetizers that include warm oysters in butter "in the style of Julia" and thin escalopes of salmon in a sorrel sauce. For a main course, we recommend duck legs served au vinaigre, thyme-scented ewe chops, Charolais beef with marrow in red-wine sauce, or superb squab. For dessert, try an assortment of cheeses or a praline soufflé. The petits fours with candied citrus peel may make you linger.

The hotel offers 19 well-furnished, air-conditioned rooms, plus 3 suites. They cost 750F to 950F ($135 to $171) for a double and 1,500F to 1,950F ($270 to $351) for a suite.

NEARBY DINING & ACCOMMODATIONS

In the satellite village of **Le Coteau** you'll find several worthy restaurants. These two are our favorites. To reach Le Coteau, take N7 2 miles from the center of Roanne.

✪ **Auberge Costelloise.** 2 av. de la Libération, Le Coteau. ☎ **04-77-68-12-71.** Reservations required. Main courses 85–155F ($15.30–$27.90); fixed-price menus 125–355F ($22.50–$63.90). AE, MC, V. Tues–Sat 12:15–2pm and 7:45–9pm. Closed Jan 2–10 and Aug 7–15. FRENCH.

Chef Daniel Alex and his wife, Solange, provide what this region needs: an attractive restaurant with fine cuisine and reasonable prices. Choose from one of the fixed-price à la carte menus, which change weekly; the cheapest one isn't available on Saturday night. Popular dishes are gâteau of chicken livers with essence of shrimp, sole filet with confit of leeks, and foie gras. You can order fine vintages of Burgundian wines by the pitcher. This is the place to head when you can't afford the dazzling but expensive food at Troisgros.

Hôtel Restaurant Artaud. 133 av. de la Libération, 42120 Le Coteau. ☎ **04-77-68-46-44.** Fax 04-77-72-23-50. Reservations recommended. Main courses 75–120F ($13.50–$21.60); fixed-price menus 98–350F ($17.65–$63). AE, V. Mon–Sat noon–2pm and 7:30–9pm. Closed July 25–Aug 15. FRENCH.

In an elegant dining room, Nicole and Alain Artaud offer traditional French cuisine. Choices include monkfish salad with saffron, beef from local farms, and a variety of desserts. There's also a good selection of French wines.

The hotel offers 25 well-appointed rooms with satellite TV; a double runs from 280F to 410F ($50.40 to $73.80).

5 Vienne

304 miles SE of Paris, 19 miles S of Lyon

Serious gastronomes know Vienne because it boasts one of France's leading restaurants, La Pyramide. But even if you can't afford the haute cuisine served there, you may want to visit Vienne for its sights. Situated on the left bank of the Rhône, it's a wine center and the southernmost Burgundian town.

ESSENTIALS

GETTING THERE   **Rail** lines connect Vienne with the rest of France. Some trips require a transfer in nearby Lyon. For train information and schedules, call ☎ **08-36-35-35-39.**

If you're **driving** from Lyon, take either N7 (which is more direct) or A7, an expressway that meanders along the banks of the Rhône River.

VISITOR INFORMATION   The **Office de Tourisme** is at 3 cours Brillier (☎ **04-74-85-12-62**).

SPECIAL EVENTS   During the first 2 weeks in July, Vienne comes to life with some of the biggest names in jazz during its annual **Festival du Jazz à Vienne.** Such notables as B. B. King, the Count Basie Orchestra, Eric Clapton, and even Little

Richard have played here. Tickets range from 150F ($27) for single performances up to 600F ($108) for seven concerts. You can get tickets and complete information from the **Théâtre de Vienne,** 4 rue Chantelouve (☎ 04-74-85-00-05).

SEEING THE SIGHTS

Vienne contains many embellishments from its past, making it a *ville romaine et médiévale*. Near the center of town on place du Palais is the **Temple d'Auguste et de Livie,** inviting comparisons with the Maison Carrée at Nîmes. It was ordered built by Claudius and turned into a temple of reason during the Revolution. Another outstanding monument is the small Pyramide du Cirque, part of the Roman circus. Rising 52 feet, it rests on a portico with four arches and is sometimes known as the tomb of Pilate.

Take rue Clémentine to the **Cathédrale St-Maurice,** place St-Maurice, dating from the 12th century even though it wasn't completed until the 15th. It has three aisles but no transepts. Its west front is built in the Flamboyant Gothic style, and inside are many fine Romanesque sculptures.

In the southern part of town near the river stands the **Eglise St-Pierre,** at place St-Pierre, a landmark that traces its origins to the 5th century, making it one of the oldest medieval churches in France. It contains a **Musée Lapidaire** (☎ 04-74-85-50-42), displaying architectural fragments and sculptures found in local excavations. The museum is open from April 1 to October 31, Tuesday through Sunday from 9:30am to 1pm and 2 to 6pm; the rest of the year, Tuesday through Saturday from 9:30am to 12:30pm and 2 to 5pm and Sunday from 2 to 6pm. Admission is 11F ($2).

A large **Théâtre Romain,** 7 rue du Cirque (☎ 04-74-85-39-23), has been excavated east of town at the foot of Mont Pipet. Once theatrical spectacles were staged here for an audience of thousands. You can visit from April 1 to August 31, daily from 9:30am to 1pm and 2 to 6pm; rest of the year, Tuesday through Saturday from 9:30am to 12:30pm and 2 to 5pm and Sunday from 1:30 to 5:30pm. Admission is 11F ($2).

If you have time to make a side trip about an hour south, in the tiny village of **Hauteville** you'll find one of the world's strangest pieces of architecture, the **Palais du Facteur Cheval** (Palace of the Mailman Cheval; ☎ 04-75-68-81-19). It represents the lifelong avocation of a French postman, Ferdinand Cheval; built of stone and concrete and elaborately decorated, often with clamshells, it's a highly unusual, highly eccentric palace of fantasy in a high-walled garden. During his lifetime, M. Cheval was ridiculed by his neighbors as a crackpot, but his palace has since been declared a national monument and a tribute to the aesthetic value, or mania, of the French individual. The work was finished in 1912, when Cheval was 76; he died in 1925. The north end of the facade is in massive rococo style. The turreted tower is 35 feet tall, and the entire building is 85 feet long. The elaborate sculptural decorations include animals such as leopards and artifacts such as Roman vases. Tours cost 26F ($4.70) per person; admission is 18F ($3.25) for adults, 17F ($3.05) for children 6 to 16, and 13F ($2.35) for children 3 to 6. The palace is open daily, mid-April to mid-September from 9am to 7pm, February to mid-April and mid-September to November from 9:30 to 5:30pm, and in December and January from 10am to 4:30pm; closed Christmas and New Year's Days.

WHERE TO STAY

✪ **Hostellerie Beau-Rivage.** 2 rue de Beau-Rivage, 69420 Condrieu. ☎ **04-74-56-82-82.** Fax 04-74-59-59-36. 25 units. MINIBAR TV TEL. 525–850F ($94.50–$153) double. AE, DC, MC, V. From Vienne, cross the Rhône on N86, then head south 7½ miles; pass through Condrieu and, on the southern outskirts, look for signs on the left.

A Relais du Silence, this place originated around 1900 as a simple inn that offered food and wine to fishers who traveled from Lyon to the well-stocked waters of this section of the Rhône. Since then, it has evolved into a stylish, nostalgic enclave of old-fashioned charm. The rooms are well furnished and, in some cases, discreetly grand and larger than you might expect.

Dining: The fast-flowing Rhône passes by the dining terrace. The cuisine is exceptional and traditional. One fixed-price menu (available only at lunch) is 180F ($32.40); the others (available anytime) range from 295F to 430F ($53.10 to $77.40). Try quenelles (fish balls) of pike; stuffed snails with new potatoes; and an intensely cultivated suprême of pigeon served on a platter with a confit of pigeon, roasted foie gras, and turnips. Also appealing are smoked salmon blinis and mousseline of lobster with chervil. The Côtes du Rhône wines complement the food well.

WHERE TO DINE

✪ **La Pyramide Fernand-Point.** 14 bd. Fernand-Point, 38200 Vienne. ☎ **04-74-53-01-96.** Fax 04-74-85-69-73. E-mail: pyramide.f.point@wanadoo.fr. Reservations required. Main courses 240–265F ($43.20–$47.70); fixed-price menus 280–630F ($50.40–$113.40). AE, DC, MC, V. Fri–Tues 12:30–2:30pm, Thurs–Tues 7–9:30pm. Closed Feb. FRENCH.

This is the area's premier place to stay and/or dine, and for many it's their preferred stopover between Paris and the Riviera. The restaurant perpetuates the memory of a superb chef, Fernand Point; many of his secrets have been preserved, especially his sauces, touted as the best in the country. Specialties are filet of lamb from the Pyrénées seasoned with fresh herbs, scallops flavored with Szechuan peppers with a ragoût of salsify and ginger-flavored endives, and filet of Charolais beef (the finest in the area). Bresse chicken studded with truffles follows Point's original recipe. The chef can appeal to the tastes of both traditionalists and adventurers.

The hotel offers 21 air-conditioned rooms and four suites, all modern and decorated with oak. Doubles are 850F to 970 F ($153 to $174.60); suites, 1,350 F ($243).

Le Bec Fin. 7 place St-Maurice. ☎ **04-74-85-76-72.** Reservations required. Main courses 80–120F ($14.40–$21.60); fixed-price menus 125–325F ($22.50–$58.50). AE, V. Tues–Sun noon–2pm, Tues–Sat 7–9:30pm. FRENCH.

The best-prepared and most generously served fixed-price meals in town are available in this rustic setting near the cathedral. A la carte specialties are somewhat more sophisticated, including salads laced with all the region's delicacies (foie gras, smoked duckling, and the like), breast of duckling with a truffled sauce, filet of turbot, and monkfish with saffron.

6 The Beaujolais Country

The vineyards of beaujolais start about 25 miles north of Lyon. This wine-producing region is small—only 40 miles long and less than 10 miles wide—yet it's one of the most famous areas in the nation and has become increasingly known throughout the world because of the beaujolais craze that began in Paris some 30 years ago. The United States is now one of the three big world markets for beaujolais. In an average year, this region produces some 30 million gallons of wine, more than 190 million bottles.

Most people don't come to the beaujolais country to visit specific sites but rather to drink the wine. There are around 180 châteaux scattered throughout this part of France, and at many of them, you can sample and/or buy bottles of the beaujolais.

This region is a colorful and prosperous rural part of France, with vineyards on sunlit hillsides, pleasant golden cottages where the vine growers live, and historic houses and castles. It has been called the Land of the Golden Stones. Don't expect many architectural monuments, though.

Unlike Alsace with its Route du Vin, the beaujolais country doesn't have a clearly defined route. You can branch off in many directions, stopping at whatever point or wine cellar intrigues you. For that reason we haven't arranged the towns in this section in any particular order. Don't be worried about losing your way after meandering off the A6 superhighway. This is one of the easiest parts of eastern France to negotiate; the road signs are very clear. If you're in doubt at any time, simply follow the signs to the region's capital and commercial center, Villefranche-sur-Saône.

However, if you're pressed for time, you can tie the highlights together in a one-way drive, beginning at the region's northern terminus, **Juliénas,** which you can access from A6 running between Mâcon and Lyon. (If you're heading south to north, follow the drive in reverse order, beginning in Villefranche, accessible via its own exit from A6.)

Start in Juliénas, marked as its own exit off A6. From Juliénas, take D266 and D68 to **Villié-Morgon.** From here, follow D68 and D37 to **Belleville-sur-Saône.** From Belleville, take D19 and D62 to **Salles-en-Beaujolais** (some maps might abbreviate the name to Salles). From Salles, take D19 to **St-Julien-sous-Montmelas** (some maps abbreviate this name to St-Julien). From there, take the meandering D20 and D504, which make sharp bends toward the west en route to **Villefranche.**

VILLEFRANCHE-SUR-SAONE—CAPITAL OF BEAUJOLAIS

In Villefranche-sur-Saône we advise you to go to the **Office du Tourisme,** 290 rue de Thizy, not far from the marketplace (☎ **04-74-68-05-18**), open Monday through Saturday from 9am to noon and 1:30 to 6:30pm. Here you can pick up a booklet on the beaujolais country containing a regional map and many itineraries; it also lists some 30 villages and the wine-tasting cellars open to the public.

ST-JULIEN-SOUS-MONTMELAS

This charming village is 6½ miles northwest of Villefranche. It was the home of Claude Bernard, the father of physiology, who was born here in 1813. The small stone house in which he lived—now the **Musée Claude-Bernard** (☎ **04-74-67-51-44**)—contains mementos of the great scholar, like instruments and books that belonged to him. The museum is open Wednesday through Sunday from 10am to noon and 2 to 6pm. Admission is 15F ($2.70) for adults and 8F ($1.45) for children. Closed in March.

SALLES-EN-BEAUJOLAIS

If you want specific sites to visit in the area, we suggest the **Eglise de Salles Arbuis-sonnas** (☎ **04-74-67-51-50**). Begun in A.D. 1090 and completed at last in the 1700s, this religious hideaway is mostly Romanesque, with an occasional Gothic overlay, especially in its doorways. Notice the Salle Capitulaire, where the ornate cappings of columns from throughout its long history are proudly displayed. The church is open daily, May to September from 9am to 7pm and October to April from 9am to 6pm. Admission is free; guided tours in French cost 10F ($1.80).

JULIENAS

This village produces a full-bodied, robust wine. People here go to the **Cellier dans l'Ancien Eglise** (☎ **04-74-04-41-43**), the old church cellar, to sip the wine. A statue of Bacchus with some scantily clad and tipsy girlfriends looks on from what used to be the altar. It's open daily from 10am to noon and 2:30 to 6:30pm (closed Tuesdays from October to June 1). Admission is 5F (90¢).

BAGNOLS-EN-BEAUJOLAIS

To reach Bagnols from Lyon, head north for 15 miles (about a half-hour drive). Take A6 to the Limonest exit, then follow the signs for Limonest/Le Bourg and turn left at the crossroads marked VILLEFRANCHE N6. Turn left once more onto D485 toward Lozanne/Le Bois d'Oingt. Go for 9 miles and take a right onto D38 heading for Bagnols.

WHERE TO STAY & DINE

✪ **Château de Bagnols-en-Beaujolais.** 69620 Bagnols. ☎ **04-74-71-40-00.** Fax 04-74-71-40-49. www.bagnols.com. 20 units. TV TEL. 2,600–3,500F ($468–$630) double; from 4,000F ($720) suite. AE, DC, V. Closed Jan 2–May 2.

This is lordly living on a grand, super-expensive scale. France's premier château/hotel, this Renaissance ruin has been restored by 400 artisans and craftspeople for Helen Hamlyn and her husband, the publisher/philanthropist Paul Hamlyn, who spent between $6 and $12 million on the project. The mansion is filled with antiques, wall paintings, and art, much from the 17th century. The rooms and suites are sumptuous; one suite is named for Mme de Sévigné, who spent a restless night here in 1673. This place is not for the young and restless—there's no gym or tennis courts, for example. Elegant continental fare is served in the Guards Room, the main dining hall.

VILLIE-MORGON

Heading south, you reach this village, which, along with the carefully delineated region around it, contains around 250 wine producers. Their product, at its best, is usually judged one of the greatest beaujolais wines in France.

In the basement of the Hôtel de Ville (town hall), place de l'Hôtel-de-Ville, is the **Caveau de Morgon** (☎ **04-74-04-20-99**), which assembles and "marries" a selection of the Villié-Morgon region's best wines into a well-respected brand name (Caveau de Morgon) whose marketing savvy benefits wine growers and consumers alike. (Whatever you do, don't use the word "blend" to describe this company's product, as it's usually received with something akin to horror.) The cellar is open for tours and sales of the product daily from 9am to noon and 2 to 7pm (closed January 1 to 15). Admission is free. The town hall that contains it, incidentally, was built during the late 1600s, destroyed during the Revolution, and reconstructed and modified several times since.

BELLEVILLE-SUR-SAONE

If you'd like another dining choice in the beaujolais country, we suggest driving south from Villié-Morgon to the junction with D37. Then head due east to Belleville-sur-Saône.

WHERE TO DINE

Le Rhône au Rhin. 10 av. du Port. ☎ **04-74-66-16-23.** Reservations required. Main courses 45–110F ($8.10–$19.80); fixed-price menus 98–260F ($17.65–$46.80). AE, MC, V. Tues–Sun noon–2pm, Tues–Sat 7–9:30pm. FRENCH.

Chef Michel Debize operates this restaurant offering impressive service and cuisine. A special feature is the wide selection of fixed-price menus, beginning inexpensively and climbing the scale for those who want to dine more elaborately. Try appetizer specialties like raw salmon terrine and foie gras in puff pastry with caramelized apples. Favored main courses are perfectly prepared frogs' legs and chicken fermier with morel-cream sauce. This restaurant doesn't seem to attract the press and guidebook acclaim it once did, but we think its cuisine remains as fine as ever.

7 Valence

417 miles SE of Paris, 62 miles S of Lyon

Valence stands on the left bank of the Rhône between Lyon and Avignon. A former Roman colony, it later became the capital of the Duchy of Valentinois, set up by Louis XII in 1493 for Cesare Borgia.

Today, Valence is the market town and the major distribution point for the mammoth fruit and vegetable market of the Rhône Valley. Perhaps it's altogether fitting that François Rabelais, who wrote of gargantuan appetites in his lusty prose, spent time here as a student.

If you'd like to follow in the footsteps of Napoléon Bonaparte, you can climb the ruined château atop the white stone **Mont Crussol.** The ruins date from the 12th century. A view of this castle is possible from the esplanade of the Champ de Mars. Valence is still the home of the Arsenal, one of France's oldest gunpowder factories.

The most interesting sight here is the **Cathédrale St-Apollinaire,** consecrated by Urban II in 1095, though it's been much restored since. Built in the Auvergnat-Romanesque style, the cathedral is on place des Clercs in the center of town. The choir contains the tomb of Pope Pius VI, who died here a prisoner at the end of the 18th century. It's open daily from 8am to 7pm.

Adjoining the cathedral is the **Musée Municipal,** 4 place des Ormeaux (☎ 04-75-79-20-80), noted for its nearly 100 red-chalk drawings by Hubert Robert done in the 18th century. It also has a number of Greco-Roman artifacts. It's open daily from 2 to 6pm. Admission is 15 F ($2.70), free for children 15 and under.

On the north side of the square, on Grand-Rue, you'll pass **Maison des Têtes,** built in 1532 with sculpted heads of Homer, Hippocrates, Aristotle, and other Greeks.

There are fast and easy rail and highway connections from Lyon, Grenoble, and Marseille. For **train** information and schedules, call ☎ 08-36-35-35-39. If you're **driving** to Valence from Lyon, take A7 south. From Grenoble, follow E711 to outside the town of Voreppe, heading southwest along E713, merging to W532 into Valence. From Marseilles, follow A7 north.

The **Office de Tourisme** is at parvis de la Gare (☎ 04-75-44-90-40).

WHERE TO STAY & DINE

✪ **Restaurant Pic.** 285 av. Victor-Hugo. ☎ **04-75-44-15-32.** Fax 04-75-40-96-03. www.pic.w3line.fr. E-mail: pic@relaischateaux.fr. Reservations required. Main courses 200–320F ($36–$57.60); fixed-price menus 290–660F ($52.20–$118.80). AE, DC, MC, V. Mon–Tues and Thurs–Sat noon–2:30pm and 8–9:30pm, Sun noon–2:30pm. Closed Aug. FRENCH.

This is the least known of France's great three-star restaurants. Both the cooking and the wine list are exceptional, the latter featuring regional selections like Hermitage, St-Péray, and Côtes du Rhône. Alain Pic took over as chef when his renowned father, Jacques, died in 1992, and he performs admirably. This charming villa has a flower-garden courtyard and a dining room with big tables and ample chairs. Appetizers include ballotine of squab, pâté de foie gras, and breast of small game bird. For a main course we recommend the sea bass filet in velvety velouté, crowned by caviar; chicken cooked in a pig's bladder; or lamb stew with basil, sweetbreads, and kidneys. In season, one of the chef's masterpieces is tender noisettes of venison in a wine-dark sauce as light as chiffon. The desserts are a rapturous experience, from the grapefruit sorbet to the cold orange soufflé.

Pic also rents 13 well-furnished doubles, costing 800F to 1,100F ($144 to $198).

8 The Ardèche

The Ardèche region began to draw significant numbers of foreign visitors only about a decade ago. Until then it was almost unknown beyond the French borders, bypassed in favor of regions with more and better monuments and museums. Its wines aren't the finest in France and its cuisine is the kind of fortifying country fare that nourishes the body but doesn't win awards. Though many districts of France contain buildings that have inspired architects around the world, the Ardèche is limited to stone-sided structures of rustic but not grandiloquent charm. But as urbanites and visitors began seeking the pleasures of escapes to the wilderness or adventures like kayaking down sublimely beautiful cliff-edged canyons, the Ardèche finally came of age.

The Ardèche occupies the eastern flank of the Massif Central (see chapter 15), a landscape of jagged, much-eroded granite and limestone highlands that ramble down to the western bank of the Rhône. It isn't the highest or most dramatic region—that honor goes to the Alps, whose peaks rise as much as three times higher. Although it defines itself as Le Midi (its southern border lies less than 25 and 31 miles from Avignon and Nîmes, respectively), its culture and landscape are more firmly rooted in the rugged uplands of France's central highlands.

Through its territory flow the streams and rivers that drain the snow and rain of the Massif Central. They include rivers with names like Ligne, Fontolière, Lignon, Tanargue, and, most important, Ardèche. They flow beside, around, and through rocky ravines, ancient lava flows, feudal ruins, and stone-sided villages perched in high-altitude sites originally chosen for their medieval ease of defense.

The most famous and oft-visited section of the Ardèche is its southern extremity, with granite-sided ravines 1,000 feet deep, gouged by millions of springtime floodings of the Ardèche River—no wonder it's called the Grand Canyon of France. This area draws thousands of tourists who, often with their children, take driving tours along the highways flanking the ravines.

We recommend that you stop in the southern Ardèche to admire the gorges only briefly, say, for a morning's drive. It's better to spend the night in the less touristy northern reaches of the Ardèche than to stay amid the honky-tonk commercialism that sometimes pervades the southern reaches.

In the northern Ardèche, in the 28 miles of hills and valleys separating the hamlets of Vals-les-Bains and Lamastre, is a soft and civilized wilderness, with landscapes that have been devoted to grape growing, sheep herding, and (more recently) hill trekking.

Vallon-Pont-d'Arc, the gateway to the gorges, was defined by one writer as a Gallic version "of honky-tonk Gatlinburg, Tennessee." (We suggest you stay in Vals-les-Bains or Lamastre instead.)

If you want to go kayaking in the gorges (from early April to late November, when the waters are green and sluggish and safer than during the floods of winter and spring), you'll find at least three dozen rental agencies for everything from plastic kayaks to horses in Vallon-Pont-d'Arc. One of the best outfitters is **Adventure Canoë,** place du Marché (B.P. 27), 07150 Vallon-Pont-d'Arc (☎ **04-75-37-18-14**), which arranges rentals of canoes and kayaks for rides through the gorges. A 3-hour *mini-descente* costs 200F ($36) for two participants riding a 4-mile route from Vallon-Pont-d'Arc to the downstream hamlet of Chames, or 115F ($20.70) for a kayak for one. A full-day *grande descente* for two riding a 19-mile downstream route from Vallon-Pont-d'Arc to St-Martin d'Ardèche costs 320F ($57.60) for two or 160F ($28.80) for one. A 2-day trip is 480F ($86.40) for two or 235F ($42.30) for one. Prices include transport by minivan back to Vallon-Pont-d'Arc at the end of the ride. Lunch is not

The Grand Canyon of France

Measuring no more than 119 miles in length, the Ardèche isn't the longest, mightiest, or most influential river in France, but it flows faster, with more geological aftereffects, than any other. Originating on the eastern edge of the Massif Central at about 5,000 feet above sea level, the Ardèche descends faster, over a shorter distance, than any of its mightier competitors. (In some sections it falls as much as 3 feet for every half mile of its length, which by the standards of such relatively placid rivers as the Seine and the Loire is positively vertiginous.) These changes in altitude, combined with cycles of heavy rainfall and drought, result in what's the most temperamental and changeable waterway in France.

The resulting ebbs and flows have created the Grand Canyon of France. Littered with alluvial deposits, strewn in ravines whose depth sometimes exceeds 950 feet, the river's lower extremity (its final 36 miles, before the waters dump into the Rhône) is one of the country's most unusual geological areas. A panoramic road (D290) runs along a rim of these canyons, providing views over an arid landscape of grasses, toughened trees, drought-resistant shrubs, and some of the most distinctively eroded deposits of granite, limestone, and basalt in Europe.

If you drive along this route, expect the type of cheap motels, family-fun emporiums, and fast-food joints you'd see near Yellowstone Park in the United States. There's no denying, however, the basic beauty of the site, which you can admire from a series of belvederes along the highway. The highway runs in a meandering line that's approximately parallel to the bluffs and corniches of the river's northwestern edge. Many of the belvederes have brown-and-white signs that encourage motorists to stop and walk for a few minutes along some of the well-marked footpaths.

The route, which you can traverse in a few hours even if you stop frequently for sightseeing, stretches southeast to northwest between the towns of Vallon-Pont-d'Arc and Pont St-Esprit. Since the meandering corniche roads are a challenge to drive, be extra-careful. Be particularly aware of other vehicles, which may weave frighteningly out of their lanes as the drivers and passengers crane their necks to admire the scenery and furiously snap photos.

included, and participants must buy and transport their own picnics. The makings for this are available at dozens of bakeries and delicatessens near each point of origin.

Despite the appeal of kayaking, most travelers stick with driving along the upper summits of the gorges.

VALS-LES-BAINS

27 miles W of Montélimar, 86 miles SW of Lyon

In a depression of the valley of the Volane River, Vals-les-Bains is surrounded by about 150 freshwater springs whose existence was discovered relatively recently—around 1600. Scientists have never really understood why each spring contains a different percentage of minerals: Most contain bicarbonate of soda, others are almost tasteless, and one—*La Source Dominique*—has such a high percentage of iron and arsenic that it's poisonous. Waters from Dominique are piped away from the town center; others are funneled into a Station Thérmale adjacent to the town's casino.

From a position in the park outside the Station Thérmale, a *source intermittante* erupts, Old Faithful–style, to a height of around 25 feet at intervals of about 6 hours. Small crowds gather for eruptions at 5:30 and 11:30am and 5:30 and 11:30pm.

A few steps away, the belle époque casino, **Parc Thermal** (☎ **04-75-37-40-29**), is open daily from noon to 3am; entrance is free. The only casino between Lyon and Aigues-Mortes, it's mobbed on weekends by local farmers and their families playing either roulette or the slot machines, the only options offered. It's not at all glamorous; this isn't Monte Carlo. There's a bistro-style theme restaurant, Le Hollywood, on the premises; it's open nightly from 7pm to midnight. There's also a 600-seat theater for occasional plays or concerts, plus a movie theater.

Other than the surrounding scenery, the town's most unusual site is about 14 miles south, beside the highway to Privas. A ruined feudal château once stood here; it was richly embellished and enlarged in the 1700s and served as the home of the comtes du Valentinois. Ironically, it escaped the ravages of the Revolution only to fall into ruin in 1820, when its bankrupt owners sold its accessories and architectural ornaments to pay their debts. Today only the 16th-century entrance gate remains relatively un-harmed. The views over the confluence of two ravines and the valley below are worth the detour.

WHERE TO STAY

Grand Hôtel des Bains. 3 Montée de l'Hôtel-des-Bains, 07600 Vals-les-Bains. ☎ **04-75-37-42-13.** Fax 04-75-37-67-02. 63 units. TV TEL. 350–495F ($63–$89.10) double; 630F ($113.40) suite. AE, DC, MC, V. Closed Dec–Mar.

This is the largest and best hotel in town, with a central wing built in 1860 in antici-pation of a visit from Empress Eugénie. (Alas, Eugénie, finding she was comfortable in the nearby resort of Vichy, canceled her visit.) Despite the snub, the hotel added two additional wings in 1870 and has survived ever since, partly because of a cordial staff and well-maintained, conservatively furnished rooms. The restaurant charges 137F to 333F ($24.65 to $59.95) for fixed-price menus, served daily at lunch and dinner.

Hôtel de l'Europe. 86 rue Jean-Jaurès, 07600 Vals-les-Bains. ☎ **04-75-37-43-94.** Fax 04-75-94-66-62. 32 units. TV TEL. 260–350F ($46.80–$63) double. V.

Built to house well-heeled patrons of the adjacent spa in 1805 and enlarged and mod-ernized many times since—most recently in 1995—this hotel retains memories of yesteryear's grandeur. There's no restaurant, but the rooms are large, high-ceilinged, and just dowdy enough to remind you of *la belle France* of another era. The staff is as courtly and well mannered as the old-fashioned setting requires. Though the hotel is open year-round, its restaurant is open only from mid-April to mid-November. The fixed-price menus begin at a bargain 90F ($16.20) and run up to 180F ($32.40).

WHERE TO DINE

Restaurant Mireille. 3 rue Jean-Jaurès. ☎ **04-75-37-49-06.** Reservations recommended. Fixed-price menus 60–170F ($10.80–$30.60). V. Thurs–Tues noon–2pm and 7–9pm. Closed 2 weeks in Apr and 2 weeks in Sept. FRENCH.

Containing only 26 seats, this restaurant occupies the space below vaulted stone ceil-ings that for centuries sheltered a herd of goats. Known for its earthy sense of warmth, the restaurant serves a carefully calibrated cuisine with an ambitious menu. It includes local pigeon roasted in honey sauce, mousse of flap mushrooms with scallops, and filet of turbot with white butter.

LAMASTRE

26 miles N of Vals-les-Bains, 18 miles W of Valence

Near the Ardèche's northern frontier, the charming hamlet of Lamastre is known for its light industry (shoes, camping gear, furniture, and light machine tools). Many connoisseurs of Ardèche architecture view it as the most unaltered and evocative village in the district. Its most important site is its church, in Macheville, in the upper part of the village. Built of pink-toned stone in Romanesque style, it boasts portions dating from the 12th century and is the frequent site of weddings, one of which you might get to view.

Don't expect lots of nightlife or razzle-dazzle here. Most visitors use the town as a base for striking out on nature walks and hikes through the surrounding hills and valleys. A network of brown-and-white signs clearly marks each trail's direction and duration.

WHERE TO STAY & DINE

Château d'Urbilhac. Rte. de Vernoux, 07270 Lamastre. ☎ **04-75-06-42-11.** Fax 04-75-06-52-75. 12 units. TEL. 1,250F ($225) double. Rates include half board. AE, DC, V. Closed Sept 30–Apr 27. From the center of Lamastre, follow the signs to the château, about 1 mile south.

This is the only château (and only château-hotel) in the Ardèche. Built in the 1500s, it was renovated in the 19th century and is sheathed in pink-toned stucco. Rated three stars, it boasts a large outdoor pool and tennis court. Its owner, Mme Marcelle Xampero, prepares evening meals and maintains the 115 acres around the building. The restaurant is open only to hotel guests.

Hôtel du Midi. Place Seignobos, 07270 Lamastre. ☎ **04-75-06-41-50.** Fax 04-75-06-49-75. 12 units. TV TEL. 410–490F ($73.80–$88.20) double. AE, DC, DISC, MC, V. Closed Jan–Feb.

Built in 1925, with slightly faded rooms that retain a vague Art Deco allure, this place has been used as an overnight stop for both Charles de Gaulle and Elizabeth Bowes-Lyon, the Queen Mother of England.

Dining: Maintained by members of the Perrier family, this place is well known for its restaurant, which serves fixed-price menus for 185F to 435F ($33.30 to $78.30). Lunch and dinner are offered daily except Sunday night and all day Monday. The food is among the region's best, including many updated takes on traditional regional specialties.

The Massif Central 15

In your race south to Biarritz or through the Rhône Valley to the Riviera, you'll pass through the Massif Central, the rugged agricultural heartland of France. Here you'll find ancient cities, lovely valleys, and a wonderful provincial cuisine. With its rolling farmland, isolated countryside, and châteaux and manor houses (in many of which you can stay and dine), this is one of the most unspoiled parts of France—your chance to see a life all too rapidly fading.

From the spa at Vichy to the volcanic puys of the Auvergne, there's much of interest here and much to learn about the art of good living. We'll begin in George Sand country in the old province of Berry, then proceed to the Auvergne and west to Limousin.

REGIONAL CUISINE Fans of this region's cuisine often praise it for its simple honesty and adherence to tradition; its critics claim that it lacks finesse and creativity. Everyone, however, agrees that this is a rural, family-inspired cuisine, based on generous quantities of fresh ingredients and few pretensions.

Characteristic dishes include soup (*une potée*) made with cabbage and about a dozen other ingredients (usually including both fresh and salted pork) and stuffed sheep's foot cooked inside a sheep's stomach. The region's cheeses include enormous wheels known as Cantal, bleu d'Auvergne, St-Nectaire, and a goats'-milk cheese called *le cabecou,* which appears on cheese trays in grand restaurants throughout France. The Massif Central is famous for its desserts, including cherry tarts (sometimes with the cherry pits still in place) and many exceptional pastries.

The climate and soil aren't conducive to grape growing, so most regional wines just pass as straightforward table wine. The best local spirits are several types of distilled alcohol traditionally served after meals. These are usually distilled from the fermented essence of flowers and herbs that include strawberries, raspberries, blossoms from the linden tree, myrtle, and a mountain flower called *gentiane.*

1 Bourges

148 miles S of Paris, 43 miles NW of Nevers, 95 miles NW of Vichy, 175 miles NW of Lyon

Once the capital of Aquitaine, Bourges lies in the heart of France; you can easily tie in a visit here from Orléans at the eastern end of the Loire Valley. The commercial/industrial center of Berry, this regional capital is still off the beaten path for most tourists, even though it boasts a rich medieval past still in evidence today. Its history goes back far beyond the Middle Ages: In 52 B.C. Caesar called it the finest city in Gaul. Today Bourges remains a rather sleepy provincial town, awakened only by the life surrounding the Institut Universitaire de Technologie.

ESSENTIALS

GETTING THERE   There are good road and rail connections from Tours and other regional cities. For example, 4 **trains** arrive daily from Paris, taking 2½ hours; sometimes a transfer is required at nearby Vierzon. Eight trains a day arrive from Tours, taking 1½ hours. For train information and schedules, call ☎ **08-36-35-35-39.**

VISITOR INFORMATION   The **Office de Tourisme** is at 21 rue Victor-Hugo (☎ **02-48-24-75-33**).

SPECIAL EVENTS   The energy level really picks up between April and August thanks to several colorful music festivals. The **Festival Printemps de Bourges** jump-starts the season in April with its dozens of concerts ranging from traditional French to international rock. Most events cost between 50F and 200F ($9 and $36), though any number of seemingly spontaneous performances always pop up along the sidewalks for everyone to enjoy at no charge. For tickets and more information, contact the **Association Printemps de Bourges,** 22 rue Henri-Sellier (☎ **02-48-24-30-50**). At the beginning of June, a younger, more free-form and high-impact music scene explodes during the **Festival International des Groupes de Musique Experimentale de Bourges,** during which groups such as U2 have appeared. For information, call ☎ **02-48-20-41-87.** Then, every year, **Un Eté à Bourges** kicks off on Bastille Day, July 14, and runs through the end of the month, during which the streets are once again filled with musical performers and actors. More structured performances also take place, with tickets ranging from 50F to 200F ($9 to $36). The Office de Tourisme (see above) has complete details on all festivals.

SEEING THE SIGHTS

✪ **Cathédrale St-Etienne.** Place Etienne-Dolet. ☎ **02-48-65-49-44.** Admission: cathedral, free; tower and crypt, 32F ($5.75) adults, 21F ($3.80) children. Combination ticket to both cathedral and Palais Jacques-Coeur 60F ($10.80) for everyone. Cathedral, Apr–Sept daily 8:30am–9pm; Oct–March daily 8:30am–6pm. Crypt cannot be visited Sun 8am–1pm during mass.

On the summit of a hill dominating the town, this is one of the largest and most beautiful Gothic cathedrals in France. Its construction began at the end of the 12th century and wasn't completed until a century and a half later; subsequent additions have been made. Flanked by asymmetrical towers, it has five magnificent doorways, including one depicting episodes in the life of St. Stephen. The cathedral has a high vaulted roof and five aisles and is remarkably long (407 feet deep); it's distinguished for its stained-glass windows, best viewed with binoculars. In rich blues and deep ruby reds, many of these windows were made between 1215 and 1225. One particularly impressive scene, *A Meal in the House of Simon,* is vividly colored, showing Jesus lecturing before Simon on the forgiveness of sins as Mary Magdalene repents at his feet.

To climb the north tower for a view of the cathedral and Bourges, you must buy a ticket from the custodian. The same ticket allows you to explore the church's 12th-century crypt, the largest in France. In the crypt rests the tomb (built between 1422 and 1438) of Jean de Berry, who ruled this duchy in the 14th century. Fanatically

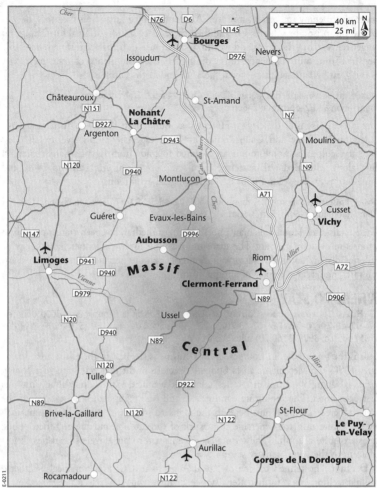

dedicated to art, he directed a "small army" of artisans, painters, and sculptors. The recumbent figure is the only part of the original tomb that has survived.

After your visit, you may want to wander through the **Jardins de l'Archevêché,** the archbishop's gardens, credited to Le Nôtre. From these gardens you'll have a good view of the eastern side of the cathedral.

Palais Jacques-Coeur. Rue Jacques-Coeur. ☎ **02-48-24-06-87.** Admission 32F ($5.75) adults, 21F ($3.80) ages 18–24 and over 60, free for children 17 and under. Combination ticket to cathedral and Palais Jacques-Coeur 60F ($10.80) for everyone. The palace can be seen only on a 60-minute guided tour in French (English-speakers receive a printed English-language text of the commentary). Tours: July–Aug daily 9, 10, and 11am and 2, 3, 4, 5, and 6pm; Apr–late June and Sept–Oct daily 9, 10, and 11am and 2, 3, 4, and 5pm; Nov–Mar daily 9, 10, and 11am and 2, 3, and 4pm.

This is one of the country's greatest secular Gothic structures. Take a guided tour through the four buildings around a central court, constructed around 1450 by the finance minister/banker Jacques Coeur, who had amassed a fortune. Monsieur Coeur never got to enjoy the palace, however. After a trial by a jury of his creditors, he was tossed into prison by Charles VII and died there in 1456. His original furnishings no longer remain, but the decor and wealth of detail inside the palace form a remarkable view of 15th-century opulence. In the dining hall is a monumental chimneypiece, and in the great hall are sculptures from the 15th and 16th centuries.

Musée du Berry. 4 rue des Arènes. ☎ **02-48-70-41-92.** Free admission. Mon and Wed–Sat 10am–noon and 2–6pm, Sun 2–6pm.

The museum is inside the elegant Hôtel Cujas, built about 1515. On display is a large collection of Celtic and Gallo-Roman artifacts; especially impressive are the 280 funerary sculptures. Some rooms are devoted to finds from Egyptian archaeological digs, along with medieval masterpieces of sculpture dating from around 1400, and some rooms on the second floor have ethnological exhibitions.

Hôtel Lallemant. 6 rue Bourbonnoux. ☎ **02-48-57-81-17.** Free admission. Tues–Sat 10am–noon and 2–6pm, Sun 2–6pm.

The Renaissance Hôtel Lallemant, north of the cathedral, has been transformed into a museum of decorative art. The mansion was built for a textile merchant; today its galleries display a colorful history of Bourges. Exhibits include china, objets d'art, ceramics, and a large display of antique furniture.

WHERE TO STAY

✪ **Hôtel Bourbon et Restaurant St-Ambroix.** Bd. de la République, 18000 Bourges. ☎ **02-48-70-70-00.** Fax 02-48-70-21-22. 59 units. A/C TV TEL. 510–750F ($91.80–$135) double; 890F ($160.20) suite. AE, DC, V.

This is the finest hotel in Bourges, and its cuisine is the best in the entire area. In the early 1990s the Mercure chain (a budget-conscious outfit that isn't otherwise known for its salvaging of historic properties) converted a ruined 17th-century abbey into this first-class hotel. The rooms are comfortable and well equipped, but—except for the half-timbered sloping rooms beneath the mansard roof on the third floor—short on style. Despite this, the venerable stonework of the exterior and the dignified public areas are quite beautiful. The setting is convenient for train travelers, as it lies almost adjacent to the town's railway station.

Dining: The refined cuisine of Pascal Auger is a draw even for locals. Under a vaulted ceiling of a former Renaissance chapel, you can select delectable main courses—perhaps baked saddle of lamb (pink and juicy) or *escalope de foie gras de canard* (duckling). The *noix de ris de veau braisée* (sweetbreads) is among the finest you're likely to sample anywhere. The menu changes four times a year but invariably offers a *crottin de chavignol* made from local goat cheese and a local almond-flavored bonbon, *des forestines.*

Le Christina. 5 rue de la Halle, 18000 Bourges. ☎ **02-48-70-56-50.** Fax 02-48-70-58-13. 71 units. TV TEL. 240–300F ($43.20–$54) double. AE, DC, MC, V. Parking 35F ($6.30).

This is a simple inn, but the rooms are comfortable and, in part, furnished with some stylish pieces. It's within an easy walk of the Palais Jacques-Coeur and the cathedral. Breakfast is the only meal served.

WHERE TO DINE

Jacques-Coeur. 3 place Jacques-Coeur. ☎ **02-48-70-12-72.** Reservations required. Main courses 65–130F ($11.70–$23.40); fixed-price menus 145–180F ($26.10–$32.40). AE, DC, MC, V. Sun–Fri noon–2:15pm, Mon–Fri 7:15–9:15pm. Closed July 25–Aug 22 and Dec 25–Jan 2. FRENCH.

François Bernard serves tasty traditional bourgeois cuisine amid a medieval Gothic decor, though the food at Bourbon et Restaurant St-Ambroix (see above) is better. Specialties here include veal kidneys berrichonne, frogs' legs sautéed with herbs, scallops *à la façon* (with a concasse of tomatoes, snail-flavored butter, and beignets of onion), and chicken *en barbouille* (with a sauce made of wine and blood). The desserts are all homemade and tempting, and service is politely efficient. The featured wines from a balanced list include Quincy and Menetou-Salon, two excellent but not-very-well-known vintages from the region. And while the competition for the dining franc in this town has heated up considerably in recent years, this place continues rather smugly doing what it's always done: serving fresh, classical cuisine. Of the two dining rooms, the one on the upper floor is more interesting, with exposed beams and plaster impressions of scallop shells on its circa 1947 ceiling.

BOURGES AFTER DARK

In general, most of the best clubs are in Bourges's old town. For the crème de la crème of your good old-fashioned drinking establishments, try **Le Pub Birdland,** 4 av. Jean-Jaurès (☎ **02-48-70-66-77**), with its wood interior, young crowd of heavy-duty beer drinkers, and jazz and rock. **Beau Bar,** rue des Beaux-Arts (☎ **02-48-24-40-49**), pulls in a very bohemian crowd—artists, poets, songwriters, and the like—whereas **La Comédie,** 10 place Mirepied (☎ **02-48-65-95-85**), has no problem packing its below-street-level dance floor with young hot bodies. The cover ranges from 50F to 70F ($9 to $12.60)—and no sneakers allowed.

For something a little different, head over to **La Soupe aux Choux,** place Gordaine (☎ **02-48-65-43-66**), where you can take in an evening of cafe-théâtre. Shows can be anything from musical performances to stand-up comics, and the ticket price runs around 70F ($12.60).

2 Nohant/La Châtre

180 miles S of Paris, 19 miles S of Châteauroux

George Sand was the pen name of Amandine Lucile Aurore Dupin, baronne Dudevant, the French novelist born in 1804. Her memory is forever connected to this little Berry hamlet near the Indre Valley.

In her early life she wrote bucolic tales of peasants, but she also penned romantic novels in which she maintained that women were entitled to as much freedom as men. Among her 80 novels, some of the best known were *François le champi* and *La Mare au diable*. She was also known for her love affairs, of which her two most notorious were with the poet Alfred de Musset, who journeyed with her to Venice, and with the composer Frédéric Chopin, with whom she traveled to Majorca. By the time of her death in Nohant in 1876, George Sand had become a legend.

ESSENTIALS

GETTING THERE   The nearest **train** station is in Châteauroux, with a connecting bus to Nohant/La Châtre. From Bourges, you can buy a combination train/bus ticket to La Châtre via Châteauroux. Five daily trains make the run to Châteauroux, where you'll then transfer to a bus to complete the 2½-hour trip. For complete train information, call ☎ **08-36-35-35-39.**

If you're **driving,** it's a 1-hour trip from Bourges to La Châtre via D940 south.

VISITOR INFORMATION   The nearest **Office de Tourisme** is on square George-Sand (☎ **02-54-48-22-64**) in La Châtre, open daily year-round.

IN THE FOOTSTEPS OF GEORGE SAND

La Maison de George Sand. 35400 Nohant-Vic. ☎ **02-54-31-06-04.** Visits only with a 45-minute guided tour in French (non-French speakers can follow the lecture with a printed text) for 35F ($6.30) adults, 23F ($4.15) children and students 12–25, free for children 11 and under. Tours depart at regular intervals according to the number of people waiting and/or the day's schedule. Apr–Oct 14 daily 9–11:15am and 2–5:30pm; Oct 16–Mar daily 10am–11:15pm and 2–3:30pm.

It was at the Château de Nohant, known today as La Maison de George Sand, that the famous novelist learned the ways and thoughts of the peasants. During her time here, she entertained some of the intellectual and artistic elite of Europe—Flaubert, Balzac, Delacroix, Liszt, and Gautier. The building, which its guides prefer to define as a large but not imperial-looking *maison bourgeoise,* set in its own 7-acre park, was constructed of stone in 1763 and purchased in 1793 by the family of George Sand. Today it houses the mementos of Sand and her admirers and friends, with ample testimonials to the literary conceits and eccentricities of one of France's most enduringly famous female writers. You can see the boudoir where she wrote *Indiana,* the popular novel published when she was 28. You can also visit her private bedchamber/study. At Nohant, George Sand staged theatricals, dramatizing several of her novels—not very successfully, according to reports. Sometimes today *fêtes romantiques de Nohant* are staged, with an impressive list of musical performers.

WHERE TO STAY & DINE

Auberge de la Petite Fadette. Nohant-Vic, 36400 La Châtre. ☎ **02-54-31-01-48.** Fax 02-54-31-10-19. 10 units. TV TEL. 300–500F ($54–$90) double. AE, MC, V.

This compound of 19th-century ivy-covered buildings abuts the château and is the focal point for one of the smallest villages in the region. Since 1890 the compound has been owned by four generations of the Chapleau family; it was renovated in 1995. A scattering of antiques decorates the interior, and the dining room serves fixed-price menus throughout the year to enthusiasts who come to worship at the shrine of Sand. Fixed-price menus are 80F to 200F ($14.40 to $36).

✪ **Château de la Vallée Bleue.** Rte. de Verneuil, St-Chartier, 36400 La Châtre. ☎ **02-54-31-01-91.** Fax 02-54-31-04-48. 13 units. MINIBAR TV TEL. 375–595F ($67.50–$107.10) double. MC, V.

This château was built in 1840 by Dr. Pestel so that he could be close to his patient, George Sand, and is now a hotel/restaurant owned by Gérard Gasquet. The rooms have been named after the doctor's former guests, including Musset, Delacroix, Flaubert, Chopin, and Liszt. There's also a 10-acre wooded park and a pool.

Dining: The excellent regional specialties are characterized as cuisine actuelle, with an accent on presentation; they include goat cheese and carp with lentils and chicken à la George Sand (with crayfish sauce). For dessert, try a delectable pear baked in pastry. Fixed-price menus cost 140F to 295F ($25.20 to $53.10); nonguests should call for a reservation. The restaurant is open daily from March 1 to November 14; it's closed completely from November 15 to February 28.

3 Vichy

216 miles S of Paris, 33 miles NE of Clermont-Ferrand, 108 miles NW of Lyon

This world-renowned spa on the northern edge of the Auvergne, in the heart of Bourbon country, is noted for its sparkling waters (said to alleviate liver and stomach ailments) and looks in part as it did a century ago when princes and industrial barons filled its rococo casino. (The casino you'll visit today isn't the one that thrived during the spa's 19th-century heyday. That edifice, at 5 rue du Casino, now functions as a convention hall. Within its premises, Diaghilev produced his first ballet and Strauss directed *Salomé*.) From 1861 Napoléon III was a frequent visitor, doing much to add to the spa's fame. During the 1980s, the hotels and baths of Vichy underwent a modernization program to keep up with the times and other baths of France, much to the pleasure of their clients and their ever-changing tastes.

The city's current reputation for health and relaxation has been aided greatly by the Perrier craze that has swept most of the world. The Perrier Company has a contract to bottle Vichy water for sale elsewhere and also runs the city's major attractions. Vichy is a sports-and-recreation center, boasting a casino, theaters, regattas, horse racing, and golf.

A promenade with covered walks, the **Parc des Sources** is the center of Vichy's fashionable life, which is at its peak from May to the end of September.

ESSENTIALS

GETTING THERE   Vichy lies on the heavily traveled Paris–Clermont-Ferrand rail line. Some 20 **trains** per day arrive from Clermont-Ferrand (trip time: 30 minutes); 10 trains per day arrive from Paris (trip time: 3 hours). For train information and schedules, call ☎ **08-36-35-35-39.** If you're **driving** to Vichy from Paris, take A10 south to Orléans, then connect to A71 south. At the Gannat/Vichy exit, follow N209 east to Vichy.

VISITOR INFORMATION   The **Office de Tourisme** is at 19 rue du Parc (☎ **04-70-98-71-94**).

WHERE TO STAY

Aletti Palace Hôtel. 3 place Joseph-Aletti, 03200 Vichy. ☎ **04-70-31-78-77.** Fax 04-70-98-13-82. 133 units. TV TEL. 530–760F ($95.40–$136.80) double; 950–1,100F ($171–$198) suite. AE, DC, MC, V.

This turn-of-the-century hotel, the largest and, in some ways, most stately in town, contains all the grand vistas and elegant accessories of the belle époque. The rooms are high-ceilinged and comfortably furnished, many with balconies overlooking the wooded park and casino; the bathrooms are especially elegant. If you ask, the staff will tell you about the role of this monument (under a different name, the Thermal Palace) during the tenure of the collaborationist Vichy government: It housed the head quarters of Vichy France's Ministry of War. The hotel has a good restaurant and offers a bar and a terrace with a view of Vichy.

Hôtel Chambord. 82–84 rue de Paris, 03200 Vichy. ☎ **04-70-31-22-88.** Fax 04-70-31-54-92. 32 units. TV TEL. 180–260F ($32.40–$46.80) double. AE, DC, MC, V.

This pleasant four-story hotel was built near the train station in the 1930s, and its bedrooms, last renovated in the 1970s, are comfortable though not stylish.

Dining: The Escargot Qui Tette restaurant offers good meals for reasonable prices. It's open Tuesday through Sunday (closed Sunday night); in July and August, it's open daily. Many visitors find the restaurant better than the hotel.

WHERE TO DINE

Brasserie du Casino. 4 rue du Casino. ☎ **04-70-98-23-06.** Reservations recommended at lunch. Main courses 75–110F ($13.50–$19.80); fixed-price menus 85F ($15.30) at lunch (Mon–Tues and Thurs–Sat), 145F ($26.10) at dinner. MC, V. Mon–Tues and Thurs–Sat noon–1:30pm and 7–10pm. Closed Nov. FRENCH.

This has been a thriving brasserie since the 1920s, and it's a preferred stopover for actors and musicians visiting from Paris to perform at the casino. The de Chassat family is charming and especially solicitous to foreigners. Their restaurant, known for its sheathing of copper and Art Deco mahogany, is busy at lunch, but the real charm comes out at night, when a pianist entertains. Specialties are sweetbreads with hazelnuts, paupiette of rabbit with shallots, and veal liver with fondue of onions.

L'Alambic. 8 rue Nicolas-Larbaud. ☎ **04-70-59-12-71.** Reservations required for certain seatings. Main courses 95–180F ($17.10–$32.40); fixed-price menus 160–280F ($28.80–$50.40). MC, V. Wed–Sun noon–2pm, Tues–Sun 7:30–10pm. Closed Feb 15–Mar 6 and Aug 20–Sept 15. FRENCH.

There are only 18 seats at this small restaurant, and they fill up quickly because the cuisine is the best in Vichy. Since 1989 Jean-Jacques Barbot has run a busy place, appealing to what one food critic called "the jaded palates of Vichy." In a pristinely elegant setting, you can enjoy ravioli stuffed with snails as a starter, then perhaps a carpaccio made with duckling and flavored with the juice of truffles. Roast lobster appears with a fondue of endives, or you might prefer cutlets of John Dory with tomato confites. The delectable meat courses feature veal sautéed with orange and basil and filet of beef Rossini. The 280F ($50.40) fixed-price menu is exceptional.

VICHY AFTER DARK

Head straight for the **Casino Elysée Palace,** passage Clémenceau (☎ **04-70-97-93-37**). What was built around 1900 as the Elysée Palace Hotel was converted into the more glamorous of the town's two casinos in the early 1990s. Don't expect imperial grandeur of the sort that would have met Napoléon III several centuries ago, as it's a lot more modern and informal. An area devoted to slot machines, where entrance is free, is open Sunday through Thursday from 11am to 3am, to 4am on Friday and Saturday. A separate area featuring roulette and blackjack is open Monday, Tuesday, and Friday from 8pm to 4am and Saturday and Sunday from 4pm to 4am. Entrance is 70F ($12.60) per person.

A less impressive place to gamble, with only whirring slot machines and roulette (no blackjack), is in an annex of the old-casino-turned-convention-center, **Le Grand Café,** 7 rue du Casino (☎ **04-70-98-32-08**). It shares its space with, as you guessed, a cafe and restaurant. Entrance is free.

4 Clermont-Ferrand

248 miles S of Paris, 110 miles W of Lyon

The ancient capital of the Auvergne, this old double city in south-central France has looked down on a long parade of history. On the small Tiretaine River, it was created in 1731 by a merger of two towns, Clermont and Montferrand. It's surrounded by hills, and in the distance looms one of the great attractions of Auvergne, **Puy-de-Dôme,** a volcanic mountain.

The city today is hardly celebrated for its ancient appearance and medieval streets. Much of the town looks as if it were created in the stark 1960s and 1970s, with unimpressive buildings, car dealerships, and plenty of shopping malls. With a population hovering around 150,000, it's an important rail hub in this region. Clermont-Ferrand, with its smoke-spitting factories, is not a town in which we'd choose to linger, although it has a number of attractions that do bring in visitors.

ESSENTIALS

GETTING THERE   The Clermont-Aulnat **airport** is 4 miles east of town. Rail lines converge on Clermont-Ferrand from all parts of France, including Paris's Gare de Lyon, Marseille, and Toulouse. Trains from small towns in the Auvergne usually require a connection. For **train** information and schedules, call ☎ **08-36-35-35-39.** Clermont-Ferrand is best approached by **car** from two cities. A lengthy drive from Paris begins along A10 south to Orléans, continuing south along A71 to Clermont-Ferrand. From Lyon, take A47 west to St-Etienne, traveling northwest on A89 to Clermont-Ferrand.

VISITOR INFORMATION   The **Office de Tourisme et des Congrès** is on place de la Victoire (☎ **04-73-98-65-00**).

SPECIAL EVENTS   If you're in town at the end of January, check out one of the 40 screenings during the **Festival du Court Métrage.** The works, by up-and-coming directors, are shown in seven theaters, mainly concentrated on boulevard François-Mitterrand. Tickets are 15F ($2.70) per showing, with discounts for packages of 20 showings, and can be purchased through Sauve Qui Peut le Court Métrage, 26 rue des Jacobins (☎ **04-73-91-65-73**).

EXPLORING THE ENVIRONS:
A SPECTACULAR VOLCANIC LANDSCAPE

The region surrounding Clermont-Ferrand is one of France's most geologically distinctive. In 1977 the government designated 946,000 acres of its undulating, dark-stoned terrain as the **Parc Naturel Régional des Volcans d'Auvergne.** The park contains 186 villages as well as farms with herds of cows and goats that produce the Auvergne's cheeses and charcuteries. Scattered among them are at least 90 extinct volcanic cones (*puys*), which rise dramatically and eerily above the pine forests.

The highest and oldest of these is **Puy-de-Dôme** (4,800 feet above sea level), a site used for worship since prehistoric times by the Gauls and the Romans. In 1648 Pascal used this mountaintop for his experiments that proved Torricelli's hypothesis about how altitudes affect atmospheric pressure. And in 1911 one of the most dramatic events in French aviation occurred at Puy-de-Dôme when Eugène Renaux, with a passenger, flew nonstop from Paris in just over 5 hours, to land precariously on its summit and collect a 100,000-franc prize. From the summit you'll have a panoramic view—on a clear day you can see as far east as Mont Blanc. Shuttle buses run daily from the base to the summit in July and August and Sundays in September from 11am to 6pm, costing 21F ($3.80) round-trip. You can drive your car to the summit daily before 11am only for 22F ($3.95).

The different areas of the park contain radically dissimilar features. **Les Puys** (also known as Monts Dômes) are a minichain of 112 extinct volcanoes (some capped with craters, some with rounded peaks) packed densely into an area 3 miles wide by 19 miles long. Each dome is unique: Some were built up by slow extrusions of upthrust rock; others were the source of vast lava flows. Those with craters at their summits were the site of violent explosions whose power stands in direct contrast to the region's peace and quiet today. The geological fury that created these hills ended between 5,000 and 6,000 years ago, but the rectangle of extinct volcanoes is aligned along one of the most potentially unstable fault lines in France, the San Andreas fault of the French mainland.

This region is relatively underpopulated, so you may not be aware of the park's boundaries during your explorations. Details about trekking and camping are available from the Parc Naturel Régional des Volcans d'Auvergne, Montlosier, 63970 Aydat (☎ **04-73-65-64-00**), 12½ miles southwest of Clermont-Ferrand. A branch office is at Château St-Etienne, 15000 Aurillac (☎ **04-71-48-68-68**). At least half a dozen guidebooks covering specific hikes and walks (from 2 to 6 hours in duration) through the park are for sale at either branch, priced at 57F to 78F ($10.25 to $14.05).

SEEING THE SIGHTS IN TOWN

To begin your tour, head for the center of Clermont, the bustling **place de Jaude,** where you can sample a glass of regional wine at a cafe under the shade of a catalpa tree. When you're ready, walk north on rue du 11-Novembre, which branches off from the main plaza. This street leads to **rue des Gras,** the most interesting artery of Clermont.

Most of the interesting old buildings are in **Vieux-Clermont,** whose focal point is **place de la Victoire,** site of the black-lava ✪ Cathédrale Notre-Dame (☎ 04-73-92-46-61). One of the great churches of central France, it dates back to the 13th and 14th centuries, and structural additions were made in the 19th century. Its most outstanding feature is the series of stained-glass windows from the 13th and 14th centuries. Admission is free; it's open Monday through Saturday from 9:30am to noon and 2 to 6:30pm.

After leaving the cathedral, explore the buildings in this historic neighborhood. In particular, look for the **Maison de Savaron,** at 3 rue des Chaussetiers, constructed in 1513. It has a beautiful courtyard and a staircase tower.

Several blocks northeast of the cathedral is the finest example of Auvergnat Romanesque architecture, made of lava from volcanic deposits in the region: the **Eglise Notre-Dame-du-Port,** rue du Port (☎ 04-73-91-32-94). Dating from the 11th and 12th centuries, the church has four radiating chapels and a transept surmounted by an octagonal tower. The crypt holds a 17th-century "black Madonna." Admission is free; it's open daily from 8am to 7pm (to 8pm in summer).

Between the two churches stands the Renaissance **Fontaine d'Amboise,** on place de la Poterne, its pyramid supporting a statue of Hercules. Nearby is square Pascal, commemorating the birth of Blaise Pascal in 1623 in a house on rue des Gras. Regrettably, the house was demolished in 1958, but a statue was erected in honor of the native son.

Musée des Beaux-Arts. Place Louis-Deteix. ☎ **04-73-23-09-49.** Admission 22F ($3.95) adults, 12F ($2.15) children 12–16 and students, free for children 11 and under.

This museum is set 2 miles north of Clermont's center in an award-winning building erected in 1992. This is the cultural showcase of the Auvergne. When it was created, multiple works of art were culled from other museums throughout the Auvergne, then reassembled into a format that displays European art and culture in chronological order. Visitors navigate their way in a circular pattern through rooms devoted to French, Italian, and Flemish works progressing from the 7th to the 20th centuries.

Musée Bargoin. 45 rue de Ballainvilliers. ☎ **04-73-91-37-31.** Admission 22F ($3.95) adults, 12F ($2.15) children 12–16 and students, free for children 11 and under. Tues–Sun 10am–6pm.

The collection here consists of objects excavated from Auvergnat sites founded by the Gallo-Romans and their predecessors: pottery shards, bronzes, wood carvings, and an array of works noteworthy for anyone interested in the primal, prehistoric, and pre-Roman origins of modern France. There's also an unusual collection of antique Oriental carpets.

Musée de Ranquet. 34 rue des Gras. ☎ **04-73-37-38-63.** Admission 13F ($2.35), free for children 11 and under. Tues–Sun 10am–6pm.

Devoted exclusively to the history of the Auvergne and local memorabilia, the Musée de Ranquet is in the Maison des Architects, a Renaissance landmark in the town center dating from 1570. The collection includes items of workaday interest (kitchen, stonemason, and carpentry tools), regional furniture, and local pottery from the 18th century. The museum owns two "arithmetical machines" that belonged to Pascal, the only two of their kind said to exist outside of private collections in France. There's also a room devoted to France's hero of the Battle of Marengo, Général Desaix.

WHERE TO STAY

Hôtel Gallieni. 51 rue Bonnabaud, 63000 Clermont-Ferrand. ☎ **04-73-93-59-69.** Fax 04-73-34-89-29. 80 units. MINIBAR TV TEL. 250–350F ($45–$63) double. AE, MC, V. Parking 20F ($3.60).

This is not the best hotel in town, but it's still a good value. The Gallieni has a completely unassuming 1960s style, with rooms that, for the most part, have been recently renovated and are comfortably furnished though somewhat uninspired. All are well maintained and clean. A simple bistro, Le Clos Maréchal, offers affordable meals: Fixed-price menus begin as low as 59F ($10.60), and plats du jour at 49F ($8.80).

Mercure Clermont-Ferrand Centre. 82 bd. François-Mitterrand, 63000 Clermont-Ferrand. ☎ **04-73-34-46-46.** Fax 04-73-34-46-36. 124 units. A/C MINIBAR TV TEL. 570F ($102.60) double. AE, DC, V. Parking 39F ($7).

This modern hotel—the best in town—was built in the early 1970s by another chain (Altea), then switched its affiliation to Mercure and was radically renovated in 1997. Its location near the lovely Jardin Lecoq is great for jogging and taking strolls. The rooms are well furnished and very clean; most are rather spacious. Everything about the hotel is functional and businesslike, but not necessarily exciting, and corporate types in town doing business with the Michelin company often stay here. The on-site restaurant, La Retirade, is a worthwhile choice.

WHERE TO DINE

✪ **Jean-Yves Bath.** Place du Marché-St-Pierre. ☎ **04-73-31-23-23.** Reservations required. Restaurant, main courses 140–160F ($25.20–$28.80); fixed-price menus 260–350F ($46.80–$63). Brasserie, main courses 60–82F ($10.80–$14.75). V. Tues–Sat noon–1:30pm and 7:30–9:30pm. Closed 3 weeks in Feb and 2 weeks in Sept. FRENCH.

Few pretensions and lots of wonderful flavors go into the locally inspired cuisine at Jean-Yves Bath's charming restaurant. Richly deserving of his Michelin star (and ours), he often caters to the demanding palates of Michelin executives working in the city.

Anyone looking for a real culinary thrill usually heads upstairs to the formal dining room, where the offerings include grandly creative dishes that change with the seasons. Examples include a modern interpretation of an old Toulouse recipe, cassoulet of lobster; and a modern version of an old peasant recipe, cabbage soup, which in this case is augmented with foie gras and perfumed salt. Also, look for the salad of stuffed morels served with asparagus tips and foie gras or the red mullet salad garnished with a tapenade of black olives. Dessert might be strawberry ravioli.

If you're in a hurry or just don't want a formal, expensive dinner, stick with the street-level brasserie, with its mahogany paneling and brass accents. Here the menu features heaping platters of bistro-style food (steaks with tagliatelle in bleu cheese sauce, confit of pig's foot with broad beans and local sausages). Unusual local vintages are sold either by the glass or bottle in both levels of this establishment.

Le Clavé. 10–12 rue St-Adjutor. ☎ **04-73-36-46-30.** Reservations required. Main courses 120–190F ($21.60–$34.20); fixed-price menus 150F ($27) at lunch, 195–490F ($35.10–$88.20) at lunch and dinner. V. Daily noon–2pm and 7:30–10:30pm. FRENCH.

This well-known restaurant brings big-city style and some of the most creative and intelligent food in the region to the heart of Clermont-Ferrand. Inside a 19th-century stone house are two monochromatic dining rooms served by an attentive staff. Menu items are both classic and contemporary, and they are invariably well prepared. Main course choices include foie gras with garnishes tailored to the seasons (fresh fruit in summer, asparagus tips in spring); warm chiffonnade of shellfish; roasted lobster served with a creamy, truffle-studded risotto; roasted rabbit with a galette of sweet polenta and tarragon sauce; and filet of Salers beef with sauce Périgueux (foie gras and truffles), accompanied with roasted potatoes drizzled with a local cheese. Alan Clavé is the owner and namesake of this well-managed place.

CLERMONT-FERRAND AFTER DARK

A very hip crowd gathers all year at **Le Blue Sport Café,** 68 place de l'Etoile (☎ 04-73-36-08-92), where jazz and rock blend with a lively pub atmosphere to create one of the most popular meeting places around.

For the best cafe/bar in town, complete with regular jazz and rock concerts, go to **Le Doppler,** 13 bis rue Jean-Jaurès (☎ 05-63-03-07-45). This place attracts a young, active, sometimes boisterous crowd. If you're really feeling rowdy, **Le Flamand,** rue de la République (☎ 05-63-66-12-20), provides the perfect balance of beer hall buzz, colorful local characters, and popular pub games.

Club l'Arlequin, 2 rue d'Etoile (☎ 04-73-37-53-88), is the trendiest disco. The doorman is selective about whom he allows in, so you're supposed to feel privileged if asked to pay the 80F ($14.40) cover. **L'Exclusif,** 12 rue des Petits Gras (☎ 04-73-37-87-69), isn't as exclusive as the Arlequin, but come to have fun with its wild, mostly male, both gay and straight crowd twisting and gyrating on the dance floor. You'll pay 50F ($9) to get into this party. The disco/dance scene is dominated by the ultra-energetic **Les Ormes,** avenue de Bordeaux (☎ 05-63-03-54-19), which has cornered the market with its two-discos-in-one concept. The under-25 crowd has a space belting out the latest in techno whereas the over-25 crowd dances the night away to more familiar rock and zouk tunes. The cover runs 50F to 80F ($9 to $14.40).

5 Le Puy-en-Velay

325 miles S of Paris, 80 miles SE of Clermont-Ferrand

Le Puy-en-Veley (usually shortened to Le Puy) is one of the most extraordinary sights of France. Steep volcanic spires, left from geological activity that ended millennia ago, were capped with Romanesque churches, a cathedral, and medieval houses that rise sinuously from the plain below. The history of Le Puy is centered around the cult of the Virgin Mary, which prompted the construction of many of the city's churches.

Le Puy today is a provincial French city of steep, cobblestone streets with lots of rather shabby buildings (many of which are now being restored). Many of the population of approximately 22,000 live off the tourist trade, today's visitors following in the footsteps of Charlemagne, "the first tourist" here. Le Puy remains a major pilgrimage destination of France, although not as famous as Lourdes.

ESSENTIALS

GETTING THERE   Passengers arriving in Le Puy from anywhere in Europe must change **trains** at the railway junction of St-Georges d'Aurac. From here, small trains, timed for convenient connections, travel along the 17-mile spur route that connects Le Puy's small railway station to the rest of the lines of the SNCF. For train information and schedules, call ☎ 08-36-35-35-39. If you're **driving,** the best way to reach Le Puy is from St-Etienne, traveling southwest along N88. From Clermont-Ferrand, drive south along N88 to Lempdes, continuing southeast along N102 to Le Puy.

VISITOR INFORMATION   The **Office de Tourisme** is on place du Breuil (☎ 04-71-09-38-41).

EXPLORING THE TOWN

Puy is the historic center of the French lace industry; you'll find lace shops on every block. But to be assured of its handmade authenticity, look for the mark carrying the words DENTELLE DU PUY. As decreed by a 1931 local government ordinance, the display of this mark on lace is a privilege reserved for the real thing. The best selections of local lace can be found at **Spécialités du Velay,** 1 bd. St-Louis (☎ **04-71-09-09-34**), and **Lucia Dentelles,** 28 place du plot (☎ **04-71-09-60-69**).

Cathédrale Notre-Dame. Place du For. ☎ **04-71-05-45-52.** Admission to cathedral free; to cloisters and Chapel of Relics 25F ($4.50) adults, 15F ($2.70) ages 12–25, free for children 11 and under. Cathedral, daily 24 hours. Cloisters and Chapel of Relics, Oct–Mar daily 9:30am–noon and 2–4pm; Apr–June daily 9:30am–12:30pm and 2–6pm; July–Sept daily 9:30am–6:30pm.

The Romanesque Cathédrale Notre-Dame was conceived as a site for shelter and prayer for medieval pilgrims heading to the religious shrines of Santiago de Compostela in northwestern Spain. Marked by vivid Oriental and Byzantine influences, it's worth a visit. The cloisters contain carved capitals dating from the Carolingian era. The Chapelle des Reliques et Trésor d'Art Religieux contains fabrics and gold and silver objects from the church treasury, as well as an unusual enameled chalice from the 12th century.

Chapelle St-Michel-d'Aiguilhe. Atop the Rocher St-Michel. ☎ **04-71-09-50-03.** Admission 10F ($1.80) adults, 5F (90¢) children 13 and under. Mid-June to mid-Sept daily 9am–7pm; late Sept to early June daily 9 or 10am–noon and 2–5 or 6pm, depending on the hours of sunrise and sunset. Dec 20–31 open 2–4pm only.

On the northwestern perimeter of Le Puy stands one of the city's most dramatic sights, requiring a very long climb up rocky stairs. When you get here you'll be struck by the Oriental influences in the floor plan, the arabesques, and the mosaics crafted from black stone. On view are some 12th-century murals and an 11th-century wooden depiction of Christ.

Musée Crozatier. In the Jardin Henri-Vinay. ☎ **04-71-09-38-90.** Admission 13F ($2.35) adults, 7F ($1.25) children. May–Sept Wed–Mon 10am–noon and 2–6pm; Oct–Apr Mon and Wed–Sat 10am–noon and 2–4pm, Sun 2–4pm.

If you appreciate handcrafts, you'll enjoy the displays of lace, some from the 16th century, at this museum, which also has a collection of carved architectural embellishments from the Romanesque era and paintings from the 14th to the 20th centuries.

WHERE TO STAY

Hôtel Brivas. Av. Charles-Massot, 43750 Vals-Près-Le-Puy. ☎ **04-71-05-68-66.** Fax 04-71-05-65-88. E-mail: brivas@aol.com.fr. 51 units. TV TEL. 294–310F ($52.90–$55.80) double. AE, V.

Set about a 2-minute drive southwest of the town center, adjacent to Le Dolaizon river, this hotel, built in 1991, is the newest and most modern in town. There's nothing antique or historic about this two-star hostel, but the rooms are clean, streamlined, and simple; it's often used by groups on bus tours. A restaurant on the premises serves many of these tour groups, offering a fixed-price menu that ranges from 95F to 190F ($17.10 to $34.20).

Hôtel Régina. 34 bd. du Maréchal-Fayolle, 43000 Le Puy-en-Velay. ☎ **04-71-09-14-71.** Fax 04-71-09-18-57. 30 units. MINIBAR TV TEL. 358F ($64.45) double. MC, V.

In 1997 a radical renovation of this four-story hotel brought it up to the best three-star standards in town. Originally built late in the 19th century and operated by extended members of a local family (the Venosinos), it offers simple but thoughtfully decorated bedrooms and a convenient location close to the heart of town. A brasserie on the premises serves affordable platters of food that begin at 78F ($14.05) and fixed-price menus at 130F to 160F ($23.40 to $28.80). Daily in midafternoon, it's transformed into a tea salon that attracts many local retirees and shopkeepers.

WHERE TO DINE

Le Bateau Ivre. 5 rue Portail-d'Avignon. ☎ **04-71-09-67-20.** Reservations recommended. Main courses 70–110F ($12.60–$19.80); fixed-price menus 105–185F ($18.90–$33.30). AE, MC, V. Tues–Sat noon–2:30pm and 7:30–10pm. Closed 1 week in June and Nov 1–15. FRENCH/AUVERGNAT.

Set in the heart of town and devoted to the traditions of the region, this restaurant occupies a pair of rustically old-fashioned dining rooms in a house whose interior is much older than its facade, which was added in the 19th century. Monsieur Datessen, your host, prepares a variety of dishes utilizing the robust wines of the region as well as lentils, which crop up in appealing and flavorful ways. Specialties include roasted versions of the Auvergne's black lambs, prepared with thyme and mashed potatoes studded with morels; beef of the Salers breed with local red wine and marrow sauce; and local whitefish (omble chevalier) served at least four different ways. Dedicated pilgrims to Le Puy always have this restaurant marked as the "serious" dining choice. Notice the lace that covers the windows and wooden tables—it was all handmade in Le Puy, mainly by elderly women who craft the material at home.

6 Limoges

246 miles S of Paris, 193 miles N of Toulouse, 58 miles NE of Périgueux

Limoges, the ancient capital of Limousin in west-central France, is world famous for its exquisite porcelain and enamel works, the latter a medieval industry revived in the 19th century. The industry is still going strong today—in fact, Limoges is the economic capital of western France. On the Vienne's right bank, the town has historically consisted of two parts: the Cité, its narrow streets and old maisons on the lower slope, and the town proper at the summit.

ESSENTIALS

GETTING THERE   Limoges has good **train** service from most regional cities, with direct trains from Toulouse, Poitiers, and Paris. Ten trains depart daily from Paris's Gare d'Austerlitz for Limoges (trip time: 3 hours). For complete train information, call ☎ **08-36-35-35-39.** If you're **driving** from Aubusson, take D941 west for the 1-hour trip.

VISITOR INFORMATION   The **Office de Tourisme** is on boulevard de Fleurus (☎ **05-55-34-46-87**).

EXPLORING THE TOWN

If you'd like to see an enameler or a porcelain factory producing its wares, ask at the tourist office (see above) for a list of workshops, or go directly to the famous Pavillon de la Porcelaine.

To stock up on local porcelain, try these three **Prestige de Limoges** shops owned by the same company: At 2 bd. Louis-Blanc (☎ **05-55-34-44-15**) you'll find Limoges's own "unblemished crystal" as well as crystal from Lalique, St. Louis, and Baccarat and silverware from Christofle and Puiforcat. At 13 and 27 bd. Louis-Blanc (☎ **05-55-34-58-61**), you can buy porcelain from Haviland, Bernardaud, Raynaud, and Lafarge, as well as slightly imperfect seconds.

For good deals on Limoges porcelain, the many factory stores in town offer good-quality seconds at reduced prices. For a thoroughly classical style of porcelain, try **Ancienne Manufacture Royale,** 7 place Horteils (☎ **05-55-70-44-82**), or **Raynaud,** 14 ancienne rte. d'Aixe (☎ **05-55-01-77-65**). If you want a larger variety in style, from the formally classic to the uniquely modern, visit **Bernardaud,** 27 rue Albert-Thomas (☎ **05-55-10-55-50**), or **Chastigner,** 20 av. des Casseaux (☎ **05-55-33-45-74**).

Pavillon de la Porcelaine. Av. John-Kennedy. ☎ **05-55-30-21-86.** Free admission. Apr–Oct daily 8:30am–7:30pm; Nov–Mar daily 9:30am–7pm.

Haviland has been exporting its porcelain to the U.S. and other countries since 1842. Over the years, it has used the designs of artists like Gauguin and Dalí. In the museum, you can see the masterpieces as well as original pieces for the U.S. White House. Later, visit an air-conditioned room where you can follow the manufacturing process with the help of a video on a giant screen. A large shop also sells the porcelain at factory prices.

Musée National Adrien-Dubouché. Av. des Lissiers. ☎ **05-55-33-08-50.** Admission 22F ($3.95) adults, 15F ($2.70) ages 18–25, free for children 17 and under. July–Aug Wed–Mon 10am–5:45pm; Sept–June Wed–Mon 10am–12:30pm and 2–5:45pm.

This museum boasts the largest public collection of Limoges porcelain. Housed in a 19th-century building, its 12,000 pieces illustrate the history of glassmaking and ceramics (porcelain, glazed earthenware, stoneware, and terra-cotta) throughout the ages. In France, its porcelain collection is second only to Sèvres. One room is devoted to the various stages of ceramics manufacturing. The main gallery contains whole dinner sets of noted figures and some contemporary Limoges ware.

Cathédrale St-Etienne. Place de la Cathédrale. ☎ **05-55-34-53-81.** Free admission. Summer daily 10am–6pm; winter daily 10am–5pm.

The cathedral was begun in 1273 but took many years to complete. The choir, for example, was finished in 1327, but work continued in the nave until almost 1890. The cathedral is the only one in the old province of Limousin to be built entirely in the Gothic style. The main entrance is through Porte St-Jean, which has beautifully carved wooden doors from the 16th century (constructed at the peak of the Flamboyant Gothic style). Inside, the nave appears so harmonious it's hard to imagine that its construction took 6 centuries. The rood screen is of particular interest, built in 1533 in the ornate style of the Italian Renaissance. The cathedral also contains some admirable bishops' tombs from the 14th to the 16th centuries.

Musée Municipal. Place de la Cathédrale. ☎ **05-55-45-61-75** or 05-55-34-44-09. Free admission. June–Sept daily 10am–noon and 2–6pm; Oct–May Wed–Mon 10am–5pm. Closed holidays.

Adjoining the cathedral in the Jardins de l'Evêché—which offer a view of the Vienne and the pont St-Etienne from the 13th century—the old archbishops' palace has been turned into the Musée Municipal. The 18th-century building, elegant in line, has an outstanding collection of Limoges enamels from the 12th century, as well as some enamel paintings by Leonard Limousin, who was born in 1505 in Limoges and went on to win world acclaim and the favor of four monarchs. Limoges was also the birthplace of Renoir, and the museum displays several works by this world-class artist.

Eglise St-Michel-des-Lions. Place St-Michel. ☎ **05-55-34-18-13.** Free admission. Mon–Sat 8am–noon and 2–6pm, Sun 8am–noon and 4–7pm.

Construction of this church was launched in the 14th century, and work continued into the 15th and 16th centuries. It boasts late Gothic stained glass, plus relics of St. Martial, including his head.

WHERE TO STAY

Hôtel La Caravelle. 21 rue Armand-Barbès, 87000 Limoges. ☎ **05-55-77-75-29.** Fax 05-55-79-27-60. E-mail: hotelcaravelle@wanadoo.fr. 29 units. TV TEL. 310–370F ($55.80–$66.60) double. AE, MC, V. Parking 30F ($5.40).

Just north of the city center, this recommendable modern hotel is the most recent manifestation of a building erected around 1900, but frequent renovations have kept the four-story site looking fresh. The rooms are simply but comfortably furnished in a modern style, calm and quiet, and accessible by elevator. Breakfast is the only meal served, but the management can direct you to the half dozen or so restaurants on rue Garibaldi, a short walk away.

Hôtel Royal Limousin. Place de la République, 87000 Limoges. ☎ **05-55-34-65-30.** Fax 05-55-34-55-21. 82 units. MINIBAR TV TEL. 480–680F ($86.40–$122.40) double; 680–1,200F ($122.40–$216) suite. AE, DC, MC, V.

This modern, six-story oasis was built in the 1960s adjacent to a municipal parking lot in the center of Limoges. It's the town's best address and welcomes virtually every large-scale buyer of Limoges's famous product. The rooms are outfitted in a neutrally modern, chain-hotel style but are generally large and sunny. Accommodations on the noisier avenue Carnot side rent for less than those on the quieter place de la République side. The only drawback is that the hotel is often booked by summer group tours. There's no restaurant, but the staff refers hotel guests to the restaurant next door, which is under separate management.

WHERE TO DINE

Philippe Redon. 3 rue Aguesseau. ☎ **05-55-34-66-22.** Reservations recommended. Fixed-price menus 140–250F ($25.20–$45). AE, DC, V. Tues–Sat noon–2:30pm and 7–10pm. Closed Aug 1–15. FRENCH.

In a 19th-century house a few steps from the produce market, this restaurant is maintained by a youthful team of waiters headed by the owner/chef, Philippe Redon, the finest cook in Limoges. It contains a 1930s Art Deco–style interior accented with exposed stone and flowers. Menu items vary with the availability of local ingredients. Examples include crayfish with spices, turbot with girolle mushrooms, filet of monkfish marinated in Szechuan pepper, and codfish with truffles in puff pastry.

NEARBY ACCOMMODATIONS & DINING
IN ST-MARTIN-DU-FAULT

✪ **La Chapelle St-Martin.** 87510 Nieul. ☎ **05-55-75-80-17.** Fax 05-55-75-89-50. www.relaischateaux.fr/chapelle. 13 units. A/C TEL. 550–980F ($99–$176.40) double; 1,500F ($270) suite. Half board 850–950F ($153–$171) per person extra. AE, V. Free parking. Closed Jan–Feb 15 (restaurant closed Mon year-round). Take N147 and D35 7 miles northeast from Limoges.

This is the best place in the environs if you enjoy turn-of-the-century-style living and superb food in the tradition of the Relais & Châteaux group. The hotel is graciously situated in a private park with two ponds. Your host, M. Dudognon, requests that you reserve well in advance. The rooms are individually decorated and tasteful, and some are suitable for those with disabilities. The food is excellent, the ingredients selected with care and deftly handled by the chefs.

IN NIEUIL

To get to Nieuil from Limoges, take N141 west of the town center (signposted Angoulême). The town of Nieuil is signposted at the town of Suaux. Follow the signs for about a mile east of the village toward Fontafie. *Note:* Don't confuse Nieuil with La Chapelle St-Martin at Nieul (with a slightly different spelling).

✪ **Château de Nieuil.** 16270 Nieuil. ☎ **05-45-71-36-38.** Fax 05-45-71-46-45. www. relaischateaux.fr/nieuil. E-mail: nieuil@relaischateaux.fr. 14 units. TEL. 850–1,500F ($153–$270) double; 1,500–2,300F ($270–$414) suite. AE, DC, MC, V. Closed Nov–Apr.

This château, built in the 16th century as a hunting lodge for François I, was transformed in 1937 into the first château-hotel in France. Restored by the comte de Dampierre early in the 1800s after its destruction in the Revolution, it has remained in the antique-collecting family of Jean-Michel Bodinaud since around 1900. Today 400 acres of park and forest lead up to a series of beautifully maintained gardens, the pride of the owners.

Dining: The cuisine, supervised by Mme Luce Bodinaud, is superb, focusing on classic traditions and regional recipes. A typical dish is stuffed cabbage (farci Charentais), though you may prefer the filet of beef du Limousine or a selection of fish that includes filet of sole in the style "pêcheurs d'Oléron," prepared with a compôte of leeks and crayfish. Fixed-price menus cost 250F to 340F ($45 to $61.20). Nonguests can dine here if they call ahead.

Amenities: Tennis courts, pool, art and antiques gallery that specializes in Art Deco furniture and old posters.

7 Aubusson

236 miles S of Paris, 55 miles E of Limoges, 59 miles NW of Clermont-Ferrand

In the Creuse Valley, the little market town of Aubusson enjoys world renown for its carpets and tapestries. Aubusson is characterized by clock towers, bridges, peaked roofs, and turrets—all of which inspired the painter Gromaire's widely reproduced cartoon *View of Aubusson.*

Against the gray granite, rainbow-hued skeins of wool hang from windows. The workshops of the craftspeople are spread throughout the town, and many are open to the public (inquire at the door). The origin of the industry is unknown. Some credit the Arabs who settled here in 732. Others think the craft came from Flanders in the Middle Ages. For years the favorite subject was *The Lady and the Unicorn,* the original of which was discovered in the nearby Château de Boussac. Many tapestry reproductions of the works of such 18th-century painters as Boucher and Watteau have also been made. Since World War II, designs by painters like Picasso, Matisse, and Braque have been stressed.

Musée Départemental de la Tapisserie, avenue des Lissiers (☎ **05-55-66-33-06**), has exhibits related to the 6-century-long tradition of the Aubusson carpet- and tapestry-weaving industry. The displays also highlight the 20th-century rebirth of the Aubusson carpet and the art of tapestry weaving. It's open Wednesday through Monday from 9:30am to noon and 2 to 6pm (in summer from 9am to 12:30pm and 2 to 6:30pm). Admission is 18F ($3.25) for adults, 12F ($2.15) for children 12 to 16, and free for children 11 and under.

La Maison du Tapissier, rue Vieille (☎ **05-55-66-32-12**), exhibits old carpets and displays a reconstruction of an old carpet-weaving studio. It's open from 9:30am to noon and 1:30 to 6pm, daily from mid-June to September and Tuesday through Saturday off-season. Admission is 17F ($3.05).

Aubusson does have rail service, much of it indirect, from Clermont-Ferrand and Paris, among other cities. Ten **trains** leave from Paris's Gare d'Austerlitz for Aubusson with a change in Limoges. From Clermont-Ferrand to Aubusson, 4 trains depart daily for a nearly 6-hour trip (with a minimum of two stops). For complete train information, call ☎ **08-36-35-35-39.**

If you're **driving** from Clermont-Ferrand, take D941 west to Aubusson. The trip takes between 1 and 1½ hours.

The **Office de Tourisme** is on rue Vieille (☎ **05-55-66-32-12**).

WHERE TO STAY & DINE

Le Lion d'Or. Place du Général-Espagne, 23200 Aubusson. ☎ **05-55-66-13-88.** Fax 05-55-66-84-73. 11 units. TV TEL. 270–300F ($48.60–$54) double. AE, MC, V.

This two-star hotel occupies a building erected around 1800 on the town's main square. It's unpretentious but still one of the town's best choices, with a polite but no-nonsense management by the Chaussoy family. The rooms are simple yet comfortable.

Dining: The street level contains a restaurant that serves the town's best food. In summer, lunch and dinner are offered daily, but between October 15 and April 15 no meals are served on Sunday nights. Menu items include stingray with cabbage and butter sauce, marinated foie gras, and beefsteaks.

The Dordogne & Périgord: Land of Prehistoric Caves, Truffles & Fine Wine

Lovers of foie gras and truffles as well as lovers of nature have always sought out the Dordogne and Périgord regions of France. Our first stop, Périgueux, was the capital of the old province of Périgord. After following the trail of the Cro-Magnon people to prehistoric caves, we'll visit Cahors, the ancient capital of Quercy, then Montauban, where the great painter Ingres was born. But the towns themselves aren't the stars—it's the unspoiled fertile countryside, of much hidden charm and antique character, that holds the fascination. In some villages the Middle Ages seem to live on. It's said that there are no discoveries to be made in France, but you can defy the experts and make many discoveries if you give yourself adequate time to visit a region too often neglected by North Americans.

REGIONAL CUISINE   Ask gastronomes about the cuisine of the Dordogne and Périgord and the first thing to come to mind will be truffles, one of the most sought-after delicacies in France. The region produces more than 30 types, growing underground, without a root or stem, at the base of one type of oak tree in light soil of a certain degree of acidity. It gives off a distinctive odor, said by one 19th-century gastronome "to epitomize the perfumed soul of the Périgord." Because truffles grow underground (they're technically classified as a "subterranean fungus"), truffle hunters have traditionally used carefully trained dogs to smell out their location. Trained pigs have also been used to find them, but they tend to eat the truffle before it can be retrieved by the hunter.

Equally famous are the region's pâtés, which, when studded with "black diamonds" (truffles), have conquered many a resistant appetite. These are made from the enlarged livers of geese that have been force-fed a diet of rich corn. Some pâtés are still made of unadulterated goose liver, but the more frequently seen version is a ballotine of foie gras. This will usually have been prepared in a factory, where the goose liver is mixed with white turkey meat and then covered with meat gelatin.

One characteristic of the region's cuisine is the stuffing of many roasts and joints. It usually includes bread crumbs, truffles, and segments of goose liver. The most famous sauce here is a sauce Périgueux, made from sweet madeira wine and truffles. Anything prepared *à la*

The Dordogne & Périgord

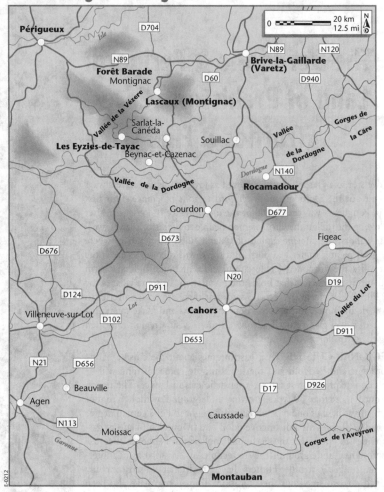

périgourdine includes a garnish of truffles to which foie gras has been added. Another staple of the cuisine is *cèpes* (flap mushrooms). Other regional specialties are *bréjaude* (a cabbage/bacon soup served with rye bread) and *lièvre en chabessal* (freshly killed rabbit stuffed with highly seasoned pork, ham, and veal).

Rich in nutrients, the soil produces huge quantities of walnuts, vegetables, and fruits, plus some of the most succulent beef and veal from the Limousin breed. This breed has been exported to Australia and South America, where it has thrived.

The most famous wines here are the red and white Bergerac, the red Pécharmant, and the deep-red Cahors. Cahors is best aged for a dozen years (some of them in an oak cask) before reaching a suitable sophistication. The Montbazillac is a sweet, tawny dessert wine whose grapes have been deliberately permeated with a whitish-green mold known as noble rot (pourriture noble). When it's fermented, this improves the flavor of the wine, partly by reducing its acidity and partly because of a mystery that only Dionysus could fully understand.

1 Périgueux

301 miles SW of Paris, 53 miles SE of Angoulême, 70 miles NE of Bordeaux, 63 miles SW of Limoges

This is the city of foie gras and truffles. Capital of the old province of Périgord, Périgueux stands on the Isle River. In addition to its food products, the region is known for its Roman ruins and medieval churches. The city is divided into three sections: the Cité (old Roman town), Le Puy St-Front (the medieval town) on the slope of the hill, and to the west, the modern town.

Périgueux today is a sleepy provincial backwater, with a population of 35,000. Its attractions probably won't hold your interest more than a day, but it's a gateway to the Dordogne Valley and the cave paintings at Les Eyzies.

ESSENTIALS

GETTING THERE   **Trains** run frequently from Paris, Lyon, and Toulouse, plus many regional towns and villages. Six trains per day arrive from Paris (trip time: 6 to 7 hours), 4 trains from Lyon (trip time: 7 hours), 10 trains from Bordeaux (trip time: 2½ hours), and 7 trains from Toulouse (trip time: 4 hours). For train information and schedules, call ☎ **08-36-35-35-39.** When **motoring** from Bordeaux, drive along N89 east. From Paris it's a much longer drive, taking A10 south to Orléans, connecting to A71 south to Vierzon, continuing along N20 south to Limoges, and then connecting to N21 south to Périgueux.

VISITOR INFORMATION   The **Office du Tourisme** is at 26 place Francheville (☎ **05-53-53-10-63**).

EXPLORING THE TOWN

You may want to rent a bike and explore the surrounding countryside; a map is available from the tourist office. Rent from **Au Tour de France,** 96 av. du Maréchal-Juin (☎ **05-53-53-41-91**), which charges 55F ($9.90) for the first and second day. You can rent mountain bikes (the French refer to them as V.T.T.—Vélos Tout Terrain) for 85F ($15.30) for the first and second day. Discounts of approximately 20% apply for rentals of 3 days or more. It's open Monday to Saturday from 9am to noon and 2 to 7pm.

Périgueux is one of the richest repositories of Gallo-Roman antiquities in France. The most visible of these is the **Tour de Vésone,** a partially ruined site that stands 85 feet tall beyond the railway station, half a mile southwest of town. The cella of a Roman temple dedicated to the goddess Vesuna, it's all that remains to conjure up images of ancient rites.

Jardin des Arènes, a vast eliptical amphitheater that once held as many as 22,000 spectators, is another reminder of Roman days. Now in ruins, the amphitheater, with a diameter of 1,312 feet, dates from the 2nd or 3rd century. The site is open daily May to August from 7:30am to 9pm and September to April from 8am to 6pm (no admission charge). Near the arena are the crumbling remains of the **Château Barrière,** rue Turenne, built in the 11th or 12th century on Roman foundations. In rare instances the tourist office conducts tours of the city's ancient sites (they call it their Circuit Gallo-Romain). Most of them are haphazardly scheduled during France's school holidays and are conducted exclusively in French.

Above all, gastronomy reigns supreme in Périgueux, especially when it comes to smooth, melt-in-your-mouth foie gras. Stores that sell this regional delicacy abound. The best foie gras emporiums include **La Maison Léon,** 9 place de la Clautre (☎ **05-**

Biking Through the Dordogne

The Dordogne's rivers meander through countryside that's among the most verdant and historic in France. This area is relatively underpopulated, but it's dotted with monuments, feudal châteaux, 12th-century villages, and charming churches.

Biking will allow you to get in sync with the pace of this rural area and really begin to understand its character. Unlike in more pretentious regions of France, no château-hotel or inn will treat you disdainfully if you show up on two rather than four wheels. (*Au contraire,* the staff will probably offer advice on suitable bike routes for your departure.) If you're ever in doubt about where your handlebars should lead you, know that you'll rarely go wrong if your route parallels the meandering riverbanks of the Lot, the Vézère, the Dordogne, or any of their ancient tributaries. Architects and builders since the 11th century have appreciated their charm and added greatly to the visual allure of their watersides.

The SNCF makes it easy to transport a bike on the nation's railways and if you don't want to bring your own wheels on the train, there are plenty of rental shops throughuot the region. (We recommend rentals in this chapter's sections on Périgueux, Les Eyzies-de-Tayac, and Montauban.)

Alternatively, you could leave the details to someone else by joining a group of cyclists led by **Backroads,** 801 Cedar St., Berkeley, CA 94710-1800 (☎ **800/ 462-2848**). The company offers a 7-day inn trip or 8-day camping trip through the Dordogne. Participants congregate in Bordeaux, then take a train to the hamlet of Tremolat, where they begin a 10-mile bike pedal, all before the end of the first day. Each day thereafter offers the option for itineraries of between 15 and 60 miles, depending on your endurance level. Accommodations include elegant châteaux-hotels, folkloric inns, or (for those willing to forgo a conventional bed) a network of campgrounds, each at a site of historic or cultural interest. Prices, depending on the degree of luxury, range from $1,198 to $2,792 per person, double occupancy, and don't include the $145 fee charged for the rental of a bicycle. You can also inquire locally about information on bike trips at **Canoé Loisin** at Sailat; call ☎ **05-53-28-23-43.**

53-53-29-96), and **A la Cathédrale,** 9 rue des Chaînes (☎ **05-53-53-47-04**). But if you want an adventure while shopping for a great goose liver, then head for a real goose farm by the name of **A la Ferme de Puy Gauthier,** about 5 minutes south of town in the village of Marsaneix (☎ **05-53-08-87-07**), where they make their own foie gras home-style.

Cathédrale St-Front. Place de la Clautre. ☎ **05-53-53-23-62.** Free admission. Daily 8am–noon and 2:30–7:30pm (closes at dusk in winter).

In Le Puy St-Front (the medieval quarter) rises the Cathédrale St-Front, which was built from 1125 to 1150, the last of the Aquitanian domed churches. Dedicated to St. Fronto, a local bishop, it's one of the largest churches in southwestern France. The cathedral's four-story bell tower rises nearly 200 feet, overlooking the marketplace; it's surmounted by a cone-shaped spire. With its five white domes and colonnaded turrets, St-Front evokes memories of Constantinople. The interior, somewhat bare, is built on the plan of a Greek cross, unusual for a French cathedral. Hearty visitors can apply to the sacristan (tip expected) for a tour of the roof. On this tour, you can walk between the domes and turrets, looking out over Vieux Périgueux with its old houses running down to the Isle. In rare cases, qualified students of art history or architecture are admitted to the crypt and cloisters, which date from the 9th century, although those are otherwise closed to the public. Mass is celebrated Saturday at 6:30pm and Sunday at 9am, 11am, and 6;30pm.

Eglise St-Etienne-de-la-Cité. 10 av. Cavaignac. ☎ **05-53-53-21-35.** Free admission. Daily 8am–5pm.

The other remarkable church—this one in the Cité area on rue de la Cité—was a cathedral until 1669, when it lost its position to St-Front. The church was built in the 12th century but has been much mutilated since. It contains a 12th-century bishop's tomb and a carved 17th-century wooden reredos depicting the Assumption of the Madonna.

Musée de Périgord. 22 cours Tourny. ☎ **05-53-06-40-70.** Admission 15F ($2.70) adults, 7.50F ($1.35) students, free for children 17 and under. Wed–Mon 10am–noon and 2–6pm.

Built on the site of an Augustinian monastery, this museum has an exceptional collection of prehistoric relics, sculptures, and Gallo-Roman mosaics. Many of the artifacts were recovered from digs in the Périgord region, which is rich in prehistoric remains.

WHERE TO STAY
L'Oison (see below) also rents rooms.

Hôtel Bristol. 39 rue Antoine-Gadaud, 24000 Périgueux. ☎ **05-53-08-75-90.** Fax 05-53-07-00-49. E-mail: bristolhotel@wanadoo.fr 29 units. A/C MINIBAR TV TEL. 350–370F ($63–$66.60) double. AE, MC, V.

This modern three-star hotel is centrally located behind a small parking lot and offers comfortable, serviceable rooms, often with sleek styling. It's your best bet among a limited, lackluster selection. Breakfast is the only meal served, but it's only a 5-minute walk to the town's best restaurants and major points of interest. The owners have spent much of their lives in North America and offer both a French and an English welcome to all international travelers.

WHERE TO DINE
✪ **L'Oison.** In the Château des Reynats, at Chancelade, 24650 Périgueux. ☎ **05-53-03-53-59.** Fax 05-53-03-44-84. Reservations recommended. Main courses 95–200F ($17.10–$36); fixed-price menus 135F ($24.30) at lunch, 180–350F ($32.40–$63) at dinner. AE, DC, MC, V. Tues–Sun noon–2pm, Tues–Sat 7:30–10pm. Closed Mon and Thurs; Mon lunch in July and Aug. FRENCH.

In 1995 the most acclaimed restaurant in Périgueux moved to the finest hotel, the 19th-century Château des Reynats, encircled by a manicured park. This slate-roofed manor offers an Empire dining room in which you can enjoy the cuisine du marché of the talented chef Régis Chiorozas, who can do more with fresh ingredients than anyone else in the area. In landlocked Périgueux he concentrates on seafood—and does it taste fresh! But his menu also includes traditional regional dishes, even a salad of fresh truffles that's among the most delectable we've ever sampled. In season, young partridge, roebuck, and hare are available. The desserts are sublime.

The château also rents 37 beautiful rooms, costing 450–800F ($81–$144) for a double.

PERIGUEUX AFTER DARK
If the weather is good, start your evening with a walk over to **place St-Stalin, place St-Louis,** and **place du Marché,** where you'll most likely stumble onto a great little bar or even a bit of live impromptu music.

If you're in the mood for a beer and a *Cheers* type of atmosphere, go to the **Gordon Pub,** 12 rue Condé (☎ **05-53-35-03-74**). A regular stop for the dance-crazed youth of town is **La Régence,** 16 rue des Chancelier-de-l'Hôpital (☎ **05-53-53-10-55**), with its booming techno-rock beat and more than ample supply of pheromones. If you prefer to while the night away over drinks and good conversation, stop by **Café Le St-Louis,** place St-Louis (☎ **05-53-53-53-90**), or the **Café La Rotonde,** 9 cours Montaigne (☎ **05-53-08-30-31**). Finally, you can always find a full house at **L'An des Rois,** 51 rue Aubarède (☎ **05-53-53-01-58**), the only gay and lesbian disco/bar in town. Dress your hottest to get noticed here, where there are separate areas for men and women. The cover is 60F ($10.80).

2 Lascaux (Montignac)

308 miles SW of Paris, 29 miles SE of Périgueux

The **Caves at Lascaux,** near the Vézère River town of Montignac in the Dordogne region, contain the most beautiful and most famous cave paintings in the world. If you weren't among the fortunate thousands who got to view the actual paintings by 1963, you may be permanently out of luck. The drawings have been closed to the general public to prevent deterioration, but a replica gives you a clear picture of the remarkable works.

They were discovered in 1940 by four boys looking for a dog and were opened to the public in 1948, quickly becoming one of France's major attractions, drawing 125,000 visitors annually. However, it became evident that the hordes of tourists had caused atmospheric changes in the caves, endangering the paintings. Scientists went to work to halt the deterioration, known as "the green sickness."

ESSENTIALS

GETTING THERE   Because of infrequent use, Montignac no longer maintains its own railway station, and consequently, rail passengers get off at the neighboring hamlet of Condat-Le-Lardin, 6 miles away. From here, taxis (☎ **05-53-51-27-62**), which usually wait at the railway station, are available to transport visitors the remaining distance to Montignac (fare: 120F). For **train information** about rail travel to Condat or anywhere else in France, call ☎ **08-36-35-35-39.**

There are no bus connections from Condat to Montignac. There are bus connections from Sarlat, but because they're relatively infrequent, the easiest way to reach Montignac is **driving** northeast from Eyzies on N704 for 12 miles.

VISITOR INFORMATION   The **Office de Tourisme** is on place Bertrand-de-Born (☎ **05-53-51-82-60**), in Montignac.

EXPLORING THE CAVES

Visits to Lascaux I by the general public ceased in 1964. Permission to visit for research purposes is given only to qualified archaeologists: Apply for permission to **Direction Régionale des Affaires Culturelles (D.R.A.C.),** Service Régional de l'Archéologie, 54 cours Magendie, 33074 Bordeaux CEDEX (☎ **05-57-95-02-02**). If you want to contact the famous cave itself, call ☎ **05-53-51-90-29,** but be warned that the staff won't let you get around the rigid protocol regarding visits to the interior.

Lascaux II. ☎ **05-53-51-95-03.** Admission 48F ($8.65) adults, 20F ($3.60) children 11 and under. May 1–Aug 31 daily 9am–7pm; Sept 1–Jan 4 Tues–Sun 10am–12:30pm and 1:30–5:30pm; Jan 26–Apr 2 daily 10am–12:30pm and 1:30–5:30pm; Apr 3–Apr 30 daily 9am–7pm. Closed Jan 5–25.

A short walk downhill from the real caves leads to Lascaux II, an impressive repro-duction of the original caves, duplicated in concrete, molded aboveground. The 131-foot-long reproduction displays some 200 paintings so that you'll at least have some idea of what the "Sistine Chapel of Prehistory" looked like. Here you can see majestic bulls, wild boars, stags, "Chinese horses," and lifelike deer, the originals of which were painted by Stone Age hunters 15,000 to 20,000 years ago.

Try to show up as close to opening time as possible—the number of visitors per day is limited to 2,000, and tickets are usually sold out within 2 hours of opening. During most of the year you can buy tickets directly at Lascaux II, but during July and August you must purchase them from a kiosk adjacent to the tourist office, place Bertran de Born, in Montignac. For information, call the number above.

Site Préhistorique de Regourdou. ☎ **05-53-51-81-23.** Admission 25F ($4.50) adults, 15F ($2.70) children 7–10, free for children 6 and under. June–Aug daily 9am–6:30pm; Jan–Feb and Nov–Dec Tues–Sun 10am–noon and 2–4:30pm; March–May and Sept–Oct Tues–Sun 9am–noon and 2–5pm.

About 500 yards uphill from the barricaded grotto of Lascaux, a narrow road branches off through a forest until it reaches this site, discovered in 1954, which produced a humanoid jawbone and other artifacts.

Le Thot. 4½ miles southwest of Montignac along D706 (follow the signs pointing to the hamlet of Les Eyzies). ☎ **05-53-50-70-44.** Admission 28F ($5.05) adults, 14F ($2.50) chil-dren 6–12. You'll save some money by buying a combination ticket that grants access to both Lascaux II and Le Thot for 55F ($9.90) for adults and 27F ($4.85) for children 6 to 12. July–Aug daily 9am–6pm; Sept–June Tues–Sun 10am–noon and 2–5:30pm.

On the premises is a zoo with live animals, two projection rooms showing short films on the discovery of cave art at Lascaux, and exhibitions relating to prehistoric com-munities in the Dordogne. After your visit to Le Thot, walk out on the terrace for a view of the Vézère Valley and the Lascaux hills.

WHERE TO STAY & DINE

✪ **Château de Puy Robert.** Rte. 65, 24290 Montignac Lascaux. ☎ **05-53-51-92-13.** Fax 05-53-51-80-11. E-mail: chateaupuyrobert@wanadoo.fr. 38 units. MINIBAR TV TEL. 1,350F ($243) double; 1,750F ($315) suite. AE, DC, MC, V. Closed Oct 15–May 5.

Set on 16 acres about a 10-minute walk from the grottoes, this mansion was built in 1860 as a country home. The handsomely furnished and comfortable guest rooms offer views of the Vézère Valley, and on the premises is an outdoor pool; mountain bikes are also available. Traditionalists prefer the rooms in the château; more modern rooms are found in the annex.

Dining: The restaurant serves imaginative meals. Chef Laurent Dufour is relatively new, but he's been good enough to retain the château's one Michelin star and delicately treads the border between regional/traditional and postnouvelle. Fixed-price menus range from 195F to 395F ($35.10 to $71.10).

Hôtel Soleil d'Or. 16 rue du 4-Septembre, 24290 Montignac Lascaux. ☎ **05-53-51-80-22.** Fax 05-53-50-27-54. 32 units. MINIBAR TV TEL. 265–430F ($47.70–$77.40) double; 650–850F ($117–$153) suite. AE, DC, MC, V.

In the heart of Montignac, this place functioned during the 1800s as a postal relay sta-tion, providing food and lodging to travelers and horses. Today, much improved, it offers traditionally furnished rooms, an outdoor pool, and a landscaped garden.

Dining: There are two restaurants, the less formal of which, Le Bistrot, offers salads, snacks, and simple platters at around 50F to 90F ($9 to $16.20). The restau-rant serves traditional Dordogne fare like fricassée of frogs' legs with a tomato concassé and a "fantasy" of sea bass with caviar butter as part of fixed-price meals costing 90F to 290F ($16.20 to $52.20). There's also a pub.

3 Les Eyzies-de-Tayac

331 miles SW of Paris, 28 miles SE of Périgueux

When prehistoric skeletons were unearthed here in 1868, the market town of Les Eyzies was launched as an archaeologist's dream. This area in the Dordogne Valley was found to be one of the richest in the world in ancient sites and deposits. Little by little, more and more caves were discovered in the region. In some of these caves our early ancestors had made primitive drawings going back some 30,000 years, the most beautiful and most famous, of course, at Lascaux (above). Many caves around Les Eyzies are open to the public.

ESSENTIALS

GETTING THERE   **Local trains** run from nearby Le Buisson, which has connections from larger cities like Bordeaux. The several daily trains from Périgueux are more direct. For train information and schedules, call ☎ **08-36-35-35-39.** A **drive** to Les Eyzies-de-Tayac will be a rural route from Périgueux, starting along D710 southeast to the town of le Bugue, then following the rural road east for a short drive. Look out for the road sign leading into Les Eyzies-de-Tayac.

VISITOR INFORMATION   The **Office de Tourisme,** place de la Mairie (☎ 05-53-06-97-05), is open year-round.

EXPLORING THE AREA

If you want to pedal around the countryside, you can rent bicycles at the tourist office, beginning at 40F ($7.20) per half day or 60F ($10.80) per full day. A 100F ($18) deposit is required.

Whether you're driving or biking, some of the loveliest villages to visit include towns like **Beynac-et-Cazenac** (9 miles southeast of Les Eyzies) and **Sarlat-la-Canéda** (4½ miles northeast of Beynac). Both routes follow country roads marked only with signs leading to the above-mentioned destinations.

Make a special effort to leave time for relaxing in the shadow of the **Château de Beynac,** where the aristocracy of Périgord used to gather. The castle is a 13th-century curiosity, but it's the view over the valley that makes a break here especially worthwhile. There's a worthy restaurant nearby, on the ground floor of a converted forge/blacksmith's shop transformed into the **Hôtel Bonnet** (☎ 05-53-29-50-01).

Sarlat-la-Canéda, 6 miles northeast, has the unusual **Cathédrale St-Sacerdos** as well as the **Maison de la Boétie,** place André-Malraux, belonging to one of France's most famous Renaissance writers, Etienne de la Boétie. You might be tempted to enjoy a meal at one of the town's most endearing restaurants, the **Hostellerie Marcel,** 8 av. de Selves (☎ 05-53-59-21-98).

Musée National de Préhistoire. ☎ **05-53-06-45-45.** Admission 22F ($3.95) adults, 15F ($2.70) ages 18–25, free for children 17 and under. Dec–Mar Wed–Mon 9:30am–noon and 2–5pm; Apr–June and Sept–Nov Wed–Mon 9:30am–noon and 2–6pm; July–Aug daily 9:30am–7pm.

Prehistoric artifacts from local excavations are on display in this late 16th-century fortress-castle on a cliff overlooking Les Eyzies. On the terrace is a statue of Neanderthal man. One building displays a reconstructed Magdalenian tomb containing a woman's skeleton.

Grotte de Font-de-Gaume. Less than a mile outside Les Eyzies on D47. ☎ **05-53-06-90-80.** Admission 38F ($6.85) adults, 26F ($4.70) ages 18–25 and over 60, 15F ($2.70) children 7–17, free for children 6 and under. Apr–Sept Wed–Mon 9am–noon and 2–6pm; Mar–Oct Wed–Mon 9:30am–noon and 2–5:30pm; Nov–Feb Wed–Mon 10am–noon and 2–5pm.

This is the only authentic cave still open to visitors, though access is very limited in summer. Unfortunately, some of the markings you see aren't from the Magdalenian ages, but from British students on a holiday back in the 18th century. Here depictions of bison, reindeer, and horses, along with other animals, reveal the skill of the prehistoric artists. Note that unless you show up very early or off-season, it may be impossible to get a ticket to look at these remarkable drawings. In season, demand far exceeds the supply of tickets, as only 200 visitors per day in groups of 20 at a time are permitted in the caves. You can reserve a ticket up to a year in advance by calling the number above.

Grotte des Combarelles. On D47 for 10½ miles north of Bergerac. ☎ **05-53-06-90-80.** Admission 35F ($6.30) adults, 23F ($4.15) ages 12–24, free for children 11 and under. Apr–Sept Wed–Mon 9am–noon and 2–6pm; Oct–Mar Wed–Mon 9:30am–noon and 2–5:30pm. Closed holidays.

Discovered at the turn of the century, the Grotte des Combarelles has many drawings of animals, including musk oxen, horses, bison, and aurochs. Think of it as a gallery of Magdalenian art but be alert to the fact that because of the deterioration of the cave art, a maximum of 100 people is allowed inside every day. (After the quota is reached, no additional tickets are sold.) Advance reservations are required—you can make reservations up to a year in advance by calling the number listed above.

Grotte du Grand-Roc (Cave of the Big Rock). On D47. ☎ **05-53-06-92-70.** Admission 35F ($6.30) adults, 20F ($3.60) children. June–Sept daily 9:30am–7pm; off-season daily 9:30am–6pm. Closed Jan.

This is one of most interesting caves. Upon entering you'll come on a tunnel of stalagmites and stalactites. The cave is northwest of the market town on the left bank of the Vézère (signs point the way on D47).

WHERE TO STAY & DINE

Hôtel du Centre. Place de la Mairie, 24620 Les Eyzies-de-Tayac. ☎ **05-53-06-97-13.** Fax 05-53-06-91-63. 20 units. TEL. 280–300F ($50.40–$54) double. MC, V. Closed Nov–Jan.

Adapted during the 1980s from the premises of a very old building on the banks of the Vézère, this well-maintained hotel contains simple but comfortable bedrooms and a restaurant with well-crafted cuisine. The fixed-price menus, as prepared by Gérard Brun and his family, represent some of the best values in town. Priced at 100F to 235F ($18 to $42.30) each, they contain such dishes as an escalope of sweetbreads with cèpes (flap mushrooms), an *assiette gourmande* with three different preparations of foie gras, and roasted pigeon with mushrooms. During clement weather, enjoy your meal on a shaded terrace.

✪ **Hôtel Le Centenaire.** Rocher de la Penne, 24620 Les Eyzies-Tayac-Sireuil. ☎ **05-53-06-68-68.** Fax 05-53-06-92-41. 24 units. MINIBAR TV TEL. 600–900F ($108–$162) double; 1,200F ($216) suite. Half board 580–850F ($104.40–$153) per person extra. DC, MC, V. Closed Nov–Apr 1.

Extensive renovation and smart decorating have made this a charming hotel with handsome but uninspired rooms. It offers a heated pool, health club, and shopping gallery.

Dining: The talented chef Roland Mazère creates a light, modern French cuisine, the finest of any restaurant mentioned in this chapter. His menu might include terrine of fresh foie gras, brochette of salmon (May to September only), noisettes d'agneau (lamb), young hare with onion purée, and lobster with truffles. The restaurant is closed Tuesday at lunch. Fixed-price dinners cost 295F to 525F ($53.10 to $94.50), with a fixed-price lunch going for 165F ($29.70).

Hôtel Les Glycines. Rte. de Périgueux (D47), 24620 Les Eyzies-Tayac-Sireuil. ☎ **05-53-06-97-07.** Fax 05-53-06-92-19. 25 units. TEL. 388–398F ($69.85–$71.65) double. Half board 420F ($75.60) per person extra. AE, MC, V. Closed Oct 15–Apr 6.

Since 1862 this establishment has offered substantial regional cuisine, comfortable accommodations, and dozens of charming touches, such as drinks served on a veranda with a grape arbor. Henri and Christiane Mercat are the hardworking owners of this 4-acre garden inn. Restaurant specialties include *émincé* of goose in confit. Fixed-price menus are 135F to 180F ($24.30 to $32.40).

4 Brive-la-Gaillarde (Varetz)

302 miles SW of Paris, 56 miles S of Limoges

Three of the old provinces of France—Limousin, Quercy, and Périgord—met near here. At the crossroads, Brive "the Bold" is an inviting town, with memories of the renowned French novelist Colette, who lived nearby when she was married to Henri de Jouvenel (see the Château de Castel-Novel under "Where to Stay," below). An important gastronomic center, Brive today is a land of fine fruits, truffles, vegetables, and liqueurs, and in some of its shops you can buy a uniquely flavored local mustard.

ESSENTIALS

GETTING THERE   Brive has rail, bus, and highway connections from all other parts of France as it lies at the intersection of the Paris–Spain and Bordeaux–Lyon rail lines. Five **trains** arrive daily from Paris (trip time: 4½ hours), and two trains daily from Périgueux (trip time: 1 hour). For train information and schedules, call ☎ **08-36-35-35-39.** There's also one daily **bus** that makes the 1-hour trip from Périgueux to Brive for 45F ($8.10).

If you're **driving,** take N89 east from Périgueux to Brive and expect to drive about 1½ hours.

The local **airport,** Laroche (☎ **05-55-86-88-37**), is 3 miles west of the town.

VISITOR INFORMATION   The **Office de Tourisme** is on place du 14-Juillet (☎ **05-55-24-08-80**).

SPECIAL EVENTS   During the middle of August, **Les Orchestrades** brings together young international musicians for instrumental and choir concert performances. These concerts are free and take place in the early evening hours at different venues around town. Call the **Office of Cultural Affairs** (☎ **05-55-92-39-39**) for detailed information.

EXPLORING THE AREA

If you have a car, we suggest that you head south of Brive on D38 for the "red village" of **Collonges.** This hamlet contains petite mansions built of dark-red stone, including one corbeled house from the 16th century dedicated to the Siren. The church nearby is Romanesque, built in the 11th and 12th centuries.

After leaving Collonges, you can continue south, passing the Puy Rouge, until you reach **Meyssac,** also built of red sandstone, known as "Collonges clay." The people here make pottery out of this clay. The village is charming with its wooden buildings, some with porch roofs and antique towers.

From Meyssac, you can take D14, which becomes D96, until you reach the intersection with D20. Take D20, which becomes D8, leading north to Brive again. On the way back, you might like to stop at the tiny village of **Turenne,** its old houses evoking long-ago provincial France.

From here, continue along D8, passing through Nazareth, until you connect with D158 leading to **Noailles.** On a hillside, the Noailles church with its Limousin-style bell tower dominates the rolling green countryside. From Noailles, it's just a short drive back into Brive.

In Brive itself is the museum listed below, as well as the nearby **Eglise St-Martin,** place Charles-de-Gaulle (☎ 05-55-24-10-82), a hodgepodge of architectural styles, with a Romanesque transept and 14th-century aisles. It's open daily from 9:30am to noon and 2 to 7pm, excluding during masses.

Musée de Brive-la-Gaillarde. In the Hôtel de Labenche, 26 bis bd. Jules-Ferry. ☎ **05-55-24-19-05.** Admission 27F ($4.85) adults, 16F ($2.90) students, free for children 16 and under. Apr–Oct Wed–Mon 10am–6:30pm; Nov–Mar Wed–Mon 1:30–6pm.

In the town center, the 16th-century residence that houses the museum is one of Brive's most beautiful monuments. The art collections inside include objects from the prehistoric, Gallo-Roman, and medieval periods; paintings, folk art, 17th-century English tapestries, and natural-history exhibits; and mementos of Brive's celebrated native daughters and sons.

WHERE TO STAY

La Crémaillère (see below) also rents rooms.

✪ **Château de Castel-Novel.** 19240 Varetz. ☎ **05-55-85-00-01.** Fax 05-55-85-09-03. 36 units. A/C TV TEL. 595–1,260F ($107.10–$226.80) double; 1,465–1,650F ($263.70–$297) suite. AE, DC, MC, V. Closed mid-Oct to Apr. Take D901 6½ miles northwest of Brive; it's half a mile outside Varetz.

The spirit of Colette lives on at this isolated old château on 25 acres. The French novelist often lived here while she was married to Henri de Jouvenel and drew many of the political and literary luminaries of her day to Varetz. Ten newer rooms are in the less luxurious annex, La Borderie, each with minibar and air-conditioning, but literary fans prefer the main building. Colette's library has been turned into a charming salon, and the old stables are now a banqueting hall.

Dining: In summer, lunch is prepared on a grill near the pool. In the restaurant, the cuisine includes temptations like filet of red mullet meunière; a combination plate of grilled veal, beef, and lamb; duckling stuffed with sorrel; ragoût of foie gras and truffles; and a salad of flap mushrooms and gizzards. Reservations are required.

Amenities: Pool, tennis courts.

Hôtel Ibis. 32 rue Marcellin-Roche, 19100 Brive-la-Gaillarde. ☎ **05-55-17-42-42.** Fax 05-55-23-54-41. 50 units. TV TEL. 310F ($55.80) double. AE, MC, V.

A 5-minute walk from the town center, this modern hotel was renovated in 1995. Since then, after several management changes, it has had three different names. The rooms are chain-hotel standardized, neutrally decorated, and comfortable but with few frills. The hotel has a bar but no restaurant. The staff helps direct hungry diners to any of a half dozen restaurants within a short walk.

WHERE TO DINE

✪ **La Crémaillère.** 53 av. de Paris, 19100 Brive. ☎ **05-55-74-32-47.** Fax 05-55-17-91-83. Reservations required. Main courses 68–220F ($12.25–$39.60); fixed-price menus 100–200F ($18–$36). V. Tues–Sun 12:30–1:30pm, Tues–Sat 7:30–9:30pm. FRENCH.

Charlou Reynal is winning increasing acclaim as an inventive chef, and he's the darling of the thriving local art colony, who treat this place as their hangout. He knows how to transform local produce into tasty dishes. Menu items include filet of perch with cèpes (flap mushrooms), poached turbot with white butter, and *chaussons aux cèpes,* which is a medley of exotic mushrooms in puff pastry and a specialty of the house. The blood sausage with chestnuts might be too robust for most tastes.

Eight well-furnished rooms are available, costing 250F ($45) double. The hotel is closed Sunday night and Monday.

BRIVE-LA-GAILLARDE AFTER DARK

This town tends to turn in early, so you won't find a very active nightlife. But as you wander the streets looking for some action, you should find a lively enough crowd at either **Le Watson Bar,** rue des Echevins (☎ 05-55-17-07-87), or **L'Europe,** 21 av. Paris (☎ 05-55-24-19-55). Both are of the brasserie/cafe genre and tend really to start hopping as the evening wears on. The only other surefire bet is the disco **La Charette,** 33 av. Ribot (☎ 05-55-87-65-73), with its techno-funk-rock mix and 18- to 30-year-old dance-floor junkies. You'll pay 60F ($10.80) to get in.

5 Rocamadour

336 miles SW of Paris, 41 miles SE of Sarlat-la-Canéda, 34 miles S of Brive, 39 miles NE of Cahors

The Middle Ages seem to live on here. After all, Rocamadour reached the zenith of its fame and prosperity in the 13th century. Make an effort to see it even if it's out of your way. The setting is striking, one of the most unusual in Europe: Towers, old buildings, and oratories rise in stages up the side of a cliff on the right slope of the usually dry gorge of Alzou.

The faithful continue to arrive today as they did more than 8 centuries ago. As a pilgrimage site, Rocamadour is billed as "the second site of France," with Mont-St-Michel ranking first, of course. Its population has held steady around 5,000 for many years. Summer visitors descend in droves, and vehicles are prohibited. Park in one of the big lots and make your way on foot.

ESSENTIALS

GETTING THERE   Rocamadour and neighboring Padirac share a **train** station that isn't really convenient to either—it's 3 miles east of Rocamadour on N140, serviced by infrequent trains from Brive in the north and Capdenac in the south. Most visitors avoid the inconvenience and drive. For train information and schedules, call ☎ 08-36-35-35-39. The best way to reach Rocamadour **by car** is from Bordeaux. Travel east along N89 to Brive-la-Gaillarde, connecting to N205 east into Cressensac, continuing along N140 south into Rocamadour.

VISITOR INFORMATION   The **Office de Tourisme,** in the Hôtel de Ville, rue Roland-le-Preux (☎ 05-65-33-62-59), is open year-round except Christmas and New Year's Day.

SEEING THE TOWN

This gravity-defying village, with its single street (lined with souvenir shops), rises abruptly along the side of a steep hill. It's best seen when approached from the road coming in from the tiny village of L'Hospitalet. Once in Rocamadour, you can take a flight of steps from the lower town (Basse Ville) to the town's **Cité Religieuse**—a cluster of chapels and churches—halfway up the cliff. The less agile are advised to take the elevator instead.

There's a fee of 25F ($4.50) one-way or 30F ($5.40) round-trip to ride both of the town's two elevators. One goes from the Basse Ville to the Cité Religieuse; the other goes from the Cité Religieuse to the panoramic medieval ramparts ("le château") high above the town (see below).

The most photogenic entrance to the Basse Ville is through the **Porte de Figuier (Fig Tree Gate),** through which many of the most illustrious Europeans of the 13th century passed.

One of the oldest places of pilgrimage in France, Rocamadour became famous as a cult center of the black Madonna. It was supposedly founded by Zacchaeus, who entertained Christ at Jericho. He's claimed to have come here with a black wooden statue of the Virgin, although some authorities have suggested that this statue was carved in the 9th century.

The Cité Religieuse. Place de la Carreta. Free admission, but donation to churches and guides appreciated. Guided tours of the chapels June–Sept 15 Mon–Sat 9am–6pm.

The entrance to the **Grand Escalier** (stairway) leads up to the town's religious centerpiece—a climb of 216 steps. Even today, devout pilgrims make this difficult journey on their knees in penance: A recent devotee was the French composer Francis Poulenc, who remained in Rocamadour after a religious conversion he experienced here, and in honor of which he composed his *Litanies à la Vierge Noire.* Climbing its weathered steps will lead to the **Parvis des Eglises,** place St-Amadour, with seven chapels.

Musée d'Art Sacré/Trésor Francis Poulenc. Parvis du Sanctuaire. ☎ **05-65-33-23-30.** Admission 35F ($6.30) adults, 20F ($3.60) children 5–12. Jan–June and Sept–Dec daily 10am–noon and 2–6pm; July–Aug daily 10am–7pm. Closed Nov–Apr except by advance appointment through the tourist board.

This artistic highlight of the religious complex, which was radically enlarged and renovated in 1996, contains a gold chalice presented by the 19th-century pope, Pius II, among other treasures.

Basilique St-Sauveur. Place St-Amadour. ☎ **05-65-33-23-23.** Daily 9am–5pm.

Against the cliff, this basilica was built in the Romanesque-Gothic style from the 11th to the 13th centuries. It's decorated with paintings and inscriptions, recalling visits of celebrated persons, including Philippe the Handsome. In the Chapelle Miraculeuse, the "holy of holies," the mysterious St. Amadour is said to have carved out an oratory in the rock. Hanging from the roof of this chapel is one of the oldest clocks known, dating back to the 8th century. Above the altar is the venerated statue of the Madonna. The Romanesque Chapelle St-Michel is sheltered by an overhanging rock; inside are two frescoes rich in coloring, dating from the 12th century. Above the door leading to the Chapelle Notre-Dame is a large iron sword that, according to legend, belonged to Roland.

Built on a cliff spur (reached by the curvy "chemin de la Croix") for chaplains in the 19th century, the château was medieval before its restoration. It's of only minor interest, but the view from its ramparts is panoramic. It's open daily: in July and August from 9am to 7pm and the rest of the year from 9am to noon and 1:30 to 6pm. Admission is 13F ($2.35) for adults and 11F ($2) for children 12 and under.

WHERE TO STAY & DINE

Hôtel Beau-Site et Le Jehan de Valon. Cité Médiévale, 46500 Rocamadour. ☎ **800/ 528-1234** in the U.S., or 05-65-33-63-08. Fax 05-65-33-65-23. E-mail: beausite. rocamadour@wanadoo.fr. 43 units. TV TEL. 380–490F ($68.40–$88.20) double; 550–690F ($99–$124.20) suite. AE, DC, MC, V. Closed Nov 12–Feb 12.

The stone walls here were built in the 15th century by an Order of Malta commander. Today the rear terrace provides a sweeping view of the Val d'Alzou. The reception area has heavy beams and a cavernous fireplace big enough to roast an ox. The rooms (in the main building and a less desirable annex) are comfortable; four are air-conditioned.

Dining: The restaurant serves flavorful regional cuisine prepared by the Menot family, who've owned the place for generations. Specialties include foie gras of duck with dark truffles, duckmeat salad, raw marinated salmon with green peppercorns, and a cake of caramelized walnuts. Fixed-price menus run 135F to 220F ($24.30 to $39.60).

Hôtel Domaine de La Rhue. 46500 Rocamadour. ☎ **05-65-33-71-50.** Fax 05-65-33-72-48. 12 units. TV TEL. 380–580F ($68.40–$104.40) double. MC, V.

The three-star Domaine de La Rhue, a renovated 19th-century stable, is between the Dordogne and Quercy. The charming owners, Christine and Eric Jooris, gutted the old stable and turned it into a series of handsome and spacious bedrooms, each individually decorated in superb taste, on the upper level. The upper level can be accessed directly from high ground, thus relieving guests of lugging heavy bags upstairs. On the lower level waits an inviting reception and breakfast with a huge, very warm and welcoming fireplace. There is also a swimming pool outside. The Joorises, who speak English, are most helpful in directing you to the best places for dinner in the center of Rocamadour, which is only a few minutes' drive away. Christine enjoys mapping out perfect tours of the nearby villages and plotting the best direction to approach each town and/or castle so as to have a commanding view from the distance and to take advantage of afternoon sun for photographs.

NEARBY ACCOMMODATIONS & DINING

Château de Roumégouse. N140, Rignac, 46500 Gramat. ☎ **05-65-33-63-81.** Fax 05-65-33-71-18. www.integra.fr/relaischateaux.fr/roumegouse. E-mail: roumegouse@relaischateaux.fr. 16 units. MINIBAR TV TEL. 650–1,000F ($117–$180) double; 1,200–1,300F ($216–$234) suite. AE, MC, V. Closed Nov–Apr 1. Take N140 to Roumégouse, 2½ miles southeast of Rocamadour.

If you prefer to be away from the tourist bustle, try this Relais & Châteaux in Roumégouse. The 15th-century château overlooking the Causse is surrounded by 12 acres of parkland. Each room is unique, in both architecture and decor, and one has a private garden.

Dining: In the lovely dining room, fixed-price menus cost 185F to 330F ($33.30 to $59.40); it's closed Tuesday at dinner except in July and August, and it's closed from December to Easter. Even the scrambled eggs come with truffles!

6 Cahors

336 miles SW of Paris, 135 miles SE of Bordeaux, 55 miles N of Toulouse

The ancient capital of Quercy, Cahors was a thriving university city in the Middle Ages, and many antiquities from its illustrious past life remain. However, Cahors is best known today for the almost-legendary red wine that's made principally from the Malbec grapes grown in vineyards around this old city in central France. Firm but not harsh, Cahors is one of the most deeply colored fine French wines.

ESSENTIALS

GETTING THERE Cahors is serviced by **train** from Toulouse, Brive, and Montauban. You may have to transfer in neighboring towns. For train information and schedules, call ☎ 08-36-35-35-39. There's infrequent bus service from some of the outlying villages, several of which are of historic interest, but it's vastly easier to drive. The **drive** to Cahors is a simple one from Toulouse. Follow A62 north to the junction of A62 and N20, continuing along N20 north into Cahors.

VISITOR INFORMATION   The **Office de Tourisme** is on place François-Mitterrand (☎ 05-65-53-20-65).

SPECIAL EVENTS   The **Festival de Blues** turns this town upside down during the last week of July when famous blues groups, including some from the United States, descend on different venues around Cahors. Tickets range from 100F to 200F ($18 to $36), and exact dates and performing artists can be obtained from the Office de Tourisme (see above).

EXPLORING THE AREA

The town is on a rocky peninsula almost entirely surrounded by a loop of the Lot River. It grew up near a sacred spring that, incidentally, still supplies the city with water. At the source of the spring, the **Fontaine des Chartreux** stands by the side of the **pont Valentré** (also called the pont du Diable), a bridge with a trio of towers, a magnificent example of medieval defensive design erected between 1308 and 1380, then restored in the 19th century. The pont, the first medieval fortified bridge in France, is the most colorful site in Cahors, with crenellated parapets, battlements, and seven pointed arches.

Dominating the old town, the **Cathédrale St-Etienne,** 30 rue de la Chanterie (☎ 05-65-35-27-80), was built beginning in 1119 and reconstructed between 1285 and 1500. It was the first cathedral in the country to have cupolas, giving it a Romanesque-Byzantine look. One remarkable feature is its finely sculptured Romanesque north portal, carved about 1135 in the Languedoc style. It's open daily from 8am (scheduled hour for daily mass) to 6 or 7pm, depending on the season. Adjoining the cathedral are the remains of a Gothic cloister from the late 15th century.

SIDE TRIPS   Cahors is a starting point for an excursion to the **Célé and Lot valleys,** a long journey that many French are fond of taking in summer, a round-trip of about 125 miles, lasting 2 days if you have plenty of time for sightseeing. The Office de Tourisme (see above) provides maps that offer itineraries.

The **Grotte du Pech-Merle** (☎ 05-65-31-27-05), a prehistoric cave near Cabrerets, 21 miles east of Cahors, was once used for ancient religious rites. The wall paintings, footprints, and carvings were discovered in 1922 and are approximately 20,000 years old. The cave may be explored only from about April 1 to November 1, daily from 9:30am to noon and 1:30 to 5pm. Admission is 38F to 44F ($6.85 to $7.90) for adults and 25F to 30F ($4.50 to $5.40) for children. There are 2 miles of chambers and galleries open to the public, especially interesting for those familiar with geology. The Aurignacian- and Magdalenian-age art includes drawings of mammoths, bison, aurochs, horses, deer, mountain goats, and women. One cave is called the picture gallery, as it's decorated with the outlines of two horses.

FOR WINE LOVERS   Woven into the fabric of Cahors's heritage is a rich tradition of wine making. The wines of Cahors are characterized by a heady robustness that mellows over time. Two wineries of exceptional merit are Jean Jouffreau's **Clos de Gamot** in Prayssac, about 20 minutes west of Cahors (☎ 05-65-22-40-26), and **Château de Gaudou** in Vire-sur-Lot (☎ 05-65-36-52-93). Their dark wines are of consistently high quality and easily hold their own with any of the region's rich, hearty dishes. The Office de Tourisme (see above) provides detailed information and maps to these wineries.

WHERE TO STAY

Hôtel France. 252 av. Jean-Jaurès, 46000 Cahors. Tel. **05-65-35-16-76.** Fax 05-65-22-01-08. 79 units. MINIBAR TEL. 250–400F ($45–$72) double. AE, DC, MC, V. Parking 40F ($7.20). Closed Dec 20–Jan 5.

This hotel, between pont Valentré and the train station, provides the best rooms in the town center. They're well furnished and well equipped, 38 with air-conditioning. The room service is efficient, and breakfast is the only meal served.

Hôtel Terminus. 5 av. Charles-de-Freycinet, 46000 Cahors. ☎ **05-65-35-24-50.** Fax 05-65-22-06-40. 22 units. TV TEL. 550–935F ($99–$168.30) double. AE, DC, MC, V. Free parking in open courtyard, 45F ($8.10) in covered garage.

On the avenue leading from the railway station into the heart of town, this hotel still oozes with the turn-of-the-century character of its original stone construction. The rooms are conservative and comfortable, last renovated in 1994. The staff is extraordinarily warm and helpful.

Dining: On the premises is a well-recommended restaurant, Le Balandre. Even if you don't opt for a meal in its Art Deco dining room or on its outdoor terrace, you might want to step into its 1920s-style bar for a drink.

WHERE TO DINE

Popular with a young crowd is **Les Terraces Valentré,** a block to the left of pont Valentré (☎ **05-65-35-95-88**). Here you can order a beer, meet some locals, and take in one of the best river views in town, especially of the flamboyant bridge.

La Taverne. Place Escorbiac. ☎ **05-65-35-28-66.** Reservations recommended. Main courses 70–110F ($12.60–$19.80); fixed-price menus 85–250F ($15.30–$45). V. Mon–Fri noon–2pm and 7–9:30pm, Sun noon–2pm. Closed Feb and Sat–Sun nights. FRENCH.

This restaurant serves outstanding local cuisine in a rustic atmosphere. The finely crafted cuisine of Quercy is featured here, along with other regional specialties. Typical dishes are truffles in puff pastry, tournedos with foie gras and truffles, duck filet, breast of chicken with morels, and fresh fish.

7 Montauban

404 miles SW of Paris, 45 miles NW of Albi, 31 miles N of Toulouse

This pink-brick capital of the Tarn-et-Garonne is the city of the painter Ingres and the sculptor Bourdelle. Montauban, on the right bank of the Tarn, is one of the most ancient of southwest France's towns, still dominated by the fortified Eglise St-Jacques. The most scenic view of Montauban is at the 14th-century brick bridge, pont Vieux, which connects the town to its satellite of Villebourbon. The bridge is supported by seven arches.

An admirer of Raphael and a student of David, Jean-Auguste-Dominique Ingres was born in 1780 in Montauban, the son of an ornamental sculptor/painter. The father recognized his son's artistic abilities early and encouraged him. Ingres lived for a time in Italy, seeking inspiration in classical motifs. He was noted for his nudes and historical paintings, now fine examples of neoclassicism. One of his first exhibitions of portraits in 1806 met with ridicule, but later generations have been more appreciative.

ESSENTIALS

GETTING THERE Seven **trains** per day arrive from Paris (trip time: 5½ hours); trains arrive every hour from Toulouse (trip time: 25 minutes). For train information and schedules, call ☎ **08-36-35-35-39.**

If you're **driving,** R.N. 20 (Paris–Toulouse–Andorra, Spain), R.N. 113 (Bordeaux–Marseille), and the A61 motorway run through the Tarn-et-Garonne.

VISITOR INFORMATION   The Office de Tourisme is on rue du Collège (☎ 05-63-63-60-60).

SPECIAL EVENTS   The two major festivals that take place in Montauban occur in May and the end of July. The **Festival Alors Chante** showcases French music and song and offers performances by some of the biggest French stars. In July, the **Festival de Jazz** fills the outdoor venues with blues and jazz concerts, including the wildly popular Baltimore Baptist Church Choir. The Office de Tourisme has information on both events, or contact **Synergie** (☎ **05-63-20-46-72**) for specifics on the Festival de Jazz.

EXPLORING THE AREA

You can rent bicycles at **Denayrolles,** 878 av. Jean-Moulin (☎ **05-63-03-62-02**), open Monday from 2 to 7pm and Tuesday to Saturday from 8:15am to noon and 2 to 7pm. A deposit of 1,500F ($270) is required.

Shoppers may want to pick up some foie gras and other goose products at the **Conserverie Artisanale Larroque,** 1300 av. de Falguières (☎ **05-63-63-45-40**). Or visit a pâtisserie for a supply of Montauriol (a chocolate-covered cherry with a shot of armagnac) and Boulet de Montauban (a chocolate-covered roasted hazelnut). For a collectible specialty of the town, go to the **Librairie Deloche,** 21 rue de la Résistance (☎ **05-63-63-22-66**), where you can buy a *pigeonnier miniature*—miniature models of "pigeon coops" that were built on local farms to attract pigeons for their "fertilizer." Deloche carries 30 models of various architectural styles and a selection of books on pigeonniers.

In addition to taking in the Ingres masterpieces in the museum listed below, head for the **Cathédrale Notre-Dame,** place Roosevelt, a classical building framed by two square towers. In the north transept is the painting the church commissioned from Ingres, *Vow of Louis XIII.* It's open daily from 9am to noon and 2 to 6pm.

✪ **Musée Ingres.** 19 rue de l'Hôtel-de-Ville. ☎ **05-63-22-12-91.** Admission 20F ($3.60) adults, 12F ($2.15) children. July–Aug daily 9:30am–noon and 1:30–6pm; Sept–June Tues–Sun 10am–noon and 2–6pm.

Although the Louvre in Paris owns many Ingres masterpieces, upon his 1867 death the artist bequeathed to Montauban more than two dozen paintings and some 4,000 drawings. These are displayed at this 17th-century bishops' palace. One painting in the collection is *Christ and the Doctors,* a work Ingres completed at 82. The *Dream of Ossian* was intended for Napoléon's bedroom in Rome. On the ground floor are works by Antoine Bourdelle, who was heavily influenced by Rodin. The two busts Bourdelle sculpted of Ingres and of Rodin are particularly outstanding.

WHERE TO STAY

The **Hôtel Orsay** (see below) also rents rooms.

Hostellerie Les Coulandrières. Rte. de Castelsarrasin, 82290 Montbeton, near Montauban. ☎ **05-63-67-47-47.** Fax 05-63-67-46-45. 22 units. TV TEL. 480F ($86.40) double. Half board 360F ($64.80) per person extra. AE, DC.

This inn, 2 miles northwest of Montauban's center in the village of Montbeton, occupies the site of an old farm, the original buildings of which form the reception area, bar, and restaurant. Set in a 10-acre park, it offers pleasant, traditionally furnished bedrooms in a nearby annex built around 1975. Facilities include a pool and miniature-golf course. The inn also makes an excellent dining choice, as first-class ingredients are deftly handled by the chefs. In summer, grills are a specialty.

Hôtel Ingres. 10 av. Mayenne, 82000 Montauban. ☎ **05-63-63-36-01.** Fax 05-63-66-02-90. 31 units. A/C MINIBAR TV TEL. 470F ($84.60) double. AE, DC, MC, V.

Many people rate the Ingres the town's finest place to stay. Streamlined and contemporary, a short walk from the rail station, it has comfortable, internationally modern rooms, some overlooking a rear garden and an outdoor swimming pool. Breakfast is the only meal served. This choice is more solid and reliable than exciting.

WHERE TO DINE

Hôtel Orsay et Restaurant La Cuisine d'Alain. Face Gare (across from the train station). ☎ **05-63-66-06-66.** Fax 05-63-66-19-39. Reservations recommended. Main courses 95–142F ($17.10–$25.55); fixed-price menus 125–280F ($22.50–$50.40). AE, DC, MC, V. Tues–Sat 12:30–2pm, Mon–Sat 7:30–9:30pm. Closed Dec 23–Jan 6 and the second and third weeks in Aug. FRENCH.

This is the best restaurant in town, as chef Alain Blanc is talented and inventive. Try his terrine of lentils flavored with the neck of a fattened goose en confit, filet of beef with liver and apple flan, or escalope of foie gras poêlée. The amazing dessert trolley offers plenty of choices.

Reasonably priced rooms also are available in the Hôtel Orsay. Doubles rent for 290F to 340F ($52.20 to $61.20).

MONTAUBAN AFTER DARK

Our favorite nightspot here is **La Santa Maria,** quai Montmurat (☎ **05-63-91-99-09**). Near the Musée d'Ingres, it's a bar loaded with ambience and offering different theme nights (salsa, merengue, rock, retro disco). The place gets lively after 9:30pm. Less stylish is **Bar Le Flamand,** 8 rue de la République, near the cathedral (☎ **05-63-66-12-20**), with an easygoing crowd and a broad roster of Belgian beers. If you're under 25 and want to party with your contemporaries, head for **Le Doppler,** 13 av. Jean-Jaurès, adjacent to the rail station (☎ **05-63-03-07-45**).

17

Bordeaux & the Atlantic Coast

From historic La Rochelle to the bordeaux wine district, the south-west of France is often glimpsed only briefly by those driving from Paris to Spain. However, this area is famous for its Atlantic beaches, medieval and Renaissance ruins, Romanesque and Gothic churches, vineyards, and charming old inns that serve up splendid regional cuisine.

In our journey through this intriguing region, we don't stay entirely on the coastline but dip inland for a snifter of cognac in Cognac and trips to nearby art cities like Poitiers and Angoulême. If you can manage it, it's great to allow a week in this region—just enough time to sample the wine, savor the cuisine, and see at least some of the major sights.

REGIONAL CUISINE   Major specialties from this region are the *huîtres* (oysters) from Arcachon or Marennes, *jambon* (ham) from Poitou, *esturgeon* (sturgeon) or *saumon* (salmon) from the Gironde, *canard* (duck) from Challans, *chapon* (capon) or *poularde* (chicken) from Barbezieux, and *agneau* (lamb) from Pauillac.

Other specialties include *mouclade* (a mussel stew prepared with cream or white wine and shallots), *lamproie* or *l'anguille à la bordelaise* (lamprey eels from local rivers, served with a blood-enriched red-wine sauce), *entrecôte à la bordelaise* (steak in a wine-laced brown sauce with shallots, tarragon, and bone marrow), *cèpes à la bordelaise* (flap mush-rooms sautéed in oil and seasoned with chopped shallots and garlic), *escargots à la vigneronne* (snails simmered in a sauce of wine, garlic, and onions), and *chaudrée* (a local fish soup). The region's most famous cheese is chabichou, a variety of goat cheese, from Poitou; its best chocolate is les duchesses d'Angoulême.

Bordeaux wines include everything from the finest French vintages to ordinary table wines found on supermarket shelves. Among the best are the incomparable wines from the Médoc and Graves. Other reds include St-Emilion and Pomerol.

1 Poitiers

207 miles SW of Paris, 110 miles SE of Nantes

This city, the ancient capital of Poitou, the northern part of Aquitaine, is filled with history. Everybody has passed through here—from Eng-land's Black Prince to Joan of Arc to Richard the Lion-Hearted.

Poitiers stands on a hill overlooking the Clain and Boivre rivers. It was this very strategic location that tempted so many conquerors. Charles Martel proved the savior of Christendom by chasing out the Muslims in 732 and altering the course of European civilization. Poitiers was the chief city of Eleanor of Aquitaine, who had her marriage to pious Louis VII annulled so she could wed England's Henry II.

For those interested in antiquity, this is one of the most fascinating towns in France. That battle we learned about in history books was fought on September 19, 1356, between the armies of Edward the Black Prince and those of King John of France. It was one of the three great English victories of the Hundred Years War, distinguished by the use of the longbow in the skilled hands of English archers.

In recent years the town has really come alive, after decades of slumber, with the opening of Futuroscope, a futuristic cinema theme park. One-third of today's population of approximately 85,000 residents consists of students.

ESSENTIALS

GETTING THERE   **Rail service** is available from Paris, Bordeaux, and La Rochelle. Some 18 of the fast TGV trains arrive from Paris daily (trip time: 1½ hours). Eighteen trains arrive daily from Bordeaux (trip time: 1¾ hours), and 11 pull in daily from La Rochelle (trip time: 2 hours). For train information and schedules, call ☎ **08-36-35-35-39.** If you're **driving,** the city of Poitiers is located on the A10 highway; from Paris, follow A10 south through the cities of Orléans and Tours, on to Poitiers.

VISITOR INFORMATION   The **Office de Tourisme** is at 8 rue des Grandes-Ecoles (☎ **05-49-41-21-24**).

SPECIAL EVENTS   The most active time to visit is in July and August during the **Poitiers l'Eté,** a festival of live jazz, opera, rock, and fireworks. Check with **Le Local** (☎ **05-49-62-84-83**) for complete information or call the tourist office. Most of the concerts are free. The cultural calendar continues into the autumn and winter, with **Rencontres Musicales de Poitiers,** 79 rue des Frères-Voisin (☎ **05-49-58-42-13**), sponsoring classical works performed in biweekly programs from late October through late April. Tickets average 60F ($10.80).

SEEING THE SIGHTS

Futuroscope. About 5½ miles north of Poitiers in Jaunay-Clan. ☎ **05-49-49-30-80.** Admission 140–185F ($25.20–$33.30) adults, 110–150F ($19.80–$27) children 5–16, free for children 4 and under. Daily 9am–6pm (to 7pm in summer). From Poitiers, bus no. 16 runs to the park; if you're driving, take N10.

Drawing some 3 million visitors annually, this science amusement park is a wonderland of technology that lets you experience new sounds, images, and sensations with the world's most advanced film-projection techniques and largest screens. Exhibitions include Kinemax (a rock crystal covered with mirrors with a 400-seat cinema); Omnimax (films projected onto a gigantic dome via a special fish-eye lens, putting you into the heart of the action); Le Tapis Magique (a cinema that lets you fly above a continent with a monarch butterfly to guide you); and a 3-D cinema that puts you close to the lions on a safari. L'IMAX 3D, added in 1996, features the first-ever fiction film presented on a 600mm flat screen. The 40-minute film, *Guillaumet: Wings of Courage,* follows a heroic episode in the history of airmail.

Cathédrale St-Pierre. Place de la Cathédrale. ☎ **05-49-41-21-24.** Free admission. Daily 8am–7pm.

Located in the eastern sector of Poitiers, the twin-towered Cathédrale St-Pierre was begun in 1162 by Henry II of England and Eleanor of Aquitaine on the ruins of a Roman basilica. The cathedral was completed much later, but it has always been

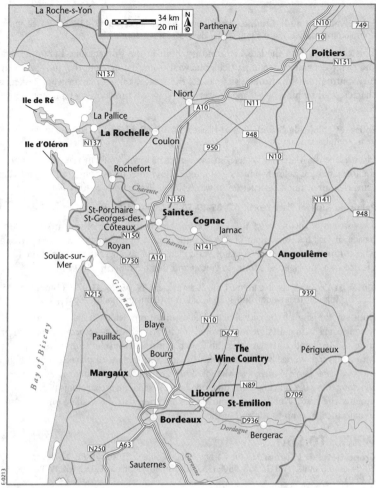

undistinguished architecturally. However, the interior, 295 feet long, contains some admirable stained glass from the 12th and 13th centuries.

Baptistère St-Jean. Rue Jean-Jaurès. Admission 4F (70¢). July–Aug daily 10am–noon and 2–6pm; Apr–June and Sept–Oct Wed–Mon 10:30am–12:30pm and 3–6pm; Nov–Mar Wed–Mon 2:30–4:30pm.

From the cathedral, you can walk to the the most ancient Christian monument in France. It was built as a baptistery in the early 4th century on Roman foundations, then extended in the 7th century. It contains frescoes from the 11th to the 14th centuries and a collection of funerary sculpture.

Eglise Ste-Radegonde. Place St-Radegonde. ☎ **05-49-41-23-76.** Free admission. Summer daily 8am–8pm; winter 8am–6pm.

A favorite place of pilgrimage in times gone by, this 11th-century structure in the eastern section of Poitiers commemorates the patroness of Poitiers. In its crypt is her black marble sarcophagus. Radegonde, who died in 587, was the consort of Clotaire, king of the Franks.

Eglise Notre-Dame-la-Grande. Place Charles-de-Gaulle. ☎ **05-49-41-22-56.** Free admission. Summer daily 8:15am–7pm; winter daily 8:15am–6:30pm.

This church is from the late 11th century, built in the Romanesque-Byzantine style and richly decorated. See in particular its west front, dating from the mid–12th century. Surrounded by an open-air market, the facade, carved like an ivory casket, is characterized by pinecone-shaped towers. Carvings on the doorway represent biblical scenes.

Eglise St-Hilaire-le-Grand. Rue St-Hilaire. ☎ **05-49-41-21-57.** Free admission. Daily 9am–7pm. Closed Sun morning.

From place du Maréchal-Leclerc, in the center of town, you can take rue Carnot to the Romanesque Eglise St-Hilaire-le-Grand. The church dates from the 11th and 12th centuries; after much destruction, it was restored in the 19th century.

Palais de Justice. Place Lepetit. ☎ **05-49-50-22-00.** Mon–Fri 9am–noon and 1–5pm.

This structure incorporates the 14th-century keep and some other parts of a ducal palace. It was here that Joan of Arc was questioned by the doctors of the university who composed the French Court of Parliament, and also here that Richard the Lion-Hearted was proclaimed comte de Poitou and duc d'Anjou in 1170.

Musée St-Croix. Accessible from 61 rue St-Simplicien. ☎ **05-49-41-07-53.** Admission 15F ($2.70). Tues–Fri 10am–noon and 1–5pm, Sat–Sun 10am–noon and 2–6pm.

Built on the site of the old abbey of St-Croix, from which it takes its name, the museum has a fine-arts section devoted mainly to painting—especially Flemish art from the 16th and 17th centuries and Dutch paintings from the 16th to the 18th centuries. Several works by Bonnard, Sisley, and Oudot are displayed, along with a bronze, *The Three Graces,* by Maillol. Our favorite painting here is *Nuit d'Enfer d'Arthur Rimbaud,* all cubed up and convulsing. A separate archaeological section documents the history of Poitou, from prehistoric times to the Gallo-Roman era, the Renaissance, and up to the end of the 19th century.

WHERE TO STAY

Grand Hôtel de l'Europe. 39 rue Carnot, 86000 Poitiers. ☎ **05-49-88-12-00.** Fax 05-49-88-97-30. 88 units. TV TEL. 330–480F ($59.40–$86.40) double. AE, DC, MC, V. Parking 20F ($3.60).

Some 200 years ago this was a coaching inn; later the stables were transformed into additional rooms. The field where the horses were watered is now a quiet courtyard with trees and shrubbery. The isolation of this place enhances its sense of 1930s civility. Many of the guest rooms were recently renovated and are much more modern than the gracefully antique public rooms suggest. Breakfast is served in an old-fashioned dining room, with tall windows and an elaborate fireplace.

Hôtel du Plat d'Etain. 7 rue du Plat-d'Etain, 86000 Poitiers. ☎ **05-49-41-04-80.** Fax 05-49-52-25-84. 24 units, 21 with bathroom. MINIBAR TV TEL. 260F ($46.80) double without bathroom, 350F ($63) double with bathroom. AE, V. Parking 15F ($2.70). Bus: 2A.

One of the best bargains in Poitiers, this renovated hotel is on a narrow alley, a few steps from place du Maréchal-Leclerc. Many restaurants and sights are nearby. Several readers have commented on the warmth of the staff. Each functional, no-frills room has one or two double beds. There's a guarded parking area.

Le Chalet de Venise. 6 rue du Square (B.P. 4), 86280 St-Benoît-Bourg. ☎ **05-49-88-45-07.** Fax 05-49-52-95-44. 12 units. MINIBAR TV TEL. 350F ($63) double. AE, DC, MC, V. Take D88 south 2½ miles from Poitiers to St-Benoît or A10 to exit 20, "Poitiers Sud."

Those who don't want to stay in the town center will enjoy this reasonably priced inn (completely renovated in 1996). It's surrounded by trees and shrubbery, and its chalet opens onto the water. The rooms are simply furnished, clean, and comfortable, each with a distinct personality.

Dining: Drinks are served on a flagstone terrace overlooking one of the many tributaries of the region. The food is among the best in the Poitiers area, and portions are generous. Fixed-price menus are offered at 150F to 295F ($27 to $53.10)—but for many of the specialties you have to order à la carte. Breakfast is served in a room overlooking a garden. The restaurant is open Tuesday through Saturday for lunch and dinner (closed February).

WHERE TO DINE

Le Saint Hilaire. 65 rue Théophraste-Renaudot. ☎ **05-49-41-15-45.** Reservations recommended. Main courses 70–130F ($12.60–$23.40); fixed-price menus 99–270F ($17.80–$48.60). DC, MC, V. Mon–Sat noon–2pm and 7:30–9:45pm. Closed Jan 1–15 and Sun and Mon in July–Aug. FRENCH/POITOU.

This is the most historic and unusual restaurant in Poitiers and would be popular with foreigners if it were more centrally located. It's on a quiet street in the southern periphery of the medieval center, in what was built during the 12th century as lodging for the plainsong singers at the nearby Eglise St-Hilaire. You can look into the exposed kitchen (and perhaps chat with the staff) on your way into a dining room whose medieval vaults are supported on four massive columns with Romanesque capitals.

The fixed-price menus offer three distinct types of cuisine: medieval, regional, and seasonal. The fare of André Point and his wife, Danielle, is superb, based on fresh ingredients that change seasonally. Examples include *pavé* of salmon, étouffée of crayfish studded with foie gras, escallopine of turbot with Chinon sauce, and a house specialty, *matelotte* of eels caught off the coast of Nantes.

Maxime. 4 rue St-Nicolas. ☎ **05-49-41-09-55.** Reservations recommended. Main courses 90–150F ($16.20–$27); fixed-price menus 100–260F ($18–$46.80). AE, MC, V. Mon–Fri noon–2pm and 7:30–10pm. Closed July 14–21 and Aug 1–15. FRENCH.

Maxime is the most sophisticated restaurant in town, and for some lucky reason it's completely ignored by the weekend crowds descending to visit Futuroscope. Start with a drink in the salon before heading to the twin upstairs dining rooms, which exude bourgeois warmth. Christian Rougier, the hardworking chef, offers a menu that varies with the seasons but always includes ravioli with hot oysters and sometimes features baked back of rabbit stuffed with eggplant, mushrooms, and fines herbes, served with chardonnay sauce; fried foie gras served with asparagus; and an herb-laden roast rack of lamb from nearby Montmorillon, a site famous for the quality of its lamb.

POITIERS AFTER DARK

The most popular student hangout is **Skylab,** 5 rue des Quatre-Roues (☎ 05-49-60-81-95), where you'll hear the latest techno grooves; **Le Confort Moderne,** 185 rue du Faubourg du Pont-Neuf (☎ 05-49-46-08-08), features techno and jazz most nights; the cover is 50F to 70F ($9 to $12.60).

The town's major disco, **Le Grand' Goule,** 46 rue du Pigeon-Blanc (☎ 05-49-50-41-36), is hot Tuesday through Saturday from 11pm to 4am; the 60F ($10.80) cover includes the first drink. The town's most popular pub is **Blues Rock Café,** 17 rue Carnot (☎ 05-49-50-55-58), decorated with vinyl records on the walls. The most frequented gay bar is **Le Georges-Sand,** 25 rue St-Pierre-le-Puellier (☎ 05-49-55-91-58). Many gay students, often from other countries, hang out at the cozy **Le Café Sixties,** 1 rue des Quatre Voues (☎ 05-49-52-19-44), which is very cruisy.

2 La Rochelle

290 miles SW of Paris, 90 miles SE of Nantes, 100 miles S of Bordeaux, 88 miles NW of Angoulême

Once known as the French Geneva, La Rochelle is a historic Atlantic port and ancient sailors' city, formerly the stronghold of the Huguenots. It was founded as a fishing village in the 10th century on a rocky platform in the center of a huge marshland. Eleanor of Aquitaine gave La Rochelle a charter in 1199, thereby freeing it from feudal dues. After becoming an independent city-state, the port capitalized on the wars between France and England. It was the departure point for the founders of Montréal and others who helped colonize Canada. From the 14th to the 16th centuries, La Rochelle enjoyed its heyday as one of France's great maritime cities.

As a hotbed of Protestant factions, it armed privateers to prey on Catholic vessels but was eventually besieged by Catholic troops. Two strong men led the fight: Cardinal Richelieu (with, of course, his Musketeers) and Jean Guiton, formerly an admiral and then mayor of the city. Richelieu proceeded to blockade the port. Although La Rochelle bravely resisted, on October 30, 1628, Richelieu entered the city. Among the almost 30,000 citizens of the proud city, he found only 5,000 survivors.

La Rochelle became the principal port between France and the colony of Canada, but France's loss of Canada ruined its Atlantic trade.

Today La Rochelle, with its population of 120,000, is the cultural and administrative center of the Charente-Maritime département. Its famous city lights have earned it the title of "City of Light," like its grander sibling, Paris. Although much of La Rochelle's sights are very old, the city is also riddled with high-rise condos and the largest pleasure-boat basin in Europe. In summer, the city is overrun with visitors.

ESSENTIALS

GETTING THERE The La Rochelle–Laleu **airport** is on the coast, north of the city. Rail connections from Bordeaux and Nantes are frequent. Six to eight **trains** from Bordeaux and Nantes arrive daily (trip time: 2 hours), and the fast TGV trains from Paris arrive 5 to 7 times per day (trip time: 3 hours). For train information and schedules, call ☎ **08-36-35-35-39.** If you're **driving** from La Rochelle, it's best to stay near the A10 highway. Follow A10 south from Poitiers to exit Niort/St-Maixent, then take N11 east to the coast and La Rochelle.

VISITOR INFORMATION The **Office de Tourisme** is on place de la Petite-Sirène, Le Gabut (☎ **05-46-41-14-68**).

SPECIAL EVENTS The busiest month is July, when the **Festival International du Film de La Rochelle** rolls in during the beginning of the month. It attracts a huge following of fans, press, actors, directors, and, of course, paparazzi. Screenings are held around town; ticket packages start at 90F ($16.20). For information, contact the festival's organizing office in Paris at ☎ **01-48-06-16-66.** Right on the heels of this festival comes **Franco Folies,** a mega–music festival with big-name as well as not-so-famous groups from the world over. The town is overrun with groupies and fans, and a festive party atmosphere prevails. Tickets range from 50F to 175F ($9 to $31.50). Call ☎ **05-46-28-28-28** for details. The Office de Tourisme can also provide details on both festivals.

EXPLORING THE CITY

There are two sides to La Rochelle: the old and unspoiled town inside the Vauban defenses and the tacky modern and industrial suburbs. Its **fortifications** have a circuit of 3½ miles with a total of seven gates.

The town, with its arch-covered streets, is great for strolling. The port is still a bustling fishing harbor and one of the major sailing centers in Western Europe. Try to schedule a visit in time to attend a fish auction at the harbor. The best streets for strolling are **rue du Palais, rue Chaudrier,** and **rue des Merciers** with its ancient wooden houses. On the last, seek out the houses at nos. 17, 8, 5, and 3.

The main shopping streets are **rue du Palais, rue de Merciers,** and **rue St-Yon,** where name-brand department stores as well as smaller shops sell everything from clothing to canned goods. If you want to explore antiques shops, art galleries, jewelry studios, and more high-end gift shops, enter the **old town.** On Saturday mornings, an **antiques market** sets up along rue St-Nicholas with a multitude of dealers carrying mainly bric-a-brac and flea market items. For one of the largest selections of beachwear, parkas, windbreakers, and great wool pullover sweaters, stop in the **Cooperative Maritime,** Port de Pêche, chef de Baie (☎ **05-46-41-31-66**).

Hôtel de Ville (city hall). Place de la Mairie, in the city center. ☎ **05-46-41-14-68.** You must visit on a guided tour by reserving in advance. Tours 17F ($3.05) adults, 11F ($2) children, free for children 3 and under. Tours Sat–Sun 3pm (also 3pm on certain school holidays).

The town's 14th-century showcase is constructed in Flamboyant Gothic style, with battlements. Inside you can admire the Henry II staircase with canopies and the marble desk of the heroic Jean Guiton. In 1996, major restoration work was needed after Corsican separatists bombed the building, causing heavy damage. Luckily, Prime Minister Alain Juppé had left the building en route to Paris before the explosion occurred.

Tour de la Chaîne. Quai du Gabut. ☎ **05-46-41-74-13.** Admission 20F ($3.60) adults, 12F ($2.15) children 14 and under. Daily 10am–noon and 2–6pm.

The tower is named for the large chain that was fastened to it and pulled across the harbor to close it against hostile warships at night. The structure dates from the 14th century.

Tour St-Nicolas. Quai du Gabut. ☎ **05-46-41-74-13.** Admission 22F ($3.95) adults, 14F ($2.50) ages 18–25, 10F ($1.80) children 12–17, free for children 11 and under. Apr–Sept daily 10am–5:30pm; Oct–Mar daily 10am–12:30pm and 2–5:30pm.

The oldest tower in La Rochelle was built between 1371 and 1382. From its second floor you can enjoy a panoramic view of the town and harbor; from the top, however, you can see only the old town and Ile d'Oléron.

Tour de la Lanterne. Opposite Tour St-Nicholas. Admission 25F ($4.50) adults, 15F ($2.70) ages 12–25, free for children 11 and under. Apr–Sept daily 10am–5:30pm; Oct–Mar daily 10am–12:30pm and 2–5:30pm.

Built between 1445 and 1476, this was once a lighthouse but was used mainly as a jail as late as the 19th century. Both the Tour de la Lanterne and the Tour St-Nicholas maintain the same hours and prices.

Musée des Beaux-Arts. 28 rue Gargolleau. ☎ **05-46-41-64-65.** Admission 19F ($3.40) adults, 14F ($2.50) students, free for children 18 and under. Wed–Mon 2–5pm.

The museum is housed in an episcopal palace built in the mid–18th century. The art spans the 17th to the 19th centuries, with works by Eustache Le Sueur, Brossard de Beaulieu, Corot, and Fromentin. Some 20th-century pieces include works by Maillol and Léger.

Musée d'Obigny-Bernon. 2 rue St-Côme. ☎ **05-46-41-18-83.** Admission 19F ($3.40) adults, free for children 17 and under. Mon and Wed–Sat 10am–noon and 2–6pm, Sun 2–6pm.

The most important artifacts pertaining to the history of ceramics and of La Rochelle are in this collection, which includes painted porcelain. Established in 1917, the museum also houses a superb collection of Far Eastern art.

Musée du Nouveau-Monde. In the Hôtel Fleuriau, 10 rue Fleuriau. ☎ **05-46-41-46-50.** Admission 19F ($3.40) adults, 14F ($2.50) students, free for children 17 and under. Wed–Mon 10:30am–12:30pm and 1:30–6pm, Sun 3–6pm.

The displays here trace the port's 300-year history with the New World. Exhibits start with the discovery of the Mississippi Delta in 1682 by LaSalle and end with the settling of the Louisiana territory. Other exhibits depict French settlements in the French West Indies, including Guadeloupe and Martinique.

Musée d'Histoire Naturelle Lafaille. 28 rue Albert-1er. ☎ **05-46-41-18-25.** Admission 20F ($3.60), free for children 18 and under. Tues–Fri 10am–12:30pm and 1:30–5:30pm, Sat–Sun 2–6pm.

This ethnography/zoology museum is housed in a handsome 18th-century building surrounded by a garden; the original paneling has been preserved. Clement de Lafaille, a former comptroller of war, assembled much of the collection, which has been enlarged since he donated it to the city. Displays include rare shellfish, an idol from Easter Island, an embalmed giraffe given to Charles X (the first of the species to be seen in France), and a parade boat encrusted with gems that was presented to Napoléon III by the king of Siam.

WHERE TO STAY

✪ **Hotel de France et d'Angleterre.** 20 rue Rambaud, 17000 La Rochelle. ☎ **800/ 528-1234** in the U.S., or 05-46-41-23-99. Fax 05-46-41-15-19. 36 units. A/C MINIBAR TV TEL. 315–560F ($56.70–$100.80) double; 685F ($123.30) suite. AE, DC, MC, V. Parking 35–48F ($6.30–$8.65).

Close to the major parks and the old port, this is the most gracious choice in La Rochelle. A former town house, it has been handsomely restored, converted, and furnished with antiques and objets d'art. Its winning feature is a romantic garden brimming with flowers, shrubbery, and shade trees. Stylish lounges and traditionally furnished, tasteful bedrooms make the place even more alluring. Breakfast is the only meal served.

Hôtel Les Brises. Chemin de la Digue de Richelieu, 17000 La Rochelle. ☎ **05-46-43-89-37.** Fax 05-46-43-27-97. 48 units. TV TEL. 420–630F ($75.60-$113.40) double; 950F ($171) suite. AE, MC, V.

This seaside hotel opposite the new Port des Minimes is most tranquil and offers a view of the soaring 19th-century column dedicated to the Virgin. You can enjoy the view from the front balconies as well as the parasol-shaded patio. The immaculate rooms have cherrywood furniture. Breakfast is the only meal served.

Novotel La Rochelle Centre. 1 av. de la Porte-Neuve, 17000 La Rochelle. ☎ **05-46-34-24-24.** Fax 05-46-34-58-32. 94 units. MINIBAR TV TEL. 570–670F ($102.60–$120.60) double. Children 15 and under stay free in parents' room. AE, DC, MC, V.

This hotel, one of the best in town, occupies a desirable verdant location in the Parc Charruyer, a greenbelt about a 5-minute walk from La Rochelle. The rooms are monochromatic, standardized, and well maintained, with generous writing desks and big windows overlooking the park. There's also an outdoor pool. A charmless in-house restaurant serves drinks and platters throughout the day, with both regional and continental dishes.

WHERE TO DINE

Les Quatre Sergents. 49 rue St-Jean-du-Pérot. ☎ **05-46-41-35-80.** Reservations required. Main courses 40–100F ($7.20–$18); fixed-price menus 80–126F ($14.40–$22.70). AE, DC, MC, V. Tues–Sun noon–2pm, Tues–Sat 7:30–10pm. FRENCH.

This restaurant is housed in a fanciful Art Nouveau greenhouse some visitors compare to the framework of the Eiffel Tower. Specialties include seafood ragoût, duxelles of turbot, mussels in curry sauce, and several regional favorites that have been going strong for the better part of 100 years.

✪ **Richard Coutanceau.** Plage de la Concurrence. ☎ **05-46-41-48-19.** Reservations required. Main courses 125–195F ($22.50–$35.10); fixed-price menus 220–420F ($39.60–$75.60). AE, DC, MC, V. Mon–Sat noon–2pm, Mon–Sat 7:30–9:30pm. FRENCH.

Delectable cuisine is served in this circular concrete pavilion in a pine-filled park. Half of the space is devoted to a tearoom, the rest to an elegant and informal dining room. This is not only the most glamorous restaurant in La Rochelle but also one of the finest along the Atlantic coast, vastly superior to the highly touted La Marmite at 14 rue St-Jean-du-Pérot. Clearly an artist, Richard Coutanceau is both the owner and the genius chef; his "modernized" cuisine often includes fresh shellfish from nearby waters, lobster-filled ravioli with zucchini flowers, roast bass, and Brittany lobster.

LA ROCHELLE AFTER DARK

To find the heart of La Rochelle's vibrant nightlife from July to September, head for **quai Duperré** and **cours des Dames.** Once the sun starts to set, cars are cleared away and the area becomes one big pedestrian zone peppered with street performers. It's a fun, almost magical area that sets the tone for the rest of the night.

Later you might find yourself at **Le Garibaldi,** rue St-Nicholas (☎ **05-46-41-05-49**), with its mixed-age crowd, and the trendier **Le Riboulding,** rue St-Nicholas (☎ **05-46-41-24-24**). Good live blues, jazz, and folk concerts regularly fill both houses. For a beer in a relaxed, laid-back atmosphere, head over to **MacEwan's,** 7 rue de la Chaîne (☎ **05-46-41-18-94**). At cour du Temple, you'll find two little hotbeds of fun. The proudly French-style **Le Piano Pub,** 12 cour du Temple (☎ **05-46-41-03-42**), hosts regular rock concerts that keep the 18- to 35-year-old crowd coming back for more, and **Le Mayflower,** 14 bis cour du Temple (☎ **05-46-50-51-39**), with its staunchly English decor of wood and leather, is just as popular with the same age group. Both places are loud, boisterous, and very friendly.

Gays are often attracted to the mixed crowds of **Le Pastel,** 33 quai Valin (☎ **05-46-41-58-81**).

3 Saintes

291 miles SW of Paris, 72 miles N of Bordeaux

The battered monuments of this town on the banks of the Charente River represent just about every civilization since the Romans, who made it the capital of southwestern France. During the Middle Ages the Plantagenets covered the city with religious monuments, many of which were visited by the pilgrims wending their way down to Santiago de Compostela in Spain. During the 18th century and continuing into the 19th, many neoclassical buildings were added, such as the national theater and a number of mansions.

Today, on its tree-lined streets bordered with shops, you're likely to enjoy an unusual stopover. Somewhat pretentiously, the Saintais refer to their left and right banks as Rive Droite and Rive Gauche, but sleepy Saintes is still no Paris.

ESSENTIALS

GETTING THERE   Saintes is a railway junction for the surrounding region, and driving is easy thanks to the nearby autoroutes. Seven or eight **trains** per day arrive from Bordeaux (trip time: 1¼ hours) and seven trains per day pull in from Cognac (trip time: 20 minutes). For train information and schedules, call ☎ **05-36-35-35-39.** If you're **driving,** Saintes is accessible from either Poitiers along A10 south or La Rochelle along N137 southwest.

VISITOR INFORMATION   The **Office de Tourisme** is in the Villa Musso, 62 cours National (☎ **05-46-74-23-82**).

SPECIAL EVENTS   During the first 2 weeks of July, **Les Académies Musicales** stages Baroque, Renaissance, and Romantic instrumental concerts throughout the town. Tickets run 60F to 240F ($10.80 to $43.20). During the middle of July, **Les Jeux Santons** packs people into different arenas for performances of folk music and dance from around the world. Expect to pay 20F to 80F ($3.60 to $14.40) for tickets to the various events. For details, contact the Office de Tourisme.

EXPLORING THE TOWN

The **Old City,** an area of winding streets with a distinctly medieval flavor, surrounds the cathedral.

Arc de Germanicus, on esplanade André-Malraux near the tourist office, was built in A.D. 19 of local limestone. In 1842 it was moved from a position near the end of a Roman bridge (which was being demolished) to its present location on the right bank of the Charente. It's dedicated to Germanicus and Tiberius.

The pedestrian parts of town, found mainly in the central area, are home to a variety of boutiques, galleries, and antiques shops. However, the main commercial streets are **cours National** and **avenue Gambetta,** where some of the more interesting stops include linen and housewares stores, jewelry and perfume shops, and bookstores.

Regional specialty items abound in Saintes. Pâtés and rabbit confits can be found at **L'Arène du Gourmet,** 11 rue Alsace-Lorraine (☎ **05-46-93-74-29**), and sweet, golden honey with a slightly herbal bouquet is sold at **Les Ruchers du Freussin,** 1 rue Peupliers, in the village of Beurlay just 20 minutes north of town (☎ **05-46-95-03-00**). Several of the town's potters sell wares in their studios, including **Poterie Le Tournaissin,** 8 rue de l'Epineuil (☎ **05-46-92-21-37**), and **Poterie Jean Alexiu,** La Chapelle-des-Pots (☎ **05-46-91-51-04**).

Abbaye aux Dames. 7 place de l'Abbaye. ☎ **05-46-97-48-48.** Free admission. June–Sept daily 10am–1:30pm and 2–7pm; Oct–May Thurs–Mon 2–6pm, Wed and Sat 10am–12:30pm and 2–7pm.

Founded in 1047 by Geoffroi Martel, comte d'Anjou, the abbey eventually became a convent, attracting women from the finest families in France; daughters of the nobility, including the future marquise de Montespan, were educated here. After the Revolution, the local people hated the church so much that it was transformed into a dress shop. In 1942, after 20 years of restoration, the church was reconsecrated. The style is Romanesque, though sections date from the 17th century. Every summer a festival of music takes place here.

Cathédrale St-Pierre. Rue St-Pierre. ☎ **05-49-41-23-76.** Free admission. Daily 9am–7pm.

Built on Roman foundations in the 12th century, the cathedral was greatly expanded in Flamboyant Gothic style in the 15th century. Parts were destroyed by the Calvinists in 1568 but then rebuilt. The enormous organs date from the 16th and 17th centuries.

Eglise St-Eutrope. Rue St-Eutrope. ☎ **05-46-74-34-58.** Free admission, but 2F (35¢) to have the crypt illuminated. Daily 9am–6pm.

This is one of the most important monuments in southwestern France, in spite of the alterations to the nave that a misdirected series of architects performed in 1803. It was built in the 1400s by Louis XI, who revered St. Eutrope, believing that the saint had cured him of a disease. The vast crypt is only half buried underground because of the slope of the land, and it's more a subterranean church than a crypt. The sarcophagus said to contain the remains of St. Eutrope is from the 4th century. In the crypt is a well nearly 150 feet deep, plus several Roman-era baptismal fonts.

Arènes Gallo-Romaines. Accessible from rues St-Eutrope and Lacurie. To visit, ring the bell for the custodian. Free admission. Apr–Sept daily 9am–7pm; Oct–Nov and Mar daily 9:30am–noon and 2–5pm; Dec–Feb daily 10am–noon and 2–4pm.

Built in the early 1st century, this is one of the oldest remaining Roman amphitheaters, though it's medium-size in comparison to others. Many of the seats are covered with wild shrubs and greenery, but in its heyday it could hold 20,000 spectators. A fountain has been built halfway up the slope of one of the sides, marking the spot where a disciple of St. Eutrope was beheaded.

Musée Dupuy-Mestreau. 4 rue Monconseil, adjacent to central place Blair. ☎ **05-46-93-36-71.** Guided tours 10F ($1.80). Tours at 2, 3, and 4pm (extra 5pm tour in summer).

This is a monumemt to the acquisitive mania of one of the town's leading citizens. The collection, once the property of M. Abel Mestreau, was taken over first by his grandson, Charles Dupuy, and then by the town of Saintes. Today it's the region's most eccentrically charming collection, a celebration of local folklore, history, and customs. You'll find 3,000 objects that include 19th-century dresses and lace headdresses, folkloric costumes, furniture, jewelry, and a poignant collection of early-20th-century objects carved from coconuts by prisoners incarcerated in the nearby prison at Rochefort.

WHERE TO STAY

Hôtel de l'Avenue. 114 av. Gambetta, 17100 Saintes. ☎ **05-46-74-05-91.** Fax 05-46-74-32-16. 15 units, 13 with bathroom. TV TEL. 177F ($31.85) double without bathroom, 250–271F ($45–$48.80) double with bathroom. MC, V. Parking 10F ($1.80). Closed Dec 26–Jan 9 and Sun Oct–Apr 1.

This budget choice was richly and comfortably renovated in 1991. Today the rooms are decorated with unusual lithographs and tasteful accessories and overlook a flowering courtyard or the garden in back.

✪ **Relais du Bois St-George.** Rue de Royan, 17100 Saintes. ☎ **05-46-93-50-99.** Fax 05-46-93-34-93. www.T3A.com/relaisdubois. E-mail: relaisdubois@T3A.com. 30 units. TV TEL. 640–950F ($115.20–$171) double; from 1,250F ($225) suite. MC, V. Parking 50F ($9).

Off the Paris–Bordeaux motorway and 2 minutes from the town center, this hotel is in the heart of a vast park with gardens and a small lake with ducks and swans. Owner/manager Jérôme Emery created it from the remains of an 11th-century farmhouse. The rooms are a well-balanced combination of modern comfort and antique furnishings, some with terraces overlooking the lake and garden.

Dining: The restaurant is in a renovated farmhouse, with a view of the park and lake. The chef prepares savory specialties like suprême of turbot in langoustine sauce, filet of Limousin beef with shallots, and a dessert trolley of homemade delicacies. Fixed-price menus are offered at 198F to 504F ($35.65 to $90.70). There's also a bistro, La Table du Bois, offering light and tasty meals at cheaper prices.

WHERE TO DINE

Brasserie Louis. 116 av. Gambetta. ☎ **05-46-74-16-85.** Reservations recommended. Main courses 40–100F ($7.20–$18); fixed-price menus 68–180F ($12.25–$32.40). MC, V. Tues–Sun noon–2pm, Tues–Sat 7–10pm. FRENCH.

This bustling brasserie is in a circa-1960 building whose interior is lined with multi-colored brick. About 100 seats are available for those craving honest, simple preparations of traditional recipes. There's also a terrace overlooking a garden, where some of the noise from the street is obscured. Menu items include platters of shellfish, mussels prepared with white-wine or curry sauce, rack of lamb with herbs, and entrecôte of beef with french fries. The cookery may not be the most inventive, but it satisfies the soul. If business merits it (and it usually does), the place is open daily in July and August.

SAINTES AFTER DARK

The best piano bar in town, **Vaudeville,** quai de la République (☎ **05-46-93-11-91**), has an English-pub decor and a crowd of hearty, happy drinkers. If you prefer to dance, no matter what your age, check out the **Complexe Saintes-Végas,** on route de Royan (☎ **05-46-93-42-76**), with its four clubs: Le Santon, for young techno fans; Le Club Disco, with its 1960s rock music and smaller dance floor; Le Romain, for the 35-to-50 crowd who like everything from rock to tango and zouk; and, finally, Le Phorum, where a more sophisticated crowd enjoys big-band music. The cover charge ranges from 60F to 80F ($10.80 to $14.40). The area's only gay and lesbian dance-club/disco is **Le Grillon,** Courcoury (☎ **05-46-74-66-98**). The DJ here continuously cranks out a hot mix of disco, techno, garage, funk, and rock that keeps the mainly male crowd pumped and buzzing. The cover is 50F ($9).

4 Cognac

297 miles SW of Paris, 23 miles NW of Angoulême, 70 miles SE of La Rochelle

The world enjoys 100 million bottles a year of the nectar known as cognac, which Victor Hugo called "the drink of the gods." Sir Winston Churchill required a bottle a day. It's worth a detour to visit one of the château warehouses of the great cognac bottlers. Martell, Hennessy, and Otard welcome visits from the public and even give you a free drink at the end of the tour.

ESSENTIALS

GETTING THERE Cognac's rail station is south of the town center. Seven **trains** per day arrive from Angoulême (trip time: 1 hour), and 7 trains pull in from Saintes (trip time: 20 minutes). For train information and schedules, call ☎ **08-36-35-35-39.** If you're **driving** to Cognac, the best route is from Saintes (which lies along the major route A10); follow N141 west.

VISITOR INFORMATION The **Office de Tourisme** is at 16 rue du 14-Juillet (☎ **05-45-82-10-71**).

SPECIAL EVENTS Cognac grapes are among the last to be picked in France. Harvesttime usually begins in mid-October. A grape harvest festival (**Salon des Vendanges**) is staged at this time, when all the town turns out for fun and celebrations, with marching bands and colorful floats.

For the ultimate in the newest whodunit movies, come to town during the first week in April for the **Festival du Film Policier.** Screenings of crime films by each year's new wave of directors are held in various theaters around town. Contact the **Bureau National de Cognac** at ☎ **05-45-35-60-89** for complete information.

EXPLORING THE TOWN

Many visitors don't realize that this unassuming town of some 22,000 people is actually a town—not just a drink. Cognac may be beautiful to drink, but it's not beautiful to make. A black fungus that lives on the vapors released by the cognac factories has turned the town's buildings an ugly gray. But while the fumes may blacken the houses, they also fill the air here with a kind of sweetness.

If you'd like to visit a distillery, go to its main office during regular business hours and request a tour. The staffs are generally receptive, and you'll see some brandies that have aged for as long as 50 or even 100 years. You can ask about guided tours at the tourist office. The best distillery tour is offered by ✪ **Hennessy,** 1 rue de la Richonne (☎ **05-45-35-72-33**). It's open daily from 10am to 6pm (closed January 1, May 1, and December 25). Guided tours cost 15F ($2.70) and last 75 minutes.

To buy bottles of cognac, you can visit one of the distilleries, take the tour, have a free taste, and then purchase a bottle or two. In addition to Hennessy, you can try **Camus,** 29 rue Marguerite-de-Navarre (☎ 05-45-32-28-28); **Martell,** place Edouard-Martell (☎ 05-45-36-33-33); and **Rémy-Martin,** domaine de Merpins, route de Pons (☎ 05-45-35-76-66). If you're short on time, opt for **La Cognathèque,** 10 place Jean-Monnet (☎ 05-45-82-43-31), where you'll find vintages from all the distilleries, though you'll pay extra for the convenience of having everything under one roof.

At the **Musée de Cognac,** 48 bd. Denfert-Rochereau (☎ **05-45-32-07-25**), you can see a collection including exhibits on popular arts and traditions (local artifacts and the cognac industry) as well as archaeological exhibits, plus a fine-arts collection (painting, sculpture, decorative arts, and furniture). It's open Wednesday through Monday, June to September from 10am to noon and 2 to 6pm and October to May from 2 to 5:30pm. Admission is 12F ($2.15), free for children 17 and under.

Cognac has two beautiful parks: the **Parc François-1er** and the **Parc de l'Hôtel-de-Ville.** The Romanesque-Gothic **Eglise St-Léger** is from the 12th century, and its bell tower is from the 15th. The town is imbued with memories of François I, who was born in the **Château de Cognac,** which today belongs to the Otard cognac firm.

WHERE TO STAY

Domaine du Breuil. 104 rue Robert-Daugas, 16100 Cognac. ☎ **05-45-35-32-06.** Fax 05-45-35-48-06. 24 units. TV TEL. 290–390F ($52.20–$70.20) double. AE, MC, V.

This 18th-century manor house, studded with magnificent windows, is set in an 18-acre landscaped park 2 minutes from the center of Cognac. Cognac aficionados and those in town to do business with the factories head here for the traditional hospitality, the good rooms, and the excellent cuisine from the southwest of France. The bedrooms have a pristine simplicity but are well furnished, well maintained, and most comfortable.

Dining: The food is reason enough to visit even if you aren't staying here, and, naturally, you finish off with a cognac in the bar to aid digestion. Fixed-price menus cost 85F, 120F, and 165F ($15.30, $21.60, and $29.70).

✪ **Hostellerie Les Pigeons Blancs.** 110 rue Jules-Brisson, 16100 Cognac. ☎ **05-45-82-16-36.** Fax 05-45-82-29-29. 7 units. TV TEL. 300–600F ($54–$108) double. AE, DC, V. Closed Jan.

This stylish hotel is named after the white pigeons that nest in its moss-covered stone walls. The angular farmhouse with sloping tile roofs was built in the 17th century as a coaching inn. For many years, it was the home of the Tachets, until three of the siblings transformed it into a hotel/restaurant in 1973. It's a mile northwest of the town center and offers elegant guest rooms. (See below for our review of its restaurant.)

Hôtel Ibis/Hôtel Urbis. 24 rue Elisée-Mousnier, 16100 Cognac. ☎ **05-45-82-19-53.** Fax 05-45-82-86-71. 40 units. TV TEL. 300F ($54) double; 500F ($90) suite. AE, DC, MC, V. Parking 20F ($3.60).

Clean, comfortable, and unpretentious, this hotel is identified by townspeople as either the Ibis or the Urbis, though management suggests the name Ibis will stick. There's a relaxed ambience in the public rooms, and the pleasant guest rooms are outfitted in a standardized modern style; some overlook a garden. Breakfast is the only meal served, but sometimes the management will prepare you a simple platter if you prefer to dine in.

WHERE TO DINE

Hostellerie Les Pigeons Blancs. 110 rue Jules-Brisson. ☎ **05-45-82-16-36.** Reservations recommended. Main courses 85–130F ($15.30–$23.40); fixed-price menus 138–250F ($24.85–$45). AE, DC, V. Daily noon–2pm, Mon–Sat 7–10pm. Closed Jan 1–15. FRENCH.

This restaurant, run by the Tachet family, has two elegant dining rooms with exposed ceiling beams and limestone fireplaces. Jacques is the chef, Jean-Michel the maître d', and Catherine the hostess. Menu offerings depend on the availability of ingredients but might include warm oysters with Vouvray-flavored sabayon, rack of suckling pig with local wine, and sole filet steamed in cognac. The flavor combinations always seem successful here.

La Marmite. 14 rue St-Jean-du-Perot. ☎ **05-46-41-17-03.** Reservations required in summer. Main courses 100–300F ($18–$54); fixed-price menus 190–385F ($34.20–$69.30). AE, DC, MC, V. Thurs–Tues noon–2:30pm and 7–9:15pm. Closed at Christmas. FRENCH.

This restaurant, in an old stone building almost adjacent to the old port of La Rochelle, is becoming better known all the time. M. and Mme Louis Marzin serve a medley of fresh fish and shellfish, with preparations based on recipes that M. Marzin learned in his apprenticeships throughout the country; they include grilled codfish served with a purée of sweet garlic, a fricassée of lobster, and monkfish with wild mushrooms and saffron sauce. The decor is a cross between a tavern and a cafe and includes lots of nautical-looking wooden panels. In one corner is a small salon where you can order an aperitif.

NEARBY ACCOMMODATIONS & DINING

Moulin de Cierzac. Rte. de Barbezieux, St-Fort-sur-le-Né, 16130 St-Gonzac-Cognac. ☎ **05-45-83-01-32.** Fax 05-45-83-03-59. 10 units. TV TEL. 195–450F ($35.10–$81) double. AE, MC, V. Closed Feb.

This former mill house, at the southern edge of the village beside a stream, has white shutters and lots of character. The guest rooms are comfortable, bright, and functional.

In the rustic dining room overlooking the park, specialties are steamed lobster in orange butter and filet of lamb in garlic-cream sauce. Local foodies flock to the place, which is noted for its accomplished classic cuisine.

5 Angoulême

275 miles SW of Paris, 72 miles NE of Bordeaux

The old town of Angoulême hugs a hilltop between the Charente and Aguienne rivers, and you can easily visit it on the same day you visit Cognac. With a population of 46,000, the town was the cradle of the French paper industry in the 17th century. The tradition is vaguely still carried out today, as Angoulême is the center of French comic-strip production. Rolling off the presses are the latest adventures of Tintin, Astérix, and Lucky Luke.

The hub of the town is **place de l'Hôtel-de-Ville,** with its town hall erected from 1858 to 1866 on the site of the old palace of the ducs d'Angoulême, where Marguerite de Navarre, sister of François I, was born. All that remains of the ducal palace are the 15th-century Tour de Valois and the 13th-century Tour de Lusignan.

The **Cathédrale St-Pierre,** place St-Pierre (☎ 05-45-95-20-38), was begun in 1128 and greatly restored in the 19th century. Flanked by towers, its facade boasts 75 statues—each in a separate niche—representing the Last Judgment. This is one of France's most startling examples of Romanesque-Byzantine style. Some of its restoration was questionable, however. The architect, Abadie (designer of Sacré-Coeur in Paris), tore down the north tower, then rebuilt it with the original materials in the same style. In the interior you can wander under a four-domed ceiling. It's open Monday through Saturday from 8am to 7pm and Sunday from 8am to 6pm.

Adjoining is the former bishops' palace, which has been turned into the **Musée Municipal,** 1 rue Friedland (☎ 05-45-95-07-69), with a collection of European paintings, mainly from the 17th to the 19th centuries. The most interesting exhibits are the African art, ethnological, and archaeological collections. It's open Monday through Friday from noon to 6pm and Saturday and Sunday from 2 to 6pm. Admission is 15 F ($2.70), free for children 17 and under.

Finally, you can take the **promenade des Remparts,** a boulevard laid down on the site of the town walls. You'll have a superb view of the valley almost 250 feet below.

Twelve regular **trains** per day arrive from Bordeaux (trip time: 1½ hours), and 8 to 10 TGVs arrive from Bordeaux each day (trip time: 55 minutes). For train information and schedules, call ☎ 08-36-35-35-39. If you're **driving,** take N10 northeast to Angoulême.

The **Office de Tourisme** is at 7 bis rue du Chat (☎ 05-45-95-16-84).

WHERE TO STAY

Mercure Hôtel de France. 1 place des Halles, 16000 Angoulême. ☎ **05-45-95-47-95.** Fax 05-45-92-02-70. 89 units. TV TEL. 430–580F ($77.40–$104.40) double; 670F ($120.60) suite. AE, DC, MC, V. Parking 40F ($7.20).

This grand hotel stands in the center of the old town on extensive grounds. Frequently renovated and kept up-to-date, it contains rooms that are generally spacious, with high ceilings and French provincial furnishings.

Dining: On the lobby level, a formal restaurant offers excellent food and polite service. Specialties include foie gras, sole meunière, and trout with almonds. Lunch is served Monday through Friday; dinner is offered nightly.

Relais Mercure Angoulême Nord. Rte. de Poitiers, 16430 Champniers. ☎ **05-45-68-53-22.** Fax 05-45-68-33-83. 103 units. A/C TV TEL. 350–380F ($63–$68.40) double. AE, DC, MC, V. Take N10 from Angoulême about 4 miles toward Poitiers.

This dependable hotel is the area's family-friendly choice. The grounds are filled with evergreens and well-maintained lawns. Inside, the rooms are simple and chain-hotel uniform, each with a double bed and a couch that transforms into a twin. The sunny modern restaurant serves a variety of local and international specialties, but the cuisine is not the reason to stay here.

WHERE TO DINE

La Ruelle. 6 rue Trois-Notre-Dame. ☎ **05-45-92-94-64.** Reservations recommended. Main courses 80–210F ($14.40–$37.80); fixed-price menus 175F ($31.50) at lunch, 185–330F ($33.30–$59.40) at dinner. AE, DC, MC, V. Mon–Fri noon–2pm, Mon–Sat 7:30–10pm. Closed Jan 1–7, Feb 19–25, Apr 8–14, and Aug 5–18. FRENCH.

This first-class restaurant, in the center of the oldest part of town, was once a pair of medieval houses separated by a narrow alley (*ruelle*) that was covered over. Jean-François Dauphin is the proprietor, and his wife, Véronique, is the cook, and they're the only shining lights in Angoulême's dim culinary scene. The menus change with the chef's mood and the availability of ingredients, but you can count on classic French recipes with a modern twist. Specialties are sole with crayfish and cucumbers, suprême of chicken in a sesame crust, and medallion of monkfish with oysters. We especially recommend the fixed-price menus.

NEARBY ACCOMMODATIONS & DINING

✪ **Le Moulin du Maine-Brun.** R.N. 141, Lieu-Dit la Vigerie, 16290 Asnières-sur-Nouère. ☎ **05-45-90-83-00.** Fax 05-45-96-91-14. 20 units. MINIBAR TV TEL. 550–750F ($99–$135) double; 1,300F ($234) suite. AE, DC, MC, V. Hotel and restaurant closed Oct 15–Apr 15. Take R.N. 141 4½ miles west of Angoulême and turn right at Vigerie.

This Relais du Silence (part of a chain of hotels noted for their tranquillity) was originally a flour mill before becoming the premier place to stay and dine in the area. It's surrounded by 80 acres of lowlands, about half of which are now devoted to the production of cognac. The maître d'hôtel's preferred brand is the one made in the hotel's distillery: Moulin du Domaine de Maine-Brun. These are the most luxurious accommodations in the area. The rooms are conservative and furnished with some antiques.

Dining: The restaurant serves splendid fare; specialties usually include foie gras per-fumed with house cognac. Fixed-price menus cost 98F to 180F ($17.65 to $32.40). The restaurant is open daily for lunch and dinner (closed Monday to nonguests).

6 Bordeaux

359 miles SW of Paris, 341 miles W of Lyon

Situated on the Garonne River, the great port of Bordeaux, the capital of Aquitaine, is the center of the world's most important wine-producing area. It attracts many visitors to the offices of wine exporters here, most of whom welcome guests. (For a trip through the surrounding bordeaux wine country, refer to the next section.)

Bordeaux is a city of warehouses, factories, mansions, and exploding suburbs, as well as wide quays 5 miles long. Now the fifth-largest French city, Bordeaux belonged to the British for 300 years, and even today is considered the most un-French of French cities.

It may not exude the joie de vivre of Paris, but Bordeaux is a major cultural center and a transportation hub between southern France and Spain. With a population of some 650,000, much of Bordeaux is looking seedy, but the worn-out docklands to the south of the center are slated for urban renewal.

ESSENTIALS

GETTING THERE   The local **airport,** Bordeaux-Mérignac (☎ **05-56-34-50-50** for flight information), is served by flights from as far away as London and New York. It's 6¾ miles west of Bordeaux in Mérignac. A shuttle bus connects the airport with the train station, departing every 30 minutes from 5:30am to 10pm (trip time: 40 minutes), and costing 33F ($5.95) one-way for adults and 25F ($4.50) for students. The railway station, Gare St-Jean, is on the west bank of the river, within a 30-minute walk (or 5-minute taxi ride) of the center of the old town. Some 12 to 15 **trains** from Paris arrive per day (trip time: 3 hours by TGV). For train information and schedules, call ☎ **08-36-35-35-39.**

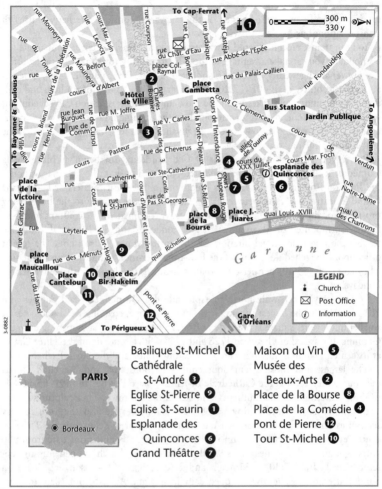

Basilique St-Michel ⑪   Maison du Vin ⑤
Cathédrale
   St-André ③   Musée des
Eglise St-Pierre ⑨   Beaux-Arts ②
Eglise St-Seurin ①   Place de la Bourse ⑧
Esplanade des   Place de la Comédie ④
   Quinconces ⑥   Pont de Pierre ⑫
Grand Théâtre ⑦   Tour St-Michel ⑩

Bordeaux is easily reached **by car.** From Paris, follow A10 south through the cities of Orléans, Tours, and Poitiers into Bordeaux. Be aware that navigating the city streets of Bordeaux is fraught with almost as many hazards as you'd face in Paris: narrow 18th-century alleys, massive traffic jams on the quays beside the Garrone, and simply too many cars and people. Consequently, expect a lack of easily available parking within the city's historic core, and head, whenever possible, for any of the blue-and-white "P" signs that indicate public garages.

VISITOR INFORMATION   The **Office de Tourisme** is at 12 cours du 30-Juillet (☎ **05-56-00-66-00**).

SEEING THE SIGHTS

Wine exporters welcome guests who come to sample wines and learn about the industry. In the next section of this chapter we take a tour of the bordeaux wine country. Plan your trip with maps and guides that are available free from the **Maison du Vin (House of Wine), 3** cours du 30-Juillet (☎ **05-56-00-22-88**), opposite the tourist office. To make the rounds of the vineyards, consider alternative forms of transportation: bus, bicycle, or walking tour.

You can traipse around the **old town** on your own, since it's a fairly compact neighborhood, or you can take advantage of the 2-hour **walking tour** that the tourist office (see above) arranges daily at 10am. Conducted in both French and English, it begins at the tourist office, costs 40F ($7.20) per adult and 30F ($5.40) for students and children 17 and under, and takes in all the most important sites. If you can schedule it, we strongly recommend it, as it corresponds to the opening hours of each of the monuments listed separately below. Reserve in advance, or at least call to confirm that the tour is on for the day of your arrival.

But if you go it alone, your tour of Old Bordeaux can begin at **place de la Comédie,** at the very heart of this venerated old city, a busy traffic hub that was once the site of a Roman temple. On this square one of the great theaters of France, the **Grand Théâtre,** was built between 1773 and 1780 as testimony to the burgeoning prosperity of Bordeaux's emerging bourgeoisie. A colonnade of 12 columns graces its facade. Surmounted on these are statues of goddesses and the Muses. If you'd like to visit the richly decorated interior, ask the porter; you can also phone the tourist office about the schedule for one of the four-times-per-month guided tours of the site. They cost 30F ($5.40) per person and are scheduled to coincide with French school holidays.

From here you can walk north to **esplanade des Quinconces,** laid out between 1818 and 1828, the largest square of its kind in Europe, covering nearly 30 acres. A smaller but lovelier square is **place de la Bourse,** bounded by quays opening onto the Garonne. It was laid out between 1728 and 1755, with a fountain of the Three Graces at its center. Flanking the square are the Custom House and the Stock Exchange.

The largest and most ostentatious church in Bordeaux, and the city's official religious centerpiece, is the **Cathédrale St-André,** place Pey-Berland (☎ **05-56-81-64-36**), standing near the southern perimeter of the old town. The sculptures on the 13th-century Porte Royale (Royal Door) are admirable; see also the 14th-century sculptures on the North Door. Separate from the rest of the church is the 155-foot **Tour Pey-Berland,** a belfry begun in the 15th century. Foundations date from 900 years ago, and 1996 witnessed its 900th birthday. The church is open July to September, daily from 7:30 to 11:30am and 2 to 6:30pm. Off-season, it's closed on Sunday afternoons. The tower is open daily in July and August from 10am to 7pm, April to June and in September from 10am to 6pm, and October to March from 10am to 5pm. Admission to the tower is 25F ($4.50) for adults and 15F ($2.70) for those 25 and under. Organ recitals are held every Tuesday in summer from 6:30 to 7:30pm. Admission is free.

Bordeaux, always a magnet for power, money, and ecclesiastical zeal, has four other important churches, each smaller than the cathedral but each with an unusual charm. Foremost among these is the **Basilique St-Michel,** place St-Michel (place Canteloup). The church itself is incredibly charming, but more impressive is the **Tour St-Michel** across the street. The belfry, erected in 1472, is the tallest stone tower in France, rising 374 feet. In some rare instances, with advance permission from the tourist office, you can climb the 228 steps for a panoramic view of the port. (When this is possible at all, it's usually only during midsummer and only as part of group tours.) In most cases you'll have to settle for a view of the tower from the ground.

Another interesting church is **Eglise St-Seurin,** place des Martyrs de la Résistance (☎ **05-56-48-22-08**), whose most ancient sections, like its crypt, date from the 5th century. See the porch left over from an earlier church; it has some capitals from the

Romanesque era. It's open daily from 8am to noon and 2 to 7:30pm. Equally appealing is **Eglise St-Pierre,** place du Parlement, dating from the 14th and 15th centuries.

Eglise Ste-Croix, place Pierre-Renaudel, gained attention in musical circles around the world when its organ, a musical marvel built by a monk, Dom Bedos, was restored to its original working order in 1996. The church itself, a severe Romanesque structure from the 11th and 12th centuries, is revered for its stately dignity.

For information about any of the four "secondary" churches above, you can call the **Presbytère de l'Eglise St-Michel** (☎ **05-56-94-30-50**), but the kindly prelates who answer are likely to speak only French. Opening hours of each vary slightly, according to the day's schedule for masses and celebrations, but are usually Monday through Saturday from 8am to 6pm and Sunday from 9am to noon.

Musée des Beaux-Arts, 20 cours d'Albret (Jardin du Palais-Rohan) (☎ **05-56-10-17-18**), has an outstanding collection ranging from the 15th to the 20th centuries. Works by Perugina, Titian, Rubens, Veronese, Delacroix, Marquet, and Lhote are displayed. The museum is open Wednesday from 11am to 8pm, and Thursday through Monday from 11am to 6pm. Admission is 20F ($3.60) for adults and 10F ($1.80) for children.

Pont de Pierre, with 17 arches, stretches 1,594 feet across the Garonne and is one of the most beautiful bridges in France. Ordered built by Napoléon I in 1813, the bridge can be crossed on foot for a fine view of the quays and the port. But for an even better view we suggest a **tour of the port,** which lasts about 1½ hours and encompasses a float up the river and all around the harbor. It departs from the Embarcadères des Quinconces, on quai Louis-XVIII in the center of town. It's open year-round. The cost is 60F ($10.80) for adults and 50F ($9) for children 9 and under. For exact times, call the tourism office (see "Essentials," above) or the boat captains' office near the quai (☎ **05-56-52-88-88**). Ask about the occasional floating concerts at night. Note that tours may be canceled without warning.

You may enjoy a **cruise** on one of France's mightiest (and least-visited) rivers, the Garonne. In July and August, **Alienor Loisirs,** Hangar 7, quai Louis-XVIII (☎ **05-56-51-27-90**), offers a Sunday-afternoon ride downriver from Bordeaux to the château town of Blaye. Boarding at the company's dock begins at around 11am for an 11:30am departure. Lunch is served on board, and between 2 and 4pm you enjoy a shore excursion in Blaye. The return to Bordeaux is usually scheduled for around 6:30pm the same day. The cost, lunch included, begins at 245F ($44.10) for adults and 110F ($19.80) for children 11 and under, depending on which fixed-price meal you opt for. The rest of the year, roughly equivalent excursions are offered, depending on the number of prepaid advance reservations. Closed each February. For more information, call the Bordeaux tourist office or Alienor Loisirs.

SHOPPING

If you want antiques, concentrate your search around **rue Bouffard, rue des Remparts,** and **rue Notre-Dame,** where you'll find a market area known as **Village Notre-Dame,** housing all sorts and sizes of antiques shops. Another haven is the neighborhood around **Eglise St-Michel.**

If you need to fill up some empty suitcases with new clothes, go to the couture quarter around **place des Grands Hommes** with its many upscale, trendy, and classic clothing emporiums. If you're out for a younger, more carefree style, patronize the shops around **place du Parlement** or the 100-plus-store **mall on rue du Château-d'Eau.**

The better-known choices include the haute couture boutique of the Bordeaux fashion designer **Jacqueline Dourthe,** 18 rue Lafaurie-de-Monbadon (☎ 05-56-52-35-78), where you can find everything from cocktail and evening dresses to the most luxurious wedding gowns, and **Le Soierie,** 27 rue du Parlement St-Pierre (☎ 05-56-51-23-75), which carries a complete line of chic women's silk garments.

Galerie Condillac, 24 rue Condillac (☎ 05-56-79-04-31), is one of the classier art houses that specializes in mostly local artists who paint with strong, vibrant colors. A well-stocked petit French crystal boutique is found at **M. Mazuque,** 4 rue du Parlement Ste-Catherine (☎ 05-56-52-94-14). For a sugar rush, head over to **Cadiot Badie,** 26 allées de Tourny (☎ 05-56-44-24-22), where you'll find everything from sinfully good pralines to creamy and decadent Bordeaux truffles.

Of course, many visitors come to Bordeaux to buy wine. There are many inexpensive wines, but it doesn't make sense to blow your one-bottle-per-adult liquor allowance on a 15F bottle. Try to pick a wine that carries personal significance because you've visited the vineyard, or chat up the experts at some of the most famous wine shops. We recommend **La Vinothèque,** 8 cours du 30-Juillet (☎ 05-56-52-32-05); **Badie,** 62 allées de Tourny (☎ 05-56-52-23-72); and **Cité Mondaile du Vin,** 23 parvis des Chatrons (☎ 05-56-01-73-44). The best spots for red bordeaux wines from small houses are **Château Lespare,** Beychac-et-Caillau, 24 miles north of Bordeaux (☎ 05-57-24-51-23); **Château Bel Air,** Naujan-et-Postiac, 9 miles east of Bordeaux (☎ 05-57-84-55-08); and **Château Les Bouzigues,** Saintes Gemmes, 47 miles south of Bordeaux (☎ 05-56-61-65-92).

WHERE TO STAY
MODERATE

Hôtel Majestic. 2 rue de Condé, 33000 Bordeaux. ☎ **05-56-52-60-44.** Fax 05-56-79-26-70. www.hotel-majestic.com. E-mail: majestic@hotel-majestic.com. 50 units. A/C MINIBAR TV TEL. 390–580F ($70.20–$104.40) double. AE, DC, V. Parking 60F ($10.80).

Set back from quai Louis-XVIII, which opens onto the Garonne, this three-star choice is sheltered in a sturdy 18th-century town house, which has been carefully restored and renovated to offer modern comforts. In the historic and commercial heart of Bordeaux, it lies on a tranquil street near the Grand Theater. Each of its bedrooms is well decorated in a traditional French provincial style and contains soundproofing and air-conditioning. A carefully prepared continental breakfast is the only meal served, but room service is always available. The street outside is one of the most bustling in Bordeaux, with boutiques, museums, cafes, and restaurants.

Mercure Bordeaux Mériadeck. 5 rue Robert-Lateulade, 33000 Bordeaux. ☎ **05-56-56-43-43.** Fax 05-56-96-50-59. www.mercure.com. 194 units. A/C MINIBAR TV TEL. 520F ($93.60) double; 800F ($144) suite. AE, DC, MC, V. Bus: 7 or 8.

A sleek geometric building facing a shopping mall in the Mériadeck business district, a 5-minute walk from the town center, this hotel offers modern comforts that are popular with business travelers and groups. The well-furnished rooms attract vine growers and wine merchants from abroad; the best rooms are on the sixth floor (some are showing signs of wear and tear). La Brasserie du Festival, the main restaurant, is one of the finest hotel grills.

Mercure Château Chartrons. 81 cours St-Louis, 33300 Bordeaux. ☎ **05-56-43-15-00.** Fax 05-56-69-15-21. www.mercure.com. 144 units. A/C MINIBAR TV TEL. 520–720F ($93.60–$129.60) double; 720F ($129.60) suite. AE, DC, MC, V. Parking 40F ($7.20).

Operated by a prestigious wine exporter, La Maison Ginneste, this is one of Bordeaux's leading hotels. Near the landmark place Tourny, it opened in 1991 behind the gracefully restored facade of an 18th-century mansion. The rooms are comfortable, outfitted with memorabilia of the wine trade.

On the premises are a bar, with an impressive array of local vintages sold by the glass, and a restaurant, Le Cabernet, where regional specialties are served. Try the seven o'clock roast leg of lamb, the veal kidneys and sweetbreads in a ramekin with a potato crust, or the Graves-style duck with peaches. A health club a few doors away opens its facilities to guests.

Novotel Bordeaux Centre. 45 cours du Maréchal-Juin, 33000 Bordeaux. ☎ **05-56-51-46-46.** Fax 05-56-98-25-56. www.novotel.com. 140 units. A/C MINIBAR TV TEL. 530F ($95.40) double; 800F ($144) suite. Children 15 and under stay free in parents' room. AE, DC, MC, V.

Built in 1989, this first-class hotel is in the heart of the city near the railway station, a short walk from the thoroughfare of Sainte Catherine, quai des Chartrons, and the cathedral. The rooms are well decorated and comfortably furnished, and some are suitable for individuals with disabilities. The hotel also offers laundry and room service.

✪ **Tulip Inn Le Bayonne Etche-Ona.** 15 cours de l'Intendance (with entrances at 4 rue Martignac and 11 rue Mautrec), 33000 Bordeaux. ☎ **05-56-48-00-88.** Fax 05-56-48-41-60. www. goldentulip.com. 64 units. A/C MINIBAR TV TEL. 430–595F ($77.40–$107.10) double; 900F ($162) suite. AE, DC, MC, V. Parking 70F ($12.60).

In 1997, two antique stone-fronted town houses, Le Bayonne Hotel and its equally antique but less elegant neighbor, Hotel Etche-Ona, were radically upgraded and connected to form this all-new, three-star entity. Today they compose part of the grand infrastructure of Bordeaux's cours de l'Intendance, and they're a great example of an intelligent use of historically important buildings. The aura of the 1930s has been retained, and many features have been added, most notably air-conditioning, sound-proofing, and comfortable furnishings. Many attractions, including several good restaurants, the cathedral, place de la Bourse, the quays, and the Grand Théâtre, are nearby. Breakfast is the only meal served.

INEXPENSIVE

Hôtel Continental. 10 rue Montesquieu, 33000 Bordeaux. ☎ **05-56-52-66-00.** Fax 05-56-52-77-97. www.hotel-le-continental.com. E-mail: continental@hotel-le-continental.com. 50 units. TV TEL. 340–430F ($61.20–$77.40) double. AE, MC, V.

To get a certain class, charm, and elegance in Bordeaux at this affordable price is a rarity. In the center of the golden triangle, on a semipedestrian mall dotted with bou-tiques, this restored 18th-century town house wins new converts every year. You'll get a warm welcome and a fine dose of Bordelaise hospitality; the rooms, although a bit small (especially the singles), are warmly decorated and comfortably furnished. A few have balconies overlooking the pedestrians below—but space in these is at an absolute minimum. Public areas are richly accessorized and furnished, and breakfasts are brunch style.

Hôtel de Sèze. 23 allées de Tourny, 33000 Bordeaux. ☎ **05-56-52-65-54.** Fax 05-56-44-31-83. 24 units. MINIBAR TV TEL. 250–420F ($45–$75.60) double. AE, DC, MC, V. Parking 40F ($7.20).

This three-star hostelry occupies an 18th-century building that's an antique in its own right, roughly equivalent to many others in its historic neighborhood. The hotel is such a well-known value that you should make reservations as early as possible. The rooms, which are scattered over four floors, are comfortable and well furnished: the cheapest with only a bed and bathroom (with shower only), the most expensive with twin beds and bathroom (with tub).

WHERE TO DINE
VERY EXPENSIVE

✪ **Le Chapon-Fin.** 5 rue Montesquieu. ☎ **05-56-79-10-10.** Reservations required. Main courses 160–240F ($28.80–$43.20); fixed-price menus 160–400F ($28.80–$72) at lunch, 260–400F ($46.80–$72) at dinner. AE, DC, V. Tues–Sat noon–2pm and 7:30–10pm. FRENCH.

Under the guidance of Francis Garcia from Barcelona, this is the leading restaurant in Bordeaux, serving an even more refined cuisine than that found at the also-highly rated La Chamade (see below). The dining room boasts elaborate latticework and several banquettes in artificial stone grottoes; a pivoting skylight lets in summer breezes. The wines are usually selected from the most respected and expensive French vintages, and menu specialties are among the best of the southwest. A meal might include truffle flan with essence of morels, gratin of oysters with foie gras, salmon steak grilled in its skin with pepper-flavored sabayon, and superb cheeses and desserts.

EXPENSIVE TO MODERATE

La Chamade. 20 rue des Piliers-de-Tutelle. ☎ **05-56-48-13-74.** Reservations required. Main courses 85–165F ($15.30–$29.70); fixed-price menus 120–350F ($21.60–$63). AE, DC, MC, V. Sun–Fri noon–2:30pm and 7:30–10:30pm, Sat 7:30–10pm. Closed Sat–Sun July–Aug. FRENCH.

You'll have a delightful time at La Chamade, in a vaulted 18th-century cellar of honey-colored stone. We highly recommend the monkfish salad—marinated, grilled, and served with leeks and Greek-style artichokes. Other specialties include roasted foie gras with confit of leeks and poached duck thighs with baby vegetables. The fish is steamed to perfection and served simply, often with warm vinaigrette of tomatoes and basil. The owner, Michel Carrère, has an impressive collection of bordeaux.

✪ **La Tupina.** 6 rue de la Porte de la Monnaie. ☎ **05-56-91-56-37.** Reservations recommended. Main courses 78–190F ($14.05–$34.20); fixed-price menus 100F ($18) at lunch, 200–250F ($36–$45) at dinner. AE, DC, MC, V. Daily noon–2pm and 7–11pm. FRENCH.

One of Bordeaux's most talented chefs runs this cozy restaurant near quai de la Monnaie. It's been called "a tribute to country kitchens and the grandmothers who cooked in them," and its entryway looks like a farmhouse larder. Jean-Pierre Xiradakis's specialty is duck, so your meal might begin with croûtons spread with duck rillettes, and his salads often use duck giblets, skin, and livers. Regional specialties include truffles and foie gras; a recently sampled potato salad contained slices of black truffles from Périgord, and the foie gras often comes steamed in parchment. Sample one of the fine wines from the cellar, and definitely ask for the *assiette grandmère,* an assortment of classic homespun desserts.

✪ **Le Vieux Bordeaux.** 27 rue Buhan. ☎ **05-56-52-94-36.** Reservations recommended. Main courses 70–180F ($12.60–$32.40); fixed-price menus 155–260F ($27.90–$46.80). AE, V. Mon–Fri noon–2pm and 8–10:15pm, Sat 8–10:15pm. Closed 2 weeks in Feb and 3 weeks in Aug. FRENCH.

Nearly a neighborhood institution, this restaurant ranks among the top five in highly competitive Bordeaux, one of the culinary capitals of France. The decor is an almost-incongruous mix of exposed wood and modern accents. Specialties include pavé of fresh salmon with warm oysters, roasted sweetbreads, and turbot with Basque pepper and strips of Basque ham. Dessert might be chocolate ice cream flavored with Izarra, the Basque liqueur.

INEXPENSIVE

La Forge. 8 rue du Chai-des-Farines. ☎ **05-56-81-40-96.** Reservations recommended. Main courses 50–85F ($9–$15.30); fixed-price menus 83–145F ($14.95–$26.10). AE, MC, V. Tues–Sat noon–1:30pm and 7:30–10:30pm. Closed mid-Aug to mid-Sept. FRENCH.

Jean-Michel Pouts, a former chef on the ocean liner *France,* owns this bistro. The well-prepared specialties include brochette of pork with Gruyère, savory grilled meats, and an excellent cassoulet. The fixed-price menus are among the best value in town. The restaurant's devotion to a regional repertoire and attempts to keep prices down are most admirable. Everything is homemade.

NEARBY ACCOMMODATIONS & DINING

✪ **Restaurant St-James/Hôtel Hautrive.** 3 place Camille-Hostein, 33270 Bouliac. ☎ **05-57-97-06-00.** Fax 05-56-20-92-58. Reservations required. Main courses 150–250F ($27–$45); fixed-price menus 255–360F ($45.90–$64.80). AE, DC, MC, V. Daily noon–2pm and 8–10pm. From Bordeaux, follow the signs to Toulouse/Bayonne, leading south; at the périphérique encircling Bordeaux, follow the signs toward Paris; take exit 23 and follow the signs to Bouliac. FRENCH.

This is the domain of Jean-Marie Amat, whose specialties are based on local seasonal ingredients. These may revolve around the abundance of *cèpes* (the district's meaty flap mushrooms), game (venison and pheasant), *girolles* (another kind of mushroom), and fruit. In an ultramodern dining room whose windows offer a view of some of the most famous vineyards in Europe, you can enjoy such dishes as tartare of salmon with olives, salad of marinated filets of quail, Pauillac lamb, and lamprey eels in a bordelaise wine sauce. Mme Amat wisely recommends the grilled pigeon. You can dine less expensively in the brasserie, Le Bistroy, where meals average 160F ($28.80) without beverage.

Adjacent is the Hôtel Hautrive, whose 15 elegant rooms and 3 suites are scattered among four modern pavilions. Doubles go for 650F to 850F ($117 to $153); suites cost 1,150F to 1,350F ($207 to $243).

BORDEAUX AFTER DARK

Pick up a copy of *Clubs et Concerts* at the Office de Tourisme or a copy of *Bordeaux Plus* at one of the newsstands; both publications detail the goings-on in and around town.

Taking in a play or an opera could make for a good start to your evening. **Grand Théâtre,** place de la Comédie (☎ 05-56-48-58-54), has a very busy and diverse performance schedule.

To pick up the pace, head for **place de la Victoire** and **place Gambetta,** alive and pulsating with hordes of students. For some of the best pubbing around, hit the **Connemara Irish Pub,** 18 cours d'Albret (☎ 05-56-52-82-57), where the Guinness flows freely and a noisy crowd gathers to hear traditional Irish music; or **Dick Turpin's Bar,** 72 rue du Loup (☎ 05-56-48-07-52), which specializes in just about every brand of whiskey imaginable. It's truly toasty in this English pub. With its white piano and live jazz, the piano/jazz club **Black Jack,** 35 place Gambetta (☎ 05-56-81-71-38), creates a soft, stylish ambience that pulls in a sophisticated middle-aged crowd.

More raucous partiers of all ages head for the immense **L'Ane Qui Tousse,** 57 rue de Bègles (☎ 05-56-92-52-98), with its two dance floors and tropical motifs, whereas the student frat types congregate at **Le Plana,** 22 place de la Victoire (☎ 05-56-91-73-23), where the space around the bar turns into a makeshift dance floor once the party gets going. An even better choice for dancing is **Sénéchal,** 57 bis quai de Paludate (☎ 05-56-85-54-80), with its classic 1970s decor and just as classic 25- to 45-year-old crowd. For a techno disco, **Le T-H,** 15 rue Montbazon (☎ 05-56-81-38-16), reverberates with the sounds of industrial music and the antics of a young, fun gay scene; the cover is 50F ($9).

Other bars for the out-and-about gay male include **Le Moyen-Age,** 8 rue des Remparts (☎ 05-56-44-12-87), with its medieval setting, and **Le 18,** 18 rue Louis-de-Foix (☎ 05-56-52-82-98); both are open Wednesday through Monday.

7 The Wine Country

The major bordeaux wine districts are Graves, Médoc, Sauternes, Entre-deux-Mers, Libourne, Blaye, and Bourg. North of the city of Bordeaux, the Garonne River joins the Dordogne. This forms the Gironde, a broad estuary at the heart of the wine country. More than 100,000 vineyards produce some 70 million gallons of wine a year—some of which are among the greatest red wines in the world. (The white wines are lesser known.)

Some of the famous vineyards are pleased to welcome visitors, providing you don't arrive at the busy harvest time. However, most vineyards aren't likely to have a permanent staff to welcome you. Don't just show up—call first or check with local tourist offices about appropriate times to visit.

VISITOR INFORMATION

The best-respected source of information about the wines of Bordeaux (and French wines in general) is the **Centre d'Information, de Documentation, et de Dégustation (CIDD),** 30 rue de la Sablière, 75014 Paris (☎ **01-45-45-32-20;** fax 01-45-42-78-20). This self-funded school presents about a dozen courses throughout the year addressing all aspects of wine tasting, producing, buying, and merchandising.

MAP   Before heading out on this wine road, make sure you get a detailed map from the Bordeaux tourist office (see section 6, earlier in this chapter, under "Essentials"), since the "trail" isn't well marked. Head toward Pauillac on D2, the wine road, called the Route des Grands-Crus.

MEDOC

The Médoc, an undulating plain covered with vineyards, is one of the most visited regions in southwestern France. Its borders are marked by Bordeaux and the Pointe de Grave. Throughout the region are many isolated châteaux producing grapes; only a handful of these, however, are worthy of your attention. The most visited château is that of Mouton-Rothschild, said to be second only to Lourdes among attractions in southwestern France, in spite of the red tape involved in visiting.

In Haut-Médoc, the soil isn't especially fertile but absorbs much heat during the day. To benefit from this, the vines are clipped close to the ground. The French zealously regulate the cultivation of the vineyards and the making of the wine. Less than 10% of the wines from the region are called bordeaux. These are invariably red, including famous labels like Château Margaux, Château Latour, Château Mouton, and Château Lafite. Most of these labels are from grapes grown some 3,000 feet from the Gironde River.

EXPLORING THE AREA

Château de Beychevelle. St-Julien, Beychevelle (10 miles beyond Margaux), 33250 Pauillac. ☎ **05-56-73-20-70.** Free admission. Apr–Sept Mon–Sat 9am–noon and 1:30–5pm; Oct–Mar call for an appointment.

The grand admiral of France, the duc d'Epernon, ordered the Château de Beychevelle built in 1757 and commanded all ships to lower their sails as they passed by. (Beychevelle means "lowered sails.")

Château Lafite. On D2. ☎ **05-56-73-18-18,** or 01-53-89-78-00 for appointments. Free admission. Tours by appointment only, Mon–Fri 9–11am and 2–5pm. Closed Aug and during grape harvest in Sept.

This site is second only to the nearby Château Mouton-Rothschild. Count on spending at least an hour here. The vinothèque contains many vintage bottles—several dating from 1797. The château was purchased in 1868 by the Rothschilds.

Château Margaux. On D2, 33460 Margaux. ☎ **05-57-88-83-83.** Vat rooms and wine cellars open by appointment only, Mon–Fri 10am–noon and 2–4pm. Closed Aug and during harvest.

Known as the Versailles of the Médoc, this Empire-style château was built in the 19th century near the village of Margaux. The estate covers more than 650 acres, of which 193 produce Château Margaux and Pavillon Rouge du Château Margaux; almost 30 acres are devoted to producing Pavillon Blanc du Château Margaux. The inhabitants of the château don't allow tours, but you may admire it from the outside. To see the vat rooms and wine cellars, make an appointment by letter or phone.

✪ **Château Mouton-Rothschild.** Le Pouyalet, 33250 Pauillac. ☎ **05-56-73-21-29.** Tours 20F ($3.60) per person without tasting, 70F ($12.60) per person with a tasting of 1996 vintage. Tours by appointment only, Apr–Oct Sat–Thurs 9:15am–4pm, Fri 9:15am–3:30pm. Call to make an appointment well in advance to see the cellars.

Thousands of tourists visit this outstanding chateau, one of the many former homes of the baron Philippe de Rothschild and his American-born wife, Pauline. Today their only daughter, Philippine de Rothschild, carries on their work. The welcoming room is beautifully furnished with a collection of sculptures and paintings that portray wine as art, plus a 16th-century tapestry depicting the grape harvest. An adjoining museum, in former wine cellars (*chai*), has art from many eras, much of it related to the cultivation of the vineyards. Note the collection of modern art, including a statue by the American sculptor Lippold.

✪ **Société Duboscq.** Château Haut-Marbuzet, 33180 St-Estephe ☎ **05-56-59-30-54.** No appointment necessary. Free admission. Tours given in English on Tues. Mon–Sat 8am–noon and 2–6pm.

Your free visit to the cellars here will be followed by a complimentary dégustation des vins of whichever product you request. A relative newcomer whose prestige has grown rapidly, Duboscq offers excellent opportunities for studying the ancient fermentation process in its modern forms and the maturation process in new oak casks.

WHERE TO DINE

Auberge André. Le Grand Port, 33880 Cambes. ☎ **05-57-97-96-60.** Reservations recommended. Main courses 70–110F ($12.60–$19.80); fixed-price menus 130–180F ($23.40–$32.40). MC, V. Daily noon–2pm and 8:30–10:30pm. FRENCH.

This charming hideaway is located at the edge of Cambes, a village with no more than 100 residents, in a century-old farmhouse whose terrace offers a sweeping view of the Garonne. Menu items might include filet of eel with parsley-butter sauce, lamprey eels in bordelaise-wine sauce, *confit de canard,* filet of sea bass infused with essence of laurel, or salmon cooked with port.

LIBOURNE

This is a sizable market town with a railway connection. At the junction of the Dordogne and Isle rivers, Libourne is roughly the center of the St-Emilion, Pomerol, and Fronsac wine districts. In the town, a large colonnaded square still contains some houses from the 16th century, including the **Hôtel-de-Ville** (town hall). You can also explore the remains of 13th-century ramparts. In the town center is the **Office de Tourisme,** 40 place Abel-Surchamp (☎ 05-57-51-15-04), where you can get details on visiting the Bordeaux vineyards.

NEARBY ACCOMMODATIONS & DINING

La Bonne Auberge. Rue du 8-Mai-1945 et av. John-Talbot, 33350 Castillon-la-Bataille. ☎ **05-57-40-11-56.** Fax 05-57-40-21-66. 10 units. TV TEL. 160–280F ($28.80–$50.40) double. AE, MC, V. From Libourne, follow the signs to Bergerac; take the highway for 18 miles to Castillon-la-Bataille, then continue to the far end of the village.

This family hotel is located near an intersection of two busy highways. Although basic, the rooms are comfortable and welcoming, and the staff keeps them well maintained. This still feels more like a restaurant avec chambres, however, than a full-fledged hotel.

Dining: The food served here is good and plentiful. Serious diners go to the restaurant at the top of the exterior stairs; there's also a brasserie on the ground level. A fixed-price menu in the brasserie is only 58F to 70F ($10.45 to $12.60), whereas the fixed-price menu in the restaurant goes for 72F to 207F ($12.95 to $37.25). Specialties are grilled salmon with shallot-flavored butter, omelets, lamb with parsley, and entrecôte in bordelaise-wine sauce. The restaurant is open daily for lunch and dinner; from November to March, closed Saturday for lunch.

ST-EMILION

Surrounded by vineyards, St-Emilion is on a limestone plateau overlooking the Valley of the Dordogne; a maze of wine cellars has been dug from the limestone beneath the town. The wine made in this world-famous district has been called "Wine of Honor," and British sovereigns nicknamed it "King of Wines." The town, constructed mostly of golden stone and dating from the Middle Ages, is also known for its macaroons.

St-Emilion still maintains the ancient tradition of La Jurade. Members of this society wear silk hats and scarlet robes edged with ermine, and the Syndicat Viticole, which watches over the quality of wine, have all been around the world to promote the wines with this appellation.

St-Emilion lies 22 miles northeast of Bordeaux between Libourne (5 miles away) and Castillon-la-Bataille (7 miles away). Trains from Bordeaux make the 45-minute trip to St-Emilion 3 times per day. Trains from other parts of France usually require transfers in either Bordeaux or Libourne, a 10-minute train ride from St. Emilion. Its **Office de Tourisme** is on place des Créneaux (☎ 05-57-55-28-28).

EXPLORING THE TOWN

At the heart of St-Emilion is **place du Marché,** between two hills. An old acacia tree marks the center.

St-Emilion is loaded with unusual monuments, some of which were dug, for defensive reasons, into the soft limestone bedrock that adds such verve to the vineyards. Foremost of these is the **Eglise Monolithe,** place du Marché (☎ 05-57-55-28-28), the largest underground church in Europe, carved by Benedictine monks during the 9th to 12th centuries. Its facade is marked by three 14th-century bay windows, and a sculpted portal from the same century depicts the Last Judgment and resurrection of the dead. The church is about 37 feet high, 67 feet wide, and 125 feet long. It can be visited only as part of organized tours, in English and French, which leave from the tourist office at 45-minute intervals every day.

Tours depart at 10:45 and 11:30am and 2, 2:45, 3:30, 4:15, and 5pm. They include a visit to the above-mentioned Eglise Monolithe, as well as the Benedictine catacombs and the 13th-century **Chapelle de la Trinité** and its underground grotto (the Hermitage, the site where St-Emilion sequestered himself for the latter part of his life).

The entire complex was kept alive during the heyday of its use by underground springs, which were surrounded in the 1500s by ornate balustrades. The tour costs 33F ($5.95) for adults, 20F ($3.60) for students, 16 F ($2.90) for children 13 to 18, and free for children 12 and under. All the above monuments are closed on December 25 and January 1.

The city contains two additional monuments that can be visited without an organized tour. The first is the **Bell Tower** (*clocher*) of the above-mentioned Eglise Monolithe. It rises from a position on place des Créneaux, near place du Marché. Built between the 1100s and the 1400s, it's the second-highest tower in La Gironde and for years after its construction was the only aboveground landmark that indicated the position of the underground church with which it's associated. You can climb the bell tower during daylight hours every day except Christmas and New Year's Day for a fee of 6F ($1.10) per person. Naturally, views from the top are panoramic.

Finally, you may want to view **Château du Roi,** founded by Henry III of the Plantagenet line in the 13th century. Until 1608 it was the town hall. From the top of the dungeon you can see St-Emilion and, on a clear day, the Dordogne. You can wander about daily from 9:30am to 12:30pm and 2 to 6:30pm. Admission iss 6F ($1.10) per person.

WHERE TO STAY & DINE

✪ **Hostellerie de Plaisance.** Place du Clocher, 33330 St-Emilion. ☎ **05-57-55-07-55.** Fax 05-57-74-41-11. 16 units. A/C TEL. 590-1,100F ($106.20–$198) double; 1,400–1,800F ($252–$324) suite. AE, DC, MC, V. Closed Jan.

This 200-year-old stone building, set on 14th-century foundations, is the best choice in this medieval town. The well-styled rooms, some with views of stone monuments and towers, welcome sophisticated wine tasters and buyers from all over the world. Some rooms are quite small, but the best doubles have terraces where you can enjoy breakfast.

Dining: The cuisine of Louis Quilain is the best known and most praised in the area. He's at his best when working with the region's bountiful seasonal ingredients. Well-seasoned specialties include various versions of foie gras, crayfish, magrêt of duckling, and fish.

18 The Basque Country

The chief interest in the Basque country, a land rich in folklore and old customs, is confined to a small corner of southwestern France, near the Spanish frontier. Here you can visit the Basque capital, Bayonne, and explore the coastal resorts, chic Biarritz and St-Jean-de-Luz. In Bayonne's Roman arena during July and August, you can see a real Spanish bullfight. The typical costume of the Basque men—beret and cummerbund—isn't as evident as it once was, but you can still spot it here and there.

The vast Pyrenean region is a land of glaciers, summits, thermal baths, subterranean grottoes and caverns, winter-sports centers, and trout-filled mountain streams. Pau is a good base for excursions in the western Pyrénées, and Lourdes is the major religious pilgrimage center in France.

REGIONAL CUISINE Several distinct culinary traditions have flourished in and around the Pyrénées: those of the Basque, the Béarn, the Catalán, and the Landes region.

The food here is simple, hearty, and fresh, traditionally served on a table draped with the roughly woven, brightly striped cloths that have always been associated with the region. Basque cuisine transforms ordinary ingredients into aromatically tantalizing concoctions, usually with the liberal addition of pepper.

One savory delicacy is tuna grilled with local herbs over a wood fire and served with chopped garlic, parsley, vinaigrette sauce, and freshly pounded pepper. Other regional specialties include *bigorneaux* (periwinkles), which diners skewer from their shells with toothpicks; *cèpes,* meaty flap mushrooms braised with garlic and sprinkled with parsley; and lamb chops, pork chops, and Basque *bourrides* (fish stews), all with dollops of garlic. Basque bouillabaisse is called *ttoro,* and *chipirones* are cuttlefish, which the Basques stuff or stew after beating the flesh to break apart its toughness.

Basque country also produces *pipérade Basque,* scrambled eggs with tomatoes, onions, green peppers, and black pepper. Sausages popular here include *tripoxa,* made from calves' blood and hot peppers; *tripotcha,* from tripe of baby veal; and *loukinkas,* small garlic-laden sausages. A local sour cider is pittara, and the region's best wine is Irouléguy. Bayonne's chocolate is famous throughout France.

In the Béarn, centered around Pau, the wines are excellent and liberally consumed with the contents of the family *toupi* (soup pot). Many kinds of onion, beet, sorrel, chicory, bacon/cabbage, and

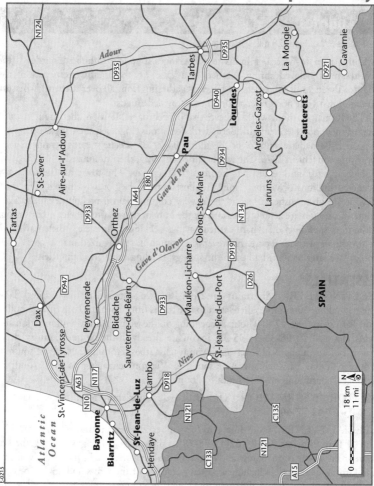

garlic/tomato soup are prepared in this pot. Thick and aromatic stews are called *garbure*, and they're not considered suitable unless the ladle can stand upright in the pot. With bread and wine, the garbure is a full meal. The wines of the Béarn are better than those of the Basque country and include its most famous vintage, Jurançon. Sadly for its regional pride, however, sauce béarnaise wasn't created here—it was invented by a Basque chef in Paris.

The Pyrénées are also inhabited by the Catalans, who do much of their cooking in olive oil with generous amounts of garlic. The Catalán national dish is *ouillade*, a constantly replenished pair of stewpots that are never emptied, washed, or cleaned. Catalán bouillabaisse is called *bouillinade* and is prepared with crayfish (among other fish) boiled in dry Banyuls wine.

Finally, in the northwestern Pyrénées, the traditional cooking medium is goose fat, which occasionally flavors the aromatic and delicious *cassoulet*. A cassoulet must always be cooked in a *cassoule* (earthenware pot), simmered in an oven for hours, and contain white beans and either goose meat, pork, lamb, partridge, or a combination of any of the above.

1 Lourdes

497 miles SW of Paris, 25 miles SE of Pau

Muslims turn to Mecca, Hindus to the Ganges, but for Catholics Lourdes is the world's most beloved shrine. Nestled in a valley in the southwestern part of the Hautes-Pyrénées, it's the scene of pilgrims gathering from all over the world. Be sure to nail down your hotel reservation in overcrowded August.

The Roman Catholic world believes that on February 11, 1858, the Virgin revealed herself to a poor shepherd girl, Bernadette Soubirous. Eighteen such apparitions were reported. Bernadette, subject of the film *Song of Bernadette* starring Jennifer Jones, died in a convent in 1879. She was beatified in 1925, then canonized in 1933.

Her apparitions literally put Lourdes on the map. The town has subsequently attracted millions of visitors, from the illustrious to the poverty-stricken. The truly devout are often disheartened at the tawdry commercialism of Lourdes today. And some vacationers are acutely disturbed by the human desperation of victims of various afflictions spending their hard-earned savings seeking a "miracle," then having to return home without a cure. However, the church has recognized many "cures" that took place after patients bathed in the springs, labeling them "true miracles."

ESSENTIALS

GETTING THERE   Six **trains** run from Pau (see section 2 in this chapter) daily, the trip taking 30 minutes; there are also five trains from Bayonne (trip time: 2 hours) and Paris, trip time: (7 to 9 hours, depending on the train). For train information and schedules, call ☎ **08-36-35-35-39.** If you are already in the Basque Country, **drive** from Toulouse along N117 west until you reach Tarbes. From here take N21 south to Lourdes. From Paris, follow A10 south to Vierzon, changing to N20 south to Limoges, continuing on N21 south to Lourdes.

VISITOR INFORMATION   The **Office de Tourisme** is on place Peyramale (☎ **05-62-42-77-40**).

SPECIAL EVENTS   From July 1 to September 20, tourists and pilgrims can join the ✪ **Day Pilgrims** (☎ **05-62-42-78-78**), a pilgrimage (in English) that gathers at 9am at the statue of the Crowned Virgin for a prayer meeting in the meadow facing the Grotto. The services include a 9:30am Stations of the Cross and an 11am mass. At 2:30pm, assembling at the same spot, pilgrims are taken on a guided visit to the Sanctuaries, or places associated with Bernadette. At 4:30pm there's a Procession of the Blessed Eucharist, starting from the Grotto. The 8:45pm Marian celebration, rosary, and torchlight procession all start from the Grotto as well. In the Sanctuaries you'll be told the story of Lourdes and of Bernadette, complete with a free slide show (in English) that runs about 15 minutes.

EXPLORING THE TOWN & ITS ENVIRONS

At the **Grotto of Massabielle** the Virgin is said to have appeared 18 times to Bernadette between February 11 and July 16, 1858. This venerated site is accessible to pilgrims both day and night, and mass is celebrated here every day. The Statue of Our Lady depicts the Virgin in the posture she is said to have taken in the place she reputedly appeared, saying to Bernadette in Pyrenean dialect, "I am the Immaculate Conception."

At the back of the Grotto, on the left of the altar, is the **Miraculous Spring** that reportedly spouted on February 25, 1858, during the ninth apparition, when Bernadette scraped the earth as instructed. The Virgin is said to have commanded her,

"Go and drink at the spring and wash there." The water from this spring is collected in several reservoirs, from which you can drink.

Other sanctuaries associated with St. Bernadette include the crypt, the first chapel built on top of the Grotto, the Basilica of the Immaculate Conception, the Rosary Basilica, and the underground Basilica of St. Pius X. In town, there is the house where Bernadette lived; the Cachot, which is the former prison that housed Bernadette and her family during the time of her visitation; the baptismal font in the parish church; and the hospital chapel where she made her first communion.

The **Upper Basilica,** at place du Rosaire, was built in the 13th-century ogival style but wasn't consecrated until 1876. It contains one nave split into five equal bays. Lining its interior are votive tablets. On the west side of the square is the Rosary Basilica, with two small towers. It was built in 1889 in the Roman-Byzantine style and holds up to 4,000. Inside, 15 chapels are dedicated to the "mysteries of the rosary."

The oval **Basilica of Pius X,** 1 ave. Monseigneur Théas, was consecrated in 1958. An enormous underground chamber covered by a concrete roof, it's 660 feet long and 270 feet wide, holding as many as 20,000. It's one of the world's largest churches. It's open daily from 7am to 7pm. International masses are conducted in six languages, including English, every Wednesday and Sunday at 9am.

Nearby, the **Musée Ste-Bernadette** (☎ **05-62-42-78-78**) contains scenes representing the life of the saint; it's open daily from 9 to 11:45am and 2 to 5:45pm (call ahead during winter). True Bernadette devotees will also seek out the **Maison Natale de Bernadette,** rue Bernadette-Soubirous (☎ **05-62-42-16-36**), where the saint was born on January 7, 1844, the daughter of a miller. Her former home is open October to March daily from 3 to 5pm and from April to September daily from 9am to noon and 2 to 6:30pm. This was actually her mother's house. Bernadette's father, François Soubirous, had his family home in another mill, **Moulin Lacadé,** at 2 rue Bernadette-Soubirous. You can visit daily from 9am to 12pm and 2 to 6:30pm in summer; in winter daily 3 to 5pm. None of these sites charges admission. For more information contact the Office de Tourisme (see above).

You can visit the privately owned and overly commercialized wax museum, **Musée Grévin,** 87 rue de la Grotte (☎ **05-62-94-33-74**), where displays retrace not only Bernadette's life but also the life of Christ, with a bad reproduction of Leonardo da Vinci's *Last Supper*. This museum in the center of Lourdes is open daily from 9 to 11:40am and 1:30 to 6:30pm (in July and August, also from 9 to 10pm). Admission is 34 F ($6.10) for adults, 17F ($3.05) for children 6 to 12, and free for children 5 and under.

If you want a panoramic view, take an elevator to the terrace of the **Château-Fort de Lourdes,** an excellent example of medieval military architecture. The castle contains the **Musée Pyrénéen,** 25 rue du Fort (☎ **05-62-42-37-37**), with regional handcrafts and costumes, including a collection of dolls in nuns' habits. In the courtyard are scale models of different styles of regional architecture. Both the château and the museum can be visited April to September, daily from 9am to noon and 1:30 to 6:30pm; off-season it closes at 5pm and is closed Tuesday. Admission is 30F ($5.40) for adults, 15F ($2.70) for children 6 to 12, and free for children 5 and under.

OUTDOOR PURSUITS   Lourdes is a good base for exploring the Pyrénées. You can take tours into the snowcapped mountains across the border to Spain or go horseback riding near **Lac de Lourdes,** 2 miles northwest of town. Outstanding sites are **Bagnères-de-Bigorre,** a renowned thermal spa; **Pic du Jer,** for a panoramic vista; **Béout,** for a view and an underground cave where prehistoric implements have been found (reached by funicular); **Pibeste,** for another sweeping view; the **Caves of**

Medous, an underground river with stalactites; and for a full-day tour, the **Heights of Gavarnie,** at 4,500 feet, one of France's great natural wonders.

WHERE TO STAY

The two restaurants reviewed below also offer rooms.

Grand Hôtel de la Grotte. 66–68 rue de la Grotte, 65000 Lourdes. ☎ **05-62-94-58-87.** Fax 05-62-94-20-50. 83 units. A/C MINIBAR TV TEL. 370–580F ($66.60–$104.40) double. AE, DC, MC, V. Closed Oct 20–Good Fri. Bus: 2.

Grand Hôtel is an old favorite, having catered to pilgrims and devout Catholics (and to an increasing degree, tourists) since 1870. It's furnished in a staid but comfortable upper-bourgeois French decor that's slowly being updated. Some of the rooms on the upper floor open onto one of the most panoramic views in town, not only of the sanctuaries and the river but also the mountains. Rooms on the basilica side seem to be noisy. The hotel has a garden set beside the banks of the river Gave de Pau. Its restaurant, open to the public, offers straightforward meals inspired by French and regional cuisine.

Hôtel Adriatic. 4 rue Baron-Duprat, 65100 Lourdes. ☎ **05-62-94-31-34.** Fax 05-62-42-14-70. 87 units. TEL. 260–395F ($46.80–$71.10) double. V. Bus: 2.

With a bright English-speaking staff, this hotel offers clean and traditional rooms; about 23 contain TVs and minibars. The in-house restaurant serves fine regional cuisine. The hotel is close to the shrines, the home of St. Bernadette, the parish church, and the town's fortified castle.

Hôtel Galilée et Windsor. 10 av. Peyramale, 65100 Lourdes. ☎ **05-62-94-21-55.** Fax 05-62-94-53-66. 163 units. TV TEL. 450F ($81) double. Rates include breakfast. Half board 300–350F ($54–$63) per person extra. AE, DC, MC, V. Closed Oct 15–Easter.

This three-star hotel, often confused with the more comfortable, more expensive Gallia et Londres, was built after World War II. The rooms are pleasant, if rather dull and anonymous-looking. As the largest hotel in Lourdes, this place is a magnet for religious groups. The restaurant serves regional and continental meals but offers nothing to challenge the tastebuds.

Hôtel Gallia et Londres. 26 av. Bernadette-Soubirous, 65100 Lourdes. ☎ **05-62-94-35-44.** Fax 05-62-42-24-64. 90 units. A/C TV TEL. 1,000F ($180) double. Rate includes breakfast. AE, V. Closed Apr–Oct 30.

This old-fashioned four-star hotel with a provincial flavor is among the most popular in Lourdes, catering to many religious groups that check in en masse. The rooms are decorated in a period style and many have balconies; some are suitable for persons with disabilities. Its restaurant is solidly reliable throughout the year, serving fixed-price menus. The hotel has a garden, plus a bar and a pub.

Hôtel Notre-Dame de France. 8 av. Peyramale, 65100 Lourdes. ☎ **05-62-94-91-45.** Fax 05-62-94-57-21. 76 units. TEL. 350F ($63) double. Half board 270F ($48.60) per person extra. AE, MC, V. Parking 50F ($9), free for half-board clients. Closed Oct 15–Mar 15. Bus: 2.

Next to the previously recommended Galilée et Windsor, this hotel is less than 100 yards from the main religious monument ("Le Sanctuaire") of Lourdes. With clean rooms and simple, almost monastic furnishings, it's a worthwhile budget choice. The meals are a good buy, with regional cuisine offered.

WHERE TO DINE

Relais de Saux. Rte. de Tarbes (N21), 65100 Lourdes. ☎ **05-62-94-29-61.** Fax 05-62-42-12-64. www.sudfr.com/relais.de.saux. E-mail: relais.de.saux@sudfr.com. Reservations recommended. Fixed-price menus 140F ($25.20) at lunch, 180–310F ($32.40–$55.80) at dinner. AE, DC, MC, V. Daily noon–2pm and 7:15–9:30pm. Take D914 1½ miles northeast of Lourdes to the village of Saux. BIGORRE.

This is the area's best restaurant, housed in an ivy-covered manor and serving the regional mountain cuisine of the Pyrénées. The carved-wood fireplaces complement the beamed ceilings, silk-upholstered walls, and rustic artifacts. Meals are supervised by innkeepers Madeleine and Bernard Heres. Begin with a selection of hot or cold hors d'oeuvres, ranging from beet flan with cheese fondue to smoked swordfish. The boneless quail is especially delectable.

Upstairs are seven guest rooms, some with large windows overlooking the garden. A double costs 550 to 580F ($99 to $104.40). Half board 850F to 950F ($153 to $171) extra for 2.

Taverne de Bigorre et Hôtel d'Albret. 21 place du Champs-Commun, 65100 Lourdes. ☎ **05-62-94-75-00.** Fax 05-62-94-78-45. Reservations recommended. Fixed-price menus 67–198F ($12.05–$35.65). AE, DC, MC, V. Daily noon–1:30pm and 7–9pm. Closed Jan 6–Feb 6 and Nov 18–Dec 23. BIGORRE.

This restaurant has some of the best food in town, with tournedos with flap mushrooms a specialty. You can also order such country dishes as escalope of hot duck foie gras with apples and duck steak kebab with green-pepper sauce. The mountain trout is especially good here.

Hôtel d'Albret is one of the best budget hotels in Lourdes, with 27 comfortable rooms. A double costs 189F to 265F ($34 to $47.70), with half board at 202F ($36.35) per person extra.

2 Pau

477 miles SW of Paris, 122 miles SW of Toulouse

High above the banks of the Gave de Pau River, this year-round resort is a good place to pause in your trek through the Pyrénées. The British discovered Pau in the early 19th century, launching such innovative practices here as fox hunting, a custom that's lingered. Even if you're just passing through, go along boulevard des Pyrénées, an esplanade erected on Napoléon's orders, for the most famous panoramic view in the Pyrénées.

Today Pau is the most cosmopolitan city in the western Pyrénées, the capital of the Pyrénées-Atlantiques département. It was once the capital of the Béarn region, the land of the kings of Navarre, the most famous and beloved of whom was Henri IV. Its population of approximately 90,000 still observes some English traditions, such as afternoon tea. At one time the English formed 15% of the population, but with the arrival of two world wars, many of them left.

ESSENTIALS

GETTING THERE   Pau-Uzein airport is 7½ miles north of town; call ☎ 05-59-33-21-29 for flight information. There are good **train connections** from Biarritz (6 per day taking 1½ hours); for train information and schedules, call ☎ 08-36-35-35-39. **Driving** to Pau is relatively easy because of its location along the N117 roadway, which is directly accessible from Toulouse. From Paris, take A10 south to Vierzon, changing to N20 south to Limoges, continuing on N21 south to Tarbes, finally turning west along N117 to Pau.

VISITOR INFORMATION   The **Office de Tourisme is on place Royale (☎ 05-59-27-27-08).

SPECIAL EVENTS In May, there's the **Grand Prix de Pau** car race. In June and early July, street festivals take over, along with theatrical, music, and dance performances. For about 4 weeks beginning in mid-July, you can take in a variety of performing arts, ranging from dance to theater and concerts, during the **Festival de Pau.** Performances are held in various locations, and tickets run between 100F to 200F ($18 to $36). The Office de Tourisme has complete details.

EXPLORING THE CITY

The heart of the commercial district is busy **place Clémenceau,** out of which radiate at least five boulevards. At the western end of town stands the **Château de Pau,** 2 rue du Château (☎ 05-59-82-38-00), dating from the 12th century and still steeped in the Renaissance spirit of the bold Marguerite de Navarre, who wrote the bawdy *Heptaméron* at 60. The castle has seen many builders and tenants. Louis XV ordered the bridge that connects the castle to the town, whereas the great staircase hall was commissioned by Marguerite herself. Louis-Philippe had all the apartments redecorated around 1840. Inside are many souvenirs, including a crib made of a single tortoise-shell for Henri de Navarre, who was born here. There's also a splendid array of Flemish and Gobelin tapestries. The great rectangular tower, **Tour de Gaston Phoebus,** is from the 14th century.

On the château's third floor is the **Musée Béarnais,** containing ethnographical collections of the Béarn, the old name of the medieval duchy of which Pau was the capital. Finally, you may want to walk through the beautiful Parc du Château, the gardens (or what's left of them) that surrounded the château in the 16th century.

The château and museum are open daily from 9:30 to 11:45am and 2 to 5:15pm. Admission is 35F ($6.30) for adults, 27F ($4.85) for students 18 to 25, and free for children 17 and under.

Musée des Beaux-Arts, rue Mathieu-Lalanne (☎ 05-59-27-33-02), displays a collection of European paintings, including Spanish, Flemish, Dutch, English, and French masters, such as El Greco, Zurbarán, Degas, and Boudin. It's open Wednesday to Monday from 10am to noon and 2 to 6pm. Admission is 10F ($1.80) for adults and 5F (90¢) for children.

SHOPPING

Pau affords ample opportunities for you to buy some authentic regional specialties, such as mouth-watering chocolates, sweet jams, and Basque antiques. The pedestrian **rue Serviez** and **rue des Cordelières** harbor an array of petit boutiques and shops that carry many of these items, as do **rue Louis-Barthou, rue Henry-IV,** and **rue du Maréchal-Foch.**

Pau is home to some of the best antiques shops in France, including **Antiquités du Sud-Ouest,** 37 rue Bayard (☎ 05-59-27-63-42), specializing in Basque art and furnishings, and **Champeau Paul,** 14 rue Castetnau (☎ 05-59-83-71-62), with its mélange of 18th- to 20th-century treasures for the home. The area around the château is well known as the antiques center of town. On Saturday, Sunday, and Monday from 10am to 6pm, you'll find a large **flea market** on place du Forail, selling everything from antiques to modern-day gadgets.

Local confectionery specialties are **armes de Pau,** the small squares of secret-recipe, medium-dark chocolate with the town's coat of arms emblazoned on top. Some of the best of these decadent morsels can be found at **Chadeuf Bouzon,** 6 rue Henri-IV (☎ 05-59-27-70-88). The **Musée de la Confiture,** 48 rue du Maréchal-Joffre (☎ 05-59-27-69-51), not only traces the rich history of jam making in this region but also has fabulously fruity jams for sale.

WHERE TO STAY

Hôtel Continental. 2 rue du Maréchal-Foch, 64000 Pau. ☎ **05-59-27-69-31.** Fax 05-59-27-99-84. www.bestwestern.com. 80 units. MINIBAR TV TEL. 395–540F ($71.10–$97.20) double. AE, DC, DISC, MC, V. Free parking in garage.

The centrally located, three-star Continental is the largest, most prominent hotel in Pau. Renovated several times since its original construction around 1900, it's the best of a lackluster lot in town. Even so, don't expect grand theatricality or even a staff that's particularly well trained. The rooms are functionally decorated, modernized, and soundproofed; some are suitable for persons with disabilities.

Hôtel de Gramont. 3 place Gramont, 64000 Pau. ☎ **05-59-27-84-04.** Fax 05-59-27-62-23. 38 units. TV TEL. 280–495F ($50.40–$89.10) double; 495F ($89.10) suite. AE, DC, DISC, MC, V.

Within walking distance of the château and the rail station, this hotel is a truly impressive building. The four-story châteaulike structure has street-level arcades and high-ceilinged soundproofed rooms, 10 of which are air-conditioned. Some are suitable for persons with disabilities.

Hôtel Le Postillon. Place de Verdun, 10 cours Camou, 64000 Pau. ☎ **05-59-72-83-00.** Fax 05-59-72-83-13. 25 units. TV TEL. 210–280F ($37.80–$50.40) double. AE, V. Bus: 1.

This is a cozy hotel, with French provincial decor and a flower-filled courtyard. The rooms are comfortably furnished, each individually decorated. Some have a balcony overlooking the garden. The reasonable price keeps the place consistently full. Breakfast is the only meal served, but there's a choice of restaurants nearby.

Hôtel-Restaurant Corona. 71 av. du Général-Leclerc, 64000 Pau. ☎ **05-59-30-64-77.** Fax 05-59-02-62-64. 20 units. TV TEL. 195–240F ($35.10–$43.20) double. AE, MC, V.

The French architect who designed this hotel had completed many commissions in Montréal. In honor of them, he added what were considered at the time many Canada-inspired touches, including the ample use of exposed pinewood. About a mile east of the center of Pau, this hotel offers comfortable accommodations and serves hearty portions of food in its two dining rooms. The restaurant (but not the brasserie) is closed on Saturday and from December 23 to January 10.

WHERE TO DINE

Au Fin Gourmet. 24 av. Gaston-Lacoste. ☎ **05-59-27-47-71.** Reservations recommended. Main courses 90–130F ($16.20–$23.40); fixed-price menus 90–165F ($16.20–$29.70). AE, DC, MC, V. Tues–Sun noon–2:15pm and 7–10pm. BASQUE.

This restaurant is maintained by Christian, Laurent, and Patrick, sons of the retired founder, Clément Ithurriague. It offers an outdoor terrace for warm-weather dining and a cuisine based almost exclusively on regional ingredients. Menu items include marinated codfish with herbs "from the kitchen garden" and bouillon-flavored potatoes, rack of lamb flavored with herbs from the Pyrénées in a parsley-enriched crust, sliced and sautéed foie gras, and braised stuffed trout. The 90F ($16.20) fixed-price menu is a crowd pleaser and one of Pau's best dining values.

✪ **Chez Pierre.** 16 rue Louis-Barthou. ☎ **05-59-27-76-86.** Reservations required. Main courses 60–160F ($10.80–$28.80); fixed-price menu 180F ($32.40). AE, DC, V. Mon–Fri noon–2:30pm, Mon–Sat 7–10pm. BEARNAISE/FRENCH.

Year after year, we're always served our finest meal in Pau at Chez Pierre, where regional products are spun into extraordinarily creative dishes. In air-conditioned comfort, you can sit downstairs at one of the eight tables or upstairs in one of three tiny salons. Chef Raymond Casau, who spent years apprenticing with some of the most successful chefs in France, is among the finest around, and his specialties are sole with white mushrooms and small new cucumbers, fresh salmon braised with Jurançon (a sweet, golden Pyrenean wine), and a Béarnais version of cassoulet. (Swimming in a marmite of white beans, it differs from the version associated with Toulouse in that the sausages are different, and there's a greater emphasis on confit of goose.) One of the most attractive bars in town, outfitted like the club room of an English golf course, lies adjacent to the dining rooms.

La Gousse d'Ail. 12 rue du Hédas. ☎ **05-59-27-31-55.** Main courses 80–115F ($14.40–$20.70); fixed-price menus 100–190F ($18–$34.20). MC, V. Mon–Fri noon–1:30pm, Mon–Sat 7–10:30pm. BASQUE.

A few blocks from the château, this restaurant has a stone, brick, and stucco interior with ceiling beams and a fireplace. Meals may include a fresh pasta with mushrooms and foie gras, escalope of fresh duck liver with apple and honey, sole cooked in champagne butter with foie gras, knuckle of ham with flap mushrooms and herbs, and filet of duck. The specialties of the southwest are deftly handled here.

NEARBY ACCOMMODATIONS & DINING

Some of the world's most discerning people head about 33 miles north of Pau, in search of the marvelous domain of Michel Guérard. The town has no rail station, so most people drive from Pau. To reach Eugénie-les-Bains from Pau, take N134 north to the town of Garlin, then follow the unmarked road west to the town of Geaune and then on to Eugénie-les-Bains.

✪ **Les Prés d'Eugénie (Michel Guérard).** Eugénie-les-Bains, 40320 Beaune. ☎ **05-58-05-06-07.** Fax 05-58-51-10-10. Reservations recommended. Main courses 220–390F ($39.60–$70.20); fixed-price menus 590–750F ($106.20–$135). AE, DC, MC, V. July–Aug daily 12:30–2pm and 7:30–10pm; Sept–June Fri–Tues 12:30–2pm, Thurs–Tues 7:30–10pm. BASQUE.

This Relais & Château is the creation of Michel Guérard, the innovative chef whose *cuisine minceur* started a culinary revolution in the early 1970s. Built during the 19th century as a spa where the Empress Eugénie could take a rest cure, it attracts a stream of diners who appreciate the calm, the much-publicized cooking, and the endless business expansions of its owner. Offered here are both cuisine minceur, so calorie counters can still enjoy well-seasoned flavors and fresh ingredients, and the heartier *cuisine gourmand*, whose traditions are influenced by Basque and classic French recipes. Specialties include cream of crayfish soup, whiting in white-wine sauce, mullet steamed with seaweed and oysters, lamb steamed with fennel, and a wide variety of simply steamed fish with fresh vegetables.

Those unwilling to pay the stratospheric prices in the main restaurant sometimes select a table in a satellite restaurant operated by M. Guérard called **La Ferme aux Grives.** The cuisine here focuses on more rural specialties of the region, offering a single fixed-price menu costing 185F ($33.30). Comfortable and rustically elegant, La Ferme aux Grives is open for lunch and dinner July 8 to September 2 from 12:30 to 2pm and 7:30 to 10pm; closed Monday night and Tuesday.

Besides the main building's 28 rooms and 7 suites—which rent for 1,350F ($243) double and 1,750 8F ($315) for a suite—8 accommodations are in an outlying annex, **La Couvent des Herbes.** These rent for 1,550F ($279) double and 1,900F ($342) for a suite. Less expensive, and deliberately geared to families are the 27 rooms and 5 apartments (each with kitchenette) in **La Maison Rose,** where doubles go for 550F ($99).

PAU AFTER DARK

A healthy portion of Pau's nightlife revolves around the youthful, fun-loving student scene. Two favorite bars are the working-class **Le Béarnais,** 3 rue Lespy (☎ **05-59-83-72-11**), with its fun staff and convivial atmosphere; and **Le Caveau,** 18 rue Castelnau (☎ **05-59-27-35-37**), more laid-back and not quite so loud. But if you need a more diverse and older crowd, check out the streets around the château, where you'll find bars like **Le Sully,** 13 rue Henri-IV (☎ **05-59-62-15-85**), blaring heavy-duty rock well into the early-morning hours. At **Le Paradis,** 11 place du Forail (☎ **05-59-84-06-73**), all ages mix, mingle, and bop the night away on the immense dance floor to the beat of popular Top-50 tunes. Covers range between 25F and 60F ($4.50 and $10.80).

3 Bayonne

478 miles SW of Paris, 114 miles SW of Bordeaux

The leading port/pleasure-yacht basin of the Côte Basque, divided by the Nive and Adour rivers, Bayonne is a cathedral city and capital of the Pays Basque. It's characterized by narrow streets, quays, and ramparts. Enlivening the scene are bullfights, *pelote* games (jai alai), and street dancing at annual fiestas. While here you may want to buy some of Bayonne's chocolate at one of the arcaded shops along rue du Port-Neuf, later enjoying a coffee at one of the cafes along place de la Liberté, the hub of town.

ESSENTIALS

GETTING THERE   Bayonne is linked to Paris by 10 **trains** per day. Regular trains take around 8 hours, though the TGV arrives in 5. Nine trains per day arrive from Bordeaux (trip time: 2½ hours). For train information and schedules, call ☎ **08-36-35-35-39.**

There's **bus service** from Biarritz. (Bus no. 1 departs from Biarritz at 12-minute intervals throughout the daylight hours, depositing passengers on place de la Mairie in Bayonne.) There's also bus service between Bayonne and outlying towns and villages not serviced by train.

Bayonne is located near the end of the N117 roadway, easily accessible from Toulouse and other cities in the south of France. From Paris, take A10 south to Vierzon, changing to N20 south to Limoges, continuing on N21 south to Tarbes, finally turning west along N117 to Bayonne.

VISITOR INFORMATION   The **Office de Tourisme** is on place des Basques (☎ **05-59-46-01-46**).

SPECIAL EVENTS   The second week of July is the traditional start of the town's jazz festival called **Jazz aux Remparts.** Great jazz musicians from as far away as the United States come here for a week of superb high-energy concerts. Tickets to most concerts range between 150F and 200F ($27 and $36) and are available along with complete details from the Théâtre Municipal (☎ **05-59-59-07-27**). During **Fête de Bayonne,** held the first weeks in August, a frenzy of music concerts and dancing fill the streets. The celebration is intense. For **free concerts** on fair-weathered Thursday evenings in July and August, head over to the gazebo on place de Gaulle where musical styles range from jazz to traditional Basque.

EXPLORING THE TOWN

The old town, **Grand Bayonne,** is inside the ramparts of Vauban's fortifications, on the left bank of the Nive. This part of town is dominated by the early 13th-century

✪ **Cathédrale Ste-Marie,** rue d'Espagne/rue des Gouverneurs (☎ **05-59-59-17-82**). This outstanding Gothic building is distinguished by its nave's stained-glass windows and many niches containing elaborate sarcophagi. From the 13th-century cloister you have a view of the cathedral's remarkable architecture. It's open daily from 8am to noon and 3 to 6pm.

The **Musée Bonnat,** 5 rue Jacques-Lafitte (☎ **05-59-59-08-52**), contains a collection of artwork that the painter Léon Bonnat donated to the city, including his own. Bonnat was especially fond of portraits, often of ladies in elegant 1890s gowns. Far greater painters whose works are represented include Degas, David, Goya, Ingres, Rubens, van Dyck, Rembrandt, Tiepolo, El Greco, and even Leonardo. The museum is open Wednesday to Monday from 10am to noon and 2:30 to 6:30pm (and until 8:30pm on Friday). Admission is 20F ($3.60) for adults and 15F ($2.70) for children 11 and under.

SHOPPING

Most of its specialty shops and boutiques lie inside the ramparts of the old town, Grand Bayonne. The pedestrian streets of **rue Pont-Neuf** (aptly nicknamed the "street of chocolate shops"), **rue Victor-Hugo,** and **rue Sarie** are the major venues. For antiques, walk over to **place Montaut,** just behind the cathedral. **Rue Thiers** and **quai de la Nive,** outside the old town, have most of the modern, everyday shops and French chain stores. In particular, visit **Maison de blanc Berrogain,** place de 5 Cantons (☎ **05-59-59-16-18**), to meet your quota of Basque bath, kitchen, and bed linens. Finally, **Cazenave,** 19 rue Pont-Neuf (☎ **05-59-59-03-16**), specializes in chocolats de Bayonne that include rich, dark, strong chocolate nougats and warm chocolate mousses in its tearoom.

You can also head for a 150-year-old shop in the shadow of Bayonne's cathedral, **La Maison Tajan,** 62-64 rue d'Espagne (☎ **05-59-59-00-39**), where you'll find the region's widest selection of glazed terra-cotta platters and pots, each oven- and microwave-proof and table-ready. Imported from nearby Spain and decorated only with a translucent earth-toned glaze, they're among the best accessories for the slow-cooking processes necessary in preparing Basque cuisine.

WHERE TO STAY

Best Western Grand Hôtel. 21 rue Thiers, 64100 Bayonne. ☎ **800/528-1234** in the U.S. and Canada, or 05-59-59-14-61. Fax 05-59-25-61-70. www.bestwestern.com. 54 units. TV TEL. 490–650F ($88.20–$117) double. AE, DC, MC, V. Parking 50F ($10).

This hotel, the best in town, was built in 1835 amid the ruins of a medieval Carmelite convent. In 1991, after a total renovation, it attained three-star status, without losing the turn-of-the-century flair of high-ceilinged guest rooms and preserving its medieval feel in the restaurant, Les Carmes. Here the original convent's bulky, carefully chiseled arcades are sheltered with a glass, greenhouse-style roof that can be opened for ventilation during warm weather. Fixed-price meals cost 90F to 200F ($16.20 to $36).

Mercure Agora. Av. Jean-Rostand, 64100 Bayonne. ☎ **05-59-63-30-90.** Fax 05-59-42-06-64. E-mail: h0953@accord-hotels.com. 109 units. A/C MINIBAR TV TEL. 360–500F ($64.80–$90) double. AE, DC, MC, V.

Widely considered the second best choice in Bayonne, the Mercure provides well-furnished rooms with views over the river Nive, which flows nearby. Drinks are served on the terrace, which was carved out of an otherwise wooded setting beside the river. The restaurant's fixed-price menus begin in the very inexpensive range, but the cuisine isn't the reason to stay here.

WHERE TO DINE

Cheval Blanc. 68 rue Bourgneuf. ☎ **05-59-59-01-33.** Reservations recommended. Main courses 95–140F ($17.10–$25.20); fixed-price menus 115–260F ($20.70–$46.80). AE, DC, V. Tues–Sun noon–2:15pm, Tues–Sat 7–9:30pm. Closed Feb 2–25 and Aug 6–10. BASQUE.

The finest restaurant in Bayonne occupies a half-timbered Basque-style house that was built in 1715 in the heart of the historic center. In a rustically elegant dining room you can enjoy the cuisine of Jean-Claude Tellechea, served by one of the most skilled maîtres d' in the Basque country, Robert Hualte. Menu items vary with the season but may include roasted merlou with finely chopped golden onions, pavé of beef prepared with madeira sauce and served with peppers stuffed with a purée of garlic, and a supremely delicious version of saltwater fish the Basques call *louvine,* cooked in a salt crust and perfumed with foie gras. Dorado might be simmered in garlic and presented with *crépinette de marmitako* (diced tuna with red and green peppers, bound by the lining of a pig's stomach). One of the best desserts is an *amandine bayonnais* with chocolate sauce.

François Miura. 24 rue Marengo. ☎ **05-59-59-49-89.** Reservations recommended. Main courses 80–115F ($14.40–$20.70); fixed-price menus 105–180F ($18.90–$32.40). AE, DC, MC, V. Thurs–Tues noon–2pm, Mon–Tues and Thurs–Sat 8–10pm. FRENCH.

Its cuisine is the most eclectic and personalized in town. Chef Miura makes creative use of fresh ingredients, and his wife, Nadine, serves the dishes with humor and style. A few steps from the Eglise St-André, the restaurant occupies a late-19th-century cloister originally built for Visitandine nuns, which has been renovated into an appealing combination of old masonry and angular postmodern design. Menu items are sophisticated and composed with intelligence, including flavorful but complicated dishes such as stuffed squid served with a confit of pig's foot flavored with squid ink and an essence of crayfish. Less daring examples include crayfish tails with galette of zucchini, tomatoes, and cumin-flavored vinaigrette; warm calamari salad with two kinds of peppers; and rack of lamb with basil, baby vegetables, and toast drenched in local ewes' cheese.

BAYONNE AFTER DARK

If you want to check out the scene, walk down **rue des Tonneliers, rue Pannecau,** or **rue des Cordeliers.** These are the liveliest areas after dark. The only pub in town is the **Killarney Pub,** rue des Cordeliers (☎ **05-59-25-75-51**), where you'll find plenty of music and hearty laughter from a carefree group of rowdies.

4 Biarritz

484 miles SW of Paris, 120 miles SW of Bordeaux

One of the most famous seaside resorts in the world, Biarritz was once a simple fishing village near the Spanish border. Favored by Empress Eugénie, the Atlantic village soon attracted her husband, Napoléon III, who truly put it on the map. Later, Queen Victoria showed up often, and her son, Edward VII, visited more than once.

In the 1930s the prince of Wales (soon to be Edward VIII, then the duke of Windsor) and the woman he loved, Wallis Simpson, did much to make Biarritz even more fashionable, as they headed south with these instructions: "Chill the champagne, pack the pearls, and tune up the Bugatti." Biarritz became the pre–jet set's favorite sun spot, though those legendary days are long gone and aren't coming back. The resort is still fashionable, but the unthinkable has happened: It now offers surf shops, snack bars, and even some reasonably priced hotels. What would the duchess have to say about that?

ESSENTIALS

GETTING THERE   Ten **trains** arrive daily from Bayonne (trip time: 10 minutes), which has rail links with Paris and other major cities in the south of France. The nearest rail station is 2 miles from the town center, in La Négresse. For train information and schedules, call ☎ **08-36-35-35-39. Bus no. 2** carries passengers at frequent intervals from the station to the center of Biarritz for a fee of 7.50F ($1.35) per person, or you can take a cab for not too much money. Biarritz is located at the end of the N117 roadway, which is the major thoroughfare for the Basque Country. From Paris, take A10 south to Vierzon, changing to N20 south to Limoges, continuing on N21 south to Tarbes, finally turning west along N117 to Biarritz.

VISITOR INFORMATION   The **Office de Tourisme** is on square d'Ixelles (☎ **05-59-22-37-10**).

SPECIAL EVENTS   If you're in town in September, check out some of the concerts and ballet performances that make up **Le Temps d'Aimer.** Events take place in different venues and tickets range from 60F to 200F ($10.80 to $36). Contact the **Biarritz Cultural Center** for details at ☎ **05-59-22-20-21.** More free activities are associated with the **International Folklore Festival** during the second week in July. The Office de Tourisme has the scoop on all of the festival's dances, music, and theater performances.

EXPLORING THE TOWN

A DAY AT THE BEACH   Along the seafront is the **Grande Plage.** During the belle époque, this was where Victorian ladies under parasols and wide-brimmed veiled hats would promenade. Today's women bathers don't dress up in such billowing skirts and often don't even bother to wear tops to their suits. The beach is also popular with surfers.

Promenade du bord de mer is still a major attraction. The paths along this walk are often carved into cliffsides. Sections have been planted with flowers growing in these rock gardens, turning the area into a well-manicured public park. From here, you can head north to **Pointe St-Martin,** where you'll find more gardens and a staircase (look for the sign DESCENTE DE L'OCEAN) leading you to allée Winston-Churchill, a paved path going along **Plage Miramar.**

La Perspective, a walk that goes up to another plateau, leads eventually to a beach that's one of the wildest and most exposed in France: **Plage de la Côte des Basques,** with breakers crashing at the base of the cliffs. This is where surfers head. For surfing rentals, contact **Ripcurl,** 2 av. de la Reine-Victoria (☎ **05-59-24-38-40**), or **Moraiz Surf Shop,** 25 rue Mazagran (☎ **05-59-24-22-09**).

If you like your beaches calmer, head for the safest beach, the small horseshoe-shaped **Plage du Port-Vieux,** lining the path from plateau de l'Atalaye. Its tranquil waters—protected by rocks—make it a favorite with families.

SEEING THE SIGHTS   **Eglise St-Martin,** rue St-Martin (☎ **05-59-23-05-19**), is one of the few vestiges of the port's early boom days. In the 12th century Biarritz grew prosperous as a whaling center until the animals left the Bay of Biscay, marking a decline in the port's fortune. The church dates from the 1100s and was restored in 1541 with a Flamboyant Gothic chancel. It's away from the center of the resort and the town's beaches. Admission is free, and it's open daily from 8am to 7:30pm.

Biarritz's turning point came with the arrival of the comtesse de Montijo, who spent lazy summers here with her two daughters. One of these, Eugénie, married Napoléon III in 1853 and prevailed on him to visit Biarritz the next year. The emperor fell under its spell and ordered the construction of the **Hôtel du Palais** (see below). The hotel remains the town's most enduring landmark, though it was originally dubbed "Eugénie's Basque folly." Edward VII stayed there in 1906 and again in 1910, only days before his death. Set in a commanding spot on Grande Plage, the hotel is worth a visit even if you're not a guest. You can at least view the palatial trappings of its public rooms.

Before the Russian Revolution of 1917, great numbers of Russian nobility arrived, so many, in fact, that they erected the **Eglise Orthodoxe Russe,** 8 av. de l'Impératrice (☎ **05-59-24-16-74**). Across from the Hôtel du Palais, this Byzantine-Russian landmark was built in 1892 so the wintering Russian aristocrats could worship when they weren't enjoying champagne, caviar, and Basque prostitutes. It's noted for its striking dome, the color of a blue sky on a sunny day.

After you pass the Hôtel du Palais, the walkway widens into **quai de la Grande Plage,** Biarritz's principal promenade. This walkway continues to the opposite end of the resort, where there's a final belvedere opening onto the southernmost stretch of beach. This whole walk would take about 3 hours.

At the southern edge of Grande Plage, steps will take you to **place Ste-Eugénie,** Biarritz's most gracious old square. Lined with terraced restaurants, it's the rendezvous point. Right below place Ste-Eugénie is the colorful **Port des Pêcheurs** (fishers' port). Crowded with fishing boats, it has old wooden houses and shacks backed up against a cliff. Here you'll find driftwood, rope, and plenty of lobster traps along with small harborfront restaurants and cafes.

The rocky **plateau de l'Atalaye** forms one side of the Port des Pêcheurs. Ordered carved by Napoléon III, a tunnel leads through the plateau to an esplanade. Here a metal footbridge stretches out into the sea to a rocky islet that takes its name **Rocher de la Vierge** (Rock of the Virgin) from the statue crowning it. Since 1865 this statue is said to have protected the sailors and fishers in the Bay of Biscay. Alexandre-Gustave Eiffel (yes, of tower fame) directed the construction of the footbridge. This walk out into the terraced edge of the rock, with crashing surf on both sides, is the most dramatic in Biarritz. From this rock you can see far to the south on a clear day, all the way to the mountains of the Spanish Basque country.

Once here, you can visit the **Musée de la Mer,** 14 plateau de l'Atalaye (☎ **05-59-24-02-59**), which houses 24 aquariums of fish native to the bay. The seals steal the show at their daily 10:30am and 5pm feedings. The museum also houses *requins* (sharks) that are fed on Tuesday and Friday at 11am and Wednesday and Sunday at 4:30pm. The museum is open May to June, Monday to Friday from 9:30am to 12:30pm and Saturday and Sunday from 9:30am to 7pm; July 1 to 13, daily from 9:30am to 8pm; July 14 to August 30, daily from 9:30am to midnight; and August 16 to September, Monday to Friday from 9:30am to 6pm and Saturday and Sunday from 9:30am to 7pm. Admission is 45F ($8.10) for adults, 40F ($7.20) for students, 25F ($4.50) for children 5 to 12, and free for children 4 and under.

SHOPPING

The major fashion boutiques, with all the big designer names from Paris, are centered around **place Clemenceau** in the heart of the resort. From this square, fan out to **rue Gambetta, rue Mazagran, avenue Victor-Hugo, avenue Edouard-VII, avenue du Maréchal-Foch,** and **avenue de Verdun.** Of particular interest are the exceptional Biarritz chocolates and confections and the select textiles that filter in from the Basque country.

The finest chocolatiers are **Pariès,** 27 place Clemenceau (☎ **05-59-22-07-52**), where you can choose from among seven varieties of tournons, ranging from raspberry to coffee; **Daranatz,** 12 av. du Maréchal-Foch (☎ **05-59-24-21-91**); and **Henriet,** place Clemenceau (☎ **05-59-24-24-15**), with its house specialty of *rochers de Biarritz*—morsels of candied orange peel and roasted almonds covered in creamy dark chocolate. At the other end of the gastronomic spectrum, try **Mille et Un Fromages,** 8 rue Victor Hugo (☎ **05-59-24-67-88**), specializing, as the name suggests, in a myriad of aromatic and tasty French cheeses as well as a host of hearty wines to accompany them.

Among antiques stores, your best bet is **Bakara,** 23 rue Mazagran (☎ **05-59-22-08-95**), with its special porcelain dolls. For the finest in Basque tablecloths, sheets, and other household linens, visit **St-Léon,** 18 av. Victor-Hugo (☎ **05-59-24-19-81**).

If a bottle of souvenir spirits appeals to you, join the stream of artists, actors, and gourmands who value **Arosteguy,** 5 av. Victor-Hugo (☎ **05-59-24-00-52**). You can procure an affordable wine or bottle of deceptively potent spirits distilled from pears, plums, or raspberries.

Incidentally, espadrilles, the canvas-topped, rope-bottomed slippers, are sold at virtually every souvenir shop and department store in the region. A simple off-the-shelf model begins at a mere 52F ($9.35), though espadrilles made to order (special sizes, special colors) rarely rise above 400F ($72) per pair. Upscale versions are made to order at **Maison Garcia,** pont de Baskutenea, in Bidart, a hamlet midway between Biarritz and St-Jean-de-Luz (☎ **05-59-26-51-27**). Opened in 1937, this is one of the last manufacturers to finish its product the old-fashioned way—by hand.

WHERE TO STAY

Café de Paris (see below) also rents rooms.

✪ **Château de Brindos.** Lac de Brindos, 64600 Anglet. ☎ **05-59-23-17-68.** Fax 05-59-23-48-47. 14 units. TV TEL. 500–900F ($90–$162) double; 1,200F ($216) suite. AE, DC, MC, V. From the town center, follow the AEROPORT signs; after the second roundabout (rond-point), follow the signs to the château; it's about 1½ miles north of Biarritz.

This is one of the most architecturally and culturally unusual homes in the southwest of France, with a history firmly entrenched in the Jazz Age. Built by the American railway heiress Virginia Gould in 1920, it occupies 27 acres of park and garden set inland from the sea. With a facade inspired vaguely by the architecture of Spain, and an interior loaded with architectural remnants such as fireplaces and staircases from the Gothic age, this is the most romantic stopover on the Côte Basque. Amenities include a private lake (where fishing can be arranged), tennis courts, and heated pool.

Dining: Set overlooking the lake, the restaurant serves a Franco-Basque cuisine. The food is superb, with a menu changing four times a year, which usually includes lobster salad, ravioli stuffed with a combination of scallops and fresh lobster, sautéed duck liver garnished with white grapes, sea bass grilled with fennel, and a mousseline of turbot in caviar sauce. The service is flawless but never intimidating.

Hôtel Atalaye. Plateau de l'Atalaye, 64200 Biarritz. ☎ **05-59-24-06-76.** Fax 05-59-22-33-51. 24 units. TV TEL. 230–380F ($41.40–$68.40) double; 300–400F ($54–$72) triple. V.

For economy with a bit of style, head here. In the heart of town on a tranquil spot overlooking the ocean, this hotel is open year-round, although it gets rather sleepy here in winter. Each bedroom is well maintained and traditionally furnished, though not a decorator's showcase. An elevator services all rooms. Breakfast is provided anytime you request it. The location is right off place Ste-Eugénie near the beaches, lighthouse, and casino.

Hôtel Carlina. Bd. du Prince-de-Galles, 64200 Biarritz. ☎ **05-59-24-42-14.** Fax 05-59-24-95-32. 15 units, 5 apts with kitchenettes. TV TEL. 350–450F ($63–$81) double; 600–1,200F ($108–$216) apt. AE, MC, V. Parking 40F ($7.20).

This hotel manages to keep its prices low by providing almost no services other than a once-per-day cleaning. There's no night watchman, no restaurant, and a staff that seems to highlight the site's disadvantages rather than its advantages. But if you're looking for a bargain and you don't mind a no-frills setting, consider emulating the French, who often check into one of the rooms or apartments for a week or more. Built in 1972, it offers an exceptional view of the Pyrénées and the Atlantic. The rooms are comfortable and well maintained if functional and uninspired, but price is the reason most guests are attracted to the place.

✪ **Hôtel du Palais.** Av. de l'Impératrice, 64200 Biarritz. ☎ **800/223-6800** in the U.S. and Canada, or 05-59-41-64-00. Fax 05-59-41-67-99. www.cotebasque.tm.fr/palais. E-mail: palais@cotebasque.tm.fr. 165 units. MINIBAR TV TEL. 1,500–2,850F ($270–$513) double; 2,600–6,350F ($468-$1,143) suite. AE, DC, MC, V. Closed Feb.

This has been the grand playground for the international elite for the past century, built in 1854 by Napoléon III for Eugénie so she wouldn't get homesick for Spain. He picked the most ideal beachfront, in view of the rocks and rugged shoreline. Of course there are elaborately furnished suites here, but even the average rooms have period furniture, silk draperies, marquetry, and bronze hardware; 95 are air-conditioned. Try to get a room facing west to enjoy the sunsets.

Dining: Villa Eugenie, a gourmet restaurant with classic columns and chandeliers, serves excellent meals. You can also dine at La Rotonde, enjoying typical Basque as well as international cuisine, and at lunch-only L'Hippocampe, a buffet restaurant around the heated seawater pool.

Hôtel Plaza. 10 av. Edouard-VII, 64200 Biarritz. ☎ **05-59-24-74-00.** Fax 05-59-22-22-01. 60 units. A/C MINIBAR TV TEL. 565–880F ($101.70–$158.40) double. AE, DC, MC, V.

Near the casino and beach, this hotel is a gorgeous Art Deco monument. Built in 1928, it has—except for discreet renovations—remained virtually unchanged, so it's classified as a historic monument and a civic treasure. The rooms contain their original Art Deco furnishings and doors; they tend to be large and high ceilinged, and some have a private terrace. Those overlooking the back and side cost less than those with full frontal sea views.

Dining: Meals are served in a formal dining room that's open for lunch and dinner daily except Monday at lunch and all day Sunday. The only inauthentic decor in the hotel is the bar, which, despite its relative newness, was designed in a—you guessed it—modernized Art Deco style.

WHERE TO DINE

Auberge de la Négresse. 10 bd. Marcel Dassault. ☎ **05-59-23-15-83.** Reservations required. Main courses 40–76F ($7.20–$13.70); fixed-price menus 60–175F ($10.80–$31.50). MC, V. Daily noon–2:30pm, Tues–Sun 7:15–10:15pm. BASQUE.

Just 1½ miles south of Biarritz, this restaurant was named for a 19th-century slave who escaped from an American plantation by hiding in the bottom of a French ship. The inn she established on this site was used by Napoléon's army on its passage to Spain, and eventually a railway station (Gare de la Négresse) was named in her honor. The inn doubles as a delicatessen, but the two dining rooms also serve flavorful meals. Typical dishes include salmon cooked in parchment, an array of homemade terrines, and fresh fish.

✪ **Café de Paris.** 5 place Bellevue, 64200 Biarritz. ☎ **05-59-24-19-53.** Fax 05-59-24-18-20. Reservations required. Restaurant, main courses 120–180F ($21.60–$32.40); fixed-price menus 250–350F ($45–$63). Bistro, main courses 85F ($15.30); fixed-price menu 165F ($29.70). AE, DC, MC, V. Daily noon–2:30pm and 7–10pm. Closed Tues and Wed lunch in winter. BASQUE.

The supercharged chef here, Didier Oudill, is the hottest in town and has rescued the Café de Paris after its long decline. Oudill was the protégé of Michel Guérard and not only learned all that fabled chef had to teach but has come up with many interesting creations of his own. He's not afraid to use Bayonne ham, Spanish merluza (hake), or even earthy fava beans. The setting is naturally elegant, from the mirrors for looking at how glamorous you are to the inevitable palm trees. If you'd like to spend less, you can go to the bistro, where the menu changes often, though fish is always a feature.

The restaurant offers 19 comfortable guest rooms, each with a sea view. Decorated in a conservatively traditional style, they cost 700F to 1,150F ($126 to $207) for a double. Half board in the restaurant is available for an additional 300F to 350F ($54 to $63) per person.

Les Flots Bleus. 41 perspective des Côtes Basques. ☎ **05-59-24-10-03.** Reservations recommended. Main courses 50–87F ($9–$15.65); fixed-price menus 80–114F ($14.40–$20.50). MC, V. Daily noon–2pm and 7:30–9:30pm. BASQUE.

On the rocky coast a 10-minute walk from the town center, in a solid-looking house originally built in the 1700s, this lighthearted and unpretentious restaurant has been the domain of Arlette Casagrande and her congenial Venice-born mother, Mami, for nearly 30 years. The food is served in generous portions that brim with the full flavor of the Basque country. Choices include duck pâté, Roquefort salad, marinated mussels, richly aromatic fish soup, Basque chicken, and dorado with garlic. The best dessert in the house is a gâteau Basque, richly laden with almonds and cream.

BIARRITZ AFTER DARK

Start the night by taking a stroll around **Port des Pêcheurs,** an ideal spot for people watching, with its stable of sport fishers, restaurants, and fascinating crowds.

Fortunes have been made and lost at the town's own municipal **Casino,** boulevard du Général-de-Gaulle (☎ 05-59-22-77-77), where you can easily catch gambling fever. While at the casino, check out its disco **Le Flamingo** (☎ 05-59-22-77-59), with its stylish crowd of movers and shakers. The cover here is 50F ($9).

Other very trendy and action-packed discos around town are **Le Copacabana,** 24 av. Edouard-VII (☎ 05-59-24-65-39), where Latin salsa music is king. **Le Play Boy,** 15 place Clemenceau (☎ 05-59-24-38-46), is a more traditional techno/rock environment that draws its share of flashy, sexy people. At **Le Caveau,** 4 place Gambetta (☎ 05-59-24-16-17), a gorgeous gay crowd mingles with a gorgeous straight crowd. The cover at any of these places ranges from 50F to 90F ($9 to $16.20).

5 St-Jean-de-Luz

491 miles SW of Paris, 9 miles S of Biarritz

This Basque country tuna-fishing port and beach resort is ideal for a seaside vacation. St-Jean-de-Luz lies at the mouth of the Nivelle opening onto the Bay of Biscay, with the Pyrénées in the background. Tourists have been flocking here since the 19th century, ever since the town was "discovered" by H. G. Wells.

ESSENTIALS

GETTING THERE Some 8 to 10 **trains** per day arrive from Biarritz (trip time: 15 minutes), and there are also 10 trains per day from Paris, a regular train taking 10 hours and the TGV arriving in only 5. For train information and schedules, call ☎ 08-36-35-35-39. St-Jean-de-Luz is a short drive from Biarritz along N10 south on the west coast of the Basque Country.

VISITOR INFORMATION The **Office de Tourisme** is on place du Maréchal-Foch (☎ 05-59-26-03-16).

SPECIAL EVENTS   On Wednesday and Saturday nights during July and August, people pile into place Louis-XIV to take part in **Toro de Fuego**—a celebration of the bull when revelers take to the streets, dancing and watching fireworks. The highlight of the festivities is when a snorting papier-mâché bull is carried through town. For a lineup of festivals, check with the Office de Tourisme.

FUN ON & OFF THE BEACH

THE BEACH   The major draw here is the wide, gracefully curving stretch of the white-sand **Plage St-Jean-de-Luz;** it's very crowded in July and August as it's one of the best beaches in France. The beach lies in a half-moon-shaped bay between the ocean and the source of the Nivelle River.

THE PORT TOWN   Though tourism accounts for most of the revenue around here, fishing is still important—in fact, the town is the major fishing port along the Basque coast. Eating seafood only recently plucked from the sea is one of the reasons to visit, especially when Basque chefs prepare the big catch into intriguing platters. This port's many narrow streets flanked by old houses are great for strolling.

ATTRACTIONS   In the town's principal church, the 13th-century **Eglise St-Jean-Baptiste,** at the corner of rue Gambetta and rue Garat (☎ 05-59-26-08-81), Louis XIV and the Spanish infanta, Marie-Thérèse, were married in 1660, as a celebration of the cessation of fighting between France and Spain over Habsburg possessions in Holland and Flanders. The interior is among the most handsome of all Basque churches. Surmounting the altar is a statue-studded gilded retable. The interior can be visited daily from 7:30am to noon and 2 to 7pm. At the harbor, the brick-and-stone **Maison de l'Infante,** in Louis XIII style, sheltered the Spanish princess.

The Sun King, meanwhile, dreamed of another woman at **La Maison de Louis XIV** (also known as the Château Lohobiague), on place Louis-XIV, the center of the old port (☎ 05-59-26-01-56). Built in 1643 by a rich shipowner, Johannis of Lohobiague, the Maison de Louis XIV received its young namesake in 1660 for more than a month. This beautiful house has been in the same family for 350 years. The noble facade is distinguished by small towers built into each corner. The interior is in old Basque style, with beams and iron nails still visible. The second-floor stairwell leads to the apartments where Louis XIV stayed when he came to sign the Treaty of the Pyrénées and get married in the church of St-Jean-de-Luz with Maria-Thérèse. It's open June to October, daily from 10:30am to noon and 2:30 to 6:30pm. Admission is 25F ($4.50) for adults and 20F ($3.60) for children.

SHOPPING

You'll find the best shopping along the pedestrian **rue Gambetta** as well as around the Eglise St-Jean-de-Luz. These are the spots where you can find just about anything from clothes and leather handbags to books, chocolates, dishes, and linens.

You can also ramble around the port, sip pastis in a harborfront cafe, and debate the virtues of the beret. Then scout out **Maison Adam,** which has sold almond-based confections since 1660 from a boutique at 6 place Louis-XIV (☎ 05-59-26-03-54). Specialties include sugared macaroons, *tournons* (an almond-paste confection flavored with everything from chocolate to confit of berries), and canougat (soft caramels).

WHERE TO STAY

✪ **Hotel de Chantaco.** Gulf de Chantaco, 64500 Chantaco, 64500 St-Jean-de-Luz. ☎ **05-59-26-14-76.** Fax 05-59-26-35-97. 23 units. A/C TV TEL. 850–1,400F ($153–$252) double. Half board 800F ($144) per person extra. Free parking. Closed Nov 15–Dec 20 and Jan 5–Feb 15. Take D918 1 mile from the town center.

There's enough memorabilia of its heyday within this mansion to remind you of the days when aristocrats from around Europe made it one of their preferred hotels. Surrounded by an 18-hole golf course and verdant parklands, within an hour from the beach, it resembles an eclectically designed country château that belonged to an erudite and somewhat eccentric industrialist. Inside, you'll find Moorish arches, a patio garden, a reception hall graced with two stone fireplaces, a salon with refectory tables and severely dignified chairs, and an upper gallery flanked with wrought-iron balustrades. Bedrooms are luxurious, with lots of personalized touches and memorabilia from the gilded age.

Dining: Breakfast is served beneath the wisteria-covered arches of an outdoor patio, and dinnertime venues are at El Patio, a restaurant well recommended for its international and regional cuisine.

Hôtel Hélianthal. Place Maurice-Ravel. ☎ **05-59-51-51-51.** Fax 05-59-51-51-54. 100 units. A/C MINIBAR TV TEL. 800–920F ($144–$165.60) double; 920–1,100F ($165.60–$198) 2-bedroom suite. AE, DC, MC, V. Parking 45F ($8.10).

Efficient, well designed, and comfortable, this three-star hotel boasts a well-recommended restaurant and lies in the commercial heart of town, near the beach. Unfortunately, none of the Art Deco–style rooms overlooks the sea, but many have terraces, bay windows, or balconies.

Dining: The hotel's big-windowed restaurant, L'Atlantique, offers a terrace overlooking the sea and a fixed-price menu at 200F and 210F ($36 and $37.80). The fare includes a spa-style light cuisine, lots of fish, and traditional dishes inspired by age-old Basque cuisine. Lunch and dinner are served daily.

Hôtel/Restaurant Lafayette. 18–20 rue de la République, 64500 St-Jean-de-Luz. ☎ **05-59-26-17-74.** Fax 05-59-51-11-78. 17 units, 16 with bathroom. TV TEL. 180F ($32.40) double without bathroom, 200–330F ($36–$59.40) double with bathroom. AE, DC, MC, V.

This utterly unpretentious hotel and restaurant occupies a central position near place Louis-XIV and the town's beaches. Its rooms evoke a dignified (now slightly battered) earlier age.

Dining: The Basque cuisine prepared by the experienced matriarch Mayie Colombet is one of the most solidly reliable in town. Tried-and-true dishes include seafood casseroles, grilled duck, sea bass with thyme and lemon-butter sauce, and roast rack of lamb. Technically, the restaurant is closed on Monday night, but during many school holidays business is so good that Ms. Colombet usually decides to remain open anyway. Fixed-price menus, served at both lunch and dinner, range from 82F to 158F ($14.75 to $28.45).

La Devinière. 5 rue Loquin, 64500 St-Jean-de-Luz. ☎ **05-59-26-05-51.** Fax 05-59-51-26-38. 10 units. TEL. 600–750F ($108–$135) double. AE, DC, MC, V. Parking 32F ($5.75).

Perhaps because of its small size, this is the best-furnished moderately priced hotel in St-Jean-de-Luz. It occupies the premises of what was originally a private town house and was brought to its present level of 18th-century elegance thanks to the unsold inventories of its antiques-dealer owner. The rooms are comfortable, well maintained, and filled, like the rest of the hotel, with attractive antiques. Although breakfast is the only meal served, the hotel contains a tea salon (L'Heure du Thé; same phone). It's open weekdays only from 4 to 6:30pm and seems to do a rollicking business every afternoon.

WHERE TO DINE

The only really grand cuisine in town is served at the **Hôtel Grand,** but you might also like to check out the restaurant at the **Hôtel Hélianthal** (see above).

Auberge Kaïku. 17 rue de la République. ☎ **05-59-26-13-20**. Reservations recommended. Main courses 90–120F ($16.20–$21.60); fixed-price menus 145–260F ($26.10–$46.80). AE, MC, V. July–Sept Tues–Sun 12:15–2:15pm, daily 7:15–10:30pm; Oct–Nov 14 and Dec 23–June Thurs–Tues 12:15–2:15pm and 7:15–10:30pm. Closed Nov 14–Dec 22. BASQUE.

On a narrow street off place Louis-XIV, Auberge Kaïku is the best restaurant in town outside the hotels. The structure, with hand-hewn beams and chiseled masonry, dates from 1540 and is said to be the oldest in town. The auberge is run by Emile and Jeanne Ourdanabia, who serve Basque cuisine that's been enhanced with modern touches. Examples are roast suckling Pyrénéan lamb, a *parrillada* of shellfish, John Dory with fresh mint, grilled shrimp, filet of beef with essence of truffles, and duckling in honey. A particularly succulent starter is the salade Kaïku, garnished with pan-fried strips of foie gras and raspberry vinegar.

Chez Maya (Petit Grill Basque). 4 rue St-Jacques. ☎ **05-59-26-80-76**. Reservations recommended. Main courses 52–96F ($9.35–$17.30); fixed-price menu 105F ($18.90). AE, DC, V. Thurs–Tues noon–2pm and 7–10pm. Closed Dec 20–Jan 20. BASQUE.

This small auberge is highly acclaimed for quality and value, with specialties that include a delectable fish soup and paella. Its fixed-price menu is the best value at the resort. The chefs cook as their grandparents did, including all the old favorites, such as squid cooked in its own ink.

La Vieille Auberge. 22 rue Tourasse. ☎ **05-59-26-19-61**. Reservations required. Main courses 59–110F ($10.60–$19.80); fixed-price menus 72–125F ($12.95–$22.50). MC, V. July–Aug Wed–Mon noon–2pm, daily 7–10pm; Apr 2–June and Sept–Nov 11 daily noon–2pm, Thurs–Mon 7–10pm. Closed Nov 12–Apr 1. BASQUE/LANDAISE.

This Basque tavern specializes in seafood, and the owners claim that the fish soup is second to none. Monsieur and Madame Daniel Grand offer good-value fixed-price menus, the most expensive of which is enormous. Generally, the recipes are part-Basque/part-Landaise, and each dish goes well with the *vin du pays,* especially mussels *à la crème.*

ST-JEAN-DE-LUZ AFTER DARK

You can start by taking a walk along the promenade to watch the sunset. If you check out **place Louis-XIV,** you'll find a hotbed of activity at the surrounding cafes and bars.

A fun spot worth a visit is **Pub du Corsaire,** 16 rue de la République (☎ **05-59-26-10-74**), one of the main places in town for simple, unpretentious merrymaking, good times, and revelry—all accompanied, of course, by copious amounts of drinking and old-fashioned rock. The disco **Challenger** is on N10 on the way out of town (☎ **05-59-51-20-56**). It's always packed with young, pretty dance floor show-offs who are willing to pay up to 70F ($12.60) for their chance to strike a pose.

19 Languedoc-Roussillon

Languedoc, one of southern France's great old provinces, is a loosely defined area encompassing such cities as Nîmes, Toulouse, and Carcassonne. It's one of the leading wine-producing areas and is fabled for its art treasures.

The coast of Languedoc—from Montpellier to the Spanish frontier—might be called France's "second Mediterranean" (first place naturally goes to the Côte d'Azur). A land of ancient cities and a generous sea, it's less spoiled than the Côte d'Azur, with an almost-continuous strip of sand stretching west from the Rhône and curving snakelike toward the Pyrénées. Back in the days of de Gaulle, the government began an ambitious project to develop the Languedoc-Roussillon coastline, and it has been a booming success, as the miles of sun-baking bodies in July and August testify.

Ancient Roussillon is a small region of greater Languedoc, forming the Pyrénées Orientales département. This is the French Catalonia, inspired more by Barcelona in neighboring Spain than by remote Paris. Over its long and colorful history it has known many rulers. Legally part of the French kingdom until 1258, it was surrendered to James I of Aragón. Until 1344 it was part of the ephemeral kingdom of Majorca, with Perpignan as the capital. By 1463 Roussillon was annexed to France again. Then Ferdinand of Aragón won it back, but by 1659 France had it again. In spite of local sentiment for reunion with the Catalans of Spain, France still firmly controls the land.

The Camargue is a marshy delta between two arms of the Rhône. South of Arles is cattle country. Strong wild black bulls are bred here for the arenas of Arles and Nîmes. The small white horses, amazingly graceful, were said to have been brought here by the Saracens. They're ridden by *gardiens,* French cowboys, who can usually be seen in wide-brimmed black hats. The whitewashed houses, plaited-straw roofs, pink flamingos that inhabit the muddy marshes, vast plains, endless stretches of sandbars—all this qualifies as Exotic France.

REGIONAL CUISINE The cuisine of Languedoc-Roussillon is heavily influenced by garlic, olive oil, and strong flavors. The region has plentiful game, trout, succulent lamb, and seafood, usually prepared with local herbs, wine, and garlic.

One of the region's legendary dishes is usually prepared on a brazier in a boat on the open sea: the tripe (intestines) of tuna mixed with white wine and herbs, accompanied by a glass of seawater, whose salt alleviates some of the unpleasantness. A vastly more palatable dish is *pouillade,* which requires the simultaneous preparation of two pots of soup (one made with cabbage, the other with white beans). Just before serving, the contents are mixed together in a serving bowl.

Other regional specialties include excellent fish stews, foie gras, truffles, escargots, exotic mushrooms from the north-central areas, pâté of thrush from Rodez, cherries from Lodève, *aigo bouillido* (a soup made with garlic, eggs, aromatic herbs, and croûtons), *aligot* (a dish with garlic-laced cream, butter, potatoes, and cheese), and cassoulet of white beans and various meats. The region's most famous cheese is pélardon, made from goat's milk. The best known pastry is the Alleluia.

As for wine, Hérault, Aude, and Garde rank first, second, and third, respectively, in total wine production in France. Most of this is ordinary table wine. A few, however, have been granted an Appellation d'Origine Contrôlée. Some of the best are Fitou, produced in the Hautes-Corbières district near Narbonne, and Minervois, from west and northwest of Narbonne.

1 Toulouse

438 miles SW of Paris, 152 miles SE of Bordeaux, 60 miles W of Carcassonne

The old capital of Languedoc and France's fourth-largest city, Toulouse (known as *La Ville Rose*) is cosmopolitan in flavor. The major city of the southwest, filled with gardens and squares, it's the gateway to the Pyrénées. Toulouse has a number of fine old mansions, most of them dating from the Renaissance, when this was one of the richest cities in Europe. Today Toulouse is an artistic and cultural center, but also a high-tech center, home to two huge aircraft makers—Airbus and Aerospatiale. Also making the city tick is its extraordinarily high population of students: some 100,000 in all, out of a total population of 600,000.

ESSENTIALS

GETTING THERE   The Toulouse-Blagnac **airport** lies in the city's northwestern suburbs, 7 miles from the center; for flight information, call ☎ **05-61-42-44-00.**

Some 9 **trains** per day arrive from Paris (trip time: 7 hours), 8 from Bordeaux (trip time: 2½ hours), and 11 from Marseille (trip time: 4½ hours). For rail information and schedules, call ☎ **08-36-35-35-39.**

The **drive** to Toulouse from Paris is a lengthy one, and the best and safest route is via the major roadways of France. From Paris, take A10 south to Bordeaux, connecting to A62 to Toulouse.

The Canal du Midi links many of the region's cities with Toulouse by waterway.

VISITOR INFORMATION   The **Office de Tourisme** is in the Donjon du Capitole, rue Lafayette (☎ **05-61-11-02-22**).

EXPLORING THE CITY

In addition to the sights listed below, the architectural highlights include the Gothic brick **Eglise des Jacobins,** parvis des Jacobins, in Old Toulouse, west of place du Capitole along rue Lakanal (☎ **05-61-22-21-92**). The convent, daring in its architecture, has been restored and forms the largest extant monastery complex in France. It's open year-round, daily from 10am to noon and 2 to 6pm. Admission to most of the complex is free, but a visit to the cloisters is 10F ($1.80) per person. Small, charming, and dating mostly from the 18th century, **Basilique Notre-Dame La Daurade** is at 7 quai de la Daurade (☎ **05-61-21-38-32**); its name derives from the gilding that covers some of its partially baroque exterior. It's open daily from 10am to noon and 2 to 6pm. Admission is free.

Languedoc-Roussillon

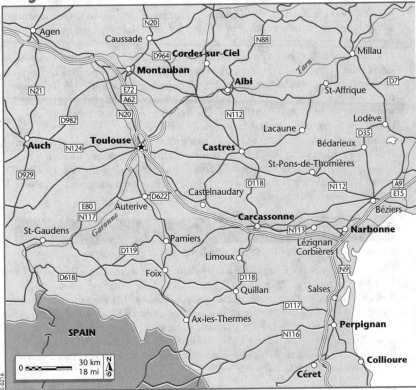

In civic architecture, **Capitole,** place du Capitole (☎ **05-61-22-29-22**), is an outstanding achievement and one of the most potent symbols of Toulouse itself. Built in 1753, it houses the **Hôtel de Ville** (city hall), plus the **Théâtre du Capitole** (☎ **05-61-22-31-31**), which is devoted to concerts, ballets, and operas. Renovated in 1996, it's outfitted in an Italian-inspired 18th-century style with shades of scarlet and gold. Admission, which usually includes a view of the theater, is free. The Capitole complex is open Monday through Friday from 9am to noon and 2 to 5pm and Saturday from 9am to noon.

After all that sightseeing, head for the oval place Wilson, a showcase 19th-century square lined with fashionable cafes.

When you're in the mood to shop, head for **rue St-Rome** and **rue d'Alsace-Lorraine.** This town has a great mall, **Centre Commercial St-Georges,** rue du Rempart St-Etienne, where you can fill your suitcases with all kinds of glittery loot. But for upscale clothing boutiques, head for **rue Croix-Baragnon** and **rue des Arts.** The pearly gates of antiques heaven can be found on **rue Fermat.** More downmarket antiques are sprawled out each Saturday and Sunday during the weekly **flea market** at the Basilique St-Sernin, the first Saturday and Sunday of each month in allée Jules-Guesde, and on the second Saturday of each month at place du Val d'Aran.

In addition, **Boutique Signatures,** 3 place St-Georges (☎ **05-61-12-07-00**), sells the most exotic and luxurious linens, and **Violets et Pastels,** 10 rue St-Pantaléon (☎ **05-61-22-14-22**), offers everything imaginable connected with violets, from violet-scented perfume to silk scarves patterned with the dainty purple flower.

Opposite St-Sernin is the **Musée St-Raymond,** place St-Sernin (☎ **05-61-22-21-85**), housed in a college reconstructed in 1523. It contains one of the finest collections of imperial busts outside Rome. Recent renovations were completed in 1998.

✪ **Basilique St-Sernin.** 13 place St-Sernin. ☎ **05-61-21-80-45.** Admission: church, free; crypt, 10F ($1.80). Church, daily 10am–noon and 2–6pm, though please refrain from pure sightseeing during Sun-morning masses; crypt, Mon–Sat 9am–noon and 2–6pm, Sun noon–6pm.

Consecrated in 1096, this is the largest and finest Romanesque church extant in the Old World. One of its most outstanding features is the Porte Miègeville, opening onto the south aisle and decorated with 12th-century sculptures. The door opening into the south transept is the Porte des Comtes, its capitals depicting the story of Lazarus. Nearby are the tombs of the comtes de Toulouse. Entering by the main west door, you can see the double side aisles that give the church five naves, an unusual feature in Romanesque architecture. An upper cloister forms a passageway around the interior. Look for the Romanesque capitals surmounting the columns.

In the axis of the basilica, 11th-century bas-reliefs depict *Christ in His Majesty.* The ambulatory leads to the crypt (ask the custodian for permission to enter), containing the relics of 128 saints, plus a thorn said to be from the Crown of Thorns. The old baroque retables and shrine in the ambulatory have been reset; the relics here are those of the Apostles and the first bishops of Toulouse.

Musée des Augustins. 21 rue de Metz. ☎ **05-61-22-21-82.** Admission 12F ($2.15), free for children 11 and under. Wed 10am–9pm, Thurs–Mon 10am–6pm.

Toulouse-Lautrec: A Giant of a Talent

Painter Henri de Toulouse-Lautrec spent his most creative years in Paris, but the pink-walled city of Albi in southwestern France, where the artist was born, clings tenaciously to his legacy. Only 5 feet tall, Toulouse-Lautrec was famous for his unfettered portraits of prostitutes and cabaret entertainers and for his brilliantly vicious caricatures of belle époque pretentions.

Born into an intermarried family of aristocrats whose ancestors could be traced back to Charlemagne, he was the only surviving child of his parents' union and the cousin of several children with epilepsy, dwarfism, neurological disorders, and alarming skeletal malformations. Toulouse-Lautrec grew into a short but relatively normal-looking young man, but his later years were marred by changes in his appearance that included violent toothaches, repeated fractures in the bones of his legs, and eventually a growth in the side of his nose and lips that led to frequent drooling.

Geneticists blame some of his problems on his genetic makeup and a propensity for pycnodysostosis (*pick*-no-did-os-*to*-sis), a sometimes painful form of dwarfism attended by such complications as underdeveloped facial bones, incomplete closure of the "soft spots" between the plates of the skull, short fingers and toes, and easily decayed teeth. But despite the cogency of scientific reasoning, no one will ever know for sure why Toulouse-Lautrec suffered as he did: His descendents have repeatedly refused to be genetically tested for the disorder or to have the artist's corpse exhumed.

Despite his physical stature, no one can debate the titanic dimensions of Toulouse-Lautrec's art. In a span of less than 20 years he executed 737 canvases, 275 watercolors, 363 prints and posters, more than 5,000 drawings, some ceramics and stained-glass windows, and more than 300 artworks classified as "pornography." Many believe that he depicted his characters in a ruthless and cruel light to get even with the world for the way those around him treated him because of his size and deformities. Yet he was brilliant in his ability to capture images, whether real or imagined, and in his ability to free colors from reality (and lines from form) to create his caricaturelike figures.

Ironically, Toulouse-Lautrec's death in 1901, at age 36, had little to do with his dwarfism: the cause was acute alcoholism.

The family's **Château du Bosc,** also known as the Fortresse Berenger-Bosc, owned during his life by the artist's grandmother, is 29 miles from Toulouse, reached from Albi by N88 (☎ **05-65-69-20-83**). Built in 1180 and renovated in the 1400s, the château is midway between Albi and Rodez (also spelled Rodes) and is open to visitors daily from 9am to 7pm. Admission is 30F ($5.40) for adults, 15F ($2.70) for children 8 to 14, and free for children 7 and under. The present owner, Mlle de Céleran, is most gracious to those interested in Toulouse-Lautrec's life. Call before you go, since visitors must be accompanied by a guide.

Originally conceived as a convent, its 14th-century cloisters contain the world's largest and most valuable collection of Romanesque capitals. The sculptures and carvings are magnificent, and there are some fine examples of early Christian sarcophagi. On the upper floors is a large painting collection, with works by Toulouse-Lautrec, Gérard, Delacroix, and Ingres. The museum also contains several portraits by Antoine Rivalz, a local artist of major talent.

Toulouse

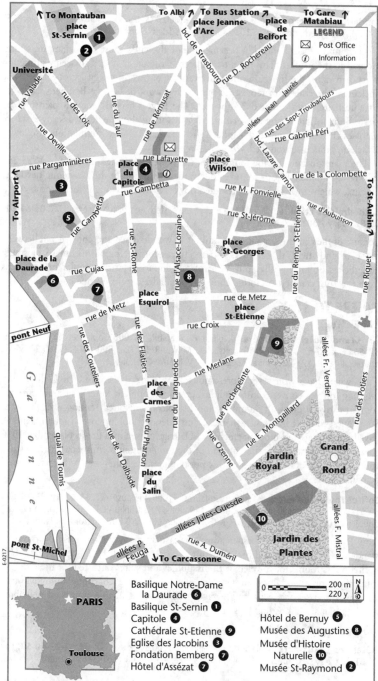

539

Fondation Bemberg. Place d'Assézat, rue de Metz. ☎ **05-61-12-06-89.** Admission 25F ($4.50). Tues–Wed and Fri–Sun 10am–6pm, Thurs 10am–9pm.

Opened in 1995, this quickly became one of the city's most important museums. Housed in the Assézat mansion, a magnificent structure that's a sightseeing attraction in its own right, the museum offers an overview of 5 centuries of European art. The nucleus of the collection represents the lifelong work of George Bemberg, collector extraordinaire, who donated 331 works. The largest bequest was 28 paintings by Pierre Bonnard, including his *Moulin Rouge.* Bemberg also donated works by Pissarro, Matisse (*Vue d'Antibes*), and Monet, plus the Fauves. The foundation also owns Canaletto's much-reproduced *Vue de Mestre.*

The mansion housing the foundation, the Hôtel d'Assézat, was built in 1555 and still has an unaltered 16th-century courtyard. It also houses the Académie des Jeux-Floraux, which since 1323 has presented flowers made of wrought metal to poets.

Cathédrale St-Etienne. Place St-Etienne, at the eastern end of rue de Metz. ☎ **05-61-52-03-82.** Daily 7:30am–7:30pm.

Because of the centuries required to build it (it was designed and constructed between the 11th and the 17th centuries), some critics scorn it for its mishmash of styles; nonetheless, it successfully conveys a solemn dignity. The rectangular bell tower is from the 16th century. A Gothic choir has been added to its unique ogival nave.

WHERE TO STAY
EXPENSIVE

✪ **Grand Hôtel de l'Opéra.** 1 place du Capitole, 31000 Toulouse. ☎ **05-61-21-82-66.** Fax 05-61-23-41-04. 50 units. A/C MINIBAR TV TEL. 890–950F ($160.20–$171) double; 1,190F ($214.20) suite. AE, DC, MC, V. Métro: Capitole.

The owners have won several prestigious awards for transforming a 17th-century building (once a convent) into a sophisticated and opulent hotel. The public rooms contain early-19th-century antiques and Napoleonic-inspired tenting over the bars. Some guest rooms contain urn-shaped balustrades overlooking formal squares, and all have high ceilings and modern amenities. Damage caused by a fire in November 1996 prompted a radical restoration, and all of the rooms are now finished. The hotel also runs a brasserie and the town's most prestigious restaurant (see "Where to Dine," below).

Sofitel Toulouse Centre. 84 allée Jean-Jaurès, 31000 Toulouse. ☎ **05-61-10-23-10.** Fax 05-61-10-23-20. E-mail: sofitel@cadrus.fr. 119 units. A/C MINIBAR TV TEL. 960F ($172.80) double; 1,700F ($306) suite. AE, DC, MC, V. Parking 60F ($10.80). Métro: Jean-Jaurès.

This 18-story hotel is the best in town, at least by many regular business travelers' standards (although we still prefer the more peaceful Grand Hôtel de l'Opéra). This Sofitel offers rooms for travelers with disabilities and suites outfitted for use either as minioffices or as lodgings for families. The hotel has a charming bilingual staff, 24-hour room service, a parking garage (much needed in this congested neighborhood), a bar, and a bustling brasserie.

MODERATE

Hôtel des Beaux-Arts. 1 place du pont-Neuf, 31000 Toulouse. ☎ **05-61-23-40-50.** Fax 05-61-22-02-27. 20 units. A/C MINIBAR TV TEL. 450–900F ($81–$162) double. AE, DC, MC, V.

Occupying a richly dignified pink-brick villa built 250 years ago on the banks of the Garonne, this is a charming hotel in the heart of town. Despite the historic facade, the well-equipped, soundproof rooms are modern and comfortable. Breakfast is the only meal served; diners often head for the Brasserie des Beaux-Arts (see "Where to Dine," below), in the same building but with an entrance around the corner.

INEXPENSIVE

Hôtel Raymond-IV. 16 rue Raymond-IV, 31000 Toulouse. ☎ **05-61-62-89-41.** Fax 05-61-61-38-01. 38 units. MINIBAR TV TEL. 230–380F ($41.40–$68.40) double. AE, DC, MC, V. Parking 25F ($4.50); free on weekends. Métro: Jean-Jaurès or Capitole.

On a quiet street close to the town center and the rail station, this antique building contains pleasantly decorated rooms that are discounted on weekends. It's within walking distance of the historic quarter's theaters, shops, and nightclubs. Although breakfast is the only meal served, the English-speaking staff will direct you to nearby restaurants.

WHERE TO DINE
VERY EXPENSIVE

✪ **Les Jardins de l'Opéra.** In the Grand Hôtel de l'Opéra, 1 place du Capitole. ☎ **05-61-23-07-76.** Reservations required. Main courses 165–280F ($29.70–$50.40); fixed-price lunch 200F ($36); fixed-price menus 295–540F ($53.10–$97.20). AE, DC, MC, V. Tues–Sat noon–2pm and Mon–Sat 8–10pm. Closed Jan 1–4, Aug 3–26, and Mon lunch year-round. Métro: Capitole. FRENCH.

The entrance to the city's best restaurant is in the 18th-century Florentine courtyard of the Grand Hôtel. Guests dine in a series of intimate salons, several of which face a winter garden and a reflecting pool. You'll be greeted by the gracious Maryse Toulousy, whose husband, Dominique, prepares what critics have called the perfect combination of modern and old-fashioned French cuisine. The outstanding menu is likely to include rack of lamb in pepper sauce with fried and poached celeriac, lobster grilled over a wood fire with artichoke and marrow ragoût, and ravioli stuffed with foie gras and a distillation of truffles.

EXPENSIVE TO MODERATE

Brasserie des Beaux-Arts. 1 quai de la Daurade. ☎ **05-61-21-12-12.** Reservations recommended. Main courses 65–152F ($11.70–$27.35); fixed-price menus 112–153F ($20.15–$27.55). AE, DC, MC, V. Daily noon–3:30pm and 7pm–1am. Métro: Esquirol. FRENCH.

This turn-of-the-century brasserie offers authentic Art Nouveau decor that's been enhanced by its connection with the Jean Bucher chain. (They're the most successful directors of Art Nouveaux French brasseries in the world, with at least a dozen similar places, some of which are classified as national historic monuments.) The carefully restored decor includes walnut paneling and mirrors, and the cuisine emphasizes well-prepared fresh seafood and all the predictable local dishes, such as cassoulet and magrêt of duckling. Try the foie gras or country-style sauerkraut, accompanied by the house Riesling, served in an earthenware pitcher. During warm weather, eat on the terrace. A menu for 106 F ($19.10) is available only after 10pm.

Chez Emile. 13 place St-Georges. ☎ **05-61-21-05-56.** Reservations recommended. Main courses 95–155F ($17.10–$27.90); fixed-price menus 115F ($20.70) at lunch, 220–245F ($39.60–$44.10) at dinner. AE, DC, MC, V. Tues–Sat noon–2pm and 7–10:30pm (also Mon 7–10:30pm in summer). Métro: Capitole or Esquirol. TOULOUSIEN.

In winter, guests dine in a cozy upstairs enclave of this old-fashioned house, overlooking one of the most beautiful squares of Toulouse; in summer, meals are served in the street-level dining room and on the flower-filled terrace. Chef Francis Ferrier's specialties include *magrêt de canard* (duck) traditional style and parillade of grilled fish with a pungently aromatic cold sauce of sweet peppers and olive oil. The wine carte is filled with intriguing surprises.

NEARBY ACCOMMODATIONS & DINING

Hôtel de Diane. 3 route de St-Simon, 31100 St-Simon. ☎ **05-61-07-59-52.** Fax 05-61-86-38-94. 22 units, 13 bungalows. MINIBAR TV TEL. 450F ($81) double; 510F ($91.80) bungalow. AE, DC, MC, V. Take D23 to exit 27, 5 miles east of Toulouse.

This hotel/restaurant surrounded by a 5-acre park is the most tranquil retreat near Toulouse. It occupies a turn-of-the-century villa with comfortable but not particularly opulent rooms that appeal to people who want to be away from the traffic and congestion of the inner city. The bungalow-style units are built side by side in a row facing the park; each has a kitchenette, private terrace, and parking. The rustic atmosphere befits this getaway, which also has a private pool and groves of pines and venerable hardwoods.

Dining: The restaurant, Saint-Simon, offers a choice of meals in the garden or the Louis XV–style dining room. The fixed-price menus at 105F to 190F ($18.90 to $34.20) offer the best value. The restaurant serves lunch Monday through Friday and dinner Monday through Saturday. In spite of the attentive service and gracious welcome, the food is somewhat uneven—sometimes delicious, other times less so. The bordeaux, however, is divine.

TOULOUSE AFTER DARK

Toulouse has theater, dance, and opera that are often on a par with that found in Paris. To stay on top of the city's arts scene, pick up a copy of *Toulouse Culture* from the Office de Tourisme.

The most notable theaters are **Théâtre du Capitole,** place du Capitole (☎ **05-61-22-31-31**); **Théâtre de la Digue,** 3 rue de la Digue (☎ **05-61-42-97-79**); and **Halle aux Grains,** place Dupuy (☎ **05-61-62-02-70**). In addition to the theatrical performances that take place here, these venues serve as stages for world-class operas from October to May as well as classical and modern ballet and dance performances by local and international companies.

The liveliest squares to wander after dark are place du Capitole, place St-Georges, place St-Pierre, and just off rue St-Rome and rue des Filatiers.

For bars and pubs, check out the Latin flair of **La Tantina de Bourgos,** 27 rue de la Garonette (☎ **05-61-55-59-29**), which is always popular with students, and the rowdier **Chez Tonton,** 16 place St-Pierre (☎ **05-61-21-89-54**), with its après-match frolicking atmosphere complete with the winning teams boozing it up. To keep the party going, stop by **Le Bikini,** route de Lacroix-Falgarde (☎ **05-61-55-00-29**), with its occasional live rock and endless supply of hot bods.

Gays and lesbians come together at **La Sige,** 6 rue de Colombette (☎ **05-61-99-61-87**). With its loud yet somewhat tame atmosphere, it has made a name for itself by offering a different style of music, from disco to techno, each night. **Le New Shanghai,** 12 rue de la Pomme (☎ **05-61-23-37-80**), feels like a gay dance club playing the latest in techno, but venture farther inside and you'll discover a darker, sexier cruise-bar environment with lots of hot men on the prowl. Plan on paying 50F to 80F ($9 to $14.40) to get in.

2 Auch

451 miles SW of Paris, 126 miles SE of Bordeaux, 40 miles W of Toulouse

On the west bank of the Gers, in the heart of the ancient Duchy of Gascony, of which it was the capital, the lively market town of Auch is divided into upper and lower quarters, connected by several flights of steps. In the old part of town the narrow streets, called *pousterles,* center on place Salinis, from which there's a good view of the Pyrénées. Branching off from here, the **Escalier Monumental** leads down to the river, a descent of 232 steps.

North of the square is the **Cathédrale Ste-Marie,** at place de la Cathédrale (☎ 05-62-05-72-71). Built from the 15th to the 17th centuries, this is one of the handsomest Gothic churches in the south of France. It has 113 Renaissance choir stalls made of carved oak and impressive stained-glass windows, also from the Renaissance. Its 17th-century organ was one of the finest in the world at the time of Louis XIV. The cathedral is open daily from 8:30am to noon and 2 to 5pm (from 9:30am to noon and 2 to 7pm in winter). A custodian will let you in for 6F ($1.10).

Next to the cathedral stands an 18th-century **archbishop's palace** with a 14th-century bell tower, the **Tour d'Armagnac,** which was once a prison.

For shops and boutiques, walk down **rue Dessoles** and **avenue de l'Alsace.** Here you'll find everything from confectionery shops to clothing stores. Also consider visiting the **Caves de l'Hôtel de France,** rue d'Etigny (☎ 05-62-61-71-71), for a bottle or two of Armagnac. It has the best selection of this firewater, with more than 100 distilleries represented.

Five to 10 SNCF **trains** or **buses** per day run between Toulouse and Auch (trip time: 1½ hours); 6 to 13 SNCF buses arrive in Auch daily from Agen, a 1½-hour trip. For more information and schedules, call ☎ 08-36-35-35-39. If you're **driving** to Auch, take N124 west from Toulouse.

The **Office de Tourisme** is at place de la Cathédrale (☎ 05-62-05-22-89).

WHERE TO STAY & DINE

✪ **Hôtel de France (Restaurant André-Daguin).** Place de la Libération, 32003 Auch CEDEX. ☎ **05-62-61-71-84.** Fax 05-62-61-71-81. 29 units. MINIBAR TV TEL. 500–800F ($90–$144) double; 1,000–1,750F ($180–$315) suite. AE, DC, MC, V. Parking 35F ($6.30) in a garage.

Built around the much-modernized 16th-century core of an old inn, this hotel in the center of town offers comfortable, conservative rooms (14 are air-conditioned) and one of the most famous restaurants in France.

Dining: The cuisine is "innovative within traditional boundaries." Choices include an assortment of preparations of foie gras from Gascony, a duo of *magrêts de canard* (duck) cooked in a rock-salt shell and served with a medley of vegetables, and stuffed pigeon roasted with spiced honey. Desserts include a platter of four chocolate dishes and café au café, a presentation of mousses and pastries unified by their coffee content. Over the years, we've had some of our most memorable meals here, yet there have also been disappointments. The restaurant is open for lunch and dinner daily.

3 Cordes-sur-Ciel

421 miles SW of Paris, 15½ miles NW of Albi

This remarkable site is like an eagle's nest on a hilltop, opening onto the Cérou valley. In days gone by, many celebrities, such as Jean-Paul Sartre and Albert Camus, considered this town a favorite hideaway.

Throughout the centuries, Cordes has been known for its textile, leather, and silk industries. Even today, it's an arts-and-crafts city, and many of the old houses on the narrow streets contain artisans—blacksmiths, enamelers, graphic artists, weavers, engravers, sculptors, and painters—plying their trades. Park outside, then go under an arch leading to the old town.

ESSENTIALS

GETTING THERE If you're coming by **train,** you'll have to get off in nearby Vindrac and either rent a bicycle or take a taxi the remaining 2 miles to Cordes. For train information and schedules, call ☎ **08-36-35-35-39.** If you're **driving,** take N88 northwest from Toulouse to Gaillac, turning north on D922 into Cordes-sur-Ciel.

VISITOR INFORMATION The **Office de Tourisme** is in the Maison Fonpeyrouse (☎ **05-63-56-00-52**).

SEEING THE SIGHTS

Often called "the city of a hundred Gothic arches," Cordes contains numerous old houses built of pink sandstone. Many of the doors and windows are fashioned of pointed (broken) arches that still retain their 13th- and 14th-century grace. Some of the best-preserved ones line **Grande-Rue,** also called **rue Droite.**

Musée d'Art et d'Histoire le Portail-Peint (Musée Charles-Portal). Grande Rue Haute. ☎ **05-63-56-00-52** for information. Admission 10F ($1.80) adults, 5F (90¢) for children. July–Aug daily 11am–noon and 3–6pm; Apr–June and Sept–Oct Sun and holidays 11am–noon and 1–6pm. Closed Nov–Mar.

Small, quirky, and relatively unvisited even by residents of Cordes, this dusty and somewhat sleepy museum is named after a nearby gateway (the Painted Gate) that pierces the fortifications surrounding the city's medieval center, and after Charles-Portal, an archivist of the Tarn region and a local historian. Set in a medieval house whose foundations date from the Gallo-Roman era, it contains artifacts of the textile industry, farming implements, samples of local embroideries, a reconstruction of an old peasant home, and a scattering of medieval pieces. Part of the museum's charm derives from its status as a holdover from small-time, bureaucratic France of long ago. If you happen to arrive when the museum is closed (which is frequently), ask someone at the tourist office to arrange a private visit at a mutually convenient time, perhaps later in the day.

Musée Yves-Brayer. Grande-Rue. ☎ **05-63-56-00-40.** Admission 10F ($1.80) adults, 2F (35¢) children 11 and under. Daily 11am–noon and 2:30–5:30pm, with extended hours, as determined by the tourist office, in July–Aug.

Maison du Grand-Fauconnier (House of the Falcon Master), named for the falcons carved into the stonework of the wall, contains a grand staircase that leads to the Musée Yves-Brayer. Brayer came to Cordes in 1940 and became one of its most ardent civic boosters. After watching Cordes fall gradually into decay, he renewed interest in its restoration. The museum contains minor artifacts relating to the town's history; the most interesting exhibits are rather fanciful scale models of the town itself.

Eglise St-Michel. Grande-Rue. Visiting hours are erratic. If the church is closed, ask at the *tabac* (tobacco shop) across from the front entrance or call the tourist office to make an appointment.

The church dates from the 13th century, but many alterations have been made since. The view from the top of the tower encompasses much of the surrounding area. Most of the lateral design of the side chapels probably comes from the cathedral at Albi. Before being shipped here, the organ (dating from 1830) was in Notre-Dame de Paris.

WHERE TO STAY & DINE

Hostellerie du Parc. Les Cabannes, 81170 Cordes. ☎ **05-63-56-02-59.** Fax 05-63-56-18-03. Reservations recommended. Main courses 75–110F ($13.50–$19.80); fixed-price menus 130–220F ($23.40–$39.60). MC, V. Daily noon–2pm, Mon–Sat 7–10pm. Closed Mon Nov–Mar. Take route de St-Antonin (D600) about 1 mile west from the town center. FRENCH.

Generous meals are served in a wooded garden or paneled dining room in this century-old stone house. Specialties include homemade foie gras, *poularde* (chicken) *occitaine*, rabbit with cabbage leaves, and calf's sweetbreads with morels.

The hotel offers 17 simply furnished rooms; a double costs 275F to 305F ($49.50 to $54.90). There's an outdoor pool, and lessons in French cuisine are offered by the chef.

✪ **Maison du Grand Ecuyer.** Rue Voltaire, 81170 Cordes. ☎ **05-63-53-79-50.** Fax 05-63-53-79-51. www.receptionfrance.com. Reservations required. Main courses 150–210F ($27–$37.80); fixed-price menus 170–440F ($30.60–$79.20). AE, DC, MC, V. July–Aug daily noon–2pm and 7–9:30pm; Easter–June and Sept–Oct 14 Wed–Sun noon–2pm, Tues–Sun 7–9:30pm. Closed Oct 15–Easter. FRENCH.

This restaurant is housed in a national historic treasure: the 15th-century hunting lodge of Raymond VII, comte de Toulouse. Despite its glamour and undeniable charm, it remains intimate and never stuffy. Chef Yves Thuriès's cuisine has made this place an almost mandatory stop. Specialties include three confits of lobster, red mullet salad with fondue of vegetables, and noisette of lamb in orange sauce. The dessert selection is about the grandest and most overwhelming in this part of France.

As a novelty, a 340F ($61.20) menu reproduces the meal served to Mitterrand during a visit, 360F ($64.80) duplicates the food offered Elizabeth II, and, grandest of all, the 440F ($79.20) menu presents a replica of what was dished up for the emperor of Japan.

The hotel contains 12 rooms and 1 suite, all with antiques discreetly combined with modern comforts. Doubles cost 550F to 850F ($99 to $153); the suite is 1,200F ($216). The most desirable room honors former guest Albert Camus and contains a four-poster bed and a fireplace.

4 Albi

433 miles SW of Paris, 47 miles NE of Toulouse

The "red city" (for the color of the building brick) of Albi straddles both banks of the Tarn River and is dominated by its brooding 13th-century cathedral. Toulouse-Lautrec was born in the Hôtel Bosc in Albi; it's still a private home and cannot be toured, but there's a plaque on the wall of the building, on rue Toulouse-Lautrec (no number) in the historic town core. The town's major attraction is a museum with a world-class collection of the artist's work.

ESSENTIALS
GETTING THERE   Fifteen **trains** per day link Toulouse with Albi (trip time: 1 hour); there's also a direct Paris-Albi night train. For rail information and schedules, call ☎ **08-36-35-35-39.** If you're **driving** from Toulouse, take N88 going northeast.

VISITOR INFORMATION   The **Office de Tourisme** is in the Palais de la Serbie, place Ste-Cécile (☎ **05-63-49-48-80**).

THE TOP ATTRACTIONS
✪ **Musée Toulouse-Lautrec.** Opposite the north side of the cathedral. ☎ **05-63-49-48-70.** Admission 24F ($4.30) adults, 12F ($2.15) children. Apr–May daily 10am–noon and 2–6pm; July–Sept daily 9am–noon and 2–6pm.

The Palais de la Berbie (Archbishop's Palace) is a fortified structure dating from the late 13th century. Inside, the Musée Toulouse-Lautrec contains the world's most important collection of the artist's paintings, more than 600 in all. His family bequeathed the works remaining in his studio. (See "Toulouse-Lautrec: A Giant of a

Talent," on p. 538, for details on the artist.) The museum also owns paintings by Degas, Bonnard, Matisse, Utrillo, and Rouault.

Cathédrale Ste-Cécile. Near place du Vigan, in the medieval center of town. ☎ **05-63-49-48-80.** Admission 5F (90¢). June–Aug daily 8:30am–7pm; Sept–May daily 8:30–11:30am and 2–5:30pm.

Fortified with ramparts and parapets and containing frescoes and paintings, this 13th-century cathedral was built by a local lord-bishop after a religious struggle with the comte de Toulouse (the crusade against Cathars). Note the exceptional 16th-century rood screen with a unique suit of polychromatic statues from the Old and New Testaments.

WHERE TO STAY

Hostellerie St-Antoine. 17 rue St-Antoine, 81000 Albi. ☎ **05-63-54-04-04.** Fax 05-63-47-10-47. E-mail: stantoine@ilink.fr. 44 units. A/C TV TEL. 550–850F ($99–$153) double; 850F ($153) suite. AE, DC, MC, V. Parking 30F ($6).

This 250-year-old hotel has been owned by the same family for five generations; today it's managed by Jacques and Jean-François Rieux. Their mother designed the hotel with a focus on Toulouse-Lautrec, since her grandfather was a friend of the painter's and was given a few of his paintings, sketches, and prints. Several are in the lounge, which opens onto a rear garden. The rooms have been delightfully decorated with some antiques, good reproductions, and a sophisticated use of color.

Dining: Even if you're not spending the night, consider dining here: the Rieuxes' culinary tradition is revealed in their traditional yet creative cuisine, and everything tastes better washed down with Gaillac wines.

✪ **La Réserve.** Rte. de Cordes à Fonvialane, 81000 Albi. ☎ **05-63-60-80-80.** Fax 05-63-47-60-60. E-mail: lareserve@ilink.fr. 28 units. MINIBAR TV TEL. 600–1,000F ($108–$180) double; 1,050–1,300F ($189–$234) suite. AE, DC, MC, V. Closed Nov–Apr. From the center of town, follow the signs to Carmaux-Rodez until you cross the Tarn, then follow the signs to Cordes; the hotel is adjacent to the main road leading to Cordes, 1¼ miles from Albi.

This country-club villa on the outskirts of Albi is managed by the Rieux family, who also run the Hostellerie St-Antoine. It was built in the Mediterranean style, with a fine garden in which you can dine. The well-furnished rooms have imaginative decor (but avoid those rooms over the kitchen); the upper-story units have sun terraces and French doors.

Dining: The restaurant's specialties are *pâté de grives* (thrush), *carré d'agneau aux cèpes* (lamb with flap mushrooms), and filet of beef with béarnaise sauce. Even if you're not a guest, consider a visit. The wine carte is rich in bordeaux, and the prices per bottle are reasonable.

Amenities: Tennis courts, pool.

Mercure. 41 bis rue Porta, 81000 Albi. ☎ **05-63-47-66-66.** Fax 05-63-46-18-40. www.hotelweb.com. 56 units. A/C MINIBAR TV TEL. 360–530F ($64.80–$95.40) double. AE, DC, V.

The modern Mercure is one of the best choices in Albi, although it's impersonal compared to La Réserve and the Hostellerie St-Antoine. It was built in an 18th-century mill on the edge of the Tarn River, and the facade and huge entryway were preserved. The rooms are well equipped, and all the bathrooms have been recently renovated.

Dining: The first-class restaurant serves superb meals—both regional and continental. Tables are set on the terrace in summer.

WHERE TO DINE

La Réserve (see above) boasts a wonderful restaurant.

Jardin des Quatre Saisons. 19 bd. de Strasbourg. ☎ **05-63-60-77-76.** Reservations recommended. Fixed-price menus 145–160F ($26.10–$28.80). AE, MC, V. Tues–Sun 12:30–2pm and 7:30–10pm. FRENCH.

The best food in Albi is served by Georges Bermond, who believes that menus, like life, should change with the seasons—thus the restaurant's name. The simple and modern dining rooms provide a pleasant setting with lighting that flatters; service is always competent and polite. Menu items have been fine-tuned to an artful science and include delicious versions of a fricassée of snails garnished with strips of the famous ham produced in the nearby hamlet of Lacoune; ravioli stuffed with pulverized shrimp and served with a truffled cream sauce; and, most delectable of all, is a pot-au-feu of the sea that contains three or four species of fish garnished with a crayfish-flavored cream sauce. The wine carte is the finest in Albi.

5 Castres

452 miles SW of Paris, 26 miles S of Albi

Built on the bank of the Agout River, Castres is the gateway for trips to the Sidobre, the mountains of Lacaune, and the Black Mountains. Today the wool industry, whose origins go back to the 14th century, has made Castres one of France's two most important wool-producing areas. The town was formerly a Roman military installation. A Benedictine monastery was founded here in the 9th century, and the town fell under the comtes d'Albi in the 10th century. During the wars of religion, it was Protestant.

ESSENTIALS

GETTING THERE   From Toulouse, there are eight **trains** per day (trip time: 1 hour); from Albi (above), there are seven trains via St-Sulpice (trip time: 2 hours). For rail information and schedules, call ☎ **08-36-35-35-39.** If you're **driving,** Castres is located on N126 east from Toulouse and along N112 south from Albi.

VISITOR INFORMATION   The **Office de Tourisme** is at 3 rue Milhau Ducommun (☎ **05-63-62-63-62**).

SEEING THE SIGHTS

Le Centre National et Musée Jean-Jaurès. 2 place Pélisson. ☎ **05-63-72-01-01.** Admission 10F ($1.80) adults, 5F (90¢) children. July–Aug Mon–Sat 9am–noon and 2–6pm, Sun 10am–noon and 2–6pm; Sept–June Tues–Sat 9am–noon and 2–5pm.

Dedicated to the workers' movements of the late 19th and early 20th centuries, this collection includes printed material issued by various Socialist factions in France during this era. See, in particular, an issue of *L'Aurore* containing Zola's famous "J'accuse" article from the Dreyfus case. Paintings, sculptures, films, and slides round out the collection.

Eglise St-Benoît. Place du 8-Mai-1945. ☎ **05-63-59-05-19.** Free admission. Mon–Sat 9am–noon and 2–6:30pm, Sun 2–4pm. Except for religious services, the church is closed to casual visitors every Sun Oct–May.

The town's most prominent and important church is an outstanding example of French baroque architecture. The architect Caillau began construction in 1677 on the site of a 9th-century Benedictine abbey, but the structure was never completed according to its original plans. The painting at the church's far end, above the altar, was executed by Gabriel Briard in the 18th century.

✪ **Musée Goya.** In the Jardin de l'Evêché. ☎ **05-63-71-59-28.** Admission 15F ($2.70) adults, 8F ($1.45) children. Apr–Aug Tues–Sat 9am–noon and 2–6pm, Sun 10am–noon and 2–6pm; Sept–Mar Tues–Sun 9am–noon and 2–5pm.

The museum is located in the town hall, an archbishop's palace designed by Mansart in 1669. Some of the spacious public rooms have ceilings supported by a frieze of the archbishops' coats-of-arms. The collection includes 16th-century tapestries and the works of Spanish painters from the 15th to the 20th centuries.

Most notable, of course, are the paintings of Francisco Goya y Lucientes, all donated to the town in 1894 by Pierre Briguiboul, son of the Castres-born artist Marcel Briguiboul. *Les Caprices* is a study of figures created in 1799, after the illness that left Goya deaf. Filling much of an entire room, the work is composed of symbolic images of demons and monsters, a satire of Spanish society.

WHERE TO STAY

Hôtel Occitan. 201 avenue Charles-de-Gaulle, 81100 Castres. ☎ **05-63-35-34-20**. Fax 05-63-35-70-32. 42 units. TV TEL. 320–430F ($57.60–$77.40) double. AE, MC, V. Bus: any bus, including no. 5, headed south or southeast from the city center.

Set about a half-mile southeast of the center of Castres, this simple two-story hotel was built in the mid-1970s in a suburban neighborhood that contains scattered private homes and large gardens. Don't expect antique charm, as the venue is contemporary and the staff can be brusque, but despite that, the Occitan offers some of the more comfortable rooms in town. Each is unpretentiously outfitted; about half contain air-conditioning and minibar. A restaurant on the premises is open daily for lunch and dinner.

Hôtel Renaissance. 17 rue Victor-Hugo, 81100 Castres. ☎ **05-63-59-30-42**. Fax 05-63-72-11-57. 20 units. TV TEL. 340–400F ($61.20–$72) double; 510–650F ($91.80–$117) suite. AE, DC, V.

The best hotel in Castres, the Renaissance was built in the 17th century as the court-house. It functioned as a colorful but run-down hotel throughout most of the 20th century, until 1993, when it was discreetly restored. Today it's a severely dignified building composed of *colombages*-style half-timbering, with a mixture of chiseled stone blocks and bricks. Some rooms have exposed timbers; all are clean and comfortable, evoking the crafts of yesteryear.

Simple platters can be prepared if you want to eat in your room, or you can dine in a recently completed restaurant and bar, Le Renaissance. Fixed-price menus are available for 95F to 250F ($17.10 to $45).

WHERE TO DINE

La Mandragore. 1 rue Malpas. ☎ **05-63-59-51-27**. Reservations recommended. Main courses 75–130F ($13.50–$23.40); fixed-price menus with wine 75F ($13.50), served at lunch and dinner, and 90–240F ($16.20–$43.20). AE, DC, V. Tues–Sat noon–2pm, Mon–Sat 7–10pm. LANGUEDOCIEN.

On an easily overlooked narrow street, this restaurant occupies a small section of one of the many wings of the medieval château-fort of Castres. The consciously simple decor sets off the stone walls and overhead beams. Sophie and Jean-Claude Belaut's regional cuisine is among the best in town. Served with charm, it might include lasagne of foie gras, roast pigeon stuffed with foie gras and accompanied with gâteau of potatoes and flap mushrooms, or monkfish flavored with basil and black olives.

6 Carcassonne

495 miles SW of Paris, 57 miles SE of Toulouse, 65 miles S of Albi

Evoking bold knights, fair damsels, and troubadours, the greatest fortress city of Europe rises against a background of the snowcapped Pyrénées. Floodlit at night, it suggests fairy-tale magic, but back in its heyday in the Middle Ages, all wasn't so romantic. Shattering the peace and quiet were battering rams, grapnels, a mobile tower (inspired by the Trojan horse), catapults, flaming arrows, and the mangonel.

Today, the city that served as a backdrop for the 1991 movie *Robin Hood, Prince of Thieves,* is overrun with hordes of visitors and tacky gift shops. But the elusive charm of Carcassone still emerges in the evening, when thousands of day-trippers have departed and floodlights bathe the ancient monuments.

ESSENTIALS

GETTING THERE   Carcassonne is a major stop for **trains** between Toulouse and destinations south and east. There are 24 trains per day from Toulouse (trip time: 50 minutes); 14 trains per day from Montpellier (trip time: 2 hours); and 12 trains per day from Nîmes (trip time: 2½ hours). For rail information and schedules, call ☎ 08-36-35-35-39. If you're **driving,** Carcassonne lies on A61 south from Toulouse.

VISITOR INFORMATION   The **Office de Tourisme** is at 15 bd. Camille-Pelletan (☎ 04-68-10-24-30) and in the medieval town at Porte Narbonnaise (☎ 04-68-10-24-36).

SPECIAL EVENTS   The town's nightlife sparkles with real pizzazz during its major summer festivals. The whole month of July is devoted to **Festival de Carcassonne,** when instrumental concerts, modern and classical dance, operas, and original theater shower the city. Tickets range from 125F to 275F ($22.50 to $49.50) and can be purchased by calling ☎ 04-68-77-71-05. For more information, contact the **Théâtre Municipal** at ☎ 04-68-25-33-13. On the night of July 14, **Bastille Day,** one of the best fireworks spectacles in all of France lights up the skies. In early August, the unadulterated merriment and good times of the Middle Ages overtake the city during the **Cité en Scènes.** For information, contact the Office de Tourisme or **Carcassonne Terre d'Histoire,** chemin de Serres (☎ 04-68-47-97-97).

EXPLORING THE TOWN

Carcassonne consists of two towns: the **Ville Basse** (Lower City) and the medieval **Cité.** The former has little interest, but the latter is among the major attractions in France and the goal of many a pilgrim. The fortifications consist of the inner and outer walls, a double line of ramparts. The inner rampart was built by the Visigoths in the 5th century. Clovis, king of the Franks, attacked in 506 but failed. The Saracens overcame the city in 728, until Pepin the Short (father of Charlemagne) drove them out in 752. During a long siege by Charlemagne, the populace of the walled city was starving and near surrender until Dame Carcas came up with an idea. According to legend, she gathered up the last remaining bit of grain, fed it to a sow, then tossed the pig over the ramparts. It's said to have burst, scattering the grain. The Franks concluded that Carcassonne must have unlimited food supplies and ended their siege.

Carcassone's walls were further fortified by the vicomtes de Trencavel in the 12th century and by Louis IX and Philip the Bold in the following century. However, by the mid–17th century its position as a strategic frontier fort was over, and the ramparts were left to decay. In the 19th century the builders of the Lower Town began to remove the stone for use in new construction. But interest in the Middle Ages revived, and the government ordered Viollet-le-Duc (who restored Notre-Dame in Paris) to repair and, where necessary, rebuild the walls. Reconstruction continued until very recently.

Within the walls resides a small populace. The **Basillique St-Nazaire,** La Cité (☎ 04-68-25-27-65), dating from the 11th to 14th centuries, contains some beautiful stained-glass windows and a pair of rose medallions. The nave is in the

Romanesque style, but the choir and transept are Gothic. The organ, one of the oldest in southwestern France, is from the 16th century. The tomb of Bishop Radulph, from 1266, is well preserved. The cathedral is open daily, in July and August from 9am to 7pm and off-season from 9:30am to noon and 2 to 5:30pm. Mass is celebrated on Sunday at 11am. Admission is free.

Carcassone, more than other French cities, is really two distinct shopping towns in one. In the modern lower city, the major streets for shopping are **rue Clemenceau** and **rue de Verdun,** particularly if you're in the market for clothing. In the walled medieval city, the streets are chock-full of tiny stores and boutiques selling mostly gift items like antiques and local arts and crafts. On the third Saturday of every month at the portail Jacobin, in the center of the modern town, a **flea market** sets up from 9am to noon.

Stores worth visiting are the **Caveau des Vins,** tour du Tréseau (☎ **04-68-25-29-38**), where you'll find a wide selection of regional wines ranging from simple table wines to those awarded the distinction of Appellation d'Origine Contrôlée; **Antiquités "Le St-Georges,"** 36 rue Victor-Hugo (☎ **04-68-47-52-66**), which specializes in antique scientific instruments and furniture from the 17th to the 19th centuries; and **Dominique Sarraute,** 15 rue Porte d'Aude (☎ **04-68-72-42-90**), for antique firearms.

WHERE TO STAY
IN THE CITÉ

✪ **Cité.** Place de l'Eglise, 11000 Carcassonne. ☎ **04-68-25-03-34.** Fax 04-68-71-50-15. 60 units. A/C TV TEL. 1,440–1,750F ($259.20–$315) double; 2,150–2,675F ($387–$481.50) suite. AE, DC, MC, V. Parking 80F ($14.40).

Originally a palace for whatever bishop or well-placed prelate happened to be in control at the time, this historically important site has thrived as the most desirable hotel in town since 1905. Massively and luxuriously renovated, it's built into the actual walls of the city, adjoining the cathedral. A long Gothic corridor/gallery leads to the lounge. Many rooms open onto the ramparts and a garden and feature antiques or reproductions; modern gadgets have been discreetly installed.

Dining: The hotel is renowned for its restaurant, La Barbacane, with its mock Gothic windows and golden fleurs-de-lis shield and lion motifs. Menu items focus on upscale versions of the region's cuisine and include sophisticated interpretations of magrêt and confit of duck, cassoulet, and cuisine du marché based on market-fresh seasonal ingredients. Fixed-price menus cost 250F ($45).

Amenities: Heated pool.

Hôtel des Remparts. 3-5 place du Grand-Puits, 11000 Carcassonne. ☎ **04-68-71-27-72.** Fax 04-68-72-73-26. 18 units. TEL. 300–330F ($54–$59.40) double. MC, V. Parking 20F ($3.60).

An abbey in the 12th century, this building at the edge of a stone square in the town center was converted into a charming hotel in 1983 after major repairs to the masonry and roof. The owners are most proud of the massive stone staircase that twists around itself. Guest rooms contain no-frills furniture. Make reservations at least 2 months ahead if you plan to stay here in summer.

AT THE ENTRANCE TO THE CITÉ

✪ **Hôtel du Donjon.** 2 rue du Comte-Roger, 11000 Carcassonne. ☎ **04-68-71-08-80,** or 800/528-1234 in the U.S. and Canada. Fax 04-68-25-06-60. E-mail: hotel.donjou. best.western@wanadoo.fr. 38 units. A/C MINIBAR TV TEL. 390–495F ($70.20–$89.10) double; 755–855F ($135.90–$153.90) suite. AE, DC, V. Parking 26F ($4.70).

This little hotel is big on charm and the best value in the moderate range. Built in the style of the old Cité, it has a honey-colored stone exterior with iron bars on the windows. The interior is a jewel, reflecting the sophistication of the owner, Christine Pujol. Elaborate Louis XIII–style furniture graces the reception lounges. A newer wing contains additional rooms in a medieval architectural style. Furnishings are in a severe style. The hotel also runs a nearby restaurant, the Brasserie Le Donjon. In summer the garden is the perfect breakfast spot.

IN VILLE-BASSE

Hôtel du Pont-Vieux. 32 rue Trivalle, 11000 Carcassonne. ☎ **04-68-25-24-99.** Fax 04-68-47-62-71. 19 units. TV TEL. 290–320F ($52.20–$57.60) double; 360F ($64.80) triple; 400F ($72) quad. AE, DC, MC, V. Parking 30F ($5.40). Closed Jan 15–31.

One of the best and most reasonably priced hotels in Carcassonne, this rustic boardinghouse lies at the foot of the medieval city. It's been completely restored but retains its provincial French charm, and is cozy and inviting from the elegantly furnished lounge to the quiet reading room. The rooms have traditional furnishings and double-glazed windows to cut down on the noise. An indoor garden provides a retreat from the crowds.

Hôtel Montségur. 27 allée d'Iéna, 11000 Carcassonne. ☎ **04-68-25-31-41.** Fax 04-68-47-13-22. 21 units. A/C TV TEL. 490F ($88.20) double. AE, DC, V.

This stately old town house with a mansard roof and dormers has a front garden that's screened from the street by trees and a high wrought-iron fence. The rooms, furnished with antiques, are cheaper than you'd imagine from the looks of the place. Modern amenities include an elevator. A continental breakfast is available, and the highly recommended Le Languedoc serves every dish with a certain flair, ranging from anglerfish to a duck cassoulet fit for a banquet.

WHERE TO DINE

Au Jardin de la Tour. 11 rue Porte-d'Aude. ☎ **04-68-25-71-24.** Reservations recommended in summer. Main courses 45–140F ($8.10–$25.20); fixed-price menus (without wine) 80F ($14.40) at lunch, 80–100F ($14.40–$18) at dinner. V. Daily noon–2pm and 8–10pm. Closed Mon Nov–Easter. FRENCH.

A culinary team labors to create authentic Languedoc cuisine served in the oldest part of the Cité, at the end of a long corridor. Menu choices include a large selection of salads, onglet of beef with shallots, confit of duckling, and the inevitable cassoulet, everybody's favorite.

✪ **La Barbacane.** In the Hôtel de la Cité, place de l'Eglise. ☎ **04-68-25-03-34.** Reservations recommended. Main courses 220–350F ($39.60–$63); fixed-price menus 340–500F ($61.20–$90). AE, DC, MC, V. Daily 7:30–11pm. Closed Jan–Feb for dinner. FRENCH.

Named after the medieval neighborhood (La Barbacane) in which it sits, this restaurant enjoys equal billing with the celebrated hotel that contains it. Its soothing dining room, whose walls are upholstered in fabric with gold fleurs-de-lis on a cerulean blue background, features the cuisine of the noted chef Christophe Turquier. Menu items, based on seasonal ingredients, include green ravioli perfumed with *seiche* (a species of octopus) and its own ink, saltwater crayfish with strips of Bayonne ham, and organically fed free-range chicken stuffed with truffles. A particularly succulent dessert is *beignets* (deep-fried fritters) of pineapple with vanilla sauce.

Le Languedoc. 32 allée d'Iéna. ☎ **04-68-25-22-17.** Reservations recommended. Main courses 95–140F ($17.10–$25.20); fixed-price menus 130F and 175F ($23.40 and $31.50); menu carte 225–240F ($40.50–$43.20). AE, DC, MC, V. Tues–Sun noon–2pm, Tues–Sat 7:30–9:30pm. Closed Dec 20–Jan 20. FRENCH.

Lucien Faugeras has passed on his carving fork to his son Didier, also an excellent chef (the family owns the Hôtel Montségur as well). The dining room's rough plaster walls, ceiling beams, and open brick fireplace create a warm Languedoc atmosphere. The specialty is cassoulet au confit de canard (the famous stew made with duck cooked in its own fat). The pièce de résistance is tournedos Rossini, with foie-gras truffles and madeira sauce. For dessert, try flambéed crêpes Languedoc. In summer, dine on a pleasant patio or in the air-conditioned restaurant.

NEARBY ACCOMMODATIONS & DINING

✪ **Domaine d'Auriac.** Rte. St-Hilaire, 11000 Carcassonne. ☎ **04-68-25-72-22.** Fax 04-68-47-35-54. E-mail: auriac@relaischateaux.fr. 27 units. A/C MINIBAR TV TEL. 550–1,500F ($99–$270) double. AE, DC, MC, V. Closed Feb 17–Mar 3 and Nov 17–Dec 8. Take D104 about 2 miles from Carcassonne.

This moss-covered, 19th-century manor house, a Relais & Châteaux, boasts gardens with reflecting pools and flowered terraces. The uniquely decorated rooms have a certain *Architectural Digest* glamour; some are in an older building with high ceilings, whereas others have more modern decor. Renovations are ongoing.

Dining: Bernard Rigaudis sets a grand table in his lovely dining room. In summer, meals are served beside the pool on the terraces. (Afterward, you might work off lunch at the tennis courts or golf course.) The menu changes about five or six times yearly but might include truffles and purple artichokes with essences of pears and olives. Meals cost 250F ($45) for the minimalist and 400F ($72) for the gourmand. The restaurant is open daily for lunch and dinner; reservations are required. Closed Sunday evening and Monday in summer.

CARCASSONNE AFTER DARK

Carcassonne nightlife is centered along **rue Omer-Sarraut** and **place Verdun.** A popular spot for an aperitif before dinner is **Le Not Café,** 18 rue de L'Aigle d'or (☎ **04-68-71-38-43**). **Le Bulle,** 115 rue Barbacane (☎ **04-68-72-47-70**), explodes with techno and rock that keep the energy pumping and the place hopping until 4am. The cover is 40F to 70F ($7.20 to $12.60).

7 Perpignan

562 miles SW of Paris, 229 miles NW of Marseille, 40 miles S of Narbonne

At Perpignan you may think you've crossed the border into Spain, for it was once Catalonia's second city, after Barcelona. Even earlier, it was the capital of the kingdom of Majorca. But when the Roussillon—the French part of Catalonia—was finally partitioned off, Perpignan became French forever, authenticated by the Treaty of the Pyrénées in 1659. However, Catalan is still spoken here, especially among the country people.

Today Perpignan is content to rest on its former glory, its residents—some 110,000 in all—enjoying the closeness of the Côte Catalane and the mountains to their north. The pace is decidedly relaxed. You'll even have time to smell the flowers that grow here in great abundance.

This is one of the sunniest places in France, but summer afternoons in July and August are a cauldron. That's when many of the locals take the 6-mile ride to the beach to cool off. There's a young scene here that brings vibrance to Perpignan, especially along the quays of the Basse River, site of impromptu nighttime concerts, beer drinking, and the devouring of endless tapas, a tradition inherited from nearby Barcelona.

ESSENTIALS

GETTING THERE   Four **trains** per day arrive from Paris (trip time: 6 to 10 hours) and 15 trains from Marseille (trip time: 5 hours). There are also three trains per day from Nice (trip time: 6 hours). For rail information and schedules, call ☎ 08-36-35-35-39. If you're **driving** and you're already on the French Riviera, continue west along A9 to Perpignan.

VISITOR INFORMATION   The **Office Municipal du Tourisme** is beside the Palais des Congrès, place Armand-Lanoux (☎ 04-68-66-30-30).

SPECIAL EVENTS   July, though terribly hot, is the time for **Les Estivales,** which causes the city to explode with a medley of music, expositions, and theater. Our favorite time to visit is during the **grape harvest** in September. If you come at this time, you may want to drive through the Rivesaltes district bordering the city to the west and north. Temperatures have usually dropped by then.

SEEING THE SIGHTS

With its inviting pedestrian streets, Perpignan is a good town for shopping. Catalan is the style indigenous to the area, and it's characterized by textiles, pottery, and furniture in strong geometric patterns and sturdy structures. For one of the best selections of Catalan pieces, including pottery, furniture, carpets, and even antiques, visit the **Galerie Sant Vicens,** rue Sant-Vicens (tel. **04-68-50-02-18**).

Castillet. Place de Verdun. ☎ **04-68-35-42-05.** Admission 25F ($4.50) adults, 10F ($1.80) students and children 17 and under. Mid-June to mid-Sept Wed–Mon 9:30am–7pm; mid-Sept to mid-June 9am–6pm.

This crenellated redbrick building is a combination gateway and fortress from the 14th century. You can climb its bulky-looking tower for a good view of the town. Also housed here is the **Musée des Arts et Traditions Populaires Catalans** (also known as La Casa Païral), which contains exhibitions of Catalan regional artifacts and folkloric items, including typical dress.

Cathédrale St-Jean. Place Gambetta/rue de l'Horloge. ☎ **04-68-51-33-72.** Free admission. Daily 8am–noon and 3–6pm.

The cathedral dates from the 14th and 15th centuries and has an admirable nave and interesting 17th-century retables. Leaving via the south door, you'll find on the left a chapel with the Devout Christ, a magnificent wood carving depicting Jesus contorted with pain and suffering, his head, crowned with thorns, drooping on his chest.

Palais des Rois de Majorque (Palace of the Kings of Majorca). Rue des Archers. ☎ **04-68-34-48-29.** Admission 20F ($3.60) adults, 10F ($1.80) students, free for children 7 and under. June–Sept daily 10am–6pm; Oct–May daily 9am–5pm.

Situated at the top of the town, the Spanish citadel encloses the Palace of the Kings of Majorca. This structure from the 13th and 14th centuries, built around a court encircled by arcades, has been restored by the government. You can see the old throne room with its large fireplaces and a square tower with a double gallery; from the tower there's a fine view of the Pyrénées. A free guided tour, in French only, departs every 30 minutes during open hours if demand warrants it.

Château de Salses. In the town of Salses, 15½ miles north of the city center. ☎ **04-68-38-60-13.** Admission 32F ($5.75) adults, 21F ($3.80) children and students 12–25, free for children under 12. July–Aug daily 9:30am–7pm; June and Sept daily 9:30am–6:30pm; Apr–May and Oct daily 9:30am–12:30pm and 2–6pm; Nov–Mar daily 10am–noon and 2–5pm.

This fort has guarded the main road linking Spain and France since the days of the Romans. Ferdinand of Aragón erected a fort here in 1497 hoping to protect the northern frontier of his kingdom. Even today, Salses marks the language-barrier point between Catalonia in Spain and Languedoc in France. This Spanish-style fort designed by Ferdinand is a curious example of an Iberian structure in France, but in the 17th century it was modified by Vauban to look more like a château. After many changes of ownership, Salses fell to the forces of Louis XIII in September 1642; its Spanish garrison left forever. Less than 2 decades later, Roussillon was incorporated into France.

WHERE TO STAY

Hôtel de la Loge. 1 rue des Fabriques-Nabot, 66000 Perpignan. ☎ **04-68-34-41-02.** Fax 04-68-34-25-13. 22 units. A/C MINIBAR TV TEL. 285–330F ($51.30–$59.40) double. AE, DC, MC, V.

This beguiling little place dates from the 16th century but has been renovated into a modern three-star hotel. It's located right in the heart of town, near not only the Loge de Mer, from which it takes its name, but also the Castillet. The cozy rooms are attractively furnished, and many are air-conditioned.

✪ **La Villa Duflot.** 109 av. Victor-Dalbiez, 66000 Perpignan. ☎ **04-68-56-67-67.** Fax 04-68-56-54-05. 24 units. A/C TV TEL. 790F ($142.20) double. Half board 530–760F ($95.40–$136.80) per person extra. AE, DC, MC, V.

This is the area's greatest hotel, yet its prices are reasonable for the luxury offered. Tranquillity, style, and refinement reign supreme. When it opened, the local mayor proclaimed, "Now we have some class in Perpignan." The Mediterranean-style dwelling, located in the suburbs, is surrounded by a 3-acre park of pine, palm, and eucalyptus. The hotel has an appealing touch to it and isn't the least bit intimidating. The guest rooms are situated around a patio planted with century-old olive trees. All are spacious and soundproofed, with solid marble bathrooms and Art Deco interiors.

Dining: The chef is a whiz, and the cuisine is reason enough to stay here. You'll surely agree after sampling his lasagne made with fresh duck liver and asparagus, grilled red mullet in anchovy butter, or (most definitely) roast lamb with a tapenade of eggplant and caviar.

Amenities: You can sunbathe in the gardens surrounding the pool and order drinks at any hour at the outside bar.

Park Hotel. 18 bd. Jean-Bourrat, 66000 Perpignan. ☎ **04-68-35-14-14.** Fax 04-68-35-48-18. 67 units. A/C MINIBAR TV TEL. 280–480F ($50.40–$86.40) double. AE, DC, MC, V. Parking 40F ($7.20).

This four-story hotel, facing the Jardins de la Ville, offers well-furnished, soundproofed rooms. There's a bit of flair and modern styling here, although rustic yet beautiful antiques are used throughout. The location is quiet, the ambience tasteful. What makes this place better than the rest in its category is the welcoming, well-trained staff.

Dining: The restaurant, Le Chapon Fin, offers both à la carte choices and fixed-price menus; the cuisine is among the finest in the area. The chef turns prime regional produce into postnouvelle choices like roast sea scallops flavored with succulent sea urchin velouté as well as penne with truffles. As an accompaniment, try one of the local wines—perhaps a Collioure or Côtes du Roussillon. The restaurant is open for lunch Monday through Saturday and for dinner Monday through Friday. The hotel also houses Le Bistrot du Park, a less expensive eatery specializing in seafood.

WHERE TO DINE

There are also wonderful restaurants in **La Villa Duflot** and the **Park Hotel** (see above).

✪ **Festin de Pierre.** 7 rue du Théâtre. ☎ **04-68-51-28-74.** Reservations required. Main courses 230–350F ($41.40–$63); fixed-price menus 150F ($27) at lunch, 150F ($27) at dinner. AE, MC, V. Wed–Sun noon–2pm, Wed–Sun 7–9:30pm. Closed 3 weeks in Feb. FRENCH.

This restaurant, housed in the 15th-century home of a former grand inquisitor for the Catholic church, attracts a conservative and exclusive crowd who come for the excellent traditional cuisine. Since Alain Boivin became chef, the restaurant has received the Golden Palms award for best restaurant in the region. In a clublike atmosphere, you can enjoy offerings like red mullet cutlets with watercress salad, filet of turbot in champagne sauce, or—especially noteworthy—veal kidneys in an aged sweet-wine sauce. It also has the best wine cellar in the region with more than 400 choices.

L'Apero. 40 rue de la Fusterie. ☎ **04-68-51-21-14.** Reservations required. Main courses 70–90F ($12.60–$16.20); fixed-price menu 72F ($12.95) Mon–Fri only. AE, V. Daily noon–2pm and 8–11pm. FRENCH.

Despite its changing ownership through the years, we've always found the best-value menus in town at this informal bistro. Many locals opt for a meal Monday through Friday, when its bargain menu of 72F ($12.95) is available. The setting is battered and very old (at least 200 years, the owners think). Menu items include filet of trout with sorrel, roast lamb with rosemary and garlic, and tournedos in roquefort sauce.

PERPIGNAN AFTER DARK

The Spanish influence permeates this town, even at night. Head for **place de Verdun,** with its cafes and bars, and you may even discover some Catalan folk dancing to enliven the evening. For a traditional Catalan-style bar with a hip staff, visit **Le Festival,** 40 place Rigaud (☎ **04-68-34-31-60**), the hot spot for tantalizing tapas and heady sangria. The bars in the center of town, including the **Républic Café,** 2 place de la République (☎ **04-68-51-11-64**), have live music and a vivacious student scene. During summer, the nearby area of **Canet-Plage** has a more vibrant, mainstream nightlife of bars and dance clubs.

8 Collioure

577 miles SW of Paris, 17 miles SE of Perpignan

You may recognize this port and its sailboats from the Fauve paintings of Lhote and Derain. It's said to resemble St-Tropez before it was overrun, attracting, in days of yore, Matisse, Picasso, and Dalí. Collioure is the most authentically alluring port of Roussillon, a gem with a vivid Spanish and Catalan image and flavor. Some visitors believe it's the most charming village on the Côte Vermeille. The town's sloping narrow streets, charming semifortified church, antique lighthouse, and eerily introverted culture make it worth an afternoon stopover. This is the ideal small-town antidote to the condo-choked Riviera.

The two curving ports are separated from each other by the heavy masonry of the 13th-century **Château Royal,** place du 8-Mai-1945 (☎ **04-68-82-06-43**). The château, now a museum of painting and folkloric artifacts, is open daily, June to September from 10am to 6pm and October to May from 9am to 5pm; closed January 1, May 1, November 1, and December 25. Admission is 20F ($3.60) for adults and 10 F ($1.80) for children. Also try to visit the **Musée Jean-Peské,** route de Port-Vendres (☎ **04-68-82-10-19**), with its collection of works by artists who migrated here to paint. It's open in July and August daily from 10am to noon and 2 to 7pm, September to June Wednesday through Monday from 10am to noon and 2 to 6pm. Admission is 12F ($2.15) for adults, 8F ($1.45) for children 12 to 16, and free for children 11 and under.

Collioure is serviced by frequent **train** and bus connections, especially from Perpignan. For train information and schedules, call ☎ **08-36-35-35-39.** Many visitors **drive** along the coastal road (R.N. 114) leading to the Spanish border.

The **Office de Tourisme** is on place du 18-Juin (☎ **04-68-82-15-47**).

WHERE TO STAY

Les Caranques. Rte. de Port-Vendres, 66190 Collioure. ☎ **04-68-82-06-68.** Fax 04-68-82-00-92. 22 units. TEL. July–Sept (including half board) 320F ($57.60) per person double; Apr–June and Oct 1–14 (without meals) 300F ($54) per person double. AE, V. Closed Oct 15–Mar.

Constructed around the core of a private villa built after World War II and enlarged in the 1960s, this hotel is well scrubbed, comfortably furnished, personalized, and one of the best bargains in town. Set on the perimeter of Collioure, away from the crush (and the charm) of the center, it features a terrace that opens onto a view of the old port. The restaurant is for guests only, almost all of whom elect to stay on the half-board plan.

✪ **Relais des Trois Mas et Restaurant La Balette.** Rte. de Port-Vendres, 66190 Collioure. ☎ **04-68-82-05-07.** Fax 04-68-82-38-08. www.chatotel.com. E-mail: chatotel @chatotel.com. 23 units. A/C MINIBAR TV TEL. 695–965F ($125.10–$173.70) double; 1,095–1,945F ($197.10–$350.10) suite. MC, V. Parking 78F ($14.05). Closed Nov 15–Dec 15.

This is not only the town's premier hotel but also the restaurant of choice. The hotel honors the famous artists who have lived at Collioure in the decor of its beautiful rooms, which all have spacious bathrooms with Jacuzzis and views of the water. Even if you aren't a guest, you may want to take a meal in the dining room, with its views of the harbor. Christian Peyre is unchallenged as the lead chef of town. His cooking is inventive—often simple but always refined. There's also an outdoor heated pool.

WHERE TO DINE

The **Restaurant La Balette** at the Relais des Trois Mas (see above) is the best dining room in town.

La Pérouse. 6 rue de la République. ☎ **04-68-82-05-60.** Reservations recommended. Main courses 75–170F ($13.50–$30.60); fixed-price menus 95–148F ($17.10–$26.65). AE, MC, V. Thurs–Tues 12:30–2pm and 7:30–9:30pm. Closed Nov 15–Dec 18. FRENCH.

This restaurant occupies the whitewashed cellar of a building in the heart of town. Small windows illuminate the enormous antique barrels and the bullfighting accessories in back, though some visitors prefer a seat on the glassed-in veranda instead. The kitchen makes few concessions to modern cuisine; instead, the food is prepared with solid authenticity, following regional traditions. Menu items may include salade catal·ne, grilled fish, spicy preparations of scallops, and bouillabaisse. Dessert might be a simple but satisfying crème catalane.

9 Narbonne

525 miles SW of Paris, 38 miles E of Carcassonne, 58 miles S of Montpelier

Medieval Narbonne was a port to rival Marseille in Roman times, its "galleys laden with riches." It was the first town outside Italy to be colonized by the Romans, but the Mediterranean, now 5 miles away, left it high and dry. For that reason it's an intriguing place, steeped with antiquity.

After Lyon, Narbonne was the largest town in Gaul. Even today you can still see evidence of the town's former wealth. Too far from the sea to be a beach town, it attracts history buffs and others aware of the memories of its glorious past. Some 50,000 Narbonnais live here, in what is really a sleepy backwater. However, many locals are trying to make a go with their vineyards. Caves are open to visitors in the surrounding area (the tourist office will advise). If you want to go to the beach, you'll have to head to the nearby sands of Gruisson-Plage or Narbonne-Plage.

ESSENTIALS

GETTING THERE Narbonne has rail, bus, and highway connections with other cities on the Mediterranean coast and with Toulouse. Rail travel is the most popular way to get here, with 14 **trains** per day arriving from Perpignan (trip time: 45 minutes), 13 per day from Toulouse (trip time: 1½ hours), and 12 per day from Montpellier (trip time: 55 minutes). For rail information and schedules, call ☎ **08-36-35-35-39.** If you're **driving,** Narbonne is located at the junction of A61 and A9, making it easily accessible from either Toulouse or the Riviera.

VISITOR INFORMATION The **Office de Tourisme** is on place Roger-Salengro (☎ **04-68-65-15-60**).

SEEING THE SIGHTS

Few other cities in France contain such a massive architectural block in their centers dating from the Middle Ages. Within Narbonne is a labyrinth of religious and civic buildings. Foremost among them is the **Cathédrale St-Just,** place de l'Hôtel-de-Ville, entrance on rue Gauthier (☎ **04-68-32-09-52**). Its construction began in 1272 but was never finished. Only the transept and a choir were completed; the choir is 130 feet high, built in the bold Gothic style of northern France. At each end of the transept are 194-foot towers from 1480. Inside is an impressive collection of Flemish tapestries. The cloisters are from the 14th and 15th centuries and connect the cathedral with the Archbishops' Palace. It's open daily, May to September from 9am to 6pm and October to April from 9am to noon and 2 to 6pm.

The cathedral is attached to the **Palais des Archevêques** (Archbishops' Palace, sometimes referred to as the Vieux-Palais), place de l'Hôtel-de-Ville (☎ **04-68-90-30-30**). It was conceived as part fortress, part pleasure palace, with three military-style towers from the 13th and 14th centuries. The Old Palace on the right is from the 12th century and the so-called New Palace on the left is from the 14th. It's said that the old, arthritic, and sometimes very overweight archbishops used to be hauled up the interior's monumental Louis XIII–style stairs on mules.

Part of the complex is devoted to the neo-Gothic **Hôtel de Ville (town hall),** which was reconstructed by Viollet-le-Duc, a 19th-century architect involved with the refurbishment of such sites as the cathedral at Paris, between 1845 and 1850.

Today the once-private apartments of the former bishops contain three museums. A **global ticket** costs 25F ($4.50) for adults, 15F ($2.70) for students and youths 12 to 18, and free for children 11 and under. It entitles you to visit all three, plus the Musée Lapidaire (below), over a period of 3 days. But if your time or interest is limited, you can buy tickets to each museum individually for 15 F ($2.70). Hours of all three are the same: May to September daily from 9:30am to 12:15pm and 2 to 6pm, October to April Tuesday to Sunday from 10am to noon and 2 to 5pm. For more information, call ☎ **04-68-90-30-54.**

Musée Archéologique contains prehistoric artifacts, Bronze Age tools, 14th-century frescoes, and Greco-Roman amphorae. Several of the sarcophagi date from the 3rd century and some of the mosaics are of pagan origin. **Musée d'Art et d'Histoire de Narbonne** is located three floors above street level in the archbishop's once-private apartments, the rooms in which Louis XII stayed during his siege of Perpignan. Their coffered ceilings are enhanced with panels depicting the nine Muses. A Roman mosaic floor and 17th-century portraits are on display. There's also a collection of antique porcelain, enamels, and a portrait bust of Louis XIV. In the **Horreum Romain,** you'll find a labyrinth of underground passageways, similar to catacombs but with none of the burial functions, dug by the Gallo-Romans and their successors for storage of food and supplies during times of siege.

If you visit between mid-June and mid-September, you might want to participate in one of the occasional hikes up the steep steps of the **Donjon Gilles-Aycelin,** place de l'Hôtel-de-Ville. Originally a watchtower and prison in the late 13th century, it has a lofty observation platform with a view of the cathedral, the surrounding plain, and the Pyrénées. Tours, at 30F ($5.40) for adults and 20 F ($3.60) for students and children 11 to 18, must be arranged through the Hôtel de Ville (☎ **04-68-90-30-66**) and are much more likely to be welcomed in summer than in winter.

You can see Roman artifacts at the **Musée Lapidaire,** place Lamourguier (☎ **04-68-65-53-58**), in the 13th-century Eglise de Lamourguier. The broken sculptures, Roman inscriptions, and relics of medieval buildings make up one of the largest (and most important) exhibits of its kind in France. Although it maintains regular hours only in July and August (daily from 9:45am to 12:15pm and 2 to 6pm), you can visit it as part of the global museum ticket described above; outside those dates, you can visit only by making special arrangements with the **Hotel de Ville Mairie de Narbonne** (☎ **04-68-90-30-30**).

A final site worth visiting is the early Gothic **Basilique St-Paul-Serge,** rue de l'Hôtel-Dieu (☎ **04-68-41-12-29**), which was built on the site of a 4th-century necropolis. It has an elegant choir with fine Renaissance wood carvings and some ancient Christian sarcophagi. The chancel, from 1229, is admirable. The north door leads to the Paleo-Christian Cemetery, part of an early Christian burial ground. It's open daily from 10am to noon and 2 to 6pm.

WHERE TO STAY

Hôtel Languedoc. 22 bd. Gambetta, 11100 Narbonne. ☎ **04-68-65-14-74.** Fax 04-68-65-81-48. 40 units. TEL. 250–450F ($45–$81) double; 480F ($86.40) suite. AE, DC, MC, V. Parking 30F ($5.40).

This turn-of-the-century hotel, near the canal de la Rhône, offers well-equipped, modernized rooms and a restaurant serving regional specialties. The hotel's wine bar, Le Bacchus, is open Monday through Saturday from 7:30pm to 2am. Specializing in the many esoteric vintages grown nearby, it sells wine by the glass and serves simple but flavorful accompaniments such as grilled salmon with anchovy butter, tender lamb cooked with beans, and sautéed chicken chasseur.

La Résidence. 6 rue du 1er-Mai, 11100 Narbonne. ☎ **04-68-32-19-41.** Fax 04-68-65-51-82. 25 units. A/C TV TEL. 320–415F ($57.60–$74.70) double. AE, MC, V. Parking 40F ($7.20).

Our favorite hotel in Narbonne is near the Cathédrale St-Just. The 19th-century La Résidence, converted from the premises of a once-stately villa, is comfortable and decorated with antiques. It doesn't have a restaurant but offers breakfast and a gracious welcome.

WHERE TO DINE

Aux Trois Caves. 4 rue Benjamin-Cremieux. ☎ **04-68-65-28-60.** Reservations required. Main courses 100–205F ($18–$36.90); fixed-price menus 99–230F ($17.80–$41.40). AE, V. Daily noon–2pm and 7:30–10:30pm. FRENCH.

This excellent restaurant occupies a trio of carefully restored, connected Romanesque cellars. (Two contain medieval but cozy-looking dining rooms; the third houses the kitchen.) The owners present a classic menu focusing on popular platters from the region. The place is known for its traditional cassoulet but also prepares confit of duckling with garlic, filet mignon with mushrooms, platters of fresh sardines cooked in white wine, grilled turbot, and gratin of John Dory—and does so exceedingly well.

L'Alsace. 2 av. Pierre-Sémard. ☎ **04-68-65-10-24.** Reservations recommended. Main courses 90–150F ($16.20–$27); fixed-price menus 98–160F ($17.65–$28.80). AE, DC, MC, V. Daily noon–2:30pm and 7:30–10pm. Across from the rail station. FRENCH.

This is the most reliable choice in the moderately priced range. The comfortable dining room is done in an English style, with wood paneling and a glass-enclosed patio. In spite of the restaurant's name, the cuisine isn't derived from Alsace-Lorraine in eastern France but is more typical of the food of southwestern France with a focus on seafood. Try the fry of red mullet, a savory kettle of bourride, or magrêt of duck with flap mushrooms. Especially noteworthy is this restaurant's expertise in baking entire fish, such as sea wolf, in a salt crust, a process that usually produces a delightfully pungent and flaky dish.

10 Aigues-Mortes

466 miles SW of Paris, 39 miles NE of Sëte, 25 miles E of Nîmes, 30 miles SW of Arles

South of Nîmes, you can explore much of the Camargue by car. The most rewarding place to focus on is Aigues-Mortes, the city of the "dead waters." In the middle of dismal swamps and melancholy lagoons, Aigues-Mortes is France's most perfectly preserved walled town. Now 4 miles from the sea, it stands on four navigable canals. Louis IX and his crusaders once set forth from Aigues-Mortes, then a thriving port, the first in France on the Mediterranean. The walls, which still enclose the town, were constructed between 1272 and 1300. The **Tour de Constance** (☎ **04-66-53-61-55**) is a model castle of the Middle Ages, its stones looking out on the marshes. At the top, which you can reach by elevator, a panoramic view unfolds. Admission is 28F ($5.05) for adults, 15F ($2.70) for youths, and free for children 11 and under. The monument is open Easter to August daily from 9am to 7pm, off-season daily from 9:30am to noon and 2 to 5:30pm.

Five **trains** per day connect Aigues-Mortes and Nîmes (trip time: 1 hour), and 4 **buses** per day arrive from Nîmes (trip time: 55 minutes). For more information and schedules, call ☎ **08-36-35-35-39.** If you're **driving** to Aigues-Mortes, take D979 south from Gallargues, or A9 from Montpellier or Nimes.

There's an **Office de Tourisme** at Porte de la Gardette (☎ **04-66-53-73-00**).

WHERE TO STAY

The **Restaurant Les Arcades** (see below) also rents rooms.

Hostellerie des Remparts. 6 place Anatole-France, 30220 Aigues-Mortes. ☎ **04-66-53-82-77.** Fax 04-66-53-73-77. 19 units. TEL. 300–475F ($54–$85.50) double. AE, DC, V.

Established about 300 years ago, this weather-worn inn lies at the foot of the Tour de Constance, adjacent to the medieval fortifications. Popular and often fully booked (especially in summer), it evokes the defensive atmosphere of the Middle Ages, albeit with charm and a sense of nostalgia. The simply furnished rooms are accessible via narrow stone staircases; 13 contain TVs. Breakfast is the only meal served.

✪ **Hôtel Les Templiers.** 23 rue de la République, 30220 Aigues-Mortes. Tel. **04-66-53-66-56.** Fax 04-66-53-69-61. 10 units. A/C TV TEL. 510-850 F ($91.80-$153) double. AE, MC, V. Closed Nov-Mar 1.

A gem of peace, tranquillity, and luxurious comfort, this is the town's leading inn; a stay here includes all the comforts of a private home. Protected by the ramparts built by Louis, king of France, this 17th-century residence has been tastefully converted to receive guests. The rooms are done in Provençal style, with just enough decorative objects to lend a homelike aura. You can relax in the courtyard, where you can also enjoy breakfast. Arrangements can be made to take half board at the Le Maguelone restaurant across the street, costing 600 F ($108) per person. The cuisine is very regional, with fresh products from the surrounding area used effectively.

Hôtel St-Louis. 10 rue de l'Amiral-Courbet, 30220 Aigues-Mortes. ☎ **04-66-53-72-68.** Fax 04-66-53-75-92. 22 units. MINIBAR TV TEL. 320–490F ($57.60–$88.20) double. AE, DC, MC, V. Parking 45F ($8.10). Closed Jan–Mar.

This small inn near place St-Louis offers attractively furnished but somewhat basic rooms—nevertheless, it's one of the most desirable addresses in town. The restaurant offers good regional cuisine that justifies its excellent reputation among local foodies; fixed-price menus range from 98F to 195F ($17.65 to $35.10).

WHERE TO DINE

Restaurant Les Arcades. 23 bd. Gambetta, 30220 Aigues-Mortes. ☎ **04-66-53-81-13.** Fax 04-66-53-75-46. Reservations recommended. Main courses 75–165F ($13.50–$29.70); fixed-price menus 128–195F ($23.05–35.10). AE, DC, MC, V. Tues 7:30–9:30pm, Wed–Sun noon–2pm and 7:30–9:45pm (also open Mon night July–Aug). Closed 2 weeks in Feb and 2 weeks in Nov. FRENCH.

This restaurant has several formal sections with ancient beamed ceilings or intricately fitted stone vaults. Almost as old as the nearby fortifications, the place is especially charming on sultry days, when the thickness of the masonry keeps the interior cool. Good food, served at reasonable prices, is likely to include fish soup, roasted monkfish in red-wine sauce, grilled filet of bull from the Camargue, and grilled duckling.

The owner also rents 10 large, comfortable rooms upstairs, each with air-conditioning, TV, and phone. A double is 480F ($86.40), breakfast included.

11 Montpellier

471 miles SW of Paris, 100 miles NW of Marseille, 31 miles SW of Nîmes

The capital of Mediterranean (or Lower) Languedoc, this ancient university city is still renowned for its medical school, founded in the 13th century. Nostradamus qualified as a doctor here, and even Rabelais studied at the school. Petrarch came to Montpellier in 1317, staying for 7 years.

Today Montpellier is a bustling metropolis, one of southern France's fastest-growing cities thanks to an influx of new immigrants. Except for some dreary suburbs, the city has a handsomely laid out core, with tree-flanked promenades, broad avenues, and historic monuments. Students make up a quarter of the population, giving the city a lively, animated feel. In recent years many high-tech corporations, including IBM, have settled in Montpellier.

ESSENTIALS

GETTING THERE Some 20 **trains** per day arrive from Avignon (trip time: 1 hour), 8 from Marseille (trip time: 1¾ hours), 1 every 2 hours from Toulouse (trip time: 2 hours), and 10 per day from Perpignan (trip time: 1½ hours). Eight trains per day arrive from Paris, calling for a change in Lyon (trip time: 4½ hours). For rail information and schedules, call ☎ **08-36-35-35-39.** Two **buses** a day arrive from Nîmes (trip time: 1¾ hours).

If you're **driving,** Montpellier lies off A9 heading west.

VISITOR INFORMATION The **Office de Tourisme** is at 30 av. Jean de Lattre de Tassigny (☎ **04-67-60-60-60**).

SPECIAL EVENTS From the end of June to the beginning of July, an array of classical and modern dance performances cascade into town for the **Festival International Montpellier Danse.** Tickets sell for 35F to 230F ($6.30 to $41.40) and can be purchased through the **Hôtel d'Assas,** 6 rue de la Vieille Aiguillerie (☎ **04-67-60-07-40**). Further information is available by calling ☎ **04-67-60-83-60.** In late July, the **Festival de Radio France et de Montpellier** presents a variety of orchestral music, jazz, and opera. Tickets range from 50F to 150F ($9 to $27) and can be purchased by calling ☎ **04-67-02-02-01;** call ☎ **04-67-61-66-81** for complete information.

EXPLORING THE TOWN

Called the Oxford of France because of its burgeoning academic community, Montpellier is a city of young people, as you'll notice if you sit at a cafe opening onto the heartbeat **place de la Comédie,** admiring the Théâtre, the 18th-century Fountain of the Three Graces, or whatever else amuses you. It's the living room of Montpellier, the ideal place to flirt, chat, people watch, cruise, or just hang out.

Before leaving town, take a stroll along the 17th-century **promenade du Peyrou,** a terraced park with views of the Cévennes and the Mediterranean. This is a broad esplanade constructed at the loftiest point of Montpellier. Opposite the entrance is an **Arc de Triomphe,** erected in 1691 to celebrate the victories of Louis XIV. In the center of the promenade is an equestrian statue of Louis XIV, and at the end, the **Château d'Eau,** a pavilion with Corinthian columns that serves as a monument to 18th-century classicism. Water is brought here by a conduit, nearly 9 miles long, and an aqueduct.

Cathédrale St-Pierre. Place St-Pierre. ☎ **04-67-66-04-12.** Free admission. Daily 9:30am–noon and 2:30–7pm.

The town's spiritual centerpiece was founded in 1364. Once associated with a Benedictine monastery, the cathedral suffered badly in religious wars. (After 1795 the monastery was occupied by the medical school.) Today it has a somewhat bleak western front with two towers and a canopied porch.

Jardin des Plantes. 163 rue Auguste-Broussonnet (reached from bd. Henri-IV). ☎ **04-67-63-43-22.** Free admission. Apr–Sept Tues–Sun 10am–7pm; Oct–Mar Mon–Fri 10am–5pm.

Paul Valéry met André Gide in the Jardin des Plantes, the oldest such garden in France, dating from the 16th century. This botanical garden, filled with exotic plants and a handful of greenhouses, was opened in 1593.

✪ **Musée Fabre.** 39 bd. Bonne-Nouvelle. ☎ **04-67-14-83-00.** Admission 20F ($3.60) adults, 10F ($1.80) students and children 11 and under. Tues–Fri 9am–5:30pm, Sat–Sun 9:30am–5pm.

One of France's great provincial art galleries occupies the former Hôtel de Massilian, where Molière once played for a season. The collection originated with an exhibition of the Royal Academy that was sent to Montpellier by Napoléon in 1803. Its most important works, however, were given by François Fabre, a Montpellier painter, in 1825. After Fabre's death, many other paintings from his collection were donated to the gallery. Several of these were of his own creation, but the more significant works were ones he had acquired—including Poussin's *Venus and Adonis* and Italian paintings like *The Mystical Marriage of Saint Catherine.* This generosity was followed by donations from other parties, notably Valedau, who in 1836 left his collection of Rubens, Gérard Dou, and Téniers.

WHERE TO STAY

The **Jardin des Sens** (see below) also rents rooms.

EXPENSIVE

Sofitel Antigone. 1 rue Pertuisanes, 34000 Montpellier. ☎ **04-67-99-72-72.** Fax 04-67-65-17-50. 91 units. A/C TV TEL. 760–960F ($136.80–$172.80) double; 1,400F ($252) suite. AE, DC, MC, V.

This hotel, built in 1991 in the heart of Montpellier, is the favorite of business travelers. In summer, however, it does quite a trade with visitors. It's particularly distinguished for its pool, which, along with a bar and breakfast room, occupies most of the top floor. The rooms are chain format but first class. The best accommodations are on a floor known as Privilège, where you get such extras as an all-marble bathroom. Some rooms are suitable for those with disabilities. It's a winning choice, with the most efficient staff in the city.

INEXPENSIVE

Hôtel du Parc. 8 rue Achille Bège, 34000 Montpellier. ☎ **04-67-41-16-49.** Fax 04-67-54-10-05. 19 units. A/C TV TEL. 295–390F ($53.10–$70.20) double. AE, V.

One of the town's more charming affordable choices lies in the heart of the city near the Palais des Congrès. It was a Languedocian residence in the 18th century but has since been turned into a hotel with a lot of grace notes and French provincial charm. The rooms have been carefully decorated and include several modern conveniences such as minibar and air-conditioning, not always found in Montpellier hotels. A garden and flowering terrace offer a venue for breakfast if you'd like to eat outside. Numerous restaurants surround the hotel.

✪ **La Maison Blanche.** 1796 av. de la Prompignane, 34000 Montpellier. ☎ **04-67-79-60-25.** Fax 04-67-79-53-39. 38 units. A/C TV TEL. 490F ($88.20) double; 780F ($140.40) suite. AE, DC, MC, V. A 5-minute drive southeast of Montpellier's center: Take bd. d'Antigone east until you reach the intersection with av. de la Pompignane and head north until you come to the hotel, on your right.

Few other hotels in the south of France can sport such a gingerbread and French Créole *Gone With the Wind* ambience. Built around 1990, it's a clapboard motel with ornate balconies and lattice-bordered gardens. The rooms are stylishly furnished in rattan and wicker. Parts of the interior, especially the dining room, might remind you of Louis XIII France more than Old Louisiana, but overall the setting is as charming and unusual as anything else in town. The in-house restaurant, open daily for lunch and dinner except Sunday and Monday nights, serves fixed-price menus from 95F to 150F ($17.10 to $27).

Les Arceaux. 33–35 bd. des Arceaux, 34000 Montpellier. ☎ **04-67-92-03-03.** Fax 04-67-92-05-09. 18 units. TV TEL. 285–315F ($51.30–$56.70) double. MC, V.

A hotel has stood at this prime location, right off the renowned promenade du Peyrou, since the turn of the century. The rooms are pleasantly but simply furnished, and a shaded terrace adjoins the hotel. Breakfast is the only meal served.

Ulysse. 338 av. de St-Maur, 34000 Montpellier. ☎ **04-67-02-02-30.** Fax 04-67-02-16-50. 28 units. MINIBAR TV TEL. 350F ($63) double. AE, DC, V. From bd. d'Antigone, head north along av. Jean-Mermoz to rue de la Pépinière; continue right for a short distance, then take a sharp left at the first intersection, which leads to av. de St-Maur.

One of the city's better bargains, Ulysse delivers a lot of bang for your buck. Despite the simplicity of the place, the owners have worked hard—on a budget—to make it as stylish as possible. Each room is individually decorated; the furnishings are original wrought-iron designs, functional but with a certain flair. The many in-room comforts include fully equipped bathrooms and extra features like a minibar, unusual for a budget hotel. The housekeeping is first rate, even though the prices aren't.

WHERE TO DINE

La Réserve Rimbaud. 820 av. de St-Maur. ☎ **04-67-72-52-53.** Reservations recommended. Main courses 100–150F ($18–$27); fixed-price menus 160–380F ($28.80–$68.40). AE, DC, MC, V. Tues–Sun noon–2pm, Tues–Sat 8-10pm. Closed Jan–Mar 20. Take N113 (av. de Nîmes) northeast toward Nîmes and follow it to the intersection with av. St-Lazare, then turn left; the restaurant is on the right. FRENCH.

The most memorable restaurant in town is housed in a bulky, rectangular manor house built in 1835 by a prosperous local family, the Rimbauds. It offers only about 30 seats in a setting that might have been plucked from the early 1900s. Menu items change with the season but are likely to include *gigot de mer* (a slab of monkfish with local herbs), warm foie gras with apples, fricassée of sole with baby vegetables, and a thin-crusted *croustillant aux pommes* served with English cream.

Note: If you request it before you begin your meal, the staff will rent you one of their rowboats for 60F ($10.80) per hour, so you can float like a character in one of Renoir's paintings beside the river's verdant banks.

Le Chandelier. Immeuble La Coupole Antigone. ☎ **04-67-15-34-38.** Reservations required. Main courses 92–205F ($16.55–$36.90); fixed-price menus 150F ($27) at lunch, 280–335F ($50.40–$60.30) at dinner. AE, DC, V. Tues–Sat noon–1:30pm, Mon–Sat 7:30–9:30pm. FRENCH.

This panoramic restaurant with large windows is a modern showcase for the cuisine of Gilbert Furland. He searches for "temptations of the palate," which means that you'll find some unusual flavor combinations, with ragoût of lobster his most delightful dish. His menu changes frequently but may include smoked eel mousse with mint-flavored mussels, lamb sweetbreads with crayfish in vinaigrette sauce, and a mosaic of hare with foie gras.

✪ **Le Jardin des Sens.** 11 av. St-Lazare, 34000 Montpellier. ☎ **04-67-79-63-38.** Reservations required. Main courses 180–250F ($32.40–$45); fixed-price lunch (Mon–Fri) 210F ($37.80); fixed-price menus 370–580F ($66.60–$104.40). AE, MC, V. Mon–Sat noon–2:30pm and 7–10pm. FRENCH.

If we could award more than one star, we'd grant two to this citadel of fine cuisine. The chefs, twins Laurent and Jacques Pourcel, have taken Montpellier by storm. Michelin has awarded them three stars, thus bestowing its divine blessing. Postnouvelle reigns here. The rich bounty of Languedoc is transformed into imaginative meals that often seem flawless, so it's no wonder the other restaurateurs of Montpellier are wishing these twins had settled in some other city. An appropriate starter might be bonbons of foie gras with new potatoes. A *tarte fine* with tomatoes, roasted monkfish, and essence of thyme is memorable, as is a filet of pigeon stuffed with pistachios. A dessert specialty is a gratin of limes with slices of pineapple en confit.

The Jardin des Sens also rents 12 deluxe guest rooms and 2 suites, each designed in cutting-edge modernist style by Bruno Borrione, a colleague of Philippe Starck. They cost 800F ($144) for a double and 1,600F to 2,500F ($288 to $450) for a suite.

✪ **L'Olivier.** 12 rue Aristide-Olivier. ☎ **04-67-92-86-28.** Reservations recommended. Main courses 68–140F ($12.25–$25.20); fixed-price menus 160–198F ($28.80–$35.65). AE, DC, MC, V. Tues–Sat noon–1:30pm and 7:30–9:30pm. Closed Aug and holidays. FRENCH.

No restaurant, with the exception of the Jardin des Sens, has improved more than this. Chef Michel Breton is making his name known in the restaurant guides to the south of France. The decor is something out of a 1950s boudoir, but you come here not for background, but for Breton's "creative statements." The menu might include salmon with oysters, warm monkfish terrine, and salad of lamb sweetbreads with extract of truffles. The welcome is warmhearted and sincere.

MONTPELLIER AFTER DARK

After the sun sets, head for **place Jean-Jaurès, rue de Verdun,** and **rue des Ecoles Laïques,** or take a walk down **rue de la Loge** for its carnival atmosphere of talented jugglers, mimes, and musical artists.

Le Notes en Bulles, 19 rue des Ecoles Laïques (☎ 04-67-60-38-21), is a great bohemian way to ease into the evening. Here you can loosen up with the locals before continuing on to something a bit more serious, like **Rockstore,** 20 rue de Verdun (☎ 04-67-58-70-10), with its 1950s rock memorabilia and live concerts drawing lots of students. Then walk up a flight of stairs to its top-story disco, which pounds out techno and rock into the wee hours. The cover for the disco is 50F ($9).

At the exotic cocktail bar **Viva Brazil,** 7 rue de Verdun (☎ 04-67-58-63-33), you can chop your way through the lush rain-forest vegetation and friendly natives to reach the mirrored sanctuary of the dance floor. For the best jazz and blues in town, check out **JAM,** 100 rue Ferdinand-de-Lesseps (☎ 04-67-58-30-30). In a noisy, smoky, and even gritty space, its regular concerts attract jazz enthusiasts from miles around. Concert tickets average 50F ($9).

Gays and lesbians start out an evening of light-hearted antics at the predominantly male **THT,** 10 rue St-Firmin (tel. 04-67-66-12-52), where a huge dance party breaks out on Saturday nights. If you're still wired around midnight, head over to **Le Rome Club,** 77 Mas de Fugières à Mauguio, in the shopping center (☎ 04-67-22-22-70), with its two levels and gargantuan dance floor, a good mix of men and women, and techno and rock music with a Diana Ross song every now and then.

You can enjoy an evening of opera or orchestra at the **Corum,** esplanade de Charles-de-Gaulle (☎ 04-67-02-02-01). For complete ticket information and schedules, contact the **Opéra Comédie,** place de la Comédie (☎ 04-67-60-19-99).

12 Nîmes

440 miles S of Paris, 27 miles W of Avignon

Nîmes, the ancient Nemausus, is one of the finest places in the world for wandering among Roman relics. The city grew to prominence during the reign of Caesar Augustus (27 B.C.–A.D. 14). Today it possesses one of the best-preserved Roman amphitheaters in the world and a near-perfect Roman temple. The city of 135,000 is more like Provence than Languedoc, in which it lies. There's a touch of Pamplona, Spain, here in the festivals of the *corridas* (bullfights) at the arena. The Spanish image is even stronger at night, when the bodegas fill, usually with students, drinking sangria and listening to the sounds of flamenco.

By 1860 the togas of Nîmes's citizenry had long given way to denim, the cloth de Nîmes. An Austrian immigrant, Leví-Strauss, exported this heavy fabric to California for use as work-pants material for gold diggers in those boomtown years. The rest, as they say, is history.

ESSENTIALS

GETTING THERE   Nîmes has bus and train service from the rest of France and is near several autoroutes. It lies on the main rail line between Marseille and Bordeaux. Six trains a day arrive from Paris, taking 4½ hours. For **train** information and schedules, call ☎ 08-36-35-35-39. If you're **driving,** Nîmes can be reached from Lyon along A7 south to the town of Orange, connecting here to A9 into Nîmes.

VISITOR INFORMATION   The **Office de Tourisme** is at 6 rue Auguste (☎ 04-66-67-29-11).

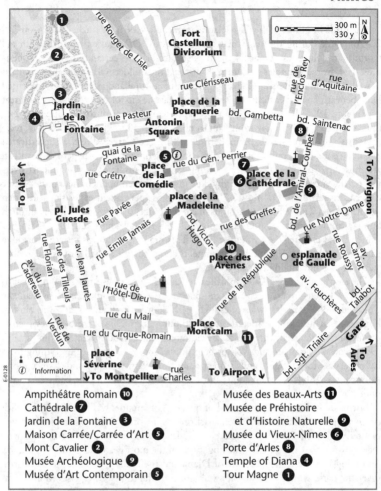

Ampithéâtre Romain ⑩	Musée des Beaux-Arts ⑪
Cathédrale ⑦	Musée de Préhistoire
Jardin de la Fontaine ③	et d'Histoire Naturelle ⑨
Maison Carrée/Carrée d'Art ⑤	Musée du Vieux-Nîmes ⑥
Mont Cavalier ②	Porte d'Arles ⑧
Musée Archéologique ⑨	Temple of Diana ④
Musée d'Art Contemporain ⑤	Tour Magne ①

SPECIAL EVENTS   Festivals, parties, and cultural events rule the summer nightlife scene in Nîmes. Once the warm weather hits, all sorts of activities take place at the arena, including concerts and theater under the stars. The Office de Tourisme has a complete listing of events and schedules, or you can contact the **Bureau de Location des Arènes,** 1 rue Alexandre-Ducros (☎ **04-66-67-28-02**). All of Nîmes's central squares burst forth with music and dancing on Thursday nights during July and August as artists, musicians, and all kinds of revelers gather in celebration of **Marchés du Soir,** where artisans sell their handicrafts.

EXPLORING THE CITY

If you really want to see all of the city's monuments and museums, consider buying a **billet global,** sold at the ticket counter of any of the local attractions. It provides access to all the cultural sites described below over a 3-day period, for an all-inclusive fee of 60F ($10.80) for adults and 30 F ($5.40) for students and children 15 and under.

The pride of Nîmes is the ✪ **Maison Carrée,** place de la Comédie (☎ **04-66-36-26-76**), built during the reign of Caesar Augustus. On a raised platform with tall Corinthian columns, it's one of the most beautiful, and certainly one of the best-preserved, Roman temples of Europe. It inspired the builders of La Madeleine in Paris as well as Thomas Jefferson. A changing roster of cultural and art exhibits is presented here, beneath an authentically preserved roof that the city of Nîmes repaired, at great expense, in 1996. It's open November to April daily from 9am to 12:30pm and 2 to 6pm, May to October daily from 9am to noon and 2:30 to 7pm. Admission is free.

Across the square stands its modern-day twin, the **Carrée d'Art,** a sophisticated research center and exhibition space that contains a library, a newspaper kiosk, and an art museum. Its understated design from 1993 was inspired by (but doesn't overpower) the ancient monument nearby. The most visible component here is the **Musée d'Art Contemporain** (☎ **04-66-76-35-35**), whose permanent expositions are often supplemented with temporary exhibits of contemporary art. It's open Tuesday through Sunday from 10am to 5:30pm, charging 24F ($4.30) for adults and 18F ($3.25) for students and children 14 and under. *Note:* This modern building's terrace provides a panorama of most of the ancient monuments and medieval churches of Nîmes, above all of the neighborhood's roaring traffic.

The elliptically shaped ✪ **Amphithéâtre Romain,** place des Arènes (☎ **04-66-76-72-77**), a better-preserved twin to the one at Arles, is far more complete than the Colosseum of Rome. It's two stories high, each floor with 60 arches, and was built of huge stones painstakingly fitted together without mortar. One of the best preserved of the arenas from ancient times, it once held more than 20,000 spectators who came to see gladiatorial combats and wolf or boar hunts. Today it's used for everything from ballet recitals to bullfights and is open daily from 9am to noon and 2 to 5:30pm. Admission is 26F ($4.70) for adults and 20F ($3.60) for students and children 15 and under.

Jardin de la Fontaine, at the end of quai de la Fontaine, was laid out in the 18th century, using the ruins of a Roman shrine as an ornamental centerpiece. It was planted with rows of chestnuts and elms, adorned with statuary and urns, and intersected by grottoes and canals—making it one of the most beautiful gardens in France. Adjoining it is the ruined **Temple of Diana** and the remains of some Roman baths. Over the park, within a 10-minute walk north of the town center, rises Mont Cavalier, a low but rocky hill on top of which rises the sturdy bulk of the **Tour Magne,** the city's oldest Roman monument. You can climb it for 12F ($2.15) for adults and 10 F ($1.80) for students and children 14 and under; it offers a panoramic view over Nîmes and its environs. It's open May to September daily from 9am to 6pm, October to April, daily from 9am to 5pm.

Nîmes is home to a great many museums. The largest and best respected, **Musée des Beaux-Arts,** rue Cité-Foulc (☎ **04-66-67-38-21**), contains French paintings and sculptures from the 17th to the 20th centuries as well as Flemish, Dutch, and Italian works from the 15th to the 18th centuries. Seek out in particular one of G. B. Moroni's masterpieces, *La Calomnie d'Apelle,* and a well-preserved Gallo-Roman mosaic. The museum is open Tuesday through Sunday from 11am to 6pm. Admission is 26F ($4.70) for adults and 20F ($3.60) for students and children 14 and under.

If time allows, visit the **Musée du Vieux-Nîmes,** place de la Cathédrale (☎ **04-66-36-00-64**), housed in an episcopal palace from the 1700s. It's rich in antiques, including pieces from the 17th century. The museum is open Tuesday through Sunday from 11am to 6pm, charging 26F ($4.70) for adults and 20F ($3.60) for children.

One of the city's busiest thoroughfares, boulevard de l'Amiral-Courbet, leads to the **Porte d'Arles**—the remains of a monumental gate built by the Romans during the reign of Augustus. Farther along, contained in the same stately building at 13 bis bd. l'Amiral-Courbet, are the **Musée de Préhistoire et d'Histoire Naturelle** (☎ **04-66-67-39-14**) and the **Musée Archéologique** (☎ **04-66-67-25-57**). Both are open Tuesday through Sunday from 11am to 6pm; a fee of 26F ($4.70) for adults and 20F ($3.60) for children admits you to both museums.

Outside the city, 14 miles to the northeast, the well-preserved, much-photographed **pont du Gard** spans the Gard River and was built without mortar; its huge stones have evolved into one of the region's most vivid reminders of the ancient glory and technical competence of the Romans. Consisting of three tiers of arches arranged into gracefully symmetrical patterns, it dates from about 19 B.C. Frédéric Mistral, national poet of Provence and Languedoc, recorded a legend alleging that the devil constructed the bridge providing he could claim the soul of the first person to cross it. To visit it, take highway N86 from Nîmes to a point 2 miles from the village of Remoulins, where signs are posted announcing its position.

If you'd rather concentrate on serious shopping, head to the center of town and **rue du Général-Perrier, rue des Marchands, rue du Chapitre,** and the pedestrian streets of **rue de l'Aspic** and **rue de la Madeleine.** You'll find a Sunday-morning **flea market** beginning at 8am in the Stade des Castières, on the boulevard Périphérique that encircles Nîmes.

One of the best purchases you can make in Nîmes, especially if you're not continuing east into Provence, is a *santon.* These wood or clay figurines are sculpted into a cast of characters from Provençal country life and can be collected together to create a uniquely country-French nativity scene. For a selection of santons in various sizes, visit the **Boutique Provençale,** 10 place de la Maison Carrée (☎ **04-66-67-81-71**), or **Au Papillon Bleu,** 15 rue du Général-Perrier (☎ **04-66-67-48-58**).

WHERE TO STAY

Atria Nîmes Centre. 5 bd. de Prague, 3000 Nîmes. ☎ **04-66-76-56-56.** Fax 04-66-76-56-59. 119 units. A/C MINIBAR TV TEL. 520–540F ($93.60–$97.20) double; 800F ($144) suite. AE, DC, MC, V.

Opened in mid-1995, this affordable member of the nationwide Novotel chain has a great location in the heart of Nîmes, adjacent to the ancient arena. Its six floors wrap around a carefully landscaped inner courtyard, providing a garden setting. Each room contains a double bed, a single bed (which converts into a sofa), a well-equipped bathroom, and a wide writing desk. The hotel offers a bar and an attractive restaurant, Les Sept Collines, which is open daily for lunch and dinner.

Note: Nîmes contains another Novotel, which is older and more remotely located on the southern perimeter of town: the **Novotel Nîmes,** chemin de l'Hostellerie, boulevard Périphérique Sud, 30000 Nîmes (☎ **04-66-84-60-20**). Here 96 rooms sell at roughly equivalent rates, with the added advantage of having an on-site pool.

Hôtel l'Amphithéâtre. 4 rue des Arènes, 30000 Nîmes. Tel. **04-66-67-28-51.** Fax 04-66-67-07-79. 17 units. TV TEL. 220–260F ($39.60–$46.80) double; 290F ($52.20) triple or quad. AE, MC, V. Closed Dec 20–Jan 25.

Behind the Arènes, this hotel dating from the 18th century sits on a narrow, quiet street. Each rather plain room has its own color scheme and is furnished with antiques or modern pieces.

Imperator Concorde. Quai de la Fontaine, 30900 Nîmes. ☎ **04-66-21-90-30.** Fax 04-66-67-70-25. www.concorde-hotels.com. 65 units. A/C MINIBAR TV TEL. 600–680F ($108–$122.40) double; 850–1,800F ($153–$324) suite. AE, DC, MC, V. Parking 70F ($12.60).

This leading hotel is near the Roman monuments, opposite the Jardin de la Fontaine. With a recent major renovation, it has been much improved. You can order lunch in the hotel's enticing rear gardens. The best rooms have Provençal pieces; others have been renewed in a traditional way to preserve their character.

Mercure Nîmes-Ouest. Parc Hôtellier Ville Active, 30900 Nîmes. ☎ **04-66-70-48-00.** Fax 04-66-70-48-01. www.hotelweb.fr. 98 units. A/C MINIBAR TV TEL. 490–610F ($88.20–$109.80) double; 800–850F ($144–$153) suite. AE, DC, MC, V. From the town center, take bd. du Sergent-Triare southwest until you reach the intersection of A9 (also marked N113) and follow this for about 2 miles.

This six-story hotel was built in 1974 as a four-star Sofitel, then downgraded to the three-star Mercure you see today. Though it's convenient if you've got a car, don't come here seeking old-world charm. The rooms are larger than you'd expect from the average three-star property. Facilities include a pool with an adjacent sun terrace, a tennis court, and a well-managed restaurant, Le Mazet, serving grilled meats and regional dishes.

New Hôtel La Baume. 21 rue Nationale, 30000 Nîmes. ☎ **04-66-76-28-42.** Fax 04-66-76-28-45. www.new-hotel.com. E-mail: info@new-hotel.com. 34 units. A/C MINIBAR TV TEL. 390–400F ($70.20–$72) double. AE, DC, MC, V.

Our favorite nest in Nîmes was created in a 17th-century mansion. The designers were careful to preserve the original architectural heritage during its creation, and the result is a winning combination of modern and traditional. The 24 rooms are fitted with exceptional charm, worthy of a Venetian palace. They're equipped with thoughtful extras like hair dryers, and the plumbing is state of the art. The hotel restaurant is also worth a visit, turning out such dishes as fresh salmon flavored with anise and chicken saltimbocca with ham.

WHERE TO DINE

The dining room at the **New Hôtel La Baume** (see above) is also a good choice.

✪ **Alexandre.** Rte. de l'Aéroport de Garons. ☎ **04-66-70-08-99.** Reservations required. Main courses 155–190F ($27.90–$34.20); fixed-price menus 275–435F ($49.50–$78.30). AE, DC, V. Tues–Sun noon–1:30pm, Tues–Sat 7:30–9:30pm. Closed Feb. From the town center, take rue de la République southwest to av. Jean-Jaurès, then head south and follow the signs to the airport in the direction of Garons. FRENCH.

The most charming, amusing, and competent restaurant around is on the outskirts of Nîmes. Its verdant setting is the elegant and rustic domain of Michel Kayser, an exceptional chef who adheres to classic tradition, with subtle improvements. He's assisted in the dining room by his charming wife, Monique. Menu items are designed to amuse as well as delight the palate. Examples are *île flottante* with truffles and *velouté* of cèpe mushrooms, roasted pigeon stuffed with purée of vegetables and liver of pigeon, and the region's most sophisticated version of an old country recipe, *pieds et paquets*. Especially appealing is the cheese trolley loaded with esoteric goat cheeses from the region and worthy cow cheeses from other parts of France. The dessert trolley is incredibly hard to resist.

Restaurant au Chapon Fin. 3 rue du Château-Fadaise. ☎ **04-66-67-34-73.** Reservations required. Main courses 79–129F ($14.20–$23.20); fixed-price menus 72F ($12.95) at lunch, 120F ($21.60) at dinner. AE, MC, V. Mon–Fri noon–2pm, Mon–Sat 7:30–10pm. Closed 2 weeks in Aug. FRENCH.

This tavern/restaurant, on a little square behind St-Paul's, is run by M. and Mme Grangier. It has beamed ceilings, small lamps, and a white-and-black stone floor. Madame Grangier is from Alsace, but don't scour the menu for many Alsatian specialties—it's more traditional and regional. From the à la carte menu you can order foie gras with truffles, coq au vin (chicken with wine), and entrecôte flambéed with morels. The proprietor makes his own *confit d'oie* (goose preserved in its own fat) from birds shipped in from Alsace.

Wine Bar Chez Michel. 11 place de la Couronne. ☎ **04-66-76-19-59.** Reservations not required. Main courses 55–130F ($9.90–$23.40); fixed-price menus 77F ($13.85) at lunch, 80–130F ($14.40–$23.40) at dinner. AE, MC, V. Tues–Sat noon–2pm and Mon–Sat 7pm– midnight. FRENCH.

This place is paneled with mahogany and has leather banquettes evocative of a turn- of-the-century California saloon. Choices include an array of salads and platters, plus dishes such as magrêt of duckling and contrefilet of steak with roquefort sauce. At lunch, you can dine on the terrace in the renovated courtyard and order a quick menu, which includes appetizer, main course, and two glasses of wine. The restaurateur extra- ordinaire Michel Hermet also makes his own wine as of the harvest of 1995, the first bottles of which were sold in May 1996. There are more than 300 other wines to choose from, by the glass or pitcher.

NIMES AFTER DARK

Popular with the intellectual set is the **Haddock Café,** 13 rue de l'Agau (☎ **04-66- 67-86-57**), with its weekly live rock concerts. But if you simply want to tank down some brew and have a rip-roaring good time, go to the **Queen's Beer,** 1 bis rue Jean- Reboul (☎ **04-66-67-81-10**).

All the town's jazz aficionados know that **Le Diagonal,** 41 bis rue Emile-Jamais (☎ **04-66-21-70-01**), hosts the area's best jazz and blues concerts. The flashy, sexy, and hip **La Comédie,** 28 rue Jean-Reboul (☎ **04-66-76-13-66**), is the hands-down best for dancing and attracts a pretty crowd of youthful danceaholics. A little less flashy, but a lot more fun, **Lulu,** 10 impasse de la Curaterie (☎ **04-66-36-28-20**), is the gay and lesbian stronghold in Nîmes. The cover at both dance clubs ranges from 50F to 70F ($9 to $12.60).

Other streets to explore for a healthy dose of good times are **impasse Porte-de- France** and **boulevard Victor-Hugo.**

20 Provence: In the Footsteps of Cézanne & van Gogh

Provence has been called a bridge between the past and the present, where yesterday blends with today in a quiet, often melancholy way. Peter Mayle's best-selling *A Year in Provence* and *Toujours Provence* have played no small part in the burgeoning popularity this sunny corner of southern France has enjoyed in recent years.

The Greeks and Romans first filled the landscape with cities boasting Hellenic theaters, Roman baths, amphitheaters, and triumphal arches. These were followed in medieval times by Romanesque fortresses and Gothic cathedrals. In the 19th century, the light and landscapes of Provence attracted illustrious painters like Cézanne and van Gogh.

Provence has its own language and its own customs. The region is bounded on the north by the Dauphine, on the west by the Rhône, on the east by the Alps, and on the south by the Mediterranean. We'll focus in the next chapter on the part of Provence known as the glittering Côte d'Azur or French Riviera.

Note: For more extensive coverage of this region, see our *Frommer's Provence & the Riviera.*

REGIONAL CUISINE   Part of the charm of Provence lies in its distinctive cuisine, which successfully marries the traditions of the mountains and the seaside. The earliest contributors to this were the ancient Italians, for strong comparisons can be made between the Provençal and the Italian emphasis on fresh fish and vegetables, olive oil, and garlic.

The best of Provençal produce includes melons from Cavaillon and elongated tube-shaped onions known as *éschalotes-bananes.* The most famous vegetable dish is *ratatouille,* a stew of tomatoes, garlic, eggplant, zucchini, onions, and peppers, liberally sprinkled with olive oil and black pepper. A slightly different version is *soupe au pistou,* with the addition of basil, pounded garlic, vermicelli, string beans, and grilled tomatoes.

Each town along the Provence coast seems to have a fish-stew specialty. In Nice, stockfish is used in *stocaficada. Bourride* is made with whitefish, garlic, onions, tomatoes, herbs, egg yolks, saffron, and grated orange rind. Toulon has its *esquinado,* with saltwater crabs, vinegar, water, and pulverized mussels. And the best and most authentic *bouillabaisse* is from Marseille.

Several Provençal meat dishes are welcome substitutes for the ubiquitous fish: *daube de boeuf* (beef stew); *fricassée de pintade* (guinea fowl), perhaps served with a mild purée of sweet garlic; and *fricassée* or

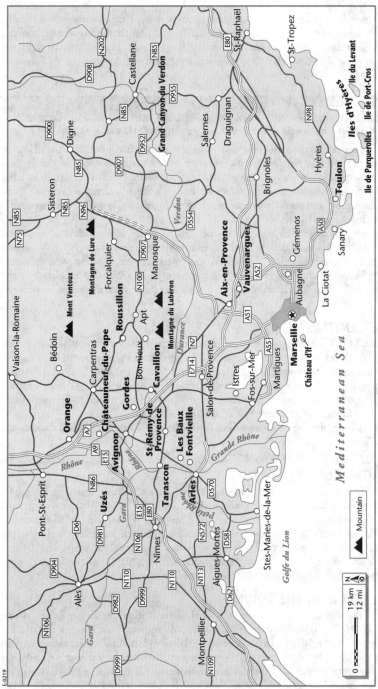

Mountain ▲

0 [ ] 19 km
[ ] 12 mi
N

E-0219

ragoût de cabri (goat). Provence boasts scores of savory cheeses, among them Picadon, Pélardon, and St-Félicien; dozens of pastries and breads; and many scented honeys.

The regional wines are almost as diverse as the cuisine. They include the vast family of the Côtes-du-Rhône, the Gigondas, Châteauneuf-du-Pape, and Château de Fonsalette.

1 Orange

409 miles S of Paris, 34 miles NE of Nîmes, 75 miles NW of Marseille, 16 miles S of Avignon

Orange gets its name from the days when it was a dependency of the Dutch House of Orange-Nassau, not because it's set in a citrus belt. Actually, the last orange grove departed 2,000 years ago. The juice that flows in Orange today comes from its fabled vineyards, which turn out a Côtes du Rhône vintage, and many caves are spread throughout the district, some of which offer *dégustations* to paying customers. (The tourist office will provide you with a list.)

Overlooking the Valley of the Rhône, today's Orange, with a somewhat sleepy population of about 30,000, boasts Europe's third-largest extant triumphal arch and best-preserved Roman theater. Louis XIV, who toyed with the idea of moving the theater to Versailles, said: "It is the finest wall in my kingdom." UNESCO has placed the arch on its World Cultural and Natural Heritage List in the hope that it can be preserved "forever."

ESSENTIALS

GETTING THERE   Orange sits on some of the major French north–south rail and highway arteries, so getting here is easy. Some 17 **trains** per day arrive from Avignon (trip time: 17 minutes) and 23 trains per day from Marseille (trip time: 1½ hours). From Paris, there are 21 trains per day (trip time: 4½ hours) by TGV, which requires a transfer at either Valence or Avignon to a conventional train into Orange. For rail information and schedules, call ☎ **08-36-35-35-39.**

If you're **driving** to Orange from Paris, take A6 south to Lyon, then connect with A7 into Orange.

VISITOR INFORMATION   The **Office de Tourisme** is on cours Aristide-Briand (☎ **04-90-34-70-88**).

SPECIAL EVENTS   From mid-July to mid-August, a drama, dance, and music festival called **Les Chorégies d'Orange** takes place at the Théâtre Antique. For information or tickets, visit the permanent office on place Sylvain, adjacent to the antique theater, or call ☎ **04-90-34-15-52.** Events for 1997 included *Tristan und Isolde* (presented in vocal and orchestral form but without costumes), *Turandot*, and *Lucia di Lammermoor.* Concert tickets range from 30F to 520F ($5.40 to $93.60); opera tickets, from 180F to 900F ($32.40 to $162).

EXPLORING THE TOWN

In the southern part of town, the ✪ **Théâtre Antique,** place des Frères-Mounet (☎ **04-90-51-17-60**), dates from the days of Augustus. Built into the side of a hill, it once held 8,000 spectators in tiered seats divided into three sections based on class. Carefully restored, the nearly 350-foot-long and 125-foot-high theater is noted for its fine acoustics and is used today for outdoor entertainment. It's open daily, April to September from 9am to 6:30pm and October to March from 9am to noon and 1:30 to 5pm. Admission is 30F ($5.40) for adults, 25F ($4.50) for children and students, and free for children 9 and under.

To the west of the theater once stood one of the biggest temples in Gaul, which, with a gymnasium and the theater, formed one of the greatest buildings in the empire. Across the street on place des Frères-Mounet, the **Musée Municipal d'Orange,** place du Théâtre-Antique (☎ **04-90-51-18-24**), displays fragments excavated in the arena. Your ticket to the ancient theater will also admit you to this museum, which is open daily, April to September from 9:30am to 7pm and October to March from 9:30am to noon and 1:30 to 5:30pm.

Even older than the theater is the ✪ **Arc de Triomphe** on avenue de l'Arc-de-Triomphe. It has decayed, but its sculptural decorations and other elements are still fairly well preserved. Built to honor the conquering legions of Caesar, it rises 72 feet and is nearly 70 feet wide. Composed of a trio of arches held up by Corinthian columns, it was used as a dungeon for prisoners in the Middle Ages.

Before leaving Orange, head for the hilltop park, **Colline St-Eutrope,** for a view of the surrounding valley with its mulberry plantations.

After exploring the town itself, you might drive south for 8 miles along A9 to **Châteauneuf-du-Pape,** where you can have lunch (any day but Monday) at the **Hostellerie du Château des Fines-Roches,** route d'Avignon (☎ **04-90-83-70-23**). Although it was built in the 19th century, it looks feudal, thanks to its many medieval features. If you're pressing on to Avignon, it's only another 8 miles south along any of at least three highways (each marked AVIGNON).

WHERE TO STAY

Hôtel Louvre et Terminus. 89 av. Frédéric-Mistral, 84100 Orange. ☎ **04-90-34-10-08.** Fax 04-90-34-68-71. 34 units. TV TEL. 320–390F ($53.45–$65.15) double; 500–650F ($90–$117) suite. AE, DC, MC, V. Parking 30F ($5.40) in garage.

Surrounded by a garden terrace, this conservatively decorated Logis de France offers good value in a much-renovated building begun around 1900. More than half the rooms are air-conditioned (you can cool off in the pool as well). The hotel also has a simple but worthy restaurant, serving both lunch and dinner daily.

Mercure Orange. 80 rte. de Caderousse, 84100 Orange. ☎ **04-90-34-24-10.** Fax 04-90-34-85-48. 99 units. MINIBAR TV TEL. 470–595F ($84.60–$107.10) double. AE, DC, MC, V. Drive half a mile west of Orange's center, following the directions to Caderousse.

This comfortable modern hotel lies about a mile west of the edge of the city, in a 22-year-old building whose wings curve around a landscaped courtyard. Its well-furnished rooms are arranged around a series of gardens, the largest of which contains a pool. Fixed-price menus are served in the poolside restaurant. This is your best bet for general overnight comfort far from the madding crowd. It was completely renovated in 1997.

WHERE TO DINE

Le Parvis. 3 cours Pourtoules. ☎ **04-90-34-82-00.** Reservations required. Main courses 65–110F ($11.70–$19.80); fixed-price menus 98–225F ($17.65–$40.50). AE, DC, V. Tues–Sun noon–2:30pm, Tues–Sat 7:30–9:30pm. Closed Sun dinner and Mon year-round and Nov 1–15. FRENCH.

Jean-Michel Berengier sets the best table in Orange, though the dining room is rather austere. He bases his cuisine not only on well-selected vegetables but also on the best ingredients from "mountain or sea." Try his escalope of braised sea bass with fennel or feuilleté of asparagus. A year-round can't-miss dish is the chef's foie gras, which could be flavorfully followed by lamb prepared according to the season. (The staff prides itself on dozens of preparations.) The service is efficient and polite. A special children's menu is offered for 65F ($11.70).

Shopping for *Brocante* in Provence

There's a big difference between antiques and fun old junk in France—they even have different names. If you're into serious purchases, you may want to stick to regular and well-established antiques stores, which are found in great abundance all over France, though concentrated mainly in Paris, naturally.

But if you prefer something more affordable, and your idea of fun is a flea market or yard sale, then you really want *brocante*. Brocante is also sold all over France; it's often featured at the regular market in town on a specific day (the markets in Cannes are a good example; see chapter 21).

If you find yourself in Provence on a Sunday, head out bright and early (9am) for **Isle-sur-la-Sorgue,** a small village that specializes in brocante. The town lies 14 miles east of Avignon, 7 miles north of Cavaillon, and 26 miles south of Orange. Though there's a brocante market on both Saturday and Sunday, Sunday is much more fun because there's also a food market. *Warning:* Everything is over by 1pm.

If you're driving, try grabbing a parking space alongside the supermarket, Marché U. The town gets jammed, especially on Sunday. The Sorgue River isn't much bigger than a canal—the heart of town lies on the far side of the river, spanned by many footbridges. The brocante is on the near side of the river, a little farther downstream from the Marché U. If you drive by and shrug at the small number of dealers who are actually outside in the street and on the curb, be aware that every building on the side of the street facing the river hosts a warehouse filled with more dealers and more loot.

Although the prices here aren't the lowest in France, this is a serious market. The market and stores offer top goods, frequently sold to dealers, and shipping can be arranged.

For lunch, there's (surprisingly for such a small place) a Michelin-starred restaurant: **La Prévôté,** 4 rue J.-J.-Rousseau (☎ **04-90-38-57-29**). You should make your reservation even before arriving in town. In the rear of a flower-filled courtyard, chef Roland Mercier wows shoppers and locals with sublime cuisine. His cannelloni filled with fresh salmon and goat cheese is reason enough to cross the river. A crème brûlée of sea urchins is aromatically served with truffles; his tender and perfectly cooked duckling is flavored with honey from bees that flew over Provençal fields of lavender. The pièce de résistance is his hot chocolate soufflé. Lunch costs from 125F ($22.50), with dinners beginning at 210F ($37.80). Closed November, Sunday nights from October to June, and Mondays year-round.

NEARBY ACCOMMODATIONS & DINING

✪ **Château de Rochegude.** 26790 Rochegude. ☎ **04-75-97-21-10.** Fax 04-75-04-89-87. 29 units. A/C MINIBAR TV TEL. 1,300F ($234) double; 2,000–2,500F ($360–$450) suite. AE, DC, V. It lies 8 miles north of Orange; take D976, following the signs toward Gap and Rochegude.

This Relais & Châteaux stands on 25 acres of parkland. The stone castle is at the edge of a hill, surrounded by Rhône vineyards. The 12th-century turreted residence has been renovated by a series of distinguished owners, ranging from the pope to the dauphin. The current owners have made many 20th-century additions, but ancient touches survive. Each room is done in traditional Provençal style, with fabrics and furniture influenced by that region's 18th- and 19th-century traditions.

Dining: The food and service are exceptional. You can enjoy meals surrounded by flowering plants in the stately dining room. There are also a barbecue by the pool and sunny terraces where refreshments are served. In the restaurant, fixed-price menus are 200F ($36) at weekday lunches; other menus (available at both lunch and dinner) are 300F to 500F ($54 to $90).

2 Avignon

425 miles S of Paris, 50 miles NW of Aix-en-Provence, 66 miles NW of Marseille

In the 14th century, Avignon was the capital of Christendom—the popes lived here during what the Romans called the Babylonian Captivity. The legacy left by that court of splendor and magnificence makes Avignon one of the most interesting and beautiful of Europe's medieval cities.

Today this walled city of some 100,000 residents is a major stopover on the route from Paris to the Mediterranean. Lately, it has become increasingly known as a cultural center. Artists and painters in growing numbers have been moving here, especially to rue des Teinturiers. Experimental theaters, painting galleries, and cinemas have brought increasing diversity to the inner city. The popes are long gone, but life goes on exceedingly well.

ESSENTIALS

GETTING THERE   Avignon is a junction for bus routes throughout the region, and train service from other towns is frequent. The TGV **trains** from Paris arrive 16 times per day (trip time: 3½ hours), and 29 trains per day arrive from Marseille (trip time: 1½ hours). For rail information and schedules, call ☎ **08-36-35-35-39.** If you're **driving** to Avignon from Paris, take A6 south to Lyon; once there, follow A7 south to Avignon.

VISITOR INFORMATION   The **Office de Tourisme** is at 41 cours Jean-Jaurès (☎ **04-90-82-65-11**).

SPECIAL EVENTS   The biggest celebration is the famous **Festival d'Avignon,** held annually during the last three weeks of July into the first week of August. With a focus on avant-garde works in the theater, dance, and music, it attracts international groups from all continents. Part of the fun is the bacchanalia that takes place nightly in the streets. Regrettably, the prices for hotel rooms and meals skyrocket, and reservations must be made far in advance. Local authorities also crack down on festival-induced vagrancy.

SEEING THE SIGHTS

Even more famous than the papal residency is the ditty "Sur le pont d'Avignon, l'on y danse, l'on y danse," echoing through every French nursery and around the world. Ironically, **pont St-Bénézet** was far too narrow for the *danse* of the rhyme. Spanning the Rhône and connecting Avignon with Villeneuve-lèz-Avignon, the bridge is now a fragmented ruin, with only 4 of its original 22 arches still extant. According to legend, it was inspired by a vision a shepherd named Bénézet had while tending his flock. Actually, the bridge was built between 1177 and 1185 and suffered various disasters from then on. (In 1669 half the bridge toppled into the river.) On one of the piers is the two-story **Chapelle St-Nicolas**—one story in Romanesque style, the other in

---

A Tale of Two Papal Cities

In 1309, a sick man named Pope Clement V, nearing the end of his life, arrived in Avignon. Lodged as a guest of the Dominicans, he died in the spring of 1314 and was succeeded by John XXII. The new pope, unlike the previous Roman popes, lived modestly in the Episcopal Palace. When Benedict XII took over, he enlarged and rebuilt the palace. Clement VI, who followed, built an even more elaborate extension called the New Palace. After Innocent VI and Urban V, Pope Gregory XI did no building. Inspired by Catherine of Siena, he wanted to return the papacy to Rome, and he succeeded. In all, seven popes reigned at Avignon. Under them, art and culture flourished—as did vice. Prostitutes blatantly went about peddling their wares in front of cardinals, rich merchants were robbed, and innocent pilgrims from the hinterlands were brutally tricked and swindled.

From 1378, during what's known as the Great Schism, one pope ruled in Avignon, another in Rome. The reign of the pope and the "antipope" continued, one following the other, until both rulers were dismissed by the 1417 election of Martin V. Rome continued to rule Avignon until it was joined to France at the time of the Revolution. The ramparts (still standing) around Avignon were built in the 14th century and are characterized by their machicolated battlements, turrets, and old gates.

Gothic. The remains of the bridge are open daily from 9am to 1pm and 2 to 5pm. Admission is 15F ($2.70) for adults and 7F ($1.25) for students and seniors.

✪ **Palais des Papes.** Place du Palais. ☎ **04-90-27-50-74.** Admission 40F ($7.20) adults; 32F ($5.75) students, children, and seniors. 6–9F ($1.10-$1.60) supplement for special exhibitions. Apr–Oct daily 9am–7pm; Nov–Mar daily 9:30am–5:45pm. Guided tours in English given whenever there's enough demand, for 40F ($7.20) adults, 32F ($5.75) children.

Dominating Avignon from a hilltop is one of the most famous, or notorious (depending on your point of view), palaces in the Christian world. Headquarters of a schismatic group of cardinals who came close to toppling the authority of the popes in Rome, this combination fortress-showplace is the monument most frequently associated with Avignon. You're shown through on a guided tour (usually lasting 50 minutes), which can be somewhat monotonous, as most of the rooms have been stripped of their once-legendary finery. The exception is the **Chapelle St-Jean,** known for its beautiful frescoes attributed to the school of Matteo Giovanetti and painted between 1345 and 1348. These frescoes present scenes from the life of John the Baptist and John the Evangelist. More Giovanetti frescoes can be found above the Chapelle St-Jean in the Chapelle St-Martial. The frescoes depict the miracles of St. Martial, the patron saint of Limousin.

The **Grand Tinel** (banquet hall) is about 135 feet long and 30 feet wide, and the pope's table stood on the southern side. The **pope's bedroom** is on the first floor of the Tour des Anges. Its walls are entirely decorated in tempera foliage on which birds and squirrels perch. Birdcages are painted in the recesses of the windows. In a secular vein, the **Studium (Stag Room)**—the study of Clement VI—was frescoed in 1343 with hunting scenes. Added under the same Clement, who had a taste for grandeur, the **Grande Audience** (Great Audience Hall) contains frescoes of the prophets, also attributed to Giovanetti and painted in 1352.

Palais des Papes

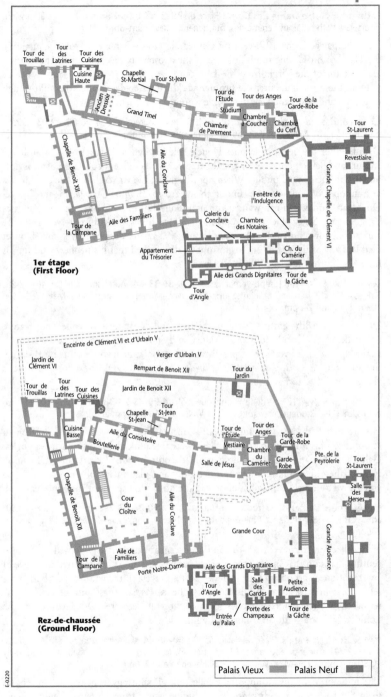

1er étage
(First Floor)

Tour de Trouillas
Tour des Latrines
Tour des Cuisines
Cuisine Haute
Ancien Dressoir
Chapelle St-Martial
Tour St-Jean
Grand Tinel
Tour de l'Étude
Tour des Anges
Tour de la Garde-Robe
Studium
Chambre à Coucher
Chambre du Cerf
Tour St-Laurent
Chambre de Parement
Revestiaire
Chapelle de Benoît XII
Aile du Conclave
Fenêtre de l'Indulgence
Galerie du Conclave
Grande Chapelle de Clément VI
Aile des Familiers
Chambre des Notaires
Tour de la Campane
Appartement du Trésorier
Ch. du Camérier
Aile des Grands Dignitaires
Tour de la Gâche
Tour d'Angle

Rez-de-chaussée
(Ground Floor)

Enceinte de Clément VI et d'Urbain V
Verger d'Urbain V
Jardin de Clément VI
Rempart de Benoît XII
Tour du Jardin
Tour de Trouillas
Tour des Latrines
Tour des Cuisines
Jardin de Benoît XII
Chapelle St-Jean
Tour St-Jean
Cuisine Basse
Aile du Consistoire
Boutellerie
Tour de l'Étude
Tour des Anges
Tour de la Garde-Robe
Vestiaire
Chambre du Camérier
Garde-Robe
Pte. de la Peyrolerie
Tour St-Laurent
Chapelle de Benoît XII
Salle de Jésus
Salle des Herses
Cour du Cloître
Aile du Conclave
Grande Cour
Grande Audience
Tour de la Campane
Aile de Familiers
Porte Notre-Dame
Tour d'Angle
Aile des Grands Dignitaires
Salle des Gardes
Petite Audience
Entrée du Palais
Porte des Champeaux
Tour de la Gâche

Palais Vieux   Palais Neuf

E-0220

577

Cathédrale Notre-Dame des Doms. Place du Palais. ☎ **04-90-86-81-01.** Free admission. Hours vary with religious ceremonies, but generally daily 9am–6pm.

Near the palace is the 12th-century Cathédrale Notre-Dame des Doms, containing the Flamboyant Gothic tomb of some of the apostate popes. Crowning the top is a gilded statue of the Virgin from the 19th century.

From the cathedral, enter the **promenade du Rocher-des-Doms** to stroll through its garden and enjoy the view across the Rhône to Villeneuve-lèz-Avignon.

✪ **La Fondation Angladon-Dubrujeaud.** 5 rue Laboureur. ☎ **04-90-82-29-03.** Admission 30F ($5.40). May–Sept Wed–Sun 1–7pm (6pm off-season).

Decades after the death of Jacques Doucet, the renowned designer of Parisian haute couture and belle époque dandy and dilettante, his magnificent collection of art is now on view to the general public. When not designing, Doucet collected the early works of a number of young artists, among them Picasso, Braque, Max Jacob, and Marcel Duchamp. Today you can wander through Doucet's former abode, viewing canvases by Cézanne, Sisley, Degas, and Modigliani (with his pink-shirted woman); rare antiques; 16th-century Buddhas; and Louis XVI chairs designed by Jacob. Doucet died in 1929 at the age of 76, his fortune so diminished that his nephew paid for his funeral—but his rich legacy lives on here.

Musée Calvet. 65 rue Joseph-Vernet. ☎ **04-90-86-33-84.** Admission 30F ($5.40) adults, 15F ($2.70) children and students. June–Sept Wed–Mon 10am–7pm; Oct–May Wed–Mon 10am–1pm and 2–6pm.

Housed in an 18th-century mansion, the fine- and decorative-arts collections feature the works of Vernet, David, Corot, Manet, and Soutine, plus the most extensive collection of ancient silverware in provincial museums. Our favorite oil is by Brueghel the Younger, *Le Cortège nuptial* (*The Bridal Procession*). Look for a copy of Bosch's *Adoration of the Magi* as well.

Musée Lapidaire. 18 rue de la République. ☎ **04-90-85-75-38.** Admission 10F ($1.80) adults, 5F (90¢) students, free for children. Wed–Mon 10am–1pm and 2–6pm.

Housed in a 17th-century Jesuit church is this important collection of Gallo-Roman sculptures. This museum has been called a veritable junkyard of antiquity. Gargoyles, Gallic and Roman statues, and broken pillars confront you at every turn. Of course, most of these pieces have known greater glory and placement (often in temples), so you'll have to use your imagination to conjure up the full splendor they once enjoyed.

Musée Louis-Vouland. 17 rue Victor-Hugo. ☎ **04-90-86-03-79.** Admission 20F ($3.60) adults, 10F ($1.80) students. June–Sept Tues–Sat 10am–noon and 2–6pm; Oct–May Tues–Sat 2–6pm.

This collection, devoted to 17th- and 18th-century fine arts, is housed in a 19th-century mansion that opens onto a lovely garden. Avignon's greatest treasure trove of lavish antiques and objets d'art includes Sèvres porcelain, the comtesse du Barry's tea set, great tapestries from Aubusson and Gobelin, Persian rugs, antique clocks, glittering chandeliers, and commodes to equal those at Versailles. Our favorites are the Louis XV inkpots with silver rats holding the lids.

Musée du Petit-Palais. Place du Palais. ☎ **04-90-86-44-58.** Admission 30F ($5.40) adults, 15F ($2.70) students and ages 12–18, free for children 11 and under. July–Aug daily 10:30am–6pm; Sept–May Wed–Mon 9:30am–noon and 2–6pm.

The museum contains an important collection of paintings from the Italian schools from the 13th to the 16th centuries, including works from Florence, Venice, Siena, and Lombardy. In addition, salons display 15th-century paintings done in Avignon, and several galleries are devoted to Roman and Gothic sculptures.

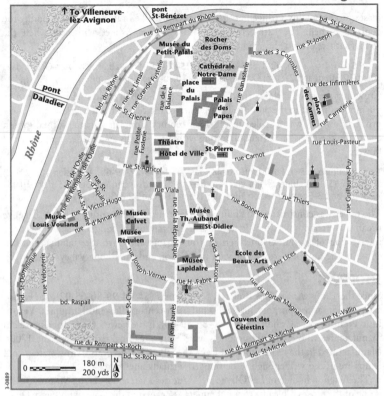

STEPPING BACK IN TIME IN VILLENEUVE-LÈZ-AVIGNON

The modern world is impinging on Avignon, but across the Rhône at Villeneuve-lèz-Avignon the Middle Ages slumber on. When the popes lived in exile at Avignon, wealthy cardinals built palaces (*livrées*) across the river. Many visitors prefer to stay or dine here rather than in Avignon.

In addition to the sights below, you might visit the **Eglise Notre-Dame**, place Meissonier, founded in 1333 by Cardinal Arnaud de Via. Its proudest possession is a 14th-century ivory Virgin, one of the great French treasures. It's open Wednesday to Monday, April to September from 10am to 12:30pm and 3 to 7pm and October to March from 10am to noon and 2 to 5:30pm. Admission is free.

Chartreuse du Val-de-Bénédiction. 60 rue de la République. ☎ **04-90-15-24-24.** Admission 32F ($5.75) adults, 21F ($3.80) ages 12–25, free for children 11 and under. Daily 9:30am–5:30pm.

Inside France's largest Carthusian monastery, built in 1352, you'll find a church, three cloisters, rows of cells that housed the medieval monks, and rooms depicting aspects of their daily lives. Part of the complex is devoted to a publicly and privately endowed workshop (the Centre National d'Ecritures et du Spectacle) for painters and writers who live in the monastic cells rent-free for up to a year to pursue their craft. Exhibitions of photography and painting are presented throughout the year.

Pope Innocent VI (whose tomb you can view) founded this charterhouse, which became the country's most powerful. Inside one of the chapels, a remarkable *Coronation of the Virgin* by Enguerrand Charonton is enshrined; painted in 1453, the masterpiece contains a fringed bottom that's Bosch-like in its horror, representing the denizens of hell. The 12th-century graveyard cloister is lined with cells where the former fathers prayed and meditated.

Fort St-André. Mont Andaon. ☎ **04-90-25-45-35.** Free admission. Apr–Oct 9 daily 10am–12:30pm and 2–6pm; Oct 10–Mar daily 10am–noon and 2–5pm.

Crowning the town is the Fort St-André, founded in 1360 by Jean-le-Bon to serve as a symbol of might to the pontifical powers across the river. The Abbaye St-André, now privately owned, was installed in the 18th century. You can visit the formal garden encircling the mansion, a tranquil setting with a rose-trellis colonnade, fountains, and flowers.

Tour Philippe le Bel. Rue Montée-de-la-Tour. ☎ **04-90-27-49-68.** Admission 10F ($1.80) adults, 6F ($1.10) students and children, free age 7 and under. Apr–Sept 15 daily 10am–12:30pm and 3–7pm; off-season Tues–Sun 10am–noon and 2–5:30pm.

The tower was constructed by Philippe the Fair in the 13th century, when Villeneuve became a French possession; it served as a gateway to the kingdom standing at the intersection of avenue Gabriel-Péri. If you're game and have the stamina, you can climb to the top for a panoramic view of Avignon and the Rhône Valley.

SHOPPING

Since the 1960s, **Antiquités Bourret,** 5 rue Limas (☎ 04-90-86-65-02), has earned a reputation as a repository for 18th- and 19th-century Provençal antiques. **Véronique Pichon,** place Crillon (☎ 04-90-85-89-00), is the newest branch of a porcelain manufacturer whose colorful products have been a regional fixture since the 1700s. Manufactured in the nearby town of Uzès, the tableware, decorative urns, statues, and lamps are priced well enough to be shipped virtually anywhere.

The Avignon branch of **Les Olivades,** 28 rue des Marchants (☎ 04-90-86-13-42), is one of the most visible of a chain of outlets associated in the States with Pierre Deux. Look for fabrics by the yard, bedcovers, slipcovers, draperies, and tablecloths. The fabrics, printed in a factory only 6 miles from Avignon, feature intricate designs in colors inspired by 19th-century models as well as Créole designs with butterflies, pineapples, bananas, and flowers. The idea behind **Les Indiens de Nîmes,** 4 rue du College-de-Roure (☎ 04-90-86-32-05), is to duplicate 18th- and 19th-century Provençal fabric patterns. They're sold by the meter as well as in clothing for men, women, and children. Also available are kitchenware and a selection of furniture inspired by Provence and the steamy wetlands west of Marseille.

The clothing at **Souleiado,** 5 rue Joseph-Vernet (☎ 04-90-86-47-67), derives from a Provençal model, and even the Provençal name (meaning "first ray of sunshine after a storm") evokes a spirit on which the owners want to capitalize. Most, but not all, of the clothing is for women. Fabrics are also sold by the meter.

WHERE TO STAY
VERY EXPENSIVE

✪ **La Mirande.** 4 place Amirande, 84000 Avignon. ☎ **04-90-85-93-93.** Fax 04-90-86-26-85. www.la-mirande.fr. 20 units. A/C MINIBAR TV TEL. 1,700–2,400F ($306–$432) double; 3,200F ($576) suite. AE, DC, MC, V.

In the heart of Avignon behind the Palais des Papes, this restored 700-year-old town house is one of Avignon's grand little luxuries, far better than anything else in town. The hotel treats you to two centuries of decorative art—from the 1700s Salon Chinois to the Salon Rouge, its striped walls in Rothschild red. In 1987 the house was acquired by Achim and Hannelore Stein, who transformed it into a citadel of opulence. All the rooms are stunning, with huge bathtubs. The loveliest is no. 20, whose lavish decor opens directly onto the garden.

Dining: The restaurant, among the finest in Avignon, deserves its one Michelin star. Chef Alain Davi has a light, sophisticated touch, with fixed-price menus at 135F to 380F ($24.30 to $68.40). The restaurant is open daily for lunch and dinner.

EXPENSIVE

✪ **Hôtel d'Europe.** 12 place Grillon, 84000 Avignon. ☎ **04-90-14-76-76.** Fax 04-90-85-43-66. www.hotel-d-europe.fr. E-mail: reservations@hotel-d-europe.fr. 47 units. A/C MINIBAR TV TEL. 650–1,900F ($117–$342) double; 2,500–3,000F ($450–$540) suite. AE, DC, MC, V. Parking 50F ($9).

The vine-covered Hôtel d'Europe has been in operation since 1799. You enter through a courtyard, where tables are set in the warmer months. The grand hall and salons boast tastefully arranged antiques and decorative elements. The good-size guest rooms have handsome decor, period furnishings, and tile or marble bathrooms. Three suites are perched on the roof with views of the Palais des Papes. Our only complaint: In some twin-bedded rooms, the beds are a bit narrow.

Dining: The restaurant, La Vieille Fontaine, is one of the best and most distinguished in Avignon. Meals are served in elegant dining rooms or in a charming inner courtyard. The wine list is impressive but celestial in price.

La Magnaneraie Hostellerie. 37 rue Camp-Bataille, 30400 Villeneuve-lèz-Avignon. ☎ **04-90-25-11-11.** Fax 04-90-25-46-37. E-mail: magnaneraie@gulliver.fr. 29 units. A/C MINIBAR TV TEL. 500–1,200F ($90–$216) double; 1,400–1,800F ($252–$324) suite. AE, DC, MC, V.

One of the most charming accommodations in the region stands on 2 acres of gardens in Villeneuve-lèz-Avignon. Tastefully renovated, the place is furnished with antiques and good reproductions. Many guests plan to stay for only a night but remain for many days to enjoy the good food and the atmosphere.

Dining: In 1993 the government rating of this inn was increased to four stars, mostly because of the excellent cuisine. Fixed-price menus range from 170F ($34) for a celebration of traditional Provençal recipes to 450F ($90) for a menu dégustation. Choices may include zucchini flowers stuffed with mushroom-and-cream purée, croustillant of red snapper with basil and olive oil, and rack of lamb with thyme. Dessert might be gratin of seasonal fruits with sabayon of lavender-flavored honey. Though the cuisine and ambience remain sublime, readers have lately noted a fall-off in the standards of service.

Amenities: Tennis court and landscaped pool.

MODERATE

Mercure Palais-des-Papes. Quartier de la Balance, rue Ferruce, 84000 Avignon. ☎ **04-90-85-91-23.** Fax 04-90-85-32-40. www.mercure.com. 87 units. A/C MINIBAR TV TEL. 545–590F ($98.10–$106.20) double. Discounts available Sat–Sun on selected winter weekends. AE, DC, MC, V. Parking 40–55F ($7.20–$9.90).

This chain hotel is a great choice if you want something modern, predictable, and affordable. Built in a contemporary three-story format in the early 1970s, it lies within the city walls, at the foot of the Palais des Papes. The rooms are well furnished but lack any particular style. There's a small bar but no restaurant, as breakfast is the only meal served.

INEXPENSIVE

Hôtel d'Angleterre. 29 bd. Raspail, 84000 Avignon. ☎ **04-90-86-34-31.** Fax 04-90-86-86-74. 38 units, 35 with bathroom. TV TEL. 180F ($32.40) double without bathroom, 270–380F ($48.60–$68.40) double with bathroom. MC, V. Free parking. Closed Dec 19–Jan 18.

In the heart of Avignon, this classical structure is the city's best budget hotel. The rooms are comfortably but basically furnished. Breakfast is the only meal served.

Hôtel Danieli. 17 rue de la République, 84000 Avignon. ☎ **04-90-86-46-82.** Fax 04-90-27-09-24. www.avignonetprovence.com/gb/danieli. 29 units. TV TEL. 390–470F ($70.20–$84.60) double. AE, DC, MC, V.

This hotel's Italian influence is clear in its arches, chiseled stone, tile floors, and baronial stone staircase. Built during the reign of Napoléon I, it's classified as a historic monument in its own right. Its small, informal public rooms are outfitted in antiques acquired by the history-conscious owner. The guest rooms, however, have mostly painted bamboo furnishings. Unless special arrangements are made for a group (and this hotel accepts many), breakfast is the only meal served at 42F ($7.55) per person.

Hôtel de l'Atelier. 5 rue de la Foire, 30400 Villeneuve-lèz-Avignon. ☎ **04-90-25-01-84.** Fax 04-90-25-80-06. 19 units. TV TEL. 250–460F ($45–$82.80) double. AE, DC, MC, V. Free parking on street, 25F ($4.50) in nearby garage.

A great budget choice in Villeneuve-lèz-Avignon is this 16th-century village house that has preserved much of its original style. Inside is a tiny duplex lounge with a large stone fireplace. Outside, a sun-filled rear garden with potted orange and fig trees provides fruit for breakfast. The immaculate accommodations are comfortable and informal but a bit dowdy. In the old bourgeois dining room, a continental breakfast is the only meal served.

WHERE TO DINE

✪ **Christian Etienne.** 10 rue Mons. ☎ **04-90-86-16-50.** Reservations recommended. Main courses 120-220F ($21.60–$39.60); fixed-price menus 170–500F ($30.60–$90). AE, DC, MC, V. July daily noon–1:30pm and 7:30–9:30pm; Aug–June Mon–Fri noon–1:30pm, Mon–Sat 7:30–9:30pm. FRENCH.

The stone house containing this restaurant was built in 1180, around the same time as the Palais des Papes next door. The dining room contains old ceiling and wall frescoes honoring the marriage of Anne de Bretagne to the French king in 1491. The owner, Christian Etienne, is the star chef of Avignon because he continues to explore the depths of his culinary repertoire. Several of the fixed-price menus present specific themes: the two 300F ($60) menus feature only tomatoes or vegetables, respectively; the 430F ($77.40) menu offers preparations of lobster; and the 500F ($90) menu relies on the chef's discretion (*menu confiance*) to come up with unique combinations. Note for strict vegetarians: The vegetable menus are among the most creative of their kind but aren't completely devoid of meat. They're flavored with small amounts of meat or fish or, sometimes, meat drippings. In summer, look for a vegetable menu where every course is based on ripe tomatoes; the main course is a mousse of lamb, eggplants, tomatoes, and herbs. A la carte specialties include filet of red snapper with a black-olive coulis and a dessert of fennel sorbet with saffron-flavored English cream sauce.

✪ **Hiély-Lucullus.** 5 rue de la République. ☎ **04-90-86-17-07.** Reservations required. Fixed-price menus 150–320F ($27–$57.60). V. Wed–Sun noon–1:30pm, daily 7:30–9:45pm. Closed June 22–30 and Mon in summer. FRENCH.

This Relais Gourmand used to reign supreme in Avignon before the arrival of Christian Etienne. It's still going strong and richly deserves its star, even if it's no longer quite as trendy. The town's most fabled chef, Pierre Hiély, has retired, but he drops in occasionally to check on his former sous chef, André Chaussy. We think he's doing just fine, still offering those reasonable fixed-price menus (no à la carte). Try one of his special appetizers, like petite marmite du pêcheur, a savory fish soup ringed with black

mussels. A main-dish specialty is *pintadeau* (young guinea hen) with ~~p~~
pièce de résistance is *agneau des Alpilles grillé* (grilled alpine lamb). Ca~~r~~
include Tavel Rosé and Châteauneuf-du-Pape.

La Fourchette. 7 rue Racine. ☎ **04-90-85-20-93.** Fixed-price menus 100–148F ($1~~8~~ $26.65) at lunch, 148F ($26.65) at dinner. MC, V. Mon–Fri 12:15–2pm and 7:15–9:45pm. Closed Aug 5–29. FRENCH.

This bistro offers creative cooking at moderate prices. Guests dine in either a summerhouselike room with walls of glass or a tavern-like space with oak beams. You might begin with fresh sardines flavored with citrus or ravioli filled with haddock, then move on to the blanquette of monkfish with endives or daube of beef prepared in the local style with a gratin of macaroni.

✪ **Le Prieuré.** 7 place du Chapitre 1, 30400 Villeneuve-lès-Avignon. ☎ **04-90-15-90-15.** Fax 04-90-25-45-39. Reservations recommended. Main courses 115–230F ($20.70–$41.40); fixed-price menus 200–480F ($36–$86.40). AE, DC, MC, V. Daily 12:30–1:45pm and 7:30–9:15pm. Closed Nov–Feb and Wed in Mar, Apr, and Oct. Bus: 11 from Avignon. FRENCH/PROVENÇAL.

This well-respected, long-established restaurant has flourished since the Mille family purchased it in 1943. Today, within a stone core originally built in 1322 as a monastery, and massively enlarged in the 1970s, you can enjoy the well-conceived cuisine of master chef Serge Chenet. You'll find the place in the heart of the village, adjacent to its most visible church, behind an ivy-covered stone facade. Inside, in richly furnished rooms that evoke prosperous, 19th-century Provence, dishes include braised scallops with a garnish of fresh pumpkin, roasted breast of pigeon with *fines herbes,* and a rack of local lamb served with a *cannelloni* of eggplant.

On the premises are 26 deluxe rooms plus 10 junior suites, each with air-conditioning, minibar, TV, phone, and accessories inspired by Old Provence. Doubles cost from 700F to 1,300F ($126 to $234); junior suites, from 1,500F to 1,800F ($270 to $324). A pool is on the premises.

AVIGNON AFTER DARK

Near the Palais des Papes is **Le Grand Café,** La Manutention (☎ **04-90-86-86-77**), a restaurant/bar/cafe that might quickly become your favorite watering hole. For dancing, head to **Les Ambassadeurs,** 27 rue Bancasse (☎ **04-90-86-31-55**), which is more animated than its subdued competitor, **Piano Bar Le Blues,** 25 rue Carnot (☎ **04-90-85-79-71**); the cover at both is 10F ($1.80). Near Le Blues is a restaurant, **Red Zone,** 27 rue Carnot (☎ **04-90-27-02-44**), whose bar area hosts live punk and rock bands.

Winning the award for having the most unpronounceable name is **Le Woolloomooloo** (it means "Black Kangaroo" in an Aboriginal dialect of Australia), 16 bis rue des Teinturiers (☎ **04-90-85-28-44**), which includes a bar and cafe in a separate room devoted to the cuisine of France and West Africa. The hottest place for gays and lesbians is **L'Esclav,** 12 rue de Limas (☎ **04-90-85-14-91**).

3 St-Rémy-de-Provence

438 miles S of Paris, 16 miles NE of Arles, 12 miles S of Avignon, 8 miles N of Les Baux

Nostradamus, the famous French physician/astrologer, was born here in 1503. Although he has many fans today, he does have detractors, like those who denounce the astrologer and his more than 600 obscure verses as psychotic. In 1922 Gertrude Stein and Alice B. Toklas found St-Rémy after "wandering around everywhere a bit," as Stein wrote to Cocteau.

ssociated with van Gogh. He committed himself to an tting off his left ear. Between moods of despair, he painted d *Cypresses.*

today not only for its memories and sights but also for a vençal life that you won't find in Aix or Avignon. It's a le charm that draws the occasional visiting celebrity trying to escape the sp

ESSENTIALS

GETTING THERE There are local **buses** from Avignon, taking 45 minutes one-way. Call ☎ **04-90-82-07-35** in Avignon for information and schedules. If you're **driving,** head south from Avignon along D571.

VISITOR INFORMATION The **Office de Tourisme** is on place Jean-Jaurès (☎ **04-90-92-05-22**).

SEEING THE SIGHTS

Monastère de St-Paul-de-Mausolée. Avenue Edgar-le-Roy. ☎ **04-90-92-77-00.** Free admission. Cloisters, Apr–Sept daily 9am–6pm; Oct–Mar daily 9am–5pm.

You can visit the 12th-century cloisters of the asylum van Gogh made famous in his paintings. Now a psychiatric hospital, the former monastery is east of D5, a short drive north of Glanum (see below). You can't visit the cell in which this genius was confined from 1889 to 1890, but it's still worth coming here to explore the Romanesque chapel and cloisters with their circular arches and columns, which have beautifully carved capitals. On your way to the church, you'll see a bust of van Gogh.

Musée Archéologique. In the Hôtel de Sade, rue du Parage. ☎ **04-90-92-64-04.** Admission 15F ($2.70) adults, 10F ($1.80) students and ages 12–17, free for children 11 and under. Feb 2–Mar 3 Tues–Sun 10am–noon and 2–5pm; Mar 4–Sept Tues–Sun 10am–noon and 2–6pm; Oct Tues–Sun 10am–noon and 2–5pm; Nov–Dec Wed, Sat, and Sun only, 10am–noon and 2–5pm; Jan by appointment only.

In the center of St-Rémy, the Musée Archéologique displays both sculptures and bronzes from the ancient Roman excavations at nearby Glanum. A combined ticket of 36F ($6.50) can be purchased at Musée Archéologique or Ruines de Glanum for admission to both.

Ruines de Glanum. Av. Vincent-van-Gogh (a mile south of St-Rémy on D5). ☎ **04-90-92-23-79.** Admission 32F ($5.75) adults, 21F ($3.80) students and ages 12–25, free for ages 11 and under. Apr–Sept daily 9am–9pm; Oct–Mar daily 9am–noon and 2–5pm. From the town center, follow the signs to Les Antiques.

A Gallo-Roman settlement thrived here during the final days of the Roman Empire. Its historic monuments include an Arc Municipal, a triumphal arch dating from the time of Julius Caesar, and a cenotaph called the Mausolée des Jules. Garlanded with sculptured fruits and flowers, the arch dates from 20 B.C. and is the oldest in Provence. The mausoleum was raised to honor the grandsons of Augustus and is the only extant monument of its type. In the area are entire streets and foundations of private residences from the 1st-century town. Some remains are from a Gallo-Greek town from the 2nd century B.C.

WHERE TO STAY

✪ **Château de Roussan.** Rte. de Tarascon, 13210 St-Rémy-de-Provence. ☎ **04-90-92-11-63.** Fax 04-90-92-50-59. E-mail: chateau.de.roussan@wanadoo.fr. 21 units. TEL. 460–600F ($82.80–$108) double. AE, MC, V.

Although there are more stylish château hotels in the district, this one is most evocative of another time and place. Its most famous resident, the Renaissance psychic Nostradamus, lived in a rustic outbuilding a few steps from the front door. Today you pass beneath an archway of 300-year-old trees leading to the neoclassical facade, which was constructed of softly colored local stone in 1701. As you wander around the grounds you'll be absorbed in the history, especially when you come across the baroque sculptures lining the basin, fed by a stream. The restaurant, open daily for lunch and dinner, serves fixed-price menus.

Les Antiques. 15 av. Pasteur, 13210 St-Rémy-de-Provence. ☎ **04-90-92-03-02.** Fax 04-90-92-50-40. 27 units. MINIBAR TEL. 370–600F ($66.60–$108) double. AE, DC, MC, V. Closed Oct 18–Apr 2.

This moderately priced, stylish 19th-century villa is set in a 7-acre park with a pool. An elegant reception lounge opens onto several salons, and all furnishings are Napoléon III. The rooms are handsomely furnished; some are in a private modern pavilion with direct access to the garden. In summer, you're served breakfast in what used to be the Orangerie.

✪ **Vallon de Valrugues.** Chemin Canto-Cigalo, 13210 St-Rémy-de-Provence. ☎ **04-90-92-04-40.** Fax 04-90-92-44-01. www.valruges-cassagne.com. E-mail: mail@valruges-cassagne.com. 53 units. MINIBAR TV TEL. 680–1,480F ($122.40–$266.40) double; 1,800–2,480F ($324–$446.40) suite. AE, DC, MC, V.

Surrounded by a park, this Mediterranean hotel has the best accommodations and restaurant in town. The owners, Françoise and Jean-Michel Gallon, offer beautifully furnished rooms and suites, all with built-in safes. The rooms have recently been enlarged and renovated, with marble bathrooms added.

Dining: The dining terrace alone may compete with the cuisine, which is winning praise for innovative light dishes.

Amenities: Pool, tennis courts, sauna, gym, golf putting green. Horseback riding ring with instructors (for which you pay extra).

WHERE TO DINE
Another great dining choice is the restaurant at **Vallon de Valrugues** (see above).

La Maison Jaune. 15 rue Carnot. ☎ **04-90-92-56-14.** Reservations recommended. Fixed-price menus 175–285F ($31.50–$51.30). MC, V. Tues–Sun noon–2pm and 7:30–10:30pm. Closed Jan–Feb. MODERN PROVENÇAL.

Offering good value and a modernized Provençal cuisine that its owners take very seriously, this restaurant occupies a blue-and-white 18th-century house that lies in the heart of St-Rémy, overlooking the château of the de Sades. Established in 1993, it contains only 35 seats in two salon-style dining rooms, or, during clement weather, a sweeping terrace whose tiles and stucco are—as you might have guessed—yellow. For the most appealing meal here, opt for the 235F ($42.30) Provençal menu, which may include a *barigoule* of artichokes, prepared with tomatoes, herbs, and olive oil; and roasted pigeon served with a sauce concocted from the heady red wine of nearby Les Baux. Dessert options invariably include an excellent version of walnut tarte with lemon marmalade. One dish that draws strong compliments, when it's available, is grilled sardines served with raw fennel and candied lemons.

Le Jardin de Frédéric. 8 bd. Gambetta. ☎ **04-90-92-27-76.** Reservations required. Main courses 95–115F ($17.10–$20.70); fixed-price menus 135–170F ($24.30–$30.60). MC, V. Thurs–Tues noon–2pm and 7:30–9:30pm. Closed Feb. FRENCH.

In a small villa close to the town center, this popular bistro is the best restaurant around. The family-run place offers rabbit with plums, duckling terrine, onion tart, and poached turbot with sorrel. It's almost the type of food you'd be served in a local Provençal home. In summer you can dine at tables in front of the house.

4 Arles

450 miles S of Paris, 22 miles SW of Avignon, 55 miles NW of Marseille

Arles has been called the soul of Provence. Art lovers, archaeologists, and historians are attracted to this town on the Rhône. Many of its scenes, painted so luminously by van Gogh in his declining years, remain to delight. The great Dutch painter left Paris for Arles in 1888, the same year he cut off part of his left ear. But he was to paint some of his most celebrated works in this Provençal town, including *Starry Night, The Bridge at Arles, Sunflowers,* and *L'Arlésienne.*

The Greeks are said to have founded Arles in the 6th century B.C. Julius Caesar established a Roman colony here in 46 B.C. Under Roman rule, Arles prospered. Constantine the Great named it the second capital of his empire in 306, when it was known as "the little Rome of the Gauls." It wasn't until 1481 that Arles was incorporated into France.

Though Arles doesn't possess quite as much charm as Aix-en-Provence, it's still rewarding to visit, with first-rate museums, excellent restaurants, and summer festivals. The city today isn't quite as lovely as it was when Picasso came here, but it has enough of the antique charm of Provence to keep the appeal alive.

ESSENTIALS

GETTING THERE   Arles lies on the Paris–Marseille and the Bordeaux–St-Raphaël rail lines, so has frequent connections from most cities of France. Ten **trains** per day arrive from Avignon (trip time: 20 minutes); 10 per day from Marseille (trip time: 1 hour); and 10 per day from Aix-en-Provence (trip time: 1¾ hours). For rail information and schedules, call ☎ **08-36-35-35-39.**

There are about four **buses** per day from Aix-en-Provence (trip time: 1¾ hours). For bus information and schedules, call ☎ **04-90-49-38-01.**

If you're **driving,** head south along N570 from Avignon.

VISITOR INFORMATION   The **Office de Tourisme,** where you can buy a billet global (see below), is on the esplanade des Lices (☎ **04-90-18-41-20**).

EXPLORING THE TOWN

Go to the tourist office (see "Essentials," above), where you can purchase a **billet global,** the all-inclusive pass that admits you to the town's museums, Roman monuments, and all the major attractions, at a cost of 55F ($9.90) for adults and 35F ($6.30) for children.

Arles is full of monuments from Roman times. The general vicinity of the old Roman forum is occupied by **place du Forum,** shaded by plane trees. The Café de Nuit, immortalized by van Gogh, once stood on this square. You can see two Corinthian columns and pediment fragments from a temple at the corner of the Hôtel Nord-Pinus. South of here is **place de la République,** the principal plaza, dominated by a 50-foot-tall blue porphyry obelisk. On the north is the impressive **Hôtel de Ville** (town hall) from 1673, built to Mansart's plans and surmounted by a Renaissance belfry.

The city's two great classical monuments are the **Théâtre Antique,** rue du Cloître (☎ **04-90-49-36-25**), and the Amphitheater (Les Arènes). The Roman theater, begun by Augustus in the 1st century, was mostly destroyed; only two Corinthian

In Search of van Gogh's "Different Ligh

What strikes me here is the transparency of the air.

—Vi

Before the Impressionists found refuge in Provence, this regio   already attracted many artists. During the pope's residency at Avignon, a flood of Italian artists frescoed the papal palace in a style worthy of St. Peter's, and even after their departure, Provençal monarchs like King René imported painters from Flanders and Burgundy to adorn his public buildings. This continued to the 18th and 19th centuries, as painters drew inspiration from the dazzling light of Provence, but it wasn't until the age of the Impressionists that Provence really became known for its role in nurturing artists.

The Dutch-born Vincent van Gogh (1853–90) moved to Arles in 1888 and spent 2 years migrating through the historic towns of Les Baux, St-Rémy, and Stes-Maries, recording through the filter of his neuroses dozens of Impressionistic scenes now prized by museums everywhere. His search, he said, was for "a different light," and when he found it, he created masterpieces like *Starry Night, Cypresses, Olive Trees,* and *Boats Along the Beach.*

Van Gogh wasn't alone in his pursuit of Provençal light: Gauguin joined him 8 months after his arrival and soon thereafter engaged him in a violent quarrel, which reduced the Dutchman to a morbid depression that sent him to a local sanitarium. Within 2 years van Gogh returned to Paris, where he committed suicide in July 1890.

Things went somewhat better for Cézanne, who was familiar with the beauties of Provence thanks to his childhood in Aix-en-Provence. He infuriated his father, a prominent Provençal banker, by abandoning his studies to pursue painting. Later, his theories about line and color were publicized around the world. Although he migrated to Paris, he rarely set foot outside Provence from 1890 until his death, in 1904. Some critics have asserted that Cézanne's later years were devoted to one obsession: recording the line, color, and texture of Montagne-St-Victoire, a rocky knoll a few hours' horse ride east of Aix. He painted it more than 60 times without ever grasping its essence the way he'd hoped. The bulk of the Provençal mountain, however, as well as the way shadows moved across its rocky planes, was decisive in affecting the Cubists, whose work Cézanne directly influenced.

columns remain. The theater was where the *Venus of Arles* was discovered in 1651. Take rue de la Calade from the city hall. Admission is 15F ($2.70) for adults and 9F ($1.60) for children. Open daily from 9am to 12:30pm and 2 to 5:30pm.

Nearby, the **Amphitheater (Les Arènes),** rond-pont des Arènes (☎ **04-90-49-36-86**), also built in the 1st century, seats almost 25,000 and still hosts bullfights in summer. The government warns you to visit the old monument at your own risk, as the stone steps are uneven, and much of the masonry is worn down to the point where it might be a problem for older travelers or for those with disabilities. For a good view, you can climb the three towers that remain from medieval times, when the amphitheater was turned into a fortress. Both the theater and Les Arènes are open daily, April 1 to September 31 from 9am to 12:30pm and 2 to 7pm; the rest of the year, daily from 9am to noon and 2 to 5pm. Admission is 15F ($2.70) for adults and 9F ($1.60) for children.

..olated position 7½ miles north of Arles, **Les Olivades Factory Store,** chemin , Indienneurs, St-Etienne-du-Grès (☎ **04-90-49-19-19**), stands beside the road leading to Tarascon. Because of the wide array of art objects and fabrics inspired by the traditions of Provence, a trek out here is worth your while. Fabric by the yard, dresses, shirts for men and women, and table linens are all available at retail outlets of the Olivades chain throughout Provence, but here the selection is a bit cheaper and more diverse.

Les Alyscamps. Rue Pierre-Renaudel. ☎ **04-90-49-36-87.** Admission 15F ($2.70) adults, 9F ($1.60) children. Dec–Jan daily 10am–noon and 2–4:30pm; Feb daily 10am–noon and 2–5pm; Mar daily 9am–12:30pm and 2–5:30pm; Apr–Sept daily 9am–7pm; Oct daily 10am–12:30pm and 2–5pm; Nov daily 10am–12:30pm and 2–5pm.

Perhaps the most memorable sight in Arles, this was once a necropolis established by the Romans. After being converted into a Christian burial ground in the 4th century, it became a setting for legends in epic medieval poetry and was even mentioned in Dante's *Inferno.* Today it's lined with poplars and the remaining sarcophagi. Arlesiens escape here to enjoy a respite from the heat.

Eglise St-Trophime. On the east side of place de la République. ☎ **04-90-96-07-38.** Admission: church, free; cloister, 15F ($2.70) adults, 9F ($1.60) students and children. Church, daily 8am–7pm; cloister, June–Sept daily 9am–7pm, Oct–May daily 9–5pm.

This church is noted for its 12th-century portal, one of the finest achievements of the southern Romanesque style. In the pediment, Christ is surrounded by the symbols of the Evangelists. Frederick Barbarossa was crowned king of Arles on this site in 1178. The cloister, in both the Gothic and Romanesque styles, is noted for its medieval carvings.

Musée de l'Arles Antique. Presqu'île du Cirque Romain. ☎ **04-90-18-88-88.** Admission 35F ($6.30) adults, 25F ($4.50) students, free for children 13 and under. Apr–Sept 15 daily 9am–7pm; Sept 16–Mar daily 9:30am–noon and 1:30–6pm.

Half a mile south of the town center, you'll find one of the world's most famous collections of Roman Christian sarcophagi, plus a rich ensemble of sculptures, mosaics, and inscriptions from the Augustinian period to the 6th century A.D. Eleven detailed models show ancient monuments of the region as they existed in the past.

Musée Réattu. 10 rue du Grand-Prieuré. ☎ **04-90-49-37-58.** Admission 15F ($2.70) adults, 9F ($1.60) children. Additional 5F (90¢) per person for special exhibits. Apr–Sept daily 9am–12:30pm and 2–7pm; Mar daily 10am–12:30pm and 2–5:30pm; Oct daily 10am–12:30pm and 2–5:30pm; Nov–Feb 10am–12:30pm and 2–5pm.

This collection of the local painter Jacques Réattu has been updated with more recent works, including etchings and drawings by Picasso. Other works are by Alechinsky, Dufy, and Zadkine. Note the Arras tapestries from the 16th century.

Museon Arlaten. 29 rue de la République. ☎ **04-90-96-08-23.** Admission 20F ($3.60) adults, 15F ($2.70) children. Apr–May and Sept Tues–Sun 9:30am–12:30pm and 2–6pm; June–Aug daily 9:30am–1pm and 2–6:30pm; Sept–Mar Tues–Sun 9:30am–12:30pm and 2–5pm.

You'll notice that the name of this museum is written in Provençal style. It was founded by Frédéric Mistral, the Provençal poet and leader of a movement to establish modern Provençal as a literary language, using the money from his Nobel Prize for literature in 1904. This is really a folklore museum, with regional costumes, portraits, furniture, dolls, a music salon, and one room devoted to mementos of Mistral. Among its curiosities is a letter (in French) from President Theodore Roosevelt to Mistral, bearing the letterhead of the Maison Blanche in Washington, D.C.

WHERE TO STAY

✪ **Hôtel Calendal.** 22 place du Docteur-Pomme, 13200 Arles. ☎ **04-90-96-11-89.** Fax 04-90-96-05-84. 27 units. TEL. 250–420F ($45–$75.60) double. AE, DC, MC, V. Bus: 4.

On a quiet square not far from the arena, this choice offers rooms with Provençal decor and some antiques, most with views of the shaded garden. The limited menu includes omelets, soups, and small dishes at conservative prices, as well as homemade desserts and pastries. The Calendal has long been the bargain hunter's favorite in Arles, and the rooms have recently been redecorated.

Hôtel d'Arlatan. 26 rue du Sauvage, 13631 Arles. ☎ **04-90-93-56-66.** Fax 04-90-49-68-45. 40 units. MINIBAR TV TEL. 465–795F ($83.70–$143.10) double; 980–1,350F ($176.40–$243) suite. AE, DC, MC, V. Parking 60F ($10.80).

In the former residence of the comtes d'Arlatan de Beaumont, near place du Forum, this hotel has been managed by the same family since 1920. It was built in the 15th century on the ruins of an old palace ordered by Constantine—in fact, there's still a wall from the 4th century. The rooms are furnished with authentic Provençal antiques, the walls covered with tapestries in the Louis XV and Louis XVI styles. Try to get a room overlooking the garden; 25 rooms are air-conditioned.

Hôtel Le Cloître. 16 rue du Cloître, 13200 Arles. ☎ **04-90-96-29-50.** Fax 04-90-96-02-88. 30 units. TEL. 250–305F ($45–$54.90) double; 375–420F ($67.50–$75.60) triple. AE, MC, V. Parking 30F ($5.40).

Between the ancient theater and the cloister, this hotel is a great value. Originally part of a 12th-century cloister, it retains the Romanesque vaultings. The restored old house has a Provençal atmosphere, pleasant rooms, and a TV lounge, though 17 rooms have their own TV as well. Parking is available nearby.

WHERE TO DINE

Hostellerie des Arènes. 62 rue du Refuge. ☎ **04-90-96-13-05.** Reservations required. Main courses 45–100F ($8.10–$18); fixed-price menus 75–129F ($13.50–$23.20). MC, V. Wed–Mon noon–2:30pm and 7–10pm. Closed Jan 10–Feb 20. PROVENÇAL.

Close to the arena, the well-prepared Provençal specialties here include seafood in puff pastry, braised duckling laced with green peppercorns, and veal marengo. Chef Didier Pirouault prepares a natively enriched bouillabaisse. Inexpensive wines, by the carafe or the bottle, provide an added element to any meal. In warm weather, meals are served on the terrace.

La Côte d'Adam (Adam's Rib). 12 rue de la Liberté. ☎ **04-90-49-62-29.** Reservations required in summer. Main courses 65–75F ($11.70–$13.50); fixed-price menus 70–106F ($12.60–$19.10). AE, MC, V. Tues–Sun noon–2pm, daily 7–10pm. May–Sept, it's likely to be open daily. Closed Nov 15–30. PROVENÇAL.

In the historic center of town, this restaurant seats 40 in its rustic interior with a beamed ceiling and high carved-stone fireplace. Choices may include aiguillettes of duck and John Dory with a confit of pear; many dishes are imbued with fragrant olive oil.

Le Vaccarès. Place du Forum, 9 rue Favorin. ☎ **04-90-96-06-17.** Reservations required. Main courses 75–155F ($13.50–$27.90); fixed-price lunch 98F ($17.65); fixed-price dinner 135–280F ($24.30–$50.40). AE, MC, V. Tues–Sun noon–2pm, Tues–Sat 7:30–9:30pm. Closed Jan 15–Feb 15, and Sun July–Aug. PROVENÇAL.

Le Vaccarès offers southern French elegance and the finest food in town, in a setting whose outdoor terrace (used during clement weather) opens onto the market of Arles. Unusual ingredients are married to create innovative Provençal dishes. Specialties are sauté of lamb with basil, croquette of squid, sea-devil soup, and sea bass steamed and garnished only with olive oil. The selection of wines is impressive (especially the Rhône Valley and Var).

ARLES AFTER DARK

The town's most appealing choice is the bar/cafe/music hall **Cargo de Nuit,** 7 av. Sadi-Carnot, route pour Barriol (☎ **04-90-49-55-99**), which plays recorded blues, salsa, reggae, and cubano music. The cover charge between 20F and 40F ($3.60 and $7.20) gets you access to a sprawling bar and a restaurant that does everything it can to break what might have become too constant a diet of southern French cooking.

Two good options farther from the city center, particularly for those in their 40s and 50s, are the very large **Le Krystal,** Route de Pont-de-Crau (☎ **04-90-98-32-40**), about 6 miles south of Arles; and **Le Baccuo,** Route des Stes-Maries-de-la-Mer, Quartier Moules (no phone), about 12½ miles south of Arles. Both combine aspects of a country picnic, cafe, bar, and dance hall into large indoor/outdoor venues.

5 Les Baux

444 miles S of Paris, 12 miles NE of Arles, 50 miles N of Marseille and the Mediterranean

Cardinal Richelieu called Les Baux a nesting place for eagles. In its lonely position high on a windswept plateau overlooking the southern Alpilles, Les Baux is a mere ghost of its former self. It was once the citadel of powerful seigneurs who ruled with an iron fist and sent their conquering armies as far as Albania. In medieval times, troubadours from all over the continent came to this "court of love," where they recited Western Europe's earliest-known vernacular poetry. Eventually, the notorious "Scourge of Provence" ruled Les Baux, sending his men throughout the land to kidnap people. If no one was willing to pay ransom for one of his victims, the poor wretch was forced to walk a gangplank over the cliff's edge.

Fed up with the rebellions against Louis XIII in 1632, Richelieu commanded his armies to destroy Les Baux. Today the castle and ramparts are a mere shell, though you can see remains of great Renaissance mansions. Although foreboding, the dry countryside around Les Baux, which is nestled in a valley surrounded by mysterious, shadowy rock formations, offers its own fascination. Vertical ravines lie on either side of the town. Vineyards—officially classified as Coteaux d'Aix-en-Provence—surround Les Baux, facing the Alpilles. If you follow the signposted route des vin, you can motor through the vineyards in an afternoon, perhaps stopping off at various growers' estates.

For the greatest drive in the area, take the panorama route along D27 for about half a mile and bear right along a steep road. From this rocky promontory you'll have the most spectacular view of Les Baux and even, in the far distance, Arles and Camargue.

Another scenic highlight is Val d'Enfer (Valley of Hell), accessed along D27 and D78 from Les Baux. This is a jagged and irregular gorge filled with caves that are the source of many legends. Young children are told of the fairies, witches, and sprites who used to reign from these caves.

From Arles, there are four **buses** Monday to Saturday from April to October, but only one bus per day the rest of the year (trip time: 30 minutes). There is no bus service on Sundays. The fare is 27.50F ($4.95) one-way. For bus information and schedules, call ☎ **04-90-49-38-01** in Arles. If you're **driving** from Arles, take N570 north and D5 east to Les Baux; from Marseille, head north along A7 to Salon de Provence and from here travel D5 west.

The **Office de Tourisme** is on Ilôt Post Tenebras Lux (☎ **04-90-54-34-39**).

WHERE TO STAY

La Riboto de Taven (see "Where to Dine," below) has two rooms for rent.

VERY EXPENSIVE

✪ L'Oustau de Beaumanière. Les Baux, 13520 Maussane-les-Alpilles. ☎ 04-90-54-33-07. Fax 04-90-54-40-46. www.relaischateaux.fr/oustau. 20 units. A/C MINIBAR TV TEL. 1,300–1,450F ($234–$261) double; 2,000–2,100F ($360–$378) suite. AE, DC, MC, V. Closed Jan 3–Mar 10; Nov–Mar both hotel and restaurant closed all day Wed and Thurs to 4pm.

This Relais & Châteaux is one of the most legendary hotels in southern France. On the premises of a Provençal *mas* (farmhouse) bought in 1945 by the late Raymond Thuilier, it became a rendezvous for the glitterati in the 1950s and 1960s and continues today, with a more subdued kind of glamour, under the founder's grandson, Jean-André Charial. The hotel consists of three stone houses, each draped in flowering vines, in the valley at the base of the rocky hill on which the fortified town rises. The plush guest rooms evoke the 16th and 17th centuries.

Dining: In the stone-vaulted dining room, the chef serves specialties like "cappuccino" of crayfish with peppers and a rossini (stuffed with foie gras) of veal with fresh truffles. The award-winning *gigot d'agneau* (lamb) *en croûte* has become this place's trademark. For dessert, consider a soufflé of red fruits. Lunch and dinner are served daily, except between November 1 and early April, when both the hotel and its restaurant are closed all day Wednesday and Thursday at lunch. Reservations are essential.

MODERATE

Auberge de la Benvengudo. Vallon de l'Arcoule, rte. d'Arles, 13520 Les Baux. ☎ 04-90-54-32-54. Fax 04-90-54-42-58. E-mail: benvengudo@aol.com. 22 units. A/C TV TEL. 600–720F ($108–$129.60) double; 800–950F ($144–$171) suite. AE, MC, V. Closed Nov–Feb. Take RD78 for a mile southwest of Les Baux, following the signs to Arles.

This auberge is a tastefully converted 19th-century farmhouse surrounded by sculptured shrubbery, towering trees, and parasol pines. Extras include a pool, a tennis court, and an expansive terrace. An annex contains attractive modern rooms with terraces, some with antique four-poster beds.

The inn serves a delectable dinner, with menu items including filet of red mullet with concassé of tomatoes, grilled lamb chops with ratatouille, and Mediterranean sole filet fried with rosemary. The 240F ($43.20) fixed-price menu changes daily and is now joined by an à la carte menu. Lunch is served in summer. Closed Sunday dinner.

INEXPENSIVE

✪ Hostellerie de la Reine-Jeanne. Grand-Rue, 13520 Les Baux. ☎ 04-90-54-32-06. Fax 04-90-54-32-33. 10 units. TV TEL. 270–570F ($48.60–$102.60) double. MC, V. Closed Nov 15–Feb 15 (open during Christmas holidays).

This warm, immaculate inn is the best bargain in Les Baux. You enter through a typical provincial French bistro, where you're welcomed by Alain Guilbard. All the rooms are comfortable, and three have their own terraces. Fixed-price menus are sumptuously prepared by chef Jean-Marc Hermann.

WHERE TO DINE

L'Oustau de Beaumanière (see above) boasts an excellent dining room.

✪ La Riboto de Taven. Le Val d'Enfer, 13520 Les Baux. ☎ 04-90-54-34-23. Fax 04-90-54-38-88. Reservations required. Main courses 120–180F ($21.60–$32.40); fixed-price menus 200–300F ($36–$54) at lunch, 300F ($54) at dinner. AE, DC, MC, V. Thurs–Tues noon–1:30pm, Thurs–Mon 7:30–9:30pm. Closed Jan 5–Mar 15. FRENCH.

This 1835 farmhouse outside the medieval section of town has been owned by two generations of the Novi family, of which Christine and Philippe Theme are the English-speaking daughter and son-in-law. In summer you can sit outdoors at the beautifully laid tables, one of which is a millstone. Jean-Pierre Novi's culinary creations are filled with brawny flavors and the heady perfumes of Provençal herbs. Menu items may include sea bass in olive oil, fricassée of mussels flavored with basil, and lamb en croûte with olives—plus homemade desserts.

Available for rent are two rooms so large they're like suites; each costs 1,100F ($198), breakfast included.

6 Aix-en-Provence

469 miles S of Paris, 50 miles SE of Avignon, 20 miles N of Marseille, 109 miles W of Nice

Founded in 122 B.C. by a Roman general, Caius Sextius Calvinus, who named it Aquae Sextiae after himself, Aix (pronounced *ex*) was first a Roman military outpost and then a civilian colony, the administrative capital of a province of the later Roman Empire, the seat of an archbishop, and the official residence of the medieval comtes de Provence. After the union of Provence with France, Aix remained until the Revolution a judicial and administrative headquarters.

The celebrated son of this old capital city of Provence, Paul Cézanne, immortalized the countryside nearby. Just as he saw it, Montagne Ste-Victoire looms over the town today, though a string of high-rises has now cropped up on the landscape. The most charming center in all Provence, this faded university town was once a seat of aristocracy, its streets walked by counts and kings.

Today this city of some 150,000 is reasonably quiet in winter but active and bustling when the summer hordes pour in. Many of the local population are international students. (The Université d'Aix dates from 1413.) Today Emile Zola's absinthe has given way to pastis in the many cafes scattered throughout the town. Summer is especially lively because of the frequent cultural events, ranging from opera to jazz, staged here from June to August. Increasingly, Aix is becoming a bedroom community for urbanites fleeing Marseille after 5pm.

ESSENTIALS

GETTING THERE   As a rail and highway junction, the city is easily accessible, with **trains** arriving hourly from Marseille (trip time: 40 minutes). For rail information and schedules, call ☎ **08-36-35-35-39.**

Independent **bus** companies service Aix-en-Provence. SATAP (☎ **04-42-26-23-78** for schedule information) operates four buses a day to and from Avignon, taking 1½ hours.

If you're **driving** from Marseille, take A51 north to Aix-en-Provence; from Avignon, travel A7 south to Senas and follow N7 southeast to Aix-en-Provence.

VISITOR INFORMATION   The **Office de Tourisme** is at 2 place du Général-de-Gaulle (☎ **04-42-16-11-61**).

SPECIAL EVENTS   Aix is more closely geared to music and its performance than virtually any other city in the south of France, and it offers at least four midsummer festivals that showcase concerts, opera, and dance. They include the **Saison d'Aix** (June to August), which focuses on symphonic and chamber music, and a well-attended **Jazz Festival** (June 28 to July 11) that brings in musicians from all over the world. For information on either of these, call the **Comité "Officielle" des Fêtes** (☎ **04-42-63-06-75**).

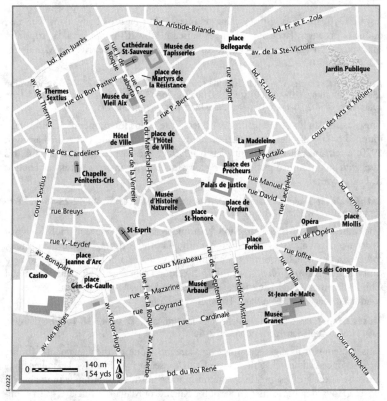

Also noteworthy is the **Festival International de Danse** (July 11 to 23), attracting classical and modern dance troupes from throughout Europe and the world. For information, call ☎ **04-42-96-05-01.**

EXPLORING THE AREA

Aix's main street, ✪ **cours Mirabeau,** is one of Europe's most beautiful. Plane trees stretch their branches across the top like an umbrella, shading it from the hot Provençal sun and filtering the light into shadows that play on the rococo fountains below. On one side are shops and sidewalk cafes, on the other richly embellished sandstone *hôtels particuliers* (mansions) from the 17th and 18th centuries. Honoring Mirabeau, the revolutionary and statesman, the street begins at the 1860 landmark fountain on place de la Libération.

The best experience in Aix is a walk along the carefully signposted ✪ **route de Cézanne (D17),** which winds eastward through the Provençal countryside toward Ste-Victoire. From the east end of cours Mirabeau, take rue du Maréchal-Joffre across boulevard Carnot to boulevard des Poilus, which becomes avenue des Ecoles-Militaires and finally D17. The stretch between Aix and the hamlet of Le Tholonet is full of twists and turns where Cézanne often set up his easel to paint. The entire route makes a lovely 3½-mile stroll. Le Tholonet has a cafe or two where you can refresh yourself while waiting for one of the frequent buses back to Aix.

After you've toured Aix, you might also consider an excursion to the **Château de Vauvenarges,** site of Pablo Picasso's last home. Reach it from Aix by driving 10 miles east on D10. You can't visit the château's interior, but Picasso's body, along with that of one of his wives, Jacqueline Roche, is buried nearby. If you opt for a day trip from Aix, you might appreciate a meal at **Au Moulin de Provence,** rue des Maquisards (☎ **04-42-66-02-22**).

Atelier de Cézanne. 9 av. Paul-Cézanne (outside town). ☎ **04-42-21-06-53.** Admission 25F ($4.50) adults, 10F ($1.80) students, free for ages 16 and under. Apr–Sept Wed–Mon 10am–noon and 2:30–6pm; Oct–Mar Wed–Mon 10am–noon and 2–5pm.

This was the studio of the painter considered the major forerunner of Cubism. Surrounded by a wall, the house was restored by American admirers. Repaired again in 1970, it remains much as Cézanne left it in 1906, "his coat hanging on the wall, his easel with an unfinished picture waiting for a touch of the master's brush," as Thomas R. Parker wrote.

Cathédrale St-Sauveur. Place des Martyrs de la Résistance. ☎ **04-42-23-45-65.** Free admission. Daily 8:30am–7:30pm.

The cathedral of Aix is dedicated to Christ under the title St-Sauveur (Holy Savior or Redeemer). Its Baptistery dates from the 4th and 5th centuries, but the architectural complex as a whole has seen many additions. It contains a brilliant Nicolas Froment triptych, *The Burning Bush,* from the 15th century. One side depicts the Virgin and Child; the other, Good King René and his second wife, Jeanne de Laval. Masses are conducted every Sunday at 9am, 10:30am, and 7pm.

Musée Granet. Place St-Jean-de-Malte (up rue Cardinale). ☎ **04-42-38-14-70.** Admission 10F ($1.80). Wed–Mon 10am–noon and 2–6pm.

This museum owns eight paintings by Cézanne, none of them major. (A former director once claimed that the walls of this museum "would never be sullied by a Cézanne"—the great painter had a famously antagonistic relationship with the people of Aix.) Housed in the former center of the Knights of Malta, the fine-arts gallery contains works by van Dyck, van Loo, and Rigaud; portraits by Pierre and François Puget; and (the most interesting) a *Jupiter and Thetis* by Ingres. Ingres also did an 1807 portrait of the museum's namesake, François Marius Granet. Granet's own works abound.

Musée des Tapisseries. 28 place des Martyrs de la Résistance. ☎ **04-42-23-09-91.** Admission 10F ($1.80). Daily 10am–noon and 2–5:45pm.

Lining the gilded walls of this former archbishop's palace are three series of tapestries from the 17th and 18th centuries, collected by the archbishops to decorate the palace: *The History of Don Quixote* by Natoire, *The Russian Games* by Leprince, and *The Grotesques* by Monnoyer. The museum also exhibits rare furnishings from the 17th and 18th centuries.

SHOPPING

For the best selection of art objects and fabrics inspired by the traditions of Provence, head for **Les Olivades,** 15 rue Marius-Reinaud (☎ **04-42-38-33-66**). It sells tasteful fabrics, shirts for women and men, fashionable dresses, and table linens.

Opened a century ago, **Bechard,** 12 cours Mirabeau (☎ **04-42-26-06-78**), is the most famous bakery in town. On the ground floor of a building on the main street, it takes its work so seriously that it refers to its underground kitchens as a *laboratoire* (laboratory). The pastries are truly delectable, in most cases made fresh every day.

La Boutique du Pays d'Aix, in the Office de Tourisme, 2 place du Général-de-Gaulle (☎ **04-42-16-11-61**), carries a wide selection of *santons* (carved figurines inspired by the Nativity of Jesus), locally woven textiles and carvings, and *calissons* (sugared confections made with almonds and a confit of melon).

Founded in 1934 on a busy boulevard about half a mile from the center of Aix, the showroom and factory of **Santons Fouque,** 65 cours Gambetta, route de Nice, RN7 (☎ **04-42-26-33-38**), stocks the largest assortment of santons in Aix. More than 1,800 figurines are cast in terra-cotta, finished by hand, then decorated with oil-based paint according to 18th-century models. Each of the trades practiced in medieval Provence is represented in the inventories, which include grizzled but awestruck shoe-makers, barrel makers, coppersmiths, ironsmiths, and rope makers, each poised to wel-come the newborn Jesus. Depending on their size and complexity, figurines range from 40F to 5,300F ($7.20 to $954).

WHERE TO STAY
VERY EXPENSIVE

✪ **Villa Gallici**. Av. de la Violette (impasse des Grands Pins), 13100 Aix-en-Provence. ☎ **04-42-23-29-23.** Fax 04-42-96-30-45. E-mail: villagallici@msn.com. 22 units. A/C MINIBAR TV TEL. 1,100–2,000F ($198–$360) double; 2,300–2,800F ($414–$504) suite. AE, DC, MC, V.

This elegant inn is the most stylishly decorated hotel in Aix, created by a trio of archi-tects and interior designers (Mssrs Dez, Montemarco, and Jouve) and acclaimed as "divinely over the top." Each room contains a private safe and an individualized decor of subtlety and charm, richly infused with the decorative traditions of Aix; some boast a private terrace or garden. The beds are hung with "waterfalls" of sprigged and striped cotton.

Dining: The villa sits in a large enclosed garden in the heart of town, close to one of the best restaurants, Le Clos de la Violette (see below). You can order lunch from this restaurant to be served beside the pool. The villa has its own in-house restaurant now, Gourmande d'Yvonne, but it still works together with La Violette.

Amenities: Spa facilities.

EXPENSIVE

Hôtel des Augustins. 3 rue de la Masse, 13100 Aix-en-Provence. ☎ **04-42-27-28-59.** Fax 04-42-26-74-87. 29 units. A/C MINIBAR TEL TV. 600–1,200F ($108–$216) double. AE, DC, MC, V. Parking 50F ($9).

Converted from the 12th-century Grands Augustins Convent, this hotel has been beautifully restored, with ribbed-vault ceilings, stained-glass windows, stone walls, terra-cotta floors, and Louis XIII furnishings. The reception desk is in a chapel, and oil paintings and watercolors decorate the public rooms. The spacious, soundproofed guest rooms—two with terrace—all have automatic alarm-call facilities. A private garage is on the other side of place de la Rotonde. This site won a place in history by sheltering an excommunicated Martin Luther on his return from Rome, but in 1892 the place was transformed from church to hotel.

✪ **Mercure Paul-Cézanne.** 40 av. Victor-Hugo, 13100 Aix-en-Provence. ☎ **04-42-26-34-73.** Fax 04-42-27-20-95. www.mercure.com. 55 units. A/C MINIBAR TV TEL. 490–595F ($88.20–$107.10) double; 700–850F ($126–$153) suite. AE, DC, MC, V. Parking 60F ($10.80).

On a street of sycamores, this member of a nationwide chain is more plush and tasteful than you'd expect, thanks to its former owner, who poured a lot of time and money into it before selling it outright. It has a refined interior, though it has lost its former top position to the more stylish and tranquil Gallici. The lounge seems more like a pri-vate sitting room than a hotel lobby. Many of the rooms have mahogany Victorian furniture, Louis XVI chairs, marble-top chests, gilt mirrors, and oil paintings. All bath-rooms have hand-painted tiles. The small breakfast room opens onto a rear courtyard.

MODERATE

Grand Hôtel Nègre Coste. 33 cours Mirabeau, 13100 Aix-en-Provence. ☎ **04-42-27-74-22.** Fax 04-42-26-80-93. 36 units. A/C MINIBAR TV TEL. 389–654F ($70–$117.70) double. AE, DC, MC, V.

This hotel, a former 18th-century town house, is so popular with the dozens of musicians who flock to Aix for the summer festivals that it's usually difficult to get a room at any price. Such popularity is understandable. Outside, flowers cascade from jardinières and windows are surrounded by 18th-century carvings. Inside, there's a wide staircase, marble portrait busts, and a Provençal armoire. The soundproofed rooms contain interesting antiques. The higher floors overlook cours Mirabeau or the old city.

Novotel Aix Point de l'Arc. Périphérique Sud, arc de Meyran, 13100 Aix-en-Provence. ☎ **800/221-4542** in the U.S., or 04-42-16-09-09. Fax 04-42-26-00-09. www.novotel.com. 80 units. A/C MINIBAR TV TEL. 460F ($82.80) double. AE, DC, MC, V. Take the ring road 2 miles south of the town center (exit at Aix-Est 3 Sautets).

At the end of a labyrinthine but well-marked route, this well-maintained member of a national chain offers large rooms. Designed for European business travelers or vacationing families in summer, each has one single and one double bed and a fully equipped bathroom. The hotel offers one of the most pleasant dining rooms in the suburbs, Côté Jardin, with big windows overlooking Rivière Arc de Méyran and an ivy-covered forest. There's an outdoor pool in the garden.

If this hotel is full, rooms may be available at the **Novotel Aix-Beaumanoir,** périphérique Sud, 13100 Aix-en-Provence (☎ **04-42-27-47-50;** fax 04-42-38-46-41). Set less than 500 yards away, it has its own outdoor pool, an in-house restaurant, and 102 rooms. Rooms and rates in both hotels are almost exactly the same.

INEXPENSIVE

✪ **Hôtel Cardinal.** 22–24 rue Cardinale, 13100 Aix-en-Provence. ☎ **04-42-38-32-30.** Fax 04-42-26-39-05. 35 units. TV TEL. 260–420F ($46.80–$75.60) double. MC, V. Parking 60F ($10.80).

To many, the Cardinal is still the best address in town. Opposite the Musée Granet and St-Jean-de-Malte, it's distinguished by a lingering air of nostalgia. Everything is Provence provincial with a vengeance. The beautifully furnished old rooms are either in the main building or in the annex up the street. Some of the annex rooms have serviceable kitchens. M. F. K. Fisher, author of *Two Towns in Provence,* lived nearby at no. 17 for many years.

Hôtel La Caravelle. 29 bd. du Roi-René (at cours Mirabeau), 13100 Aix-en-Provence. ☎ **04-42-21-53-05.** Fax 04-42-96-55-46. 32 units. A/C TV TEL. 260–390F ($46.80–$70.20) double. AE, DC, MC, V.

A 3-minute walk from the center, this conservatively furnished three-star hotel has a bas-relief of a three-masted caravelle on its beige stucco facade. The hotel is run by M. and Mme Henri Denis, who offer breakfast in the stone-floored lobby, part of their continuing tradition of warm hospitality. Most rooms were renovated in 1995; they have double-glazed windows to help muffle the noise.

WHERE TO DINE
VERY EXPENSIVE

Le Clos de la Violette. 10 av. de la Violette. ☎ **04-42-23-30-71.** Reservations required. Main courses 185–200F ($33.30–$36); fixed-price menus 250–500F ($45–$90) at lunch, 500F ($90) at dinner. AE, MC, V. Tues–Sat noon–1:30pm, Mon–Sat 7:30–9:30pm. FRENCH.

In an elegant residential neighborhood, which most visitors reach by taxi, Le Clos de la Violette is a creative and innovative restaurant whose cuisine is usually a bit better than the attention span of its sometimes inexperienced staff. This imposing Provençal villa has an octagonal reception area and several modern dining rooms. Jean-Marc and Brigitte Banzo celebrate the bounty of Provence with a menu that changes every 2 months and may include an upside-down tart of snails with parsley juice, a pissaladière of local fish, and a slow-cooked version of lamb with brown sauce. Filet of pigeon with foie gras is always appealing, as is the sophisticated array of desserts.

MODERATE

Chez Maxime. 12 place Ramus. ☎ **04-42-26-28-51.** Reservations recommended. Main courses 80–280F ($14.40–$50.40); fixed-price menus 130–270F ($23.40–$48.60). MC, V. Tues–Sat noon–2pm, Mon–Sat 8–10:30pm. Closed Jan 15–31. GRILLS/PROVENÇAL.

In the pedestrian-only part of town, this likable restaurant reflects the skills and personality of its owner/chef/namesake, Felix Maxime. There's a terrace on the sidewalk in front, plus a wood-trimmed stone interior where the most important element is the cuisine. The appetizer most redolent of the flavors of Provence is a *tian*—layers of eggplant, peppers, and Mediterranean herbs in a terra-cotta pot, infused with garlic, aromates, and olive oil, and baked until bubbly. Another superb beginning is *rillettes* (similar to a roughly textured pâté) of sea wolf with rouille (a garlicky mayonnaise). Specialties include as many as 19 kinds of grilled meat or fish, cooked over an oak-burning fire, and several preparations of lamb (M. Maxime will dress your cut of meat adjacent to your table). The wine list features more than 530 vintages, many esoteric bottles from the region.

Trattoria Chez Antoine Côte Cour. 19 rue Mirabeau. ☎ **04-42-93-12-51.** Reservations recommended. Main courses 60–140F ($10.80–$25.20). DC, MC, V. Tues–Sat noon–2:30pm and Mon–Sat 7:30pm–midnight. PROVENÇAL/ITALIAN.

In 1997 this popular trattoria moved into new quarters—an 18th-century town house a few steps from place Rotonde—and managed to lure most of its regulars along. These include Emanuel Ungaro and many film and fashion types who mingle smoothly with old-time "Aixers." Despite the grandeur of the setting, the ambience is deliberately unpretentious, even jovial. Crusty bread and small pots of aromatic purées (anchovy and basil) are placed at your table before a staff member takes your order. A simple wine, such as Côtes du Rhône, will go nicely with the kind of hearty Mediterranean food that's de rigueur. Examples are a memorable version of pastis (pasta Romano flavored with calf's liver, flap mushrooms, and tomato sauce), osso bucco (veal shank layered with salty ham), a selection of *légumes farcies* (such as eggplant and zucchini stuffed with minced meat and herbs), and at least half a dozen kinds of fresh fish.

INEXPENSIVE

✪ **Le Bistro Latin.** 18 rue de la Couronne. ☎ **04-42-38-22-88.** Reservations recommended. Main courses 85–125F ($15.30–$22.50); fixed-price menus 75F ($13.50) at lunch, 119–139F ($21.40–$25) at dinner. AE, V. Tues–Sat noon–2pm, Mon–Sat 7–10:30pm. PROVENÇAL.

The best little bistro in Aix (for the price) is run by Bruno Ungaro and his partner, Gilles Holtz, who pride themselves on their fixed-price menus. The intimate street-level and cellar dining rooms are decorated in Greco-Latin style; the staff is young and enthusiastic; and Provençal music plays in the background. Try the chartreuse of mussels or crêpe of hare with basil sauce. We've enjoyed the classic cuisine on all of our visits, particularly the scampi risotto.

The management has opened a second restaurant, **Amphitryon** (☎ 04-42-26-54-10), in the center of the old town about 100 yards away; it concentrates on reasonably priced Provençal fare.

AIX AFTER DARK

Because Aix is a university town, and one of the largest towns in Provence, you're guaranteed an animated nightlife.

Rockers head for **Le Mistral,** 3 rue Frédéric-Mistral (☎ 04-42-38-16-49), where techno and house music blare long and loud. Its slightly more subdued competitor, **Le Richelme,** 24 rue de la Verrerie (☎ 04-42-23-49-29), plays the same music but sometimes dips into 1970s and 1980s disco. Nearby is a woodsy-looking English pub that plays rock videos, **Bugsy,** 25 rue de la Verrerie (☎ 04-42-38-25-22), where the good times are punctuated with bouts at billiard tables.

The over-30 set heads for the **Scat Club,** 11 rue de la Verrerie (☎ 04-42-23-00-23), where rock and funk provide music to drink to. A similar choice is **Hot Brass,** chemin de la Pleine des Vergueiers (☎ 04-42-21-05-57), attracting lots of off-duty photographers, artists, actors, and literary types who appreciate the drinks and live music in the rock and country vein. Both these places boast two floors, each with its own bar, and live acts that include healthy doses of rhythm and blues.

If you're a student or want to act like one, head for the **Jungle Café,** 4 bd. Carnot (☎ 04-42-21-47-44), where live music enhances an everyday preoccupation with dating and mating. The town's most animated gay bar is **M. P. Aix Vidéo Pub,** 38 rue des Bernadines (☎ 04-42-27-66-90).

7 Marseille

479 miles S of Paris, 116 miles SW of Nice, 19 miles S of Aix-en-Provence

Bustling Marseille, with more than a million inhabitants, is the second-largest city in France (its population surpassed that of Lyon in the early 1990s) and the country's premier port. A crossroads of world traffic, it's an ancient city, founded by Greeks from the city of Phocaea in the 6th century B.C., and a place of unique sounds, smells, and sights. It has seen wars and much destruction, but its life has always revolved around trade and commerce.

Perhaps its most common association is with the national anthem of France, "La Marseillaise." During the Revolution, 500 volunteers marched to Paris, singing this rousing song along the way. The rest is history.

Although in many respects Marseille is big and sprawling, dirty and slumlike in some places, there's elegance and charm to be found here as well—if you know where to look. Vieux-Port, the old harbor, is especially colorful, somehow compensating for the dreary industrial dockland nearby. Marseille has always symbolized danger and intrigue, and that reputation is somewhat justified. It's now the home of thousands of North and sub-Saharan African immigrants, who have created a lively mix of races and creeds.

Marseille today actually occupies twice the amount of land space as Paris, and its age-old problems remain, including drugs, smuggling, corruption (often at the highest levels), the Mafia, and racial tension. Unemployment, as always, is on the rise. But in spite of it all, it's a bustling, always-fascinating city unlike any other in France.

ESSENTIALS

GETTING THERE   The Marseille **airport** (☎ 04-42-14-14-14), 18 miles north of the center, receives international flights from all over Europe. From the airport,

Marseille

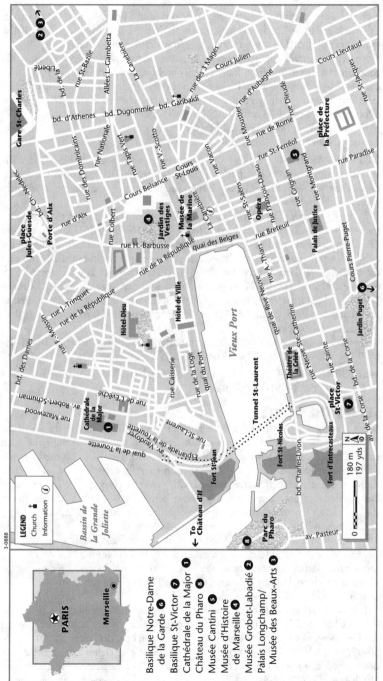

LEGEND
+ Church
ⓘ Information

Bessin de
la Grande
Joliette

Bassin de
la Grande
Joliette

Gare St-Charles

bd. de la Liberté

rue St-Bazile

Allées L.-Gambetta

La Canebière

rue des 3 Mages

Cours Julien

Cours Lieutaud

rue St-Jacques

bd. d'Athenes   bd. Dugommier   bd. Garibaldi

rue Moustier   rue d'Aubagne

rue de Rome   rue Dieudé

place de
la Préfecture

rue Paradise

rue des Dominicains

rue Nationale

rue Tapis Vert

rue V.-Scotto

Cours
St-Louis

rue Vacon

rue St-Ferréol

rue Grignan

rue Montgrand

place
Jules-Guesde   bd. Ch.-Nédélec

rue d'Aix

Porte d'Aix

rue Colbert

Cours Belsance

Jardin des
Vestiges

Musée de
la Marine

La Canebière

rue St-Säens

Opéra   rue François-Daviso

Palais de Justice

rue H.-Barbusse

rue de la République

quai des Belges

rue Breteuil

Cours Pierre-Puget

rue F.-Moisson

rue I. Trinquet
rue de la République

Hôtel-Dieu

Hôtel de Ville

quai de Rive Neuve

rue A.-Thiars

Jardin Puget

bd. des Dames

rue de la Loge   quai du Port

rue Caisserie

rue Neuve Ste-Catherine

Théâtre de
la Criée

rue Sainte

bd. de la Corse

av. Robert-Schuman

rue de l'Evêché

rue St-Laurent

Vieux Port

Tunnel St-Laurent

place
St-Victor

av. de la Corse

rue Mazewood

Cathédrale
de la Major

av. Vaudoyer
Esplanade de la Tourette

quai de la Tourette

Esplanade de la Tourette

Fort St-Jean

Fort St-Nicolas

bd. Charles-Livon

Fort d'Entrecasteaux

To
Château d'If

N

180 m
197 yds

0

Parc du
Pharo

av. Pasteur

3-0888

PARIS

Marseille

Basilique Notre-Dame
de la Garde ⑥

Basilique St-Victor ⑦

Cathédrale de la Major ①

Château du Pharo ⑧

Musée Cantini ⑤

Musée d'Histoire
de Marseille ④

Musée Grobet-Labadié ②

Palais Longchamp/
Musée des Beaux-Arts ③

blue-and-white minivans (*navettes*) make the trip from a point in front of the arrivals hall to Marseille's St-Charles rail station, near the Vieux-Port, for a one-way fee of 45F ($8.10) per person. The minivans run daily from 6:20am to 10:50pm.

Marseille has **train** connections from hundreds of European cities, with especially good connections to and from Italy. The city is also the terminus for the TGV bullet train, which departs daily from Paris's Gare de Lyon (trip time: 4¾ hours). Local trains leave Paris almost every hour, making a number of stops before reaching Marseille. For information and schedules, call ☎ **08-36-35-35-39.**

If you're **driving** from Paris, follow A6 south to Lyon; then continue south along A7 to Marseille.

GETTING AROUND   Parking and car safety are such potential hazards in Marseille that your wisest bet is to put your car in a garage and rely on public transportation during your visit here. The city is sprawling, and public transportation will help you avoid the hassle of traffic.

Marseille is serviced by **Métro** lines 1 and 2, both of which stop at the main train station, Gare St-Charles, place Victor Hugo (☎ **08-36-35-35-35**). The Métro runs daily from 5am to 9pm. At the tourist office, pick up a free brochure outlining the public transportation routes of Marseille. If you're going to be in Marseille for 2 or 3 days, purchase a **Carte Liberté** for 50F ($9). These tickets are available from RTM, 6–8 rue de Fabres (☎ **04-91-91-92-10**), open Monday to Friday from 8:30am to 5:30pm and Saturday from 9am to 5:30pm. Otherwise, you can purchase tickets at Métro and bus stops, costing 8F ($1.45) for a ride good for 70 minutes. After that, you need another ticket.

If you can't face the hassle of public transportation, call Taxi Plus at ☎ **04-91-03-60-03** or Marseille Taxi at ☎ **04-91-02-20-20.**

VISITOR INFORMATION   The **Office de Tourisme** (Métro: Vieux-Port) is at 4 La Canebière (☎ **04-91-13-89-00**).

SEEING THE SIGHTS

Many visitors never bother to visit the museums, preferring to absorb the life of the city on its busy streets and at its sidewalk cafes, particularly those along the main street, **La Canebière.** Known as "can of beer" to World War II GIs, it's the heart and soul of Marseille, even if it is the seediest main street in France. Lined with hotels, shops, and restaurants, the street is filled with sailors of every nation and people of every nationality, especially Algerians. (In fact, some 100,000 North Africans live in the city and its tenement suburbs, often in communities that resemble *souks*.)

Canebière winds down to the **Vieux-Port,** dominated by the massive neoclassical forts of St-Jean and St-Nicholas. The port is filled with fishing craft and yachts and ringed with seafood restaurants. For a panoramic view, head for the **Parc du Pharo,** a promontory facing the entrance to the Vieux-Port. From a terrace overlooking the Château du Pharo, built by Napoléon III for his Eugénie, you can clearly see Fort St-Jean and the old and new cathedrals.

From quai des Belges at the Vieux-Port you can take a motorboat for a 20-minute ride to **Château d'If** for 50F ($9) round-trip. Boats leave about every hour. Contact the **Groupement des Armateurs Côtiers;** its office on quai des Belges (☎ **04-91-55-50-09,** Métro: Vieux-Port) is open daily from 7am to 7pm. Depending on the season, boats depart at intervals between 60 and 90 minutes. On the sparsely vegetated island of Château d'If (☎ **04-91-59-02-30** for information), François I built a fortress to defend Marseille and its port. The site later housed a state prison; carvings by Huguenot prisoners can still be seen inside some of the cells. Alexandre Dumas used the château as a setting for *The Count of Monte Cristo,* though the adventure never really took place. Its most famous association—with the legendary Man in the Iron Mask—is also apocryphal. The château is open April to September daily from 9am to 6pm, October to March Tuesday to Sunday from 9am to 1pm and 2 to 5:30pm. Admittance to the island costs 25F ($4.50) for adults and 15F ($2.70) for children.

If you're driving, continue along from the old port to the **corniche Président-J.-F.-Kennedy,** a promenade running for about 3 miles along the sea. You pass villas and gardens along the way and have a good view of the Mediterranean. To the north, the **Port Moderne,** the "gateway to the East," is man-made. Its construction began in 1844, and a century later the Germans destroyed it. Motorboat trips are conducted along the docks.

Basilique Notre-Dame-de-la-Garde. Rue Fort-du-Sanctuaire. ☎ **04-91-13-40-80.** Free admission. Mid-June to mid-Sept daily 7am–8pm; late Sept to early June daily 7am–7pm. Métro: Vieux-Port. Bus: 60.

This landmark church crowns a limestone rock overlooking the southern side of the Vieux-Port. It was built in the Romanesque-Byzantine style popular in the 19th century and topped by a 30-foot gilded statue of the Virgin. Visitors come here not so much for the church as for the view—best seen at sunset—from its terrace. Spread out before you are the city, the islands, and the sea.

Basilique St-Victor. Place St-Victor. ☎ **04-91-33-25-86.** Admission to crypt 10F ($1.80). Crypt daily 8am–6:30pm. Head west along quai de Rive-Neuve (near the Gare du Vieux-Port). Métro: Vieux-Port.

This semifortified basilica was built above a crypt from the 5th century, when the church and abbey were founded by St. Cassianus. You can visit the crypt, which also reflects work done in the 10th and 11th centuries.

Cathédrale de la Major. Place de la Major. ☎ **04-91-90-53-57.** Free admission. Mid-June to mid-Sept Tues–Sat 9–7pm, Sun–Mon 9am–noon; late Sept to early June Tues–Sun 9am–noon and 2:30–6pm. Métro: Joliette.

This was one of the largest cathedrals (some 450 feet long) built in Europe in the 19th century. Its interior is adorned with mosaic floors and red-and-white marble banners, and the exterior is in a bastardized Romanesque-Byzantine style. The domes and cupolas may remind you of Istanbul. This vast pile has almost swallowed its 12th-century Romanesque predecessor (originally a baptistery) built on the ruins of a Temple of Diana.

Musée des Beaux-Arts. In Palais Longchamp, on place Bernex. ☎ **04-91-14-59-30.** Admission 10F ($1.80), free for children and seniors. June 15–Sept 15 Tues–Sun 11am–6pm; Sept 16–June 14 Tues–Sun 10am–5pm. Metro: Cinq avenue Longchamp or Réfomés.

One of the most scenic sights is Palais Longchamp, with its spectacular fountain and colonnade, built during the Second Empire. This museum, housed in a northern wing of the palace, displays a vast array of paintings from the 16th to the 19th centuries. They include works by Corot, Millet, Ingres, David, and Rubens. Some 80 sculptures and objets d'art were bequeathed to the museum as well; particularly interesting is a gallery of Pierre Puget sculpture. One salon is devoted to Honoré Daumier, born in Marseille in 1808.

Musée Cantini. 19 rue Grignan. ☎ **04-91-54-77-75.** Admission 12F ($2.15), free for seniors and children 10 and under. June–Sept Tues–Sun 11am–6pm; Oct–May Tues–Sun 10am–5pm. Métro: Estrangin Préfecture.

The temporary exhibitions of contemporary art staged here are often as good as the permanent collection. This museum is devoted to modern art, with masterpieces by

Derain, Marquet, Ernst, Masson, Balthus, and others. It also owns a selection of works by important young international artists.

Musée Grobet-Labadié. 140 bd. Longchamp. ☎ **04-91-62-21-82.** Admission 12F ($2.15) adults, free for children. Call the tourist office or the number above for more information. Métro: Réfomés.

This private collection, bequeathed to the city in 1919, includes exquisite Louis XV and Louis XVI furniture, as well as an outstanding collection of medieval Burgundian and Provençal sculpture. Other exhibits are 17th-century Gobelin tapestries; 15th- to 19th-century German, Italian, French, and Flemish paintings; and 16th- and 17th-century Italian and French faïence.

Musée d'Histoire de Marseille. Centre Bourse, square Belsunce. ☎ **04-91-90-42-22.** Admission 10F ($1.80) adults, 5F (90¢) children. Mon–Sat noon–7pm. Métro: Vieux-Port.

You're allowed to wander through an archaeological garden where excavations are still going on, as scholars attempt to learn more about the ancient town of Massalia, founded by Greek sailors. Of course, many of the exhibits, such as old coins and fragments of pottery, only suggest their former glory. To help you more fully realize the era, you're aided by audiovisual exhibits and a free exhibition room. A medieval quarter of potters has been discovered, and the Louis XIV town is open to the public. You can also see what's left of a Roman wreck that was excavated from the site.

SHOPPING

Only Paris and Lyon can compete with Marseille in the breadth and diversity of merchandise. Your best bet is a trip to the **Vieux-Port** and the streets surrounding it to check out the folkloric items that literally pop out of the boutiques. Many are loaded with souvenirs like crèche-style *santons* (carved wooden figurines of saints appropriate for display at Christmas). But the best place for acquiring these artifacts is just above the Vieux-Port, behind the Théâtre National de la Criée. At **Ateliers Marcel Carbonel,** 49 rue Neuve-Ste-Catherine (☎ **04-91-54-26-58;** Métro: Vieux-Port), more than 600 Nativity-related figures, available in half a dozen sizes, sell at prices beginning at 50F ($9).

At **Amandine,** 69 bd. Eugène-Pierre (☎ **04-91-47-00-83;** Métro: Timone), every theatrical agent in Marseille has benefited from the way chocolate syrup can be "photo-reproduced" onto delicious layer cakes in virtually any flavor you specify in advance. Even if you don't happen to have your scrapbook with you for something important to duplicate, you'll find a roster of artfully rich cakes, emblazoned with scenes of the Vieux-Port or whatever. A traditional inventory of pastries and chocolates is available at **Puyricard,** 25 rue Francis-Davso (☎ **04-91-54-26-25;** Métro: Vieux-Port), with another location at 155 rue Jean-Mermoz (☎ **04-91-77-94-11;** Métro: Rondpoint du Prado). The treats available here include chocolates stuffed either with almond paste (*pâté d'amande*) or confits de fruits, along with a type of biscuit (*une Marseillotte*).

Since medieval times, Marseille has thrived on the legend of *Les Trois Maries*—three saints named Mary, including everyone's favorite ex-sinner, Mary Magdalene. Assisted by awakened-from-the-dead St. Lazarus, they reportedly came ashore at a point near Marseille to Christianize ancient Provence. In commemoration of their voyage, small boat-shaped cookies (*les navettes*) flavored with secret ingredients that include tons of orange zest, orange-flower water, and sugar, are forever associated with Marseille. They're sold throughout the city, most notably at **Le Four des Navettes,** 136 rue Sainte (☎ **04-91-33-32-12;** Métro: Vieux-Port). Opened in 1791, it sells the cookies for 40F ($7.20) per dozen—and does very little else except perpetuate the city's most cherished (and dubious) medieval myth and ferociously guard the secret of how the pastries are made.

Two of the city's most sophisticated emporiums for food are **Traiteur Blanc,** 19 av. du Prado, 8e (☎ **04-91-79-21-09;** Métro: Castellane), where you can acquire many of the ingredients for a picnic; and its long-time rival, **Benette,** 7 place Notre-Dame-du-Mont (☎ **04-91-48-66-23;** Métro: Cours-Julien Notre-Dame-du-Mont). For a staggering selection of cheeses, there's **La Fromagerie des Alpes,** place Notre-Dame-du-Mont (☎ **04-91-47-06-23;** Métro: Cours-Julien Notre-Dame-du-Mont).

Marseille has a handful of well-respected art galleries. The most internationally minded of the lot is **Galerie Cargo,** 55 rue Grignan (☎ **04-91-54-84-84;** Métro: Préfecture), which sells paintings by medium- to top-echelon artists from all over the world. Its most powerful competitor is **Galerie Roger-Pailhas,** 20 quai Rive Neuve (☎ **04-91-54-02-22;** Métro: Vieux-Port).

Antiques from around Provence are sold at **Galerie Wulfram-Puget,** rue Wulfram-Puget (☎ **04-91-76-42-85;** Métro: Périer), and **Antiquités François-Décamp,** 302 rue Paradis (☎ **04-91-81-18-00;** Métro: Périer).

Looking for a Provençal version of a sunny indoor-outdoor California-style mall? Head for the most talked-about real-estate development in the city's recent history, **L'Escale Borély,** avenue Mendès-France. A 25-minute trip south of Marseille (take the Métro to rond-point du Prado, then transfer to bus no. 19), it incorporates shops, cafes, bars, and restaurants. As you relax on a terrace sipping pastis, note the newest fad to hit France: in-line skating.

WHERE TO STAY
VERY EXPENSIVE

✪ **Résidence Le Petit Nice.** Corniche Président-J.-F.-Kennedy/Anse-de-Maldormé, 13007 Marseille. ☎ **04-91-59-25-92.** Fax 04-91-59-28-08. www.integra.fr/relaischateaux/passedat. E-mail: petitnice.passedat@wanadoo.fr. 17 units. A/C MINIBAR TV TEL. 1,000–2,200F ($180–$396) double; 2,900–3,900F ($522–$702) suite. AE, DC, MC, V. Parking in garage 100F ($18). Métro: Vieux-Port.

The best hotel in Marseille, the Résidence opened in 1917, when the Passédat family joined two suburban villas in a secluded area below the street, paralleling the beach. The beautiful, tasteful guest rooms are in the main building or an annex; all open onto views of the sea and boast the best and roomiest bathrooms in town (nearly all of which have a separate shower). Rooms also contain a number of thoughtful extras, including modem capabilities.

Dining: The restaurant is panoramic, with a view of the Marseille shore and the rocky islands off its coast. In summer, dinner is served in the garden facing the sea. Jean-Paul Passédat and his son, Gerald, create imaginative culinary dishes like Breton lobster with thyme, vinaigrette of rascasse (hogfish), and sea devil with saffron and garlic. This is the finest restaurant in Marseille.

Amenities: Seawater pool and solarium.

EXPENSIVE

Sofitel Marseille Vieux-Port. 36 bd. Charles-Livon, 13007 Marseille. ☎ **04-91-15-59-00.** Fax 04-91-15-59-50. www.sofitel.com. 130 units. A/C MINIBAR TV TEL. 890–1,190F ($160.20–$214.20) double; 2,200–2,650F ($396–$477) suite. AE, DC, MC, V. Parking 65F ($11.70). Métro: Vieux-Port.

This seven-story Sofitel looms above the massive embankments. It's not loaded with charm or atmosphere, but it's a fine chain hotel offering good value. The rooms look out on either boulevard traffic or on one of the best panoramic views of the port of Old Marseille. They're fairly generous in size, comfortable, and recently furnished in a Provence style. In 1987 its owner, the Accor hotel giant, turned over 93 rooms to a new three-star Novotel (see below). Today the two entrances, staffs, and dining/drinking facilities exist in the same building.

Dining: There's an elegant bar, and Les Trois Forts, a restaurant with views of the harbor and its defenses, serves lunch and dinner daily.

Amenities: Pool.

MODERATE TO INEXPENSIVE

La Résidence du Vieux-Port. 18 quai du Port, 13001 Marseille. ☎ 04-91-91-91-22. Fax 04-91-56-60-88. 53 units. A/C MINIBAR TV TEL. 550F ($99) double; 1,250F ($225) suite. AE, DC, MC, V. Métro: Vieux-Port.

Old-fashioned, with a touch of raffish charm and an unbeatable location directly beside the harbor, this eight-story hotel contains a cafe and a breakfast room on the second floor; a bar is behind the lobby. The guest rooms have loggia-style terraces opening onto the port; they're simple but serviceable thanks to a renovation completed in 1997. The conscientious staff tends appropriately to guests.

New Hôtel Vieux-Port. 3 bis rue Reine-Elisabeth, 13001 Marseille. ☎ 04-91-90-51-42. Fax 04-91-90-76-24. www.new-hotel.com. E-mail: info@new-hotel.com. 47 units. A/C MINIBAR TV TEL. 420F ($75.60) double. AE, DC, MC, V. Parking 30F ($5.40) nearby. Métro: Vieux-Port.

This stylish hotel near the port is a good value, particularly since its complete renovation in 1995. The attractively furnished rooms with views of the port are no more expensive than the others but must be reserved far in advance. Breakfast is the only meal served.

Novotel Vieux-Port. 36 bd. Charles-Livon, 13007 Marseille. ☎ 04-91-59-22-22. Fax 04-91-31-15-48. www.novotel.com. 90 units. A/C MINIBAR TV TEL. 550–650F ($99–$117) double. AE, DC, MC, V. Parking 40F ($7.20). Métro: Vieux-Port.

As mentioned above, this Novotel was created in 1987 out of the Sofitel. You don't receive the services offered at the Sofitel, but the prices are much more reasonable. Each room contains a double and a single bed (which serves as a couch) and a desk; some, however, look a little tired. Those with views of the Old Port tend to fill up first. The lattice-decorated restaurant serves good basic meals, daily from 6am to midnight.

WHERE TO DINE
EXPENSIVE

Au Pescadou. 19 place Castellane. ☎ 04-91-78-36-01. Reservations recommended. Main courses 90–120F ($16.20–$21.60); fixed-price menus 168–210F ($30.25–$37.80). AE, DC, MC, V. Daily noon–2pm, Mon–Sat 7–11pm. Closed July–Aug. Métro: Castellane. SEAFOOD.

Maintained by three multilingual sons of the original owner, Barthélémy Mennella, this is one of Marseille's finest seafood restaurants. Don't expect elaborate scraping and bowing—the service is civil but down-to-earth and not at all stuffy. Beside a busy traffic circle downtown, it overlooks a fountain, an obelisk, and a sidewalk display of fresh oysters. For an appetizer, try almond-stuffed mussels or "hors d'oeuvres of the fisherman." Main-dish specialties are bouillabaisse, *gigot de lotte* (monkfish stewed in cream sauce with fresh vegetables), and scallops cooked with morels.

Next to the main restaurant and under the same management are two informal newcomers, with rapid service and lower prices. In **Le Coin Bistrot,** straightforward and flavorful platters are served to a mostly young crowd for 100F to 120F ($18 to $21.60). **La Brasserie,** the least formal of all, serves platters of nonfish dishes, with menu items like blanquettes of veal, steak *à la pizzaiola,* and pastas, costing 40F to 50F ($7.20 to $9) for the plat du jour.

Les Echevins. 44 rue Sainte. ☎ **04-91-33-08-08.** Reservations recommended. Main courses 82–170F ($14.75–$30.60); fixed-price menus 120–280F ($21.60–$50.40). AE, DC, MC, V. Mon–Fri noon–2:30pm, Mon–Sat 7:30–11:30pm. Métro: Vieux-Port. PROVENÇAL/ SOUTHWESTERN FRENCH.

On the opposite side of the same building that contains Les Arcenaulx (see below), this restaurant occupies what was built as a dorm for the prisoners who were forced to row the ornamental barges of Louis XIV during his rare inspections of Marseille's harbor facilities. Today the setting contains crystal chandeliers, plush carpets, an enviable collection of antiques, and massive rocks and thick beams. You'll get a lot for your money, as the Moréni family charges relatively reasonable prices and insist on using fresh ingredients prepared at the last possible minute. Inspiration for menu items (cassoulet, magrêt of duckling, and foie gras) derives from either the southwest of France or from Provence, specifically Marseille. Provençal dishes include a delectable version of baked sea wolf that's prepared as simply as possible—just with herbs and olive oil. There's also roast codfish with aioli, and a succulent version of baudroie (a simpler version of bouillabaisse).

MODERATE

✪ **Les Arcenaulx.** 25 cours Etienne-d'Orves, 1er. ☎ **04-91-59-80-30.** Reservations recommended. Main courses 65–100F ($11.70–$18); fixed-price menus 135–280F ($24.30–$50.40). AE, DC, MC, V. Mon–Sat noon–2:30pm and 8–11:30pm. Métro: Vieux-Port. PROVENÇAL.

These bulky stone premises were built by the navies of Louis XIV. Close to the water near the Vieux-Port, they contain this restaurant as well as two bookstores (one for French classics, one for modern titles), all directed by hardworking and charming sisters, Simone and Jeanne Laffitte. Expect authentic and hearty Provençal cuisine with a Marseillais accent in dishes like a *baudroie* (kettle of seasonal fish) *à la Raimu*— named for a popular 20th-century actor, it's equivalent to bouillabaisse. Equally tempting are artichokes *barigoule* (loaded with aromatic spices and olive oil) and a worthy assortment of *petites légumes farcies* (slit-open Provençal vegetables stuffed with chopped meat and herbs).

INEXPENSIVE

Chez Angèle. 50 rue Caisserie (on the route between Marseille and Aix). ☎ **04-91-90-63-35.** Reservations recommended. Pizzas, pastas, and salads 45–95F ($8.10–$17.10); fixed-price menu 95F ($17.10). MC, V. Mon–Fri noon–2:30pm and Mon–Sat 7:30–11:30pm. Closed July 20–Aug 20. Métro: Vieux-Port. PROVENÇAL/PIZZA.

A local friend guided us here, and though many of Marseille's cheap eating places aren't recommendable, this one is worthwhile if you're watching your francs. Small, unpretentious, and amiable, it defines itself as a pizzeria-restaurant, with a menu that's much more comprehensive than the average pizzeria's. You can get pizza (the versions with pistou, fresh seafood, or flap mushrooms are among the best) or well-prepared ravioli, tagliatelle, osso bucco, and grilled versions of shrimp, squid, and daurade Provençal style. If you're looking for something really ethnic, ask for Francis's version of *pieds et paquets*, a country recipe savored by locals that includes equal portions of grilled sheep's foot and sheep's intestines stuffed with garlic-flavored bread crumbs, herbs, and chopped vegetables.

Dar Djerba. 15 Cours Julien. ☎ **04-91-48-55-36.** Reservations recommended. Main courses 85–110F ($15.30–$19.80). MC, V. Daily 11:30am–2:30pm and 7:30–11:30pm. Métro: Nouailles or Cours Julien. TUNISIAN.

Known to local residents as one of the best-managed of the Arab restaurants in Marseilles, this place celebrates the cuisine and the aesthetics of the historic Tunisian coastal settlement of Dar Djerba, a popular holiday destination for French and Italian tourists. The dining room is ringed with meticulously crafted ceramic mosaics and hammered artifacts of copper and brass, all centered around a splashing fountain. An attentive staff is well-versed in teaching newcomers about the nuances of Tunisian cuisine. The menu includes at least four kinds of couscous; a succulent *pastilla* that combines roasted pigeon with sugar and gravy; and an array of slow-cooked *tagines,* whereby lamb, chicken, or fish is baked in a covered clay pot. Meals taste best when accompanied by *méchouia,* a traditional salad of grilled vegetables drenched in herbs and olive oil. Any of the strong and heady red wines of Morocco, Tunisia, or Algeria makes a fine accompaniment.

NEARBY ACCOMMODATIONS & DINING

Relais de la Magdeleine. Route d'Aix, 13420 Gemenos. ☎ **04-42-32-20-16.** Fax 04-42-32-02-26. www.chatotel.com. E-mail: chatotel@chatotel.com. 24 units. TV TEL. 610–870F ($109.80–$156.60) double; 1,040–1,260F ($187.20–$226.80) suite. MC, V. Closed Dec–Mar 15. Take A50 east of Marseille for 15 miles.

In a stone-sided country mansion built in the early 18th century, at the foot of the Ste-Baume mountain range, this hotel, surrounded by open fields and woodlands, is near the venerated spot where, according to medieval legend, Mary Magdalene is believed to have died. Built of gray stone, with an upscale decor loaded with antiques and worthy reproductions, the inn has pleasant architectural details, like a carving above the entrance that depicts St. Roch with his dog. The guest rooms are individually decorated, each in a different motif such as Directoire, Provençal, and some of the Louis styles.

Dining: Good meals are served daily at lunch and dinner. Fixed-price menus cost 250F ($45); at lunch Monday through Friday, there's also a menu at 160F ($28.80). Specialties include lamb cooked with Provençal herbs and filet of sole Beau Manoir.

Amenities: A good-size pool is on the premises, and tennis courts, a golf course, and the beach are nearby.

MARSEILLE AFTER DARK

You can get an amusing (and relatively harmless) exposure to the town's saltiness during a walk around the Vieux-Port, where cafes and restaurants angle their sightlines for the best possible view of the harbor. Select any of them that strikes your fancy (or just park yourself by the waterfront for a view of the passing parade). But for a sure bet, head for the bar area of the previously recommended **Brasserie Vieux-Port New-York,** 33 quai des Belges (☎ **04-91-33-91-79**). You'll most likely be joined by a wide roster of Marseille's arts community, who are more interested in chatting with friends than in eating the well-presented cuisine.

A modern-day equivalent of the Vieux-Port is a 20-minute Métro ride away: **Escale Borély,** avenue Mendès-France, a waterfront development south of the town center. About a dozen cafes as well as restaurants of every possible ilk present a wide choice of cuisines, views of in-line skaters on the promenade in front, and a chance to strike up a friendly chat with someone. An especially worthwhile place here is **L'Assiette Marine** (☎ **04-91-71-04-04**), a seafood restaurant with a separate bar area where fresh oysters, clams, and chilled lobster might accompany your drink.

Unless the air-conditioning is very powerful, you'll work up a sweat in Marseille's dance clubs. The best of them is the **Café de la Plage,** in the above-mentioned Escale Borély (☎ **04-91-71-21-76**), where a 35-and-under crowd dances in an environment that's a lot less seedy than many places around town. Closer to the Vieux-Port, you can dance and drink at the **Metal Café,** 20 rue Fortia (☎ **04-91-54-03-03**), where 20- to 50-year-olds listen to current music; or the nearby **Trolley Bus,** 24 quai de Rive-Neuve (☎ **04-91-54-30-45**), best known for its wide variety of music but especially appreciated by the arts community for the dramatic readings and philosophical debates held the first Tuesday of every month (call ahead for schedules). Also very appealing, if only because people here seem to have so much fun, is **Pêle-Mêle,** 8 place aux Huiles (☎ **04-91-54-85-26**), a many-faceted bar/disco/cafe and host of occasional live music.

If you miss free-form modern jazz and don't mind taking your chances in the somewhat scary neighborhood adjacent to the city's rail station (La Gare St-Charles), consider dropping into **Jazz la Samaritaire,** 2 quai du Port (☎ **04-91-90-31-21;** Métro: Vieux-Port). You might want to take a taxi both coming and going, though.

If you're a single, straight male, two disco/pickup bars you might check out are **The Bunny Club,** 2 rue Corneille (☎ **04-91-54-09-20**), and **Le Victoria Club,** 3 rue Pythéas (☎ **04-91-54-15-17**).

Gay and hopeful? **L'Enigme (Le Kempson),** 22 rue Beauvau (☎ **04-91-33-79-20**), is the kind of bar where over-40 gay males might appreciate the jokes and randiness more than twentysomethings. It has the ambience of a French-speaking British pub where 98% of the crowd happens to be gay, male, and into either denim or leather. The youth-conscious **New Can Can,** 3–5 rue Sénac (☎ **04-91-48-59-76**), is an enormous venue that's everybody's favorite place for dancing till dawn. Looking for an appropriate way to kick off your evening at Can Can, just a short walk away? Head for **L'Eden,** 7 rue Curiol (☎ **04-91-47-30-06**), where lesbians and gays mingle freely in the most whimsical and playful gay environment in town. Don't be surprised at the many cross-dressers, who feel perfectly at home here.

8 Toulon

519 miles S of Paris, 79 miles SW of Cannes, 42 miles E of Marseille

This fortress and modern town is the principal naval base of France: the headquarters of the Mediterranean fleet, with hundreds of sailors wandering the streets. It's not as seedy or as intriguing as Marseilles. A beautiful harbor, it's surrounded by hills and crowned by forts, protected on the east by a large breakwater and on the west by the great peninsula of Cap Sicié. Separated by the breakwater, the outer roads are known as the Grande Rade and the inner roads the Petite Rade. A winter resort colony lies on the outskirts. Like Marseilles, Toulon has a large Arab population from North Africa. Note that there's racial tension here, worsened by the closing of the shipbuilding yards.

Park your vehicle underground at place de la Liberté, then go along boulevard des Strasbourg, turning right onto rue Berthelot. This will take you into the pedestrian-only area in the core of the old city. It's filled with shops, hotels, restaurants, and cobblestone streets (but it can be dangerous at night). The best beach, **Plage du Mourillon,** is 1¼ miles east of the heart of town.

ESSENTIALS

GETTING THERE & GETTING AROUND **Trains** arrive from Marseille about every 30 minutes (trip time: 1 hour). If you're on the Riviera, frequent trains arrive from Nice (trip time: 2 hours) and from Cannes (trip time: 80 minutes). For rail information and schedules, call ☎ **08-36-35-35-39.**

Four **buses** per day arrive from Aix-en-Provence (trip time: 75 minutes). For bus information and schedules, call ☎ **04-94-18-93-40** or 04-94-93-11-39.

If you're **driving** from Marseille, take A50 east to Toulon. When you arrive in Toulon, it's best to park your car and get around on foot, as the vieille ville (old town) and most of the attractions are easy to reach. A municipal **bus** system serves the town as well. Tickets cost 8F ($1.45) each, and a map of bus routes is available at the tourist office.

VISITOR INFORMATION The **Office de Tourisme** is at place des Riaux (☎ 04-94-18-53-00).

EXPLORING THE TOWN

In **Vieux Toulon,** between the harbor and boulevard des Strasbourg (the main axis of town), are many remains of the port's former days. Visit the **Poissonerie,** the typical covered market, bustling in the morning with fishmongers and buyers. Another colorful market, the **Marché,** spills over onto the narrow streets around cours Lafayette. Also in old Toulon is the **Cathédrale Ste-Marie-Majeure,** built in the Romanesque style in the 11th and 12th centuries, then much expanded in the 17th. Its badly lit nave is Gothic, and the belfry and facade are from the 18th century. It's open daily from 9am to 5pm.

In contrast to the cathedral, tall modern buildings line quai Stalingrad, opening onto **Vieille d'Arse.** On place Puget, look for the *atlantes* (caryatids), figures of men used as columns. These interesting figures support a balcony at the **Hôtel de Ville** (city hall) and are also included in the facade of the naval museum.

Musée de la Marine, place du Ingénieur-Général-Monsenergue (☎ 04-94-02-02-01), contains many figureheads and ship models. It's open in July and August, daily from 9:30am to noon and 3 to 7pm, September to June Wednesday through Monday from 9:30am to noon and 2 to 6pm. Admission is 29F ($5.20) for adults and 19F ($3.40) for students and children. **Musée de Toulon,** 113 bd. du Maréchal-Leclerc (☎ 04-94-93-15-54), contains works from the 16th century to the present. There's a particularly good collection of Provençal and Italian paintings, as well as religious works. The latest acquisitions include New Realism pieces and minimalist art. It's open daily from 1 to 6pm; admission is free.

Once you've covered the top attractions, we suggest taking a drive, an hour or two before sunset, along the **corniche du Mont-Faron.** It's a scenic boulevard along the lower slopes of Mont Faron, providing views of the busy port, the town, the cliffs, and, in the distance, the Mediterranean.

Earlier in the day, consider boarding a funicular near the Altéa La Tour Blanche Hôtel. This *téléphérique* **(cable car)** operates daily from 9 to 11:45am and 2:15 to 6:30pm, costing 37F ($6.65) for adults and 25F ($4.50) for children round-trip. It is not in service during windy conditions, however. At the top, enjoy the view and then visit the **Memorial du Débarquement en Provence,** Mont Faron (☎ 04-94-88-08-09), which documents, among other exhibits, the Allied landings in Provence in 1944. It's open in summer Tuesday through Sunday from 9:30 to 11:30am and 2 to 5pm, in winter Tuesday through Sunday from 9:30 to 11:30am and 2:30 to 5:45pm. Admission is 25F ($4.50) for adults, 10F ($1.80) for children 5 to 12, and free for children 4 and under.

WHERE TO STAY

La Corniche. 1 littoral Frédéric-Mistral (at Le Mourillon), 83000 Toulon. ☎ **04-94-41-35-12.** Fax 04-94-41-24-58. www.bestwestern.com. 23 units. A/C MINIBAR TV TEL. 380–470F ($68.40–$84.60) double; 420–650F ($75.60–$117) suite. AE, DC, MC, V. Parking 40F ($7.20). Bus: 3, 13, or 23.

You'll find this place near the town's beaches, in the neighborhood known as Le Mourillon, a 15-minute walk from the congested commercial center of Toulon. An attractive hotel with an interior garden, La Corniche offers a pleasant staff, two restaurants, and comfortable accommodations. Those opening onto the front have sea views and loggias and are more expensive. Rooms are decorated in the Provençal style.

Dining: Ironically, the more formal of the two restaurants is referred to as the Bistro; it features a trio of pine trees growing upward through the roof and a large bay window overlooking the port. The simpler restaurant is the cramped but cozy Rôtisserie. Both emphasize fish dishes. A fairly good but limited wine list complements the food, which is perfectly adequate.

New Hôtel Tour Blanche. Bd. de l'Amiral-Vence, 83200 Toulon. ☎ **04-94-24-41-57.** Fax 04-94-22-42-25. www.new-hotel.com. E-mail: info@new-hotel.com. 91 units. A/C MINIBAR TV TEL. 380–535F ($68.40–$96.30) double. AE, DC, MC, V. Bus: 40. From the town center, follow the signs to the Mont Faron téléphérique and you'll pass the hotel en route.

With excellent modernized accommodations, attractive gardens with terraces, and a pool, this seven-story hotel is the best in Toulon. It lies in the rocky hills about 2 miles north of the center of town, a position that affords sweeping views from even the lower floors out over the town to the port facilities and the sea. Many rooms have balconies, and each is comfortably and simply outfitted in modern style.

Dining: The restaurant, Les Terrasses, offers a panoramic view and food and wine whose selection is inspired by the culinary traditions of Provence and the Midi.

WHERE TO DINE

✪ **La Chamade.** 25 rue Denfert-Rochereau. ☎ **04-94-92-28-58.** Reservations recommended. Fixed-price menu 185F ($33.30). AE, MC, V. Mon–Fri noon–2:30pm, Mon–Sat 7:30–9:30pm. Closed Aug 1–25. Bus: 1 or 21. FRENCH.

In the town center, in a relatively nondescript building whose thick walls hint at its age, this restaurant offers only one option—a fixed-price menu that includes a changing choice of three appetizers, three main courses, and three desserts. In a labyrinth of several small, appealingly modern dining rooms, you can enjoy the carefully cultivated cuisine of Francis Bonneau, former disciple of some of the grandest restaurants of Paris and Brittany. Menu items change with the seasons and the availability of ingredients but might include stuffed and deep-fried zucchini blossoms, filet of sea bass with basil-flavored butter sauce, and roast whitefish garnished with ham and risotto with local herbs. Desserts often include a *craqueline* of dates served with *gentian,* a herb that flourishes on Provence's arid hillsides, or frozen custard garnished with local strawberries marinated in red wine.

TOULON AFTER DARK

Options in the town center include **Le Cocotier,** 330 av. Claret (☎ **04-94-92-78-76**), a disco for ages 20 to 45. One of the Azure Coast's best-known gay discos is **Boy's Paradise,** 1 bd. Pierre-Toesca (☎ **04-94-09-35-90**), where the gay men include lots of French sailors—and to a lesser degree, women.

Adjacent to the port are **Bar La Lampa,** Port de Toulon (☎ **04-94-03-06-09**), where Spanish-style tapas and live music accompany your bottles of beer and scotch; and **Bar à Thym,** 32 bd. Cuneo (☎ **04-94-41-90-10**), a less formal hangout where everybody seems to drink beer and listen to the live shows featuring local rock bands. For jazz, try **113 Bar,** 113 avede L'Infanterie de Olarine (☎ **04-94-03-42-41**), which offers live performances on Tuesday nights.

But if you feel claustrophobic in a town noted for its heavy industry and want something more resorty, you might be happier at **Hyère,** about 16 miles east of Toulon, where there's an upscale disco, **Le Fou du Roy,** in the Casino des Palmiers (☎ **04-94-12-80-80**). It attracts a more animated crowd than the nearby casino games. About 9 miles west of Toulon, in the small port town of **Sanary,** is a disco appealing to dancers under age 30: **Mai-Tai,** route de Bandol (☎ **04-94-74-23-92**).

9 Iles d'Hyères

24 miles ESE of Toulon, 74 miles SW of Cannes

Off the Riviera in the Mediterranean is a little group of islands enclosing the southern boundary of the Hyères anchorage. During the Renaissance they were called the Iles d'Or, from a golden glow sometimes given off by the rocks in the sunlight. Today, the tranquil but increasingly touristy islands give no indication of the periods of attacks suffered by pirates and Turkish galleys, British fleet activity, and the landing of Allied troops during World War II.

Mass tourism's discovery of these sun-baked Mediterranean islands has added a dose of tackiness. Fortunately, because cars are forbidden on all three of the archipelago's major islands (except for delivery and repair services), they cannot be transported on any of the ferryboats. Expect a summer holiday spirit (think of it as a Gallic version of Nantucket). Thousands of midsummer day-trippers arrive, often skimpily clad and with children in tow, for a day of sun, sand, and people watching.

Which island is the most appealing? Ile des Porquerolles is the most beautiful. Thinking of heading to Le Levant? Be warned that only 25% of that strategic island is accessible to visitors, as three-quarters of the landmass there belongs to the French army, which uses it frequently for the test blasts of missiles. Consequently, you may want to steer clear of it.

ESSENTIALS

GETTING THERE   Though ferryboats head for the Ile de Porquerolles from at least three points along the Côte d'Azur, by far the most frequent and most convenient connection from the French mainland is from the peninsula of Gien (the harbor of La Tour Fondue), a 20-mile drive east of Toulon. Depending on the season, there are 4 to 20 departures a day for a crossing that takes only 15 minutes. Round-trip fares are 78F ($14.05) per person. For information, call the **Transports Maritimes et Terrestres du Littoral Varois,** La Tour Fondue, 83400 Giens (☎ 04-94-58-21-81).

The next-best option involves longer, less convenient ferryboat rides from Toulon. Even worse are the infrequent boats (usually only twice a day, and only during July and August) from the French mainland ports of Le Lavandou and Cavalaire. For information on rides from the ports of Toulon, Le Lavandou, and Cavalaire, call **Trans-Med 2000,** quai Stalingrad, Toulon (☎ 04-94-91-98-57).

The most popular maritime route to Ile de Port-Cros is the 35-minute crossing from Le Lavandou, departing four to six times daily, depending on the season. For information, call the **Compagnie Maritime des Vedettes "Iles d'Or,"** 15 quai Gabriele-Peri, 83980 Le Lavandou (☎ 04-94-71-01-02). Round-trip fares are 122F ($21.95) for adults and 80F ($14.40) for children 4 to 12. The same company also offers less convenient, longer, and more tedious crossings to Ile du Port-Cros, usually in midsummer only, from the mainland port of Cavalaire.

VISITOR INFORMATION   Other than temporary, summer-only kiosks, without phones, that distribute brochures and advice near the ferry docks of Porquerolles and Port-Cros, there are no tourist bureaus on the islands. Consequently, the mainland tourist offices in Toulon and Hyères try to fill in the gaps. Contact the **Office de Tourisme,** Rotonde J.-Salusse, avenue de Belgique, Hyères (☎ 04-94-65-18-55), or the **Office de Tourisme,** place des Riaux, Toulon (☎ 04-94-18-53-00).

ILE DE PORQUEROLLES

This is the largest and westernmost of the Iles d'Hyères. It has a rugged south coast and a north strand made up of sandy beaches bordered by heather, scented myrtles, and pine trees. The island is about 5 miles long and 1¼ miles wide and is 3 miles from the mainland; it has a population of only 400.

The island is said to receive 275 days of sunshine annually. It's a land of rocky capes, pine forests twisted by the mistral, sun-drenched vineyards, and pale ocher houses. The hot spots, if there are any, are the cafes around place d'Armes where everybody gathers.

The island has had a bloody history of raids, attacks, and occupation by everybody from the Dutch and English to the Turks and Spaniards. Ten forts, some in ruins, testify to a violent past. The most ancient is Fort Ste-Agathe, built in 1531 by François I. In time, it served as a penal colony and a retirement center for soldiers of the colonial wars.

In 1971 the French government purchased the largest hunk of the island and turned it into a national park and botanical garden. The best beaches are along the north coast facing mainland France.

WHERE TO STAY & DINE

✪ **Mas du Langoustier.** 83400 Porquerolles. ☎ **04-94-58-30-09.** Fax 04-94-58-36-02. 50 units. TV TEL. 963–1,552F ($173.35–$279.35) double. Rates include half board. AE, DC, MC, V. Closed Oct–Apr.

In a large park on the island's western tip, this is a tranquil resort hotel—actually an old Provençal *mas* (farmhouse)—with a view of a lovely pine-ringed bay. The staff greets guests in a covered wagon by the jetty.

Dining: If you visit only for a meal, prices begin at 320F ($57.60). The menu is the finest in the islands, offering mainly seafood in a light nouvelle style. Try the loup (sea bass) with Noilly Prat in puff pastry or tender kid with dried tomatoes roasted in casserole. The house wine is an agreeable rosé. You can drink and dine on the terraces.

Amenities: Tennis courts.

ILE DE PORT-CROS

Lush subtropical vegetation reminiscent of a Caribbean island makes this a green paradise, 3 miles long and 1¼ miles wide. No cars are allowed on the island.

The most mountainous of the archipelago, Port-Cros has been a French national park since 1963. Although a fire in 1892 devastated the island, it has bounced back with pine forests and ilexes. **Bird-watchers** in France flock here to observe nearly 100 different species. Many **trails** are marked on the island, mainly for day-trippers. The most walked and the most scenic is *sentier botanique.* More adventurous and athletic visitors take the 6-mile *circuit historique* (you'll need a packed lunch for this one). **Divers** follow a 300-yard trail from Plage de la Palud to the islet of Rascas. A plastic guide sheet identifies the underwater flora. Thousands of pleasure craft call here annually, which does little to help the fragile environment of the island.

WHERE TO STAY & DINE

Le Manoir. 83400 Ile de Port-Cros. ☎ **04-94-05-90-52.** Fax 04-94-05-90-89. 23 units. TEL. 1,500–2,100F ($270–$378) double. Rates include half board. MC, V. Closed Oct–May 8.

This 18th-century colonial-style mansion, set in a park with a large pool, is the best choice on the island. The terrace overlooks the bay of Port-Cros, shaded by bamboo, eucalyptus, and oleander. Chef Sylvain Chaduteau serves lobster-and-fish terrine, several seasoned meats, and fresh local fish with baby vegetables, as well as regional goat cheese and velvety mousses. Dinner is served daily; the fixed-price menu costs 250F ($45).

21 The French Riviera

Each resort on the Riviera, known as the Côte d'Azur, offers its own unique flavor and special charms. This narrow strip of fabled real estate, which is less than 125 miles long and is located between the Mediterranean and a trio of mountain ranges, has always attracted the jet set, with its clear skies, blue waters, and orange groves.

A trail of modern artists captivated by the brilliant light and setting of the Côte d'Azur has left a rich heritage: Matisse in his chapel at Vence, Cocteau at Menton and Villefranche, Picasso at Antibes and seemingly everywhere else, Léger at Biot, Renoir at Cagnes, and Bonnard at Le Cannet. The best collection of all is at the Maeght Foundation in St-Paul-de-Vence.

The Riviera's high season used to be winter and spring only. However, with changing tastes, July and August have long been the most crowded, and reservations are imperative. The average summer temperature is 75°F; the average winter temperature, 49°F.

The corniches of the Riviera, depicted in countless films, stretch from Nice to Menton. The Alps here drop into the Mediterranean, and roads were carved along the way. The lower road, about 20 miles long, is the Corniche Inférieure. Along this road are the ports of Villefranche, Cap-Ferrat, Beaulieu, and Cap-Martin. Built between World War I and the beginning of World War II, the Moyenne Corniche (Middle Road), 19 miles long, also runs from Nice to Menton, winding spectacularly in and out of tunnels and through mountains. The highlight is at mountaintop Eze. The Grande Corniche—the most panoramic—was ordered built by Napoléon in 1806. La Turbie and Le Vistaero are the principal towns along the 20-mile stretch, which reaches more than 1,600 feet high at Col d'Eze.

Note: For more extensive coverage of this region, check out the book *Frommer's Provence & the Riviera.*

REGIONAL CUISINE   In the 19th century an undeveloped coastal strip of eastern Provence was deemed "the Riviera." Technically, the Riviera is part of Provence, and all the culinary traditions of that region (see chapter 20) apply here, albeit in slightly diluted forms.

On the Riviera you'll find high-toned bastions of French cuisine right alongside budget joints catering to the latest culinary fads, juxtaposed in sometimes-uncomfortable proximity. Outside Paris, the Riviera has more different types of restaurants and greater numbers of

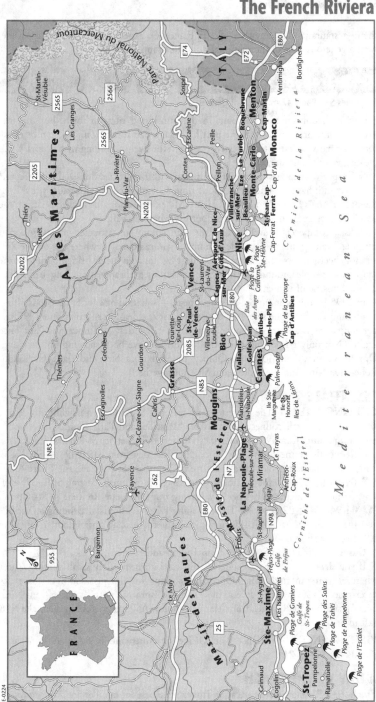

theme restaurants than anywhere else in France. So expect to find Provençal cuisine, with a generous dose of international sophistication.

1 St-Tropez

543 miles S of Paris, 47 miles SW of Cannes

An air of hedonism runs rampant in this sun-kissed carnival town, but the true Tropezian resents the fact that the port has such a bad reputation. "We can be classy too," one native has insisted. Creative people in the lively arts along with ordinary folk create a volatile mixture.

St-Tropez was really put on the tourist map with Brigitte Bardot's *And God Created Woman,* but it has been known for a long time. Colette lived here for many years. Even the diarist Anaïs Nin, confidante of Henry Miller, posed for a little cheesecake on the beach here in 1939 in a Dorothy Lamour–style bathing suit.

Artists, composers, novelists, and the film colony are attracted to St-Tropez in summer. Trailing them is a parade of humanity unmatched anywhere else on the Riviera for sheer flamboyance. Some of the most fashionable yachts bringing some of the most chic people around, anchor here in summer, disappearing long before the dreaded mistral of winter.

In 1995 Bardot pronounced St-Tropez dead—"squatted by a lot of no-goods, drugheads, and villains." She swore she'd never go back, at least in summer. But 1997 saw her return, as headlines in France flashed the news that St-Tropez was "hot once again." Not only Bardot but also other celebrities have been showing up, including Oprah Winfrey, Don Johnson, Quincy Jones, Barbra Streisand, Jack Nicholson, Robert De Niro, and even Elton and Sly (not together!).

ESSENTIALS

GETTING THERE The nearest rail station is at St-Raphaël, a neighboring resort, which has good rail connections to Nice, Marseille, and Paris. **Trains** arrive about every 30 minutes from Nice (via Cannes). Riviera trains service St-Raphaël from Paris, and frequently connections arrive throughout the day from Marseille. At the Vieux Port, 4 or 5 boats per day leave the Gare Maritime de St-Raphaël, rue Pierre-Auble (☎ **04-94-95-17-46**), for St-Tropez (trip time: 50 minutes), costing 50F ($9) each way. Some 15 Sodetrav buses per day, leaving from the Gare Routière in St-Raphaël (☎ **04-94-95-24-82**), go to St-Tropez, taking 1½ to 2¼ hours, depending on the bus and the traffic density, which during midsummer is usually horrendous. A one-way ticket costs 55F ($9.90).

Buses run directly to St-Tropez from Toulon and Hyères.

If you **drive,** you'll have to squeeze your car into impossibly small parking spaces wherever you can find them. One large parking lot lies just south of place des Lices/place du XVe Corps, several blocks inland from the port. To drive from Nice, take A8 south to St-Raphaël; from Marseille, follow A50 east to Toulon then take N98 east to St-Raphaël.

VISITOR INFORMATION The **Office de Tourisme** is on quai Jean-Jaurès (☎ **04-94-97-45-21**).

A DAY AT THE BEACH

The hottest Riviera beaches are at St-Tropez. The best for families are those closest to the center, including the amusingly named **Plage de la Bouillabaisse** and **Plage des Graniers.** The more daring are the 6-mile sandy cresents at **Plage des Salins** and **Plage de Pampellone,** beginning some 2 miles from the town center and best reached

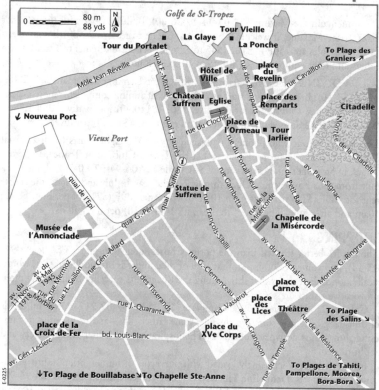

by bike (see below) if you're not driving. Called "notoriously decadent," ✪ **Plage de Tahiti** occupies the north end of the 3½-mile-long Pampellone, lined with concessions, cafes, and restaurants. It's a strip of golden sand that has long been favored by exhibitionists wearing next to nothing (or truly nothing) and crusing shamelessly. If you ever wanted to go topless, this is the place to do it. Vive la France!

OUTDOOR PURSUITS

BIKING The largest outfitter for bikes and motor scooters is **Louis Mas,** 5 rue Josef-Quaranta (☎ **04-94-97-00-60**). You'll be required to leave a deposit of 1,000F ($180), payable with American Express, MasterCard, or Visa, plus 50F ($9) per day for a bike and 190F to 275F ($34.20 to $49.50) per hour for a motor scooter (deposit of 6,000F [$1,080], depending on its size).

BOATING The well-recommended **Suncap Company,** 15 quai de Suffren (☎ **04-94-97-11-23**), rents boats from 18 to 40 feet. The smallest can be rented to qualified sailors without a captain, but the larger ones come with a captain at the helm. Prices per day begin at 3,000F ($540).

GOLF The nearest golf course, at the edge of Ste-Maxime, across the bay from St-Tropez, is the **Golf Club de Beauvallon,** boulevard des Collines (☎ **04-94-96-16-98**), a popular 18-hole course. Its terrain allows you to walk rather than rent a cart. Greens fees are 250F to 300F ($45 to $54) for 18 holes.

Sprawling over a rocky, vertiginous landscape that requires a golf cart and a lot of physical labor is the Don Harradine–designed **Golf de Ste-Maxime-Plaza,** route du

Débarquement, Ste-Maxime (☎ 04-94-49-26-60). Built in 1991 with the four-star Plaza de Ste-Maxime, it welcomes nonguests; phone to reserve tee-off times. Greens fees for 18 holes are 250F to 310F ($45 to $55.80) per person; rental of a cart for two golfers and their equipment is 130F ($23.40) per 18 holes.

SCUBA DIVING   Head for **Octopussy,** village Léo Lagrange at Ramatuelle (☎ 04-94-56-53-10). Beginner dives start at 250F ($45) including equipment; more experienced divers pay 150F ($27) for one dive, 780F ($140.40) for six dives, and 1,380F ($248.40) for 12 dives. Equipment rental an extra 70F ($12.60) per dive.

TENNIS   Anyone who phones in advance can use the eight courts (both artificial grass and "Quick," a form of concrete) at the **Tennis-Club de St-Tropez,** route des Plages, in St-Tropez's industrial zone of St-Claude (☎ 04-94-97-80-76), about half a mile from the resort's center. Open throughout the year, in July and August the courts rent for 100F ($18) per hour from 10am to 5pm and 120F ($21.60) per hour before 10am and after 5pm. The rest of the year, it's 100F ($18) per hour all day.

SHOPPING

Though it's better stocked than the norm, **Choses,** quai Jean-Jaurès (☎ 04-94-97-03-44), is a women's clothing store typical of the hundreds of middle-bracket, whimsically nonchalant shops that thrive along the Riviera. Its specialty is clingy and often provocative t-shirt dresses.

Galeries Tropéziennes, 56 rue Gambetta (☎ 04-94-97-02-21), crowds hundreds of unusual gift items—some worthwhile, some rather silly—and textiles into its rambling showrooms near place des Lices. The inspiration is Mediterranean, breezy and sophisticated.

In a resort that's increasingly loaded with purveyors of suntan lotion, touristy souvenirs, and t-shirts, **Jacqueline Thienot,** 12 rue Georges-Clemenceau (☎ 04-94-97-05-70), maintains an inventory of Provençal antiques that's prized by dealers from as far away as Paris. The one-room shop is in a late-18th-century building that shows the 18th- and 19th-century antiques to their best advantage. Also sold are antique examples of Provençal wrought iron and rustic farm and homemaker's implements.

SIGHTSEEING

Château Suffren is east from the port at the top end of quai Jean-Jaurès. Now home to occasional art exhibits, it was built in 980 by Comte Guillame I of Provence.

Near the junction of quai Suffren and quai Jean-Jaurès stands the bronze *Statue de Suffren,* paying tribute to Vice-Admiral Pierre André de Suffren. This St-Tropez hometown boy became one of the greatest sailors of 18th-century France, though he's largely forgotten today. And in the Vieille Ville, one of the most interesting streets is **rue de la Misércorde.** At the corner of rue Gambetta is the **Chapelle de la Misércorde,** with a blue, green, and gold tile roof.

Two miles from St-Tropez, **Port Grimaud** makes an interesting outing. From St-Tropez, drive 3 miles west on A98 to Route 98, then 1 mile north to the Port Grimaud exit. If you approach the village at dusk, when it's softly bathed in Riviera pastels, it'll look like some old hamlet, perhaps from the 16th century. But this is a mirage. Port Grimaud is the dream fulfillment of its promoter, François Spoerry, who carved it out of marshland and dug canals. Flanking these canals, fingers of land extend from the main square to the sea. The homes are Provençal style, many with Italianate window arches. Boat owners can anchor right at their doorsteps. One newspaper called the port "the most magnificent fake since Disneyland."

Musée de l'Annonciade (Musée St-Tropez). Place Grammont. ☎ **04-94-97-04-01.** Admission 30F ($5.40) adults, 15F ($2.70) children. June–Sept Wed–Mon 10am–noon and 3–7pm; Oct and Dec–May Wed–Mon 10am–noon and 2–6pm. Closed Nov.

Near the harbor, this museum was installed in the former chapel of the Annonciade. It boasts one of the finest modern art collections on the Riviera. Many of the artists, including Paul Signac, depicted the port of St-Tropez. The collection includes such works as Van Dongen's yellow-faced *Women of the Balustrade* and paintings and sculpture by Bonnard, Matisse, Braque, Dufy, Utrillo, Seurat, Derain, and Maillol.

WHERE TO STAY
VERY EXPENSIVE

✪ **Hôtel Byblos.** Av. Paul-Signac, 83990 St-Tropez. ☎ **04-94-56-68-00.** Fax 04-94-56-68-01. www.interactive.line.com/lead. 98 units. A/C MINIBAR TV TEL. 1,500–3,070F ($270–$552.60) double; 3,325–7,500F ($598.50–$1,350) suite. AE, DC, MC, V. Parking 140F ($25.20) in garage. Closed Oct 15–Easter.

The builder said he created "an anti-hotel, a place like home." That's true if your home resembles a palace in Beirut with salons decorated with Phoenician gold statues from 3000 B.C. Located on a hill above the harbor, this deluxe complex has intimate patios and courtyards and seductive retreats filled with antiques and rare decorative objects, including polychrome carved woodwork on the walls, marquetry floors, and a Persian-rug ceiling. Every room is unique. In one, for example, there's a fireplace on a raised hearth, paneled blue-and-gold doors, and a bed recessed on a dais. Le Hameau also contains 10 duplex suites built around a small courtyard with an outdoor spa. Some rooms have balconies overlooking an inner courtyard; others open onto a terrace of flowers.

Dining/Diversions: You can dine by the pool at Les Arcades, enjoying Provençal food, or try an Italian restaurant offering an antipasti buffet, many pasta courses, and other typical fare from France's neighbor. Later in the evening you can dance on a circular floor surrounded by bas-relief columns in the hotel's nightclub, Caves du Roy. There are also two bars.

Amenities: "High-fashion" pool, sauna, 24-hour room service, same-day laundry/valet, beauty salon.

EXPENSIVE TO MODERATE

Hôtel Ermitage. Av. Paul-Signac, 83990 St-Tropez. ☎ **04-94-97-52-33.** Fax 04-94-97-10-43. 26 units. TEL. 590–990F ($106.20–$178.20) double. V.

Attractively isolated amid the rocky heights of St-Tropez, this hotel was built in the 19th century as a private villa. Today its red-tile roof and green shutters shelter a plush hideaway. A walled garden is illuminated at night, and a cozy corner bar near a wood-burning fireplace takes the chill off blustery evenings. The guest rooms are pleasantly but simply furnished, and the staff can be charming. Breakfast is the only meal served.

Hôtel La Tartane. Route des Salins, 83990 St-Tropez. ☎ **04-94-97-21-23.** Fax 04-94-97-09-16. 14 units. A/C MINIBAR TV TEL. 650–900F ($117–$162) double. AE, MC, V. Closed Oct 15–Easter.

This small-scale hotel is midway between the center of St-Tropez and the Plage des Salins, about a 3-minute drive from each. There's a stone-rimmed pool set into the garden, attractively furnished public rooms with terra-cotta floors, and an attentive management that works hard to keep everything pulled together. The guest rooms are well-furnished bungalows centered around the pool. Breakfast is elaborate and attractive; lunch and dinner are also offered. Bouillabaisse and fresh fish from the Mediterranean are the specialties, and in addition to the à la carte dishes, there's a fixed-price menu at 120F ($21.60).

✪ **La Bastide de St-Tropez.** Route des Carles, 83990 St-Tropez. ☎ **04-94-97-58-16.** Fax 04-94-97-21-71. www.bastidesaint-tropez.com. E-mail: bst@wanadoo.fr. 26 units. A/C MINIBAR TV TEL. 980–1,900F ($176.40–$342) double; 1,400–3,500F ($252–$630) suite. AE, DC, MC, V. Closed Jan.

Near the landmark place des Lices, this tile-roofed replica of a Provençal manor house looks deliberately severe, but the interior is far more opulent. It contains a monumental staircase leading from a sun-filled living room to the upper floors. The guest rooms are named according to their unique decor, including "Rose of Bengal," "Fuschia," and "Tangerine Dawn." Each has a terrace or private garden, and some have a Jacuzzi. Several, however, are quite small. The hotel is noted for its restaurant, L'Olivier.

La Ponche. 3 rue des Remparts, 83990 St-Tropez. ☎ **04-94-97-02-53.** Fax 04-94-97-78-61. 18 units. A/C MINIBAR TV TEL. 950–2,400F ($171–$432) double. AE, MC, V. Closed Nov–Mar 15.

Overlooking the old fishing port, this has long been a cherished address, run by the same family for more than half a century. The hotel is filled with the original, airy paintings of Jacques Cordier, which adds to the elegant atmosphere. Each room has been newly redecorated and is well equipped, opening onto views of the sea. The hotel restaurant is big on Provençal charm and cuisine, and on almost any given night, a sophisticated crowd can be found on its terrace.

WHERE TO DINE

The restaurant at the **Résidence de la Pinède** (see above) serves wonderful Provençal dishes.

Chez Maggi. 7 rue Sibille. ☎ **04-94-97-16-12.** Reservations recommended. Fixed-price menu (including wine) 130F ($23.40). MC, V. Daily 8pm–3am. Closed Nov–Easter weekend. PROVENÇAL/ITALIAN.

Across from Chez Nano (below), this restaurant retained the name it was given by two women during its earlier incarnation as a lesbian bar. Since its acquisition by the present owners, it has emerged as St-Tropez's most flamboyant gay restaurant/bar. At least half its floor space is devoted to a very busy bar, with patrons between the age of 25 and 35 who when space gets tight often flow out of the bar into the street.

Meals are served in an adjoining dining room. Menu items include chicken salad with ginger, goat-cheese salad, *petits farcis provençaux* (local vegetables stuffed with minced meat and herbs), brochettes of sea bass with lemon sauce, and a well-recommended chicken curry with coconut milk, capers, and cucumbers.

Chez Nano. Place de la Mairie. ☎ **04-94-97-01-66.** Reservations recommended. Main coures 100–400F ($18–$72). AE, MC, V. May–Sept daily noon–2:30pm and 8pm–midnight; Oct–Apr Wed–Mon noon–2:30pm and 8pm–midnight. Closed Jan–Feb. FRENCH.

This restaurant/bar has been a stylish fixture on the St-Tropez scene since it was founded by Nano (an omnipresent celebrity who seems to know every show-biz personality in France) many ages ago. The cozy bar is outfitted with varnished wooden panels, oil paintings, and photos of Nano welcoming the stylish and famous (Elton John, George Michael, Michael Bolton); the crowd is heavily gay and fashionable. Glasses of champagne are 65F ($11.70) and served to an animated crowd that seems to remain in place every night from 7pm to 6am the next morning. (Like the restaurant, the bar is closed Tuesday off-season.)

Adjacent to the bar is a restaurant of about 35 tables, giving you lots of opportunities for table gazing. Menu items are consciously gastronomic and artful, like lobster salad, an adventurous tartare of salmon and lobster that's advisable only for the strong and the brave, tournedos Rossini, grilled jumbo shrimp, and fricassée of scallops. Except for one or two costly seafood dishes, most prices are quite reasonable.

L'Echalotte. 35 rue Allard. ☎ **04-94-54-83-26.** Reservations recommended in summer. Main courses 80–130F ($14.40–$23.40); fixed-price menus 98–160F ($17.65–$28.80). AE, MC, V. Thurs 8–11:30pm, Fri–Wed 12:30–2pm and 8–11:30pm. Closed Nov 15–Dec 15. FRENCH.

This charming restaurant, with a tiny garden and simple dining room, serves consistently good food for fairly reasonable prices. It may be tough to get in here, especially in peak summer weeks. The cuisine is solidly bourgeois, including grilled veal kidneys, crayfish with drawn-butter sauce, filet of turbot with truffles, and some of the classic dishes of southwestern France, like three preparations of foie gras and magrêt of duckling. The menu includes several species of fish, like sea bass and daurade royale, which can be cooked in a salt crust.

Le Girelier. Quai Jean-Jaurès. ☎ **04-94-97-03-87.** Main courses 150–250F ($27–$45); fixed-price menu 185F ($33.30). AE, DC, MC, V. Daily noon–2:30pm and 7–11pm. Closed Jan to mid-Feb and Nov 1–Dec 15. PROVENÇAL.

The Rouets own this portside restaurant whose blue-and-white color scheme has become its own kind of trademark. Filled with rattan furniture and boasting a large glassed-in veranda, it serves well-prepared grilled fish in many versions, as well as bouillabaisse (served only for two). Also available is brochette of monkfish, a kettle of mussels and *pipérade* (a Basque omelet with pimientos, garlic, and tomatoes).

ST-TROPEZ AFTER DARK

On the lobby level of the Hôtel Byblos, **Les Caves du Roy,** avenue Paul-Signac (☎ **04-94-97-16-02**), is the most self-consciously chic nightclub in St-Tropez. There's no cover, but drink prices begin at a shocking 130F ($23.40)!

Le Papagayo, in the Résidence du Nouveau-Port, rue Gambetta (☎ **04-94-97-07-56**), is one of the largest nightclubs in town, with two floors, three bars, and lots of attractive women and men from throughout the Mediterranean eager to pursue their bait. The decor was inspired by the psychedelic 1960s. Cover is 90F ($16.20) and includes the first drink.

Discothèque l'Esquinade, 2 rue Dufour (☎ **06-94-97-87-45**), immediately became a gay sensation when it opened in 1998 to fill the gap caused by the closing of Le Pigeonnier, one of the Riviera's most celebrated gay bars. In fact, Philippe Pager, who operated Le Pigeonnier for a decade, is in charge of this new disco, luring a crowd that is at least 80% gay, the rest gay-friendly. The age group, in all sorts of attire, ranges from 20 to 50, and it's the hottest address in St-Tropez on a summer night. Music is recorded, including techno. No cover is charged: you pay only for your drinks.

Located below the Hôtel Sube, the **Café de Paris,** sur le Port (☎ **04-94-97-00-56**), is one of the most consistently popular hangouts. An attempt has been made to dress the rather utilitarian room with turn-of-the-century globe lights, an occasional 19th-century bronze, masses of artificial flowers, and a long zinc bar. The crowd is irreverent and animated. Busy even in winter, after the yachting crowd departs, it's open daily.

The reporter Leslie Maitland once described the kind of crowd attracted to the **Café Sénéquier,** sur le Port (☎ **04-94-97-00-90**), at cocktail hour: "What else can one do but gawk at a tall, well-dressed young woman who appears comme il faut at Sénéquier's with a large white rat perched upon her shoulder, with which she occasionally exchanges little kisses, while casually chatting with her friends?"

2 La Napoule-Plage

560 miles S of Paris, 5 miles W of Cannes

This secluded resort is on the sandy beaches of the Golfe de la Napoule. In 1919 the once-obscure fishing village was a paradise for the eccentric sculptor Henry Clews and his wife, Marie, an architect. Fleeing America's "charlatans," whom he believed had profited from World War I, this New York banker's son emphasized the fairy-tale qualities of his new home. His house is now the **Musée Henry-Clews**—an inscription over the entrance reads ONCE UPON A TIME.

Château de la Napoule, boulevard Henry-Clews (☎ **04-93-49-95-05**), was rebuilt from the ruins of a medieval château. Clews covered the capitals and lintels with his own grotesque menagerie—scorpions, pelicans, gnomes, monkeys, lizards—the revelations of a tortured mind. Women, feminism, and old age are recurring themes in the sculptor's work, as exemplified by the distorted suffragette depicted in his *Cat Woman.* The artist admired chivalry and dignity in man as represented by *Don Quixote*—to whom he likened himself. Clews died in Switzerland in 1937, and his body was returned to La Napoule for burial. Marie Clews later opened the château to the public as a testimonial to the inspiration of her husband. You can visit on a guided French-English language tour, conducted March 1 to October 31 Wednesday to Monday at 3 and 4pm. In July and August, there is an extra tour at 5pm. They cost 25F ($4.50) for adults and 20F ($3.60) for children.

La Mandelieu Napoule-Plage lies on the **bus** and **train** routes between Cannes and St-Raphaël. For information and schedules, call ☎08-36-35-35-39. If you're **driving,** La Mandelieu Napoule-Plage is best reached from A8 west from Cannes.

The **Office de Tourisme** is at 274 bd. Henry-Clews (☎ **04-93-49-95-31**).

WHERE TO STAY

✪ **La Calanque.** Bd. Henry-Clews, 06210 La Napoule. ☎ **04-93-49-95-11.** Fax 04-93-49-67-44. 17 units, 11 with bathroom. TEL. 390–440F ($70.20–$79.20) double without bathroom, 500–700F ($90–$126) double with bathroom. Rates include half board. MC, V. Closed Nov–Mar.

The foundations of this charming hotel date from the Roman Empire, when an aristocrat built a villa here. The present hotel, run by the same family since 1942, looks like a hacienda, with salmon-colored stucco walls and shutters. Register in the bar in the rear (through the dining room). The hotel's simple restaurant spills onto a terrace and offers some of the cheapest fixed-price meals in La Napoule, at 95F to 135F ($17.10 to $24.30). Nonguests are welcome.

Royal Hôtel Casino. 605 av. du Général-de-Gaulle, 06212 Mandelieu La Napoule. ☎ **04-92-97-70-00.** Fax 04-92-97-70-49. 210 units. A/C MINIBAR TV TEL. 690–1,650F ($124.20–$297) double; from 2,500F ($450) suite. AE, DC, MC, V. Parking 60F ($10.80).

This Las Vegas–style hotel, a member of the upscale Sofitel chain, is on the beach near a man-made harbor, about 5 miles from Cannes. It was the first French hotel to include a casino and the last (just before the building codes changed) to be allowed to have a casino directly on the beach. The hotel has one of the most contemporary designs on the Côte d'Azur. The interior is dramatically modern, with plush touches, warm shades, and lots of marble. Most of the attractive modern rooms are angled toward a view of the sea. Those facing the street are likely to be noisy in spite of soundproofing.

Dining/Diversions: Le Féréol is recommended below. An informal cafe (Le Poker) serves both Tex-Mex and specialties of Provence, and a nightclub offers live music. The casino (open daily from 8pm to 4am) offers blackjack, craps, and roulette.

Amenities: Pool, tennis courts, sauna, 27-hole golf course.

WHERE TO DINE

The restaurant in **La Calanque** (see above) is open to nonguests.

Le Féréol. In the Royal Hôtel Casino, 605 av. du Général-de-Gaulle. ☎ **04-92-97-70-00.** Reservations recommended. Main courses 95–170F ($17.10–$30.60); buffet lunch (June–Sept only) 190F ($34.20); fixed-price dinner 260F ($46.80). AE, DC, MC, V. July–Aug daily noon–3:30pm and 7:30–11pm; Sept–June daily noon–2:30pm and 7:30–10:30pm. FRENCH.

This well-designed restaurant is located in the largest hotel in town. Outfitted in an upscale nautical style, it offers one of the most impressive lunch buffets in the neighborhood. At night the place is candlelit and more elegant, and the view through bay windows over the pool is more soothing. Well-prepared, often flawless menu items include foie gras, scampi tails fried with ginger, zucchini flowers with mousseline of lobster, mignon of veal with Parma ham and tarragon sauce, and an émincé of duckling baked under puff pastry with cèpe mushrooms. The dessert buffet lays out a wide array of sophisticated pastries, some light and fruity summer dishes, others designed as irresistable temptations for chocoholics.

✪ **L'Oasis.** Rue Honoré-Carle. ☎ **04-93-49-95-52.** Reservations required. Main courses 180–280F ($32.40–$50.40); fixed-price lunch (including wine) 275F ($49.50); fixed-price lunch or dinner (without wine) 290–650F ($52.20–$117). AE, DC, MC, V. Daily noon–1:30pm and 8–10pm. FRENCH.

At the entrance to the harbor of La Napoule, in a 40-year-old house with a lovely garden and an unusual re-creation of a mock-medieval cloister, this restaurant became world famous under the tutelage of the now-retired Louis Outhier. Today chef Stéphane Raimbault prepares the most sophisticated cuisine in La Napoule. Michelin rates it two stars. Raimbault learned everything Outhier had to teach him and now charts his own culinary course, and does so exceedingly well. Because Raimbault cooked in Japan for 9 years, many of his dishes are of the "East Meets West" variety. In summer meals are served in the shade of the plane trees in the garden. Menu specialties may be taboulette of crayfish with tamarind juice, warm foie gras of duckling with *verdure de blettes* (a Provençal vegetable similar to spinach), filet of pork with sage oil, and John Dory roasted with herbs in the traditional style. The wine cellar houses one of the finest collections of Provençal wines anywhere.

3 Cannes

562 miles S of Paris, 101 miles E of Marseille, 16 miles SW of Nice

When Coco Chanel went here and got a suntan, returning to Paris bronzed, she startled the milk-white society ladies. However, they quickly began copying her. Today the bronzed bodies—clad in nearly nonexistent swimsuits—that line the sandy beaches of this chic resort continue the late fashion designer's example.

ESSENTIALS

GETTING THERE   Cannes is connected to each of the Mediterranean resorts, Paris, and the rest of France by rail and bus lines.

Cannes lies on the major coastal rail line along the Riviera, with **trains** arriving frequently throughout the day. The train from Antibes takes only 15 minutes (it's 35 minutes from Nice). The TGV from Paris going via Marseille also serves Cannes. (Transit from Paris to Cannes via TGV takes only about 3 breathless hours.) For rail information and schedules, call ☎ **08-36-35-35-39.**

Buses pick up passengers at the Nice **airport** every 40 minutes during the day, delivering them to Cannes at the Gare Routière, place de la Gare (☎ **04-93-39-18-71**). Because of stopovers it's a 1½-hour drive and costs 48.50F ($8.70). Express

Cannes

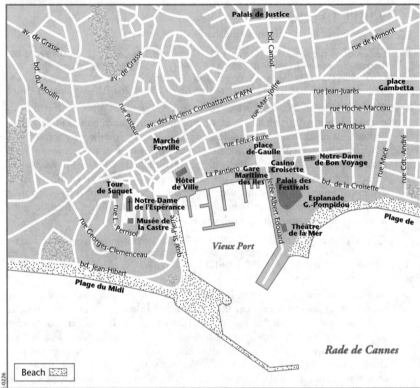

buses to Cannes take 45 minutes and cost 70F ($12.60). At Cannes, there are also buses to Antibes that leave frequently for the 30-minute trip; cost is 16F ($2.90).

By car, Cannes can be easily approached by two cities along the Riviera. From Marseille, take A51 north to Aix-en-Provence, continuing along A8 east to Cannes. From Nice, follow A8 southwest to Cannes.

VISITOR INFORMATION   The **Office de Tourisme** is in the Palais des Festivals, bd. de la Croisette (☎ **04-93-39-24-53**).

SPECIAL EVENTS   Cannes is at its most frenzied during the **International Film Festival** at the Palais des Festivals on promenade de la Croisette. Held in either April or May, it attracts not only film stars but also their hangers-on, as well as seemingly every photographer in the world. On the seafront boulevards, flashbulbs pop as the stars and wanna-bes emerge and pose and pose and pose. The festival's stellar activities are closed to most visitors, who are forced to line up in front of the Palais des Festivals. Known as "the bunker," this concrete structure is the venue for premieres that draw some 5,000 spectators. With paparazzi shouting ("Bruce, Demi, over here!") and shooting away and a guard of gendarmes holding back the fans, the guests parade along the red carpet into the building, stopping for a moment or two to strike a pose and chat with a journalist. C'est Cannes!

From international regattas, to galas, concours d'élégance, and even a Mimosa Festival in February—something's always happening at Cannes, except in November, traditionally a dead month.

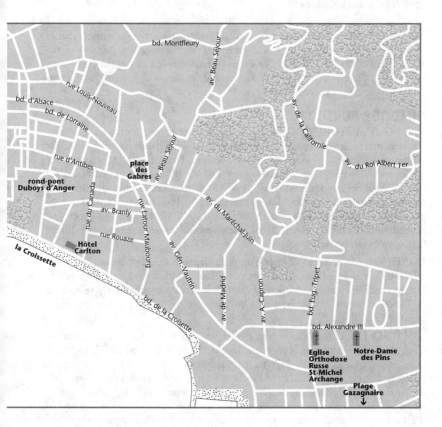

A DAY AT THE BEACH

Beachgoing in Cannes has more to do with exhibitionism and voyeurism than with actual swimming.

Plage de la Croisette extends between the Vieux Port and the Port Canto. Though the beaches along this billion-dollar stretch of sand aren't in the strictest sense private, they're *payante,* meaning that you must pay between 90F and 100F ($16.20 and $18). You don't need to be a guest of the Noga Hilton, Martinez, Carlton, or Majestic to use the beaches associated with those hotels, though if you are you'll usually get a discount of around 50% off the admission fee. Each beach is separated from its neighbors by a wooden barricade that stops several feet from the sea, making it easy for you to stroll from one to another.

Why should you pay a fee at all? Well, it includes a full day's use of a mattress, a chaise longue (the seafront isn't particularly sandy or even soft, covered as it is with pebbles and dark-gray shingle), and a parasol, as well as easy access to freshwater showers and kiosks selling beverages. There are also outdoor restaurants where no one minds if you appear in your bathing suit.

For nostalgia's sake, our favorite beach is the one associated with the Carlton—it was the first beach we ever went to, as teenagers, in Cannes. The relative merits of each of the 20 or so beaches along La Croisette vary daily depending on the crowd. And since every beach here allows topless bathing (and is absolutely adamant that you keep your bottom covered), you're likely to find the same forms of décolletage along the entire strip.

Looking for a free public beach where you'll have to survive without rentable chaises or parasols? Head for **Plage du Midi,** sometimes called Midi Plage, just west of the Vieux Port (☎ 04-93-39-92-74), or **Plage Gazagnaire,** just east of the Port Canto (no phone). Here you'll find greater numbers of families with children and lots of caravan-type vehicles parked nearby.

OUTDOOR PURSUITS

BIKING & MOTOR SCOOTERING   Despite the roaring traffic, the flat landscapes between Cannes and nearby resorts such as La Napoule are well suited for riding a bike or motor scooter. **Cannes Location Deux Roues,** 11 rue Hélène-Vagliano (☎ 04-93-39-46-15), across from the Gray-d'Albion, rents pedal bikes for 62F ($11.15) per day and requires a 1,000F ($180) deposit (payable with American Express, MasterCard, or Visa). Motor scooters rent for 160F to 200F ($28.80 to $36) per day and require a deposit of 5,000F to 8,000F ($900 to $1,440) per day, depending on their value. None of the motor scooters rented here requires a driver's license or special permit.

BOATING   **Motor Yacht Charter,** Port de la Napoule, Baie de Cannes (☎ 04-93-49-74-04), is in Mandelieu, 4 miles west of Cannes. With a good reputation and an excellent staff, they maintain a fleet of more than 30 motor yachts, ranging from 12 to 70 feet in length. Smaller boat rentals start at 1,250F ($225) per day, and yachts begin at 11,000F ($1,980) per day.

GOLF   ✪ One of the region's most challenging and interesting courses, **Country-Club de Cannes-Mougins,** 175 rte. d'Antibes, Mougins (☎ 04-93-75-79-13), 4 miles north of Cannes, was a 1976 reconfiguration by Dye & Ellis of an overly plain course laid out in the 1920s. Noted for the olive trees and cypresses that adorn a relatively flat terrain, it has many water traps and a deceptively tricky layout loaded with technical challenges. It has a par of 72 and a much-envied role, since 1981, as host to the Cannes-Mougins Open, an important stop on the PGA European Tour. The course is open to anyone with proof of his or her handicap willing to pay greens fees of 380F to 430F ($68.40 to $77.40), depending on the day of the week. An electric golf cart rents for 280F ($50.40), and golf clubs can be rented for 150F ($27) per set. Reservations are recommended.

TENNIS   Its 10 tennis courts are one of the highlights of the **Complexe Sportif Montfleury,** 23 av. Beauséjour (☎ 04-93-38-75-78). You'll find eight hard-surfaced courts, at 70F ($12.60) per hour, and two clay-surfaced courts, at 90F ($16.20) per hour.

SHOPPING

Cannes, a highly commercial blend of resort-style leisure, luxury glamour, and media glitz, boasts branch outlets of virtually every stylish Paris retailer. There's every big-name designer you can think of (Saint Laurent, Rykiel, Hermès) as well as big-name designers you may or may not have heard of (Claude Bonucci, Durrani). But, more important, there are real-people shops, resale shops for gently worn star-studded castoffs, two flea markets for fun junk, and a fruit, flower, and vegetable market.

ANTIQUES & *BROCANTE*   Looking for top-notch antiques dealers whose merchandise will wow you? Two of the city's most noteworthy dealers are **Hubert Herpin,** 20 rue Macé (☎ 04-93-39-56-18), and **Marc Franc,** 142 rue d'Antibes (☎ 04-93-43-86-43). You'll find a wide selection of bronze and marble statues, marquetry, and 18th- and 19th-century furniture.

Things are a lot less stuffy at Cannes's two regular flea markets. Casual, dusty, and filled with the castaways from various estate sales, **Marché Forville,** conducted in the Marché Forville neighborhood, near the Palais des Festivals, is a battered stucco structure with a roof and a few arches but no sides. It usually functions as the fruit-and-vegetable market that supplies the raw materials for dozens of grand restaurants. But Monday is *brocante* day, when the market fills with offhanded, sometimes strident antiques dealers selling everything from *grandmère's* dishes to bone-handled carving knives.

Every Saturday, a somewhat disorganized and invariably busy **flea market** is held outdoors, along the edges of the allée de la Liberté, across from the Palais des Festivals. Exact hours depend on the whims of whatever dealer happens to haul in a cache of merchandise, but they usually begin around 8am and run out of steam by around 4:30pm. Note that the vendors at the two flea markets may or may not be the same.

DEPARTMENT STORES   Near the train station in the heart of Cannes, **Galeries Lafayette** has a small branch at 6 rue du Maréchal-Foch (☎ **04-93-39-27-55**). It's noted for the self-consciously upscale fashion available in carefully arranged interiors. You'll save some francs and check out a French versions of a five-and-dime, **Monoprix,** across the street at no. 9 (☎ **04-92-99-61-61**). Monoprix contains a grocery store as well.

DESIGNER SHOPS   Most of the big names in designer fashion, for both men and women, line promenade de la Croisette, known as La Croisette, the main drag facing the sea. These stores are all in a row, stretching from the Hôtel Carlton almost to the Palais des Festivals, with the best names closest to the high-rise **Gray-d'Albion,** 17 La Croisette (☎ **04-92-99-79-79**), which is both a mall and a hotel (how convenient). The stores in the Gray-d'Albion mall include Hermès and Souleiado. The mall is broken into two parts, so you go outdoors from the first part of the building and then enter again for the second part. It serves as the shopper's secret cutaway from the primary expensive shopping street, La Croisette, to the less expensive shopping street, rue d'Antibes.

FOOD   There are several famous chocolatiers in Cannes; try **Maiffret,** 31 rue d'Antibes (☎ **04-93-39-08-29**). But the real local specialty is *fruits confits* (jellied fruits, also called crystallized fruits), which became the rage in the 1880s. Maiffret sells these as well, especially in summer, when the chocolates tend to melt. Pâtés and confits of fruit, some of which decorate cakes and tarts, are also sold as desirable confections. Look for the Provençal national confection, *calissons,* crafted from almonds, a confit of melon, and sugar. A block away is **Chez Bruno,** 50 rue d'Antibes (☎ **04-93-39-26-63**). Opened in 1929 and maintained today by a matriarchal descendent of its founder, the shop is famous throughout Provence for fruits confits as well as its recipe for glazed chestnuts (*marrons glacés*), made fresh daily.

A charmingly old-fashioned shop, **Cannolive,** 16–20 rue Vénizelos (☎ **04-93-39-08-19**), is owned by the Raynaud family, who founded the place in 1880. It sells Provençal olives and their by-products-purées (*tapenades*) that connoisseurs refer to as "Provençal caviar," black "olives de Nice," and green "olives de Provence," as well as three grades of olive oil from several regional producers. Oils and food products are dispensed from no. 16, but gift items (fabrics, porcelain, and Provençal souvenirs) are sold next door.

PERFUME   The best shop is **Bouteille,** 59 rue d'Antibes (☎ **04-93-39-05-16**), but it's also the most expensive. Its prices are high because it stocks more brands, has a deeper selection, gives away many more free samples, and presents you with a tote

Ferrying to the Iles de Lérins

Across the bay from Cannes, the Lérins Islands are the most interesting excursion from the port. Ferryboats depart at 30-minute intervals throughout the day, beginning at 7:30am and lasting until 30 minutes before sundown, from the **Compagnies Esterel-Chanteclair,** Gare Maritime des Iles, 06400 Cannes (☎ **04-93-39-11-82**). Round-trip passage is 50F ($9) per person.

Ile Ste-Marguerite is named after St. Honorat's sister, Ste. Marguerite, who lived here with a group of nuns in the 5th century. Today this is a youth center whose members (when they aren't sailing and diving) are dedicated to the restoration of the fort. From the dock where the boat lands, you can stroll along the island (signs point the way) to the Fort de l'Ile, built by Spanish troops from 1635 to 1637.

Below is the 1st-century B.C. Roman town where the unlucky man immortalized in *The Man in the Iron Mask* was imprisoned. One of French history's most perplexing mysteries is the identity of the man who wore the masque du fer, a prisoner of Louis XIV who arrived at Ste-Marguerite in 1698. Dumas fanned the legend that he was a brother of Louis XIV, and it has even been suggested that the prisoner and a mysterious woman had a son who went to Corsica and "founded" the Bonaparte family. However, the most common theory is that the prisoner was a servant of the superintendent, Fouquet, named Eustache Dauger. At any rate, he died in the Bastille in Paris in 1703.

You can visit his cell at Ste-Marguerite, in which every visitor seemingly has written his or her name. As you stand listening to the sound of the sea, you realize what a forlorn outpost this was.

Musée de la Mer, Fort Royal (☎ **04-93-43-18-17**), traces the history of the island, displaying artifacts of Ligurian, Roman, and Arab civilizations, plus the remains discovered by excavations. These include paintings, mosaics, and ceramics. It's open June to September, daily from 10:30am to 12:15pm and 2:15 to 6:30pm; the rest of the year, it closes between 4:30 and 5:30pm, depending on sundown. Admission is 10F ($1.80) for adults, free for children and students.

Only a mile long, **Ile St-Honorat** is even lonelier than its neighbor. St. Honorat founded a monastery here in the 5th century. Since the 1860s the Cistercians have owned the ecclesiastical complex, consisting of both an old fortified monastery and a contemporary one. You can spend the day wandering through the pine forests on the west side of the island—the other part is reserved for silent prayer.

bag. A selection of other perfume shops dots rue d'Antibes. Any may feature your favorite fragrance in a promotional deal (they rotate the deals). If you hit it right, you'll save money at **Starlett,** 18 rue d'Antibes (☎ **04-93-39-23-77**).

SIGHTSEEING

Some 16 miles southwest of Nice, Cannes is sheltered by hills. For many visitors, it might as well consist of only one street, **promenade de la Croisette** (or just La Croisette), curving along the coast and split by islands of palms and flowers.

A port of call for cruise liners, the seafront of Cannes is lined with hotels, apartment houses, and chic boutiques. Many of the bigger hotels, some dating from the 19th century, claim part of the beaches for the private use of their guests. But there are also public areas. Above the harbor, the old town of Cannes sits on Suquet Hill, where you'll see a 14th-century tower, **Tour de Suquet,** which the English dubbed the Lord's Tower.

Nearby is the **Musée de la Castre,** in the Château de la Castre, Le Suquet (☎ **04-93-38-55-26**), containing paintings, sculpture, examples of decorative arts, and a section on ethnography. The latter includes relics and objects from everywhere from the Pacific islands to Southeast Asia, including both Peruvian and Maya pottery. There's also a gallery devoted to relics of ancient Mediterranean civilizations, from the Greeks to the Romans, from the Cypriots to the Egyptians. Five rooms are devoted to 19th-century paintings. The museum is open Wednesday to Monday: April to June from 10am to noon and 2 to 6pm, July to September from 10am to noon and 3 to 7pm, and October to March from 10am to noon and 2 to 5pm. Admission is 10F ($1.80), free for students and children.

WHERE TO STAY
VERY EXPENSIVE

✪ **Hôtel Carlton Intercontinental.** 58 bd. de la Croisette, 06400 Cannes. ☎ **800/327-0200** in the U.S., or 04-93-06-40-06. Fax 04-93-06-40-25. www.interconti.com. E-mail: cannes@interconti.com. 354 units. A/C MINIBAR TV TEL. 1,290–3,915F ($232.20–$704.70) double; from 4,025F ($724.50) suite. AE, DC, MC, V. Parking 160F ($28.80).

One of the most amusing sights in Cannes is the view from under the vaguely Art Deco grand gate of the Carlton. Here you'll see vehicles of every description pulling up to drop off piles of luggage and vast numbers of oh-so-fashionable (and sometimes not-so-fashionable) guests. Located right on the beach, it's the epitome of luxury and has become such a part of the scene that to ignore it would be to miss the spirit of Cannes.

Shortly after it was built in 1912, the Carlton attracted the most prominent members of Europe's haut monde, including royalty. They were followed decades later by battalions of screen stars. Today the hotel hosts lots of conventions and tour groups; however, in summer (especially during the Film Festival) the public rooms still are filled with all the frenzied posing that seems so much a part of the Riviera. The guest rooms were renovated in 1990. Double-glazing, big combination baths with hair dryers, and luxurious appointments are standard. The most spacious rooms are in the west wing, and many of the upper-floor rooms open onto balconies fronting the sea.

Dining: The hotel contains five restaurants. The most expensive and sophisticated is La Belle Otéro, on the seventh floor, followed by the elegant but less spectacular Restaurant du Casino and Restaurant de la Côte, which was renovated in 1997. A ground-floor Brasserie doles out less expensive fare, and at the waterfront Restaurant de la Plage, virtually everyone seems to arrive in bathing suits.

Amenities: Health club with spa facilities, glass-roofed indoor pool, room service, sauna, Jacuzzi, casino, conference rooms, boutique, concierge.

✪ **Hôtel Martinez.** 73 bd. de la Croisette, 06400 Cannes. ☎ **800/888-4747** from the U.S. or Canada, 212/752-3900 in the U.S., 04-92-98-73-00, or 0800/181591 in the U.K. Fax 04-93-39-67-82. E-mail: martinez@concorde-hotels.com. 430 units. A/C MINIBAR TV TEL. 1,920–3,680F ($345.60–$662.40) double; from 3,520F ($633.60) suite. AE, DC, MC, V. Parking 100F ($18).

When this landmark Art Deco hotel was built on the beach in the 1930s, it rivaled any other hotel along the coast in sheer size alone. Over the years, however, it has fallen into disrepair and closed and reopened several times. But in 1982 the Concorde chain returned the hotel and its restaurants to their former luster, and today it competes with the Carlton and Noga Hilton. Despite its grandeur, the hotel is a little too convention-oriented for our tastes, but the rooms remain in good shape. The aim of the decor was a Roaring Twenties style, and all units boast private safes, marble bathrooms, tasteful carpets, and pastel fabrics.

Dining: La Palme d'Or, among the finest restaurants in Cannes, is reviewed below. The poolside restaurant, Le Relais Martinez, serves light, low-calorie meals in a decor of azure and white lattices.

Amenities: Waterskiing school, cabanas, octagonal pool, seven tennis courts, 24-hour room service, same-day laundry/valet.

✪ **Noga Hilton Cannes.** 50 bd. de la Croisette, 06414 Cannes. ☎ **800-445-8667** in the U.S., or 04-92-99-70-00. Fax 04-92-99-70-11. 229 units. A/C MINIBAR TV TEL. 990–4,790F ($178.20–$862.20) double; from 1,950F ($351) suite. AE, DC, MC, V.

The owners were able to procure one of Cannes's most sought-after building sites, the seafront lot occupied by the old (since demolished) Palais des Festivals. Finished in 1992, the Hilton was the first major hotel to open in Cannes since the 1930s. This six-story deluxe palace, with massive amounts of exposed glass, boasts a contemporary design. You register in a soaring lobby sheathed with a semitranslucent white marble. The guest rooms are stylish, containing impeccable soundproofing and all the electronic gadgets you'll ever need. All the rooms are the same; rates vary based on whether you have a sea view.

Dining/Diversions: The most expensive dining venue is La Scala, a smart restaurant that specializes in the cuisines of the Riviera—both French and Italian. La Plage is an informal lunch restaurant on the beach. There's also a casino and an 800-seat theater for cabarets and conventions.

Amenities: Health club with sauna, outdoor pool, shopping arcade with about 30 boutiques, waterfront pier for mooring yachts, business center, access to nearby golf course, 24-hour room service, baby-sitting.

MODERATE

Hôtel Gray-d'Albion. 38 rue des Serbes, 06400 Cannes. ☎ **04-92-99-79-79.** Fax 04-93-99-26-10. 186 units. A/C MINIBAR TV TEL. 700–1,750F ($126–$315) double; from 2,600F ($468) suite. AE, DC, MC, V.

The smallest of the major hotels here isn't on La Croisette, but this building contains pastel-colored rooms, each outfitted with all the luxury a modern hotel can offer—some critics even consider the Gray-d'Albion among France's most luxurious hotels. Groups form a large part of its clientele, but it also caters to the individual guest. Rooms on the eighth and ninth floors have views of the Mediterranean. Dining selections include Le Royal Gray, one of the best in Cannes and a beach-club restaurant.

Hôtel Le Fouquet's. 2 rond-point Duboys-d'Angers, 06400 Cannes. ☎ **04-92-59-25-00.** Fax 04-92-98-03-39. 10 units. A/C MINIBAR TV TEL. 480–850F ($86.40–$153) double. AE, DC, MC, V. Parking 50F ($9). Closed Nov 30–Mar.

This is an intimate low-rise hotel drawing a discreet clientele, often from Paris, who'd never think of checking into the grand palace hotels, even if they could afford them. Very "Riviera French" in design and decor, it's several blocks from the beach, behind the Noga Hilton. Each of the attractive, airy rooms is decorated in bold colors, containing a loggia, a dressing room, and a hair dryer. Most rooms are spacious. There's no restaurant.

Hôtel Villa de l'Olivier. 5 rue des Tambourinaires, 06400 Cannes. ☎ **04-93-39-53-28.** Fax 04-93-39-55-85. 24 units. TV TEL. 495–715F ($89.10–$128.70) double. Extra bed 120–150F ($21.60–$27). AE, DC, V. Free parking.

In a verdant compound whose palms, figs, and shrubs shield it from the commercial neighborhood surrounding it, this hotel grew from what was a private villa around

1900. Because of its beige stucco walls and terra-cotta roof, it evokes a Provençal farm-house. The rooms open onto views of the free-form pool or the sea and are thought-fully decorated. Beaches and the diversions of La Croisette are within a 15-minute walk. Breakfast is the only meal served. Your hosts, the Schildknecht family, do every-thing they can to make your stay in their home comfortable.

INEXPENSIVE

Hôtel de Provence. 9 rue Molière, 06400 Cannes. ☎ **04-93-38-44-35.** Fax 04-93-39-63-14. 30 units. A/C MINIBAR TV TEL. 310–460F ($55.80–$82.80) double. AE, MC, V. Parking 35F ($6.30). Closed Nov 20–Dec 20.

Built in the 1930s and renovated into its present comfortable but simple format in 1992, this hotel is small scale and unpretentious. Most of the rooms have balconies, and many overlook the carefully tended shrubs and palms of the hotel's walled garden. In warm weather, breakfast is served under the vines and flowers of an arbor.

Hotel La Madrilène. 15 bd. Alexandre III, 06400 Cannes. ☎ **04-97-06-37-37.** Fax 04-93-94-38-78. 17 units. A/C TV TEL. May–Sept 490F ($88.20) double; Oct–Apr 340F ($61.20) double. AE, MC, V. Free parking. Bus: 1.

Set less than 150 yards from Port Canto, the city of Cannes's newer dock facilities and close to the much more expensive Hotel Martinez, this pleasant and unpretentious guesthouse is in the turn-of-the-century villa that belonged to a long-ago mayor of Cannes. Each of its three floors is accessorized with a different color. As you rise upward, the walls remain the same roughly textured plaster, although color schemes change from cherry to Provençal yellow to light brown. Throughout, you'll find sim-plicity, unpretentiousness, and a sense of large numbers of rather loud guests coming and going. Despite that, rooms are comfortable, and the prices are a lot more afford-able than at more grandiloquent places nearby. Orange and lemon trees in the walled garden provide nostalgic hints of another era. There's a simple restaurant on the premises, open daily from 1 to 3pm and 7:30 to 10pm, serving French and Provençal platters.

Hôtel Le Florian. 8 rue Commandant-André, 06400 Cannes. ☎ **04-93-39-24-82.** Fax 04-92-99-18-30. 20 units. A/C TV TEL. 200–350F ($36–$63) double. AE, MC, V. Parking 45F ($8.10) in nearby public facility.

This hotel is on a busy but narrow commercial street that leads directly into La Croisette, less than 100 yards from the beach and the Palais des Festivals. Built about a century ago, it has been maintained by three generations of the Giordano family since the 1950s. In 1992 many (much-needed) improvements were made. The effect is basic but adequate and even comfortable. You'll get the sense that the strong and not particularly subtle doorman is keeping a careful eye on things. Breakfast is the only meal served.

WHERE TO DINE
VERY EXPENSIVE

✪ **La Palme d'Or.** In the Hôtel Martinez, 73 bd. de la Croisette. ☎ **04-92-98-74-14.** Reser-vations required. Main courses 180–480F ($32.40–$86.40); fixed-price menus 295F ($53.10) (Mon–Sat lunch only) and 350–580F ($63–$104.40). AE, DC, MC, V. Wed–Sun 12:30–2pm and 7:30–10:30pm; mid-June to mid-Sept Tues 7:30–10:30pm. Closed Nov 20–Dec 20. FRENCH.

When this hotel was renovated by the Taittinger family (of champagne fame), one of their primary concerns was to establish a restaurant that could rival the tough compe-tition in Cannes. And they've succeeded. The result is this light-wood-paneled, Art Deco marvel with bay windows, a winter garden theme, and outdoor and enclosed terraces overlooking the pool, the sea, and La Croisette. Your experience will be artfully handled by Vincent Rouard, maître d'hôtel, and the Alsatian-born chef Christian Willer. Menu items change with the seasons but are likely to include warm foie gras with fondue of rhubarb; filets of fried red mullet with a beignet of potatoes, zucchini, and an olive-cream sauce; or a medley of crayfish, clams, and squid marinated in peppered citrus sauce. The most appealing dessert is wild strawberries from nearby Carros, with a Grand Marnier–flavored nage and a "cream sauce of frozen milk." The service is sensitive, sophisticated, and worldly, without being stiff.

EXPENSIVE

Gaston-Gastounette. 7 quai St-Pierre. ☎ **04-93-39-49-44.** Reservations required. Main courses 130–200F ($23.40–$36); fixed-price menus 170F ($30.60) at lunch, 200F ($36) at dinner. AE, DC, MC, V. Daily noon–2pm and 7–11pm. Closed Dec 1–20. FRENCH.

This is the best restaurant to offer views of the marina. Located in the old port, it has a stucco exterior with oak moldings and big windows and a sidewalk terrace surrounded by flowers. Inside you'll be served bouillabaisse, breast of duckling in garlic-cream sauce, grilled sea bass with herbs, stuffed mussels, *pot-au-feu de la mer* (a stew of seafood), and such fish platters as turbot and sole. Sorbet, after all that savory Mediterranean food, is appropriate for dessert.

✪ **La Mère Besson.** 13 rue des Frères-Pradignac. ☎ **04-93-39-59-24.** Reservations required. Main courses 75–140F ($13.50–$25.20); fixed-price menus 100F ($18) at lunch, 145–170F ($26.10–$30.60) at dinner. AE, DC, MC, V. Tues–Fri 12:15–2pm, Mon–Sat 7:30–10:30pm (also open Sun in summer). PROVENÇAL.

The culinary traditions of the late Mère Besson, who opened her restaurant in the 1930s, are carried on in one of Cannes's favorite places. All the specialties are prepared with respect for Provençal traditions and skill and served up in great steaming portions. Most delectable is *estouffade provençal* (beef braised with red wine and rich stock flavored with garlic, onions, herbs, and mushrooms). You can also sample an old-fashioned platter with codfish, fresh vegetables, and dollops of the famous garlic mayonnaise (aioli) that Provence produces by the tubful. Other specialties are fish soup and, whenever the chef feels inspired, *lou piech*, a Niçois name for veal brisket stuffed with white-stemmed vegetables, peas, ham, eggs, rice, grated cheese, and herbs.

MODERATE

Le Monaco. 15 rue du 24-Août. ☎ **04-93-38-37-76.** Reservations required. Main courses 50–90F ($9–$16.20); fixed-price menus 90–115F ($16.20–$20.70). MC, V. Mon–Sat noon–4:30pm and 7–10:30pm. Closed Nov 10–Dec 10. FRENCH/ITALIAN.

This is a local favorite, crowded but always cheap, and conveniently located near the train station. The likable ambience features closely placed tables and a staff dressed in bistro-inspired uniforms. Menu choices include osso bucco with sauerkraut, spaghetti bolognese, paella, couscous, roast rabbit with mustard sauce, mussels, trout with almonds, and minestrone with basil. Another specialty is grilled sardines, which many restaurants won't serve anymore, considering them too messy and old-fashioned.

CANNES AFTER DARK

The largest and most legendary casino in Cannes is the **Casino Croisette,** in the Palais des Festivals, 1 jetée Albert-Edouard, near promenade de la Croisette (☎ **04-93-38-12-11**). Within its glittering confines you'll find all the gaming tables you'd expect—open daily from 5pm to 4 or 5am—and one of the best nightclubs in town, **Jimmy's de Régine** (☎ **04-93-68-00-07**). Jimmy's is open Wednesday to Sunday from 11pm to dawn. You must present your passport to enter the gambling room. Admission is 100F ($18) and includes a drink.

On the eighth floor (seventh in France) of the Hôtel Carlton Intercontinental, 58 bd. de la Croisette, is **Le Carlton Casino Club** (☎ **04-92-99-51-00**). It's considerably smaller than the Casino Croisette, but many people prefer its modern decor. Jackets are required for men, and a passport or government-issued identity card is required for admission. It's open daily from 7:30pm to 4am. Admission is 70F ($12.60).

Jane's is in the cellar of the Hôtel Gray-d'Albion, 38 rue des Serbes (☎ **04-92-99-79-79**). This is a stylish and appealing nightclub with an undercurrent of coy permissiveness. The crowd is well dressed (often with the men wearing jackets and ties) and from a wide gamut of ages. The cover is 50F to 100F ($9 to $18), depending on business, and on some slow nights women enter free.

Gays and lesbians should check out the action in **Disco 7,** 7 rue Rouguiéres (☎ **04-93-39-10-36**), open Tuesday to Sunday until 3am. Attracting an older gay crowd, **Zanzi-Bar,** 85 rue Felix-Faure, opposite Vieux Port (☎ **04-93-39-30-75**), charges a 50F to 100F ($9 to $18) cover.

4 Mougins

561 miles S of Paris, 7 miles S of Grasse, 5 miles N of Cannes

This once-fortified town on the crest of a hill provides an alternative for those who want to be near the excitement of Cannes but not in the midst of it. Picasso and other artists appreciated the rugged, sun-drenched hills covered with gnarled olive trees. The artist arrived in 1936 and in time was followed by Jean Cocteau, Paul Eluard, and Man Ray. Picasso decided to move here permanently, choosing as his refuge an ideal site overlooking the Bay of Cannes, near the Chapelle Notre-Dame de Vie, which Winston Churchill once painted. Here Picasso continued to work and spend the latter part of his life with his wife, Jacqueline. Fernard Léger, René Clair, Isadora Duncan, and even Christian Dior have lived at Mougins.

Mougins is the perfect haven for those who feel that the Riviera is overrun, spoiled, and overbuilt. It preserves the quiet life even though it's a stone's throw from Cannes. The wealthy come from Cannes to golf here. Though Mougins looks serene and tranquil, it's actually part of the industrial park of Sophia Antipolis, a technological center where more than 1,000 national and international companies have offices.

ESSENTIALS

GETTING THERE   There's frequent daily **bus** service from Cannes every half hour to Mougins. Call ☎ **04-93-39-11-39** for information and schedules. To **drive** from Cannes, take the signposted road heading north to Mougins.

VISITOR INFORMATION   The **Syndicat d'Initiative** (tourist office) is at 15 av. Jean-Charles-Mallet (☎ **04-93-75-87-67**).

SEEING THE SIGHTS

For a look at the history of the area, **Musée Municipal,** place du Village (☎ **04-92-92-50-42**), is in the Saint Bernardin Chapel, built in 1618. It traces the local history of life in the area from 1553 to the 1950s and is open December to October, Monday to Friday from 10am to noon and 2 to 6pm; free admission.

You can also visit the **Chapelle Notre-Dame de Vie,** a mile southeast of Mougins, where Picasso spent the last 12 years of his life next to the chapel that Churchill painted. It was a priory from the 12th century that was rebuilt in 1646. It was an old custom at one time to bring stillborn babies here to have them baptized.

Musée de l'Automobiliste. Aire des Bréguières. ☎ **04-93-69-27-80.** Admission 40F ($7.20) adults, 25F ($4.50) ages 12–18, free for children 11 and under. Daily 10am–6pm. Closed Nov 15–Dec 15.

This is one of the top attractions on the Riviera. Founded in 1984 by Adrien Maeght, this ultramodern concrete-and-glass structure rises out of a green clearing. It houses temporary exhibitions but also owns one of Europe's most magnificent collections of original and prestigious automobiles—more than 100 vehicles from 1894 until the present.

WHERE TO STAY
Le Moulin de Mougins (see below) offers charming rooms and suites.

Manoir de l'Etang. Aux Bois de Font-Merle, allée du Manoir, 06250 Mougins. ☎ **04-93-90-01-07.** Fax 04-92-92-20-70. 14 units, 2 apts. TV TEL. 600–1,000F ($108–$180) double; 1,300–1,600F ($234–$288) apt. AE, MC, V. Closed Nov–Jan.

In the midst of olive trees and cypresses, this is one of the choice places to stay on the Riviera, housed in a 19th-century Provençal building. It boasts all the romantic extras associated with some Riviera properties, including "love goddess" statuary in the garden and candlelit dinners around a pool, but it charges reasonable rates. The rooms are bright and modern—you'll feel almost as if you're staying in a private home, which this place virtually is. Some rooms are extremely spacious.

Dining: In winter meals are served around a wood-burning fireplace. The chef bases his menu on the freshest ingredients available in any season, with fixed-price menus for 150F to 190F ($27 to $34.20).

WHERE TO DINE
L'Amandier de Mougins Café-Restaurant. Place du Commandant-Lamy. ☎ **04-93-90-00-91.** Reservations recommended. Main courses 70–100F ($12.60–$18). Fixed-price menus 140–180F ($25.20–$32.40). AE, DC, MC, V. Daily noon–2:15pm and 8–10pm. NIÇOISE/PROVENÇAL.

The illustrious founder of this relatively inexpensive bistro, in an airy stone house, is the world-famous Roger Vergé, whose much more expensive Le Moulin de Mougins is described below. This is your chance to sample his cuisine without paying a fortune. You'll get simple platters, usually based on traditional recipes, such as tuna and swordfish carpaccio, tagliatelli with truffle-cream sauce, magrêt of duckling, or veal kidneys with fricassée of mushrooms.

✪ **Le Moulin de Mougins.** Notre-Dame de Vie, 06250 Mougins. ☎ **04-93-75-78-24.** Fax 04-93-90-18-55. Reservations required. Main courses 180–400F ($32.40–$72); fixed-price menus 250–740F ($45–$133.20) at lunch, 520–740F ($93.60–$133.20) at dinner. AE, DC, MC, V. Tues–Sun noon–2:30pm and 7–10:30pm. Closed Jan 29–Mar 8. FRENCH.

This place, 4 miles north of Cannes, is among France's top 20 restaurants. From the moment you enter and are greeted by a burst of flowers, you know you're headed for one of the special experiences along the Riviera. This is the kingdom of Roger Vergé, and he's one of France's outstanding chefs, although not in the class of Alain Ducasse in Monte Carlo. Nevertheless, he will astound you with his cuisine, providing you brought along a fat wallet. Vergé is a knowledgeable professional, insisting on the finest of ingredients, which he fashions into dishes that leave favorable and often lasting culinary memories. The man's an artist in the kitchen, as the chic and fashionable who make their way to his door agree.

A 10-foot-wide stone oil vat, with a wooden turnscrew and a grinding wheel, is near the entrance. His forte is fish from the Mediterranean, bought fresh each morning. His specialties include *filets de rougets* (red mullet) with artichokes; *noisettes d'agneau* (lamb) *de Sisteron* with an eggplant cake in thyme-flavored sauce and *poupeton* (zucchini flowers) stuffed with a mixture of truffles and pulverized mushrooms, served with truffle-flavored butter sauce; fricassée of lobster with sweet wine, cream sauce, and sweet peppers; and pepper steak "à la Mathurin," with grapes, pepper, and brandy. Dessert might be a lemon soufflé. Monsieur Vergé offers a lot of fantastic, even historic wines but also has a good selection of local vintages.

The old mill offers four beautiful suites and three rooms, with air-conditioning, minibar, TV, phone, and fax machine. The rooms are decorated with French antiques. These cost 800F to 1,500F ($144 to $270).

5 Grasse

563 miles S of Paris, 11 miles N of Cannes, 6 miles NW of Mougins, 14 miles NW of Antibes

It has a tacky modern look, but Grasse, a 20-minute drive from Cannes, is the most fragrant town on the Riviera. Surrounded by jasmine and roses, it has been the capital of the perfume industry since the 19th century. It was once a famous resort, attracting such royalty as Queen Victoria and Princess Pauline Borghese, Napoléon's lascivious sister.

Today some three-quarters of the world's essences are produced here from foliage that includes violets, daffodils, wild lavender, and jasmine. It takes 10,000 flowers to produce 2.2 pounds of jasmine petals. Another statistic: Almost a ton of petals is needed to distill 1½ quarts of essence. That explains the high price tag on a bottle of perfume!

ESSENTIALS

GETTING THERE   Some 21 **buses** per day pull in from Cannes (trip time: 45 minutes), at a one-way fare of 21.50F ($3.85), and 20 per day from Nice (trip time: 1¼ hours), at 37F ($6.65) one-way. For bus information, call ☎ **04-93-85-61-81** in Nice, **04-93-39-18-71** in Cannes. To **drive** from Cannes, take N85 north to Grasse.

VISITOR INFORMATION   The **Office de Tourisme** is in the Palais des Congrès on place du Cours (☎ **04-93-36-66-66**).

SEEING THE SIGHTS

✪ **Parfumerie Fragonard.** 20 bd. Fragonard. ☎ **04-93-36-44-65.** Summer daily 9am–6:30pm; winter Mon–Sat 9am–12:30pm and 2–6pm.

One of the best-known perfume factories is named after an 18th-century French painter. This factory has the best villa, the best museum, and the best tour. An English-speaking guide will show you how "the soul of the flower" is extracted. After the tour, you can explore the museum of perfumery, which displays bottles and vases that trace the industry back to ancient times. Of course, if you're shopping for perfume and want to skip the tour, that's okay with the factories.

Villa Fragonard. 23 bd. Fragonard. ☎ **04-93-40-32-64.** Admission 20F ($3.60) adults, 10F ($1.80) children. June–Sept Wed–Sun 10am–7am; Oct–May Wed–Sun 10am–noon and 2–5pm.

The collection displayed here includes the paintings of Jean-Honoré Fragonard; his sister-in-law, Marguerite Gérard; his son, Alexandre; and his grandson, Théophile. Fragonard was born in Grasse in 1732. The grand staircase was decorated by Alexandre.

Parfumerie Molinard. 60 bd. Victor-Hugo. ☎ **04-93-36-01-62.** Free admission. May–Sept daily 9am–6:30pm; Oct–Apr Mon–Sat 9am–noon and 2–6pm.

The firm is well known in the United States, and its products are sold at Saks, Neiman Marcus, and Bloomingdale's. In the factory you can witness the extraction of the essence of the flowers, and the process of converting flowers into essential oils is explained in detail. You can admire a collection of antique perfume-bottle labels as well as see a rare collection of perfume *flacons* (bottles) by Baccarat and Lalique.

Musée d'Art et d'Histoire de Provence. 2 rue Mirabeau. ☎ **04-93-36-01-61.** Admission 20F ($3.60) adults, 10F ($1.80) children 8–16, free for children 7 and under. June–Sept daily 10am–12:30pm and 1:30–7pm; Oct and Dec–May Wed–Sun 10am–noon and 2–5pm. Closed Nov.

This museum is in the Hôtel de Clapiers-Cabris, built in 1771 by Louise de Mirabeau, the marquise de Cabris and sister of Mirabeau. The collection includes paintings, four-poster beds, marquetry, ceramics, brasses, kitchenware, pottery, urns, and even archaeological finds.

WHERE TO STAY

Hôtel Les Arômes. 115 rte. de Cannes, 06130 Grasse. ☎ **04-93-70-42-01.** 7 units. TV TEL. 360F ($64.80) double. Rate includes breakfast. AE, MC, V.

Although Les Arômes is near a noisy highway between Grasse and Cannes, it's private and calm thanks to the surrounding wall and gravel-covered courtyard. Half a mile south of the center of Grasse, this modern building was designed in the 1950s in a Provençal style, with beige stone, pink stucco, and terra-cotta tiles.

Dining: The dining room, with three large arched windows overlooking the courtyard, is open daily for lunch and dinner (except Saturday lunch); nonguests are welcome. Fixed-price menus are 80F to 140F ($14.40 to $25.20). Don't expect high style or spit-and-polish glamour, as this place is deliberately laid-back and informal.

WHERE TO DINE

The dining room at the **Hôtel Les Arômes** (see above) is open to nonguests.

✪ **La Bastide St-Antoine (Restaurant Chibois).** 48 av. Henri-Dunant. ☎ **04-93-09-16-48.** Reservations recommended. Main courses 190–280F ($34.20–$50.40); fixed-price menus 230F ($41.40) (Mon–Sat lunch) and 480–600F ($86.40–$108). AE, MC, V. Daily noon–2pm and 8–10:30pm. FRENCH/PROVENÇAL.

The fame that this restaurant has attracted since it opened in 1996 is viewed with amazement and envy by every restaurateur in France. It occupies a 200-year-old Provençal farmhouse surrounded by 7 acres of stately trees and verdant shrubbery. The aspect that intrigued the French press was Jacques Chibois, formerly employed in the dining room of Cannes's Hôtel Gray-d'Albion; his elevation to superstar came in 1997 through awards lavished on him by the controversial Gault-Millau group.

With a hardworking team directed by the maître d'hôtel Herve Domenge, the restaurant serves a sophisticated array of dishes that aren't as much composed as they are "harmonized," according to Domenge. To begin, you might try a salad of red snapper with parsley, Provençal vegetables, and olive oil. Main courses to look for are roast rack of lamb with brochettes of rosemary and basil juice, veal kidneys with an émincé of purple artichokes and risotto, and an exotic recipe for veal chops cooked in laurel leaves and flavored with sherry. Dessert might be sliced apples in puff pastry with a caramel sauce or frozen rhubarb flavored with oranges, wild strawberries, and rhubarb sorbet.

Restaurant Amphitryon. 16 bd. Victor-Hugo. ☎ **04-93-36-58-73.** Reservations recommended. Main courses 98–160F ($17.65–28.80); fixed-price menus 120–252F ($21.60–$45.35). AE, DC, MC, V. Mon–Sat noon–1:30pm and 7:30–9:30pm. Closed Aug and Dec 23–Jan 3. FRENCH.

Many of the buildings that line this street, including the premises of this restaurant, functioned as stables in the 19th century. Today, amid fabric-covered walls and soothing grays and off-whites, you can enjoy the flavorful cuisine of Michel André. The food is inspired by southwestern France, with plenty of foie gras and duckling, as well as lamb roasted with thyme and a ragoût of fish in red wine that in recent years has become one of the chef's most popular dishes.

6 Biot

570 miles S of Paris, 6 miles E of Cagnes-sur-Mer, 4 miles NW of Antibes

Biot has been famous for its pottery ever since merchants began to ship earthenware jars to Phoenicia and destinations throughout the Mediterranean. Biot was first settled by Gallo-Romans and has had a long, war-torn history. Somehow the potters still manage to work at their ancient craft. Biot is also the place Fernand Léger chose to paint until the day he died. A magnificent collection of his work is on display at a museum here.

ESSENTIALS

GETTING THERE   Biot's **train station** is 2 miles east of the town center. There's frequent service from Nice and Antibes. For rail information and schedules, call ☎ 08-36-35-35-35. The **bus** from Antibes is even more convenient than the train. For bus information and schedules, call ☎ 04-93-34-37-60 in Antibes. To **drive** to Biot from Nice, take N7 west. From Antibes, follow N7 east.

VISITOR INFORMATION   The **Office de Tourisme** is on place de la Chapelle (☎ 04-93-65-05-85).

EXPLORING THE TOWN

If you have time, you might explore the village. Begin at the much-photographed **place des Arcades,** where you can see the 16th-century gates and the remains of the town's former ramparts. The town also is known for its carnations and roses, which are sold on this lovely square. **Eglise de Biot,** place des Arcades (☎ 04-93-65-00-85), dates from the 15th century, when it was built by Italian immigrants who arrived to resettle the town after its population was decimated by the black death. The church is known for two stunning 15th-century retables: the red-and-gold *Retable du Rosaire* by Ludovico Bréa and the recently restored *Christ aux Plaies* by Canavesio.

In the late 1940s, glassmakers created a bubble-flecked glass known as *verre rustique.* It comes in brilliant colors like cobalt and emerald and is displayed in many store windows on the main shopping street, **rue St-Sebastien.** The best place to watch the glassblowers and buy glass, aside from the shops along rue St-Sebastien, is **Verrerie de Biot,** 5 chemin des Combes (☎ 04-93-65-03-00), at the edge of town. Prices are about the same as in town. Hours are Monday to Saturday from 9am to 7pm. You can also visit the showroom on Sunday from 10:30am to 1pm and 2:30 to 7pm. While you're here, you can call at **Galerie International du Verre,** where beautifully displayed glass works are for sale, often at exorbitant prices. Even if you don't buy, you can admire these one-of-a-kind collector pieces.

There's also the **Galerie Jean-Claude Novaro** (also known as Galerie de la Patrimoine), place des Arcades (☎ 04-93-65-60-23). Its namesake is known as the Picasso of glass artists. His works are pretty and colorful though sometimes lacking the diversity and intellectual flair of works by some of the artists displayed at the Galerie International du Verre. Most of his glass art, except for some exhibition pieces, is for sale.

You may also want to shop at **La Poterie Provençale,** 1689 rte. de la Mer (☎ **04-93-65-63-30**). Set nearly adjacent to the Musée Fernand-Léger, about 2 miles southeast of town, it's one of the last potteries in Provence to specialize in the tall amphoralike containers known as *jarres.*

The **Musée d'Histoire Locale et de Céramique Biotoise,** place de la Chapelle (☎ 04-93-65-54-54), over the years has assembled the best work of local glass-blowing artists, potters, ceramists, painters, and silver- and goldsmiths. It's open Thursday to Sunday from 2:30 to 6:30pm, charging 10F ($1.80) admission.

✪ **Musée National Fernand-Léger.** Chemin du Val-de-Pome (on the eastern edge of town, beside the road leading to Biot's rail station). ☎ **04-92-91-50-30.** Admission 30F ($5.40) adults, 20F ($3.60) ages 18–24 and seniors over 60, free for children 17 and under. Guided tours can be arranged by calling ☎ 04-92-91-50-20. Wed–Mon 10am–12:30pm and 2–6pm (to 5:30pm in winter).

This collection was assembled by the artist's widow, Nadia Léger, who donated its contents to the French government after the artist's death. The stone-and-marble facade is enhanced by Léger's mosaic-and-ceramic mural. On the grounds is a polychrome ceramic sculpture, *Le Jardin d'enfant.* Inside are two floors of geometrical forms in pure flat colors. The collection includes gouaches, paintings, ceramics, tapestries, and sculptures—showing the development of the artist from 1905 until his death. His paintings abound in cranes, acrobats, scaffolding, railroad signals, buxom nudes, casings, and crankshafts. From his first cubist paintings, Léger was dubbed a "Tubist." The most unusual work depicts a Léger Mona Lisa (*La Giaconde aux Clés*) contemplating a set of keys, a wide-mouthed fish dangling at an angle over her head.

WHERE TO DINE

✪ **Les Terraillers.** 11 rte. du Chemin-Neuf. ☎ **04-93-65-01-59.** Fax 04-93-65-13-78. Reservations required, as far in advance as possible. Main courses 170–190F ($30.60–$34.20); fixed-price menus 180–310F ($32.40–$55.80) at lunch, 250–360F ($45–$64.80) at dinner. AE, MC, V. Thurs–Tues noon–2pm and 7–10pm. July–Aug closed Thurs lunch and closed Wed throughout the year. Take rte. du Chemin-Neuf, following the signposts to Antibes. MEDITERRANEAN.

Deeply evocative of Provence, this restaurant is about half a mile south of Biot, in what was built in the 1500s as a studio for the production of clay pots and ceramics. Today, under the guidance of chef Claude Jacques, it's a well-respected restaurant. The menu may include terrine of foie gras with Armagnac, sea wolf roasted in a salt crust, ravioli stuffed with foie gras and essence of morels, and saddle of rabbit with wild mushrooms. There are those who say his cookery could use a bit of simplification, but that didn't prevent Michelin and us from awarding him a star.

7 Golfe-Juan & Vallauris

Golfe-Juan: 567 miles S of Paris, 4 miles E of Cannes; Vallauris: 565 miles S of Paris, 4 miles E of Cannes

Napoléon and 800 men landed at Golfe-Juan in 1815 to begin his Hundred Days. Protected by hills, this spot beside the coast was also the favored port for the American navy. Today it's primarily a family resort known for its beaches and boasting a noteworthy restaurant (Chez Tétou).

The 1¼-mile-long R.N. 135 leads inland from Golfe-Juan to Vallauris. Once merely a stopover along the Riviera, Vallauris (noted for its pottery) owes its reputation to Picasso, who "discovered" it. The master came to Vallauris after World War II and occupied a villa known as "The Woman from Wales."

ESSENTIALS

GETTING THERE   **Buses** travel to both Vallauris and Golfe-Juan from Cannes, and other buses connect the two towns. In Cannes, call ☎ **04-93-39-18-71** for information and schedules. To **drive** to Golfe-Juan, take N7 east from Cannes.

VISITOR INFORMATION   There's an **Office de Tourisme** at 84 av. de la Liberté in Golfe-Juan (☎ **04-93-63-73-12**) and another on square 8-Mai in Vallauris (☎ **04-93-63-82-58**).

EXPLORING THE AREA

BEACHES   Because of its position beside the sea, Golfe-Juan developed long ago into a warm-weather resort. The town's twin strips of beach are **Plages du Soleil** (east of the Vieux Port and the newer Port Camille-Rayon) and **Plages du Midi** (west of those two). Each stretches half a mile and charges no entry fee, with the exception of small areas administered by concessions that rent mattresses and chaises and offer access to kiosks dispensing snacks and cold drinks. Regardless of which concession you select (on Plage du Midi they sport names like Au Vieux Rocher, Palma Beach, and Corail Plage; on Plage du Soleil, Plage Nounou and Plage Tétou), you'll pay around 70F ($12.60) for a day's use of a mattress. Plage Tétou is associated with the upscale Chez Tétou (see "Dining," below). If you don't want to rent a mattress, you can cavort unhindered anywhere along the sands, moving freely from one area to another. Golfe-Juan indulges bathers who remove their bikini tops, but in theory it forbids nude sunbathing.

ATTRACTIONS   Picasso's *Homme et Mouton* (Man and Sheep) is the outdoor statue at which Aly Kahn and Rita Hayworth were married. The council of Vallauris had intended to ensconce this statue in a museum, but Picasso insisted that it remain on the square "where the children could climb over it and the dogs water it unhindered."

SHOPPING

Landlocked Vallauris depends on the sale of tourist items and ceramics—many the color of rich burgundy—for part of its livelihood. Merchants selling the colorful wares line both sides of **avenue Georges-Clemenceau,** which begins at a point adjacent to the Musée Picasso and slopes downhill and southward to the edge of town. Frankly, at least some of the pieces displayed in these shops are in poor taste, though in recent years the almost-universal emphasis on the traditional deep-red color has been replaced with a wider variety geared to modern tastes.

One shop that rises far above its neighbors is **Galerie Madoura,** av. des Anciens-Combattants-d'Afrique-du-Nord in Vallauris (☎ **04-93-64-66-39**); it's the only shop licensed to sell Picasso reproductions. The master knew and admired the work of the Ramie family, who founded Madoura. Some of the reproductions are limited to 25 to 500 copies.

Other galleries to seek out are **Galerie Jean Marais,** av. des Martyrs de la Résistance (☎ **04-93-63-85-74**); and **Galerie Sassi-Milici,** 65 bis av. Georges-Clemenceau (☎ **04-93-64-65-71**), displaying works by contemporary artists.

Market day at Vallauris takes place Saturday and Sunday in the morning at place de l'Homme au Mouton, with its flower stalls and local produce. For a souvenir, you may want to visit a farming cooperative, **Cooperative Nérolium,** 12 av. Georges-Clemenceau (☎ **04-93-64-27-54**), and purchase some locally made perfumes direct from the producers. Another outlet is **Parfumerie Bouis,** 50 av. Georges-Clemenceau (☎ **04-93-64-38-27**).

Musée Magnelli/Musée de la Céramique/Musée National Picasso La Guerre et La Paix. Place de la Libération. ☎ **04-93-64-16-05.** Admission 17F ($3.05) adults, 8.50F ($1.55) students, free for children 15 and under. Sept–June Wed–Mon 10am–noon and 2–6pm; July–Aug Wed–Mon 10am–12:30pm and 2–6:30pm.

A chapel of rough stone shaped like a Quonset hut is the focal point of a three-in-one sightseeing highlight. The museum grew from the site of a chapel that Picasso decorated with two paintings: *La Paix* (Peace) and *La Guerre* (War). The paintings offer contrasting images of love and peace on the one hand and violence and conflict on the other. In 1970 a housepainter gained illegal entrance to the museum one night and substituted one of his own designs, after whitewashing a portion of the original. When the aging master inspected the damage, he said, "Not bad at all." In July 1996 the site was enhanced with a permanent exposition devoted to the works of the Florentine-born Alberto Magnelli, a pioneer of abstract art whose first successes were acclaimed in 1915 and who died in 1971, 2 years before Picasso. A third section showcases ceramics, both traditional and innovative, from potters throughout the region.

WHERE TO DINE

✪ **Chez Tétou.** Av. des Frères-Roustand, sur la Plage, Golfe-Juan. ☎ **04-93-63-71-16.** Reservations required. Bouillabaisse 400–480F ($72–$86.40); fixed-price menus 500–700F ($90–$126). No credit cards. Thurs–Tues noon–1:45pm and 7:30–10:30pm. Closed Nov–Apr. SEAFOOD.

In its own amusing way, this is one of the Côte d'Azur's most famous restaurants, still trading on the fame of the glittering celebrity set that frequented it during the 1950s and 1960s. Retaining its Provençal earthiness despite its incredibly high prices, it has thrived in a white-sided beach cottage for more than 65 years. It still serves a bouillabaisse often remembered years later by diners. Other items on the deliberately limited menu are grilled sea bass with tomatoes Provençal, sole meunière, and several preparations of lobster—the most famous of which is grilled and served with lemon-butter sauce, fresh parsley, and a bed of basmati rice. The appetizers are limited to platters of *charcuterie* (cold cuts) or several almost-perfect slices of fresh melon, as most diners order the house specialty, bouillabaisse. Your dessert might be a special powdered croissant with grandmother's jams (winter) or a homemade raspberry and strawberry tart (summer).

8 Antibes & Cap d'Antibes

567 miles S of Paris, 13 miles SW of Nice, 7 miles NE of Cannes

On the other side of the Baie des Anges (Bay of Angels), across from Nice, is the port of Antibes. This old Mediterranean town has a quiet charm unique on the Côte d'Azur. Its little harbor is filled with fishing boats and pleasure yachts, and in recent years it has emerged as a new hot spot. The marketplaces are full of flowers, mostly roses and carnations. If you're in Antibes in the evening, you can watch fishers playing the popular Riviera game of boule.

Spiritually, Antibes is totally divorced from Cap d'Antibes, a peninsula studded with the villas and pools of the superrich. In *Tender Is the Night,* F. Scott Fitzgerald described it as a place where "old villas rotted like water lilies among the massed pines." Photos of film and rock stars lounging at the Eden Roc have appeared in countless magazines.

ESSENTIALS

GETTING THERE   Trains from Cannes arrive every 30 minutes (trip time: 10 minutes), and trains from Nice pull in every 30 minutes (trip time: 18 minutes). For rail information and schedules, call ☎ **08-36-35-35-39.** To **drive** to Antibes, the best route is from Nice. Take N7 east; from Cannes, follow N7 west.

VISITOR INFORMATION   The **Office de Tourisme** is at 11 place du Général-de-Gaulle (☎ **04-92-90-53-00**).

SEEING THE SIGHTS

✪ **Musée Picasso.** Place du Château. ☎ **04-92-90-54-20** for recorded message or 04-92-90-54-26 for an attendant. Admission 30F ($5.40) adults, 18F ($3.25) students and ages 15–24 and over 60, free for children 14 and under. June–Sept Tues–Sun 10am–6pm; Oct–May Tues–Sun 10–11:50am and 2–5:50pm.

On the ramparts above the port is the Château Grimaldi, once the home of the princes of Antibes of the Grimaldi family, who ruled the city from 1385 to 1608. Today it houses one of the world's greatest Picasso collections. Picasso came to the small town after his bitter war years in Paris and stayed in a small hotel at Golfe-Juan until the museum director at Antibes invited him to work and live at the museum. Picasso then spent 1946 painting here. When he departed, he gave the museum all the work he'd done—24 paintings, 80 pieces of ceramics, 44 drawings, 32 lithographs, 11 oils on paper, 2 sculptures, and 5 tapestries. In addition, there's a gallery of contemporary art, which exhibits Léger, Miró, Ernst, and Calder, among others. (Be warned in advance that some of the works by those other artists might be in storage at the time of your visit, based on whatever temporary exhibition is being displayed.)

Musée Naval et Napoléonien. Batterie du Grillon, bd. J.-F.-Kennedy. ☎ **04-93-61-45-32.** Admission 20F ($3.60) adults, 10F ($1.80) students, free for children 14 and under. Mon–Fri 9:30am–noon and 2–6pm, Sat 9:30am–noon.

In a stone-sided fort and tower that was built in stages between the 17th and 18th centuries, there's an interesting collection of Napoleonic memorabilia, naval models, paintings, and mementos, many of which were donated to the museum by at least two world-class collectors. A toy soldier collection depicts various uniforms, including one used by Napoléon in the Marengo campaign. A wall painting on wood shows Napoléon's entrance into Grenoble; another tableau shows him disembarking at Golfe-Juan on March 1, 1815. In contrast to Canova's Greek-god image of Napoléon, a miniature pendant by Barrault reveals the Corsican general as he really looked, with pudgy cheeks and a receding hairline. In the rear rotunda is one of the many hats worn by the emperor. You can climb to the top of the tower for a view of the coast that's worth the admission price.

WHERE TO STAY
VERY EXPENSIVE

✪ **Hôtel du Cap-Eden Roc.** Bd. J.-F.-Kennedy, 06160 Cap d'Antibes. ☎ **04-93-61-39-01.** Fax 04-93-67-76-04. www.edenroc.hotel.fr. 130 units, 10 suites. A/C TEL. 2,050–4,000F ($369–$720) double; 4,800–6,400F ($864–$1,152) suite. No credit cards. Closed mid-Oct to mid-Apr. Bus: A2.

Legendary for the glamour of both its setting and its clientele, this Second Empire hotel, opened in 1870, is surrounded by 22 splendid acres of gardens. It's like a great country estate, with spacious public rooms, marble fireplaces, scenic paneling, chandeliers, and richly upholstered armchairs. Some guest rooms and suites have regal period furnishings. It's a seriously glamorous place, as you might expect from those astronomical prices. Even though the guests snoozing by the pool might appear artfully undraped during daylight hours, evenings here are intensely upscale, with lots of emphasis on clothing and style. The staff is well drilled, but regardless of how important you are, they can always claim they've dealt with bigger and more famous names.

Dining: The world-famous Pavillon Eden Roc, near a rock garden apart from the hotel, has a panoramic Mediterranean view. Venetian chandeliers, Louis XV chairs, and elegant draperies add to the drama. Lunch is served on an outer terrace, under umbrellas and an arbor. Dinner specialties include bouillabaisse, lobster Thermidor, and sea bass with fennel.

Amenities: The swimming pool here was blasted out of the cliffside at enormous expense; it's one of the most famous on the Riviera; concierge, 24-hour room service, dry cleaning and laundry service, massage, secretarial services, baby-sitting.

MODERATE

Hôtel La Gardiole-Lagaroupe. Chemin de la Garoupe, 06160 Cap d'Antibes. ☎ **04-93-61-35-03.** Fax 04-93-67-61-87. 40 units. A/C MINIBAR TV TEL. 340–590F ($61.20–$106.20) per person double. AE, DC, MC, V. Closed Nov–Feb. Bus: A2.

M. and Mme Morlay run this country inn with a delightful personal touch. The large villa, surrounded by gardens, is in an area full of private estates. The charming rooms, on the upper floors of the inn and in the little buildings in the garden, contain personal safes.

Dining: The owners buy the food and supervise its preparation; the cuisine is French/Provençale with fixed-price menus at 100F to 150F ($18 to $27). The cheerful dining room has a fireplace and hanging pots and pans, and in good weather you can dine under a wisteria-covered trellis.

INEXPENSIVE

Le Cameo. Place Nationale, 06600 Antibes. ☎ **04-93-34-24-17.** 8 units (3 with shower only, 5 with bathtub). TEL. 250F ($45) double with shower only, 300F ($54) double with bathtub. Rates include breakfast. DC, MC, V. Closed Jan–Feb. Bus: A2.

On a historic square, this 19th-century Provençal villa is the best-known inn in the center of town. The rooms are old-fashioned and admittedly not for everyone, perhaps typical of the place where Picasso might have stayed when he first hit town.

Dining: Locals gather every afternoon and evening in the bar, often taking a meal in the adjacent home-style dining room. Amid bouquets of flowers and crowded tables, you'll enjoy local fish, stuffed mussels, bouillabaisse, and fried scampi. The restaurant is open daily, and the staff provides a more authentic exposure to the essence of Provence than what you get at larger, less personalized hotels.

WHERE TO DINE

La Bonne Auberge. Quartier de Brague, rte. N7. ☎ **04-93-33-36-65.** Reservations required. Fixed-price menu 200F ($36). MC, V. Tues–Sun noon–2pm and 7–10pm. Closed mid-Nov to mid-Dec. Take the coastal highway (N7) 2½ miles from Antibes. FRENCH.

For many years following its 1975 opening, this was one of the most famous restaurants on the French Riviera. In 1992, in the wake of the death of its famous founder, Jo Rostang, his culinary heir, Philippe Rostang, wisely limited its scope and transformed it into a worthwhile but less ambitious restaurant. The fixed-price menu offers a wide selection. Choices vary but may include a Basque-inspired pipérade with poached eggs, savory swordfish tart, chicken with vinegar and garlic, and perch-pike dumplings Jo Rostang. Dessert might be an enchanting peach soufflé.

Les Vieux Murs. Promenade de l'avenue de l'Amiral-de-Grasse. ☎ **04-93-34-06-73.** Reservations recommended. Main courses 100–200F ($18–$36); fixed-price menu 200F ($36). AE, MC, V. Daily noon–2pm and 7:30–10pm. Closed Mon Oct–Apr. Bus: A2. FRENCH/SEAFOOD.

This charming Provençal tavern occupies a room inside the 17th-century ramparts that used to fortify the old seaport. Close to the Picasso Museum, the space contains soaring stone vaults and a simple decor painted for the most part in white. There's also a glassed-in front terrace that offers a pleasant view of the water. Menu specialties are a warm salad of mullet, sophisticated arrays of crudités that reflect the bounty of the local harvest, artichoke hearts with a confit of tomatoes, and fresh filets of such fish as daurade, hogfish, sole, salmon, and red mullet, prepared dozens of ways. Especially appealing is the roast *chapon,* a local seafish, with a simple but ultrafresh fricassée of vegetables and olive oil. Suzanne and Georges Romano often have more hungry diners than tables, so try to book early. Their fixed-price menu is one of the best values on the coast.

✪ **Restaurant de Bacon.** Bd. de Bacon. ☎ **04-93-61-50-02.** Reservations required. Fixed-price menus 250–400F ($45–$72). AE, DC, MC, V. Tues–Sun 12:30–2pm and 8–10pm (open Mon dinner July–Aug). Closed Nov–Jan.

Set among ultraexpensive residences, this restaurant on a rocky peninsula has a panoramic coast view. Bouillabaisse aficionados claim that Bacon offers the best version in France. In its deluxe version, saltwater crayfish float atop the savory brew; we prefer the simple version—a waiter adds the finishing touches at your table. If bouillabaisse isn't to your liking, try fish soup with the traditional garlic-laden rouille sauce, fish terrine, sea bass, John Dory, or something from an exotic collection of fish unknown in North America. Many visitors are confused by the way fish dishes are priced by the gram, but be prepared before you order fish and find yourself with a huge bill: A guideline is that light lunches cost around 250F to 400F ($45 to $72); substantial dinners go for 550F to 800F ($99 to $144)!

9 Juan-les-Pins

567 miles S of Paris, 6 miles S of Cannes

This suburb of Antibes is a resort in its own right, attracting young Europeans from many economic backgrounds in pursuit of sex, sun, and sea in that order. Juan-les-Pins is often called a honky-tonk town or the Coney Island of the Riviera (but anyone who calls it that hasn't seen Coney Island in a long time). It's a lively, boisterous, middle-class resort. Long ago, F. Scott Fitzgerald decried it as a "constant carnival." If he could see it now, he would know that he was a prophet.

ESSENTIALS

GETTING THERE   Juan-les-Pins is connected by rail and bus to most other Mediterranean coastal resorts, especially Nice, from which frequent **trains** arrive throughout the day (trip time: 30 minutes). For rail information and schedules, call ☎ **08-36-35-35-39.** There are also **buses** that arrive from Nice and its airport at 40 minute intervals throughout the day. To **drive** to Juan-les-Pins from Nice, travel along N7 south; from Cannes, follow the signposted roads—Juan-les-Pins is just outside of Cannes.

VISITOR INFORMATION   The **Office de Tourisme** is at 51 bd. Charles-Guillaumont (☎ **04-92-90-53-05**). The staff here can sell you tickets to the annual **Festival International de Jazz,** which descends at the end of July, attracting stellar jazz masters and their devoted fans. Tickets range from 110F to 200F ($19.80 to $36).

EXPLORING THE TOWN

Part of the reason people flock here is that the town's beaches actually have sand, unlike many of the other resorts along this coast, which have pebbly beaches. **Plage de Juan-les-Pins** is the town's most central beach. Its subdivisions, all public, include

Plage de la Salis and **Plage de la Garoupe.** Many people opt to tote their own blankets, chairs, and picnic hampers, but if you're interested in renting a chaise with a mattress, go to the concessions operated by each of the major beachfront hotels, even if you're not a guest; they cost between 60F and 70F ($10.80 and $12.60). The most chic of the lot is the area maintained by the Hôtel des Belles-Rives. Competitors more or less in the same category are La Jetée and La Voile Blanche, both opposite the tourist information office. Topless sunbathing is permitted, but total nudity isn't.

If you're interested in scuba diving, check with your hotel concierge or one of these companies: the **Spondyle Club,** 62 av. des Pins-du-Cap (☎ **04-93-61-45-45**); **Club de la Mer,** Port Gallice (☎ **04-93-61-26-07**); or **EPAJ,** embarcadère Courbet (☎ **04-93-67-52-59**). **Waterskiing** is available at virtually every beach in Juan-les-Pins, including one outfit that's more or less permanently located on the beach of the Hôtel des Belles-Rives. Ask any beach attendant or bartender and he or she will guide you to the waterskiing representatives who station themselves on the sands. The cost for a 10-minute session is about 150F ($27).

WHERE TO STAY
VERY EXPENSIVE

Belles-Rives. 33 bd. Baudoin, 06160 Juan-les-Pins. ☎ **04-93-61-02-79.** Fax 04-93-67-43-51. 45 units. A/C MINIBAR TV TEL. 990–2,550F ($178.20–$459) double; 3,240–4,400F ($583.20–$792) suite. Half board 390F ($70.20) per person extra. AE, MC, V. Closed Oct–Mar.

This is one of the Riviera's fabled beachfront addresses, on a par with the equally famous Juana, though the Juana boasts a somewhat superior cuisine. Once it was a holiday villa occupied by Zelda and F. Scott Fitzgerald, so it was the scene of many a drunken brawl. In the following years it hosted the illustrious, like the duke and duchess of Windsor, Josephine Baker, and even Edith Piaf. A certain 1930s aura still lingers. A major restoration was completed in 1990, with subsequent, less comprehensive upgrades made at 2-year intervals since. Double-glazing and a new air-conditioning system help a lot.

Dining: The lower terraces are devoted to garden dining rooms and a waterside aquatic club with a snack bar/lounge and a jetty extending into the water. Dinners are served in a romantic setting on the terrace with a panoramic bay view; lunches are stylish but somewhat less formal and offered overlooking the beach.

Amenities: Landing dock, car-rental desk, concierge, room service, dry cleaning/laundry, baby-sitting, courtesy car, private beach.

✪ **Hôtel Juana.** La Pinède, av. Gallice, 06160 Juan-les-Pins. ☎ **04-93-61-08-70.** Fax 04-93-61-76-60. www.french-riviera.com or www.travelfirst.com. 50 units. A/C TV TEL. 950–2,050F ($171–$369) double; 1,600–3,500F ($288–$630) suite. AE, MC, V. Parking 50F ($9). Closed Nov–Mar.

This balconied Art Deco four-star hotel, owned by the Barache family since 1931, is separated from the sea by the park of pines that gave Juan-les-Pins its name and that was so beloved by F. Scott Fitzgerald. The hotel has a private swimming club where you can rent a "parasol and pad" on the sandy beach at reduced rates. Nearby is a park with umbrella tables and shady palms. The hotel is constantly being refurbished, as reflected in the attractive rooms, with mahogany pieces, well-chosen fabrics, tasteful carpets, and large rooms in marble or tile imported from Italy. The rooms also have such extras as safes and (in some) balconies.

Dining: We review La Terrasse restaurant below. There's a bar in the poolhouse.

Amenities: Private beach club and a heated marble outdoor pool with a solarium; concierge, room service, dry cleaning and laundry service, massage, bicycle rentals, baby-sitting, secretarial services.

MODERATE

Hôtel des Mimosas. Rue Pauline, 06160 Juan-les-Pins. ☎ **04-93-61-04-16.** Fax 04-92-93-06-46. 36 units. TV TEL. 500–680F ($90–$122.40) double. AE, MC, V. Closed Sept 30–Apr 26. From the town center, drive a quarter mile west, following N7 toward Cannes.

This elegant 1870s-style villa sprawls in a tropical garden on a hilltop. The decor is a mix of high-tech and Italian-style comfort, with antique and modern furniture. There's a bar but no restaurant. The rooms have balconies. A pool is set, California style, amid huge palm trees. The hotel is fully booked in summer, so reserve far in advance.

Hôtel Le Pré Catelan. 22 av. des Palmiers, 06160 Juan-les-Pins. ☎ **04-93-61-05-11.** Fax 04-93-67-83-11. 18 units. TV TEL. 450–600F ($81–$108) double. AE, DC, MC, V.

In a residential area near the town park, this circa-1900 Provençal villa has a garden with rock terraces, towering palms, lemon and orange trees, large pots of pink geraniums, trimmed hedges, and outdoor furniture. The atmosphere is casual, the setting simple and not at all stuffy. The more expensive rooms open onto terraces, and the furnishings are durable and rather basic. Despite the setting in the heart of town, the garden here manages to provide a sense of isolation. No meals are served other than breakfast.

INEXPENSIVE

Hôtel Cecil. Rue Jonnard, 06160 Juan-les-Pins. ☎ **04-93-61-05-12.** Fax 04-93-67-09-14. 21 units. TV TEL. 150–400F ($27–$72) double. AE, MC, V. Parking 60F ($10.80). Closed Nov–Jan 1.

Located 50 yards from the beach, this well-kept hotel is one of the best bargains in Juan-les-Pins. The owner/chef Michel Courtois provides a courteous welcome and good meals beginning at 80F ($14.40). The rooms are well worn yet clean. In summer you can dine on a patio.

WHERE TO DINE

La Romana. 21 av. Dautheville. ☎ **04-93-61-05-66.** Pizzas 35–55F ($6.30–$9.90); main-course salads and platters 50–138F ($9–$24.85). MC, V. June–Sept daily noon–2:30am; Oct to early Nov, late Dec to early Jan, and late Mar to May daily noon–2:30pm and 5pm–midnight. Closed mid-Nov to mid-Dec and mid-Jan to mid-Mar. FRENCH/INTERNATIONAL.

Behind the town's casino, this is a completely unpretentious and informal joint that successfully caters to the thousands of vacationers who flood the town every season with pizzas, meal-size salads, fried fish and fried scampi, grilled steaks with french fries, and plats du jour that change every day.

✪ **La Terrasse.** In the Hôtel Juana, La Pinède, av. Gallice. ☎ **04-93-61-20-37.** Reservations required. Main courses 260–350F ($46.80–$63); fixed-price menus 275F ($49.50) at lunch, 420–640F ($75.60–$115.20) at dinner. AE, MC, V. Thurs–Tues 12:30–2pm and 7:30–10:30pm. Also open same hours on Wed in July–Aug. Closed Nov–Mar. FRENCH/MEDITERRANEAN.

Bill Cosby loves this place so much that he's been known to fly chef Christian Morisset and his Dalí mustache to New York to prepare dinner for him. Morisset, who trained with Vergé and Lenôtre, cooks with a light, precise, and creative hand. His cuisine is the best in Juan-les-Pins. The setting is lively and sophisticated, with a conservatively modern decor overlooking the verdant garden and a glassed-in terrace whose roof opens for midsummer ventilation and a view of the stars. Scampi-stuffed ravioli, roast turbot with crusty mashed potatoes studded with Périgord truffles, or pink roasted crayfish with risotto and asparagus are examples of a flavorful, satisfying cuisine that's invariably delectable. We have to mention the crunchy, fresh "baby vegetables" (for eating baby vegetables is what distinguishes the rich from the rest of us, according to the late Truman Capote).

✪ **Le Bijou.** Bd. Charles-Guillaumont. ☎ **04-93-61-39-07.** Reservations recommended. Main courses 150–190F ($27–$34.20); fixed-price menus 165–280F ($29.70–$50.40); shellfish platters 270F ($48.60); bouillabaisse 300F ($54). AE, DC, MC, V. Daily noon–2:30pm and 7:30–10:30pm (to 11:30pm June to mid-Sept). FRENCH/PROVENÇAL.

This upscale brasserie has flourished beside the seafront promenade for almost 80 years. The marine-style decor includes lots of varnished wood and bouquets of blue and white flowers in a mostly blue-and-white interior. Windows overlook a private beach whose sands are much less crowded than those of the public beaches nearby. Menu items are succulent, sophisticated, but very expensive. The bouillabaisse will leave you clamoring for more. You might also enjoy platters of grilled sardines, steamed mussels with sauce *poulette* (frothy cream sauce with herbs and butter), grilled John Dory with a vinaigrette enriched with a tapenade of olives and fresh basil, and a supersize *plateau des coquillages et fruits de mer* (shellfish).

The management also runs a separate operation on its beachfront terrace, open only from April to September every day from noon to 4pm. Here a lunch buffet—served to diners in swimsuits, which are strictly forbidden in the main restaurant several paces uphill—is 70F ($12.60) per person.

JUAN-LES-PINS AFTER DARK

The town offers some of the best nightlife on the Riviera, and the action reaches its frenzied height during the annual jazz festival.

For starters, visit the **Eden Casino,** boulevard Baudoin in the heart of Juan-les-Pins (☎ **04-92-93-71-71**), and try your luck at the roulette wheel or at one of the slot machines. For a more tropical experience, head to **Le Pam Pam,** route Wilson (☎ **04-93-61-11-05**), where you can sip rum drinks in an exotic ambience created by live reggae, Brazilian, and African music and dance.

If you prefer some high-energy reveling, check out the town's many discos, the best of which are **Whisky à Gogo,** bd. de la Pinède (☎ **04-93-61-26-40**), with its young trendsetters and pounding rock beat; **Vertigo,** guy de Maupassant (☎ **04-93-67-78-87**), where everyone bumps and grinds to a stellar house and techno mix; the richly dramatic **Le Bureau,** av. Georges-Gallica (☎ **04-93-67-22-74**), keeping the fast and frenzied beat going with anything from Latin salsa to disco; and **Voom Voom,** 1 bd. de la Pinède (☎ **04-93-61-18-71**), which boasts an action-packed dance floor and hip DJs spinning the latest from the international music scene. The cover charge at these clubs is a stiff 100F ($18).

For a more relaxed evening, go to the British pub **Le Ten's Bar,** 25 av. du Dr.-Hochet (☎ **04-93-67-20-67**), where you'll find 56 brands of beer and a sociable crowd of young and old merrymakers. You could even choose the tranquil piano bar **New Orléans,** in the Garden Beach Hotel (☎ **04-92-93-57-57**), with its older, more sophisticated crowd, or **Le Madison,** 1 av. Alexandre-III (☎ **04-93-67-83-80**), with the town's best jazz and blues.

10 Cagnes-sur-Mer

570 miles S of Paris, 13 miles NE of Cannes

Cagnes-sur-Mer, like the Roman god Janus, has two faces. Perched on a hill in the "hinterlands" of Nice, **Le Haut-de-Cagnes** is one of the most charming spots on the Riviera. Naomi Barry of *The New York Times* wrote that it "crowns the top of a blue-cypressed hill like a village in an Italian Renaissance painting." At the foot of the hill is an old fishing port and rapidly developing beach resort called **Cros-de-Cagnes,** between Nice and Antibes.

For years Le Haut-de-Cagnes attracted the French literati, including Simone de Beauvoir, who wrote *Les Mandarins* here. A colony of painters also settled here; Renoir said the village was "the place where I want to paint until the last day of my life." Today the racecourse is one of the finest in France.

ESSENTIALS

GETTING THERE   **Buses** from Nice and Cannes stop at Cagnes-Ville and at Béal/Les Collettes, within walking distance of Cros-de-Cagne. For bus information, call ☎ **04-93-39-18-71** in Cannes or **04-93-85-61-81** in Nice. The climb from Cagnes-Ville to Le-Haut-de-Cagnes is very strenuous, so there's a minibus running about every 30 minutes from place du Général-de-Gaulle in the center of Cagnes-Ville to Le-Haut-de-Cagnes. To **drive** to Cagnes-sur-Mer from Nice, travel along N7 west.

VISITOR INFORMATION   The **Office de Tourisme** is at 6 bd. Maréchal-Juin, Cagnes-Ville (☎ **04-93-20-61-64**).

SPECIAL EVENTS   The **International Festival of Painting** is presented by the Musée d'Art Moderne Méditerranéen from November 22 to January 20 in the Château-Musée, 7 place Grimaldi; 40 nations participate. For information, call ☎ **04-93-20-87-29.**

EXPLORING THE TOWN

Cros-de-Cagnes is known for 2¼ miles of seafront evenly covered with light-gray pebbles (the French refer to it as galet) that've been worn smooth by centuries of wave action. These beaches are collectively identified as **Plages de Cros-de-Cagnes.** The expanse is punctuated by five concessions that rent beach mattresses and chaises for around 85F ($15.30). The best, or at least the most centrally located, are **Tiercé Plage** (☎ **04-93-20-13-89**), **Le Cigalon** (☎ **04-93-07-74-82**), and **La Gougouline** (☎ **04-93-31-08-72**). As usual, toplessness is accepted but full nudity isn't.

The orange groves and fields of carnations of the upper village provide a beautiful setting for the narrow cobblestone streets and 17th- and 18th-century homes. Drive your car to the top, where you can enjoy the view from **place du Château** and have lunch or a drink at a sidewalk cafe.

Musée de l'Olivier (Museum of the Olive Tree)/Musée d'Art Moderne Méditer-ranéen (Museum of Modern Mediterranean Art). 7 place Grimaldi. ☎ **04-93-20-85-57.** Admission to both museums 20F ($3.60) adults, 10F ($1.80) students. May–Sept Wed–Mon 10am–noon and 2–6pm; Oct and Dec–Apr Wed–Mon 10am–noon and 2–5pm. Closed Nov.

This structure was originally a fortress built in 1301 by Rainier Grimaldi I, a lord of Monaco and a French admiral (see the portrait inside). Charts reveal how the defenses were organized. In the early 17th century, the dank castle was converted into a more gracious Louis XIII château, which now contains two museums. The ethnographic museum shows the steps in cultivating and processing the olive.

The modern art gallery displays works by Kisling, Carzou, Dufy, Cocteau, and Seyssaud, among others, with temporary exhibitions. In one salon is an interesting trompe-l'oeil fresco, *La Chute de Phaeton.*

From the tower you get a panoramic view of the Côte d'Azur. The International Festival of Painting (see above) takes place here.

Les Collettes. 19 chemin des Collettes. ☎ **04-93-20-61-07.** Admission 20F ($3.60) adults, 10F ($1.80) children. May–Oct 14 daily 10am–noon and 2–6pm; Oct 15–April Wed–Mon 10am–noon and 2–5pm. Ticket sales end 30 min before the lunch and evening closing hour.

Les Collettes has been restored to what it looked like when Renoir lived here from 1908 until his death in 1919. He continued to sculpt here, even though he was crippled by arthritis and had to be helped in and out of a wheelchair. He also continued to paint, with a brush tied to his hand and with the help of assistants.

The house was built in 1907 in an olive and orange grove. There's a bust of Mme Renoir in the entrance room. You can explore the drawing room and dining room on your own before going up to the artist's bedroom. In his atelier are his wheelchair, easel, and brushes. From the terrace of Mme Renoir's bedroom is a stunning view of Cap d'Antibes and Le Haut-de-Cagnes. On a wall hangs a photograph of one of Renoir's sons, Pierre, as he appeared in the 1932 film *Madame Bovary.*

Although Renoir is best remembered for his paintings, it was in Cagnes that he began experimenting with sculpture. The museum has 20 portrait busts and portrait medallions, most of which depict his wife and children. The curators say they represent the largest collection of Renoir sculpture in the world.

WHERE TO STAY
IN CAGNES-SUR-MER

Hôtel Le Chantilly. Chemin de la Minoerie, 06800 Cagnes-sur-Mer. ☎ **04-93-20-25-50.** Fax 04-92-02-82-63. 18 units. MINIBAR TV TEL. 300–350F ($54–$63) double. V.

This is the best bargain for those who prefer to stay at a hotel near the beach instead of an inn in the hills. It won't win any architectural awards, but the owners have landscaped the property and made the interior as homelike and inviting as possible, using Oriental rugs and potted plants, including dwarf palms, as grace notes. In fair weather you can enjoy breakfast, the only meal served, on an outdoor terrace. The rooms, for the most part, are small but cozily furnished and well kept, often opening onto balconies. The owners, Monique and Jean-Claude Barran, will direct you to nearby restaurants.

IN LE HAUT-DE-CAGNES

✪ **Le Cagnard.** Rue du Pontis-Long, Le Haut-de-Cagnes, 06800 Cagnes-sur-Mer. ☎ **04-93-20-73-21.** Fax 04-93-22-06-39. E-mail: cagnard@relaischateaux.fr. 28 units. A/C MINIBAR TV TEL. 800–950F ($144–$171) double; 950–1,700F ($171–$306) suite. AE, DC, MC, V.

Several village houses have been joined to form this handsome hostelry owned by Félix Barel. The dining room is covered with frescoes, and there's a vine-draped terrace. The rooms and salons are furnished with family antiques, such as provincial chests, armoires, and Louis XV chairs. Each room has its own style: Some are duplexes; others have terraces and views of the countryside.

Dining: The cuisine of chef Jean-Yves Johany is reason enough to make the trip here. Fresh ingredients are used in the delectable dishes placed on one of the finest tables set in Provence. This talented chef features Sisteron lamb (*carré d'agneau*) spit-roasted with Provençal herbs for two, as well as tender côte de boeuf. The pièce de résistance dessert is the extravagant mousseline of ice cream.

WHERE TO DINE
IN LE HAUT-DE-CAGNES

Josy-Jo. 8 place du Planastel. ☎ **04-93-20-68-76.** Reservations required. Main courses 150–170F ($27–$30.60). AE, MC, V. Mon–Fri 11:30am–1:30pm and 7:30–10pm, Sat 7:30–10pm. Closed Aug 1–15 and Jan 15–31. FRENCH.

Sheltered behind a 200-year-old facade covered with vines and flowers, this restaurant on the main road to the château used to be the home and studio of Modigliani and Soutine, when they borrowed it from a friend during their hungriest years. Today it belongs to the cheerful Bandecchi family, who have lined the dining room with art. Their cuisine is simple, fresh, and excellent, featuring grilled meats and a roster of fish. You can enjoy brochette of gigot of lamb with kidneys, four succulent varieties of steak, calves' liver, a homemade terrine of foie gras of duckling, and an array of salads.

✪ **Restaurant des Peintres.** 71 montée de la Bourgade. ☎ **04-93-20-83-08.** Reservations required. Main courses 140–200F ($25.20–$36); fixed-price menus 200–420F ($36–$75.60). AE, DC, MC, V. Tues and Thurs–Sun noon–2pm, Thurs–Mon 7:30–10:30pm. Closed Mar. FRENCH.

About half a mile north of the town center, on the rocky hillside above the center of Cagnes, this 200-year-old building contains an undeniable sense of Provençal authenticity, and Patrice Reignault presents a well-choreographed cuisine. Menu items include foie gras, vegetarian risotto, filets of fried red mullet with eggplant caviar, and stuffed pigeon *en cocotte*.

IN CROS-DE-CAGNES

✪ **Loulou (La Réserve).** 91 bd. de la Plage. ☎ **04-93-31-00-17.** Reservations recommended. Main courses 140–325F ($25.20–$58.50); fixed-price menu 210F ($37.80). AE, MC, V. Mon–Fri noon–2pm, Mon–Sat 7–9:45pm. Closed for lunch daily July 14–Aug 15. FRENCH.

Run by the Campo family, whose brothers perform various functions inside, this place is named for a famous long-departed chef and sits across from the sea. It is one of the few restaurants that specialize in line-caught (as opposed to net-caught) fish, which Eric Campo prepares with gusto and flair. Specialties are rockfish soup (in season); aiguillettes of duckling with herbs, baby squid with just a drizzling of olive oil and balsamic vinegar, and a selection of grilled meats. Though many of the French gastronomic guides continue to ignore this talented chef, Michelin has bestowed a star, of which Campo is rightly proud. Everything is solid and reliable, yet he also knows how to be inventive in bringing out the inherent flavor in every dish. In front is a glassed-in veranda perfect for people-watching.

11 St-Paul-de-Vence

575 miles S of Paris, 14 miles E of Grasse, 17 miles E of Cannes, 19 miles N of Nice

Of all the perched villages of the Riviera, St-Paul-de-Vence is the best known. It was popularized in the 1920s when many noted artists lived here, occupying the 16th-century houses flanking the narrow cobblestone streets. The feudal hamlet grew up on a bastion of rock, almost blending into it. Its ramparts (allow about 30 minutes to circle them) overlook a peaceful setting of flowers and olive and orange trees. They remain somewhat as they were when they were constructed from 1537 to 1547 by François I. From the ramparts to the north you can look out on Baou de St-Jeannet, a sphinx-shaped rock that was painted into the landscape of Poussin's *Polyphème*.

ESSENTIALS

GETTING THERE   Some 20 **buses** per day leave from Nice's Gare Routière, taking 55 minutes and costing 20F ($3.60) one-way. For bus information and schedules, call ☎ **04-93-85-61-81.** To **drive** to St-Paul-de-Vence from Nice, travel along N7 west to Cagnes-sur-Mer, then connect to D236 north to St-Paul-de-Vence.

VISITOR INFORMATION   The **Office de Tourisme** is at Maison Tour, rue Grande (☎ **04-93-32-60-27**).

EXPLORING THE TOWN

The pedestrian-only **rue Grande** is the most interesting street, running the entire length of St-Paul. Most of the stone houses along it are from the 16th and 17th centuries, many still bearing the coats-of-arms placed here by the original builders. Today most of the houses are antiques shops, art-and-craft galleries, and souvenir and gift shops; some are still artists' studios.

The village's chief sight is **La Collégiale de la Conversion de St-Paul,** constructed in the 12th and 13th centuries though much altered over the years. The Romanesque choir is the oldest part, containing some remarkable stalls carved in walnut in the 17th century. The bell tower built in 1740, but the vaulting was reconstructed in the 1600s. Although the facade today isn't alluring, the church is filled with art, notably a painting of *Ste-Cathérine d'Alexandrie* attributed to Tintoretto and hanging to the left as you enter. The Trésor de l'Eglise is one of the most beautiful in the Alpes-Maritimes, with a spectacular ciborium. Look also for a low relief of the Martyrdom of St-Clément on the last altar on the right. In the baptismal chapter is a 15th-century alabaster Madonna.

Near the church is the **Musée d'Histoire de St-Paul,** place de Castre (☎ **04-93-32-41-13**), a minor museum in a 16th-century village house. It was restored and refurnished in a 1500s style, with many artifacts illustrating the history of the village. It's open daily from 10am to 7pm (to 5:30pm in winter). Admission is 20F ($3.60) adults, 12F ($2.15) children and students.

✪ **Fondation Maeght.** Outside the town walls. ☎ **04-93-32-81-63.** Admission 40F ($7.20) adults, 30F ($5.40) students and ages 10–18, free for children 9 and under. 5F (90¢) supplement charged during some special exhibits. July–Sept daily 10am–7pm; Oct–June daily 10am–12:30pm and 2:30–6pm.

The is one of the most modern art museums in Europe. On a hill in pine-studded woods, the Maeght Foundation is like a Shangri-La. Not only is the architecture avant-garde, but also the building houses one of the finest collections of contemporary art along the Riviera. Nature and the creations of men and women blend harmoniously in this unique achievement of the architect José Luís Sert. Its white concrete arcs give the impression of a giant pagoda.

A stark Calder rises like some futuristic monster on the grassy lawns. In a courtyard, the elongated bronze works of Giacometti form a surrealistic garden, creating a hallucinatory mood. Sculpture is also displayed inside, but it's at its best in a natural setting of surrounding terraces and gardens. The museum is built on several levels, its many glass walls providing an indoor-outdoor vista. The foundation, a gift "to the people" from Aimé and Marguerite Maeght, also provides a showcase for new talent. Exhibitions are always changing. Everywhere you look, you see 20th-century art: mosaics by Chagall and Braque, Miró ceramics in the "labyrinth," and Ubac and Braque stained glass in the chapel. Bonnard, Kandinsky, Léger, Matisse, Barbara Hepworth, and many other artists are well represented.

There are a library (open only to scholars and only by appointment), a cinema, and a cafeteria here. In one showroom you can buy original lithographs by artists like Chagall and Giacometti and limited-edition prints.

WHERE TO STAY

La Colombe d'Or also rents deluxe rooms (see below).

VERY EXPENSIVE

✪ **Hôtel le St-Paul.** 86 rue Grande, 06570 St-Paul-de-Vence. ☎ **04-93-32-65-25.** Fax 04-93-32-52-94. 18 units. A/C MINIBAR TV TEL. 850–1,500F ($153–$270) double;

1,200–2,400F ($216–$432) suite. Half board 380F ($68.40) per person extra. AE, DC, MC, V.

Converted from a 16th-century Renaissance residence and retaining many original features, this four-star Relais & Châteaux is in the heart of the medieval village. The rooms, decorated in a sophisticated Provençal style, have safe-deposit boxes, satellite TVs, and many extras. One woman wrote us that while sitting on the balcony of Room 30 she understood why Renoir, Léger, Matisse, and even Picasso were inspired by Provence. Many rooms enjoy a view of the valley with the Mediterranean in the distance.

Dining: The restaurant has a flower-bedecked terrace sheltered by the 16th-century ramparts as well as a superb dining room with vaulted ceilings. Menus may include locally inspired dishes like cream of salt cod with a thin slice of grilled pancetta, risotto of crayfish and broadbeans, roast veal chop with morels and barley, and a delightful crème brûlée with a hint of rosemary.

Le Mas d'Artigny. Rte. de la Colle et des Hauts de St-Paul, 06570 St-Paul-de-Vence. ☎ **04-93-32-84-54.** Fax 04-93-32-95-36. www.french-riviera/hotels/p/paulmas.html. E-mail: mas-artigny@wanadoo.fr. 54 units, 29 suites. A/C MINIBAR TV TEL. 800–1,800F ($144–$324) double; 1,760–6,000F ($316.80–$1,080) suite. AE, DC, MC, V. Parking garage 60F ($10.80). From the town center, follow the signs west about 1¼ miles.

This elegant hotel, one of the Riviera's grandest and a member of the exclusive Relais & Châteaux organization, evokes a sprawling Provençal homestead set in an acre of pine forests. In the lobby is a constantly changing exhibition of art. Each of the comfortably large rooms has its own terrace or balcony, and private suites with a private pool are on a slope below the blue-tile pool, with hedges for privacy.

Dining: For such an elegant hotel, the restaurant is a bit lackluster in decor and has a staff that isn't always too alert, but it does have great views of the garden. Chef Francis Scordel regales you with his flavors of Provence, everything tasting as if it ripened in the sun. Only quality ingredients are used to shape this harmonious and rarely complicated cuisine. The wine cellar deserves a star for its vintage collection, but watch those prices!

MODERATE TO INEXPENSIVE

Les Bastides St-Paul. 880 rte. des Blaquières (rte. Cagnes–Vence), 06570 St-Paul-de-Vence. ☎ **04-92-02-08-07.** Fax 04-93-20-50-41. 17 units. MINIBAR TV TEL. 450–650F ($81–$117) double; 620F ($111.60) triple. AE, DC, MC, V. From the town center, follow the signs to Cagnes-sur-Mer for 1 mile south.

This hotel is in the hills outside town, a mile south of St-Paul and 2½ miles south of Vence. Divided into three buildings, it offers clean and comfortably carpeted rooms, each accented with regional artifacts and a terrace and garden. On the premises is a pool shaped like a cloverleaf, a cozy breakfast area, and a sensitive management staff headed by the longtime hoteliers Marie José and Maurice Giraudet. Breakfast is served anytime you want it.

Les Orangers. Chemin des Fumerates, rte. de la Colle (D107), 06570 St-Paul-de-Vence. ☎ **04-93-32-80-95.** Fax 04-93-32-00-32. 9 units. TEL. 650–680F ($117–$122.40) double; 850F ($153) suite. Rates include breakfast. MC, V. From the town center, follow the signs to Cagnes-sur-Mer for half a mile south.

Monsieur Franklin has created a beautiful "living oasis" in his villa. The scents of roses, oranges, and lemons waft through the air. The main lounge is impeccably decorated with original oils and furnished in a provincial style. Expect to be treated like a guest in a private home. The rooms, with antiques and Oriental carpets, have panoramic views. On the sun terrace are banana trees and climbing geraniums.

WHERE TO DINE

La Colombe d'Or. 1 place du Général-de-Gaulle, 06570 St-Paul-de-Vence. ☎ **04-93-32-80-02.** Fax 04-93-32-77-78. Reservations required. Main courses 120–180F ($21.60–$32.40). AE, DC, MC, V. Daily noon–2pm and 7–10pm. Closed Nov–Dec 15. FRENCH.

"The Golden Dove" has for decades been St-Paul's most celebrated restaurant, famous for its remarkable art collection: You can dine amid Mirós, Picassos, Klees, Dufys, Utrillos, and Calders. In fair weather everyone tries for a seat on the terrace—trying to soak up the view. You won't find cutting-edge cuisine or wildly exotic experiments here. You may begin with smoked salmon or foie gras from Landes if you've recently won at the casino. Otherwise, you can count on a soup made with the fresh seasonal vegetables. The best fish dishes are poached sea bass with mousseline sauce and sea wolf baked with fennel. Tender beef comes with *gratin dauphinois* (potatoes), or you may prefer lamb from Sisteron. A classic finish to any meal is a *soufflé flambé au Grand-Marnier.*

The 26 guest rooms in this three-star hotel contain French antiques and fabrics and accessories inspired by the traditions of Provence. They're scattered among three areas: the original 16th-century stone house, a more recent wing that stretches into the garden adjacent to the pool, and an even more modern annex built in the 1950s and upgraded several times since. Some have exposed stone and heavy ceiling beams; all are very comfortable and clean, with air-conditioning, minibar, TV, and phone. Prices are 1,350F ($243) for a double and 1,550F ($279) for a suite.

12 Vence

575 miles S of Paris, 19 miles N of Cannes, 15 miles NW of Nice

Travel up into the hills northwest of Nice—across country studded with cypresses, olive trees, and pines, where bright flowers, especially carnations, roses, and oleanders, grow in profusion—and Vence comes into view. Outside the town, along boulevard Paul-André, two olive presses carry on with their age-old duties. But the charm lies in the **Vieille Ville** (Old Town). Visitors invariably have themselves photographed on place du Peyra in front of the urn-shaped **Vieille Fontaine** (Old Fountain), a background shot in several motion pictures. The 15th-century square tower is also a curiosity.

If you're wearing the right kind of shoes, the narrow, steep streets of the Old Town are worth exploring. Dating from the 10th century, the cathedral on place Godeau is unremarkable except for some 15th-century Gothic choir stalls. But if it's the right day of the week, most visitors quickly pass through the narrow gates of this once-fortified walled town to where the sun shines more brightly—to see one of Matisse's most remarkable achievements

ESSENTIALS

GETTING THERE Frequent **buses** (no. 400 or 410) from Nice take 1 hour and cost 21.50F ($3.85) one-way. Call ☎ **04-93-58-37-60** for schedules. To **drive** to Vence from Nice, travel along N7 west to Cagnes-sur-Mer, then connect to D236 north to Vence.

VISITOR INFORMATION The **Office de Tourisme** is on place Grand-Jardin (☎ **04-93-58-06-38**).

A MATISSE MASTERPIECE

Chapelle du Rosaire. Av. Henri-Matisse. ☎ **04-93-58-03-26.** Admission 10F ($1.80); contributions to maintain the chapel are welcomed. Unless special arrangements are made, the chapel is open only Tues and Thurs 10–11:30am and 2:30–5:30pm.

It was a beautiful golden autumn along the Côte d'Azur. The great Henri Matisse was 77, and after a turbulent introspective time he set out to design and decorate his masterpiece—"the culmination of a whole life dedicated to the search for truth," as he said. Just outside Vence, Matisse created the Chapelle du Rosaire for the Dominican nuns of Monteils. (Part of his action was a gesture of thanks for Sister Jacques-Marie, a member of the order who nursed him back to health after a debilitating illness.) From the front you might find it unremarkable and pass it by—until you spot a 40-foot crescent-adorned cross rising from a blue-tile roof.

Matisse wrote: "What I have done in the chapel is to create a religious space . . . in an enclosed area of very reduced proportions and to give it, solely by the play of colors and lines, the dimensions of infinity." The light picks up the subtle coloring in the simply rendered leaf forms and abstract patterns: sapphire blue, aquamarine, and lemon yellow. In black-and-white ceramics, St. Dominic is depicted in only a few lines. The most remarkable design is in the black-and-white tile Stations of the Cross, with Matisse's self-styled "tormented and passionate" figures. The bishop of Nice came to bless the chapel in the late spring of 1951 when the artist's work was completed. Matisse died 3 years later.

The price of admission includes entrance to **L'Espace Matisse,** a gallery devoted to the documentation of the way Matisse handled the design and construction of the chapel during its construction (1949–51). It also contains lithographs and religious artifacts that concerned Matisse in one way or another.

WHERE TO STAY
VERY EXPENSIVE

✪ **Le Château du Domaine St-Martin.** Rte. de Coursegoules, 06140 Vence. ☎ **04-93-58-02-02.** Fax 04-93-24-08-91. www.chateau-st-martin.com. E-mail: st-martin@weastore.fr. 38 units. A/C MINIBAR TV TEL. 2,800–3,000F ($504–$540) double; 3,500–4,500F ($630–$810) suite. AE, DC, MC, V. Closed Oct–Apr. From the town center, follow the signs to Coursegoules and Col-de-Vence for 1 mile north.

This château, in a 35-acre park, was built in 1936 on the grounds where the Golden Goat treasure was reputedly buried. It is built on the site of a former millionaire's palace, which allows you to live with all the splendor of the gilded age, although at a high price tag. A complex of tile-roofed villas with suites was built in the terraced gardens. You can walk through the gardens on winding paths lined with tall cypresses, past the ruined chapel and olive trees. Accommodations are beautifully decorated, often with antiques and brocades. Those units in the on-site tower are smaller and not as costly, although perfectly adequate in every way. Sheltered from the dreaded mistral, the residence has been converted into a deluxe gem that often attracts some of the rulers of the world. The staff is among the best trained on the Riviera, and the setting in a splendid grove of cypress and olive trees is regal. This is a citadel of French taste and elegance for those whose annual income equals the world gross of *Titanic.*

Dining: The restaurant has a view of the coast and offers superb French cuisine. In summer, many guests prefer the poolside grill.

Amenities: Room service, pool, two championship tennis courts.

MODERATE

✪ **Hôtel La Roseraie.** Avenue Henri Giraud, 06140 Vence. ☎ **04-93-58-02-20.** Fax 04-93-58-99-31. 14 units. 460–630F ($82.80–$113.40) double. AE, MC, V.

This charming small hotel, lying a 5-minute walk from the historic center of Vence, lies in a totally renovated 19th-century manor house. Marc Chagall lived for many years on a hill across from the hotel, which is within an easy walk of the Matisse Chapel. Monica and Maurice Garnier are among the most charming hosts at Vence, and they've furnished their home with old-fashioned pieces, often antiques. The garden offers perfect southern exposure, and contains a moon-shaped swimming pool. The "Rose Garden" (its English name) is studded with magnolias, yucca, eucalyptus, banana trees, palms, and, of course, roses. Bedrooms are decorated in a homelike Provençal style. Try for accommodations 4, 5, or 8, which contain balconies. Bathrooms are coated with Provençal tiles from neighboring Salernes. There's no better way to start the day here than by sampling one of the fresh house-baked croissants.

INEXPENSIVE

Auberge des Seigneurs (Inn of the Noblemen). Place du Friene, 06140 Vence. ☎ **04-93-58-04-24.** Fax 04-93-24-08-01. 6 units. TEL. 344–374F ($61.90–$67.30) double. AE, DC, MC, V. Closed Nov 15–Mar 15.

This 400-year-old stone hotel gives you a taste of Old Provence. Fascinating decorative objects and antiques are everywhere. The guest rooms are well maintained and comfortable, though management gives priority to the running of the restaurant here, as that generates far more revenue.

Dining: Inside is a long wooden dining table, in view of an open fireplace with a row of hanging copper pots and pans. The cuisine of François I is served in an antique atmosphere with wooden casks of flowers and an open spit for roasting and grilling.

WHERE TO DINE

The **Auberge des Seigneurs** (see above) is an excellent place to dine at reasonable prices.

La Farigoule. 15 rue Henri-Isnard. ☎ **04-93-58-01-27.** Reservations recommended. Main courses 70–82F ($12.60–$14.75); fixed-price menus 120–150F ($21.60–$27). MC, V. Wed–Mon 12:30–2pm, Sat–Thurs 7:30–10:30pm (also open for lunch on Sat in summer). Closed Nov 10–Dec 15. PROVENÇAL.

In summer you can enjoy regional cuisine in the garden under a rose arbor. Owners Patrick and Dominique Brout grill much of the food over an open fire. A long line forms on Sunday afternoon. The least expensive fixed-price menu may include fish soup, trout meunière, a vegetable, and cheese or dessert—service and drinks are extra. The most expensive fixed-price menu is far more enticing and may include asparagus vinaigrette, mussels marinara, a tender rabbit with seasonal vegetables, cheese, and dessert—drinks and service extra.

13 Nice

577 miles S of Paris, 20 miles NE of Cannes

The Victorian upper class and tsarist aristocrats loved Nice in the 19th century, but it's solidly middle class today, not as chichi and astronomically expensive as Cannes. In fact, of all the major resorts of France, from Deauville to Biarritz to Cannes, Nice is the most affordable. It's also the best place to base yourself on the Riviera, especially if you're dependent on public transportation. For example, you can go to San Remo, "the queen of the Italian Riviera," and return to Nice by nightfall. From the Nice airport, the second largest in France, you can travel by bus along the entire coast to resorts like Juan-les-Pins and Cannes.

Nice is the capital of the Riviera, the largest city between Genoa and Marseille. It's also one of the most ancient, having been founded by the Greeks, who called it Nike, or Victory. Because of its brilliant sunshine and relaxed living, artists and writers have been attracted to Nice for years. Among them were Dumas, Nietzsche, Flaubert,

Nice

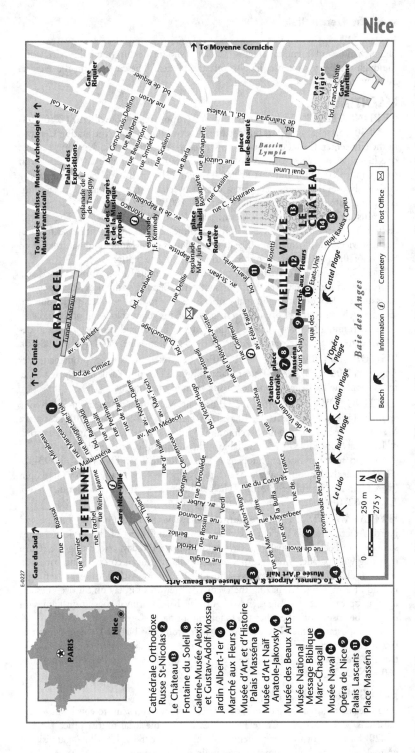

To Moyenne Corniche ↑

↑ To Cimiez

To Musée Matisse, Musée Archéologie & ↑
Musée Franciscain

Gare
Riquier

Parc
Vigier

Gare
Maritime

CARABACEL

Palais des
Expositions

rue A. Gal

rue de Riquier

bd. de Riquier

rue Arson

bd. Gero-Louis-Delfino

rue Barberis

rue Beaumont

rue Smolett

rue Scaliero

bd. L. Walesa

rue Barla

rue Bonaparte

place
Ile-de-Beauté

bd. de Stalingrad

bd. Franck-Pilatte

Bassin
Lympia

Palais des Congrès
et de la Musique
Acropolis

Monaco ①

esplanade de L.
de Tassigny

esplanade
J.F. Kennedy

av. de la République

rue Guizol

place
Bonaparte

rue Cassini

rue C. Ségurane

quai Lunel

Tunnel Malraux

av. E. Biekert

bd. de Cimiez

bd Carabacel

rue Delille

esplanade
Mar. Juin

Gare
Routière

place
Garibaldi

rue Rossetti

LE
CHÂTEAU

⑬

⑭

⑮

quai Rauba Capeu

VIEILLE VILLE

⑫

Marché aux Fleurs

Castel Plage

Baie des Anges

① Monaco

② Cathédrale Orthodoxe
Russe St-Nicolas

⑬ Le Château

⑧ Fontaine du Soleil

⑥ Galerie-Musée Alexis
et Gustav-Adolf Mossa

⑥ Jardin Albert-1er

⑫ Marché aux Fleurs

⑤ Musée d'Art et d'Histoire
Palais Masséna

④ Musée d'Art Naïf
Anatole-Jakovsky

③ Musée des Beaux Arts

① Musée National
Message Biblique
Marc-Chagall

⑭ Musée Naval

⑨ Opéra de Nice

⑪ Palais Lascaris

⑦ Place Masséna

rue Gioffredo

rue de l'Hôtel-des-postes

rue Pastorelli

bd. Dubouchage

bd. Victor-Hugo

av. Notre-Dame

rue de Paris

rue Pertinax

rue Assalit

bd. Raimbaldi

rue Rouget-de-l'Isle

rue Marceau

rue Gioffredo

av. Félix Faure

bd. Jean-Médecin

av. Georges-Clemenceau

rue d'Italie

av. Jean Médecin

⑪

Station
Centrale

place
Masséna

cours Selaya

⑦ ⑧

⑨ quai des
États-Unis

⑩

l'Opéra
Plage

av. de Verdun

⑥

Galion Plage

Ruhl Plage

rue Masséna

av. de Verdun

av. Tibère

av. Reine-Jeanne

rue Trachel

rue C. Roassal

rue Vernier

ST-ETIENNE

Gare Nice-Ville

Gare du Sud ↗

av. Malausséna

rue Paganini

av. Jean Médecin

bd. Victor-Hugo

av. Auber

av. Georges-Clemenceau

rue de France

rue du Congrès

rue de la Buffa

rue Verdi

rue Meyerbeer

rue Rossini

rue Gounod

rue Berlioz

rue Herold

rue Guigia

rue de Rivoli

rue de Mar.

promenade des Anglais

⑤

③

④

Le Lido

Musée d'Art Naïf

To Cannes, Airport & ↗ To Musée des Beaux-Arts

PARIS

Nice

Beach ← | Information ⓘ | Cemetery ✝✝ | Post Office ⊠

N

0   250 m
    275 y

E-0227

653

Hugo, Sand, and Stendhal. Henri Matisse, who made his home in Nice, said, "Though the light is intense, it's also soft and tender." The city has, on the average, 300 days of sunshine a year.

ESSENTIALS

GETTING THERE   Visitors who arrive at **Aéroport Nice-Côte d'Azur** (☎ 04-93-21-30-30) can take an airport bus departing every 20 minutes to the Station Centrale in the city center. (Delta offers nonstop service to this airport from New York; there's one flight per day from JFK. All other flights are routed through Paris.) Buses run from 6am to 10:30pm and cost 8F ($1.45). For 21F ($3.80) you can take a *navette* (airport shuttle) that goes several times a day between the train station and the airport. A taxi ride into the city center will cost at least 180F ($32.40).

Trains arrive at Gare Nice-Ville, av. Thiers (☎ 08-36-35-35-39). There's four daily trains from Paris (trip time: 6½ hours); Cannes, Monaco, and Antibes feature frequent service. An information office at the station is open Monday to Saturday from 8am to 6:30pm and Sunday from 8am to noon and 2 to 5:30pm.

Nice is a comfortable **drive** from virtually anywhere in the Riviera; from Cannes, take N7 east; from Monaco, travel along N7 southwest. Because of the heavy traffic conditions and the lack of parking in many places, it's best to drive to Nice, park your car, and then rely on your feet or public transportation for your exploration of the old city.

Buses running between Nice and other parts of France and Europe arrive and depart from the Intercars Terminal, Gare Routière, 5 bd. Jean-Jaurès (☎ 04-93-80-08-70).

VISITOR INFORMATION   The **Office de Tourisme** is at 5 promenade des Anglais (☎ 04-93-87-07-07), near place Masséna. This office will make you a hotel reservation; the fee depends on the classification of the hotel.

GETTING AROUND   Most local buses in Nice form connections with one another at the **Station Centrale,** 10 av. Félix-Faure (☎ 04-93-16-52-10), near place Masséna. Take bus no. 6 to the beach for 8F ($1.45). To save money, purchase a carnet of 10 tickets for 68F ($12.25), available at the tourist office (see above).

You can rent bicycles and mopeds at **Nicea Rent,** 9 av. Thiers (☎ 04-93-82-42-71), near the Station Centrale. March to October, it's open daily from 9am to 6pm (closed Sunday November to April). The cost begins at 120F ($21.60) per day, plus a 1,500F ($270) deposit. Credit cards are accepted.

SPECIAL EVENTS   The **Nice Carnaval** draws visitors from all over Europe and North America to this ancient spectacle. This "Mardi Gras of the Riviera" begins sometime in February, usually 12 days before Shrove Tuesday, celebrating the return of spring with parades, floats (*corsi*), masked balls (*veglioni*), confetti, and battles in which young women toss flowers—and only the most wicked throw rotten eggs instead of carnations. Climaxing the event is a fireworks display on Shrove Tuesday, lighting up the Baie des Anges (Bay of Angels). King Carnival goes up in flames on his pyre but rises from the ashes the following spring.

Also important is the **Nice Festival du Jazz,** from July 11 to 20, where a roster of jazz artists perform in the ancient Arène de Cimiez. For information and tickets, contact the **Comité des Fêtes,** Mairie (town hall) de Nice, 5 rue de l'Hôtel-de-Ville, 06000 Nice (☎ 04-93-13-20-00).

EXPLORING THE CITY

If you decide to forgo the pleasures of the pebbly beach and want to check out several museums, you can buy a **Carte Passe-Musée** from the local tourist office for 40F ($7.20) for adults or free for students and children under 18. It'll allow you visits to up to 15 of the city's museums, over an unlimited time period.

In 1822 the orange crop at Nice was bad and the workers faced a lean time. So the English residents put them to work building the **promenade des Anglais,** a wide boulevard fronting the bay, split by "islands" of palms and flowers and stretching for about 4 miles. Fronting the beach are rows of grand cafes, the Musée Masséna, villas, and hotels—some good, others decaying.

Crossing this boulevard in the briefest of bikinis or thongs are some of the world's most attractive, bronzed bodies. They're heading for the **beach**—"on the rocks," as it's called here. Tough on tender feet, the beach is shingled, one of the least attractive aspects of the cosmopolitan resort city. Many bathhouses provide mattresses for a fee.

In the east, the promenade becomes **quai des Etats-Unis,** the original boulevard, lined with some of the best restaurants in Nice, all specializing in bouillabaisse. Rising sharply on a rock is the site known as **Le Château,** the spot where the ducs de Savoie built their castle, which was torn down in 1706. All that remains are two or three stones—even the foundations have disappeared in the wake of Louis XIV's deliberate destruction of what was viewed as a bulwark of Provençal resistance to his regime. The steep hill has been turned into a garden of pines and exotic flowers. To reach the panoramic site, you can take an elevator; indeed, many prefer to take the elevator up, then walk down. The park is open daily from 8am to 7:30pm.

At the north end of Le Château is the famous old **graveyard** of Nice, visited primarily for its lavishly sculpted monuments that form their own enduring art statement. It's the largest one in France and the fourth largest in Europe. To reach it, you can take a small canopied **Train Touristique de Nice** (☎ **04-93-92-45-59**), which departs from the Jardin Albert-1er. Rolling on rubber wheels, it makes a 40-minute sightseeing transit past many of Nice's most heralded sites—like place Masséna, promenade des Anglais, and quai des Etats-Unis. Trains operate daily: June to August from 10am to 6pm, April to May and September to October from 10am to 6pm, and November to March from 10am to 5pm. The price is 30F ($5.40) per person.

Continuing east from "the Rock" you reach the **harbor,** where the restaurants are even cheaper and the bouillabaisse is just as good. While sitting here lingering over a drink at a sidewalk cafe, you can watch the boats depart for Corsica. The port was excavated between 1750 and 1830. Since then an outer harbor—protected by two jetties—has abeen created.

The "authentic" Niçois live in **Vieille Ville,** the Old Town, beginning at the foot of "the Rock" and stretching out from place Masséna. Sheltered by sienna-tiled roofs, many of the Italianate facades suggest 17th-century Genoese palaces. The old town is a maze of narrow streets, teeming with local life and studded with the least expensive restaurants in Nice. Buy an onion pizza (*la pissaladière*) from one of the local vendors. Many of the old buildings are painted a faded Roman gold, and their banners are multicolored laundry flapping in the sea breezes.

While here, try to visit the **Marché aux Fleurs,** the flower market at cours Saleya. The vendors set up their stalls Tuesday to Sunday at noon, then conduct the serious business of adorning the interiors of homes and businesses with bouquets until sometime between 2 and 4pm, depending on the vendor. A flamboyant array of carnations, violets, jonquils, roses, and birds of paradise is hauled in by vans or trucks, then displayed in the greatest regularly scheduled market in town.

Nice's commercial centerpiece is **place Masséna,** with pink buildings in the 17th-century Genoese style and the **Fontaine du Soleil** (Fountain of the Sun) by Janoit, from 1956. Stretching from the main square to the promenade is the **Jardin Albert-1er,** with an open-air terrace and a Triton Fountain. With palms and exotic flowers, it's the most relaxing oasis in town.

✪ **Cathédrale Orthodoxe Russe St-Nicolas à Nice.** Av. Nicolas-II (off bd. du Tzaréwitch). ☎ **04-93-96-88-02.** Admission 12F ($2.15). June–Sept daily 9am–noon and 2:30–6pm; Oct–May daily 9:30am–noon and 2:30–5pm. From the central rail station, head west along av. Thiers to bd. Gambetta; then go north to av. Nicolas-II.

Ordered built by none other than Tsar Nicholas II, this is the most beautiful religious edifice of the Orthodoxy outside Russia and is the perfect expression of Russian religious art abroad. It dates from the belle époque, when some of the Romanovs and their entourage turned the Riviera into a stomping ground (everyone from grand dukes to ballerinas walked the promenade). The cathedral is richly ornamented and decorated with lots of icons. You'll easily spot the building from afar because of its collection of ornate onion-shaped domes. Church services are held on Sunday morning.

✪ **Musée des Beaux-Arts.** 33 av. des Baumettes. ☎ **04-92-15-28-28.** Admission (includes entry to the Galerie-Musée Raoul-Dufy) 25F ($4.50) adults, 15F ($2.70) children. Tues–Sun 10am–noon and 2–6pm. Bus: 9, 12, 22, 23, or 38.

The collection is housed in the former residence of the Ukrainian Princess Kotchubey. There's an important gallery devoted to the masters of the Second Empire and belle époque, with an extensive collection of the 19th-century French experts. The gallery of sculptures includes works by J. B. Carpeaux, Rude, and Rodin. Note the important collection by a dynasty of painters, the Dutch Vanloo family. One of its best-known members, Carle Vanloo, born in Nice in 1705, was Louis XV's premier *peintre*. A fine collection of 19th- and 20th-century art is displayed, including works by Ziem, Raffaelli, Boudin, Renoir, Monet, Guillaumin, and Sisley.

Galerie-Musée Alexis et Gustav-Adolf Mossa. 59 quai des Etats-Unis. ☎ **04-93-62-37-11.** Admission 15F ($2.70). Tues–Sat 10am–noon and 2–6pm, Sun 2–6pm. Bus: 8.

Here you can admire the dynamic lines of a veritable family dynasty of Nice-born artists. Among them is Alexis Mossa, famous for local landscapes and scenes of the Nice carnival. He's one of the early symbolist painters, a representative of a movement that brought a definitive end to the romantic movement of the late 19th century and a harbinger of surrealism. Also here are the works of Alexis's son, Gustav-Adolf Mossa, who continued his father's work. One series of works executed between 1903 and 1919 gracefully serves as a precursor to surrealism.

Musée International d'Art Naïf Anatole-Jakovsky (Museum of Naïve Art). Av. Val-Marie. ☎ **04-93-71-78-33.** Admission 25F ($4.50) adults, 15F ($2.70) students and seniors, free for children 17 and under. Wed–Mon 10am–noon and 2–6pm. Bus: 9, 10, or 12; the walk from the bus stop takes 10 minutes.

This museum is housed in the beautifully restored Château Ste-Hélène in the Fabron district. The collection was once owned by the namesake of the museum, for years one of the world's leading art critics. His 600 drawings and canvases were turned over to the institution and made accessible to the public. Artists from more than two dozen countries are represented here—from primitive painting to contemporary 20th-century works.

Musée d'Art et d'Histoire Palais Masséna. 65 rue de France. ☎ **04-93-88-11-34.** Admission 25F ($4.50) adults, 15F ($2.70) children; free for everyone one Sun per month. Tues–Sun 10am–noon and 2–6pm. Bus: 3, 7, 8, 9, 10, 12, 14, or 22.

The fabulous villa housing this collection was built in 1900 in the style of the First Empire as a residence for Victor Masséna, the prince of Essling and grandson of Napoléon's marshal. The city of Nice has converted the villa, next door to the Hôtel Négresco, into a museum of local history and decorative art. A remarkable First Empire drawing room furnished in the opulent taste of that era, with mahogany-veneer pieces and ormolu mounts, is on the ground floor. Of course there's the representation of Napoléon as a Roman Caesar and a bust by Canova of Maréchal Masséna. The large first-floor gallery exhibits a collection of Niçois primitives and also has a display of 14th- and 15th-century painters, as well as a collection of 16th- to 19th-century masterpieces of plates and jewelry decorated with enamel (Limoges). There are art galleries devoted to the history of Nice and the memories of Masséna and Garibaldi. Yet another gallery is reserved for a display of views of Nice during the 18th and 19th centuries.

Musée Naval (Naval Museum). Parc du Château. ☎ **04-93-80-47-61.** Admission 15F ($2.70) adults, 9F ($1.60) students and children. June–Sept Wed–Sun 10am–noon and 2–7pm (closes at 5pm off-season).

In the Tour Bellanda is the Naval Museum, sitting on "the Rock." The tower stands on a precariously perched belvedere overlooking the beach, the bay, the old town, and even the terraces of some of the nearby villas. Of the museum's old battle prints, one depicts the exploits of Caterina Segurana, the Joan of Arc of the Niçois. During the 1543 siege by Barbarossa, she ran along the ramparts, raising her skirt to show her shapely bottom to the Turks as a sign of contempt, though the soldiers were reported to have been more excited than insulted.

Palais Lascaris. 15 rue Droite. ☎ **04-93-62-05-54.** Admission 25F ($4.50) adults, 15F ($2.70) children, free for everyone one Sun per month. Tues–Sun 10am–noon and 2–6pm. Bus: 1, 2, 3, 5, 6, 14, 16, or 17.

The baroque Palais Lascaris in the city's historic core is intimately linked to the Lascaris-Vintimille family, whose recorded history predates the year 1261. Built in the 17th century, it contains elaborately detailed ornaments. An intensive restoration undertaken by the city of Nice in 1946 brought back its original beauty, and the palace is now classified a historic monument. The most elaborate floor is the *étage noble*, retaining many of its 18th-century panels and plaster embellishments. A circa-1738 pharmacy, complete with many of the original Delftware accessories, is on the premises. Every Wednesday between 2 and 4pm, the museum focuses attention on children of any age: Various craftspeople are invited to show the details of how they accomplish their art forms through live demonstrations.

NEARBY ATTRACTIONS IN CIMIEZ

In the once-aristocratic hilltop quarter of Cimiez, Queen Victoria wintered at the Hôtel Excelsior and brought half the English court with her. Founded by the Romans, who called it Cemenelum, Cimiez was the capital of the Maritime Alps province. To reach this suburb, take bus no. 15 or 17 from place Masséna. Recent excavations have uncovered the ruins of a Roman town, and you can wander among the diggings. The arena was big enough to hold at least 5,000 spectators, who watched contests between gladiators and wild beasts shipped in from Africa.

Monastère de Cimiez (Cimiez Convent). Place du Monastère. ☎ **04-93-81-00-04.** Free admission. Museum Mon–Sat 10am–noon and 3–6pm; church daily 8:30am–noon and 2–6:30pm.

The convent embraces a church that owns three of the most important works from the primitive painting school of Nice by the Bréa brothers. See the carved and gilded wooden main altarpiece. In a restored part of the convent where some Franciscan friars still live, the Musée Franciscain is decorated with 17th-century frescoes. Some 350 documents and works of art from the 15th to the 18th century are displayed, and a monk's cell has been re-created in all its severe simplicity. See also the 17th-century chapel. In the gardens you can get a panoramic view of Nice and the Baie des Anges. Matisse and Dufy are buried in the cemetery.

Musée Matisse. In the Villa des Arènes-de-Cimiez, 164 av. des Arènes-de-Cimiez. ☎ **04-93-81-08-08.** Admission 25F ($4.50) adults, 15F ($2.70) children; free for everyone one Sun per month. Wed–Mon 10am–6pm.

This museum honors the great artist who spent the last years of his life in Nice; he died here in 1954. Seeing his nude sketches today, you'll wonder how early critics could have denounced them as "the female animal in all her shame and horror." The museum has several permanent collections, most painted in Nice and many donated by Matisse and his heirs. These include *Nude in an Armchair with a Green Plant* (1937), *Nymph in the Forest* (1935/1942), and a chronologically arranged series of paintings from 1890 to 1919. The most famous of these is *Portrait of Madame Matisse* (1905), usually displayed near a portrait of the artist's wife by Marquet, painted in 1900. There's also an ensemble of drawings and designs (*Flowers and Fruits*) he prepared as practice sketches for the Matisse Chapel at Vence. The most famous are *The Créole Dancer* (1951), *Blue Nude IV* (1952), and around 50 dance-related sketches he did between 1930 and 1931.

✪ **Musée National Message Biblique Marc-Chagall.** Av. du Dr.-Ménard. ☎ **04-93-53-87-20.** Admission 30F ($5.40) adults, 20F ($3.60) ages 18–24, free for children 17 and under. Fees may be higher for special exhibits. July–Sept Wed–Mon 10am–6pm, Oct–June Wed–Mon 10am–5pm.

In the hills of Cimiez above Nice, this handsome museum, surrounded by shallow pools and a garden planted with thyme, lavender, and olive trees, is devoted to Marc Chagall's treatment of biblical themes. Born in Russia in 1887, Chagall became a French citizen in 1937. The artist and his wife donated the works—the most important collection of Chagall ever assembled—to France in 1966 and 1972. Displayed are 450 of his oils, gouaches, drawings, pastels, lithographs, sculptures, and ceramics; a mosaic; three stained-glass windows; and a tapestry. A splendid concert room was especially decorated by Chagall with brilliantly hued stained-glass windows. Temporary exhibitions are organized each summer featuring great periods and artists of all times. Special lectures in the rooms are available in both French and English (call ☎ **04-92-91-50-20** for a reservation).

OUTDOOR PURSUITS

GOLF   The oldest golf course on the Riviera is about 10 miles from Nice: **Golf Bastide du Roi** (also known as the Golf de Biot), av. Jules-Grec, Biot (☎ **04-93-65-08-48**). Open daily throughout the year, this is a flat, not particularly challenging seafronting course. (Regrettably, it's necessary to cross over a highway midway through the course to complete the full 18 holes.) Tee-off times are 8am to 6pm, with the understanding that players then continue their rounds as long as the daylight allows. Reservations aren't necessary, though on weekends you should probably expect a delay. Greens fees are 220F ($39.60) for 18 holes, and clubs can be rented for 50F ($9). No carts are available.

HORSEBACK RIDING   The **Club Hippique de Nice,** 368 rte. de Grenoble (☎ **04-93-71-24-34**), contains about 40 horses, 13 of which are available for rental. About 3 miles from Nice, near the airport, it's hemmed in on virtually every side by busy roads and highways and conducts all its activities in a series of riding rinks. Riding sessions should be reserved in advance, last about an hour, and cost 65F ($11.70).

SCUBA DIVING   The best outfit is the **Centre International de Plongée de Nice,** 2 ruelle des Moulins (☎ **04-93-55-59-50**), adjacent to the city's old port, midway between quai des Docks and boulevard Stalingrad. A baptême (initiatory dive for first-timers) costs 150F ($27) and a one-tank dive for experienced divers, with all equipment included, is 180F ($32.40).

TENNIS   The oldest tennis club in Nice is the **Nice Lawn Tennis Club,** Parc Impérial, 5 av. Suzanne-Lenglen (☎ **04-93-96-17-70**), near the rail station. It's open daily June to September from 8:30am to 9pm; the rest of the year daily 8:30am to 8pm, and charges 120F ($21.60) per person for 2 noncontiguous hours of court time, or a reduced rate ranging from 150F to 500F ($27 to $90) per person for unlimited access to the courts for 1 week. The club has a cooperative staff, a loyal clientele, 13 clay courts, and 6 hard-surfaced courts. Reservations should be made the evening before.

SHOPPING

You might want to begin with a stroll through the streets and alleys of Nice's historic core. The densest concentrations are along **rue Masséna, place Magenta,** and **rue Paradis,** as well as on the streets funneling into and around them. Examples are **Gigi,** 7 rue de la Liberté (☎ **04-93-87-81-78**), and **Trabaud,** 10 rue de la Liberté (☎ **04-93-87-53-96**). Still alluring after all these years are the products of **Yves Saint Laurent,** 4 av. de Suède (☎ **04-93-87-70-79**).

Opened in 1949 by Georges Fuchs, the grandfather of the present English-speaking owners, **Confiserie du Vieux-Nice,** 14 quai Papacino (☎ **04-93-55-43-50**), is near the Old Port. The specialty here is glazed fruits crystallized in sugar or artfully arranged into chocolates. Look for exotic jams (rose-petal preserves or mandarin marmalade) and the free recipe leaflet as well as candied violets, verbena leaves, and rosebuds.

Façonnable, 7–9 rue Paradis (☎ **04-93-87-88-80**), is the site that sparked the creation of what is today several hundred Façonnable menswear stores around the world. This is one of the largest stores, with a wide range of men's suits, raincoats, overcoats, sportswear, and jeans. The look is youthful and conservatively stylish, for relatively slim (French) bodies.

If you're thinking of indulging in a Provençal pique-nique, **Nicola Alziari,** 14 rue St-François-de-Paule (☎ **04-93-85-76-92**), will provide everything you'll need: from olives, anchovies, and pistous to aiolis and tapenades. It's one of Nice's oldest purveyors of olive oil, with a house brand that comes in two strengths—a light version that aficionados claim is vaguely perfumed with Provence and a stronger version suited to the earthy flavors and robust ingredients of a Provençal winter. Also look for a range of objects crafted from olive wood.

Other shopping recommendations are **La Couquetou,** 8 rue St-François-de-Paule (☎ **04-93-80-90-30**), selling *santons,* the traditional Provençal figurines. The best selection of Provençal fabrics is found at **Les Olivades,** 7 rue de la Boucherie (☎ **04-93-85-85-19**).

Nice is also known for its colorful street markets. The flower market, **Marché aux Fleurs,** cours Saleya, is open from 6am to 5:30pm except Monday and Sunday afternoon. The main Nice flea market, **Marché à la Brocante,** also at cours Saleya, takes place every Monday from 8am to 5pm. There's another flea market on the port, **Les Puces de Nice,** place Robilante, open Tuesday to Saturday from 10am to 6pm.

WHERE TO STAY
VERY EXPENSIVE

✪ **Hôtel Négresco.** 37 promenade des Anglais, 06007 Nice CEDEX. ☎ **04-93-16-64-00.** Fax 04-93-88-35-68. E-mail: negresco@nicematin.fr. 150 units. A/C MINIBAR TV TEL. 1,700–2,450F ($306–$441) double; from 3,950F ($711) suite. AE, DC, MC, V. Parking 160F ($28.80) in the garage. Bus: 9, 10, or 11.

The Négresco is one of the Riviera's many superglamorous hotels, though those pockets of posh in Beaulieu and St-Jean-Cap-Ferrat are even more regal and certainly more peaceful, as the Négresco stands in the heart of noisy Nice. Jeanne Augier has taken over the place and has triumphed. This Victorian wedding-cake hotel is named after its founder, Henry Négresco, a Romanian who died francless in Paris in 1920. It was built on the seafront, in the French château style, with a mansard roof and domed tower; its interior design was inspired by the country's châteaux and the decorators scoured Europe to gather antiques, tapestries, paintings, and art. Some guest rooms have personality themes: The Chambre Impératrice Joséphine 1810 regally re-creates an Empire bedroom, with a huge rosewood swan bed set in a fleur-de-lis–draped recess. The Napoléon III room has swagged walls and a half-crowned canopy in pink, with a leopard-skin carpet. The most expensive rooms with balconies face the Mediterranean. (There are a few jarring notes, like clear plastic toilet seats flecked with glitter.) The staff wears 18th-century costumes.

Dining: Reasonably priced meals are served in La Rotonde, but the featured restaurant—one of the Riviera's greatest—is Chantecler (see below).

Amenities: Concierge, room service, maid service, massage, baby-sitting, secretarial services.

✪ **Palais Maeterlinck.** Basse Corniche, 06300 Nice. ☎ **04-92-00-72-00.** Fax 04-92-04-18-10. www.webstore.fr/maeterlinck. E-mail: maeterlinck@webstore.fr. 28 units. A/C MINIBAR TV TEL. 1,450–2,500F ($261–$450) double; 2,700–10,000F ($486–$1,800) suite. AE, DC, MC, V. Closed Jan 5 to mid-Mar. Drive 4 miles east of Nice along the Basse Corniche.

On 9 landscaped acres east of Nice, this "the jewel of the Côte d'Azur" occupies a villa that was inhabited between the world wars by the Belgian-born writer Maurice Maeterlinck, winner of the Nobel Prize for literature. The setting is sumptuous and is more tranquil than the hotels in more central locations. This pocket of posh offers verdant terraces and a large outdoor pool, set amid banana trees, gnarled olive trees, and soaring cypresses. Each of the elegant guest rooms is outfitted in a different monochromatic color scheme and neoclassical Florentine styling, with a terrace opening onto views of such chic enclaves as Cap d'Antibes and Cap-Ferrat.

Dining: The restaurant Mélisande offers excellent French and international cuisine with Provençal specialties.

Amenities: Outdoor pool, concierge, room service, baby-sitting, laundry service. A funicular will carry you down to the rock-strewn beach and nearby marina.

EXPENSIVE

Westminster Concorde. 27 promenade des Anglais, 06000 Nice. ☎ **04-93-88-29-44.** Fax 04-93-82-45-35. www.concorde-hotels.com. 120 units. A/C MINIBAR TV TEL. 950–1,300F ($171–$234) double; from 1,500F ($270) junior suite. AE, DC, MC, V. Parking 100F ($18). Bus: 9, 10, or 11.

This 1880 hotel stands prominently along the famous promenade. Its elaborate facade was restored in 1986 to its former grandeur, and many renovations were made, including the installation of air-conditioning. The contemporary rooms are comfortable and have soundproofed windows; a few open onto balconies. The dining and drinking facilities include plant-ringed terraces with a view of the water and a simple in-house restaurant, Le Farniente.

MODERATE

Grand Hôtel Aston. 12 av. Félix-Faure, 06000 Nice. ☎ **04-92-17-53-00.** Fax 04-93-80-40-02. 156 units. 600–1,100F ($108–$198) double. AE, DC, MC, V. Parking 90F ($16.20).

One of the most alluring in its price bracket, this elegantly detailed 19th-century hotel has been radically renovated. Most rooms overlook the splashing fountains of the city's showcase, L'Espace Masséna, a few blocks from the water. The rooftop garden offers dance music and a bar on summer evenings and has a panoramic coastline view.

Hôtel Busby. 36–38 rue du Maréchal-Joffre, 06000 Nice. ☎ **04-93-88-19-41.** Fax 04-93-87-73-53. 80 units. A/C TV TEL. 500–700F ($90–$126) double. AE, DC, MC, V. Closed Nov 15–Dec 20. Bus: 9, 10, 12, or 22.

Dating from around 1910, this hotel has a rather faded grandeur. The owners, the Busby family, refer to the hotel's ornate facade as style Garibaldi and have retained the balconies and the shutters at the tall windows. Totally renovated, the guest rooms are dignified yet colorful, and some contain pairs of mahogany twin beds and white-and-gold wardrobes. There's a cozy bar on the premises; however, faced with stiff competition from neighboring places, the hotel's restaurant closed in 1997.

✪ **La Pérouse.** 11 quai Rauba-Capéu, 06300 Nice. ☎ **04-93-62-34-63.** Fax 04-93-62-59-41. www.hroy.com/la-perouse. E-mail: la@hroy.com. 67 units. A/C MINIBAR TV TEL. 695–920F ($125.10–$165.60) double; 1,700–2,290F ($306–$412.20) suite. AE, DC, MC, V. Parking 60F ($10.80).

Once a prison, La Pérouse has been reconstructed and is now a unique Riviera hotel. Set on a cliff, it overlooks the sea and is entered through a lower-level lobby, where an elevator takes you up to the gardens and a pool. There's no hotel in Nice with a better view over both the old city and the Baie des Anges. In fact, La Pérouse is built right into the gardens of an ancient château-fort. Inside, the hotel is like an old Provençal home, with low ceilings, white walls, and antiques. Most of the lovely rooms have loggias overlooking the bay. The restaurant, with a different menu every day, specializes in a Niçoise cuisine and is open for lunch and dinner in summer (in winter, guests rely on room service).

INEXPENSIVE

Flots d'Azur. 101 promenade des Anglais, 06000 Nice. ☎ **04-93-86-51-25.** Fax 04-93-97-22-07. 21 units. A/C TEL. 250–500F ($45–$90) double. V. Bus: 8.

This three-story villa-hotel is next to the sea, a short walk from the more elaborate and costlier promenade hotels. The rooms vary in size and decor, but all have good views and sea breezes, and 12 contain TV and minibar. Double-glazed windows were recently added to cut down on the noise. There's a small sitting room and sun terrace in front, where a continental breakfast is served.

Hôtel de la Mer. 4 place Masséna, 06000 Nice. ☎ **04-93-92-09-10.** Fax 04-93-85-00-64. 12 units. MINIBAR TV TEL. 250–380F ($45–$68.40) double. AE, MC, V. Parking 70F ($12.60) in nearby covered garage. Bus: 1, 5, or 12.

In the center of Old Nice, this place was built around 1910, transformed into a hotel in 1947, and renovated in 1993. Despite that, it manages to keep its prices low. Feri Forouzan, the owner, welcomes you with personalized charm. Most guest rooms are of good size and have such items as a minibar and TV, not often found in inexpensive Nice hotels. From the hotel it's a 2-minute walk to promenade des Anglais and the seafront. Breakfast is served in one of the public salons or your room.

Hôtel du Centre. 2 rue de Suisse, 06000 Nice. ☎ **04-93-88-83-85.** Fax 04-93-82-29-80. E-mail: hotel-centre@webstore.fr. 28 units, 20 with bathroom. TV TEL. 186–206F ($33.50–$37.10) double without bathroom, 296–320F ($53.30–$57.60) double with bathroom. AE, DC, MC, V. Parking 10F ($1.80). Bus: 23.

Near the rail station, this hotel was built in 1947 and today welcomes gay travelers among others. Rooms are simple and clean, and you'll be located very near the attractions and bars of downtown Nice. The staff knows the city well and is happy to provide guests with inside information and advice.

Hôtel Excelsior. 19 av. Durante, 06000 Nice. ☎ **04-93-88-18-05.** Fax 04-93-88-38-69. 45 units. TV TEL. 330–490F ($59.40–$88.20) double. Rates include breakfast. AE, MC, V.

Its ornate corbels and chiseled stone pediments—evidence of its original function as a private villa in the 1880s—rise grandly a few steps from the railway station. Inside you'll find a pleasantly modern decor with comfortably upholstered armchairs. There's a reflecting pool in the large lobby, a larger one (with fish) in the rear garden, and high-ceilinged and cozy guest rooms. The beach is a 20-minute walk from the hotel through the residential and commercial center of Nice.

Hôtel Magnan. Square du Général-Ferrié, 06200 Nice. ☎ **04-93-86-76-00.** Fax 04-93-44-48-31. 25 units. TV TEL. 280–360F ($50.40–$64.80) double. AE, MC, V. Parking 35F ($6.30). Bus: 12, 23, or 24.

This well-run modern hotel was built around 1945 and renovated frequently during its long and busy life. It's a 10-minute bus ride from the heart of town but only a minute or so from promenade des Anglais and the bay. Many of the simply furnished rooms have a balcony facing the sea, and some contain a minibar. The owner, Daniel Thérouin, occupies the apartment on the top floor, guaranteeing a closely supervised setup. Breakfast can be served in your room.

✪ **Hôtel Villa Eden.** 99 bis promenade des Anglais, 06000 Nice. ☎ **04-93-86-53-70.** Fax 04-93-97-67-97. 15 units. A/C TV TEL. 200–390F ($36–$70.20) double. AE, DC, MC, V. Bus: 3, 9, 10, 22, 23, or 24 from the center, or 12 from the train station.

In 1925 an exiled Russian countess built this Art Deco villa on the seafront, surrounded it with a wall, and planted a tiny garden. The pastel-pink villa still remains, despite the construction of much taller modern buildings on both sides. You can enjoy the ivy and roses in the garden and stay in old-fashioned, partly modernized rooms whose sizes vary greatly. The owner maintains a wry sense of humor and greets you at breakfast, the only meal served.

Le Petit Palais. 10 av. Emile-Bieckert, 06000 Nice. ☎ **04-93-62-19-11.** Fax 04-93-62-53-60. www.bestwestern.com. 25 units. TV TEL. 430–780F ($77.40–$140.40) double. AE, DC, V. Parking 50F ($9).

This whimsical hotel occupies a mansion built around 1890; in the 1970s it was the home of the actor/writer Sacha Guitry, a name that's instantly recognized in millions of French households. It lies about a 10-minute drive from the city center in the Carabacel residential district. Much of its architectural grace remains, as evoked by the Art Deco/Italianate furnishings and Florentine moldings and friezes. The preferred rooms, and the most expensive, have balconies for sea views during the day and sunset watching at dusk. You can order light food from room service until midnight, and breakfast is served in a small but pretty salon.

WHERE TO DINE
VERY EXPENSIVE

✪ **Chantecler.** In the Hôtel Négresco, 37 promenade des Anglais. ☎ **04-93-16-64-00.** Reservations required. Main courses 210–280F ($37.80–$50.40); fixed-price menus 235F ($42.30) at lunch, 395–590F ($71.10–$106.20) at dinner. AE, DC, MC, V. Daily 12:30–2:30pm and 7:30–10:30pm. Closed mid-Nov to mid-Dec. Bus: 9, 10, or 11. FRENCH.

This is Nice's most prestigious restaurant. In 1989 a massive redecoration sheathed its walls with panels removed from a château in Puilly-Fussé, a Regency-style salon was installed for before- or after-dinner drinks, and a collection of 16th-century paintings, executed on leather backgrounds in the Belgian town of Malines, was imported. The much-respected chef, Alain Llorca, creates the most sophisticated and creative dishes in Nice. They change almost weekly but usually include fresh asparagus with

Parmesan cheese and a sabayon of black truffles, roast suckling lamb with beignets of vegetables and ricotta-stuffed ravioli, and a melt-in-your-mouth fantasy of marbled hot chocolate drenched in an almond-flavored cream sauce. Gourmands take note: The most expensive fixed-price dinner menu includes a well-orchestrated banquet followed by three separate desserts.

EXPENSIVE

Chez Michel (Le Grand Pavois). 11 rue Meyerbeer. ☎ **04-93-88-77-42.** Reservations required. Main courses 125–160F ($22.50–$28.80); bouillabaisse 320–450F ($57.60–$81); fixed-price menus 185–295F ($33.30–$53.10). MC, V. Daily noon–2:30pm and 7–11pm. Bus: 8. SEAFOOD.

Chez Michel is nestled under an Art Deco apartment building near the water. One of the partners, Jacques Marquise, is from Golfe-Juan, where for 25 years he managed the famous fish restaurant Chez Tétou. At Golfe-Juan, M. Marquise became celebrated for his bouillabaisse, which he now prepares here. Other delectable specialties are baked sea bass in white wine, herbs, and lemon sauce and grilled flambé lobster. The wine list has a number of reasonably priced bottles.

Don Camillo. 5 rue des Ponchettes. ☎ **04-93-85-67-95.** Reservations recommended. Main courses 120–150F ($21.60–$27); fixed-price menu 140F ($25.20). AE, MC, V. Tues–Sat noon–2pm, Mon–Sat 8–10:30pm. Bus: 8. PROVENÇAL.

This nine-table restaurant promises (and delivers) some of Nice's most authentic Provençal food. The dining room is adorned with the modern paintings of the Niçois painter Laurent Gerbert, and Franck Cerutti, assisted by his wife, Véronique, apply the gilded training he learned during stints at some of the grandest restaurants of the Côte d'Azur. Staples of the menu are fava beans, Swiss chard, goat cheese, stockfish, cuttlefish, and a medley of herbs produced on the region's dry hillsides. Every dish bears the mark of a master chef who's almost guaranteed to become much better known among Provence's gastronomes. Do your best to sample the selections from the cheese tray. Each derives from a small local farm, with goodly numbers fermented from sheep's or goat's milk.

Restaurant Barale. 39 rue Beaumont. ☎ **04-93-89-17-94.** Reservations imperative. Fixed-price menu 250F ($45). Dinner Tues–Sat by special request only, often between 7:30 and 8:30pm. Bus: 8. PROVENÇAL.

You can't just drop in here: Advance reservations are absolutely required. At the helm here is Hélène Barale, who has spent more than 80 years learning about and crafting the culinary specialties of Provence. Nothing here is innovative: The *pissaladière* and *sautée de veau aux champignons* (veal with mushrooms) are prepared exactly the way they were when Mme Barale was a girl. Even if the food is occasionally scorched or reheated (which some locals suspect it occasionally might be), the evocative dining room lined with copper pots, the wood-fired oven, and the old-fashioned Provençal accent and allure of Mme Barale herself add to what might be a memorable cultural experience.

MODERATE

Flo. 2–4 rue Sacha-Guitry. ☎ **04-93-13-38-38.** Reservations recommended. Main courses 80–100F ($14.40–$18); fixed-price menus 106F ($19.10) at lunch, 153F ($27.55) all day, and 106F ($19.10) after 10pm. AE, DC, MC, V. Daily noon–3pm and 7pm–12:30am. Bus: 1, 2, or 5. FRENCH.

With high ceilings covered with their original frescoes, Flo is brisk, stylish, reasonably priced, and fun. Menu items include an array of grilled fish, choucroute (sauerkraut) Alsatian style, steak with brandied pepper sauce, and fresh oysters and shellfish.

✪ **La Merenda.** 4 rue Terrasse. No phone. Reservations required. Main courses 160–220F ($28.80–$39.60). No credit cards. Mon–Fri noon–2pm and 7–9:30pm. Closed Aug 4–18, Dec 24–Jan 4, and Feb 16–22. Bus: 8. NIÇOISE.

Since there's no phone, you have to go by this place twice: once to make a reservation and once to dine. However, it's worth the extra effort, as this is the best bistro in Nice. We wish we could eat here every day.

Forsaking his two-star crown at the renowned Chantecler (see above), chef Dominique Le Stanc opened up this tiny bistro serving a sublime cuisine. "A no-star hole in the wall," the press screamed. But that's what Le Stanc wanted. Born in Alsace, his heart and soul belong to the Mediterranean, the land of black truffles, seasonal wild morels, fat sea bass, and plump asparagus. His food has been called a lullaby of gastronomic unity, with texture, crunch, richness, and balance. "I've known my days of glory in the gastronomic world. Now I'm doing family cooking, which is what I always like to eat." Le Stanc never knows what he's going to serve until he goes to the market. Look for his specials on a chalkboard. Perhaps you'll find stuffed cabbage, fried zucchini flowers, or oxtail flavored with fresh oranges. Lamb from the Sisteron is cooked until it practically falls from the bone. Raw artichokes are paired with a salad of mâche. Service is discreet and personable.

INEXPENSIVE

Acchiardo. 38 rue Droite. ☎ **04-93-85-51-16.** Reservations not needed. Main courses 60–100F ($10.80–$18). No credit cards. Mon–Fri noon–1:30pm and 7–9:30pm, Sat noon–1:30pm. Closed Aug. NIÇOISE.

One of your best bets for a meal in Vieux Nice is Acchiardo, a time-tested bistro that looks like a setting for one of those Riviera movies of the '50s, the type that starred Jean Seberg and was called *Bonjour Tristesse*. You don't really come here for the decor, although there are all the rustic artifacts you would need to remake a Ma and Pa Kettle movie, right down to the corncobs hanging from the ceiling beams.

At one of the red-and-white checked oilcloth-covered tables, you might ask for the plat du jour. Ours was boeuf daube, and it was perfectly tasty and well seasoned. The fish soup is one of the best in the old town. You might follow with the homemade ravioli or the tournedos with gorgonzola. Old-timers meet here to gossip in the Niçois dialect. The wine cellar was constructed during the reign of Louis XIV, and nothing much has been changed since. This atmospheric place is run by a family, including the father, Joseph, his wife, Evelyne, aided by their English-speaking daughter, Virgine.

Le Baron Ivre. 6 rue Maraldi. ☎ **04-93-89-52-13.** Reservations recommended. Main courses 70–110F ($12.60–$19.80); fixed-price menu 100F ($18). DC, MC, V. Daily 7:30pm–midnight. Closed Wed Oct–Mar. Bus: 2. GERMAN/FRENCH.

Behind Nice's enormous exhibition center, this is a highly reputable restaurant whose clientele happens to be about 80% gay. It's a cosmopolitan spot offering a blend of Teutonic and Gallic food that's one of the most appealing on the Riviera. Menu items are affordably priced, flavorful, and served in generous portions. They include filets of beef with peppercorns, magrêt of duckling with honey sauce, and such German specialties as rouladen of beef, goulash soup, schnitzels in cream sauce, and (in winter) Berliner leber (Berlin-style calf's liver). More than 40 vintages of wine are in stock, and the original paintings decorating the place are for sale.

✪ **Le Safari.** 1 cours Saleya. ☎ **04-93-80-18-44.** Reservations recommended. Main courses 60–135F ($10.80–$24.30); fixed-price menu 150F ($27). AE, DC, MC, V. Daily noon–2:30pm and 7–11:30pm. Bus: 1. PROVENÇAL/NIÇOISE.

The decor couldn't be simpler: a black ceiling, white walls, and an old-fashioned terra-cotta floor. The youthful staff is relaxed, sometimes in jeans, and always alert to the waves of fashion. Look for mobs here, many of whom prefer the outdoor terrace over-looking the Marché aux Fleurs and all of whom appreciate the earthy, reasonably priced meals that appear in generous portions. Menu items include a pungent bagna cauda, where vegetables are immersed in a sizzling brew of hot oil and anchovy paste; grilled peppers bathed in olive oil; daube (stew) of beef; fresh pasta with basil; an omelet with blettes (tough but flavorful greens); and the unfortunately named *merda de can* (dog shit), which is actually a gnocchi stuffed with spinach.

Restaurant L'Estocaficada. 2 rue de l'Hôtel-de-Ville. ☎ **04-93-80-21-64.** Reservations recommended. Pizzas 33–48F ($5.95–$8.65); main courses 50–95F ($9–$17.10); fixed-price menus 58–89F ($10.45–$16). AE, DC, MC, V. Tues–Sun noon–2pm and Tues–Sat 7–10pm. Bus: 1, 2, or 5. NIÇOISE.

Estocaficada is the Provençal word for stockfish, the ugliest fish in Europe. You can see one for yourself—there might be a dried-out, balloon-shaped version on display in the cozy dining room. Brigitte Autier is the owner/chef, and her busy kitchens are visible from everywhere in the dining room. Descended from a matriarchal line (since 1958) of mother-daughter teams who have managed this place, she's devoted to the preser-vation of recipes prepared by her Niçoise grandmother. Examples are gnocchi, beignets, several types of *farcies* (tomatoes, peppers, or onions stuffed with herbed fill-ings), grilled sardines, or bouillabaisse served as a main course or in a miniversion. As a concession to popular demand, the place also serves pizzas and pastas.

NICE AFTER DARK

Nice has some of the most active nightlife along the Riviera, with evenings usually beginning at a cafe. The newspaper *La Semaine des Spectacles* is available at kiosks around town and outlines the week's diversions.

The major cultural center along the Riviera is the **Opéra de Nice,** 4 rue St-François-de-Paul (☎ **04-92-17-40-44**), with a busy season in winter. A full repertoire is pre-sented, with special emphasis on serious, large-scale operas. In one season you might see *La Bohème,* as well as a *saison symphonique,* dominated by the Orchestre Philhar-monique de Nice. The opera hall is also the major venue for concerts and recitals. The box office is open Tuesday to Saturday from 10am to 6pm. Tickets cost from 40F ($7.20) for a high-altitude, low-visibility seat to 380F ($68.40) for front-and-center seats.

Near the Hotel Ambassador, **L'Ambassade,** 18 rue des Congrès (☎ **04-93-88-88-87**), was deliberately designed in a mock-Gothic style that includes the wrought-iron accents you'd expect to find in a château, two bars, and a dance floor. The cover is 80F ($14.40), including the first drink. **Niel's Club,** 10 rue Cité-du-Parc (☎ **04-93-80-49-84**), is a double-tiered nightclub with live rock in its 200-year-old vaulted cellar during the week and a modern disco on its street level on weekends. There's a cover of 50F ($9), including the first drink.

Le Cabaret du Casino Roule (La Madonette), in the Casino Roule, 1 promenade des Anglais (☎ **04-93-87-95-87**), is Nice's answer to the cabaret glitter of Monte Carlo and Las Vegas. It includes just enough flesh to titillate; lots of spangles, feathers, and sequins; a medley of cross-cultural jokes and nostalgia for the good old days of French *chanson;* and an acrobat or juggler. The regular cover of 70F ($12.60) includes the first drink. Shows are presented on Friday and Saturday at 10pm with a cover of 140F ($25.20).

Le Relais American Bar, in the Hotel Négresco, 37 promenade des Anglais (☎ **04-93-16-64-00**), is the most beautiful bar in Nice, filled with white columns, an oxblood-red ceiling, Oriental carpets, English paneling, Italianate chairs, and tapestries. With its piano music and white-jacketed waiters, the bar still attracts a chic crowd.

Near the Hôtel Négresco and promenade des Anglais, **Le Blue Boy,** 9 rue Spinetta (☎ 04-93-44-68-24), is the oldest gay disco on the Riviera. With two bars and two floors, it's a vital nocturnal stopover for passengers aboard the dozens of all-gay cruises (most of which are administered from Holland) that make regular stopovers at Nice and such nearby ports as Villefranche. The cover is 50F ($9) on Saturday, 30F ($5.40) other days.

A SIDE TRIP TO PEILLON

The fortified medieval town of Peillon, 12 miles northwest of Nice, is the most spectacular "perched village" along the Côte d'Azur. At 1,000 feet above the sea, it's also unspoiled, unlike so many of the perched villages that have become filled with day-trippers and souvenir shops.

The main sightseeing interest is the semifortified architecture of the town itself. You can also visit the **Eglise du St-Sauveur,** a simple parish church built in a country-baroque style in the early 1700s, near the highest point of the village, and the 15th-century **Chapelle des Pénitents-Blancs,** on place Auguste-Arnuls. The parish church is always open, but local authorities don't encourage interior visits to the chapel unless tours, usually for groups of art historians, are arranged several weeks in advance through officials at the town hall (☎ 04-93-79-91-04). Instead, most of the interior is visible through an iron gate. If you plunk 2F (35¢) into a machine near the iron gate, lights will illuminate the interior's noteworthy frescoes. Painted in 1491 by Jean Cannavesio, they represent eight stages of the passion of Christ.

Each of the town's narrow streets, some of which are enclosed with vaulting and accented with potted geraniums and strands of ivy, radiates outward from the town's "foyer," **place Auguste-Arnuls,** which is shaded by rows of plantain trees centered around a fountain that has splashed water from its basin since 1800.

Suggested diversions? Consider a 2-hour, 7½-mile northward hike across the dry and rocky landscapes of eastern Provence to Peillon's remote twin, **Peille,** a smaller version of what you'll find in Peillon.

GETTING THERE

Few other towns in Provence are as easy to reach **by car** and as inconvenient to reach by public transport. It's an easy drive northeast from Nice—take D2204 to D21 and you'll arrive in about 20 minutes, depending on traffic.

Only two **trains** a day stop near Peillon, at St-Techle, a rarely used station along an antique-looking train spur that connects Nice with Coni, a town across the border in Italy. For rail information and schedules, call ☎ 08-36-35-35-39. You'll find lots of dilapidated local color at St-Techle. Know in advance that no taxis will be waiting in line. There's also no bus service to carry you on to Peillon. Most backpackers continue into Peillon by hitchhiking.

The Santa Azur **bus** line operates four buses from Nice every day, with multiple stops en route and transit time of around 25 minutes each way. Don't expect it to be convenient, as you'll be dropped off about 2 miles from Peillon's center, at a tiny crossroads known as Le Moulin. Many hardy souls opt to continue on to the center by foot, as there's no other regularly scheduled transit, and taxis simply aren't available. For bus information, call ☎ 04-93-85-61-81.

The **Syndicat d'Initiative** (tourist office) is in the village center (☎ 04-93-79-91-04).

WHERE TO STAY & DINE

The only hotel/restaurant in town is a magnet in its own right for urban escapists who want a view of the Provence of long ago.

Auberge de la Madone. 06440 Peillon. ☎ **04-93-79-91-17.** Fax 04-93-79-99-36. 20 units. TEL. 420–720F ($75.60–$129.60) double; 800–1,300F ($144–$234) suite. MC, V. Closed Oct 20–Dec 20; restaurant closed Wed.

This hotel, with its well-recommended restaurant, has thrived here since the 1930s, when it was installed in a stone-sided complex of buildings whose oldest sections dated from the 12th century. Evocative of a sprawling *mas provençal* (Provençal farmhouse), it's capped with terra-cotta tiles and draped with a small version of the Hanging Gardens of Babylon. The auberge is on the opposite side of place Auguste-Arnuls from the rest of the village and boasts a wide terrace offering one of the best views of the town's vertical and very angular architecture. The guest rooms are comfortable and rustic, each outfitted with Provençal themes and fabrics. The hotel operates an annex within a 5-minute walk, with seven additional rooms. Expect accommodations much simpler than those in the main building, many without bathrooms, and rates of between 210F and 380F ($37.80 and $68.40) per night, depending on the plumbing and views.

Dining: The hotel restaurant is by far the most formal in town, serving lunch and dinner daily except Wednesday and during the annual closing noted above. Menu items are based on cuisine that developed in this pocket of Provence over the centuries and include unusual dishes like tourton des pénitents, a salty tart enriched with 17 herbs, almonds, eggs, and cream; suckling lamb with garlic-enriched mashed potatoes and a tapenade of olives; farm-raised guinea fowl with a confit of pears; and pot-au-feu, a savory kettle of seafood served with aioli.

14 St-Jean-Cap-Ferrat

583 miles S of Paris, 6 miles E of Nice

Of all the oases along the Côte d'Azur, no place has the snob appeal of Cap-Ferrat. It's a 9-mile promontory sprinkled with luxurious villas, outlined by sheltered bays, beaches, and coves. The vegetation is lush. In the port of St-Jean, the harbor accommodates yachts and fishing boats.

ESSENTIALS

GETTING THERE   Most visitors drive or take a bus or taxi from the **rail station at nearby Beaulieu.** Buses from Beaulieu depart at hourly intervals for Cap-Ferrat from the rail station. There's also bus service from Nice. For bus information and schedules, call ☎04-93-85-61-81. **By car,** St-Jean-Cap-Ferrat is best reached from Nice by driving along N7 east.

VISITOR INFORMATION   The **Office de Tourisme** is on av. Denis-Séméria (☎ 04-93-01-02-21).

SEEING THE SIGHTS

There are few public paths to enjoy the scenery. The most scenic goes from **Plage de Paloma** to **Pointe St-Hospice,** at which point a panoramic view of the Riviera landscape unfolds.

You can also spend time wandering around St-Jean, a colorful fishing village with bars, bistros, and simple inns. The beaches, although popular, are shingly. The best and most luxurious one belongs to the Grand Hôtel du Cap-Ferrat (see below), and it is open to nonguests who pay 100F ($18) to rent a mattresses and an umbrella.

Everyone tries to visit the **Villa Mauresque,** av. Somerset-Maugham, but it's closed to the public. Near the cape, it's where Maugham spent his final years, almost begging for death. When tourists tried to visit him, he loudly proclaimed that he wasn't one of the local sights. One man did manage to crash through the gate, and when he encountered the author, Maugham snarled, "What do you think I am, a monkey in a cage?"

Once the property of King Leopold II, of Belgium, the **Villa Les Cèred** lies directly west of the port of St-Jean. Although the villa is in private hands and can't be visited, you can go to the **Parc Zoologique,** boulevard du Général-de-Gaulle, northwest of the peninsula, near Villa Les Cèdres (☎ **04-93-76-04-98**). It's open daily: April to October from 9:30am to 7pm, to 5:30pm in winter. Admission is 25F ($4.50). This private zoo is set in the basin of a now-drained lake and was Leopold's private domain. It houses a wide variety of reptiles, birds, and animals in outdoor cages. Six times a day there's a chimps' tea party, which explains Maugham's remark.

✪ **Musée Ile-de-France.** Av. Denis-Séméria. ☎ **04-93-01-33-09.** Admission 45F ($8.10) adults, 33F ($5.95) ages 9–24, free for children 8 and under. July–Aug daily 10am–7pm; Sept–June daily 10am–6pm.

Built by Baronne Ephrussi, this is one of the Côte d'Azur's most legendary villas. Born a Rothschild, she married a Hungarian banker and friend of her father, M. Ephrussi, about whom even the curator of the museum says that very little is known. She died in 1934, leaving the stately Italianate building and its magnificent gardens to the Institut de France on behalf of the Académie des Beaux-Arts. The wealth of her collection is preserved: 18th-century furniture; Tiepolo ceilings; Savonnerie carpets; screens and panels from the Far East; tapestries from Gobelin, Aubusson, and Beauvais; drawings by Fragonard; canvases by Boucher; rare Sèvres porcelain; and more. Covering 12 acres, the gardens contain fragments of statuary from churches, monasteries, and torn-down palaces. One entire section is planted with cacti.

WHERE TO STAY

✪ **Grand Hôtel du Cap-Ferrat.** Bd. du Général-de-Gaulle, 06230 St-Jean-Cap-Ferrat. ☎ **04-93-76-50-50.** Fax 04-93-76-04-52. www.grand-hotel-cap-ferrat.com. E-mail: reserv@grand-hotel-cap-ferrat.com. 70 units. A/C MINIBAR TV TEL. 1,900–4,800F ($342–$864) double; 5,400–12,500F ($972–$2,250) suite. AE, DC, MC, V. Free parking.

One of the best features of this turn-of-the-century palace is its location at the tip of the peninsula in the midst of a 14-acre garden of semitropical trees and manicured lawns. It has been the retreat of the international elite since 1908, and it occupies the same celestial status as the Réserve and Métropole in Beaulieu. Its cuisine even equals the Métropole's. Parts of the exterior have open loggias and big arched windows, and you can enjoy the views from the elaborately flowering terrace over the sea. The guest rooms are conservatively modern, with dressing rooms, and rates include admission to the pool, Club Dauphin. The beach is accessible via funicular from the main building.

Dining: The hotel's indoor/outdoor restaurant serves *cuisine du marché,* which might include salad of warm foie gras and chanterelle mushrooms, nage of crayfish and lobster, or breast of duckling with honey and cider vinegar. The dining room is one of the last of the great belle époque palaces on the Côte d'Azur. The meals and service are flawless but come at a very high price. The American-style bar opens onto the garden.

Amenities: Olympic-size heated pool, tennis courts, bikes, 24-hour room service, same-day laundry.

Hôtel Brise Marine. Av. Jean-Mermoz, St-Jean-Cap-Ferrat, 06230 Villefranche-sur-Mer. ☎ **04-93-76-04-36.** Fax 04-93-76-11-49. E-mail: bmarine@nicematin.fr. 16 units. A/C TV TEL. 670–750F ($120.60–$135) double. AE, MC, V. Closed Nov–Jan.

This circa-1878 villa with front and rear terrace is on a hillside. A long rose arbor, beds of subtropical flowers, palms, and pines provide an attractive setting. The atmosphere is casual and informal, and the rooms are comfortably but simply furnished. You can have breakfast either in the beamed lounge or under the rose trellis.

✪ **Hôtel Clair Logis.** 12 av. Centrale, 06230 St-Jean-Cap-Ferrat. ☎ **04-93-76-04-57.** Fax 04-93-76-11-85. 18 units. MINIBAR TV TEL. 390–650F ($70.20–$117) double. AE, DC, MC, V. Closed Jan–Feb and Nov–Dec 15.

A rare find here, this hotel occupies what was a 19th-century villa surrounded by 2 acres of semitropical gardens. The pleasant rooms are scattered over three buildings in the confines of the garden. The hotel's most famous guest was de Gaulle, who lived in a room called Strelitzias (Bird of Paradise) during many of his retreats from Paris. Each room is named after a flower. The most romantic and spacious accommodations are in the main building; the rooms in the annex are the most modern but have the least character.

✪ **La Voile d'Or.** 31 av. Jean-Mermoz, St-Jean-Cap-Ferrat, 06230 Villefranche-sur-Mer. ☎ **04-93-01-13-13.** Fax 04-93-76-11-17. voiledor@calva.net. 49 units. A/C MINIBAR TV TEL. 1,050–3,600F ($189–$648) double; 2,500–5,000F ($450–$900) suite. Rates include continental breakfast. No credit cards. Closed Nov–Mar 12.

The "Golden Sail" is a brilliant tour de force offering intimate luxury in a converted villa. As a deluxe hotel it's absolutely equal to the Grand Hôtel, though its cuisine isn't quite as superb. An antique collector turned hôtelier, Jean R. Lorenzi owns this hotel at the edge of the little fishing port and yacht harbor, with a panoramic view of the coast and a nice stretch of beach. The guest rooms, the lounges, and the restaurant open onto terraces. The rooms are individually decorated with hand-painted reproductions, carved gilt headboards, baroque paneled doors, parquet floors, antique clocks, and paintings.

Dining: Guests gather on the canopied outer terrace for lunch and in the evening dine in a stately room with Spanish armchairs and white wrought-iron chandeliers. The sophisticated menu offers regional specialties and international dishes, as well as classic French cuisine. The drawing room is richly decorated. Most intimate is a little bar, with Wedgwood-blue paneling and antique mirroring.

Amenities: Two pools.

WHERE TO DINE

✪ **Le Provençal.** 2 av. Denis-Séméria. ☎ **04-93-76-03-97.** Reservations required. Main courses 230–450F ($41.40–$81). Fixed-price menus 250–350F ($45–$63). AE, MC, V. Apr to mid-Oct Thurs–Mon noon–2:30pm, Wed–Mon 7:30–11pm; Mar daily noon–2:30pm and 7:30–11pm. Closed mid-Oct to Feb. FRENCH.

With the possible exception of the Grand Hôtel's dining room, this is the best restaurant in town. Near the top of the resort's highest peak, it has the most panoramic view, with sight lines that, on good days, sweep as far away as Menton and the Italian border. Many of the menu items are credited directly to the inspiration of "the Provençal" in the kitchens, who in this case is the well-trained Jean-Jacques Jouteux. Menu items include marinated artichoke hearts presented beside half a lobster, a tarte fine of potatoes with deliberately undercooked foie gras, rack of lamb with local herbs and tarragon sauce, and crayfish asparagus and black-olive tapenade. The best way to appreciate the desserts is to order the house sampler, *"les cinq desserts du Provençal"*— a potpourri of five petits desserts that usually includes macaroons with chocolate and crème brûlée. With the passage of years here, the cooking seems more inspired than ever.

Le Sloop. Au Nouveau Port. ☎ **04-93-01-48-63.** Reservations recommended. Main courses 110–155F ($19.80–$27.90); fixed-price menu 155F ($27.90). AE, MC, V. Thurs–Tues noon–2:30pm, daily 7–10:30pm. Closed Nov 15–Dec 15 and Wed dinner in off-season. FRENCH.

This is the most popular and most reasonably priced bistro in this very expensive area. Outfitted in blue and white inside and out, it sits directly at the edge of the port, overlooking the yachts in the harbor. The best of regional produce is handled deftly by the chefs, who present dishes like salmon tartare with baby onions; warm salad of red mullet; salad of fresh mozzarella, avocados, and lobster; John Dory with fresh pasta and basil; turbot with lobster sauce and calamari; and filet of veal with basil sauce. The regional wines are reasonably priced.

15 Villefranche-sur-Mer

581 miles S of Paris, 4 miles E of Nice

According to legend, Hercules opened his arms and Villefranche was born. It sits on a big blue bay that looks like a gigantic bowl, large enough to attract U.S. Sixth Fleet cruisers and destroyers. Quietly slumbering otherwise, Villefranche takes on the appearance of an exciting Mediterranean port when the fleet's in. Four miles from Nice, it's the first town you reach along the Lower Corniche.

Rue Obscure is vaulted, one of the strangest streets in France (to get to it, take rue de l'Eglise). In spirit it belongs more to a North African casbah. People live in tiny houses on this street, protected from the elements. Occasionally, however, there's an open space, allowing for a tiny courtyard.

Once popular with such writers as Katherine Mansfield and Aldous Huxley, the town is still a haven for artists, many of whom take over the little houses—reached by narrow alleyways—that climb the hillside.

One artist who came to Villefranche left a memorial: Jean Cocteau, the legendary painter, writer, filmmaker, and well-respected dilettante, spent a year (1956 to 1957) painting frescoes on the 14th-century walls of the **Romanesque Chapelle St-Pierre,** quai de la Douane/rue des Marinières (☎ **04-93-76-90-70**). He eventually presented it to "the fishermen of Villefranche in homage to the Prince of Apostles, the patron of fishermen." One panel pays homage to the gypsies of the Stes-Maries-de-la-Mer. In the apse is a depiction of the miracle of St. Peter walking on the water, not knowing that he's supported by an angel. On the left side of the narthex Cocteau honored Villefranche's young women in their regional costumes. The chapel, which charges 12F ($2.15) admission, is open Tuesday to Sunday: July to September from 10am to noon and 4 to 8:30pm, October to March from 9:30am to noon and 2 to 5pm, and April to June from 9:30am to noon and 3 to 7pm (closed mid-November to mid-December).

ESSENTIALS

GETTING THERE   **Trains** arrive from most towns on the Côte d'Azur, especially Nice, every 30 minutes, but most visitors **drive** via the Corniche Inférieure (Lower Corniche). For more rail information and schedules, call ☎ **08-36-35-35-39**. Villefranche-sur-Mer is best reached from Nice by driving along N7 east.

VISITOR INFORMATION   The **Office de Tourisme** is on Jardin François-Binon (☎ **04-93-01-73-68**).

WHERE TO STAY

Hôtel Versailles. Av. Princesse-Grace-de-Monaco, 06230 Villefranche-sur-Mer. ☎ **04-93-01-89-56.** Fax 04-93-01-97-48. www.pagezoom.com/leversaille. 49 units. A/C TV TEL. 450–600F ($81–$108) double; 700–800F ($126–$144) suite. Rates include breakfast. AE, DC, MC, V. Free parking. Closed late Nov to Dec.

Several blocks from the harbor and outside the main part of town, this three-story hotel gives you a perspective of the entire coast. The hotel offers comfortably furnished rooms and suites (suitable for up to three) with big windows and panoramas. Guests congregate on the roof terrace, where they can order breakfast or lunch under an umbrella. The hotel's pool has a terrace and is surrounded by palms and bright flowers.

Hôtel Welcome. 1 quai Courbet, 06230 Villefranche-sur-Mer. ☎ **04-93-76-27-62.** Fax 04-93-76-27-66. 32 units. A/C MINIBAR TV TEL. 495–950F ($89.10–$171) double. Rates include breakfast. Half board 150F ($27) per person extra. AE, DC, MC, V. Closed Nov 15–Dec 20. Parking 100F ($18).

Involving you instantly in Mediterranean port life, the Welcome was a favorite of Jean Cocteau and is the best hotel at the port. In this six-floor villa hotel, with shutters and balconies, everything has recently been modernized. Try for a fifth-floor room over-looking the water. Once Pope Paul III embarked from this site with Charles V, but nowadays the departures are more casual—usually for fishing expeditions. The side-walk cafe is the focal point of town life. The lounge and the restaurant, St-Pierre, have open fireplaces and fruitwood furniture.

WHERE TO DINE

La Mère Germaine. Quai Courbet. ☎ **04-93-01-71-39.** Reservations recommended. Main courses 125–460F ($22.50–$82.80); fixed-price menu 195F ($35.10). AE, MC, V. Daily noon–2:30pm and 7–10:30pm. Closed Nov 16–Dec 24. FRENCH/SEAFOOD.

Relax here over lunch while watching fishers repair their nets, as this is the very best of a string of restaurants on the port. The cuisine is prepared by the grandson (the lik-able Thierry Blouin) of the matriarch, mère Germaine, who opened the place in the 1930s. It's popular with U.S. Navy officers, who've discovered the bouillabaisse made with tasty morsels of freshly caught fish and mixed in a cauldron with savory spices. We recommend the grilled loup (sea bass) with fennel, salade niçoise, sole Tante Marie (stuffed with mushroom purée), and beef filet with three peppers. The perfectly roasted *carré d'agneau* (lamb) is for two.

✪ **La Trinquette.** Port de la Darse. ☎ **04-93-01-71-41.** Reservations recommended. Main courses 50–140F ($9–$25.20); fixed-price menus 99–180F ($17.80–$32.40); bouillabaisse 220F ($39.60). No credit cards. Thurs–Tues noon–2:15pm and 7:30–10pm. Closed Dec–Jan. PROVENÇAL/SEAFOOD.

Charming and traditional, in a pre-Napoleonic building that rises a few steps from the harborfront, this restaurant prides itself on its fish. These are hauled out of a back-room, on platters, for anyone skeptical enough to ask to see the actual fish before it's cooked. You can choose from among 15 to 20 kinds, prepared any way you specify, with a wide variety of well-flavored sauces. Bouillabaisse is an enduring favorite that's much cheaper here than at many other places. There's even a roasted version of chapon de mer, served with a Provençal sauce. How do the hardworking owners, Paul and Monique Osiel, recommend their John Dory? Roasted in as simple and fresh a means as possible, served only with a hint of white butter. Alternatives for this or any of the other offerings include aioli, the region's garlic-enriched mayonnaise.

16 Beaulieu

583 miles S of Paris, 6 miles E of Nice, 7 miles W of Monte Carlo

Protected from the cold north winds blowing down from the Alps, Beaulieu-sur-Mer is often referred to as "La Petite Afrique" (Little Africa). Like Menton, it has the mildest climate along the Côte d'Azur and is especially popular with wintering wealthy. Originally, English visitors staked it out, after an English industrialist founded a hotel here between the rock-studded slopes and the sea. Beaulieu is graced with lush vegetation, including oranges, lemons, and bananas, as well as palms.

ESSENTIALS

GETTING THERE   **Train** service connects Beaulieu with Nice, Monaco, and the rest of the Côte d'Azur. For rail information and schedules, call ☎ **08-36-35-35-39.** Most visitors **drive** from Nice via the Moyenne Corniche or the coastal highway.

VISITOR INFORMATION   The **Office de Tourisme** is on place Georges-Clemenceau (☎ **04-93-01-02-21**).

EXPLORING THE TOWN

Beaulieu does have a beach, but don't expect soft sands. Some seasons might have more sands than others, depending on tides and storms, but usually the surfaces are covered with light-gray gravel whose texture is finer than at beaches at other resorts nearby. The longer of the town's two beaches is **Petite Afrique,** adjacent to the yacht basin; the shorter is **Baie des Fourmis,** beneath the casino. Both are free public beaches. If you want to rent a mattress for the day and have easy access to a beachfront kiosk selling snacks and drinks, the two most visible purveyors of comfort on the sands are on Petite Afrique: **Africa Plage** (☎ **04-93-01-11-00**) and **Banana Beach** (☎ **04-93-01-14-36**). Mattresses rent for 80F ($14.40).

The town boasts an important church, the late 19th-century **Eglise de Sacré-Coeur,** a quasi-Byzantine, quasi-Gothic mishmash at 13 bd. du Maréchal-Leclerc (☎ **04-93-01-18-24**). With the same address and phone is the 12th-century Romanesque chapel of Santa Maria de Olivo, used mostly for temporary exhibits of painting, sculpture, and civic lore.

As you walk along the seafront promenade, you can see many stately belle époque villas that evoke the days when Beaulieu was the very height of fashion. Although you can't go inside, you'll see signs indicating **Villa Namouna,** which once belonged to Gordon Bennett, the owner of the *New York Herald,* who sent Stanley to find Livingstone, and **Villa Léonine,** former home of the marquess of Salisbury.

For a memorable 2-hour walk, start directly north of boulevard Edouard-VII, where a path leads up the Riviera escarpment to **Sentier du Plateau St-Michel.** A belvedere here offers panoramic views from Cap d'Ail to the Estérel. A 1-hour alternative is the stroll along **promenade Maurice-Rouvier.** The promenade runs parallel to the water, stretching from Beaulieu to St-Jean. On one side you'll see the most elegant of mansions set in well-landscaped gardens; on the other you'll get views of the distant Riviera landscape and the peninsular point of St-Hospice.

Casino de Beaulieu, av. Fernand-Dunan (☎ **04-93-76-48-00**), built in the Art Nouveau style in 1903, was revitalized with new management in 1997. Open every night from 8pm to dawn, it charges 70F ($12.60) admission, requests that men wear jackets and ties into the gaming rooms, and maintains a bar and disco in a separate area. At this writing, there were no slot machines.

Villa Kérylos. Rue Gustave-Eiffel. ☎ **04-93-01-01-44.** Admission 35F ($6.30) adults, 20F ($3.60) children and seniors. Daily 10:30am–12:30pm and 2–6pm (to 7pm July–Aug).

This is a replica of an ancient Greek residence, painstakingly designed and built by the archaeologist Theodore Reinach. Inside, the cabinets are filled with a collection of Greek figurines and ceramics. But most interesting is the reconstructed Greek furniture, much of which would be fashionable today. One curious mosaic depicts the slaying of the minotaur and provides its own labyrinth (if you try to trace the path, expect to stay for weeks).

WHERE TO STAY
VERY EXPENSIVE

✪ **La Réserve de Beaulieu.** 5 bd. du Maréchal-Leclerc, 06310 Beaulieu-sur-Mer. ☎ **04-93-01-00-01.** Fax 04-93-01-28-99. 37 units. A/C MINIBAR TV TEL. 1,550–3,850F ($279–$693) double; 3,100–7,350F ($558–$1,323) suite. AE, DC, MC, V. Closed Nov–Mar.

One of the Riviera's most famous hotels, this pink-and-white fin-de-siècle palace is on the Mediterranean. Here you can sit having a cocktail as the sun sets over the Riviera while a pianist treats you to Mozart. A number of the public lounges open onto a courtyard with bamboo chairs, grass borders, and urns of flowers. The social life centers around the main drawing room, much like the grand living room of a country estate. The hotel has been rebuilt in stages, so the rooms range widely in size and design; however, all are deluxe and individually decorated, with a beautiful view of either the mountains or the sea.

Dining: The dining room has a coved frescoed ceiling, parquet floors, crystal chandeliers, and picture windows facing the Mediterranean. Specialties are sea bass with thin slices of potatoes in savory tomato sauce, sea bream stuffed with local vegetables, and roast rack of lamb.

Amenities: Private harbor for yachts, submarine fishing gear, sauna, thalasso-therapy, seawater pool.

✪ **Le Métropole.** 15 bd. du Maréchal-Leclerc, 06310 Beaulieu-sur-Mer. ☎ **04-93-01-00-08.** Fax 04-93-01-18-51. www.relaischateaux.fr/metropole. E-mail: metropole@relaischateaux.fr. 49 units. A/C MINIBAR TV TEL. 1,700–3,900F ($306–$702) double; 3,000–6,300F ($540–$1,134) suite. Rates include half board. AE, DC, MC, V. Closed Oct 20–Dec 20.

This Italianate villa, a Relais & Châteaux, offers some of the most luxurious accommodations along the Côte d'Azur and as a hotel is on equal rank with the fabled Réserve. It's set on 2 acres of grounds that are discreetly shut off from the traffic of the resort. Here you'll enter a world of polished French elegance, with lots of balconies opening onto sea views. The marble, Oriental carpets, and polite staff members set a pervasive grace note. The guest rooms are furnished in tasteful fabrics and flowery wallpapers. The bathrooms are elegantly spacious, most often tiled, and have double sinks.

Dining: Though the in-house restaurant lost a star from the Michelin judges in the late 1990s, the food is nonetheless superb. The restaurant has a seaside terrace/bar, which elegantly retreats inside when the weather turns chilly.

Amenities: Room service (24 hours), concrete jetty for sunning, heated pool; tennis and golf nearby.

INEXPENSIVE

Hôtel Frisia. Bd. Eugène-Gauthier, 06310 Beaulieu-sur-Mer. ☎ **04-93-01-01-04.** Fax 04-93-01-31-92. 32 units. A/C MINIBAR TV TEL. 450–690F ($81–$124.20) double. AE, MC, V. Closed Nov 15–Dec 6.

Frisia's rooms, decorated in a modern style, most often open onto views of the harbor, with sea-view rooms the most expensive. English is spoken, and the American ownership makes foreign guests feel especially welcome. The hotel has a sunny garden and inviting lounges. Breakfast is the only meal served, but many reasonably priced dining places are nearby.

Hôtel Marcellin. 18 av. Albert-1er, 06310 Beaulieu-sur-Mer. ☎ **04-93-01-01-69.** Fax 04-93-01-37-43. 22 units, 15 with bathroom. TV TEL. 160–180F ($28.80–$32.40) double without bathroom, 250–300F ($45–$54) double with bathroom; 500–700F ($90–$126) suite. MC, V. Closed Nov–Dec 15.

A good budget selection in an otherwise high-priced resort, the turn-of-the-century Marcellin rents restored rooms with homelike amenities, each with a southern exposure. It has been run by the same family since 1938. The hotel stands amid the town's congestion, near its western periphery, a 5-minute walk to the beach. Its only breathing space consists of a small outdoor terrace. Despite that, it's a pleasant, well-maintained place to stay. The government has given the Marcellin a well-deserved two stars. Breakfast is the only meal served, but many restaurants are nearby.

WHERE TO DINE

La Pignatelle. 10 rue de Quincenet. ☎ **04-93-01-03-37.** Reservations recommended. Main courses 55–130F ($9.90–$23.40); fixed-price menus 85–188F ($15.30–$33.85). AE, MC, V. Thurs–Tues 12:15–1:30pm and 7:15–9:30pm. Closed mid-Nov to mid-Dec. FRENCH.

Even in this superexpensive resort, you can find an excellent and affordable Provençal bistro. Despite its relatively low prices, it prides itself on the fact that all the products that go into its robust cuisine are fresh. As a result, it's usually crowded. Specialties are salade niçoise, a succulent version of *soupe de poissons* where someone has labored to remove the bones, cassolette of mussels, monkfish steak garnished only with olive oil and herbs, scampi Provençal, tripe niçoise, scallops, and a *"petite friture du pays"* that incorporates very small fish with Provençal traditions that are many hundreds of years old.

17 Eze & La Turbie

585 miles S of Paris, 7 miles NE of Nice

The hamlets of Eze and La Turbie, though 4 miles apart, have so many similarities that most of France's tourist officials speak of them as if they're one. Both boast fortified feudal cores high in the hills overlooking the Provençal coast, and both were built during the early Middle Ages to stave off raids from corsairs who wanted to capture harem slaves and laborers. Clinging to the rocky hillsides around these hamlets are upscale villas, many of which were built since the 1950s by retirees from colder climes. Closely linked, culturally and fiscally, to nearby Monaco, Eze and La Turbie have full-time populations of fewer than 3,000, and the medieval cores of both contain art galleries, boutiques, and artisans' shops that have been restored.

Eze is accessible via the Moyenne (Middle) Corniche, La Turbie via the Grande (Upper) Corniche. Signs are positioned along the coastal road indicating the direction motorists should take to reach either of the hamlets.

The leading attraction in Eze is the **Jardin Exotique,** bd. du Jardin-Exotique (☎ **04-93-41-10-30**), a lushly landscaped showcase of exotic plants set in Eze-Village, at the pinnacle of the town's highest hill. Entrance is 12F ($2.15), free for children 11 and under. In July and August, it's open daily from 8:30am to 8pm; the rest of the year, it opens at 9am and closes between 6 and 7:30pm, depending on sunset.

La Turbie boasts a ruined monument erected by the ancient Roman emperor Augustus in 6 B.C., the **Trophée des Alps** (Trophy of the Alps). (Many locals call it La Trophée d'Auguste.) It rises near a rock formation known as La Tête de Chien, at the highest point along the Grand Corniche, 1,500 feet above sea level. The monument, restored with funds donated by Edward Tuck, was erected by the Roman Senate to celebrate the subjugation of the people of the French Alps by the Roman armies. A short distance from the monument is the **Musée du Trophée des Alps,** rue Albert-1er, La Turbie (☎ **04-93-41-20-89**), a minimuseum containing finds from archaeological digs nearby and information about the monument's restoration. It's open daily: April to June from 9:30am to 6pm, July to September from 9:30am to 7pm, and

October to March from 9:30am to 5pm. Entrance is 25F ($4.50) for adults, 15F ($2.70) for students and ages 12–25, and free for children 11 and under. Closed January 1, May 1, November 1–11, and December 25.

The **Office de Tourisme** is on place du Général-de-Gaulle, Eze-Village (☎ **04-93-41-26-00**).

WHERE TO STAY & DINE

Auberge Eric Rivot. 44 av. de la Liberté, 06360 Eze-Bord-de-Mer. ☎ **04-93-01-51-46.** Fax 04-93-01-58-40. 10 units. TV TEL. 280F ($50.40) double. Half board 280F ($50.40) per person extra. AE, DC, MC, V. Closed mid-Nov to Dec 1.

This straw-yellow stucco villa is a few steps from the Basse Corniche. It has a quiet rear terrace, and the interior is filled with rattan chairs, exposed brick, and lots of brass. The simply furnished doubles draw mainly a summer crowd, though the inn is open most of the year. Half board is a good deal here—the meals are satisfying, and wine is included.

✪ **Hostellerie du Château de la Chèvre d'Or.** Rue du Barri, 06360 Eze-Village. ☎ **04-92-10-66-66.** Fax 04-93-41-06-72. 30 units. A/C MINIBAR TV TEL. 1,700–3,700F ($306–$666) double; 2,900–3,700F ($522–$666) suite. AE, DC, MC, V. Closed late Nov to Mar 1.

This is a miniature village retreat built in the 1920s in neo-Gothic style, but without a beach. On the side of a stone village off the Moyenne Corniche, this Relais & Châteaux is a complex of village houses, all with views of the coastline. The owner has had the interior of the "Golden Goat" flawlessly decorated to maintain its old character while adding modern comfort. Even if you don't stop in for a meal or a room, try to visit for a drink in the lounge, which has a panoramic view.

Dining: Le Grill du Château is a traditional restaurant where you can enjoy grilled fish and meat. Other choices are Chez Justin, for informal meals, and La Chèvre d'Or, known for its menu dégustation at 560F ($100.80).

18 Monaco

593 miles S of Paris, 11 miles E of Nice

Monaco, according to a famous quote from Somerset Maugham, is defined as 370 sunny acres peopled with shady characters. The outspoken Katharine Hepburn once called it "a pimple on the chin of the south of France." She wasn't referring to the principality's lack of beauty but rather to the preposterous idea of having a little country, a feudal anomaly, taking up some of the choicest coastline along the Riviera. Monaco became a property of the Grimaldi clan, a Genoese family, as early as 1297. With shifting loyalties, it has maintained something resembling independence ever since. In a fit of impatience the French annexed it in 1793, but the ruling family recovered it in 1814.

Hemmed in by France on three sides and facing the Mediterranean, tiny Monaco staunchly maintains its independence. Even Charles de Gaulle couldn't force Prince Rainier to do away with his tax-free policy. As almost everybody in an overburdened world knows by now, the Monégasques do not pay taxes. Nearly all their country's revenue comes from tourism and gambling.

Monaco—or rather its capital of Monte Carlo—has for a century been a symbol of glamour. Its legend was enhanced by the 1956 marriage of the world's most eligible bachelor, Prince Rainier III, to the American actress Grace Kelly. She had met the prince when she was in Cannes for the film festival to promote *To Catch a Thief*, the Hitchcock movie she made with Cary Grant; a journalist friend had arranged a *Paris*

Match photo shoot with the prince—and the rest is history. A daughter, Caroline, was born to the royal couple in 1957; a son, Albert, in 1958; and a second daughter, Stephanie, in 1965. The Monégasques welcomed the birth of Caroline but went wild at the birth of Albert, a male heir. According to a 1918 treaty, Monaco would become an autonomous state under French protection should the ruling dynasty become extinct. However, the fact that Albert is still a bachelor has the entire principality concerned.

Though not always happy in her role, Princess Grace soon won the respect and adoration of her people. In 1982 a sports car she was driving, with her daughter Stephanie as a passenger (not as the driver, as was viciously rumored), plunged over a cliff, killing Grace instantly. The Monégasques still mourn her death.

The second-smallest state in Europe (Vatican City is the tiniest), Monaco consists of four parts. The old town, **Monaco-Ville,** on a promontory, "the Rock," 200 feet high, is the seat of the royal palace and the government building, as well as the Oceanographic Museum. To the west of the bay, **La Condamine,** the home of the Monégasques, is at the foot of the old town, forming its harbor and port sector. Up from the port (walking is steep in Monaco) is **Monte Carlo,** once the playground of European royalty and still the center for wintering wealthy, the setting for the casino and its gardens and the deluxe hotels. The fourth part, **Fontvieille,** is a neat industrial suburb. Ironically, **Monte-Carlo Beach,** at the far frontier, is on French soil. It attracts a chic crowd, including movie stars in the skimpiest bikinis and thongs.

No one used to go to Monaco in summer, but now that has totally changed—in fact, July and August tend to be so crowded it's hard to get a room. Further, with the decline of royalty and multimillionaires, Monaco is developing a broader base of tourism (you can stay here moderately—but definitely not cheaply). The Monégasques very frankly court an affluent crowd. And at the casinos here you can also lose your shirt. "Suicide Terrace" at the casino, though not used as frequently as in the old days, is still a real temptation to many who have gambled away family fortunes.

Life still focuses around the Monte Carlo Casino, which has been the subject of countless legends and the setting for many films (remember Lucy Ricardo and the chip she found lying on the casino floor?). High drama is played to the fullest here. Depending on the era, you might've seen Mata Hari shooting a tsarist colonel with a jewel-encrusted revolver when he tried to slip his hand inside her bra to discover her secrets (military, not mammary). The late King Farouk, known as "The Swine," used to devour as many as 8 roast guinea hens and 50 oysters before losing thousands at the table. And Richard Burton presented Elizabeth Taylor with the obscenely huge Koh-i-noor diamond here.

ESSENTIALS

GETTING THERE   Monaco has rail, bus, and highway connections from other coastal cities, especially Nice. **Trains** arrive every 30 minutes from Cannes, Nice, Menton, and Antibes. For more rail information and schedules, call ☎ **08-36-35-35-39.** There are no border formalities for anyone entering Monaco from mainland France. Monaco is a rather lengthy **drive** from Paris. Take A6 south to Lyon. At Lyon, connect with A7 south to Aix-en-Provence; from here, take A6 south directly to Monaco. If you're already on the Riviera, drive from Nice along N7 northeast.

VISITOR INFORMATION   The **Direction du Tourisme** office is at 2A bd. des Moulins (☎ **92-16-61-16**).

TELEPHONE   If you're calling Monaco from within France, dial 00 (the new international access code for all international long-distance calls placed from mainland

Collection des Voitures Anciennes de S.A.S. 1e Prince de Monaco ❹

Jardin Exotique ❶

Monte Carlo Casino ❻

Musée d'Anthropologie Préhistorique ❷

Musée National de Monaco ❽

Musée de l'Océanographie ❺

Palais du Prince/Musée du Palais/Les Grands Appartements du Palais ❸

Sun Casino ❼

France), followed by Monaco's new country code, 377, and then the eight-digit local phone number. (Don't dial the 33 code; this is the country code for France and no longer applies to Monaco.) To call Monaco from North America, dial the international access code, 011, followed by the country code, 377, plus the local eight-digit Monaco number.

If you're calling France from within Monaco, dial all the necessary national codes. For example, to call Cannes, dial 00 (international access code), 33 (country code for France), 4 (without the zero), and the eight-digit number.

SPECIAL EVENTS Some of the most-watched car-racing events in Europe are held every January (**Le Rallye**) and May (the **Grand Prix**). One of the Riviera's most famous tennis tournaments takes place in mid-April.

FUN ON & OFF THE BEACH

BEACHES Just outside the border, on French (not Monacan) soil, the **Monte-Carlo Beach** adjoins the Monte-Carlo Beach Hotel, 22 av. Princesse-Grace

(☎ **04-93-28-66-66**). Permeated with intricate social rituals that might not be immediately visible to first-timers, the beach club has thrived for years as an integral part of Monaco's social life. Princess Grace used to come here in flowery swimsuits, greeting her friends and subjects with humor and style. The sand is replenished at regular intervals, and you'll find two large pools (one for children), beach cabanas, a restaurant, a cafe, and a bar. As the temperature drops in late August, expect the beach to close for the winter. The admission is 150F ($27). As usual, topless is acceptable but bottomless isn't.

Monaco itself, the quintessential kingdom by the sea, also offers sea bathing at its most popular beach, the **Plage de Larvotto,** off av. Princesse-Grace (☎ **93-30-63-84**). There's no charge for entering this strip of beach, whose sands are frequently replenished with sand hauled in by barge. The beach is open to public access at all hours.

GOLF The prestigious **Monte Carlo Golf Club,** Route N7, La Turbie (☎ **04-93-41-09-11**), on French soil, is a par-72 golf course with scenic panoramas. Certain perks (including use of electric golf buggies) are reserved for members. Before they're allowed to play, nonmembers are asked to show proof of membership in another golf club and provide evidence of their handicap ratings. Greens fees for 18 holes are 350F ($63) Monday through Friday and 450F ($81) Saturday and Sunday. Clubs can be rented for 120F ($21.60). The course is open daily from 8am to sunset.

SPA TREATMENTS In 1908 the Societé des Bains de Mer launched a seawater (thalassotherapy) spa in Monte Carlo. It was inaugurated by Prince Albert I himself. However, in World War II it was bombed and reopened only in 1996. **Les Thermes Marins de Monte-Carlo,** 2 av. de Monte-Carlo (☎ **04-92-16-40-40**), is one of the largest spas in Europe. Spread over four floors are a gigantic pool, a Turkish haman, a diet restaurant, a juice bar, two tanning booths, a fitness center, a beauty center, and private treatment rooms.

SWIMMING Of course, you can try the beaches mentioned above. But if you're looking for a pool instead, you might want to try these two. Built to overlook the yacht-clogged harbor, the stupendous **Stade Nautique Rainier-III,** quai Albert-1er, at La Condamine (☎ **93-15-28-75**), a pool frequented by the Monégasques, was a gift from the prince to his loyal subjects. It's open May to October daily from 9am to 7pm; closed the rest of the year. Admission is 25F ($4.50).

If you're not here in summer, you can still go swimming indoors. The **Piscine du Prince Héréditaire Albert** lies in the Stade Louis II, at 7 av. de Castellane (☎ **92-05-42-13**). It's open Monday, Tuesday, Thursday, and Friday from 7:30am to 2:30pm; Saturday from 2 to 6pm; and Sunday from 9am to 1pm. Closed in August. Admission is 15F ($2.70).

TENNIS & SQUASH The **Monte Carlo Country Club,** in France on av. Princesse-Grace, Roquebrune-St-Roman (☎ **04-93-41-30-15**), includes 23 tennis courts (21 clay and 2 concrete). The 215F ($38.70) entrance fee provides access to a restaurant, a health club with Jacuzzi and sauna, a putting green, a beach, squash courts, and the well-maintained tennis courts. Plan to spend at least half a day, ending a round of tennis with use of any of the other facilities. It's open daily from 8am to 8 or 9pm, depending on the season.

SHOPPING

Rising costs and an increase in crime have changed women's tastes in jewelry, perhaps forever. **Bijoux Cascio,** in Les Galeries du Métropole, 207 av. des Spélugues

(☎ **93-50-17-57**), sells only imitation gemstones. They're rather shamelessly copied from the real McCoys sold by Cartier and Van Cleef & Arpels. Made in Italy of gold-plated silver, the fake jewelry costs between 200F and 2,000F ($36 and $360).

Boutique du Rocher, 1 av. de la Madone (☎ **93-30-91-17**), is the largest of two roughly equivalent boutiques opened in 1966 by Princesse Grace as the official retail outlets of her charitable foundation. The organization merchandizes Monégasque and Provençal handcrafts. A short walk from place du Casino, the shop sells carved frames for pictures or mirrors; housewares; gift items crafted from porcelain, textiles, and wood; toys; and dolls. On the premises are workshops where local artisans produce the goods you find for sale.

Old River, 17 bd. des Moulins (☎ **93-50-33-85**), is a menswear store aiming at a middle-class crowd of men who simply want to dress appropriately and look good. You can pick up a swimsuit, shorts, slacks, a blazer, and a pair of socks to replace the ones you ruined by too many walking tours, at prices that won't require that you remortgage your house.

You don't have to be Princesse Caroline to be able to afford to shop in Monaco, especially now that **FNAC** (☎ **93-10-81-81**), a member of the big French chain that sells records, CDs, tapes, and books, has opened in the heart of town at the Centre Commercial Le Métropole, in the Jardins du Casino, alongside the Hôtel Métropole and across from the casino.

If you insist on ultrafancy stores, you'll find them cheek by jowl with the Hôtel de Paris and the casino and lining the streets leading to the Hôtel Hermitage or across from the gardens at the minimall Park Palace. **Allée Serge-Diaghilev** is just that, an alley, but a very tony one filled with designer shops.

There's also the **Centre Commercial,** 17 av. des Spélugues. It has a few specialty shops worth visiting (especially if you aren't going into France). Check out **Geneviève Lethu** (☎ **93-50-09-41**) for colorful and country tabletop design or **Manufacture de Monaco** (☎ **93-50-64-63**) for glorious bone china and elegant tabletop design. If the prices send you to bed, two doors away is a branch of the chic but often affordable French linen house **Yves Delorme** (☎ **93-50-08-70**). **Marché Royal** (☎ **93-15-05-04**) is a tiny gourmet grocery store down a set of curving stairs hidden in the side entrance of the mall; here you can buy gifts or stock up for *le picque-nique* or for your day trips. This market is open Monday to Saturday from 9am to 8pm.

For real-people shopping, stroll **rue Grimaldi,** the principality's main commercial street, near the fruit, flower, and food market (see below) and **boulevard des Moulins,** closer to the casino, where glamorous boutiques specialize in international chicness. There's also an all-pedestrian thoroughfare with shops less forbiddingly chic than those along boulevard des Moulins: **Rue Princesse-Caroline** is loaded with bakeries, flower shops, and the closest thing you'll find to funkiness in Monaco. Also check out the **Formule 1 shop,** 15 rue Grimaldi (☎ **93-15-92-44**), where everything from racing helmets to specialty key chains and t-shirts celebrates the roar of high-octane racing machines.

If you are looking for the heart and soul of the real Monaco, get away from the glitz and head to place des Armes for the **fruit, flower, and food market** held daily from 9am to noon; it has an indoor and an outdoor market complete with a fountain, cafes, and hand-painted vegetable tiles set beneath your feet. While the outdoor market packs up promptly at noon, some dealers at the indoor market stay open to 2pm. If you prefer bric-a-brac, there's a small but very funky (especially for Monaco) **flea market,** Les Puces de Fontvieille, held Saturday from 9am to 6pm at the Espace Fontvieille, a panoramic open-air site near the heliport in Monaco's Fontvieille district.

SEEING THE SIGHTS

Les Grands Appartements du Palais. Place du Palais. ☎ **93-25-18-31**. Combination ticket 40F ($7.20) adults, 20F ($3.60) children 8–14, free for children 7 and under. Palace, June–Sept daily 9:30am–6:30pm; Oct daily 10am–5pm. Closed Nov–May. Museum, June–Sept daily 9:30am–6:30pm; Oct–Nov 11 daily 10am–5pm; Dec 17–May Tues–Sun 10:30am–12:30pm and 2–5pm. Closed Nov 12–Dec 16.

During summer, most visitors—many over from Nice for the day—want to see the Italianate home of Monaco's royal family, the Palais du Prince, dominating the principality from "the Rock." When touring Les Grands Appartements, you're shown the Throne Room and allowed to see some of the art collection, including works by Brueghel and Holbein, as well as Princesse Grace's stunning state portrait. The palace was built in the 13th century, and part dates from the Renaissance. You're also shown the chamber where England's George III died. The ideal time to arrive is 11:55am to watch the 10-minute **Relève de la Garde** (changing of the guard).

In a wing of the palace, the **Musée du Palais du Prince (Souvenirs Napoléoniens et Collection d'Archives),** place du Palais (☎ **93-25-18-31**), contains a collection of mementos of Napoléon and Monaco itself. When the royal residence is closed, this museum is the only part of the palace the public can visit.

Jardin Exotique. Bd. du Jardin-Exotique. ☎ **93-30-33-65**. Admission to museum 40F ($7.20) adults, 18F ($3.25) children 6–18, free for children 5 and under. June–Sept daily 9am–7pm; Oct–May daily 9am–6pm.

Built on the side of a rock, the gardens are known for their cactus collection. They were begun by Prince Albert I, who was a naturalist and a scientist. He spotted some succulents growing in the palace gardens, and knowing that these plants were normally found only in Central America or Africa, he created the garden from them. You can also explore the grottoes here, as well as the **Musée d'Anthropologie Préhistorique** (☎ **93-15-80-06**). The view of the principality is splendid.

Musée de l'Océanographie. Av. St-Martin. ☎ **93-15-36-00**. Admission 60F ($10.80) adults, 30F ($5.40) children 6–18, free for children 5 and under. July–Aug daily 9am–8pm; Apr–June and Sept daily 9am–7pm; Mar and Oct daily 9:30am–7pm; Nov–Feb daily 10am–6pm.

This museum was founded in 1910 by Albert I, great-grandfather of the present prince. In the main rotunda is a statue of Albert in his favorite costume—that of a sea captain. Displayed are specimens he collected during 30 years of expeditions aboard his oceanographic ships. The aquarium—one of the finest in Europe—contains more than 90 tanks.

Prince Albert's collection is exhibited in the zoology room. Some of the exotic creatures here were unknown before he captured them. You'll see models of the oceanographic ships aboard which he directed his scientific cruises from 1885 to 1914. The most important part of its laboratory has been preserved and reconstituted as closely as possible. The cupboards contain all the equipment and documentation necessary for a scientific expedition. Skeletons of specimens are on the main floor, including a giant whale that drifted ashore at Pietra Ligure in 1896—it's believed to be the same one the prince harpooned earlier that year. The skeleton is remarkable for its healed fractures sustained when a vessel struck the animal as it was drifting asleep on the surface. An exhibition devoted to the discovery of the ocean is in the physical-oceanography room on the first floor. Underwater movies are shown continuously in the lecture room.

Collection des Voitures Anciennes de S.A.S. le Prince de Monaco. Les Terrasses de Fontvieille. ☎ **92-05-28-56**. Admission 30F ($5.40) adults, 15F ($2.70) students and children 8–14, free for children 7 and under. Daily 10am–6pm.

Prince Rainier III has opened a showcase of his private collection of more than 100 exquisitely restored vintage autos, including the 1956 Rolls-Royce Silver Cloud that carried the prince and princess on their wedding day. It was given to the royal couple by Monaco shopkeepers as a wedding present. A 1952 Austin Taxi on display was once used as the royal "family car." Other exhibits are a Woodie, a 1937 Ford station wagon once used by Prince Louis II when on hunting trips, and a 1925 Bugatti 35B, winner of the Monaco Grand Prix in 1929. Other outstanding autos are a 1903 De Dion Bouton and a 1986 Lamborghini Countach.

Musée National de Monaco. 17 av. Princesse-Grace. ☎ **93-30-91-26.** Admission 26F ($4.70) adults, 15F ($2.70) children 6–14, free for children 5 and under. Easter–Sept daily 10am–6:30pm; Oct–Easter daily 10am–12:15pm and 2:30–6:30pm.

This museum features "automatons and dolls of yesterday," along with sculptures in the rose garden. In a villa designed by Charles Garnier (architect of Paris's Opéra Garnier), this museum houses one of the world's greatest collections of mechanical toys and dolls. See especially the 18th-century Neapolitan crib, which contains some 200 figures. This collection, assembled by Mme de Galea, was presented to the principality in 1972; it stemmed from the 18th- and 19th-century trend of displaying new fashions on doll models.

WHERE TO STAY
VERY EXPENSIVE

✪ **Hôtel de Paris.** Place du Casino, 98000 Monaco. ☎ **92-16-30-00.** Fax 93-16-38-50. www.sbm.mc. E-mail: hp@sbm.mc. 180 units. A/C MINIBAR TV TEL. 2,100–3,200F ($378–$576) double; 5,700–9,000F ($1,026–$1,620) suite. AE, DC, MC, V. Parking 180F ($32.40).

On the resort's ornate main plaza, opposite the casino, this is one of the world's most famous hotels and most spectacular beaux-arts monuments. Linked with the sybaritic, high-spending image of Monte Carlo, it's the principality's choice address, more famous and legendary even than the Hermitage. At least two dozen movie companies have used its lobby as a background. The ornate facade has marble pillars, and the impressive lounge has an Art Nouveau rose window at the peak of the dome. The hotel is furnished with a dazzling decor that includes marble pillars, statues, crystal chandeliers, sumptuous carpets, Louis XVI chairs, and a wall-size fin-de-siècle mural. The guest rooms are fashionable and, in many cases, sumptuous. Unlike most hotels, the rooms opening onto the sea aren't as spacious as those in the rear.

Dining: The evening usually begins in the bar. The hotel's most famous dining options are Le Louix XV (see below) and Le Grill. Both restaurants benefit from a collection of rare fine wines kept in a dungeon chiseled out of the rocks. The less formal Restaurant Côté Jardin offers a daily lunch buffet whose rich offerings are inspired by the Mediterranean.

Amenities: Thermes Marins spa, directly connected to both the Hôtel de Paris and the Hôtel Hermitage, offers complete cures of thalassotherapy under medical supervision, (including "antismoking," "anticellulite thighs," and "postnatal" cures); a large indoor pool; two saunas; fitness center; beauty center; room service; concierge; babysitting; valet parking.

✪ **Hôtel Hermitage.** Square Beaumarchais, 98005 Monaco CEDEX. ☎ **92-16-40-00.** Fax 92-16-38-52. www.sbm.mc. 227 units. A/C MINIBAR TV TEL. 1,600–2,900F ($288–$522) double; from 4,300F ($774) suite. High-season rates charged during Christmas, New Year's, Easter, and July–Aug. AE, DC, MC, V. Parking 120F ($21.60).

Picture yourself sitting in a wicker armchair, being served drinks under an ornate stained-glass dome with an encircling wrought-iron balcony. You can do this at the clifftop Hermitage, with its "wedding cake" facade. The "palace" was the creation of

Jean Marquet (who created marquetry). Large brass beds anchor every room, wherein decoratively framed doors open onto balconies. You have a choice of rooms in the Prince wing, where accommodations are more traditional and old-fashioned, or in the more modern Costa or Excelsior wing, with a choice of either contemporary or period furnishings. The most expensive rooms open onto the water.

Dining/Diversions: The stylish dining room has Corinthian columns and chandeliers and serves a refined modern cuisine. The Bar Terrasse is a chic rendezvous that at night is a piano bar.

Amenities: Concierge, room service, massage, maid service, gym, Jacuzzi, sauna, tennis courts, 18-hole golf course.

MODERATE

Hôtel Alexandra. 33 bd. Princesse-Charlotte, 98000 Monaco. ☎ **93-50-63-13.** Fax 92-16-06-48. 56 units. A/C TV TEL. 800–850F ($144–$153) double. AE, DC, MC, V. Parking 45F ($8.10) per day.

The Alexandra attracts those who'd like to visit the principality without spending a fortune. This hotel is in the center of the business district, on a busy and often-noisy street corner. Its comfortably furnished guest rooms don't generate much excitement, but they're reliable and respectable.

INEXPENSIVE

Hôtel Cosmopolite. 4 rue de la Turbie, 98000 Monaco. ☎ **93-30-16-95.** Fax 93-30-23-05. 24 units, none with toilet, all with sink, some with shower. 222F ($39.95) double without shower or toilet, 310F ($55.80) double with shower but without toilet. No credit cards. Free parking on street.

When it was built in the 1930s, this hotel was sited in the then-fashionable neighborhood a few steps downhill from the railway station. Today it's an appealingly dowdy Art Deco monument with three floors, no elevator, and comfortable but anonymous-looking rooms. Mme Gay Angèle, the English-speaking owner, is proud of her "Old Monaco" establishment. Her more expensive rooms have showers, but the cheapest way to stay here is to request a room without a shower—there are adequate facilities in the hallway.

Hôtel de France. 6 rue de la Turbie, 98000 Monaco. ☎ **93-30-24-64.** Fax 92-16-13-34. 26 units. TV TEL. 380F ($68.40) double; 450F ($81) triple. V. Parking 40F ($7.20).

Not all Monégasques are rich, as a stroll along this street will convince you. Here you'll find some of the cheapest living and eating places in the high-priced principality. This 19th-century hotel, 3 minutes from the rail station, has modest furnishings but is clean and comfortable.

WHERE TO DINE
VERY EXPENSIVE

✪ **Le Louis XV.** In the Hôtel de Paris, place du Casino. ☎ **92-16-30-01.** Fax 92-16-69-21. Reservations recommended. Jacket and tie required for men. Main courses 195–755F ($35.10–$135.90); fixed-price menus 810–920F ($145.80–$165.60). AE, DC, MC, V. Thurs–Mon noon–2pm, Wed–Mon 8–10pm. Closed Dec 8 to mid-Feb. FRENCH/ITALIAN.

On the lobby level of the five-star Hôtel de Paris, the three-star and astoundingly expensive Louis XV offers what one critic called "down-home Riviera cooking within a Fabergé egg." Despite the place's regal trappings (or as a reaction against them?), the culinary star chef/namesake Alain Ducasse creates a refined but not overly adorned cuisine, which is served by the finest staff in Monaco. Ducasse has claimed that the real gastronomic genius is Mother Nature and that "more than half of my cuisine is the quality of her products." Everything is light, attuned to the seasons, with an intelligent and modern interpretation of both Provençal and northern Italian dishes. Surprisingly, he dares to serve "a fish from the local catch of the day cooked whole as one likes it on the Riviera, dotted with bits of oil and butter and a little bitter." Begin, perhaps, with his arugula ravioli with crisp slices of deep-fried artichoke and sheep-milk curd, all in a beef consommé. The flavors and textures of every dish come shooting out at you, including such delights as large prawns roasted and placed on slivers of artichoke and strips of rhubarb (yes, rhubarb). His soft, fresh pasta with black truffles, fresh basil leaves, and tomatoes prepared in three different ways is without equal on the Riviera. The service is superb. Ducasse is now dividing his time between this glittering enclave and his new restaurant in Paris. The latter also wins three stars, making the celebrated chef the only Michelin six-star chef in France.

EXPENSIVE

Café de Paris. Place du Casino. ☎ **92-16-20-20.** Main courses 88–200F ($15.85–$36). AE, DC, MC, V. Daily 8am–4am (last order at 2am). INTERNATIONAL.

Frankly, we've always found this place cramped, glittery, and relatively devoid of charm, but it provides one of the best front-row seats in town for observing the non-stop carnival that is Monte Carlo. Set across from the casino and the Hôtel de Paris, it's owned by the Société des Bains de Mer and was completely rebuilt in the late 1980s, when a reproduction belle époque–style brasserie was created. Come here for an ongoing jangle of about a hundred slot machines, English-style or continental breakfasts, and brasserie-style meals that begin at noon and are served continuously throughout the afternoon until very late in the evening. The premises also contains the Monte Carlo branch of Le Drugstore, that trendsetting and somewhat claustrophobic temple to impulse buying that seems to have changed little since the concept made its debut in Paris in the 1970s.

INEXPENSIVE

Stars 'n Bars. 6 quai Antoine-1er. ☎ **93-50-95-95.** Reservations recommended. Sandwiches 50–75F ($9–$13.50); dinner salads and platters 70–130F ($12.60–$23.40). AE, DC, MC, V. Tues–Sun 11am–midnight. AMERICAN.

Modeled on the sports bars popular in the States, this place features two distinct dining and drinking areas devoted to American-style food, as well as a third-floor space, The Club, which is a sports bar with memorabilia donated by many athletes of note and even a disco every night after 10:30pm (sometimes with live performances). No one will mind if you drop in just for a drink—they cost a hefty 40F to 80F ($7.20 to $14.40) each—but if you're hungry, menu items read like an homage to the macho American experience. Try an Indy 500 or a Triathlon salad, a Wimbledon or a Slam Dunk sandwich, or a breakfast of champions (eggs and bacon and all the fixings). If your children happen to be in tow and are feeling nostalgic for the ballpark back home, order a little leaguer's platter (for those under 12). Unless an artist of international note appears, there's never a cover charge.

MONACO AFTER DARK

The ✪ **Monte Carlo Casino,** place du Casino (☎ **92-16-21-21**), is the most famous in the world. Over the years, it's attracted the exiled aristocracy of Russia, Sarah Bernhardt, Mata Hari, King Farouk, and Aly Khan (Onassis used to own a part interest). The architect of Paris's Opéra Garnier, Charles Garnier, built the oldest part of the casino, and it remains an extravagant example of the 19th century's most opulent architecture. It's rather schizophrenically divided into an area devoted to the casino and other different kinds of nighttime entertainment, including a theater (see below) presenting opera and ballet.

Baccarat, roulette, and chemin-de-fer are the most popular games, though you can play le craps and blackjack as well.

Salle Américaine, containing only Las Vegas–style slot machines, opens at noon, as do doors for roulette and *trente-quarente.* A section for roulette and chemin-de-fer opens at 3pm. Most of the facilities inside are operational by 4pm, when additional rooms open with more roulette, craps, and blackjack. The gambling continues until very late/early, the closing depending on the crowd. The casino classifies its "private rooms" as the more demure, nonelectronic areas devoid of slot machines. To enter the casino, you must carry a passport, be at least 21, and pay an admission of between 50F and 100F ($9 and $18), depending on where you want to go. In lieu of a passport, an identity card or driver's license will suffice. After 9pm, the staff will insist that gentlemen wear jackets for entrance into the private rooms.

The premises also contains a **Cabaret in the Casino Gardens,** where the show is usually preceded by the music of a well-rehearsed orchestra. A sexy cabaret featuring lots of feathers, glitter, jazz dance, ballet, and Riviera-style seminudity is presented at 10pm Wednesday to Monday from mid-September to the end of June. If you want dinner as part of the show, service begins at 9pm and, with the show included, costs 420F ($75.60) per person. If you want to see just the show, your drinks will cost from 150F ($27) each! For reservations, call ☎ **92-16-36-36.**

In the casino's **Salle Garnier,** where lots of gilt and belle époque accents evoke the 19th-century opera house of Paris, concerts are held periodically; for information, contact the tourist office (see above) or the Atrium du Casino. The music is usually classical, featuring the Orchestre Philharmonique de Monte Carlo.

The casino also contains the **Opéra de Monte-Carlo,** whose patron is Prince Rainier. This world-famous house, opened in 1879 by Sarah Bernhardt, presents a winter and spring repertoire that traditionally includes Puccini, Mozart, and Verdi. The famed Ballets Russes de Monte-Carlo, starring Nijinsky and Karsavina, was created in 1918 by Sergei Diaghilev. The national orchestra and ballet company of Monaco appear here. Tickets can be hard to come by; your best bet is to ask your hotel concierge. You can make inquiries about tickets on your own at the Atrium du Casino (☎ **92-16-22-99**), open Tuesday to Sunday from 10am to 12:15pm and 2 to 5:30pm. Standard tickets are 100F to 600F ($18 to $108).

Sun Casino, in the Loews Monte-Carlo, 12 av. des Spélugues (☎ **93-50-65-00**), is a huge room filled with one-armed bandits. It also features blackjack, craps, and American roulette. Additional slot machines are available on the roof starting at 11am—for those who want to gamble with a wider view of the sea. It's open daily from 4pm to 4am (to 5am for slot machines). Admission is free.

Tiffany, av. des Spélugues (☎ **93-50-53-13**), is a favorite of the 25- to 40-year-old crowd who like a glamorous modern setting. On Sunday a bevy of showgirls is featured. Cover is 100F ($18) with first drink included. **Le Symbole,** rue du Portier (☎ **93-25-09-25**), is a hot spot for those over 30. The decor glitters in a high-tech gloss, and the music is disco. Free admission.

Les Folies Russes, in the Loews Monte-Carlo, 12 av. des Spélugues (☎ **93-50-65-00**), is a dinner-dance cabaret. Many viewers like its shows much more than those staged at the cabaret of the Monte Carlo casino. Vaudeville acts are thrown in to ease the "monotony" of all those nude dancers. There's a dinner dance Tuesday to Saturday with food served from 8:30 to 9:30pm, and a floor show, La Folie Russe, is presented Tuesday to Sunday at 11pm. Jackets for men are mandatory. The show with dinner is 580F ($104.40); 250F ($45) gets you only the show.

19 Roquebrune & Cap-Martin

Roquebrune: 592 miles S of Paris, 3 miles W of Menton, 36 miles NE of Cannes, 2 miles E of Monaco; Cap-Martin: 3 miles W of Menton, 1½ miles W of Roquebrune

Roquebrune, along the Grande Corniche, is a charming mountain village with vaulted streets. It has been restored, though some critics have found the restoration artificial. Today its rue Moncollet is lined with artists' workshops and boutiques with inflated merchandise.

Three miles west of Menton, Cap-Martin is a satellite of the larger resort that's been associated with the rich and famous since the empress Eugénie wintered there in the 19th century. In time the resort was honored by the presence of Sir Winston Churchill, who came here often in his final years. Two famous men died here—William Butler Yeats in 1939 and Le Corbusier, who drowned while swimming off the cape in 1965. Don't expect to find a wide sandy beach—you'll encounter plenty of rocks, against a backdrop of pine and olive trees.

ESSENTIALS

GETTING THERE   Cap-Martin has **train and bus connections** from the other cities of the Mediterranean coast, including Nice and Menton. To reach Roquebrune, you'll have to take a taxi or bus from the small rail station at Cap-Martin or the nearby hamlet of Carnoles. From Cap-Martin or Carnoles, buses to Roquebrune travel at 15-minute intervals along the length of RN7, stopping in Roquebrune en route. They're marked DIRECTION MENTON; buses from the rail station of Menton headed for Roquebrune are marked DIRECTION NICE. If you arrive by TGV from any other city in France, you'll be routed through Menton and not through Cap-Martin or Carnoles. For more information and schedules, call ☎ **08-36-35-35-39.** To **drive** to Roquebrune and Cap-Martin, follow N7 16 miles east of Nice.

VISITOR INFORMATION   The **Office de Tourisme** is at 20 av. Paul-Doumer in Roquebrune (☎ **04-93-35-62-87**).

SEEING THE SIGHTS

IN ROQUEBRUNE   It'll take you about an hour to explore Roquebrune. You can stroll through its colorful covered streets, which retain their authentic look even though the buildings are now devoted to handcrafts, gift and souvenir shops, or art galleries. From the parking lot at place de la République, you can head for place des Deux-Frères, turning left into rue Grimaldi. Then head left to **rue Moncollet.** This long, narrow street is covered with stepped passageways and filled with houses that date from the Middle Ages, most often with barred windows. Rue Moncollet leads into **rue du Château,** where you may want to explore the château.

The only one of its kind, **Château de Roquebrune** (☎ **04-93-35-07-22**) was originally a 10th-century Carolingian castle; the present structure dates in part from the 13th century. Dominated by two square towers, it houses a historic museum. From the towers there's a panoramic view along the coast to Monaco. The castle gates are open daily from 10am to noon and 2 to 6pm. Admission is 20F ($3.60) for adults, 15F ($2.70) for seniors, and 10F ($1.80) for students and children. From mid-September to mid-June it's open daily from 10am to noon and 2 to 6pm (to 7pm the rest of the year).

Rue du Château leads to place William-Ingram. After crossing this square, you reach rue de la Fontaine. Take a left. This will lead you to the **Olivier millénaire** ("millennary olive tree"), said to be one of the oldest in the world, having survived for at least 1,000 years.

Back on rue du Château you can reach **Eglise Ste-Marguerite,** which hides behind a relatively common baroque facade. But this exterior merely masks the church from the 12th century. It's not entirely from that time, however, having seen many alterations over the years. The interior is of polychrome plaster. Look for two paintings by a local artist, Marc-Antoine Otto, who in the 17th century painted a Crucifixion (in the second altar) and a Pietà (above the entrance door).

IN CAP-MARTIN   Cap-Martin is a rich suburb. At the center of the cape is a feudal tower that's today a telecommunications relay station. At its base you can still see the ruins of the **Basilique St-Martin,** the only evidence remaining of a priory constructed here by the monks of the Lérins Islands in the 11th century. After repeated pirate raids in the centuries to come, notably around the 15th century, it was destroyed and abandoned. If you follow the road (by car) along the eastern shoreline of the cape, you'll be rewarded with a view of Menton set against a backdrop of mountains. In the far distance looms the coastline of the Italian Riviera, and you can see as far as the resort of Bordighera.

Although it takes about 3 hours, you can take one of the most interesting walks along the Riviera here. The coastal path, called **Sentier Touristique,** leads from Cap-Martin to Monte Carlo Beach. If you have a car, you can park it in the lot at av. Winston-Churchill and begin your promenade. The path is marked by a sign labeled PROMENADE LE CORBUSIER. As you go along you'll be able to take in a view of Monaco set in a natural amphitheater. In the far distance, you'll view Cap-Ferrat and even Roquebrune with its château. The scenic path comes to an end at Monte Carlo Beach.

If you have a car, you can also take a **scenic 6-mile drive,** taking about an hour. Leave by D23, following the signs to Gorbio, a perched village on a hill and reached by this narrow, winding road. Along the way you'll pass homes of the wealthy and view a verdant setting with pines and silvery olives. The site is wild and rocky, the buildings having been constructed as a safe haven from pirate attacks. The most interesting street is rue Garibaldi, which leads past an old church to a panoramic belvedere.

WHERE TO STAY

Hôtel Victoria. 7 promenade du Cap, 06190 Roquebrune/Cap-Martin. ☎ **04-93-35-65-90.** Fax 04-93-28-27-02. 32 units. A/C MINIBAR TV TEL. 418–588F ($75.25–$105.85) double. Rates include breakfast. AE, DC, V. Parking 30F ($5.40).

This rectangular low-rise building is set behind a garden in front of the beach. Built in the 1970s, it was renovated in the mid-1990s in a neoclassical style that weds tradition and modernity. The casual bar/lounge near the entrance sets a stylishly relaxed tone. Breakfast is the only meal served.

✪ **Hôtel Vista Palace.** Grande Corniche, 06190 Roquebrune/Cap-Martin. ☎ **800/223-6800** in the U.S., or 04-92-10-40-00. Fax 04-93-35-18-94. E-mail: vistapalace@ webstore.fr. 71 units. A/C MINIBAR TV TEL. 950–2,300F ($171–$414) double; from 2,000F ($360) suite. AE, DC, MC, V. Parking 100F ($18) in garage.

This extraordinary hotel/restaurant stands on the outer ridge of the mountains running parallel to the coast, giving an "airplane view" of Monaco that's spectacular. And the design of the Vista Palace is just as fantastic: three levels are cantilevered out into space so every room seems to float. Nearly all the rooms have balconies facing the Mediterranean.

Dining: If you don't want to stay here, at least consider stopping by for a meal—it's expensive but worth it. Le Vistaero is open daily from noon to 2pm and 8 to 10pm; three fixed-price menus are available featuring Mediterranean cuisine envied by the region's other restaurateurs.

Amenities: Pool, sauna, masseuse, indoor squash court, fitness center, boutique, helipad, and 9-acre landscaped Mediterranean garden.

WHERE TO DINE

You might also like to try **Le Vistaero** at the Hôtel Vista Palace (see above).

Au Grand Inquisiteur. 18 rue du Château. ☎ **04-93-35-05-37.** Reservations required. Main courses 82–135F ($14.75–$24.30); fixed-price menus 147F and 243F ($26.45 and $43.75). MC, V. Wed–Sun noon–1:30pm and Tues–Sun 7:30–10pm. Closed Nov–Dec 25. FRENCH.

This culinary find is a miniature restaurant in a two-room cellar near the top of the medieval mountaintop village of Roquebrune. On the steep, winding road to the château, this climate-controlled building is made of rough-cut stone, with large oak beams. The cuisine, though not the area's most distinguished, is quite good, especially the chef's duck special or scallops meunière. Most diners opt for one of the fresh fish choices. The wine list is exceptional—some 150 selections, most at reasonable prices.

20 Menton

596 miles S of Paris, 39 miles NE of Cannes, 5 miles E of Monaco

Menton is more Italianate than French. Right at the border of Italy, Menton marks the eastern frontier of the Côte d'Azur. Its climate, incidentally, is the warmest on the Mediterranean coast, which attracts a large, rather elderly British colony throughout the winter. Because these senior citizens form a large part of the population of 130,000, Menton today is called "the Fort Lauderdale of France." Menton experiences a foggy day every 10 years—or so they say.

According to a local legend, Eve was the first to experience Menton's glorious climate. Expelled from the Garden of Eden along with Adam, she tucked a lemon in her bosom, planting it at Menton because it reminded her of her former stomping grounds. The lemons still grow in profusion here, and the fruit of that tree is given a position of honor at the Lemon Festival in February. Actually, the oldest Menton visitor may have arrived 30,000 years ago. He's still around—or at least his skull is—in the Municipal Museum.

Don't be misled by all those "palace-hotels" studding the hills. No longer open to the public, they've been divided up and sold as private apartments. Many of these turn-of-the-century structures were erected to accommodate elderly Europeans, mainly English and German, who arrived carrying a book written by one Dr. Bennett in which he extolled the joys of living at Menton.

ESSENTIALS

GETTING THERE Many visitors arrive by **car** along one of the corniche roads. More specifically, you can follow N7 east from Nice and arrive within 45 minutes.

There are good **bus and rail connections** that make stops at each resort along the Mediterranean coast, including Menton. Two trains per hour pull in from Nice (trip time: 35 minutes), and two trains per hour from Monte Carlo (trip time: 10 minutes). For rail information and schedules, call ☎ **08-36-35-35-39.** A local company, **Autocars Broch** (☎ **04-93-31-10-52**), runs buses between Nice and Menton, one almost every hour. The same frequent bus service is offered between Monte Carlo and Menton. **Rapide Côte d'Azur** also offers bus service (☎ **04-93-85-64-44**).

VISITOR INFORMATION The **Office de Tourisme** is in the Palais de l'Europe, 8 av. Boyer (☎ **04-92-41-76-76**).

EXPLORING THE TOWN

On the Golfe de la Paix (Gulf of Peace), Menton, which used to belong to Monaco, is on a rocky promontory, dividing the bay in two. The fishing town, the older part with narrow streets, is in the east; the tourist zone and residential beltare in the west.

Menton's beaches stretch for 2 miles between the Italian border and the city limits of Roquebrune and are interrupted only by the town's old and new ports. Collectively, they're known as **La Plage de la Promenade du Soleil** and with rare exceptions are public and free. Don't expect soft sands or even any sand at all; as the beaches are narrow, covered with gravel (or more charitably, big pebbles), and notoriously uncomfortable to lie on. Don't expect big waves or tides either. Who goes there? In the words of one nonswimming resident, mostly Parisians or residents of northern France, who are grateful for any escape from their urban milieux. Topless bathing is widespread, but complete nudity is forbidden.

Unlike in Cannes, where tens of thousands of chaises pepper the beaches, there aren't many options in Menton for renting mattresses and parasols; most people bring their own. Two exceptions are **Le Splendid Plage** (☎ **04-93-35-60-97**) and **Les Sablettes** (☎ **04-93-35-44-77**), both charging around 50F ($9) for use of a mattress. They're immediately to the east of the Vieux Port.

Musée Jean-Cocteau. Bastion du Port, quai Napoléon-III. ☎ **04-93-57-72-30.** Free admission. Wed–Mon 10am–noon and 2–6pm.

The writer/artist/filmmaker Jean Cocteau liked Menton, and this museum, in a 17th-century fort, contains the death portrait of Cocteau sketched by MacAvoy, as well as MacAvoy's portrait of Cocteau. Some of the artist's memorabilia is here—stunning charcoals and watercolors, ceramics, signed letters, and 21 brightly colored pastels.

La Salle des Mariages. In the Hôtel de Ville (town hall), rue de la République. ☎ **04-92-10-50-50.** Admission 5F (90¢). Mon–Fri 8:30am–12:30pm and 1:30–5pm.

Here Cocteau painted frescoes depicting the legend of Orpheus and Eurydice, among other things. A tape in English helps explain them. The room contains red-leather seats and leopard-skin rugs and is used for civil marriage ceremonies.

Musée de Préhistoire Régionale. Rue Lorédan-Larchey. ☎ **04-93-35-84-64.** Free admission. Wed–Mon 10am–noon and 2–6pm.

This collection presents human evolution on the Côte d'Azur for the past million years. It emphasizes the prehistoric era, including the 25,000-year-old head of the Nouvel Homme de Menton (sometimes known as "Grimaldi Man") found in 1884 in the Baousse-Rousse caves. Audiovisual aids, dioramas, and videocassettes enhance the exhibition.

Musée des Beaux-Arts. Palais Carnoles, 3 av. de la Madone. ☎ **04-93-35-49-71.** Free admission. Wed–Mon 10am–noon and 2–6pm.

Here you'll find 14th-, 16th-, and 17th-century paintings from Italy, Flanders, Holland, and the French schools, as well as modern paintings, including works by Dufy, Valadon, Derain, and Leprin—all acquired by a British subject, Wakefield-Mori.

WHERE TO STAY

Hôtel Aiglon. 7 av. de la Madone, 06500 Menton. ☎ **04-93-57-55-55.** Fax 04-93-35-92-39. 30 units. A/C MINIBAR TV TEL. 420–755F ($75.60–$135.90) double; 750–1,010F ($135–$181.80) suite. Half board 380–676F ($68.40–$121.70) per person extra. AE, DC, MC, V. Closed Nov 4–Dec 20.

A gem along the coast, this three-star hotel was coverted from a stately Riviera villa. In a large park filled with Mediterranean vegetation, it offers a more intimate and homelike environment than any other hotel in Menton in its league. The former private residence has been skillfully converted to receive guests, and each room is tastefully furnished. The magnet of the hotel is a heated pool surrounded by a 1900 veranda. The garden setting is beautifully maintained, and other facilities include a solarium and a children's game area. An excellent Provençal and international cuisine is offered in a restaurant with windows opening onto the pool and garden.

Hôtel Princess et Richmond. 617 promenade du Soleil, 06500 Menton. ☎ **04-93-35-80-20.** Fax 04-93-57-40-20. www.oda.fr/aa/hotel-princess. E-mail: princess.hotel@wanadoo.fr. 46 units. A/C MINIBAR TV TEL. 350–575F ($63–$103.50) double; 690–850F ($124.20–$153) suite. AE, DC, V. Parking 40F ($7.20). Closed Nov 7–Dec 18.

At the edge of the sea near the commercial district, this hotel boasts a facade of warm Mediterranean colors, with a sunny garden terrace. The owner rents comfortable soundproofed rooms with modern and French traditional furnishings and balconies. Drinks are served on the roof terrace, where you can enjoy a view of the curving shoreline. A restaurant in the garden of the nearby Hôtel Aiglon, under the same ownership, offers lunch and dinner beside a heated pool you may use as well. There's also an open-air Jacuzzi, plus a small fitness room in the solarium. The staff organizes sightseeing excursions.

WHERE TO DINE

✪ **La Calanque.** 13 square Victoria. ☎ **04-93-35-83-15.** Reservations required. Main courses 85–95F ($15.30–$17.10); fixed-price menus 97–140F ($17.45–$25.20). MC, V. Daily noon–2:30pm and 7:15–11pm. FRENCH/SEAFOOD.

Of the restaurants along the port, La Calanque is the best for the budget. In fair weather, tables are set under shade trees in full view of the harbor. We recommend the spaghetti napolitaine, tripe niçoise, *soupe de poissons* (fish soup), and fresh sardines (grilled over charcoal and very savory), with the focus on locally harvested seafood. Two specialties are bouillabaisse and barba giuan, small biscuits cooked in olive oil after having been stuffed with a variety of local greens.

Petit Port. 1 place Fontana. ☎ **04-93-35-82-62.** Reservations recommended. Main courses 80–130F ($14.40–$23.40); fixed-price lunch 85F ($15.30); fixed-price menus 120–150F ($21.60–$27). AE, MC, V. Sept 16–Jan 14 Thurs–Tues noon–3pm and 7pm–midnight; Jan 15–Sept 15 daily noon–3pm and 7pm–midnight. FRENCH.

Small and charming, employing many members of an extended family, this restaurant serves well-prepared portions of fresh fish in a century-old house near the medieval port. Everything is homemade, even the bread. Specialties are grilled sardines (succulent and increasingly difficult to find), fish soup, several kinds of grilled meats and fish, and (in honor of the northern France origins of its owner) tripe in the style of Caen. The place prides itself on its location—less than a mile from the Italian border.

Appendix A

Glossary of Useful Terms

A well-known character is the American or lapsed Canadian who returns from a trip to France and denounces the ever-so-rude French. But it is often amazing how a word or two of halting French will change their dispositions. At the very least, try to learn a few numbers, basic greetings, and—above all—the life raft, "Parlez-vous anglais?" ("Do you speak English?"). As it turns out, many people do speak a passable English and will use it liberally, if you demonstrate the basic courtesy of greeting them in their language. Go out, try our glossary on, and don't be bashful. *Bonne chance!*

BASICS

English	French	Pronunciation
Yes / No	Oui / Non	wee / nohn
OK	D'accord	dah-*core*
Please	S'il vous plaît	seel voo *play*
Thank you	Merci	mair-*see*
You're welcome	De rien	duh ree-*ehn*
Hello (during daylight hours)	Bonjour	bohn-*jhoor*
Good evening	Bonsoir	bohn-*swahr*
Good-bye	Au revoir	o ruh-*vwahr*
What's your name?	Comment vous appellez-vous?	ko-mahn-voo-za-pell-ay-*voo?*
My name is	Je m'appelle	jhuh ma-*pell*
Happy to meet you	Enchanté(e)	ohn-shahn-*tay*
How are you?	Comment allez-vous?	kuh-mahn-tahl-ay-*voo?*
Fine, thank you, and you?	Très bien, merci, et vous?	tray bee-ehn, mare-ci, ay *voo?*
So-so	Comme ci, comme ça	kum-*see*, kum-*sah*
I'm sorry / excuse me	Pardon	pahr-*dohn*
I'm so very sorry	Désolé(e)	day-zoh-*lay*
That's all right	Il n'y a pas de quoi	eel nee ah pah duh *kwah*

GETTING AROUND/STREET SMARTS

English	French	Pronunciation
Do you speak English?	Parlez-vous anglais?	par-lay-voo-ahn-*glay?*
I don't speak French	Je ne parle pas français	jhuh ne parl pah frahn-*say*
I don't understand	Je ne comprends pas	jhuh ne kohm-*prahn* pas
Could you speak more loudly / more slowly?	Pouvez-vous parler un peu plus fort / plus lentement?	Poo-*vay* voo par-lay un puh ploo for / ploo lan-te-*ment?*
Could you repeat that?	Répetez, s'il vous plait	ray-pay-*tay,* seel voo *play*
What is it?	Qu'est-ce que c'est?	kess-kuh-*say?*
What time is it?	Qu'elle heure est-il?	kel uhr eh-*teel?*
What?	Quoi?	kwah?
How? *or* What did you say?	Comment?	ko-*mahn?*
When?	Quand?	kahn?
Where is?	Où est?	ooh-eh?
Who?	Qui?	kee?
Why?	Pourquoi?	poor-*kwah?*
Here / There	ici / là	ee-*see* / lah
Left / Right	à gauche / à droite	a goash / a drwaht
Straight ahead	tout droit	too-drwah
I'm American / Canadian / British	Je suis amèricain(e) / canadien(e) / anglais(e)	jhe sweez a-may-ree-*kehn*/ can-ah-dee-*en* / ahn-*glay* (*glaise*)
Fill the tank (of a car), please	Le plein, s'il vous plaît	luh plan, seel-voo-*play*
I'm going to	Je vais à	jhe vay ah
I want to get off at	Je voudrais descendre à	jhe voo-*dray* day-son drah-ah
I'm sick	Je suis malade	jhuh swee mal-*ahd*
airport	l'aéroport	lair-o-*por*
bank	la banque	lah bahnk
bridge	pont	pohn
bus station	la gare routière	lah gar roo-tee-*air*
bus stop	l'arrêt de bus	lah-*ray* duh boohss
by means of a bicycle	en vélo/par bicyclette	uh *vay*-low, par bee-see-*clet*
by means of a car	en voiture	ahn vwa-*toor*
cashier	la caisse	lah *kess*
cathedral	cathédral	ka-tay-*dral*
church	église	ay-*gleez*
dead end	une impasse	ewn am-*pass*
driver's license	permis de conduire	per-*mee* duh con-*dweer*
elevator	l'ascenseur	lah sahn *seuhr*
entrance (to a building or a city)	une porte	ewn port
exit (from a building or a freeway)	une sortie	ewn sor-*tee*
gasoline	du pétrol / de l'essence	duh pay-*trol* / de lay-*sahns*
ground floor	rez-de-chausée	ray-de-show-*say*
highway to	la route pour	la root por
hospital	l'hôpital	low-pee-*tahl*

insurance	les assurances	lez ah-sur-*ahns*
luggage storage	consigne	kohn-*seen*-yuh
museum	le musée	luh mew-*zay*
no entry	sens interdit	sehns ahn-ter-*dee*
no smoking	défense de fumer	day-*fahns* de fu-may
on foot	à pied	ah pee-*ay*
one-day pass	ticket journalier	tee-kay jhoor-nall-ee-*ay*
one-way ticket	aller simple	ah-*lay* sam-pluh
police	la police	lah po-*lees*
rented car	voiture de location	vwa-*toor* de low-ka-see-*on*
round-trip ticket	aller-retour	ah-*lay* re-*toor*
second floor	premier étage	prem-ee-*ehr* ay-*taj*
slow down	ralentir	rah-lahn-*teer*
store	le magazin	luh ma-ga-*zehn*
street	rue	roo
suburb	banlieu, environs	bahn-*lieu,* en-veer-*ohn*
subway	le métro	le may-tro
telephone	le téléphone	luh tay-lay-*phone*
ticket	un billet	uh *bee*-yay
ticket office	vente de billets	vahnt duh bee-*yay*
toilets	les toilettes / les WC	lay twa-*lets* / les vay-*say*
tower	tour	toor

NECESSITIES

English	**French**	**Pronunciation**
I'd like	je voudrais	jhe voo-*dray*
a room	une chambre	ewn *shahm*-bruh
the key	la clé (la clef)	la clay
How much does it cost?	C'est combien? / Ça coûte combien?	say comb-bee-*ehn?* / sah coot comb-bee-*ehn?*
That's expensive	C'est cher/chère	say share
Do you take credit cards?	Est-ce que vous acceptez les cartes de credit?	es-kuh voo zaksep-*tay* lay kart duh creh-*dee?*
I'd like to buy	Je voudrais acheter	jhe voo-dray ahsh-*tay*
aspirin	des aspirines / des aspros	deyz ahs-peer-*een* / deyz ahs-*proh*
cigarettes	des cigarettes	day see-ga-*ret*
condoms	des préservatifs	day pray-ser-va-*teef*
dictionary	un dictionnaire	uh deek-see-oh-*nare*
dress	une robe	ewn robe
envelopes	des envelopes	days ahn-veh-*lope*
gift (for someone)	un cadeau	uh kah-*doe*
handbag	un sac	uh sahk
hat	un chapeau	uh shah-*poh*
magazine	une revue	ewn reh-*vu*
map of the city	un plan de ville	unh plahn de *veel*
matches	des allumettes	dayz a-loo-*met*
necktie	une cravate	uh cra-*vaht*
newspaper	un journal	uh zhoor-*nahl*
phone-card	une carte téléphonique	uh cart tay-lay-fone-*eek*
postcard	une carte postale	ewn carte pos-*tahl*

road map	une carte routière	ewn cart roo-tee-*air*
shirt	une chemise	ewn che-*meez*
shoes	des chaussures	day show-*suhr*
skirt	une jupe	ewn jhoop
soap	du savon	dew sah-*vohn*
socks	des chaussettes	day show-*set*
stamp	un timbre	uh *tam*-bruh
trousers	un pantalon	uh pan-tah-*lohn*
writing paper	du papier à lettres	dew pap-pee-*ay* a *let*-ruh

IN YOUR HOTEL

English	**French**	**Pronunciation**
Are taxes included?	Est-ce que les taxes sont comprises?	ess-keh lay taks son com-*preez*?
balcony	un balcon	uh bahl-cohn
bathtub	une baignoire	ewn bayn-*nwar*
for two occupants	pour deux personnes	poor duh pair-*sunn*
hot and cold water	l'eau chaude et froide	low showed ay fwad
Is breakfast included?	Petit déjeuner inclus?	peh-*tee* day-jheun-*ay* ehn-*klu*?
room	une chambre	ewn *shawm*-bruh
shower	une douche	ewn dooch
sink	un lavabo	uh la-va-*bow*
suite	une suite	ewn sweet
We're staying for . . . days	On reste pour . . . jours	ohn rest poor . . . jhoor
with	avec	ah-*vek*
with air-conditioning	avec climatization	ah-*vek* clee-mah-tee-zah-ion
without	sans	sahn
youth hostel	une auberge de jeunesse	oon oh-bayrge-duh-jhe-*ness*

IN THE RESTAURANT

English	**French**	**Pronunciation**
I would like	Je voudrais	jhe voo-*dray*
to eat	manger	mahn-*jhay*
to order	commander	ko-mahn-*day*
Please give me	Donnez-moi, s'il vous plaît	doe-nay-*mwah*, seel voo play
an ashtray	un cendrier	uh sahn-dree-*ay*
a bottle of	une bouteille de	ewn boo-*tay* duh
a cup of	une tasse de	ewn tass duh
a glass of	un verre de	uh vair duh
a plate of	une assiette de	ewn ass-ee-*et* duh
breakfast	le petit-déjeuner	luh puh-*tee* day-zhuh-*nay*
cocktail	un apéritif	uh ah-pay-ree-*teef*
check/bill	l'addition/ la note	la-dee-see-*ohn*/la noat
dinner	le dîner	luh dee-*nay*
knife	un couteau	uh koo-*toe*
napkin	une serviette	ewn sair-vee-*et*
platter of the day	un plat du jour	uh plah dew jhoor
spoon	une cuillère	ewn kwee-*air*

Cheers!	A votre santé!	ah vo-truh sahn-*tay!*
Can I buy you a drink?	Puis-je vous acheter un verre?	*pwee*-jhe voo *zahsh*-tay uh *vaihr?*
fixed-price menu	un menu	uh may-*new*
fork	une fourchette	ewn four-*shet*
Is the tip / service included?	Est-ce que le service est compris?	ess-ke luh ser-*vees* eh com-*pree?*
Waiter! / Waitress!	Monsieur! / Mademoiselle!	mun-*syuh* / mad-mwa-*zel*
wine list	une carte des vins	ewn cart day *van*
appetizer	une entrée	ewn en-*tray*
main course	un plat principal	uh plah pran-see-*pahl*
tip included	service compris	sehr-*vees* cohm-*pree*
wide-ranging sampling of the chef's best efforts	menu dégustation	may-*new* day-gus-ta-see-*on*
drinks not included	boissons non comprises	bwa-*sons* no com-*pree*

SHOPPING

English	**French**	**Pronunciation**
antiques store	un magasin d'antiquités	uh maga-*zan* d'on-tee kee-*tay*
bakery	une boulangerie	ewn boo-lon-zhur-*ree*
bank	une banque	ewn bonk
bookstore	une librairie	ewn lee-brehr-*ree*
butcher	une boucherie	ewn boo-shehr-*ree*
cheese shop	une fromagerie	ewn fro-mazh-*ree*
dairy shop	une crémerie	ewn krem-*ree*
delicatessen	une charcuterie	ewn shar-koot-*ree*
department store	une grande magasin	ewn gronde maga-*zan*
drugstore	une pharmacie	ewn far-mah-*see*
gift shop	un magasin de cadeaux	uh maga-*zan* duh ka-*doh*
greengrocer	un marchand de légumes	uh mar-*shon* duh lay-*goom*
hairdresser	un coiffeur	uh kwa-*fuhr*
market	un marché	uh mar-*shay*
pastry shop	une pâtisserie	ewn pa-tee-*sree*
supermarket	un supermarché	uh soo-pehr-mar-*shay*
tobacconist	un tabac	uh ta-*bah*
travel agency	une agencie de voyages	ewn azh-on-*see* duh vwa-*yazh*

COLORS, SHAPES, SIZES, ATTRIBUTES

English	**French**	**Pronunciation**
black	noir	nwahr
blue	blue	bleuh
brown	marron/brun	mar-*rohn*/bruhn
green	vert	vaihr
orange	orange	o-*rahnj*
pink	rose	rose
purple	violette	vee-o-*let*
red	rouge	rooj
white	blanc	blahnk
yellow	jaune	jhone
bad	mauvais(e)	moh-*veh*

big	grand(e)	gron / gronde
closed	fermé(e)	fer-*meh*
down	en bas	on *bah*
early	de bonne heure	duh bon *urr*
enough	assez	as-*say*
far	loin	lwan
free, unoccupied	libre	*lee*-bruh
free, without charge	gratuit(e)	grah-*twee* / grah-*tweet*
good	bon/bonne	boa/bun
hot	chaud(e)	show / shoad
near	près	preh
open (as in a museum or store)	ouvert(e)	oo-*ver*
small	petit(e)	puh-*teel*/puh-*teet*
up	en haut	on *oh*
well	bien	byehn

NUMBERS & ORDINALS

English	French	Pronunciation
zero	zéro	*zare*-oh
one	un	uh
two	deux	duh
three	trois	twah
four	quatre	*kaht*-ruh
five	cinq	sank
six	six	seess
seven	sept	set
eight	huit	wheat
nine	neuf	nuf
ten	dix	deess
eleven	onze	ohnz
twelve	douze	dooz
thirteen	treize	trehz
fourteen	quatorze	kah-*torz*
fifteen	quinze	kanz
sixteen	seize	sez
seventeen	dix-sept	deez-*set*
eighteen	dix-huit	deez-*wheat*
nineteen	dix-neuf	deez-*nuf*
twenty	vingt	vehn
twenty-one	vingt-et-un	vehnt-ay-*uh*
twenty-two	vingt-deux	vehnt-*duh*
thirty	trente	trahnt
forty	quarante	ka-*rahnt*
fifty	cinquante	sang-*kahnt*
sixty	soixante	swa-*sahnt*
sixty-one	soixante-et-un	swa-*sahnt*-et-*uh*
seventy	soixante-dix	swa-sahnt-*deess*
seventy-one	soixante-et-onze	swa-sahnt-et-*ohnze*
eighty	quatre-vingts	kaht-ruh-*vehn*
eighty-one	quatre-vingt-un	kaht-ruh-vehn-*uh*

ninety	quatre-vingt-dix	kaht-ruh-venh-*deess*
ninety-one	quatre-vingt-onze	kaht-ruh-venh-*ohnze*
one hundred	cent	sahn
one thousand	mille	meel
one hundred thousand	cent mille	sahn meel
first	premier	*preh*-mee-ay
second	deuxième	*duhz*-zee-em
third	troisième	*twa*-zee-em
fourth	quatrième	*kaht*-ree-em
fifth	cinquième	*sank*-ee-em
sixth	sixième	*sees*-ee-em
seventh	septième	*set*-ee-em
eighth	huitième	*wheat*-ee-em
ninth	neuvième	*neuv*-ee-em
tenth	dixième	*dees*-ee-em
eleventh	onzième	*ohnz*-ee-em
twelfth	douzième	*dooz*-ee-em
thirteenth	treizième	*trehz*-ee-em
fourteenth	quatorzième	kah-*torz*-ee-em
twentieth	vingtième	*vehnt*-ee-em
thirtieth	trentième	*trahnt*-ee-em
one hundredth	centième	*sant*-ee-em

THE CALENDAR

English	French	Pronunciation
Sunday	dimanche	dee-*mahnsh*
Monday	lundi	luhn-*dee*
Tuesday	mardi	mahr-*dee*
Wednesday	mercredi	mair-kruh-*dee*
Thursday	jeudi	jheu-*dee*
Friday	vendredi	vawn-druh-*dee*
Saturday	samedi	sahm-*dee*
Yesterday	hier	ee-*air*
Today	aujourd'hui	o-jhord-*dwee*
This morning / this afternoon	ce matin / cet après-midi	suh ma-*tan* / set ah-preh mee-*dee*
Tonight	ce soir	suh *swahr*
Tomorrow	demain	de-*man*

Appendix B

Glossary of Basic Menu Terms

You're hungry, you don't want brains, but you don't understand a thing on the menu. What to do? Use the following list of menu terms (organized by food type) to help determine what exactly you're ordering.

Note: To order any of these items from a waiter, simply preface the French-language name with the phrase, "Je voudrais" (jhe voo-*dray*), which means, "I would like . . ." *Bon appetit!*

MEATS

French	English	Pronunciation
De l'agneau	Lamb	Duh l'ahn-*nyo*
Des ailes de poulet	Chicken wings	Dayz ehl duh poo-lay
De l'aloyau	Sirloin	Duh l'ahl-why-*yo*
Du bifteck	Steak	Dew beef-*tek*
De la blanquette	Stewed meat with white sauce, enriched with cream and eggs	Duh lah blon-*kette*
Du boeuf à la mode	Marinated beef braised with red wine and served with vegetables	Dew bewf ah lah *mhowd*
De la cervelle	Brains	Duh lah ser-*vel*
Du Chateaubriand	Double tenderloin, a long muscle from which filet steaks are cut	Dew sha-tow-bree-*ahn*
Du coq au vin	Chicken, stewed with mushrooms and wine	Dew cock o vhaihn
Des cuisses de grenouilles	Frogs' legs	*Day cweess duh gre noo yuh*
Du gigot	Haunch or leg of an animal, especially that of a lamb or sheep	Dew *jhi*-goh
Du jambon	Ham	*Dew jham*-bohn
Du lapin	Rabbit	*Dew lah*-pan
Du pot au feu	Beef stew	*Dew poht o* fhe

French	English	Pronunciation
Du poulet	Chicken	*Dew poo*-lay
Des quenelles	Rolls of pounded and baked chicken, veal, or fish, often pike, usually served warm	*Day ke*-nelle
Des ris de veau	Sweetbreads	*Day ree duh* voh
Des rognons	Kidneys	*Day row*-nyon
Un steak au poivre	Filet steak, embedded with fresh green or black peppercorns, flambéed and served with a cognac sauce	*Uh stake o pwah*-vruh
Du veau	Veal	*Dew voh*

FISH

French	English	Pronunciation
De l'anguille	Eel	Duh l'ahn-*ghwee*-uh
De la bouillabaisse	Mediterranean fish soup or stew made with tomatoes, garlic, saffron, and olive oil	Duh lah booh-ya-*besse*
Du brochet	Pike	Dew broh-*chay*
Des crevettes	Shrimp	Day kreh-*vette*
Du hareng	Herring	*Dew ahr*-rahn
Du homard	Lobster	*Dew oh*-mahr
Des huîtres	Oysters	*Dayz hoo-ee-truhs*
Du loup de mer	Wolffish, a Mediterranean sea bass	*Dew loo-duh*-mehr
Des moules	Mussels	*Day moohl*
Des moules marinières	Mussels in herb-flavored white wine with shallots	*Day moohl mar-ee-nee*-air
Du poisson de rivière, or poisson d'eau douce / du poisson de mer	Fish (freshwater) and fish (saltwater)	*Dew pwah-sson duh ree-vee*-aire, *dew pwah-sson d'o dooss/ dew pwah-sson duh* mehr
Du saumon fumé	Smoked salmon	*Dew sow-mohn fu*-may
Du thon	Tuna	*Dew tohn*
De la truite	Trout	*Duh lah tru*-eet

SIDES/APPETIZERS

French	English	Pronunciation
Du beurre	Butter	Dew bhuhr
De la choucroute	Sauerkraut	Duh lah chew-*kroot*
Des escargots	Snails	Dayz ess-car-*goh*
Du foie	Liver	Dew fwoh
Du foie gras	Goose liver	Dew fwoh grah
Du pain	Bread	Dew pan
Des rillettes	Potted and minced pork and pork by-products, prepared as a roughly chopped pâté	*Day ree*-yett
Du riz	Rice	*Dew* ree

FRUITS/VEGETABLES

French	English	Pronunciation
De l'ananas	Pineapple	Duh l'ah-na-*nas*
De l'aubergine	Eggplant	Duh l'oh-ber-*jheen*
Du choux	Cabbage	Dew *shoe*
Du citron / du citron vert	Lemon / lime	Dew cee-*tron* / dew cee-*tron* vaire
Des épinards	Spinach	Dayz ay-pin-*ar*
Des fraises	Strawberries	Day frez
Des haricots verts	Green beans	*Day ahr-ee-coh* vaire
Une orange	Orange	*Ewn or-an*-jhe
Un pamplemousse	Grapefruit	*Uh pahm-pluh*-moose
Des petits pois	Green peas	*Day puh-tee-* pwah
Des pommes frites	French fried potatoes	*Day puhm* freet
Des pommes de terre	Potatoes	*Day puhm duh* tehr
Du raisin	Grapes	*Dew ray*-zhan

SOUPS/SALADS

French	English	Pronunciation
Une salade de concombres	Cucumber salad	*Ewn sah-lahd duh con-con*-bruh
Une salade de fruit /une macédoine de fruits	Fruit salad	*Ewn sah-lahd duh* fwee/ *ewn mah-say*-doine *duh* fwee
Une salade de laitue	Lettuce salad	*Ewn sah-lahd duh lay*-tew
Une salade Niçoise	Salad, native to Nice, composed of lettuce, tuna, anchovies, capers, tomatoes, olives, olive oil, wine vinegar, and herbs	*Ewn sah-lahd nee*-swaz
Une salade verte	Green salad	*Ewn sah-lahd* vairt
De la soupe à l'oignon	Onion soup	*Duh lah soop ah low*-ñon

BEVERAGES

French	English	Pronunciation
De la bière	Beer	Duh lah bee-*aire*
Boissons non compris	Drinks not included	*Bwa-son nohn com*-pree
Un café	Coffee	Uh-ka-*fay*
Un café au lait	Coffee (with milk)	Uh ka-fay o *lay*
Un café crème	Coffee (with cream)	Uh ka-fay krem
Un café decaffeiné (un déca; *slang*)	Coffee (decaf)	Un ka-fay ka-fay day-kah-fay-*e-nay* (uh day-kah)
Un café noir	Coffee (black)	Uh ka-fay-nwahr
Un espresso (*un express*)	Coffee (espresso)	Un ka-fay ek-*sprehss*-o (uh ek-*sprehss*)
Du jus d'orange	Orange juice	*Dew joo d'or-an*-jhe
De l'eau	Water	Duh lo
Du lait	Milk	*Dew* lay
Du thé	Tea	*Dew* tay

Une tisane	Herbal tea	*Ewn tee*-zahn
Du vin blanc	White wine	*Dew vhin blahn*
Du vin rouge	Red wine	*Dew vhin rooj*

DESSERTS

French	**English**	**Pronunciation**
De la crème brulée	Thick custard dessert with a caramelized topping	Duh lah krem bruh-*lay*
Du fromage	Cheese	*Dew fro* mahjz
Du gâteau	Cake	*Dew gha*-tow
De la glace à la vanille	Vanilla ice cream	*Duh lah glass a lah vah*-ne- *yuh*
Une tarte	Tart	*Ewn tart*
Une tarte tatin	Caramelized upside-down apple pie	*Ewn tart tah*-tihn

SPICES/CONDIMENTS

French	**English**	**Pronunciation**
De la crème fraîche	Sour heavy cream	Duh lah krem *fresh*
De la moutarde	Mustard	*Duh lah moo*-tard-*uh*
Du poivre	Pepper	*Dew pwah*-vruh
Du sel	Salt	*Dew* sel
Du sucre	Sugar	*Dew suh*-kruh

COOKING METHODS

French	**English**	**Pronunciation**
Bourgignon/ à la bourguignonne	In the style of Burgundy, usually with red wine, mushrooms, bacon, and onions	Boor-geehn-*nyon*/ a lah boor-geeh-ny-*uhn*
Un confit	Method of cooking whereby anything (including fish, meat, fruits, or vegetables) is simmered in a reduction of its own fat or juices	Uh khon-feeh
Cuit au feu de bois	Cooked over a wood fire	Kwee o fhe duh *bwoi*
A la Lyonnaise	A method of food preparation native to Lyon and its region, that usually includes wine sauce accented with shredded and sautéed onions.	*Ah lah lee-ohn*-nehz
En papillotte	Cooked in parchment paper	*Ehn pah-pee*-yott
Une terrine	Minced and potted meat, seasoned and molded into a crock	*Ewn tair*-een
Vol-au-vent	Puff pastry shell	*Vhol-o-*vhen

Index

Page numbers in italics refer to maps.

FROMMER'S® COMPLETE TRAVEL GUIDES

(Comprehensive guides with selections in all price ranges—from deluxe to budget)

Alaska
Amsterdam
Arizona
Atlanta
Australia
Austria
Bahamas
Barcelona, Madrid & Seville
Belgium, Holland &
  Luxembourg
Bermuda
Boston
Budapest & the Best of
  Hungary
California
Canada
Cancún, Cozumel & the
  Yucatán
Cape Cod, Nantucket &
  Martha's Vineyard
Caribbean
Caribbean Cruises &
  Ports of Call
Caribbean Ports of Call
Carolinas & Georgia
Chicago
China
Colorado
Costa Rica
Denver, Boulder &
  Colorado Springs
England
Europe
Florida

France
Germany
Greece
Hawaii
Hong Kong
Honolulu, Waikiki & Oahu
Ireland
Israel
Italy
Jamaica & Barbados
Japan
Las Vegas
London
Los Angeles
Maryland & Delaware
Maui
Mexico
Miami & the Keys
Montana & Wyoming
Montréal & Québec City
Munich & the Bavarian Alps
Nashville & Memphis
Nepal
New England
New Mexico
New Orleans
New York City
Nova Scotia, New
  Brunswick &
  Prince Edward Island
Oregon
Paris
Philadelphia & the Amish
  Country

Portugal
Prague & the Best of the
  Czech Republic
Provence & the Riviera
Puerto Rico
Rome
San Antonio & Austin
San Diego
San Francisco
Santa Fe, Taos &
  Albuquerque
Scandinavia
Scotland
Seattle & Portland
Singapore & Malaysia
South Pacific
Spain
Switzerland
Thailand
Tokyo
Toronto
Tuscany & Umbria
USA
Utah
Vancouver & Victoria
Vermont, New Hampshire &
  Maine
Vienna & the Danube Valley
Virgin Islands
Virginia
Walt Disney World &
  Orlando
Washington, D.C.
Washington State

FROMMER'S® DOLLAR-A-DAY GUIDES

(The ultimate guides to comfortable low-cost travel)

Australia from $50 a Day
California from $60 a Day
Caribbean from $60 a Day
England from $60 a Day
Europe from $50 a Day
Florida from $60 a Day
Greece from $50 a Day
Hawaii from $60 a Day
Ireland from $50 a Day

Israel from $45 a Day
Italy from $50 a Day
London from $70 a Day
New York from $75 a Day
New Zealand from $50 a Day
Paris from $70 a Day
San Francisco from $60 a Day
Washington, D.C., from
  $60 a Day

FROMMER'S® MEMORABLE WALKS

Chicago
London

New York
Paris

San Francisco

FROMMER'S® PORTABLE GUIDES

Acapulco, Ixtapa/ Zihuatanejo	Dublin	Puerto Vallarta, Manzanillo & Guadalajara
Bahamas	Las Vegas	San Francisco
California Wine Country	London	Sydney
Charleston & Savannah	Maine Coast	Tampa Bay & St. Petersburg
Chicago	New Orleans	Venice
	New York City	Washington, D.C.
	Paris	

FROMMER'S® NATIONAL PARK GUIDES

Grand Canyon	Yosemite & Sequoia/ Kings Canyon
National Parks of the American West	Zion & Bryce Canyon
Yellowstone & Grand Teton	

THE COMPLETE IDIOT'S TRAVEL GUIDES
(The ultimate user-friendly trip planners)

Cruise Vacations	Las Vegas	New York City
Planning Your Trip to Europe	Mexico's Beach Resorts	San Francisco
Hawaii	New Orleans	Walt Disney World

SPECIAL-INTEREST TITLES

The Civil War Trust's Official Guide to the Civil War Discovery Trail	Outside Magazine's Adventure Guide to the Pacific Northwest
Frommer's Caribbean Hideaways	Outside Magazine's Guide to Family Vacations
Israel Past & Present	Places Rated Almanac
New York City with Kids	Retirement Places Rated
New York Times Weekends	Washington, D.C., with Kids
Outside Magazine's Adventure Guide to New England	Wonderful Weekends from Boston
	Wonderful Weekends from New York City
Outside Magazine's Adventure Guide to Northern California	Wonderful Weekends from San Francisco
	Wonderful Weekends from Los Angeles

THE UNOFFICIAL GUIDES®
(Get the unbiased truth from these candid, value-conscious guides)

Atlanta	Florida with Kids	Miami & the Keys	Skiing in the West
Branson, Missouri	The Great Smoky & Blue Ridge Mountains	Mini-Mickey	Walt Disney World
Chicago		New Orleans	Walt Disney World Companion
Cruises		New York City	
Disneyland	Las Vegas	San Francisco	Washington, D.C.

FROMMER'S® IRREVERENT GUIDES
(Wickedly honest guides for sophisticated travelers)

Amsterdam	London	New Orleans	San Francisco
Boston	Manhattan	Paris	Walt Disney World
Chicago			Washington, D.C.

FROMMER'S® DRIVING TOURS

America	Florida	Ireland	Scotland
Britain	France	Italy	Spain
California	Germany	New England	Western Europe

WHEREVER YOU TRAVEL, *H*ELP IS NEVER FAR AWAY.

From planning your trip to

providing travel assistance along

the way, American Express®

Travel Service Offices are

always there to help

you do more.

American Express Travel Service
Offices are found in central locations
throughout France.

Travel

http://www.americanexpress.com/travel